HANDBOOK OF EMOTIONS
Second Edition

HANDBOOK OF EMOTIONS

Second Edition

Edited by
Michael Lewis
Jeannette M. Haviland-Jones

The Guilford Press
NEW YORK   LONDON

© 2000 The Guilford Press
A Division of Guilford Publications, Inc.
72 Spring Street, New York, NY 10012
www.guilford.com

Printed in the United States of America

This book is printed on acid-free paper.

Last digit is print number: 9 8 7 6 5 4 3 2 1

Library of Congress Cataloging-in-Publication Data

Handbook of emotions / edited by Michael Lewis and Jeannette M. Haviland-Jones
— 2nd ed.
    p. cm.
  Includes bibliographical references and indexes.
  ISBN 1-57230-529-0 (hardcover : alk. paper)
  1. Emotions.   2. Emotions—Sociological aspects.   I. Lewis, Michael, 1937 Jan. 10—   II.
Haviland-Jones, Jeannette M.

  BF561.H35 2000
  152.4—dc21

                                            99-086558

About the Editors

Michael Lewis, PhD, is the University Distinguished Professor of Pediatrics and Psychiatry, and Director of the Institute for the Study of Child Development at Robert Wood Johnson Medical School, University of Medicine and Dentistry of New Jersey. Dr. Lewis has written or edited over 30 books on developmental psychology and was rated as number one in scholarly impact in the field of developmental psychology in a survey published in *Developmental Review* in 1995. He is coeditor of *The Handbook of Developmental Psychopathology,* and his book *Altering Fate: Why the Past Does Not Predict the Future* was a finalist for the Maccoby Book Award.

Jeannette M. Haviland-Jones, PhD, is Professor of Psychology at Rutgers—The State University of New Jersey. Her research has focused on normal and deviant emotional development across the lifespan, with emphasis on transitional periods such as adolescence. She is coauthor of *Contemporary Adolescence,* with Hollis Scarborough, and coeditor, with Michael Lewis, of the first edition of *Handbook of Emotions.* Her upcoming book, with Carol Magai, *The Matrix of Emotion and Life Trajectories,* integrates scientific approaches to order, complexity, and chaos with the development of emotion and personality. As a founding member of the International Society for Research on Emotion, she has participated in national and international symposia, and has lectured in Europe and North America on emotional development. She is the author of numerous research and review articles that point to the role of nonverbal emotional signals, ranging from facial expression to odors or pheromones, as well as narrative signals of emotion.

Contributors

Brian P. Ackerman, PhD, Department of Psychology, University of Delaware, Newark, Delaware

James R. Averill, PhD, Department of Psychology, University of Massachusetts, Amherst, Massachusetts

Carol Barr-Zisowitz, MD, PhD, Department of Psychiatry, University of Pittsburgh School of Medicine, Pittsburgh, Pennsylvania

John E. Bates, PhD, Department of Psychology, Indiana University, Bloomington, Indiana

Brian T. Bedell, MS, Department of Psychology, Yale University, New Haven, Connecticut

Gary G. Berntson, PhD, Department of Psychology, The Ohio State University, Columbus, Ohio

Roger J. Booth, PhD, Department of Molecular Medicine, Faculty of Medical and Health Sciences, The University of Auckland, Auckland, New Zealand

Leslie R. Brody, PhD, Department of Psychology, Boston University, Boston, Massachusetts

George W. Brown, PhD, Academic Department of Psychiatry, Socio-Medical Research Centre, St. Thomas' Hospital, London, England, United Kingdom

John T. Cacioppo, PhD, Department of Psychology, University of Chicago, Chicago, Illinois

Susan D. Calkins, PhD, Department of Psychology, University of North Carolina at Greensboro, Greensboro, North Carolina

Leda Cosmides, PhD, Department of Psychology and Center for Evolutionary Psychology, University of California at Santa Barbara, Santa Barbara, California

Jerusha B. Detweiler, MS, Department of Psychology, Yale University, New Haven, Connecticut

Ed Diener, PhD, Department of Psychology, University of Illinois at Urbana–Champaign, Champaign, Illinois

Kenneth A. Dodge, PhD, Center for Child and Family Policy, Duke University, Durham, North Carolina

Nancy Eisenberg, PhD, Department of Psychology, College of Liberal Arts and Sciences, Arizona State University, Tempe, Arizona

Paul Ekman, PhD, Department of Psychiatry, University of California at San Francisco, San Francisco, California

Joseph P. Forgas, DPhil, DSc, School of Psychology, University of New South Wales, Sydney, New South Wales, Australia

Nathan A. Fox, PhD, Institute for Child Study, Department of Human Development, University of Maryland, College Park, Maryland

Nico H. Frijda, PhD, Department of Psychology, University of Amsterdam, Amsterdam, The Netherlands

Jonathan Haidt, PhD, Department of Psychology, University of Virginia, Charlottesville, Virginia

Judith A. Hall, PhD, Department of Psychology, Northeastern University, Boston, Massachusetts

Paul L. Harris, DPhil, Department of Experimental Psychology, University of Oxford, Oxford, England, United Kingdom

Elaine Hatfield, PhD, Department of Psychology, University of Hawaii at Manoa, Honolulu, Hawaii

Jeannette M. Haviland-Jones, PhD, Department of Psychology, Rutgers—The State University of New Jersey, New Brunswick, New Jersey

Ursula Hess, PhD, Department of Psychology, University of Quebec at Montreal, Montreal, Quebec, Canada

Alice M. Isen, PhD, Department of Psychology and Johnson Graduate School of Management, Cornell University, Ithaca, New York

Tiffany A. Ito, PhD, Department of Psychology, University of Colorado, Boulder, Colorado

Carroll E. Izard, PhD, Department of Psychology, University of Delaware, Newark, Delaware

P. N. Johnson-Laird, PhD, Department of Psychology, Princeton University, Princeton, New Jersey

Tom Johnstone, PhD candidate, Department of Psychology, University of Geneva, Geneva, Switzerland

Patricia Kahlbaugh, PhD, Department of Psychology, Southern Connecticut State University, New Haven, Connecticut

Dacher Keltner, PhD, Department of Psychology, University of California at Berkeley, Berkeley, California

Theodore D. Kemper, PhD, Department of Sociology, St. John's University, Jamaica, New York

Gilles Kirouac, PhD, School of Psychology, Laval University, Quebec, Quebec, Canada

Jeff T. Larsen, MA, Department of Psychology, The Ohio State University, Columbus, Ohio

Joseph E. LeDoux, PhD, Center for Neural Science, New York University, New York, New York

Ghyslaine Lemay, PhD, Department of Psychology, University of British Columbia, Vancouver, British Columbia, Canada

Elizabeth A. Lemerise, PhD, Department of Psychology, Western Kentucky University, Bowling Green, Kentucky

Howard Leventhal, PhD, Institute of Health, Health Care Policy and Aging Research, Rutgers—The State University of New Jersey, New Brunswick, New Jersey

Michael Lewis, PhD, Institute for the Study of Child Development, Robert Wood Johnson Medical School, University of Medicine and Dentistry of New Jersey, New Brunswick, New Jersey

Maria D. Liwag, PhD, Atteneo University, Quezon City, The Philippines

Richard E. Lucas, MA, Department of Psychology, University of Illinois at Urbana–Champaign, Champaign, Illinois

John D. Mayer, PhD, Department of Psychology, University of New Hampshire, Durham, New Hampshire

Clark R. McCauley, PhD, Department of Psychology, Bryn Mawr College, Bryn Mawr, Pennsylvania

Suzanne M. Miller, PhD, Division of Population Science, Psychosocial and Behavioral Medicine Program, Fox Chase Cancer Center, Cheltenham, Pennsylvania

Thomas A. More, PhD, U.S. Forest Service, Northeastern Research Station, Burlington, Vermont

Keith Oatley, PhD, Centre for Applied Cognitive Science, Ontario Institute for Studies in Education, University of Toronto, Toronto, Ontario, Canada

Arne Öhman, PhD, Department of Clinical Neuroscience, Section of Psychology, Karolinska Institute and Hospital, Stockholm, Sweden

Jaak Panksepp, PhD, Department of Psychology, Bowling Green State University, Bowling Green, Ohio

W. Gerrod Parrott, PhD, Department of Psychology, Georgetown University, Washington, DC

Linda Patrick-Miller, PhD, Institute of Health, Health Care Policy and Aging Research, Rutgers—The State University of New Jersey, New Brunswick, New Jersey

James W. Pennebaker, PhD, Department of Psychology, University of Texas, Austin, Texas

Elizabeth A. Phelps, PhD, Department of Psychology, New York University, New York, New York

Kirsten M. Poehlmann, PhD, Department of Psychology, University of Houston, Houston, Texas

Richard L. Rapson, PhD, Department of History, University of Hawaii at Manoa, Honolulu, Hawaii

Richard Rende, PhD, Department of Psychology, Rutgers—The State University of New Jersey, Piscataway, New Jersey

Paul Rozin, PhD, Department of Psychology, University of Pennsylvania, Philadelphia, Pennsylvania

James A. Russell, PhD, Department of Psychology, University of British Columbia, Vancouver, British Columbia, Canada

Carolyn Saarni, PhD, Department of Counseling, Sonoma State University, Rohnert Park, California

Peter Salovey, PhD, Department of Psychology, Yale University, New Haven, Connecticut

Klaus R. Scherer, PhD, Department of Psychology, University of Geneva, Geneva, Switzerland

Robert A. Schnoll, PhD, Division of Population Science, Psychosocial and Behavioral Medicine Program, Fox Chase Cancer Center, Cheltenham, Pennsylvania

Richard A. Shweder, PhD, Committee on Human Development, University of Chicago, Chicago, Illinois

Robert C. Solomon, PhD, Department of Philosophy, University of Texas, Austin, Texas

Matthew P. Spackman, PhD, Department of Psychology, Brigham Young University, Provo, Utah

Peter N. Stearns, PhD, Department of History, George Mason University, Fairfax, Virginia

Nancy L. Stein, PhD, Department of Psychology, University of Chicago, Chicago, Illinois

Ed S. Tan, PhD, Arts Department, Vrije Universiteit, Amsterdam, The Netherlands

John Tooby, PhD, Department of Anthropology and Center for Evolutionary Psychology, University of California at Santa Barbara, Santa Barbara, California

Tom Trabasso, PhD, Department of Psychology, University of Chicago, Chicago, Illinois

Patrick T. Vargas, PhD, School of Psychology, University of New South Wales, Sydney, New South Wales, Australia

Geoffrey M. White, PhD, Department of Anthropology, University of Hawaii, Honolulu, Hawaii

Preface

When we published the first edition of the *Handbook of Emotions* in 1993, research in emotion was beginning to blossom. Since then, its study has been recognized as an essential aspect of any study of humankind. At the beginning of the new century, the study of emotion—as it interfaces with cognition, with personality, and with social and health issues—has become obvious to all. This second edition of the *Handbook* is an attempt to meet this new challenge by allowing us to consider the work already accomplished and to begin exploring the new work that lies ahead.

The first edition was rated by *Choice* as an "Outstanding Academic Book" in 1995. This edition seeks to continue this tradition by serving as a resource for those beginning to investigate the field, as well as for those who wish to examine how the study of emotion has extended into new areas. For those who are just beginning to take an interest in the field of emotion research, this volume should propel their interest further, with new areas to investigate and old questions to be viewed in a new way. For those of us who continue to work in the field, and who once labored as isolated scientists, it demonstrates the strength and vitality of the field as new areas open up and new investigators make notable contributions. Such a development reflects the large community of scholars who are now invested in research and conceptual questions about emotions. These research activities are only enhanced when such a gathering of scholars reaches a critical mass.

This second edition contains new chapters by authors who made different contributions to the first edition, updates to chapters in the first edition that reflect the research of the last decade, and chapters by new contributors that reflect the expanding understanding of how emotions interface with other aspects of behavior. Thus the new edition takes into account work by pioneers of the field as they continue to expand their original ideas, as well as efforts by new investigators whose contributions to the study of emotion are well documented. We have expanded the section on psychophysical aspects of emotion; this reflects, in part, the tremendous and continuing advances in technology and new findings about brain–behavior relationships.

Especially important is the new section on emotions and health. Research about the emotion–illness connection is a rapidly expanding area of inquiry, and ways of thinking about the connection between stress, mediated through emotional reaction, and illness not only represent important advances in our theories, but have important implications for health services. They thus provide another arena for testing models and generating data.

In addition to this new section, we have expanded our net in looking at the relation of emotions to the arts and to the fields of history, philosophy, genetics, and anthropology. Our efforts are to look at emotions from a broad as well as a more focused perspective, allowing the reader access to the role of emotion in diverse fields, as well as allowing for a more focused view when we come to addressing work in specific emotions. Even here we have expanded our list of specific emotions—something we will continue to do as additional empirical work is generated.

Although this second edition of the *Handbook* follows the same basic organization of the first edition, there has been such an increase in the possible topics that could have been included that we greatly regretted omitting some areas. We chose some areas because we believe that they will emerge as significant; others because they have already been enormously productive; and still others simply to provide balance to the various perspectives. Bringing together the broadening content of the *Handbook* and working with this large, diverse group of scholars were great challenges and privileges. It is to our contributors that the volume owes its strength.

We continue to hope that scholars, clinicians, and students from a variety of disciplines will find our efforts helpful. Finally, we would like to express our appreciation to Despi Laverick, who helped put this edition together.

MICHAEL LEWIS
JEANNETTE M. HAVILAND-JONES

Contents

PART III. DEVELOPMENTAL CHANGES

PART IV. SOCIAL/PERSONALITY ISSUES

PART I

INTERDISCIPLINARY FOUNDATIONS

CHAPTER 1

The Philosophy of Emotions

Robert C. Solomon

"What is an emotion?" That question was asked in precisely that form by William James, as the title of an essay he wrote for *Mind* over 100 years ago (James, 1884). But philosophers have been concerned about the nature of emotion since Socrates and the "pre-Socratics" who preceded him, and although the discipline has grown up (largely because of Socrates and his student Plato) as the pursuit of reason, the emotions have always lurked in the background—often as a threat to reason and a danger to philosophy and philosophers. One of the most enduring metaphors of reason and emotion has been the metaphor of master and slave, with the wisdom of reason firmly in control and the dangerous impulses of emotion safely suppressed, channeled, or (ideally) in harmony with reason. But the question "What is an emotion?" has proved to be as difficult to resolve as the emotions have been to master. Just when it seems an adequate definition is in place, some new theory rears its unwelcome head and challenges our understanding.

The master–slave metaphor displays two features that still determine much of the philosophical view of emotion today. First and foremost, there is the inferior role of emotion—the idea that emotion is as such more primitive, less intelligent, more bestial, less dependable, and more dangerous than reason, and thus needs to be controlled by reason (an argument that Aristotle and other enlightened Athenians used to justify the political institution of slavery as well). Second, and more profoundly, there is the reason–emotion distinction itself—as if we were dealing with two different natural kinds, two conflicting and antagonistic aspects of the soul. Even those philosophers who sought to integrate them and reduce one to the other (typically reducing emotion to an inferior genus of reason, a "confused perception" or "distorted judgment") maintained the distinction and continued to insist on the superiority of reason. It was thus a mark of his considerable iconoclasm that the Scottish skeptic David Hume (1739/1888), in the 18th century, famously declared that "reason is, and ought to be, the slave of the passions." But even Hume, despite an ingenious analysis of the structure of emotions, ultimately fell back on the old models and metaphors. His work remains an exemplary celebration of reason, even while challenging its limits.

Philosophy is a historical discipline. It is constrained and defined as much by its past as by any particular field of phenomena. Philosophical theories and debates today cannot be understood or appreciated without some understanding of philosophy's rich and convoluted past. Even when a philosopher pretends to understand the phenomenon of emotion "in itself," or to analyze the language of emotion without reference to history or to any earlier attempts at analysis, both the wisdom and the folly of generations of accumulated reflection and argument are nevertheless inescapable. Although one might impatiently demand from the outset that one "define the terms" before the current discussion commences, the truth is that a definition emerges only at the end of a long discussion, and even then it is always tentative and appropriate only within a limited context and certain models of culture and personal character.

In what follows, I have tried to sketch a somewhat selective history of philosophical attempts to understand emotion, followed by a brief summary of questions still central to philosophical debate. Given the nature of philosophy and its emphasis on reason, however, we would expect that the focus of most philosophical analysis has been and remains the more cognitive aspects of emotion, with the physiological and to a certain extent the social and behavioral dimensions of emotion diminished or in many cases even denied. The dialectic in philosophy, accordingly, tends to go back and forth in its rediscovery of these often neglected dimensions. Sometimes emotions are dismissed as mere feelings and physiology, utterly unintelligent, even sub-human. In reaction, emotions are then ascribed the virtues of true wisdom; they are defended as the proper masters of reason and even the very foundation of our being-in-the-world. Most philosophers, however, try to find some more moderate, multidimensional position.

One might object that philosophical theories of emotion tend to be "armchair" speculation, devoid of the empirical support supplied by social scientists. However, this objection ignores the fact that philosophers, contrary to their own self-styled reputations as men and women of pure reason, have emotions themselves, and in most (but not all) cases a sufficiently rich repertoire of emotions to fund and support a dozen theories of emotion. As Descartes (1649/1989) said in his introduction to the subject, "everyone has experience of the passions within himself, and there is no necessity to borrow one's observations from elsewhere in order to discover their nature." Ultimately, there is no justification for the century-old feud between philosophy and psychology. Their history is in fact the same, and the phenomenon of emotion lies equally open to both of them.

THE HISTORY OF THE PHILOSOPHY OF EMOTION

Although the history of philosophy has often been described as the history of the development of reason—for example, by the great 19th century German philosopher G. W. F. Hegel—philosophers have never entirely neglected emotion, even if they have almost always denied it center stage. It would be a mistake, however, to put too much emphasis on the term "emotion," for its range and meaning have altered significantly over the years, due in part to changes in theories about emotion. So too, the word "passion" has a long and varied history, and we should beware of the misleading assumption that there is a single, orderly, natural class of phenomena that is simply designated by different labels in different languages at different times. The language of "passion" and "emotion" has a history into which various feelings, desires, sentiments, moods, attitudes and more explosive responses enter and from which they exit, depending not on arbitrary philosophical stipulation but on an extensive network of social, moral, cultural, and psychological factors. Thus we will often find that the focus is not emotion as such, but rather some particular class of emotions or particular emotion and its role in the manners or morals of the time.

The emotions as such, accordingly, do not form one of the three aspects of Plato's (c. 428–347 B.C.) tripartite soul as defined in *The Republic* (1974). There are reason, spirit, and appetite; not only does what we call emotion seem divided between spirit and appetite, but, considering Plato's discussion of *eros* as the love of the Good in his dialogue *The Symposium* (1989), there are emotions involved in reason as well. Aristotle (384–322 B.C.), by contrast, did seem to have a view of emotion as such, but although he had a mania for taxonomies, he spent relatively little time listing or analyzing the emotions—as he did, for example, the virtues and the various kinds of birds. In his *Rhetoric*, (1941) however, he defined emotion "as that which leads one's condition to become so transformed that his judgment is affected, and which is accompanied by pleasure and pain. Examples of emotion include anger, fear, pity, and the like, as well as the opposites of these."[1] (He did not tell us what these "opposites" might be.) Aristotle discussed certain emotions at length, notably anger, which he described in remarkably modern terms. In the *Rhetoric* he defined anger as "a distressed desire for conspicuous vengeance in return for a conspicuous and unjustifiable contempt of one's person or friends." He added that "anger is always directed towards someone in particular, e.g. Cleon, and not towards all of humanity," and mentioned (if only in passing) the physical distress that virtually always accompanies such emotion.

The key to Aristotle's analysis, however, is the notion of a "slight." This is the cause of anger, and it may be an instance of "scorn, spite, or insolence." Aristotle made allowances for only imagined slights (in other words, unwarranted anger is nevertheless anger), and he gave a central place to the desire for revenge, thus introducing a behavioral component at the heart of the emotion. We might note that Aristotle, who was so precocious in so many disciplines, seems to have anticipated most of the main contemporary theories. His analysis of anger includes a distinctive cognitive component, a specified social context, a behavioral tendency, and a recognition of physical arousal. He even noted that physical or psychological discomfort—sickness, poverty, love, war, breached expectations, or ingratitude—yields a predisposition for anger. It is worth noting that Aristotle had little to say of "feeling," presumably not because the Greeks were anesthetic, but rather because what we (inconsistently) call "affect" and inner sensation generally held little interest for them and played no significant role in their language or their psychology.

Perhaps the most important single point to make about Aristotle's view of emotion is the fact that his analyses make sense only in the context of a broader *ethical* concern. Anger was of interest to him because it is a natural reaction to offense and a moral force, which can be cultivated and provoked by reason and rhetoric. (Thus its inclusion in a book on that topic.) Anger (and several other emotions, notably pride) are also prominent in Aristotle's classical list of virtues in his *Nicomachean Ethics*, (1941) where he discussed in some detail those circumstances in which it is appropriate to get angry, those in which it is not, and what amount or intensity of anger is justified. He suggested that forgiveness may be a virtue, but only sometimes. He also insisted that only fools don't get angry, and that although overly angry people may be "unbearable," the absence of anger (aimed at the right offenses) is a vice rather than a virtue. In this as in all else, Aristotle defended moderation, the "mean between the extremes." So too, he discussed fear at length in the *Ethics* with regard to courage, which is not fearlessness or "overcoming" fear so much as it is having just the right amount of fear—not being foolhardy or a coward either.

The emotions, in other words, are central and essential to the good life, and the analysis of their nature is part and parcel of an ethical analysis.

So too, in Roman times, we find the conjunction of ethics and emotion in the philosophy of the Stoics (see Rist, 1969, and Nussbaum, 1994). But whereas Aristotle took emotion to be essential to the good life, the Stoics analyzed emotions as conceptual errors, conducive to misery. In modern terms, the Stoics Seneca and Chrysippus developed a full-blooded cognitive theory of the emotions, two millennia ago (see especially Seneca, 1963). Emotions, in a word, are judgments—judgments about the world and one's place in it. But the world of Roman society was not a happy or a particularly rational place. (Seneca served under the Emperor Nero, and ultimately commited suicide at his behest.) And as the Stoics saw the world they lived in as out of control and beyond any reasonable expectations, they saw the emotions, which impose such expectations on the world, as misguided judgments about life and our place in the world. The emotions consequently make us miserable and frustrated. Accordingly, the Stoics made a careful study of the component judgments that compose the emotions—the presumptuousness of moral judgment in anger, the vulnerability of love, the self-absorption of security in fear. The alternative was seen as "psychic indifference," or *apatheia* (apathy). The Stoics believed in a "higher" reason, one transcending the vanities of the social world. But they felt that the best life in that world could be achieved only by getting straight about the ultimate pointlessness of emotional attachments and involvement.

Throughout the Middle Ages, the study of emotion was again typically attached to ethics, and it was central to Christian psychology and the theories of human nature in terms of which the medievals understood themselves (see Hyman & Walsh, 1973). There were elaborate, quasi-medical studies of the effects of the various "humours" (gall, spleen, choler, and blood itself) on emotional temperament, but there were (as there were among the Stoics) especially rich studies of the cognitive and "conative" aspects of the emotions. Emotions were essentially linked with desires, particularly self-interested, self-absorbed desires. And so the Christian preoccupation with sin led to elaborate analyses of those emotions, passions, and desires designated as sins (notably greed, gluttony, lust, anger, envy, and pride; sloth, perhaps, is a special case). The tight linkage between the study of emotion and ethics is particularly evident in the curious observation that the highest virtues, such as love, hope, and faith, were not classified as emotions as such, but were rather elevated to a higher status and often (e.g., by Thomas Aquinas) equated with reason. The old master–slave metaphor remained alive and well, and as some emotions were seen as sins, the highest virtues could hardly be counted among the mere emotions.

Reviewing the ancient and medieval literature on emotion, René Descartes (1596–1650) was provoked to write that what they taught was "so slight, and for the most part so far from credible, that I am unable to entertain any hope of approximating the truth excepting by shunning the paths they followed" (1649/1989). Descartes is typically recognized as the "father" of modern philosophy, and, in a more scholarly vein, as the bridge between the scholastic world of the Middle Ages and our own. But Descartes was fundamentally a scientist and a mathematician, awed by "the natural light of reason" and fascinated by the unique autonomy of the human mind. Accordingly, he disdained the bodily and the bestial, insisting that the mind is a separate "substance" from the body (and that beasts therefore do not have minds). The separation of mind and body proved to be a famously difficult problem for Descartes and his successors, however, and nowhere was that problem more evident than in his attempt to deal with the emotions. Thoughts about mathematics may be clearly "in" the mind, as stomach contractions are in the body, but an emotion seems to require the interaction of mind and body in an undeniable way. Accordingly, Descartes defended a theory in his treatise *On the Passions of the Soul* (1649/1989), in which the mind and body "meet" in a small gland at the base of the brain (now known as the pineal gland), and the latter affects the former by means of the agitation of "animal spirits" (minute particles of blood), which bring about the emotions and their physical effects in various parts of the body. But the emotions also involve not only sensations caused by this physical agitation, but perceptions, desires, and beliefs as well. Thus over and above the physical agitation and familiar sensations, the emotion of hatred ultimately arises from the perception of an object's potential harmfulness and involves a desire to avoid it. Accordingly, it is not as if an emotion is merely a perception of the body; it may also be, as Descartes put it, a perception of the soul (e.g., a perception of desire), and some perceptions (as in dreams) may in fact be of things that do not exist at all.

An emotion is one type of "passion," for Descartes defined the passions in general as "the perceptions, feelings or emotions of the soul which we relate specifically to it, and which are caused, maintained, and fortified by some movement of the [animal] spirits." The passions in general are distinguished from "clear cognition," and render judgment "confused and obscure." Emotions are particularly disturbing passions. And yet emotions can be influenced by reason. For example, writing of courage, Descartes stated:

> To excite courage in oneself and remove fear, it is not sufficient to have the will to do so, but we must also apply ourselves to consider the reasons, the objects or examples which persuade us that the peril is not great; that there is always more security in defense than in flight, that we should have the glory and joy of having vanquished, while we should expect nothing but regret and shame for having fled, and so on.

And so the physiological account gives way to a cognitive account, and the emotions move from being merely bodily to becoming an essential ingredient in wisdom: "The utility of the passions consists alone in their fortifying and perpetuating in the soul thoughts which it is good that it should preserve, and which without that might easily be effaced from it." How then can there be "bad" emotions? "The harm is that they fortify these thoughts more than necessary, or they conserve others on which it is not good to dwell." Somewhat bewildered by the physiology (though he was at the cutting edge of the science of his times), Descartes ultimately tended to a value-oriented analysis of emotion. His six "primitive" passions—wonder, love, hatred, desire, joy, and sadness—are not meaningless agitations of the animal spirits, but ingredients in the good life.

Baruch (Benedict) Spinoza (1632–1677) might well be considered to be a latter-day Stoic, like Chrysippus and Seneca in ancient Rome. Just as the Stoics saw the emotions as misguided judgments about life and our place in the world, Spinoza too saw the emotions as a form of "thoughts" that, for the most part, misunderstand the world and consequently make us miserable and frustrated. But unlike the Stoics,

Spinoza did not aspire to that "psychic indifference" known as *apatheia;* rather, in his *Ethics* (1677/1982), he urged the attainment of a certain sort of "bliss," which can be achieved only once we get straight our thinking about the world. In particular, we have to give up the idea that we are or can be in control of our own lives, and adopt instead the all-embracing idea of ourselves and our minds as part of God. Most of the emotions, which are passive reactions to our unwarranted expectations of the world, will leave us hurt, frustrated, and enervated. The active emotions, by contrast, emanate from our own true natures and heighten our sense of activity and awareness. Spinoza, like the Stoics, developed an early version of the cognitive theory of emotion. But Spinoza also defended a grand and complex metaphysics, in which all substance is one and mind and body are but dual "aspects" of one and the same being. Accordingly, he did not face Descartes's formidable "mind–body" problem; although he himself would not have predicted this, he anticipated some of the subtle emotion–brain research that is being carried out today.

David Hume (1711–1776) was one of the most outspoken defenders of the Enlightenment, that very vocal and often rebellious intellectual movement that challenged old orthodoxies, elevated science and put religion on the defensive, attacked superstition and irrationality in all quarters, practiced and encouraged vigorous debate and discussion, and put a premium on the virtues of reason. But Hume, in carrying out the directives of reason to challenge, debate, and question, came to question the role and capacities of reason itself, and in particular the power of reason to motivate even the most basic minimum of moral behavior. "It is not against reason," he declared in one of his most outrageous proclamations, "to prefer the destruction of half the world to the scratching of my finger (1739/1888)." What motivates us to right (and wrong) behavior, Hume insisted, were our passions, and rather than being relegated to the margins of ethics and philosophy, the passions deserve central respect and consideration. Accordingly, he gave the passions the large middle portion of his great first book, *A Treatise of Human Nature* (1739/1888). Unfortunately, however, most philosophers then and since have preferred to read the first and third parts, on knowledge and ethics, and to ignore the central position of the passions.

Hume's theory is especially important not only because he challenged the inferior place of passion in philosophy and questioned the role of reason. He also advanced a theory of the passions that, although limited and encumbered by his general theory of mind, displayed dazzling insight and a precocious attempt to grapple with problems that would only be formulated generations later. Hume, like many of his contemporaries and predecessors, defined an emotion as a certain kind of sensation, or what he called an "impression," which (as in Descartes) is physically stimulated by the movement of the "animal spirits" in the blood. Such impressions are either pleasant or unpleasant, but the differentiation of the many emotions is not to be found in the nature of these impressions as such. Rather, the impressions that constitute our emotions are always to be located within a causal network of other impressions and, importantly, ideas. Ideas cause our emotional impressions, and ideas are caused in turn by them. The pleasant impression of pride, for example, is caused by the idea that one has achieved or accomplished something significant, and the impression in turn causes another idea, which Hume described as an idea of the self, *simpliciter*. The emotion, in other words, cannot be identified with the impression or sensation alone, but can only be identified by the whole complex of impressions and ideas. What Hume acknowledged with his emphasis on the essential place of ideas in emotion is what we now call the cognitive dimension of emotion, in addition to the physiological ("animal spirits") and merely sensational ("impression") aspects of emotion. Moreover, his inclusion of the second idea of the self in his analysis of pride indicates his grappling with the notion of intentionality (the "aboutness" of emotions)—an effort further reinforced by his somewhat obscure insistence that the connection between an emotion (the impression) and this consequent idea is "original" or "natural," or something more than the merely causal associations that form the usual bonds between ideas and impressions.

The emotions, for Hume, form an essential part of ethics. There are good emotions and bad emotions. Pride, he declared, is a good emotion. Humility, its opposite (an unpleasant feeling brought about by the idea that we are inadequate or deeply flawed beings), is a bad emotion, a "monkish" emotion. Here we can see again the extent to which, as so often, a theory of emotion serves to grind some larger philosophical ax—in this case, Hume's Enlightenment attack on religion. In this regard too, we might mention another aspect of Hume's moral philosophy, followed in kind by his illustrious Edinburgh friend and colleague Adam Smith (1723–1790, also the author of *The Wealth of Nations* [1776/1976], the bible of modern capitalism). Hume and Smith both defended the importance of what they called "the moral sentiments" (see Smith, 1759/1976), the foremost of which is sympathy, our ability to "feel with" other people and appreciate (if not suffer with) their misfortunes. Sympathy, they argued, is a universal feature of human nature (countering and mitigating the self-interest that Smith in particular famously championed in *The Wealth of Nations*), and it is the bedrock foundation of society and morality. Emotion, in other words, is not an embarrassment or part of the refuse of the human psyche but rather the very essence of human social existence and morality. It is not to be unfavorably contrasted and opposed to reason, but, on the contrary, is to be celebrated and defended along with it.

Immanuel Kant (1724–1804) was also a champion of the Enlightenment, but though he too questioned the capacities and limits of reason, he was uncompromising in its defense—against Hume's skepticism, against any attempt to replace reason by irrational faith, and against any attempt to ground ethics on fleeting human feeling instead of the universal and necessary dictates of reason. Thus Kant reinforced the crucial distinction between reason and what he called "the inclinations" (emotions, moods, and desires) and dismissed the latter (including the moral sentiments) as inessential to morals at best and intrusive and disruptive at worst. And yet, although Kant felt no need to develop a theory of emotion to accompany his elaborate and brilliant "critiques" of reason, his position on the "inclinations" is more ambiguous than is usually supposed, and his respect for "feeling" more significant. It was Kant, a quarter-century before Hegel (who is credited with it), who insisted that "nothing great is ever done without passion," and it was Kant, in his *Critique of Judgment* (1793/1951, concerned in part with art and aesthetics) who celebrated the importance of shared ("intersubjective") feeling in the appreciation of beauty and the awe with which we try to comprehend the wonder of God's creation. Indeed, even Kant's central notions of respect and human dignity, the very heart of his rationalist ethics, are sometimes suggested to be matters of feeling as well as reason, thus calling into question the harshness of his ruthlessly divided self. When his successor Hegel took over the reins of German philosophy in the early 19th century, the overstated distinction between reason and passion was again called into question, and Hegel's own odyssey of reason (in a epochal book called *The Phenomenology of Spirit* (1807/1977) has rightly been called a "logic of passion" as well.

Friederich Nietzsche (1844–1900) was a philosopher for whom passion was the watchword and reason a source of suspicion. He was the culmination of a long line of "Romantics," beginning with the *Sturm und Drang* poets of the previous century and continuing through the philosophy of Nietzsche's own favorite influence, the neo-Kantian pessimist Arthur Schopenhauer. Nietzsche anticipated the global skepticism and conceptual chaos of the 20th century; like Freud, who admired him, he described (and celebrated) the darker, more instinctual, and less rational motives of the human mind. Accordingly, in his *On the Genealogy of Morals* (1887/1967), he praised the passions and, in an ironic twist, described the passions as themselves having more reason than Reason. But this was not to say that all passions are wise; some, he declares, "drag us down with their stupidity," and others, notably the "slave morality" emotion of resentment, are devious and clever but to a disastrous end—the "leveling" of the virtuous passions and the defense of mediocrity. Nietzsche never developed a "theory" of emotions, but his distinctions were remarkable in their insight and subtlety. His celebration of passion scared the wits out of a great many philosophers in Europe, however, who saw more than enough passion and irrationality in the Great War and then the rise of National Socialism in Germany. Accordingly, the ancient celebration of reason would once more rule philosophy, and emotion was again relegated to the sidelines.

In the 20th century, one can trace the fate of emotion in Western philosophy through two very different tracks. In North America and in England, the emotions were given short *shrift*, in large part because of the newly exaggerated emphasis on logic and science. The great British philosopher Bertrand Russell gave elaborate praise to love and passion in the opening pages of his autobiography (1967), but in his philosophy he said virtually nothing about them. Of course, the nature of emotion was a major concern of William James and the young John Dewey in the early years of the century, but with James's emphasis on the physiological nature of emotion (he argued [1884] that an emotion is a sensation or set of sensations caused by a physiological disturbance, which in turn is prompted by some "perception" or other), coupled with the subsequent and quite unfortunate split between philosophy and psychology as academic disciplines, questions about emotion were relegated to the realm of psychology (where they were also treated with less than the full respect due them). Indeed, the first major attention to emotion in Anglo-American philosophy came in midcentury, when an ethical theory named "emotivism" came to dominate both the English and the North American scene. But emotivism, which was part and parcel of an across-the-board philosophical purgative known as "logical positivism," was essentially a dismissal of ethical (and many other) questions in philosophy as "meaningless" (i.e., unscientific and without verifiable solutions). Emotion came back onto the stage of philosophy but only as the butt of the argument: Ethical statements were viewed as meaningless because they were seen as *nothing but* expressions of emotion.

During the same period in Europe, however, the emotions enjoyed more attention. Franz Brentano (1874–1971) succeeded the British "moral sentiment" theorists in attempting to found an ethics on a foundation of emotions. (Sigmund Freud was one of his students.) Following the "phenomenology" of Edmund Husserl (1838/1960) (another Brentano student and a mathematician who showed little or no interest in emotion), Max Scheler (1916/1970), Martin Heidegger (1927/1962), and more recently, Paul Ricouer (1950/1966) developed ambitious philosophies in which emotions were given a central place in human existence and accorded with considerable respect. Heidegger, in particular, defended what he generally called "moods" as our way of "being tuned" to the world. In the shadow of World War II, Jean-Paul Sartre offered the slim but important *The Emotions: Sketch of a Theory* (1939/1948), followed by his magnificent tome *Being and Nothingness* (1943/1956), which includes embedded within its many pages a number of detailed "phenomenological" analyses of emotion. Sartre's conception of emotions as "magical transformations of the world"— willful strategems for coping with a difficult world—added a new "existential" dimension to the investigation of emotion. But, predictably, philosophy in both France and Germany turned again to other interests, though the study of emotion continued despite the perennial shift in fashions.

In Anglo-American philosophy, however, the fortunes of emotion were also to change. In an article simply entitled "Emotion" (indicating how rarely the topic had even been broached), Errol Bedford (1956/1964) addressed the Aristotelean Society in London on the nature of emotion and the errors of thinking of emotions as "feelings." The essay might have sat on the shelves gathering dust except for the fact that the then dean of Oxford philosophers, J. L. Austin (1956–1957/1964), took it upon himself to remark on one of Bedford's claims. (Austin's own essay was not about emotions at all.) Austin's attention kept the article alive and occasionally anthologized until the 1960s, when the subject seemed to come to life again.

Today, one finds a rich variety of arguments about emotions on both sides of the Atlantic Ocean and the English Channel. Given the nature of philosophy and its current concern with epistemological matters, it is again not surprising that the focus is on the conceptual structures of emotion, rather than the sensory, social, or physiological aspects of emotion. But there has been a reaction even within philosophy to the "hypercognizing" of emotion; consequently, there has been a serious effort to join forces with psychologists, neurologists, anthropologists, and moral philosophers to obtain a more holistic theory of emotion.

SOME PHILOSOPHICAL QUESTIONS ABOUT EMOTION

What is an emotion? Because philosophy is a discipline concerned with the essential nature and the "definition" of things, the basic question facing theories of emotion in philosophy is still the question posed by James and answered, in a fashion by Aristotle. It is, on the face of it, a quest for a definition, a conceptual analysis. But it is also a much larger quest for an orientation: How should we think about emotion—as intrusive, as essential to our rationality, as constitutive of meaning, as dangerous, as dispensable, as an excuse for irresponsibility, or as a mode of responsibility? Which of the evident aspects of emotion—that is, the various sensory, physiological, behavioral, cognitive and social phenomena that typically correspond with an emotion—should we take to be essential? Many philosophers hold onto the old "Cartesian" view that an emotion cannot lack its "subjective" or "introspective" aspect, although what this means (and how accessible or articulate an emotion must be on inspection) is itself a subject of considerable dispute, for instance, in Freud (1915/1935), Sartre (1943/1956), Lyons (1980), and de Sousa (1987). But many philosophers have become skeptical about such subjective essentialism and, like their associates in the social sciences have pushed the analysis of emotion toward more public, observable criteria. Accordingly, philosophers have formulated their own versions of behaviorism, physiologism, and social construction theory, for example, although there has not always been mutual awareness with their counterparts in the social sciences.

The seemingly self-evident Cartesian demand that first-person experience is ineliminable is evident, nevertheless, even in the most radical philosophical behaviorists. For instance, Gilbert Ryle (1951) chastised philosophers for their "myth of the ghost in the machine" and suggested that many emotions are mere "agitations" (much as Descartes had insisted) and dispositions to behave in certain ways. But Ryle did not give up the idea that some of the symptoms of emotion consist of "tingles and itches."

Can one have an emotion without feeling? What is a "feeling"? The virtue of the Jamesian theory is that it ties down the nature of emotional sensation to quite particular and therefore verifiable visceral responses. Unfortunately, the Jamesian theory is wrong, at least in its details. How specifically are emotional feelings tied to physiological processes? To be sure, whatever goes on in the mind must now be supposed to have some correlate and cause in the brain, but can we not and should we not describe the "phenomenology" of those feelings quite apart from their brain correlations and causes? Some theorists have tried to save feeling theory by employing the vague, general (and technical) notion of "affect" and its cognates ("affective tone"). But do such terms do anything more than cover up the problem with another word, whose meaning can only be explained by "the kind of feeling you get when you have emotion X"? It is a heuristic mistake to suppose that such feelings are indescribable

or "ineffable," whether out of excessive romanticism (as if understanding undermines passion) or dismissive scientism (why talk about feelings if we can't experimentally test them?) Most feelings have at least an "as if" recognizability ("It feels as if I'd known him for years" or "It felt as if he had shot me through the heart, it was so sudden and so traumatizing").

Many feelings have a distinctive structure, which (not surprisingly) emerges in the thoughts (and then in the verbal expressions) of the emotions. In general, one must ask how much cognition and learning are presupposed in the feelings that we identify as emotions. One does not need an elaborate Schachter and Singer (1962) scenario to do the *Gedanken* experiment, which shows that certain feelings typical of, say, fear and anger do not actually constitute fear and anger if there are no appropriate beliefs accompanying them. A person may well feel flushed, uncomfortable, and "as if" he or she wanted to flee or start a fight with someone, but if there is no fearful object (more precisely, if the person has no sense of a fearful object) or if there is nothing objectionable, frustrating, or offensive (to the person), then those feelings do not count as fear and anger (or even as "feeling afraid" or "feeling angry"). Whatever else we may say about the place of feeling in emotion, feeling is not sufficient to yield emotion. Of course, this same term "feeling" can be expanded to include all sorts of thoughts, cognitions, and attitudes about the immediate situation, and not only tendencies to behave but even the behavior itself (as subjective experience rather than observable action). But this only shows that the seemingly innocuous notion of "feeling" also needs careful analysis, and the common-sense notion that an emotion is basically a feeling (perhaps a feeling in a certain context or brought about by a certain kind of cause) is accordingly still a prominent focus in philosophy. (For example, see Kraut, 1987; Stocker, 1996.)

Recent advances in neurology disclose structural and functional patterns in the central nervous system that are correlated with, and that under experimental conditions bring about, certain emotional reactions. Do these patterns dictate the structure of an adequate theory of emotion, or are those findings but one more set of (contingent) considerations for inclusion in an all-embracing theory? Whatever the case, it is now clear that philosophers cannot ignore or neglect the rich neurophysiological literature on emotions. Indeed, there is now a interdisciplinary subfield in philosophy called "neurophilosophy," which makes the new neurology central to any adequate analysis of emotion and "the mind" Churchland, 1986). Philosophers may continue to argue that Aristotle knew all about emotions even though he did not know anything about the brain, but they do so at their peril—and in the face of the obvious fact that among the factors that have altered the history of philosophy and its concepts most radically have been new advances in previously unknown or undeveloped sciences.

Virtually all emotions get expressed (however minimally) in behavior. Should behavioral tendencies or sequences of actions or certain basic gestures be taken as essential? A great deal of detailed work in psychology has shown the enormous subtlety and the seemingly "hard-wired" nature of basic patterns of facial expression. Philosophers remain skeptical. (Neu, 1987). The data are not in question, but the implied shift in conception from the emotion to the symptom of emotions is. What is it that causes a twitch or a gesture? The emotion would seem to be the perception, the awareness, the realization that is expressed, not the expression itself. On the other hand, many philosophers of a somewhat behaviorist bent (following Wittgenstein's later *Philosophical Investigations* [1953] and Gilbert Ryle's *The Concept of Mind* [1951]) have suggested that an emotion is nothing but its behavioral expression, though certainly not a single gesture but an open-ended sequence of actions. An emotion is not a "ghostly inner event," according to Ryle, but a "multitrack disposition" to behave in any number of recognizable ways. So too, philosophers have tried to understand emotion not as an inner feeling but as a value-laden description of a social situation. Thus Errol Bedford (1956/1964), in his pioneering article in the1950s, suggested that the difference between shame and embarrassment, for example, is not some shade of difference between internal *qualia* but the difference between descriptions of the situation.

What remains at the core of all such theories, however, is an awareness that all emotions presuppose or have as their preconditions certain sorts of cognitions—an awareness of danger in fear, recognition of an offense in anger, appreciation of someone or something lovable in love. Even the most hard-headed neurological or behavioral theory must take account of the fact that no matter what the neurology or the behavior, if a person is demonstrably ignorant of a certain state of affairs or facts, he or she cannot have certain emotions. If neurologically induced rage does not include some object of anger, that rage (whatever else it may be) cannot be anger. So too, Freud's "free-floating anxiety" would count as an emotion only insofar as it does indeed (as Freud [1915/1935] argued) have an object, albeit "unconscious." Philosophers (following Aristotle and the scholastics of the Middle Ages) have come to call this the "formal object" of emotion, and one might well think of this as the minimum essential set of "beliefs" defining an emotion and an emotional experience. The formal object of fear, to take an obvious case, is a fearful object, together with the beliefs that constitute the awareness of the presence or threat of such an object.

Other emotions are more complicated and, accordingly, are more often topics of debate and disagreement. Anger would seem to require a formal object involving an offense, but some authors would allow frustration alone to count as anger (Gordon, 1987). Jealousy is more difficult still, for its object seems to involve not only a threatened loss but a perpetrator as well (perhaps the threatened object as a perpetrator too), and possibly the larger social situation in which jealousy involves not only loss but humiliation as well (Neu, 1980). But though the exact natures of the formal objects and requisite beliefs of various emotions are matters of lively debate (and there is some doubt and debate over the very possibility of a generalized formal object for all emotions or emotions *sui generis*), the presumption is that every emotion must have a cognitive basis and an object. (There is some corollary debate concerning the status of moods and mood-like emotions [e.g., joy], which do not have a determinate object.)

There is also considerable debate over the nature of cognition itself. Beliefs seem to be established states and therefore lack the spontaneity that characterizes many emotions. Beliefs also seem to be too fully articulate for the unreflective reaction that characterizes most emotions. For that reason, some theorists prefer the concept of "judgment" (e.g., the ancient Stoics), while others prefer the term "thought" (e.g., Spinoza) (see Solomon, 1976; Neu, 1977). Some have simply stuck with the notion of evaluation (Pitcher, 1965) while others have preferred the less cognitively committal notion of a way of seeing ("seeing as")—sometimes as a rejection of the cognitive view, but more appropriately, perhaps, as a refinement of it (Calhoun, 1984). The nature of an emotional cognition, and whether it must be fully conscious or capable of articulation, remain matters of considerable debate. Indeed, if certain holistic suggestions can be worked out, it may be that the very distinctions that philosophers have so long presupposed among cognition, behavior, physiology, and feeling are themselves inadequate and ought to be integrated into a single picture (Damasio, 1994).

One way of putting the point that emotions must have a cognitive component—that they cannot be simply feelings or physiological processes or even "mindless" bits of behavior—is to insist that they have *intentionality*. "Intentionality" is a technical notion, but its common-sense meaning can be captured by the idea that emotions are always "about" something or other; one is always angry about something, one is always in love with someone or something (even if one is also "in love with love"), one is always afraid of something (even if one doesn't know what it is). Thus we can understand the "formal object" of an emotion as its essential intentionality—the kind of object (event, person, state of affairs) to which it must be directed if it is to be that emotion. But intentionality has also been the object of philosophical consternation for over a century now, because despite its appeal as a way of understanding the nature of perception and other mental "acts" (which gets us away from the image of images or representations "in" the mind), intentionality has its own peculiar complications (Kenny, 1963; Searle, 1983). Most troubling for philosophers is the obvious fact that an emotion may be "about" some nonexistent, merely imagined object. The object of fear may be nowhere around. The imagined threat in jealousy may not exist. The person one still loves may be dead. (Indeed, the problem seems to remain whether the lover knows of the death or not. In either case, the emotion is directed at a person who is in no position to receive it.) Moreover, the object of an emotion would seem to be one and the same object, whether it exists or not. (It is one and the same devil that is the object of a child's fear, whether the devil exists or not.) Thus the ontological status of the intentional object of emotion causes considerable commotion. In recent decades, many Anglo-American language-oriented or "analytic" philosophers have reduced the seemingly mysterious notion of intentionality to the supposedly more manageable notion of "intensionality," a precisely defined feature of certain sorts of sentences (Dennett, 1978, 1991). But whether intensionality does in fact capture the necessary features of intentionality is itself a topic of considerable debate and at least seems to confuse the language with which we ascribe emotions with the nature of the emotions themselves (Searle, 1983).

Philosophers have also become concerned with the "why?" of emotions—their function and their explanation. Most of the work here has been done on the explanation of particular instances of emotion, although a few investigators have recently tackled the much larger question of the evolution and function of emotions as such (de Sousa, 1987; Gibbard, 1990). Particular instances of emotion seem to be subject to two different sorts of explanation. On the one hand, because they are intentional and essentially involve beliefs (also desires, needs, attitudes, and values), emotions seem to require an explanation that invokes a person's belief and attitudes toward the world. A person is angry because he believes that so-and-so wronged him, or someone is saddened because she has found out that she has just lost a loved one, and so on. But this cannot be a complete account of emotional explanation. We also explain emotions by citing the fact that a person has been sleepless all week, or is ill, or has been given some medication. In other words, explanation of emotion may cite an underlying cause that may or may not make mention of the object of emotion. The cause may be physiological—for example, an underlying state of irritability, an ingested drug, or a direct surgical stimulation of the brain. The cause may be some state of affairs or incident that "triggered" the person's emotion, but this may not be the object of the person's emotion, nor need he or she have any memory or awareness of it. ("Subliminal" messages presumably work this way.)

How is causal explanation to be reconciled with an explanation in terms of beliefs and attitudes? Many philosophers have tended to emphasize the importance of one form of explanation over the other, or to reduce all explanations to either causal explanations or belief-and-desire, "reason"-type explanations. The latter sort of explanation provides a fuller account of the intentionality of an emotion by describing not only its formal object ("He's angry because he's been offended") but the specific details of the situation, as well as the person's beliefs and various attitudes. The former sort of explanation invokes an underlying cause that may or may not make mention of the object of emotion. Very often, however, the citation of a cause of emotion (its initiating stimulus or "trigger") and the account of the object of the emotion will be nominally the same ("He got mad because she stepped on his toe"). The problem that has been addressed by many philosophers (and has been the subject of several weighty studies) has been the relation between these two and the various problems in understanding them together (Wilson, 1972; Rorty, 1980; Nissenbaum, 1985).

The cognitive basis of emotions also raises another question, one that was often a matter of deep concern for earlier philosophers: the question of the *rationality* of emotions. Many thinkers have written as if the emotions were not only irrational but also nonrational—not even candidates for intelligence. Accounts of emotions as mere feelings or physiological processes would make them no more than nonrational (one cannot have a "stupid" headache, except by way of a roundabout complaint about its inconvenience.) Aristotle, on the other hand, simply assumed that an emotion can be appropriate or inappropriate, foolish or prudent, not just on the basis of whether or not it is acceptable in the circumstance in question (though that social dimension is certainly essential), but on the basis of the perceptions, beliefs, and desires of the individual. The fact that emotions consist at least in part of cognitions means that they can be evaluated in terms of the same epistemic and ethical criteria that we use to evaluate beliefs and intentions: Are they appropriate to the context? Do they consider the facts of the matter? Are their perceptions fair and their evaluations reasonable? Indeed the argument is now prevalent and persuasive that emotions cannot be understood without grasping their reasons, and these reasons in turn give us a basis for evaluation (de Sousa, 1987; Greenspan, 1988). The current debate, however, concerns how these reasons are to be understood, and whether the rationality of emotions can indeed be fairly compared to the evaluation of more fully deliberative, articulate activities.

The rationality of emotions also moves to center stage the question of emotions and ethics that we have been following through the history of philosophy. How does emotion enter into ethical understanding, and how do our ethics affect our emotions? One thing is clear: The commingling of emotions and ethics is not grounds for dismissing either ethics or emotion, as the old emotivists suggested. It is worth noting that a new conception of the emotional foundations of ethics has taken root in the Anglo-American tradition and, an appropriate irony, has taken the name "emotivism" (Gibbard, 1990). Of course, one of the questions that remains, left over from the old rationalist charges that emotions are "merely subjective," is that emotions vary too much from culture to culture to provide a firm basis for ethics; in other words, they are "relative." But though philosophers cannot (and should not try to) answer the empirical question of the universality or relativity of emotions, they can and should clear away the dogmatic assumptions and mistaken conceptions that have often occupied philosophy in the past. There is nothing in the nature of emotion (including the human brain, which changes significantly with experience and varies considerably from person to person) that assures universality, but neither is it so obvious that emotions differ so much from place to place either. (This is indicated not only by studies of facial expression, but by the logic of the "human condition" and its more general features.) This also raises the question of emotions and choice, the supposed passivity of emotions. Sartre (1939/1948, 1943/1956) suggested that the emotions are willful, but many philosophers who do not share Sartre's extreme voluntarism would agree that emotions are indeed ways of coping, whether inherited through natural selection or cultivated in the less articulate practices of a society. But are we at the mercy of our emotions? Do we simply "have" them, or do we perhaps to some extent cultivate them and "do" them ourselves? Obviously, a good deal of ethics and our attitudes toward ourselves depend on this. The study of emotion in philosophy is, accordingly, not a detached and marginal discipline, but the very core of our inquiry into ourselves and our own natures. It was Socrates, the great champion of reason, who took as his mottos the slogan at Delphi ("Know thyself") and the rather extreme injunction that "The unexamined life is not worth living." But part of that knowledge, surely, is our understanding and appreciation of our emotions, which are, after all, much of what makes life worth living.

NOTE

1. This and other quotations from Aristotle in this chapter have been newly translated by Jon Solomon.

REFERENCES AND FURTHER READING

Aristotle. (1941). *The basic works of Aristotle* (R. McKeon, Ed.). New York: Random House. See also W. Fortenbaugh (1975). *Aristotle on emotion.* London: Duckworth.

Austin, J. L. (1964). Pretending. In D. Gustafson (Ed.), *Essays in philosophical psychology.* Garden City, NY: Doubleday/Anchor. (Original work published 1956–1957)

Bedford, E. (1964). Emotion. In D. Gustafson (Ed.), *Essays in philosophical psychology.* Garden City, NY: Doubleday/Anchor. (Original work published 1956)

Brentano, F. (1971). *Psychology from the empirical standpoint.* London: Routledge. (Original work published 1874)

Calhoun, C. (1984). Cognitive emotions? In C. Calhoun & R. C. Solomon (Eds.), *What is an emotion?* New York: Oxford University Press.

Churchland, P. S. (1986). *Neurophilosophy.* Cambridge, MA: MIT Press.

Damasio, A. (1994). *Descartes' error.* New York: Putnam.

Dennett, D. (1978). *Brainstorms.* Cambridge, MA: MIT Press.

Dennett, D. (1991). *Consciousness explained.* Boston: Little, Brown.

Descartes, R. (1989). *On the passions of the soul.* (S. Voss, Trans.). Indianapolis, IN: Hackett, (Original work published 1649)

de Sousa, R. (1989). *The rationality of emotion.* Cambridge: MIT Press.

Freud, S. (1935). The unconscious (C. M. Baines, Trans.). In *Essays in Metapsychology.* London: Liveright. (Original work published 1915)

Gibbard, A. (1990). *Wise choices, apt feelings: A theory of normative judgment.* Cambridge, MA: Harvard University Press.

Gordon, R. M. (1987). *The structure of emotion.* Cambridge, England: Cambridge University Press.

Greenspan, P. (1988). *Emotions and reasons.* New York: Routledge.

Griffiths, P. (1998). *What emotions really are.* Chicago: University of Chicago Press.

Hamlyn, D. W. (1978). The phenomenon of love and hate. *Philosophy, 53.* Includes a discussion of Brentano's theory.

Hegel, G. W. F. (1977). *The phenomenology of spirit.* (A. N. Miller, Trans.). Oxford, England: Oxford University Press. (Original work published 1807)

Heidegger, M. (1962). *Being and time.* New York: Harper & Row. (Original work published 1927) See also the following explications of Heidegger: C. Guignon (1984). Moods in Heidegger's *Being and time.* H.

Dreyfus, (1991). *Being-in-the-world: A commentary on Heidegger's Being and Time.*

Hume, D. (1888). *A treatise of human nature* (L. A. Selby-Bigge, Ed.). Oxford, England: Oxford University Press. (Original work published 1739) See also A. Baier (1991). *A progress of sentiments: Reflections on Hume's treatise.* Cambridge, MA: Harvard University Press. And see also D. Davidson (1976). Hume's cognitive theory of pride. *Journal of Philosophy, 73,* 733–757.

Husserl, E. (1960). *Cartesian meditations* (D. Cairns, Trans.). The Hague: Nijhoff. (Original work published 1938)

Hyman, A., & Walsh, J. (1973). *Philosophy in the Middle Ages.* Indianapolis, IN: Hackett.

James, W. (1884). What is an emotion? *Mind, 9,* 188–205.

Kant, I. (1953). *Critique of judgment* (J. H. Bernard, Trans.). New York: Hafner. (Original work published 1793)

Kenny, A. (1963). *Action, emotion and will.* London: Routledge & Kegan Paul.

Kraut, R. (1986). Feelings in context. *Journal of Philosophy, 83.* See R. C. Solomon (1990). Emotions, feelings and contexts: A reply to Robert Kraut. *Dialogue, 29,* 277–284.

Lyons, D. (1980). *Emotion.* Cambridge, England: Cambridge University Press. An excellent attempt to bring together philosophical and psychological views of emotion.

Neu, J. (1977). *Emotion, thought and therapy.* Berkeley: University of California Press.

Neu, J. (1980). Jealous thoughts. In A. Rorty (Ed.), *Explaining emotions.* Berkeley: University of California Press.

Neu, J. (1987). A tear is an intellectual thing. *Representations, 19,* 35–61.

Nietzsche, F. (1967). *On the genealogy of morals* (W. Kaufmann, Trans.). New York: Random House. (Original work published 1887)

Nissenbaum, H. (1985). *Emotions and focus.* Stanford, CA: CSLI.

Nussbaum, M. (1994). *The therapy of desire.* Princeton, NJ: Princeton University Press. A sympathetic and detailed discussion of the Stoics on the place of emotion in life.

Pitcher, G. (1965). Emotion. *Mind, 74.*

Plato. (1974). *The Republic* (E. M. A. Grube, Trans.). Indianapolis, IN: Hackett.

Plato. (1989). *The symposium* (A. Nehamas & P. Woodruff, Trans.). Indianapolis, IN: Hackett.

Ricouer, P. (1966). *The voluntary and the involuntary* (E. Kohak, Trans.). Evanston IL: Northwestern University Press. (Original work published 1950)

Rist, J. M. (1969). *Stoic philosophy.* Cambridge, England: Cambridge University Press.

Rorty, A. (1980). Explaining emotions. In A. Rorty, (Ed.), *Explaining emotions.* Berkeley: University of California Press.

Russell, B. (1967). *The autobiography of Bertrand Russell* (Vol. 1). Boston: Little, Brown.

Ryle, G. (1951). *The concept of mind.* New York: Barnes & Noble.

Sartre, J.-P. (1948). *The emotions: Sketch of a theory*

(B. Frechtman, Trans.). New York: Philosophical Library. (Original work published 1939) See the commentary in R. C. Solomon (1988). *From Hegel to existentialism.* Oxford: Oxford University Press.

Sartre, J.-P. (1956). *Being and nothingness* (H. Barnes, Trans.). New York: Washington Square Press. (Original work published 1943) See also J. Fell (1965). *Sartre's theory of the passions.* New York: Columbia University Press.

Schachter, S., & Singer, J. (1962). Cognitive, social and physiological determinants of emotional state. *Psychological Review, 69*(5), 379–399. For a good philosophical rejoinder, see R. M. Gordon (above), Chapter 5.

Scheler, M. (1970). *The nature of sympathy.* New York: Archon. (Original work published 1916)

Searle, J. (1983). *Intentionality: An essay in the philosophy of mind.* Cambridge, England: Cambridge University Press.

Seneca. (1963). *De ira.* Oxford, England: Loeb Classical Library, Oxford University Press.

Smith, A. (1976). *Theory of the moral sentiments.* Oxford, England: Oxford University Press. (Original work published 1759)

Smith, A. (1976). *An inquiry into the nature and causes of the wealth of nations.* Indianapolis, IN: Liberty Classics. (Original work published 1776) For a good study of the relation between Smith's ethics and his economic theory, see P. Werhane (1991). *Ethics and economics: The legacy of Adam Smith for contemporary capitalism.* Oxford, England: Oxford University Press.

Solomon, R. C. (1976). *The passions.* Notre Dame, IN: University of Notre Dame Press. See also R. C. Solomon (1988). *About love.* New York: Simon & Schuster; R. C. Solomon & K. Higgins (Eds.). (1991). *The philosophy of (erotic) love.* Lawrence: University of Kansas Press.

Spinoza, B. (1982). *Ethics.* (S. Shirley, Trans.). Indianapolis, IN: Hackett. (Original work published 1677) See also A. Rorty (1991). Spinoza on the pathos of love. In R. C. Solomon & K. Higgins (Eds.), *The philosophy of (erotic) love.* Lawrence: University of Kansas Press.

Stocker, M. (1996). *Valuing emotions.* Cambridge, England: Cambridge University Press. A particularly rich and varied discussion of the various connections between emotions and ethics.

Thalberg, I. (1977). *Perception, emotion and action.* New Haven, CT: Yale University Press.

Williams, B. (1973). Morality and the emotions. In *Problems of the self.* Cambridge, England: Cambridge University Press.

Wilson, J. R. S. (1972). *Emotion and object.* Cambridge, England: Cambridge University Press. Perhaps the best and most extended discussion of the "intentionality" of emotion.

Wittgenstein, L. (1953). *Philosophical investigations.* London: Routledge & Kegan Paul.

CHAPTER 2

History of Emotions:
Issues of Change and Impact

Peter N. Stearns

Historical work on emotions, though relatively new as an explicit subfield, is expanding rapidly. Historians' additions to the facets of emotions research and to connections with other topics and approaches gain ground steadily. The challenge for additional work remains great, but solid results can already be tallied.

The principal focus of historical research on emotions is straightforward: The history of emotions deals with processes of change in emotional standards and emotional experience, or, somewhat more complexly, with emotional continuities amid changing contexts. Historians may also be interested in a third focus—seeking to grasp the characteristic emotional styles of a particular period, in and of themselves, as a means of enriching the portrayal of that past time and launching the process of comparing one previous period to another. Ultimately, however, the analytical goals center on change, either in emotions themselves or in the environments in which they operate. Here, correspondingly, is the central justification for adding history to the list of disciplines seriously engaged in emotions research. For if emotions change in significant ways—and historians and others have conclusively demonstrated that they do—then the process must be grappled with as part of evaluating emotional expressions even in the present time. Adding change to the variables involved in emotions research means adding complexity, but it is empirically inescapable

and provides an essential perspective for assessing the results of other social science research on emotion, such as those emanating from sociology and anthropology.

Examining change involves establishing baselines, so that new trends can be carefully evaluated against real, rather than assumed or imagined, past standards—a task historians at their best handle quite well. It involves assessing the causes of change and also its results, in personal emotional lives but also in larger institutions such as law or education.

THE DEVELOPMENT
OF EMOTIONS HISTORY

Explicit historical research is still a relative newcomer. Theorists from other social science disciplines provided frameworks for historical assessment long ignored by most historians themselves. Thus Norbert Elias's (1938/1982) classic work on how new levels of "civilization" began to constrain spontaneous emotional expressions, beginning with the Western European aristocracy by the 18th century, focused attention on a key turning point now being widely explored. Until recently Elias's research was more widely utilized by European sociologists dealing with emotion than by any other group. More generally, the constructivist theory of emotion, generated by several social psychologists as well as sociologists, argues that emotions should be interpreted primarily in terms of the social functions they serve; constructivists also correctly note that as social functions frequently change, emotions will shift substantially as well (Averill, 1980, 1982). Some emotions may disappear as part of this process, and others may newly emerge. Here is a richly suggestive historical framework—only rarely, however, fleshed out by detailed historical research, and largely ignored by professional historians. The constructivist view, including the common attention to cultural context as a functional area or as an intermediary between function and emotion, independently affecting ideas about emotional experiences and the vocabularies used to phrase them (Gordon, 1989), in fact tallies closely with recent historical work.

Historians themselves moved into research on emotion hesitantly. The great French social historian Lucien Febvre called almost 70 years ago for a "historical psychology" that would "give up psychological anachronism" and "establish a detailed inventory of the mental equipment of the time" (Febvre, 1933/1973). His appeal was not quickly heeded. A number of cultural historians dealt with past styles and rituals that had strong emotional components. Johann Huizinga's (1927) masterful portrayal of the late Middle Ages contained a wealth of data relevant to emotions history, and even more limited studies of popular protest or religious life offered important emotional insight into the past periods involved (Stearns with Stearns, 1985). Explicit focus on emotion, however, was lacking. Most historians continued to emphasize the conscious actions and rational decisions of their subjects—particularly, of course, when they dealt with political and diplomatic history, with an eye toward formal policy decisions. Even the advent of social history in the United States, bent on detailing the activities and interests of groups of ordinary people, did not quickly break this mold. Indeed, it could confirm it, as social historians were bent on rescuing ordinary people from accusations of mob impulsiveness and so stressed their transcendent rationality (e.g., in protest situations). Ordinary people may have mental worlds different from those of elites, according to the pioneer social historians, but they are no less careful in choosing methods appropriate to their goals. Emotion, in this formulation, was not a significant variable.

The advent of psychohistory in the 1960s brought attention to the role of emotions in the past, but on a very limited scale. Most psychohistorians, from the great Erik Erikson (1958) to more recent practitioners, have concentrated on biography and have utilized a largely Freudian theoretical framework. They have linked emotional characteristics to historical developments—thus Erikson translates Luther's tense relationship with his harsh father into Lutheranism's preoccupation with an angry and omnipotent God—but they have not dealt with emotional change, and they have tended to enmesh emotional factors in a rigid and unchanging psychodynamic. Furthermore, while psychohistorians continue to generate interesting work, their approach has never won wide acceptance within the historical discipline, and (because of pervasive Freudianism) has had a limited reception in other fields as well. Overall, the difficulties of dealing with change and the characteristic inability to go beyond individual case studies have constrained the impact of self-styled psychohistory in emotions research.

It remains true, however, that prior to the development of explicit historical work on emotion, several theories pointed to promising lines of inquiry, and several sociological schools were sketching possible patterns of change over time; a good bit of general cultural history suggested topics in the emotions area and provided a wealth of relevant detail; and psychohistory highlighted the significance of certain kinds of emotional dynamics in the past while again contributing significant evidence. It was psychohistory, for example, that inspired the pioneering study of David Hunt (1970) on parent–child relations in 17th-century France, in turn one of the first direct studies of emotional socialization in the past. It was hardly surprising that as emotions research revived in many disciplines by the late 1970s, historians began to contribute significantly to the agenda.

The direct antecedents of historical research on emotion, however, awaited a final ingredient, provided by the 1970s through the maturation of social history as the leading branch of historical research (a development anticipated, however, in France, as the insight by Lucien Febvre demonstrated). By the 1970s historians throughout the United States and Western Europe increasingly focused not only on the activities and value systems of ordinary people, but also on institutions and behaviors in addition to formal politics, as the central stuff of the past. New topics meant new materials, and also promoted the analysis of change as the dominant mode of historical presentation, displacing the mere narration of political and military events.

From social history, in turn, the issues emerged that led a number of historians to consider emotional patterns as central to their task and that produced increasing confluence with other disciplines dealing with the social contexts of emotional life. Social historians inevitably developed a strong interest in family history. Initially they focused on "objective" features of family organization—size, household composition, marriage age, and the like—where indeed important changes could be traced. Quickly, however, concern about the emotional quality of family relationships began to shape research agendas. Discussion of affective parental ties with children followed, for example, from analysis of the impact of changes in family size. A general linkage emerged between reductions in birth rate and greater affectionate intensity between parents and individual children, although which came first was (and is) not always easy to discern. Other aspects of household composition related to emotional factors. When the property power of older family members began to decline, in a more commercial economy in which independent jobs for younger adults became more abundant, affective links between young adults and older parents might well improve. Finally, efforts to explain changes in marriage patterns—in rates of marriage, ages at marriage, and age ratios between partners—generated attention to the emotional implications of courtship behaviors and subsequent spousal relationships. (For a solid survey of the family history field, see Mintz & Kellogg, 1989.) The social history of emotion—the effort to trace emotional norms in groups of relatively ordinary people and their impact on key institutions of daily life—was born above all from the progressive extension of family history.

By the late 1970s various studies were directly confronting the emotional aspects of family history. Historians working on France, Britain, Germany, and colonial North America uncovered a pronounced increase in familial affection in the late 17th and 18th centuries, contrasting with the more restrained emotional tone seemingly characteristic of families in earlier centuries. John Demos (1970), a historian dealing with colonial New England, noted an effort in 17th-century Plymouth to keep families free from the angry bickering more readily tolerated among neighbors; this effort to control anger was accompanied by the encouragement of conjugal love. European families may have tolerated outbursts of anger as part of appropriate family hierarchy for a slightly longer time—it is possible that in the unsettled conditions of the colonies, preservation of family harmony proved particularly important in North America—but a similar evolution set in throughout much of Western Europe by the 18th century (Stone, 1977; Flandrin, 1979; Trumbach, 1978; Shorter, 1975). Child-rearing methods that had focused on breaking children's wills, reflecting parental anger at animal-like offspring and generating intense if necessarily repressed anger in turn, yielded to greater reliance on affectionate persuasion, though the change was gradual and uneven. Mothers began to be defined as central ingredients of the network of familial affection. Romantic love began to influence courtship and marital expectations; the absence of love even served, by the 18th century, as a valid reason for the dissolution of engagements. On the eve of its decline as an economic unit, the family began taking on important new emotional functions and began to generate new expectations (Leites, 1986). Although the rise of various kinds of love headed the innovation list (Stone, 1977), other emotions entered in. Here was the context in which 18th-century family manuals began to urge repression of anger within the family, particularly enjoining men to treat their wives, children, and servants with appropriate decorum. Anger and love did not mix, and love was now becoming more important than anger-implemented maintenance of traditional hierarchies within the household.

While the expansion of family history began to introduce emotional change as an explicit historical topic—indeed, a central issue in dealing with the rise of new kinds of family relationships in the 17th and 18th centuries—another kind of social history promoted attention to other emotional issues. Here French historians led the way, in contrast to Anglo-Saxon dominance in the pioneering family history studies. A field of "mentalities" research emerged, focusing on deeply held popular beliefs about self, environment, and society, which were expressed more frequently in ritual behavior than in formal declarations of principle. Historians of mentalities probed what ordinary people really meant by their religious observances, often discovering that beneath a Christian veneer a variety of magical ingredients still held sway. Emotional beliefs, or emotional components of other beliefs, increasingly engaged this field of inquiry. Robert Muchembled (1985) and Jean Delumeau (1978, 1989) emphasized the high level of fear characteristic of French peasants from the Middle Ages to the 18th century, expressed in a variety of religious and magical practices and in festival rituals. Anxiety about death, about crop failure, and about violence generated intense community practices that might relieve fears of the outside world. Delumeau, in particular, painted a picture of popular religion dominated by the need to control constantly overspilling fear. Delumeau also argued, however, that as with family emotion, the 18th century saw a pronounced change in popular emotional life: Growing confidence about measures that could control the natural and social environment reduced the need for fear-managing rituals, leading to a shift in religious emphasis and a redefinition of fear that (in a process Delumeau did not himself trace) would lead ultimately to the 20th-century formulation of fear as an interior emotion focused on inward demons.

Mentalities historians also dealt with relationships between elite and popular belief systems. Here too they emphasized a significant change opening up in the early modern period, particularly again in the 17th and 18th centuries. Elite Europeans, increasingly influenced by Renaissance culture, began to look askance at a popular leisure tradition in which they had once willingly shared. A key focus of their dismay was emotional spontaneity—those occasions where emotion generated physical actions, such as crowd frenzy, ribald dances, or dangerously exuberant sports, that now seemed both vulgar and disorderly. Correspondingly, the elite launched a variety of disciplinary and legal measures designed to curb spontaneity, and won some success in denting the traditional festival culture of European peasants and artisans (Burke, 1978; Mitzman, 1987). A historian dealing with colonial Virginia has subsequently traced a somewhat similar process of elite–mass divergence over emotional spontaneity, taking shape in the later 18th century in parts of North America (Isaac, 1982).

In various ways, in sum, analysis of emotional change and its impact had become inescapable by the late 1970s. Without launching a specific subfield concentrating on the history of emotions, social historians of several types were vigorously engaged in dealing with several facets of emotional change, with familial emotions, fear, and spontaneity heading the list. Several topical inquiries, initially directed toward other issues, pointed conclusively both to the existence of substantial emotional change in the past and to the importance of this change in grasping key passages in social history. Attention centered particularly on the early modern period, with demonstrations that in several different ways Europeans and North Americans were changing their emotional rules or seeing these rules changed during the 17th and 18th centuries. The link between these findings and Elias's earlier theory about increasing civilized restraint was not immediately drawn, but it soon added a theoretical ingredient to the emerging picture.

A MATURING FIELD

The history of emotions emerged as an explicit and increasingly polished research area during the 1980s. Earlier findings continued to vivify the field, but a number of features were added or redrawn. In the first place, growing numbers of social historians began dealing with the history of emotions in and of itself, rather than as an adjunct to family or mentalities study. Changes in a particular emotion, and the relationship between these changes and other aspects of a historical period, began to constitute respectable (if still clearly innovative) historical topics. Social historians have also expanded the list of emotions that can be subjected to historical scrutiny. Along with love and fear, anger, envy, jealousy, shame, guilt, grief, disgust, and sadness have received significant historical attention, and interest in augmenting the range of emotions considered as part of research on historical change continues strong.

The contexts in which emotional change can be explored have also been elaborated. Predominant attention, particularly in Anglo-American research, continues to go to family settings and related emotional socialization, but studies of emotional change have now dealt with workplace relations, religion, leisure and its emotional symbolism, and legal standards and uses of the law to reflect new emotional norms.

The maturation of emotions history has also involved growing recognition of a need to modify some of the impulses toward reifying stark contrasts that characterized much of the initial work. Premodern families, for example, are no longer seen as emotionally cold. Affection for children is not a modern invention, nor—despite the fascinating argument of a feminist French historian (Badinter, 1980)—is mother love. Recognition of some biological constants in emotional expressions, and simply more extensive data probes, have modified the earlier picture of sharp premodern–modern emotional dichotomies. Better use of theory has come into play. Historians using Jerome Kagan's (1979) findings on child rearing can understand that evidence of severe physical discipline in the past, once taken as a sign of emotional distancing, is in fact compatible with real affection. Change has continued to organize historical research on emotion, but change is now seen as more subtle than was previously the case.

The process of reassessing initial overstatements generated some interesting byways. Some revisionists began to argue that certain emotional relationships do not change; Linda Pollock (1983), most notably, tried to demonstrate that European parents manifested consistent love for their children from the 16th century onward, though in fact her evidence clustered around 1700. In another important variant, Philip Greven (1977; see also the later extension of the argument, Greven, 1991) posited three basic emotional socialization styles in colonial North America, which have since persisted; change was involved in establishing the initial variety, but thenceforward continuity has prevailed. Angry parents in the 1990s have been trapped in the same culture that generated their predecessors in 1750. These approaches have not captured dominant historical attention, however, which continues to emphasize change, but in more complex guise.

Love offers a clear illustration of the current approach. Historians now realize that their initial effort to contrast economically arranged marriages with modern romance was overly simple. Economics remains a factor in modern love, and love entered into premodern courtship. The nature and experience of love were different, however. Love in 17th-century Western Europe was less intense, less individually focused, and less physically controlled than would become the norm in the 18th and 19th centuries. The system of arranged marriage led to groups of young men and young women stimulating each other emotionally, for an indi-

vidual could not be singled out prior to final arrangement. The 18th-century decline of arranged marriages cut into the group-oriented experience of premarital excitement; this shift soon led to an unprecedented association of love with privacy and with one-on-one intensity. Finally, expressions of love pulled away from a traditional range of vigorous bodily manifestations. Suitors in Wales stopped urinating on their fiancées' robes as a sign of affection; kissing became gentler, biting far less common. The relationship of love and the body, in other words, changed substantially (Gillis, 1985; Leites, 1986; Stearns & Stearns, 1988). This means that a new definition of love—a modern kind of romantic love—did indeed emerge in the late 17th and 18th centuries. The significance of the change is, if anything, enhanced by its fuller definition, even if the complexity increases as well. Similar modifications of initial generalizations about grief (e.g., over infant death) and parent–child affection have generated more subtle, but also richer, definitions of what emotional change entails (Lofland, 1985; Rosenblatt, 1983).

A crucial part of this increased sophistication has resulted from historians' growing recognition of distinctions between emotional standards—the "feeling rules" or emotionology that describes socially prescribed emotional values, and often the criteria individuals themselves use to evaluate their emotional experience—and emotional experience itself. Both topics are important, but they are not the same. The rise of official approval of love in courtship and marriage is genuinely significant—it began to influence legal reactions to marital distress, for example (Griswold, 1986)—but it is not the same thing as a rise of experienced love. The actual experience may have changed less, or at least differently, than the new standards imply. Historians of emotion still try to deal with both aspects of their subject, but in distinguishing between culture and experience they greatly improve their precision.

Finally, maturation of emotions history has involved increasing interaction between historians and other scholars working on the social context of emotion. The revival of attention to emotions research in sociology brought new interest in the issue of emotional change from this camp, inspired to an extent by demonstrated historical work on emotional reformulations over time but augmenting this work as well. North American sociologists and social psychologists dealt with a number of changes and patterns in emotional standards in the 20th century, using many of the same materials historians themselves relied upon (Cancian, 1987; Shields & Koster, 1989; Cancian & Gordon, 1988). European sociologists, particularly in the Netherlands, took a somewhat longer view. Relying heavily on the Elias (1938/1982) framework, they dealt with new forms of emotional control in earlier centuries and particularly tried to place 20th-century patterns of emotional management, including a new informality, in the context of earlier shifts (de Swaan, 1981; Wouters, 1991). Systematic interaction between emotions historians and psychologists remains limited, but the rise of a minority school, deeply committed to exploring the cultural construction of mental states, provides one vigorous connection. Interdisciplinary concern for the relationship between language and emotion, including linguistic change, is another connection that involves psychology, though also cultural studies and other social sciences (Harré & Stearns, 1995; Gergen, 1998). Finally, although most anthropologists dealing with emotions continued to focus on durable cultural traditions several major studies, such as Robert Levy's (1973) work on Tahiti, dealt with alterations in emotional expression under the impact of such changes as missionary contact. Historians, for their part, became more aware of relevant work in other fields and more explicitly interested in theories of emotional expression, ranging from Elias's statement (easily assimilable to historical concerns) to Sylvan Tomkins's work (1962–1963); and Peter Gay (1984–1986), essaying an extensive historical survey of the sexual and emotional life of the Victorian bourgeoisie on both sides of the Atlantic, continued to plump for a Freudian approach (applied, however, to group experience).

THE FINDINGS

Growing interest in the history of emotions has generated research in a variety of historical areas, and a handful of classical historians have begun to take up the cause. Several medievalists have contributed explicitly. A substantial literature exists on the rise and subsequent impact of chivalric love (Lantz, 1982). A recent study contrasts this Western impulse with the Orthodox Christian tradition in Eastern Europe, which left less opening for love (Levin, 1989). Other emotions are beginning to receive attention for this period, as the rich vein of research on medieval culture extends to further uses (Morrison, 1988). A 1997 presidential address to the American Historical Association, by a leading medievalist, specifically invoked the importance of changes in emotional forms between medieval and early modern Europe (Bynum, 1997). The literature on emotions history has also been extended actively to scholarship on China. In 1989 Mark Elvin called for "the history of ideas and emotions," and has advanced his work on this subject in recent publications offering sketches of the emotions in modern China (Elvin, 1989, 1991). A history of Maoism notes the Chairman's need to appeal for emotional reconfiguration on the part of peasants, toward releasing the anger necessary to fuel the revolution he sought (Solomon, 1971). Forthcoming research on grief and mourning practices in the Middle East promises to provide findings relevant to the history of emotions in this society as well. Although existing examples remain limited, one can expect growing understanding of various facets of emotions history in cultures outside the West, and for periods prior to the last five centuries.

The richest literature on emotions history continues to apply, however, to modern Western history—defined as beginning about 1500 and extending to the present, and as applying to Western Europe and North America. Within this range, three periods command primary attention and generate the most extensive findings, in a pattern that also demonstrates the sporadic bursts rather than the steady development of significant emotional change.

Historical research continues to embellish the picture of a fundamental transformation in emotional standards during the early modern centuries, and particularly the 17th and 18th centuries. Imaginative research on the German peasantry has even discerned some symptoms of emotional change, toward fuller identification of an emotional self, in the century after 1500 (Sabean, 1984). In addition to refinements in the understanding of changes in parental and marital love, and to the ongoing work on fear and spontaneity, historians have made a number of other changes to the early modern transformation model. John Demos (1988), treating New England in the colonial and early national periods, traces a shift from pervasive use of shame in dealing with children and miscreant adults to guilt, from the 18th to the early 19th century. As community cohesion declined, parents had to find new ways to internalize behavioral guidelines; they were able to use newly intense love as the basis for instilling a greatly heightened level of guilt. A comparable shift, toward guilt rather than public shaming, describes innovations in the principles of social discipline and criminal justice in the same period. Carol Stearns (1988), dealing with the 17th and 18th centuries, emphasizes a decline in the acceptability of sadness or melancholia, traditionally acknowledged as an appropriate badge of human baseness and an indirect expression of anger. In England and colonial North America, a growing number of diarists after 1700 began to be able to describe emotions in new detail, to assume that they could be managed as part of developing an individual personality, and to argue that an individual owed those around him or her a normally cheerful demeanor. On yet another front, Alain Corbin (1986) describes a vast transformation in the emotion of disgust, as Frenchmen from the 18th century onward began to manifest intense disgust at a new range of objects and to use the emotion to motivate a variety of new sanitary and cosmetic behaviors and to justify new social distinctions between the washed and the unwashed. Here emotional change is directly linked to altered experience of the senses. This kind of emotions research, linked to the mentalities approach, is expanding into historical inquiries about changes in gestures and humor (Bremmer & Roodenburg, 1997).

The notion of a substantial redefinition of emotional range, with new meanings and new values placed on a variety of emotions, thus continues to define a growing amount of work on the 17th and 18th centuries. Some of this work amplifies Norbert Elias's insight about a new level of civilization in manners (see also Kasson, 1990), but other findings (e.g., those on guilt and cheerfulness) strike out in newer directions, building on previous research on family emotions and on emotional selfhood.

Research on 19th-century emotions history has become increasingly active, but it lacks the focus of the early modern framework. To some extent, the very notion of a great transformation in the 17th and 18th centuries overshadows findings on the 19th century, as many developments served to amplify and disseminate to new social groups the basic trajectories established earlier. Yet amplification can carry important new messages. North American studies on the apotheosis of mother love go well beyond 18th-century findings concerning new expectations for parental affection (Lewis, 1989), and the standards applied to children, in terms of anticipated emotional reward, escalated as well (Zelizer, 1985). Several important studies on the 19th-century version of romantic love similarly point to novel and distinctive features (Stearns, 1989; Lystra, 1989). Love became a virtually religious ideal, involving self-abnegation and worshipful devotion to the other; 18th-century standards had not sought so much. Jealousy was redefined in this process, as a largely female emotion and a contradiction of proper selflessness in love; older ideas of jealousy in defense of honor fell by the wayside. Grief gained new attention and vast new symbolic expression in Victorian funeral practices (Houlbrooke, 1989). Anger received more explicit condemnation, particularly in the family setting. Gender distinctions urged total suppression of anger on women, but an ability to channel anger toward competition and righteous indignation on men (Stearns & Stearns, 1986).

Victorian emotional patterns thus provided no overall new direction, but they did adjust prior trends to the new sanctity of the family in an industrial world; to new social class divisions; and to the new need to define emotional distinctions between boys and girls, men and women. Whereas love was seen as uniting men and women in common emotional goals, negative emotions became highly gender-linked; in addition to jealousy and anger, the conquest of fear was redefined to serve purposes of gender identity (Stearns & Haggerty, 1991). Although most current attention is riveted on the new standards urged in 19th-century Western society and within the middle class, spelled out in a surge of new kinds of prescriptive literature, various evidence suggests considerable behavioral impact. Men and women did have, with some frequency, the kind of love experiences now recommended; they did work toward appropriate training of children concerning anger and fear. Still not entirely defined, the 19th century stands as a rich source of materials on emotional history and as the scene of a number of significant modifications in norms and experience.

The 20th century, finally, has received sharper definition from the historical perspective. Several emotions historians, to be sure, trace a variety of oscillations in 20th-century standards without an overarching theme. Some analysis concentrates on the need to refute facile modernization ideas that urge—against virtually all available findings—that the 20th century should be seen simply in terms of increasing openness of emotional expression, as older repressions have gradually fallen away. Significant work also stresses continuities from the 19th century, particularly in the gender-linked quality of certain emotional standards; women, for example, continue to be held to a particularly self-sacrificing image of love, even as male standards may have changed (Cancian, 1987). A few historians plump for continuity pure and simple, from the 19th or even the 18th century (Kasson, 1990; Flandrin, 1979).

Two related approaches focus a number of the most important current findings about the 20th century. The first, emanating particularly from several Dutch sociologists, grapples with the problem of growing emotional informality and apparent liberalization, in a context that continues to insist on a great deal of self-control. Spontaneity has revived, but within strict (if unacknowledged) limits. The general argument is that most Westerners have learned so well the lessons of restraint of violence and of unwanted sexuality that they can be allowed (indeed, must be allowed) a good bit of informal emotional idiosyncrasy as part of personal style. Rules of emotional expression have become more complex, and judgments are made about appropriate emotional personalities on the basis of a variety of individual interactions rather than rigid and hierarchical codes (de Swaan, 1981; Wouters, 1991; Gerhards, 1989). Increasing democratization is also part of this shift, as emotional standards used in the 19th century to separate respectable and unrespectable classes are now more widely enjoined (Wouters, 1995).

The second approach similarly urges that the 20th century constitutes a period of considerable, and reasonably coherent, change in emotional standards. It focuses on implicit attacks on 19th-century emotional formulas, becoming visible by the 1920s and extending over a transition period of several decades (Stearns, 1994). Hostility to negative emotions has increased. Gender linkages, though by no means absent, have been muted in favor of more uniform standards of emotional control. The importance of managing emotions through talking out rather than active expression has become a dominant theme, as emotional intensity becomes suspect. Relatedly, reference to embarrassment in front of others has come to supplement guilt and shame as enforcement for emotional normality (Stearns & Stearns, 1986; Stearns, 1989). Amid a host of specific changes, including new emphasis on avoiding rather than mastering fear as part of building character, the dominant theme is a new aversion to undue emotional intensity (Shields & Koster, 1989; Stearns & Haggerty, 1991). The decline of the acceptability of open grief is a key index to the new emotional regime. Even good emotions have dangers; earlier icons of intense emotion, such as the idealized Victorian mother as well as lavish grief, have come in for substantial criticism.

Recent work on 20th-century change enhances what is now a well-established focus. Tensions between the overall discouragement of emotional intensity and a new emphasis on husband–wife intimacy are being explored. In this context, Arlie Hochschild (1997) has recently noted how work sometimes provides an easier emotional climate than home life. Also vital is the relationship between increasingly overt sexuality and emotional formulations; sexual prowess may compete with emotional links. Growing approval of envy has adjusted 19th-century standards to the needs of a consumer economy (White, 1993; Shumway, 1998; Seidman, 1991; Matt, 1998; Hochschild, 1997).

PROBLEMS AND RESPONSES

None of the three chronological focal points of historical research on emotion is entirely worked out. Gaps, disagreements, and issues of synthesis persist. One of the obvious current challenges involves pulling together diverse findings on emotional transformation, even for the early modern period, toward a fuller understanding of relationships among different facets of change. Historians also grapple with indications of late-20th-century change, where their perspective needs to be combined with data emanating from the social and behavioral sciences: How fast, and how fundamentally, are emotional formulations changing now in a society such as the United States? The lack of substantial research on non-Western emotions history limits theoretical potential and comparative inquiry. Comparative work is lamentably lacking even for modern Western societies. European sociologists use trans-Atlantic data but they assume commonalities, at least in recent trends (Melucci, 1989); no explicit comparative effort of any magnitude has yet been attempted. Yet current studies—for example, on jealousy—reveal substantially different national reactions that beg for exploration and explanation through history (Salovey, 1991).

Tentative linkages between historical and social science approaches to the topic have yet to be fleshed out; despite their timely rejections of simplistic modernization schemes, American sociologists, for example, continue to emphasize purely 20th-century patterns, sometimes implying an undifferentiated traditionalism before 1900. Emotions history constitutes a relatively new field still, and though it offers important findings concerning three major time periods, there are limits to the established wisdom available.

Contacts with psychology are theoretically crucial, but not in fact well developed aside from the maverick "discursive" or constructionist school. In principle, case studies could be developed that examine cultural context and change along with more durable emotional expressions and functions (comparative work could be revealing here), to determine more precisely where the boundary lines are and to improve the statement of what changes in emotions and emotional standards involve. But the dominant cultures and funding sources of history and its disciplinary allies (such as anthropology and much sociology) on the one hand, and psychology on the other, so far inhibit the desirable interactions. What should be a knowledge frontier awaits its first settlers.

Furthermore, some obvious problems are endemic to the history field itself. Finding data appropriate for dealing with the emotional standards, and even more the emotional experience, of dead people is no easy task. The distinction between professed values and actual emotions helps. Historical research has become progressively more inventive in finding materials on emotional standards and in interpreting them through nuances of language and choices of metaphor, as well as through explicit message. Changes in word meanings ("temper," "lover") and outright neologisms ("sissy," "tantrum") provide direct testimony. Absence of comment may sometimes prove revealing, as in the avoidance of elaborate jealousy discussions in Victorian culture. Utilization of diary evidence, available in Western society from the 17th century and also in 19th-century Japan (Walthall, 1990), provides insight into internalization of standards and self-evaluations, though there are problems of representativeness. A growing number of historians utilize rituals and various ethnographic evidence to get at emotional expressions in the past (Gillis, 1988). History adds greatly to the cases available for assessing the social contours of emotion, and while its service as laboratory has some undeniable empirical complexities, major strides in data sources continue.

Emotions history also enters researchers into versions of debates important in other social science fields. The results complicate the field, but also allow historical work to contribute to larger issues. Research on emotional change obviously provides yet another confrontation between definitions of basic emotions, biologically predetermined though perhaps variable in target and expression, and emphasis on the cultural preconditions of emotional experience. Like other emotions researchers, historians, as they have gained in theoretical sophistication, participate in these discussions from various vantage points; the fact of significant change in aspects of emotional perception adds a vital dimension to the larger debates, challenging excessive focus on inherent basic responses.

Grasping the emotional arsenal of a past culture involves historians in another set of issues, already familiar in anthropology: Is the task merely to record the emotional language of a past age, or can we legitimately interpret past emotions in light of current categories? Again, dispute has been vigorous, with some historians explicitly renouncing efforts to translate earlier terminology into contemporary parlance even as a means of highlighting differences in time (Clark, 1983), and other agreeing with anthropologists like Melford Spiro in contending that we must translate from one culture to another in order to understand variance or change (Stearns, 1988).

Emotions history also generates some theoretical issues of its own, associated with the focus on tracing change. These issues merit further exploration, not only in history but in other emotions research as historical findings are increasingly taken into account. Problems of timing constitute one example. When emotional standards begin to change in a society, how long does it take for key groups to internalize the changes, at least to some significant extent? Are there generalizable factors that speed or delay the response? For example, advice givers in the United States began early in the 19th century to urge that parents not use fear as a disciplinary tool with children. But manualists were still arguing against the "bogeyman" style a century later, implying that many parents still held out; and studies of rural areas in the 1930s reveal explicit and only mildly embarrassed use of the ploy. Yet change did come: By the 1950s, most prescriptive literature no longer judged the warnings necessary. The issue is not whether change occurred, but at what pace, and what factors determined the timing. Another instance involves implementation of standards in a more public sphere: Available findings in the 19th and 20th centuries, again in the United States, suggest a three- to five-decade lag between significant middle-class acceptance of new standards (about marital love, jealousy, or grief) and translation of these standards into relevant laws about divorce, jealousy-provoked crime, or grief-related damage suits (Stearns, 1994). Again, can we devise more general models to describe the probable speed of change, at least in modern societies, or will we be confined (as is currently inescapable) to case-by-case judgments? A similar problem arises in dealing with the interaction of dominant prescriptions, issued by leading religious (or, in modern cases, scientific) popularizers, and the effective emotional standards of subcultures (ethnic or social class). Historians have done much better with middle- and upper-class emotions history than with immigrant or lower-class.

A second set of historically generated theoretical issues involves the relationship between recreations and emotions. Historical work makes it increasingly clear that cultural expressions—in theater, or reading matter, or ritual, or sports—sometimes serve to train individuals in dominant emotional norms. Middle-class parents in the United States around 1900 believed that boxing was a good way to teach boys to retain and express anger, while confining its intensity to appropriate targets. In other instances, however, culture can be used in reverse fashion, as an outlet for emotions that are proscribed in daily life. Chinese love poems issued from a society highly intolerant of love in actual youth relationships (Goode, 1959). Twentieth-century spectator sports allow men to vent emotions that they know are normally inappropriate, despite greater acceptability in the past. Historians of leisure talk about "compensa-

tions" for the daily restrictions of contemporary life, but their approach needs further integration with emotions history. The historical perspective is not the only means of entry into these issues of cultural–emotional relationships, but it provides a growing list of significant and diverse examples.

THE STRENGTHS OF THE HISTORICAL APPROACH

Emotions history, despite the limitations of novelty, has already generated a number of important findings about changes in standards and their relationship to aspects of emotional experience. The direction of changes in three major periods in modern Western history, although by no means fully captured, is becoming increasingly clear. The results in turn add evidence and issues to a number of basic discussions in emotions research, and generate additional theoretical problems associated with the phenomenon of change.

History also permits deeper exploration of the causation operating in the social context of emotions, an area suggested by constructivist theory but not systematically probed. Historical research deals with the factors that induce new emotional formulations, permitting a kind of causation analysis that differs from and is more extensive than that possible in cross-cultural comparisons of relevant variables. In the major cases explored thus far, historians have picked up on the role of shifts in larger beliefs in inducing new emotional standards. For example, the Protestant Reformation encouraged reevaluation of emotions within the family, while new elite culture prompted reassessment of popular spontaneity. The role of changing expertise in the 20th century provides an opportunity to assess cultural causation of another sort. Economic and organization systems provide the second major strand of causation. Increased commercialization prompted new attention to family emotionality in the early modern period, as relationships among other adults became more competitive (Nelson, 1969). The separation of home and work prompted emotional reevaluations in the 19th century. Most of the leading judgments on basic shifts in the 20th century point to the impact of new organizational experiences and styles, attendant on the rise of a service economy, corporate management hierarchies, and mass consumerism. The effects of prior emotional change, in setting standards that gradually affect other facets or other groups, and of changes in sources of expertise also play a role in assessments of shifts in emotional perceptions in the 19th and 20th centuries. Definitive statements of causation remain elusive, particularly in terms of assigning priority and precedence to one set of variables over another, but the analytical task has been engaged. It involves evaluations that, though rooted in history, inevitably apply to other social research on emotion as well.

Historical research also encourages renewed attention to the impact of emotion and emotional standards, again in a context of change. Emotions research in other disciplines sometimes assumes that further understanding of emotions themselves constitutes a sufficient end result. The growing group of researchers interested in emotions history certainly seeks to add to this understanding, and accepts it as a major goal. Historians, however, are typically interested in relating one facet of the human experience to others, so it is natural that they seek to discuss the results of emotional change on other aspects of society, whatever the time period involved. The effort to distinguish between emotional standards and outright experience adds to this inclination, for new standards often have measurable impact—on the law, for example—even when basic emotional experience may remain more obdurate.

Historians of emotion have consistently commented on the interaction between emotional change and other facets of family life. History is proving to be a crucial means of improving the articulation between gender and emotion. Because gender is in large measure a cultural construct and varies greatly over time, historical research is central to the determination of the origins and results of particular gender formulas for emotional expression. One of the key findings of researchers dealing with the 19th and 20th centuries thus involves recognizing the central importance of gender distinctions in Victorian emotional prescriptions, and then their reconfiguration beginning in the 1920s. Emotional standards also intertwine with power relationships, even aside from gender. Emotions are used regularly to enforce, and sometimes to conceal, such relationships. Research on emotion in the early modern period deals extensively with the interrelationship between changes in this area and revision of family hierarchies. Research on differences in rates and di-

rections of emotional change, even in the 20th century, provides new insight into the often hidden hierarchies of contemporary social and economic life. It also explains the changing emotional bases for collective protest within the configuration of power—including the decline of emotionally charged protest, the late 1960s excepted, from the 1950s to the present in Western society (Moore, 1978).

Historical research on emotion generates important new data, evaluative tools, and theoretical perspectives for emotions research more generally. It provides prior examples of emotional reassessments and an explicit historical vantage point for evaluating current directions of change. Emotions history, increasingly ensconced in the broader field of social history despite its newcomer status, thus becomes part of an interdisciplinary inquiry into the constituents of emotional experience and the role of emotion in social life. The history of emotions adds challenge and complexity to the study of emotion by introducing the factor of change as a central ingredient. Emotions history also provides many of the tools necessary to deal with the issue of change and to use its analysis toward fuller understanding of the ways in which emotions develop and function.

GROWING MOMENTUM

Recent work in emotions history suggests how the field is gaining ground, beginning to tackle some of the major items on the research agenda. Use of findings by historians not explicitly concerned with emotion also suggests important cross-fertilization—for example, in recent work on changing patterns of spousal abuse (Del Mar, 1996). Although the breakthrough in interdisciplinary collaboration with psychologists has not yet occurred, particularly in real collaborative research, the discussions with social psychologists as well as avowed constructionists are encouraging. New research also provides sophisticated treatment of changes in scientific paradigms of emotion and their impact on wider emotional expectations (Dror, 1998).

Equally important are the extensions within history itself, including the coverage of additional emotions such as envy, the new attention to medieval history, and the fuller explorations of the complexities of 20th-century change. Some big tasks still await attention, such as comparison and wider exploration of emotions history in Asian, African, and Latin American contexts. But emotions historians in the United States are beginning to grapple with one vital task: the evaluation of the relations of subgroups to dominant, white-middle-class standards. Emergence of a distinctive African American religious–emotional subculture took on new significance around 1900, for example, because its trajectory contrasted so markedly from changing patterns in middle-class emotionology (Phillips, 1998). Differences in timing between Catholic emotional culture and its Protestant counterpart provide important insights into uses of fear (Kelly & Kelly, 1998; Griffith, 1998).

A final growth area involves extending the inquiry in the consequences of emotional culture and emotional change. Here, as in exploring change itself, historians offer considerable experience in dealing with causation and with interlocking factors. Corbin's (1986) work has shown the impact of emotional reactions in helping to shape social class relations, but also sanitary policies, in 19th-century France. New research on changing patterns of friendship suggests another vital impact area (Rotundo, 1989; Rosenzweig, 1998). Fuller understanding of 20th-century change in emotional expectations is being applied to parent–child relations, as well as to wider phenomena such as consumerism (Stearns, 1998). Recent American work extends the idea of changes in emotional culture as links between large structural shifts—the rise of a corporate, service-based economy, for example—and alterations in law, political behavior, and even military policy (Stearns, 1997, 1999; Wouters, 1992). Connections between changes in emotional style (Wouters, 1996) and shifts in the crime rate are also being explored. Clearly, this diverse use of emotional patterns as cause, though still tentative, is a major new frontier in the field.

Emotions history has carved a noticeable (though hardly dominant) niche in the larger history discipline, and a measurably greater role in interdisciplinary work. It has considerably expanded available knowledge about the range of emotional cultures and behaviors. It has fed important theories about processes of change and, increasingly, the consequences of change. Its interactions with other relevant disciplines have produced mutually significant results. Real challenges remain—in societies, periods, and topics still unexplored, as well as in

the pressing need for comparative work and for fuller cross-disciplinary collaboration. The vitality of the subfield suggests the possibility of addressing these broader research needs.

REFERENCES

Averill, J. R. (1980). A constructivist view of emotion. In R. Plutchik & H. Kellerman (Eds.), *Emotion: Theory, research, and experience: Vol. 1. Theories of emotion* (pp. 305–339). New York: Academic Press.

Averill, J. R. (1982). *Anger and aggression: An essay on emotion.* New York: Springer-Verlag.

Badinter, E. (1980). *L'amour en plus: Histoire de l'amour maternel.* Paris: Flammarion.

Bremmer, J., & Roodenburg, H. (Eds.). (1997). *A cultural history of humor.* Cambridge, MA: Polity Press.

Burke, P. (1978). *Popular culture in early modern Europe.* New York: New York University Press.

Bynum, C. (1997). Wonder. *American Historical Review, 102,* 1–26.

Cancian, F. M. (1987). *Love in America: Gender and self development.* Cambridge, England: Cambridge University Press.

Cancian, F. M., & Gordon, S. (1988). Changing emotion norms in marriage: Love and anger in U.S. women's magazines since 1900. *Gender and Society, 2*(3), 303–342.

Clark, S. (1983). French historians and early modern culture. *Past and Present, 100,* 62–99.

Corbin, A. (1986). *The foul and the fragrant: Odor and the French imagination.* Cambridge, MA: Harvard University Press.

Del Mar, D. (1996). *What trouble I have seen: A history of violence against wives.* Cambridge, MA: Harvard University Press.

Delumeau, J. (1978). *La peur en Occident, XIVe–XVIIe siècles: Une cité assiégée.* Paris: Fayard.

Delumeau, J. (1989). *Rassurer et proteger: Le sentiment de sécurité dans l'Occident d'autrefois.* Paris: Fayard.

Demos, J. (1970). *A little commonwealth: Family life in Plymouth Colony.* New York: Oxford University Press.

Demos, J. (1988). Shame and guilt in early New England. In C. Z. Stearns & P. N. Stearns (Eds.), *Emotion and social change: Toward a new psychohistory* (pp. 69–86). New York: Holmes & Meier.

de Swaan, A. (1981). The politics of agoraphobia: On changes in emotional and relational management. *Theory and Society, 10*(3), 359–385.

Dror, O. E. (1998). Creating the emotional body: Confusion, possibilities, and knowledge. In P. N. Stearns & J. Lewis (Eds.), *Emotional history of the United States* (pp.173–196). New York: New York University Press.

Elias, N. (1982). *The history of manners* (E. Jephcott, Trans.). New York: Pantheon Books. (Original work published 1938)

Elvin, M. (1989). Tales of the Shen and Xien: Body-personal and heart-mind in China during the last 150 years. *Zone, 4,* 266–349.

Elvin, M. (1991). The inner world of 1830. *Daedalus, 120*(2), 33–61.

Erikson, E. (1958). *Young man Luther.* New York: Norton.

Febvre, L. (1973). *A new kind of history.* New York: Harper & Row. (Original work published 1933)

Flandrin, J. L. (1979). *Families in former times* (R. Southern, Trans.). Cambridge, England: Cambridge University Press.

Gay, P. (1984–1986). *The bourgeois experience: Victoria to Freud* (2 vols.). New York: Oxford University Press.

Gergen, K. J. (1998). History and psychology: Three weddings and a future. In P. N. Stearns & J. Lewis (Eds.), *Emotional history of the United States* (pp. 15–32). New York: New York University Press.

Gerhards, J. (1989). The changing culture of emotions in modern society, *Social Science Information, 28,* 737–754.

Gillis, J. R. (1985). *For better, for worse: British marriages, 1600 to the present.* New York: Oxford University Press.

Gillis, J. R. (1988). From ritual to romance: Toward an alternate history of love. In C. Z. Stearns & P. N. Stearns (Eds.), *Emotion and social change: Toward a new psychohistory* (pp. 87–122). New York: Holmes & Meier.

Goode, W. J. (1959). The theoretical importance of love. *American Sociological Review, 24*(1), 38–47.

Gordon, S. L. (1989). The socialization of children's emotion: Emotional culture, competence, and exposure. In C. Saarni & P. Harris (Eds.), *Children's understanding of emotion* (pp. 319–349). Cambridge, England: Cambridge University Press.

Greven, P. J., Jr. (1977). *The Protestant temperament: Patterns of child-rearing, religious experience and the self in early America.* New York: Knopf.

Greven, P. J., Jr. (1991). *Spare the child: The religious roots of punishment and the psychological impact of physical abuse.* New York: Knopf.

Griffith, R. M. (1998). "Joy unspeakable and full of glory": The vocabulary of pious emotion in the narratives of American Pentecostal women, 1910–1945. In P. N. Stearns & J. Lewis (Eds.), *Emotional history of the United States* (pp. 218–240). New York: New York University Press.

Griswold, R. L. (1986). The evolution of the doctrine of mental cruelty in Victorian American divorce, 1790–1900. *Journal of Social History, 20,* 127–148.

Harré, R., & Stearns, P. N. (Eds.). (1995). *Discursive psychology in practice.* London: Sage.

Hochschild, A. R. (1997, April 20). There's no place like work. *The New York Times Magazine,* pp. 50–55, 81–84.

Houlbrooke, R. (Ed.). (1989). *Death, ritual and bereavement.* New York: Routledge/Chapman & Hall.

Huizinga, J. (1927). *The waning of the Middle Ages.* London: E. Arnold.

Hunt, D. (1970). *Parents and children in history: The psychology of family life in early modern France.* New York: Basic Books.

Isaac, R. (1982). *The transformation of Virginia, 1740–1790.* Chapel Hill: University of North Carolina Press.

Kagan, J. (1979). *The growth of the child: Reflections on human development.* New York: Norton.

Kasson, J. F. (1990). *Rudeness and civility: Manners in nineteenth-century urban America.* New York: Hill & Wang.

Kelly, T., & Kelly, J. (1998). American Catholics and the discourse of fear. In P. N. Stearns & J. Lewis (Eds.), *Emotional history of the United States* (pp. 259–282). New York: New York University Press.

Lantz, H. R. (1982). Romantic love in the pre-modern period: A social commentary. *Journal of Social History,* 15, 349–370.

Leites, E. (1986). *The Puritan conscience and modern sexuality.* New Haven, CT: Yale University Press.

Levin, E. (1989). *Sex and society in the world of the Orthodox Slavs, 900–1700.* Ithaca, NY: Cornell University Press.

Levy, R. I. (1973). *Tahitians: Mind and experience in the Society Islands.* Chicago: University of Chicago Press.

Lewis, J. (1989). Mother's love: The construction of an emotion in nineteenth-century America. In A. E. Barnes & P. N. Stearns (Eds.), *Social history and issues in human consciousness* (pp. 209–229). New York: New York University Press.

Lofland, L. (1985). The social shaping of emotion: The case of grief. *Symbolic Interaction, 8*(2), 171–190.

Lystra, K. (1989). *Searching the heart: Women, men, and romantic love in nineteenth-century America.* New York: Oxford University Press.

Matt, S. J. (1998). Frocks, finery, and feelings: Rural and urban women's envy, 1890–1930. In P. N. Stearns & J. Lewis (Eds.), *Emotional history of the United States* (pp. 377–395). New York: New York University Press.

Melucci, A. (1989). *Nomads of the present: Social movements and individual needs in contemporary society.* Philadelphia: Temple University Press.

Mintz, S., & Kellogg, S. (1989). *Domestic revolutions: A social history of American family life.* New York: Free Press.

Mitzman, A. (1987). The civilizing offensive: Mentalities, high culture and individual psyches. *Journal of Social History, 20,* 663–688.

Moore, B. (1978). *Injustice: The social basis of obedience and revolt.* White Plains, NY: M. E. Sharpe.

Morrison, K. F. (1988). *I am you: The hermeneutics of empathy in Western literature, theology and art.* Princeton, NJ: Princeton University Press.

Muchembled, R. (1985). *Popular culture and elite culture in France, 1400–1750* (L. Cochrane, Trans.). Baton Rouge: Louisiana State University Press.

Nelson, B. (1969). *The idea of usury: From tribal brotherhood to universal brotherhood.* Princeton, NJ: Princeton University Press.

Phillips, K. L. (1998). "Stand by me": Sacred quartet music and the emotionology of African American audiences, 1900–1930. In P. N. Stearns & J. Lewis (Eds.), *Emotional history of the United States* (pp. 241–258). New York: New York University Press.

Pollock, L. A. (1983). *Forgotten children: Parent–child relations from 1500 to 1900.* Cambridge, England: Cambridge University Press.

Rosenblatt, P. C. (1983). *Bitter, bitter tears: Nineteenth-century diarists and twentieth-century grief theories.* Minneapolis: University of Minnesota Press.

Rosenzweig, L. W. (1998). "Another self'"?: Middle-class American women and their friends, 1900–1960. In P. N. Stearns & J. Lewis (Eds.), *Emotional history of the United States* (pp. 357–376). New York: New York University Press.

Rotundo, A. (1989). Romantic friendship: Male intimacy and middle-class youth in the northern United States, 1800–1900. *Journal of Social History, 23,* 1–25.

Sabean, D. (1984). *Power in the blood: Popular culture and village discourse in early modern Germany.* Cambridge, England: Cambridge University Press.

Salovey, P. (Ed.). (1991). *The psychology of jealousy and envy.* New York: Guilford Press.

Seidman, S. (1991). *Romantic longings: Love in America, 1830–1980.* New York: Routledge.

Shields, S. A., & Koster, B. A. (1989). Emotional stereotyping of parent in child rearing manuals, 1915–1980. *Social Psychology Quarterly, 52*(1), 44–55.

Shorter, E. (1975). *The making of the modern family.* New York: Basic Books.

Shumway, D. R. (1998). Something old, something new: Romance and marital advice in the 1920s. In P. N. Stearns & J. Lewis (Eds.), *Emotional history of the United States* (pp. 305–318). New York: New York University Press.

Solomon, R. H. (1971). *Mao's revolution and Chinese political culture.* Berkeley: University of California Press.

Stearns, C. Z. (1988). "Lord help me walk humbly": Anger and sadness in England and America, 1570–1750. In C. Z. Stearns & P. N. Stearns (Eds.), *Emotion and social change: Toward a new psychohistory* (pp. 39–68). New York: Holmes & Meier.

Stearns, C. Z., & Stearns, P. N. (1986). *Anger: The struggle for emotional control in America's history.* Chicago: University of Chicago Press.

Stearns, C. Z., & Stearns, P. N. (Eds.). (1988). *Emotion and social change: Toward a new psychohistory.* New York: Holmes & Meier.

Stearns, P. N. (1989). *Jealousy: The evolution of an emotion in American history.* New York: New York University Press.

Stearns, P. N. (1994). *American cool: Constructing a twentieth-century emotional style.* New York: New York University Press.

Stearns, P. N. (1997). Emotional change and political disengagement in the 20th-century United States. *Innovation—The European Journal of Social Sciences, 10*(4), 361–380.

Stearns, P. N. (1998). Consumerism and childhood: New targets for American emotions. In P. N. Stearns & J. Lewis (Eds.), *Emotional history of the United States* (pp. 396–416). New York: New York University Press.

Stearns, P. N. (1999). Perceptions of death in the Korean War. *War in History, 6,* 72–87.

Stearns, P. N., & Haggerty, T. (1991). The role of fear: Transitions in American emotional standards for children, 1850–1950. *American Historical Review, 96*(1), 63–94.

Stearns, P. N., with Stearns, C. Z. (1985). Emotionology: Clarifying the history of emotions and emotional standards. *American Historical Review, 90*(4), 813–836.

Stone, L. (1977). *The family, sex and marriage in England, 1500–1800.* New York: Harper & Row.

Tomkins, S. (1962–1963). *Affect, imagery, consciousness* (2 vols.). New York: Springer.

Trumbach, R. (1978). *The rise of the egalitarian family: Aristocratic kinship and domestic relations in eighteenth century England.* New York: Academic Press.

Walthall, A. (1990). The family ideology of the rural entrepreneurs in nineteenth-century Japan. *Journal of Social History, 23,* 463–484.

White, K. (1993). *The first sexual revolution: The emergence of male heterosexuality in modern America.* New York: New York University Press.

Wouters, C. (1991). On status competition and emotion management. *Journal of Social History, 24*(4), 690–717.

Wouters, C. (1992). On status competition and emotion management: The study of emotions as a new field. *Theory, Culture and Society, 9,* 229–252.

Wouters, C. (1995). Etiquette books and emotion management in the 20th century. *Journal of Social History, 29,* 107–124, 325–340.

Wouters, C. (1996). *Changing patterns of social controls and self-controls: On the rise of crime since the 1950s.* Paper presented at the "Causes of Crisis" symposium, Edinburgh, Scotland.

Zelizer, V. (1985). *Pricing the priceless child.* New York: Basic Books.

CHAPTER 3

Representing Emotional Meaning: Category, Metaphor, Schema, Discourse

Geoffrey M. White

What can be learned about emotion from the study of emotion language, including ordinary emotion talk? Focusing on "emotional meaning" rather than simply "emotion" underscores the importance of the *interpreted* aspects of emotion as it enters into ordinary social life (Shweder, 1994). At the same time, however, it is important to resist the tendency to dichotomize the world into separate realms of cognitive and affective phenomena (White, 1994). Challenging this separation is made difficult by the fact that it is deeply entrenched both in the English language and in common-sense folk models of the mind (D'Andrade, 1987). Scientific paradigms themselves frequently rely on European and American models of emotion that smuggle implicit cultural concepts into supposedly universal theorizing.

For example, dominant scientific and popular paradigms have historically located emotion in the brain. This view finds regular expression in newspaper and magazine stories about the latest neurophysiological research on sites of emotion in the brain. Examples include the cover story of the June 24, 1991 issue of *U.S. News and World Report,* titled "Where Emotions Come From: Unlocking the Biological Secrets of Joy, Fear, Anger and Despair" (Where Emotions Come From, 1991), or a front-page story in the March 28, 1995 issue of *The New York*

Times under the heading "Inside the Brain: New View of Emotion" (Goleman, 1995). The latter article includes two brain scan diagrams graphically displaying sites of neurological activity associated with the emotions "happiness" and "sadness." Under the "happiness" label the caption reads, "Brain scans show that a happy thought produces a lull in nerve activity in specific areas." Under "sadness" is the following: "A sad thought produces an increase in nerve activity in different areas." The article itself, back in the science section of the newspaper, begins thus: "The essence of emotion . . . is hard enough for a poet to capture, let alone a neuroscientist. Now brain researchers, in their own fashion, have begun to do so" (p. B9). Reports such as these affirm popular understandings of emotions as neurological essences in the brain that work their way up and out in symbolic, linguistic, and social forms. Despite the fact that cognitive and social factors are central to common-sense models of "happiness" or "sadness," the representational apparatus of digital imaging easily renders them peripheral, if not irrelevant, to scientific explanation.

In contrast to popular and scientific views of emotions as physiological essences, research on common-sense understandings of emotions shows that people widely talk about emotions primarily in terms of social relations and situations (see, e.g., Rosaldo [1980] on the Ilongot of the Philippines, and Lutz [1988] on the Ifaluk in the Pacific). Although people also talk about emotions as bodily states, they are more likely to define them in terms of their significance for social situations and transactions. It is important to note, however, that such social-relational theories of emotion do not necessarily exclude a role for bodily states in folk theories of emotion. One way of sorting out these issues is to examine common-sense conceptions of emotion in comparative perspective—a task most often taken up in anthropology and linguistics, with increasing interest in cultural psychology (Kitayama & Markus, 1994a).

Exercises in comparison and translation run the risk of being seen as *only* concerned with making distant, foreign cultures familiar or comprehensible. In a more fundamental way, however, comparative work raises questions about the symbolic and constructed aspects of English-language emotion concepts. For example, when Catherine Lutz (1988) claimed that the Ifaluk differ from Americans in seeing emotions as concerned with relations between persons and events rather than with feeling states, Shaver, Wu, and Schwartz (1992) responded with research showing that American emotion concepts are also about social relations. In a comparative study of reports of emotional experience, they found that American accounts "are concerned with the same general issue that Oceanic people's emotion accounts are concerned with: the relationship between a person (with desires, goals, and values) and an event, *usually an event involving at least one other person*" (p. 201; italics added).

If nothing else, the kinds of questions being asked in this exchange, and the type of data brought to bear on them, reflect useful interdisciplinary interest in the problem of emotional meaning and how to interpret it. By focusing on the problem of emotional meaning, this chapter examines some of the ways implicit theories of language reinforce assumptions about the location of emotion—whether in the body, in the mind, in communicative action, or in social interaction. In general, the more a research paradigm focuses on linguistic and social factors, the more likely it is to argue for the importance of discursive processes in emotional experience (Edwards, 1997). Rather than essentialize definitions of emotion by locating them on one side or the other of such classic binaries as mind–body or individual–society, it is more

productive to view emotions and emotion talk as communicative signs that mediate body, mind, and society in ongoing interaction. This chapter takes up these issues, using examples of distinct approaches to emotional meaning drawn from research in a non-Western language of the Southwest Pacific.

A great deal of emotion theory is built upon assumptions about irreducible oppositions between thought and feeling, mind and body, rationality and irrationality, conscious and unconscious, nurture and nature, and so forth. Although it would be impossible to collapse or dispense with these distinctions, theories of emotion have been caught in an overly dichotomous separation of emotion and culture, as well as the more fundamental opposition of nature and culture; such theories must then puzzle over ways to reconnect them. The phrase "emotional meaning" is usefully ambiguous in relation to these polarities. It can be read as referring to the emotional aspects of meaning, as well as to the meaningful aspects of emotion. The phrase can refer to the ways biologically based affects are interpreted (given meaning) or to the manner in which language and other communicative acts obtain affective force. One goal of a theory of emotional meaning is to bring these problems within a single explanatory framework.

Without minimizing the role of feeling states or facial expressions, an approach to emotion that takes emotional meaning seriously leads to research on the linkages between affect, cultural models, and social practices—all of which may be viewed as constitutive elements of emotional experience. Rather than seeing cognitive and social dimensions of emotion as secondary effects, however, a theory that focuses on emotional meaning takes these phenomena as core elements of emotion.

Much of the research on the meanings of emotion has separated the problem of *concepts* of emotion from the study of emotional *experience* by conceptualizing the former as ideas about emotion and the latter as hard-wired, biological affects. In this view, interpretive constructions get laid on top of prior physiological processes such as feeling states or facial expressions. Again, once emotion and culture have been separated in this way, theories of emotion must then grapple with the problem of reconnecting them. This has been an enduring problem for most emotion theories, from Freudian theory to Schachter and Singer's

(1962) study of emotional labeling. Despite their differences, most emotion theories articulate some kind of dual-phase model of emotion that begins with "primary" biological affects and then adds "secondary" cultural or cognitive processes.

The question of basic or universal emotions has provided an important connection between research on the biological bases of emotion and research on emotional meaning. A great deal of comparative research has proceeded from the premise that cross-cultural commonalities in emotion concepts and categories provide evidence for underlying universals (for reviews, see Lutz & White, 1986; Mesquita & Frijda, 1992; Russell, 1991a). Given the difficulties of making direct comparisons of emotion concepts across languages, most such studies have relied on lexical approaches, which represent emotional meaning solely in terms of referential meaning or denotative function. In short, emotion words are viewed as labels for feelings or categories of feeling. Although these approaches have the advantage of enabling comparisons, they rely upon implicit theories of language that constrict the representation of emotional meaning, stripping out more complex cognitive, communicative, and interactional functions of language.

In this respect, referential theories of language and biological theories of emotion collude in mutually reinforcing a view of emotion as consisting of discrete feeling states, and of emotional meaning as primarily a matter of labeling them. In other words, a theory that sees emotion primarily as the expression of basic affects is more likely to see emotion words as labels for natural objects. Furthermore, approaching emotional meaning as a matter of words denoting feeling states or categories has the added effect of erasing the pragmatic functions of emotion language when used in social and psychological context.

Comparative research from Ekman's (1992) studies of facial expression to more recent work on emotion lexicons by Romney, Moore, and Rusch (1997) has produced evidence for cross-cultural convergence in the expression and recognition of emotions. But the significance of these studies for emotional meaning is unclear, given that they pay little attention to ordinary language or to problems of interpretation and translation. As Wierzbicka (e.g., 1992) has asked persistently, what does it mean to label non-English emotion categories or clusters with English terms such as "anger," "sadness," and so forth, given the dense semantic complexity of those terms and the wide range of contexts in which they are put to use? By taking words out of context, lexical models apply a form of methodological individualism that ignores the communicative and social functions of emotion language.

A more comprehensive approach to emotional meaning would pursue multimethod strategies capable of representing the significance of emotion talk in terms of more complex cultural models and situated practices. Without this type of more detailed cognitive and social research, explanations of commonalities in emotion vocabularies across cultures will continue to make recourse to hypothetical basic affects defined, by default, by English-language categories. Given the current state of knowledge about the relative physiological and social determinants of emotion concepts, it is at least as plausible that cross-cultural convergences in emotion vocabularies derive from cultural and social-institutional structures as they do from biological substrates. As Kitayama and Markus (1994b, p. 6) state, "It may be more accurate and more fruitful for social science research to hypothesize that the commonality of emotional configuration reflects, at least in part, the commonality of social and cultural processes in which the workings of the psychological component processes are situated" (cf. Lutz & White, 1986). At the level at which people understand and experience emotions, we know that the emotions are fundamentally integrated into cognitive and social functioning, at multiple levels of awareness and degrees of cultural coding. Ultimately, a fuller psychological account requires defining emotion in a manner that encompasses, at a minimum, feeling states, cognitive processes, and sociocultural context.

This chapter attempts to go beyond perennial definitional issues to consider some of the methodological implications of focusing on emotional meaning. In addition to anthropological studies of emotion (Bowlin & Stromberg, 1997; Lyon, 1995; Reddy, 1997), social-constructionist theories and cultural psychology have long been concerned with these issues. My strategy is to examine several forms of language-centered analysis, asking how each represents emotional meaning. It is instructive to consider the distinct aspects of linguistic meaning that emerge from looking first at one term among others within a lexicon of emotion words, then at the elaboration of its meaning in metaphorical expressions and event schemas, and finally at the socially situated practices within which it obtains pragmatic force. Although the progression from category to metaphor, schema, and discourse is easily represented as moving from static to process-oriented models or from cognitive-psychological to sociocultural approaches. I don't want to imply that one type of analysis subsumes the next or that one excludes another.

The remainder of this chapter takes up a number of strategies or methodologies that have been used to determine what people are talking about (or what they are doing) when they talk about or with emotions. The discussion is grounded in examples drawn from a non-Western language of the Southwest Pacific: Cheke Holo (also called A'ara) on the island of Santa Isabel in the Solomon Islands.

EMOTION AS CATEGORY: LEXICAL MODELS

Historically, much of the anthropological and social-psychological work on emotional meaning has focused on the significance of specific emotion words. The dominant approach in cognitive anthropology of the 1960s and 1970s was word-centered: It focused on the denotative meaning of word sets, represented in terms of category structure for specific domains of terminology. Techniques were devised to tease out features of referential meaning for domains as diverse as plant names and kinship terms. With the development of methods such as cluster analysis and multidimensional scaling, it became possible to use lexical techniques to map terms on the basis of judged similarity, and then to attempt to infer dimensions of meaning from derived configurations of similarity relations. Emotion, like color or kinship, offers an appealing domain in which to apply these methods, given that most if not all languages have identifiable vocabularies of emotion—even if these are fuzzy around the edges.

The cross-cultural literature on emotion contains repeated references to the possibility of an analogy between the domains of color and emotion, suggesting that basic emotion concepts might be analyzed in a fashion similar to the way color terms have been represented as physiologically based prototype categories (Kay & Berlin, 1997). Although this analogy is highly suggestive, it is limited by the fact that ordinary emotion language conveys complex social and moral meanings that far exceed the referential significance of emotion terms. In other words, emotion language entails semantic and pragmatic dimensions that differ sharply from the largely referential function of color terms, used primarily to discriminate sections of the visible light spectrum. The success of lexical models in representing color terminology follows from the appropriateness of denotative semantics for representing the meanings of words used largely as descriptors or labels. As a result, researchers have been able to construct a universal or "etic" grid to represent the color spectrum. A particularly apt analogy in the emotion domain is the research of Ekman and his associates in utilizing universal features of facial expressions to develop a pancultural system for comparing emotion terms on the basis of their denotation of similar faces.

As stated earlier, referential theories of language and biological theories of emotion jointly reinforce a view of emotion words as labels for objects and categories that, at base, represent feeling states and their behavioral correlates, much as color terms refer to frequencies in the visible light spectrum. Given the feeling-state model of emotion, another approach to emotion words in terms of underlying physiological correlates has sought to recover underlying dimensions of feeling or sensation by measuring judgments about facial expressions and/or the meanings of emotion words.

Interpretations such as these make sense if the goal is to reduce emotional meaning to a small number of discrete categories (usually thought of as denoting biological states, but conceivably also social). However, conceiving of emotional meaning in this way has only a distant relation to the more specific meanings of emotion words in ordinary speech, as revealed by a now considerable amount of ethnographic research (Mesquita & Frijda, 1992; Russell, 1995; Wierzbicka, 1992). The usefulness—and limitations—of lexical semantics in representing emotional meaning can be illustrated with examples drawn from my own work with the Cheke Holo (or A'ara) language, spoken by about 18,000 people on the island of Santa Isabel in the Solomon Islands.

In order to explore the meanings of common emotion words in this society, I have used several distinct approaches, including a set of techniques known in anthropology as "cultural domain analysis" (Bernard, 1995). This approach is based on the premise that linguistic terminologies represent bounded domains of knowledge that can be mapped by exploring the semantics of core terms in a given domain. Once an assumption about the validity of a "domain" is made, the first step in analysis is to derive a set of core or basic terms that can be said to represent the range of discriminations or meanings relevant to the domain. Typically this is accomplished by a free-listing task in which a small number of informants are asked to list examples of "*X*," where "*X*" is the name of the domain. The results of these listings are then compared, and the most salient terms (measured by frequency or rank) are selected as core terms for the analysis. The derivation of core terms (frequently regarded as a simple, mechanical procedure) is crucial to the final results of domain analysis, which depends entirely on the specific terms selected. This is particularly problematic for a vocabulary as large and complex as emotion, where an enormous diversity and range of terminology must somehow be reduced to a smaller set of representative terms that can be subjected to formal analysis.

In this case, I asked five people to list words used to talk about "feelings" (*nagnafa*, literally "heart"). Using their listings, I selected all the words mentioned by at least three of the five, producing a list of 15 emotion terms. I next asked a sample of 11 adult men between the ages of 32 and 55 to sort words into groupings according to similarity in meaning. For this purpose, the words were written on 3″ × 5″ index cards, one to a card. I asked each person to sort the terms into any number of piles according to which were judged "similar in meaning" (literally, *kaisei gaogatho di,* "have the same thought").

Using the frequency with which each pair of terms were grouped together as a measure of similarity, I next analyzed the resulting matrix of correspondences with the nonmetric multivariate techniques of multidimensional scaling and cluster analysis (D'Andrade, 1978; Kruskal, Young, & Seery, 1972). Using scaling techniques that plot semantic similarities in terms of spatial distance, one can look for conceptual dimensions that organize relations among terms across the entire domain. Because multidimensional scaling models inevitably produce "best-fit" spatial diagrams in just two or three dimensions, such dimensions remain at a very high level of generality. For the emotion domain, spatial models repeatedly show two or three dimensions resembling those of Osgood's (1964) semantic differential, interpreted as an evaluative factor often labeled "pleasure," and as an activity/strength factor often labeled "arousal" (Russell, 1980, 1983).

Consider the way the Cheke Holo emotion words appear when mapped as a two-dimensional diagram produced by multidimensional scaling. Figure 3.1 represents the "best-fit" configuration that emerges from analysis of the pattern of similarities resulting from sorting the 15 terms. If discussion of this diagram is based on English glosses of the original Cheke Holo terms used in the sorting task, it is possible to interpret the first (horizontal) dimension as evaluative: defined by the opposition of positive emotions to "be happy" and to "love" with negative emotions of to "be shamed" and to "be sad." Similarly, the second (vertical) axis can be interpreted as a dimension of strength/activity by contrasting the emotions to "be angry," to "be disgusted," and to have a "tangled heart" with a cluster of "fear" and "surprise."

At the same time, however, the dimensions of Figure 3.1 can also be interpreted with labels more relevant to the social, interpersonal meanings of emotion. Thus "evaluation" can be read as "solidarity" versus "conflict," and "strength" can be interpreted as "power" or "dominance" versus "submission." Cross-cultural research with pronouns as well as personality and emotion terms has shown that these dimensions recur widely in ordinary language applied to social interaction (Brown & Gilman, 1960; White, 1980).

Similarity diagrams such as Figure 3.1 have been derived for numerous languages, especially in the Pacific (see, e.g., Lutz [1982] on Ifaluk, and Gerber [1985] on Samoa) and Asia (see, e.g., Heider [1991] on Indonesia, and Romney et al. [1997] on Japan). These have produced some interesting speculations about basic or universal emotions, but do not give much information about the significance of emotion words for native speakers. Research focusing on universal aspects of emotional meaning tends to limit analysis to word-centered techniques that rarely go beyond referential meaning to more complex conceptual or pragmatic functions of language. As noted earlier, an emphasis on single words lends itself to a view of emotions as discrete psychological entities such as feeling states and correlated facial expressions.

Research on the cognitive processes that un-

FIGURE 3.1. Two-dimensional scaling of 15 Cheke Holo/A'ara (Solomon Islands) emotion words.

derlie judgments of similarity among emotion concepts has explored the conceptual basis for perceptions of similarity and difference among emotion words (Oatley & Jenkins, 1996). In general, emotion researchers attending to emotional meaning assume that people make judgments about the similarity and difference among emotion words on the basis of implicit knowledge of word meanings. Wierzbicka, who has developed a theory for representing emotional meaning in terms of "cognitive scenarios" (see below), puts the matter succinctly: "It is the cognitive scenario associated with an emotion term . . . which allows us to distinguish one presumed emotion from another" (Wierzbicka, 1995, p. 232). Schimmack and Reisenzein (1997) compare several alternative explanations for similarity judgments, comparing "dimensional" theories, "semantic feature" theories, and "episodic knowledge" of the co-occurrence of emotions in experiential memory (their preferred model). They argue against the explanatory utility of semantic models of emotion words, but in so doing divorce "semantics" from "episodic knowledge"—a separation that

relies on a highly abstract "semantics" insulated from cultural models and experience.

If one pays attention to what people *say* about their own reasoning in making similarity judgments of emotion terms (data that some theorists find irrelevant), it is apparent that people's accounts frequently indicate a reliance on knowledge about the social contexts of emotion. Such knowledge is both episodic and semantic. By definition, accounts of experience can only be produced in the language and conceptual apparatus available for remembering and talking about experience. One way to interpret Figure 3.1 is to see the distances between terms as a measure of overlap in common-sense understandings about the (proto)typical situations in which emotions occur in social life (Russell, 1991b; Shaver, Schwartz, Kirson, & O'Connor, 1987; Wierzbicka, 1995). So, for example, the fact that "be angry," "be disgusted," and "be fed up" all cluster together in Figure 3.1 might be interpreted as evidence that Cheke Holo speakers see them as entailing negative appraisals of actions offensive to the self or social norms. Of course, they also differ in certain ways, such that "being angry" involves a desire for harm or retribution, whereas "being disgusted" implies rejection or avoidance, and "being fed up" implies impatience and reprimand.

Note that the terms arrayed in Figure 3.1 are verbs, not nouns. Such differences are common in lexical studies of emotion, but rarely affect the treatment of words in terms of denotative meaning. For example, Romney et al. (1997) observe that Japanese emotion words take the form of adjectives, but compare them on a one-to-one basis with English nouns. Noun forms reinforce the view of emotions as labels for things (states of the brain or body) rather than processes, especially social processes. Cheke Holo emotion terms, for example, are mostly stative verbs (hence "be angry," "be surprised," etc., instead of "anger," "surprise," etc.). They function in a manner similar to adjectives, but syntactically require temporal markers of a process in which the subject (the person experiencing the emotion) is also the object or recipient of emotional process. Emotions are conceptualized in Cheke Holo as something that happen *to* the experiencing subject. In general, Cheke Holo speakers do not talk about emotions as abstract or discrete states of mind independent of these contextual linkages. Talk that takes the form of "psychologizing" is almost always embedded in talk about interpersonal interactions and events. The verbal-processual nature of Cheke Holo emotion words reflects the syntactic role they play in sentences and larger stretches of discourse, where they usually occupy a strategic place in interactive episodes or scripts that link personal responses to both antecedent events and possible consequences.

EMOTION AS METAPHOR

Whereas lexical models such as that in Figure 3.1 can only assess the social meanings of emotion indirectly, analyses of emotion language as metaphor have opened up a more complex format for representing word-centered meaning (e.g., Kövecses, 1990). Analyzing emotion words as metaphors widens the analytical lens to include a wider range of conceptual schemas than are normally included in "cultural domain analysis." Utilizing metaphor and schema theory to represent emotional meaning leads to a more direct engagement with the social aspects of emotion concepts. Although few people on Santa Isabel could articulate an explicit "theory" of emotion, a great deal of ordinary thinking and talking about emotion are expressed in terms of figurative language or "conventional metaphor" (Lakoff & Kövecses, 1987).

Consider the term *fifiri nagnafa* ("tangled heart"), located in the top center of the similarity diagram depicted in Figure 3.1. Similar to the English metaphor "heart = feeling," the term *nagnafa* means both "heart" and "feeling." Syntactically, *fifiri nagnafa*, like other emotion terms, is attributed to self or others by using possessive pronouns ("my," "his," etc.). Thus *fifiri nagnafagu* ("tangled heart" + first-person singular possessive) says "My feelings are tangled." This usage of the first-person possessive suggests that Cheke Holo emotions are "inside" the person or body. In fact, this is a significant premise of much of Cheke Holo reasoning about emotions, which uses container metaphors to express concerns about negative emotions that get metaphorically "stuck" inside and remain hidden as potential causes of illness and misfortune.

A particularly notable aspect of the positioning of *fifiri nagnafa* in Figure 3.1 is that it mediates two evaluatively opposed clusters—the anger/disgust grouping in the upper right, and the happiness/love grouping on the left. Judged solely in terms of its location in the scaling diagram, we would conclude that "tangled heart" is evaluatively neutral. In fact, when the phrase is used in ordinary language, it is precisely the evaluative ambiguity of the phrase that is important, making it one of the most commonly used phrases in Cheke Holo emotion language.

The metaphor of "entanglement" is a generative concept in Cheke Holo culture, used variously to talk about the nature of persons, emotions, and social relations (White, 1990a). To be "tangled" (or "knotted," *haru*) is to be in a state of social and psychological conflict, yielding this metaphorical proposition: TO BE IN CONFLICT IS TO BE TANGLED. Talk of "tangled feelings" refers to personal emotional turmoil, usually associated with interpersonal conflict. As a result, talk of emotion provides an idiom for talking about interpersonal conflict. In Santa Isabel society, this is especially useful as an indirect means for discussing difficult social conflicts or "entanglements." Open, direct talk about interpersonal relations is always difficult in small-scale societies, where social life is organized around densely cross-cutting relations between people who reside in close proximity to one another.

In ordinary speech the phrase *fifiri nagnafa* may substitute for other, more specific terms such as "anger," "sadness," or "shame." To say that one's heart is "tangled" is to make a generalized statement about problematic feelings associated with some social, moral dilemma. Not only does the metaphor of entanglement tend to displace or dilute more specific negative feelings; it also carries implications for culturally prescribed means of resolving conflict. Just as tangled objects such as fishing nets or threads require straightening out before they can be useful, so tangled emotions require "straightening" or "disentangling." As it turns out, the term "disentangling" refers to a culturally prescribed practice in which people "entangled" in conflict meet together to "talk out" recent conflicts and pent-up grievances, much like group therapy (Watson-Gegeo & White, 1990). This type of cultural logic is expressed in this metaphorical proposition: TO UNTANGLE IS TO RESOLVE CONFLICTS.

The location of "tangled heart" in Figure 3.1, between the clusters of anger/disgust and happiness/compassion, reflects the mediating role of entanglement—and of disentangling—as a process that transforms ill feeling into something more positive. Key metaphors, such as entanglement, encode aspects of larger event structures and cultural models (Holland & Quinn, 1987). More than a static image, Cheke Holo talk of entanglement activates broader understandings of interpersonal conflict and its transformation. Evidence of the salience of these understandings may be found in the elaboration of a variety of conventional metaphors used to conceptualize the transformation of conflict. A series of binary oppositions (including "tangled–untangled," "blocking–clearing," and "sticking–freeing") are all associated with verbs that metaphorically describe the transformation of conflicted feelings ("disentangle," "clear away," "pry out"):

TANGLED (*fifiri*)–UNTANGLED (*krutha*)
→
disentangle (*ruarutha*)

BLOCKED (*nagra*)–CLEAR (*snagla*)
→
clear away (*fasnasnagla*)

STUCK (*chakhi*)–UNSTUCK (*snagla*)
→
pry out (*suisukhi*)

In connection with the premise that bad feelings kept inside are dangerous, a parallel set of metaphors conceptualizes the process of making thoughts and emotions public by moving them "outside." This process is expressed in metaphoric images of "opening up" and "talking out" that make hidden thoughts and feelings "visible":

1. TALKING IS PUTTING [THOUGHTS] OUTSIDE.
   INSIDE (*lamna*)–OUTSIDE (*kosi*)
   →
   talk out (*cheke fajifla*)

2. TALKING IS OPENING UP.
   CLOSED (*botho*)–OPEN (*thora*)
   →
   open up (*toatora*)

3. TALKING IS MOVING [THOUGHTS] UP TO THE SURFACE.
   DOWN (*pari*)–UP (*haghe*)
   →
   talk up (*cheke haghe*)
   float up (*thagra*)

4. TALKING IS MAKING [THOUGHTS] VISIBLE.
   HIDDEN (*poru*)–VISIBLE (*kakhana*)
   →
   reveal (*fatakle*)

In each of the verbs above ("talk out," "open up," "float up," and "reveal"), a spatial metaphor represents a social-psychological process of expressing emotions in the service of a desired transformation. As Lakoff and Kövecses (1987) show in their study of metaphors of American anger, conventional English-language expressions for anger are also not static, but rather represent elements of prototypic event sequences associated with anger scenarios or scripts.

EMOTION AS EVENT SCHEMA

In addition to work on emotion metaphors, studies in linguistics (Wierzbicka, 1992), anthropology (Lutz, 1987; White, 1990b), and psychology (Ortony, Clore, & Collins, 1988; Stein, Trabasso, & Liwag, 1993) have all used script-like event schemas to represent emotional meaning. These models go beyond the function of emotion terms to denote feeling states or facial expressions. Instead they represent more complex psychological and social scenarios associated with specific emotions. In their most general, simplified form, emotion schemas represent emotions as mediating antecedent and consequent events.

EVENT → FEELING → THOUGHT/ACTION
                              RESPONSE

Once schemas are represented in this fashion, it is possible to see how emotion theories differ in their emphasis, or exclusion, of particular components of this processual model (cf. Mesquita & Frijda, 1992). Whereas some theories choose to define emotion strictly as embodied feelings or affect, leaving associated actions, thoughts, and events as secondary, others see emotion as constituted in entire action sequences, such that shifts in antecedents or consequents imply different feelings.

Schema models represent emotion as *process*—as embedded in social and psychological scenarios that not only contextualize emotion, but define it in relation to sequences of thoughts and actions. Insofar as event schemas link emotions to social scenarios and modes of thought, they locate emotions in a broader field of significance than typically represented in lexical models. By asking what talk of emotions says implicitly about minds, persons, actions, and events, it is possible to probe emotion talk for unspoken assumptions about subjectivity and social action (in other words, about the premises of folk psychology; see White, 1992).

Even word-centered definitions of emotion terms inevitably represent them as a temporal sequence of events in which feelings mediate specific antecedents and consequents. Thus the cognitivist approaches of both Lakoff and Wierzbicka, using quite different formalisms, each utilize event schemas to represent prototypic word meanings. Lakoff and Kovecses (1987, p. 214), for example, describe a "prototypical scenario" for American English "anger" that consists of five stages, from "offending event" through affective and psychological responses to a performative act, "retribution." Wierzbicka (1992, p. 141), using the format of a proposed semantic metalanguage, represents the abstract meaning of English-language "angry" as an ordered set of propositions as follows:

X thinks something like this:
this person (Y) did something bad
I don't want this

I would want to do something bad to this person because of this, X feels something bad toward Y because of this, X wants to do something

Note that the sequential ordering of propositions in both proposed anger scenarios follows the schematic structure cited above as a universal framework for common-sense reasoning about emotion: EVENT → FEELING → RESPONSE. To further illustrate the utility of event schemas as a representational format capable of linking the analysis of emotional meaning with more situated uses of emotion language, I now briefly consider the representation of several key Cheke Holo emotion words as event schemas.

In discussing the scaling diagram of Cheke Holo emotion words in Figure 3.1, I have noted that negative, undesirable emotions are arrayed generally to the right side of the diagram. "Tangled heart," "be angry," "be sad," and "be shamed" are all located in this space, yet each "says" something quite specific about the kinds of events that precede and follow. To represent these words in event-schematic form, one could begin by noting that all of these terms describe responses to transgressions or violations of the self and the social order. Their similarity as alternative responses in a similar narrative "slot" can be represented as a series of causal event schemas:

Just as "be shamed" and "be sad" are used almost interchangeably by the speaker in the transcript to be presented later, they are also close together in the similarity judgments represented in Figure 3.1, reflecting overlap in knowledge about their occurrence in everyday life. To oversimplify greatly: Both "shame" and "sadness" are associated with transgressions that disturb relations between the self and another person *with whom the self has an important, valued relation*. Unlike "be angry" (*di'a tagna*), which implies some form of serious rupture or break in a relationship, and which is ideally not expressed between closely related people, both *mamaja* and *di'a nagnafa* foreground the value of relations and the need for restoring harmony. Talk of *mamaja* constitutes a kind of relational calculus that works to calibrate or mark social distance and boundaries. In all these cases, it is common for Cheke Holo speakers to use plural pronouns ("we," "us") in making emotional attributions; they often prefer to talk about collective emotional propensities rather than those of individuals.

In Figure 3.1, *mamaja* ("be shamed") is scaled as the most negative emotion on the evaluative dimension. Here the liabilities of lexical models become more obvious. In fact, *mamaja* is a central concept in the Cheke Holo language and has multiple evaluative meanings. It may be good, bad, or both, depending upon context. A primary theme of most usages of *mamaja* is the importance of recognizing or maintaining proper social relations (social distance). Rather than signifying an internal feeling of discomfort evoked by an exposure of the self, or a violation of societal standards of comportment, *mamaja* is much more commonly talked about in the context of interpersonal relations. In particular, *mamaja* is typically evoked in situations where a person inappropriately breaches a social boundary or relationship of respect and distance.

In such situations, *both* parties may report feeling "shame" (or, more correctly, "being shamed"). In Santa Isabel society, the most typical context for eliciting or experiencing shame is the violation of expectations surrounding the sharing or nonsharing of food. To give or exchange food is to affirm the value of enduring relations. In other words, sharing food is a potent index of social relationships. To move about with ease and share food is *not* to feel shame. Conversely, to feel constricted and observant of the proper respect associated with distant relationships *is* to feel shame. The appropriate response to shame situations is withdrawal or avoidance. At the same time, talk of "shame" or its absence also presupposes a certain type of relation between self and other.

CLOSE → NOT *MAMAJA* → APPROACH
RELATION

RELATION → *MAMAJA* → WITHDRAW/AVOID
VIOLATION

If speakers share these understandings about the meanings of *mamaja*, the attribution of *ma-maja* in speech allows listeners to infer unstated propositions about the nature of social actions and relations being described. By chaining together such inferences, emotion schemas constitute a cognitive framework for reasoning about social events. For much the same reason, emotion talk provides an idiom for speaking about social relations and events. These examples illustrate ways in which research on emotion schemas links the study of emotion concepts with the study of the social and pragmatic force of emotion language. Interest in representing emotional meaning in terms of script-like or "scenario" models cuts across a variety of theoretical commitments in the study of emotion, bridging work on emotion cognition with research on more situated uses of emotion language.

EMOTION AS DISCOURSE

To study emotional meaning as it emerges in everyday social life is to study emotion as *discourse*—that is, as a tool for actively shaping the construction of social reality (Lutz & Abu-Lughod, 1990). Discursive approaches to emotional meaning necessarily go beyond strictly psychological or cognitive models to examine the function of emotion signs, especially emotion talk, as it works to create or reproduce social identities and relationships (Bailey, 1983). In semiotic terms, to study emotion as discourse is to focus on the pragmatics of emotion—on what emotion talk *does* in social life, in addition to what it says. As one author puts it, a discourse of emotions involves "the use of verbal formulae for actions, feelings, and motives . . . , with regard to interpersonal judgments and attitudes, all located within local moral orders of authority and responsibility" (Edwards, 1997, p. 187).

Talk about emotions in everyday life frequently has the effect of moral commentary, delivering at least an implicit evaluation of the desirability of specific actions and their consequences for self and society. To talk about feeling a certain way in a certain context is to talk about inclinations to think or act in a certain way. As Ortony et al. (1988) and others have noted, emotion words are always valenced, signifying an evaluation of events and a desire to maintain or adjust some state of affairs (as suggested by the strong evaluative dimension

that emerges in scaling studies of emotion terminology, exemplified by the horizontal dimension of Figure 3.1). Whereas positive emotions
express an acceptance or willingness to maintain a situation, negative emotions function as
signs of discontent, signifying a desire to
change the situation, the self, or both. The
moral work done by emotion language is reflected in the preponderance of negative terms
in emotion lexicons across cultures.

Research on emotion discourse requires an
account of the ecology of emotion talk and expression, identifying the distribution of culturally appropriate ways of talking about the self
in a range of situations and settings. Identifying
culturally constituted contexts for speaking is a
useful step in analyzing the social and moral
force of emotional expression. Attending to the
recurrent social environments for emotion talk
and expression makes it possible to focus attention on the interaction of affective, cognitive,
and social-interactional processes that ultimately constitute emotional meaning in everyday
life. Most research on emotion discourse to
date has focused on well-structured social contexts such as therapy, courts, or meetings,
where social roles and interactive purposes can
be specified with greater certainty, thus identifying the influence of "context," even as context itself may be negotiated in participants'
talk. Consider briefly the role of several key
Cheke Holo emotion words when used in the
context of "disentangling" meetings mentioned
above.

In the Cheke Holo lexicon, several of the
words in Figure 3.1 are used frequently in the
context of the disentangling activities. Two of
the most salient usages in this context are the
terms "be shamed" (*mamaja*) and "be sad"
(*di'a nagnafa*). The significance of these terms
for purposes of disentangling can be illustrated
with a portion of a transcript of a disentangling
session, in which several members of a village
community spoke about interpersonal conflicts
in an effort to "talk out" lingering troubles (for
more details, see White, 1990a). In the passage
below (given in translation), a middle-aged
man describes an incident in which his younger
brother had cut himself after being berated by
his girlfriend's parents (who were also the two
men's uncle and aunt). This passage illustrates
the role of emotion talk as a rhetoric for interpreting past events and restoring social harmony. It begins with the speaker talking about
feeling "knotted up":

1 "Allright, it was his wrongdoing that brought
2 this on," I thought, but got all *haru* [knotted
3 up] inside about it.

4 It was the statement "Don't set foot in [our vil-
5 lage]" that made me *mamaja* [shamed] with
6 him [the girlfriend's father]

7 Hey! But this is our uncle. The two of us
8 [speaker and younger brother] would go into
9 their house. The sweet potatoes were our food,
10 these houses and these beds. "Sleep! Eat, you
11 all!" [they would say]. . . . That's what made
12 me *di'a nagnafa* [sad]. . . .

13 . . . It's just that when my real uncle came out
14 and said that ["Don't set foot here any more"]
15 that I was sad and came to talk to the old lady
16 [aunt]. I was just ashamed is all. I didn't mean
17 "You all don't come up to [our village]." That
18 was just from my sadness and my shame. . . .

19 . . . Now I'm in front of my mothers and sis-
20 ters. These houses are for entering, for drink-
21 ing water. It was when that talk ["Don't set
22 foot here!"] started coming from my uncle
23 that I was sad.

Disentangling meetings allow speakers extended stretches of time for uninterrupted narration,
thus producing more explicit statements about
antecedents, feelings, intentions, and responses
than is typical in ordinary conversation. Speakers make explicit a greater proportion of implicit knowledge by verbalizing aspects of emotion scenarios that might otherwise be inferred.
By talking about preceding events, mediating
feelings, intentions, and so forth, each speaker
works to instantiate a desired reading of events
as a public account. In the example above, the
speaker's talk of his "shame," *mamaja*, punctu-
ates a longer narrative about the nature of his
relationship with the other principals in the
conflict episode.

A notable aspect of the speaker's narrative is
the interplay of attributions of "sadness" and
"shame," at times used almost interchangeably
as emotional descriptions of responses that
foreground valued relations. This has to do not
only with the fact that both emotions concern
social transgressions (as represented in the
schematic formulas listed earlier), but that both
also pertain to conflict between closely related
persons. In addition, it can be hypothesized that
talk of "sadness" and "shame" has the effect of
rhetorically displacing "anger" (*di'a tagna*),
which might otherwise be expected to arise in
such conflict situations (see White, 1990b).

By hypothesizing that Cheke Holo speakers understand *mamaja* in terms of event schemas such as those sketched above linking antecedents and responses, it is possible to analyze the implicational structure of these attributions. Thus, if talk of "shame" entails understandings about degrees of "closeness" in social relations, the speaker's reference to his ability to move about freely and be offered food in the home of his uncle and aunt (lines 7–10, 19–23) implies a close relationship. Similarly, asserting that he felt "shame" in their presence implies a breakdown in these relations associated with the incident at hand.

The present discussion of emotional meaning as a social-psychological scenario has begun by considering the processual form of cognitive, semantic models, and has then moved to consider emotional meaning as it emerges in situated uses of emotion talk. A fuller account of the discursive psychology of "disentangling" and the emotion talk that occurs in this context is not possible in the limited space available here. However, brief consideration of the emotion "shame" will further expand issues that arise in the study of emotional meaning as discourse.

Despite the salience of shame in emotion lexicons worldwide, it has not been extensively researched in work on "basic" emotions. "Shame" is included in Ekman's studies of facial expression (Ekman, 1992), but typically gets low reliability scores and is usually left off lists of basic affects. One study of English emotion terms, for example, represented "shame" as subsumed within a "sadness" cluster that also included "suffering," "disappointment," "loneliness," and "sympathy" (Shaver et al., 1987). Michael Lewis (Chapter 39, this volume) describes shame as a "self-conscious evaluative" emotion that emerges later in development than emotions such as joy, anger, fear, or sadness and requires more complex cognitive elicitors than the latter, which are regarded as more basic emotions. In other words, the largely social and moral significance of shame and its non-English analogues does not fit the more individuated, physiological conception of basic emotions.

Investigation of the emotional meanings of English-language "shame" and "embarrassment" highlight the significance of social relations for this class of emotions in ways that parallel arguments about the salience of shame in non-Western cultures. Using interview data to examine American concepts of shame and embarrassment, Holland and Kipnis (1995) found that "public exposure" is a key metaphor in stories about embarrassment. More importantly, however, the "exposure" in these stories was not bodily exposure, but exposure of some kind of contradiction in the presentation of self for specific audiences. Thus, for Americans as for many non-Western peoples, embarrassment has a prototypically social-relational meaning. In the words of Holland and Kipnis (1995), "in every embarrassment story we heard the social context was specified. In no story was it taken for granted, or even spoken of metaphorically. The social contexts had to be spoken of explicitly, because the social context is what stories are about. . . . One cannot discuss embarrassment without social context because the stories are *about the social presentation of the self*" (p. 195; italics added).

Despite their marginal or secondary position in English-language studies of basic emotions, shame-like emotions are ubiquitous in emotion lexicons and ideologies around the world (see Mesquita & Frijda, 1992, for a review). In a volume of essays surveying Pacific islands ethnopsychologies (White & Kirkpatrick, 1985), for example, "anger" and "shame" are the most frequently mentioned emotion words (as measured, unsystematically, by the size of index entries for English glosses). In many of these societies, "shame" often takes the form of an action or performance, "shaming," rather than a noun or label for a type of feeling. As a transitive verb, "shaming" practices performatively direct and enforce desired social behavior. To understand the emotional meanings of shame and its importance cross-culturally, it is necessary to examine the social and emotional work of shame and shame talk as these occur in everyday interaction.

Much of the research on the emotional meanings of shame has focused on socialization practices where shame talk functions as a rhetorical device in the speech of caregivers attempting to sanction or direct the actions of children. Caregiver–child speech has been the subject of intensive sociolinguistic research, such as that of Schieffelin (1990) on shaming and teasing routines among the Kaluli of Papua New Guinea, or Ochs (1986) on Samoan family interactions. Their work demonstrates the function of emotion words and routines in creating specific, desired forms of social behavior. The discourse approach is effective in analyzing the interaction of emotion concepts (in this case, Pacific variants of "shame"), interactive "scripts," and normative social relations. This research analyzes emotional meaning as essentially social in nature—as constituted in speech acts that index key dimensions of social identity.

The other context in which shame emotions have been studied extensively concern practices of conflict resolution (Watson-Gegeo & White, 1990). In Santa Isabel society, as in many cultures worldwide, a typical response to shame situations is avoidance. Avoidance, however, creates its own problems, especially in small communities where avoidance places a burden on people and implies the existence of unresolved conflict and bad feeling. Many conflict resolution practices in the Pacific islands are in fact primarily concerned with "avoidance resolution"—with (rhetorically) transforming shame so as to reestablish a more desired form of social relations. Indeed, many societies have institutionalized culturally defined contexts that make it possible to talk openly about social conflict for this purpose. These contexts enable talk that does *not* activate troublesome emotions because of the definition of the situation, the purpose of talk, and relations among participants. For example, in meetings of chiefs in Samoa studied by Duranti, the formality of the occasion "permits direct talk about the transgressions of chiefs that would be highly shaming in other settings. Talk of chiefly transgressions is allowed and encouraged by defining the situation as one of decorous discussion among chiefs aimed at reconciliation" (cited in Watson-Gegeo & White, 1990, p. 17).

Such culturally organized practices as caregiver–child interaction, conflict resolution activities, or meetings of chiefs are examples of institutionalized forms of emotion discourse. Here emotion talk is a kind of communicative practice that links conceptual models, narrative accounts, and speech acts in the context of purposive activities. In these contexts emotional meaning is embedded in institutionalized practices concerned with facilitating goal-oriented actions, especially collective actions. Activities such as these may be seen as "emotion institutions," in which ordinary talk instantiates emotion schemas in the service of transforming social realities. Other examples would include therapy practices, religious and healing rituals, memorial ceremonies, pilgrimages, and so forth. In the Pacific and elsewhere, one finds a multitude of culturally constituted practices for transforming anger, from gossip to apology rituals. The potential variety of representational means used in the service of forming and transforming emotional meaning is seemingly limitless (cf. Besnier, 1995).

CONCLUSION

Lutz (1988) describes emotional meaning as a "social rather than an individual achievement" (p. 5). This chapter has explored the proposition that the meaningful world of emotion is preeminently social. When several distinct styles and methods of analysis are traced from strictly word-centered approaches to clearly social, discursive ones, it is possible to see that each entails a different range of constraints on the representation of emotional meaning. Instead of viewing these approaches as exclusive, however, it is more useful to see them as related in complex ways. So, for example, socially constructed emotional meaning also depends on cognitive emotion schemas, conceived as processual and emergent in interaction. Although there are points of contradiction in the various approaches to emotional meaning discussed here (such that differing methodological preferences reinforce conflicting theoretical commitments), there are also points of complementarity where one approach to emotional meaning may be embedded or presupposed in another. For example, the more limited formalisms of lexical methods and cognitive semantics provide opportunities for comparison not easily pursued with the more contextualized approaches to emotion as discourse. On the other hand, any approach to emotional meaning that seeks to represent the common-sense (cultural) significance of ordinary emotion words and categories will need to take account of the actual discursive practices within which emotion talk (and, more generally, communicative action) occurs. As Edwards (1997) puts it, "Emotion categories are not graspable merely as individual feelings or expressions, and nor is their discursive deployment reducible to a kind of detached, cognitive sense-making. They are discursive phenomena and need to be studied as such, as part of how talk performs social actions" (p. 187).

Research on emotion and emotional meaning that seeks to avoid being caught in self-limiting dichotomies will require multiple methods for representing the ways emotions are conceptualized, talked about, and manipulated in everyday life. There seems little to be gained in playing these realms off against one another, or in characterizing entire socioemotional systems as *either* individual or social (collective) in orientation. It is important to note that research on cultural differences in emotional meaning does not imply some kind of "radical otherness" or incommensurability of culturally relative forms. To the contrary, one of the aims of comparative research on emotional meaning is to articulate points of similarity and difference in terms of a common (revisable) framework. The introduction of a variety of cognitive, linguistic, and ethnographic methods for exploring emotional meaning is expanding the focus of emotion research beyond its historical focus on basic emotions conceived in terms of biopsychological essences. Employing a variety of representational schemes to investigate emotional meaning at multiple levels of analysis makes it possible to define emotion in a way that encompasses greater social and psychological complexity.

REFERENCES

Bailey, F. (1983). *The tactical uses of passion: An essay on power, reason and reality*. Ithaca, NY: Cornell University Press.

Bernard, H. R. (1995). *Research methods in anthropology: Qualitative and quantitative approaches*. Walnut Creek, CA: AltaMira Press.

Besnier, N. (1995). *Literacy, emotion and authority: Reading and writing on a Polynesian atoll*. New York: Cambridge University Press.

Bowlin, J. R., & Stromberg, P. G. (1997). Representation and reality in the study of culture. *American Anthropologist, 99*, 123–134.

Brown, R., & Gilman, A. (1960). The pronouns of power and solidarity. In T. Sebeok (Ed.), *Style in language* (pp. 253–276). Cambridge, MA: Harvard University Press.

D'Andrade, R. G. (1978). U-statistic hierarchical clustering. *Psychometrika, 43*, 59–67.

D'Andrade, R. G. (1987). A folk model of the mind. In D. Holland & N. Quinn (Eds.), *Cultural models in language and thought* (pp. 112–148). Cambridge, England: Cambridge University Press.

Edwards, D. (1997). *Emotion, discourse and cognition*. Thousand Oaks, CA: Sage.

Ekman, P. (1992). An argument for basic emotions. *Cognition and Emotion, 6*, 169–200.

Gerber, E. (1985). Rage and obligation: Samoan emotions in conflict. In G. White & J. Kirkpatrick (Eds.), *Person, self and experience: Exploring Pacific ethnopsychologies* (pp. 121–167). Berkeley: University of California Press.

Goleman, D. (1995, March 28). The brain manages happiness and sadness in different centers. *The New York Times,* pp. B9–10.

Heider, K. (1991). *Landscapes of emotion: Mapping three cultures in Indonesia*. Cambridge, England: Cambridge University Press.

Holland, D., & Kipnis, A. (1995). American models of embarrassment: The not-so-egocentric self laid bare. In J. Russell, A. Manstead, & J. Wellenkamp (Eds.), *Everyday conceptions of emotion: An introduction to the psychology, anthropology and linguistics of emotion* (pp. 181–202). Dordrecht, The Netherlands: Kluwer.

Holland, D., & Quinn, N. (Eds.). (1987). *Cultural models in language and thought*. Cambridge, England: Cambridge University Press.

Kay, P., & Berlin, B. (1997). Science not = imperialism: There are nontrivial constraints on color naming. *Behavioral and Brain Sciences, 20*, 196–203.

Kitayama, S., & Markus, H. (Eds.). (1994a). *Emotion and culture: Empirical studies of mutual influence*. Washington, DC: American Psychological Association.

Kitayama, S., & Markus, H. (1994b). Introduction to cultural psychology and emotion research. In S. Kitayama & H. Markus (Eds.), *Emotion and culture* (pp. 1–19). Washington, DC: American Psychological Association.

Kövecses, Z. (1990). *Emotion concepts*. Berlin: Springer-Verlag.

Kruskal, J., Young, F., & Seery, J. (1972). *How to use KYST-2, a very flexible program to do multidimensional scaling and unfolding*. Murray Hill, NJ: Bell Laboratories.

Lakoff, G., & Kövecses, Z. (1987). The cognitive model of anger inherent in American English. In N. Quinn & D. Holland (Eds.), *Cultural models in language and thought* (pp. 194–221). Cambridge, England: Cambridge University Press.

Lutz, C. (1982). The domain of emotion words on Ifaluk. *American Ethnologist, 9*, 113–128.

Lutz, C. (1987). Goals, events and understanding in Ifaluk emotion theory. In D. Holland & N. Quinn (Eds.), *Cultural models in language and thought* (pp. 290–312). Cambridge, England: Cambridge University Press.

Lutz, C. (1988). *Unnatural emotions: Everyday sentiments on a Micronesian atoll and their challenge to Western theory*. Chicago: University of Chicago Press.

Lutz, C., & Abu-Lughod, L. (Eds.). (1990). *Language and the politics of emotion*. Cambridge, England: Cambridge University Press.

Lutz, C., & White, G. (1986). The anthropology of emotions. *Annual Review of Anthropology, 15*, 405–436.

Lyon, M. L. (1995). Missing emotion: The limitations of cultural constructionism in the study of emotion. *Cultural Anthropology, 10*(2), 244–263.

Mesquita, B., & Frijda, N. H. (1992). Cultural variations in emotions: A review. *Psychological Bulletin, 112*, 179–204.

Oatley, K., & Jenkins, J. M. (1996). *Understanding emotions*. Oxford, MA: Blackwell.

Ochs, E. (1986). From feelings to grammar: A Samoan case study. In B. B. Schieffelin & E. Ochs (Eds.), *Language socialization across cultures* (pp. 251–272). Cambridge, England: Cambridge University Press.

Ortony, A., Clore, G., & Collins, A. (1988). *The cognitive structure of emotions.* Cambridge, England: Cambridge University Press.

Osgood, C. (1964). The semantic differential technique in the comparative study of cultures. *American Anthropologist, 66,* 171–200.

Reddy, W. M. (1997). Against constructionism: The historical ethnography of emotions. *Current Anthropology, 38*(3), 327–351.

Romney, A. K., Moore, C., & Rusch, C. (1997). Cultural universals: Measuring the semantic structure of emotion terms in English and Japanese. *Proceedings of the National Academy of Sciences USA, 94,* 5489–5494.

Rosaldo, M. (1980). *Knowledge and passion: Ilongot notions of self and social life.* Cambridge, England: Cambridge University Press.

Russell, J. A. (1980). A circumplex model of affect. *Journal of Personality and Social Psychology, 39,* 1152–1168.

Russell, J. A. (1983). Pancultural aspects of the human conceptual organization of emotion. *Journal of Personality and Social Psychology, 45,* 1281–1288.

Russell, J. A. (1991a). Culture and the categorization of emotions. *Psychological Bulletin, 110,* 426–450.

Russell, J. A. (1991b). In defense of a prototype approach to emotion concepts. *Journal of Personality and Social Psychology, 60,* 37–47.

Russell, J. A. (Ed.). (1995). *Everyday conceptions of emotion.* Dordrecht, The Netherlands: Kluwer.

Schachter, S., & Singer, J. E. (1962). Cognitive, social and physiological determinants of emotional state. *Psychological Review, 69,* 379–399.

Schieffelin, B. (1990). *The give and take of everyday life.* Cambridge, England: Cambridge University Press.

Schimmack, U., & Reisenzein, R. (1997). Cognitive processes involved in similarity judgments of emotions. *Journal of Personality and Social Psychology, 73*(4), 645–661.

Shaver, P. R., Schwartz, J. C., Kirson, D., & O'Connor, C. (1987). Emotion knowledge: Further explorations of a prototype approach. *Journal of Personality and Social Psychology, 52,* 1061–1086.

Shaver, P. R., Wu, S., & Schwartz, J. C. (1992). Cross-cultural similarities and differences in emotion and its representation. In M. Clark (Ed.), *Review of personality and social psychology* (Vol. 13, pp. 175–212). Newbury Park, CA: Sage.

Shweder, R. (1994). "You're not sick, you're just in love": Emotion as an interpretive system. In P. Ekman & R. J. Davidson (Eds.), *The nature of emotion: Fundamental questions* (pp. 32–44). New York: Oxford University Press.

Stein, N. L., Trabasso, T., & Liwag, M. (1993). The representation and organization of emotional experience: Unfolding the emotion episode. In M. Lewis & J. M. Haviland (Eds.), *Handbook of emotions* (pp. 279–300). New York: Guilford Press.

Watson-Gegeo, K. A., & White, G. M. (Eds.). (1990). *Disentangling: Conflict discourse in Pacific societies.* Stanford, CA: Stanford University Press.

Where emotions come from: Unlocking the biological secrets of joy, fear, anger and despair. (1991, June 24). *U.S. News and World Report,* pp. 54–62.

White, G. M. (1980). Conceptual universals in interpersonal language. *American Anthropologist, 82,* 759–781.

White, G. M. (1990a). Emotion talk and social inference: Disentangling in Santa Isabel, Solomon Islands. In K. A. Watson-Gegeo & G. M. White (Eds.), *Disentangling: Conflict discourse in Pacific societies* (pp. 53–121). Stanford, CA: Stanford University Press.

White, G. M. (1990b). Moral discourse and the rhetoric of emotions. In C. Lutz & L. Abu-Lughod (Eds.), *Language and the politics of emotion* (pp. 46–68). Cambridge, England: Cambridge University Press.

White, G. M. (1992). Ethnopsychology. In T. Schwartz, G. M. White, & C. Lutz (Eds.), *New directions in psychological anthropology* (pp. 21–46). Cambridge, England: Cambridge University Press.

White, G. M. (1994). Affecting culture: Emotion and morality in everyday life. In S. Kitayama & H. Markus (Eds.), *Emotion and culture: Empirical studies of mutual influence* (pp. 219–239). Washington, DC: American Psychological Association.

White, G. M., & Kirkpatrick, J. (Eds.). (1985). *Person, self and experience: Exploring Pacific ethnopsychologies.* Berkeley: University of California Press.

Wierzbicka, A. (1992). *Semantics, culture, and cognition.* Oxford: Oxford University Press.

Wierzbicka, A. (1995). Emotion and facial expression: A semantic perspective. *Culture and Psychology, 1*(2), 227–258.

CHAPTER 4

Social Models in the Explanation of Emotions

Theodore D. Kemper

In primacy of interest, disciplinary seemliness, and volume of empirical work, psychologists "own" the topic of emotions. Yet, given the scope, span, and ramifications of emotion phenomena, many other disciplines are also legitimately concerned with affective life. Physiologists link emotions to anatomical structures and processes; anthropologists tie emotions to particular cultural logics and practices; historians trace emotions of today to emotions of the past; ethologists seek what is phylogenetically given as well as distinctively human in emotions; and sociologists examine how emotions are triggered, interpreted, and expressed by virtue of human membership in groups. In this chapter, several major social models of emotions are presented.

The sociological interest in emotions is manifold, spanning such topics as the emotional foundation of social solidarity in groups, whether large or small; the determination of emotions by outcomes of social interaction; the normative regulation of emotional expression and the management of emotional deviance; the socialization of emotions through transfer of meaning to physiological experience; the linkage of emotion to socially derived conceptions of identity and the self; the variation in emotional experience according to categories of social organization such as social class, occupation, gender, race/ethnicity, and the like; and emotions in large-scale societal processes of

stability and change. Sociological models of emotion often dovetail with psychological and even physiological approaches to emotion. But the sociological examination of emotions is valid in its own right.

Put baldly, there can be no individual as the subject of psychological study without the social. Survival itself is socially dependent. The acquisition of any but the most rudimentary abilities and motives is socially determined. The development of a large portion of what we call "personality" is a social product. Even when there is a recognized hereditary contribution (Tellegen et al., 1988; Neubauer & Neubauer, 1990), the socially caused variance in personality and behavior is large. Identity, the self, and self-esteem are social outcomes. Even the capacity of mind to reflect and to rehearse alternative courses of action—that is, the ability to think—is socially given (Mead, 1934). Threading through, between, and around these elements of the person are emotions.

Although a substantial part of the emotional anlage is biological, the social overlay in every culture is so substantial that without it we would not identify the person as truly human. The groups and group categories that matter for the production of emotions include social class; occupation, gender, and racial/ethnic groups; and peer groups, families, communities, crowds, audiences, and nations. Each of these memberships provides the individual with identity, motives, goals, roles, and interaction partners.

Given that the individual is the locus of emotion—we can measure emotion nowhere but in the individual—the containment of the individual in the social matrix determines *which emotions are likely to be expressed when and where, on what grounds and for what reasons, by what modes of expression, by whom.* As the social matrix changes, so do all of the parameters of the emotion formula just presented. Sociological models of emotion theorize the social matrix and its parameters. The sociological models of emotions presented here are marked by their scope, substantive diversity, and comprehensiveness. They display the broad range of inquiry that a sociological address to emotions makes possible. (For additional sociological approaches to emotions, see Kemper, 1991b.)

SOCIAL RELATIONS AND EMOTIONS

There can be no argument that social relations produce emotions. Indeed, emotions have an evolutionary function precisely because they allow the individual to adapt to environmental contingencies (Plutchik, 1991), a substantial portion of which entail social relations. If there is an argument, it is over how to characterize the social environment or social relations. Elsewhere (Kemper, 1978; Kemper & Collins, 1990), I have proposed that social relations can be usefully expressed in two dimensions, "power" and "status," and that a very large number of human emotions can be understood as reactions to the power and/or status meanings and implications of situations.

Power is understood as a relational condition in which one actor actually or potentially compels another actor to do something he or she does not wish to do. The means of power in a relationship include threatened or actual use of force or deprivation of valued material or symbolic goods and experiences. Noxious behavioral stimuli, including shaking of fists, facial grimacing, raised voice, speech interruptions, and the like, are hallmarks of power use. Lies, deceit, and manipulation also fall within the power category.

Status, on the other hand, is understood as the relational condition of voluntary compliance with the wishes, interests, and desires of another person. One actor accords status to another through acts of recognition of the other's value. These include considerateness, sociability, caring, respect, esteem, and, at its ultimate, love.

Support for the power and status delineation of social relations derives from a large number of factor analyses of interaction in small groups; ethological analyses of primate behavior; studies of cross-cultural roles and behavior; semantic analysis; studies of interpersonal vectors of personality; and the dimensions of learning theory (details in Kemper & Collins, 1990). The weight of evidence for the power and status dimensions of social relationship has led to the surmise that these are perhaps the theoretically optimum dimensions by which any relationship may usefully be characterized.

I have proposed (Kemper, 1978) the following implication for emotions: *A very large class of human emotions results from real, anticipated, imagined, or recollected outcomes of social relations.* From the perspective of any actor, any episode of interaction in a social relationship may have the following outcomes: increase, decrease, or no change in the self's own power and status vis-à-vis the other; and increase, decrease, or no change in the other's power and status vis-à-vis the self. All together, there are 12 possible outcomes, only 4 of which will occur; that is, both the self's own and the other's power and status position will be affected. Emotions will ensue depending on the particular power and status outcomes, taking into account also the factor of "agency"—namely, the attribution of who is responsible for the relational outcome (self, other, or a third party).

The extensive results on emotions obtained in surveys and laboratory experiments support the following conclusions about emotions and power and status outcomes in social relations:

1. *Own power.* Power increase leads to feelings of security because one can better protect oneself if necessary from the power incursions of the other, but excess use of power leads to feelings of guilt for having wronged the other, and fear/anxiety concerning the other's possible retaliation. Power decrease leads to feelings of fear/anxiety because the other has greater ability to compel one to do what one does not want to do.

2. *Other's power.* Increase in the other's power has the same effect as decrease of one's own power—namely, fear/anxiety. Decrease of

the other's power has the same effect as increase in one's own power—namely, security.

3. *Own status*. Status increase in the amount felt as deserved leads to satisfaction or happiness/contentment. If the self was the agent, pride is also likely. If the agent was the other or a third party, one will feel gratitude. Increase in status beyond what was expected results in joy, with the corresponding effects of agency, as above. To accept more status than one feels one deserves leads to shame/embarrassment. Decrease in status leads to anger if the agent is the other, shame if the agent is the self, and depression if the situation is deemed irremediable.

4. *Other's status*. One's own emotions in respect to the other's status depend on one's liking for the other. Liking is a summary feeling that reflects the degree to which other has conferred sufficient status on the self and has not used excessive power against the self (Kemper, 1989). If one likes the other, increase in the other's status, regardless of agency, leads to satisfaction. If one dislikes the other, the agent is not likely to be self. The other or a third party as the agent leads to envy or jealousy, depending on whether the other has something one desires, or the other has taken away something of one's own. If one likes the other, and the other's status decreases, agency by the self leads to either guilt or shame, depending on whether one caused the status decrease by use of power or by failing to act according to the standards that apply to one's own level of deserved status. If the agent of the decrease is the other or a third party, one's own feeling is sorrow or pity. If one does not like the other, the other's status decrease where the agent is the self leads to satisfaction. When the agent of the decrease is the other or a third party, the feeling is called *Schadenfreude*—a German term for the satisfaction one feels at the discomfiture of another.

Anticipatory emotions are based on a combination of past relational (power and status) experience, which affects optimism–pessimism, and one's estimate of present relational conditions, which arouses some degree of confidence–lack of confidence. Taken together the two sentiments give rise to four feelings: optimism + confidence = serene confidence or happiness/contentment; optimism + lack of confidence = guarded optimism or anxiety; pessimism + confidence = grudging optimism or anxiety; and pessimism + lack of confidence = hopelessness or depression.

Within the power–status framework, I have proposed (Kemper, 1978) a socialization paradigm for the assumption of the four major negative emotions (guilt, shame, anxiety, and depression) as characteristic moods and dispositions. The elements of the model are three dichotomous punishment parameters: type (is it power-oriented punishment, e.g., physical, or status-oriented punishment, e.g., shaming?); proportionality (is the punishment roughly proportional or excessive with respect to the seriousness of the punished act?); and affection (is the punisher a major source of affection or status?). Tracing the several branches of this model leads to a set of eight outcome hypotheses about how each of the negative emotions is socialized as a characteristic personality trait, as well as the usual coping response when the negative emotion is activated. For example, a status-based punishment in proportion to the seriousness of the act socializes shame as a characteristic emotion. If the punisher is also the major source of affection (which is more than likely if he or she is a parent), coping will be oriented toward compensation of those toward whom the subject acts in a shameful manner. If the punisher does not control affection, the coping response is hypothesized to be a characteristic hypercritical perfectionism.

Finally, the power–status model affords an insight into love relations and the difference between loving and liking. "Love" can be defined as a relationship in which one actor gives or is prepared to give extremely high amounts of status to another. This definition yields seven different types of love relationships—romantic, brotherly, charismatic, unfaithful, unrequited, adulation by fans, and parent–infant—which vary according to whether one or both actors are conferring extreme amounts of status, and on the power positions of each actor (power is not excluded from love relations, except in two of the types). Evolution and devolution of love relationships are examined in light of the dynamics of power use and status accord (Kemper, 1978). Liking is distinguished from love by the following: Love is experienced when the attributes of the other match one's own standards. This match produces a sense of pleasurable harmony between self and other that is labeled "love." Liking, on the other hand, is felt for another who gives adequate status and uses very little power. From this perspective, one can like and not love another, can not like and love another, or can both like and love (Kemper, 1989; Kemper & Reid, 1997).

In an empirical test of the power–status approach to the determination of emotions, I (Kemper, 1991a) found a good fit between the theory and the relational conditions antecedent to the four primary emotions about which data were gathered in the eight-nation study conducted by Scherer, Wallbott, and Summerfield (1986): anger, fear, sadness, and joy.

INTERACTION RITUAL CHAINS: MAKING SOCIAL CLASS

A fundamental question for anyone who reflects on social life is what keeps a group, whether a society or a marriage, cohesive and together. One possible answer would be coercion. Stronger members force weaker members to remain, usually to serve the stronger ones. From another perspective, self-interest may be used to explain the pattern of continued interaction among group members. In contrast to these explanations, Émile Durkheim (1912/1954) proposed that the force of cohesion resides in shared emotions. Groups cohere because they undertake ritual activities (e.g., of a religious nature), which leads to heightened emotions among the participants. Those who share arousal also respond positively to it, and hence seek the experience again with the same coparticipants. Emotional rewards thus bind us to groups.

This idea was taken further by Erving Goffman (1967), who postulated the ritual nature of all interactions, including those between two participants in a small group. The enacted ritual is not focused on religious symbols, as in Durkheim's example, but on an equally sacred object—namely, the *self* of each interaction participant. Small-group interactions, which consist mainly of conversation, are able when successful to enhance the self of each participant. Although social conversation appears to have an unstructured and perhaps even random or meandering character, Goffman pointed out that it is strongly guided in the minds of all participants by the need to protect the esteem and standing of all other participants. Ordinarily, this is accomplished without incident. But when the rules fail (a social solecism has occurred), and someone's integrity has been violated (either by one's own unwitting doing or by another's), the result is a commonly felt emotion of embarrassment. Indeed, this emotion reveals that the group has failed in its effort to rouse emotions in common, especially in their focus on a sacred object—the self of each participant. Goffman detailed the great lengths to which group members are likely to go to preserve themselves and others from embarrassment, including taking people's claims about themselves (except if egregiously questionable) at face value. To challenge such a claim is to cause a possible loss of face to the other, but also to oneself, since in addition to denying credibility to another, one has violated the cardinal rule of group coherence—namely, to preserve intact the ritual objects that are the focus of group attention.

Randall Collins (1975, 1981, 1990) has mobilized the ideas of Durkheim and Goffman into a theory of "interaction ritual chains," designed to explain emotion at both the micro (or small-group) and the macro (or large-group) levels. The key concept for Collins is "emotional energy." This is a feeling of confidence and enthusiasm that is experienced after successful ritual interaction. Such interaction requires several elements:

1. Group members' attention must be focused on a common object of ritual interest. It could be the self of one or more members, or other symbols of interest, such as the work being done together, or the sports contest all are watching, or the flag being lowered at the end of a day.

2. A common emotion is engendered by whatever activities the members are engaged in. Any emotion will do—even anger, if the common activity is an argument. In the course of common emotional arousal, members begin to resonate in tune with each other's emotional frequency, so that there is not only a cognitive commonality but also a physiological entrainment. Each member becomes more and more attuned to the rhythms of talk and action of the other members.

3. The result, over and above all others, is a feeling of solidarity with other members. More often than not, the initial emotion (of step 2 above) is transient. What remains is the long-term satisfaction of membership. Those who emote together tend to stay together.

Solidarity, according to Collins, is not an abstract notion, but one that is rooted in the body of each participant in the form of emotional energy. Emotional energy derived from such ritual interaction encounters provides the emotional capital with which to undertake other interactions, where one has again the opportunity (if the proper attention has been paid to the requirements of ritual interaction) to renew one's stock of emotional resources or to gain even more of them.

In optimum interaction episodes, all members gain emotional energy because the proper respect has been accorded to the common symbols all hold dear, or to each person's own most cherished symbol (namely, the self, as discussed above). But interactions are optimum only some of the time. More often, some members come away with surplus emotional energy, while others experience a deficit. Each individual enters the interaction with his or her own stock of emotional energy and other resources attained in prior interactions. The group itself is more or less able to organize the conditions of interaction so as to generate optimum outcomes for the members. For example, one thinks of a seminar with too many participants, or a party with too few. In each case, the proper critical mass for the purposes of the ritual occasion has been missed, and the interaction that proceeds is likely to be strained, uncomfortable, and unable to mobilize the members into the mutually resonating sets that successful groups accomplish. But beyond these individual or ecological deficits or obstacles to optimum outcomes for members are the relational conditions of power and status, which stratify opportunities for emotional energy. By virtue of their power and status standing in groups, individuals are able to accumulate greater or lesser amounts of emotional resonance with the group and its sacred objects.

Power Interaction

Interactions in the power domain occur between those Collins calls "order givers" and "order takers." The former are the established institutional leaders of the group, the latter their subordinates: managers and workers, officers and enlisted personnel, teachers and students, government officials and citizens, and so on. In the ritual interactions that any such pair engages in, the order giver is ordinarily more committed to the particular sacred symbols that are the focus of the interaction—the production schedule, the war strategy, the homework assignment, the tax law. Hence the order giver, who is ordinarily able to enforce his or her view

of how the interaction should proceed, is more likely to derive a charge of emotional energy from the interaction. The order taker assists at this process by assenting to the commands of the order giver, and at the same time is likely to lose emotional energy because his or her sacred symbols are being violated or ignored. Order givers thus derive the enthusiasm and confidence to go on to other interaction ritual occasions filled with the expectation of obtaining even more benefits. *In toto,* these chains of ritual interaction in which there is differential power sum to the stratification system of society, with each interaction in the power domain confirming and reinforcing the existing pattern of differential benefit.

Status Interaction

Social life is differentiated not only by the dimension of giving and taking orders, but by membership in groups where one shares identity with others. These include race, ethnicity, gender, social class, occupation, and community (which are standard sociological categories), but also peer groups, sociability groups, and ad hoc groups with a transient life. Shared identity is the criterion, and membership in and of itself is a basis for emotional energy. This is because each group provides members with a sense of inclusion, which is a valued enhancement of self.

But group members differ in the amount of emotional energy they derive from their status group memberships. One consideration is centrality–peripherality. Some members are always present when the group convenes, interacting intensely with many other members. They become sociometric stars, the focus of much interest and attention. Their presence and their conversation are sought, and they come to personify the group's values and interests. Their emotional energy is thus constantly being renewed. On the other hand, some members are isolated, rarely in attendance, and little likely to stir interest in other members by their actions or verbal sallies. Such peripheral members derive only the minimal amount of emotional energy from their membership in the group.

Together, power and status constitute a grid of social relations that underlies all social interactions, providing the individual with greater or lesser amounts of emotional resources of a relatively stable nature. Thus, at the high end are the emotions of confidence, enthusiasm, and trust, while at the low end are depression and distrust. Collins (1990) has proposed that the more intense short-term or dramatic emotions, such as fear, anger, joy, and the like, are like spikes superimposed on a tonic or baseline level of emotional energy that is characteristic for the person.

For example, joy is the sharply heightened experience of successful ritual interaction, as when one is participating in a rollicking party among good friends; or when one's team is winning at a sports event; or even when one has been recognized by other members as exemplary, as in winning an award. Anger is of several kinds. "Dominating" anger is the high-energy aggression of order givers who employ it to overcome obstacles that order takers may put in their way. "Disruptive" anger is manifested by order takers who believe, correctly or otherwise, that they have enough resources to resist the demands of an order giver. "Righteous" anger is felt by those who believe that a sacred symbol has been violated, and thus that the ritual integrity of the group is in peril. Fear is a response to another person's anger, reflecting the expectation that one will be hurt.

According to Collins, these short-term emotions are governed to a great extent by the tide of emotional energy upon which they ride. Those who are high in emotional energy are seldom likely to experience anger, except of the righteous kind. Those low in emotional energy are more likely to experience fear, because of their frequent occasions of subordination in the power settings where they are order takers.

SHAME AND SOCIAL ORDER

Charles Horton Cooley (1902) created the "looking-glass" metaphor by which we are most likely to understand the source of self-evaluation:

> In imagination we perceive in another's mind some thought of our appearance, manners, aims, deeds . . . and are variously affected by it. A self-idea of this sort seems to have three principal elements: the imagination of our appearance to the other person; the imagination of his judgment of that appearance; and some sort of self-feeling, such as pride or mortification. (p. 184)

Cooley alluded to the process as something like standing before a "looking glass," giving rise to the notion of the "looking-glass self."

For Thomas Scheff (1988, 1990a, 1990b), the emotions that underlie the looking-glass self give rise to a theory of social control, which is fundamental to the maintenance of society. Scheff contends that we are continually in a state of either pride or shame with respect to the judgments of others about our adherence to their and society's moral strictures. When we obey, we experience pride; when we disobey, we experience shame. Since pride is a pleasurable emotion and shame unpleasurable, the effect is to produce conformity in society, and hence a high degree of social stability. Pride and shame thus ensure social control without the need for external surveillance and regulation.

If pride and shame are as prevalent as Scheff requires them to be, why is there not more evidence of their presence? To answer this question, Scheff relies on the work of Helen Block Lewis (1971), who has proposed that there are two forms of shame that go unrecognized by those who experience them. These are "overt, undifferentiated" shame and "bypassed" shame.

According to Lewis, overt, undifferentiated shame is marked by efforts to disguise or hide the shame from others, including the self. It takes the form of speech disruption (stammering, repetition, long vocal pauses), lowered head and averted gaze, blushing, or barely audible speech. This form of shame also tends toward the use of avoidant self-references, such as "foolish," "stupid," "incompetent," "inept," "insecure," and other terms that do not directly identify shame. On the other hand, in bypassed shame there is no overt disturbance of communication, but rather an obsession with the disturbing incident; this leads to continual internal replay and absorption in the event, to the exclusion of required concentration on presently ongoing events. Notwithstanding, in the bypassed as in the overt form of shame, the emotional pain is present. That shame (in whatever version) is present is less important than that it is unacknowledged, which means that it cannot be discharged.

But even if one is aware of the presence of shame, one may become ashamed of one's shame, or angry at oneself for feeling shame, and then ashamed again of this self-directed anger. Scheff calls this a "shame spiral." Furthermore, the shame–anger spiral may engage two parties, leading to cycles of vengeance, humiliation, and countervengeance, all because the original shame experience was unacknowledged. Scheff contends that even nations may become engrossed in such spirals; he cites the example of French and German shame and motives of revenge, inaugurated by the French defeat in the war of 1870 and ending only with the German defeat in 1945.

But shame is consequential in practical contexts and has an important locus in the socialization experiences of childhood (Scheff, 1990b), as well as in psychotherapy (Scheff, 1996). In training children to acquire various skills, teachers and parents are themselves variably skilled. When they are uncertain of their own skills, they are more likely to feel ashamed and to shame the children, thus setting up an emotional tone that is antagonistic to learning. In therapy, practitioners must bring clients to an awareness of how conventional defense against verbal attack—usually a counterattack that is designed to shame the attacker—may meet a momentary need for self-protection and provide transient status equilibration, but leads to further deterioration of the social bond.

For Scheff, shame, which is mainly unacknowledged, is the emotional pivot of social life, since it underlies social order. Coming at the question of shame and social order from an antipodal direction, Michael Lewis (1992) first distinguishes between a "we-self" and an "I-self." Historically, the we-self preceded the I-self, which is a relatively late development. In earlier times, when strict social hierarchies (such as church and aristocracy) were dominant, individuals were submerged in their social roles and were relatively undifferentiated. Failure to abide by prescribed rules aroused feelings of guilt, which Lewis explains as arising from failure to observe standards and rules, with a focus on the specific behavioral fault or on the other who was the victim of it. As the grip of traditional social controls loosened in the progressive changes marked by the Renaissance, the Reformation, industrialization, urbanization, the Enlightenment, and political democratization, the I-self emerged. Freed from the bonds of rigid social contexts, the I-self claimed more territory for itself in consciousness, to the detriment of social cohesion. For Lewis, the I-self carries with it the burden of shame, since this more available emotion, by contrast with guilt, is evoked by a global sense of unworthiness of the now imperial I-self. Taken to its limits, the I-self shades into narcissism. For Scheff shame operates to support the social bond, whereas for Lewis the absence of

the social bond is an important foundation for shame.

EMOTION WORK AND EMOTION MANAGEMENT

An ongoing debate in the social sciences deals with the respective influence of social structure and of culture. The former consists of social arrangements, such as power and status relations; the latter of "conceptions of the desirable" (Kluckhohn, 1951), as detailed in values, norms, and rules. Some sociologists of emotions (e.g., Collins and myself) lean toward social-structural considerations in the determination of emotions; others, such as Arlie Russell Hochschild (1979, 1983, 1990), Steven Gordon (1990), and Peggy Thoits (1990), lean toward the cultural. The differences between the two approaches are reflected in the degree to which social norms are introduced into the emotional experience to manage or change it.

Hochschild views emotion as having a signaling function—indicating to us where we stand in the world, and defining relationships to others and to our own goals, motives, and interests. Emotional experience is a compound of how we feel, how we wish we felt, how we try to feel, how we classify feelings, and how we express them. How we feel is initially determined by how we appraise the situation, and this is guided to a great extent by social-structural considerations of social class, occupation, gender, race, and similar categories. But almost immediately, cultural considerations enter: There are "feeling rules" and "expression rules," which inform us that what we feel may be inappropriate (too intense or too mild, too long or too short in duration, suitable or unsuitable for someone with our social identity) or that our manner of expressing our feeling is acceptable or outré. Emotional life, therefore, consists of moments in which a good deal of emotion management necessarily takes place in order to maintain conformity with the normative regime.

Managing emotions requires "emotion work," which includes both "surface acting" and "deep acting." Surface acting is accomplished when an individual purposely puts on a suitable emotion—for example, smiling when he or she feels like crying, in order to swing the feeling away from sadness. Deep acting is done when the individual attempts to change the feeling by changing the determinants of feeling—mainly the mental construction or appraisal that gave rise to the feeling, but also including such underlying physical elements as muscle tone and heart rate. Hochschild (1983) examined a variety of these emotion management strategies in her study of airline flight attendants. Beyond this occupation (which is heavily dependent on the ability to do "emotional labor," or emotion work prescribed as a condition of holding down the job), Hochschild determined that about a quarter of predominantly male jobs and about half of all predominantly female jobs in the U.S. labor force require heavy amounts of emotional labor—that is, the ability to modify or change one's emotions in light of employer requirements. Although emotional labor is seen to satisfy employer interests, Hochschild described some of her flight attendant respondents for whom the burden of emotion suppression or management on the job led to "emotional numbing" off the job.

Hochschild has proposed that how and whether or not one chooses to do emotion work is a function of certain ideologies that emerge from and guide the emotional resonances of social class, gender, occupational, racial, and other identities. Hochschild's major concern has been with gender ideologies, those conceptions of male and female gender role that guide emotional response in situations involving gender. Gender ideologies determine the feeling rules that are deemed to apply, and the emotional pathways that allow one to realize the goals of a gender ideology.

Hochschild's approach brings into play many of the cognitive elements in the creation and expression of emotions: culture, norms, rules, and ideologies. These help to define what is emotionally acceptable or deviant, and whether or not emotion work should be undertaken.

Thoits (1990) has obtained data from a college population indicating that the amount of emotional deviance is relatively small (just under 20%), with about half reporting guilt or shame over their departure from emotion norms. Thoits proposed that emotional deviance is likely to occur more frequently under the conditions of multiple role occupancy (e.g., a physician's becoming emotionally involved in the illness of a patient), subcultural marginality (e.g., a "swinging" couple's having to deal with jealousy), occasions of role transition (e.g., postpartum depression in a new mother), and

occasions when ceremonial or other rigid rules govern (e.g., feeling sad at a wedding).

Occasions of emotional deviance also evoke the need for emotion management or coping strategies. Here Thoits (1990) has proposed a typology entailing behavioral and cognitive strategies applied either to the situation evoking the emotion or to physiological, expressive, or labeling aspects of the emotion. For example, a behavioral–expressive strategy might be to engage in hard exercise, or initiate relaxation techniques, or take drugs. A cognitive–situational strategy might be to reinterpret the situational cues, or fantasize an escape, or distract oneself. Where emotional deviance continues, the label of mental illness may be assigned. Thoits (1985) calculated that nearly half of the 210 disorders described in the third edition of the *Diagnostic and Statistical Manual of Mental Disorders* (DSM-III; American Psychiatric Association, 1980) are identified by deviant emotions. This suggests that to a significant extent, treatment of mental illness involves the acquisition of techniques of emotion management.

EMOTIONS, SELVES, AND ROLES

Cognate with Cooley's "looking-glass" metaphor on the development of self-feelings (see above) is the theory of self proposed by American social-behaviorist philosopher George Herbert Mead (1934). Mead proposed that the self is a social creation, formed through the process of "role taking"—that is, putting oneself in the position of another and looking back at oneself as if one were an object. Social experience develops the capacity to take the role of another, and hence to obtain a sense of self. Role taking enables individuals to formulate courses of action by providing advance understanding of how a particular course of action will affect the self. Since language is the main vehicle of role taking, the Meadian approach has been called "symbolic interaction": Role taking is an interactive process that takes place cognitively, as opposed to actually, through the use of language symbols. Another term for the role-taking process and its effects is "reflexivity," which connotes acting back on oneself. A distinct sociological position on emotions and the self derives from the symbolic-interactionist perspective.

Rosenberg (1990) has proposed that reflexivity is necessarily involved in such fundamental processes as emotional identification, emotional display, and emotional experience. Since emotions do not come readily labeled, there is always to some degree a problem of emotional identification. Role taking or reflexivity allows for the interpretation of the ambiguous situational and physiological conditions of the emotional state by attending to three possible identifiers. First is a cause–effect logic that social experience provides and that individuals in a given culture learn to employ to reflect on the meaning of their inner experience (e.g., "My dog died; no wonder I'm so depressed"). Second is the recognition of a social consensus about the situation in the responses of others (e.g., "Everyone at the party is excited; no wonder I'm excited too"). Third are cultural scenarios that provide information about emotions (e.g., "I can't wait until I see her again; I must be in love").

Reflexivity operates in decisions concerning emotional display, since the intention of display is to persuade others that one is experiencing a given emotion. Although this is fundamentally "impression management," as Goffman (1959) has referred to it, the stakes are high. According to Coulter (1986), to fail to show the proper emotion in a given situation is to be accounted morally deficient, or even mentally ill.

Although emotional experience originates as a direct result of a situation that activates an autonomically based response, reflexivity enters into the process of moderating or managing the experience, or facilitating or inhibiting the likelihood of its occurrence in the first place. Reflexive judgments can be applied to enhancing or changing the initial stimulus conditions for the emotion, or to modifying one's thoughts about those conditions. In this way, the individual actively partakes in the alteration of the content of emotional experience.

Shott (1979) applies the role-taking perspective directly to the identification of specific emotions. She differentiates between "reflexive" role-taking emotions and "empathic" role-taking emotions. The former include guilt, shame, and embarrassment. In each case, in order to experience these emotions, one must put oneself mentally in the place of another to obtain his or her view of oneself. Guilt entails the other's judgment of moral inadequacy; shame entails the other's unwillingness to accept one's ideal conception of one's action; and embarrassment entails the other's low regard for one's

self-presentation. Because these are painful emotions, they motivate efforts to regain the good opinion of others through a variety of compensatory acts, often of an altruistic nature.

The empathic role-taking emotions are even better at eliciting altruistic behavior. Empathic role taking provides *vicarious* emotional experience, through putting the individual in the place of another who may be suffering and who can be relieved or assisted. Clearly, empathic role taking can also lead to emotional contagion.

AFFECT CONTROL THEORY

Affect control theory is a major effort to bridge the gap between structural and cultural approaches to the sociological explanation of emotions, as well as a unique synthetic strategy in its own right (Heise, 1979; Smith-Lovin, 1990; Smith-Lovin & Heise, 1988; MacKinnon, 1994). Initiated by David Heise, this approach derives from several sources. First is the classic work with the semantic differential (SD) by Osgood, Suci, and Tannenbaum (1957), who found that three dimensions underlie the universe of word content examined by SD methods: evaluation (E), or goodness; potency (P), or power; and activity (A), or arousal. Second is the approach to a mathematical representation of the stimulus value of objects as developed by Gollub (1968; Gollub & Rossman, 1973). This involves obtaining parameter estimates of the cultural value of objects through use of the SD. The results are series of equations in which objects are located in the three-dimensional SD space and carry a tripartite EPA score profile. Samples of college students, for the most part, have provided the SD evaluations that form the basis of the EPA parameters tagged to a large number of items. The items consist of words designating social statuses (e.g., "policeman," "wife," "child," "criminal," etc.); behaviors (e.g., "helps," "fights," "forgives," "assists," etc.); and emotions (e.g., "happy," "sad," "angry," etc.). The outcome of these basic data collection and analysis procedures is a dictionary of terms, each identified by its EPA profile. The equations can be solved for results in status, behavior, or emotion terms from input specified in the other two types of terms.

The basic behavioral theorem of the affect control approach is derived in part from a symbolic-interactionist view of the self and holds that individuals act in more or less homeostatic ways to maintain their identity. Thus, if a parent assists a child, this conforms to the basic cultural notion of how a parent should treat a child. But if, for whatever reason, the parent acts contraculturally (e.g., ignores the child), this represents a deviation or deflection from the culturally approved identity of (good) parent. This creates a transient identity for the parent and for the child too, since the child, in the situation of being ignored, is no longer able to experience him- or herself as a (loved) child.

Both the original identities and the transient identities can be represented by EPA profiles. The mathematical distance between the original and transient identities opens the door to emotions, which carry their own EPA profiles. Heise theorizes that the arousal of emotion is a direct result of the discrepancy between the original and transient identities.

Since the basic motive, as postulated in the theory, is the maintenance of the original identity, the emotion is a cue and a source of energy for certain reparative behaviors to restore the original identity. A new set of equations provides a set of possible reparative actions—that is, behaviors with the requisite EPA profiles that, when applied to the discrepant identity, will restore it to its original EPA values. In the example at hand, the behaviors might include consoling, appreciating, apologizing, and the like. These behaviors are also likely to restore the child's original identity as well. If the reparative behaviors are not undertaken, then both the holder of the original identities (here, parent and child), as well as any observers of the discrepant action, may need to recast the original identities in the direction of the transient ones. Thus the original (good) parent may be reconfigured into an EPA profile that reflects the identity of (neglectful) parent. The child is also recast from (loved) child to (unloved) child.

Heise's approach takes account of both structural and cultural elements in the determination of emotions. The EPA dimensions are themselves structural features of social identities. In fact, the potency (P) and evaluation (E) dimensions have close affinity with the power and status dimensions in my own work (Kemper, 1978, 1991a; Kemper & Collins, 1990). But the stimulus value of these dimensions is sought in a straightforward cultural fashion, through developing what are essentially normative descriptions in SD terms from participants in the culture. Concern with the maintenance of identity also engages fundamental issues in the symbolic-interactionist perspective, which also relies heavily on cultural notions in the determination of behavior.

Research on emotions and identities suggests a linkage between the two that is obscured in other traditions—namely, that identities with certain EPA profiles are likely to manifest emotions with compatible profiles. For example, an identity high in potency (P) is likely to manifest high-potency emotions, such as anger and pride, while low-potency identities are more likely to manifest low-potency emotions, such as anxiety and sadness (Smith-Lovin, 1990).

The affect control approach also differentiates between emotion and mood. As described above, an emotion emerges as a consequence of a discrepancy between a normal and a transient identity, such as the (good) parent and the (neglectful) parent; this discrepancy may produce unhappy emotions such as guilt, sorrow, or shame. Given certain reparative acts, the original (good) parent identity is restored and the negative emotions abrogated. But if the original identity combines an emotion with an identity (e.g., unhappy parent), this defines a mood, and behavior consistent with this mood could be expected to occur. For example, the parent may attack or neglect the child (Averett & Heise, 1988).

The affect control approach has also extended its reach beyond the strict mathematical examination and prediction of identity, behavior, and emotion outcomes. A number of studies derived from affect control principles lend empirical support to some of the fundamental notions. Robinson, Smith-Lovin, and Tsoudis (1994) used simulations based on the theory to predict the effect of emotion displays on identity attributions in a setting involving sentencing recommendations after criminals had confessed to certain crimes. A display of remorse after confession affected the severity of the sentence through its impact on the assessment of the identity of the confessor, as predicted by the theory. Robinson and Smith-Lovin (1992) also applied affect control theory derivations to propose a counterintuitive set of hypotheses about the effect of self-esteem (a mood indicator) on the tendency to solicit identity-supporting sentiments and behaviors from others. They found that experimental subjects reacted homeostatically to maintain their identity as either high or low in self-esteem. Both high- and low-esteem subjects felt good when praised and bad when criticized, but the low-esteem subjects felt the criticism was accurate and liked the critics more than did the high-esteem subjects. When given a chance to choose interaction partners, high- and low-esteem subjects tended to select those who would support their view of themselves.

The most complete statement of affect control theory is contained in MacKinnon's (1994) work, where 24 fundamental propositions are cited, along with substantial arguments suggesting affinities between the theory and a number of other approaches (including role theory, attribution theory, and symbolic interactionism).

EMOTIONS AND MACROPROCESSES

Most sociological examinations of emotion are social-psychological; that is, social structures, processes, or outcomes of these are seen to produce emotions in the individuals involved, with emotions differing according to where in a structure, process, or outcome an individual stands. Jack Barbalet (1998) provides an important exception to this social-psychological approach. Rather, Barbalet conceives of emotion as integral to social relations and social processes themselves. Emotion is felt by individuals—this cannot be escaped—but as an aspect of societal patterns of social organization in terms of class, gender, race, and the like. This leads to another perspectival difference: Most sociological approaches to emotion examine social processes and social relations as the independent variables (they cause or produce emotions). Barbalet reverses this and examines how emotions cause or produce social processes and social relations. Furthermore, this is conceived at the macro level, engaging societal as opposed to interpersonal processes.

For example, members of the working class might be expected to feel social resentment against those who are better off, but such resentment is in fact scant, and in the United States it has led to no effective political movements. Following Bensman and Vidich (1962), Barbalet tries to explain this in part by locating different sectors of the working class in different places in normal trade cycles in capitalist societies. A dynamic economy contains both expanding industries (e.g., computers) and contracting ones (e.g., textiles), and workers in the different industries cannot be expected to experience the same emotions; this vitiates any theory or program that views workers in a monolithic way.

In another venture into the macrosociology of emotions, Barbalet (1996) examines the emotion, mood, or feeling of confidence as an important feature of social process. Particularly in the business community, confidence is a necessary condition of investment. Indeed, in Barbalet's view, confidence dominates even rational calculation. This is because rational business planning is limited by the fact that it is future-oriented, and the information that rational assessment requires is unavailable; it can only unfold in the future. Therefore, to undertake action under conditions of limited rationality, the business community must rely on its intuition that investment will be profitable. Put otherwise, it must have confidence. Government is an important constituent of the situation, sometimes enhancing and sometimes depressing business confidence. Barbalet proposes that what differentiates these effects of government policy is whether they reflect "acceptance and recognition" of the business community. For example, government spending on infrastructure or on the bailout of the savings and loan industry reflect such appreciation. On the other hand, business interests feel slighted when the government proposes strict policies to reduce global warming, and business confidence falls accordingly.

In both instances—the working class and the business community—the emotions are aggregated products of many individuals, which then act as a discrete force in society.

EXPECTATIONS AND SANCTIONS

In a relatively new approach, Robert Thamm (1992) has built a theory of emotions on the foundations of Parsons and Shils's (1951) scheme for a general theory of action. The main elements of that scheme, in which social actors are linked in reciprocal forms of action and response, are expectations and sanctions. Individuals in social settings have expectations of each other, and in light of those expectations they reward or fail to reward each other's behavior. From the perspective of each actor, this leads to four questions: (1) Is the self meeting expectations? (2) Is the self receiving rewards? (3) Is the other meeting expectations? (4) Is the other receiving rewards? These constitute the fundamental social matrix for the production of emotions. Because the answers to these questions vary from "yes" (+) to "no" (–) to "don't know" (0), different emotions result. A given state of the system of self's and other's expectations and sanctions can be coded by a pertinent series of pluses, minuses, and zeroes. For example, if the answer to all four questions is "yes," the coding is [++++]; if the answer to all four is "no," the coding is [– – – –]; if the answer to the first two is "yes" and the last two is "no," the coding is [++– –].

Based on the permutations of the many possible states of the expectations–sanctions system, Thamm hypothesizes a variety of emotional results. For example, when the self meets expectations [+000], the self feels pleased with the self. When the self does not meet expectations [–000], the self feels disappointed with the self. When the other does not meet expectations [00–0], the self feels disappointed in the other. When the self meets expectations but is not rewarded [+–00], the self feels powerless. When the other does not meet expectations so that the self is not rewarded [0– –0], the self feels anger at the other. Many additional hypotheses follow from the variations along the spectrum of expectations–sanctions possibilities. Thus far, Thamm has tested his hypotheses by asking respondents (college students) to imagine that "you and a friend were expected to do something and you planned to share the rewards." The students have then been given a set of possible expectations–sanctions outcomes and asked to select a suitable emotion for each outcome from a list of hypothesized emotions. Chi-square results have been uniformly highly significant in this kind of statistical testing.

OTHER MODELS

The efflorescence of interest in emotions among sociologists does not end with the models detailed here. Additional approaches include a contrasociobiological model of how the need for emotional gratification gives rise to systems of stratification (Hammond, 1990); a postmodernist phenomenological analysis of emotions as "lived experience" (Denzin, 1984, 1990); an approach to emotions through the sociology of knowledge (McCarthy, 1989); a model of the social construction of emotions

via "emotion culture" and the socialization process (Gordon, 1989, 1990); and an examination of how emotions are employed as political counters in the microinteractions that determine social rank (Clark, 1990). Clark (1997) has also focused specific attention on sympathy and "sympathy entrepreneurs," such as blues musicians, greeting card writers, organizers of charity drives, and social scientists, who construct the implicit social rules that govern definitions of "bad luck" and other circumstances that ought to elicit sympathy.

REFERENCES

American Psychiatric Association. (1980). *Diagnostic and statistical manual of mental disorders* (3rd ed.). Washington, DC: Author.

Averett, C., & Heise, D. R. (1988). Modified social identities: Amalgamations, attributions, and emotions. In L. Smith-Lovin & D. R. Heise (Eds.), *Analyzing social interaction: Advances in affect control theory* (pp. 103–122). New York: Gordon & Breach.

Barbalet, J. M. (1996). Social emotions: Confidence, trust and loyalty. *International Journal of Sociology and Social Policy, 16*, 75–96.

Barbalet, J. M. (1998). *Macrosociology: Emotion, social theory and social structure.* Cambridge, England: Cambridge University Press.

Bensman, J., & Vidich, A. (1962). Business cycles, class and personality. *Psychoanalysis and Psychoanalytic Review, 49*, 30–52.

Clark, C. (1990). Emotions and micropolitics in everyday life: Some patterns and paradoxes of "place." In T. D. Kemper (Ed.), *Research agendas in the sociology of emotions* (pp. 305–333). Albany: State University of New York Press.

Clark, C. (1997). *Misery and company: Sympathy in everyday life.* Chicago: University of Chicago Press.

Collins, R. (1975). *Conflict sociology: Toward an explanatory science.* New York: Academic Press.

Collins, R. (1981). On the micro-foundations of macrosociology. *American Journal of Sociology, 86*, 984–1014.

Collins, R. (1990). Stratification, emotional energy, and the transient emotions. In T. D. Kemper (Ed.), *Research agendas in the sociology of emotions* (pp. 27–57). Albany: State University of New York Press.

Cooley, C. H. (1902). *Human nature and the social order.* New York: Scribner.

Coulter, J. (1986). Affect and social context: Emotion definition as a social task. In R. Harré (Ed.), *The social construction of emotions* (pp. 120–134). Oxford: Blackwell.

Denzin, N. (1984). *On understanding emotion.* San Francisco: Jossey-Bass.

Denzin, N. (1990). On understanding emotion: The interpretive–cultural agenda. In T. D. Kemper (Ed.), *Research agendas in the sociology of emotions* (pp. 85–116). Albany: State University of New York Press.

Durkheim, É. (1954). *The elementary forms of the religious life.* New York: Free Press. (Original work published 1912)

Goffman, E. (1959). *The presentation of self in everyday life.* Garden City, NY: Doubleday/Anchor.

Goffman, E. (1967). *Interaction ritual.* Garden City, NY: Doubleday/Anchor.

Gollub, H. (1968). Impression formation and word combinations in sentences. *Journal of Personality and Social Psychology, 10,* 341–353.

Gollub, H., & Rossman, B. B. (1973). Judgments of actors' "power and ability to influence others." *Journal of Personality and Social Psychology, 19,* 391–406.

Gordon, S. (1989). The socialization of children's emotions: Emotional culture, competence, and exposure. In C. I. Saarni & P. L. Harris (Eds.), *Children's understanding of emotion* (pp. 319–349). Cambridge, England: Cambridge University Press.

Gordon, S. (1990). Social structural effects on emotions. In T. D. Kemper (Ed.), *Research agendas in the sociology of emotions* (pp. 145–179). Albany: State University of New York Press.

Hammond, M. (1990). Affective maximization: A new macro-theory in the sociology of emotions. In T. D. Kemper (Ed.), *Research agendas in the sociology of emotions* (pp. 58–81). Albany: State University of New York Press.

Heise, D. (1979). *Understanding events: Affect and the construction of social action.* New York: Cambridge University Press.

Hochschild, A. R. (1979). Emotion work, feeling rules, and social structure. *American Journal of Sociology, 85,* 551–575.

Hochschild, A. R. (1983). *The managed heart: The commercialization of human feeling.* Berkeley: University of California Press.

Hochschild, A. R. (1990). Ideology and emotion management: A perspective and path for future research. In T. D. Kemper (Ed.), *Research agendas in the sociology of emotions* (pp. 117–142). Albany: State University of New York Press.

Kemper, T. D. (1978). *A social interactional theory of emotions.* New York: Wiley.

Kemper, T. D. (1989). Love and like and love and *love.* In D. D. Franks & E. D. McCarthy (Eds.), *The sociology of emotions: Original essays and papers* (pp. 249–268). Greenwich, CT: JAI Press.

Kemper, T. D. (1991a). Predicting emotions from social relations. *Social Psychology Quarterly, 54,* 330–342.

Kemper, T. D. (1991b). An introduction to the sociology of emotions. In K. T. Strongman (Ed.), *International review of studies on emotion* (Vol. 1, pp. 301–349). Chichester, England: Wiley.

Kemper, T. D., & Collins, R. (1990). Dimensions of microinteraction. *American Journal of Sociology, 96,* 32–68.

Kemper, T. D., & Reid, M. T. (1997). Love and liking in the attraction and maintenance phases of long term relationships. In B. Cuthbertson-Johnson & R. J. Erickson (Eds.), *Social perspectives on emotions* (Vol. 4, pp. 37–69). Greenwich, CT: JAI Press.

Kluckhohn, C. (1951). Values and value orientations in the theory of action: An exploration in definition and classification. In T. Parsons & E. A. Shils (Eds.), *Toward a general theory of action* (pp. 388–433). New York: Harper & Row.

Lewis, H. B. (1971). *Shame and guilt in neurosis.* New York: International Universities Press.

Lewis, M. (1992). *Shame: The exposed self.* New York: Free Press.

MacKinnon, N. (1994). *Symbolic interaction as affect control.* Albany: State University of New York Press.

McCarthy, D. (1989). Emotions are social things: An essay in the sociology of emotions. In D. D. Franks & E. D. McCarthy (Eds.), *The sociology of emotions: Original essays and research papers* (pp. 51–72). Greenwich, CT: JAI Press.

Mead, G. H. (1934). *Mind, self and society.* Chicago: University of Chicago Press.

Neubauer, P. B., & Neubauer, A. (1990). *Nature's thumbprint: The new genetics of personality.* Reading, MA: Addison-Wesley.

Osgood, C. E., Suci, G. J., & Tannenbaum, P. H. (1957). *The measurement of meaning.* Urbana: University of Illinois Press.

Parsons, T., & Shils, E. A. (1951). *Toward a general theory of action.* New York: Harper & Row.

Plutchik, R. (1991). Emotions and evolution. In K. T. Strongman (Ed.), *International review of studies on emotion* (Vol. 1, pp. 37–58). Chichester, England: Wiley.

Robinson, D. T., & Smith-Lovin, L. (1992). Selective interaction as a strategy for identity maintenance: An affect control model. *Social Psychology Quarterly, 55,* 12–28.

Robinson, D. T., Smith-Lovin, L., & Tsoudis, O. (1994). Heinous crime or unfortunate accident?: The effects of remorse on responses to criminal confession. *Social Forces, 73,* 175–190.

Rosenberg, M. (1990). Reflexivity and emotions. *Social Psychology Quarterly, 53,* 3–12.

Scheff, T. J. (1988). Shame and conformity: The deference–emotion system. *American Sociological Review, 53,* 395–406.

Scheff, T. J. (1990a). *Microsociology: Discourse, emotion, and social structure.* Chicago: University of Chicago Press.

Scheff, T. J. (1990b). Socialization of emotions: Pride and shame as causal agents. In T. D. Kemper (Ed.), *Research agendas in the sociology of emotions* (pp. 281–304). Albany: State University of New York Press.

Scheff, T. J. (1996). Self-defense against verbal assault: Shame, anger, and the social bond. *Family Process, 34,* 271–286.

Scherer, K. R., Walbott, H. G., & Summerfield, A. B. (1986). *Experienceing emotion: A cross-cultural study.* Cambridge, England: Cambridge University Press.

Shott, S. (1979). Emotion and social life: A symbolic interactionist analysis. *American Journal of Sociology, 84,* 1317–1334.

Smith-Lovin, L. (1990). Emotion as the confirmation and disconfirmation of identity. In T. D. Kemper (Ed.), *Research agendas in the sociology of emotions.* Albany: State University of New York Press.

Smith-Lovin, L., & Heise, D. R. (Eds.). (1988). *Analyzing social interaction: Advances in affect control theory.* New York: Gordon & Breach.

Tellegen, A., Lykken, D. T., Bouchard, T. J., Wilcox, K. J., Segal, N. L., & Rich, S. (1988). Personality similarity in twins reared apart and together. *Journal of Personality and Social Psychology*, *54*, 1088–1039.

Thamm, R. (1992). Social structure and emotion. *Sociological Perspectives*, *35*, 649–671.

Thoits, P. A. (1985). Self-labeling processes in mental illness: The role of emotional deviance. *American Journal of Sociology*, *92*, 221–249.

Thoits, P. A. (1990). Emotional deviance: Research agendas. In T. D. Kemper (Ed.), *Research agendas in the sociology of emotions*. Albany: State University of New York Press.

CHAPTER 5

The Psychologists' Point of View

Nico H. Frijda

As Magda Arnold, one of the first psychologists to devote herself to the study of emotion (Arnold, 1960), stated in 1970, there are a number of "perennial problems in the field of emotion." These problems cause recurrent discussion and divergence of theories, and of course they give rise to research. In many respects, these perennial problems define the psychology of emotion. In this chapter I discuss the prominent problems, such as how we define the task of the psychology of emotion, how we define "an" emotion or delimit the concept of emotions generally, and how we distinguish different emotions and the elicitors of emotions. Then I turn to defining the boundaries of emotion, to considering the relations between emotion and motivation, to pondering where nature or nurture have their effects, and to determining the relation between emotion and reason. Finally, I discuss the functions of emotions as psychologists present them.

DEFINING THE FIELD OF EMOTION STUDY

A first and major problem is how to define our field of interest. What is an emotion? "Emotion" is not a natural class. Then why did the concept emerge? There must be certain phenomena that imposed themselves and required a designation and an explanation. These phenomena include those of feelings, of shifts in the control of behavior and thought, of involuntary and impulsive behaviors, of the emergence

or tenacity of beliefs, of changes in an individual's relationship with the environment, and of physiological changes not caused by physical conditions.

Feeling is a striking kind of phenomenon. It represents a different kind of experience from other kinds. Feeling indeed looms large in many definitions of emotion (see Kleinginna & Kleinginna, 1981). But it is not the only phenomenon that might have motivated forming and using the concept of emotion. I even doubt that it was the major one. Other phenomena, I think, were more conspicuous, and feelings were not emphasized in discourse on emotion before the 17th century.

There is, for instance, the phenomenon that salient events intrude upon ongoing goal-directed behavior and thought, and may interrupt it (Elster, 1999). They also elicit unplanned behavior and thought. The events concerned appear to "affect" the person. This is the phenomenon that gave rise to the very notions of "affect" and its predecessors, the Greek *pathèma*, the Latin *affectus*, and the early French and English "passion." They all indicate some sort of passivity—a form of control of behavior that differs from "action," to which passion and affect were contrasted. The intrusions often extend to desires, thoughts, plans, and behaviors that persist over time. They may lead to performing behaviors regardless of costs, external obstacles, and moral objections. These are the characteristics of passion in the more modern sense—the desires, behaviors, and thoughts that suggest urges with considerable force.

Yet another phenomenon that strikes the eye is that an individual's relationship with the environment, and particularly with other people, often changes. The individual draws back, or turns away, or approaches with eagerness. Such changes frequently appear due to the meaning of some aspect of the environment rather than to its physical characteristics.

Another phenomenon consists of recurrent patterns of behavior, such as smiling, laughter, weeping, or outbursts of violent movements. These frequently accompany the relationship changes and appear predictive of future behavior. For example, smiling makes one expect further friendly contact, crying the seeking or needing of help, and an angry voice forthcoming hostility.

Finally, there are the phenomena of bodily upset and of disorganization of organized behavior and thought. They are what led to the term "emotion" itself. It was borrowed in the 17th century by Descartes (1649/1970) from a French word meaning something like "riot" or "unruliness," to supplement "passion" in its original sense.

All these phenomena require explanations from "within" the person. They demand hypotheses about possible causal factors. "Emotion," whether taken as feeling or just as some inner state or process, serves that purpose; it fulfills the function of rendering the phenomena intelligible and their consequences more predictable.

The notion of emotion fulfills the same role in explaining discrepancies of various sorts. Different people react in different ways to the same situations, and one person may react in different ways to one given situation on different occasions. Also, people entertain many beliefs that have only slim justifications in fact, but that persist in the face of contrary evidence. There further exist contradictions between how people act at different times, or how they act and say they will act, so that a person may "smile and smile and be a villain." Hence emotion allows us to develop hypotheses about the reasons that different people have for the same actions; it also allows us to account for contradictions in acting.

These, then, are the various sources for a concept of emotion. They correspond to the phenomena that usually occur in definitions of emotion: feelings, shifts in the control of behavior and thought, involuntary and impulsive behaviors (including "expressive" behaviors),

the emergence or tenacity of beliefs, changes in the relationship with the environment, and physiological changes not caused by physical conditions. All these phenomena usually occur in response to external events, to a person's own actions, or to thoughts. The events usually have appreciable consequences for the person's goals or conduct of life.

These different kinds of phenomena tend to occur in conjunction, for which reason emotions are sometimes referred to as "multicomponent phenomena." They are the phenomena that lead to the assumption of "states" of the individual, called "emotions" or some equivalent. They are the phenomena that the psychology of emotion tries to deal with.

THE TASK OF THE PSYCHOLOGY OF EMOTION

The task of the psychology of emotion is to analyze these "states" of the individual and to explain them at the level of the individual. That is to say that psychology seeks explanations in terms of cognitive, motor, and emotional facilities and processes that are attributes of individuals, together with their capacities for goal setting and planning, their attentional and energy resources, and the like. The explanations include the various kinds of information that the processes have to work with and that are stored within the individual, such as innate sensitivities, stored facts, cognitive schemas, prescriptions, associations, habits, and so forth.

The psychology of emotion also includes among its explanatory tools the individual's actual, dynamic interactions with the environment. These dynamic interactions bring in sensory stimuli and what is picked up from them, effects of the environment upon how well the facilities and processes function, effects of the individual's actions upon the environment and their feedback, changes over time in both the environment and the individual's functioning, and finally the individual's anticipations concerning all of this.

Psychological explanations thus are composed of three terms: the structure of the individual, stored information, and dynamic interaction with the environment. How the emotional phenomena emerge from what corresponds to these three terms raises several of the other perennial problems that Arnold (1970) alluded to. For instance, the three terms leave an indefinite number of ways that one might emphasize one or another of them, and the fact that they play a role provides little guidance about the amount of variance that each might explain. The leeway for variance is well illustrated by Simon's (1981) parable of the ant. One can explain the erratic path of an ant on a stretch of soil by assuming the ant to be equipped with a highly complex mental program. But the same erratic behavior can be explained by assuming a very simple mental program that allows the animal to respond to the complexities of the environment, such as pebbles and grains of sand. In emotion psychology, the assumptions of basic emotions (e.g., Ekman, 1992) and of innate, prepared stimulus sensitivities (e.g., Öhman, Chapter 36, this volume) illustrate the pole of complex structure, since both require structural provisions. The other end of the pole—simple structure with openness to complexity in the environment—is illustrated in the hypotheses that all emotions are variants of very general affect and arousal mechanisms (Russell, 1991) or that they all result from a general sensitivity to goal interruption (Mandler, 1984). In both approaches, finer differentiation is supposed to come from the complexities of the environment or from language.

Theorizing generally tries to find an optimal balance between structure and adaptation to information. This search is guided by the principle of Occam's razor—that is, by the effort to be as stingy with structure as possible. What is considered an optimal balance depends upon the empirical data, as well as upon the investigator's overall perspectives and taste. Within those aims, there are important differences in the kinds of explanation being sought. One can seek explanations in the intentional mode (Dennett, 1987)—that is, in terms of aims, subject–object relations, and the meanings of events. One can also seek for explanations on the psychological or functional level—that is, in terms of psychological mechanisms and transformation functions. And one can seek them at the structural level—that is, in terms of neurophysiological and biochemical processes. The various modes can coexist in psychology and, in principle, are mutually compatible.

The different modes each also leave room for quite different explanatory approaches. On the intentional level one can seek regularities, or laws dealing with general relationships between variables. An example of such a regularity is to view anger as the inevitable outcome of frustration. Of great interest is an alternative to laws, recently proposed by Elster (1999), in which explanatory rules have a more limited scope and are subject to unspecified restrictions. They are rules, not laws; Elster calls them "mental mechanisms." Their major point is their lack of specification of the conditions under which each applies. Elster gives the following illustrative example of a pair of rules: Rule 1, "Tyranny decreases the likelihood of rebellion," and Rule 2, "Tyranny increases the likelihood of rebellion." Both are true. This, Elster argues, is not so much due to limited knowledge of the conditions for each, but to the context dependency of these conditions—that is, the chaotic nature of the processes.

WHAT IS "AN" EMOTION?

Whatever the kind of psychological explanation chosen, its aim is to understand the phenomena of emotion and their conditions of occurrence. However, it is not fully obvious what the phenomena to be explained are. The observable phenomena can be described and analyzed in very different ways and at very different levels of abstraction and integration; hence the recurrent discussion and divergence of theories.

Efforts to describe "an" emotion in the sense of a type, such as "joy" or "anger," illustrate very clearly the issue of choosing one's level of description. Different theoretical approaches represent different views of how this should be done. Some may focus on one component—for instance, on feeling or on physiological arousal. Others describe emotions as sets of components, with a deterministic or probabilistic structure. Approaches may also differ in that some view emotions as states, and others as processes that may cover the entire sequence from appraising an event to making a response or set of responses. The term "jealousy," for instance, can be understood to refer to a particular feeling, or to the process that runs from the appraisal of a particular three-person constellation as a threat to feelings of anger or distress and to the desire to do something about that threat.

An important difference concerns the level of conceptualization of emotions that is considered optimal. Emotions can be viewed primarily as intrapersonal states, such as feelings, states of arousal, or activation of certain motor patterns. They may also be viewed as interactive states involving the subject and an object, and their relationship. The chosen level has considerable theoretical implications. The focus upon feelings as intrapersonal *qualia*, for instance, abandons sight of the intentional nature of emotional experience or considers it to be secondary. Within the field of psychology, different views of the nature of an emotion are thus possible, and several of these views appear equally valid.

In attempts to define "an" emotion in the sense of what constitutes an individual emotion occurrence, a similar situation is met. One can describe emotion instances at different levels. Which level is being chosen has important consequences. It matters, for instance, for how long one thinks emotions last, and for whether they can be seen as fast emergency provisions. One can describe occurrences of emotions at a transactional level, as emotion episodes dealing with a particular issue. Alternatively, one can describe them at the level of interaction patterns, defined by a particular core relational theme or overall appraisal, such as loss or threat (Lazarus, 1991). One can also describe them at the level of the prevailing mode of action readiness—for instance, as states of hostile or defensive inclination. Finally, one can describe and distinguish them at the level of elementary emotion phenomena, as sequences of facial expressions or particular states of autonomic arousal.

What subjects report when asked to recall some emotion instance, (e.g., one of anger or of joy) is usually an episode at the transactional level. Such reported episodes may have lasted from 5 seconds to several days (Frijda, Mesquita, Sonnemans, & Van Goozen, 1991). During the episode, appraisals may change (e.g., from threat to its resolution), and when emotions are being distinguished at a lower level (by a feeling or by a mode of action readiness), different emotions co-occur or succeed one another during such an instance of an emotion. If "an" emotion is defined by the occurrence of a particular facial expressions, then emotions last for 5 seconds at most (Ekman, 1992).

Which level one selects as representing "an" emotion is largely arbitrary, and should be no topic for disagreement. Emotion units as defined at higher levels are complexes made up of basic processes, such as feelings of pleasure or pain, individual facial expression components, particular appraisals, and particular action plans and activation states. Those processes would seem to form the psychological bedrock that any theory of emotions ultimately rests upon, and the ingredients of which any emotion is composed.

Analyses at different levels are not incompatible with each other. However, there may well be incompatibility between emotion categorizations based on different levels. Descriptions at higher levels cannot always be reduced to those at lower levels without loss. Likewise, higher-level categorizations cannot always be built up from the lower-level phenomena. Higher-level categorizations often, or perhaps usually, include more phenomena (e.g., the nature of the emotional object or of a particular environment), as well as more interactions between the lower level-phenomena or feedback from them.

WHAT ARE EMOTIONS?

The question remains whether the phenomena for which the word "emotion" is being used form or include a class of events with sufficient functional specificity and functional unity to justify a single concept. Do emotions indeed exist? Do the phenomena require or justify assuming a distinct function of "Emotion," separate from "Cognition" and "Conation," as an older psychology would have it? It has always been a major issue how to characterize what the states or processes called Emotions might have in common, and what sets them off from Cognition or Conation, or from whatever functional categories are being distinguished.

Specificity and unity of "emotion" are commonly assumed. The assumptions are not necessarily correct, however, nor are they universally held. James (1884) assumed that emotional behavior is no different from any other behavior called forth by key stimuli; he thought that it originates in the cerebral cortex, just as all other behavior does. Emotional experience, he also proposed, is nothing but the experienced feedback from such behavior. Other prominent investigators have also argued that there is nothing specific in emotional experience. "Emotional experience is a highly variable state [and] often partakes of the complicated nature of a judgement," wrote Landis and Hunt (1932, quoted by Hebb, 1949, p. 237). Duffy (1941) also took the nonspecificity position, but in a different way. According to her, organisms always vary in level of activation;

what are being called "emotions" are just the high and low levels, and no sharp boundary separates them from the so-called "nonemotional" middle range.

One may also deny the unity assumption. Hebb (1949), for one, denied that reactions involving goal-directed action, such as those called "angry," have anything in common with those involving upset, mere excitement, or disintegration of behavioral organization. More recently, LeDoux (1996) has suggested that the various emotions may not derive from shared mechanisms.

There is good reason to raise the unity and specificity issues. Little agreement exists about the features that might characterize unity and specificity. In 1928, Bentley wrote a paper with the title "Is 'Emotion' More Than a Chapter Heading?" He concluded:

> Well, emotion is at least a topic! It is something to talk about and to disagree upon. To me, its essential characteristic is a progressive activity of the organism when faced with a predicament. . . . But to another psychologist, emotion means . . . a type of external bodily activity or deportment; or again a pleasant or unpleasant reaction upon events or a "mental state." (pp. 21–22)

There are indeed several rather specific features that qualify for defining emotions. The problem is that these features define overlapping but nonidentical sets of phenomena. For many theorists, the essence of emotion is feeling, and notably "affect," here used in the sense of a feeling of pleasure or pain. These feelings are experiences that cannot be reduced to body sensations or cognitive judgments (Arnold, 1960). What sets affects apart from other experiences is that they are evaluative. They are good or bad, or signal the eliciting stimulus to be so. They imply acceptance or non-acceptance of the experience or of the stimulus event involved. Affect thereby represents something specific and special in psychology, apart from its phenomenology. It introduces value in a world of fact, to echo Wolfgang Köhler (1938). It involves evaluations that may have no cognitive basis; a rose smells good because it smells good. Emotions can therefore be viewed as processes that include affect (Russell, 1991), or as "valenced reactions" (Ortony, Clore, & Collins, 1988).

To explain the arousal of affect, one has to assume some process that turns an event into an evaluated event. The process is often being referred to as one of appraisal or appraising (Lazarus, 2000). Appraisal may be the automatic outcome of certain stimuli (e.g., the smell of roses), or the result of a cognitive assessment of the meaning of the stimulus event. In an influential view, emotions are the results of appraising events as promoting or obstructing one's well-being, concerns, motives, or current goals (Lazarus, 1991; Oatley, 1992; Stein & Trabasso, 1992). Appraising events may be considered one of the basic abilities of human and animal systems. Emotions can therefore be viewed as processes that involve appraisal.

Other authors have given the central place to desire, or the impulse to act. Among them are Thomas Aquinas, Arnold (1960), McDougall (1923), Shand (1920), Tomkins (1962), and Wallon (1942). Impulses to act imply assumptions of forms of action instigation and action control that are neither automatic and habitual nor planned. They are among the main reasons to consider emotions as "affecting" the individual. Impulsive action control, in turn, requires assumptions about the psychological apparatus that are not required to understand paradigmatic phenomena of cognition and decision making. It thus sets emotion apart from cognition, and even from conation. Emotions can therefore be viewed as processes that involve involuntary, nonhabitual action control—or, as I call it, "action readiness" (Frijda, 1986).

Impulsive action instigation (including involuntary loss of instigation, as in apathetic sadness) is conspicuous in certain reactions that a definition of emotions in terms of affect leaves out. Desire itself is the clearest instance, with its variants such as greed, lust, or interest. Surprise and amazement (i.e., behavioral interruption with reorientation activity) are others. Emotion as defined by affect and by action instigation thus delimit overlapping but nonidentical domains.

As I have mentioned earlier, the history of emotion theories began with noting that certain reactions affect the individual. The individual does not produce feelings of pleasure or pain at will, except by submitting to selected stimulus events; and he or she does not produce impulsiveness at will by definition. One can give this involuntary nature of "passions" a somewhat more positive accent when noting that emotional reactions tend to overrule ongoing actions and processes. I have termed this feature "control precedence" (Frijda, 1986). This passivity and the voluntary–involuntary distinction, which defined what were called "emotions" in older times, are notions that current psychology does not feel at ease with. They imply some notion of "agency" that, like "will," is difficult to fit into the cognitive science perspective, and therefore attracts little interest in psychology. This is wrong, I think. These notions are basic for the major psychological category of responsibility. Assigning, accepting, or carrying responsibility does not seem just to be an arbitrary moral, juridical, or cultural convention. Sense of responsibility implies that one accepts blame or praise as being justified, and some sense that one was free to have acted as one did. Assigning and accepting responsibility have pronounced emotional as well as ethical implications, as does the loss of feeling responsible.

What specifies and unifies emotional phenomena may not be one or the other of the various components. It may be the process that connects the components. One may reserve the word "emotion" for states of synchronization of the various components (Scherer, 1999), or may restrict it to occurrences of affect that produce a change in action readiness (all hunger may be unpleasant, but hunger would be considered an emotion only when it leads to restlessness and an imperative urge to find food). The emotion category can also be restricted to the various response components or their patters, when these are elicited by cognitive appraisal of the meaning of events (e.g., Elster, 1999; Lazarus, 1991). Such restrictions are meaningful. Each in its own way sets those reactions that, in principle, involve some impact of events upon the individual's life and behavior apart from those that are being caused by mere affect without personal consequence, such as a hunger pang or a toothache. Such connections between components may make the domain of what are considered to be emotions smaller within the larger domain of affect phenomena, but it renders the smaller domain more coherent.

Just as there are arguments to restrict the domain of emotion, there are arguments to enlarge it. Many investigators distinguish between "emotions" and "emotional attitudes" or "sentiments" (Arnold, 1960; Shand, 1920). Being frightened by a dog and being afraid of dogs is not the same sort of thing. The distinction corresponds with that between occurrent states and inclinations or dispositions. Emotions have a limited duration; sentiments may persist over a lifetime. Nevertheless, occurrent emotions and sentiments are not that different. They have the same structure. Emotions and sentiments can both be characterized by an object, its appraisal, and a particular propensity to act in relation to the object. Also, sentiments are not all that dispositional. One may feel that one fears dogs and loves one's beloved. Also one may know these sentiments and act accordingly—by avoiding places where one knows a dog to live, or by going upstairs to embrace the beloved. One may also know that the sentiment may turn into an emotion at the slightest provocation. One may, in other words, join sentiments and occurrent emotions together in one emotion category, contrary to what Kenny (1963) proposed.

All the preceding discussion in this section involves the definition of emotions, as does much of the debate and divergence in emotion theory. One may consider this an unprofitable pastime and believe that definitions are a mere matter of taste. Yet whether an individual has or does not have an emotion is sometimes a meaningful issue, and one that is hard to avoid. For instance, the question may come up whether a given reaction represents a "false emotion" or a "faked emotion." Can emotions be false or faked? And if they can, in what respect is a false or faked emotion different from a true one? There also is the moral or legal issue of whether some act has been committed "coolly" or "with emotion." Finally, there are imagined and empathic emotions, as well as anticipated emotions (e.g., anticipated guilt, shame, or regret), which belong to the powerful forces in the social control of behavior (Harré & Parrott, 1996) and which may be absent in some individuals. But perhaps it is better to replace the questions of whether or not a given state is an emotion by the more analytic question of which of the various components (e.g., appraisal, action readiness, control precedence) are or are not involved.

HOW ARE WE TO DISTINGUISH DIFFERENT EMOTIONS?

What makes one emotion different from another has been a prominent recurrent question. It has led to a search for information sources that might account for emotion differentiation.

Such sources can be found in any of the components or in their combinations; there is information aplenty. In the past, the sources were sought in irreducible *qualia* (Izard, 1977; Oatley, 1992); in patterns of physiological autonomic response and their feedback (James, 1884); or in feeling states as defined by affect and state of activation (Wundt, 1902; Russell, 1980). Work over the last several decades has emphasized many other possibilities, such as states of action readiness and their awareness (Arnold, 1960; Frijda, 1986); overt or covert motor behavior, including facial expression, and its feedback (Tomkins, 1962; Izard, 1977); and felt patterns of appraisal (Lazarus, 1991; Scherer, 1992). Distinctions also come from the type of eliciting event or core relational theme (Lazarus, 1991). There is evidence for each of these that they tend to correspond to distinctions between emotion categories. Jointly, they may do still better.

Which of the components should be preferred for distinguishing emotions? The answer depends upon the assumptions one makes about the relationships among the components. I can discern three kinds of assumptions. One is that one component has causal priority over the others; that is, it may be supposed to cause all others. Such an assumption has been made for assumed irreducible feeling *qualia* (Oatley, 1992) and for the dimensions of affect and activation (Russell, 1980, 1991).

A second assumption holds that there exist hypothetical dispositions that underlie all components together. Supposedly, activating the disposition activates the set of corresponding components as a whole. This corresponds to major versions of the basic-emotions hypothesis (Buck, 1988; Tomkins, 1962; Ekman, 1992; Izard, 1977). Such an assumption makes most sense if the dispositions are defined in functional terms, as systems for dealing with particular types of contingencies. It finds support in the identification of dedicated brain circuits and neurochemicals (Panksepp, 1998).

A third assumption starts from the moderate correlations among components. It views emotions as more or less unordered collections of components. In those collections, each component is activated by separate external conditions or habits, in addition to the common eliciting event (Ortony & Turner, 1990; Scherer, 1992). This third assumption provides the option of abandoning the very notion of distinct emotion types. Emotions may just be loose bundles of component processes. Such looseness is not necessarily absolute; the various components are to some extent interdependent. Readiness

for vigorous motor response requires sympathetic energy arousal; feeling consists in part of feedback from autonomic and skeletal responses and from felt states of action readiness; and so forth.

Several investigators have taken this third option. They view emotion labels as arbitrary distinctions in a more or less unstructured domain (Mandler, 1984). These labels are felt to represent more or less arbitrary ecological, cultural, or linguistic prototypes or scripts (Russell, 1991). The prototypes may reflect frequent or socially important patterns of components (as in Scherer's [1992] conception of "modal emotions"). They may also correspond to cognitive elaborations of states defined by given fuzzily delimited areas in bidimensional affect space (Russell, 1980).

An unstructured multicomponent view seems better able to deal with cultural differences in emotion categories (e.g., Lutz, 1988), as well as with differences in the precise semantic content of similar categories in different languages, such as "anger" in English and *ikari* (translated as "anger") in Japanese. It also deals easily with the appreciable differences in the structure of given emotions that appear to exist within a culture. On the other hand, a basic-emotions view more readily handles evidence suggesting that certain emotion categories are very common or even universal (Mesquita, Frijda, & Scherer, 1997). Moreover, that view too has room for many of the cultural differences. Basic emotions can be considered to represent functionally defined classes (Ekman, 1992). Within each class, the precise antecedents, the nature of the objects, the full gamut of appraisal components, the precise type of action goal or action to deal with the appraised contingency, and emotion significance (see below) all may vary. They all provide the leeway that cultural and individual differences require. So far, the issue is far from settled.

Indeed, the moderate correlations between components can also be accommodated within a basic-emotions conception. Each component may have its own facilitating conditions, in addition to being called up by a central emotion process. For instance, respiration rate is determined by the variable need for oxygen before it is marshaled by the activation of an emotion mechanism. Display rules and other regulatory processes, too, may affect each component separately or differentially.

So far, I have treated emotion categories realistically. I have viewed the labels as reflecting structure among the phenomena, or prototypical ordering of those phenomena in fuzzy sets. A different approach is possible. One may consider emotion labels as reflecting prototypes or scripts of cultural origin that to some extent prescribe the phenomena. One behaves as the script for a given circumstance—say, personal loss or threat—demands. This is the social-constructionist view, represented, for instance, by Harré and Parrott (1996). A strong form of this view is implausible in the face of the evidence suggesting a biological basis for emotions. However, it points to one of the forces that might shape the patterns of phenomena. It also points to a formative role of emotion labels. Labels not only reflect; the "significance" of emotions is attached to the labels in the first place. "Significance" refers to the complex of social norms about having or expressing a given emotion, as well as to the subject's personal evaluation of having a given emotion, and to the emotions that having a given emotion is likely to arouse. Emotion labels are a major entry point for processes of emotion regulation by way of such significance. How far all this goes has yet to be determined.

The multicomponent nature of emotional phenomena thus reflects a looseness in structure that fits viewing emotion categories as fictions. Similar considerations apply to the distinctions between different categories of affective phenomena, such as emotions, feelings, moods, and sentiments. These issues reflect a deeper and more general one: that of using substance concepts instead of function concepts in efforts to understand phenomena. Cassirer (1908) introduced this distinction when discussing the development of physics. There, for instance, Aristotle's distinction between heavy and light substances came to be replaced by the function relating the respective masses of object and medium. Substances are static; functions allow for change over time. The distinction between substance and function parallels that between states or things and processes.

Emotions are often treated as states or things. Language supports this because, at least in those languages I am familiar with, they are referred to by nouns. It appears useful to do so in social communication. For psychological analysis at a functional level, however, it may be better to treat emotions as the variable phenomenal results of processes that can perhaps be better referred to by verbs. "One is joying" might not be a bad expression, as it would indicate current and variable activation of the disposition for dealing with playful encounters. In general, the phenomena discussed so far, the response components, may be more profitably understood as the outcomes of processes, if only because their interactions occur at the process level and not at that of the phenomena.

From this perspective, the very notions of emotion and of the different emotions may even be abandoned. That they are indispensable in social interaction does not imply that they are optimal in psychological analysis (Mandler, 1984). One can describe the various phenomena directly in terms of the processes. It would avoid needless discussions about categorical boundaries ("Is this a mood or an emotion?"), because processes are graded in strength, and making cuts at certain levels of strength is arbitrary. That, of course, was the moral of Duffy's (1941) attack on the emotion concept, although her analysis was limited by its focus on activation. Further process parameters may be added—for instance, those relevant for the emotion–mood distinction. The degree of articulation of an intentional object and process duration can both be considered as such parameters. They would turn the distinction between emotions and moods into a continuum of "emotionness" or "moodness."

Replacing categories by processes may be extended to emotions themselves, and even to their components. Ortony and Turner (1990), Smith and Scott (1997), and Scherer (1992) have all advocated it at the level of individual response components. These authors have argued that one can best describe facial expressions as assemblies of separate facial expression components. These components can be defined functionally—for example, as protective, attentional, or force-assembling actions (eye narrowing, eye widening, and vertical frowning respectively)—or topographically in terms of facial action units. Efforts can then be made, as Smith and Scott (1997) have done, to link those component processes directly to appraisal component processes.

Employing the process level rather than a category level turns the relationships between components into a subject for unprejudiced empirical research. From this perspective, several basic questions can be addressed: Which processes are linked to which other processes, and to which degree? Which linkages are due to joint response to the same antecedent contingencies, and which to joint response to different contingencies that are themselves correlated, such as suddenness and unexpectedness? Which linkages represent functional dependence, as in the example of vigorous action and respiration rate, and which represent the effects of a joint command system, as a basic-emotions view suggests?

All these questions are relevant for another recurrent question in emotion theory: Which of the phenomena discussed belong to emotion itself, and which are its antecedents or consequences? In older stages of emotion research, discussions raged over whether motivation or action impulse belongs to emotion proper or is merely one of the results (e.g., Dumas, 1948). I return to this issue below. Similar problems occur elsewhere—for instance, in discussions of facial expression. Is it indeed "expression" that communicates something with independent existence, or is expression an integral aspect of what emotion is about, such as action impulse or social interaction? The contributions in Russell and Fernández-Dols (1997) provide much that is relevant to this discussion.

The question of whether certain phenomena belong to emotions, or are among their antecedents and consequences, loses much of its sense when "emotion" is understood to refer to a collection of processes and not to a single or a solidly integrated entity. It yields, however, three additional fruitful questions. The first of these is this: How strictly do stimuli or thoughts determine particular processes? Expressions may turn out to occur without preceding feelings, and even without preceding action readiness. These and other emotional reactions may even occur without antecedent external stimulus, appraisal, or relevant thought. They can occur spontaneously, due to neural irritations, to hormonal overstimulation, or to diffuse excitement (see Izard, 1993).

The second question that emerges from viewing emotions as collections of processes is this: To what extent may processes that logically or prototypically follow the component processes influence those latter processes? May facial expressions influence appraisals, and may the expected effect of an emotion upon others influence occurrence of that emotion? They probably may. Emotion processes are probably not linearly organized. A nonlinear dynamic model may be more adequate (Lewis, 1996). Such a model better accounts for the fact that emotion elicitation sometimes indeed seems to depend upon the feedback from the subject's own actual or anticipated response.

The third question is this: How solidly do given subprocesses follow each other? For instance, how solid is the relationship between certain stimuli and certain responses, or that between certain appraisals and certain emotions? What this third question really asks is how strongly secondary conditions—such as personality, mood, the state of the organism, and coincidences in the physical and social situation—determine the appearance of a particular response. These secondary conditions may be so important that, for this reason too, a model involving chaotic determination may turn out to be more satisfactory than the usual linear model.

WHAT ARE THE RELATIONS BETWEEN EMOTION AND MOTIVATION?

The relations between motivation and emotion constitute another of the perennial problems. Discussions of that relation are usually drowning in a conceptual quagmire. Small wonder: The term "motivation" suffers from a polysemy similar to that for "emotion." It, too, has an occurrent as well as a dispositional reading. One may be motivated to visit the bathroom; while doing that, one is motivated by a concern for propriety; and, after one's actions, one is motivated to leave things as proper as one found them. The first is an occurrent reading, the second is a dispositional one, and the third is ambiguous.

One can view motivation as a cause of emotions, as one of its major aspects, and as one of its consequences. The mutual osmosis of these applications of the motivation concept has led some investigators (e.g., Bindra, 1959) to advocate abandoning the emotion–motivation distinction. However, both notions can be kept apart by the dispositional–occurrent distinction. Many emotions are occurrent motivational states, since they involve action readiness that arouses behavior and drives it forth. An upsurge of lust is one example. And many of these emotions are instigated by a dispositional motivational readiness for achieving a particular valued end state, which becomes occurrent because of its urgency or because an event promises its satisfaction or frustration. Mc-

Dougall (1923) called such dispositional readiness "instincts," with emotions as their actualizations. Buck (1988, 1999) speaks of emotions as the readouts of motivation. Oatley (1992) and others use the more cognitive term "goals," with emotions the responses to contingencies in achieving or not achieving them.

Some have argued that emotions such as fear and lust, and motivations such as the desire to escape and the desire to possess, are related as causes and consequences (e.g., Oatley & Johnson-Laird, 1987). As already noted, such separation between emotion and the induction of activity has appeared artificial to other authors. Again, the problem largely disappears when one conceives the domains in process terms. It changes into the question of under which conditions action readiness change does or does not depend upon prior occurrence of appraisal or feeling, or perhaps may be triggered by stimulus perception directly.

Closer to the heart of the emotion–motivation relation is the question of whether every emotion involves some motivational change. Joy and sadness have always offered problems in this regard, because they are not easily seen as including some motivational goal. The same applies to emotional shock, surprise, and excitement. Wider conceptions of motivational changes may seem needed to bring these into a common perspective with fear, anger, and the like. Further confusion arises because many emotions also do create motives of both dispositional and occurrent kinds. Having fallen in love is perhaps the emotion for which this is most clearly the case. Love comes from the need for intimacy or sex, it consists of the urge for union, and it leads to the urge to get hold of its target and to please it. But one may fill in "it" more precisely with process designations.

WHAT ELICITS EMOTIONS?

Emotions are generally regarded as being caused by external events or by thoughts, apart from physiological causes such as biochemical changes and neural discharges caused by tumors (Izard, 1993). Emotions are therefore often defined as responses to events. What is the nature of those events that are the antecedents to emotion? Can one reduce the multitude of emotion antecedents to simple principles?

As usual, there have been several approaches to finding an answer to this question. A first approach proposes that emotions are responses to certain unconditioned stimuli; other events may evoke emotions by conditioning. Different emotions may correspond to different unconditioned stimuli. This was Watson's (1929) view; however, the proposal has seemed to account for only a fraction of what actually elicits emotions.

A second approach came from later behaviorism. It considered emotions to be aroused not by particular stimuli, but by contingencies consisting of the actual or signaled arrival or termination of pleasant or unpleasant events, or, as the behaviorist authors said, of positive or negative reinforcers (Millenson, 1967; Mowrer, 1960). Gray (1987) and others have extended this line of thought by including stimulus omission and interactions with the subject's resources—in particular, the availability or absence of action programs (habits, responses) to deal with the contingencies. "Coping resources" are thus included among the emotion antecedents.

A third approach has given the subject–event interaction a still stronger role in three ways. First, one may seek to explain the pleasant or unpleasant nature of events depending upon whether they promote or obstruct the subject's concerns (motives, well-being, major goals). Second, these concerns may differ from one individual to another. Third, what is causally effective may be whether and how the subject has appraised the relevance of events to concerns, and how he or she has appraised the eliciting contingency. Emotion arousal is thus viewed as depending upon the individual's cognitive or associative appraisal processes: A loss is a loss when the subject feels it is a loss (Lazarus, 1991; Oatley, 1992). This is the core of the cognitive approach to emotions.

The view that emotion arousal is determined by the meaning of events for the individual's concerns has been a common element in all classical writings on emotion from Plato onward. What causes pleasure is the achievement of the goal of a concern, and pain results from its nonachievement. Such an explanation of emotions, ancient and respectable as it is, has always encountered problems. The evidence for concerns often emerges only after the occurrence of emotions; for example, the idea of death presumably evokes anxiety. The explanation invokes a goal of self-preservation. Such a goal, however, is inferred primarily from the fear of death and is obviously circular. Such circularity formed the objection raised, for instance, against McDougall's (1923) conception of instinct. Another problem is that people's actions are often motivated by the goal of achieving pleasure or of escaping from pain. Hedonism explains much human effort. The conflict between the hedonic and what Duncker (1941–1942) called the "hormic" approaches constitutes a recurrent issue in treatments of the relation between emotions and motives. Finally, the structure of concerns is largely unclear. What makes a concern a concern, or a motive a motive, if not ultimate pleasure? Currently, the term "goal" is often used for what I here refer to as "concern." However, the achievement or nonachievement of a goal does not always lead to an emotion, so again the hedonic may be hidden in those goals that do. Clarification is still needed.

Furthermore, the various approaches mentioned fail to account for the "cognitive" emotions, such as surprise and boredom. An alternative to the concern–satisfaction view is that emotions (or many emotions) result from meeting or thwarting expectancies. Hebb's (1949) analysis of emotional distress was of this sort; so is that of Mandler (1984).

The various approaches may not represent mutually exclusive alternatives. Emotions may spring from various sources: from innately hedonic stimuli and their associations, from the actual and possible acquisition or loss of such stimuli, from nonhedonic concerns (including values), and from the fate of expectancies.

NATURE OR NURTURE?

How much, and what, in emotional phenomena are due to constraints and patternings laid down in the mechanisms with which humans are by nature equipped? How much, and what, result from individual learning and from prescriptions and models provided by the social environment?

That emotions have a biological basis is something that probably nobody contests. The evidence for neurological and neurochemical mechanisms is fairly compelling (see Buck, 1999; Panksepp, 1998). The precise nature of what they are mechanisms for, however, remains unclear. Do the limbic mechanisms control motivational states and the bases for impulses or states of action readiness? Or do they control integration of behavioral patterns? Or

do they determine affective sensitivity to particular stimuli or contingencies? Or do they control all of these?

In any case, the capacity for affect is rooted in the human (and animal) constitution, since affect can neither functionally nor phenomenally be reduced to cognitions and judgments. The processes of elementary appraisal, by which inputs come to evoke affect, likewise rest upon innate capabilities (LeDoux, 1996). There are also strong indications that there exist innate dispositions related to specific emotions, or at least to forms of action readiness such as satisfaction seeking, hostility, and self-protection. The evidence comes from neuropsychological findings (Panksepp, 1998), as well as the findings on the universality of such action patterns, including (Ekman, 1994) but not limited to facial expressions. Also, one can make a strong case for the universality or near-universality of major emotion categories as defined by such patterns, as well as for the universality or near-universality of the contingencies that typically elicit those emotions, and for the universal or near-universal presence of corresponding lexical terms in different languages (Shaver, Wu, & Schwartz, 1992; but see Russell, 1991).

By itself, universality does not prove biological origin. Major emotions may correspond to universal contingencies or "core relational themes" (Lazarus, 1991), such as threat, loss, or success. Universal contingencies present universal occasions for learning. They also present constellations for universally similar problem solving, or dynamic compilations of action patterns. Take revenge, for example. Why should it come from an innate disposition? Is it not enough that harm is universally painful, and that people are familiar with several sorts of actions that can modify the behavior of others who harm them? Those actions—kicking, shouting, throwing objects—are familiar both within emotional contexts (as when chasing intruders) and outside such contexts (as when cracking eggshells, breaking branches, and playing boisterously with companions). One can discover that such actions are effective in the dynamic context of hostile, playful, and instrumental interactions, in the same way that a baby discovers the possibility of walking when body weight and muscle strength have reached the right proportion (Fogel & Thelen, 1987). There is thus more than one way to explain instances of universality, as there is more than one way to explain instances of cultural specificity.

Biological dispositions and cultural determinants, as we all know, are neither incompatible nor mutually exclusive. It may only be useful to stress that the role of cultural differences in emotional phenomena depends to an important degree upon one's level of analysis (Mesquita et al., 1997). The phenomena as well as the social role of shame, for instance, differ strongly in Western and in Arabic societies; yet both may represent the same sensitivity to social acceptance and involve the same motivation to correct deviations from norms and efforts to prevent such deviations from occurring. Universality may lurk behind cultural specificity without detracting from the specific meanings of each cultural form. Conversely, culture determines not only specifics, but also universals. Sensitivity to social acceptance is itself cultural. Human grief is like primate or elephant grief (De Waal, 1996), although to a limited extent. One shares it with others, and builds one's shrine or puts souvenirs on the bookshelf and nods at them every morning. Symbolic capacities and social interactions both penetrate every phenomenon, its occasions for appearing, and its duration. Their implications remain to be explored.

Still, it is usually not very clear how biological dispositions and cultural determinants interact. It is also unclear how emotions that have an important cognitive component, such as regret and revenge, relate to biological mechanisms and basic emotion dispositions. How does learning make use of what is given, or does what is given constrain what is learned? These questions, to my knowledge, have hardly been treated with any depth.

EMOTION AND REASON

The traditional contrast of emotion and reason is still very much with us in some form or other. "Reason" is being used to denote several quite different things—for instance, the use of complex thought processes such as logical inference, as well as efforts to achieve optimal solutions. Both have been regarded as being opposed to emotion. It has frequently been argued that emotions do not employ reasoning and may even confuse it. Indeed, emotions often lead to behavior or thought that is suboptimal and that the individual may regret at a later moment.

Both contrasts have been attenuated in modern theory. The notion that emotion does not employ reasoning is weakened by the renewed emphasis upon the role of cognition in emotional appraisal (Aristotle, Spinoza, and many other philosophers stressed this role before) and in particular emotions such as regret (Landman, 1993). The emphasis upon emotion-induced suboptimal behavior was weakened by recognizing the "rationality of emotions" (de Sousa, 1987), the importance of emotion for rational behavior (Damasio, 1994; de Sousa, 1987; Frank, 1988; Solomon, 1993), and the functional nature of emotional reactions themselves. Emotional behavior is often considered appropriate to the eliciting event as appraised by the person (Lazarus, 2000). I return to that point in the next section.

Yet both contrasts between emotion and rationality remain. Affect can be aroused without a cognitive antecedent, as in the response to simple affective stimuli such as pain and smells, to "prepared" stimuli (Öhman, Chapter 36, this volume), and to the conditioned stimuli in traumatic conditioning (LeDoux, 1996). It has been forcefully argued that emotion, or at least affect, does not always need inferences. Many early theorists, such as Dumas (1948) defended this thesis; Zajonc (1980) did this more recently. It is also clear that not all cognitions that are relevant for well-being actually elicit or modify emotions. Demonstrating to a person with a spider phobia that spiders are harmless rarely helps. Which cognitions are emotionally effective, and which are not? Maybe we need to distinguish different kinds of cognition, such as knowledge-by-acquaintance as opposed to knowledge-by-description (Buck, 1999) or propositional versus implicational cognition (Teasdale & Barnard, 1993).

The irrationality of emotions, too, is still there. The rationality of emotions is at best restricted to "local rationality," as de Sousa (1987) has called it. Local rationality is not incompatible with irrationality from a wider or long-term perspective. That irrationality lurks in every emotion is suggested by the almost ubiquitous presence of emotion regulation and self-control. Rationality has an ally, built into the very emotion mechanisms in those functions. It is increasingly being recognized that regulation belongs to the emotion mechanisms as much as appraisal does, and that it is not there merely to satisfy social convention (De Waal, 1996). It also serves self-interest at many levels.

Emotions can be irrational, in the sense of

producing suboptimal results. They may be harmful in the long run, but even in the short run. People in panic press through too-narrow exits, stage fright spoils performance, nervousness spoils precision of movement, and rage may lead to childish behavior and upset social harmony (De Waal, 1996). Such detrimental effects dominated earlier emotion theorizing. Kant designated emotions as illnesses of the mind; Claparède (1928) interpreted emotions as forms of primitivization; and Darrow (1939) designated emotion as "functional decortication."

It is true that one can always think of some function for any behavior. One can explain stage fright as a show of helplessness that invites indulgence, or perhaps as a sensible escape impulse in view of the danger of ridicule. One can understand grief upon bereavement as a mechanism to achieve detachment from the obsolete attachment. Many emotions seem irrational only when the individual's appraisals are neglected (although it is true enough that these may themselves be irrational). Explaining irrationality away in this fashion suggests a Panglossian perspective. Pangloss, as readers may recall, is the philosopher in Voltaire's *Candide* who upon every misfortune echoes Leibniz's dictum that we live in the best of all possible worlds (Gould & Lewontin, 1979). But do we? Whatever the possible functions, the fact remains that restricting attention to short-term gains and focusing upon proximal appraisals are both often irrational, and that the disturbance of optimal functioning is dysfunctional.

The topics of emotional irrationality and primitivization have gone out of fashion in current emotion psychology. Nevertheless, they are there. They have to be dealt with and may be beginning to receive renewed attention (e.g., Parrott, 1998).

THE FUNCTIONS OF EMOTIONS

The negative aspects of emotions dominated earlier theorizing in both philosophy and psychology. In present theorizing, the tides have turned: Emotions are being viewed as adaptively useful. The functional perspective now dominates.

The functional perspective upon emotions is plausible because of biological data and evolutionary explanations. It is also plausible because the range of possible functions of emotions appears wider than only dealing with opportunities and threats that the individual faces. Joy may serve readiness for new exploits, may assist in recovery from previous stress, and may invite others to participate. Shame and guilt are powerful regulators of social interaction (Harré & Parrott, 1996). Seemingly irrational emotions such as compassion and revenge may serve as signs of commitment that are adaptive in long-term interactions, and thus may outweigh occasional costs in short-term interaction (Frank, 1988).

One has to be careful with functional interpretations, though, because they exist in two kinds that are not always kept distinct. There are evolutionary and proximal functions. Emotions may have been functional for dealing with the contingencies that made them come into existence in evolution. Sex serves the survival of the species, for instance. Emotions may also be functional for what they accomplish once they are there, and in relation to proximal elicitors, as when sex is indulged in to obtain pleasure and intimacy. Many emotions are functional in this latter sense. Guilt feelings can be used to blackmail others, and are indeed often used for that aim (Baumeister, Stillwell, & Heatherton, 1994). Grief provides the satisfaction that others will grieve after one's death, and thus strengthens attachment. One's own emotions and those in others are sources of social bonding and sources of human interest.

The evolutionary perspective almost obliges one to see emotions as functional provisions. Moreover, evolutionary hypotheses for emotional phenomena tend to come very easily these days. Anger? Small wonder if it is innate, since it helps in protecting one's territory and offspring. Apathy in grief? Again, small wonder, because it saves useless expenditure of energy and allows detachment from the broken attachment. Heart rate increases in sex and fear? They were obviously useful when those emotions developed, under threat of rivals and predators; one always had to be ready to climb a tree. However, nobody was around then to gauge these benefits against the costs that anger, apathy, and the wear and tear caused by heart rate increases might entail. Evolutionary hypotheses often resemble lazy thinking, failure to examine implications, or failure to consider alternative possibilities. Such possibilities include dynamic explanations (emotions' developing on the spot as a result of their immediate material and social effects) and the notion that certain emotional phenomena may be mere "spandrels"—chance offshoots of something quite different (Gould & Lewontin, 1979). "Anger," as I have indicated, may be a by-product of provisions for power deployment that developed to help individuals crack nuts.

One may nevertheless grant that, all in all, emotions are functional for adaptation. How does one begin to reconcile this with the instances of irrationality and disturbance of optimal functioning? Some authors tried to solve the problem of the irrationality of emotion by distinguishing different types of emotion. Claparède (1928) distinguished emotions and feelings by the features of irrationality versus constructiveness. Dumas (1948) separated "emotional shock" from the organized emotions such as anger and fear, as did Hebb (1949) in his earlier work. Later, Hebb (1970) linked the organizing or disruptive nature of emotions to their intensity, in the inverted-U-curve hypothesis. One can think of additional principles of explanation. Some dysfunction may come from limited resources for emotion regulation, from exhaustion, and from the fact that certain emotional predicaments are simply inescapable. One may even give this a functional twist by saying that dysfunction is the price to pay for not weighing more than we do, and for requiring only 9 months of gestation.

Many irrational or dysfunctional instances of emotion are due to a common feature of functioning. Reactions that are in principle functional are being applied far beyond the contexts in which they are of use. Grief upon bereavement, for instance, may serve no purpose. It is merely a response to loss and pain. But grief is useful when it prompts retrieving a lost person, such as a mother who has walked out of the room. This usefulness makes the grief of bereavement comparable to, and as meaningless as, the pain of incurable cancer or pain in a phantom limb.

A further major hypothesis is that human intellectual and cultural development have outrun evolution. Emotions may have been adaptive for coping with the risks and opportunities of the savannah, and with the use of fists and stone tools. They may not be adaptive any more for dealing with present-day interactions with the technological infrastructure and the almost unlimited availability of resources. Present-day anger and present-day greed may have turned into perversions because the emotion systems did not develop along with those cultural conditions. Here, too, the psychology of emotion will have to progress slowly toward a balanced answer to the perennial questions.

CONCLUDING REMARKS

Will the perennial problems in the psychology of emotion be truly perennial? Will they remain with us forever? Perennial problems are often not resolved because they reflect particular world views or limits in capacities for conceptualization. The wave–particle dilemma in physics would seem to be a problem of the latter sort, and the contrast between social constructivism and explanations of emotions via laws and mechanisms would seem to be one of the former sort. But perhaps the scope of the perennial problems in emotion psychology can be considerably narrowed by achieving more insight into how their proposed solutions are related to each other.

As I have remarked at the beginning of this chapter, psychological explanations of emotional phenomena are being sought at different levels. Those levels are the levels of explanation as distinguished by Dennett (1987), as well as the levels of what one seeks to explain—the levels of complexity of the phenomena—as alluded to above in the section titled "What Is 'an' Emotion?" Answers to some questions may seem incompatible when in fact they are answers to different questions, answers at different levels of explanation, or answers at different levels of the phenomena.

I also think that the study of emotion will be advanced when Dennett's (1987) functional or psychological level receives more attention. In current analyses of emotion antecedents, little is being said about what constitutes a reinforcement and why. Only the first efforts are now being made to construct models of the processes of appraisal and of the inner structure of goals or concerns, which play such a pivotal role in explaining emotions. Ultimately, intentional phenomena such as experiences, desires, and goals should be clarified in terms of subpersonal, functionally defined processes. Such clarification is scarce. As far as I know, for instance, there exist no detailed hypotheses at the functional level of how innate affective stimuli evoke affect. I have no idea how sugar evokes not only the sensation of sweetness but also the experience of pleasantness. As a consequence, jumps are being made from the intentional level to the hardware or neurophysiological level, and vice versa. Fear arousal is mediated by the amygdala, but how exactly is the amygdala supposed to do that, and which fear mechanisms is it supposed to harbor or affect?

All this is important for advances in emotion research, for a general and common reason. There is no guarantee that categories of analysis at one level will project onto coherent categories at another level. There is no guarantee that emotions as defined experientially or behaviorally will all involve one mechanism or one coherent set of mechanisms. The same may apply to a single emotion category, such as fear. The mechanisms of fear of failure may have little in common with the mechanisms of fear of the unknown or fear of spiders, except that they all share the final common pathway of trying to escape or of behavioral inhibition. That all stimuli that evoke emotions are in some way appraised (they receive affective valence) does not imply the existence of one coherent appraisal process or mechanism. And so on.

Of course, the relationships between explanations at different levels depend upon the findings at different levels. It would be profitable if researchers in different areas and on different levels talked more to one another. It would be profitable if they knew more about what happened at these other areas and levels. Experimental investigators of emotions often know little about the social and cultural psychology of emotions, and vice versa. This painfully restricts the range of emotion elicitors considered in explanatory hypotheses. Students of the neuropsychology of emotion often know little about the contemporary psychology of emotion, and they frequently write as if the paradigm of what causes emotions is an electric shock, and as if the paradigm of motivation is thirst or hunger or something weird like "survival." To most psychological researchers, the limbic area is merely somewhere in the brain, and the amygdala is an amorphous blob of tissue. There is no real reason why all this should remain that way—and countering this situation, of course, is one of the main purposes of this handbook.

REFERENCES

Arnold, M. B. (1960). *Emotion and personality* (2 vols.). New York: Columbia University Press.

Arnold, M. B. (1970). Perennial problems in the field of emotion. In M. B. Arnold (Ed.), *Feelings and emotions: The Loyola symposium.* (pp. 169–186). New York: Academic Press,

Baumeister, R., Stillwell, A. M., & Heatherton, T. F. (1994). Guilt: An interpersonal approach. *Psychological Bulletin, 115,* 243–267.

Bentley, M. (1928). Is "emotion" more than a chapter heading? In M. L. Reymert (Ed.), *Feelings and emotions: The Wittenberg symposium* (pp. 17–23). Worcester, MA: Clark University Press.

Bindra, D. (1959). *Motivation: A systematic reinterpretation.* New York: Ronald Press.

Buck, R. (1988). *Human motivation and emotion* (2nd ed.). New York: Wiley.

Buck, R. (1999). The biological affects: A typology. *Psychological Review, 106,* 301–336.

Cassirer, E. (1908) *Substanzbegriff und Funktionsbegriff* [*Substance concepts and function concepts*]. Leipzig: B. Cassirer.

Claparède, E. (1928). Emotions and feelings. In M. L. Reymert (Ed.), *Feelings and emotions: The Wittenberg symposium* (pp. 124–139). Worcester, MA: Clark University Press.

Damasio, A. (1994) *Descartes' error: Emotion, reason, and the human brain.* New York: Putnam.

Darrow, C. W. (1939). Emotion as relative functional decortication. *Psychological Review, 42,* 566–578.

Dennett, D. C. (1987). *The intentional stance.* Cambridge, MA: MIT Press.

Descartes, R. (1970). *Les passions de l'âme* [*The passions of the soul*]. Amsterdam: Elzevier. (Original work published 1649)

de Sousa, R. (1987). *The rationality of emotions.* Cambridge, MA: MIT Press.

De Waal, F. B. M. (1996). *Good natured.* Cambridge, MA: Harvard University Press.

Duffy, E. (1941). An explanation of "emotional" phenomena without the use of the concept "emotion." *Journal of General Psychology, 25,* 283–293.

Dumas, G. (1948). *La vie affective* [*The life of emotion*]. Paris: Presses Universitaires de France.

Duncker, K. (1941–1942). On pleasure, emotion, and striving. *Philosophy and Phenomenological Research, 1,* 391–430.

Ekman, P. (1992). An argument for basic emotions. *Cognition and Emotion, 6,* 169–200.

Ekman, P. (1994). Strong evidence for universals in facial expression: A reply to Russell's mistaken critique. *Psychological Bulletin, 115,* 268–287.

Elster, J. (1999). *Alchemies of the mind.* Cambridge, England: Cambridge University Press

Fogel, A., & Thelen, E. (1987). Development of early expressive and communicative action: Reinterpreting the evidence from a dynamic systems perspective. *Developmental Psychology, 23,* 747–761.

Frank, R. H. (1988). *Passions within reason: The strategic role of the emotions.* New York: Norton.

Frijda, N. H. (1986). *The emotions.* Cambridge, England: Cambridge University Press

Frijda, N. H., Mesquita, B., Sonnemans, J., & Van Goozen, S. (1991). The duration of affective phenomena, or emotions, sentiments and passions. In K. Strongman (Ed.), *International review of emotion and motivation* (Vol. 1, pp. 187–225). Chichester, England: Wiley.

Gould, S. J., & Lewontin, R. C. (1979). The spandrels of San Marco and the Panglossian paradigm: A critique of the adaptationist programme. *Proceedings of the Royal Society of London, 205,* 581–598.

Gray, J. A. (1987). *The psychology of fear and stress* (2nd ed.). Cambridge, England: Cambridge University Press.

Harré, R., & Parrott, W. G. (Eds.). (1996). *The emotions: Social, cultural and biological dimensions.* Thousand Oaks, CA: Sage.

Hebb, D. O. (1949). *The organization of behavior.* New York: Wiley.

Hebb, D. O. (1970). *Textbook of psychology* (3rd ed.). Philadelphia: Saunders.

Izard, C. E. (1977). *Human emotions.* New York: Plenum Press.

Izard, C. E. (1993). Four systems of emotion activation. *Psychological Review, 100,* 68–90.

James, W. (1884). What is an emotion? *Mind, 9,* 188–205.

Kenny, A. (1963). *Action, emotion and will.* London: Routledge & Kegan Paul.

Kleinginna, P. R., & Kleinginna, A. M. (1981). A categorized list of emotion definitions, with suggestions for a consensual definition. *Motivation and Emotion, 5,* 345–379.

Köhler, W. (1938). *The place of value in a world of facts.* New York: Liveright.

Landis, C.,& Hunt, W. A. (1932). Adrenalin and emotion. *Psychological Review, 39,* 467–485.

Landman, J. (1993). *Regret: The persistence of the possible.* Oxford: Oxford University Press.

Lazarus, R. S. (1991). *Emotion and adaptation.* New York: Oxford University Press.

Lazarus, R. S. (2000). Appraisal, relational meaning, stress, and emotion. In K. R. Scherer, A. Schorr, & T. Johnstone (Eds.), *Appraisal processes in emotion: Theory, methods, research.* New York: Oxford University Press.

LeDoux, J. (1996). *The emotional brain.* New York: Simon & Schuster.

Lewis, M. (1996). Self-organizing cognitive appraisals. *Cognition and Emotion, 10,* 1–26.

Lutz, C. (1988). *Unnatural emotions: Everyday sentiments on a Micronesian atoll and their challenge to Western theory.* Chicago: University of Chicago Press.

Mandler, G. (1984). *Mind and body: The psychology of emotion and stress.* New York: Norton.

McDougall, W. (1923). *Outline of psychology.* New York: Scribner.

Mesquita, B., Frijda, N. H., & Scherer, K. R. (1997). Culture and emotion. In P. R. Dasen & T. S. Saraswathi (Eds.), *Handbook of cross-cultural psychology* (Vol. 2, pp. 255–298). Boston: Allyn & Bacon.

Millenson, J. R. (1967). *Principles of behavioral analysis.* New York: Macmillan.

Mowrer, O. H. (1960). *Learning theory and behavior.* New York: Wiley.

Oatley, K. (1992). *Best laid schemes: The psychology of emotions.* Cambridge, England: Cambridge University Press.

Oatley, K., & Johnson-Laird, P. (1987). Towards a cognitive theory of emotion. *Cognition and Emotion, 1,* 51–58.

Ortony, A., Clore, G., & Collins, A. (1988). *The cognitive structure of emotions.* Cambridge, England: Cambridge University Press.

Ortony, A., & Turner, T. (1990). What's basic about basic emotions? *Psychological Review, 97,* 315–331.

Panksepp, J. (1998). *Affective neuroscience.* Oxford: Oxford University Press.

Parrott, G. (1998). Multiple goals, self-regulation, and functionalism. In A. Fischer (Ed.), *ISRE '98: Proceedings of the 10th Conference of the International Society for Research on Emotion* (pp. 37–400). Amsterdam: International Society for Research on Emotion.

Russell, J. A. (1980). A circumplex model of affect. *Journal of Personality and Social Psychology, 39,* 1161–1178.

Russell, J. A. (1991). Culture and the categorization of emotions. *Psychological Bulletin, 110,* 426–450.

Russell, J. A., & Fernández-Dols, J.-M. (Eds.). (1997). *The psychology of facial expression.* Cambridge, England: Cambridge University Press.

Scherer, K. R. (1992). What does facial expression express? In K. T. Strongman (Ed.), *International review of studies of emotion* (Vol. 2, pp. 139–165). Chichester, England: Wiley.

Scherer, K. R. (1999). Appraisal theory. In T. Dalgleish & M. Power (Eds.), *Handbook of cognition and emotion* (pp. 637–663). Chichester, England: Wiley.

Shand, A. F. (1920). *The foundations of character: A study of the emotions and sentiments.* London: Macmillan.

Shaver, P., Wu, S., & Schwartz, J. C. (1992). Cross-cultural similarities and differences in emotion and its representation: A prototype approach. In M. Clark (Ed), *Review of personality and social psychology* (Vol. 13, pp. 175–212). Newbury Park, CA: Sage.

Simon, H. A. (1981). *The sciences of the artificial.* Cambridge, MA: MIT Press.

Smith, C. A., & Scott, H. H. (1997). A componential approach to the meaning of facial expressions. In J. A. Russell & J.-M. Fernández-Dols (Eds.), *The psychology of facial expression* (pp. 229–254). Cambridge, England: Cambridge University Press.

Solomon, R. C. (1993). *The passions* (2nd ed.). Indianapolis, IN: Hackett.

Stein, N., & Trabasso, T. (1992). The organization of emotional experience: Creating links between emotion, thinking, and intentional action. *Cognition and Emotion, 6,* 225–244.

Teasdale, J. D., & Barnard, P. (1993). *Affect, cognition, and change.* Hillsdale, NJ: Erlbaum.

Tomkins, S. S. (1962). *Affect, imagery and consciousness: Vol. 1. The positive affects.* New York: Springer.

Wallon, H. (1942). *De l'acte à la pensée.* Paris: Flammarion.

Watson, J. B. (1929). *Psychology from the standpoint of a behaviorist* (3rd ed.). Philadelphia: Lippincott.

Wundt, W. (1902). *Grundzüge der pysiologischen Psychologie* (5th ed., Vol. 3). Leipzig: Engelmann.

Zajonc, R. B. (1980). Thinking and feeling: Preferences need no inferences. *American Psychologist, 35,* 151–175.

CHAPTER 6

Emotion and Clinical Depression: An Environmental View

George W. Brown

There is now an extensive literature on stress and the etiology of a variety of psychiatric disorders, and there is not much doubt that emotion can play some role as a mediating factor. However, the processes involved remain surprisingly obscure. Most discussion is theoretical, or, less generously, speculative. Although particular emotions are related to specific disorders—for example, disgust with eating disorders (Phillips, Senior, Fahy, & David, 1998)—the range of symptoms involved suggests that such disorders are clearly a good deal more than complications of such emotions. Depression, the subject of this chapter, is no exception. Women found to be suffering from "clinically relevant depression"—which is comparable to *Diagnostic and Statistical Manual of Mental Disorders,* third edition, revised (DSM-III-R) "major depression" (Finlay-Jones et al., 1980; Dean, Surtees, & Sashidharan, 1983)—in a random sample of London women had on average 18.1 symptoms out of a possible 40 covered by a clinical interview (Brown, Craig, & Harris, 1985). Recognized core symptoms of depression (such as hopelessness, weight loss, early waking, loss of interest, and inertia) were always present, but so almost always were nondepressive ones (such as tension and free-floating anxiety). What is clear about a depressive disorder is that usually there has been a fundamental change in everyday behavior; this has been described in terms of "the paralysis of depres-

sion, the demobilization, including the changes in behaviour and mental ability, and the negative views of self" (Gilbert & Allan, 1998, p. 586). Nonetheless, it is also heterogeneous in character. For example, despite such demobilisation, as many as a quarter of the depressed London women just cited were without a negative view of self or, for that matter, self-blame (Brown, Andrews, Bifulco, & Veiel, 1990, Table 8). Also, despite highly debilitating symptoms, a number had persistently struggled to deal with the adverse circumstances they saw as bringing about their depression. Despite this overabundance of "emotion," I argue here that it is not foolhardy to search for an emotion-producing meaning (or an appraisal) capable of provoking a serious depressive episode.

FUNCTIONALIST AND LIFE-EVENT PERSPECTIVES COMPARED

The way forward, taken by the research to be outlined in this chapter, has been to move away from considering internal states to considering the environmental events that may have provoked the disorder. This has been made possible by the fact that the majority of clinically relevant depressive episodes appear to be "reactive" rather than "endogenous." Circumstances surrounding the event have been reconstructed by the investigator from the vantage point of an interview after the onset of any disorder. Using research with depression as an example, I outline an approach to this task of reconstruction that has been developed over a period of 25 years. The perspective is similar in several ways to a "functionalist" one on emotion that views it as typically "reactive" (as is depression). Both perspectives then take as their starting point the interweaving between person and environment, and they play down the importance of intrapersonal factors—the traditional domain of emotional theory (Campos & Campos, 1989).

A functionalist perspective assumes that an *appraisal* of an event is essential if emotion is to occur, and that this results from recognition of its implications for the satisfaction of goals, motives, or concerns, with different emotions corresponding to different patterns of appraisal (Frijda, 1993). The event → appraisal → emotion sequence is again similar to that taken by life-event research if "clinical depression" is substituted for "emotion." And since an event can be dated and juxtaposed in time with the start of an episode of depression or emotion, it is possible to envisage causal inquiries (Brown & Harris, 1978). For this it is necessary to establish appraisal, and it is at this point that research on emotion has run into difficulties. Frijda (1993) notes that the literature is confused about how far appraisal differs from the emotional experience itself. Joy may be no more than the experience of an event appraised in a joyful way; in other words, appraisal may often be coterminous with the emotion. An obvious but nonetheless telling example is the anger that may be directed at a hammer that has struck a finger (perhaps with a violent casting of it aside), with the appraisal of blame the result of the anger rather than its cause. In an impressive argument, Frijda (1993) suggests, as in this example, that appraisal preceding an emotion may typically be much simpler than that conveyed by a self-report. However, this simplicity does not necessarily hold for the cognitive elaborations that may follow such an initial appraisal, where the emotions provoked by the event may in turn lead to further cognitive elaborations.

This position once again comes fairly close to that emerging from life-event research on depression. The relevant appraisal leading to a depressive episode may well be essentially a simple one, but unfortunately not one necessarily revealed by a self-report. Certainly the cognitive elaborations that can follow an event seriously complicate the task of isolating any such core appraisal. A woman experiencing an event of a kind that is capable of provoking a depressive disorder (say, discovery of a husband's infidelity) will typically describe in convincing detail a number of different emotions and cognitions that followed the discovery—ranging from anger, a sense of humiliation, anxiety about the future, and/or relief at the thought she will no longer have to put up with his violence, to a completely contrasting sense of hope that a reconciliation may be possible. And none of this will necessarily occur in a linear fashion. With such contrasts, and with the kind of variability already noted in the symptomatology of depression itself, it may be asked why we should even try to uncover a core appraisal. Perhaps the most honest answer is that without attempting to document such an appraisal, it is difficult to see how systematic research can proceed in exploring the role of the environment. Moreover, the picture I have outlined is not necessarily incompatible with such a core appraisal. The variability in emotional response, even on the assumption that it is the result of genetic, constitutional, or personality differences, may in practice play no etiological role or at most may only influence the form of the depressive response.

The presence of a core appraisal is also compatible with the possibility that common psychiatric disorders such as depression have their origins in an evolution-based response that in the past was selected to deal with a situation of relevance for survival. (However, here there is no good reason for the use of the singular; more than one survival-linked situation may be relevant.) In particular, it is possible that clinical depression has its roots in a behavioral system dealing with social rank, in contrast to the various anxiety disorders, some of which appear to reflect a defense system associated with threat from predators and others a defense system linked with threat from a social source (Gilbert, 1992). John Price (1972) was the first to suggest that depression evolved to limit fighting and conflict among conspecifics, and that without such a biologically based deescalation strategy, animals would engage in conflicts they could not win—with the risk of resulting harm. The strategies that have evolved appear for the most part to have been associated with some form of submissive behavior (Gilbert, 1992). There is, for example, experimental evidence that loss of status of a dominant male marsupial sugar glider (a highly social mammal) is quickly followed by withdrawn, nonexploratory behavior, which is in turn followed by lower testosterone titers and raised cortisol titers (Jones, Stoddart, & Mallick, 1995). It does not follow, however, that such a submissive state is in any way equivalent to human clinical depression; for example, the behavioral and biological characteristics of the dominant male sugar glider once he is introduced to the new group are more or less equivalent to those of the rest of the colony, other than the dominant resident male. Nor does it follow that, given that there is an animal equivalent to human depression, either state has ever been adaptive. Nonetheless, it still may be the case that the basic appraisal of importance for the kind of submissive states seen in the sugar gliders is also of relevance for the genesis of human depression. But, even given such assumptions, an evolutionary perspective is unfortunately compatible with other evolutionary possibilities. The most obvious—and probably the most important where depression is concerned—is the role of loss, which Bowlby (1980) saw as critical for depression via its link with the attachment system. I consider both possibilities.

EVENT APPRAISAL

In a radical attempt to avoid the kind of problems so far outlined in dealing with appraisal, the *contextual* measures to be described ignore self-reports concerning the impact of particular events. The approach is based on the Life Events and Difficulties Schedule (LEDS), which uses a semistructured interview employing investigator-based ratings to reflect the likely "stress" of an event or an ongoing difficulty. The internal world is approached via the external one and it is at this point that the functionalist and LEDS/life-event approach to the problem of documenting appraisal diverge. The life-event approach is much closer to ethological work relying on the observation of behavior, from which such concepts as submission, conflict, and defeat can be operationalized. The intellectual origin of the context-based approach of the LEDS stems from the early 19th-century debate concerning *Verstehen*, or understanding. This debate was based on the proposition that by taking account of a much broader context than that of the event itself, a common-sense

judgment can be made about its *likely* meaning. Max Weber (1964) made clear that this must take account of a person's values, plans, and goals—or as Frijda (1986) puts it, "concerns"—and here there is no difference with a functionalist perspective. But while the idea of concerns returns us to the internal world, as already intimated, I argue that an effective estimate of likely meaning can be made via an investigator-based judgment excluding any consideration of internal states.

Plans and Concerns

Frijda (1993) has firmly linked the process of appraisal of an event to relevant concerns, and the contextual measurement of events of the LEDS has throughout its development made exactly the same assumption (Brown & Harris, 1978; Brown, 1989b). However, concerns are not necessarily any more easy to document than the process of appraisal itself. In his short story "Albert Nobbs," George Moore (1985) describes the discovery of the secret of a woman who, in order to obtain a livelihood, has spent much of her adult life disguised as a male waiter in a Dublin hotel. On contemplating her life until that point, she muses, "I thought I would never cry again. . . . It is much sadder than I thought it was, and if I had known how sad it was I shouldn't have been able to live through it." The story conveys how people often manage to adapt reasonably well to adversity and deprivation. For this woman, there would probably have been over many years a persistent sense of dissatisfaction, but with dysphoric emotions kept within tolerable limits. It is in this kind of situation that a life event can tell us something that in a sense has been known all along—but nonetheless at times with devastating consequences. Such accommodation to adversity and the failure of the round of daily experience to provoke the kind of intensity of emotion that might be expected may be said to be fairly commonplace. It can, for instance, be seen in accounts of habit and routinization. Tomkins (1979, p. 212) notes how a husband and wife can become too skilled in knowing each other, and as a result can enter the same valley of perceptual skill and become hardly aware of each other.

If it can take a life event to bring home to us what is significant, is it possible to establish relevant concerns in a way that does not run the risk of being contaminated by the fact of the occurrence of the event itself? Once the discovery was made, the Dublin waiter would probably have told an interviewer of her deeply felt commitment to radically changing her way of life, but would she have conveyed this *before* the crisis? And given a discrepancy in the two accounts, which would be the correct one? To take another literary example, in *Albertine Gone* (*Albertine Disparue*; Proust, 1989), Marcel has for some time hoped that Albertine, his lover, will leave him and has indulged in fantasies of new liaisons; however, he experiences turmoil within seconds of learning of her departure from her room in his apartment: "And what I had believed to mean nothing to me was quite simply my whole life!" (p. 1). Nonetheless, his earlier dominant concern, as far as his conscious life was involved, has been met rather than obstructed by the event. It is possible to consider establishing what is important for a person before the occurrence of such an event. But this is likely to be a costly undertaking, and not one that is in any case always possible. I therefore continue to deal with the task of reconstruction faced by an investigator once an event has occurred.

Solomon (1991) has argued for the importance of viewing emotions in just the terms provided by my two literary examples—in terms of "taking something personally," experiencing something as particularly important and personally meaningful. Because of this, he argues, emotions are best seen as enduring structures of consciousness as much as transient passionate outbursts, and he suggests that the critical need is to deal with degree of *investment*. Frijda (1986) makes much the same point in his discussion of source and surface concerns. One way of looking at the LEDS measurement of threat or unpleasantness can be seen as an attempt to reflect such investment (or lack of it). However, less emphasis is placed on the part played by consciousness: The need is for an approach that can assess investment even when background problems have been "routinized' (as with the Dublin waiter) or even largely denied (as with Proust's Marcel), and to do so in a way that is methodologically acceptable.

As mentioned earlier, *Verstehen*, or understanding, attempts to do just this by using a common-sense judgment on the part of an outside observer about likely meaning. The investigator is used as the measuring instrument. The idea arose at the turn of the century in the context of the new cultural sciences, the *Geisteswissenschaften*, where the meaning to be tackled typically concerned historical data that afforded no possibility of asking questions about internal experience. (In his 1946 book *The Idea of History*, R. G. Collingwood, a historian, philosopher, and archaeologist, emphasized a similar approach to estimating intention or meaning.) Although there is no specific reason why a subject, if available, should not also be questioned directly about the significance of a life event, doing this would open up the formidable problem of possible bias, particularly where the questioning takes place *after* the "outcome" to be explained (e.g., depressive onset). There has therefore been a sound basis for continuing to restrict the approach to an investigator-based one—and in so doing, of course, to rule out the use of a questionnaire, the mainstay of most psychosocial research. This was the route taken with the LEDS, which was the first instrument to systematize the idea of *Verstehen* and in doing so to take account of the medley of events faced by most of us in the course of our lives.

The most basic contextual rating used in the LEDS deals with the degree of threat presented by a particular event. The investigator is expected to take account of relevant plans and concerns, and to do this indirectly by considering what appear to be relevant aspects of the person's biography and circumstances (Brown, 1989b). The event of a medical student's finding herself pregnant after she had broken up with her boyfriend would take into account the fact that she had a Catholic upbringing, as well as the fact that she was doing well in her studies and gave every appearance of being a dedicated student. In this instance, the pregnancy would almost certainly be rated as a highly threatening event. The rating is *contextual* in the sense of dealing with biographical and current circumstances of possible relevance. The rating is intended to reflect a person's likely appraisal of a particular event, and the research challenge has been to develop a set of ratings that are accurate enough to use any apparent event–depression link as a basis for building a fuller etiological model. However, it would be a mistake to see the probabilistic approach involved as simply a response to methodological problems. It is now established, for example, that only a minority of those experiencing a seriously threatening life event go on to develop a depressive disorder; and here a totally accurate assessment of the degree of threat actually experienced might well handicap any understanding of why this should be so. If, say, social support reduced threat enough to ward off a depressive response, our ability to demonstrate this would be reduced to the extent that the impact of support was taken into account in characterizing the threat of the event. What is ideally required, if the role of other factors such as support is to be explored, is a measure of *potential* threat. It is just this that is provided by contextual ratings (Brown, 1989b).

Three Types of Appraisal

In dealing with event appraisal, I discuss the three different types of meaning shown in Figure 6.1. The first two, "social meaning" and "specific meaning," are integral aspects of the LEDS. The first refers to severity of threat, and, as already outlined, concentrates on the likely impact of an event on plans and concerns (Brown, 1989b). It is *social* in the sense that core roles such as that of wife or mother are almost always involved. (A possible exception concerns atypical events, discussed later.) It is probabilistic in its attempt to deal with appraisal in terms of the level of the threat *likely* to have been involved. In practice, when describing an event, the interviewer withholds from a consensus team of raters anything in the reports about what was felt in response to the event and whether or not a depressive episode followed. Concerns that could be expected to be involved are estimated, as in the example of the medical student, on the basis of biographical detail and current circumstances that appear to be relevant. As in this instance, the information used is usually fairly straightforward. The members of the consensus team are allowed to ask questions about background material they think may be relevant, and there are extensive notes and numerous examples to guide raters. (Training in the use of the LEDS takes about 1 week.) However, an event is only judged severe if, as in the example of the medical student, its threatening implications are apparently still present some 10 to 14 days after its occurrence. Events with only short-term threat have not proved to be of etiological significance for depression (Brown & Harris, 1978). If this approach were used, Albertine's disappearance would be rated as severely threatening, given Marcel's obsession with her possible infidelity and the fact of his spying on her via his friends when she was away from home. The status of the threat involved in the discovery of the waiter's secret is less clear and probably would depend on circumstances such as the threat to her job and whether any alternative ways of life were possible. Only a small proportion of events capable of producing significant emotions are, in fact, defined as severe in this long-term sense (Brown & Harris, 1978). This is so despite the fact that everyday "hassles" are not defined as events by the LEDS (Brown, 1989a).

Keith Oatley (1992) has contrasted such an emphasis on plans with a mechanistic view of etiology not concerned with meaning. But if we see as part of the idea of mechanism some element of marked constraint, in contrast to "the infinity of what can be wished for or intended" (Oatley, 1992, p. 167) in a plan or goal, a relatively mechanistic aspect of meaning is taken into account in box 2 of Figure 6.1. This deals with more specific meanings, but with particu-

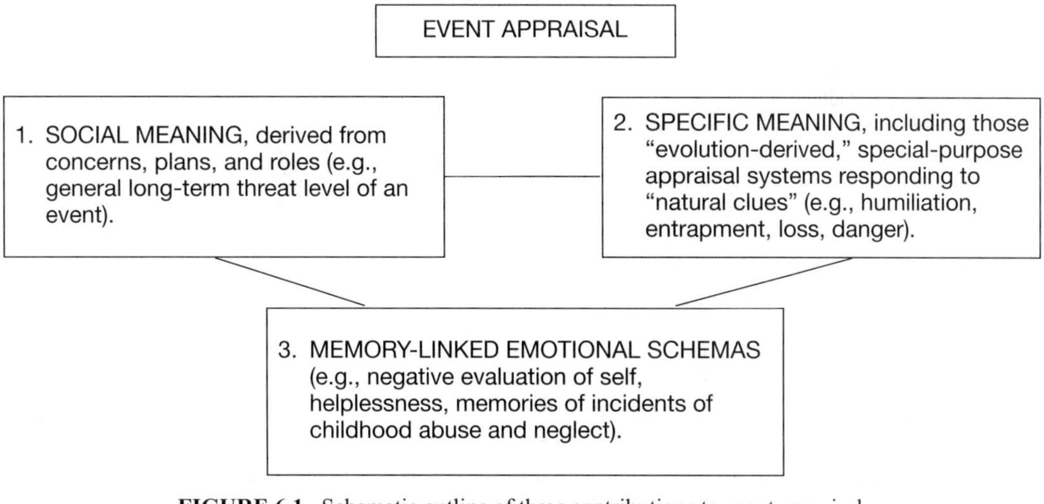

FIGURE 6.1. Schematic outline of three contributions to event appraisal.

lar emphasis on possible *evolution-derived meanings*—that is, the triggering of special-purpose appraisal systems by the kind of "natural clues" discussed by Bowlby (1973). Once again, self-reports of experience are ignored by raters. A good deal of research has now suggested that the social meanings of box 1 are relatively nonspecific in etiological terms. The onset of a range of disorders has been shown to be associated with the occurrence of a severely threatening event; depression, most anxiety disorders, functional and organic gastrointestinal disorders, multiple sclerosis, and menorrhagia are just some of these (Brown & Harris, 1989). By contrast, the evolution-derived meanings of box 2 go some way to determine the type of disorder that develops.

The third box refers to yet another source of meaning—"memory-linked emotional schemas." Events as such are not involved, but in so far as they are etiologically relevant, the schemas are activated by an event. Internal representations laid down in early attachment relationships are of particular importance where psychopathology is concerned (Harris, Brown, & Bifulco, 1986, 1990). Tomkins's (1979) "nuclear scenes," which "capture the individual's most urgent and unsolved problems and continue to grow by recruiting even more thought, feeling and action" (p. 212) would belong here. Self-esteem also belongs, although it is substantially influenced by the current environment and particularly by the quality of core ties (Brown, Bifulco, & Andrews, 1990; Andrews & Brown, 1995).

Figure 6.2 outlines the three types of measurement for the three types of meaning depicted in Figure 6.1. I have already dealt with the contextual ratings of box 1. The more specific (evolution-derived) meanings of box 2 are also judged contextually in terms of the *likelihood* of experiencing a particular appraisal, such as loss or humiliation. But these judgments differ from those in box 1, because only the *immediate* circumstances surrounding an event are considered. These are therefore simpler ratings; plans and concerns, as such, are not taken into account. It would be enough for the mother of a hyperactive boy to be criticized for her son's behavior by a school teacher in a parent meeting for it to be rated "humiliating."

It is important to note that the LEDS takes into account the possible multiplicity of meanings of the *same* event. An event may, for example, be rated higher on short-term than on long-term threat (box 1) and may involve loss, danger, and humiliation (box 2).

By contrast, the investigator-based ratings of the third box are not contextual and are designed to reflect as accurately as possible what is going on—how many negative remarks about self were made in the course of a particular interview, and so on. There is no question of withholding material, as with the two types of event ratings. Confidence in the validity of box 3 measures therefore will often depend a good deal on whether or not they have been used as part of a prospective design capable of controlling for the kind of artifacts inherent in a cross-sectional inquiry that involves self-report measures.

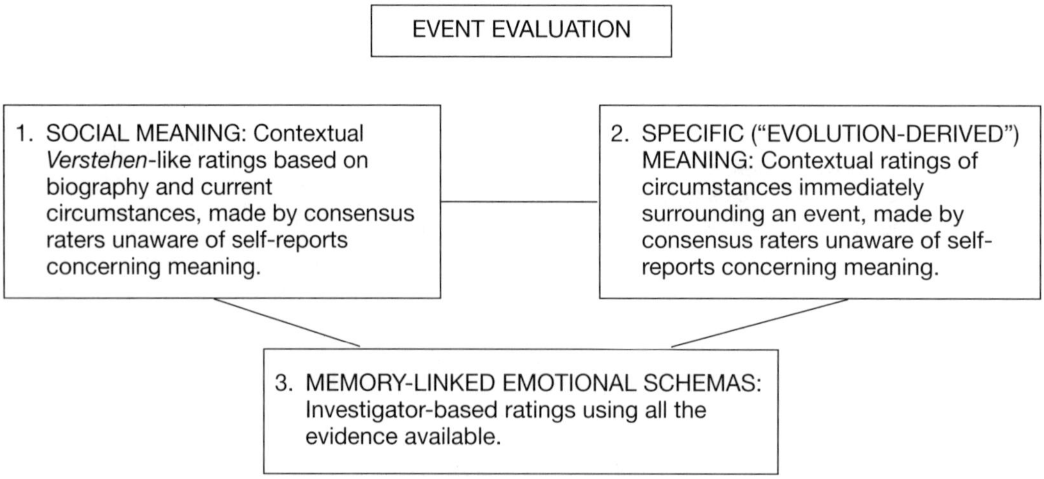

```
┌─────────────────────────┐
│     EVENT EVALUATION     │
└─────────────────────────┘
```

┌──────────────────────────────────┐   ┌──────────────────────────────────┐
│ 1. SOCIAL MEANING: Contextual   │   │ 2. SPECIFIC ("EVOLUTION-DERIVED") │
│   *Verstehen*-like ratings based on │   │   MEANING: Contextual ratings of │
│   biography and current   │   │   circumstances immediately   │
│   circumstances, made by consensus │   │   surrounding an event, made by │
│   raters unaware of self-reports │   │   consensus raters unaware of self-│
│   concerning meaning.   │   │   reports concerning meaning.   │
└──────────────────────────────────┘   └──────────────────────────────────┘

        ┌──┐
        │ 3. MEMORY-LINKED EMOTIONAL SCHEMAS: │
        │   Investigator-based ratings using all the │
        │   evidence available.   │
        └──┘

FIGURE 6.2. Contributions to event evaluation by type of measures employed.

THE ONSET OF DEPRESSION— SOME FINDINGS

Social Meaning

Studies using the LEDS have shown that as many as 90% of depressive episodes occurring in the community have a severe event within 6 months of onset, with most within a matter of weeks (Brown & Harris, 1986, 1989). Typical findings are those from a largely working-class sample of mothers with a child living at home in Islington, an inner-city area of London. Although women with these two characteristics are particularly likely to be at risk (Brown & Harris, 1978), the findings concerning the role of events has been replicated in a wide range of populations (Brown & Harris, 1989). The study was prospective. A total of 303 women were without depression at a "caseness" level (equivalent to DSM-III-R "major depression") at the time of first contact, and 32 developed a depressive episode during the follow-up year. Of these 32, 29 had a prior severe event, usually within a matter of weeks of the onset (Brown, Bifulco, & Harris, 1987). In terms of the 303 women as a whole, 29 of the 130 who had a severe event had both a depressive onset and an event within 6 months, whereas of the 173 without any severe event, only 3 had an onset. Unexpectedly learning of a husband's infidelity, or learning that a child has been defined as in need of special schooling, conveys the level of threat involved in a severe rating. (Severe difficulties, which had to have lasted at least 2 years, play a minor role and are be ignored in this account.)

The Role of Commitment or Investment in Plans and Goals

The importance of background plans and concerns reflected in the contextual ratings of severe threat was confirmed when a more sensitive set of ratings dealing with emotional *commitment* in various role domains on the part of each woman was taken into account (Brown et al., 1987). The ratings were made at the time of our first contact, and the fact that the survey was prospective enabled such "soft" material to be used. The ratings of commitment (or investment, to use Solomon's [1991] term) were based on a tape recording of what each woman told us, or expressed spontaneously, when talking about her life in the lengthy interview. Degree of emotional commitment was rated for role domains, such as marriage, motherhood, or employment (Brown et al., 1987). Particular account was taken of the amount of enthusiasm spontaneously expressed. On average, a woman was rated "marked" (on a 4-point scale) on only one and a half of the possible six domains.

The risk of depression trebled when a severe event in the follow-up year *matched* an area of high role commitment—for example, when a woman highly committed to motherhood found out that her adolescent son was sniffing glue. Forty percent (16/40) of those with such a matching severe event had a depressive onset, compared with 14% (13/90) of those with a nonmatching one. There was no hint that events of lesser severity contributed to an increased risk in this way (Brown et al., 1987). The result is, of course, an endorsement of the assumption built into the contextual threat ratings of the role played by plans and concerns in determining the threat of an event. The result also underlines the fact that the contextual ratings, making only an indirect assessment of commitment, have been good enough to document major etiological effects.

Specific Meaning

Where specific meaning (box 2) is concerned, the most clear-cut finding for depressive disorder until recently has been the role of loss when defined in a broad sense—that is, not only loss of a person, but loss of a role, an important plan, or a cherished idea about self or someone close. About three-quarters of severe events provoking depression involve a loss in this broad sense (Finlay-Jones & Brown, 1981; Brown, 1993). But on the assumption that an evolution-derived response pattern is involved in the etiology of depression, recent evidence suggests that it may not be the key "natural clue" of importance for depression. This possibility was hinted at in the increased risk associated with a second form of matching, involving a linkage between a severe event in the follow-up year and a severe ongoing difficulty present at first contact. Such a match was again associated among Islington women with a considerably increased risk, and one largely independent of that involving commitment (Brown et al., 1987). However, the very presence of such an ongoing difficulty, which had usually gone on for well over a year, might be said to suggest that nothing specific had been "lost" as a result of the event. One woman with a hyperactive son had had full knowledge of his behavior for several years and had earlier discussed him on several occasions at some length with various members of the staff at the school. It would seem unlikely that the matching difficulty event, involving a meeting of mothers at the school where a teacher criticized her son, would have led to any loss of a cherished idea about him. It might well, however, have underlined her helplessness in the situation, together with a sense of being humiliated. In contrast to the literature's focus on the role of loss, the importance of the experience of hopelessness in the genesis of depression was emphasised by Edward Bibring, a psychoanalyst, almost 50 years ago (Bibring, 1953). As already noted, more recently the possible role of defeat has been underlined by those focusing on the role of evolution-derived response tendencies concerning ranking (Price & Sloman, 1987; Price, Sloman, Gardner, Gilbert, & Rohde, 1994). This is clearly related to a concept such as hopelessness, but is picked up from the behavior of an animal and its immediate context rather than from a self-report of feelings. With this perspective in mind, Gilbert (1989) has outlined a number of depressogenic situations that follow closely those emerging over a number of years from life-event research with the LEDS:

- Direct attacks on a person's self-esteem, forcing him or her into a subordinate position.
- Events undermining a person's sense of rank, attractiveness, and value, particularly via the consequences of the event for core roles.
- Blocked escape.

With such conclusions in mind, a contextual rating system has recently been developed as part of the LEDS package to characterize *severe* events in terms of four experiences: "humiliation," "entrapment," "loss," or "danger" (Brown, Harris, & Hepworth, 1995). The general idea in designing the scale has been that a person would, in common-sense terms, be expected to experience a sense of powerlessness or marked devaluation of self following the experience of an event rated as humiliating or entrapping, with this once again rated in probabilistic terms (in this instance, on a 9-point scale). There are three subtypes of humiliation: "separation," "other's delinquency," and "putdown." Typical events for the women we have

studied would be a boyfriend's saying he was not interested in continuing a relationship ("humiliation:separation"), discovery of a husband's infidelity ("humilation:other's delinquency"), or the event mentioned earlier of hyperactive boy's mother's being demeaned in front of other mothers ("humiliation:putdown"). Entrapment, by contrast, involves an event underlining the fact of imprisonment in a punishing situation that has gone on for some time—for example, a woman's being told by a hospital doctor that nothing could be done to relieve her crippling arthritis. (At a minimum, entrapment events have to meet the requirement for the kind of difficulty-matching event already outlined.) There are, in addition, four types of loss: "death" of a core tie, a "separation" initiated by the subject, another "key loss," or a "lesser loss." All by definition have to be rated as severely threatening—a typical key loss, for example, would be a woman's only daughter's marrying and emigrating to Australia, with the implication that the woman would perhaps never see her daughter again. A final rating concerns danger—that is, a severe event conveying the threat of a future loss.

Table 6.1 presents results for the Islington women again, but now in terms of severe events and depression occurring over a 2-year period (only periods free from depression were examined) (Brown et al., 1995). Each event was dealt with in terms of a hierarchy running from the top to the bottom of the scale; for example, an event involving both "humiliation: putdown" and "loss," was characterized by the former. Related events, such as a father's diagnosis of cancer (danger) and later death (loss), were dealt with as a sequence, with the highest event type taken to characterize it. As predicted, events involving humiliation or entrapment preceded the bulk of episodes of depression. By contrast, the experience of a loss *without* one of these two characteristics was relatively uncommon. Only severe events involving the experience of the death of someone close were at all highly related to risk. A severe event involving only danger, such as a husband's diagnosis of cancer, rarely preceded depression. These findings have been replicated in a patient series (Brown et al., 1995) and in a population survey of Shona-speaking women in a township in Harare, Zimbabwe (Broadhead & Abas, 1998).

Extensive analysis has so far failed to reveal convincing evidence for additivity in risk across events, once those that are part of a se-

TABLE 6.1. Onset by Type of Severe Event over a 2-Year Period in the Islington Community Series

Hierarchical event classification	No. of onsets	% onset rate
A. All "humiliation" events	31/102	30
1. Humiliation: separation	12/34	35
2. Humiliation: other's delinquency	7/36	19
3. Humiliation: putdown	12/32	38
B. All "entrapment"-alone events (i.e., not A)	10/29	34
C. All "loss"-alone events (i.e., not A or B)	14/157	9
1. Death	7/24	29
2. Separation (subject-initiated)	2/18	11
3. Other key loss	4/58	7
4. Lesser loss	1/57	2
D. All "danger"-alone events (i.e., not A, B, or C)	3/89	3
All severe events	58/377	15

Note. Adapted from Brown, Harris, and Hepworth (1995). Copyright 1995 by Cambridge University Press. Adapted by permission.

quence are taken into account (Brown, 1989b). On the basis of present evidence, the characteristics of one severe event (or of a series of related severe events) appear to be critical. This is a somewhat surprising result, as quite unrelated threatening events may well have been expected from a cognitive perspective on depression to summate to produce a general sense of helplessness. It possibly reflects the etiological importance of the special appraisal systems of box 2, which respond to a limited range of stimuli.

The Role of Loss

Oatley and Bolton (1985) have seen the issue of onset of depression in terms of "a loss of a sense of self via loss of key role which is experienced either as not having a self at all or of having a self without worth, or having a self that is guilty or defective in some way" (p. 380). I think this is a correct emphasis. The key point of my argument is that loss of a core role alone does not usually appear to be critical. In the context of the loss, experiencing an inability to move forward, being stuck, or being defeated and humiliated appears to be more salient. Often involved is entrapment in a role that cannot readily be given up—or, on occasions, being trapped by the recognition of the likely persistent *lack* of a core role.

Nonetheless, there remains a certain ambiguity about the part played by loss. In terms of the word itself, it is possible to lose something in

the ordinary sense and to lose in the sense of a defeat. The two meanings understandably at times are intertwined, and occasionally an apparently ordinary loss will be experienced as a defeat. This may be one reason why the risk of depression associated with bereavement is higher than the risk associated with other losses. With bereavement, there can be hopelessness about restoring a core identity intimately linked with the presence of the person lost—and, along with this, a sense of being trapped within a self that is deeply unwelcome. It follows that, given the approximate nature of the humiliation–entrapment–loss–danger ratings, the conclusions about the importance of humiliation and entrapment may have been too conservative. Some of the losses could in practice have been appraised in terms of defeat. However, it is equally important to emphasize that the link of loss with depression has also been confirmed—that three-quarters of the provoking humiliation and entrapment events were *also* losses in terms of the broad definition of the LEDS. I also suspect that it is too soon to rule out a significant etiological role for loss in the usual sense of this term. There were certainly some depressive episodes in Islington following a loss where entrapment or humiliation would seem most unlikely to have been involved—for example, following the death of a father whose relationship with his grown daughter was reported by the woman not to be particularly close.

Events and Remission of an Episode

A distinct approach to life events has dealt with their role in the course taken by a disorder. Once an episode has lasted 20 weeks, various kinds of positive events (again rated contextually) appear to relate to chances of remission. Indeed, the results are roughly a mirror image of those for onset (Brown, Adler, & Bifulco, 1988; Brown, Lemyre, & Bifulco, 1992; Brown, 1993). The key experiences are "fresh starts" (e.g., meeting a new boyfriend), "delogjamming"' (e.g., managing to leave a violent husband), and "difficulty reduction" (e.g., moving from an overcrowded flat). All are assessed as likely to have conveyed an exit from a situation of deprivation or entrapment, or hope of doing so. The association is somewhat less strong for those receiving psychiatric treatment (Brown, 1993). This probably relates to the fact that many receive adequate doses of antidepressive medication, but it may also relate to the fact that receiving treatment as such has not so far been counted in the LEDS as a "positive" event, since its role (say, as some kind of "placebo" response) could only be convincingly assessed in the context of an experimental design. It is also worth noting in this context that about a third of the "positive" events associated with a remission were also rated as severely threatening. (As noted earlier, the LEDS is designed to reflect the possibility that an event can have several "meanings.") The husband of one woman in Islington, with the help of a bullying solicitor, forced her to agree to an unwanted divorce settlement regarding their jointly owned house. This was rated as severely threatening. But it was judged that her accepting the settlement would enable this woman, after many months of uncertainty, to begin once more to plan for her future. It was therefore also rated as a "delogjamming" event—that is, as positive in the sense of offering a possible way forward. It is therefore possible that an event such as entry to psychiatric care, which is thought to be essentially negative in contextual terms, can also have an important positive connotation.

SOME POSSIBLE EXCEPTIONS

Endogenous Depressive Conditions

Most systematic research using LEDS or a related instrument has concluded that the majority of depressive episodes, whether or not an individual is seen by a psychiatrist, have had a provoking life event (Brown & Harris, 1989). On the other hand, there can be little doubt about the occurrence of depressive episodes that have not been provoked by a life event or difficulty—and these appear particularly likely to be found among psychiatric patients. But at the same time, it has proved highly puzzling that no study has been able to identify a majority of depressed patients defined in *clinical* terms who are without a provoking life event. In this sense, systematic research has produced modest evidence at best for the existence of an endogenous depressive disorder defined in clinical terms.

Some recent work based on a sample of depressed North London women receiving psychiatric care suggests a possible explanation. Among women with a melancholic–psychotic depressive episode (defined in clinical terms) and a *prior* depressive episode, a provoking severe event was much less likely to be present (Brown, Harris, & Hepworth, 1994); this finding perhaps indicates some kind of "kindling" or "sensitization" effect, perhaps similar to what has been suggested for bipolar conditions (Post, 1990). However, there is nothing to suggest that the rate of events in first episodes involving a melancholic–psychotic condition differs from the high rate of events found in other depressive episodes. It is also of interest that among nonmelancholic patients, who form the bulk of depressed conditions seen by psychiatrists, as many as 1 in 10 are without any hint of a provoking event or difficulty (Brown, Harris, & Hepworth, 1994). This second type of "endogenous" episode appears to be only partly explained by the presence of postpartum conditions.

Atypical Severe Events

The North London depressed sample of women receiving psychiatric care was based on women aged between 18 and 60. This difference from the series of Islington mothers appeared to relate to a second interesting contrast: The descriptive accounts of a quarter of the severe events occurring before depressive onsets of the patients suggested that they fell somewhat short of the threat of those provoking depression in the general population sample of mothers. In particular in this quarter, a major crisis in an active core relationship was not involved, although this was mostly the case among the Islington mothers. Because of this, these severe events in the North London patient sample have been labeled "atypical." The event of one single woman in her 50s, for example, had been the fact that she had been prevented from going to work for several months after construction scaffolding fell on her on her way to work. What may have been important about such events is that they underlined the fact that the women involved were typically leading restricted lives and often living alone. The woman who had the accident, for example, lived alone and had no really close tie; her sexual relationship had obvious shortcomings in terms of intimacy and support. The event had been rated as severe, though not leading to any permanent handicap, because of its financial implications and its impact on her everyday social contacts. When talking about the event, she revealed, "It made me wonder who would look after me when I couldn't work," perhaps reflecting her concern about her "marginal" status. It is possible that a sense of exclusion, of not belonging, was also at times involved in atypical events—leading to an adverse response that might also have evolutionary roots (Gilbert, 1989; Gardner, 1988). For example, one woman had been brought up in France and for 10 years had been leading a lonely life in London, again in the context of a clearly inadequate sexual relationship. The provoking severe event was her sister's writing some months after her father's death to say that the family had decided that since she saw so little of the family, it was inappropriate for her to inherit any part of the family property. Although this was rated contextually as a "minor loss," it is possible that a sense of exclusion, of not belonging, may have been involved. Therefore, given that the large majority of the North London women with an atypical event were without children and often living alone, it is possible that what was often evoked was a sense of basic needs' not being met or ever likely to be met—something akin to what might have been experienced by the Dublin waiter in George Moore's story after the discovery of her secret.

However, in terms of the measurement issues discussed earlier, it remains an open question how far, if we were to have seen such women before the occurrence of the event, we would have been able to reflect the degree to which they had invested (if only in fantasy) in a more attractive way of life. There may prove to be similar problems of recognizing the relevant concerns of adolescents and perhaps the elderly. In measurement terms, a good deal remains to be done. It is encouraging, however, as far as the elderly are concerned, that recent cross-sectional and prospective population studies of depression among the elderly in a working-class population in Kentish Town in North London have shown that by far the greatest risk factor for depression is handicap arising from a physical illness (Prince, Harwood, Blizard, Thomas, & Mann, 1997; Prince, Harwood, Thomas, & Mann, 1998). This suggests a clear link with the findings on entrapping events established for younger women, although the relevance of the notion of investment has yet to be established.

VULNERABILITY

The Concept of Vulnerability

In considering appraisal, I now turn to consider the memory schemas of box 3 in Figures 6.1 and 6.2. Here the concept of "vulnerability," covering risk factors that only increase chances of depression once a relevant stressor has occurred, has proved critical. This concept is similar to that of diathesis–stress interactions, but extended to cover nonbiological factors (Monroe & Simons, 1991). There is ample evidence that measures of the kind noted in box 3 do increase risk in this sense (Brown & Harris, 1986). To return to the basic event–depression link, only about a fifth of Islington women with a severe event developed a depressive episode, and a number of inquiries have concluded that an onset appears to result in large part from the additional presence of the kind of psychosocial factors reflected in box 3 of Figure 6.1. For example, for Islington mothers, the presence of low self-esteem (or negative evaluation of self) at the time of first interview doubled the risk of an onset in the follow-up year once a severe event had occurred (Brown, Andrews, Harris, Adler, & Bridge, 1986). The vulnerability model was confirmed by the fact that without the presence of a severe event, risk of an onset was negligible, regardless of the presence of low self-esteem. (For the measure of low self-esteem, all negative comments a woman made about herself in a lengthy interview were listed, and an overall judgment was made in terms of their number and the degree of conviction conveyed in making them.)

A Full Etiological Model
of Depression

The breadth of the issues involving vulnerability is illustrated by setting the self-esteem result in the context of a broader set of findings. Two fairly straightforward psychosocial indices collected at the time of our first contact with Islington mothers predicted onset of depression surprisingly well. These were (1) a *negative psychological index*, consisting of either negative evaluation of the self (just dealt with) or chronic subclinical symptoms of anxiety or depression; and (2) a *negative environmental index*, consisting of fairly marked negative interaction in the home (or, for single mothers, lack of a close confiding relationship with someone seen regularly). Both indices were additive in effect. Their predictive power can be judged by the fact that although at first contact only a quarter of the 303 nondepressed women had both risk factors, three-quarters of those developing depression in the follow-up year belonged to this small group (Brown, Andrews, Bifulco, & Veiel, 1990). The findings have recently been replicated (Bifulco, Brown, Moran, Ball, & Campbell, 1998).

The two background indices behaved in the same manner as self-esteem. A severe event rarely led to an onset without the presence of at least one of these two background risk factors. This is shown in Figure 6.3, which includes consideration of the humiliation–entrapment–loss–danger ratings (again dealt with hierarchically) (Brown, 1996b). As expected, the two background risk factors did not raise risk without occurrence of a severe event. (Unlike the earlier analysis, only a 1-year follow-up period is considered, since self-esteem was measured only at the time of first interview.)

Risk of depression approached 50% following a severe event involving humiliation or entrapment when both background risk factors were present, compared with half this level of risk in the presence of one factor and none in their absence. Risk associated with a loss event (without humiliation or entrapment) was about 20% with both factors and practically absent otherwise, whereas danger (without humiliation, entrapment, or loss) was unassociated with onset, regardless of the presence of a risk factor.

One reason why the negative environmental and psychological risk factors are able to pre-

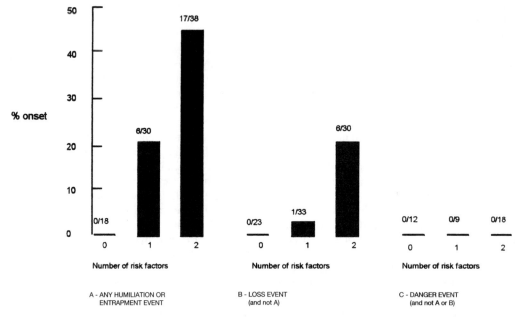

FIGURE 6.3. Rates of onset of depression in follow-up year by severe event type and background risk among 130 Islington women. All onsets and severe events (or sequences) taken. Only event nearest onset considered provoking. From Brown (1996b). Copyright 1996 by Royal College of Psychiatrists. Reprinted by permission.

dict the onset of depression so well relates to their link with a subsequent failure to receive help with a severe event in the follow-up year (judged in terms of a detailed reconstruction of the support received at the time). However, findings concerning support are particularly complex (Brown, 1992; Harris, 1992). Although support is undoubtedly important (e.g., Edwards, Nazroo, & Brown, 1998), working out a comprehensive picture of all of the processes linking background risk factors and depression remains a major challenge and will probably necessitate some experimental work (For an example, see Harris, Brown, & Robinson, 1999a, 1999b).

In an account of event evaluation, it is only possible to hint at the wider issues raised by the findings concerning vulnerability just presented. One of the most significant to emerge is the importance of a lifespan perspective. Among Islington mothers, for example, there was a marked improvement in their level of self-esteem when seen 8 years later, and this was highly associated with improvements in their lives, such as taking on an interesting job or a violent husband's leaving home (Andrews & Brown, 1995). Adverse childhood experiences have proved to be particularly important. For Islington mothers, parental loss, parental antipathy (involving criticism and rejection from parents), and discord in the home were related to adult depression. However, the presence in severe form of "childhood adversity"—that is, either parental neglect or physical abuse in the home, or sexual abuse from anyone—proved to be particularly critical (Bifulco, Brown, & Harris, 1994; Harris et al., 1990). Parental neglect included behavior such as a child's not being properly fed and clothed, lack of concern about the child, or lack of emotional availability when the child was upset or ill; physical abuse involved a child's being hit with an instrument or being beaten up; sexual abuse involved physical contact, excluding contact with a teenage peer. Nearly a third of the Islington women were positive on this index in the sense of experiencing at least one of these three factors. Parental neglect and physical abuse were each experienced by one in five women, and sexual abuse (the least common) by one in nine. In terms of the issue of the role of loss discussed earlier, it is of interest that although loss of mother before the age of 11 is an important predictor of adult depression, the fact that this relates to an increased risk of abuse and neglect,

particularly after the loss, is of crucial etiological importance (Harris et al., 1986). To be speculative, the experience of humiliation and entrapment would appear even at this early age to be more crucial than the experience of loss itself.

In overall terms, risk of adult depression was doubled among those with childhood adversity. An even greater association emerged for women with "chronic" depression (depressive episodes lasting a year or longer). Nearly half of the depressive episodes among Islington women with childhood adversity took a chronic course, compared with a sixth among the remaining women. A study of depressed psychiatric patients in London has shown a similar relationship (Brown & Moran, 1994; Brown, Harris, Hepworth, & Robinson, 1994). There is also suggestive evidence that almost all the impact of such childhood experiences is mediated through the kind of current background risk factors outlined earlier (Brown, Bifulco, & Andrews, 1990). Just what role emotional schemas originating in childhood play in creating adult vulnerability remains to be elucidated.

FINAL COMMENTS

The overall thrust of the etiological perspective outlined in this chapter emphasizes the naturalness of the occurrence of much clinical depression, given the coming together of a particular set of adverse circumstances. In psychology, there has understandably been a greater emphasis on the role of maladaptive thoughts. My own view is that although these are of relevance, their role has been exaggerated—particularly when they are studied without attention to the impact of the current social milieu. This view gains support from the marked differences in the rates of clinically relevant depression that can on occasion occur across populations. Two recent epidemiological inquiries using the semistructured Present State Examination (PSE) have revealed a 10-fold difference in 1-year prevalence of "caseness" of depression—3% among women in a Basque-speaking rural population (Gaminde, Uria, Padro, Querejeta, & Ozamiz, 1993), and 30% among a Shona-speaking sample living in a township in Harare, Zimbabwe (Broadhead & Abas, 1998). The rates of severe events also differed dramatically across the two populations. Even when such extremes are put aside, the rate of clinically relevant depression can vary a good deal by demographic characteristics. In Europe, both lone mothers (Brown & Moran, 1997) and those living in inner-city areas have higher rates; rates are also higher in rural areas among those not following a traditional way of life (e.g., living in flats rather than farms and not going to church regularly) (Gaminde et al., 1993; Brown & Prudo, 1981; Prudo, Brown, Harris, & Dowland, 1981; Prudo, Brown, & Harris, 1984). Since such differences are also fairly closely paralleled by levels of environmental adversity, the implications must be that the differences are largely driven by what has been occurring in the external environment (Brown, 1998). This does not necessarily rule out a significant genetic contribution, but it does suggest that this will be found to be largely restricted to explaining risk *within* a population in terms of who responds to adversity with depression, rather than explaining differences across populations (Brown, 1996a).

Where emotion is concerned, the research illustrates, I believe, the advantages of studying it in social context and of seeing it in functional terms. More controversially, it illustrates the heuristic value of evolutionary ideas, despite the fact that as yet they lack much by way of empirical underpinning in relation to ourselves (e.g., Stevens & Price, 1996). It should be recognized that severe depressive states do not need to have been adaptive for evolutionary ideas to be useful. What appear to be severe depressive states in animals may well be largely the result of artificial conditions in captivity. Martin Eales (personal communication, July 1997) has pointed out the paucity of evidence for real pathological states in free-ranging primates after the experience of defeat with a conspecific. Nonetheless, this does not detract from the suggestive evidence that ancient responses to this kind of experience are in some way involved in human depression. There is a possibility that the experiences of defeat and entrapment are particularly depressogenic for us because of our greatly expanded cognitive abilities and parallel cultural developments, which result in our awareness of our entrapment and powerlessness in terms of the future. Also involved are likely to be our greater facility for the development of emotional commitments, especially in a family setting (MacDonald, 1992), and the fact that "axiomatic" relationships such as that of mother and child are not easily put aside (Park, 1974).

The importance of animal research in the development of an evolutionary perspective on human depression raises the more general question of how far there can be an interchange of ideas. The concept of entrapment has been relevant for animal research because it can be based on the observation of behavior; it has proved relevant for the study of life events because it can be judged to be present or not on the basis of the circumstances surrounding an event and the history of the environmental difficulties that have preceded it. Gilbert and Allan (1998) note the inappropriateness of the related idea of hopelessness for animals, since it involves looking into the future. But in a study of depressed patients, they attempted to measure both concepts by means of a self-report questionnaire. A clear-cut distinction failed to emerge. Given our highly developed capacity to view the future (Nunn, 1996), this was perhaps inevitable; self-reports about entrapment and hopelessness are probably bound to be highly related. There is therefore much to be said for continuing, as with LEDS research, to see entrapment in objective terms and to view a sense of hopelessness in terms of personal experience as reflected by self-report measures. Indeed, now that a reasonably convincing etiological model of depression has emerged from research using measures that avoid self-reports of experience, the time is ripe for a more sustained attempt to incorporate "softer" measures. I have doubts, however, about the profitability of employing such measures outside the framework of the kind of contextual measures that I have outlined.

ACKNOWLEDGMENT

A version of this chapter was presented at the 8th Conference of the International Society for Research on Emotions, Fitzwilliam College, University of Cambridge, England, Cambridge. July 14–17, 1994.

REFERENCES

Andrews, B., & Brown, G. W. (1995). Stability and change in low self-esteem: The role of psychosocial factors. *Psychological Medicine, 25*, 23–31.

Bibring, E. (1953). Mechanisms of depression. In P. Greenacre (Ed.), *Affective disorders: Psychoanalytic contributions to their study* (pp. 154–181). New York: International Universities Press.

Bifulco, A., Brown, G. W., & Harris, T. O. (1994). Childhood Experience of Care and Abuse (CECA): A retrospective interview measure. *Journal of Child Psychology and Psychiatry, 35,* 1419–1435.

Bifulco, A., Brown, G. W., Moran, P., Ball, C., & Campbell, C. (1998). Predicting depression in women: the role of past and present vulnerability. *Psychological Medicine, 28,* 39–50.

Bowlby, J. (1973). *Attachment and loss: Vol. 2. Separation: Anxiety and anger.* London: Hogarth Press.

Bowlby, J. (1980). *Attachment and loss: Vol. 3. Loss: Sadness and depression.* London: Hogarth Press.

Broadhead, J., & Abas, M. (1998). Life events and difficulties and the onset of depression amongst women in an urban setting in Zimbabwe. *Psychological Medicine, 28,* 29–38.

Brown, G. W. (1989a). What about the real world?: Hassles and Richard Lazarus. *Psychological Inquiry, 1,* 19–22.

Brown, G. W. (1989b). Life events and measurement. In G. W. Brown & T. O. Harris (Eds.), *Life events and illness* (pp. 3–45). New York: Guilford Press.

Brown, G. W. (1992). Social support: An investigator-based approach. In H. O. F. Veiel & U. Baumann (Eds.), *The meaning and measurement of social support* (pp. 235–257). Washington, DC: Hemisphere.

Brown, G. W. (1993). Life events and affective disorder: Replications and limitations. *Psychosomatic Medicine, 55,* 248–259.

Brown, G. W. (1996a). Genetics and depression: A social science perspective. *International Review of Psychiatry, 8,* 387–401.

Brown, G. W. (1996b). On act and course of depressive disorders. In C. Mundt, M. J. Goldstein, K. Hahlwey, & P. Fiedler (Eds.), *Interpersonal factors in the origin and course of affective disorders* (pp. 151–167). London: Royal College of Psychiatrists.

Brown, G. W. (1998). Genetic and population perspectives on life events and depression. *Social Psychiatry and Psychiatric Epidemiology, 33,* 363–372.

Brown, G. W., Adler, Z. & Bifulco, A. (1988). Life events, difficulties and recovery from chronic depression. *British Journal of Psychiatry, 152,* 487–498.

Brown, G. W., Andrews, B., Bifulco A., & Veiel, H. O. F. (1990). Self-esteem and depression: 1. Measurement issues and prediction of onset. *Social Psychiatry and Psychiatric Epidemiology, 25,* 200–209.

Brown, G. W., Andrews, B., Harris, T. O., Adler, Z., & Bridge, L. (1986). Social support, self-esteem and depression. *Psychological Medicine, 16,* 813–831.

Brown, G. W., Bifulco, A., & Andrews, B. (1990). Self-esteem and depression: 3. Aetiological issues. *Social Psychiatry and Psychiatric Epidemiology, 25,* 235–243.

Brown, G. W., Bifulco, A., & Harris, T. O. (1987). Life events, vulnerability and onset of depression: Some refinements. *British Journal of Psychiatry, 150,* 30–42.

Brown, G. W., Craig, T. K. J., & Harris, T. O. (1985). Depression: Disease or distress? Some epidemiological considerations. *British Journal of Psychiatry, 147,* 612–622.

Brown, G. W., & Harris, T. O. (1978). *Social origins of depression: A study of psychiatric disorder in women.* London: Tavistock.

Brown, G. W., & Harris, T. O. (1986). Establishing causal links: The Bedford College studies of depression. In H. Katschnig (Ed.), *Life events and psychiatric disorders* (pp. 107–187). Cambridge, England: Cambridge University Press.

Brown, G. W., & Harris, T. O. (Eds.). (1989). *Life events and illness.* New York: Guilford Press.

Brown, G. W., Harris, T. O., & Hepworth, C. (1994). Life events and 'endogenous' depression: A puzzle re-examined. *Archives of General Psychiatry, 51,* 525–534.

Brown, G. W., Harris, T. O., & Hepworth, C. (1995). Loss, humiliation and entrapment among women developing depression: A patient and non-patient comparison. *Psychological Medicine, 25,* 7–21.

Brown, G. W., Harris, T. O., Hepworth, C., & Robinson, R. (1994). Clinical and psychosocial origins of chronic depressive episodes: 2. A patient enquiry. *British Journal of Psychiatry, 165,* 457–465.

Brown, G. W., Lemyre, L., & Bifulco, A. (1992). Social factors and recovery from anxiety and depressive disorders: A test of the specificity hypothesis. *British Journal of Psychiatry, 161,* 44–54.

Brown, G. W., & Moran, P. (1994). Clinical and psychosocial origins of chronic depressive episodes: 1. A community survey. *British Journal of Psychiatry, 165,* 447–456.

Brown, G. W., & Moran, P. (1997). Single mothers, poverty and depression. *Psychological Medicine, 27,* 21–33.

Brown, G. W., & Prudo, R. (1981). Psychiatric disorder in a rural and an urban population: 1. Etiology of depression. *Psychological Medicine, 11,* 581–599.

Campos, J. J., & Campos, R. G. (1989). Emergent themes in the study of emotional development and emotion regulation. *Developmental Psychology, 25,* 394–402.

Collingwood, R. G. (1946). *The idea of history.* Oxford: Oxford University Press.

Dean, C., Surtees, P. G., & Sashidharan, S. D. (1983). Comparison of research diagnostic systems in an Edinburgh community sample. *British Journal of Psychiatry, 142,* 247–256.

Edwards, A. C., Nazroo, J. Y., & Brown, G. W. (1998). Gender differences in marital support following a shared life event. *Social Science and Medicine, 46,* 1077–1085.

Finlay-Jones, R., & Brown, G. W. (1981). Types of stressful life event and the onset of anxiety and depressive disorders. *Psychological Medicine, 11,* 803–815.

Finlay-Jones, R., Brown, G. W., Duncan-Jones, P., Harris, T., Murphy, E., & Prudo, R. (1980). Depression and anxiety in the community. *Psychological Medicine, 10,* 445–454.

Frijda, N. H. (1986). *The emotions.* Cambridge, England: Cambridge University Press.

Frijda, N. H. (1993). The place of appraisal in emotion. *Cognition and Emotion, 3–4,* 357–387.

Gaminde, I., Uria, M., Padro, D., Querejeta, I., & Ozamiz, A. (1993). Depression in three populations in the Basque country—a comparison with Britain. *Social Psychiatry and Psychiatric Epidemiology, 28,* 243–251.

Gardner, R. (1988). Psychiatric syndromes as infrastructure for intra-specific communication. In M. R. A. Chance (Ed.), *Social fabrics of the mind*. Hillsdale, NJ: Erlbaum.

Gilbert, P. (1989). *Human nature and suffering*. Hillsdale, NJ: Erlbaum.

Gilbert, P. (1992). *Depression: The evolution of powerlessness*. Hillsdale, NJ: Erlbaum.

Gilbert, P., & Allan, S. (1998). The role of defeat and entrapment (arrested flight) in depression: An exploration of an evolutionary view. *Psychological Medicine, 28*, 585–598.

Harris, T. O. (1992). Some reflections of the process of social support, and nature of unsupportive behaviours. In H. O. F. Veiel & U. Baumann (Eds.), *The meaning and measurement of social support* (pp. 171–189). Washington, DC: Hemisphere.

Harris, T. O., Brown, G. W., & Bifulco, A. (1986). Loss of parent in childhood and adult psychiatric disorder: The role of lack of adequate parental care. *Psychological Medicine, 16*, 641–659.

Harris, T. O., Brown, G. W., & Bifulco, A. (1990). Loss of parent in childhood and adult psychiatric disorder: A tentative overall model. *Development and Psychopathology, 2*, 311–328.

Harris, T. O., Brown, G. W., & Robinson, R. (1999a). Befriending as an intervention for chronic depression among women in an inner city: 1. Randomised controlled trial. *British Journal of Psychiatry, 174*, 219–224.

Harris, T. O., Brown, G. W., & Robinson, R. (1999b). Befriending as an intervention for chronic depression among women in an inner city: 2. Role of fresh-start experiences and baseline psychosocial factors in remission from depression. *British Journal of Psychiatry, 174*, 225–232.

Jones, I. H., Stoddart, D. M., & Mallick, J. (1995). Towards a sociobiological model of depression: A marsupial model (*Petancus breviceps*). *British Journal of Psychiatry, 166*, 475–479.

MacDonald, K. (1992). Warmth as a developmental construct: An evolutionary analysis. *Child Development, 63*, 753–773.

Monroe, S. M., & Simons, A. D. (1991). Diathesis–stress theories in the context of life-stress research: Implications for the depressive disorders. *Psychological Bulletin, 110*, 406–425.

Moore, G. (1985). Alfred Nobbs. In D. B. Eakin & H. E. Gerber (Eds.), *Minor keys: The uncollected short stories of George Moore*. Syracuse, NY: Syracuse University Press.

Nunn, K. P. (1996). Personal hopefulness: A conceptual review of the relevance of the perceived future to psychiatry. *British Journal of Medical Psychology, 69*, 227–246.

Oatley, K. (1992). Integrative action of narrative. In D. J. Stein & J. E. Young (Eds.), *Cognitive science and clinical disorders* (pp. 151–170). Orlando, FL: Academic Press.

Oatley, K., & Bolton, W. (1985). A social-cognitive theory of depression in reaction to life events. *Psychological Review, 92*, 372–388.

Park, G. (1974). *The idea of social structure*. New York: Doubleday/Anchor.

Phillips, M. L., Senior, C., Fahy, T., & David, A. S. (1998). Disgust—the forgotten emotion of psychiatry. *British Journal of Psychiatry, 172*, 373–375.

Post, R. M. (1990). Sensitization and kindling perspectives on the course of affective illness: Toward a new treatment with the anticonvulsant carbamazepine. *Pharmophychiatry, 23*, 3–17.

Price, J. S. (1972). The dominance hierarchy and the evolution of mental illness. *Lancet, 7502*, 243–246.

Price, J. S., & Sloman, L. (1987). Depression as a yielding behaviour: An animal model based on Schjelderup-Ebbe's pecking order. *Ethology and Sociobiology, 8*, 85–98.

Price, J. S., Sloman, L., Gardner, R., Jr., Gilbert, P., & Rohde, P. (1994). The social competition hypothesis of depression. *British Journal of Psychiatry, 164*, 309–315.

Prince, M. J., Harwood, R. H., Blizard, R. A., Thomas, A., & Mann, A. H. (1997). Impairment, disability and handicap as risk factors for depression in old age: The Gospel Oak Project V. *Psychological Medicine, 27*, 311–321.

Prince, M. J., Harwood, R. H., Thomas, A., & Mann, A. H. (1998). A prospective population-basis cohort study of the effects of disablement and social milieu on the onset and maintenance of late-life depression: The Gospel Oak Project VII. *Psychological Medicine, 28*, 337–350.

Proust, M. (1989). *Albertine gone*. (T. Kilmartin, Ed. and Trans.). London: Chatto and Winders.

Prudo, R., Brown, G. W., & Harris, T. O. (1984). Psychiatric disorder in a rural and an urban population: 3. Social integration and the morphology of affective disorder. *Psychological Medicine, 14*, 327–345.

Prudo, R., Brown, G. W., Harris, T. O., & Dowland, J. (1981). Psychiatric disorder in a rural and an urban population: 2. Sensitivity to loss. *Psychological Medicine, 11*, 601–616.

Solomon, R. C. (1991). E-type judgements, emotions, and desire. In D. Ozer, J. M. Healy, A. J. Stewart, & R. Hogan (Eds.), *Perspectives in personality* (Vol. 3, Part A, pp. 169–190). London: Jessica Kingsley.

Stevens, A., & Price, J. (1996). *Evolutionary psychiatry*. London: Routledge.

Tomkins, S. S. (1979). Script theory: Differential magnification of affects. In H. E. Howe, Jr., & R. A. Dienstbier (Eds.), *Nebraska Symposium on Motivation* (Vol. 26, pp. 201–236). Lincoln: University of Nebraska Press.

Weber, M. (1964). *The theory of social and economic organisation* (T. Parson, Ed. and Trans.). London: Collier–Macmillan.

CHAPTER 7

Evolutionary Psychology and the Emotions

Leda Cosmides
John Tooby

Evolutionary psychology is an approach to the psychological sciences in which principles and results drawn from evolutionary biology, cognitive science, anthropology, and neuroscience are integrated with the rest of psychology in order to map human nature. By "human nature," evolutionary psychologists mean the evolved, reliably developing, species-typical computational and neural architecture of the human mind and brain. According to this view, the functional components of this architecture were designed by natural selection to solve adaptive problems faced by our hunter–gatherer ancestors, and to regulate behavior so that these adaptive problems were successfully addressed (for discussion, see Cosmides & Tooby, 1987; Tooby & Cosmides, 1992). Evolutionary psychology is not a specific subfield of psychology, such as the study of vision, reasoning, or social behavior. It is a *way of thinking* about psychology that can be applied to any topic within it—including the emotions.

The analysis of adaptive problems that arose ancestrally has led evolutionary psychologists to apply the concepts and methods of the cognitive sciences to scores of topics that are relevant to the study of emotion, such as the cognitive processes that govern cooperation, sexual attraction, jealousy, aggression, parental love, friendship, romantic love, the aesthetics of landscape preferences, coalitional aggression,

incest avoidance, disgust, predator avoidance, kinship, and family relations (for reviews, see Barkow, Cosmides, & Tooby, 1992; Crawford & Krebs, 1998; Daly & Wilson, 1988; Pinker, 1997). Indeed, a rich theory of the emotions naturally emerges out of the core principles of evolutionary psychology (Tooby, 1985; Tooby & Cosmides, 1990a; see also Nesse, 1990). In this chapter we (1) briefly state what we think emotions are and what adaptive problem they were designed to solve; (2) explain the evolutionary and cognitive principles that led us to this view; and (3) using this background, explicate in a more detailed way the design of emotion programs and the states they create.

AN EVOLUTIONARY-PSYCHOLOGICAL THEORY OF THE EMOTIONS

An evolutionary perspective leads one to view the mind as a crowded zoo of evolved, domain-specific programs. Each is functionally specialized for solving a different adaptive problem that arose during hominid evolutionary history, such as face recognition, foraging, mate choice, heart rate regulation, sleep management, or predator vigilance, and each is activated by a different set of cues from the environment. But the existence of all these microprograms itself creates an adaptive problem: Programs that are individually designed to solve specific adaptive problems could, if simultaneously activated, deliver outputs that conflict with one another, interfering with or nullifying one another's functional products. For example, sleep and flight from a predator require mutually inconsistent actions, computations, and physiological states. It is difficult to sleep when your heart and mind are racing with fear, and this is no accident: Disastrous consequences would ensue if proprioceptive cues were activating sleep programs at the same time that the sight of a stalking lion was activating programs designed for predator evasion. To avoid such consequences, the mind must be equipped with superordinate programs that override some programs when others are activated (e.g., a program that deactivates sleep programs when predator evasion subroutines are activated). Furthermore, many adaptive problems are best solved by the simultaneous activation of many different *components* of the cognitive architecture, such that each component assumes one of several alternative states (e.g., predator avoidance may require simultaneous shifts in both heart rate and auditory acuity; see below). Again, a superordinate program is needed that coordinates these components, snapping each into the right configuration at the right time.

Emotions are such programs. To behave functionally according to evolutionary standards, the mind's many subprograms need to be orchestrated so that their joint product at any given time is functionally coordinated, rather than cacophonous and self-defeating. This coordination is accomplished by a set of superordinate programs—the emotions. They are adaptations that have arisen in response to the adaptive problem of mechanism orchestration (Tooby & Cosmides, 1990a; Tooby, 1985). In this view, exploring the statistical structure of ancestral situations and their relationship to the mind's battery of functionally specialized programs is central to mapping the emotions. This is because the most useful (or least harmful) deployment of programs at any given time will depend critically on the exact nature of the confronting situation.

How did emotions arise and assume their distinctive structures? Fighting, falling in love, escaping predators, confronting sexual infidelity, experiencing a failure-driven loss in status, responding to the death of a family member, and so on each involved conditions, contingen-cies, situations, or event types that recurred innumerable times in hominid evolutionary history. Repeated encounters with each kind of situation selected for adaptations that guided information processing, behavior, and the body adaptively through the clusters of conditions, demands, and contingencies that characterized that particular class of situation. This can be accomplished by engineering superordinate programs, each of which jointly mobilizes a subset of the psychological architecture's other programs in a particular configuration. Each configuration should be selected to deploy computational and physiological mechanisms in a way that, when averaged over individuals and generations, would have led to the most fitness-promoting subsequent lifetime outcome, given that ancestral situation type.

This coordinated adjustment and entrainment of mechanisms constitutes a *mode of operation for the entire psychological architecture*, and serves as the basis for a precise computational and functional definition of each emotion state (Tooby & Cosmides, 1990a; Tooby, 1985). Each emotion entrains various other adaptive programs—deactivating some, activating others, and adjusting the modifiable parameters of still others—so that the whole system operates in a particularly harmonious and efficacious way when the individual is confronting certain kinds of triggering conditions or situations. The conditions or situations relevant to the emotions are those that (1) recurred ancestrally; (2) could not be negotiated successfully unless there was a superordinate level of program coordination (i.e., circumstances in which the independent operation of programs caused no conflicts would not have selected for an emotion program, and would lead to emotionally neutral states of mind); (3) had a rich and reliable repeated structure; (4) had recognizable cues signaling their presence;[1] and (5) were of a type in which an error would have resulted in large fitness costs (Tooby & Cosmides, 1990a; Tooby, 1985). When a condition or situation of an evolutionarily recognizable kind is detected, a signal is sent out from the emotion program that activates the specific constellation of subprograms appropriate to solving the types of adaptive problems that were regularly embedded in that situation, and deactivates programs whose operation might interfere with solving those types of adaptive problems. Programs directed to remain active may be cued to enter subroutines that are specific to that emotion mode and that were tailored by natural selection to solve the problems inherent in the triggering situation with special efficiency.

According to this theoretical framework, an emotion is a superordinate program whose function is to direct the activities and interactions of the subprograms governing perception; attention; inference; learning; memory; goal choice; motivational priorities; categorization and conceptual frameworks; physiological reactions (e.g., heart rate, endocrine function, immune function, gamete release); reflexes; behavioral decision rules; motor systems; communication processes; energy level and effort allocation; affective coloration of events and stimuli; recalibration of probability estimates, situation assessments, values, and regulatory variables (e.g., self-esteem, estimations of relative formidability, relative value of alternative goal states, efficacy discount rate); and so on. An emotion is not reducible to any one category of effects, such as effects on physiology, behavioral inclinations, cognitive appraisals, or feeling states, because it involves evolved instructions for all of them together, as well as other mechanisms distributed throughout the human mental and physical architecture.

All cognitive programs—including superordinate programs of this kind—are sometimes mistaken for "homunculi," that is, entities endowed with "free will." A homunculus scans the environment and freely chooses successful actions in a way that is not systematic enough to be implemented by a program. It is the task of cognitive psychologists to replace theories that implicitly posit such an impossible entity with theories that can be implemented as fixed programs with open parameters. Emotion programs, for example, have a front end that is designed to detect evolutionarily reliable cues that a situation exists (whether or not these cues reliably signal the presence of that situation in the modern world). When triggered, they entrain a specific set of subprograms: those that natural selection "chose" as most useful for solving the problems that situation posed in ancestral environments. Just as a computer can have a hierarchy of programs, some of which control the activation of others, the human mind can as well. Far from being internal free agents, these programs have an unchanging structure regardless of the needs of the individual or her circumstances, because they were designed to create states that worked well in ancestral situations, regardless of their consequences in the present.

FEAR: AN EXAMPLE

Consider the following example. The ancestrally recurrent situation is being alone at night, and a situation detector circuit perceives cues that indicate the possible presence of a human or animal predator. The emotion mode is a fear of being stalked. (In this conceptualization of emotion, there might be several distinct emotion modes that are lumped together under the folk category "fear," but that are computationally and empirically distinguishable by the different constellation of programs each entrains.) When the situation detector signals that you have entered the situation "possible stalking and ambush," the following kinds of mental programs are entrained or modified:

1. There are shifts in perception and attention. You may suddenly hear with far greater clarity sounds that bear on the hypothesis that you are being stalked, but that ordinarily you would not perceive or attend to, such as creaks or rustling. Are the creaks footsteps? Is the rustling caused by something moving stealthily through the bushes? Signal detection thresholds shift: Less evidence is required before you respond as if there were a threat, and more true positives will be perceived at the cost of a higher rate of false alarms.

2. Goals and motivational weightings change. Safety becomes a far higher priority. Other goals and the computational systems that subserve them are deactivated: You are no longer hungry; you cease to think about how to charm a potential mate; practicing a new skill no longer seems rewarding. Your planning focus narrows to the present: Worries about yesterday and tomorrow temporarily vanish. Hunger, thirst, and pain are suppressed.

3. Information-gathering programs are redirected: Where is my baby? Where are others who can protect me? Is there somewhere I can go where I can see and hear what is going on better?

4. Conceptual frames shift, with the automatic imposition of categories such as "dangerous" or "safe." Walking a familiar and usually comfortable route may now be mentally tagged as "dangerous". Odd places that you normally would not occupy—a hallway closet, the branches of a tree—suddenly may become salient as instances of the category "safe" or "hiding place."

5. Memory processes are directed to new retrieval tasks: Where was that tree I climbed before? Did my adversary and his friend look at me furtively the last time I saw them?

6. Communication processes change. Depending on the circumstances, decision rules might cause you to emit an alarm cry, or to be paralyzed and unable to speak. Your face may automatically assume a species-typical fear expression.

7. Specialized inference systems are activated. Information about a lion's trajectory or eye direction may be fed into systems for inferring whether the lion saw you. If the inference is "yes," then a program automatically infers that the lion knows where you are; if "no," then the lion does not know where you are (the "seeing-is-knowing" circuit identified by Baron-Cohen, 1995, and inactive in individuals with autism). This variable may automatically govern whether you freeze in terror or bolt. Are there cues in the lion's behavior that indicate whether it has eaten recently, and so is unlikely to be predatory in the near future? (Savannah-dwelling ungulates, such as zebras and wildebeests, commonly make this kind of judgment; Marks, 1987.)

8. Specialized learning systems are activated, as the large literature on fear conditioning indicates (e.g., LeDoux, 1995; Mineka & Cook, 1993; Pitman & Orr, 1995). If the threat is real, and the ambush occurs, you may experience an amygdala-mediated recalibration (as in posttraumatic stress disorder) that can last for the remainder of your life (Pitman & Orr, 1995).

9. Physiology changes: Gastric mucosa turn white as blood leaves the digestive tract (another concomitant of motivational priorities changing from feeding to safety); adrenalin spikes; heart rate may go up or down (depending on whether the situation calls for flight or immobility); blood rushes to the periphery, and so on (Cannon, 1929; Tomaka, Blascovich, Kibler, & Ernst, 1997); instructions to the musculature (face, and elsewhere) are sent (Ekman, 1982). Indeed, the nature of the physiological response can depend in detailed ways on the nature of the threat and the best response option (Marks, 1987).

10. Behavioral decision rules are activated. Depending on the nature of the potential threat, different courses of action will be potentiated: hiding, flight, self-defense, or even tonic immobility (the latter is a common response to actual attacks, both in other animals and in humans[2]).

Some of these responses may be experienced as automatic or involuntary.

From the point of view of avoiding danger, these computational changes are crucial: They are what allowed the adaptive problem to be solved with high probability, on average over evolutionary time. Of course, in any single case they may fail, because they are only the evolutionarily computed best bet, based on ancestrally summed outcomes; they are not a sure bet, based on an unattainable perfect knowledge of the present.

Whether individuals report consciously experiencing fear is a separate question from whether their mechanisms have assumed the characteristic configuration that, according to this theoretical approach, defines the fear emotion state. Individuals often behave as if they are in the grip of an emotion, while denying that they are feeling that emotion. We think it is perfectly possible that individuals sometimes remain unaware of their emotion states, which is one reason we do not use subjective experience as the *sine qua non* of emotion. At present, both the function of conscious awareness, and the principles that regulate conscious access to emotion states and other mental programs, are complex and unresolved questions. Mapping the design features of emotion programs can proceed independently of their resolution, at least for the present.

With the preceding view of emotions in mind, in the next two sections we outline the evolutionary and cognitive principles that led us to it (detailed arguments for these positions can be found in Tooby & Cosmides, 1990a, 1990b, 1992, and in Cosmides & Tooby, 1987, 1992, 1997).

EVOLUTIONARY FOUNDATIONS

Chance and Selection

For reasons researchers have only recently come to appreciate fully, every species has a universal, species-typical evolved architecture (Tooby & Cosmides, 1990b).[3] These designs are largely conserved through genetic inheritance from generation to generation (accounting over the long term for homologous similarities among related species). Nevertheless, over the long run, evolutionary change takes place, and this design modification is governed by two kinds of processes: chance and selection.

Random mutations are always being injected into species. What ultimately happens to each mutation is shaped both by chance and by the stable consequences the mutation has on the design of the organism—selection. A mutational modification to a design feature will often alter how well it functions (e.g., improving the optics of the lens, or reducing a liver enzyme's detoxification efficiency). Those alterations in a design feature that improve the machine's ability to solve reproduction-promoting tasks (compared to the earlier model design feature) will increase their own frequency over the generations, until (usually) they become universally incorporated into the species design. The accumulated effects of this positive feedback is one reason why species tend to have universal, species-typical evolved architecture in their functional components (see Tooby & Cosmides, 1990b, for details and exceptions). Other modifications interfere with replication; these act to edit themselves from the population and the species design (negative feedback). Still others have no systematic effect: Neutral alterations randomly drift in frequency, sometimes disappearing and sometimes becoming species-typical. These processes—chance and selection—explain how species acquired their designs.

For researchers seeking to understand organic design, natural selection is the most important component to consider, because it is the only force in nature that can build functional organization into organisms. Natural selection is a hill-climbing feedback process that chooses among alternative designs *on the basis of how well they function.* This is what biologists mean when they say that function determines structure. Natural selection is a causal process in which a structure spreads *because of* its functional consequences. This causal relationship is what gives theories of adaptive function their heuristic power for psychologists and biologists. If investigators know what adaptive problems our ancestors faced generation after generation, they can look for mechanisms that are well engineered for solving them.

Because of the different roles played by chance and selection, the evolutionary process builds three different types of outcomes into organisms: (1) adaptations—that is, functional machinery built by selection (usually species-typical); (2) by-products of adaptations, which are present in the design of organisms because they are causally coupled to traits that were se-

lected for (usually species-typical); and (3) random noise, injected by mutation and other random processes (often not species-typical) (Tooby & Cosmides, 1990a, 1990b, 1992; Williams, 1966). The emotion of sexual jealousy is an adaptation (Daly, Wilson, & Weghorst, 1982; Buss, 1994); stress-induced physical deterioration is arguably a by-product of the flight–fight system; and heritable personality variation in emotional functioning (e.g., extreme shyness, morbid jealousy, bipolar depression) is probably noise (Tooby & Cosmides, 1990b). Evidence of the presence (or absence) of high degrees of coordination between adaptive problems and the design features of putative adaptations allows researchers to distinguish adaptations, by-products, and noise from one another (Williams, 1966; Cosmides & Tooby, 1997).

How Well Designed Are Emotion Adaptations Expected to Be?

Organisms, as a result of millions of years of selection, are full of evolved adaptations that are improbably well engineered to solve the adaptive problems the species encountered repeatedly during its evolution. Biologists have found that selection has routinely produced exquisitely engineered biological machines of the highest order, at all scales—from genetic error correction and quality control in protein assembly to photosynthetic pigments, the immune system, the vertebrate eye and visual system, efficient bee foraging algorithms, echolocation, and color constancy systems. Although Stephen Jay Gould (1997) and his followers have energetically argued in the popular science literature that natural selection is a weak evolutionary force, evolutionary biologists, familiar with the primary literature, have found it difficult to take these arguments seriously (Tooby & Cosmides, 1999).

In fact, whenever the adaptive problem can be well specified (as in color constancy, object recognition, grammar acquisition, word meaning induction, tactile perception, or chemical identification), natural computational adaptations have consistently and strikingly outperformed the best artificial devices that teams of engineers, after decades of effort and millions of dollars of funding, have produced (consider, e.g., artificial vision or speech recognition programs). So while adaptations are in some abstract sense undoubtedly far from optimal, they are nevertheless extremely well engineered, and their performance on the problems they evolved to solve is unrivaled by any machine yet designed by humans. The empirical evidence falsifies the claim that evolved computational adaptations tend to be crude or primitive in design, and supports the opposite view: that our mental machinery, including the emotions, is likely to be very well designed to carry out evolved functions. For emotion researchers, this means that working hypotheses (which are always open to empirical revision) should begin with the expectation of high levels of evolutionary functionality, and that research methods should be sensitive enough to detect such organization. This does not mean that emotions are well designed for the modern world—only that their functional logic is likely to be sophisticated and well engineered to solve ancestral adaptive problems.

Adaptive Problems

Over evolutionary time, design features are added to or discarded from the species' design because of their consequences. A design feature will cause its own spread over generations if it has the consequence of solving adaptive problems such as detecting predators, deterring sexual rivals, helping sisters, or ejecting toxin-laden food. "Adaptive problems" are evolutionarily long-enduring recurring clusters of conditions that constitute either reproductive opportunities (e.g., the arrival of a potential mate, the reflectant properties of light) or reproductive obstacles (e.g., the speed of a prey animal, the actions of a sexual rival, limited food supplies for relatives). Adaptations were designed by selection to exploit these opportunities and to circumvent these obstacles. A design feature may be said to solve an adaptive problem to the extent that its presence in an organism (when compared to alternative designs) increases the organism's net lifespan reproduction, and/or the reproduction of kin (who are likely to carry the same genetically based design feature; Hamilton, 1964).

Researchers less familiar with evolutionary psychology often equate adaptive problems exclusively with short-run threats to physical survival. However, survival is not central to evolution; indeed, all individual organisms die sooner or later. In contrast, genes—which can be thought of as particles of design—are potentially immortal, and design features spread by promoting the reproduction of the genes that participate in building them. Survival is significant only insofar as it promotes the reproduction of design features. It is no more significant than anything else that promotes reproduction, and is often advantageously risked or sacrificed in the process of promoting reproduction in self, children, or other relatives.

Because events and conditions in the organism's local world are causally linked, the enhancement of its reproduction reaches out to encompass, in a network of causal linkages, all of human life—from the subtleties of facial expression to attributions of responsibility to the intrinsic rewards of projectile games to the ability to imagine alternatives. The realm of adaptive information-processing problems is not limited to one area of human life, such as sex, violence, or resource acquisition. Instead, it is a dimension cross-cutting all areas of human life, as weighted by the strange, nonintuitive metric of their cross-generational statistical effects on direct and kin reproduction.

Moreover, it is important to remember that the consequences at issue in a good design are *total lifetime fitness consequences*, not just what happens in the short run. The design features of every program have been shaped by the answer to the question: Given the situation the organism is in at each given present moment, what is the deployment at that moment of the modifiable characteristics of the individual (physiology, action, knowledge states, etc.) that will net the best return on own and kin reproduction, as accrued over the expected remainder of the individual's lifespan? Emotion programs that incline the individual to engage in seemingly pointless activities over the near-term (e.g., grief, playfulness, fascination, guilt, depression, feeling triumphant) need to be analyzed in terms of how they modify the psychological architecture for benefits that are accrued probabilistically over the long run (e.g., gains in knowledge; recalibration of motivational priorities; the recomputation of a huge body of choice-variables in the face of information that the local world has dramatically changed).[4]

The Environment of Evolutionary Adaptedness

Behavior in the present is generated by evolved information-processing mechanisms that were constructed in the past because they solved adaptive problems in the ancestral environments in which the human line evolved. For this reason, evolutionary psychology is both environment-oriented and past-oriented in its functionalist orientation. Adaptations become increasingly effective as selection makes their design features more and more complementary to the long-enduring structure of the world. The articulated features of the adaptation are designed to mesh with the features of the environment that were stable during the adaptation's evolution, so that their interaction produced functional outcomes. The regulation of breathing assumes the presence of certain long-enduring properties of the atmosphere and the respiratory system. Vision assumes the presence of certain evolutionarily stable properties of surfaces, objects, and terrestrial spectral distributions. The lactase digestive enzyme presupposes an infant diet of milk with lactose. And each emotion presupposes that certain cues signal the presence of a structure of events and conditions that held true during the evolution of that emotion. Disgust circuits presume a world in which rotten smells signal toxins or microbial contamination, for example.

Accordingly, to understand an adaptation as a problem solver, one needs to model the enduring properties of the task environment that selected for that adaptation—the "environment of evolutionary adaptedness," or EEA. Although the hominid line is thought to have first differentiated from the chimpanzee lineage on the African savannahs and woodlands, the EEA is not a place or time. It is the statistical composite of selection pressures that caused the genes underlying the design of an adaptation to increase in frequency until they became species-typical or stably persistent (Tooby & Cosmides, 1990a). Thus statistical regularities define the EEA for any given adaptation. The conditions that characterize the EEA are usefully decomposed into a constellation of specific environmental regularities that had a systematic (though not necessarily unvarying) impact on reproduction and that endured long enough to work evolutionary change on the design of an adaptation. These regularities can include complex conditionals (e.g., if one is a male hunter–gatherer *and* one is having a sexual liaison with someone else's mate *and* that is discovered, then one is the target of lethal retributory violence 37% of the time). Descriptions of these statistical regularities are essential for constructing a task analysis of the adaptive problem that a hypothesized adaptation evolved

to solve (Tooby & Cosmides, 1990a). Conceptualizing the EEA in statistical terms is fundamental to the functional definition of emotion that we presented above and will elucidate below.

COGNITIVE FOUNDATIONS

The Cognitive Science Resolution of the Mind–Body Problem

Evolutionary psychology starts with a fundamental insight from cognitive psychology: The brain is a machine designed to process information. From this perspective, one can define the "mind" as a set of information-processing procedures (cognitive programs) that are physically embodied in the neural circuitry of the brain. For cognitive scientists, "brain" and "mind" are terms that refer to the same system, which can be described in two complementary ways— either in terms of its physical properties (the neural) or in terms of its information-processing operation (the mental). The mind is what the brain does, described in computational[5] terms (Jackendoff, 1987; Cosmides & Tooby, 1987; Pinker, 1997). This approach allows mental operations to be described with great precision: One is led to specify what information is extracted from the environment; what procedures act to transform it; what formats are involved in its representation or storage; and what operations access it to govern decision making, physiological or behavioral regulation, or further information integration (Marr, 1982). Also, because it provides an intelligible way of relating physical and mental phenomena, discoveries in brain science (e.g., from dissociation studies and neuroimaging) can be used in making inferences about the mind, and vice versa—a process that is leading to a principled mapping between brain and mind (for reviews, see Gazzaniga, 1995).

An evolutionary perspective makes clear why the cognitive or computational level of description is more than an analogy. Whereas other parts of the body were designed for lifting loads, grinding food, chemically extracting nutrients, and so on, the brain was designed by evolution to use information derived from the environment and the body to functionally regulate behavior and the body. The brain came into existence and accreted its present complex structure over evolutionary time because, in ancestral populations, mutations that created or altered cognitive programs such that they carried out adaptively consequential information-processing tasks more successfully were differentially retained, replicated, and incorporated into our species' neural design.

The ancestral world posed recurrent information-processing problems, such as What substances are best to eat? or What is the relationship between others' facial expressions and their mental states? Information-processing programs—food preferences and aversions, or rules for inferring emotions from facial expressions—acquired one set of design features rather than many others because the retained features better computed solutions to these information-processing problems. Over evolutionary time, it was the *computational* properties of alternative neural circuits—their relative ability to solve adaptive information-processing tasks—that caused some neural circuits to be selected for and others to be selected out. So, from an evolutionary and a functional point of view, the brain is intrinsically and by its nature an organ of computation—a set of information-processing devices realized in neural tissue (Cosmides & Tooby, 1987; Tooby & Cosmides, 1992; Pinker, 1997). Key tasks for psychologists, then, are to discover, inventory, and map the "circuit logic" of the collection of programs that constitute the human mind, and to relate how that adaptive logic maps onto the suite of informational problems faced by our hunter–gatherer ancestors.

Emotion and Computation

It may strike some as odd to speak about love or jealousy or disgust in computational terms. "Cognition" and "computation" have affectless, flavorless connotations. In everyday language, the term "cognition" is often used to refer to a particular *subset* of information processing—roughly, the effortful, conscious, voluntary, deliberative kind of thinking one does when solving a mathematics problem or playing chess: what is sometimes called "cold cognition." This use of "cognition" falls out of the folk-psychological classification of thinking as distinct from feeling and emotion, and it appears in a few subfields of psychology as well (particularly those concerned with education and the acquisition of skills that must be explicitly taught). As a result, one sometimes sees articles in the psychological literature on how emotion, affect, or mood influence "cognition."

However, from an evolutionary cognitive perspective, one cannot sensibly talk about emotion affecting cognition because "cognition" refers to a language for describing all of the brain's operations, including emotions and reasoning (whether deliberative or nonconscious), and not to any particular subset of operations. If the brain evolved as a system of information-processing relations, then emotions are, in an evolutionary sense, best understood as information-processing relations (i.e., programs) with naturally selected functions. Initially, the commitment to exploring the underlying computational architecture of the emotions may strike one as odd or infelicitous, but it leads to a large number of scientific payoffs, as we sketch out below.

Thus the claim that emotion is computational does not mean that an evolutionary-psychological approach reduces the human experience to bloodless, affectless, disembodied ratiocination. Every mechanism in the brain—whether it does something categorizable as "cold cognition" (such as inducing a rule of grammar or judging a probability) or as "hot cognition" (such as computing the intensity of parental fear, the imperative to strike an adversary, or an escalation in infatuation)—depends on an underlying computational organization to give its operation its patterned structure, as well as a set of neural circuits to implement it physically.

Of course, shifting terminology (e.g., from "cognition" as thinking to "cognition" as everything mental) does nothing to invalidate research done with the old terminology, and valuable research exploring how various emotion states modify performance on tasks that require deliberative thinking has been done (e.g., Isen, 1987; Mackie & Worth, 1991). But an evolutionary and computational view of emotion can open up for exploration new empirical possibilities obscured by other frameworks. An evolutionary perspective breaks categories such as "thinking" into a large set of independent domain-specific programs, and so opens up the possibility that distinct emotions affect separate inference programs in diverse yet functionally patterned ways, rather than in a single, aggregate way.[6]

Domain Specificity and Functional Specialization

A basic engineering principle is that the same machine is rarely capable of solving two different problems equally well. Corkscrews and cups have different properties because they are solutions to different problems, and each therefore solves its targeted problem better than the other. Similarly, natural selection has constructed different tissues and organs (e.g., the heart for pumping blood, the liver for detoxifying poisons) for exactly this reason. This same principle applies to our evolved cognitive programs and neural circuitry. Different information-processing problems usually require different procedures for their successful solution. For example, to solve the adaptive problem of selecting a good mate, one's choices must be guided by qualitatively different standards than when one is choosing the right food, or the right habitat, or the right meaning for an unfamiliar word. Implementing different solutions requires different, functionally distinct mechanisms (Sherry & Schacter, 1987; Gallistel, 1995). Speed, reliability, and efficiency can be engineered into specialized mechanisms because they do not need to make tradeoffs between mutually incompatible task demands, and because they can use problem-solving principles that work in one domain but not in others. (For detailed arguments, both on the weakness of domain-general architectures and on the many advantages of architectures that include a large number of domain-specific computational devices, see Cosmides & Tooby, 1987, 1994; Tooby & Cosmides, 1990a, 1992).

The application of these principles to the design of the mind has convinced many scientists, including most evolutionary psychologists, that the human cognitive architecture is *multimodular*—that it is composed of a large number of information-processing programs, many of which are functionally specialized for solving a different adaptive problem. These adaptations appear to be domain-specific expert systems, equipped with "crib sheets": inference procedures, regulatory rules, motivational priorities, goal definitions, and assumptions that embody knowledge, regulatory structure, and value weightings specific to an evolved problem domain. These generate correct (or at least adaptive) outputs that would not be warranted on the basis of perceptual data processed through some general-purpose decisional algorithm. In the last two decades, many cognitive researchers have found evidence for the existence of a diverse collection of inference systems, including specializations for reasoning about objects, physical causality, number, language, the

biological world, the beliefs and motivations of other individuals, and social interactions (for reviews, see Hirschfeld & Gelman, 1994; *Cognitive Science*, Volume 14, 1990; and Barkow et al., 1992). These domain-specific inference systems have a distinct advantage over domain-independent ones, akin to the difference between experts and novices: Experts can solve problems faster and more efficiently than novices because they already know a lot about the problem domain, and because they are equipped with specialized tools and practices.

Each adaptive problem recurred millions of times in the EEA, and so manifested a statistical and causal structure whose elements were available for specialized exploitation by design features of the evolving adaptation. For example, predators used darkness and cover to ambush. Physical appearance varied with fertility and health. Other children regularly fed by one's mother were usually one's genetic siblings. Specialized programs—for predator fear, sexual attraction, and incest avoidance, respectively—could evolve whose configuration of design features embodied and/or exploited these statistical regularities, allowing these adaptive problems to be solved economically, reliably, and effectively. Such specializations, by embodying "innate knowledge" about the problem space, operate better than any general learning strategy could. A child did not have to wait to be ambushed and killed in the dark to prudently modulate his or her activities. Adults did not need to observe the negative effects of incest, because the Westermarck mechanism mobilizes disgust toward having sex with probable siblings (Shepher, 1983).

Selection Detects the Individually Unobservable

Animals subsist on information. The single most limiting resource to reproduction is not food or safety or access to mates, but what makes them each possible: the information required for making adaptive behavioral choices. However, many important features of the world cannot be perceived directly. Cognitive adaptations can use perceivable events as cues for inferring the status of important, nonperceivable sets of conditions, provided that a predictable probabilistic relationship between them was maintained over evolutionary time. Natural selection can extract statistical relationships that would be undetectable to any individual organism (Cosmides & Tooby, 1987; Tooby & Cosmides, 1990a). It does this by testing randomly generated alternative designs, each of which embodies different assumptions about the structure of the world, and retaining the ones that succeed most effectively. The most effective design will be the one that best embodies design features that reflect most closely the actual long-term statistical structure of the ancestral world. Designs whose features exploited these real but ontogenetically unobservable relationships outperformed those that depended on different relationships, or that only responded to conditions an individual could observe during his or her lifetime.

This is why *tabula rasa* models of human and nonhuman minds are evolutionary impossibilities (Cosmides & Tooby, 1987). For example, the negative effects of incestuous conceptions are difficult for any individual to observe in the absence of a modern controlled study with numerous participants, much less to integrate rationally into one's motivational system. Fortunately, the consequences of incest over evolutionary time selected for specialized disgust mechanisms that reflected the ancestral distribution of choice–consequence pairings, and so are designed to guide humans away from incestuous unions between fertile adults, given appropriate cues of familial connection such as coresidence in the first years of life (Shepher, 1983). Evolved psychological adaptations are selected to use cues that (1) can be reliably and easily detected by the individual, and (2) reliably predicted the hidden structure of conditions relevant to determining which course of action one should take.

The Functional Structure of an Emotion Program Evolved to Match the Evolutionarily Summed Structure of Its Target Situation

The set of human emotion programs assumed their evolved designs through interacting with the statistically defined structure of human EEAs. Each emotion program was constructed by a selective regime imposed by a particular evolutionarily recurrent situation. By an "evolutionarily recurrent situation," we mean a cluster of repeated probabilistic relationships among events, conditions, actions, and choice consequences that endured over a sufficient stretch of evolutionary time to have had selec-

tive consequences on the design of the mind, and that were probabilistically associated with cues detectable by humans.

For example, the condition of having a mate plus the condition of one's mate copulating with someone else constitutes a situation of sexual infidelity—a situation that has recurred over evolutionary time, even though it has not happened to every individual. Associated with this situation were cues reliable enough to allow the evolution of a "situation detector" (e.g., observing a sexual act, flirtation, or even the repeated simultaneous absence of the suspected lovers were cues that could trigger the categorization of a situation as one of infidelity). Even more important, many necessarily or probabilistically associated elements tended to be present in the situation of infidelity as encountered among our hunter–gatherer ancestors. Additional elements included (1) a sexual rival with a capacity for social action and violence, as well as allies of the rival; (2) a discrete probability that one's mate has conceived a child with the sexual rival; (3) changes in the net lifetime reproductive returns of investing further in the mating relationship; (4) a probable decrease in the degree to which the unfaithful mate's mechanisms value the victim of infidelity (the presence of an alternative mate lowers replacement costs); (5) a cue that the victim of the infidelity is likely to have been deceived about a range of past events, leading the victim to confront the likelihood that his or her memory is permeated with false information; (6) the likelihood that the victim's status and reputation for being effective at defending his or her interests in general will plummet, inviting challenges in other arenas. These are just a few of the many factors that constitute a list of elements associated in a probabilistic cluster, and that constitute the evolutionary recurrent structure of a situation of sexual infidelity. The emotion of sexual jealousy evolved in response to these properties of the world, and there should be evidence of this in its computational design.

Emotion programs have evolved to take such elements into account, whether they can be perceived or not. Thus not only do cues of a situation trigger an emotion mode, but embedded in that emotion mode is a way of seeing the world and feeling about the world related to the ancestral cluster of associated elements. Depending on the intensity of the jealousy evoked, less and less evidence will be required for an individual to believe that these conditions apply to his or her personal situation. Individuals with morbid jealousy, for example, may hallucinate counterfactual but evolutionarily thematic contents.

To the extent that situations exhibit a structure repeated over evolutionary time, their statistical properties will be used as the basis for natural selection to build an emotion program whose detailed design features are tailored for that situation. This is accomplished by selection, acting over evolutionary time, differentially incorporating program components that dovetail with individual items on the list of properties probabilistically associated with the situation.

For example, if in ancestral situations of sexual infidelity there was a substantially higher probability of a violent encounter than in the absence of infidelity, then the sexual jealousy program will have been shaped by the distillation of those encounters, and the jealousy subroutines will have been adjusted to prepare for violence in proportion to the raised probability in the ancestral world. (Natural selection acts too slowly to have updated the mind to post-hunter–gatherer conditions.) Each of these subelements and the adaptive circuits they require can be added together to form a general theory of sexual jealousy.

The emotion of sexual jealousy constitutes an organized mode of operation specifically designed to deploy the programs governing each psychological mechanism so that each is poised to deal with the exposed infidelity. Physiological processes are prepared for such things as violence, sperm competition, and the withdrawal of investment; the goal of deterring, injuring, or murdering the rival emerges; the goal of punishing, deterring, or deserting the mate appears; the desire to make oneself more competitively attractive to alternative mates emerges; memory is activated to reanalyze the past; confident assessments of the past are transformed into doubts; the general estimate of the reliability and trustworthiness of the opposite sex (or indeed everyone) may decline; associated shame programs may be triggered to search for situations in which the individual can publicly demonstrate acts of violence or punishment that work to counteract an (imagined or real) social perception of weakness; and so on.

It is the relationship between the summed details of the ancestral condition and the detailed structure of the resulting emotion program that makes this approach so useful for emotion researchers. Each functionally distinct emotion state—fear of predators, guilt, sexual jealousy, rage, grief, and so on—will correspond to an integrated mode of operation that functions as a solution designed to take advantage of the particular structure of the recurrent situation or triggering condition to which that emotion corresponds. This approach can be used to create theories of each individual emotion, through three steps: (1) reconstructing the clusters of properties of ancestral situations; (2) constructing engineering analyses about how each of the known or suspected psychological mechanisms in the human mental architecture should be designed to deal with each ancestral condition or cluster of conditions, and integrating these into a model of the emotion program; (3) conducting experiments and other investigations to test (and, if necessary, revise) the models of emotion programs.

It is also important to understand that evolutionarily recurrent situations can be arrayed along a spectrum in terms of how rich or skeletal the set of probabilistically associated elements defining the situation is. A richly structured situation, such as sexual infidelity or predator ambush, will support a richly substructured emotion program in response to the many ancestrally correlated features: Many detailed adjustments will be made to many psychological mechanisms as instructions for the mode of operation. In contrast, some recurrent situations have less structure (i.e., they share fewer properties in common), and so the emotion mode makes fewer highly specialized adjustments, imposes fewer specialized and compelling interpretations and behavioral inclinations, and so on. For example, a surge of happiness or joy reflects an emotion program that evolved to respond to the recurrent situation of encountering unexpected positive events (as will be explained). The class of events captured by "unexpectedly positive" is extremely broad, and such events have only a few additional properties in common. Emotion programs at the most general and skeletal end of this spectrum correspond to what some call "mood" (happiness, sadness, excitement, anxiety, playfulness, homesickness, etc.).

HOW TO CHARACTERIZE
AN EMOTION

To characterize an emotion adaptation, one must identify the following properties of environments and of mechanisms:

1. *An evolutionarily recurrent situation or condition.* A "situation" is a repeated structure of environmental and organismic properties, characterized as a complex statistical composite of how such properties covaried in the EEA. Examples of these situations include being in a depleted nutritional state, competing for maternal attention, being chased by a predator, being about to ambush an enemy, having few friends, experiencing the death of a spouse, being sick, having experienced a public success, having others act in a way that damages you without regard for your welfare, having injured a valued other through insufficient consideration of self–other behavioral tradeoffs, and having a baby.

2. *The adaptive problem.* Identifying the adaptive problem means identifying which organismic states and behavioral sequences will lead to the best average functional outcome for the remainder of the lifespan, given the situation or condition. For example, what is the best course of action when others take the products of your labor without your consent? What is the best course of action when you are in a depleted nutritional state? What is the best course of action when a sibling makes a sexual approach?

3. *Cues that signal the presence of the situation.* For example, low blood sugar signals a depleted nutritional state; the looming approach of a large fanged animal signals the presence of a predator; seeing your mate having sex with another signals sexual infidelity; finding yourself often alone, rarely the recipient of beneficent acts, or actively avoided by others signals that you have few friends.

4. *Situation-detecting algorithms.* A multimodular mind must be full of "demons"—algorithms that detect situations. *The New Hacker's Dictionary* defines a "demon" as a "portion of a program that is not invoked explicitly, but that lies dormant waiting for some condition(s) to occur" (Raymond, 1991, p. 124). Situation-detecting subprograms lie dormant until they are activated by a specific constellation of cues that precipitates the analysis of whether a particular ancestral situation has arisen. If the assessment is positive, it sends the signal that ac-

tivates the associated emotion program. Emotion demons need two kinds of subroutines:

a. *Algorithms that monitor for situation-defining cues.* These programs include perceptual mechanisms, proprioceptive mechanisms, and situation-modeling memory. They take the cues in point 3 above as input.

b. *Algorithms that detect situations.* These programs take the output of the monitoring algorithms and targeted memory registers in point *a* as input, and through integration, probabilistic weighting, and other decision criteria, identify situations as absent or present with some probability.

The assignment of a situation interpretation to present circumstances involves a problem in signal detection theory (Swets, Tanner, & Birdsall, 1961; see also Gigerenzer & Murray, 1987). Animals should be designed to "detect" what situation they are in on the basis of cues, stored variables, and specialized interpretation algorithms. Selection will not shape decision rules so that they act solely on the basis of what is most likely to be true, but rather on the basis of the weighted consequences of acts, given that something is held to be true. Should you walk under a tree that might conceal a predator? Even if the algorithms assign a 51% (or even 98%) probability to the tree's being predator-free, under most circumstances an evolutionarily well-engineered decision rule should cause you to avoid the tree—to act as if the predator were in it. The benefits of calories saved via a shortcut, scaled by the probability that there is no predator in the tree, must be weighed against the benefits of avoiding becoming catfood, scaled by the probability that there is a predator in the tree. Because the costs and benefits of false alarms, misses, hits, and correct rejections are often unequal, the decision rules may still treat as true situations that are unlikely to be true. In the modern world, this behavior may look "irrational" (as is the case with many phobias), but people engage in it because such decisions were adaptive under ancestral conditions.

Situation-detecting algorithms can be of any degree of complexity, from demons that monitor single cues (e.g., "snake present") to algorithms that carry out more complex cognitive assessments of situations and conditions (LeDoux, 1995; Lazarus & Lazarus, 1994; Tooby & Cosmides, 1990a). Inherent in this approach is the expectation that the human mind has a series of evolved subsystems designed to represent events in terms of evolutionarily recurrent situations and situational subcomponents. The operation of these representational systems is not necessarily consciously accessible. By their structure, they impose an evolutionary organization on representational spaces that are updated by data inputs. When the representational space assumes certain configurations, an interpretation is triggered that activates the associated emotion program—corresponding approximately to what others have called a cognitive appraisal (see, e.g., Lazarus & Lazarus, 1994). It is important to recognize that the evolutionary past frames the experienced present, because these situation-detecting algorithms provide the dimensions and core elements out of which many cross-culturally recurring representations of the world are built. To some extent, the world we inhabit is shaped by the continuous interpretive background commentary provided by these mechanisms.

5. *Algorithms that assign priorities.* A given world state may correspond to more than one situation at a time; for example, you may be nutritionally depleted *and* in the presence of a predator. The prioritizing algorithms define which emotion modes are compatible (e.g., hunger[7] and boredom) and which are mutually exclusive (e.g., feeding and predator escape). Depending on the relative importance of the situations and the reliability of the cues, the prioritizing algorithms decide which emotion modes to activate and deactivate, and to what degree. Selection, through ancestral mutant experiments, would have sorted emotions based on the average importance of the consequences stemming from each and the extent to which joint activation was mutually incompatible (or facilitating). (Prioritizing algorithms can be thought of as a supervisory system operating over all of the emotions.)

6. *An internal communication system.* Given that a situation has been detected, the internal communication system sends a situation-specific signal to all relevant programs and mechanisms; the signal switches them into the appropriate adaptive emotion mode. In addition, information is fed back into the emotion program from other programs and systems that assess body states, which may govern the intensity, trajectory, supplantation, or termination of the emotion.

Some modes of activation of the cognitive system are accompanied by a characteristic feeling state, a certain quality of experience. The fact that we are capable of becoming aware of certain physiological states—our hearts thumping, bowels evacuating, stomachs tightening—is surely responsible for some of the qualia evoked by emotion states that entrain such responses. The fact that we are capable of becoming aware of certain mental states, such as retrieved memories of past events, is probably responsible for other qualia. But it is also possible that in some cases, the characteristic feeling state that accompanies an emotion mode results (in part) from mechanisms that allow us to sense the *signal* that activates and deactivates the relevant programs. Such internal sensory mechanisms—a kind of cognitive proprioception—can be selected for if there are mechanisms that require as input the information that a particular emotion mode has been activated. (This might be true, for example, of mechanisms designed to inhibit certain stimulus-driven actions when the conditions are not auspicious.)

7. *Each program and physiological mechanism entrained by an emotion program must have associated algorithms that regulate how it responds to each emotion signal.* These algorithms determine whether the mechanism should switch on or switch off, and if on, what emotion-specialized performance it will implement. For example, there should be algorithms in the auditory system that, upon detecting the fear signal (see point 6), reset signal detection thresholds, increasing acuity for predator-relevant sounds.

WHAT KINDS OF PROGRAMS CAN EMOTIONS MOBILIZE?

Any controllable biological process that, by shifting its performance in a specifiable way, would lead to enhanced average fitness outcomes should have come to be partially governed by emotional state (see point 7 above). Some examples are discussed in this section.

Goals

The cognitive mechanisms that define goal states and choose among goals in a planning process should be influenced by emotions. For example, vindictiveness—a specialized subcategory of anger—may define "injuring the offending party" as a goal state to be achieved.

(Although the evolved functional logic of this process is deterrence, this function need not be represented, either consciously or unconsciously, by the mechanisms that generate the vindictive behavior.)

Motivational Priorities

Mechanisms involved in hierarchically ranking goals or calibrating other kinds of motivational and reward systems should be emotion-dependent. What may be extremely unpleasant in one state, such as harming another, may seem satisfying in another state (e.g., aggressive competition may facilitate counterempathy). Different evolutionarily recurrent situations predict the presence (visible or invisible) of different opportunities, risks, and payoffs, so motivational thresholds and valences should be entrained. For example, a loss of face should increase the motivation to take advantage of opportunities for status advancement, and should decrease attention to attendant costs.

Information-Gathering Motivations

Because establishing which situation one is in has enormous consequences for the appropriateness of behavior, the process of detection should in fact involve specialized inference procedures and specialized motivations to discover whether certain suspected facts are true or false. What one is curious about, what one finds interesting, and what one is obsessed with discovering should all be emotion-specific.

Imposed Conceptual Frameworks

Emotions should prompt construals of the world in terms of concepts appropriate to the decisions that must be made. When one is angry, domain-specific concepts such as social agency, fault, responsibility, and punishment will be assigned to elements in the situation. When one is hungry, the food–nonfood distinction will seem salient. When one is endangered, safety categorization frames will appear. The world will be carved up into categories based partly on what emotional state an individual is in.

Perceptual Mechanisms

Perceptual systems may enter emotion-specific modes of operation. When one is fearful, acuity of hearing may increase. Specialized perceptual inference systems may be mobilized as well: If you've heard rustling in the bushes at night, human and predator figure detection may be particularly boosted, and not simply visual acuity in general. In fact, nonthreat interpretations may be depressed, and the same set of shadows will "look threatening"—given a specific threatening interpretation such as "a man with a knife"—or not, depending on emotion state.

Memory

The ability to call up particularly appropriate kinds of information out of long-term memory ought to be influenced by emotion state. A woman who has just found strong evidence that her husband has been unfaithful may find herself flooded by a torrent of memories about small details that seemed meaningless at the time but that now fit into an interpretation of covert activity. We also expect that what is stored about present experience will also be differentially regulated. Important or shocking events, for example, may be stored in great detail (as has been claimed about "flashbulb memories," for example), but other, more moderate emotion-specific effects may occur as well.

Attention

The entire structure of attention, from perceptual systems to the contents of high-level reasoning processes, should be regulated by emotional state. If you are worried that your spouse is late and might have been injured, it is hard to concentrate on other ongoing tasks (Derryberry & Tucker, 1994), but easy to concentrate on danger scenarios. Positive emotions may broaden attentional focus (Fredrickson, 1998).

Physiology

Each organ system, tissue, or process is a potential candidate for emotion-specific regulation, and "arousal" is an insufficiently specific term to capture the detailed coordination involved. Each emotion program should send out a different pattern of instructions (to the face and limb muscles, the autonomic system, etc.), to the extent that the problems embedded in the associated situations differ. This leads to an expectation that different constellations of effects will be diagnostic of different emotion states

(Ekman, Levenson, & Friesen, 1983). Changes in circulatory, respiratory, and gastrointestinal functioning are well known and documented, as are changes in endocrinological function. We expect thresholds regulating the contraction of various muscle groups to change with certain emotion states, reflecting the probability that they will need to be employed. Similarly, immune allocation and targeting may vary with disgust, with the potential for injury, or with the demands of extreme physical exertion.

Communication and Emotional Expressions

Emotion programs are expected to mobilize many emotion-specific effects on the subcomponents of the human psychological architecture relevant to communication. Most notably, many emotion programs produce characteristic species-typical displays that broadcast to others the emotion state of the individual (Ekman, 1982). Ekman and his colleagues have established in a careful series of landmark studies that many emotional expressions are human universals; that is, they are both generated and recognized reliably by humans everywhere they have been tested (Ekman, 1994). Indeed, many emotional expressions appear to be designed to be informative, and these have been so reliably informative that humans have coevolved automated interpreters of facial displays of emotion that decode these public displays into knowledge of others' mental states. It is surely true that people sometimes "lie" with their faces. But programs for inferring emotion states from facial displays would not have evolved unless doing so created a net advantage for the inferrer, suggesting that these inferences were warranted more often than not.

Two things are communicated by an authentic emotional expression:[8] (1) that the associated emotion program has been activated in an individual, providing observers with information about the state of that individual's mental programs and physiology (e.g., "I am afraid"); and (2) the identity of the evolutionarily recurrent situation being faced, in the estimation of the signaler (e.g., the local world holds a danger). Both are highly informative, and emotional expressions provide a continuous commentary on the underlying meaning of things to companions.[9] This provokes a question: Why did selection build facial, vocal, and postural expressions at all? More puzzlingly, why are

they often experienced as automatic and involuntary?

From an evolutionary perspective, sometimes it is beneficial to provide information to others and at other times it is injurious, so most evolved communication systems involve close regulation of whether to transmit information or not. Usually this leads to a system, such as language, in which the decision to communicate something (or not) can be made by the individual in detailed response to the immediate circumstances. The apparent selective disadvantages of honestly and automatically broadcasting one's emotional state have led Fridlund (1994), for example, to argue that expressions must be voluntary and intentional communications largely unconnected to emotion state. Undoubtedly they sometimes are. But even when a person deliberately lies, microexpressions of face and voice often leak out (Ekman, 1985), suggesting that certain emotion programs do in fact create involuntarily emitted signals that reliably broadcast the person's emotion state. Why?

Natural selection has shaped emotion programs to signal their activation, or not, on an emotion-by-emotion basis. For each emotion program considered by itself (jealousy, loneliness, disgust, predatoriness, parental love, sexual attraction, gratitude, fear), there was a net benefit or cost to having others know that mental state, averaged across individuals over evolutionary time. For those recurrent situations in which, on average, it was beneficial to share one's emotion state (and hence assessment of the situation) with those one was with, species-typical facial and other expressions of emotion were constructed by selection. For example, fear was plausibly beneficial to signal, because it signaled the presence of a danger that might also menace one's kin and cooperators, and also informed others in a way that might recruit assistance.

Nevertheless, averaged across individuals over evolutionary time, it was functional for an organism to signal the activation of only *some* emotion states. The conditions favoring signaling an emotion are hard to meet, so only some emotions out of the total species-typical set are associated with distinctive, species-typical facial expressions.[10] There should be a larger set of emotions that have no automatic display. Jealousy, guilt, and boredom are all genuine emotions lacking distinctive signals. This changes the question from: "Why are emotions automatically signaled?" to "Why are *some* emotions automatically signaled?" When selection is neutral, the signs of an emotion should only be the by-products of whatever is necessary to run the emotion program, without any selection to make the cues informative. When selection disfavors others' knowing the organism's internal state, selection should suppress and obscure external cues identifying internal states. Precisely because they publicly signal themselves, our attention goes disproportionately to the subset of emotions that do come equipped with emotional expressions. We think it likely that this has had an impact on the history of emotion research.

Three factors govern whether transmitting information will be beneficial or harmful: the signaler's relationship to the audience; the nature of the information that an emotion signal would release; and the computational overhead of computing the benefits and costs of information sharing on a case-by-case basis, in order to regulate whether to make a broadcast (Tooby & Cosmides, 1996). In general (but with some notable exceptions), the closer the cooperative relationship and shared fitness interests, the more beneficial it is to share information; the more distant and adversarial the relationship, the more harmful it is. For this reason, we expect that circuits have evolved that regulate global emotional expressiveness depending on whether one is (apparently) alone, with people one shares interests with, or with social antagonists (e.g., enemies or higher-ranking individuals) where leakage of damaging information should be suppressed. This global regulation may be largely automatic and nonconscious, and may involve open parameters set culturally and developmentally. Other things being equal, individuals will be shyer and less spontaneous with strangers (creating problems in public speaking), and more expressive with intimates. Similarly, it may be that male–female differences in emotional expressiveness arise from an evolutionary history in which males were on average more often in the presence of potential adversaries. Of course, it is beneficial to the transmitter to share certain types of information with adversaries, such as anger, triumph, or surrender, but many other types (fear of adversaries, pain, anxiety about weaknesses) ought to be suppressed.

The nature of the information broadcast has two components: (1) reliable consequences, predicted by the identity of the emotion; and (2) context-specific consequences (Tooby & Cosmides, 1996). The first component can be handled by automating the broadcast of the identity of those emotions that, on average, reliably produced a benefit when shared: Approval or disapproval assist in communicating to social interactants one's values; fear communicates the nature of a common danger; disgust communicates avoidance and spoilage; anger signals a conflict of values, with a willingness to enforce one's values with a sanction. The second, context-specific component requires computational circuitry to calculate the consequences of releasing a piece of information into the social world—a very complex set of computations. The benefit gained by inhibiting release of an expression on a case-by-case basis must be large enough to offset the cost of such computations for selection to favor the evolution of such regulatory circuits.[11] The overall result of these selection pressures would be that some emotions would evolve to be automatically broadcast, others would not evolve a signal, and a third category would evolve circuits that regulate the broadcast to some extent, just as in language.

Nevertheless, the automatic, involuntary expression of many emotions is a key feature of the biology and social life of our species, and their presence provides powerful evidence that ancestral humans spent a large portion of their time with close cooperators, as opposed to antagonists and competitors. Indeed, species ought to vary in the magnitude of automatic emotion signaling and in which emotions are signaled, based on the social ecology of the species. Highly cooperative social species, such as canids, are expected to (and appear to) have a rich repertoire of emotion signals, while more solitary species, such as felids, should have fewer emotion signals.

Behavior

All psychological mechanisms are involved in the generation and regulation of behavior, so obviously behavior will be regulated by emotion state. More specifically, however, mechanisms proximately involved in the generation of actions (as opposed to processes such as face recognition, which are only distally regulatory) should be very sensitive to emotion state. Not only may highly stereotyped behaviors of certain kinds be released (as during sexual arousal or rage, or as with species-typical facial expressions and body language), but more complex action generation mechanisms should be regulated as well. Specific acts and courses of action will be more available as responses in some states than in others, and more likely to be implemented. Emotion mode should govern the construction of organized behavioral sequences that solve adaptive problems.

Biologists, psychologists, and economists who adopt an evolutionary perspective have recognized that game theory can be used to model many forms of social interaction (Maynard Smith, 1982). If the EEA imposes certain evolutionarily repeated games, then the "strategies" (the evolved cognitive programs that govern behavior in those contexts) should evolve in the direction of choices that lead to the best expected fitness payoffs. The strategy activated in the individual should match the game (e.g., exchange) and the state of play in the game (e.g., having just been cheated)—a process that requires the system of cues, situation detection, and so on, already discussed. So different emotion and inference programs or subprograms may have evolved to correspond to various evolved games, including zero-sum competitive games, positive-sum exchange games, coalitional lottery games, games of aggressive competition corresponding to "chicken," and so on (for exchange, see Cosmides, 1989; Cosmides & Tooby, 1992). Corresponding emotion programs guide the individual into the appropriate interactive strategy for the social "game" being played, given the state of play. Surprisingly, for some games, rigid obligatory adherence to a prior strategy throughout the game is better than the ability to revise and change strategies ("voluntarily") in the light of events. If an individual contemplating a course of action detrimental to you knew you would take revenge, regardless of how costly this is to you, then that individual will be less likely to take such harmful action. This may translate into emotion programs in which the desire to attempt certain actions should be overwhelming, to the point where the actions are experienced as compulsory. In the grip of such programs, competing programs, including the normal integration of prudential concerns and social consequences, are muted or terminated. For example, the desire to avenge a murder or an infidelity is often experienced in this way, and crimes resulting from this desire are even culturally recognized as "crimes of passion" (Daly & Wilson, 1988). In modern state societies, where there are police who are paid to punish and otherwise enforce agreements, it is easy to underestimate the importance that deterrence based on the actions of oneself and one's coalition had in the Pleistocene. Hirshleifer (1987) and Frank (1988) are evolutionary economists who have pursued this logic the furthest, arguing that many social behaviors evolved to solve such "commitment problems."

Specialized Inference

Research in evolutionary psychology has shown that "thinking" or reasoning is not a unitary category, but is carried out by a variety of specialized mechanisms. So, instead of emotion activating or depressing "thinking" in general, the specific emotion program activated should *selectively* activate appropriate specialized inferential systems, such as cheater detection (Cosmides, 1989; Cosmides & Tooby, 1989, 1992), bluff detection (Tooby & Cosmides, 1989), precaution detection (Fiddick, Cosmides, & Tooby, in press), attributions of blame and responsibility, and so on. We are presently conducting research to see whether, as predicted, fear influences precautionary reasoning, competitive loss regulates bluff detection, and so on.

Reflexes

Muscular coordination, tendency to blink, threshold for vomiting, shaking, and many other reflexes are expected to be regulated by emotion programs to reflect the demands of the evolved situation.

Learning

Emotion mode is expected to regulate learning mechanisms. What someone learns from stimuli will be greatly altered by emotion mode, because of attentional allocation, motivation, situation-specific inferential algorithms, and a host of other factors. Emotion mode will cause the present context to be divided up into situation-specific, functionally appropriate categories so that the same stimuli and the same environment may be interpreted in radically different ways, depending on emotion state. For example, which stimuli are considered similar should be different in different emotion states, distorting the shape of the individual's psychological "similarity space" (Shepard, 1987). Highly specialized learning mechanisms may be activated, such as those that control food aversions (Garcia, 1990), predator learning (Mineka & Cook, 1985), or fear conditioning (LeDoux, 1995). Happiness is expected to signal the energetic opportunity for play, and to allow other exploratory agendas to be expressed (Frederickson, 1998).

Affective Coloration of Events and Stimuli as a Form of Learning

A behavioral sequence is composed of many acts. Each of these acts can be thought of as an intermediate "factor" in the production of a behavioral sequence (to use economic terminology). Determining which courses of action are worthwhile and which are not is a major informational problem. The payoff of each "factor of production"—of each act in the sequence—must be computed before an agent can determine whether the whole sequence would be worthwhile. Every time there is a change in the world (e.g., death of a spouse, the acquisition of a better foraging tool) that affects the probable payoff of an act, or new information that allows a better evaluation of payoffs, this value needs to recomputed. Evaluating entire chains as units is not sufficient, because each item in a chain (staying behind from the hunt, making a tool, borrowing materials from a friend, etc.) may be used in another unique sequence at a later time. Therefore, effort, fitness token payoffs (rewards), opportunity costs, risks, and many other components of evaluation need to be assigned continually to classes of acts. For this reason, there should be mechanisms that assign hedonic and other motivationally informative values to acts (e.g., "dangerous," "painful," "effort-consuming," "informative," "fun," "socially approved"), tallied as intermediate weights in decision processes. Our stream of actions and daily experiences will be affectively "colored" by the assignment of these hedonic values. If our psychological mechanisms were not using present outcomes to assign a common internal currency of hedonic weights to classes of acts, there would be no function to suffering, joy, and so on. Emotion mode obviously impacts the assignment of hedonic values to acts.

Energy Level, Effort Allocation, and Mood

Overall metabolic budget will be regulated by emotion programs, as will specific allocations to various processes and facilitation or inhibition of specific activities. The effort that it takes to perform given tasks will shift accordingly, with things being easier or more effortful depending on how appropriate they are to the situation reflected by the emotion (Tooby & Cosmides, 1990a). Thus fear will make it more difficult to attack an antagonist, whereas anger will make it easier. The confidence with which a situation has been identified (i.e., emotional clarity) should itself regulate the effortfulness of situation-appropriate activities. Confusion (itself an emotional state) should inhibit the expenditure of energy on costly behavioral responses and should motivate more information gathering and information analysis. Nesse (1990) has suggested that the function of mood is to reflect the propitiousness of the present environment for action, a hypothesis with many merits. We hypothesized (Tooby & Cosmides, 1990a) a similar function of mood, based on recognizing that the action–reward ratio of the environment is not a function of the environment alone, but an interaction between the structure of the environment and the individual's present understanding of it. (By "understanding," we mean the correspondence between the structure of the environment, the structure of the algorithms, and the weightings and other information they use as parameters.) The phenomenon that should regulate this aspect of mood is a perceived discrepancy between expected and actual payoff. The suspension of behavioral activity accompanied by very intense cognitive activity in depressed people looks like an effort to reconstruct models of the world so that future action can lead to payoffs, in part through stripping away previous valuations that led to unwelcome outcomes. Depression should be precipitated by (1) a heavy investment in a behavioral enterprise that was expected to lead to large payoffs that either failed to materialize or were not large enough to justify the investment; or (2) insufficient investment in maintaining a highly valued person or condition that was subsequently lost (possibly as a consequence); or (3) gradual recognition by situation detectors that one's long-term pattern of effort and time expenditure has not led to a sufficient level of evolutionarily meaningful reward, when implicitly compared to alternative life paths (the condition of Dickens' Scrooge). Discrepancies between expected and actual payoffs can occur in the other direction as well: Joy, or a precipitated surge of happiness, reflects an emotion program that evolved to respond to the condition of an unexpectedly good outcome. It functions to recalibrate previous value states that had led to underinvestment in, or underexpectation for, the successful activities or choices. Moreover, energy reserves that were being sequestered under one assumption about future prospects can be released, given new, more accurate expectations about a more plentiful or advantageous future. Similarly, one can be informed of bad outcomes to choices not made: For example, one may discover that a company one almost invested in went bankrupt, or that the highway one almost took was snowed in. Information of this kind leads to a strengthening of the decision variables used (experienced as pleasure), which is sometimes mistaken for pleasure in the misfortune of others. Reciprocally, one can be informed of good outcomes to choices not made, which will be experienced as unpleasant.

Recalibrational Emotions, Evolved Regulatory Variables, and Imagined Experience

Information about outcomes is not equally spread throughout all points in time and all situations. Some situations are information-dense, full of ancestrally stable cues that reliably predicted the fitness consequences of certain decisions or revealed important variables (e.g., discovering who your father really is or how good a friend someone has been to you) and could therefore be used to alter weightings in decision rules.

Indeed, we expect that the architecture of the human mind is full of evolved variables whose function is to store summary magnitudes that are useful for regulating behavior and computation. These are not explicit concepts, representations, or goal states, but rather registers or indices that acquire their meaning by the evolved behavior-controlling and computation-controlling procedures that access them. Such regulatory variables may include measures of: how valuable to the individual a mate is, a child is, one's own life is, etc.; how stable or variable the food productivity of the habitat is; the distribution of condition-independent mortality in the

habitat; one's expected future lifespan or period of efficacy; how good a friend someone has been to you; the extent of one's social support; one's aggressive formidability; one's sexual attractiveness; one's status or self-esteem; the status of the coalition one belongs to; present energy stores; present health; the degree to which subsistence requires collective action; and so on.

Most evolutionarily recurrent situations that select for emotion programs involve the discovery of information that allows the recomputation of one or more of these variables. Recalibration (which, when consciously accessible, appears to produce rich and distinct feeling states) is therefore a major functional component of most emotion programs. Jealousy, for example, involves several sets of recalibrations (e.g., dimunition in estimate of one's own mate value, diminution of trust). Indeed, "recalibrational emotion programs" are emotion programs such as guilt, grief, depression, shame, and gratitude, whose primary function is to carry out such recomputations (Tooby & Cosmides, 1990a) rather than to orchestrate any short-run behavioral response. These are emotion programs that have appeared puzzling from a functional perspective, because the feelings they engender interfere with short-term utilitarian action that an active organism might be expected to engage in.

Consider guilt. Hamilton's (1964) rule defines the selection pressures that acted to build the circuits governing how organisms are motivated to allocate benefits between self and kin. This rule says nothing, however, about the procedures by which a mechanism could estimate the value of, say, a particular piece of food to oneself and one's kin. The fitness payoffs of such acts of assistance vary with circumstances. Consequently, each decision about where to allocate assistance depends on inferences about the relative weights of these variables. These nonconscious computations are subject to error. Imagine a mechanism that evolved to allocate food according to Hamilton's rule, situated (for example) in a hunter–gatherer woman. The mechanism in the woman has been using the best information available to her to weight the relative values of meat to herself and her sister, perhaps reassuring her that it is safe to be away from her sister for a while. The sudden discovery that her sister, since she was last contacted, has been starving and has become sick functions as an information-dense situation allowing the recalibration of the algorithms that weighted the relative values of the meat to self and sister. The sister's sickness functions as a cue that the previous allocation weighting was in error and that the variables need to be reweighted—including all of the weightings embedded in habitual action sequences. We believe that guilt functions as an emotion mode specialized for recalibration of regulatory variables that control tradeoffs in welfare between self and other (Tooby & Cosmides, 1990a).

One significant subcomponent of these recomputational bouts is imagined experience, including both factual and counterfactual elements to potentiate branching decision points and the variables that govern them (Cosmides & Tooby, in press). Previous courses of action are brought to mind ("I could have helped then; why didn't I think to?"), with the effect of resetting choice points in decision rules. The negative valence of depression may be explained similarly: Former actions that seemed pleasurable in the past, but that ultimately turned out to lead to bad outcomes, are reexperienced in imagination with a new affective coloration, so that in the future entirely different weightings are called up during choices.

Recalibrational Releasing Engines

The EEA was full of event relationships (e.g., "Mother is dead") and psychophysical regularities (e.g., "Blood indicates injury") that cued reliable information about the functional meanings and properties of things, events, persons, and regulatory variables to the psychological architecture. For example, certain body proportions and motions indicated immaturity and need, activating the emotion program of experiencing cuteness (see Eibl-Ebesfeldt, 1970). Others indicated sexual attractiveness (Symons, 1979; Buss, 1994). To be moved with gratitude, to be glad to be home, to see someone desperately pleading, to hold one's newborn baby in one's arms for the first time, to see a family member leave on a long trip, to encounter someone desperate with hunger, to hear one's baby cry with distress, to be warm while it is storming outside—these all *mean* something to us. How does this happen? In addition to the situation-detecting algorithms associated with major emotion programs such as fear, anger, or jealousy, we believe that humans have a far

larger set of evolved specializations that we call "recalibrational releasing engines." These also involve situation-detecting algorithms, but their function is to trigger appropriate recalibrations, including affective recalibrations, when certain evolutionarily recognizable situations are encountered. By coordinating the mental contents of two individuals in the same situation (since both intuitively know, for example, that the loss of one's mother is, as a default, experienced as a sad and painful event), these programs also facilitate communication and culture learning, both of which depend on a shared frame of reference. Although these pervasive microprograms construct a great deal of our world, investigations into adaptations of this nature are only beginning.

The Role of Imagery and Emotion in Planning

Imagery is the representation of perceptual information in a format that resembles actual perceptual input. In the evolution of animal nervous systems, simpler designs preceded more complex designs. The evolutionary designs of all modern species, including humans, use distinctive constellations of perceptual inputs as signals of states of affairs (for a rabbit, the outline of a hawk silhouette means a hawk is swooping in). Consequently, the key to unlocking and activating many complex evolved decision and evaluation programs was chained to the present—to being in an environment displaying specific perceptually detectable cues and cue constellations (sweetness, predators, running sores, emotion expressions).

There is a large inventory of wisdom stored in such programs, but this information initially could only be used by organisms in the environment displaying the activating cues—a profound limitation. An important design advance was achieved when psychological architectures evolved in which these programs could be accessed by feeding a decoupled fictional or counterfactual set of perceptual images, or event relations, so that the response of these programs could be experienced and analyzed as part of planning and other motivational and recalibrational functions (Tooby & Cosmides, 1990a; Cosmides & Tooby, in press). For example, the earlier design would go into a fear emotion mode, and flee the predator when encountered. The new design could imagine that a planned course of action would, as a side effect, bring it into confrontation with a predator; experience (in appropriately attenuated and decoupled form) the fear program; and recognize that prospective, potential course of action as one to be avoided.

Recreating cues through imagery in a decoupled mode triggers the same emotion programs (minus their behavioral manifestations), and allows the planning function to evaluate imagined situations by using the same circuits that evaluate real situations. This allows alternative courses of action to be evaluated in a way similar to the way in which experienced situations are evaluated. In other words, image-based representations may serve to unlock, for the purposes of planning, the same evolved mechanisms that are triggered by an actual encounter with a situation displaying the imagined perceptual and situational cues. For example, imagining the death of your child can call up the emotion state you would experience had this actually happened, activating previously dormant algorithms and making new information available to many different mechanisms. As many have recognized, this simulation process can help in making decisions about future plans: Even though you have never actually experienced the death of a child, for example, an imagined death may activate an image-based representation of extremely negative proprioceptive cues that "tell" the planning function that this is a situation to be avoided. Paradoxically, grief provoked by death may be a by-product of mechanisms designed to take imagined situations as input: It may be intense so that, if triggered by imagination in advance, it is properly deterrent. Alternatively (or additionally), grief may be intense in order to recalibrate weightings in the decision rules that governed choices prior to the death. If your child died because you made an incorrect choice (and, given the absence of a controlled study with alternative realities, a bad outcome always raises the probability that you made an incorrect choice), then experiencing grief will recalibrate you for subsequent choices. Death may involve guilt, grief, and depression because of the problem of recalibration of weights on courses of action. You may be haunted by guilt, meaning that courses of action retrospectively judged to be erroneous may be replayed in imagination over and over again, until the reweighting is accomplished. Similarly, joyful experiences may be savored—that is, replayed with attention to all of the details of the experience, so that every step of the course of action can be colored with positive weightings as it is rehearsed, again until the simulated experience of these pseudo-"learning trials" has sufficiently reweighted the decision rules. The same principle may explain why rape victims often report experiencing horrifying unbidden images of the attack for 6-18 months after it has happened: The mind is replaying the trauma; running it through various decision rules and inference procedures; sifting it for clues of how to avoid such situations in the future; giving a different affective coloration to some of the locations, behaviors, and decisions that preceded the attack; and connecting them to a weighting of just how bad the consequent outcome was. After the 6- to 18-month period, the unbidden images suddenly stop, in a way that is sometimes described as "like a fever breaking." This would be the point at which either the calibration is finished or there is no more to be learned from the experience (on unbidden images after trauma, see Horowitz, 1978). One might expect the same phenomenon in combat veterans, with posttraumatic stress disorder being an extreme version in which, for some reason, the shutoff mechanism malfunctions (Pitman & Orr, 1995).

Culture, Ontogeny, and Individual Differences

How this theory of emotion can be integrated with models of culture, models of human development, and models of individual differences must be treated elsewhere (see Tooby & Cosmides, 1990b, for an extended analysis of the relationship between emotions and individual differences; see Tooby & Cosmides, 1992, for a discussion of culture). It is important to recognize, however, that the claim that evolved emotion programs are reliably developing aspects of a universal human nature does not necessarily imply fixed and uniform outcomes either for individuals or for cultures. Computational programs often have large numbers of open parameters, allowing their expression in adults to be highly variable; until the mapping of the emotion programs is done, and tested cross-culturally (as Ekman and his associates did for facial expression), the range of variation will not be known.

HEURISTIC FUNCTIONS
OF THE THEORY

The discussion so far should give some indications of how this theoretical approach allows the construction of testable, functional models for each emotion, and for the relations between emotion programs and other aspects of psychological functioning. The existence of such a theory also allows the discovery of previously unsuspected emotion states. Consideration of recurrent situations our ancestors would have had to be good at solving can prompt one to look for emotion modes even if one has never experienced them oneself (Cosmides & Tooby, 1994). A possible example is hunting. Humans are not just prey, equipped with fear emotions; they have also been predators for millions of years. A hunting emotion mode (predatoriness) may involve a special state of alert attention; suppression of any desire to talk (even before a particular animal is being stalked); heightened ability to read the minds of companions; heightened sense of hearing; and activation of abilities to make inferences about the presence, mental states, and activities of prey.[12]

Moreover, the functional definition of emotion given here invites the possibility that many well-known mental states should be recognized as emotion states, such as the malaise engendered by infectious illness; coma; shock; the appreciation of beauty; homesickness; sexual arousal; confusion; nausea; and so on. For example, when you are sick, initiating actions and going about your daily activities is more effortful than usual; your impulse is to stay home and lie still. Although you feel as if your energy reserves are depleted, at a physical level the same fat reserves and digestively delivered glucose are available. Malaise is a computational state, not a physical one, and is designed to cope with the adaptive problem of illness, shunting energy from behavior to the immune system and possibly signaling the need for aid. Similarly, when situation-detecting algorithms detect the presence of a very grave internal injury, or the potential for one as indicated by a major blow, these may trigger coma—a mode of operation of the cognitive system that is designed to prevent *any* discretionary movement. The functions of coma, in a world before hospitals, were to prevent further injury from being done, to minimize blood loss and internal hemorrhaging, and to allow the mobilization of the body's resources toward repair of immediate threats to life. Note that a coma is not a physically mandated state of paralysis; it is a computational state—technically, "a state of unconsciousness from which the patient cannot be roused" (Miller, 1976, p. 46), or "unarousable unresponsiveness" (Berkow, 1992, p. 1398)—which occurs even when there has been no damage to the motor system.

PUZZLES OF CONSCIOUSNESS
AND PHENOMENOLOGY

Emotions have a species-typical computational design, even if the quality of people's conscious experience in an emotion state varies. Phenomena such as hypnotic blindness and blindsight—where people lack the conscious experience of seeing, yet can be shown to be processing visual information—demonstrate that a computational state can exist without a person's being aware of it. Moreover, there are many double dissociations between awareness and physiological states. That amputees experience phantom limbs shows that one can be aware of a nonexistent physiological state (such as the presence of a nonexistent leg!), whereas anosagnosics are unaware of having a paralyzed limb and deny that it is true, even in the face of evidence (Prigatano & Schacter, 1991). Phenomena such as these show that whether a person becomes aware of an internal state is governed by machinery quite separate from that which creates the state itself. Hence awareness of a state such as an emotion cannot be what defines the presence of that state. The theoretical approach to the emotions described in this chapter provides criteria for assessing whether a person is in an emotion state (i.e., is running a particular emotion program), regardless of whether the person admits it or is aware of it (or whether their culture has a word for it). The study of emotion can coexist with individual differences in the extent to which people metacognize about, or otherwise become aware of, their own emotion states (see, e.g., Weinberger, 1990, on repressors). At present, there is no validated, widely agreed-upon theory of the nature or function of consciousness. Although an eventual scientific understanding of consciousness will be an important breakthrough, the study of the emotions can proceed without becoming entangled in the limitations of our present lack of understanding of consciousness.

ACKNOWLEDGMENTS

We would like to thank Daphne Bugental, David Buss, Martin Daly, Paul Ekman, Alan Fridlund, Steve Pinker, Don Symons, and Margo Wilson for many stimulating discussions of the issues discussed in this chapter. The financial support for this chapter was generously provided by National Science Foundation Grant No. BNS9157-449 to John Tooby, by the James S. McDonnell Foundation, and by the Research Across Disciplines program of the Office of Research, University of California, Santa Barbara.

NOTES

1. If there is no repeated structure, or no cues to signal the presence of a repeated structure, then selection cannot build an adaptation to address the situation.
2. Marks (1987, pp. 68–69) vividly conveys how many aspects of behavior and physiology may be entrained by certain kinds of fear:

   During extreme fear humans may be "scared stiff" or "frozen with fear." A paralyzed conscious state with abrupt onset and termination is reported by survivors of attacks by wild animals, by shell-shocked soldiers, and by more than 50% of rape victims (Suarez & Gallup, 1979). Similarities between tonic immobility and rape-induced paralysis were listed by Suarez & Gallup (features noted by rape victims are in parentheses): (1) profound motor inhibition (inability to move); (2) Parkinsonian-like tremors (body-shaking); (3) silence (inability to call out or scream); (4) no loss of consciousness testified by retention of conditioned reactions acquired during the immobility (recall of details of the attack); (5) apparent analgesia (numbness and insensitivity to pain); (6) reduced core temperature (sensation of feeling cold); (7) abrupt onset and termination (sudden onset and remission of paralysis); (8) aggressive reactions at termination (attack of the rapist after recovery); (9) frequent inhibition of attack by a predator. . . .

3. In Tooby and Cosmides (1990b), we show why a universal, species-typical design for adaptations (but not for functionless traits) is a necessary outcome of the evolutionary process in species like humans, who are long-lived, reproduce sexually, and exhibit an open population structure.
4. Of course, there are some situations involving high likelihoods of immediate death, such as confrontation with a lion or with an armed, murderous adversary. In such a situation, the long-term effects may be dwarfed by the magnitude of short-term effects: A fear emotion program may mobilize nearly all of the resources of the individual, with little regard to saving reserves for the future, because failure to escape will eliminate any future. Indeed, one expects that one important evolved regulatory variable that governs emotions as well as other programs will be an "efficacy discount rate": Given the evidence available to the individual at any given present moment, specialized machinery can compute and store an internalized expectation about how long the organism will continue to live and/or be efficacious. Such a regulatory variable can be used in a number of psychological machines that need to calibrate, in some form, the answer to this question: How are present returns valued compared to future returns? The steeper the discount rate, the more the individual's emotion programs will be calibrated to choose present payoffs over activities that lead to deferred but larger fitness payoffs (e.g., individuals with steep discount rates will find impulse control more difficult) (see Wilson and Daly, 1997).
5. We use "information-processing," "cognitive," and "computational" interchangeably.
6. We are presently researching how various emotion-provoking situations differentially activate specialized reasoning circuits for cheater detection, bluff detection, and precaution detection.
7. We see no principled reason for distinguishing drive states from other emotion programs, and suspect that this practice originated from outdated notions of natural selection that separated "survival-related" functions (hunger, thirst) from other functions, such as mate acquisition or reciprocity.
8. The evolutionary purpose of deceitful emotional expressions is to (falsely) communicate the same two things.
9. Some emotions may be communicative as an essential part of their function. For example, certain forms of happiness (as distinct from pleasure) as a program may have evolved to handle the situation in which something good has happened and the organism is benefited by informing those present (perhaps by gaining their approval or support).
10. For this reason, the existence of a distinctive expression is not a necessary aspect of an emotion, or part of its definition.
11. Because many types of information may be used over and over again in unforeseeable contexts (e.g., about personal preferences), the best decision rule for whether to release such categories of information will be one that takes into account how much overlap in interest there is between the recipient of the emotion signal and the sender. A deceit that places false information in the mind of a cooperator may help initially, but as it spreads outside of the initial context, it may lead to an endless subsequent series of well-intended acts directed toward the deceiver that go awry because of the falsehood. This may help answer the deep puzzle of why it is easier to change the degree of emotion communication than it is to be deceitful with emotional expression (top actors are paid enormous sums for this unusual talent)—indeed, the puzzle of why modifying one's facial expression should pose *any* difficulty, while choosing different words is effortless.
12. Studies investigating adaptations for hunting are being conducted by Larry Sugiyama, Department of Anthropology, University of Oregon, and H. Clark Barrett, Center for Evolutionary Psychology, University of California at Santa Barbara.

REFERENCES

Barkow, J., Cosmides, L., & Tooby, J. (Eds.) (1992). *The adapted mind: Evolutionary psychology and the generation of culture.* New York: Oxford University Press.

Baron-Cohen, S. (1995). *Mindblindness: An essay on autism and theory of mind.* Cambridge, MA: MIT Press.

Berkow, R. (Ed.). (1992). *The Merck manual of diagnosis and therapy* (16th ed.). Rahway, NJ: Merck.

Buss, D. M. (1994). *The evolution of desire.* New York: Basic Books.

Cannon, W. (1929). *Bodily changes in pain, hunger, fear and rage: Researches into the function of emotional excitement.* New York: Harper & Row.

Cosmides, L. (1989). The logic of social exchange: Has natural selection shaped how humans reason? Studies with the Wason selection task. *Cognition, 31,* 187–276.

Cosmides, L., & Tooby, J. (1987). From evolution to behavior: Evolutionary psychology as the missing link. In J. Dupre (Ed.), *The latest on the best: Essays on evolution and optimality* (pp. 276–306). Cambridge, MA: MIT Press.

Cosmides, L., & Tooby, J. (1989). Evolutionary psychology and the generation of culture, Part II. Case study: A computational theory of social exchange. *Ethology and Sociobiology, 10,* 51–97.

Cosmides, L., & Tooby, J. (1992). Cognitive adaptions for social exchange. In J. Barkow, L. Cosmides, & J. Tooby (Eds.), *The adapted mind: Evolutionary psychology and the generation of culture* (pp. 163–228). New York: Oxford University Press.

Cosmides, L., & Tooby, J. (1994). Beyond intuition and instinct blindness: The case for an evolutionarily rigorous cognitive science. *Cognition, 50,* 41–77.

Cosmides, L., & Tooby, J. (1997) Dissecting the computational architecture of social inference mechanisms. In G. Bock & G. Cardeco (Eds.), *Characterizing human psychological adaptations* (Ciba Symposium No. 208, pp. 132–156). Chichester, England: Wiley.

Cosmides, L., & Tooby, J. (in press). Consider the source: The evolution of cognitive adaptations for decoupling and metarepresentation. In D. Sperber (Ed.), *Metarepresentations: A multidisciplinary perspective.* New York: Oxford University Press.

Crawford, C., & Krebs, D. (Eds.). (1998). *Handbook of evoluionary psychology.* Mawah, NJ: Erlbaum.

Daly, M., & Wilson, M. (1988). *Homicide.* New York: Aldine.

Daly, M., Wilson, M., & Weghorst, S. J. (1982). Male sexual jealousy. *Ethology and Sociobiology, 3,* 11–27.

Derryberry, D., & Tucker, D. (1994). Motivating the focus of attention. In P. M. Neidenthal & S. Kitayama (Eds.), *The heart's eye: Emotional influences in perception and attention* (pp. 167–196). San Diego, CA: Academic Press.

Eibl-Ebesfeldt, I. (1970). *Ethology: The biology of behavior.* New York: Holt, Rinehart & Winston.

Ekman, P. (Ed.). (1982). *Emotion in the human face.* (2nd ed.). Cambridge, England: Cambridge University Press.

Ekman, P. (1985). *Telling lies.* New York: Norton.

Ekman, P. (1994). Strong evidence for universals in facial expressions. *Psychological Bulletin, 115,* 268–287.

Ekman, P., Levenson, R., & Friesen, W. (1983). Autonomic nervous system activities distinguishes between emotions. *Science 221,* 1208–1210.

Fiddick, L., Cosmides, L., & Tooby, J. (in press). No interpretation without representation: The role of domain-specific representations and inferences in the Wason selection task. *Cognition.*

Frank, R. (1988). *Passions within reason: The strategic role of the emotions.* New York: Norton.

Fredrickson, B. (1998). What good are positive emotions? *Review of General Psychology, 2,* 300–319.

Fridlund, A. (1994). *Human facial expression: An evolutionary view.* San Diego, CA: Academic Press.

Gallistel, C. R. (1995). The replacement of general-purpose theories with adaptive specializations. In M. S. Gazzaniga (Ed.), *The cognitive neurosciences* (pp. 1255–1267). Cambridge, MA: MIT Press.

Garcia, J. (1990). Learning without memory. *Journal of Cognitive Neuroscience, 2,* 287–305.

Gazzaniga, M. S. (Ed.). (1995). *The cognitive neurosciences.* Cambridge, MA: MIT Press.

Gigerenzer, G., & Murray, D. (1987). *Cognition as intuitive statistics.* Hillsdale NJ: Erlbaum.

Gould, S. J. (1997 June 12). Darwinian fundamentalism. *New York Review of Books*, pp. 34–38.

Hamilton, W. D. (1964). The genetical evolution of social behaviour. *Journal of Theoretical Biology, 7,* 1–52.

Hirschfeld, L., & Gelman, S. (Eds.). (1994). *Mapping the mind: Domain specificity in cognition and culture.* New York: Cambridge University Press.

Hirshleifer, J. (1987). On the emotions as guarantors of threats and promises. In J. Dupre (Ed.), *The latest on the best: Essays on evolution and optimality* (pp. 307–326). Cambridge, MA: MIT Press.

Horowitz, M. (1978). *Image formation and cognition.* New York: Appleton-Century-Crofts.

Isen, A. (1987). Positive affect, cognitive processes, and social behavior. In L. Berkowitz (Ed.), *Advances in experimental social psychology* (Vol. 20, pp. 203–253. San Diego: Academic Press.

Jackendoff, R. (1987). *Consciousness and the computational mind.* Cambridge, MA: MIT Press.

Lazarus, R., & Lazarus, B. (1994). *Passion and reason.* New York: Oxford University Press.

LeDoux, J. (1995). In search of an emotional system in the brain: Leaping from fear to emotion to consciousness. In M. S. Gazzaniga (Ed.), *The cognitive neurosciences* (pp.1049–1061). Cambridge, MA: MIT Press.

Mackie, D., & Worth, L. (1991). Feeling good, but not thinking straight: The impact of positive mood on persuasion. In J. Forgas (Ed.), *Emotion and social judgments* (pp. 201–219). Oxford: Pergamon Press.

Marks, I. (1987). *Fears, phobias, and rituals.* New York: Oxford University Press.

Marr, D. (1982). *Vision: A computational investigation*

into the human representation and processing of visual information. San Francisco: Freeman.

Maynard Smith, J. (1982). *Evolution and the theory of games.* Cambridge England: Cambridge University Press.

Miller, S. (Ed.). (1976). *Symptoms: The complete home medical encyclopedia.* New York: Crowell.

Mineka, S., & Cook, M. (1993). Mechanisms involved in the observational conditioning of fear. *Journal of Experimental Psychology: General, 122,* 23–38.

Nesse, R. (1990). Evolutionary explanations of emotions. *Human Nature, 1,* 261–289.

Pinker, S. (1997). *How the mind works.* New York: Norton.

Pitman, R., & Orr, S. (1995). Psychophysiology of emotional and memory networks in posttraumatic stress disorder. In J. McGaugh, N. Weinberger, & G. Lynch (Eds.), *Brain and memory: Modulation and mediation of neuroplasticity* (pp. 75–83). New York: Oxford University Press.

Prigatano, G., & Schacter, D. (1991). *Awareness of deficit after brain injury.* New York: Oxford University Press.

Raymond, E. S. (1991). *The new hacker's dictionary.* Cambridge, MA: MIT Press.

Shepard, R. N. (1987). Evolution of a mesh between principles of the mind and regularities of the world. In J. Dupre (Ed.), *The latest on the best: Essays on evolution and optimality* (pp. 251–275). Cambridge, MA: MIT Press.

Shepher, J. (1983). *Incest: A biosocial view.* New York: Academic Press.

Sherry, D., & Schacter, D. (1987). The evolution of multiple memory systems. *Psychological Review, 94,* 439–454.

Suarez, S. D., & Gallup, G. G. (1979). Tonic immobility as a response to rage in humans: A theoretical note. *Psychological Record, 29,* 315–320.

Swets, J. A., Tanner, W. D., & Birdsall, T. G. (1961). Decision processes in perception. *Psychological Review, 68,* 301–340.

Symons, D. (1979). *The evolution of human sexuality.* Oxford: Oxford University Press.

Tomaka, J., Blascovich, J., Kibler, J., & Ernst, J. (1997). Cognitive and physiological antecedents of threat and challenge appraisal. *Journal of Personality and Social Psychology, 73,* 63–72.

Tooby, J. (1985). The emergence of evolutionary psychology. In D. Pines (Ed.), *Emerging Syntheses in Science: Proceedings of the Founding Workshops of the Santa Fe Institute.* Santa Fe, NM: Santa Fe Institute.

Tooby, J., & Cosmides, L. (1990a). The past explains the present: Emotional adaptations and the structure of ancestral environments. *Ethology and Sociobiology, 11,* 375–424.

Tooby, J., & Cosmides, L. (1990b). On the universality of human nature and the uniqueness of the individual: The role of genetics and adaptation. *Journal of Personality, 58,* 17–67.

Tooby, J., & Cosmides, L. (1992). The psychological foundations of culture. In J. Barkow, L. Cosmides, & J. Tooby (Eds.), *The adapted mind: Evolutionary psychology and the generation of culture* (pp.19–136). New York: Oxford University Press.

Tooby, J., & Cosmides, L. (1996). *The computational theory of communication.* Paper presented at the meeting of the Human Behavor and Evolution Society, University of Arizona, Tuscon, AZ.

Tooby, J., & Cosmides, L.(1999). *On evolutionary psychology and modern adaptationism: A reply to Stephen Jay Gould.* Manuscript submitted for publication.

Weinberger, D. A. (1990). The construct validity of the repressive coping style. In J. L. Singer, (Ed.), *Repression and dissociation: Implications for personality theory, psychopathology, and health* (pp. 337–386). Chicago: University of Chicago Press.

Williams, G. C. (1966). *Adaptation and natural selection: A critique of some current evolutionary thought.* Princeton NJ: Princeton University Press.

Wilson, M., & Daly, M. (1997). Life expectancy, economic inequality, homicide, and reproductive timing in Chicago neighborhoods. *British Medical Journal (Clinical Research Ed.), 314*(7089), 1271–1274.

CHAPTER 8

Emotion, Art, and the Humanities

Ed S. Tan

THE CONTRIBUTION OF THE HUMANITIES TO THE STUDY OF EMOTION

Relevant 20th-Century Developments in the Humanities

What can the humanities contribute to an understanding of aesthetic emotions? At least according to one common view, the humanities lend their essential conceptions and methods to the scrutiny of written texts. Humanist scholars have developed elaborate conceptual systems for the critical analysis of political, moral, religious, scholarly, historical, fictional, poetical, and all other types of writings, literary or nonliterary. Their aim has been and still is to uncover the ideas underlying texts, and to separate right from wrong. In clarifying texts they come across the issues that have fueled intellectual debates over the centuries and have stirred the emotions, and they scrutinize how texts, relate to and even control the emotions.

In the 20th century three developments that are relevant for the study of emotion, have altered the humanities. First, the activities of humanists, like those of scientists, have branched into a multitude of highly specialized studies—ranging from the study of the King's position in early Celtic poetry to that of adverbs of degree in newspaper ads. They can nevertheless be grouped into the following conventional clus-

ters: philosophy, linguistics, history, and the studies of literature and the arts. Second, the humanists' attention has widened to include more than texts. The ideas conveyed by texts as cultural forms and practices, and also cultural artifacts other than texts—speech (including dialogue and conversation), images (still and moving) and musical and theatrical performances—have all become crucial objects of study. Contextual factors determining an artifact's meaning, such as a recipient's gender, have been studied as well. Third, and most recently, an exclusive focus on elitist texts and artifacts has shifted into a broader one, giving way to the study of popular—culture, notably film, television, and other new media. Taken together, these changes have added to what was already a wealth of specialized knowledge.

Social scientists need this knowledge in order to deepen their understanding of the emotional stimulus and the mechanisms of emotional appraisal. People relate to art works, to texts, and to ideas. Much of what is meaningful to their lives may include political, aesthetic, and religious ideas; books; artifacts such as paintings and photographs; television programs; fashion in dress; and lifestyle. The world of ideas and artifacts can mean just as much to them as the world of real people or the world of nature. It comes as no surprise, then, that a considerable amount of emotion in daily life appears to stem from dealing with cultural artifacts. Oatley and Duncan (1992) report a figure of 7%, and Oatley (1995) summarizes findings indicating that the emotions people experience during reading short stories are as intense as ones related to emotion episodes in daily life.

A Reverse-Design Approach to Aesthetic Emotion

Humanist, or critical, theories of art forms can be used to describe the works of art, in order to understand their design as emotional stimuli The social scientist's task is to reconstruct the emotional process from the characteristics of the stimuli that have been analyzed by the humanist, more or less in the way the archeologist attempts to reconstruct ways of life and behavior of prehistoric peoples by inference from the design of their utensils. This "reverse-design approach" to art provoked emotion is complementary to two established research traditions in psychological aesthetics and the psychology of the arts, which I will not describe systematically in this chapter. I refer the reader to the journal *Empirical Studies of the Arts*, that represents major research in psychological aesthetics more or less in the tradition of Berlyne's (1971; 1974) "new experimental aesthetics" (and more cognitive and social-psychological approaches as well). It is less easy to delineate the psychology of the arts, which integrates many psychological research areas. However, the following sources offer a reasonable overview: Crozier and Chapman (1984), Kreitler and Kreitler (1972), Langer (1953), and Winner (1982).

In this chapter I review humanist knowledge according to a number of very general categories of art works content and form: themes, style, tropes, levels of meaning, and genre. I focus on art works and leave cultural ideas aside because of space limitations. It should be noted that I cannot do justice to the intricacies and sophistication of present humanist theorizing, and thus limit myself to a global discussion of relevant topics. Without pretending to be complete in this respect, I also review some influential theoretical ideas from philosophical aesthetics relating to some of these categories. Finally, I refer to related empirical research, carried out either by scholars from the humanities or by social scientists with an interest in the questions current in the humanities, which will make

clear that the two disciplines have already begun to meet.

Before turning to the detailed review of these aspects of the emotional stimulus, I sketch the larger picture of emotion produced by art works, and the major questions related to the topic.

EMOTION IN EXPERIENCING ART WORKS: THE LARGE PICTURE AND BROAD QUESTIONS

What Is Art?

A discussion of what art is lies beyond the scope of this contribution and far beyond my own competence.[1] I take pragmatic position here by maintaining the following criteria: (1) Art works are human-made artifacts resulting from some deliberate design; (2) art works attract attention to themselves as objects; (3) art works represent a meaning that extends beyond themselves; (4) art works can have various functions, ranging from purely aesthetic to religious and entertainment or plainly functional uses. An art work can have an immediate aesthetic effect on a naïve beholder, as the romanticist conception of art would have it, but this is not necessarily so. Many if not most art works require some knowledge in the beholder, the nature of which will be discussed later. In general, I consider art works that have been accepted by experts from the humanities as valuable instances of an art form. Examples include widely varying works as the *Book of Celts,* Giotto's work, Raymond Loewy's locomotive, Peter Brooks' plays, Bruckner's symphonies, and Jane Campion's films.

Emotion in Experiencing Art and in Real Life

The major question underlying all discussion on aesthetic emotion is whether or not art works elicit genuine emotions—that is, emotions as we know them in the reality of life. If we call all cognitive and feeling states caused by art works "aesthetic," we can then ask whether there are "aesthetic emotions"—that is, emotions in the proper sense of the word, caused by a work of art.

The functional view of emotion suggests a set of criteria for distinguishing emotion from other cognitive and feeling states. The most complete elaboration of the functional perspective can be found in Frijda's (1986) theory of the emotions. In addition, this theory is eminently suited to this chapter's purposes because it gives an account of emotional experience, focusing especially on the meaning of the stimulus and on the way it is being appraised by the subject. (For the latter aspect, see also Frijda 1993, and Chapter 5 of the present volume.) The core of the theory can be summarized in a number of basic tenets or laws (see Frijda, 1986, Ch. 9, and Frijda, 1988), which together constitute the definition of "emotion." The shortest possible definition is that emotion is a system for the realization of an individual's concerns. Events are appraised as relevant for concerns. The emotional response consists of a change in action readiness and the experience of the event's meaning in terms of concerns. The response is difficult to resist; in other words, it has "control precedence."

Table 8.1 offers an overview of these laws of emotion. Each offers a starting point for comparing aesthetic emotion with emotion in real life, and each raises questions of what is special in art-provoked emotion. Most of these questions have been addressed by humanist scholars, and the third column of Table 8.1 summarizes these. The fourth column offers some examples of the issues raised in the comparison.

In conclusion, if we consider the issues raised by comparing art-provoked with real-life emotion, it seems that art may be both an intensifying and a weakening condition in the operation of the laws. For instance, a suspension of disbelief in the reality of fiction opens the way for strong R-emotion, but it may also be argued that suspension is a willful act that has its price in terms of a decrease in perceived reality.

A- and R-emotions; Interest as a Characteristic Response

Emotions have objects. Art works can be appraised in at least two ways, each resulting in a possible distinct object of emotion. One is the art work as a man made, material artifact ("Oh, what a lovely painting!"). Emotions related to the artifact may be called "A-emotions." The other object is the representation of something besides the artifact itself ("Yech, what an ugly man!"). Figurative paintings represent persons and objects in another time and place, a novel conjures up a fictional world; a sculpture may mimic a human figure, a piece of music may evoke reveries and memories; and so on. Theories of art can help in classifying the relation between a particular artifact and the world it represents. "Mimesis," "diegesis," "symbolization," "make-believe," and "expression" are examples of relevant theoretical concepts. Emotions resulting from appraisals involving elements of the represented world are called "R-emotions."[2] The relations between the materiality of the art work and the represented elements, or the solutions to the problems that this relationship poses to the artist are subject to A-appraisal. Ascribing intentions, failures, or successes to the artist is also part of A-appraisal.

As an example, consider Robert Capa's 1936 photograph "Death of a Loyalist Soldier." We see a soldier falling over at the moment he is hit by a bullet. We can have A pleasure ("Excellent picture. Dramatic composition, high symbolic value, extremely realistic as such a picture should be"), A-surprise (when we have never seen such a photograph) A-admiration ("A great picture by Capa"), and A-wonder ("The soldier was caught exactly when he was hit. Was that lucky timing? Capa must have

TABLE 8.1. Overview of the Laws of Emotion According to Frijda (1986, 1988) and Questions Raised

Law of emotion	Summary of tenets	Selected issues raised as to art-provoked (a.p.) emotion	Representative questions
1. Law of concern	Emotion signals activation of a concern; there is no emotion without concern. Source	What are the concerns addressed by art works? If the art experience involves a "disinterested attitude," there	Why do some people cry upon hearing a Beethoven sonata? Is "psychical distance" a necessary

(continued)

TABLE 8.1. *(continued)*

Law of emotion	Summary of tenets	Selected issues raised as to art-provoked (a.p.) emotion	Representative questions
	concerns include curiosity, proximity, coherence, and values.	cannot be any a.p. emotion. Is there a concern for beauty?	element of the art experience (Bullough, 1912–1913)?
2. Law of situational meaning	Emotions reflect the meaning of events. Components of emotional meaning relate to concerns and to action possibilities. Core components common to all emotions include valence, difficulty, and reality. "Primary appraisal" is an elementary process and antecedent of emotion. "Secondary appraisal" is part of the emotional response, the content of emotion; it requires more cognitive elaboration.	Does art provoke an immediate appreciation? Does secondary appraisal predominate? Is secondary appraisal at variance with primary? Does a.p. emotion feed back onto the beholder's self? What are the typical components of emotional meaning in art? What about the action possibilities appraised in an art work?	Why does an initially repelling scene in a Francis Bacon painting fascinate a viewer in the second examination? Do readers understand themselves because of having sympathetic emotion in reading a novel? Does art involve ambiguity, conflict, retardation, etc.?
3. Law of apparent reality	Some reality must be recognized by the subject in the stimulus, if concerns are to be activated.	What is the reality of art? What is the beholder's share in it? What is the role of perceived artist intention? Is suspension of disbelief a mediating factor?	What is real about abstract art? Is illusion in such arts as film taken for real? Do art experts experience less emotion, or other emotions, than nonexperts?
4. Law of comparative feeling	Stimuli are emotional by reference to something else—for instance, the near future in acute fear, or what should have been done in guilt. Change may result in emotion.	Does the structure of art works contain internal reference points serving comparative feeling? Does the relation between the art work and the represented contribute to emotion? Do other art works serve as a reference?	Do expectancies that are built into sonatas and novel plots contribute to emotion? Does the Aristotelian cathartic effect of drama exist, and does it depend on an ordering of spectator emotions?
5. Law of closure	Emotions tend to persist. Once elicited, appraisal and action readiness of an emotion are difficult to resist.	Do a.p. emotions persist over time, and are they subject to change?	Do beholders continue or resume their appraisals after initial exposure to an art work?
6. Law of care for consequence	Emotions tend to elicit a secondary impulse toward moderation (e.g., blind rage is rare). Anticipation of adverse consequences acts as a stimulus.	Do art works have built-in emotion regulation? Does art (temporarily) liberate the beholder from care for consequences?	Is art style (e.g., abstraction) a means to moderate emotion caused by other elements of the work, e.g., theme? Are cinema viewers free to live through their sympathy, fears, etc.?

been under heavy fire himself. How did he do this?"). The appraisal of the artifact can end in emotionally laden conflict ("Is this art or moral propaganda?"). Of course, the represented element invokes emotion as well, and possibly even in the first place, for instance R-compassion ("Poor fellow"), R-sadness (when realizing that the man could have lived a happy life, or contemplating the uselessness of war), and R-disgust ("I hate to see this happen"). The examples of R-emotions demonstrate an appraisal in various stages, but always of the represented world.

Within the R-emotions we can distinguish empathetic from non-empathetic feelings. In empathetic R-emotion, the beholder imagines what the represented situation means to some represented or implied person or character. In nonempathetic R-emotion, the situation is viewed from outside, stripped of its personal meaning to anyone within the represented world. Obviously, in most cases the two kinds of R-emotion occur in combination. Capa's soldier is pitied because the situation depicted in the photograph meant the abrupt end of his life, but at the same time we are struck by the view of death in war *as a spectacle*.

Appraisal of the art work *as* an art work and appraising its content are, of course, intimately linked. A-emotion is impossible without some appraisal of the represented contents, and in more complex art we cannot get at the represented element and its implications without some analysis of style, technique, and possibly even intentions of the artist.

R-emotion is a response to an imagined situation, as the emotional stimulus is a representation. What this means is a complex problem in itself, for if no reality at all is perceived, there can be no emotion. I return to this problem shortly. Here it suffices to say that the emotional response is a feeling—that is, an emotion with a virtual action tendency, because the action repertoire is essentially empty. The reader of literature cannot act in the world of Jane Austen. In the suspense scene of the action thriller, we would like to warn the protagonist who is about to be ambushed, but we are well aware that this would be pointless, and ultimately enjoy this. A-emotion, on the contrary, is a response to a reality, but this type of aesthetic emotion faces us with the problem of the response all the same.

Most art works call for passivity, and although there may be a tendency to touch artworks such as sculptures, most art (and not only the classic genres) does not invite viewers to take action. Looking, listening, and reading are the appropriate responses—the ones art works have been designed for (e.g., Walton, 1994). What responses to all art works have in common is a tendency toward paying attention to the art work, and this tendency may be an emotional action tendency when the beholder cannot resist exploring the artwork in a search for further understanding and enjoyment of its meaning, form, and style. The response is close to "fascination," but since this term has too strong a connotation of irrational and complete surrender, which are not necessarily present or dominant in the experience of art, "flow" is a better description. (Csikszentmihalyi, 1990).

The core of the appraisal, then, is challenge mixed with promise; the action tendency is a search for understanding; the emotion is *interest*, understood as more than a merely cognitive state. (See Izard, 1977; Panksepp, 1982; Tan, 1995; Tomkins, 1984; but see also Ortony & Turner, 1990, and Lazarus, 1991b, who oppose the view of interest as an emotion.) The difference from the purely cognitive state is that there is an emotional action tendency to spend attention and effort, which has control precedence (Frijda, 1986 and Chapter 5, this volume), in the sense that it persists in the face of distracting stimuli. Interest provoked by art works results from primary appraisal, in which some promise is recognized that relates to prospects of insight into the art work itself and into the things it represents. In experiencing a work of art, the law of closure manifests itself as a search for structure and meaning. It may continue in the absence of the art work, in some cases for weeks. An event in reality, or another work of art, may remind a person of his or her unfinished experience with that particular painting or novel, adding further meaning to it.

Furthermore, my claim is that interest is the dominant emotion in experiencing all kinds of art works. The content of a representational artifact can only be grasped when it has been understood as an artifact, and to the degree that this poses a challenge, it elicits interest. Of course, mixture with other emotions alters the experience to the point of hiding the role of interest. First, there is enjoyment in various forms. The (A-)pleasure of discovering balance in a choreography differs from the sensual (R-)pleasure of experiencing a camera movement in a lyrical part of a film. Second, in the case of representational art, all sorts of R-emotions (e.g., sympathy for a protagonist on stage or in a novel, and amusement because of a comic situation) mix with interest.

EMOTION AND EXPLANATORY CONCEPTS FROM THE HUMANITIES

In this section I review some concepts that are central to the description, interpretation, and explanation of art works by scholars in the humanities. I cannot do full justice to the complexity of the theoretical issues, as this would require a lengthy discussion by specialists from many fields of scholarship.

Themes and Emotion

Can we (re)construct the beholder's emotion from the theme of an art work—for instance, the subject of a painting or the central conflict of a drama? In a most simplified view of the operation of emotional themes in art, "themes" are materials available in the physical and cultural world that have an emotion potential, that are already on people's minds—ready, as it were, to be launched wrapped up in some representation. Themes, then, are the major causes of R-emotions.

A major challenge to this view is that art may be about anything, in principle and in practice. It follows that not all themes dealt with in art works have an emotion potential by themselves—that is, regardless of the way they are represented in some art form. An anatomical lesson, featuring a corpse being dissected, is exciting per se. The fish, fruits, and vases gathered in a still life do not provoke any emotion in everyday life; skillfully portrayed, however, they may evoke an emotional kind of contemplation. Nevertheless, there seem to be popular themes (or, rather, themes in popular art) that have an appeal because of their emotion potential, almost regardless of the particular art form.

1. *Popular themes.* Studies of myth and folk tales—for instance, those of Campbell (1949) and Propp (1968)—have laid bare recurrent patterns in the organization and texture of ideas that provoke certain emotions. Well-known examples are the incest theme (as in the Oedipus myth) and the theme of the revenge of the gods angered or made envious by humans, both of which are supposed to inspire fear (see

Kerényi, 1981). The popular culture of our time also has emotional themes that seem to be universal. The nostalgic portrayal of nature scenes without any sign of human presence seems attractive to viewers from varying educational backgrounds (Lindauer, 1990). Eternal themes (death, sex, violence, good versus evil, fate, threat, error, betrayal, love, fortune, misfortune, hubris, etc.) have the potential for eliciting emotion, because they can be hypothesized to touch on *basic concerns* and contain *core components of emotional meaning*, such as valence (including loss and gain) and difficulty (Frijda, 1986). One could also say that they overlap with the core relational themes proposed by Lazarus (1991a) in his theory of emotion, such as "having failed to live up to an ego-ideal," (related to shame) and "taking in or being too close to an indigestible object or idea" (related to disgust). It should be added that many themes in figurative and narrative arts portray the fate of others, and that the beholder's self is only obliquely addressed. Many themes invoke "fortune-of-others" emotions in the first place, as Ortony, Clore, and Collins (1988) have dubbed these. Relevance to basic concerns and reflection of core components of emotional meaning may in part explain the frequency of such themes as leave taking, death, victory, defeat, suffering, redemption, liberation, wealth, prosperity, virture, vice, hope, and fear.

2. *Emotion as a theme.* Some art works portray happy or sad persons, or suggest their inner world. Other art works represent an emotion without showing any person having it. In both cases the works of art are about emotion, but only in the latter case do we call the art work "expressive." At first sight an expressive work of art would seem more effective in eliciting emotion in the beholder than a work portraying a person with an emotion, other things being equal, but I do not know of any studies that directly confirm this assumption.

3. *Themes specific for art works.* Some recurring themes in the arts have been given specific emotion labels for a very long time. These have no equals in qualifying for being called the emotional themes of art and literature, and seem to be tailored to the needs of a reverse-design approach to aesthetic emotion. We all know that the comic makes us laugh, the tragic weep, the fantastic wonder, and the uncanny shiver; most of us also know that humanistic knowledge about the stimulus is widely available. But there are many of other, comparable themes that derive from art rather than from the physical or so-

cial world, and that deserve study by social scientists because of the particular appraisal that appears to be related to their functioning. What is the emotion provoked by the "grotesque," the absurd," the "holy," the "picturesque," or the "sentimental"?[3] In these cases, a thorough analysis of what is meant by such classifications is called for. My favorite candidate is the "sublime," a theme that at least in the 18th century stood for materials that overwhelm and threaten the beholders, making them feel insignificant in the first instance, and then enabling them to recover and regain mastery over their imagination and negative emotion. The two stages may alternate, resulting in a series of attractions and repulsions. Kant (1977), whose description I have just borrowed from, called the sublime in art that which causes delight. Delight differs from pleasure, as it involves a lessening of negative valence rather than a positive valence of the stimulus. Danger and pain coupled with an awareness that these are not happening to ourselves but to others, are delightful. (Delight could be a response to Capa's photograph we just discussed!) It has been observed that although hardly any critic, let alone a common beholder of art works, uses the term "sublime" today, the combination of terror with some distancing element is far from obsolete (von der Thüsen, 1997). The distancing elements often include humor (e.g., Quentin Tarantino's film *Pulp Fiction,*) and always a third-person, or witness perspective, rather than a first-person, one. The example of the sublime offers an example of a critical notion pointing at essentials of the design of the art work as an emotional stimulus. Valuable hypotheses are obtained about the complexity of the multistage appraisal that may be characteristic of art.

Reconstructing emotion provoked by art contents other than represented events, such as deeper layers of thematic meaning, is often extremely difficult. Do men and women appraise the Oedipus theme in the same way, and could there have been a gender difference in antiquity? Does the "defying authority" theme in Sophocles's *Antigone* elicit less fear in democratic than in autocratic societies? Will Capa's photograph soon be part of a gallery of cliché emblems for the concept of war, instead of inciting awe in the viewer? Beholders may have extensive knowledge and strong attitudes about themes that determine their appraisal of a particular art work, and this knowledge is used in what may be a complex and gradual process of appraisal.

A proper understanding of aesthetic emotion, then, requires extensive knowledge of the meanings themes have for artists and their particular audiences. The humanities have yielded a wealth of interpretative studies on the meaning of art works—for instance, within the tradition of iconology established by Panofsky (1939/1962). Translating this knowledge into hypotheses about the quality and strength of particular emotions produced by art works in a given group of beholders may proceed by identifying culture-related elements of concerns and appraisal.[4]

Finally, a question most relevant for the study of emotion is whether non-representational arts, such as music and abstract sculpture or experimental film, can convey content themes that contribute to aesthetic emotion—in interaction with style, of course. At least since Plato it has been argued that music has an immediate emotional effect, with one key arousing excitement, and another provoking a serene mood.[5] It may be that music has a direct effect on motor programs that are part of basic emotions, such as joy, sadness, and love. That is, music may match with movements and associated kinesthetic sensations that are part of the expression of basic emotions. The work of Clynes (Clynes, 1980; Clynes & Nettheim, 1982) has empirically demonstrated such a match.

It is a most interesting question whether visual arts such as dance and abstract film are expressive in the same way,[6] and one could even propose that static visual art, such as abstract paintings, might touch directly on expressive motor programs in the viewer. For example, it has often been suggested that Mondrian's last paintings, such as *Victory Boogie-Woogie,* may provoke a synesthetic sense of rhythm.[7] Other researchers have suggested that there is some minimal cognitive process in appraising music. Levinson (1990) holds that the musical theme that is recognized is a concept of an emotion (e.g., sadness). The listener subsequently identifies with the music, and then imagines that he or she is sad.

Style and Emotion

Style as a Characteristic Choice of Techniques

The most simplified view of the relationship between style and emotion assumes that style functions as a necessary but irrelevant container of thematic materials that really matter. Style then acts as a transparent window for passing the emotion potential that the theme has by itself. The major reason why this view is wrong is that it underestimates the functions of style, and hence its emotional effects. The concept of A-emotion is in large part based on the assumption that style is a source of emotion in its own right, whereas themes induce R-emotion in the first place.

What is "style"? If we attempt to isolate the way thematic content is presented from the content itself, a definition of style may be derived from art forms where the role of themes in experiencing a work is relatively weak, (e.g., abstract art, decorative art, music) and generalized to all art. Meyer's (1989, p. 3) definition in his work on style in music emphasizes an abstract patterning that one particular art work shares with another. Closely following Meyer, style, whether it is defined for schools, *oeuvres,* or individual works, is *a characteristic pattern in the choice of techniques made within some set of constraints.* The choice is not necessarily a deliberate one, and the constraints may arise from a number of different sources, including historical convention specific to an art form or genre, the availability of technological means, and contemporary ideology and tastes. The constraints diminish the number of options available to the artist.

The definition of style just given has been originally elaborated and proven fruitful in Gombrich's (1959/1992) history of art, which gives an account of the solution to the problem of rendering a convincing illusion of reality.

An example from the cinema may clarify this line of reasoning. Robert Bresson's film style has been characterized as "ascetic" because of the following recurrent patterns: (1) concentrating on selected details of the action, such as objects, hands, and feet; (2) leaving out or playing down of major plot events; (3) preventing the viewer from easily reading actors' expressions and behaviors; (4) abrupt cutting and short scenes; and (5) laconic use of sound (Schrader, 1972; Thompson & Bordwell, 1994) The problem to which Bresson's style is a solution can be described as (1) how to portray "a solitary individual's struggle to survive a spiritual or physical ordeal" (Thompson & Bordwell, 1994, p. 446) or (2) how to suggest a spiritual world behind the reality that is shown (Schrader, 1972). A particular artist's style is dependent on his or her freedom. There were options in solv-

ing Bresson's problem other than the ones chosen, but not everything was possible in his day, in his circle, and within his own conceptions of film art in general and his projects in particular.

The definition above may also be of help in understanding appraisal in aesthetic emotion. If style as conceived here is a psychologically real phenomenon, and I believe that it is, it can result in an emotion by itself. This must be an A-emotion, as the artifact is the emotional stimulus.

The appraisal process in style-evoked emotion has two components. One is relatively primary—the perception of some pattern or gestalt within an art work, in terms of techniques. The other is secondary and involves understanding the nature of the problem and its solution. The first takes relatively little time; the second is a slower process.[8] The primary appraisal process, the perception of patterns, is affectively pleasing, as it may answer a concern for order ("the sense of order," as Gombrich [1959/1992]claims). But not all patterns are equally pleasing. The effort needed for identifying them may be a crucial factor here. Finding structure in a painting, or completing patterns that unfold in time in arts such as music, narrative, and film, offers both difficulty or challenge and promise to the beholder. Some optimum ratio between difficulty and promise may provoke and sustain interest, followed by enjoyment. How exactly the optimum ratio is composed is the subject of research in experimental aesthetics. Features such as symmetry, balance, harmony, *Praegnanz*, typicality, and the like have been proposed as equivalents of order. Incongruity, irregularity, ambiguity and deviation from thematic prototypes (the "collative" variables, in Berlyne's [1971, 1974] aesthetics). are thought to work against order. Appraisal, then, according to this approach, involves finding unity in variety.[9]

The precise ways in which a particular artist realizes unity in variety can be appraised as his or her style. There is some evidence that style in the sense of a set of regularities (which may consist of both gestalt-like order and its opposite) across a number of works of art can readily be identified by nonexperts and even by children.[10]

The other component of appraising style is secondary, in the sense that it presupposes the first, and that it involves an awareness and understanding of (1) the options that the artist has had, (2) the degree to which the art work's patterned use of techniques is shared across some set of art works, and (3) the nature of the constraints determining the options.[11] Understanding these three elements requires a progressive knowledge of context that is not always immediately available. It requires some reflection and an additional search for sources of knowledge, such as titles, reviews, and talks with other people. Evidence is available that knowledge of canons, styles, and principles of form mediates experts' enjoyment of various works of art (see e.g., Cupchik & Gebotys, 1990, Hekkert & van Wieringen, 1996, and Winston & Cupchik, 1991, for visual art; Gaver & Mandler, 1987, for music; and Purcell, 1984, for buildings). However, the view that knowledge of the art work's background and style may contribute to its appreciation is not unequivocally documented yet (see, e.g., Temme, 1983; Russell & Milne, 1997).

To return to the example of Bresson's work, in watching his 1951 film *Diary of a Country Priest,* viewers may immediately enjoy the narrow framing of the protagonist and the repetition of camera setups in short scenes featuring him (primary appraisal of characteristic pattern of techniques). Perhaps they soon realize that the priest could have been filmed differently (other options), and only gradually and slowly —if at all—do they arrive at an understanding of why the framing is as narrow as it is ("the problem"). If their conclusion parallels Schrader's (1972) analysis, they recognize a prison metaphor, and the assignment Bresson set himself to render visible the idea of spiritual liberation. The connoisseur will recognize the "cell" as a stylistic motive in Bresson's *oeuvre.* The aesthetic emotion that any viewer may have is enjoying the gain of insight. Meanwhile, the emotion potential of the film's theme is also unfolded, and R-emotions may develop in parallel. At first, surprise, wonder, pity and aversion may be a response to the priest's self-inflicted sufferings; in the second instance, understanding of a more encompassing and problematic theme may arise, deepening R-emotion into compassion and contemplation.[12] And in the end, admiration may be felt for the film's complex symbolism and the filmmaker's skill and inventiveness.

This example illustrates how humanistic knowledge—in this case the interpretation of a film's theme and style—may help the social scientist to reconstruct aesthetic appraisal. Use of secondary sources in finding out the problems for which a particular style is the answer, and why themes may have mattered to contemporary beholders, is another type of expertise that the humanities offer to the social sciences. Many monographs on particular periods or oeuvres in the history of art are available to this end.[13]

A striking case of successful cooperation between the two academic fields is Kubovy's (1986) study of the function of perspective in Renaissance art. Kubovy argues for the robustness of perspective in art, and deals with distortions resulting from a vantage point that does not coincide with the center of projection. Drawing on relevant historical studies in art and architecture, he discusses examples of such a discrepancy. One concerns Leonardo da Vinci's *The Last Supper,* painted over a 3-year period (1495–1498). Leonardo created a discrepancy between a lower vantage point and a higher center of projection, corroborated by an illusion of continuity between the refectory room where the fresco actually is and the represented room. Kubovy shows that the continuity of the real and the virtual architecture is perfect when the fresco is seen from the center of projection, a position 4.5 meters above the real floor level. The inconsistency "pushes" you away from the low vantage point to which your body confines you, and "pulls" you up toward the center of projection." (p. 145) "thus *achieving a feeling of spiritual elevation*" (p. 148, italics added). Kubovy here exposes the artist's design from an analysis of the work of art. Like Bresson, Da Vinci may have set himself the assignment of implying a spiritual reality. See Willats (1997) for other lucid analyses of style and its relation to the meaning of an art work that are most relevant for social scientists.

Bringing to light the creative solution to artistic problems, and reconstructing the beholder's appraisal of these, are perhaps even more difficult than establishing the emotion potential of a theme. Nevertheless, the critical analysis of art works is an alternative to the naive view of the functioning of style, in that style is shown to interact with theme and cultural context in shaping aesthetic emotion. It thus refines the questions of what is universal in aesthetic emotion and what is variable. Some of the techniques making up a particular style may not lose their immediate effects on the beholder with the passage of time, but a complete understanding of the appraisal and the final emotional experience of historical beholders requires studying of additional sources.

The Contribution of Critical Theories of Art Forms and Genres

Since antiquity poetical and critical traditions have existed, and in more recent times styles of the various periods have been accompanied and led by influential writings by artists, critics, and philosophers. It is not always easy to interpret critical notions, but the debates about the meaning of *catharsis* in Aristotle, *Verfremdung* in Brecht's writings, *photogénie* in early French film criticism, or the "organicity of form" in essays on abstract postwar paintings—to name just a few examples—seem to contain valuable insights concerning essential elements of art works in aesthetic emotion. A comparative study of critical writings in relation to art works and the psychology of the period has not been undertaken so far, to my knowledge, but it may be especially valuable.

Of all critical theories of art, literary criticism is the most sophisticated. The analysis of style in relation to emotion in the reader or hearer has been the domain of classical rhetoric. Today it has branched into studies of persuasion and argumentation as part of discourse linguistics. Style in literature and its implications for emotion are studied under the rubrics of "rhetoric of fiction" (e.g., Booth, 1961; Chatman, 1990; Richards, 1929/n.d., Sternberg, 1978) and the "theory of narrative" (e.g., Genette, 1983; Prince, 1982). Topics dealt with include types of narrator and mediation of the story, and the related issue of narrative perspective; characterization; description; narrative structure, including plot structures and temporal ordering of events; realism and the role of convention; and more. As can be seen, not all parameters of literary style are equally relevant for emotion in the reader, but most do apply in one way or another to the appraisal process, probably because of the aims of traditional rhetoric (i.e., to describe the essentials of texts as emotional stimuli). For instance, perspective and type of narrator may either filter or amplify components of emotional meaning structure. Characterization may introduce distance from the protagonist, as in a comic narrative. First person narration can perfectly communicate the significance of an event for a protagonist (in case he or she is aware of it), whereas authorial narration puts events in a context, often enhancing comparative feeling. (See the fourth law of emotion in Table 8.1.)

More than any other theories of art, theories of literature have been the subject of empirical research, in which literary scholars—and affiliated researchers in theatre and film—collaborate with psychologists (especially researchers in the field of discourse processes) and sociologists. Research relevant for readers' emotions, such as interest and R-emotions, mostly has to do with the rhetoric of narration. I cannot give a complete review of the studies concerned, but the research topics listed in Table 8.2 may give an impression of the field.

TABLE 8.2. Selected Empirical Research into Various Literary Phenomena

Topic	Selected studies
1. Plot structures and manipulation of reader or viewer expectations	Brewer & Lichtenstein (1982); de Wied (1991); de Wied, Zillmann, & Ordman (1995); Cupchik & Làszló (1994); Gerrig (1989); Magliano, Dijkstra, & Zwaan (1996); Tan & Diteweg (1996)
2. Perspective and point of view	Andringa (1996); Andringa, Tan, van Horssen, & Jacobs (in press); Bourg, Risden, Thompson, & Davis (1993); Làszló (1986); Mummendey, Linneweber, & Loeschper (1984); Pitchert & Anderson (1977); Sanders & Redeker (1996); van Peer & Pander-Maat (1996)
3. Empathy	Albritton & Gerrig (1991); Davis, Hull, Young, & Warren (1987); Hakemulder (1998); Konijn (in press); Schoenmakers (1988); Tannenbaum & Gaer (1965); van der Bolt & Tellegen (1992–1993); Zillmann (1991)
4. Characterization	Hoffner & Cantor (1985); Jose & Brewer (1984); Potter (1992); Scherer (1971)
5. Imagery	Esrock (1994); Sadowski, Goetz, & Kangiser (1988)
6. Genre-defined text characteristics and genre expectations	Goldman & Kantor (1993); Halasz (1991, 1997); Zwaan (1993)

Representation and Realism

Realism is an issue that has recurred in poetics, rhetoric, and (normative) theories of art and is of utmost importance to an understanding of aesthetic emotion. For in the present view, emotion cannot exist if the stimulus does not have some reality value. To limit the discussion to representational art, the problem is that art works are distinguished from reality by the beholder, but at the same time they clearly elicit R-emotions. No viewer of the Goya etching *Bobabilicon* will claim to have seen a nightmarish giant in reality, but most will admit that they were shocked when they saw the picture for the first time. Can this shock be called a real emotion? And if so, what reality is perceived in the stimulus?

Humanistic studies have pointed to two complementary factors, mimesis and the role of learning. Art may be real to the degree that it imitates reality, and to the degree that the beholder has internalized conventions pertaining to the meaning of art works and knows how to interpret signs. However, more recently another explanation has gained currency—the "imagination hypothesis" or "make-believe theory." It holds that the beholder of an art work engages in an act of imagination or make-believe (e.g. Currie, 1995; Gombrich, 1963; Oatley, 1992; Walton, 1990, 1994). Gombrich (1963) introduced the notion that elements of an art work are substitutes for reality, rather than imitations or signs, just as a stick is a substitute for a horse in child's play. According to Walton (1990), viewers of art and readers of literature engage in imagining that they are part of the represented world. Emotion is a response that is both part of the imagination, and a result of the vividness of the imagination. Beholders are conscious of their active imagination, but imagining is not always a deliberate choice; a beholder cannot help engaging in it. Most interesting events in art and literature do not happen to the beholder but to some character in the world of make-believe. The beholder, imagines that he or she sees events happening to characters. Make-believe, then, is a condition for empathy, and empathy involves feelings that the subject has about other people (Walton, 1994). A somewhat similar theory of imagination has been put forward by Currie (1990, 1995).

Before I became familiar with Walton's work, I proposed an explanation of emotion in the film viewer that is quite similar to Walton's account of emotion (Tan, 1996). I suggested that the film viewer imagines him- or herself to be physically present in a fictional world, and that it is very difficult to resist this illusion. I also proposed that the film viewer's imaginary position in the fictional world is identical to the witness positions people take or are forced to take in the reality of daily life. For instance, when you see an accident happen from behind a window, you watch; that is all you do or can do, and that condition is part of the emotion you have. In my view, the film viewer's emotion is an instance of the broader class of witness emotions, which are real emotions in the sense defined above. As I understand Walton, his view, like mine, implies that the beholders' awareness of the imagined nature of the characters they empathize with is not relevant for the existence of empathetic feeling. The beholders pretend to see people, but they actually feel for the pretended people; they do not pretend to feel.

The make-believe theory seems plausible for three reasons. First, it does not require any likeness between substitutes and what they stand for. The stick is far removed from the hobby-horse, which in turn only catches some features of real horses. In contrast, photographic realism is relatively rare in art at large. To put the argument more generally, illusion-oriented techniques that imitate a perceptual experience, such as *trompe-l`oeil,* can only be used in art and the theatre, and even there they do not abound. Quasi-sensory likeness plays only a marginal role in literature. Not surprisingly, then, R-emotions in readers of literature have been explained by active imagination on the reader's part. Oatley (1995) has argued that objects of literature are not imitative, but instead stimulate an imaginative act. At its core is simulating characters' plans, and interpreting the events as variables and outcomes in terms of plans.

Second, the make-believe theory does not imply, as less sophisticated explanations of perceived realism seem to do, that beholders hold representations for the represented. The implication that the viewer who sees a dying soldier, rather than a picture of the death of a soldier, has a delusion is of course an implication that has to be avoided, at the cost of a rather ad hoc solution—the best-known way out probably being the hypothesis of temporary suspension of disbelief. It may still be possible that make-believe gives occasionally way to belief; that is, beholders may forget that it is only a game they are in, and can have very intense emotions, as Currie (1990) proposes. But this is not permanently the case, and the theory does not need a claim to this effect.

Third, and most relevant for our purposes, the make-believe theory links imagination to emotion. From a functional perspective, it is obvious that imagination in the sense of simulation of events and other people's mental states can result in real emotion, because being aware of the relevance for concerns of an imaginary situation (and ensuing mandatory and possible courses of actions) before the fact rather than afterward, has adaptive value (see Klinger, 1971, for a discussion of concern-related fantasies). The intensity of any R-emotion in the experience of an art work may then be a function of the imagined possibility that it opens up to the beholder. This is how art works may interact with the law of apparent reality in producing an R-emotion (cf. Frijda, 1989). It has also been proposed that fiction makes us aware of the discrepancies between reality and possibility, and thus may affect our moral beliefs (Nussbaum, 1991).

The concept of make-believe seems a priori better suited to describe the imagination process in the reader of fiction and in the viewer of theatre and film than in the viewer of painting and sculpture. In regard to painting, various historians have stressed that one of the functions that art has had is to provide lifelike, realistic depictions of people and events (cf. Freedberg, 1989). And we have some evidence that today also realism is an important determinant of preference (e.g. Berlyne & Ogilvie, 1974; Knapp, 1964), although some qualifications seem to hold.[14] In recent years "prototypicality" rather than realism has been identified as an important factor in the attractiveness of paintings. When applied to subject matter rather than to style of painting, prototypicality leaves a lot more room for the beholder's imagination than realism. Abstract attributes, perhaps as abstract as the stick in Gombrich's (1963) make-believe hobbyhorse—may contribute to prototypicality.

The make-believe theory leaves open a number of other questions. Perhaps the most important one is this: How general is the make-believe theory of realism in art? After all, representation in many art works is profoundly symbolic, metaphorical, allegorical or emblematic. Abstract concepts such as Virtue, the Sins, or Prosperity can only be represented by making use of such tropes. This fact should render us hesitant to reject theories that explain the beholder's realistic experience by referring to tacit convention and automated response to symbolism. Could make-believe theory be expanded as to incorporate the use of sophisticated, highly conventional knowledge in the process of imagination, and still account for the fairly immediate emotional appraisal of reality? And do art works contain cues or signs as to what specific game of make-believe the beholder needs to play in order to get the most emotional satisfaction out of the experience? In particular, the distinction between genres that do allow for make-believe and those that do not seems most relevant for theories of art-provoked emotion. That mistakes can be made is illustrated by public debates and court cases about novels, plays, and films that implicitly or explicitly refer to politicians, society figures, or historical events, such as the Holocaust.[15]

Stylistics

Aspects of Literary Stylistics

I have discussed earlier how style as a pattern of global techniques, pertaining to art works as a whole may control emotion. In literature, genre and plot structure shape emotional responses to the work as a whole. In addition to this macro-level control, the appraisal process is fine-tuned at the level of sentences, expressions, and words. Once the writer of a comedy has opted for an ironic characterization of a protagonist, the particular words chosen may still effect amusement, exhilaration, or yet another feeling state. At this point, the second form of study of style comes into play—literary stylistics in a narrower sense (see, e.g., Leech & Short, 1981). Comparable stylistic knowledge has not yet developed in other areas of humanist art studies.

Aspects of literary stylistics include choice of words, lexical cohesion, word order, and phonemic phenomena (e.g., alliteration, rhythm, and rhyme). These aspects do not by themselves relate to emotion in the reader. Again, style is a characteristic use of these, in which the problem is to arrive at some effect while obeying a number of formal constraints. It can be assumed that the reader has A-interest and A-enjoyment in identifying patterns in language use; this has been found to be typical of literary reading. Several empirical studies in foregrounding or estrangement effects in poetry illustrate the assumption (de Beaugrande, 1985; Miall & Kuiken, 1994; van Peer, 1986).

Levels of Meaning and Tropes

Some phenomena of style occur in several art forms. Tropes are most familiar to us as figures of speech in language, but variants of these are to be found in other art forms; for this reason, they seem to be highly interesting for an understanding of aesthetic emotion. In all representational art forms, a distinction is made between literal and nonliteral meaning. The distinction is basic, as it is found in language use in general. Clark (1996) has recently offered the most comprehensive account of what he calls "layering" in language use. He shows that very different phenomena occurring in daily speech communication are based on a distinction between two related sets of meaning; these phenomena include make-believe, storytelling, and such rhetorical devices as irony, teasing, and understatement.

What tropes have in common is that they traverse the distinction between two or more levels of meaning. Tropes are one way to make communications, including works of art, more interesting. The hypothesized effect of tropes is that, by shifting levels of meaning, they add some complexity or difficulty to the stimulus that requires an increase in the beholder's attention. Literary scholars have described this added complexity as "tension," paired with an instant reward because of a deeper or richer understanding.[16] Contradictions between meanings at various levels do not always have to be resolved. Resolved or not, they signal an attitude to be shared between speaker and hearer or between artist and beholder (Berntsen & Kennedy, 1996). The hypothesis implies that tropes are aesthetic emotional stimuli par excellence, and there is nothing against considering them as art works in themselves.

In addition to attracting interest, tropes may be a vehicle for emotional meaning. It seems probable that some meanings can be eminently or even exclusively expressed by way of tropes. One reason for this is that subtle features of a represented event, which are decisive for a particular emotion, can only be articulated through an interaction process between the meanings of the topic and the vehicle (e.g. Black, 1979).[17] In line with this assumption is the privileged status that tropes have had in rhetorics. Current descriptions of tropes also suggest that they are delicate instruments effective in specifying emotional meaning.

Let me present views of the emotional effect of metaphor in more detail. Metaphor is the most intensively studied trope at present. A common element of speech in daily life, it is particularly frequent in literary language use. Metaphor in a broad sense, like some other tropes, applies to various linguistic units of analysis, such as the word, sentence, and discourse level. Some literary and other art works as a whole are interpreted as metaphorical, or in some cases allegorical. In metaphor, predicates (i.e., qualities, attributes, or properties) belonging to the vehicle are transferred to the target, either rendering some of the target's original attributes more salient, or adding new ones to it. Ortony (1975) discusses aspects of transferred predicates. They include emotive aspects—for instance, when some person (the target) is compared with a well-known person (the vehicle) who is loved or hated for specific reasons. If I am called "Atilla the Hun," then this person's proverbial bad manners are transferred to me. Steen (1992) has experimentally demonstrated such emotive effects in an experiment.

Transferred predicates often have a high degree of concreteness and perceptual value, also increasing the target's emotion potential. For instance, disgust and appetite are facilitated by the presence of such attributes in a description.

Some metaphors are assumed to enhance clarity of the target, whereas others (especially literary ones) may contribute to the opposite, the target's semantic ambiguity. Lakoff (1980, p. 141) gives the example "Love is like a collaborative art work." This metaphor not only reflects a positive attitude, but also captures the connotations of delicate efforts and demand for creativity. Both are readily recognized as emotional meanings. Lakoff points out that the insight may assume an immediate quality of truth, when the added predicates entail what is essential in the target to the reader.

It has also been suggested that metaphor is not linguistic in nature but conceptual, and hence it is also used in pictorial communication and arts. Visual metaphors abound in advertising (Forceville, 1996), painting (Hausman, 1989), and film (Carroll, 1996). Carroll (1994) describes a nice example—Man Ray's 1924 photograph of a woman's bare back with a cello's f-holes superimposed on it. According to Carroll, the visual metaphor is "food for thought" without expressing any fixed propositional meaning. The viewer is invited to explore the meanings. The exploration includes considering the possibility of bidirectional transfer of predicates—a possibility that is excluded in verbal metaphor. Another difference is that visual metaphors are "creative" by definition, and hence invariably attract the beholder's attention. "Creative" in this sence means that transferred predicates add a new property to the target. It may be, then, that visual metaphors produce surprise as the outcome of the first stage of appraisal. We can add to this analysis, as Forceville's (1996) approach implies, that the visual metaphor has more powerful emotional effects when the visual elements help in directly addressing the concerns of a particular group of target receivers.

Classification of Art Works According to Emotion Potential

What constitutes a genre differs widely across the arts. There is wide consensus in the humanities that the concept of "genre" does not refer to stable categories, but instead to classifications of art works that can be made on the basis of widely differing criteria. The still life and the detective genres are based on common themes and on some kind of realism. Symphonies, ballets, and one-act plays owe their status as genre to numerical attributes (e.g., in the case of symphonies, the number of players and the concomitant structural complexity).

Classification of art works according to any of these criteria may result in genres that differ in emotion potential, but at least two current genre definitions appear to be based exclusively on the art works' capacity for provoking emotions. One is the distinction between fiction and nonfiction, which seems to be crucial for the kind of emotion provoked by an art work, and which has been discussed earlier. The other is the explicitly emotion-based concept of genre. Some of the most common genre labels explicitly refer to an emotion or a mixture of emotions, which is not surprising if we assume that some art works are especially designed for provoking specific emotions. Thrillers, tragedies, comedies, tearjerkers, horror movies, and the blues are common examples of these. Preference for such genres may be dependent not only on liking the emotions involved, but also on the views of life that they imply as possibilities.

Furthermore, there may be a current distinction between "high" and "low" genres that relates to their characteristic emotion potential above all. Some value scale seems to correlate with the spectrum of emotions produced by art works. Laughter is less valuable than weeping for serious reasons, and therefore comedy is "low," and tragedy "high."

In sum, it seems worth trying to extrapolate the existing emotion-based classifications of art works, and so to identify genres in the arts according to the emotion potential that sets of art works share with respect to some representative beholder. We can conceive of an emotion-based genre as a set of art works that elicit the same emotions, in the sense that the variability of the emotional response to the works within the set is smaller than the variability between this set and any other one. By "emotional response" I mean the type and intensity of emotion, as well as the specific blend of emotions (e.g., the mixture between amusement and sadness in a tragicomedy, or that of hopes and fears in a thriller). Genres based on emotion potential could be identified by collecting standardized emotion questionnaire data for a variety of art works and in some way classifying these. The resulting classes would be emotional fingerprints of art works as experienced by their beholders, and could be related to critical analyses of the works involved.

CONCLUSION

Emotion in general involves at least some degree of comprehension (Frijda, 1993); an emotion provoked by an art work requires lots of it more often than not. Humanist expertise in each of the arts may provide a starting point for the social scientist who attempts to grasp what is understood in aesthetic emotion. The expert's analysis of an art work may have correlates in the general beholder's appraisal. However, as yet there is very little research starting from the assumption that a critic's description of an art work's style pinpoints elements that correspond to situational meaning components appraised by more representative beholders. Available humanist knowledge of art works has been underexplored with respect to the following issues.

First, art works contain clues about concerns that are addressed. Why people care about art works, or about what they represent, is dealt with in numerous case studies in the history and interpretation of the various arts. My conjecture is that a thorough inventory of these proposals may enrich the set of acknowledged source and surface concerns that are current in the theory and research of emotion, and that concerns may be added that cannot be straightforwardly connected to adaptive needs, thus adding new fuel to the old nature-versus-nurture debate on emotion.

In the second place, the humanities can inform the researcher about the meaning of art. One of the observations Winner (1982) made in concluding her psychology of the arts is that psychology has not made much progress in studying the ways people make sense of art works. More recently, Funch (1997) arrived at a similar conclusion in a comprehensive survey of current psychological approaches to art appreciation, arguing that the richness of the art experience remains largely unexplained. There is a wealth of ideas in the humanities about what art signifies in particular instances or in a more general sense; some of these ideas are better documented than others. These may be the only starting points for research into semantically deep interpretation by the general beholder of art, which is particularly scarce (both relative to studies of perception, categorization, appreciation, and comprehension, and in a more absolute sense).

In the third place, as I have tried to illustrate, studies of style should be exploited in explaining how the perception of order and the evaluation of artistic intentions and constraints go together in aesthetic appreciation. Here again, an inventory may add to or refine the features that have been subject to psychological theory and research so far, such as psychophysical dimensions, symmetry, collative properties, typicality, and so on. If it were possible to summarize what the humanities may contribute to this theory and research, it would be the conviction that interpretation plays an indispensable role in aesthetic emotion, and the suggestion that pleasure in art generally depends on the use of complex knowledge. In this conviction, the importance of extreme forms of immediate appreciation is relatively minor. Furthermore, discovering the meaning of art works is, as a cognitively complex and variable process, subject to influences from other beholders. The beholder of art typically searches actively for such influences, as the pleasure of experiencing art is in large part discovering meanings; the humanist's view implies that an exchange of ideas is an essential part of the appraisal process, if only because polyvalence and multiple interpretation are in the humanist's view the hallmarks of all art, and especially modern art.

Getting at a reverse-design account of aesthetic emotion, then, seems to be a common endeavor. The humanities deliver mostly case studies of effective emotional design, describing the art works' and the beholder's share in this. The challenge to the emotion researcher is to determine both, testing as much as possible of the richness of humanist description in elegant models and creative experiments. I believe that the exciting part of the collaboration still lies ahead, but is within reach.

ACKNOWLEDGMENT

The author wishes to thank Dick Schram and Paul Hekkert for their fruitful comments on an earlier version of this chapter.

NOTES

1. I refer, first, to Goodman's (1976) well-known philosophical treatment of the problem, to which my pragmatic proposal owes more than a few notions; and, second, to Kristeller's (1965) reconstruction of the meaning of the term "art" throughout the European history of culture.
2. Elsewhere (Tan, 1995, 1996), I have referred to this type of emotions as "F-emotions," where F stands for "fictional world." In these cases all the represented contents are part of a fictional world, constructed by the viewer of narrative film.
3. For a discussion of the sentimental film, see Tan and Frijda (1999).
4. It would seem that "focality of concerns in a cultural group" and "felt obviousness of appraisal" (Mesquita, 1993) are determinants of emotion that can be estimated from available humanistic sources. Emotion scripts or schemas, conventional forms for expressing emotion (e.g., Lutz, 1987), can also be reconstructed from humanistic sources.
5. See, for instance, Vellekoop (1994).
6. A compelling case for a nonconceptual bodily representation of music and dance structures, which is basic for affect, is made by Jackendoff (1989, pp. 236–239).
7. For a thorough treatment of synesthesia as an explanation of the interaction of music and painting, see Marks (1978); see Simon and Wohlwill (1968) for a study on matching of visual patterns and sequences of music.
8. A study by Ognjenovic (1991) may serve as an illustration of the time course of the two appraisal processes. The researcher presented three versions of paintings, varying as to harmony, beauty of de-

tails, and authenticity of individual style, with various presentation durations. Gestalt-like harmony determined aesthetic preference at the shortest durations, whereas beauty of detail and characteristic style governed preference at the longer and longest viewing times, respectively.

9. The principle dates back at least to Fechner (1876). Well-known formulations can be found in Arnheim (1971), Birkhoff (1933), and Boselie and Leeuwenberg (1985).

10. For instance, Avital and Cupchik (1998) found that untrained viewers could reproduce a hierarchical system of paintings based on ordering and transformations of color known to the artist but not to them. Leontiev and Yemeyanov (1994) reported significant correlation between semantic judgments of poems of the same author, which in addition exceeded the ones between poems with the same theme and with the same plot. And findings such as those by McManus, Cheema, and Stoker (1993) can be considered as illustrative of emotional appraisal of style. They demonstrated that untrained subjects preferred abstract paintings by Mondrian to facsimiles in which proportional relations of compositional lines had been modified.

11. As a simple example, we may consider the denotation systems (Willats, 1997) that any drawing artist can choose among. For instance, an artist may choose points or regions rather than lines as basic means of pictoral representation, and he or she may be constrained by norms for a particular genre in his or her time.

12. At the time of the film's release in France, there was a revival of religious interest after World War II, and the role of the clergy in French society was being intensively discussed. The idea of spiritual ordeal followed by liberation may thus have had a particular appeal to viewers, even inspiring awe.

13. It is impossible to list even a sample of titles of interest here. Two completely arbitrary examples are Baxendall's (1972) study of conventions and experience in the quattrocento, and Moxey's (1994) paper on the attractiveness of Hieronymus Bosch's imagery to his contemporaries.

14. Realism's impact differs across art genres (Kettlewell, Lipscomb, Evans, & Rosston, 1990) and is reduced among experts (e.g., Hekkert & van Wieringen, 1996).

15. Intuitions about genre have been shown to affect strategies in dealing with art works. For instance, Zwaan (1993) presents evidence showing that a narrative text labeled as "literature" is read more slowly, with more attention devoted to its surface characteristics, than the same text labeled as "news."

16. Not all empirical research on tropes confirms this hypothesis. The most encompassing model comparison and related set of experiments in the processing of literary metaphors were carried out by Hoorn (1997), who has proposed a model in which a race is run between parallel literal and figurative interpretations after detection of an anomaly.

17. Unfortunately, there have been no psychological studies of emotional inference on the part of the be-

holder in metaphor processing (Steen, 1992), or even in narrative text processing (Graesser, Singer, & Trabasso, 1994).

REFERENCES

Albritton, D. W., & Gerrig, R. J. (1991). Participatory responses in text and understanding. *Journal of Memory and Language, 30,* 603–626.

Andringa, E. (1996). Effects of narrative distance on readers' emotional involvement and response. *Poetics, 23,* 431–452.

Andringa, E., Tan, T. E., van Horssen, P., & Jacobs, A. (in press). Effects of focalization in film narration. In W. van Peer & S. Chatman (Eds.), *New perspectives on narrative perspective.* Albany: State University of New York Press.

Arnheim, R. (1971). *Entropy and art.* Berkeley: University of California Press.

Avital, T., & Cupchik, G. (1998). Perceiving hierarchical structures in non-representational paintings. *Empirical Studies of the Arts, 16,* 59–70.

Baxendall, M. (1972). *Painting and experience in fifteenth century Italy: A primer in the social history of pictorial style.* Oxford: Oxford University Press.

Berlyne, D. E. (1971). *Aesthetics and psychobiology.* New York: Appleton-Century-Crofts.

Berlyne, D. E. (Ed.) (1974). *Studies in the new experimental aesthetics: Steps toward an objective psychology of aesthetic appreciation.* New York: Wiley.

Berlyne, D., & Ogilvie, J. C. (1974). Dimensions of perception of paintings. In D. E. Berlyne (Ed.), *Studies in the new experimental aesthetics: Steps toward an objective psychology of aesthetic appreciation* (pp. 181–227). New York: Wiley.

Berntsen, D., & Kennedy, J. M. (1996). Unresolved contradictions specifying attitudes—in metaphor, irony, understatement and tautology. *Poetics, 24,* 13–29.

Birkhoff, G. (1933). *Aesthetic measure.* Cambridge, MA: Harvard University Press.

Black, M. (1979). More about metaphor. In A. Ortony (Ed.), *Metaphor and thought* (pp. 19–43). Cambridge, England: Cambridge University Press.

Booth, W. L. (1961). *The rhetoric of fiction.* Chicago: University of Chicago Press.

Boselie, F., & Leeuwenberg, E. (1985). Birkhoff revisited: Beauty as a function of effect and means. *American Journal of Psychology, 98,* 1–39.

Bourg, T., Risden, K., Thompson, S., & Davis, E. C. (1993). The effects of an empathy-building strategy on 6th graders' causal inferencing in narrative text comprehension. *Poetics, 22,* 117–133.

Brewer, W. F., & Lichtenstein, E. H. (1982). Stories are to entertain: A structural-affect theory of stories. *Journal of Pragmatics, 6,* 473–486.

Bullough, E. (1912–1913). Psychical distance as a factor in art and an aesthetic principle. *British Journal of Psychology, 5,* 88–118.

Campbell, J. (1949). *The hero with a thousand faces.* New York: Pantheon.

Carroll, N. (1994). Visual metaphor. In J. Hintikka

(Ed.), *Aspects of metaphor*, (pp. 189–218). Dordrecht, The Netherlands: Kluwer.

Carroll, N. (1996). *Theorizing the moving image*. Cambridge, England: Cambridge University Press.

Chatman, S. (1990). *Coming to terms*. Ithaca, New York: Cornell University Press.

Clark, H. H. (1996). *Using language*. Cambridge, England: Cambrdige University Press.

Clynes, M. (1980, August). *Expressive brain codes common to emotion, music, and dance*. Paper presented at the Third Workshop on Physical and Neuropsychological Foundations of Music, Ossiac, Austria.

Clynes, M., & Nettheim, N. (1982). The living quality of music: Neurobiological basis of communicative feeling. In M. Clynes (Ed.), *Music, mind and brain* (pp. 47–82). New York: Plenum Press.

Crozier, W. R., & Chapman, A. J. (Eds.). (1984). *Cognitive processes in the perception of art*. Amsterdam: North-Holland.

Csikszentmihalyi, M. (1990). *The art of seeing: An interpretation of the aestetic encounter*. Malibu, CA: Paul Getty Museum.

Cupchik, G., & Gebotys, R. J. (1988). The search for meaning in art: Interpretive styles and judgments of quality. *Visual Arts Research*, 14, 38–50.

Cupchik, G., & László, J. (1994). The landscape of time in literary reception: Character experience and narrative action. *Cognition and Emotion*, 8, 297–312.

Currie G. (1990). *The nature of fiction*. Cambridge, England: Cambridge University Press.

Currie, G. (1995). *Image and mind: Film, philosophy, and cognitive science*. Cambridge, England: Cambridge University Press.

Davis, M. H., Hull, J. G., Young, R. D., & Warren, G. G. (1987). Emotional reactions to dramatic film stimuli: The influence of cognitive and emotional empathy. *Journal of Personality and Social Psychology*, 52, 126–133.

de Beaugrande, R. (1985). Poetry and the ordinary reader: A study of immediate responses. *Empirical Studies of the Arts*, 3, 1–21.

de Wied, M. A. (1991). *The role of temporal structures in the production of suspense and duration experience*. Unpublished doctoral dissertation, University of Amsterdam, Amsterdam, The Netherlands.

de Wied, M. A., Zillmann, D., & Ordman, V. (1995). The role of empathetic distress in the enjoyment of cinematic tragedy. *Poetics*, 23, 91–106.

Esrock, E. (1994). *The reader's eye*. Baltimore: Johns Hopkins University Press.

Fechner, G. T. (1876). *Vorschule der Ästhetik*. Leipzig: Breitkopf.

Forceville, C. (1996). *Pictorial metaphor in advertising*. London: Routledge.

Freedberg, D. (1989). *The power of images: Studies in the history and theory of response*. Chicago: University of Chicago Press.

Frijda, N. H. (1986). *The emotions*. Cambridge, England: Cambridge University Press.

Frijda, N. H. (1988). The laws of emotion. *American Psychologist*, 43, 349–358.

Frijda, N. H. (1989). Aesthetic emotions and reality. *American Psychologist*, 44, 1546–1547.

Frijda, N. H. (1993). The place of appraisal in emotion. *Cognition and Emotion*, 7, 357–387.

Funch, B. S. (1997). *The psychology of art appreciation*. Copenhagen: Museum Tusculanum Press.

Gaver, W. W., & Mandler, G. (1987). Play it again Sam: On liking music. *Cognition and Emotion*, 1, 259–282.

Genette, G. (1983). *Nouveau discours du récit*. Paris: Seuil.

Gerrig, R. J. (1989). Suspense in the absence of uncertainty. *Journal of Memory and Language*, 28, 633–648.

Goldman, S. R. & Kantor, R. J. (1993). The limits of poetic license: When shouldn't an ending be happy? *Poetics*, 22, 135–150.

Gombrich E. H. (1963). *Meditations on a hobby horse and other essays*. London: Phaidon.

Gombrich, E. H. (1992). *Art and illusion*. London: Phaidon. (Original work published 1959)

Goodman, N. (1976). *Languages of art: An approach to a theory of symbols* (2nd ed.). Indianapolis, IN: Hackett.

Graesser, A. C., Singer, M., & Trabasso, T. (1994). Constructing inferences during narrative text comprehension. *Psychological Review*, 101, 371–395.

Hakemulder, F. (1998). *The moral laboratory*. Unpublished doctoral dissertation, Utrecht University, Utrecht, The Netherlands.

Halasz, L. (1991). Emotional effect and reminding in literary processing. *Poetics*, 20, 247–272.

Halasz, L. (1997). Expectations from and characteristics of literature vs. historiography: A comparative study of genre and text. In L. Dorfman, C. Martindale, D. Leontiev, G. Cupchik, V. Petrov, & P. Machotka (Eds.), *Emotion, creativity and art* (Vol. 2, pp. 101–116). Perm, Russia: Perm Institute of Arts.

Hausman, C. (1989). *Metaphor and art*. Cambridge, England: Cambridge University Press.

Hekkert, P., & van Wieringen, P. C. W. (1996). The impact of level of expertise on the evaluation of original and altered versions of post-impressionist paintings. *Acta Psychologica*, 94, 117–131.

Hoffner, C., & Cantor, N. (1985). Developmental differences in responses to a television character's appearance and behavior. *Developmental Psychology*, 21, 1065–1074.

Hoorn, J. (1997). *Metaphor and the brain: A behavioral and psychophysiological research into literary metaphor processing*. Unpublished doctoral dissertation, Vrije Universiteit, Amsterdam, The Netherlands.

Izard C. E. (1977). *Human emotions*. New York: Plenum Press.

Jackendoff, R. (1989). *Consciousness and the computational mind*. Cambridge, MA: MIT Press.

Jose, P. E., & Brewer, W. F. (1984). Development of story liking: Character identification, suspense and outcome resolution. *Developmental Psychology*, 20, 911–924.

Kant, I. (1977). *Kritik der Urteilskraft* (Critique of judgment). Frankfurt am Main, Suhrkamp. (Original work published 1790)

Kerényi, K. (1981). *Die Mythologie der Griechen*, (5th ed., 2 vols.), München: Deutsche Taschenbuch Verlag

Kettlewell, N., Lipscomb, S., Evans, L., & Rosston, K.

(1990). The effect of subject matter and degree of re-alism on aesthetic preferences for paintings. *Empirical Studies of the Arts, 8,* 85–93.

Klinger, E. (1971). *Structure and function of fantasy.* New York: Wiley.

Knapp, R. H. (1964). An experimental study of a triadic hypothesis concerning the sources of aesthetic imagery. *Journal of Projective Techniques and Personality Assessment, 28,* 49–54.

Konijn, E. A. (in press). *Acting emotions.* Amsterdam: Amsterdam University Press.

Kreitler, H., & Kreitler, S. (1972). *Psychology of the arts.* Durham, NC: Duke University Press.

Kristeller, P. O. (1965). *Renaissance thought and the arts,* New York: Harper & Row.

Kubovy, M. (1986). *The psychology of perspective and Renaissance art.* Cambridge, England: Cambridge Univeristy Press.

Lakoff, G. (1980). *Metaphors we live by.* Chicago: University of Chicago Press.

Langer, S. (1953). *Feeling and form.* New York: Scribner.

László, J. (1986). Same story with different point of view. *SPIEL: Siegener Periodicum zur Internationalen Empirischen Literaturwissenschaft, 5,* 1–22

Lazarus, R. S. (1991a). *Emotion and adaptation.* New York: Oxford University Press

Lazarus, R. S. (1991b). Progress on a cognitive–motivational–relational theory of emotion. *American Psychologist, 46,* 819–834.

Leech, G. N., & Short, M. H. (1981). *Style in fiction.* London: Longman.

Leontiev, D. A., & Yemeyanov, G. A. (1994). Catching psychological effects of poetic form: Experiments with parodies and translations. *SPIEL: Siegener Periodicum zur Internationalen Empirischen Literaturwissenschaft, 13*(1), 101–113.

Levinson, J. (1990). *Music, art, and metaphysics.* Ithaca, NY: Cornell University Press.

Lindauer, M. S. (1990). Reactions to cheap art. *Empirical Studies of the Arts, 8,* 95–110.

Lutz, C. (1987). Goals, events and understanding in Ifaluk emotion theory. In D. Holland & N. Quinn (Eds.), *Cultural models of language and thought.* Cambridge, England: Cambridge University Press.

Marks, L. E. (1978). *The unity of the senses.* New York: Academic Press.

Magliano, J. P., Dijkstra, K., & Zwaan, R. (1996). Generating predictive inferences when viewing a movie. *Discourse Processes, 22,* 199–224.

McManus, I. C., Cheema, B., & Stoker, J. (1993). The aesthetics of composition: A study of Mondrian. *Empirical Studies of the Arts, 11,* 83–94.

Mesquita, B. (1993). *Cultural variations in emotions.* Unpublished doctoral dissertation, University of Amsterdam, Amsterdam, The Netherlands.

Meyer, L. (1989). *Style and music: Theory, history and ideology.* Philadelphia: University of Pennsylvania Press.

Miall, D., & Kuiken, D. (1994). Beyond text theory: Understanding literary response. *Discourse Processes, 17,* 337–352.

Moxey, K. (1994). Hieronymus Bosch and the "world upside down": The case of the *Garden of Earthly Delights.* In N. Bryson, M. A. Holly, & K. Moxey (Eds.), *Visual culture. Images and interpretations,* (pp. 104–140). Hanover, NH: University Press of New England.

Mummendey, A., Linneweber, V., & Loeschper, G. (1984). Actor or victim of aggression: Different perspectives. *European Journal of Social Psychology, 14,* 297–311.

Nussbaum, M. (1991). The literary imagination in public life. *New Literary History, 22,* 877–910.

Oatley, K. (1992). *Best laid schemes.* Cambridge, England: Cambridge University Press.

Oatley, K. (1995). A taxonomy of the emotions of literary response and a theory of identification in fictional narrative. *Poetics, 23,* 1–2, 53–74.

Oatley, K., & Duncan, E. (1992). Structured diaries for emotions in daily life. In K. T. Strongman (Ed.), *International review of studies in emotion,* (Vol. 2, pp. 250–293). Chichester, England: Wiley.

Ognjenovic, P. (1991). Processing of aesthetic information. *Empirical Studies of the Arts, 9,* 1–9.

Ortony, A., (1975). Why metaphors are necessary and not just nice. *Educational Theory, 25,* 45–53.

Ortony, A., Clore, G., & Collins A. (1988). *The cognitive structure of emotions.* Cambridge, England: Cambridge University Press.

Ortony, A, & Turner, T. J. (1990). What's basic about basic emotions? *Psychological Review, 97,* 315-331.

Panksepp, J. (1982). Towards a general psychological theory of emotions. *Behavioral and Brain Sciences, 5,* 407-467.

Panofsky, E. (1962). *Studies in iconology.* New York: Harper and Row. (Original work published 1939 as *Ikonologische Studien*)

Pitchert, J. W., & Anderson R. C. (1977). Taking different perspectives on a story. *Journal of Educational Psychology, 69,* 309–315.

Potter, R. (1992). Reader response to dialogue. In E. F. Nardocchio (Ed.), *Reader response to literature: The empirical dimension* (pp. 15–33). New York: Mouton.

Prince, G. (1982). *Narratology: The form and functioning of narrative.* New York: Mouton.

Propp, V. (1968). *Morphology of the folk tale* (2nd ed.). Austin: University of Texas Press. (Original work published 1928)

Purcell, A. T. (1984). The aesthetic experience and mundane reality. In W. R. Crozier, & A. J. Chapman (Eds.), *Cognitive processes in the perception of art* (pp. 189–210). Amsterdam: North-Holland.

Richards, I. A. (n.d.). *Practical criticism.* San Diego: Harcourt, Brace (Original work published 1929).

Russell, P. A., & Milne, S. (1997). Meaningfulness and hedonic value of paintings: Effects of titles. *Empirical Studies of the Arts, 15,* 61–73.

Sadowski, M., Goetz, E., & Kangiser, S. (1988). Imagination in story response: Relationships between imagery, affect, and structural importance. *Reading Research Quarterly, 23,* 320–336.

Sanders, J., & Redeker, G. (1996). The representation of speech and thought in narrative texts. In G. Fauconnier & E. Sweetser (Eds.) *Spaces, worlds and grammar* (pp. 290–317). Chicago: University of Chicago Press.

Scherer, K.R. (1971). Stereotype change following exposure to counter-stereotypical media heroes. *Journal of Broadcasting, 15*, 91–100.

Schoenmakers, H. (1988). To be, wanting to be, forced to be: Identification processes in theatrical situations. In W. Sauter (Ed.), *New directions in audience research*, (Vol. 2, pp. 138–163). Utrecht, The Netherlands: Utrecht University, Instituut voor Theaterwetenschap.

Schrader, P. (1972). *Transcendental style in film: Ozu, Bresson, Dreyer*. Berkeley: University of California Press.

Simon, C. R., & Wohlwill, J. F. (1968). The role of expectation and variation in music. *Journal of Research in Music Education, 16*, 227–238.

Steen, G. (1992). *Metaphor in literary reception: A theoretical and empirical study of understanding metaphor in literary discourse*. Unpublished doctoral dissertation, Vrije Universiteit, Amsterdam, The Netherlands.

Sternberg, M. (1978). *Expositional modes and temporal ordering in fiction*. Baltimore: Johns Hopkins University Press.

Tan, E. S. (1995). Emotion in film viewing. *Poetics, 23*, 7–32.

Tan, E. S. (1996). *Emotion and the structure of narrative film*. Mahwah, NJ: Erlbaum.

Tan, E. S., & Diteweg, G. (1996). Suspense, predictive inference and emotion in film viewing. In P. Vorderer, H. J. Wulff & M. Friedrichsen (Eds.), *Suspense* (pp. 149–188). Mahwah, NJ: Erlbaum.

Tan, E. S. & Frijda, N. H. (1999). Sentiment in film viewing. In C. Plantinga, & G. Smith (Eds.), *Passionate views* (pp. 48–64). Baltimore: Johns Hopkins University Press.

Tannenbaum, P. H., & Gaer, E. P. (1965). Mood change as a function of stress of protagonist and degree of identication in a film viewing situation. *Journal of Personality and Social Psychology, 2*, 612–616.

Temme, E. (1983). *Over smaak valt te twisten.[Accounting for taste]*.Unpublished doctoral dissertation, Utrecht University, Utrecht, The Netherlands.

Thompson, K., & Bordwell, D. (1994). *Film history*. New York: McGraw-Hill.

Tomkins, S. S. (1984). Affect theory. In K. R. Scherer & P. Ekman (Eds.), *Approaches to emotion* (pp. 163–195. Hillsdale NJ: Erlbaum.

van der Bolt, L., & Tellegen, S. (1992–1993). Involvement while reading: An empirical exploration. *Imagination, Cognition and Personality, 12*(3), 273–285.

van Peer W. (1986). *Stylistics and psychology: Investigations of foregrounding*. London: Croom Helm.

van Peer, W., & Pander-Maat, H. (1996). Perspectivation and sympathy: Effects of point of view. In R.J. Kreuz & M.S. MacNealy (Eds.), *Empirical approaches to literature and aesthetics* (pp. 143–154). Norwood, NJ: Ablex.

Vellekoop, C. (1994). *Musica movet affectus. [Music sets the affects into motion]*. Inaugural lecture, Occasion of accepting the function of professor. Utrecht, Utrecht University, The Netherlands.

von der Thüsen, J. (1997). *Het verlangen naar huivering. [Desire for shivering]*. Amsterdam: Querido.

Walton, K. (1990). *Mimesis as make-believe: On the foundations of the representational arts*. Cambridge, MA: Harvard University Press.

Walton, K. (1994). Make-believe, and its role in pictorial representation and the acquisition of knowledge. *Philosophic Exchange, 24*, 81–95.

Willats, J. (1997). *Art and representation: New principles in the analysis of pictures*. Princeton, NJ: Princeton University Press.

Winner, E. (1982). *Invented worlds: The psychology of the arts*. Cambridge, MA: Harvard University Press.

Winston, A., & Cupchik, G. (1992). The evaluation of high art and popular art by naïve and experienced viewers. *Visual Arts Research, 18*, 1–14.

Zillmann, D. (1991). Empathy: Affect from bearing witness tot the emotions of others. In J. Bryant & D. Zillmann (Eds.), *Responding to the screen: Reception and reaction processes* (pp. 103–134). Hillsdale, NJ: Erlbaum.

Zwaan, R. (1993). *Aspects of literary comprehension*. Amsterdam: John Benjamins.

PART II

BIOLOGICAL AND NEUROPHYSIOLOGICAL APPROACHES TO EMOTION

CHAPTER 9

Emotions as Natural Kinds within the Mammalian Brain

Jaak Panksepp

Many aspects of emotions emerge from genetically ingrained brain processes that are homologous in all mammals. Other aspects emerge from the epigenetic interaction of those processes with ecological and social environments, and yet others from our human ability to semantically conceptualize issues of importance to us. There is precious little agreement that any of these levels of analysis is more important than any other for a scientific understanding of emotions. Confusion and controversy are bound to prevail until we begin to anchor our ideas about emotion to empirically falsifiable neuroscience concepts. This is a tall order for the many disciplines, from anthropology to sociology, where brain perspectives remain poorly cultivated. However, the emerging brain views (e.g., Damasio, 1994; Gray, 1990; LeDoux, 1996; MacLean, 1990; Panksepp, 1998a) are harmonious with many perspectives emerging from the psychosocial sciences.

My aim in this chapter is to provide a synopsis of the brain lessons that all other levels of analysis may need to consider if they are going to fully understand how basic emotional systems resonate and elaborate through the diverse dimensions of human institutions and human lives. My assumption is that the basic emotional processes, which we inherit as evolutionary birthrights, are the essential integrative components from which the vast complexity of human emotional life ultimately emerges. Most certainly, the driving forces behind the fundamental feeling tones and autonomic/behavioral/cognitive tendencies that we commonly recognize as distinct types of emotional arousal (Ekman, 1998) arise primarily from the neurodynamics of specific types of subcortical circuits. According to this view, the basic emotions are "natural kinds" that have specifiable neural substrates within the mammalian brain. If we do not come to terms with such foundation principles, we will have impoverished views of psychological and cultural complexities that ultimately arise from emotional learning.

Let me first highlight an obvious, but not well-appreciated, brain issue: There is no single "motivational" circuit in the brain, and there is no unitary "emotional" circuit there either. In fact, there are many brain circuits, especially neuropeptidergic ones (Panksepp, 1993), that mediate many different emotions and motivations, and many others, like noradrenergic and serotonergic ones, that nonspecifically modulate all of them (Panksepp, 1986a). Hence, if there is any common theme that allows us to place various emotions under a single conceptual umbrella, it must be found among the shared psychoneurological properties of basic emotional systems. I have suggested (Panksepp, 1982 to 1998a) that such neural properties will constitute a general definition of emotions and will probably consist of at least six attributes, including: (1) a need to focus on the underlying neuroanatomical trajectories, (2) their autonomic and motor controls, (3) their effects on sensory-perceptual systems, (4) their neurodynamic properties, (5) their ability to control learning, and (6) their interactions with other higher brain functions (see Table 4.1 in Panksepp, 1986b). In addition, there is a most problematic property that makes emotions so important to us phenomenologically—namely, their affective valence. These seven properties allow emotional processes to interact with many other psychoneural functions, leading to levels of complexity that will be most difficult to dissect in fine detail.

Darwin (1872/1998) realized that emotions had certain basic properties: Namely, each basic emotional system of the brain (i.e., his "principle of action," due to the constitution of the nervous system) interacts with other systems (his "principle of antithesis") and is also accompanied by the vast baggage of accumulated learning (his "principle of serviceable associated habits"). He also realized that the key feature of emotions is a feeling tone, a property of emotional neurodynamics that still defies our understanding. Neuroscientists commonly neglect affective properties when they seek to provide a scientific understanding of how emotions are elaborated by the brain. However, it may well turn out that such properties are not simply a by-product of higher brain functions, as some investigators assume (e.g., LeDoux, 1996), but essential attributes of how emotionality is generated by subcortical and higher limbic neural activities (Panksepp, 1998a,c).

In any event, most investigators recognize that concepts such as "emotions," "motivations," and "the limbic system" are class identifiers that help us circumscribe conceptual groupings of the various natural/evolutionary integrative systems (i.e., innate affective knowledge structures) of the brain. However, caution and parsimony are called for when we try to specify what types of "natural kinds" actually exist within the brains of newborn animals before they become modified by individual experiences. Just as one branch of modern evolutionary epistemology suggests that there are no real "genera," "classes," or "kingdoms" in the animate world, only individual species (Ghiselin, 1997), those interested in emotions will need to distinguish the real entities that exist within the brain from the many elaborations on basic themes that emerge via the experiences of each organism. Unfortunately, there is

no consensus on, or even much discussion of, how we should discriminate the basic entities that emerge directly from the genetically guided neurodynamics of brain from those that emerge from subsequent learning and the many conceptual "needs" of our linguistic faculties.

The ontological status of many concepts is bound to remain inherently ambiguous because they straddle both basic and derivative usages. For instance, it is likely that affective concepts such as "guilt," "shame," and "sympathy" do not really exist as fundamental processes, even in the human brain, but they can easily arise as derivative processes based on social learning that weaves such basic feelings as separation distress and social bonding into more complex sociocultural realities. Once evolution endowed our ancestors with a basic "integrative system for social affect" (Panksepp, 1998a), along with a certain amount of complex, multimodal association cortex, the emergence of language could construct many concepts from the bipolar dimensional feelings engendered by social isolation and social warmth/solidarity. Through the analysis of the behavioral indicators of separation distress and social comfort in a few species of laboratory animals, we now know a great deal about the neural circuits that mediate such emotions in all mammals (Panksepp, Newman & Insel, 1992), and it is not difficult to generate predictions and to see implications for human emotional life (Panksepp, 1998a).

Perhaps the best criterion for the existence of certain natural affective kinds within the brain is the specification of brain circuits that generate coherent emotional behaviors along with valenced states in animal models that have homologous counterparts in human brains. In other words, the core concepts for basic-emotion theory must arise from defensible ideas concerning the types of affective arousal that can emerge naturally from the underlying brain activities. This, of course, is the traditional folk-psychological perspective, which was also Darwin's (1872/1998) preferred view. As Figure 9.1 summarizes, most people consider feelings to be among the most important aspects of emotion. However, recognizing the nature of the problem is not the same as being able to deal with it, and Darwin, like most investigators who followed him, sought to characterize only the external signs rather than the internal processes that mediate emotions. There are few alternatives unless we choose to remain in the realm of surface manifestations (Ortony &

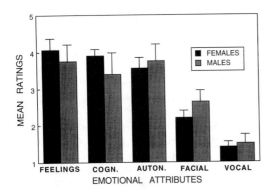

FIGURE 9.1. Average (± *SEM*) opinions of 40 psychology graduate and undergraduate students who were requested to prioritize five major attributes of emotions from least important (rating of 1) to most important (rating of 5). The options were listed in the following order: "facial expressions," "vocal expressions," "feeling states," "cognitive changes," and "autonomic changes," with an open space for any other options, which was never used. Although feeling states had the highest overall rating, cognitive changes and autonomic changes were not far behind. However, these results are not representative for the population at large. When 10 music majors were asked the same questions, the ratings were more clearly skewed for feeling states (mean = 4.6) compared to cognitive changes (mean = 2.9) (*p* < .01). In contrast, the responses generated by 10 philosophy students were essentially just the opposite (*p* < .05). Opinions from the less-intellectual strata of society were also evaluated: Of 35 drivers incarcerated for drinking and driving, 30 listed feeling states as the most important attribute of emotions. In sum, most people probably believe that feeling states are the most important attributes of emotions, but this opinion is not necessarily shared by highly cognitivized individuals and/or those who have been exposed to the intellectual biases that are traditional in psychology.

Turner, 1990). How affective arousal is truly generated can only be resolved by understanding the intrinsic evolutionary epistemology embedded within brain circuits.

CONCEPTUAL ISSUES IN THE STUDY OF THE BRAIN SUBSTRATES OF EMOTIONS

Affective experience and how it may be constructed in the brain continue to constitute the most neglected aspect of emotion research. My personal perspective on this troublesome issue is that credible answers to our affective ques-

tions will gradually come as we unravel the integrated brain substrates that mediate the best external signs of emotionality we can agree upon. A deep understanding may emerge through an understanding of the neurochemical underpinnings of instinctive emotional responses—the evolutionary operants that animals naturally exhibit in affectively engaging situations. Neurochemical facts will provide the easiest and most direct ways to manipulate the underlying systems in humans—the only species that can give us propositional descriptions of their feelings. In other words, a triangulation among psychological, neurological, and behavioral indicators of emotions is an essential strategy for us to fathom the basic nature of emotions (Panksepp, 1991, 1998a).

A wider recognition of this epistemological principle should serve as a clarion call for psychology to become "neurologized" in the many new and interesting ways that recent advances in neuroscience permit (Panksepp, 1996a). This does not mean that we need to abandon psychological, social, and cultural studies of what it means to have subjective affective experiences. These levels of analysis can operate harmoniously without denigrating each other. We will all have to tolerate and respect many vague and successive approximations if we are ever to achieve a satisfactory level of understanding in this troubled area. Testable theoretical positions must be taken, and we must be willing to make the types of necessary mistakes that can lead to progress.

A focus on the perennially troubled "limbic system" concept can be instructive here. An increasing number of investigators have advocated discarding this concept, since it does not adequately describe a clear structural entity within the nervous system (Brothers, 1997; LeDoux, 1996). Their reasoning is compelling from a certain harsh positivistic vantage, but from a more realistically tolerant vantage, it is misplaced. The "limbic system" has never been anything more than a high-order conceptual entity that helps us designate and discuss the general location of the families of functional neural systems that contribute most heavily to dynamic processes commonly placed under the conceptual umbrella of "emotions." It was never meant to be as straightforward an anatomical convention as the "amygdala." However, we should remember that even such seemingly precise anatomical terms for groupings of neurons have no intrinsic meaning or any exact borders.

They are stipulative labels created for our communicative convenience. Such labels merely help us speak clearly when we have specific communicative purposes in mind. If we wished to push such strident criticisms to their limits, we might do away with all artificial anatomical concepts, such as "amygdala," "habenula," and "hippocampus," and simply talk about neurons A_i to Z_j. After all, amygdalas do not really exist in human brains; they are only distributed fields of neurons and glia. But if we insisted on such austerity, we would paralyze our ability to communicate effectively with each other as well as with a broader educated citizenry that wishes to appreciate our findings.

If we remember that all words are simply symbolic communicative tools, we may be less likely to banish useful concepts when they seem to have outlived their precision in one domain of inquiry but not another. General concepts can continue to serve didactic purposes even when they no longer serve major empirical ends. This, I believe, is the major role that the "limbic system" has always played, and that it should continue to play within the communicative needs of our educational endeavors. It points us toward a general conceptual understanding, not to a molecular description of underlying neural events. The "limbic system" has the same taxonomic status as "genus," "family," and "kingdom" in our attempts to systematically describe organization of species. Although those concepts no longer have much substantive ontological status in modern biology (Ghiselin, 1997), they still provide an abstract conceptual ordering that is a useful way to summarize and systematize the complexity of the world.

The limbic system concept allowed us to talk about the general brain areas that are especially influential in elaborating emotions, and to do so more effectively than the Papez circuit or earlier views permitted. It encouraged us to initiate productive neuroscientific inquiries at a time when other less productive modes of thought, such as the James–Lange theory, were pointing us toward the idea that the cortex mediates emotional feelings by harvesting eruptive sensations emerging from the periphery. In fact, certain neuronal properties of the limbic system suggest that there may be physiological coherence to the limbic system concept, including unique chemical features (such as the high concentration of certain peptidergic circuits), a high preponderance of slowly firing neurons

(see Figure 4.4 in Panksepp, 1998a); and some functional compartmentalization indicated by the existence of neurally restricted types of epilepsy, such as limbic seizures (MacLean, 1990). Indeed, these facts, such as the relatively slow firing patterns in most limbic neurons as compared to those in thalamic–neocortical systems, helps explain why modern forms of brain imaging often fail to highlight the participation of diencephalic and mesencephalic circuits in emotions. The glare from the metabolically active cortices tends to wash out changes in brain areas with much more modest neuronal activities. This "lighting problem" is similar to that experienced by stargazers under bright city lights.

Although controversy over the best strategies for understanding emotions (see Ekman & Davidson, 1994) is bound to continue for some time, in my estimation the most robust empirical approach continues to be a categorical one that assumes the existence of "affect programs" within the human brain (Ekman, 1998). Indeed, my allegiance to this approach arose from a totally orthogonal intellectual tradition—namely, the neuroscientific view that "sensory-motor command systems" for various basic emotions do exist in the brain (Panksepp, 1982, 1998a). The compelling nature of the "affect program" view has been affirmed by certain modern philosophical lines of thought (Griffiths, 1997). However, it probably cannot be overemphasized that the existence of basic emotional circuits in the brain does not diminish the need for complementary perspectives: Social-constructivist, categorical, and propositional attitude theories all have important roles in rounding out the real-life complexities that emotional systems can create, especially in highly encephalized human brains (Panksepp, 1992). It would be desirable to have a formal "concilience," not to mention "consilience," among these competing views, especially since our ignorance concerning emotions so grossly outweighs our knowledge.

Now that such conceptual issues have been aired, my aim is to summarize what we know about the basic emotional command circuits that are so important in regulating basic survival/adaptive tendencies of the mammalian brain. However, before I delve into these neural complexities, let me first share some general arguments about the various theoretical approaches most often taken in the analysis of brain substrates of emotions.

TYPES OF BRAIN APPROACHES TO UNDERSTANDING EMOTIONS

The same three general approaches to emotions that have traditionally existed at the psychological level of analysis—namely, constructivist, basic-emotion theory, and hybrid componential approaches—are also represented in brain theorizing. I now present a brief outline of these three views.

1. Those who focus on the point of view that emotions are constructed from a variety of raw parts via learning mechanisms (e.g., Davis, 1996; LeDoux, 1984, 1996) generally devote little effort to taxonomies, for they see emotions within the accepted cognitive framework of understanding mind. Let us call this approach "generalized emotion theory" (GET), since generalized processes such as learning and working memory are seen as the quintessential attributes of emotions. Presumably, general learning principles will translate from one emotional process to any other. Hence GET theorists commonly work on a single prototypical emotional system, usually fear, as a source of general principles. Most are not very receptive to the claim that affective feelings are essential attributes of emotional functions in the brain. They usually stick to a careful analysis of a limited set of well-accepted behaviors, and if they consider the issue, they typically regard emotional feelings as simply another potential content of a global consciousness-generating (e.g., working memory) mechanism of the brain.

2. Those who argue that there are central affective programs (e.g., MacLean, 1990; Panksepp, 1982, 1998a) believe that evolution created intrinsic mechanisms in the brain for generating specific types of emotionality. Let us call this approach "central affective programs" (CAP) theory (e.g., MacLean, 1990, Panksepp, 1998a), since individuals ascribing to this view believe that emotions are global brain states that ultimately emerge from intrinsic brain processes. Although emotional systems are essential ingredients in memory and learning, emotions are not created from such processes. For CAP theorists, taxonomizing is an essential part of the game, as is discussion of the nature of emotional feelings. However, some still remain so conservative as only to acknowledge the general dimensions of arousal and degrees of approach or avoidance. In my estimation, such dimensional views can only be advocated if theorists blind themselves to the mass of neurobehavioral evidence that suggests otherwise. Most theorists who believe in the existence of basic emotions in the brain typically assume that the neuroanatomical, neurophysiological, and neurochemical core of each emotional system needs to be fully understood before we can claim to understand any emotion. The manner in which emotional systems learn is somewhat less important than how they are intrinsically organized. Some CAP theorists are prone to conceptualize emotions as foundation processes in the evolution of consciousness, so that emotions deserve a distinct ontological status in our studies of the brain (Panksepp, 1998a,c).

3. Several hybrid approaches have emerged that focus on the many component parts (COPs) from both brain and body that contribute to emotionality. Although it is difficult to designate any major brain theorists who might be sterling representatives of this group, for didactic purposes we might place in this group investigators such as Damasio (1994) and Lang (1995), who generally espouse sophisticated brain views linked to the analysis of many critical bodily processes: All the relevant COPs go into a combinatorial neural stew to yield the fascinating complexity of emotions. Investigators from the COP point of view are typically not fond of taxonomizing emotions, and tend to focus heavily on the empirical relationships between psychophysiological and brain measures.

Finally, I might add that the majority of neuroscientists seem to believe that emotions are simply socially constructed figments of our imagination and not worthy of neuroscientific attention. Indeed, this mainline social-constructivist view—which has led to a massive neglect of emotionality in modern neuroscience, has been formalized by Brothers (1997), who argues that since emotions are largely social constructions, talk of emotions in animals borders on the absurd.

Surrounding and interpenetrating with all these approaches is the self-evident psychological perspective that emotions, whatever their fundamental nature, must be major ingredients within the global operational (GO) workspaces of consciousness (see the electronic seminar moderated by Watt, 1998).

In sum, there is emerging variety in brain emotion theory. My personal bias is that it is long past time to GET a CAP for our COPs, but obviously all views have something going for them. It is largely a matter of choosing a strategy that will take us most rapidly to a lasting understanding of the intrinsic nature of emotionality in the mammalian brain, and this depends completely on who is generating the most interesting empirically verifiable predictions. It is a pity that the proponents of the various approaches tend to ignore the findings and perspectives of other approaches, but this is probably little more than a reflection on human nature, as investigators vie for their own stakes in this underdeveloped territory. As I have argued before, such approaches do not need to fight for primacy; all should be tolerated, since they probably work best in different arenas of inquiry (Panksepp, 1982). Some of the empirical and theoretical findings from the GET-GO and COP-GO perspectives are fascinating (Baars, 1998; Damasio, 1994; LeDoux, 1996), but my own research strategy has crystallized around the CAP approach, and in my estimation it is laying the broadest and deepest foundation of knowledge in the area (Panksepp, 1998a). Accordingly, I focus briefly on the conceptual and empirical bases of the taxonomies that have been created within the categorical approach.

NEURAL TAXONOMIES OF EMOTIONS

Taxonomies can serve many functions in science, but the most important is to dissect the world into natural rather than artificial categories. Because of the difficulty of such enterprises for even seemingly straightforward pursuits such as the categorization of species (Ghiselin, 1997), most neuroscientists have been loath to conceptualize the fracture lines within the "great intermediate net" of the brain that elaborates the neuropsychological processes that reside between the inputs and the outputs.

Of course, our taxonomies have to be based upon observable attributes of brain systems, and there are many ways to view such complexities. We can focus on the face or the voice, on cognitive or bodily postures, on peripheral autonomic changes, or on the types of feelings that we can experience. Because of the neuroscience revolution, we can also now carefully look at the brain and attempt to determine how

"feelings" emerge from the neural interactions (Panksepp, 1982, 1998a,b,c). If we carefully look at the evidence, we can agree that certain controversial items, such as a generalized positive SEEKING/expectancy/interest state (see below), are fundamental processes of the brain (Panksepp, 1986a, 1992). To the extent that more and more levels of analysis match up, we may eventually be able to agree on a lasting taxonomy of emotions. As long as we fail to do so, confusion and controversy are bound to prevail.

Fortunately, the taxonomies derived directly from neuroscience data (Gray, 1990; Panksepp, 1998a) match fairly well with many of the other existing taxonomies, but there are also some troublesome incongruities. For instance, even though most taxonomies accept fear, anger, sadness, and joy as major species, it remains hard to agree on items such as surprise, disgust, interest, love, guilt, and shame. It is also hard to understand why strong feelings such as hunger, thirst, and lust should be excluded. My view, which is concordant with some recent philosophical analyses (Griffiths, 1997), is that there are several distinct kinds of affective processes within the brain, but that only some have the neural properties of bonafide emotional systems. I have suggested that affective processes be divided into at least three conceptual categories (Panksepp, 1994), which may allow us to make distinctions that are essential for discussing affective matters more clearly. I do not wish to suggest that all of these categories are "natural kinds" that should have equal ontological status, but simply that they are useful conceptual categories for discussing affective systems that may have certain similarities and dissimilarities in their underlying neural control structures. The following three general levels of complexity seem evident to me:

Category 1 (the Reflexive Affects)

Certain eruptive and transient emotive responses are reasonably closely time-locked to precipitating conditions. For instance, the startle reflex, gustatory disgust, pain, and the various homeostatic distresses (e.g., hungers) and pleasures (e.g., good tastes) appear to have comparatively simple circuitries. Many of these basic affective states are organized in quite low regions of the brainstem, even though they may come to have metaphoric representations within our higher cognitive associative abilities, as in socially constructed positive affective surprise, social disgust, and contempt.

Category 2 (the Blue-Ribbon, Grade-A Emotions)

There appears to be a set of circuits situated in intermediate areas of the brain (linking higher limbic zones for cingulate, frontal, and temporal cortices with midbrain emotion integrator zones such as the periaqueductal gray [PAG]) that have been conceptualized as sensory–motor emotional command circuits. That is, they orchestrate coherent behavioral, physiological, cognitive, and affective consequences that can markedly outlast precipitating conditions. The items in this category appear to be present in rather homologous fashion in all mammalian species, even though they will most assuredly differ in fine detail if not in general principle. They are emotions like fear, anger, sadness, joy, affection and interest. They are the main focus of this chapter.

Category 3 (the Higher Sentiments)

Finally, there are emotional/affective processes that emerge from the recent evolutionary expansion of the forebrain. In this category, we find many of the more subtle social emotions that are so common in humans, including shame, guilt, contempt, envy, humor, empathy, sympathy, and certain forms of jealousy. Some of these higher affects may be constituted completely from intermixtures of the lower affects with higher cognitive processes, while some may be unique because of intrinsic local circuitries in the higher reaches of the brain. Some of these may be intrinsic to the types of associations those higher regions tend to make, while others may be completely socially learned. For instance, it is among these systems that humans may aspire to create art—ranging from various folk crafts to great music, dance, and poetry—from our emotional urges and yearnings. The notion that there are some strictly cognitive affects related to our aesthetic experiences (see Tan, Chapter 8, this volume), remains a distinct possibility wide open for neuroscientific speculation and perhaps inquiry. Thus, if one wished, one could view items in the previous two categories as "components" for constructing emotional processes in this category.

My aim for the rest of this chapter is to provide sketches of the various basic emotional systems

that exist in subcortical regions of the brain. All of these systems seem to coordinate behavioral, physiological, affective, and cognitive responses to major adaptive problems faced by all mammalian species. Although it is premature to conclude that each system generates distinct affective feelings within the brain, this should become a major research area in the future. It will require careful analysis of the differential approach–avoidance patterns of animals as the underlying neural systems are manipulated, along with attempts to determine whether animals can discriminate the various forms of affective arousal from each other. Obviously, at the neuroscience level, all taxonomies remain open-ended until our knowledge is more complete.

THE BASIC (CATEGORY 2) EMOTIONAL SYSTEMS OF THE BRAIN

The following review is a synopsis of the extensive discussion of emotional systems available in *Affective Neuroscience* (Panksepp, 1998a). Although there are many connections of this view to those put forward by nonbiologically oriented emotion theorists, the present conceptualizations have emerged largely independently of those schools of thought, which may also help explain some of the unusual semantic usages. To highlight the fact that we are talking about the necessary neural substrates for various emotional constructs rather than any comprehensive sets of attributes of such systems operating in the real world, the labels for the various systems are given in small capital letters. In other words, the labels refer to specific neural systems that remain incompletely understood.

There is space only to provide a thumbnail sketch of each system, along with several key references. An overview of key neuroanatomical areas and neurochemical factors that help create these emotions is provided in Table 9.1. This is not meant to be anywhere close to a comprehensive list. However, until demonstrated otherwise, it is assumed that these systems constitute the core processes for the "natural kinds" of emotions, and they probably also provide the raw materials for many socially constructed emotional complexities that arise through learning and cultural experiences. It should be emphasized that all emotions power-

TABLE 9.1. General Summary of the Key Neuroanatomical and Neurochemical Factors That Contribute to the Construction of Basic Emotions within the Mammalian Brain

Basic emotional systems	Key brain areas	Key neuromodulators
General + motivation SEEKING/expectancy	Nucleus accumbens–VTA Mesolimbic mesocortical outputs Lateral hypothalamus–PAG	DA (+), glutamate (+), many neuropeptides, opioids (+), neurotensin (+)
RAGE/anger	Medial anygdala to BNST Medial and perifornical hypothalamus to dorsal PAG	Substance P (+), ACh (+), glutamate (+)
FEAR/anxiety	Central and lateral amygdala to medial hypothalamus and dorsal PAG	Glutamate (+), many neuropeptides, DBI, CRF, CCK, alpha-MSH, NPY
LUST/sexuality	Corticomedial amygdala BNST Preoptic and ventromedial hypothalamus Lateral and ventral PAG	Steroids (+), vasopressin and oxytocin, LH-RH, CCK
CARE/nurturance	Anterior cingulate, BNST Preoptic area, VTA, PAG	Oxytocin (+), prolactin (+), DA (+), opioids (+/–)
PANIC/separation	Anterior cingulate BNST and preoptic area Dorsomedial thalamus Dorsal PAG	Opioids (–), oxytocin (–), prolactin (–), CRF (+), glutamate (+)
PLAY/joy	Dorsomedial diencephalon Parafascicular area Ventral PAG	Opioids (+/–), glutamate (+), ACh (+); any agent that promotes negative emotions reduces play

Note: The monoamines serotonin and norepinephrine are not indicated since they participate in nonspecific ways in all emotions. The higher cortical zones devoted to emotionality, mostly in frontal and temporal areas are not indicated. ACh, Acetylcholine; BNST, bed nucleus of stria terminalis; CCK, cholecystokinin; CRF, corticotropin-releasing factor; DA, dopamine; DBI, diazepam-binding inhibitor; LH-RH, luteinizing hormone-releasing hormone; MSH, melanocyte-stimulating hormone; NPY, neuropeptide Y; PAG, periaqueductal gray; VTA, ventral tegmental area; – , inhibits prototype; +, activates prototype. Data from Panksepp (1998a) and Watt (1998).

fully arouse cortical processes (e.g., see Beck & Fibiger, 1995; Kollack-Walker, Watson, & Akil, 1997), but this does not mean that the cortex is essential for generating affect—only that lots of cognitive information processing is related to affective arousal. In fact, neonatal decortication does not compromise the development of basic emotional responsivity, even though the animals are cognitively rather dull (Panksepp, Normansell, Cox, & Siviy, 1994)

Also, to help highlight the many remaining conundrums that need to be empirically addressed, at the end of each section I identify some **key issues** that deserve concerted empirical attention. References are used sparingly, since a detailed description of the relevant literature is available in Panksepp (1998a).

A general key issue: Probably the main conundrum for the neuroscience view has been

our ability to dissect neural components, without being able to evaluate clearly how these components are coordinated into an integrated response. We still do not have adequate methods for analyzing the broad neurodynamics of coherent brain functions, but great progress has been made at the neuroanatomical level. Probably the most impressive tool is the visualization of oncogenes such as *c-fos,* which manufacture growth-regulating proteins in the brain (e.g., the protein c-Fos arising from the *c-fos* gene), which in turn can serve as neuronal markers for identifying brain systems that are especially strongly aroused during distinct psychobehavioral states. Some striking recent emotion-relevant examples from this type of work can be found in Beckett, Duxon, Aspley, and Marsden (1997) and Kollack-Walker et al. (1997). Unfortunately, this technique (like all brain-imaging techniques) does not allow one to easily sift the essential neural components for psychobehavioral states from the many correlated consequences that reflect widespread broadcasting of emotional influences through many emotionally nonessential regions of the brain. Those types of discriminations can only be generated by causal rather than correlative types of experiments.

The SEEKING System

I have changed the name of this system from "expectancy" to SEEKING, to help reduce the semantic ambiguity that had troubled certain cognitively oriented investigators (Ortony & Turner, 1990). This affectively valenced system has been studied for almost half a century under the guise of electrical self-stimulation of the brain. However, it is well known by investigators that self-stimulation can be generated by activating many distinct neural systems, and the SEEKING response reflects arousal of the system that mediates the most energized forms of self-stimulation along the ascending brain dopamine system (Figure 9.2). Descending components in this system are as important as the various ascending ones, and the type of affective arousal generated when this system is active appears to be psychologically homogeneous. It is one that accompanies the urge of all mammals to explore their environments (Ikemoto & Panksepp, 1994; Panksepp, 1986b). When aroused in this way, animals learn about the sources of rewards using trial-and-error learning that is not all that

different, at a fundamental level, from the trial-and-error manner in which good scientists acquire knowledge from experience.

The "reinforcement" within the fluctuating dynamics of this system may be linked more integrally to reductions rather than increments in the arousal of this system. Fluctuations of activity within this system can mediate many goal-directed behaviors through intrinsic learning mechanisms, which in humans can generate false beliefs (i.e., affirmations of consequences), such as those represented in schizophrenic delusions. A great deal of work has recently been done indicating that this system is activated by various positive incentives, especially when animals are still in the early foraging phases of behavior (Schultz, Apicella, & Ljungberg, 1993). Most investigators now agree with the once controversial notion that this system may be best conceptualized as a generalized positive appetitive motivation system. The transition to this view has been achieved with little acknowledgment in the literature that the older views—namely, that that this system directly encodes reward, reinforcement, or pleasure—were seriously flawed. The absence of any official acknowledgment of a shift in understanding continues to leave most of psychology in the perplexing position of not knowing exactly what to do with such powerful and important psychobehavioral systems of the brain.

A key issue in the field is whether both anticipatory approach and avoidance responses are aroused by this system. At present, preliminary

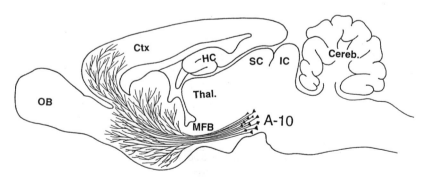

FIGURE 9.2. A midsagittal chematic summary of the mesolimbic and mesocortical dopamine system, where the most vigorous forms of self-stimulation are obtained. This medial forebrain bundle (MFB) system allows the frontal cortex and the ventral striatum to process appetitive information effectively, regardless of the reward. The system mediates many forms of drug addiction, including addiction to psychostimulants and opiates, and is also excessively active in certain forms of schizophrenia. OB, olfactory bulb; Ctx, cortex; HC, hippocampus; Thal., thalamus; SC, superior colliculus, IC, inferior colliculus; Cereb., cerebellum. Adapted from Panksepp (1998a). Copyright 1998 by Oxford University Press. Adapted by permission.

results tend to suggest that much larger effects are seen with positive rewards, but that some arousal is also present with aversive contingencies. This is not a conceptual embarrassment if we recognize that aspects of successful avoidance may eventually also arouse positive incentive processes within the brain (i.e., approach to safety is a desired state).

The RAGE System

The decline in research on the neurological basis of aggression, not to mention anger, has been dramatic in the past few decades. This may be because of a growing antipathy to the notion that such "natural kinds" exist in human brains. However, several investigators, most notably Allan Siegel and colleagues (Siegel & Schubert, 1995), have continued to highlight the underlying mechanism with the modern techniques of neuroscience. Most investigators have chosen to place their work under the behaviorist concept of "defense system." In my estimation, this often mixes the contributions of two distinct but interactive nearby systems—namely, those of FEAR and RAGE. However, the ongoing research has provided detailed descriptions of how the underlying neural circuitries are organized, including anatomical organizations in lower reaches such as the PAG that suggest distinct functional domains for different emotions (Bandler & Keay, 1996).

As summarized in Figure 9.3 and Table 9.1,

much of the executive structure of this hierarchically arranged system is built around excitatory amino acid neurotransmitters such as glutamate, with several neuropeptide modulators. The amygdala exerts descending inhibitory control over anger via met-enkephalin circuits and excitatory control via substance P circuits. This suggests that through the development of orally effective substance P antagonists, it may be possible to develop selective antianger agents. Considering the importance of defense in organizing interspecies relationships, we should keep open the possibility that the brain does, in fact, contain a distinct DEFENSE system that is somewhat independent of FEAR and RAGE. If so, I would anticipate that it generates a certain type of aroused immobility, with mixed affective valence, in which all the animal's senses are directed toward an imminent threat. If such a system exists, I would, on the basis of behavioral observations, tend to place it near the border of the thalamus and hypothalamus, in the region of the zona incerta.

Key issue: Is RAGE intrinsically a positive or a negative emotion? Most investigators assume that anger is a negative emotional state, but it is easy to envision that consistent winning may make this a positive emotional state. If so, we should consider that the positive aspects of this emotion emerge via gradual appetitive conditioning of the SEEKING system, which is normally related to RAGE through the "principle of antithesis," but may become an appetitive instrumental response through the molding of

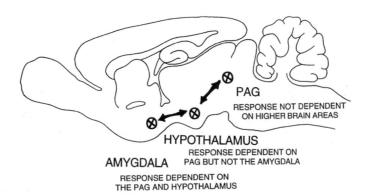

FIGURE 9.3. Hierarchical control of RAGE in the brain. Lesions of higher areas do not diminish responses from lower areas, while damage of lower areas compromises the functions of higher areas. The connections from the amygdala to the medial hypothalamus (MH) convey information via substance P. The connections from the amygdala and MH convey excitatory information to the PAG via the excitatory amino acid glutamate, and inhibitory information via the pentapeptide leu-enkephalin, as described in Siegel & Schubert (1995). Adapted from Panksepp (1998a). Copyright 1998 by Oxford University Press. Adapted by permission.

"serviceable associated habits" via reinforcement processes aroused by fluctuations of activity in the SEEKING system and associated consummatory behaviors.

The FEAR System

A major FEAR system, arranged very similarly to the RAGE system depicted in Figure 9.3, courses between the amygdala and the PAG essentially in parallel with the RAGE system (Panksepp, 1990, 1996b; Rosen & Schulkin, 1998). However, in addition to having a glutamatergic component at its core, as do most emotional systems, the major neuromodulators appear to be different, including corticotropin-releasing factor (CRF), neuropeptide Y, NPY, and the endogenous benzodiazepine-type systems (for reviews, see Fanselow, 1994; Panksepp, Sacks, Crepeau, & Abbott, 1991). Unfortunately, there has been very little effort to untangle how affective states of trepidation emerge from the neurodynamics of this emotional system.

Most of the work has been devoted to analyzing how learned inputs, or Darwin's "serviceable associated habit," emerge from the convergence of thalamic and cortical inputs into the lateral amygdala, which then sends information concerning the cues that predict aversive events to the central amygdaloid nucleus and down to various integrative and output components in the centromedial diencephalon and mesencephalon (LeDoux, 1996). It is recognized that other forms of information, such as the contextual cues associated with aversive events, enter the system from the hippocampus (Kim & Fanselow, 1992), and that yet others emerge from other higher areas of the brain. Whether there are several distinct anxiety/fear systems in the brain, or whether there are only multiple cognitive/informational inputs into one integrative FEAR system is already being partially answered by the analysis of *c-fos* expression within the brain. It seems that naturalistic fears, such as fears of being in elevated open spaces (Silveira, Graeff, & Sandner, 1994) and of social defeat (Kollack-Walker et al., 1997) as well as classically conditioned fear (Beck & Fibiger, 1995), can arouse very widespread areas of the brain. However, there is certainly a distinct system in the brain that mediates separation anxiety (see discussion of the PANIC system below).

One of the serious dilemmas in the field right now is the relative neglect of the functional nature of the FEAR circuitry below the amygdaloid level. There has been a regrettable tendency for behavioral neuroscientists to view this trunk line of the FEAR system as consisting of mere output components, without any integrative or affective functions. This view is most certainly wrong; there are good reasons to believe that the existential nature of angst will be clarified as much through a study of the neurodynamics of the circuitry below the amygdala as of the associative-learning circuits of the amygdala and associated cortical zones (Panksepp, 1990, 1996b). It is likely that the FEAR circuitry below the amygdala is also capable of exhibiting learning/plasticity resulting in behavioral habits, even though the ability of all emotional systems to mediate the learning of discrete responses probably increases markedly as one moves upward within each of the basic command circuits.

A key issue for current brain research in the area should be this: What is the functional nature of the vast neural system between the amygdala and the PAG? Is it simply a set of behavioral and autonomic output units, or is it an integrative system whose activity is essential for the affective experience of fear?

The LUST Systems

Although sexuality has commonly been neglected by emotion theorists, many agree that this is a short-sighted view of the concept of emotionality. One of the spectacular revelations of modern behavioral neuroscience has been the organization of distinct neural systems that elaborate male and female sexuality in all mammalian species that have been studied. The center of gravity for male sexuality consists of sexually dimorphic, preoptic areas of the hypothalamus, while the epicenter for female sexuality is the ventromedial hypothalamus (Becker, Breedlove, & Crews, 1992). Of course, each epicenter is modulated by many higher inputs, especially those arising from the corticomedial amygdala, septal area, and bed nucleus of the stria terminalis, to name the most well-studied zones. Although the male and female LUST systems have many neurochemical components, including many distinct hormonal regulators (Crenshaw & Goldberg, 1996), it is clear that male sexuality is organized around vasopressingeric circuits that help energize the appetitive phase of male eagerness. Female sexuality is organized more around the cycling dynamics of oxytocinergic and leuteinizing hormone-releasing hormone (LH-RH) systems (Moss & Dudley, 1984). The orgasmic component of both males and females appears to be accompanied by strong surges of oxytocin and endogenous opioid release within the brain (Petersen, Caldwell, Jirikowski, & Insel, 1992).

Though human investigators are still prone to believe that gender identity is a matter of choice (Bem, 1996), the biological data affirm that there are strong evolutionary/biological constraints over such matters. However, because of the nature of the early organizational processes that help determine gender identity after birth, many combinations of urges are possible, including equal interest for male and female sexual activities. Thus it should come as no surprise that there are distinct systems of the brain for male and female sexual consummatory urges, and for the preceding appetitive components, even in the animal brain. For instance, even though preoptic hypothalamic damage severely compromises sexual competence in males, it does not produce a comparable reduction in their desire for female companionship (Everitt, 1990).

It will be a most interesting chapter of future neuroscience when we finally decipher what it means, in neurodynamic terms, to have sexual feelings within the brain. There are bound to be surprises, such as the degree of overlap with other emotional processes. Thus, a *key issue may be this: To what extent is the male* LUST *system independent and overlapping with aggression systems? Should rape be considered biologically simply as an aggressive response or also a sexual response? Recent c-Fos data suggest that there is substantial overlap between aggression and sexuality systems in the rodent brain (Newman, 1999).*

The CARE System

It was a momentous passage in biological evolution when neural circuits emerged in the brain that encouraged animals to take care of each other. The fact that these urges evolved from preexisting sexual circuits should come as no surprise to those who appreciate the tinkering ways of evolution. Thus, one of the key neuromodulators that helps sustain female sexuality —namely, oxytocin—is also a key player in the initiation of maternal urges in first-time mothers. In addition to mediating orgasmic feelings in both males and females, oxytocin helps de-

liver milk to babies as they nurse. When babies stimulate the maternal breast, the touch signals run up to neurons of the hypothalamic paraventricular nucleus, the axons of which releases oxytocin from the posterior pituitary. However, there are other widespread oxytocin neural systems in the brain, which also promote nurturance. For instance, if first-time mothers (at least of the animal variety) cannot feel the surges of their brain oxytocin systems, then they do not rapidly develop maternal competence (Petersen et al., 1992). Indeed, the ancestral form of this hormone—namely, vasotocin—already helped deliver babies long before mothers cared for their offspring, as in sea turtles.

It is a finding of considerable aesthetic appeal that the same hormones that control the bodily aspects of birthing and delivery of food to the baby are also essential for generating nurturant feelings in the mother. In addition to oxytocin, which promotes the smooth muscle contractions in the uterus and breasts that help deliver and feed mammalian babies, the other major hormone of motherhood, prolactin, also helps take care of the baby by modulating psychological states. A few days before a baby is born, the breasts are already gearing up milk production by increasing prolactin synthesis and release from the anterior pituitary. In breasts prolactin promotes the synthesis of milk, while in the brain this peptide primes maternal urges. How these neuropeptides control the subtle feelings of nurturance and love that characterize the mother–infant bond remains a provocative idea for future investigations (Krasnegor & Bridges, 1990; Nelson & Panksepp, 1998).

A key issue: Can the arousability of this system in males be increased to approach the levels characteristic of females? If so, how can this be achieved?

The PANIC System

Separation distress circuits have been mapped by identifying brain sites that yield the cries young animals typically make when isolated from social companionship (Jürgens, 1976; Panksepp, Normansell, Herman, Bishop, & Crepeau, 1988). In the forebrain, the circuits are heavily represented in the bed nucleus of the stria terminalis, dorsal preoptic area, and ventral septal area. In the diencephalon, the circuits are most heavily concentrated in medial thalamic areas; in the mesencephalon, the heaviest concentrations are in the dorsal parts of the rostral PAG. As one descends to more caudal reaches, the relative PAG areas that generated separation calls begin to generate cries of pain, suggesting that separation distress emerged evolutionarily from more primal pain mechanisms (Panksepp et al., 1988). In the cortex, the anterior cingulate has been implicated in the higher integration of social feelings (Devinsky, Morrell, & Vogt, 1995; MacLean, 1990). Presumably this system provides a special psychic energy to social motivation: It psychologically hurts to be alone.

The fine interconnectivities of these systems are not known, but many of the neurochemistries have been identified. One can activate this emotional response by injections of glutamate into the brain, and blockade of glutamate receptors can markedly reduce separation calls (Panksepp, 1996a, 1998a). Another important activator of this emotion is CRF, while several other peptides dramatically reduce separation distress, especially opioids, oxytocin, and prolactin. It is believed that the chemistries that modulate this emotion will be prominent among those that mediate social bonds, but definitive data are scarce. This system has been implicated in the genesis of early childhood autism, with some benefits observed following treatment of children with the opiate receptor antagonist naltrexone (Bouvard et al., 1995; Kolmen, Feldman, Handen, & Janosky, 1997).

Key issue: Is there a positive social affect response that is completely independent of this system, or does positive social affect always entail a reduction of arousal of the separation distress system?

The PLAY System

That basic brain systems for rough-and-tumble play exist in mammalian brains is a certainty. It is likely that this constitutes a basic system for joy in the mammalian brain. The neural aspects of this system are not well understood, but the evidence suggests that critical components are closely associated with separation distress systems, which makes good sense. The processes of joy and sadness are closely intertwined in the brain.

The most definitive brain evidence is that the parafasicular area integrates somatosensory signals that instigate play, and that essential components probably lie in the PAG—probably ventrorostral areas, where positive affective responses have been produced with brain stimulation. In general, the chemistries that activate separation distress tend to reduce play, while several chemistries that reduce separation distress, especially opioids, increase play (Panksepp, Siviy, & Normansell, 1984; Vanderschuren, Niesink, & Van Ree, 1997).

Recently we have discovered a tickling-induced vocalization pattern in young rats that may reflect a primitive form of mammalian laughter. Animals exhibit strong appetitive conditioning and preference for stimuli associated with the tickling (Panksepp & Burgdorf, 1998, 1999). This type of vocalization is present in abundance when young animals play (Knutson, Burgdorf, & Panksepp, 1998). Since this response measure is much easier to study than play itself, it may provide a special avenue into the analysis of the brain mechanisms of social joy.

It appears likely that a great deal of social dominance is also learned through the dictates of play sytems. Whether there is an intrinsic brain system for the independent generation of DOMINANCE remains unknown. There are many implications in the study of such ludic systems of the brain—for instance, understanding childhood disorders such as attention-deficit/hyperactivity disorder (ADHD), which may reflect excessive activity in the rough-and-tumble play systems of the brain (Panksepp, 1998b,d). Hence a *key issue* is this: *What are the consequences of this system for mental health issues? Is overactivity in this system one of the major causes of ADHD? Can ADHD be diminished by more systematic exercise of this system?*

AFFECTIVE FEELINGS AND EMOTIONAL COMMAND SYSTEMS

Should any one of the many aspects of emotions—facial, vocal, feeling, cognitive, autonomic, neurological—have primacy within our conceptualization of the nature of emotions? Some of us would say that the neurological dimensions, taken in conjunction with a careful psychological analysis, will ultimately be decisive in framing proper conceptualizations, but this is not a view that is common currency in the psychological sciences. Among the public at large, the understanding of the nature of "feelings" is generally deemed to be the essential issue (e.g., Figure 9.1). I also agree with that, but no true understanding of the nature of feelings can be achieved without a neurological analysis. Regrettably, this topic is not being vigorously pursued, since there is no unambiguous or agreed upon way to experimentally analyze subjective states. Since the neural causes of our various emotional feelings lie hidden among neurodynamics that we cannot clearly envision, most neuroscientists consider "feelings" to be outside the realm of reductive scientific analysis. Indeed, talk about such matters is often deemed inappropriate in polite scientific discussions and philosophical arguments.

Still, most of us, as deeply feeling individuals, know that there is something very powerful under the veneer of our external actions and surface appearances that speaks to us directly about the deep biological values within our lives. Animals' behavior is strongly suggestive that their behavior is governed by similar processes. Do we need any more reason than that to accept feelings as an equal partner among all the other dimensions we must focus on to consider in understanding emotions? Indeed, by carefully triangulating among (1) the analysis of instinctive and learned emotional behaviors that suggest the operation of such emotional processes, (2) a study of the underlying brain substrates, and (3) an attempt to validate the findings and hypotheses so derived by studying human subjective experience, we can construct a sufficiently robust strategy to seek a lasting understanding of the nature of affective feelings within mammalian brains (Panksepp, 1991, 1998a)

Considering the likelihood that the basic emotional feeling states are natural consequences of ancient brain functions, we must develop model systems to systematically study the neurological nature of feelings. Out of necessity, the most penetrating lines of evidence must come from brain research in other animals, where the relevant brain systems can be modified and studied in sufficiently precise molecular detail, using sensitive behavioral measures such as place preference and avoidance tests (Schechter & Calcagnetti, 1993).

Connections from such work to human issues will emerge largely from the implementation of neuropharmacological approaches, where homologous neurochemical systems are modified with pharmacological agents, so that ensuing mood states and emotional responsivity are systematically monitored (Panksepp,

1986a). Already we have abundant data that facilitation of serotonin activity in the brain can take the emotional edge off most negative moods, and can thereby promote positive feelings and confident social interchange (Knutson, Wolkowitz, et al., 1998). Equally fascinating trends are emerging from the study of other brain chemistries, especially those drugs of abuse that promote brain dopamine arousal (Blum, Cull, Braverman, & Comings, 1996).

At present only a few neuropeptides can be modulated in a comparable manner (largely because of the availability of nonpeptide congeners that can enter the brain). Opiates have long been known to produce transient positive mood states, but the opponent processes that emerge when such agents dissipate, result in strikingly negative moods (Panksepp, Siviy, & Normansell, 1985). Antianxiety agents working through CRF blockade have emerged as promising antifear and antistress drugs (Perrin, M.H., Sutton, Bain, Berggren, & Vale, 1998). NPY receptor stimulants may prove to have similar effects (Kask, Rago, & Harro, (1998). Recently blockade of substance P has yielded robust antidepressant effects (Kramer et al., 1998), and these finding were based on separation distress models developed decades ago (Panksepp, Herman, Villberg, Bishop, & De-Eskinazi, 1980). We can anticipate that molecules that will block vasopressin may reduce male sexual cravings, while those that stimulate oxytocin receptors may promote social warmth and bonding (for reviews, see Carter, Kirkpatrick, & Lederhendler, 1997).

There are a remarkable number of other exciting possibilities on the horizon, but we should remember that therapeutic effects of such maneuvers will require that the agents get to the proper receptors in the proper amounts. Many neuropeptide receptor systems change dynamically as a function of environmental events and bodily conditions that organisms are exposed to (Insel, 1992), and at present we have no assurance that the right receptors will be available for modulation at the times such agents are given. The classic example of this principle was the discovery that the onset of birth, which is characterized by high oxytocin activity on uterine muscles, is due not to increased secretion of oxytocin within the body, but to the massive proliferation of oxytocin receptors in the uterus of the parturient female (Soloff, Alexandrova, & Fernstrom, 1979). Thus the use of some peptide receptor stimulants may require prior priming of the relevant brain receptive fields so that a receptor agonist can have a desired effect.

ON THE OBJECTIVE MEASUREMENT OF EMOTIONAL FEELINGS

Considering that feelings are neurodynamic states of the brain that respond to certain types of external stimuli as well as cognitive attributions, the only option until recently was to measure such states indirectly though behavioral changes in animals and verbal reports in humans. Neither is a fully satisfactory approach. It is still widely assumed that all animal behaviors can be explained without resort to ephemeral neurodynamic concepts such as feelings. Indeed, various emotional behaviors, such as threat display, may be useful acts that are not necessarily accompanied by affective states. Likewise, it is well appreciated how effectively humans can deceive others as well as themselves, unintentionally as often as not. Since the priorities of the nonspeaking, less emotional right hemisphere are commonly overridden by the speaking left hemisphere which is more adept at putting on a social front (Ross, Homan, & Buck, 1994), there is also a special barrier to studying feelings in humans through verbal reports—of which we must always remain wary. This makes it all the more important to seek more objective brain measures of emotional states.

Great progress has been made in the brain imaging of emotional states (George, Kettner, Kimbrell, Steedman, & Post, 1996; Lane et al., 1997; Paradiso, Robinson, Andreasen, Downhill, & Davidson, 1997), but we will also need more routine measures such as electroencephalographic (EEG) ones to detect affective signatures in the brain (Freeman, 1960, 1995). To some extent this has been achieved by monitoring frontal cortical alpha power (Davidson, 1993; Davidson & Fox, 1989; Henriques & Davidson, 1991; Dawson, Panagiotides, Klinger, & Spieker, 1997), as well as related approaches (Ahren & Schwartz, 1985; Smith, Meyers, Kline, & Bozman, 1987). We have applied variants of EEG algorithms to similar ends, but have detected only modest differential effects of happy and sad music segments on topographic EEG signals (Panksepp & Bekkedal, 1997). There was some tendency of

sad music to promote cerebral arousal (desynchronization), and for happy pieces to promote cerebral synchronization, but the effects were not robust enough for routine detection of emotion-specific responses from the cerebral surface. A similar lack of discriminability was observed with brief emotional sounds (joy, anger, pleasure, and sadness), even though there were interesting gender differences—such as the greater tendency of female brains to exhibit synchronization to anger, and of male brains to exhibit greater desynchronization to pleasure sounds (Bekkedal, 1997).

It may well be that surface recordings are so far from the generators of emotion that distinct cortical signatures for the basic emotions cannot be achieved in that way. This problem is especially clearly highlighted by the inability of sleep EEG researchers to detect powerful subcortical storms characteristic of rapid-eye-movement sleep, such as pontine–geniculate occipital cortex spikes, which are not evident from recordings off the cortical surface. Thus, if we are going to achieve EEG signals indicative of discrete emotional processes, we will probably have to situate our electrodes astride the subcortical systems and attempt to characterize the signatures of the individual systems when various emotions are aroused—preferably under strict stimulus control, as might be achieved with electrical stimulation of discrete brain loci. Obviously, this will entail a great deal of animal brain research that remains to be initiated (Panksepp, in press).

Emotional Memories

Although great progress has been made recently in unraveling the manner in which FEAR systems come under the conditional control of associated world events (LeDoux, 1996), there is one quite perplexing characteristic of emotional memories. If everyday human reports are to be believed, it appears that the brain is much more skilled in remembering the world events associated with arousal of emotional states than the intensity of the affective processes themselves. This would suggest that emotional feelings are not simply reflections of information functions in working memory.

In my estimation, emotional feelings must be elaborated in parts of the brain other than the areas of the cortex that mediate memories. The possibility that one can establish long-term habitual changes in emotional systems is largely unstudied, even though there is some evidence that one can modify the emotional temperament of animals by chronically stimulating certain emotional circuits (Adamec, 1991, 1993).

What Is an Affective Feeling?

At present, there are few proposals of how feelings are created in the brain. The classic James–Lange view, which guided thinking during most of the 20th century, was that emotional feelings arise from the cortical readout of the sensory commotion that transpires in our peripheral visceral organs during various energized behaviors. Although peripherally initiated feelings surely exist, the peripheralist view is quite incomplete and probably largely misleading. It is more probable that feelings emerge more directly from the neurosymbolic and neurodynamic representations of viscera and other body components within the brain (Panksepp, 1998a,c).

A few theorists have vigorously defended the position that higher brain functions are essential for the generation of feelings (e.g., LeDoux, 1996), but the evidence against such position is substantial. One of the most compelling is the failure of direct neocortical stimulation to promote affective states. By contrast, direct experimental evidence for various brainstem areas for the mediation of affect is very substantial (David & Cazal, 1996; Olmstead & Franklin, 1997; Panksepp, 1985). Damage to the cortex only modulates the degree of emotionality, not the ability to have emotional feelings. In general, decorticate animals are just as emotional as, and perhaps more emotional than, normal ones (Panksepp et al., 1994). Clearly, what the cortex allows is ever more sophisticated ways for organisms to regulate their emotions—to extend and shorten emotional episodes in time, to focus their emotional resources via learning, and in humans to parse basic emotional concepts in increasingly sophisticated ways.

So how might we now conceptualize feelings to emerge from brain dynamics? One proposal is to assume that it arises from the arousal of specific emotional circuits that course through the brain interacting with neurosymbolic bodily representations: The primal source of emotional feelings may be the fluctuating neurodynamics of a "virtual body" image that is constructed primarily by spontaneously active neural nets representing "selfness" in the midbrain and lower brainstem (Panksepp, 1998a,c). Such an endogenous pattern of neural activity may serve to maintain a resting tone within the musculature, and may provide a homeostatic reference point for various types of disturbances that are ultimately felt as affective states by interacting with many higher strata of the nervous system. In other words, there may be an "actor" rather than an "observer" at the center of the "Cartesian theater"—the widely ramifying workspace of consciousness (Baars, 1997; Newman, 1997).

The very core of the virtual bodily representation upon which emotional systems operate, may be constructed more in terms of motor than of sensory coordinates (Panksepp, 1998c). Of course, to yield any adaptive behaviors, it would obviously have to be strongly influenced by sensory inputs. As a working hypothesis, I am willing to assume that such a virtual motor representation may have been an essential neural prerequisite for the emergence of the ability of the evolving nervous system to generate simple goal-directed and avoidant behaviors. In short, I am assuming that the initial evolution of sensory guidance systems had to be based on certain preexisting levels of motor competence. Presumably some type of primitive motor representation—an evolutionary given for organisms—provided a solid foundation for additional psychobehavioral developments, and the initial varieties of approach and avoidance movements established an essential foundation of intrinsic values for future affective developments.

The epicenter of such a fundamental brain process has been conceptualized to reside in primitive centromedial zones of the diencephalon and mesencephalon such as the PAG (Panksepp, 1998a,c). Indeed, there is massive convergence of emotional circuits into the PAG, and the rich ascending and descending connectivities of this brain area (Cameron, Khan, Westlund, Cliffer, & Willis, 1995; Cameron, Khan, Westlund, & Willis, 1995; Mantyh, 1982) may control a great deal of brain activity (Depaulis & Bandler, 1991; Holstege, Bandler, & Saper, 1996). For instance, by interacting with adjacent neural systems for exteroceptive attention and consciousness, such as the Extended Reticulo Thalamic Activating System (ERTAS; Baars, 1998; Newman, 1997), such integrative systems establish global affective states throughout the nervous system. This view of brain organization has recently been rather fully discussed (Watt, 1998).

Although this idea needs to be fleshed out with additional empirical findings, I would hazard some fairly radical predictions. For instance, I would assume that the foundation of higher forms of consciousness is based on primitive affective foundations, and that if one damaged those foundations, higher forms of consciousness would be severely compromised. This, in fact, has long been known to be true for complete PAG damage (Bailey & Davis, 1942, 1943). Also, if this area of the brain sustains an endogenous, evolutionarily provided center of gravity for other brain activities, it would be expected to sustain neural reverberations most clearly after the brain is disconnected from inputs and outputs and sustained in tissue culture.

Indeed, it may be worth enunciating criteria that we may utilize for helping us identify brain tissues that sustain primary-process or core consciousness within the brain. An empirical focus on three neuroempirical attributes seems reasonable: (1) At key brain areas, global psychobehavioral abilities should be compromised to the greatest extent with the smallest amounts of brain damage across a diversity of species; (2) the most intense and coherent affective/ emotional behavioral states should be capable of being provoked with the lowest levels of exogenously applied brain stimulation, whether it be electrical or chemical; (3) anatomically, such information-rich convergence zones should receive the greatest concentrations of inputs from other brain areas, and they should also have, neuron for neuron, the most prolific outputs. At the present time the premiere candidate for such a brain area consists of the PAG and nearby surrounding tectal and tegmental tissues. This brain zone contains critical neural tissue for creating emotional feelings in the brain, even though many higher areas closely linked to these tissues, such as the anterior cingulate and other frontal areas where emotion-regulating circuits are concentrated (Devinsky et al., 1995), may be equally important in bringing these bodily feelings fully into human consciousness.

REFERENCES

Adamec, R. E. (1991). Partial kindling of the ventral hippocampus: Identification of changes in limbic physiology which accompany changes in feline aggression and defense. *Physiology and Behavior, 49,* 443–453.

Adamec, R. E. (1993). Lasting effect of FG-7142 on anxiety, aggression and limbic physiology in the rat. *Journal of Neurophysiology, 3,* 232–248.

Ahren, G. L., & Schwartz, G. E. (1985). Differential lateralization for positive and negative emotion in the human brain: EEG spectral analysis. *Neuropyschologia, 23,* 745–755.

Baars, B. J. (1998). *In the theater of consciousness. The workspace of the mind.* Cambridge, MA: MIT Press.

Bailey, P., & Davis, E. W. (1942). Effects of lesions of the periaqueductal gray matter in the cat *Proceedings of the Society for Experimental Biology and Medicine, 351,* 305–306.

Bailey, P., & Davis, E. W. (1943). Effects of lesions of the periaqueductal gray matter on the *Macaca mulatta. Journal of Neuropathology and Experimental Neurology, 3,* pp. 69–72.

Bandler, R., & Keay, K. A. (1996). Columnar organization in the midbrain periaqueductal gray and the integration of emotional expression. *Progress in Brain Research, 107,* 287–300.

Beck, C. H. M., & Fibiger, H. (1995). Conditioned fear-induced changes in behavior and the expression of the immediate early gene *c-fos:* With and without diazepam pretreatment. *Journal of Neuroscience, 15,* 709–720.

Becker, J. B., Breedlove, S. M., & Crews, D. (Eds.). (1992). *Behavioral endocrinology.* Cambridge, MA: MIT Press.

Beckett, S. R., Duxon, M. S., Aspley, S., & Marsden, C. A. (1997). Central c-Fos expression following 20kHz/ultrasound induced defence behaviour in the rat. *Brain Research Bulletin, 42,* 421–426.

Bekkedal, M. Y. V. (1997). *Emotion in the brain: EEG changes in response to emotional vocalizations.* Unpublished doctoral dissertation, Bowling Green State University, Bowling Green, OH.

Bem, D. J. (1996). Exotic becomes erotic: A developmental theory of sexual orientation. *Psychological Review, 103,* 320–335.

Blum, K., Cull, J. G., Braverman, E. R., & Comings, D. E. (1996). Reward-deficiency syndrome. *American Scientist, 84,* 132–145.

Bouvard, M. P., Leboyer, M., Launay, J. M., Recasens, C., Plumet, M. H., Waller-Perotte, D., Tabuteau, F., Bondoux, D., Dugas, M., Lensing, P., & Panksepp, J. (1995). Low-dose naltrexone effects on plasma chemistries and clinical symptoms in autism: A double-blind, placebo-controlled study. *Psychiatry Research. 58,* 191–201.

Brothers, L. (1997). *Friday's footprint: How society shapes the human mind.* New York: Oxford University Press.

Cameron, A. A., Khan, I. A., Westlund, K. N., Cliffer, K. D., & Willis, W. D. (1995). The efferent projections of the periaqueductal gray in the rat: a *Phaseolus vulgaris*–leucoagglutinin study. I. Ascending projections. *Journal of Comparative Neurology, 351,* 568–584.

Cameron, A. A., Khan, I. A., Westlund, K. N. & Willis, W. D. (1995b), The efferent projections of the periaqueductal gray in the rat: A *Phaseolus vulgaris*–leucoagglutinin study. II. Descending projections. *Journal of Comparative Neurology, 351,* 585–601.

Carter, S., Kirkpatrick, B., & Lederhendler, I.I. (Eds.).

(1997). Neurobiology of affiliation. *Annals of the New York Academy of Sciences, 807.*

Crenshaw, T., & Goldberg, J. P. (1996). *Sexual pharmacology: Drugs that affect sexual functioning.* New York: Norton.

Damasio, A. R. (1994). *Descartes' error.* New York: Putnam.

Depaulis, A., & Bandler, R. (Eds.). (1991). *The midbrain periaqueductal gray matter: Functional anatomical and neurochemical organization.* New York: Plenum Press.

Darwin, C. (1998). *The expression of the emotions in man and animals* (3rd ed.). New York: Oxford University Press. (Original work published 1872)

David, V., & Cazal, P. (1996). Preference for self-administration of a low dose of morphine into the ventral tegmental area rather than into the amygdala of mice. *Psychobiology, 24,* 211–218.

Davidson, R. J. (1993). The neuropsychology of emotion and affective style. In M. Lewis & J. M. Haviland (Eds.), *Handbook of emotions* (pp. 143–154). New York: Guilford Press.

Davidson, R. J., & Fox, N. A. (1989). Frontal brain asymmetry predicts infants response to maternal separation. *Journal of Abnormal Psychology, 98,* 127–131.

Davis, M. (1996). Fear-potentiated startle in the study of animal and human emotion. In R. Kavanaugh, B. Zimmerberg, & S. Fine (Eds.) *Emotion: An interdisciplinary approach* (pp. 61–89). Hillsdale, NJ: Erlbaum.

Dawson, G., Panagiotides, H., Klinger, L. G., & Spieker, S. (1997). Infants of depressed and nondepressed mothers exhibit differences in frontal brain electrical activity during the expression of negative emotions. *Developmental Psychology, 33,* 650–656.

Devinsky, O., Morrell, M.J., & Vogt, B.A. (1995). Contributions of anterior cingulate cortex to behavior. *Brain, 118,* 279–306.

Ekman, P. (1998). Universality of emotional expression?: A personal history of the dispute. In C. Darwin (1872/1998), *The expression of the emotions in man and animals* (3rd ed., pp. 363–393). New York: Oxford University Press.

Ekman, P. & Davidson, R. (Eds.). (1994). *Questions about emotions.* New York: Oxford University Press.

Everitt, B. J. (1990). Sexual motivation: A neural and behavioral analysis of the mechanisms underlying appetitive and copulatory responses of male rats. *Neuroscience and Biobehavioral Reviews, 14,* 217–232.

Fanselow, M. S. (1994). Neural organization of the defensive behavior system responsible for fear. *Psychonomic Bulletin Reviews, 1,* 429–438.

Freeman, W. J. (1960). Correlation of electrical activity of prepyriform cortex and behavior in cat. *Journal of Neurophysiology, 23,* 111–131.

Freeman, W. J. (1995). *Societies of brain: A study in the neuroscience of love and hate.* Hillsdale, NJ: Erlbaum.

George, M. S., Kettner, T. A., Kimbrell, T. A., Steedman, J. M., & Post, R. M. (1996). What functional imaging has revealed about the brain basis of mood and emotion. In J. Panksepp (Ed.). *Advances in bio-logical psychiatry* (Vol. 2, pp. 63–114). Greenwich, CT: JAI Press.

Ghiselin, M. T. (1997). *Metaphysics and the origin of species.* Albany: State University of New York Press.

Gray, J. A. (1990). Brain systems that mediate both emotion and cognition *Cognition and Emotion,* 269–288.

Griffiths, P. E. (1997). *What emotions really are.* Chicago: University of Chicago Press.

Henriques, J. B., & Davidson, R.J. (1991). Left frontal hypo-activation in depression. *Journal of Abnormal Psychology, 100,* 535–545.

Holstege, G., Bandler, R., & Saper, C. B. (Eds.). (1996). The emotional motor system. *Progress in Brain Research, 107.*

Ikemoto, S., & Panksepp, J. (1994). The relationship between self-stimulation and sniffing in rats: Does a common brain system mediate these behaviors? *Behavioural Brain Research, 61,* 143–162.

Insel, T. R. (1992). Oxytocin: A neuropeptide for affiliation—evidence from behavioral, autoradiographic and comparative studies. *Psychoneuroendocrinology, 17,* 3–35.

Jürgens, U. (1976). Reinforcing concomitants of electrically elicited vocalizations. *Experimental Brain Research, 26,* 203–214.

Kask, A., Rago, L., & Harro, J. (1998). Anxiolytic-like effect of neuropeptide Y (NPY) and NPY13-36 microinjected into vicinity of locus coeruleus in rats. *Brain Research, 788,* 345–348.

Kim, J. J. & Fanselow, M. S. (1992). Modality-specific retrograde amnesia of fear. *Science, 256,* 675–677.

Knutson, B., Burgdorf, J., & Panksepp, J. (1998). Anticipation of play elicits high-frequency ultrasonic vocalizations in young rats. *Journal of Comparative Psychology, 112,* 1–9.

Knutson, B., Wolkowitz, O. W., Cole, S. W., Chan, T., Moore, E. A., Johnson, R. C., Terpstra, J., Turner, R. A., & Reus, V. I. (1998) Serotonergic intervention selectively alters aspects of personality and social behavior in normal humans. *American Journal of Psychiatry, 155,* 373–379.

Kolmen, B. K., Feldman, H. M., Handen, B. L., & Janosky, J. E. (1997). Naltrexone in young autistic children: replication study and learning measures. *Journal of the American Academy of Child and Adolescent Psychiatry, 36,* 1570–1578.

Kollack-Walker, S., Watson, S. J., & Akil, H. (1997). Social stress in hamsters: Defeat activates specific neurocircuits within the brain. *Journal of Neuroscience, 15,* 8842–8855.

Kramer, M. S., Cutler, N., Feighner, J., Shrivastava, R., Carman, J., Sramek, J. J., Reines, S. A., Liu, G., Snavely, D., Wyatt-Knowles, E., Hale, J. J., Mills, S. G., MaCross, M., Swain, C. J., Harrison, T., Hill, R. G., Hefti, F., Scolnick, E. M., Cascieri, M. A., Chicchi, G. G., Sadowski, S., William, A. R., Hewson, L., Smith, D., Carlson, E. J., Hargreaves, R. J., & Rupnikak, N. M. J. (1998). Distinct mechanism for antidepressant activity by bolckade of central substance P receptors. *Science, 281,* 1640–1645.

Krasnegor, N. A., & Bridges, R. S. (Eds.). (1990). *Mammalian parenting.* New York: Oxford University Press.

Lane, R. D., Reiman, E. M., Bradley, M. M., Lang, P. J., Ahern, G. L., Davidson, R. J., & Schwartz, G. E. (1997), Neuroanatomical correlates of pleasant and unpleasant emotion. *Neuropsychologia, 35,* 1437–1444.

Lang, P. J. (1995). The emotion probe. *American Psychologist, 50,* 372–385.

LeDoux, J. (1984). Cognition and emotions: Processing functions and brain systems. In M. S. Gazzaniga (Ed.), *Handbook of cognitive neuroscience* (pp. 357–368). New York: Plenum Press.

LeDoux, J. (1996). *The emotional brain. The mysterious underpinnings of emotional life.* New York: Simon & Schuster.

MacLean, P. D. (1990). *The triune brain in evolution: Role in paleocerebral functions.* New York: Plenum Press.

Mantyh, P. W. (1982). Forebrain projections to the periaqueductal gray in the monkey, with observations in the cat and rat. *Journal of Comparative Neurology, 206,* 146–158.

Moss, R. L., & Dudley, C. A. (1984). The challenge of studying the behavioral effects of neuropeptides. In. L. L. Iversen, S. D. Iversen, & S. H. Snyder (Eds.), *Handbook of psychopharmacology* (Vol. 18, pp. 397–454). New York: Plenum Press.

Nelson, E., & Panksepp, J. (1998). Brain substrates of infant–mother attachment: Contributions of opioids, oxytocin, and norepinephrine. *Neuroscience and Biobehavioral Reviews, 22,* 237–452.

Newman, J. (1997). Putting the puzzle together: Towards a general theory of the neural correlates of consciousness. *Journal of Consciousness Studies, 4,* 47–66, 101–121.

Newman, S. W. (1999). The medial extended amygdala in male reproductive behavior. A node in the mammalian social behavior network. *Annals of the New York Academy of Sciences, 877,* 242–257.

Olmstead, M. C., & Franklin, K. B. (1997). The development of a conditioned place preference to morphine: Effects of microinjections into various CNS sites. *Behavioral Neuroscience, 111,* 1324–1334.

Ortony, A., & Turner, T. J. (1990). What's basic about basic emotions? *Psychological Review, 97,* 315–331.

Panksepp, J. (1982). Toward a general psychobiological theory of emotions. *Behavioral and Brain Sciences, 5,* 407–467.

Panksepp, J. (1985). Mood changes, In P. J. Vinken, G. W. Bruyn, & H. L. Klawans (Eds.), *Handbook of clinical neurology: Vol. 1. Clinical neuropsychology* (pp. 271–285). Amsterdam: Elsevier.

Panksepp, J. (1986a). The neurochemistry of behavior. *Annual Review of Psychology, 37,* 77–107.

Panksepp, J. (1986b). The anatomy of emotions. In R. Plutchik & H. Kellerman (Eds.), *Emotion: Theory, research, and experience. Vol. 3. Biological foundations of emotions* (pp. 91–124). New York: Academic Press.

Panksepp, J. (1990). The psychoneurology of fear: Evolutionary perspectives and the role of animal models in understanding anxiety, In G. D. Burrows, M. Roth, & R. Noyes Jr. (Eds.), *Handbook of anxiety: Vol. 3. The neurobiology of anxiety* (pp. 3–58). Amsterdam: Elsevier.

Panksepp, J. (1991). Affective neuroscience: A conceptual framework for the neurobiological study of emotions. In K. Strongman (Ed.), *International review of emotion research* (Vol. 1, pp. 59–99). Chichester, England: Wiley.

Panksepp, J. (1992). A critical role for "affective neuroscience" in resolving what is basic about basic emotions. *Psychological Review, 99,* 554–560.

Panksepp, J. (1993). Neurochemical control of moods and emotions: Amino acids to neuropeptides. In M. Lewis and J. Haviland (Eds.), *Handbook of emotions* (pp. 87–107). New York: Guilford Press.

Panksepp, J. (1994). The basics of basic emotions In R. Davidson & P. Ekman (Eds.), *Questions about emotions* (pp. 20–24). New York: Oxford University Press.

Panksepp, J. (1996a). Affective neuroscience: A paradigm to study the animate circuits for human emotions. In R. Kavanaugh, B. Zimmerberg, and S. Fine (Eds.), *Emotion: An interdisciplinary approach* (pp. 29–60). Hillsdale, NJ: Erlbaum.

Panksepp, J. (1996b). Modern approaches to understanding fear: From laboratory to clinical practice. In J. Panksepp (Ed.), *Advances in biological psychiatry* (Vol. 2, pp. 209–230). Greewich, CT: JAI Press.

Panksepp, J. (1998a). *Affective neuroscience: The foundations of human and animal emotions.* New York: Oxford University Press.

Panksepp, J. (1998b). The quest for long-term health and happiness: To play or not to play, that is the question. *Psychological Inquiry, 9,* 56–66.

Panksepp, J. (1998c). The periconscious substrates of consciousness: Affective states and the evolutionary origins of the SELF. *Journal of Consciousness Studies, 5,* 566–582.

Panksepp, J. (1998d). A critical analysis of ADHD, psychostimulants, and intolerance of childhood playfulness: A tragedy in the making? *Current Directions in Psychology, 7,* 91–98.

Panksepp, J. (in press). The neurodynamics of emotions: An evolutionary–neurodevelopmental view. In M. D. Lewis & I. Granic (Eds.), *Emotion, self-organization, and development.* New York: Cambridge University Press.

Panksepp, J., & Bekkedal, M. Y. V. (1997). The affective cerebral consequence of music: Happy vs. sad effects on the EEG and clinical implications. *International Journal of Arts Medicine, 5,* 18–27.

Panksepp, J., & Burgdorf, J. (1998). Laughing rats?: Playful tickling arouses 50KHz ultrasonic chirping in rats. *Society for Neuroscience Abstracts, 24,* 691.

Panksepp, J., & Burgdorf, J. (1999). Laughing rats?: Playful tickling arouses high frequency ultrasonic chirping in young rodents. In S. Hameroff, D. Chalmers, & A. Kazniak (Eds.), *Toward a science of consciousness III* (pp. 231–244). Cambridge, MA: MIT Press.

Panksepp, J., Herman, B. H., Villberg, T., Bishop, P., & DeEskinazi, F. G. (1980). Endogenous opioids and social behavior. *Neuroscience and Biobehavioral Reviews, 4,* 473–487.

Panksepp, J., Newman, J. D., & Insel, T. R. (1992). Critical conceptual issues in the analysis of separation distress systems of the brain. In K. T. Strongman

(Ed.), *International review of studies on emotion* (Vol. 2, pp. 51–72), Chichester, Encland: Wiley.

Panksepp, J., Normansell, L., Cox, J. F., & Siviy, S. M. (1994). Effects of neonatal decortication on the social play of juvenile rats. *Physiology and Behavior, 56,* 429–443.

Panksepp, J. , Normansell, L. , Herman, B., Bishop, P., & Crepeau, L. (1988). Neural and neurochemical control of the separation distress call. In. J. D. Newman (Ed.), *The physiological control of mammalian vocalizations* (pp. 263–300). New York: Plenum Press.

Panksepp, J., Sacks, D. S., Crepeau, L. J., & Abbott, B. B. (1991). The psycho- and neuro-biology of fear systems in the brain. In M. R. Denny (Ed.), *Aversive events and behavior* (pp. 7–59). Hillsdale, NJ: Erlbaum.

Panksepp, J., Siviy, S. M., & Normansell, L. A. (1984). The psychobiology of play: Theoretical and methodological perspectives. *Neuroscience and Biobehavioral Reviews, 8,* 465–492.

Panksepp, J. , Siviy, S. M., & Normansell, L.A. (1985). Brain opioids and social emotions. In M. Reite and T. Fields (Eds.), *The psychobiology of attachment and aeparation* (pp. 3–49). New York: Academic Press.

Paradiso, S., Robinson, R.G ., Andreasen, N. C., Downhill, J. E., & Davidson R. J. (1997). Emotional activation of limbic circuitry in elderly normal subjects in a PET study. *American Journal of Psychiatry. 154,* 384–389.

Perrin, M. H., Sutton, S., Bain, D. L., Berggren, W. T., & Vale, W. W. (1998). The first extracellular domain of corticotropin releasing factor-R1 contains major binding determinants for urocortin and astressin. *Endocrinology. 139,* 566–570.

Petersen, C. A., Caldwell, J. D., Jirikowski, G. F., & Insel, T. R. (Eds.). (1992). Oxytocin in maternal, sexual, and social behaviors. *Annals of the New York Academy of Sciences, 652.*

Rosen, J. B., & Schulkin, J. (1998). From normal fear to pathological anxiety. *Psychological Review, 105,* 325–350.

Ross, E. D., Homan, R. W., & Buck, R. (1994). Differential hemispheric lateralization of primary and social emotions. *Neuropsychiatry, Neuropsychology and Behavioral Neurology, 7,* 1–19.

Schechter, M. D., & Calcagnetti, D. J. (1993). Trends in place preference conditioning with a cross-indexed bibliography: 1957–1991. *Neuroscience and Biobehavioral Reviews, 17,* 21–41.

Schultz, W., Apicella, P., & Ljungberg, T. (1993). Responses of monkey dopamine neurons to reward and conditioned stimuli during successive steps of learning a delayed response task. *Journal of Neuroscience, 13,* 900–913.

Siegel, A., & Schubert, K. (1995). Neurotransmitters regulating feline aggressive behavior. *Reviews of Neuroscience, 6,* 47–61.

Silveira, M. C., Graeff, F. G., & Sandner, G. (1994). Regional distribution of Fos-like immunoreactivity in the rat brain after exposure to fear-inducing stimuli. *Brazilian Journal of Medical and Biological Research, 27,* 1077–1081.

Smith, B. D., Meyers, M., Kline, R., & Bozman, A. (1987). Hemispheric asymmetry and emotion: Lateralized parietal processing of affect and cognition. *Biological Psychology, 25,* 247–260.

Soloff, M. S., Alexandrova, M., & Fernstrom, M. J. (1979). Oxytocin receptors: Triggers for parturition and lactation? *Science, 204,* 1313–1314.

Vanderschuren, L. J., Niesink, R. J., & Van Ree, J. M. (1997). The neurobiology of social play behavior in rats. *Neuroscience and Biobehavioral Reviews, 21,* 309–326.

Watt, D. (1998), *The Association for the Scientific Study of Consciousness electronic seminar on emotion and consciousness, Sept. 21, 1998–Oct. 9, 1998* [Online]. Available: http: //www. phil. vt. edu/ assc/ esem. html [1998, Oct. 9].

CHAPTER 10

Emotional Networks in the Brain

Joseph E. LeDoux
Elizabeth A. Phelps

Contemporary neuroscientists have available a vast arsenal of tools for understanding brain functions, from the level of anatomical systems to the level of molecules. Localization of function at the anatomical level is the oldest but also the most basic approach. Until the function in question can be localized to a specific set of structures and their connections, application of cellular and molecular approaches is the neurobiological equivalent of a search for a needle in a haystack. Fortunately, considerable progress has been made in understanding the anatomical organization of one emotion, fear, and this chapter focuses on this work. Whereas most of the progress in the past came from studies of experimental animals, recent studies in humans, some capitalizing on new techniques for imaging the human brain, have confirmed and extended the animal work.

IN SEARCH OF
THE EMOTIONAL BRAIN

Our understanding of the brain mechanisms of emotion has changed radically over the past 100 years. In the late 19th century, William James (1884) suggested that emotion is a function of sensory and motor areas of the neocortex, and that the brain does not possess a special system devoted to emotional functions. This idea was laid low by studies showing that emotional reactions require the integrity of the hypothalamus (Cannon, 1929; Bard, 1929). On the basis of such observations, Papez (1937) proposed a circuit theory of emotion involving the hypothalamus, anterior thalamus, cingulate gyrus, and hippocampus. MacLean (1949, 1952) then named the structures of the Papez circuit, together with several additional regions (amygdala, septal nuclei, orbito-frontal cortex, portions of the basal ganglia), the "limbic system"; he viewed the limbic system as a general-purpose system involved in the mediation of functions required for the survival of the individual and the species.

MacLean's writings were very persuasive, and for many years the problem of relating emotion to brain mechanisms seemed solved at the level of anatomical systems. However, the limbic system concept came under fire beginning in the 1980s (see Brodal, 1982; Swanson, 1983; LeDoux, 1987, 1991; Kotter & Meyer, 1991). It is now believed that the concept suffers from imprecision at both the structural and functional levels. For example, it has proven impossible to provide unequivocal criteria for defining which structures and pathways should be included in the limbic system (Brodal, 1982; Swanson, 1983). A standard criterion, connectivity with the hypothalamus, extends the limbic system to include structures at all levels of the central nervous system, from the neocortex to the spinal cord. Furthermore, classic limbic areas, such as the hippocampus and mammillary bodies, have proven to be far more important for cognitive processes (such as declarative memory) than for emotional processes (e.g., Squire & Zola, 1996; Cohen & Eichenbaum, 1993).

Nevertheless, one limbic area that has been consistently implicated in emotional processes in a variety of situations is the amygdala (e.g., Gloor, 1960; Mishkin & Aggleton, 1981; Aggleton & Mishkin, 1986; LeDoux, 1987, 1996; Rolls, 1986, 1992; Halgren, 1992; Aggleton, 1992; Davis, 1992; Kapp, Whalen, Supple, & Pascoe, 1992; Ono and Nishijo, 1992; Damasio, 1994; Everitt & Robbins, 1992; McGaugh et al., 1995). Interestingly, the amygdala was not part of the Papez circuit model and was clearly a second-class citizen, relative to the hippocampus at least, in the limbic system hypothesis. However, the survival of the limbic system hypothesis for so long may be largely due to the inclusion of the amygdala (LeDoux, 1992). Otherwise, the relation between emotional functions and classic limbic areas would have been far less prominent over the years.

THE AMYGDALA AS AN EMOTIONAL COMPUTER

The contribution of the amygdala to emotion emerged from studies of the Kluver–Bucy syndrome, a complex set of behavioral changes brought about by damage to the temporal lobe in primates (Kluver & Bucy, 1937). Following such lesions, animals lose their fear of previously threatening stimuli, attempt to copulate with members of other species, and attempt to eat a variety of things that "normal" primates find unattractive (feces, meat, rocks). Studies by Weiskrantz (1956) then determined that lesions confined to the amygdala and sparing other temporal lobe structures produce the emotional components of the syndrome. Weiskrantz proposed that amygdala lesions interfere with the ability to determine the motivational significance of stimuli. A host of subsequent studies have shown that the amygdala is a key structure in the assignment of reward value to stimuli (Jones & Mishkin, 1972; Spiegler & Mishkin, 1981; Gaffan & Harrison, 1987; Gaffan, Gaffan, & Harrison, 1988; Everitt & Robbins, 1992; Ono & Nishijo, 1992; Rolls, 1992), in the conditioning of fear to novel stimuli (Blanchard & Blanchard, 1972; Kapp et al., 1992; Davis, 1992, 1994; LeDoux, 1996; Maren & Fanselow, 1996), in the self-administration of rewarding brain stimulation (Kane,

Coulombe, & Miliaressis, 1991; Olds, 1977), and in the elicitation by brain stimulation of a host of behavioral and autonomic responses typical of emotional reactions (Hilton & Zbrozyna, 1963; Fernandez de Molina & Hunsperger, 1962; Kapp, Pascoe, & Bixler, 1984; Iwata, Chida, & LeDoux, 1987). These and other findings have led a number of authors to conclude that the amygdala plays an important role in the assignment of affective significance to sensory events.

As important as the various studies described above have been in establishing that the amygdala plays a role in emotional processes, most of the studies were done with little appreciation for the anatomical organization of the amygdala. It is generally believed that there are at least a dozen diffferent nuclei, and that each has several subdivisions, each with its own set of unique connections (e.g., Pitkänen, Savander, & LeDoux, 1997). If we are to understand how the amygdala participates in computation of emotional significance, we need to take these distinctions into account.

NEURAL PATHWAYS INVOLVED IN FEAR PROCESSING

Much of our understanding of the role of different regions of the amygdala in emotional processes has come from studies of fear conditioning, where an auditory stimulus, a conditioned stimulus (CS), is paired with footshock, the unconditioned stimulus (US). The reason this task has been so successful in mapping the pathways is, in large part, the simplicity of the task itself. It involves a discrete, well-defined CS and stereotyped autonomic and behavioral conditioned responses (CRs), both of which are very helpful when one is trying to relate brain function to brain structure. Also, fear conditioning can and has been used similarly in animal and human studies, which has allowed the establishment of commonalities in the underlying brain systems. Fear conditioning may not be able to tell us everything we need to know about emotions and the brain, or even about fear and the brain, but it has been an excellent starting point.

Basic Circuits

The pathways involved in conditioning of fear responses to a single-tone CS are shown in Figure 10.1. The CS is transmitted through the auditory system to the medial geniculate body (MGB), the auditory relay nucleus in the thalamus (LeDoux, Sakaguchi, & Reis, 1984). The signal is then transmitted from all regions of the auditory thalamus to the auditory cortex, and from a subset of thalamic nuclei to the amygdala. The thalamo-amygdala pathway originates primarily in the medial division of the MGB and the associated posterior intralaminar nucleus (LeDoux, Cicchetti, Xagoraris, & Romanski, 1990). The auditory association cortex also gives rise to a projection to the amygdala (Romanski & LeDoux, 1993; Mascagni, McDonald, & Coleman, 1993). Both the thalamo-amygdala and thalamo-cortico-amygdala pathways terminate in the sensory input region of the amygdala, the lateral nucleus (LA) (see Turner & Herkenham, 1991; LeDoux, Cicchetti, et al., 1990; Romanski & LeDoux, 1993; Mascagni et al., 1993). In fact, the two pathways converge onto single neurons in LA (Li, Stutzman, & LeDoux, 1996). Damage to LA interferes with fear conditioning (LeDoux, Cicchetti, et al., 1990), which can be mediated by either the thalamo-amygdala or thalamo-cortico-amygdala pathways (for discussions, see Romanski & LeDoux, 1993; Campeau & Davis, 1995; Corodimas & LeDoux, 1995). Temporary inactivation of LA and the adjacent basal nucleus (Helmstetter & Bellgowan, 1994; Muller, Corodimas, Fridel, & LeDoux, 1997) or pharmacological blockade of excitatory amino acid receptors in this region (Miserendino, Sananes, Melia, & Davis, 1990; Kim & Fanselow, 1992; Maren & Fanselow, 1996;

Gewirtz & Davis, 1997) also disrupts the acquisition of conditioned fear, and facilitation of excitatory amino acid transmission enhances the rate of fear learning (Rogan, Staubli, & LeDoux, 1997).

Although the auditory cortex is not required for the acquisition of conditioned fear to a simple auditory stimulus (Romanski & LeDoux, 1992; Armony, Servan-Schreiber, Romanski, Cohen, & LeDoux, 1997), processing of the CS by cells in the auditory cortex is modified as a result of its pairing with the US (Weinberger, 1995; Quirk, Armony, & LeDoux, 1997). In situations involving more complex stimuli that must be discriminated, recognized, and/or categorized, the auditory cortex may be an essential link to the amygdala (e.g., Cranford & Igarashi, 1977; Whitfield, 1980).

The dual sensory inputs to the amygdala are depicted in Figure 10.2, which shows the thalamic projections as the "low road" and the cortical inputs as the "high road." What are the advantages of the parallel processing capabilities of this system? First, the existence of a subcortical pathway allows the amygdala to detect threatening stimuli in the environment quickly, in the absence of a complete and time-consuming analysis of the stimulus. This "quick and dirty" processing route may confer an evolutionary advantage to the species. Second, the rapid subcortical pathway may function to "prime" the amygdala to evaluate subsequent information received along the cortical pathway (LeDoux, 1986a, 1986b; Li et al., 1996). For example, a loud noise may be sufficient to alert the amygdala at the cellular level to pre-

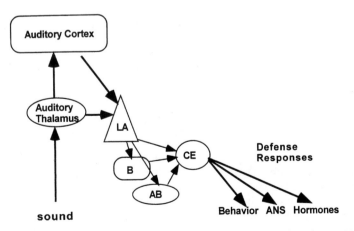

FIGURE 10.1. Auditory pathways to amygdala circuits. AB, accessory basal nucleus; ANS, autonomic nervous system; B, basal nucleus; CE, central nucleus; LA, lateral nucleus.

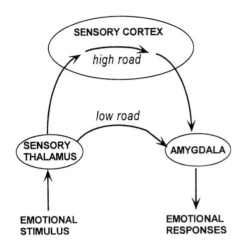

FIGURE 10.2. The dual sensory inputs to the amygdala.

pare to respond to a dangerous predator lurking nearby, but defensive reactions may not be fully mobilized until the auditory cortex analyzes the location, frequency, and intensity of the noise, to determine specifically the nature and extent of this potentially threatening auditory signal. The convergence of the subcortical and cortical pathways onto single neurons in the LA (Li et al., 1996) provides a means by which the integration can take place. Third, recent computational modeling studies show that the subcortical pathway can function as an interrupt device that enables the cortex, by way of amygdalo-cortical projections, to shift attention to dangerous stimuli that occur outside the focus of attention (Armony, Servan-Schreiber, Cohen, & LeDoux, 1996).

As noted, sensory information from both the thalamus and the cortex enters the amygdala through the LA. Information processed by the LA is then transmitted via intra-amygdala connections (Pitkänen et al., 1997) to the basal and accessory basal nuclei, where it is integrated with other incoming information from other areas and further transmitted to the central nucleus. The central nucleus is the main output system of the amygdala. Damage to the central amygdala or structures that project to it interferes with the acquisition and expression of all CRs, whereas lesions of areas to which the central amygdala projects interfere with individual responses, such as blood pressure changes, freezing behavior, or hormone release (e.g., see LeDoux,1996).

Contextualization of Fear

Whether a stimulus signals danger, and thus elicits fear reactions, often depends on the situation (context) in which it occurs. For example, the sight of a bear in the zoo poses little threat, but the same bear seen while on a walk in the woods would make us run away in fear. Furthermore, contexts may themselves acquire aversive value through prior experiences. If we are mugged, we are very likely to feel "uneasy" when we return to the scene of the crime. The relationship between environmental situations and fear responses can been investigated in the laboratory through contextual fear conditioning: When a rat is conditioned to expect a footshock in the presence of a tone CS, it will also exhibit fear reactions to the chamber where the conditioning took place, even in the absence of the CS (Kim & Fanselow, 1992; Phillips & LeDoux, 1992). Several studies have shown that the formation and consolidation of contextual fear associations depend on the hippocampus. Lesions of the hippocampus made prior to training interfere with the acquisition of CRs to the context without having any effect on the conditioning to the CS (Maren, Anagnostaras, & Fanselow, 1998; Frankland, Cestari, Filipkowski, McDonald, & Silva, 1998; Phillips & LeDoux, 1992, 1994; Selden, Everitt, Jarrard, & Robbins, 1991). Furthermore, hippocampal lesions made after training interfere with the consolidation and retention of contextual fear associations (Kim & Fanselow, 1992). Bidirectional projections between the hippocampal formation and the amygdala (Amaral, Price, Pitkänen, & Carmichael, 1992; Canteras & Swanson, 1992; Ottersen, 1982) provide anatomical channels through which the attachment of emotional value to context may take place. The fibers from the hippocampus to the amygdala terminate extensively in the basal and accessory basal nuclei, and to a much lesser extent in the LA, suggesting why lesions of the LA have little effect on context conditioning, but lesions of the basal nucleus and/or accessory basal nucleus seem to be disruptive (Maren, Aharonov, Stote, & Fanselow, 1996; Majidishad, Pelli, & LeDoux, 1996). The role of the hippocampus in the evaluation of contextual cues in fear conditioning is consistent with current theories of spatial, configural, and/or relational processing in the hippocampus (Cohen & Eichenbaum, 1993; O'Keefe & Nadel, 1978; Sutherland & Rudy, 1989). The different inputs involved in conditioning to a discrete tone CS and to context are shown in Figure 10.3.

Getting Rid of Fear

Fear responses tend to be very persistent. This has obvious survival advantages, as it allows us to keep a record of previously encountered threatening experiences, and thus allows us to respond quickly to similar situations in the future. Nonetheless, it is also important to be able to learn that a stimulus no longer signals danger. Otherwise, unnecessary fear responses will be elicited by innocuous stimuli and may potentially become a liability, interfering with other important routine tasks. In humans, the inability to inhibit unwarranted fear responses can have devastating consequences, as observed in phobias, posttraumatic stress disorder, generalized anxiety disorder, and other anxiety disorders. In laboratory experiments, learned fear responses can be reduced (extinguished) by repeatedly presenting the CS without the US. It is important to note, however, that extinction of conditioned fear responses is not a passive forgetting of the CS-US association, but an active process, possibly involving a new learning (Bouton & Swartzentruber, 1991). In fact, CS-elicited responses can be spontaneously reinstated following an unrelated traumatic experience (Pavlov, 1927; Jacobs & Nadel, 1985; Rescorla & Heth, 1975). Experimental observations in fear conditioning studies suggest that neocortical areas, particularly areas of the prefrontal cortex, are involved in the extinction process. Lesions of the medial prefrontal cortex lead to a potentiation of fear responses and a retardation the extinction (Morgan, Romanski, & LeDoux, 1993; Morgan & LeDoux, 1995; but see Gewirtz & Davis, 1997). These findings complement electrophysiological studies showing that neurons

within the orbito-frontal cortex are particularly sensitive to changes in stimulus–reward associations (Thorpe, Rolls, & Maddison, 1983; Rolls, 1996). Lesions of sensory areas of the cortex also retard extinction (LeDoux, Romanski, & Xagoraris, 1989; Teich et al., 1989), and neurons in auditory cortex exhibit extinction-resistant changes to an auditory CS (Quirk et al., 1997). Thus the medial prefrontal cortex, possibly in conjunction with other neocortical regions, may be involved in regulating amygdala responses to stimuli based on their current affective value. These findings suggest that fear disorders may be related to a malfunction of the prefrontal cortex that makes it difficult for patients to extinguish fears they have acquired (Morgan et al., 1993; Morgan & LeDoux, 1995; LeDoux, 1996). Recent studies have shown that stress has the same effects as lesions of the medial prefrontal cortex (fear exaggeration) (Corodimas, LeDoux, Gold, & Schulkin, 1994; Conrad, Margarinos, LeDoux, & McEwen, 1997). Given that stress is a common occurrence in psychiatric patients, and that such patients can have functional changes in the prefrontal cortex (Drevets et al., 1997; Bremner et al., 1995), it is possible that the exaggeration of fear in anxiety disorders results from stress-induced alterations in the medial prefrontal region.

Emotional Action

The defensive responses we have considered so far are hard-wired reactions to danger signals. These are evolution's gifts to us; they provide a first line of defense against danger. Some animals rely mainly on these. But mammals, especially humans, can do much more. We are able to take charge. Once we find ourselves in a dangerous situation, we can think, plan, and make decisions. We make the transition from

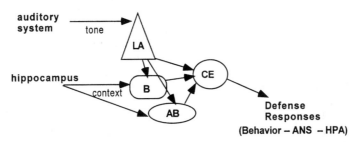

FIGURE 10.3. Discrete cues and contextual stimuli enter the amygdala differently. HPA, hypothalamic–pituitary–adrenal axis; other abbreviations as in Figure 10.1.

reaction to action. Considerably less is understood about the brain mechanisms of emotional action than reaction, due in part to the fact that emotional actions come in many varieties and are limited only by the ingenuity of the actor. For example, once we are freezing and expressing physiological responses to a dangerous stimulus, the rest is up to us. On the basis of our expectations about what is likely to happen next and our past experiences in similar situations, we make a plan about what to do. We become instruments of action. Instrumental responses in situations of danger are often studied using avoidance conditioning procedures.

Avoidance is a multistage learning process (Mowrer & Lamoreaux, 1946). First, fear CRs responses are acquired. Then the CS becomes a signal that is used to initiate responses that prevent encounters with the US. Finally, once avoidance responses are learned, animals no longer show the characteristic signs of fear (Rescorla & Solomon, 1967). They know what to do to avoid the danger and simply perform the response in a habitual way. Consistent with this is the fact that the amygdala is required for avoidance learning (for the fear conditioning part) but not for the expression of well-trained avoidance responses (the instrumental part) (Parent, Tomaz, & McGaugh, 1992). The involvement of an instrumental component to some aversive learning tasks may explain why these are not dependent on the amygdala for long-term storage (Packard, Williams, Cahill, &McGaugh, 1995; McGaugh et al., 1995).

Because avoidance learning involves fear conditioning, at least initially, it will be subject to all the factors that influence fear conditioning and conditioned fear responding. However, because avoidance learning involves more than simple fear conditioning, it is to be expected that avoidance will be subject to influences that have little or no effect on conditioned fear. Much more work is needed to understand how fear and avoidance interact, and thus how emotional actions emerge out of emotional reactions. From what we know so far, it appears that, as in other habit systems (Mishkin, Malamut, & Bachevalier, 1984), interactions among the amygdala, basal ganglia, and neocortex are important in avoidance (Everitt & Robbins, 1992; Gray, 1987; Killcross, Robbins, & Everitt, 1997) (see Figure 10.4).

The avoidance circuits may be the means through which emotional behaviors are performed initially as voluntary responses and then converted into habits. Emotional habits can be useful, but can also be quite detrimental. Successful avoidance is known to prevent extinction of conditioned fear, since the opportunity to experience the CS in the absence of the US is eliminated by the avoidance. In real life, this can perpetuate anxiety states. The panic patient who never leaves home as a means of avoiding having a panic attack is but one example.

Modulation of Fear

The circuits described above do not by any means exhaust the systems involved in emotional functions. Processing in these pathways is influenced by a number of other systems. The contribution of these other systems is best viewed as modulating the processing that occurs in the through processing systems. Modulating influences arise both from within the brain and from the periphery. A thorough discussion of modulatory systems is beyond the scope of this chapter; we will therefore focus on studies that have shown how modulatory systems interact with amygdala functions.

Modulatory networks within the brain include the various chemically identified neuronal groups that innervate widespread areas of the forebrain. Some of these, such as the norepinephrine containing neurons of the locus coeruleus, the dopamine-containing neurons of the ventral tegmental area, and the cholinergic brainstem neurons in the dorsal tegmentum, are in the brainstem. Others, such as the cholinergic cells in the nucleus of Meynert, are in the forebrain. As an illustration, we focus on the basal forebrain cholinergic system.

It has long been known that cholinergic cells in the basal forebrain regulate cortical functions (see Shepherd, 1997). Related to this fact, Weinberger and colleagues found that the processing of auditory signals—specifically, the regulation of auditory cortex during fear conditioning—is modulated by cholinergic modulation (see Weinberger, 1995). They proposed that the amygdala plays an important role in activating the cholinergic system, which then modulates cortical arousal and conditioning. Experimental studies have shown that this may occur. Kapp et al. (1992), for example, found that stimulation of the amygdala can change cortical arousal (as measured by EEG patterns), and that cholinergic blockade prevents this. Furthermore, during the presentation of a CS,

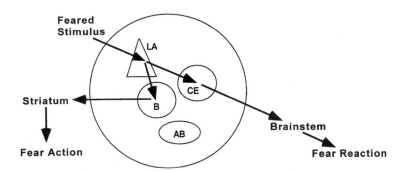

FIGURE 10.4. Emotional action versus reaction. Abbreviations as in Figure 10.1.

cells in the auditory cortex become very active at the time just preceding the occurrence of the US, and lesions of the amygdala prevent this anticipatory response (Quirk et al., 1997; Armony, Quirk, & LeDoux, 1998). Through projections to the cortex, either directly (see Amaral et al., 1992) or by way of the cholinergic system, the amygdala may direct attentional resources toward environmental stimuli that are eliciting amygdala activity.

The amygdala also appears to be involved in the triggering the release of so-called stress hormones, including epinephrine (adrenaline) and glucocorticoids, from the adrenal gland. The glucocorticoids circulate to the brain, where they bind to specific receptors in the hippocampus, medial prefrontal cortex, other cortical areas, and the amygdala. Epinephrine does not enter the brain directly from the bloodstream, but studies by McGaugh and colleagues suggest that it nevertheless influences areas in the brain by changning the activity of the vagus nerve, which then, through several relays in the brain, affects the amygdala and other areas (see McGaugh et al., 1995, Cahill & McGaugh, 1998). Their work in both animals and humans suggests that peripheral hormones, such as glucocorticoids and epinephrine, can modulate the strength of memories (especially conscious or declarative memories) formed in other brain regions (especially the hippocampus and neocortex). In brief, intermediate levels of these hormones tend to facilitate declarative memory for events while high levels tend to impair it. This may account for why emotional arousal sometimes leads to an enhancement of memory and sometimes a memory impairment for an event.

Glucocorticoids are particularly interesting for their contrasting effects on the amygdala and hippocampus. As noted, these are released when the amygdala detects dangerous or otherwise threatening events. When they reach the brain, they inhibit hippocampus-dependent processes (e.g., spatial memory), but enhance amygdala-dependent processes (e.g., fear conditioning) (Corodimas et al., 1994; Conrad, Margarinos, et al., 1997; Conrad, Lupien, Thanosoulis, & McEwen, 1997). Given that conscious or declarative memory is one of the prime functions of the hippocampus, we may conclude that during periods of intense stress the brain's ability to form conscious memories is impaired, but its ability to form unconscious emotional memories is potentiated. This observation has important implications for understanding such processes as memory loss during trauma and stress, and may account for memory disturbances in patients with depression and posttraumatic stress disorder.

EMOTIONAL SYSTEMS IN THE HUMAN BRAIN

In the past decade, traditional studies on patients have been combined with new neuroimaging techniques to ask questions about neural circuits of emotion in human subjects. This approach has been used especially in the study of fear, and the findings so far are largely consistent with the animal models described above.

Taking the lead from animal research, most studies on the neural basis of fear in humans have focused on the amygdala. The fear conditioning paradigm has been the standard means of investigating amygdala function across species. In humans, the paradigm is essentially the same as in other species. Typical CSs include colored squares, pictures of faces, or tones. The most commonly used USs are noise or mild shock. The unconditioned response (UR) and CR most often reported is the skin conductance response.

Studies of fear conditioning have found that the human amygdala plays a critical role in acquisition and expression. Two of the early studies on amygdala function in humans examined fear conditioning in patients with amygdala damage (Bechara et al., 1995; LaBar, LeDoux, Spencer, & Phelps, 1995). Both studies found that such patients exhibited normal URs to the US, but that they failed to acquire a normal fear response to the CS. Like nonhuman animals with amygdala damage, the patients showed no evidence of a CR.

Subsequent studies used neuroimaging techniques to learn more about the pattern of the human amygdala activity during fear conditioning. Two recent papers reported activity in the amygdala during a fear conditioning paradigm as measured by functional magnetic resonance imaging (fMRI) (Buchel, Morris, Dolan, & Friston, 1998; LaBar, Gatenby, Gore, LeDoux, & Phelps, 1998). The LaBar et al. (1998) study found that the activity in the amygdala was greatest when the CS and US were initially paired and that the activity dropped off after a few acquisition trials, at about the time the CR was reliably produced. In addition, this activity in early acquisition was strongly correlated with the strength of the CR, suggesting that this activity was linked to the later expression of the CR. Surprisingly, the activity in the amygdala, which diminished during the late acquisition trials, picked up again in the beginning of extinction, when the CS and US were no longer paired. The amygdala seemed to be most active when there was a change in the relationship between the CS and US, either during initial pairing or when they ceased to be paired. This pattern of amygdala responding is similar to that observed when recording from the amygdala in rats (Quirk, Repa, & LeDoux, 1995). Results from both lesion and neuroimaging studies in humans suggest that the role of the amygdala during fear conditioning is preserved across species.

Although the amygdala plays a critical role in signaling the aversive property of events, other brain systems are necessary for normal fear responses. The studies with nonhuman animals cited above suggest that the amygdala interacts with the hippocampus to affect fear responses across a variety of situations. In particular, research with rats has found that the

hippocampus is necessary to learn to fear the environmental situation, or context, where the aversive event occurred. The role of the hippocampus in contextual conditioning has not been studied in humans. However, several human studies have examined the relationship between the amygdala and hippocampus in the production of normal fear responses and emotional memory.

The hippocampus in humans is thought to be necessary for the acquisition of declarative or explicit memories (Squire, 1987a, 1987b)—in other words, the ability to acquire memories that can declared and are available to conscious awareness. In humans, it has been found that this ability is independent of the ability to acquire a CR in the fear conditioning paradigm. Patients with lesions to the amygdala who do not show fear conditioning are able to report verbally that the CS is followed by the US (Bechara et al., 1995; LaBar et al., 1995). They are able to use their hippocampal memory system to explicitly learn the relationship between the CS and US, even though they do not demonstrate a fear response to the CS. In addition, patients with hippocampal damage who have intact amygdalae are not able to explicitly report the relationship between the CS and US, but will demonstrate a CR, as measured by skin conductance (Bechara et al., 1995). These studies suggest that the hippocampus and amygdala can operate independently to acquire different kinds of representations of the aversive properties of events. These different kinds of representations, explicit/hippocampal and implicit/amygdala, are likely to be useful in different types of situations.

But what would happen if we acquired one form of representation of the aversive property of an event without the other? We humans often acquire explicit knowledge about the aversive properties of events without actually experiencing the event, or having a fear response when we acquire this knowledge. For instance, we might be told that a given neighborhood is dangerous without ever having been to the neighborhood. Just hearing and learning this information do not make us afraid. However, we might have a fear response if we find ourselves in that neighborhood at a later time. The hippocampus is necessary to acquire explicit knowledge about the aversive properties of an event. We may not have a fear response when you acquire this knowledge. However, if we have this explicit knowledge or representation, our fear response to this event when it occurs seems to be mediated by the amygdala. In a recent study, subjects were told that there was a possibility they would get a shock when they saw a colored square (Funayama, Grillon, Davis, & Phelps, 1998). All subjects acquired explicit knowledge about the aversive properties of the colored square. Although no one ever received a shock, normal subjects demonstrated a fear response when the colored square was presented. Patients with amygdala damage did not exhibit normal fear responses to the colored square, in spite of their explicit knowledge about the possible relationship between the square and the shock. A recent fMRI study also found that the activity in the amygdala was strongly correlated with the strength of the fear response in this type of situation (Phelps, O'Connor et al., 1998).

These results suggests that an explicit, hippocampus-dependent representation of the aversive properties of an event may modulate amygdala activity. The research with nonhuman animals cited above indicates that this relationship may go either way. That is, amygdala activity may facilitate or impair the storage of hippocampus-dependent memories. There is extensive evidence that low levels of stress or arousal associated with emotional events improves explicit or declarative memories for these events in humans (see Christianson, 1992). There are several factors contributing to the enhanced memory observed for arousing events, one of them being the amygdala's modulation of hippocampal processing (see Phelps, LaBar et al., 1998). Recent studies of patients with amygdala damage have found that under some circumstances these patients do not show the normal enhancement of explicit memory with emotion (Cahill, Babinsky, Markowitsch, & McGaugh, 1995), although they are often able to compensate for this deficit (Phelps, LaBar et al., 1998). Further support for this modulatory effect of the amygdala on hippocampus-dependent memories comes from neuroimaging. Cahill et al. (1996) used positron emission tomography to examine glucose metabolism in the amygdala while subjects viewed emotional and neutral film clips. They found that the rate of glucose metabolism in the amygdala was correlated with the ability to later recall the emotional, but not the neutral, film clips.

There may be several mechanisms through which the emotion can modulate hippocampus-dependent memories, only some of which may be related to amygdala activity (Phelps, LaBar et al., 1998). Research with nonhuman animals suggests that the amygdala's primary contribution to the enhanced memory observed with emotion may be the modulation of hippocampal consolidation (Packard, Cahill, & McGaugh, 1994). Consolidation is a process occurring over time, after the event is encoded, by which hippocampus-dependent memories become more or less permanent. Since consolidation occurs over time, the relative strength of memories for emotional and neutral stimuli should differ at different points in time after encoding. Consistent with this hypothesis, there is evidence that stressful or arousing events are not forgotten as rapidly as neutral events, if they are forgotten at all (Kleinsmith & Kaplan, 1963). A recent study by LaBar & Phelps (1998) examined the rate of forgetting for arousing and neutral words in patients with amygdala damage and normal controls. Consistent with previous studies, normal subjects showed different forgetting curves for the arousing and neutral words. They remembered fewer of the neutral words over time, but actually remembered more of the arousing words over time. Patients with amygdala damage not did demonstrate different forgetting curves for the neutral and arousing words; for both types of words, they remembered fewer over time. These results support the idea that the human amygdala may help modulate hippocampal consolidation.

All of the studies examining hippocampus-dependent memories for fearful or arousing events in humans have used relatively low levels of stress or arousal. For ethical reasons, it is not possible to induce high levels of stress or fear in humans in the laboratory. The animal research discussed earlier in this chapter found that high levels of stress may enhance amygdala function, while hippocampal function under these circumstances is impaired. There is evidence that high levels of stress or fear may impair hippocampus-dependent memory processes in humans who have naturally been exposed to extremely stressful or fearful events (Loftus & Kaufman, 1992). In fact, there is evidence that prolonged exposure to stress will eventually lead to hippocampal damage in humans (Bremner et al., 1995). The animal models described earlier suggest that this impairment in hippocampal processing or damage is most likely due to exposure to glucocorticoids, which are released as a reaction to fear or stress.

The studies described thus far have focused on the role of the amygdala in memory for fearful events. Specifically, the amygdala seems to be critical for us to express a fear response to an event, when we have learned that this event is linked to an aversive event. The amygdala may also affect the formation of hippocampus-dependent memories. But does the amygdala have a role beyond learning and memory? There are stimuli in the environment that we may have a predisposition to interpret as signaling threatening or aversive situations. Researchers have begun to examine the amygdala's role in evaluating these naturally occurring stimuli, and have found that the amygdala may play a crucial role in the evaluation of one type of stimuli of this class—fearful faces.

Adolphs, Tranel, Damasio, and Damasio (1994) reported the case of a woman with damage to the amygdala who did not have any difficulty recognizing faces, and who also responded normally to most facial expressions. However, when shown a face expressing fear, she would invariably report that it did not appear very fearful. Evidence of the amygdala's importance in responding to fearful faces has also been observed with neuroimaging. Several studies have reported greater amygdala activity in response to fearful faces than to faces with other expressions (Breiter et al., 1996; Morris et al., 1996). In an intriguing study, Whalen et al. (1998) found that subjects did not have to be aware of seeing the fearful face to elicit activity in the amygdala. They presented faces in such a way that subjects could not report the expression on the face. Even though subjects were not aware of seeing a fearful face, there was still greater activity in the amygdala for these faces. Whalen and colleagues suggest that this activity in the amygdala may act as an early warning system to get us ready to respond to threat, before we are even aware that a threat could possibly exist.

The studies with fearful faces suggest that the amygdala may play a separate role in the evaluation of certain classes of stimuli, in addition to emotional learning and memory. These are stimuli that may be evolutionary important for survival. However even though these stimuli have a biological significance, there is some reason to think that the amygdala's role in interpreting fearful faces could be related to learn-

ing the emotional significance of these faces. Although other researchers have replicated the results of Adolphs et al. (1994), who reported that amygdala damage leads to impaired processing of fearful faces (Calder, Young, Hellawell, Van De Wal, & Johnson, 1996; Young et al., 1995), there are also several cases of patients with amygdala damage who respond to fearful faces normally (Hamann, Stefanacci, Squire, Adolphs, & Damasio, 1996). It has been proposed that the crucial difference between those patients with amygdala damage who do and do not show deficits in evaluating fearful faces is the age at which the amygdala damage occurred. Patients with damage to the amygdala early in life are more likely to show a deficit in the evaluation of fearful faces. There is some evidence to suggest that our ability to interpret facial expressions changes during development, and that learning may be required to become an "expert" (Kolb, Wilson, & Taylor, 1992; Nelson & DeHaan, 1997). It is possible that the amygdala is necessary early in development to learn to interpret fearful faces normally. After this is learned, the amygdala may no longer be crucial for the normal interpretation of fearful faces, so that if the amygdala is damaged later in life, no deficit will be observed (Anderson, LaBar, & Phelps, 1996; Phelps & Anderson, 1997). However, this learning explanation for the amygdala's involvement in evaluating fearful faces is not without its controversy. Others have suggested that damage to the amygdala at any age leads to deficits in evaluating fearful facial expressions, depending on the task (Broks et al., 1998). Clearly, more research is needed to understand the importance of the human amygdala in evaluating fearful and emotional stimuli.

We are just beginning to examine the neural circuits involved in human emotion. The studies presented above highlight the role of the human amygdala and hippocampus in processing the emotion of fear. As mentioned earlier, fear is a good model for studying emotion because there is a consistent pattern of responding across species. What has been learned so far is largely consistent with animal research described earlier in this chapter. However, this research has also been extended to examine behaviors that are more relevant to human emotional responses. As we develop new techniques to study both the behavior of human emotion and the human brain, we will achieve a better understanding of the differences and similarities in emotional processing across species.

FEELINGS AND THE BRAIN

How do we become consciously aware that an emotion system in our brains is active? This is the problem that most emotion studies and theories, especially psychological studies of and theories about humans, have focused on (e.g., Lewis & Michalson, 1983). However, we have examined the neural basis of emotion in this chapter without really mentioning feelings. Our hypothesis is that the mechanism of consciousness is the same for emotional and nonemotional subjective states, and that what distinguishes these states is the brain system that consciousness is aware of at the time. This is why we have focused on the nature of the underlying emotion systems throughout the chapter. Now, however, we consider feelings and their relation to consciousness.

Several theorists have proposed that consciousness has something to do with "working memory," a serially organized mental workspace where things can be compared, contrasted, and mentally manipulated (Johnson-Laird, 1988; Kihlstrom, 1984; Schacter, 1989; Shallice, 1988). Working memory allows us, for example, to compare an immediately present visual stimulus with information stored in long-term (explicit) memory about stimuli with similar shapes and colors or stimuli found in similar locations.

Various studies of humans and nonhuman primates point to the prefrontal cortex, especially the dorsolateral prefrontal areas as being involved in working memory processes (Baddeley & Della Sala, 1996; Fuster, 1989; Goldman-Rakic, 1987). Immediately present stimuli and stored representations are integrated in working memory by way of interactions among prefrontal areas, sensory processing systems (which serve as short-term memory buffers as well as perceptual processors), and the long-term explicit (declarative) memory system involving the hippocampus and related areas of the temporal lobe. Working memory may involve interactions between several prefrontal areas, including the anterior cingulate and orbital cortical regions, as well as dorsolateral prefrontal cortex (D'Esposito et al., 1996; Gaffan, Murray, & Fabre-Thorpe, 1993).

If a stimulus is affectively charged (say, a

trigger of fear), the same sorts of processes will be called upon as for stimuli without emotional implications; in addition, however, working memory will become aware of the fact that the fear system of the brain has been activated. This further information, when added to perceptual and mnemonic information about the object or event, may the condition for the subjective experience of an emotional state of fear (Figure 10.5).

But what is the further information that is added to working memory when the fear system is activated? As noted, the amygdala projects to many cortical areas, even some from which it does not receive inputs (Amaral et al., 1992). It can thus influence the operation of perceptual and short-term memory processes, as well as processes in higher-order areas. Although the amygdala does not have extensive connections with the dorsolateral prefrontal cortex, it does communicate with the anterior cingulate and orbital cortex, two other components of the working memory network. But in addition, the amygdala projects to nonspecific systems involved in the regulation of cortical arousal, such as the various modulatory system described earlier. And the amygdala controls bodily responses (behavioral, autonomic, endocrine), which then provide feedback that can influence cortical processing indirectly, such as the adrenal hormones mentioned above. Thus working memory receives a greater number of inputs, and receives inputs of a greater variety, in the presence of an emotional stimulus than in the presence of other kinds of stimuli. These extra inputs may just be what is required to add affective charge to working memory represen-

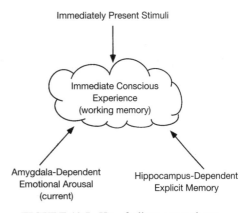

FIGURE 10.5. How feelings come about.

tations, and thus to turn subjective experiences into emotional experiences.

Though described in terms of the fear system, the present hypothesis about feelings is a general one that applies to any emotion. That is, an emotional feeling results when working memory is occupied with the fact that an emotion system of the brain is active. The difference between an emotional state and other states of consciousness, then, is not due to different underlying mechanisms that give rise to the qualitatively different subjective experiences. Instead, there is one mechanism of consciousness, and it can be occupied by either mundane events or emotionally charged ones.

REFERENCES

Adolphs, R. A., Tranel, D., Damasio, H., & Damasio, A. R. (1994). Impaired recognition of emotion in facial expressions following bilateral amygdala damage to the human amygdala. *Nature, 372,* 669–672.

Aggleton, J. P. (Ed.). (1992) *The amygdala: Neurobiological aspects of emotion, memory, and mental dysfunction.* New York: Wiley-Liss.

Aggleton, J. P., & Mishkin, M. (1986). The amygdala: Sensory gateway to the emotions. In R. Plutchik & H. Kellerman, (Eds.), *Emotion: Theory, research and experience. Vol. 3. Biological foundations of emotions* (pp. 281–299). New York: Academic Press.

Amaral, D. G., Price, J. L., Pitkänen, A., & Carmichael, S. T. (1992). Anatomical organization of the primate amygdaloid complex. In J. P. Aggleton, (Ed.), *The amygdala: Neurobiological aspects of emotion, memory, and mental dysfunction* (pp. 1–66). New York: Wiley–Liss.

Anderson, A. K., LaBar, K. S., & Phelps, E. A. (1996). Facial affect processing abilities following unilateral temporal lobectomy. *Society for Neuroscience Abstracts, 22,* 1866.

Armony, J. L., Quirk, G. J., & LeDoux, J. E. (1998). Differential effects of amygdala lesions on early and late plastic components of auditory cortex spiketrains during fear conditioning. *Journal of Neuroscience 18,* 2592–2601.

Armony, J. L., Servan-Schreiber, D., Cohen, J. C., & LeDoux, J. E. (1996). Emotion and cognition interactions in the thalamo-cortico-amygdala network: Theory and model. *Cognitive Neuroscience Society Abstracts, 3,* 76.

Armony, J. L., Servan-Schreiber, D., Romanski, L. M., Cohen, J. D., & LeDoux, J. E. (1997). Stimulus generalization of fear responses: Effects of auditory cortex lesions in a computational model and in rats. *Cerebral Cortex, 7,* 157–165.

Baddeley, A., & Della Sala, S. (1996) Working memory and executive control. *Philosophical Transactions of the Royal Society of London. Biological Science, 351,* 1397–1403 (discussion 1403–1404).

Bard, P. (1929). The central representation of the sym-

pathetic system: as indicated by certain physiological observations. *Archives of Neurolology and Psychiatry, 22,* 230–246.

Bechara, A., Tranel, D., Damasio, H., Adolphs, R., Rockland, C., & Damasio, A. R. (1995). Double dissociation of conditioning and declarative knowledge relative to the amygdala and hippocampus in humans. *Science, 269,* 1115–1118.

Blanchard, D. C., & Blanchard, R. J. (1972). Innate and conditioned reactions to threat in rats with amygdaloid lesions. *Journal of Comparative and Physiological Psychology, 81,* 281–290.

Bouton, M. E., & Swartzentruber, D. (1991). Sources of relapse after extinction in Pavlovian and instrumental learning. *Clinical Psychology Review, 11,* 123–140.

Bremner, J. D., Randall, T., Scott, T. M., Brunen, R. A., Seibyl, J. P., Southwick, S.M., Delaney, R. C., McCarthy, G., Charney, D. S., & Innis, R. B. (1995). MRI-based measurement of hippocampal volume in patients with combat-related posttraumatic stress disorder. *American Journal of Psychiatry, 152,* 973–981.

Breiter, H. C., Etcoff, N. L., Whalen, P. J., Kennedy, W. A., Rauch, S. L., Buckner, R. L., Strauss, M. M., Hyman, S., & Rosen, B. (1996). Response and habituation of the human amygdala during visual processing of facial expression. *Neuron, 17,* 875–887.

Brodal, A. (1982) *Neurological anatomy.* New York: Oxford University Press.

Broks, P., Young, A. W., Maratows, E. J., Coffey, P. J., Calder, A. J., Isaac, C. L., Mayes, A. R., Hodges, J. R., Montaldi, D., Cezayirli, E., Roberts, N., & Hadley, D. (1998). Face processing impairments after encephalitis: Amygdala damage and recognition of fear. *Neuropsychologia, 36,* 59–70.

Buchel, C., Morris, J., Dolan, R. J., & Friston, K. J. (1998). Brain systems mediating aversive conditioning: An event-related fMRI study. *Neuron 20,* 947–957.

Cahill, L., Babinsky, R., Markowitsch, H. J., & McGaugh, J. L. (1995). The amygdala and emotional memory. *Science, 377,* 295–296.

Cahill, L., Haier, R. J., Fallon, J., Alkire, M. T., Tang, C., Keator, J., Wu, J., & McGaugh, J. L. (1996). Amygdala activity at encoding correlated with long-term, free recall of emotional information. *Proceedings of the National Academy of Sciences USA, 93,* 8016.

Cahill, L., & McGaugh, J. L. (1998). Mechanisms of emotional arousal and lasting declarative memory. *Trends in Neurosciences 21,* 294–299.

Calder, A. J., Young, A. W., Hellawell, D. J., Van De Wal, C., & Johnson, M. (1996). Facial expression processing after amygdalectomy, *Neuropsychologia, 34,* 31–39.

Campeau, S., & Davis, M. (1995). Involvement of subcortical and cortical afferents to the lateral nucleus of the amygdala in fear conditioning measured with fear-potentiated startle in rats trained concurrently with auditory and visual conditioned stimuli. *Journal of Neuroscience, 15,* 2312–2327.

Cannon, W. B. (1929). *Bodily changes in pain, hunger, fear, and rage.* New York: Appleton.

Canteras, N. S., & Swanson, L. W. (1992). Projections of the ventral subiculum to the amygdala, septum, and hypothalamus: A PHAL anterograde tract-tracing study in the rat. *Journal of Comparative Neurology, 324,* 180–194.

Christianson, S. A. (1992).*The handbook of emotion and memory: Research and theory.* Mahwah, NJ: Erlbaum.

Cohen, N. J., & Eichenbaum, H. (1993). *Memory, amnesia, and the hippocampal system.* Cambridge, MA: MIT Press.

Conrad, C. D., Lupien, S. J., Thanosoulis, L. C., & McEwen, B. S. (1997). The effects of type I and type II corticosteroid receptor agonists on exploratory behavior and spatial memory in the Y-Maze. *Brain Research, 759,* 76–83.

Conrad, C. D., Margarinos, A. M., LeDoux, J. E., & McEwen, B. S. (1997). Chronic restraint stress enhanced contextual and cued fear conditioning in rats. *Society for Neuroscience Abstracts, 718,* 4.

Corodimas, K. P., & LeDoux, J. E. (1995). Disruptive effects of posttraining perirhinal cortex lesions on conditioned fear: Contributions of contextual cues. *Behavioral Neuroscience, 109,* 613–619.

Corodimas, K. P., LeDoux, J. E., Gold, P. W., & Schulkin, J. (1994). Corticosterone potentiation of learned fear. *Annals of the New York Academy of Sciences, 746,* 392–393.

Cranford, J. L., & Igarashi, M. (1977). Effects of auditory cortex lesions on temporal summation in cats. *Brain Research, 136,* 559–564.

Damasio, A. (1994). *Descartes' error: Emotion, reason, and the human brain.* New York: Putnam.

Davis, M. (1992). The role of the amygdala in conditioned fear. In J. P. Aggleton (Ed.) *The amygdala: Neurobiological aspects of emotion, memory, and mental dysfunction* (pp. 255–306). New York: Wiley–Liss.

Davis, M. (1994). The role of the amygdala in emotional learning. *International Review of Neurobiology, 36,* 225–266.

D'Esposito, M., Detre, J. A., Alsop, D. C., Shin, R. K., Atlas, S., & Grossman, M. (1996). The neural basis of the central executive system of working memory. *Nature, 378,* 279–281.

Drevets, W. C., Price, J. L., Simpson, J. R., Jr., Todd, R. D., Reich, T., Vannier, M., & Ralchle, M. E. (1997). Subgenual prefrontal cortex abnormalities in mood disorders. *Nature, 386,* 824–827.

Everitt, B. J., & Robbins, T. W. (1992). Amygdala–ventral striatal interactions and reward-related processes. In J. P. Aggleton (Ed.), *The amygdala: Neurobiological aspects of emotion, memory, and mental dysfunction* (pp. 401–429). New York: Wiley–Liss.

Fernandez de Molina, A., & Hunsperger, R. W. (1962). Organization of the subcortical system governing defense and flight reactions in the cat. *Journal of Physiology, 160,* 200–213.

Frankland, P. W., Cestari, V., Filipkowski, R. K., McDonald, R. J., & Silva, A. (1998). The dorsal hippocampus is essential for context discrimination, but not for contextual conditioning. *Behavioral Neuroscience, 112,* 863–874.

Funayama, E. S., Grillon C., Davis M., & Phelps E. A. (1998). Impaired fear-potentiated startle following unilateral temporal lobectomy. *Society for Neuroscience Abstracts, 24,* 163.

Fuster, J. M. (1989). *The prefrontal cortex.* New York: Raven Press.

Gaffan, D., & Harrison, S. (1987). Amygdalectomy and disconnection in visual learning for auditory secondary reinforcement by monkeys. *Journal of Neuroscience, 7,* 2285–2292.

Gaffan, D., Murray, E. A., & Fabre-Thorpe, M. (1993). Interaction of the amygdala with the frontal lobe in reward memory. *European Journal of Neuroscience, 5,* 968–975.

Gaffan, E. A., Gaffan, D., & Harrison, S. (1988). Disconnection of the amygdala from visual association cortex impairs visual reward–association learning in monkeys. *Journal of Neuroscience, 8*(9), 3144–3150.

Gewirtz, J. C., & Davis, M. (1997). Second-order fear conditioning prevented by blocking NMDA receptors in amygdala. *Nature, 388,* 471–474.

Gloor, P. (1960). Amygdala. In J. Field, H. W. Magoun & V. E. Hall (Eds.), *Handbook of physiology: Neurophysiology. Section I. The nervous system. Vol. 2* (pp. 1395–1420). Washington, DC: American Physiological Society.

Goldman-Rakic, P. S. (1987). Circuitry of primate prefrontal cortex and regulation of behavior by representational memory. In F. Plum (Ed.), *Handbook of physiology. Section I: The nervous system. Vol. 5. Higher functions of the brain* (pp. 373–418). Bethesda, MD: American Physiological Society.

Gray, J. A. (1987). *The psychology of fear and stress* (Vol. 2). New York: Cambridge University Press.

Halgren, E. (1992). Emotional neurophysiology of the amygdala within the context of human cognition. In J. Aggleton (Ed.), *The amygdala: Neurobiological aspects of emotion, memory, and mental dysfunction* (pp. 191–228). New York: Wiley–Liss.

Hamann, S. B., Stefanacci, L., Squire, L. R., Adolphs, R., & Damasio, A. R. (1996). Recognizing facial emotion. *Nature, 379,* 497.

Helmstetter, F. J., & Bellgowan, P. S. (1994). Effects of muscimol applied to the basolateral amygdala on acquisition and expression of contextual fear conditioning in rats. *Behavioral Neuroscience, 108,* 1005–1009.

Hilton, S. M., & Zbrozyna, A. W. (1963). Amydaloid region for defense reactions and its efferent pathway to the brainstem. *Journal of Physiology, 165,*160–173.

Iwata, J., Chida, K., & LeDoux, J. E. (1987). Cardiovascular responses elicited by stimulation of neurons in the central amygdaloid nucleus in awake but not anesthetized rats resemble conditioned emotional responses. *Brain Research, 418,*183–188.

Jacobs, W. J., & Nadel, L. (1985). Stress-induced recovery of fears and phobias. *Psychological Review, 92,* 512–531.

James, W. (1984). What is an emotion? *Mind, 9,* 188–205.

Johnson-Laird, P. N. (1988). *The computer and the mind: An introduction to cognitive science.* Cambridge, MA: Harvard University Press.

Jones, B., & M. Mishkin (1972). Limbic lesions and the problem of stimulus–reinforcement associations. *Experimental Neurololgy, 36,* 362–377.

Kane, F., Coulombe, D., & Miliaressis, E. (1991). Amygdaloid self-stimulation: A movable electrode mapping study. *Behavioral Neuroscience, 105,* 926–932.

Kapp, B. S., Pascoe, J. P., & Bixler, M. A. (1984). The amygdala: A neuroanatomical systems approach to its contributions to aversive conditioning. In N. Butters & L. R. Squire (Eds.), *Neuropsychology of memory* (pp. 473–488). New York: Guilford Press.

Kapp, B. S., Whalen, P. J., Supple, W. F., & Pascoe, J. P. (1992). Amygdaloid contributions to conditioned arousal and sensory information processing. In J. P. Aggleton (Ed.), *The amygdala: Neurobiological aspects of emotion, memory, and mental dysfunction* (pp. 229–254). New York: Wiley–Liss.

Kihlstrom, J. F. (1984). Conscious, subconscious, unconscious: A cognitive perspective. In K. S. Bowers & D. Meichenbaum (Eds.), *The unconscious reconsidered* (pp. 149–211). New York: Wiley.

Killcross, S., Robbins, T. W., & Everitt, B. J. (1997). Different types of fear-conditioned behavior mediated by separate nuclei within amygdala. *Nature, 388,* 377–380.

Kim, J. J., & Fanselow, M. S. (1992). Modality-specific retrograde amnesia of fear. *Science, 256,* 675–677.

Kleinsmith, L. J., & Kaplan, S. (1963). Paired-associate learning as a function of arousal: An interpolated interval. *Journal of Experimental Psychology, 67,* 124–126.

Kluver, H., & Bucy, P. C. (1937). "Psychic blindness" and other symptoms following bilateral temporal lobectomy in rhesus monkeys. *American Journal of Physiology, 119,* 352–353.

Kolb, B., Wilson, B., & Taylor, L. (1992). Developmental changes in recognition and comprehension of facial expression: Implications for frontal lobe function. *Brain and Cognition, 20,* 74–84.

Kotter, R., & Meyer, N. (1992). The limbic system: A review of its empirical foundation. *Behavioural Brain Research, 52,* 105–127.

LaBar, K. S., Gatenby, C., Gore, J. C., LeDoux, J. E., & Phelps, E. A. (1998). Amygdolo-cortical activation during conditioned fear acquisition and extinction: A mixed trial fMRI study. *Neuron, 20,* 937–945.

LaBar, K. S., LeDoux, J. E., Spencer, D. D., & Phelps, E. A. (1995). Impaired fear conditioning following unilateral temporal lobectomy in humans. *Journal of Neuroscience, 15,* 6846–6855.

LaBar, K. S., & Phelps, E. A. (1998). Role of the human amygdala in arousal mediated memory consolidation. *Psychological Science, 9,* 490–493.

LeDoux, J. E. (1986a). Neurobiology of emotion. In J. E. LeDoux & W. Hirst (Eds), *Mind and brain* (pp. 301–354). New York: Cambridge University Press.

LeDoux, J. E. (1986b). Sensory systems and emotion. *Integrative Psychiatry, 4,* 237–248.

LeDoux, J. E. (1987). Emotion. In F. Plum (Ed.), *Handbook of physiology: Section I. The nervous system. Vol 5. Higher functions of the brain* (pp. 419–460). Bethesda, MD: American Physiological Society.

LeDoux, J. E. (1991). Emotion and the limbic system concept. *Concepts in Neuroscience, 2,* 169–199.

LeDoux, J. E. (1992). Emotion and the amygdala. In J. P. Aggleton (Ed.), *The amygdala: Neurobiological aspects of emotion, memory, and mental dysfunction.* (pp. 339–351). New York: Wiley–Liss.

LeDoux, J. E. (1996). *The emotional brain.* New York: Simon & Schuster.

LeDoux, J. E., Cicchetti, P., Xagoraris, A., & Romanski, L. R. (1990). The lateral amygdaloid nucleus: Sensory interface of the amygdala in fear conditioning. *Journal of Neuroscience, 10,* 1062–1069.

LeDoux, J. E., Romanski, L. M., & Xagoraris, A. E. (1989). Indelibility of subcortical emotional memories. *Journal of Cognitive Neuroscience, 1,* 238–243.

LeDoux, J. E., Sakaguchi, A., & Reis, D. J. (1984). Subcortical efferent projections of the medial geniculate nucleus mediate emotional responses conditioned by acoustic stimuli. *Journal of Neuroscience, 4,* 683–698.

Lewis. M., & Michalson, L. (1983). *Children's emotions and moods: Developmental theory and measurement.* New York: Plenum Press.

Li, X. F., Stutzmann, G. E., & LeDoux, J. L. (1996). Convergent but temporally separated inputs to lateral amygdala neurons from the auditory thalamus and auditory cortex use different postsynaptic receptors: *in vivo* intracellular and extracellular recordings in fear conditioning pathways. *Learning and Memory, 3,* 229–242.

Loftus, E. F., & Kaufman, L. (1992). Why do traumatic experiences sometimes produce good memory (flashbulbs) and sometimes no memory (repression)? In E. Winograd & U. Neisser (Eds.), *Affect and accuracy in recall* (pp. 212–223). New York: Cambridge University Press.

MacLean, P. D. (1949). Psychosomatic disease and the "visceral brain": Recent developments bearing on the Papez theory of emotion. *Psychosomatic Medicine, 11,* 338–353.

MacLean, P. D. (1952). Some psychiatric implications of physiological studies on frontotemporal portion of limbic system (visceral brain). *Electroencephalography and Clinical Neurophysiology 4,* 407–418.

Majidishad, P., Pelli, D. G., & LeDoux, J. E. (1996). Disruption of fear conditioning to contextual stimuli but not to a tone by lesions of the accessory basal nucleus of the amygdala. *Society for Neuroscience Abstracts, 22,* 1116.

Maren, S., Aharonov, G., Stote, D. L., & Fanselow, M. S. (1996). N-methyl-D-aspartate receptors in the basolateral amygdala are required for both acquisition and expression of conditional fear in rats. *Behavioral Neuroscience, 110,* 1365–1374.

Maren, S., Anagnostaras, S. G., & Fanselow, M. S. (1998). The startled seahorse: is the hippocampus necessary for contextual fear conditioning? *Trends in Cognitive Sciences, 2,* 39–41.

Maren, S., & Fanselow, M. S. (1996). The amygdala and fear conditioning: Has the nut been cracked? *Neuron, 16,* 237–240.

Mascagni, F., McDonald, A. J., & Coleman, J. R. (1993). Corticoamygdaloid and corticocortical projections of the rat temporal cortex: A *Phaseolus vulgaris* leucoagglutinin study. *Neuroscience, 57,* 697–715.

McGaugh, J. L., Mesches, M. H., Cahill, L., Parent, M. B., Coleman-Mesches, K., & Salinas, J. A. (1995). Involvement of the amygdala in the regulation of memory storage. In J. L. McGaugh, F. Bermudez-Rattoni

& R. A. Prado-Alcala (Eds.), *Plasticity in the central nervous system* (pp. 18–39). Hillsdale, NJ: Erlbaum.

Miserendino, M. J. D., Sananes, C. B., Melia, K. R., & Davis, M. (1990). Blocking of acquisition but not expression of conditioned fear-potentiated startle by NMDA antagonists in the amygdala. *Nature, 345,* 716–718.

Mishkin, M., Malamut, B., & Bachevalier, J. (1984). Memories and habits: Two neural systems. In J. L. McGaugh, G. Lynch, & N. M. Weinberger (Eds.), *The neurobiology of learning and memory.* New York: Guilford Press.

Mishkin, M., & Aggleton, J. (1981). Multiple functional contributions of the amygdala in the monkey. In Y. Ben-Ari (Ed.), *The amygdaloid complex* (pp. 409–420). Amsterdam: Elsevier/North-Holland.

Morgan, M., & LeDoux, J. E. (1995). Differential contribution of dorsal and ventral medial prefrontal cortex to the acquisition and extinction of conditioned fear. *Behavioral Neuroscience, 109,* 681–688.

Morgan, M. A., Romanski, L. M., & LeDoux, J. E. (1993). Extinction of emotional learning: Contribution of medial prefrontal cortex. *Neuroscience Letters, 163,* 109–113.

Morris, J. S., Frith, C. D., Perret, D. I., Rowland, D., Young, A. W., Calder, A. J., & Dolan, R. J. (1996). A differential neural responce in the human amygdala to fearful and happy facial expressions. *Nature, 383,* 812–815.

Mowrer, O. H., & Lamoreaux, R. R. (1946). Fear as an intervening variable in avoidance conditioning. *Journal of Comparative Psychology, 39,* 29–50.

Muller, J., Corodimas, K. P., Fridel, Z., & LeDoux, J. E. (1997). Functional inactivation of the lateral and basal nuclei of the amygdala by muscimol infusion prevents fear conditioning to an explicit CS and to contextual stimuli. *Behavioral Neuroscience, 111,* 683–691.

Nelson, C. A., & DeHaan, M. (1997). A neurobehavioral approach to the recognition of facial expressions in infancy. In J. A. Russell & J. M. Fernandez-Dols (Eds.), *The psychology of facial expression: Studies in emotion and social interaction* (pp. 176–204). New York: Cambridge University Press.

O'Keefe, J. & Nadel, L. (1978). *The hippocampus as a cognitive map.* Oxford: Clarendon Press.

Olds, J. (1977). *Drives and reinforcement.* New York: Raven Press.

Ono, T., & Nishijo, H. (1992). Neurophysiological basis of the Kluver–Bucy syndrome: Responses of monkey amygdaloid neurons to biologically significant objects. In J. P. Aggleton (Ed.), *The amygdala: Neurobiological aspects of emotion, memory, and mental dysfunction* (pp. 167–190). New York: Wiley–Liss.

Ottersen, O. P. (1982). Connections of the amygdala of the rat: IV. Corticoamygdaloid and intraamygdaloid connections as studied with axonal transport of horseradish peroxidase. *Journal of Comparative Neurology, 205,* 30–48.

Packard, M. G., Cahill, L., & McGaugh, J. L. (1994). Amygdala modulation of hippocampal-dependent and caudate nucleus-dependent memory processes.

Proceedings of the National Academy of Sciences USA, 91, 8477–8481.

Packard, M. G., Williams, C. L., Cahill, L., & McGaugh, J. L. (1995). The anatomy of a memory modulatory system: From periphery to brain. In N. E. Spear, L. P. Spear, & M. L. Woodruff (Eds.), *Neurobehavioral plasticity: Learning, development,and reponse to brain insults* (pp. 149–150). Hillsdale, NJ: Erlbaum.

Papez, J. W. (1937). A proposed mechanism of emotion. *Archives of Neurology and Psychiatry, 79,* 217–224.

Parent, M. B., Tomaz, C., & McGaugh, J. L. (1992). Increased training in an aversively motivated task attenuates the memory-impairing effects of posttraining *N*-methyl-D-aspartate-induced amygdala lesions. *Behavioral Neuroscience, 106*(5), 789–798.

Pavlov, I. P. (1927). *Conditioned reflexes.* New York: Dover.

Phelps, E. A., & Anderson, A. K. (1997). Emotional memory: What does the amygdala do? *Current Biology, 7,* 311–314.

Phelps, E. A., LaBar, K. S., Anderson, A.K., O'Connor, K. J., Fulbright, R. K., & Spencer, D. S. (1998). Specifying the contributions of the human amygdala to emotional memory: A case study. *Neurocase, 4,* 527–540.

Phelps, E. A., O'Connor, K.J., Gatenby, J. C., Anderson, A.K., Grillon, C., Davis, M., & Gore, J.C. (1998). Activation of the human amygdala by a cognitive representation of fear. *Society for Neuroscience Abstracts 24,* 1524.

Phillips, R. G. & LeDoux, J. E. (1992). Differential contribution of amygdala and hippocampus to cued and contextual fear conditioning. *Behavioral Neuroscience, 106,* 274–285.

Phillips, R. G., & LeDoux, J. E. (1994). Lesions of the dorsal hippocampal formation interfere with background but not foreground contextual fear conditioning. *Learning and Memory, 1,* 34–44.

Pitkänen, A., Savander, V., & LeDoux, J. L. (1997). Organization of intra-amygdaloid circuitries: an emerging framework for understanding functions of the amygdala. *Trends in Neurosciences 20,* 517–523.

Quirk, G. J., Armony, J. L., & LeDoux, J. E. (1997). Fear conditioning enhances different temporal components of tone-evoked spike trains in auditory cortex and lateral amygdala. *Neuron, 19,* 613–624.

Quirk, G. J., Repa, J. C., & LeDoux, J. E. (1995). Fear conditioning enhances short-latency auditory responses of lateral amygdala neurons: Parallel recordings in the freely behaving rat. *Neuron, 15,* 1029–1039.

Rescorla, R. A., & Heth, C. D. (1975). Reinstatement of fear to an extinguished conditioned stimulus. *Journal of Experimental Psychology: Animal Behavior Processes, 104,* 88–96.

Rescorla, R. A., & Solomon, R. L. (1967). Two process learning theory: Relationships between Pavlovian conditioning and instrumental learning. *Psychological Review, 74,* 151–182.

Rogan, M., Staubli, U., & LeDoux, J. E. (1997). AMPA-receptor facilitation accelerates fear learning without altering the level of conditioned fear acquired. *Journal of Neuroscience, 17,* 5928–5935.

Rolls, E. T. (1986). A theory of emotion, and its application to understanding the neural basis of emotion. In Y. Oomur (Ed.), *Emotions: Neural and chemical control* (pp. 325–344). Tokyo: Japan Scientific Societies Press.

Rolls, E. T. (1992). Neurophysiology and functions of the primate amygdala. In J. P. Aggleton, (Ed.), *The amygdala: Neurobiological aspects of emotion, memory, and mental dysfunction* (pp. 143–165). New York: Wiley–Liss.

Rolls, E. T. (1996). *The orbitofrontal cortex.* Unpublished manuscript, Department of Experimental Psychology, University of Oxford.

Romanski, L. M., & LeDoux, J. E. (1992). Bilateral destruction of neocortical and perirhinal projection targets of the acoustic thalamus does not disrupt auditory fear conditioning. *Neuroscience Letters 142,* 228–232.

Romanski, L. M., & LeDoux, J. E. (1993). Information cascade from primary auditory cortex to the amygdala: Corticocortical and corticoamygdaloid projections of temporal cortex in the rat. *Cerebral Cortex, 3,* 515–532.

Schacter, D. L. (1989). On the relation between memory and consciousness: Dissociable interactions and conscious experience. In H. L. I. Roediger & F. I. M. Craik (Eds), *Varieties of memory and consciousness: Essays in honour of Endel Tulving* (pp. 355–389). Hillsdale, NJ: Erlbaum.

Selden, N. R. W., Everitt, B. J., Jarrard, L. E., & Robbins, T. W. (1991). Complementary roles for the amygdala and hippocampus in aversive conditioning to explicit and contextual cues. *Neuroscience 42*(2), 335–350.

Shallice, T. (1988). Information processing models of consiousness. In A. Marcel & E. Bisiach (Eds.), *Consciousness in contemporary science* (pp. 305–333). Oxford: Oxford University Press.

Shepherd, G. (1997). *Neurobiology.* New York: Oxford University Press.

Spiegler, B.J., & Mishkin, M. (1981). Evidence for the sequential participation of inferior temporal cortex and amygdala in the acquisition of stimulus–reward associations. *Behavioural Brain Research, 3,* 303–317.

Squire, L.R. (1987a). Memory: Neural organization and behavior. In F. Plum, (Ed.), *Handbook of physiology: Section I. The nervous system. Vol. 5. Higher functions of the brain* (pp. 295–371). Bethesda, MD: American Physiological Society.

Squire, L. R. (1987b). *Memory and the brain.* New York: Oxford University Press.

Squire, L. R., & Zola S. M. (1996). Structure and function of declarative and nondeclarative memory systems. *Proceedings of the National Academy of Sciences, USA, 93,* 13515–13522.

Sutherland, R. J., & Rudy, J. W. (1989). Configural association theory: The role of the hippocampal formation in learning, memory, and amnesia. *Psychobiology 17,* 129–144.

Swanson, L. W. (1983). The hippocampus and the concept of the limbic system. In W. Seifert (Ed.), *Neurobiology of the hippocampus* (pp. 3–19). London: Academic Press.

Teich, A. H., McCabe, P. M., Gentile, C. C., Schneiderman, L. S., Winters, R. W., Liskowsky, D. R., & Schneiderman, N. (1989). Auditory cortex lesions prevent the extinction of Pavlovian differential heart rate conditioning to tonal stimuli in rabbits. *Brain Research, 480,* 210–218.

Thorpe, S. J., Rolls, E. T., & Maddison, S. (1983). The orbitofrontal cortex: Neuronal activity in the behaving monkey. *Experimental Brain Research, 49,* 93–115.

Turner, B., & Herkenham, M. (1991). Thalamoamygdaloid projections in the rat: a test of the amygdala's role in sensory processing. *Journal of Comparative Neurology, 313,* 295–325.

Weinberger, N. M. (1995). Retuning the brain by fear conditioning. In M. S. Gazzaniga (Ed.), *The Cognitive Neurosciences* (pp. 1071–1090). Cambridge, MA: MIT Press.

Weiskrantz, L. (1956). Behavioral changes associated with ablation of the amygdaloid complex in monkeys. *Journal of Comparative and Physiological Psychology, 49,* 381–391.

Whalen, P. J., Rauch, S. L., Etcoff, N. L., McInerney, S. C., Lee, M. B., & Jenike, M. A. (1998). Masked presentations of emotional facial expressions modulate amygdala activity without explicit knowledge. *Journal of Neuroscience, 18,* 411–418.

Whitfield, I. C. (1980). Auditory cortex and the pitch of complex tones. *Journal of the Acoustical Society of America, 67,* 644–647.

Young, A. W., Aggleton, J. P., Hellawell, D. J., Johnson, M., Broks, P., & Hanley, J. R. (1995). Face processing impairments after amygdalotomy. *Brain, 118,* 15–24.

CHAPTER 11

The Psychophysiology of Emotion

John T. Cacioppo
Gary G. Berntson
Jeff T. Larsen
Kirsten M. Poehlmann
Tiffany A. Ito

Humans have walked the surface of the earth for about 2 million years, and for all but the last 2,000 or 3,000 years, humans have been hunter–gatherers (Ackerman, 1990). In a strikingly brief span, human civilization has achieved the engineering of the Great Pyramids, the elegance of Beethoven's Ninth Symphony, the refinement of Dom Perignon, the efficiency of mass production, the triumph of modern medicine, the cognizance of heterotic string theory, and the wonder of space exploration. Perhaps we can be excused for tending to see our achievements as the outcome of pure reason and our distant past "through a reverse telescope that compresses it: a short time as hunter–gatherers, a long time as 'civilized' people" (Ackerman, 1990, p. 129).

Despite the constraints of civilization, however, humans are also the source of less rarified achievements: the relentless exploitation of fossil fuels and rainforests, the apocalyptic peril of biological and nuclear warfare, and the savage horror of torture and genocide, to name but a few. We may sing in choirs and bridle our rages behind placid countenances, but we patrol the world under the auspices of an affect system sculpted over millennia of evolutionary forces.

Emotions are shared across species—an observation that has long fueled the concern that emotions are an obstacle to fulfilling human potential (Brazier, 1960). We may sit in quiet repose contemplating the diversity of the linguistic expressions for emotions, but emotions predate language and the human species.

Individuals are revered for cultivated tastes and seemingly dispassionate responses to life's challenges. Yet emotions, however archaic in origin, saturate human existence throughout the lifespan. Emotions guide, enrich, and ennoble life; they provide meaning to everyday existence; they render the valuation placed on life and property. Emotions promote behaviors that protect life, form the basis for the continuity in life, and compel the termination of life. They can be essential ingredients for, as well as overwhelming obstacles to, optimizing human potential, and they often serve as the engines for intellectual development. Given their evolutionary heritage and daily currency, there is little wonder that emotions have preoccupied humankind throughout recorded history, and there is little doubt that emotions are both biologically rooted and culturally molded.

Affect and emotion in human studies have

been treated as the conscious subjective aspect of an emotion considered apart from bodily changes (e.g., Osgood, Suci, & Tannenbaum, 1957; Green, Salovey, & Truax, 1999; cf. Cacioppo, Gardner, & Berntson, 1999; LeDoux, 1996). Like the organization and processes underlying the undeniable percept that the sun circles the earth, however, the organization and processes underlying affective experiences may be far subtler than their apparent manifestations might lead one to suspect (Cacioppo, Gardner, & Berntson, 1997). Although rich in emotional terms (Clore, Ortony, & Foss, 1987; Frijda, Markam, Sato, & Wiers, 1995; Russell, 1978), language sometimes fails to capture affective experiences—especially intense affective experiences—so metaphors become more likely vehicles for rendering these conscious states of mind (Fainsilber & Ortony, 1987; Ortony & Fainsilber, 1989; Hoffman, Waggoner, & Palermo, 1991).

Affective reports have also long been recognized as subject to a host of motivational influences and contextual distortions, as well as being only modestly related to other aspects of affective reactions, such as somatovisceral events and behavior. Dating back to Freud, research from clinical psychology has underscored the dissociation between reportable aspects and affective states (e.g., Bradley, 2000; Davidson, 1998; Lang, 1971); research in neuropsychology and the neurosciences has shown that emotional feelings are neither necessary nor sufficient for the evocation of emotional processes (Gazzaniga & LeDoux, 1978; Tranel & Damasio, 2000); and research from social and cognitive psychology has shown that emotions are capable of being elicited quickly, effortlessly, automatically, or even unconsciously upon exposure to the relevant stimulus (e.g., Bargh, Chaiken, Govender, & Pratto, 1992; Pratto & John, 1991). Zajonc (1980) observed:

> When we meet a stranger, we know within a fraction of a second whether we like the person or not. The reaction is instantaneous and automatic. Perhaps the feeling is not always precise, perhaps we are not always aware of it, but the feeling is always there. . . . Perhaps we have not developed an extensive and precise verbal representation of feeling just because in the prelinguistic human this realm of experience had an adequate representation in the nonverbal channel . . . if affect is not always transformed into semantic content but is instead often encoded in, for example, visceral or muscular symbols, we would expect information contained in feelings to be acquired, organized, categorized, represented, and retrieved somewhat differently than information having direct verbal referents. (pp. 157–158).

Zajonc's point that interpersonal judgments and emotional experiences are fundamentally organized in terms of the dimension(s) of positivity and negativity has strong empirical support (see review by Cacioppo & Gardner, 1999). His proposition that emotion is meaningfully associated with, and possibly encoded in, somatovisceral events is more speculative; however, at least when limited to positive and negative processes, it has received preliminary support (Cacioppo, Priester, & Berntson, 1993). The study of the somatovisceral links to emotion, however, has perhaps been fueled most by the common experience that different visceral sensations underlie different emotions. If individuals were to say that they felt butterflies in their stomachs or that they felt they were ready to boil, few observers would fail to understand that the individuals were experiencing fear and anger, respectively. These interoceptive sensations are so distinct and compelling that it is hard to believe that these emotions are *not* differentiated peripherally as well as centrally. In this chapter we examine the psychophysiology of emotions, with a special emphasis on subtle mechanisms by which somatovisceral events may contribute to human emotions. Because of the centrality of hedonic tone in studies of emotion, we examine both the physiological differentiation of discrete emotions and the differentiation of positive and negative states.

HEURISTIC PERSPECTIVES

More than a century ago, William James (1884, 1890/1950) argued that emotional feelings are consequences rather than antecedents of peripheral physiological changes brought about by some stimulus. James (1884) also viewed emotions as being multiply determined. Individuals may recall earlier emotional episodes, including their feelings, and in so doing they may reexperience the emotion. If the remembered emotion was weak originally (e.g., it involved little or no somatovisceral activation), reexperiencing the emotion may occur in the absence of significant peripheral bodily disturbances. James (1884) therefore stated at the outset that "the only emotions I propose expressly to consider here are those that have a distinct bodily expression" (p. 189). James maintained that within this class of emotional phenomena, discrete emotional experiences can be identified with unique patterns of bodily changes, and that the perception of one of these specific patterns of peripheral physiological changes *is* the emotional experience.

James's (1884) hypothesis that autonomic nervous system (ANS) activity produces the percepts of discrete emotional states implies that emotion-specific somatovisceral patterns generate emotional experiences, and that a somatovisceral pattern begins before the experience of the corresponding emotion. In an early critique of this position, Cannon (1927) provided evidence from animal studies that autonomic events are too slow, too insensitive, and too undifferentiated to contribute to emotions. This critique appeared devastating and led to the notion that emotional experience is the exclusive province of central networks. Consistent with this notion, research on the influence of cognitive appraisals in emotion (e.g., Ellsworth, 1994) and on emotions in the spinal-cord-injured (e.g., Chwalisz, Diener, & Gallagher, 1988) suggests that afferent information from peripheral activity is not a necessary condition for emotional experience. Recently, however, the pendulum appears to have begun to swing in the other direction, as investigations suggest that autonomic processes *can* contribute to the encoding and recall (if not the experience) of emotional information (e.g., see review by Cahill, 1996; see also Demaree & Harrison, 1997).

To the extent that emotional experiences are multiply determined, the experience of a discrete emotion can occur in the absence of the "corresponding" somatovisceral pattern, even if somatovisceral afference can be an antecedent of the emotion. A recent neurobiological model of anxiety emphasizes the reciprocal relations between ascending and descending systems (Berntson, Sarter, & Cacioppo, 1998). This model recognizes not only that affective states may be primed by either top-down (cognition) or bottom-up (visceral reactivity) processes, but that these alternative activational modes may mutually reinforce one another (e.g., as in panic disorder). For this reason, it is more informative to ask under what conditions and for what emotions differential physiological activity is observed than to search for an invariant relationship between emotional experience (or expressions) and physiological response. For instance, Schachter and Singer (1962) shaped thinking about emotions when they suggested that undifferentiated autonomic activity *can* subserve discrete emotions. The mechanism by which this is accomplished, according to Schachter and Singer (1962; see also Mandler, 1975; Reisenzein, 1983), is the perception of neutral, unexplained physiological arousal, which creates an "evaluative need" and motivates the individual to understand and label cognitively the arousal state. The consequent attributional processes were thought to produce discrete feeling states and influence emotional behavior.

Figure 11.1 depicts a general framework summarizing mechanisms by which somatovisceral afference may influence emotional experience (Cacioppo, Berntson, & Klein, 1992). At one end of the continuum (Figure 11.1, top left column), discrete emotional experiences result from the apperception of distinct somatovisceral patterns (e.g., Ekman, Levenson, & Friesen, 1983; James, 1884; Levenson, 1988; Levenson, Ekman, & Friesen, 1990). At the other end of the continuum (Figure 11.1, bottom left column), discrete emotional experiences derive from attributional processes that are initiated by the perception of undifferentiated physiological arousal (e.g., Mandler, 1975; Schachter & Singer, 1962). Falling between these extremes is yet another process by which peripheral bodily reactions may contribute to emotional experience—"somatovisceral illusions," an active perceptual process by which an ambiguous pattern of somatovisceral afference is disambiguated to produce an immediate, spontaneous, and indubitable emotional percept (Figure 11.1, middle left column).

The essential feature of the proposition that discrete emotions can result from somatovisceral illusions can be illustrated by analogy using the ambiguous visual figure depicted in Figure 11.2 (see Cacioppo, Berntson, & Klein, 1992, for a more complete description of the model). Even though there is only one set of visual contours and features in Figure 11.2, top-down processes make it possible for a person looking at this picture to see or experience two very different perceptual images: a young woman facing left or an old woman facing right. Once these images have been identified, the viewer may find that he or she can alternate quickly between seeing these discrete images,

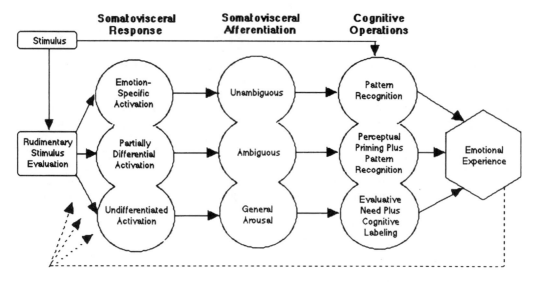

FIGURE 11.1. The somatovisceral afference model of emotion (SAME). The same pattern of somatovisceral activity has been associated with surprisingly different emotions, and the same emotion has been associated with quite different patterns of somatovisceral activity. These results have been viewed as evidence against the importance of somatovisceral afference in emotion. The SAME, depicted above and described in the text, encompasses both of these findings while emphasizing the instrumental role of somatovisceral afference and cognitive/perceptual processes in producing emotion. From Cacioppo, Berntson, and Klein (1992). Copyright 1992 by Sage Publications. Reprinted by permission.

but cannot see both at once. That is, the same visual afference can lead to two different, discrete, and indubitable perceptual experiences, just as the same physiological afference may lead to two different, discrete, and indubitable emotions.

Ambiguous visual figures such as the one depicted in Figure 11.2 are constructed by using elements from two (or more) unambiguous images in such a way that the figure created by overlapping or slightly modifying the elements of the unambiguous images can be interpreted in multiple discrete ways (Sekuler & Blake, 1985). Because the same sensory information in an ambiguous figure can produce such strikingly different, immediately obvious, and unambiguous perceptions, Leeper (1935) referred to ambiguous figures as "reversible illusions." There is little reason to suppose that somatovisceral illusions can not operate similarly. The active perceptual processes underlying reversible visual illusions are not limited to visual information processing, but can also operate on interoceptive (e.g., visceral) and proprioceptive (e.g., postural, facial, vocal) input. Indeed, the architecture of the somatovisceral apparatus may be better suited to produce ambiguous afference than is the visual system (Reed, Harver,

& Katkin, 1990). For instance, in the perception of ambiguous visual figures, the stimulus is a visual array outside the body. However, the central nervous system serves to create and interpret both the stimulus and the response to somatovisceral information. In this regard, visual processes are somewhat more like somatic instrumental processes than like visceral processes. Both of the former differ from visceral perception, for instance, in the distinctiveness of the reafference. In the somatic case, the accuracy of response is readily ascertainable, and correctable, by somatosensory and visual feedback. In the visceral domain, there is no "intended" outcome in the conscious sense (although there are target outcomes in an automatic or homeostatic sense). In the case of all three, feedback can importantly shape subsequent action without conscious awareness. Hence visceral perception differs from somatic and visual perception in that there is no discrete criterion (or "correct" perception) for which an individual is consciously looking. For this reason, visceral afference may be particularly prone to misperceptions and "illusions." Furthermore, it seems likely that events as important and commonplace as the emotions have cognitive representations that include somato-

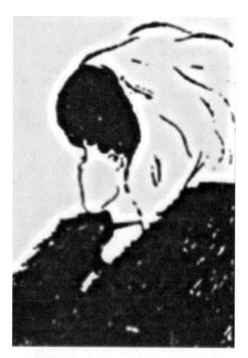

FIGURE 11.2. This ambiguous figure is called "My wife and mother-in-law" and is constructed from overlapping unambiguous elements. The perceptual system tends to group like or related information together. Rather than presenting some odd mixture of the two alternative pictures, partial identification of a young woman or an old woman in this figure supports a stable perception of a single coherent image. The identification of wholes and of parts is reciprocally supportive, contributing further to the locking-in process. A shift in gaze is not necessary for a perceptual change to occur. In what may be analogous to discrete emotional feelings' being spawned by the same ambiguous pattern of somatovisceral information, ambiguous visual figures demonstrate that discrete images can derive from the same ambiguous pattern of visual information. From Boring (1930).

formation flow (Cacioppo, Berntson, & Klein, 1992). The extent of the cognitive elaboration of the somatovisceral afference required to produce an emotional experience ranges from simple informational analyses such as pattern recognition (e.g., James's theory of emotion as the perception of discrete patterns of somatovisceral afference) to much more complex attributional analyses and hypothesis testing (e.g., Mandler's theory of emotion), with simple cognitive appraisals of the stimulus and perceptual priming of an emotion schema falling between these two endpoints. Note that quite different patterns of somatovisceral afference (see Figure 11.1, left column) can lead to the same emotional experience via three very different psychophysiological mechanisms (see Figure 11.1, right column), whereas the same pattern of somatovisceral afference can lead to discrete emotional experiences by two distinct psychophysiological mechanisms: (1) somatovisceral "illusions" when the afference is ambiguous and an emotion schema has been primed (see Figure 11.2); and (2) cognitive labeling when the perception of the afference is undifferentiated with respect to an emotion and there is an evaluative need. The framework outlined in Figure 11.1 argues against the tendency to view the psychophysiological mechanisms underlying emotion in terms of a simple central–peripheral dichotomy. It also is in accord with robust findings in the literature that discrete emotional percepts can occur even when the autonomic changes do not discriminate fully the emotions that are experienced, and that autonomic activation can alter the intensity if not the nature of emotional experience. In the sections that follow, we examine the nature of the expressive patterns associated with discrete emotions.

FACIAL ELECTROMYOGRAPHY

Scientific studies of the link between facial expressions and emotions originated with Darwin's (1872) seminal analysis and were reinvigorated by Tomkins's (1962) proposition that facial movement and feedback play an important role in the experience of emotion. Tomkins suggested that high-speed filming could be used to perform microscopic analyses of facial expressions and emotion. These proposals led to important methodological advances in the coding of facial expressions (e.g., Ekman &

visceral attributes. Thus several important features required for the production of somatovisceral illusions are plausibly in place.

The nodes along the continuum in the left column of Figure 11.1 represent important transitions in the constitution of the autonomic response, but the openings between these nodes underscore the continuous nature of this dimension. The pattern of somatovisceral activation produces a parallel continuum of somatovisceral sensory input to the brain. The arrows between nodes denote the major pathways for in-

Friesen, 1978; Izard, 1971, 1977). Building on this foundation, investigators have provided provocative evidence that (1) at least some discrete emotions are associated with distinct overt facial expressions; (2) induced states in which individuals report positive and negative emotions are associated with distinctive facial actions; and (3) displays similar to those of adults can be found in neonates and the congenitally blind, suggesting that these displays are inherently linked with basic emotions (e.g., see Ekman, 1973; Ekman & Friesen, 1978; Izard, 1977).

Although facial expressions may seem intuitively to reveal the nature of underlying emotions, many emotional and affect-laden information processes are not accompanied by visually perceptible facial actions. This fact has limited the utility of analyses of facial actions in understanding emotions. Furthermore, although observers across cultures attribute the same emotional meaning to the expressions of happiness, sadness, fear, anger, surprise, and disgust, these attributions are not perfect (Russell, 1994). Complicating research in this area, the specific emotion that is evoked by a stimulus may vary across individuals and cultures. Finally, individuals can invoke display rules to mask or hide the emotion they are feeling, and observers can confuse the meaning of expressions (e.g., fear and surprise; Ekman, 1973; cf. Cacioppo, Bush, & Tassinary, 1992). For these reasons, the coding of overt facial expressions can be a less than perfect measure of affective state. An important complement to visual inspection of facial expression has been the measurement of patterns of activity in facial muscles. This technique—facial electromyography (EMG)—has made it possible to index muscle activity even in the absence of observable facial expressions (Cacioppo & Petty, 1981; Cacioppo, Tassinary, & Fridlund, 1990).

In pioneering research, Schwartz and colleagues demonstrated differences related to emotional imagery in EMG activity over the brow (corrugator supercilii), cheek (zygomaticus major), and perioral (depressor anguli oris) muscle regions. Schwartz, Fair, Salt, Mandel, and Klerman (1976), for instance, asked participants to imagine positive or negative events in their lives. Results revealed that people showed more EMG activity over the brow region and less over the cheek and perioral regions when imagining sad as compared to happy events. Schwartz, Ahern, and Brown (1979) asked subjects to engage in thought and imagery tasks that involved happiness, excitement, sadness, fear, and neutral emotional states. Facial EMG was recorded over two sites, the brow and cheek. The only significant main effects for discrete emotional states indicated higher EMG activity over the cheek and lower EMG activity over the brow during positive than negative emotions.

Although the number of studies is limited, research has consistently shown that EMG activity over the brow (corrugator supercilii, frown muscle) region is lower and EMG activity over the cheek (zygomaticus major, smile muscle) and periocular (orbicularis oculi) muscle regions is higher when emotions that are mildly positive, as opposed to mildly negative, are evoked. These opposing effects are more apparent at the group (nomethetic) level than at the individual (idiographic) level of analysis. In early reports, the facial EMG patterns associated with emotional states were characterized as "miniature representations" of those occurring during overt facial expressions (Schwartz, Fair, Greenberg, Foran, & Klerman, 1975). The evidence for covert emotion-specific facial expressions has been far weaker than the evidence for overt emotion-specific facial expressions, however. In a comprehensive study, for instance, Brown and Schwartz (1980) had participants go through imagery conditions designed to elicit happiness, sadness, fear, and anger at three levels of intensity while EMG activity was recorded over the brow, cheek, forehead, and jaw muscle regions. Results revealed that the imagery of negative emotions (fear, anger, and sadness) was associated with higher EMG activity over the brow muscle regions than was the imagery of the positive emotion (happiness). EMG activity over the cheek region was highest during happy imagery but also was elevated at least somewhat during fear and anger imagery. Whether these latter elevations reflect some participants engaging in miserable or distress smiling (Ekman, Friesen, & Ancoli, 1980), "cross-talk" from other muscles of the middle and lower facial regions, or the putative phylogenetic origin of smiling and laughter in primitive agonistic displays (Andrew, 1963; van Hooff, 1972) is unclear. EMG activity over the jaw and forehead muscle regions did not vary significantly (see also Brown & Schwartz, 1980; Hess, Kappas, McHugo, Lanzetta, & Kleck, 1992; Schwartz et al., 1976). Finally, increasing emotional intensity led to increased

EMG activity, especially over the brow muscle regions during sad, angry, and fearful imagery, and over the cheek muscle region during happy imagery (see, also, Cacioppo, Martzke, Tassinary, & Petty, 1988).

Fridlund, Schwartz, and Fowler (1984), using a unique classification analysis, reported evidence for emotion-specific facial EMG patterns. Subjects were instructed to imagine 48 emotional scenes designed to elicit happiness, fear, sadness, or anger, and EMG activity was recorded over the frontalis, corrugator supercilii, orbicularis oculi, and orbicularis oris muscle regions. A one-way multivariate analysis of variance was performed separately on the data from each subject. The parameter of EMG activity (e.g., mean, peak) that yielded the discriminant function with the clearest separation of emotion categories was selected on a subject-by-subject basis. A linear discriminant analysis differentiated among the emotion categories at better than chance level: Hit rates were 51% for happiness, 49% for sadness and anger, and 38% for fear. Posed expressions were also tested, yielding hit rates ranging from 83% to 89%. The covert facial EMG patterns that best differentiated among the emotions may have varied across subjects, and we have found no subsequent study in which an approach such as this produced evidence for distinctive (and generalizable) incipient facial expressive actions associated with discrete emotional states. Thus the bulk of the evidence to date suggests that the simple differentiation of hedonic tone has a lower threshold for activation than emotion-specific facial displays across individuals. That is, emotions can be characterized as a coalition of normally loosely coupled control mechanisms that are temporally recruited in a hierarchical sequence in order to meet an environmental challenge (imagined or real). The global distinction between hospitable (positive) or hostile (negative) stimuli, which is among the first information extracted from stimuli (Zajonc, 1980), may be one of the first aspects of an emotional response to be reflected in peripheral physiological activation in the form of rudimentary facial efference.

Although facial EMG research has proven to be a sensitive measure of hedonic tone, most psychophysiological research on discrete emotions has focused on the ANS. This emphasis is attributable to several factors. First, and as noted above, different emotions appear to be associated with signature visceral sensations (e.g.,

feeling steamed when one is angry, feeling butterflies in one's stomach when one is frightened). Second, whether or not visceral responses contribute to emotional experiences, they are clearly involved in emotion—as, for instance, demonstrated by the visceral changes that are observed when central networks associated with emotions are activated (LeDoux, 1996). Third, emotions, like the viscera, are common to all animals and fall largely outside of direct voluntary control. Consequently, the links between emotions and the ANS have been the topic of much research. Much of this research has been influenced by James's (1884) proposal that peripheral physiological changes are antecedents rather than consequences of the perception of emotional experience. Because of the close links between emotions and ANS activity, many researchers have focused their search for emotion-specific patterning on the ANS. We turn to this research next.

AUTONOMIC ACTIVITY

Early research on autonomic activity and affective reactions appeared to be characterized by a lack of replicability or generalizability. Despite the lack of consistency in early findings, the notion that visceral responses differentiate discrete emotions remained popular. In an important development in this area, Ekman, Levenson, and colleagues (Ekman et al., 1983; Levenson, 1988) attributed much of the inconsistency in prior results to various methodological problems. Among the problems they cited are the failure to verify independently that an emotional state has been aroused (e.g., through self-report or behavioral observation); the failure to equate the intensity of the emotions; and the mistiming of physiological recordings, given the likely onset and offset of the emotion. Furthermore, Ekman, Levenson, and colleagues argued that differentiation requires simultaneous examination of a number of indices of ANS activity. They maintained that emotion-specific autonomic differentiation would be obtained if these shortcomings were eliminated.

Ekman's group first presented evidence for the differentiation of discrete emotions in an article in *Science* in 1983 (Ekman et al., 1983). Heart rate, left- and right-hand finger temperature, skin resistance, and forearm flexor muscle tension were recorded during the manipulation of the emotional states of anger, fear, sadness, happiness, surprise, and disgust. One method for evoking emotions involved a directed facial action task, in which a participant was induced to form a facial expression associated with a discrete emotion through muscle-by-muscle contraction instructions that omitted any reference to the emotional state. For example, a participant might be told to pull the eyebrows down and together, to raise the upper eyelid, to push the lower lip up, and to press the lips together. These instructions corresponded to the facial expression associated with anger.

Emotion was also evoked in this experiment with an imagery task, in which participants were asked to relive a past emotional experience for 30 seconds. Physiological responses during a relived emotion period were compared to a nonimagery resting baseline, revealing higher skin resistance during sadness than during fear, anger, or disgust. Together, the results from the two emotion induction techniques generated considerable enthusiasm for the idea of emotion-specific autonomic patterning, especially because emotions of the same valence (e.g., anger and fear) appeared distinguishable. Similar results were obtained by Levenson et al. (1990), using the directed facial action task, leading these researchers to propose that each discrete emotion is associated with an innate affect program whose role is to coordinate changes in the organism's biological states. They further argued that these changes are directed at supporting the behavioral adaptations and motor programs most likely associated with a particular emotion (e.g., fleeing in the case of fear), and can be recorded as emotion-specific changes in ANS activity (Levenson et al., 1990).

There is now a significant body of research relevant to this hypothesis, and several reviews have been performed (Cacioppo, Klein, Berntson, & Hatfield, 1993, Cacioppo, Berntson, Klein, & Poehlmann, 1997; Zajonc & McIntosh, 1992). These reviews reveal that whereas some reliable autonomic differentiation has been obtained across studies, the results are far from definitive regarding emotion-specific autonomic patterning. Table 11.1 lists in chronological order published research that has contrasted the effects of at least two discrete emotions on two or more autonomic measures in humans.

We (Cacioppo, Berntson, et al., 1997) conducted a meta-analysis providing data relevant to the question of whether emotion-specific autonomic patterning exists. We updated the database (see Table 11.1) and repeated the meta-analyses based on this more complete dataset. Our inclusion criteria yielded numerous effect sizes involving 22 measures across almost two dozen studies. A word of caution is in order before we turn to the results. These meta-analyses allow one to examine statistically the differentiation of discrete emotions by individual measures. It is possible that discrete emotions differ in terms of the patterns of autonomic responses associated with each, even if no single measure is found to differentiate these emotions. Still, the literature is replete with claims of differentiating emotions using individual autonomic measures, and meta-analyses provide a more rigorous test of such assertions. Furthermore, a meta-analytic approach to this literature points to particularly fertile areas of research as well as to barren areas.

Consistent with Ekman et al.'s (1983) finding, greater heart rate acceleration was obtained to anger, fear, and sadness as compared to disgust. There was also a tendency for happiness to be associated with greater heart rate acceleration than disgust. However, disgust was associated with the same heart rate response as control conditions; indeed, disgust did not differ from control conditions on any autonomic measure. The meta-analysis also revealed heart rate responses to be larger in (1) anger than happiness, (2) fear than happiness (which also differed on finger pulse volume), and (3) fear than sadness (which also differed on respiration rate). Emotion-specific differentiation for cardiorespiratory measures other than heart rate was less reliable (e.g., measures of bodily tension, facial temperature, respiration amplitude, inspiration volume, or cardiac stroke volume; (Cacioppo, Berntson, et al., 1997). The only other replicable autonomic differentiation noted by Levenson et al. (1990; Levenson, Carstensen, Friesen, & Ekman, 1991) was that finger temperature decreased less in anger than in fear. Meta-analyses revealed that this effect did not achieve statistical significance when the results of all studies were considered. A study by Boiten (1996) also raises the possibility that at least some of the cardiac differentiation of emotions that has been observed may be secondary to effort and respiratory changes.

Several other reliable results emerged from our meta-analyses. Consistent with prior claims, diastolic blood pressure was higher in anger than in fear, but meta-analyses also re-

TABLE 11.1. Studies Comparing Two or More Physiological Measures as a Function of Two or More Discrete Emotions

Study	Age range (mean or mode)	Emotions [Induction]	Dependent variables
Ax (1953)	21–55 (27) $n = 43^*$	Anger, fear [Real life]	SBP, DBP, SV, HR, FCT, FT, NNSCR, NMTP, SCL, EMG, RR
Funkenstein, King, & Drollette (1954)	19–24 $n = 52^*$	Anger in (21 Ss), anger out (22 Ss), fear (anxiety; 9 Ss) [Psychological stressor]	HR, SBP, DBP, SV, CO
Schachter (1957)	(Normotensives, 38; potential hypertensives, 41; hypertensives, 42) $n = 48^a$	Anger, fear, pain [Real life]	HR, SBP, DBP, FCT, HT, SCL, EMG, II, RR, SV, CO, TPR
Sternbach (1962)[b]	All 8 years old $n = 10$	Fear, happiness, humor, sadness [Film]	SRL, gastric motility, RR, HR, EOG, FPV
Averill (1969)	17–24 (18) $n = 54$	Happiness, sadness, control [Film]	HR, SBP, DBP, FCT, FT, SCL, FPV, NNSCR, RR, RI
Tourangeau & Ellsworth (1979)	Undergrads $n = 123$	Fear, sadness, neutral [Film[c]] crossed with fear, sadness, neutral expression, undirected as to expression [DFA]	HR, SRL, NNSCR
Schwartz, Weinberger, & Singer (1981)	Undergrads $n = 32$	Anger, fear, happiness, sadness, relaxation, control [Imagery[d]]	HR, SBP, DBP
Roberts & Weerts (1982)	Undergrads $n = 16^*$	Anger, fear, neutral [Imagery]	HR, SBP, DBP
Ekman, Levenson, & Friesen (1983)[c]	Nonundergrads $n = 16$ Only "best faces" and "best imagery" trials were reported	Anger, disgust, fear, happiness, sadness, surprise [DFA, relived emotion]	HR, FT, SRL, EMG
Stemmler (1989)	(23) $n = 42$	Anger, fear, happiness, control [Real life, imagery]	HR, FT, SCL, EMG, MVT (finger and head acceleration), RR, PTT, FPV, BV, NNSCR, FCT
Tassinary, Cacioppo, & Geen (1989)	Undergrads and grads $n = 15$	Anger, happiness, control [DFA]	SCL, HR
Levenson, Ekman, & Friesen (1990)	18–30 $n = 62^f$	Anger, disgust, fear, happiness, sadness, surprise [DFA]	HR, FT, SCL, EMG, MVT
Levenson, Carstensen, Friesen, & Ekman (1991)	71–83 (77) $n = 20^*$ Only "best faces" and "best imagery" were reported	Anger, disgust, fear, happiness, sadness, surprise [DFA, relived emotion]	HR, FT, SCL, MVT
Hess, Kappas, McHugo, Lanzetta, & Kleck (1992)	Undergrads $n = 27$	Anger, happiness, peacefulness, sadness [Feel, express, feel-and-express]	Facial EMG, SCL, HR

(continued)

TABLE 11.1 *(continued)*

Study	Age range (mean or mode)	Emotions [Induction]	Dependent variables
Levenson, Ekman, Heider, & Friesen (1992)	16–27 $n = 46^g$ Only "best faces" were reported.	Anger, disgust, fear, happiness, sadness [DFA]	HR, FT, SCL, PTT, FPV, RD, RR
Sinha, Lovallo, & Parsons (1992)	21–35 $n = 26*$	Anger, fear, joy, sadness, neutral state [Imagery]	HR, SBP, DBP, SV, CO, TPR, PEP, LVET
Vrana (1993)	Undergrads $n = 50$	Anger, disgust, pleasure (happiness), joy [Imagery]	HR, SCL, facial EMG
Boiten (1996)	Undergrads $n = 15*$ Data also broken down into emotional and nonemotional responders	Anger, disgust, fear, happiness, sadness, surprise, nonemotion, standard control [DFA]	RSP (T_i, T_e, P_i, T_{tot}, V_t, FRC), HR
Sinha & Parsons (1996)	21–35 $n = 27^h$	Anger, fear, neutral [Imagery]	FT, HR, SBD, DBP, SCL, facial EMG
Collet, Vernet-Maury, Delhomme, Dittmar (1997)	19–26 (22) $n = 30$	Happiness, surprise, sadness, fear, disgust, anger [Imagery]	EDR-Dur, HT, RR, SBF-Nod, SCL
Alaoui-Ismaili, Robin, Rada, Dittmar, & Vernet-Maury (1997)	20–28 (25) $n = 44$	Happiness, surprise, sadness, ear, disgust, anger [Odorants ^{i}]	EDR-Dur, HR, HT, RR, SBF-Nod
Miller & Wood, 1997	8–17 $n = 24^j$	Happiness, sadness, sadness/happiness, neutral [Film ^{k}]	HR, HRV, OS

Note. BV, blood volume; CO, cardiac output; DBP, diastolic blood pressure; DFA, directed facial action; EMG, muscle activity; EOG, eyeblink rate; EDR-Dur, electrodermal response duration; FCT, face temperature; FPV, finger pulse volume; FRC, functional residual capacity; FT, finger temperature; HR, heart rate; HRV, heart rate variability; HT, hand temperature; II, inspiratory index; LVET, left ventricular ejection time; MVT, movement; NMTP, number of muscle tension peaks; NNSCR, number of nonspecific skin conductance responses; OS, oxygen saturation of the blood; PEP, preejection period; Pi, postinspiratory pause; PTT, pulse transit time; RD, respiration depth; RSP, respiration; RI, respiration irregularity; RR, respiration rate; SBF-Nod, nonoscillatory duration of the skin blood flow response; SBP, systolic blood pressure; SCL, skin conductance level; SRL, skin resistance level; SV, stroke volume; T_i, inspiratory time; T_e, expiratory time; TPR, total peripheral resistance; T_{tot}, total cycle duration; V_t, tidal volume. An asterisk that indicates that participants were selected based on ability to control facial muscles, on ability to produce appropriate imagery, or on whether they experimented the emotions of interest.

^{a}18 hypertensives, 8 potential hypertensives, and the same 15 normotensives as in Ax (1953).

^{b}Although this study is included in this descriptive table, it is not included in the meta-analyses because no interemotion comparisons were reported.

^{c}No significant effects were found for differences in facial expressions during the film.

^{d}Participants imagined a scene in which they felt the appropriate emotion as they were (in their imaginations) exercising on a one-step exercise machine.

^{e}The DFA results of this study were subsequently incorporated into Levenson et al. (1990).

^{f}Article combined results from three experiments: Ekman et al. (1983); a group of 16 Ss selected from 103 screened; and a group of 30 Ss selected from 109 screened.

^{g}Participants were from the Minangkabau community in West Sumatra.

^{h}Only males with Minnesota Multiphasic Personality Inventory *T*-scores between 30 and 70 were selected.

^{i}Ss inhaled vanillin, menthol, eugenol, propionic acid, and dental resin. Vanillin and propionic acid evoked happiness and disgust, respectively; the other odorants did not reliably evoke the intended emotions and were not included in the meta-analyses.

^{j}All Ss were asthmatics; no comparison sample was reported.

^{k}Ss viewed clips from the film *E.T.: The Extra-Terrestrial*. The sadness/happiness clip was a farewell scene; the data from this condition were not included in the meta-analyses.

vealed that anger was associated with more nonspecific skin conductance responses, smaller increases in heart rate, smaller increases in stroke volume and cardiac output, larger increases in total peripheral resistance, larger increases in facial temperature, and larger increases in finger pulse volume than fear. Thus anger appears to act more on the vasculature and less on the heart than fear. Whether these differences generalize to other conditions of evocation requires further research.

The diastolic blood pressure response was also higher in anger than in sadness or happiness, and in sadness than in happiness (which also differed on the measure of systolic blood pressure). No other differences were reliable. Most of these meta-analytic results were characterized by high heterogeneity, however; this suggests that anger, fear, sadness, and happiness may have differential effects on peripheral vascular function, but that one or more unspecified variables are also likely to be moderating these relationships.

Meta-analyses showed that skin conductance level increased less in happiness than in disgust, but as noted above, disgust did not differ from control conditions in terms of any autonomic response. Fear was associated with greater increases in nonspecific skin conductance responses and smaller increases in skin conductance level than sadness. Too few data exist on several other measures (e.g., systolic time intervals, finger pulse volume, pulse transit time, body movement) to permit us to draw strong conclusions (see also Cacioppo, Berntson, et al., 1997, Tables 2.2 and 2.3).

Several reviews have also noted the failure of imagery to produce differentiation reliably or to produce the same pattern of differentiation as other operationalizations; this is problematic for the notion of *emotion*-specific patterning (e.g., Cacioppo, Berntson, et al., 1997; Zajonc & McIntosh, 1992). Skin resistance level, for instance, has been observed to decrease more during sadness than during fear, anger, or disgust, but these comparisons were not significant when requested facial actions were used to manipulate discrete emotions (Ekman et al., 1983).

The notion that ANS activity is mobilized in response to perceived or expected metabolic demands is consistent with a distinction made by Lang and colleagues (Lang, Bradley, & Cuthbert, 1990; Bradley, 2000) between "strategic" and "tactical" aspects of emotions.

Tactics are specific, context-bound patterns of action. Although affective reactions can be organized into a finite set of discrete emotions, tactical demands may vary among situations, making it possible for the same emotion to be associated with a range of behavior and varying patterns of somatovisceral activation. For example, Lang et al. (1990) note that the behaviors associated with fear can range from freezing to vigilance to flight. This tactical variability may account in part for the poor reliability of emotion-specific autonomic patterning unless one considers the modulation of ANS substrates by these factors.

In contrast to tactics, strategies are viewed as underlying organizations that direct actions in the pursuit of broad end goals. The dimensions of valence (appetitive or aversive) and intensity are viewed by Lang and colleagues as strategic aspects of emotion. The ability of the ANS to mobilize metabolic resources in response to hostile and hospitable stimuli is crucial to survival. Despite unreliable emotion-specific autonomic patterning, valuence-specific patterning may exist. A variety of theoretical and empirical work suggests that, all else being equal, negative emotions may be characterized by greater autonomic activation than that found in positive emotions (Cacioppo, Berntson, et al., 1997; Taylor, 1991). Among the ways in which negative and positive affective processes appear to differ, for instance, is the tendency for the change in negative motivational output to be larger than the change in positive motivational output per unit of activation. This effect, which has been observed in animal learning (Miller, 1961), human affective judgments (Ito, Cacioppo, & Lang, 1998), attitudes and impression formation (Cacioppo & Berntson, 1994; Skowronski & Carlson, 1989), and late positive brain potentials to affectively discrepant stimuli (Ito, Larsen, Smith, & Cacioppo, 1998), is termed the "negativity bias" (Cacioppo & Berntson, 1994; Cacioppo et al., 1999).

To examine whether autonomic responses differed for positive and negative discrete emotions, we conducted moderated meta-analyses of the data from the studies in Table 11.1. The results are depicted in Table 11.2. Diastolic blood pressure, blood volume, cardiac output, left ventricular ejection time, preejection period, pulse transit time, and heart rate all showed significantly greater activation during negative than during positive discrete emotions. The effect size for systolic blood pressure was comparable to that found for heart rate, but the effect size was not significant given the relatively small number of comparisons that went into this meta-analysis. Inspection of Table 11.2 further reveals that electrodermal measures did not differentiate positive from negative states, with the exception that negative emotions were associated with shorter-duration electrodermal responses than was happiness. A similar effect was found for cutaneous blood flow responses (see Table 11.2). The tests for heterogeneity suggest caution in interpreting the effects for the measures of diastolic blood pressure, blood volume, nonoscillary duration of the skin blood flow response, and electrodermal response duration. Thus, of the 22 measures that were meta-analyzed, 5 showed clearly greater activation to negative than to positive emotions, and none showed the reverse.

In sum, the meta-analyses indicated that even a limited set of discrete emotions such as happy, sad, fear, anger, and disgust cannot be fully differentiated by visceral activity alone, but follow-up meta-analyses did suggest that the negative emotions in this literature are associated with stronger ANS responses than are the positive emotions. Thus the evidence for the visceral differentiation of emotion, like that for incipient facial differentiation, is clearer when positive and negative emotions are contrasted than when discrete emotions are contrasted. To return to the heuristic portrayed in Figure 11.1, a stimulus is depicted as initially undergoing a rudimentary evaluation. Although not sufficient to produce emotion-specific somatovisceral activation, the rudimentary evaluation of the stimulus may at least identify it as one that is to be approached or avoided, producing a cascade of central and peripheral responses. We have thus far covered somatovisceral processes. We turn in the final section to central processes, where it has been found that anterior hemispheric asymmetries differentiate motivational dispositions and responses.

TABLE 11.2. Number of Comparisons, Combined Effect Size, and p Value for Comparisons of Negative (Anger, Fear, Disgust, Sadness) and Positive (Happiness[a]) Emotions by Physiological Measure

Measure	k	$d+$	$p(d+)$	$p(Q)$
DBP	7	0.54	.01	.01
BV	2	0.50	.01	.01
CO	3	0.47	.01	.14
LVET[b]	3	0.32	.05	.48
PEP[b]	3	0.32	.05	.42
PTT[b]	6	0.22	.01	.18
SBP	5	0.18	.15	.39
HR	32	0.17	.01	.10
RSP-Dur[b]	11	0.11	.14	.03
FPV[b]	7	0.09	.27	.82
FT[b]	15	0.07	.22	.82
RSP-Amp	7	0.04	.65	.75
SCL	26	0.03	.49	.04
NNSCR	3	0.02	.87	.95
MVT	2	0.01	.97	.58
SV	3	−0.03	.85	.89
FCT[b]	3	−0.11	.44	.01
EMG	10	−0.12	.08	.52
HT[b]	4	−0.12	.34	.60
TPR	3	−0.14	.04	.13
SBF-Nod	5	−0.25	.02	.02
EDR-Dur	5	−0.29	.01	.01

Note. k, = number of comparisons; $d+$, the average d weighted by the inverse of the variance of the measure ($d+$ > 0 indicates greater activation by negative emotion rela-

tive to positive emotion); $p(d+)$, the probability of obtaining the $d+$ by chance; $p(Q)$, the probability that heterogeneity of the k effect sizes is due to chance (a significant test of heterogenity indicates heterogeneity among the effect sizes). Variables representing the same construct were all given the same abbreviation, regardless of the name used in the original article. Abbreviations are as follows: DBP, diastolic blood pressure; BV, blood volume (includes head blood volume); CO, cardiac output (includes average height of IJ wave × pulse rate); LVET, left ventricular ejection time; PEP, preejection period, PTT, pulse transit time; SBP, systolic blood pressure; HR, heart rate; RSP-Dur, respiration duration (includes respiration rate, respiratory period, postinspiratory pause, expiratory time, inspiratory time, total cycle duration, respiratory intercycle interval); FPV, finger pulse volume (includes finger pulse volume amplitude, finger blood volume); FT, finger temperature; RSP-Amp, respiratory amplitude (includes respiratory depth, tidal volume, increase in functional capacity); SCL, skin conductance level (includes log conductance change, log palmar conductance); NNSCR, number of nonspecific skin conductance responses (includes number of galvanic skin responses, rate of galvanic skin responses); MVT, movement; SV, stroke volume (includes ballistocardiogram); FCT, face temperature; EMG, muscle activity (includes number of muscle tension peaks, maximum muscle tension increase); HT, hand temperature; TPR, total peripheral resistance (includes peripheral vascular resistance); SBF-Nod, nonoscillatory duration of the skin blood flow response; EDR-Dur, electrodermal response duration.

[a]Includes four comparisons involving Vrana's (1993) joy condition.

[b]Indicates measures coded such that lower values represent greater activation.

ELECTROENCEPHALOGRAPHIC ASYMMETRY

The left anterior region of the brain appears to be involved in the expression and experience of approach-related emotions, and the right anterior region appears to be involved in the expression and experience of avoidance-related emotions (see reviews by Davidson, 1992, 1993). Speculation relating hemispheric asymmetry to affective reactions was originally spurred by clinical observations linking depressive symptomology to hemispheric damage. Left anterior brain lesions, for instance, are more likely to produce major depression, whereas right anterior brain lesions are more likely to produce mania (Robinson & Downhill, 1995). Particularly compelling evidence was provided by Robinson and colleagues (Robinson, Kubos, Starr, Rao, & Price, 1984; Robinson & Downhill, 1995), who used computerized tomography to link stroke-related lesion location with the severity and valence of affective symptomatology. Severity of poststroke depression was positively related to lesion proximity to the left frontal pole, but negatively related to lesion proximity to the right frontal pole. Moreover, patients with right lateralized infarctions were more likely than their left-hemisphere-lesioned counterparts to display inappropriate cheerfulness.

These clinical observations are supported by experimental research suggesting that stable individual differences in activation of left and right anterior cortical areas result in a predisposition to experience approach-related positive affective states and withdrawal-related negative affective states, respectively. Davidson (1993, 1998) and colleagues have integrated these findings into a diathesis–stress model linking individual differences in anterior cortical asymmetry to dispositional affective tendencies. An important feature of this model is the requirement of an affective elicitor (e.g., Davidson, 1992; Davidson & Tomarken, 1989). That is, differences as a function of cerebral asymmetry are expected only when a stressor or affective challenge is experienced.

In studies illustrative of this body of research, emotionally evocative film clips served as the affective challenge, and self-reported reactions to the films were related to anterior cortical activity that was measured prior to film exposure (e.g., Wheeler, Davidson, & Tomarken, 1993; Tomarken, Davidson, & Henriques, 1990). In these studies, as in much of the research in this area, cortical asymmetry was quantified via scalp electroencephalographic (EEG) recordings. The dependent measure of interest in this and other studies was power in the alpha band (8–13 Hz), which is inversely related to hemispheric activation (Lindsley & Wicke, 1974). Consistent with the diathesis stress model, relative left anterior cortical asymmetry in the resting EEG was positively correlated with intensity of positive reactions reported to positive film clips, but negatively correlated with intensity of negative reactions in response to negative film clips. Importantly, this relationship between asymmetry and affective responses was valence-dependent, and not simply a function of greater affective reactivity associated with one or the other hemispheres. That is, global reactivity, computed as the sum of the positive reactions to the positive films and the negative reactions to the negative films, was uncorrelated with cerebral asymmetry.

Differences in temperament as a function of cortical asymmetry are also apparent in children. For example, behaviorally inhibited toddlers tend to show relative right midfrontal activation, whereas their uninhibited counterparts display relative left midfrontal activation (Davidson, 1993). A similar relation between anterior cortical asymmetry and childhood temperament was observed in infants as young as 10 months (Davidson & Fox, 1989), with maternal separation serving as the affective challenge. Those children who cried during the 60-second separation had greater relative right-hemisphere activation in a resting EEG period that preceded the separation, whereas infants who did not cry showed relative left-hemisphere activation.

The studies reviewed thus far have sought to relate cortical asymmetry to phasic differences in the tendency to activate either approach- or withdrawal-related motivation. It is also possible to classify affective states as resulting from a hypoactivation of one of these systems. Depression, in particular, may result from a hypoactivation of approach-related motivation. This characterization of depression is supported by differences in resting EEG asymmetry recorded from clinically depressed and control participants (Henriques & Davidson, 1991). Whereas the two groups did not differ in right midfrontal activation, the clinically depressed participants showed decreased left midfrontal activation relative to controls. Similar results have been obtained with currently normothymic participants with a history of depression (Henriques & Davidson, 1990). It is important to note that in this latter study, previously depressed and control participants did not differ in their current self-reported mood—a result that has been interpreted to mean that left-hemisphere hypoactivation renders individuals vulnerable to depressive episodes. Similarly, the studies comparing resting EEG asymmetry to reactions elicited by emotionally evocative films in nondepressed populations reveal relations between left-hemisphere activation and positive affective states and between right-hemisphere activation and negative affective states, even when the effects of baseline mood are statistically removed (Tomarken et al., 1990; Wheeler et al., 1993).

Phasic shifts in cortical asymmetry have also been observed during the actual experience of affective reactions. Davidson, Ekman, Saron, Senulis, & Friesen (1990) recorded EEG during the presentation of film clips chosen to elicit the approach-related positive states of amusement and happiness and the withdrawal-related state of disgust. Surreptitious video recording of the participants as they watched the films allowed for offline coding of facial expressions. EEG epochs corresponding to the facial expressions of either happiness or disgust were retained for analysis. Disgusted as compared to happy expressions were associated with greater activation over right midfrontal and anterior temporal regions, similar activation over left midfrontal regions, and less activation over left anterior temporal regions. Analyses conducted across all artifact-free EEG data (i.e., including those times in which a facial expression was not present) failed to reveal any relation between positive or negative film clips and cerebral asymmetry. Thus it may be that only emotional experiences strong enough to produce overt facial expressions are associated with measurable concomitant cortical asymmetry.

Cerebral asymmetry was measured as the difference between log alpha power in the right and left hemisphere (for an exception, see Wheeler et al., 1993)—a computation that implies a single continuum of activation. As evidence suggesting separable motivational systems has grown within cerebral asymmetry research (e.g., Sutton & Davidson, 1997) and other areas of neurophysiology, theoretical accounts of cerebral asymmetry have similarly evolved, and now explicitly incorporate separable systems (c.f. Sutton & Davidson, 1997). Anterior EEG asymmetries have not differentiated discrete emotions, however; instead, they appear more generally to differentiate approach-related emotions (e.g., happiness, anger) from withdrawal-related emotions (e.g., sadness, fear; Harmon-Jones & Allen, 1998).

EPILOGUE

As the varied perspectives represented in this volume suggest, the study of emotion can be informed from a wide range of viewpoints. One of the more interesting questions concerning the psychophysiology of emotions is the role of somatovisceral afference in emotional experience. The research on the somatovisceral differentiation of emotions is provocative, but th cumulative evidence for emotion-specific patterns remains inconclusive (Wagner, 1989). The psychophysiological research reviewed in this chapter suggests the following conclusions. Facial EMG activity over the cheek (zygomaticus major) and periocular (orbicularis oculi) muscle regions varies as a function of positivity, whereas EMG activity over the brow (corrugator supercilii) muscle region varies as a function of negativity, and research on EEG asymmetries similarly suggests that anterior brain regions are differentially involved in approach-related versus avoidance-related behavioral processes. Although autonomic activation differs as a function of the energetic (e.g., metabolic action) components of affective states, meta-analyses have revealed that negative emotions are additionally associated with larger changes than positive states on several autonomic indices.

Emotions—particularly *negative* emotions—have also been linked to increases in health problems, including an enhanced susceptibility to infection (see review by Herbert & Cohen, 1993), poorer response to an influenza vaccine (Kiecolt-Glaser, Glaser, Gravenstein, Malarkey, & Sheridan, 1996), and impaired wound healing (Kiecolt-Glaser, Marucha, Malarkey, Mercado, & Glaser, 1995). The mechanisms underlying the relationship between emotion and health are complex and are not yet fully understood, but several different mechanisms are likely to be involved, some of which imply autonomic differentiation of positive from negative affective states. Health problems increase with aging as well, with negative emotions augmenting age-related declines in health and well-being (e.g., Kiecolt-Glaser, Dura, Speicher, Trask, & Glaser, 1991) and positive emotions having less impact (Ewart, Taylor, Kraemer, & Agras, 1991). Given this backdrop, it is understandable why investigators have been receptive to the idea that the emotions have distinct somatovisceral effects.

The psychophysiology of emotion might benefit from an expansion to include neuroendocrine systems, as these may serve as a gateway by which different emotions influence health. In addition, the potential elements and patterns of autonomic activity have not been exhaustively examined. Potential patterns may not be describable in terms of gross measures of end-organ response (e.g., heart rate), for instance. Among the possible obstacles to identifying autonomic patterning as a function of emotion, particularly for dually and antagonistically innervated organs such as the heart, are the many-to-one mappings between neural changes and organ response. Emotional stimuli do not invariably evoke reciprocal activation of the sympathetic and parasympathetic branches of the ANS. For instance, the presentation of an aversive conditioned stimulus can produce coactivation of the sympathetic and parasympathetic nervous systems, with the consequent heart rate response being acceleratory, deceleratory, or unchanged from prestimulus levels, depending upon which activational input is greater (see Berntson, Cacioppo, & Quigley, 1991). Berntson et al. (1991) have proposed a theory of autonomic control and modes of autonomic activation that resolves the loss of fidelity in the translation between changes in sympathetic and parasympathetic activation and organ responses. It is possible that emotions (e.g., disgust) or components of emotions (e.g., attention) could be differentiated if the focus were on indices of the sympathetic and the parasympathetic innervation of the viscera, rather than on visceral responses per se.

Whether or not the conditions for and the elements of emotion-specific peripheral patterns of activity can be identified, what does seem clear from this research is that discrete emotional percepts can occur even when the autonomic changes do not discriminate fully the emotions that are experienced. If discrete emotional percepts can occur even when the autonomic changes do not discriminate fully the emotions that are experienced, does it necessarily follow that somatovisceral afference plays no role in defining these discrete emotional percepts? Whereas Cannon's (1927) answer to

this question was "yes," we have outlined three routes by which somatovisceral afferentiation may influence emotional experience—emotion-specific ANS patterns, somatovisceral illusions, or cognitive labeling of unexplained feelings of arousal. Perhaps the most important implications of the model, however, are twofold: First, undifferentiated (or incompletely differentiated) physiological activation can still be an essential determinant of discrete emotional experiences. This can occur through any route except the first. Second, the traditional tendency to view the mechanisms underlying emotion in terms of a simple central–peripheral dichotomy appears no longer to be tenable.

Finally, studies of the "psychophysiology" of emotion have tended to focus on autonomic and, to some extent, somatic responses, as reflected by the content of the current chapter. Given recent advances on the interactions among the autonomic, neuroendocrine, and immune systems and the role of neuropeptides in integrating these systems, this focus is unnecessarily restrictive. Similarly significant advances in human brain imaging have now placed measures of central processes squarely within the psychophysiologist's armamentarium as well. Although experimental studies of discrete emotion are still new to these areas, it is our hope that by the next edition of the *Handbook* the chapter on the psychophysiology of emotions will be able to broaden the coverage from single somatovisceral measures to patterns of reactions across central and multiple peripheral (e.g., somatic, autonomic, endocrinological, and immunological) systems. Such an approach should provide a more complete picture of the central and peripheral processes associated with discrete emotions, and should enrich our understanding of the interactions among these central and peripheral processes.

ACKNOWLEDGMENTS

Preparation of this manuscript was supported by National Science Foundation Grant No. SBR-9512459.

REFERENCES

Ackerman, D. (1990). *A natural history of the senses.* New York: Vintage Books.

Alaoui-Ismaili, O., Robin, O., Rada, H., Dittmar, A., & Vernet-Maury, E. (1997). Basic emotions evoked by odorants: Comparison between autonomic responses and self-evaluation. *Physiology and Behavior, 62,* 713–720.

Andrew, R. J. (1963). The origin and evolution of the calls and facial expressions of the primates. *Behaviour, 20,* 1–109.

Averill, J. R. (1969). Autonomic response patterns during sadness and mirth. *Psychophysiology, 5,* 399–414.

Ax, A. F. (1953). The physiological differentiation between fear and anger in humans. *Psychosomatic Medicine, 15,* 433–442.

Bargh, J. A., Chaiken, S., Govender, R., & Pratto, F. (1992). The generality of the automatic attitude activation effect. *Journal of Personality and Social Psychology, 62,* 893–912.

Berntson, G. G., Cacioppo, J. T., & Quigley, K. S. (1991). Autonomic determinism: The modes of autonomic control, the doctrine of autonomic space, and the laws of autonomic constraint. *Psychological Review, 98,* 459–487.

Berntson, G. G., Sarter, M., & Cacioppo, J. T. (1998). Anxiety and cardiovascular reactivity: The basal forebrain cholinergic link. *Behavioural Brain Research, 94,* 225–248.

Boiten, F. (1996). Autonomic response patterns during voluntary facial action. *Psychophysiology, 33,* 123–131.

Boring, E. G. (1930). A new ambiguous figure. *American Journal of Psychology, 42,* 444.

Bradley, M. (2000). Emotion and motivation. In J. T. Cacioppo, L. G. Tassinary, & G. G. Berntson (Eds.), *Handbook of psychophysiology.* New York: Cambridge University Press.

Brazier, M. A. (1960). The historical development of neurophysiology. In J. Field, H. W. Magoun, & V. E. Hall (Eds.), *Handbook of physiology: The nervous system. Vol. 2. Section I. Neurophysiology* (pp. 1–58). Washington, DC: American Physiological Society.

Brown, S. L., & Schwartz, G. E. (1980). Relationships between facial electromyography and subjective experience during affective imagery. *Biological Psychology, 11,* 49–62.

Cacioppo, J. T., & Berntson, G. G. (1994). Relationship between attitudes and evaluative space: A critical review, with emphasis on the separability of positive and negative substrates. *Psychological Bulletin, 115,* 401–423.

Cacioppo, J. T., Berntson, G. G., & Klein, D. J. (1992). What is emotion? The role of somatovisceral afference, with special emphasis on somatovisceral "illusions." *Review of Personality and Social Psychology, 14,* 63–98.

Cacioppo, J. T., Berntson, G. G., Klein, D. J., & Poehlmann, K. M. (1997). The psychophysiology of emotion across the lifespan. *Annual Review of Gerontology and Geriatrics, 17,* 27–74.

Cacioppo, J. T., Bush, L. K., & Tassinary, L. G. (1992). Microexpressive facial actions as a function of affective stimuli: Replication and extension. *Personality and Social Psychology Bulletin, 18,* 515–526.

Cacioppo, J. T., & Gardner, W. L. (1999). Emotion. *Annual Review of Psychology, 50,* 191–214.

Cacioppo, J. T., Gardner, W. L., & Berntson, G. G. (1997). Beyond bipolar conceptualizations and measures: The case of attitudes and evaluative space. *Personality and Social Psychology Review, 1,* 3–25.

Cacioppo, J. T., Gardner, W. L., & Berntson, G. G. (1999). The affect system: Form follows function. *Journal of Personality and Social Psychology, 76,* 839–855.

Cacioppo, J. T., Klein, D. J., Berntson, G. G., & Hatfield, E. (1993). The psychophysiology of emotion. In M. Lewis & J. M. Haviland (Eds.), *Handbook of emotions* (pp. 119–142). New York: Guilford Press.

Cacioppo, J. T., Martzke, J. S., Petty, R. E., & Tassinary, L. G. (1988). Specific forms of facial EMG response index emotions during an interview: From Darwin to the continuous flow hypothesis of affect-laden information processing. *Journal of Personality and Social Psychology, 54,* 592–604.

Cacioppo, J. T., & Petty, R. E. (1981). Electromyograms as measures of extent and affectivity of information processing. *American Psychologist, 36,* 441–456.

Cacioppo, J. T., Priester, J. R., & Berntson, G. G. (1993). Rudimentary determinants of attitudes: II: Arm flexion and extension have differential effects on attitudes. *Journal of Personality and Social Psychology, 65,* 5–17.

Cacioppo, J. T., Tassinary, L. G., & Fridlund, A. J. (1990). The skeletomotor system. In J. T. Cacioppo & L. G. Tassinary (Eds.), *Principles of psychophysiology: Physical, social, and inferential elements* (pp. 325–384). New York: Cambridge University Press.

Cahill, L. (1996). Neurobiology of memory for emotional events: Converging evidence from infra-human and human studies. *Cold Spring Harbor Symposia on Quantitative Biology, 61,* 259–264.

Cannon, W. B. (1927). The James–Lange theory of emotions: A critical examination and an alternative theory. *American Journal of Psychology, 39,* 106–124.

Chwalisz, K., Diener, E., & Gallagher, D. (1988). Autonomic arousal feedback and emotional experience: Evidence from the spinal cord injured. *Journal of Personality and Social Psychology, 54,* 820–828.

Clore, G. L., Ortony, A., & Foss, M. A. (1987). The psychological foundations of the affective lexicon. *Journal of Personality and Social Psychology, 53,* 751–766.

Collet, C., Vernet-Maury, E., Delhomme, G., & Dittmar, A. (1997). Autonomic nervous system response patterns specificity to basic emotions. *Journal of the Autonomic Nervous System, 62,* 45–57.

Darwin, C. (1872). *The expression of the emotions in man and animals.* New York: Appleton.

Davidson, R. J. (1992). Anterior cerebral asymmetry and the nature of emotion. *Brain and Cognition, 20,* 125–151.

Davidson, R. J. (1993). Childhood temperament and cerebral asymmetry: A neurobiological substrate of behavioral inhibition. In K. H. Rubin & J. B. Asendorpf (Eds.), *Social withdrawal, inhibition, and shyness in childhood* (pp. 31–48). Hillsdale, NJ: Erlbaum.

Davidson, R. J. (1998). Affective style and affective disorders: Perspectives from affective neuroscience. *Cognition and Emotion, 12,* 307–330.

Davidson, R. J., Ekman, P., Saron, C. D., Senulis, J. A.,

& Friesen, W. V. (1990). Approach–withdrawal and cerebal asymmetry: Emotional expression and brain physiology I. *Journal of Personality and Social Psychology, 58*, 330–341.

Davidson, R. J., & Fox, N. A. (1989). Frontal brain asymmetry predicts infants' response to maternal separation. *Journal of Abnormal Psychology, 98*, 127–131.

Davidson, R. J., & Tomarken, A. J. (1989). Laterality and emotion: An electrophysiological approach. In F. Boller & J. Grafman (Eds.), *Handbook of neuropsychology* (Vol. 3, pp. 419–441). New York: Elsevier.

Demaree, H. A., & Harrison, D. W. (1997). A neuropsychological model relating self-awareness to hostility. *Neuropsychology Review, 7*, 171–185.

Ekman, P. (1973). Cross-cultural studies of facial expression. In P. Ekman (Ed.), *Darwin and facial expression: A century of research in review* (pp. 1–83). New York: Academic Press.

Ekman, P., & Friesen, W. V. (1978). *The Facial Action Coding System: A technique for the measurement of facial movement.* Palo Alto, CA: Consulting Psychologists Press.

Ekman, P., Friesen, W. V., & Ancoli, S. (1980). Facial signs of emotional experience. *Journal of Personality and Social Psychology, 39*, 1125–1134.

Ekman, P., Levenson, R. W., & Friesen, W. V. (1983). Autonomic nervous system activity distinguishes among emotions. *Science, 221*, 1208–1210.

Ellsworth, P. C. (1994). William James and emotion: Is a century of fame worth a century of misunderstanding? *Psychological Review, 101*, 222–229.

Ewart, C. K., Taylor, C. B., Kraemer, H. C., & Agras, W. S. (1991). High blood pressure and marital discord: Not being nasty matters more than being nice. *Health-Psychology, 10*, 155–163.

Fainsilber, L., & Ortony, A. (1987). Metaphorical uses of language in the expression of emotions. *Metaphor and Symbolic Activity, 2*, 239–250.

Fridlund, A. J., Schwartz, G. E., & Fowler, S. C. (1984). Pattern recognition of self-reported emotional state from multiple-site facial EMG activity during affective imagery. *Psychophysiology, 21*, 622–637.

Frijda, N. H., Markam, S., Sato, K., & Wiers, R. (1995). Emotions and emotion words. In J. A. Russell, J. Fernandez-Dols, A. S. R. Manstead, & J. C. Wellenkamp (Eds.), *NATA ASI Series D: Behavioural and social sciences. Vol. 81. Everyday conceptions of emotion: An introduction to the psychology, anthropology and linguistics of emotion.* (pp. 121–143). Dordrecht, The Netherlands: Kluwer.

Funkenstein, D. H., King, S. H., & Drollette, M. (1954). The direction of anger during a laboratory stress-inducing situation. *Psychosomatic Medicine, 16*, 404–413.

Gazzaniga, M. S., & LeDoux, J. E. (1978). *The integrated mind.* New York: Plenum Press.

Green, D. P., Salovey, P., & Truax, K. M. (1999). Static, dynamic, and causative bipolarity of affect. *Journal of Personality and Social Psychology, 76*, 856–867.

Harmon-Jones, E., & Allen, J. J. B. (1998). Anger and frontal brain activity: EEG asymmetry consistent with approach motivation despite negative affective

valence. *Journal of Personality and Social Psychology, 74*, 1310–1316.

Henriques, J. B., & Davidson, R. J. (1990). Regional brain electrical asymmetries discriminate between previously depressed and healthy control subjects. *Journal of Abnormal Psychology, 99*, 22–31.

Henriques, J. B., & Davidson, R. J. (1991). Left frontal hypoactivation in depression. *Journal of Abnormal Psychology, 100*, 535–545.

Herbert, T. B., & Cohen, S. (1993). Depression and immunity: A meta-analytic review. *Psychological Bulletin, 113*, 472–486.

Hess, U., Kappas, A., McHugo, G. J., Lanzetta, J. T., & Kleck, R. E. (1992). The facilitative effect of facial expression on the self-generation of emotion. *International Journal of Psychophysiology, 12*, 251–265.

Hoffman, R. R., Waggoner, J. E., & Palermo, D. S. (1991). Metaphor and context in the language of emotion. In R. R. Hoffman & D. S. Palermo (Eds.), *Cognition and the symbolic processes: Applied and ecological perspectives* (pp. 163–185). Hillsdale, NJ: Erlbaum.

Ito, T. A., Cacioppo, J. T., & Lang, P. J. (1998). Eliciting affect using the International Affective Picture System: Bivariate evaluation and ambivalence. *Personality and Social Psychology Bulletin, 24*, 855–879.

Ito, T. A., Larsen, J. T., Smith, N. K., & Cacioppo, J. T. (1998). Negative information weighs more heavily on the brain: The negativity bias in evaluative categorizations. *Journal of Personality and Social Psychology, 75*, 887–900.

Izard, C. E. (1971). *The face of emotion.* New York: Appleton-Century-Crofts.

Izard, C. E. (1977). *Human emotions.* New York: Academic Press.

James, W. (1884). What is an emotion? *Mind, 9*, 188–205.

James, W. (1950). *Principles of psychology* (Vol. I). New York: Dover. (Original work published 1890)

Kiecolt-Glaser, J. K., Dura, J. R., Speicher, C. E., Trask, O. J., & Glaser, R. G. (1991). Spousal caregivers of dementia victims: Longitudinal changes in immunity and health. *Psychosomatic Medicine, 53*, 345–362.

Kiecolt-Glaser, J. K., Glaser, R., Gravenstein, S., Malarkey, W. B., & Sheridan, J. (1996). Chronic stress alters the immune response to influenza virus vaccine in older adults. *Proceedings of the National Academy of Sciences USA, 93*, 3043–3047.

Kiecolt-Glaser, J. K., Marucha, P. T., Malarkey, W. B., Mercado, A. M., & Glaser, R. (1995). Slowing of wound healing by psychological stress. *Lancet, 346*, 1194–1196.

Lang, P. J. (1971). The application of psychophysiological methods to the study of psychotherapy and behavior change. In A. E. Bergin & S. L. Garfield (Eds.), *Handbook of psychotherapy and behavior change: An empirical analysis* (pp. 75–125). New York: Wiley.

Lang, P. J, Bradley, M. M., & Cuthbert, B. N. (1990). Emotion, attention, and the startle reflex. *Psychological Review, 97*, 377–395.

LeDoux, J. (1996). *The emotional brain.* New York: Simon & Schuster.

Leeper, R. (1935). A study of a neglected portion of the

field of learning—the development of sensory organization. *Journal of Genetic Psychology, 46,* 41–75.

Levenson, R. W. (1988). Emotion and the autonomic nervous system: A prospectus for research on autonomic specificity. In H. L. Wagner (Eds.), *Social psychophysiology and emotion: Theory and clinical applications* (pp. 17–42). Chichester, England: Wiley.

Levenson, R. W., Carstensen, L. L., Friesen, W. V., & Ekman, P. (1991). Emotion, physiology, and expression in old age. *Psychology and Aging, 6,* 28–35.

Levenson, R. W., Ekman, P., & Friesen, W. V. (1990). Voluntary facial action generates emotion-specific autonomic nervous system activity. P*sychophysiology, 27,* 363–384.

Levenson, R. W., Ekman, P., Heider, K., & Friesen, W. V. (1992). Emotion and autonomic nervous system activity in the Minangkabau of West Sumatra. *Journal of Personality and Social Psychology, 62,* 972–988.

Lindsley, D. B., & Wicke, J. D. (1974). The electroencephalogram: Autonomous electrical activity in man and animals. In R. Thompson & M. N. Patterson (Eds.), *Bioelectric recording techniques* (pp. 3–79). New York: Academic Press.

Mandler, G. (1975). M*ind and emotion.* New York: Wiley.

Miller, B. D., & Wood, B. L. (1997). Influence of specific emotional states on autonomic reactivity and pulmonary function in asthmatic children. *Journal of the American Academy of Child and Adolescent Psychiatry, 36,* 669–677.

Miller, N. E. (1961). Some recent studies on conflict behavior and drugs. A*merican Psychologist, 16,* 12–24.

Ortony, A., & Fainsilber, L. (1989). The role of metaphors in descriptions of emotions. In Y. Wilks (Ed.), *Theoretical issues in natural language processing* (pp. 178–182). Hillsdale, NJ: Erlbaum.

Osgood, C. E., Suci, G. J., & Tannenbaum, P. H. (1957). *The measurement of meaning.* Urbana, IL: University of Illinois Press.

Pratto, F., & John, E. (1991). Automatic vigilance: The attention-grabbing power of negative social information. *Journal of Personality and Social Psychology, 61,* 380–391.

Reed, S. D., Harver, A., & Katkin, E. S.(1990). Interoception. In J. T. Cacioppo & L. G. Tassinary (Eds.), *Principles of psychophysiology: Physical, social, and inferential elements* (pp. 253–294). New York: Cambridge University Press.

Reisenzein, R. (1983). The Schachter theory of emotion: Two decades later. *Psychological Bulletin, 94,* 239–264.

Roberts, R. J., & Weerts, T. C. (1982). Cardiovascular responding during anger and fear imagery. *Psychological Reports, 50,* 219–230.

Robinson, R. G., & Downhill, J. E. (1995). Lateralization of psychopathology in response to focal brain injury. In R. J. Davidson & K. Hugdahl (Eds.), *Brain asymmetry* (pp. 693–711). Cambridge, MA: MIT Press.

Robinson, R. G., Kubos, K. L., Starr, L. B., Rao, K., & Price, T. R. (1984). Mood disorders in stroke patients. *Brain, 107,* 81–93.

Russell, J. A. (1978). Evidence of convergent validity on the dimensions of affect. *Journal of Personality and Social Psychology, 36,* 1152–1168.

Russell, J. A. (1994). Is there universal recognition of emotion from facial expressions?: A review of the cross-cultural studies. *Psychological Bulletin, 115,* 102–141.

Schachter, J. (1957). Pain, fear, and anger in hypertensives and normotensives: A psychophysiological study. *Psychosomatic Medicine, 19,* 17–29.

Schachter, S., & Singer, J. E. (1962). Cognitive, social, and physiological determinants of emotional state. *Psychological Review, 69,* 379–399.

Schwartz, G. E., Ahern, G. L., & Brown, S. L. (1979). Lateralized facial muscle response to positive and negative emotional stimuli. *Psychophysiology, 16,* 561–571.

Schwartz, G. E., Fair, P. L., Greenberg, P. S., Foran, J. M., & Klerman, G. L. (1975). Self-generated affective imagery elicits discrete patterns of facial muscle activity. *Psychophysiology, 12,* 234. (abstract)

Schwartz, G. E., Fair, P. L., Salt, P., Mandel, M. R., & Klerman, G. R. (1976). Facial muscle patterning to affective imagery in depressed and nondepressed subjects. *Science, 192,* 489–491.

Schwartz, G. E., Weinberger, D. A., & Singer, J. A. (1981). Cardiovascular differentiation of happiness, sadness, anger, and fear following images and exercise. *Psychosomatic Medicine, 43,* 343–364.

Sekuler, R., & Blake, R. (1985) *Perception.* New York: Knopf.

Sinha, R., Lovallo, W. R., & Parsons, O. A. (1992), Cardiovascular differentiation of emotions. *Psychosomatic Medicine, 54,* 422–435.

Sinha, R., & Parsons, O. A. (1996), Multivariate response patterning of fear and anger. *Cognition and Emotion, 10,* 173–198.

Skowronski, J. J., & Carlson, D. E. (1989). Negativity and extremity biases in impression formation: A review of explanations. *Psychological Bulletin, 105,* 131–142.

Stemmler, G. (1989). The autonomic differentiation of emotions revisited: Convergent and discriminant validation. *Psychophysiology, 26,* 617–632.

Sternbach, R. A. (1962). Assessing differential autonomic patterns in emotion. *Journal of Psychosomatic Research, 6,* 87–91.

Sutton, S. K., & Davidson, R. J. (1997). Prefrontal brain asymmetry: A biological substrate of the behavioral approach and inhibition systems. *Psychological Science, 8,* 204–210.

Tassinary, L. G., Cacioppo, J. T., & Geen, T. R. (1989). A psychometric study of surface electrode placements for facial electromyographic recording: I. The brow and cheek muscle regions. *Psychophysiology, 26,* 1–16.

Taylor, S. E. (1991). Asymmetrical effects of positive and negative events: The mobilization-minimization hypothesis. *Psychological Bulletin, 110,* 67–85.

Tomarken, A. J., Davidson, R. J., & Henriques, J. B. (1990). Resting frontal asymmetry predicts affective responses to films. *Journal of Personality and Social Psychology, 59,* 791–801.

Tomkins, S. S. (1962). *Affect, imagery, and consciousness: Vol. 1. The positive affects.* New York: Springer.

Tourangeau, R., & Ellsworth, P. C. (1979). The role of facial response in the experience of emotion. *Journal of Personality and Social Psychology, 37,* 1519–1531.

Tranel, D., & Damasio, A. (2000). Neuropsychology and behavioral neurology. In J. T. Cacioppo, L. G. Tassinary, & G. G. Berntson (Eds.), *Handbook of psychophysiology.* New York: Cambridge University Press.

van Hooff, J. A. R. A. M. (1972). A comparative approach to the phylogeny of laughter and smiling. In R. Hinde (Ed.), *Non-verbal communication* (pp. 129–179). London: Royal Society and Cambridge University Press.

Vrana, S. R. (1993). The psychophysiology of disgust: Differentiating negative emotional contexts with facial EMG. *Psychophysiology, 30,* 279–286.

Wagner, H. (1989). The physiological differentiation of emotions. In H. Wagner & A. Manstead (Eds.), *Handbook of social psychophysiology* (pp. 77–89). New York: Wiley.

Wheeler, R. E., Davidson, R. J., & Tomarken, A. J. (1993). Frontal brain asymmetry and emotional reactivity: A biological substrate of affective style. *Psychophysiology, 30,* 82–89.

Zajonc, R. B. (1980). Feeling and thinking: Preferences need no inferences. *American Psychologist, 35,* 157–193.

Zajonc, R. B., & McIntosh, D. N. (1992). Emotions research: Some promising questions and some questionable promises. *Psychological Science, 3,* 70–74.

CHAPTER 12

Emotion and Behavior Genetics

Richard Rende

WHY BRING A BEHAVIORAL GENETIC PERSPECTIVE TO THE STUDY OF EMOTIONS?

John Loehlin, an eminent figure in the history of behavioral genetic research, began a book on the study of personality with the words "People differ" (Loehlin, 1992). This deceptively simple and elegant statement captures exactly the thrust of behavioral genetic research: to understand the origins of individual differences in the population, specifically in terms of both genetic and nongenetic influences on such variation. Indeed, the foundation of behavior genetics is quantitative genetic theory, which provides a conceptual framework for understanding etiological contributions to individual differences. Given this, a behavioral genetic perspective, when applied to the study of emotions, will be concerned with the extent to which individuals *differ* in some aspect of emotional development, be it in the expression, understanding, or regulation of emotions. As a corollary of this statement, behavior genetics is not concerned with the origins of emotions per se. Although there are undoubtedly numerous genetic and nongenetic processes that have been driven by evolutionary forces to produce the capacity for emotions in humans (and nonhumans), this topic is not the province of behavior genetics, which is called into play only when we consider why individuals differ in their emotional development.

The potential yield of a behavioral genetic perspective on emotional development can be seen by considering that developmentalists' current interest in naturally occurring, early differences in emotionality in infancy (e.g., Fox, 1994). Given that pronounced individual differences in the frequency or intensity of different emotions may be reliably assessed, it is reasonable to speculate on the origins of these differences, and especially on the implications of such differences for later development. Furthermore, as developmental psychopathology has broadened the study of development to include "the development of deviation, the definition of deviation, and individual differences" (Lewis, 1992, p. 487), theoretical and methodological approaches geared toward understanding the origins of variation in emotional development provide an essential component to the study of emotions. This chapter coalesces current trends in behavioral genetic research that contribute to this task.

WHAT METHODS ARE USED IN BEHAVIORAL GENETIC RESEARCH?

Before I discuss knowledge derived from behaviorial genetic approaches to emotional development, it is important to briefly review the core methods, their subtle variations, and new approaches that have been used. At the core of behavior genetics is a theory devoted to exploring the etiology of individual differences in the population—quantitative genetic theory (Plomin, DeFries, McClearn, & Rutter, 1997). Quantitative genetic theory postulates underlying or latent factors that may operate to produce phenotypic variation for a given trait, which in the broadest sense, are genetic and nongenetic (or environmental) influences. Within this theory of individual differences, "genetic" influences refer specifically to what is typically thought of as "inheritance," meaning genomic information transmitted from generation to generation. This is a particular way of studying genetic influence, as an individual's genetic code may be affected by nonheritable events, such as intracellular and extracellular stimuli. Hence, genetic influence, in the quantitative genetic model, refers specifically to the biological process by which genetic information is transmitted from parents to offspring at conception. In conjunction with the specificity of the definition of genetic influence in the quantitative genetic model, "nongenetic" or "environmental" influences also have a particular meaning, as they refer to noninherited factors, whether they be biological or psychosocial in origin.

Modern quantitative genetic theory makes more fine-grained distinctions in sorting out effects of genetic and environmental influences on individual differences. In terms of the theory, "genetic influences" typically refer to what are known as "additive genetic effects," which are theoretically the combined impact of a number of genes that each explain a small amount of population variance in a trait (see Plomin et al., 1997; Rende & Plomin, 1995). "Environmental influences" are of two primary types: those that contribute to similarity in individuals exposed to them (typically labeled "shared" or "common" environmental factors), and those that have a unique effect on individuals (typically labeled "unique" or "nonshared" environmental factors). The purpose of the theory is to postulate that all three latent variables—additive genetic effects, common environmental effects, and unique environmental effects—may contribute to individual differences in a trait. As an example, consider the idea that individual differences may exist in some form of emotional expression in infants (e.g., scores on the trait that approach a normal distribution in a representative sample of infants). Quantitative genetic theory would set out to describe the potential role that all three

latent factors may have in producing such individual differences.

It is critical to recognize that the purpose of quantitative genetic theory is not to prescribe which factors are most important. Rather, the point is to utilize methods that are capable of detecting each type of influence, and to attempt to quantify the effect size of each of these traits. The two most commonly used paradigms are the twin and adoption paradigms. Twin studies are natural experiments in which the resemblance of monozygotic (MZ) twins, who may be described as having a genetic relatedness of 100%, is compared to the resemblance of dizygotic (DZ) twins, who are first-degree relatives whose coefficient of genetic relatedness is 50%. If heredity affects a behavioral trait, MZ twins will resemble each other on the trait to a greater extent than will DZ twins, as was postulated in 1924 in the first explicit statements of the classical twin method (Rende, Plomin, & Vandenberg, 1990). If a trait is influenced by common environmental factors, then MZ and DZ twins will have similar coefficients of resemblance, assuming that the rearing environment of MZ and DZ twins is similar. This assumption, which is known as the "equal environments assumption," has received empirical study, and there is reasonable support for it (Plomin et al., 1997).

In addition to the twin paradigm, the adoption paradigm provides a number of methods for examining quantitative genetic parameters. Genetically related individuals adopted apart provide evidence of the degree to which familial resemblance is attributable to genetic similarity. The other fundamental side of the adoption paradigm tests the influence of the common environment by studying the resemblance of genetically unrelated individuals living together in adoptive families. The potential difficulty in the adoption paradigm is selective placement, in which children are placed with adoptive parents who resemble the birth parents. As is the case with the equal environments assumption in twin studies, the impact of this complication can be assessed empirically (Plomin et al., 1997).

A number of related designs complement both the twin and adoption paradigms. Stepfamilies provide opportunities to assess variations in genetic relatedness (e.g., by comparing the similarity of full biological siblings to that of half-siblings and unrelated siblings living together in a reconstituted family). Twin and adoption designs can be combined by studying twins reared apart as well as control twins reared together. Although the classic twin and adoption paradigms, as well as such variations, have methodological limitations endemic to being natural experiments, the various methods—each of which has unique strengths and weaknesses—allow for the opportunity of convergence (or lack thereof) in the estimation of quantitative genetic parameters.

Behavioral genetic methods employ what is referred to as "biometrical model fitting" to assess the statistical significance and magnitude of effect for each parameter, as derived from the informative designs reviewed above. "Heritability" is a descriptive statistic that assigns an effect size to genetic influence. For example, the correlation for MZ twins reared apart in uncorrelated environments directly estimates heritability. If hereditary influence was unimportant for a trait of interest, their correlation would be low; however, their correlation would be high if heredity was primarily responsible for phenotypic variance. Similarly, if common environmental influence was important for a given trait, then adoptive siblings would be expected to be highly correlated, whereas if they were uncorrelated it would suggest a negligible influence of common environment. Within each informative quantitative genetic design, such statements are translated into equations that decompose phenotypic variance into effect sizes of each parameter of interest—namely, additive genetic effects, common environmental effects, and unique environmental effects (see Plomin et al., 1997). Although various limitations and complications arise in the application of this approach (see Plomin et al., 1997; Rende & Plomin, 1995), the basic information reviewed in this chapter is the more straightforward interpretation of the relative impact of these sources of influence on individual differences in emotional development through the lifespan.

WHAT HAVE BEHAVIORAL GENETIC STUDIES TOLD US ABOUT INDIVIDUAL DIFFERENCES IN EMOTIONAL DEVELOPMENT?

Until recently, behavioral genetic studies have focused on individual differences in emotional development through the related constructs of temperament and personality. The key trait of interest for the purposes of this chapter is emotionality, which is one of the three fundamental temperamental traits posited by Buss and Plomin (1984). "Emotionality" refers to an individual's predominant *intensity* of emotional reactivity, and typically has encompassed emotional reactions to stress (Eley & Plomin, 1997). Emotionality has most frequently been assessed via questionnaires, which have been adapted for parent and teacher reports for infants and children, and for self-reports in studies of adolescents and adults (Buss & Plomin, 1984). An examination of the items used reveals that "emotionality" has most typically encompassed negative emotionality, as indicated by questions from the EAS Temperament Survey for Children (see Buss & Plomin, 1984):

> Child cries easily.
> Child tends to be somewhat emotional.
> Child often fusses and cries.
> Child gets upset easily.
> Child reacts intensely when upset.

This construct of emotionality, as assessed by questionnaire, has been included in behavioral genetic studies for over two decades. Key findings, which have been reviewed numerous times in recent years (Eley & Plomin, 1997; Eaves, Eysenck, & Martin, 1989; Loehlin, 1992; Rende & Plomin, 1995), have been replicated across paradigms, samples, and age periods. One finding is the consistent evidence of genetic influence in twin studies. Self-report studies of the personality trait called "neuroticism" (which is closely related to the construct of emotionality) suggest that genetic factors may account for nearly half of the population variance of this trait (Loehlin, 1992). Similar findings exist for emotionality, and comparable findings have been reported in studies of twins reared apart (Loehlin, 1992). Furthermore, a number of studies suggest substantial heritability of parent-rated emotionality in toddlerhood and childhood (see Goldsmith, Buss, & Lemery, 1997), and recent studies have extended the evidence of heritability of emotionality to adolescence (Saudino, McGuire, Reiss, Hetherington, & Plomin, 1996). Although the actual estimates of heritability may fluctuate across studies (as would be expected, since "heritability" is a descriptive statistic), a large body of evidence from twin studies indicates that emotionality and related personality dimensions are moderately heritable traits throughout the entire lifespan.

A second key finding, which is a corollary of the first finding described above, is that twin studies have also suggested that genetic influence is only half of the story: Because heritability estimates only approach .50, twin studies of emotionality and related traits clearly indicate the critical role of nongenetic factors as well. Twin studies indicate that the environmental contribution does not reflect the impact of a common rearing environment, but rather effects of unique or nonshared environment (which reflects lack of similarity between twins). Although "unique environment" may include error variance (which is, in essence, variance not explained by either genetic or common environmental factors), there has been much theorizing on the potential importance of uncorrelated or unique nongenetic effects on many behavioral traits, including emotionality (Loehlin, 1992).

A third key finding in the literature, however, is that the results of twin studies, though highly replicated, may be questioned. One issue is that the prototypical quantitative genetic model used (one that specifies as latent traits additive genetic influence, common environmental influence, and unique environmental influence) does not always provide the best fit to the collected data. The problem is that in many studies, the observed correlation for DZ twins is too low, as compared to the correlation for MZ twins. Specifically, although the MZ correlations exceed the DZ correlations (which is consistent with a model that yields a significant heritability estimate), the DZ correlations sometimes are near zero (which does not make sense, since DZ twins share half of their segregating genes). In addition, adoption studies have not yielded as much evidence for genetic effects as have twin studies (Eley & Plomin, 1997; Loehlin, 1992). Two different explanations have been offered. One speculation is that the type of genetic effect observed is not reflective of additive genetic effects, but rather of a different type of genetic effect referred to as "nonadditivity" (Plomin et al., 1997). A different explanation is that the unexplained divergence between MZ and DZ twin similarity may be due to "contrast effects," in which raters of emotionality (especially parents) may exaggerate either the similarity of MZ twins or the dissimilarity of DZ twins. To date, both explanations remain plausible, and the issue requires more empirical study.

Recent behavioral genetic studies have gone beyond the latent trait of emotionality to explore the etiology of individual differences in more specific indices of emotional development not captured by traditional measures of temperament and personality (see Emde et al., 1992). One advance comes from expansions of traditional temperament questionnaires, which include more specific indices of emotional development, especially in terms of differentiating positive and negative emotions. In this work, two newer measures of temperament—the Toddler Behavior Assessment Questionnaire and the Children's Behavior Questionnaire—have been used in a study of toddler and preschool-age twin pairs (Goldsmith et al., 1997). A first finding of this study was that more specific indicators of negative emotionality showed evidence of genetic influence; these included "anger proneness" in toddlerhood and "negative affectivity" in childhood. However, an interesting result was that positive emotionality (as measured by a construct of "pleasure") showed strong evidence of shared environmental influence, with little contribution from genetic factors. This result is important for a number of reasons: It demonstrates that the twin paradigm may capture both genetic and environmental influences on emotional development, that different domains of emotional development may have very different etiological architectures, and that there is much to be gained by including more specific indicators of "emotionality" in behavioral genetic studies. Goldsmith et al. (1992) discuss possible shared environmental factors (such as attachment security) that may be implicated as potential shapers of positive affectivity but that may not have similar effects on negative affectivity, which appears to reflect, in part, genetic contributions.

Goldsmith et al. (1992), in discussing the findings of the study described above, also suggest that behavioral genetic studies of emotion regulation may profit by moving away from questionnaire measures to more operational assessments. Another recent twin study, the MacArthur Longitudinal Twin Study (Emde et al., 1992), has used such paradigms with interesting results. In this study of 200 twins assessed at 14 months of age, several strategies were used to elicit the twins' emotional reactions in the home, to be captured on videotape. For example, a brief episode of restraint (in which each child was videotaped while lying still for physical measurement) was used to elicit reactivity, while a toy removal episode was designed to elicit anger. In addition, other videotaped activities during the home visit (which lasted less than 3 hours) were coded for hedonic tone and mood via time-sampling procedures, and raters also coded occurrences of empathy during the home visit. Notable here is the use of videotaping to achieve direct observation (rather than relying on parental report) of emotional behavior, as well as the use of behavior paradigms designed to elicit naturally occurring emotions. Another key addition to this study was the inclusion of parental reports on the infants' emotional behavior, as assessed using the Differential Emotions Scale, which measures the frequency of 10 basic emotions (Fuenzalida, Emde, Pannabecker, & Stenberg, 1981; Johnson, Emde, Pannabecker, Stenberg, & Davis, 1982).

The observational measures of emotions showed diverse results, but in general did not provide overwhelming evidence for genetic influence. For example, the heritability estimate for negative hedonic tone was .10; heritability estimates for positive hedonic tone and overall mood were moderate (between .33 and .34) but not significant, given the sample size; and the measure of empathy also yielded a moderate heritability (.36), which was significant. There was little evidence of shared environmental influence on any of these observational measures of emotional behavior. Hence, in most cases, the fundamental behavioral genetic model did not explain substantial amounts of variance, suggesting that twin resemblance in general was low.

Perhaps surprisingly, parental reports of their twins' emotional expression yielded more clear-cut findings. Similar to the results of the Goldsmith et al. (1992) study, parental reports of positive emotionality showed substantial influence of shared environment, whereas negative emotionality was highly heritable. Although these results clearly converge with other published data on parental reports, they also do not match well the model-fitting results derived from the observational measures of emotional expression. Emde et al. (1992) present a thorough discussion of this discrepancy, in which they emphasize the differences between observational measures (which are direct but limited to brief sampling time frames) and parental report measures (which may be more subject to bias but also reflect longer time frames of observation by the parents). As these authors argue, it is most reasonable at this point to consider both types of data (observational and parental report) of value, and to use further research to help elucidate the underlying phenotypes captured by the different methodologies.

In summary, behavioral genetic research on emotional development is very much in a beginning stage. Most studies have focused on broad temperamental or personality traits, with less effort devoted to more specific indicators of emotional expression or understanding. There is evidence, primarily from twin studies, of a moderate genetic contribution to emotionality, which has been shown from infancy to adulthood. However, issues in this area await resolution, including the mechanism responsible for excessive disparity between MZ and DZ similarity, as well as lack of convergence between twin and adoption paradigms. There is some suggestion that the putative genetic influence on emotionality is specific to the expression of negative emotionality, as positive emotionality appears to be shaped in part by shared environmental factors. Finally, more specific measures of emotional expression and understanding have only recently received attention in behavioral genetic designs; they require more intensive study, especially in terms of longitudinal frameworks. As demonstrated by current approaches (Emde et al., 1992; Goldsmith et al., 1997), there are new and innovative ways for researchers to study individual differences in emotional development via behavioral genetic designs, and more studies of this type are necessary to give a more complete picture on how genetic and nongenetic factors contribute to variability in emotional behavior throughout the lifespan.

WHAT HAVE BEHAVIORAL GENETIC STUDIES TOLD US ABOUT INDIVIDUAL DIFFERENCES IN THE DEVELOPMENT OF PSYCHOPATHOLOGY?

The studies reviewed in the preceding section of this chapter have focused on individual differences in emotional development without reference to boundaries of adaptive and maladaptive behavior. However, much of our interest in the etiological architecture underlying variability in emotionality is derived from the applications that may be made to deviations from normality. Although not specifically conceptualized as behavioral genetic studies of emotional development, there is a large literature on psychopathology that is clearly related to the broad construct of emotionality (Eley & Plomin, 1997).

Most relevant studies have applied behavioral genetic methods to the study of internalizing symptomatology in children and adolescents, and of mood and anxiety disorders in adults. The youngest age group studied has been toddlerhood, with two studies to date that have obtained conflicting results. Schmitz, Cherny, Fulker, and Mrazck (1994) reported that most of the variance in parent reported internalizing symptoms could be attributed to shared environmental factors, with little evidence for genetic contributions. In contrast, van der Valk, Verhulst, Stroet, and Boomsma (1998) found that internalizing symptoms were highly heritable (with a reported heritability of 68%) in a sample of 3,620 twin pairs aged 2–3 years.

This issue of two different models—a shared environmental model and a genetic model—has been a theme in studies of later childhood and adolescence. Overall, the picture that currently emerges is that shared environmental factors are more important in childhood, whereas evidence for genetic influence becomes apparent during adolescence. Thapar and McGuffin (1994, 1996) explored this issue in a study of 411 twin pairs aged 8–16 years; they reported strong evidence for shared environmental factors in the middle childhood sample, but evidence for high heritability of depressive symptoms in the adolescent sample. The finding of shared environmental influence on depressive symptoms in childhood has been replicated in an adoption design that compared the similarity of biological and adoptive sibling pairs (Eley, Deater-Deckard, Fombonne, Fulker, & Plomin, 1998). Replication of heritability of depressive symptoms in adolescence has come from other twin samples (Eley, 1997), as well as from a combined twin–sibling design (Rende, Plomin Reiss, & Hetherington, 1993) that included MZ and DZ twins, full biological siblings, biological half-siblings, and biologically unrelated siblings (stepsiblings). Interestingly, one twin study, which focused primarily on twin pairs making the transition to adolescence, found evidence for both genetic and shared environmental influence (Edelbrock, Rende, Plomin, & Thompson, 1995).

An important addition to the literature is the Virginia Twin Study of Adolescent Behavioral Development, which is a population-based study of 1,412 twin pairs between 8 and 16 years of age. This study is using multiple raters (parents, teachers, and children), as well as a combination of clinical interviewing and questionnaire measures, in order to incorporate multiple perspectives on adolescent behavior problems. In addition, the project will eventually yield longitudinal data on the genetic and environmental architecture of behavioral problems throughout adolescence. A number of intriguing results have begun to emerge (Eaves et al., 1997) with respect to symptoms of anxiety and depression. Both maternal and paternal reports of symptoms of anxiety and depression have shown evidence of genetic influence, as well as a potential impact of shared environmental influence. Adolescent self-reports, in contrast, have not yielded evidence of genetic influence, but have shown stronger indications of the importance of shared environment. The overall pattern of results has been replicated using parental and adolescent responses to face-to-face clinical interviews. Of special interest will be the results of longitudinal and age-restricted analyses, to determine whether they are consistent with cross-sectional analyses from other datasets indicating that shared environmental factors are notable in middle childhood, and that genetic factors affect phenotypic variation in adolescence.

The suggestion that heritable influences on internalizing disorders is "turned on" in adolescence may be expanded to include the proposition that genetic factors are of importance for the expression of mood and anxiety disorders in adulthood. Recent evidence has come from a series of papers focused on a large population study of adult female twins in Virginia by Kendler and colleagues. This group has demonstrated the importance of heritable factors for major depressive disorder (Kendler, Neale, Kessler, Heath, & Eaves, 1992a), generalized anxiety disorder (Kendler, Neale, Kessler, Heath, & Eaves, 1992b), and phobias (Kendler, Neale, Kessler, Heath, & Eaves, 1992d).

To date, then, behavioral genetic methods have been applied to both internalizing symptomatology and clinical manifestations of mood and anxiety disorders, with study populations ranging from infants to adults. Overall, there is reasonable evidence for both genetic influence and the importance of shared environmental factors, although the actual mix of these factors may vary according to developmental epoch.

WHAT SHOULD FUTURE BEHAVIORAL GENETIC STUDIES TELL US ABOUT EMOTIONAL DEVELOPMENT?

The review of studies in this chapter has thus far fallen along traditional lines in behavioral genetic research, as research on temperamental and personality traits has been conducted, for the most part, independently of research on clinical symptomatology and disorders. However, in recent years, the application of developmental psychopathology has been integrated with quantitative genetic theory (Rende & Plomin, 1995), providing new directions for research focused on individual differences in emotional development.

One new direction is to consider ways in which the study of "normative" traits (e.g., emotionality) may be integrated with investigations of "clinical" traits (e.g., major depressive disorder). A major advance that has occurred over the past decade in behavioral genetic research is the refinement of multivariate techniques that can decompose *covariation* across traits into genetic and environmental components (see Plomin et al., 1997). To take the twin paradigm as an example, the basis for multivariate genetic analysis is the "cross-twin" resemblance between one twin on trait X and the cotwin on trait Y. The phenotypic correlation between X and Y is assumed to be mediated genetically to the extent that MZ cross-twin resemblance exceeds DZ cross-twin similarity. A bottom line of interest is referred to as the "genetic correlation," which provides an index of the extent to which genetic effects on one trait overlap with genetic effects of the other trait.

In recent years, multivariate genetic techniques have been put to good use in revealing underlying etiological connections between different traits. For example, much of the observed covariation between symptoms of anxiety and depression in adolescence has been adequately explained by a model that postulates a common set of genes or high genetic correlation between the two traits (Thapar & McGuffin, 1997). A similar picture has emerged in studies of comorbidity between generalized anxiety disorder and major depressive disorder in adulthood (Kendler, Neale, Kessler, Heath,

& Eaves, 1992c; Kendler et al., 1996). Interestingly, these studies have converged on the notion that there may be an underlying genetic propensity for either anxiety or depression, but that the actual phenotypic expression is shaped by environmental factors specific to individual experience.

Multivariate genetic strategies are of special interest for the purposes of this chapter because they provide a methodology for examining covariation between temperamental traits and psychopathology, or, more generally speaking, etiological links between normal variation and behavioral deviance. With respect to childhood, the oft-noted empirical relationship between emotionality and behavioral problems (e.g., Rende, 1993) has been studied via multivariate approaches in the twin paradigm, with model-fitting results suggesting some genetic overlap between temperament and psychopathology (Gjone & Stevenson, 1997). A similar result has been found in research on adults, as multivariate approaches have identified substantial genetic correlations between the personality trait of neuroticism and clinical manifestations of anxiety and depressive disorders (Kendler, Neale, Kessler, Heath, & Eaves, 1993; Eaves et al., 1989; Kendler, Kessler, Neale, Heath, & Eaves, 1993). The implication from this emerging body of work is that genetic influences on emotionality may function as underlying biological propensities for psychopathology, especially in the form of mood and anxiety disorders. Such a finding is critical because it suggests that the study of variation in fundamental aspects of emotional development may convey important information about biological risk factors for maladaptation, which is the thrust of arguments for the merger of quantitative genetic methods with theoretical frameworks derived from developmental psychopathology (Rende & Plomin, 1995).

A second new direction is the consideration of etiological models that attempt to incorporate the joint effects of genetic and environmental influence. Note that discussions about genetic covariation across traits have been framed in terms such as "underlying genetic propensity." Such terms convey that the most sophisticated multivariate biometrical models have provided strong evidence that *both* genetic and environmental factors are critical for explanations of phenotypic variation in personality, psychopathology, and essentially most forms of behavioral expression (Rende & Plomin, 1995).

This is not to say that separate effect sizes for each are not possible to discern, but rather that the effect sizes for both types of influence are typically notable (except in the case of rare behavioral conditions, such as Huntington's disease or fragile-X syndrome, which have clear genetic determinants). Hence behavioral genetic researchers are now embarking on a new stage of research that attempts to specify multiple models by which genetic and environmental factors may come together to shape complex phenotypes.

Three types of models may be considered. A first model is the prototypical model used in behavioral genetic research, which is an additive model in the sense that genetic and environmental factors are conceptualized as being independent contributors to phenotypic variation. Two additional models, however, represent different scenarios of *dependence* between genetic and environmental factors (Kendler, 1995; Plomin et al., 1997; Rende & Plomin, 1992). A gene–environment (GE) interaction model postulates that the effects of the environment are conditional on genetic propensities. An example of this is to postulate that the heritable components of emotionality will contribute to the way an individual responds to a psychosocial stressor, literally taking the form of a *statistical interaction* between the two constructs of interest (emotionality and stressor). In contrast to GE interaction, a GE correlation model adds that genetic and environmental factors are not independent, so that genetic propensities not only will condition the response to the environment, but will also affect the *likelihood* of environmental exposure. To use the example of emotionality again, a GE correlation model postulates that genetically mediated high emotionality will help contribute to the elicitation of certain forms of psychosocial stress. Full discussion of the implications of these models for research on developmental psychopathology are available in Rutter et al. (1997).

Although several empirical advances in behavior genetics have been made by researchers using GE interaction and correlation models (Plomin, Owen, & McGuffin, 1994; Rutter et al., 1997), there are few data to report in terms of the substantive themes of this chapter. However, given the complexity of the etiological architecture of emotional development throughout the lifespan, it seems not only reasonable but necessary to suggest that these models should receive more thorough attention in future studies. For example, a common theme in developmental research is the interplay between the behavior of an infant and parent. Developmental theorists have long argued that both infant and parent shape each other's behavior. GE models may add depth to the study of dyadic interaction by asking whether phenotypic variation in specific behavioral tendencies of infants (e.g., distress) in response to a psychosocial stimulus (e.g., negative tone of voice) reflects in part GE interaction (so that only some infants respond with high distress because of genetic predispositions to negative emotionality). Furthermore, an alternate (but not necessarily mutually exclusive) GE correlation model may be tested, to determine whether heritable components of negative emotionality in infancy in fact elicit the parental behavior of interest. The utility of these models is to examine empirically alternate mechanisms by which both genetic and environmental influences come together to produce reliable individual differences in complex phenotypes (see Rutter et al., 1997).

Perhaps the most intriguing new direction will be the incorporation of molecular genetic strategies into behavioral genetic paradigms aimed at understanding the etiology of individual differences in emotional development throughout the lifespan (Eley & Plomin, 1997). Molecular genetic techniques are now being aimed at genes that theoretically account for only small portions of population variance on complex behavioral and disease phenotypes (Plomin, et al.,1994; Risch & Merikangas, 1996). This approach is in contrast to more traditional genetic methods, which attempted to find single genes with "sledgehammer" affects on rare diseases (see Rende & Plomin, 1995), and is consistent with quantitative genetic theory. Indeed, this effort may be seen as an attempt to elucidate the actual genetic mechanisms that underlie the "black box" or latent trait of heritability in behavioral genetic designs. As there are now methods for collecting DNA in a noninvasive and pragmatic manner from large samples (Freeman et al., 1997), as well as statistical techniques for assessing the association between genomic and phenotypic variation (Risch & Merikangas, 1996), it is worth considering that molecular genetic strategies will become a critical approach within the broader domain of behavior genetics (Plomin et al., 1994).

What are the implications for the study of emotional development? A key consideration is that as candidate genes have begun to be associated with various personality dimensions (see Eley & Plomin, 1997), it is likely that the study of the biology of individual differences in emotional expression may be revolutionized. However, such a revolution comes with a number of caveats that may guide future research studies. One caveat is that genetic studies will not progress without appropriate attention to the definition and assessment of the *phenotype* (e.g., Risch & Merikangas, 1996). Research on molecular genetics will thus require the active involvement of experts in emotional development, in order to carve out the precise nature of "emotional" phenotypes that may be influenced in part by genetic factors. A second caveat is that, consistent with quantitative genetic theory, the genes that may be identified will only account for small proportions of variance on the traits of interest (Plomin et al., 1994), and thus progress in molecular genetics should not be mistaken as arguments for genetic determinism (Rende & Plomin, 1995). Relatedly, a third caveat is that in order for us to understand more completely the etiology of individual differences in emotional development, studying measured indicators of environmental influence will be as important as including assessments of candidate genes.

It may be proposed that the inclusion of measured indicators of both genetic and environmental factors will not only help fill in the "black box" components of variance derived from more traditional behavioral genetic paradigms, but also will make more likely the prospect of studying directly the interplay between genes and environment (Plomin & Rutter, 1998). As discussed by Lewis (1997), the task of finding such predictive relations will be difficult, given the combinational possibilities of the human genome, as well as the importance of random and chance events that affect development. The promise of future behavioral genetic work is to search empirically for markers of probabilistic rather than fixed patterns of development, even if such markers account for small proportions of variance in the traits of interest. In addition, behavioral genetic strategies do incorporate a component of variance that may reflect in part the effect of chance on development. This component, referred to as "nonshared" or "unique" enviroment, is the overall proportion of variance not accounted for by common genetic or environmental effects. Although many potential sources of influence may be captured by this construct, including error of measurement and systematic environmental events that are specific to an individual, behavior geneticists have long recognized that chance and random effects that may have a profound influence on development fall empirically within this category of variance (Rende & Plomin, 1995). It is informative to conclude that in many behavioral genetic studies conducted to date, this component of variance is often the largest, and often surpasses the variance explained by common genetic and environmental influence. In this sense, the yield of behavioral genetic research may be to explain the predictable, which, despite being of obvious importance, will not be confused with explaining all of the key sources of influence on human development.

ACKNOWLEDGMENTS

The support received from the Charles and Johanna Busch Memorial Fund at Rutgers, The State University of New Jersey, is gratefully acknowledged.

REFERENCES

Buss, A. H., & Plomin, R. (1984). *Temperament: Early developing personality traits.* Hillsdale, NJ: Erlbaum.

Eaves, L. J., Eysenck, H., & Martin, N. G. (1989). *Genes, culture, and personality· An empirical approach.* London: Academic Press.

Eaves, L. J., Silberg, J. L., Meyer, J. M., Maes, H. H., Simonoff, E., Pickles, A., Rutter, M., Neale, M. C., Reynolds, C. A., Erikson, M. T., Heath, A. C., Loeber, R., Truett, K. R., & Hewitt, J. K. (1997). Genetics and developmental psychopathology: 2. The main effects of genes and environment on behavioral problems in the Virginia Twin Study of Adolescent Behavioral Development. *Journal of Child Psychology and Psychiatry, 38,* 965–980.

Edelbrock, C., Rende, R., Plomin, R., & Thompson, L. (1995). A twin study of competence and behavioral problems in adolescence. *Journal of Child Psychology and Psychiatry, 36,* 775–785.

Eley, T. C. (1997). Depressive symptoms in children and adolescents: Etiological links between normality and abnormality: a research note. *Journal of Child Psychology and Psychiatry, 38,* 861–866.

Eley, T. C., Deater-Deckard, K., Fombonne, E., Fulker, D. W., & Plomin, R. (1998). An adoption study of depressive symptoms in middle childhood. *Journal of Child Psychology and Psychiatry, 39,* 337–346.

Eley, T. C., & Plomin, R. (1997). Genetic analyses of

emotionality. *Current Opinion in Neurobiology, 7,* 279–284.

Emde, R. N., Plomin, R., Robinson, J., Corley, R., DeFries, J., Fulker, D. W., Reznick, J. S., Campos, J., Kagan, J., & Zahn-Waxler, C. (1992). Temperament, emotion, and cognition at fourteen months: The MacArthur Longitudinal Twin Study. *Child Development, 63,* 1437–1455.

Fox, N. (Ed.). (1994). The development of emotion regulation: Biological and behavioral considerations. *Monographs of the Society for Research in Child Development, 59* (2–3, Serial No. 240).

Freeman, B., Powell, J., Ball, D., Hill, L., Craig, I., & Plomin, R. (1997). DNA by mail: an inexpensive and noninvasive method for collecting DNA samples from widely dispersed populations. *Behavior Genetics, 27,* 251–257.

Fuenzalida, C., Emde, R. N., Pannabecker, B. J., & Stenberg, C. (1981). Validation of the Differential Emotions Scale in 613 Mothers. *Motivation and Emotion, 5,* 37–45.

Gjone, H., & Stevenson, J. (1997). A longitudinal twin study of temperament and behavior problems: Common genetic or environmental influences? *Journal of the American Academy of Child and Adolescent Psychiatry, 36,* 1448–1456.

Goldsmith, H. H., Buss, K. A., & Lemery, K. S. (1997). Toddler and childhood temperament: Expanded content, stronger genetic evidence, new evidence for the importance of the environment. *Developmental Psychology, 33,* 891–905.

Johnson, W. F., Emde, R. N., Pannabecker, B. J., Stenberg, C., & Davis, M. (1982). Maternal perception of infant emotion from birth through 18 months. *Infant Behavior and Development, 5,* 313–322.

Kendler, K. S. (1995). Genetic epidemiology in psychiatry: Taking both genes and environment seriously. *Archives of General Psychiatry, 52,* 895–899.

Kendler, K. S., Kessler, R. C., Neale, M. C., Heath, A. C., & Eaves, L. J. (1993). The prediction of major depression in women: Toward an integrated etiologic model. *American Journal of Psychiatry, 180,* 1138–1148.

Kendler, K. S., Neale, M. C., Kessler, R. C., Heath, A. C., & Eaves, L. J. (1992a). A population-based twin study of major depression in women: The impact of varying definitions of illness. *Archives of General Psychiatry, 49,* 257–266.

Kendler, K. S., Neale, M. C., Kessler, R. C., Heath, A. C., & Eaves, L. J. (1992b). Generalized anxiety disorder in women: A population-based twin study. *Archives of General Psychiatry, 49,* 267–272.

Kendler, K. S., Neale, M. C., Kessler, R. C., Heath, A. C., & Eaves, L. J. (1992c). Major depression and generalized anxiety disorder: Same genes, (partly) different environments? *Archives of General Psychiatry, 49,* 718–722.

Kendler, K. S., Neale, M. C., Kessler, R. C., Heath, A. C., & Eaves, L. J. (1992d). The genetic epidemiology of phobias in women: The interrelationship of agoraphobia, social phobia, situational phobia, and simple phobia. *Archives of General Psychiatry, 49,* 273–281.

Kendler, K. S., Neale, M. C., Kessler, R. C., Heath, A.

C., & Eaves, L. J. (1993). A longitudinal twin study of personality and major depression in women. *Archives of General Psychiatry, 50,* 853–862.

Kendler, K. S., Walters, E. E., Neale, M. O., Kessler, R. C., Heath, A. C., & Eaves, L. J. (1996). The structure of the genetic and environmental risk factors for six major psychiatric disorders in women; Phobias, generalized anxiety disorder, panic disorder, bulimia, major depression, and alcoholism. *Archives of General Psychiatry, 52,* 374–383.

Lewis, M. (1992). Developing developmental psychopathology. *Journal of Applied Developmental Psychology, 13,* 483–488.

Lewis, M. (1997). *Altering fate: Why the past does not predict the future.* New York: Guilford Press.

Loehlin, J. (1992). *Genes and environment in personality development.* Newbury Park, CA: Sage.

Plomin, R., DeFries, J. C., McClearn, G. E., & Rutter, M. (1997). *Behavioral genetics* (3rd ed). New York: Freeman.

Plomin, R., Owen, M. J., & McGuffin, P. (1994). The genetic basis of complex human behaviors. *Science, 264,* 1733–1739.

Plomin, R., & Rutter, M. (1998). Child development and molecular genetics: What do we do with genes once they are found? *Child Development, 69,* 1223–1242.

Rende, R. (1993). Longitudinal relations between temperamental traits and behavioral syndromes in middle childhood. *Journal of the American Academy of Child and Adolescent Psychiatry, 32,* 287–290.

Rende, R., & Plomin, R. (1992). Diathesis–stress models of psychopathology: A quantitative genetic perspective. *Applied and Preventive Psychology, 1,* 177–182.

Rende, R., & Plomin, R. (1995). Nature, nurture, and the development of psychopathology. In D. Cicchetti & D. J. Cohen (Eds.), *Developmental psychopathology: Vol. 1. Theory and Methods.* New York: Wiley.

Rende, R., Plomin, R., Reiss, D., & Hetherington, E. M. (1993). Genetic and environmental influences on depressive symptomatology in adolescence: Individual differences and extreme scores. *Journal of Child Psychology and Psychiatry, 34,* 1387–1398.

Rende, R., Plomin, R., & Vandenberg, S. (1990). Who discovered the twin method? *Behavior Genetics, 20,* 277–285.

Risch, N., & Merikangas, K. R. (1996). The future of genetic studies of complex human diseases. *Science, 273,* 1515–1517.

Rutter, M., Dunn, J., Plomin, R., Simonoff, E., Pickles, A., Maughan, G., Ormel, J., Meyer, J., & Eaves, L. (1997). Integrating nature and nurture: Implications of person–environment correlations and interactions for developmental psychopathology. *Development and Psychopathology, 9,* 335–364.

Saudino, K. J., McGuire, S., Reiss, D., Hetherington, E. M., & Plomin, R. (1996). Parent ratings of EAS temperaments in twins, full siblings, half siblings, and stepsiblings. *Journal of Personality and Social Psychology, 68,* 723–733.

Schmitz, S., Cherny, S. S., Fulker, D. W., & Mrazek, D. A. (1994). Genetic and environmental influences on early childhood behavior. *Behavior Genetics, 24,* 25–34.

Thapar, A., & McGuffin, P. (1994). A twin study of depressive symptoms in childhood. *British Journal of Psychiatry, 165,* 259-265.

Thapar, A., & McGuffin, P. (1996). The genetic etiology of childhood depressive symptoms: A developmental perspective. *Development and Psychopathology, 8,* 751–760.

Thapar, A., & McGuffin, P. (1997). Anxiety and depressive symptoms in childhood: A genetic study of comorbidity. *Journal of Child Psychology and Psychiatry, 38,* 651–656.

van der Valk, J. C., Verhulst, F. C., Stroet, T. M., & Boomsma, D. I. (1998). Quantitative genetic analysis of internalising and externalsing problems in a large sample of 3-year-old twins. *Twin Research, 1,* 25–33.

CHAPTER 13

Multiple-Measure Approaches to the Study of Infant Emotion

Nathan A. Fox
Susan D. Calkins

Research on the development of infant emotion has focused primarily on the expression of emotion, charting the ontogeny of particular emotions such as anger and fear (Campos, Hiatt, Ramsay, Henderson, & Svejda, 1978). In recent years, a number of important changes in the field have allowed researchers to broaden the scope of their inquiries. First, vastly improved methodologies for the study of biological components of emotion have led to more detailed and comprehensive descriptions of infant emotional experience. The application of noninvasive psychophysiological procedures for measuring brain electrical activity or cortisol changes have produced a number of important findings, which provide a clearer conception of the relations between emotion and physiology. At the same time, developmental psychology has experienced a renewed interest in the study of individual differences in infancy (see Columbo & Fagan, 1990). With respect to the study of infant emotion, this implies examining the phenomenon with special attention both to endogenous infant traits, and to the interaction of these traits with socialization experiences to produce particular patterns of behavior. This approach has led theorists and researchers to consider emotion, temperament, and social behavior as elements of an emotion

system that interact dynamically (Campos, Barret, Lamb, Goldsmith, & Stenberg, 1983). Moreover, recent research on the regulation of emotion demonstrates quite convincingly that infant emotional reactivity is at the core of the infant's personality or temperament, and that the display of affect and affect regulation are powerful mediators of interpersonal relationships and socioemotional adjustment in the first few years of life (Calkins & Fox, 1992; Calkins, 1994; Cicchetti, Ganiban, & Barnett, 1991; Malatesta, Culver, Tesman, & Shephard, 1989; Rothbart, 1989; Thompson, 1990, 1994).

These two developments in the area of infant emotion—improvements in psychophysiological assessment and analysis, and an interest in infant temperament and its role in developing affiliative relationships—have led to new approaches to the study of infant emotion, ones that consider the interrelation of both behavioral and biological systems. These approaches assume that emotion is neither exclusively expression nor physiology, but is best understood as a combination of the two (Davidson & Cacioppo, 1992; Fox & Davidson, 1984). Such perspectives have led to the establishment of programs of research whose aim is to assess these systems during the period of infancy, and to observe convergence among them. The aim of this chapter is to describe the methodologies currently being used in these programs, and to describe some of the early findings.

The chapter is divided into three sections. First, we briefly discuss psychophysiological assessment, with special emphasis on methodologies used in conjunction with infant emotion. Second, we discuss the interrelations among the domains of emotion and temperament and social behavior. Finally, we bring together these two areas by reviewing some of the most recent research that has undertaken to measure emotion in infancy, using a variety of behavioral and physiological measures.

ISSUES IN PSYCHOPHYSIOLOGICAL MEASUREMENT OF INFANT EMOTION

What Is Being Measured?

The history of psychophysiological measurement in the study of emotion is a long and complex one. Many studies have approached the study of relations between emotion and physiology by using classical theories of arousal. This work has viewed physiological change as either accompanying and intensifying affective experience or being the source of emotion experience itself. Measurement of heart rate is an obvious example. Numerous early studies recorded heart rate during different emotion-eliciting situations and interpreted the change in heart rate to reflect the degree to which a subject became aroused by the stimulus. Increases in heart rate were viewed as reflecting arousal, whereas decreases in heart rate or no change were viewed as reflecting lack of arousal. Thus subjects who exhibited increases in heart rate were thought to be experiencing emotion, while those with little change were not. Emotion experience was seen as a function of the degree to which the person was aroused by the stimulus.

This unidimensional view of emotion and arousal was replaced by one that specifically interpreted directional heart rate changes within a psychological framework. Graham and Clifton (1966) viewed increases in heart rate as reflecting a defensive response to noxious stimuli and decreases in heart rate as reflecting orienting responses. Changes in heart rate were not thought to reflect general arousal or activa-

tion; rather, these changes were linked to specific psychological states. An example from the developmental literature that used these concepts is a study by Campos, Emde, Gaensbauer, and Henderson (1975) in which changes in infant heart rate in response to stranger approach and maternal separation were reported. Campos et al. (1975), described increases in heart rate that occurred with the increasing proximity of the stranger and with the departure of the mother. Increases in heart rate were interpreted to reflect a defensive emotional response, while decreases were thought to signify orienting, attention, and interest to the novel event.

Contrast this type of study with the research of Ekman and colleagues (and the earlier research of Ax, 1953), who examined specific patterns of autonomic change associated with the expression of certain discrete emotions. They reported the ability to distinguish between the emotion expressions of anger and fear by using measures of finger temperature and heart rate. Ekman and colleagues interpreted these data as indicating that there are unique patterns of autonomic activity for each discrete emotion. The patterning of autonomic responses was seen as specific to an emotion rather than merely reflecting an undifferentiated state of arousal (Ekman, Levenson, & Friesen, 1983; Levenson, Ekman, & Friesen, 1990).

The majority of these studies—both those focusing on undifferentiated arousal of the autonomic nervous system, and those attempting to identify specific physiological changes associated with discrete emotions—utilized measurement of the autonomic nervous system. As such these studies recorded changes in the cardiac and vascular systems with measures of heart rate, skin conductance/resistance/potential, skin temperature, blood pressure, and respiration. In general, one or more of these responses were chosen for measurement, and in the best of studies, patterning among these measures was reported (e.g. Ekman et al., 1983).

However, a number of technical issues relevant to these studies and to the research on physiological measurement in general have often been overlooked. Perhaps the most important one is the issue of time course of change in each of these systems. It is clear from the physiological literature that each of the various autonomic responses has quite a different time course, ranging from milliseconds to seconds and in some cases minutes before change in the response can be measured. The fact that each of these systems elicits a different time course of change would seem problematical to the different approaches for study of emotion. For example, if physiological measurement is to describe patterns of arousal, then choice of measure will obviously influence the conclusion as to whether the subject has indeed become aroused by the emotional stimulus or not. Changes in cortisol are only noted some 15 minutes after the eliciting event. If cortisol is measured during an emotion, one would not conclude that the subject has become aroused during that emotion. Similarly, if one is measuring patterns of physiological change during the expression of discrete emotions, the time course for these changes may preclude finding these patterns if ecologically valid expressive responses are utilized. Ekman and colleagues, for example, have used a task in which subjects hold the facial musculature changes associated with certain emotions (the "directed facial action" task) for long periods of time for just this reason.

The differing time course of physiological systems may also be helpful in understanding certain aspects of emotion experience. Fox (1991) has suggested that the slower-changing autonomic responses that are associated with the expression of certain discrete emotions may be more related to the intensive aspects of the experience than to the central feeling state. Certain emotions may be intensified by the contribution of changing autonomic and visceral tone. Certain emotional states, which last over prolonged periods of time, may do so because of the slow changing physiological systems that are involved in the expression of the emotion. Of course, the degree to which these states last may be a function of individual differences in physiological lability. To the best of our knowledge, these issues have not been thoroughly explored in the literature, although the time courses of these systems have been well defined.

A parallel issue in the use of multiple physiological measures is the degree to which we understand the relations among different physiological systems. There are a number of levels in which this problem may be approached. Perhaps the most simple and direct one is to record more than one measure and to examine simple bivariate correlations among the measures. If one system goes up in response to or during an emotion, does the other go up or down? Patterning of this nature among systems that share

some similarity (e.g., among autonomic measures) has had a long history in psychophysiology. Classical approaches emphasizing the role of arousal maintained that there should be a correspondence among physiological systems in their response to emotional stimuli. Physiological arousal should, it was argued, be reflected in multiple measures. These responses should all go up or down together. However, researchers were quick to discover that this was not the case. Indeed, Lacey and colleagues (Lacey & Lacey, 1970) revealed different directional patterns to autonomic measures in response to a stressor. The concept of a unitary notion of arousal as measured by multiple systems could not be supported.

Perhaps a more informative strategy is to understand the particular physiological systems that are being tapped, and consequently the underlying physiology and anatomy of those systems, so that particular patterns of relationship among measures can be interpreted with greater depth and understanding. As an example, consider the research on blood pressure and heart rate. There has been a good deal of work attempting to clarify the physiological mechanisms that relate these two systems, in order to elucidate both the unique nature of each and the manner in which these two systems overlap. The unique feedback systems between blood pressure and heart rate via baroreceptor mechanisms have allowed scientists to understand how blood pressure and heart rate covary. Use of both measures together can illuminate issues regarding the nature of interaction among these physiological systems, rather than just between emotion and a single autonomic index.

Synchrony of Emotion and Physiology

A second issue in the study of multiple response measures of emotion involves the nature of emotion behavior–physiology synchronization. As discussed above, different physiological systems have differing time courses. Measuring more than one involves understanding the manner in which these different time courses overlap and interact. But what of measurement of the emotion itself? What is its time course and how does it factor into the pattern that is being described? Again, the history of efforts to answer this question is long and complex. There are many definitions of emotion, and there have been multiple attempts at measurement of emotion. One theoretical position that may be helpful in studying emotion–physiology relationships is presented by Ekman (1984). Emotion, in Ekman's conceptualization, is a fast-occurring event linked directly to changes in facial expression and autonomic activity. The time course of emotion may be viewed on the order of seconds. Feeling states that occur over longer periods of time are thought of as mood states rather than emotions. If one accepts these definitional distinctions, one can begin to find ways to link physiology to emotion behavior. For example, we have utilized facial expression as an anchor in determining the presence of specific central nervous system states in infants. In our studies of brain electrical activity and its relation to emotion, we have synchronized changes in the ongoing electroencephalogram (EEG) to changes in facial expression (Fox & Davidson, 1987). This has been possible because the resolution and time course of the EEG are on the order of milliseconds, as are the resolution and time course of facial expressive change. Thus, it is not unreasonable to link the two together; their time changes are compatible.

But what about linking expressive changes to autonomic activity? Again, since most autonomic change is on the order of seconds, it is difficult to find instances of expressive change that match this temporal level. Ekman et al. (1983) developed the directed facial action task for just this purpose. In this task, a subject is required to move his or her facial muscles into a pattern resembling a discrete emotion. The subject must then hold that expression for a long period of time, so that changes in autonomic activity may be recorded. Although such a pattern is interesting in the abstract and can inform us about the relations between certain behaviors and physiology its direct relation to ecologically valid changes in facial activity is dubious. Seldom are facial expressions of discrete emotion in "real life" held for such long periods of time. It is therefore difficult if not impossible in ecologically valid situations to synchronize emotion and autonomic behavior, if emotion is solely defined by the presence of specific facial behaviors.

One can define emotion by the stimulus condition itself. However, the obvious drawback here is that individuals may respond quite differently to the same condition, and if physiology and behavior are linked one may not find clear relations when differing emotions are elicited across individuals. For example, we have recorded physiology in young infants in response to maternal separation (Fox, Bell, & Jones, 1992). Not all infants cry at separation or are distressed. Indeed, we have found that the physiology of infants who are distressed is quite different from that of infants who are not upset by this identical stimulus situation. Collapsing data across individual subjects would obscure these differences. As an alternative to either collapsing data across individuals or anchoring emotion to facial expression, which is a fast-changing response, one could interview subjects as to their emotion response or have subjects rate their individual responses. Subjects could then be grouped by the type of emotion that they report. Alternatively, other response measures of emotion may be used. For example, in the case of infant response to maternal separation we have grouped infants into those who cry and those who do not cry at this event (e.g., Davidson & Fox, 1989). Interestingly, the discrete facial expression does not discriminate physiological activity within individual infants who cry at separation. We have found, for example, that some infants cry and exhibit anger expressions, while others cry and exhibit distress/sadness. Physiologically (at least with regard to the EEG measures we have utilized), these two subgroups do not differ. Thus vocal measures of emotion have proved to be more successful in parsing emotion behavior–physiology relations than have facial expressions of emotion.

Physiological Approaches to the Study of Infant Emotion

Although the study of central and autonomic nervous system substrates of emotion has a long history within the adult personality literature (Davidson, 1984; Porges, 1991), relatively little has been done in the area of infant emotions. Three primary types of measures have been used to study relations between physiology and emotional responsivity to a variety of elicitors: measures of heart rate, brain electrical activity, and adrenocortical activity. Excellent reviews of the use of these three measures in both the adult and child literature are to be found in Fox and Davidson (1986), Porges (1991), and Gunnar (1989; Stansbury & Gunnar, 1994). In this section, we briefly describe the application of these measures to the study of infant emotion.

Heart Rate

Assessment of heart rate among infant and child populations is a nonintrusive, painless procedure. Whereas methods of collecting heart rate data from infants have proven to be relatively straightforward, methods of analyzing these data have proven to be more complex. Traditionally, studies examined changes in heart rate (deceleration and acceleration) in response to particular emotion-eliciting events. In particular, a number of studies have examined the changes in heart rate accompanying fear-inducing situations, such as the visual cliff and the approach of an unfamiliar adult (Campos et al., 1978; Emde, Gaensbauer & Harmon, 1976). These studies were patterned after Graham and Clifton's (1966) reinterpretation of the meaning and significance of directional changes in heart rate.

Another dimension of cardiac activity that has been linked to emotionality and individual differences in emotionality is heart rate variability. Although there are multiple ways to measure heart rate variability, Porges and colleagues (Porges & Byrne, 1992; Porges, 1996) have developed a method that measures the amplitude and period of the oscillations associated with inhalation and exhalation. Thus this measure refers to the variability in heart rate that occurs at the frequency of breathing (respiratory sinus arrythmia or RSA) and is thought to reflect parasympathetic influence via the vagus nerve. Porges has termed this measure of heart rate variability "vagal tone" (Porges & Byrne, 1992; Porges, 1996). In characterizing the theoretical relation between RSA and behavior, Porges (1991) has speculated that the vagal tone measure reflects appropriate reactivity to, and awareness of, one's environment. For example, high resting RSA is one index of autonomic functioning that has been associated with appropriate emotional reactivity (Stifter & Fox, 1990) and good attentional ability (Richards, 1985, 1987; Suess, Porges, & Plude, 1994). Several studies have linked high RSA in newborns with good developmental outcomes, suggesting that it may be an important physiological component of appropriate engagement with the environment (Hoffheimer, Wood, Porges, Pearson, & Lawson, 1995; Richards & Cameron, 1989). Children with low RSA may be at risk because they may have difficulty attending and reacting to environmental stimulation (Porges, 1991).

Most of the research examining relations between RSA and behavior has examined relations between baseline measures of RSA and laboratory or parent report assessments of temperamental reactivity (Calkins & Fox, 1992; Fox, 1989; Gunnar, Porter, Wolf, Rigatuso, & Larson, 1995; Stifter & Fox, 1990; Stifter, Fox, & Porges, 1989). Recently, however, several studies have examined a second dimension or measure of cardiac RSA—the degree to which an individual displays suppression of RSA during an attention-demanding or cognitively challenging task. Porges and colleagues have recently speculated on the two functional roles of vagal tone (Porges, Doussard-Roosevelt, Portales, & Greenspan, 1996). During periods of low external or environmental stress, vagal tone works to promote homeostasis and activities related to growth; in situations of environmental challenge, the vagal system works to regulate metabolic output such that the external demands may be met. The first of these two functions, homeostasis, may be indexed by steady-state or baseline measures of RSA. During periods of stress or challenge, the vagus functions as a "brake" to regulate cardiac output (Porges et al., 1996). Control of the vagal brake may be measured in terms of suppression or decreases in RSA in response to various types of environmental challenge. This suppression may act to increase an individual's orientation to external stimuli, allowing the individual to balance internal, homeostatic needs with environmental demands (Porges, 1991; Porges et al., 1996). Thus studies of cardiac correlates of temperament, emotion, and social behavior have begun to look at multiple measures of cardiac activity, including basal and challenge measures of both heart rate and heart rate variability.

Electroencephalogram

A second physiological measure that has recently been utilized in the study of infant emotion is the ongoing EEG. The EEG is low-level electrical activity recorded off the scalp. First noticed by Berger (1929), the EEG has been routinely recorded in adults during cognitive tasks and during situations designed to elicit different emotions. The advent of powerful and fast computers made it possible to collect large amounts of EEG data, sample the signal quickly, and spectral-analyze the signal, decomposing the signal into energy at different frequency bands. Berger (1929) had noticed that the energy in the EEG decreased when patients were attending to the environment. This phenomenon later detailed by Lindsley and Wicke (1974), is known as "alpha desynchronization" or "alpha blocking." Greater desynchronization (decreased energy in a frequency band) is associated with increased activation.

Researchers interested in the pattern of activation between the right and left hemispheres have computed ratio scores of the difference in power or energy between the two hemispheres. These ratio or difference scores present relative differences in power and a score reflecting the degree to which one hemisphere or region in a hemisphere exhibits greater activation than a homologous region. There is an extensive literature on EEG asymmetry patterns during verbal versus spatial tasks (Davidson, Chapman, Chapman, & Henriques, 1990) and during the expression and perception of different emotions (Davidson, 1984; Fox & Davidson, 1988).

In applying these methods to the study of infant emotion, Fox and Davidson (Davidson & Fox, 1982, 1989; Fox & Davidson, 1986, 1987, 1988) have addressed two issues. The first issue, addressed in their early research, concerned the relation between the experience of a given emotion and the hemispheric activation associated with that emotion experience. In their studies of infants presented with videotaped facial expressions of happiness and sadness, for example, they found that infants displayed greater relative left frontal activation during happy than during sad expressions (Davidson & Fox, 1982). In a study of newborns, they found that different tastes produced both different facial expressions (interest vs. disgust) and different patterns of brain activity (Fox & Davidson, 1986). The second issue addressed in Fox and Davidson's research is whether differences in hemispheric asymmetry are markers for individual differences in emotionality, or temperament in infancy (Davidson & Fox, 1989; Fox & Davidson, 1991). In their study of infants' reactions to maternal separation they found that infants who displayed less left-sided activation in the frontal region during a baseline condition were more likely to cry at a brief separation (Fox & Davidson, 1987). Fox & Davidson (1991) argue that infants who show a characteristic right-sided frontal activation may have a lower threshold for negative emotion. More recently, this work has been extended to examine differences among behav-

iorally inhibited and uninhibited children. Data from the Maryland Infant Study suggest that infants selected for temperamental characteristics predictive of inhibition are more likely to exhibit greater relative right frontal activation (Calkins, Fox, & Marshall, 1996).

Adrenocortical Activity.

A third physiological measure that has recently been applied to the study of infant emotion is adrenocortical activity as measured in plasma and salivary cortisol. Cortisol is the primary hormone of the hypothalamic–pituitary–adrenocortical (HPA) system, whose production varies fairly rhythmically during the course of the 24-hour day–night cycle. In addition, however, cortisol levels change in response to both physiological and psychological elicitors, and help the organism to mount a response to both physical and emotional challenges. In using cortisol as a measure of stress or emotional reactivity, then, the aim is to compare changes in cortisol levels from basal to stressor conditions, with consideration of the activity of the system relative to its daily cycle (Stansbury & Gunnar, 1994). Measurement of adrenocortical activity in infants is further complicated by the developmental changes occurring in the pattern of daily cortisol activity during the first year of life. For example, Lewis and Ramsay (1995a, 1995b) report that a predictable decline in cortisol response between 2 and 6 months of age. They also report that although the response is not stable from the early months of life to toddlerhood, stability can be observed from 6 to 18 months of age. Despite the potential difficulties associated with this developmental shift, recent improvements in the radioimmune assays used to analyze salivary cortisol make this method of obtaining psychophysiological data from very young infants quite feasible.

In examining the relations between measures of cortisol and emotion, researchers have debated whether observed increases in cortisol reflect reactivity to stress or whether changes in cortisol level reflect reactivity to novelty and uncertainty. The first hypothesis implies that elevations in cortisol levels will be observed consistently in response to stressors producing negative affect, whereas the second hypothesis predicts habituation of the adrenocortical response once the novelty of the event or stimulus has dissipated (Gunnar, 1990). A third hypothesis, more recently proposed, suggests that control or regulation of the affective response may be the critical factor related to observed changes in cortisol (Stansbury & Gunnar, 1994).

Issues and Problems

This brief introduction to the kinds of psychophysiological measures currently being used with infants to study emotional development raises several issues. First, although these studies have undertaken the study of the biological component to emotion, it is clear that these emotion responses occur within a social context. Responsivity to the approach of a stranger and maternal separations, for example, are not simple biological responses independent of a child's history and experience in dyadic interactions. Other systems, such as attachment and/or social learning histories, are at work as well. The emotion the infant displays, then, is a function of both the event and the process of socialization experienced by the infant. The second important issue raised by these studies is that temperamental individuality plays a role in infant behavioral and physiological responsivity. That is, as the studies of Fox (1991) suggest, emotions may occur as certain predictable biological events occur in response to particular situational elicitors. Given a certain degree of novelty or stress, certain patterns of biological responsivity may be a characteristic response of an individual. Both pieces of information are critical to the understanding of the relations between physiology and behavior. In the next section, we explore the idea that infant emotions are reflected in both temperament and social behavior.

LINKS BETWEEN EMOTION AND TEMPERAMENT, ATTACHMENT, AND SOCIAL DEVELOPMENT

The interrelations among emotion, temperament, and social behavior are most dramatically observed in infancy. Infants display a varied repertoire of emotional expressions very early in life (Malatesta et al., 1989), and this repertoire serves as the infants' primary means of communication with their caretakers. Infant emotion expression and regulation of that expression are key elements in the formation of primary attachments and early social relationships (Thompson, 1990). Infants use distress signals to alert the caretaker to their needs;

caretakers become adept at interpreting the infants' signals in order to fulfill those needs. And there are rapid developments in the infants' ability to acquire the necessary skills to regulate their own emotions and monitor their own behaviors. Very young infants are able to use gaze aversion and self-comforting to manage affective experience; as motor and cognitive abilities grow, so too will the range of behaviors infants use to regulate themselves. These developments in self-regulation, which follow a fairly predictable path in infancy and early childhood (Kopp, 1982), are clearly the result of dyadic interactions with the caretaker (Tronick, 1989).

Although there are normative trends in the development of emotion regulation during infancy, there are also individual differences in the way infants learn to regulate affective states and the rate at which this process occurs. Infants bring to the dyadic interactions with caretakers their own personalty style, or "temperament." The notion of temperament suggests that infant characteristics are a function of biological predispositions (Rothbart & Derryberry, 1981). Most temperament theorists see emotionality as a core construct, although other traits are measured as well (Buss & Plomin, 1984). The tendency to be fussy, difficult to soothe, easily distressed by novelty or frustration, and unable to adapt is often tapped by both experimental observations and maternal assessments of infant temperament (Matheny & Wilson, 1981; Rothbart, 1981). Clearly, an infant's tendency to be easily distressed will have an impact on interactions with the caretaker. Furthermore, the infant's success or failure at managing states of emotional reactivity will have implications for future interactions with caregivers, and eventually with others as well. The role of both emotional reactivity and regulation in personality and social development is thus clearly an important one, and one that is influenced not simply by the infant's tendencies, but by the caregiver's input as well.

Fogel (1982) has suggested that an infant's ability to manage distress, coupled with caregiver support, may be predictive of an ability to self-comfort and rely less on caregivers, as well as the development of a growing sense of security. Alternatively, an inability to develop distress tolerance may lead to both withdrawn behavior and feelings of insecurity on the part of the infant. The role of a secure attachment in the development of self-regulation seems, then, to be a function of both an infant's own capacity for utilizing necessary mechanisms of affective regulation and a caregiver's ability to meet the regulatory needs of the infant. Attachment theorists use the term "working model" (Bretherton, 1985) to describe the infant's sense of caretaker responsivity. A secure attachment is a function of positive interactions that allow the child to anticipate that regulation needs will effectively be met by the caretaker. An insecure attachment results when regulation needs are not fulfilled, either because the caretaker is neglecting and unavailable, or because the caretaker is inconsistent in meeting the affective needs of the infant. This process is clearly bidirectional, and its success depends on whether an infant is able to elicit the appropriate caregiver behaviors to help manage distress and how competently the caregiver is able to fulfill the role of emotion regulator for the child. Thus one way to examine linkages among temperament, emotion, and social relationships is to study the way each contributes to early emotion regulation. However, although these conceptual linkages seem strong, the measurement of these separate but interrelated domains may be more difficult, as is the measurement of emotion regulation abilities.

Given the obvious intersections among emotion, temperament, social development, and emotion regulation, an approach to the study of these domains ought to include multiple behavioral or observational measures which may provide a more complete picture than a technique that relies on a single measure may give. In this way, the relative contributions of temperament, attachment, and social responsivity to emotionality may be assessed with respect to one another. Moreover, the strategy of considering multiple indicators of emotion in infancy is further strengthened by application of the types of psychophysiological measures discussed earlier. In the next section, we review research that has taken the approach of exploring emotion–physiology relations by studying behaviors reflecting temperament and social behavior, as well as emotional displays.

MULTIPLE MEASURES OF INFANT EMOTION

Studies Assessing Autonomic Activity

Several recent studies comparing measures of heart rate to temperament, attachment, and so-cial behaviors have recently been conducted. Using measures of heart period and vagal tone, Porges and colleagues have observed both normative changes and individual differences related to various aspects of behavior. For example, Porges, Doussard-Roosevelt, Portales, & Suess (1994) followed a group of infants from the first to the third year of life. Assessments of temperament were made via both maternal questionnaires and laboratory observations at 9, 20, and 36 months of age. Normative increases in heart rate measures were found across the three ages. Stability of both behavioral measures of difficultness and the heart rate measures was also found. The most interesting finding, however, was that concurrent measures of vagal tone and difficultness did not correlate highly. Rather, earlier measures of vagal tone tended to predict changes in maternal assessments of infant difficultness. Infants with higher vagal tone at 9 months were perceived by their mothers to be less difficult at 36 months than infants with low vagal tone. These findings support Porges's contention that vagal tone is a reflection of physiological and behavioral regulation (Porges, 1991). Infants with high heart rate variability, or vagal tone, seem to be responsive to stimuli in a way that assists them in regulating their state. Reports by mothers that these infants became less difficult over time supports the notion that, in fact, they became better able to manage their own emotional reactivity. More recently, Stifter and Jain (1996) reported that infants who displayed negative affect in response to frustration, but who also displayed high levels of regulation, had higher vagal tone than infants who were not engaging in regulatory behaviors. What these studies may indicate is that infants with high vagal tone are physiologically reactive and have developed appropriate strategies for behavioral regulation. Behavioral regulation is a dynamic process requiring management of distress by both caretaker and infant, and underlying physiological reactivity and regulation are clearly what the infant contributes to this process early in development.

We have examined a similar hypothesis regarding emotional reactivity and regulation in a longitudinal study (Fox, 1989; Stifter & Fox, 1990; Calkins & Fox, 1992) that examined the relations among heart rate measures on the one hand and temperament, attachment, and inhibited behavior on the other. In examining these data, Fox (1989) and Stifter and Fox (1990) demonstrated stable individual differences in reactivity during the first year of life. Infants who cried in response to pacifier withdrawal at 2 days were likely to cry in response to arm restraint at 5 months, and were likely to be rated by their mothers as being more active. These differences in reactivity were associated with individual differences in autonomic patterning: Infants who cried in the newborn period had a higher vagal tone then did noncriers. Five-month-old infants who cried in response to arm restraint had a higher vagal tone than did noncriers. Infants who cried at both events had higher vagal tone and heart period than those who did not cry at both events, and were rated by their mothers as being more distressed to limitations. Fox and Stifter (1989) have argued that infant negative affect in response to mildly stressful and frustrating events is related to individual differences in vagal tone. However, these infants did not display difficult behavior at later assessments. Indeed, Fox (1989) found that infants displaying high frustrative reactivity in the lab at 5 months were likely to display positive approach social behaviors toward strangers and novel events at 14 months, compared to those infants who were less reactive to frustration. Moreover, infants from this sample who displayed high heart rate variability across the first three age points demonstrated more sociable and less distressed behavior at 14 months. These findings support the finding of Porges et al. (1994) that early reactivity as indexed by high vagal tone may be a sign of good emotional and behavioral regulation.

The stability in autonomic reactivity reported by Stifter and Fox (1990) was confirmed in the later assessments of this same sample (Calkins & Fox, 1992). However, no relations were found between earlier or concurrent measures of heart period and vagal tone, and attachment and inhibition at 14 months and 24 months of age, respectively. Examination of the behavioral data at these later ages did indicate, however, that there was a relation between attachment and temperament. Infants whose attachment to their mothers was classified as insecure/resistant at 14 months of age tended to be inhibited at 24 months of age, while infants whose attachment was classified as insecure/avoidant at 14 months of age tended to be uninhibited by 24 months. We have also concluded that some types of emotional reactivity may be related to insecure attachments. Emotional reactivity may be influenced by interactions with

the parent to produce particular sorts of adaptive or regulatory patterns in early toddlerhood (Calkins & Fox, 1992). Infants whose early distress at frustrations or limits is met with a degree of freedom by their parents may appear to be avoidantly attached, but may in fact be regulating their state of arousal by high amounts of exploratory behavior. Infants whose early distress at novelty is dealt with by parental intervention may be more distressed in a situation where attachment is assessed, and may be managing their reactivity by spending large amounts of time in close contact with their parents.

Although our longitudinal study of autonomic reactivity, temperament, and attachment found no relations between heart rate and temperament in the second year of life, Kagan and colleagues have observed such relations (Garcia-Coll, Kagan, & Reznick, 1984; Kagan, Reznick, & Snidman, 1987). For almost 20 years, their research program has focused on the developmental course of inhibited behavior from early infancy through childhood, and has made assessments of the possible psychophysiological correlates of this behavior. For example, Kagan and colleagues, in two separate samples, have reported associations between heart period and heart period variability, and inhibited behavior observed in the laboratory. Infants with high and stable heart rates tend to be more fearful or reticent during encounters with novel people, objects, and events than infants with low and variable heart rates (Kagan et al., 1987). One important difference, however, between this research and ours (Calkins & Fox, 1992) is that Kagan et al. selected samples of infants that they believed represented the extremes of the population in terms of inhibited behavior, whereas we reported findings from an unselected sample. The correlations Kagan's group reports may thus be high because of the use of extreme samples of the distribution.

Another dimension of cardiac activity that may be relevant to a study of the psychophysiological correlates of aggression consists of *changes* in cardiac activity in response to an external stress or challenge. Heart rate changes are thought to be a primary indicator of attention. Typically, deceleration of heart rate reflects attention directed outward (e.g., processing novel stimulation), while acceleration reflects attention directed inward (e.g., during problem-solving conditions) (Ruff & Rothbart, 1996). Eisenberg et al. (1996) found an association between boys' problem behavior and changes in heart rate during a distressing film stimuli, but argued that this relation was due to the lower resting heart rate measure as opposed to any independent change in heart rate. In addition, other researchers have begun to examine changes in RSA in response to challenge or stress. Change or suppression of RSA during demanding tasks may be a physiological strategy that allows a child to shift focus from internal homeostatic demands to demands that require internal processing or the generation of coping strategies to control affective or behavioral arousal (Calkins, 1997; DeGangi, DiPietro, Greenspan, & Porges, 1991; Porges, 1996; Fracasso, Porges, Lamb, & Rosenberg, 1994). This ability may foster the development of adaptive behavioral strategies that influence early self-regulated behavior.

Recent research indicates that suppression of RSA during challenging situations is related to better state regulation in infancy (DeGangi et al., 1991), fewer behavior problems and more appropriate emotion regulation in preschool (Calkins, 1997; Porges et al., 1996), and sustained attention in school-age children (Suess et al., 1994). The extension of these research findings is that while the ability to suppress RSA may be related to complex responses involving the regulation of attention and behavior, a deficiency in this ability may be related to early behavior problems, particularly problems characterized by a lack of behavioral and emotional control (Porges, 1996). Such a relation has been identified recently in a study of problem toddlers. Children with early-identified externalizing problems displayed less suppression of RSA than children with no behavior problems during several emotion tasks requiring attention and regulation (Calkins, 1997). There were no baseline RSA differences between the average children and the externalizing children, nor was there a difference in heart rate between these groups. Moreover, physiological regulation, in the form of RSA suppression, may be influenced by early caregiving experiences. In one recent study, maternal negative and interfering behavior was found to be related to low RSA suppression during an emotion task (Calkins, Smith, Gill, & Johnson, 1998).

Studies of autonomic activity, then, are moving toward indexing both temperamental reactivity and emotional regulation along with RSA and RSA changes. In a study conducted by Calkins (1997), basal measures of RSA were correlated with both positive (positively correlated) and negative (negatively correlated) affect in response to emotion-eliciting situations, while suppression of RSA was correlated with emotion-regulating behaviors observed during the tasks. Thus both types of physiological measures are proving to be useful predictors of emotional and social functioning, primarily because both emotional reactivity and emotion regulation appear to play a role in early social behavior and social adjustment problems (Cole, Michel, & O'Donnell, 1994; Eisenberg et al., 1996).

Studies of Brain Electrical Activity

Although the first research relating brain electrical activity to emotions in infants involved the use of videotaped stimuli (see Davidson & Fox, 1982), more recent research has examined more complex emotion processes. Fox and colleagues, for example, have conducted several studies examining both infants' response to brief maternal separation and their response to unfamiliar adults (Fox ct al., 1992; Fox & Davidson, 1987, 1988). Both are strong affect elicitors by the end of the first year of life, and may continue as such during toddlerhood. And, responses to both events may produce individual differences in affective display and approach–avoidance behaviors.

In the first of these studies, Fox and Davidson (1987) observed the responses of 10-month-old infants to the approach of an unfamiliar adult female, the approach and reach of the mother, and departure of the mother from the testing room. Comparisons of the pattern of EEG activation and behavior revealed relations to conditions as well as to individual differences in behavioral response. Greater relative left frontal activation was observed during the mother-reach condition (compared with the mother-enter epoch). And infants who cried at maternal separation showed a larger increase in relative right frontal activation during separation. Interestingly, no association between the stranger approach epoch and EEG activation was observed. Given the differences between infants who cried at maternal separation and those who did not cry, Fox and Davidson conclude that infants who cry and have greater relative right frontal activation may be displaying a lower threshold to stressful events.

In the subsequent analysis of the data from this study, Fox and Davidson (1988) distinguished felt smiles from unfelt (wary) smiles in response to both the mother's and the stranger's approach. Infants were more likely to display felt smiles to the mother and unfelt smiles to the stranger. Moreover, felt smiles were associated with greater relative left frontal activation, while unfelt smiles were associated with greater relative right frontal activation. Fox and Davidson (1991) suggest that this pattern of findings may indicate early indications of behavioral regulation in response to emotion-eliciting events.

To provide additional evidence that differences in patterns of brain electrical activity may be a marker for individual differences in temperament, Fox et al. (1992) examined maternal separation data from two separate samples. Study 1 examined infants at ages 14 and 24 months, whereas Study 2 involved monthly assessments of infants from 7 to 12 months. Across both studies, infants exhibiting greater relative right frontal activation were more distressed to maternal separation than those exhibiting greater relative left frontal activation. Among the infants who were observed from 7 to 12 months, there was stability in both the tendency to be distressed by maternal separation and frontal asymmetry. This study provides additional evidence for the hypothesis proposed by Fox (1991; Fox & Davidson, 1991) that temperamental differences in tendencies to approach or withdraw from certain elicitors may originate in differences in brain asymmetry; it also underscores the role that the frontal region plays in the regulation of emotion in infancy.

Additional evidence for the role of the frontal lobes in the regulation of affective states in infancy comes from the work of Dawson and colleagues (Dawson, Hessl, & Frey, 1994; Dawson, Klinger, Panagiotides, Hill & Spieker, 1992). Dawson's work is notable for its attempt to examine affect across a number of events eliciting both positive and negative affect. She and her colleagues have been especially interested in affective tone and hemispheric differences in infants of mothers exhibiting depressive symptoms. In this work, infants of depressive mothers exhibited less relative left frontal activation during a playful interaction (and potential positive elicitor) with their mothers, and did not exhibit the expected greater relative right frontal activation during maternal separation, during which they showed less distress. These findings indicate that the affective

differences between mothers with and without depressive symptoms may be reflected in both their interactions with their infants, and in the infants' frontal lobe activity. Such a conclusion supports the evidence that interactions with the caretaker both elicit emotional reactivity and provide a forum for the development of affective regulation.

Dawson has further explored the consequences of disturbances in mother–infant affective synchrony in a study of attachment and brain electrical activity in infants of mothers with depressive symptoms (Dawson, Klinger, Panagiotides, Spieker, & Frey, 1992). The findings indicated that more disorganized behavior was observed among infants of mothers with depressive symptoms. No EEG differences were found with respect to either of the two attachment classification systems used, although an interaction of symptomatology and attachment was found. Reduced left frontal activation was found among securely attached infants of mothers with depressive symptoms. Dawson et al. (1994) argue that for some children, the risk for depression derives from the parent's inability to respond to emotional signals and meet emotional needs.

It is clear from these findings that the relation between attachment and patterns of brain activity may be mediated by other factors. One possible mediating factor is emotion regulation, which is likely to be influenced by both biological and behavioral factors and to influence subsequent social behavior (Dawson et al., 1994; Calkins, 1994). We and our colleagues have conducted longitudinal studies of individual differences in EEG, emotion, and social behavior, and this work may help to clarify the role of emotion regulation (Calkins et al., 1996; Fox, Calkins, & Bell, 1994; Fox, Schmidt, Calkins, Rubin, & Coplan, 1996). In the most recent longitudinal study, infants were screened in their homes at 4 months of age; a battery of procedures designed to elicit negative affect, positive affect, and motor activity (Kagan, 1997; Kagan & Snidman, 1991) was used. This screening procedure was designed to select infants who would display inhibited behavior and negative affect at later ages. In the initial phase of the study (Calkins et al., 1996), from a sample of 200 infants seen at 4 months, 81 infants were selected for follow-up visits at 9 and 14 months. At 9 months, EEG was collected during a baseline procedure, and at 14 months, infant behavior was observed in a series of episodes designed to elicit inhibited versus un-inhibited behavior.

The infants who were selected for the follow-up phases of the study were clustered into three groups: (1) infants high on motor activity and negative affect and low on positive affect, (2) infants high on motor activity and positive affect and low on negative affect, and (3) infants who were low on all dimensions. The data from this study reveal that these behavioral tendencies are accompanied by specific patterns of brain electrical activity. Infants selected at 4 months because they displayed high amounts of negative affect and motor activity exhibited greater relative right frontal activation at 9 months. Infants who displayed high amounts of positive affect and motor activity at 4 months exhibited greater relative left frontal activation at 9 months (Calkins et al., 1996). These findings are consistent with findings from the adult literature, which demonstrate that adults with resting right frontal asymmetry are more likely to rate video film clips with negative affect than are adults with left frontal asymmetry. Differences in frontal asymmetry may reflect the fact that the left and right hemispheres are differentially specialized for the expression of emotions associated with either approach or withdrawal (Fox, 1991).

To what degree are these early asymmetry differences stable, and what behavioral consequences are associated with stability? We (Fox et al., 1994) examined this issue and concluded that asymmetry is modestly stable over time and related in important ways to behavioral outcomes. In the follow-up of our selected sample at 24 months of age, we observed that children who maintained a pattern of right frontal asymmetry over the first 2 years of life were more likely to be inhibited, compliant, less impulsive, and high on a measure of frustration tolerance. We speculate that the behavioral display of inhibition is actually a coping response that enables children to manage high levels of biologically based fear. We acknowledge, however, that these emotion regulation behaviors, which are critical to social interaction and social adjustment, are likely to be a consequence of *both* early biological tendencies and patterns of caregiving behaviors (Calkins, 1994; Fox & Calkins, 1993; Fox et al., 1994).

We also speculate that patterns of frontal EEG asymmetry may reflect early dispositions to approach versus withdraw, as well as the capacity for the development of adaptive regula-tory behavior (Fox, 1994; Fox et al., 1996). The frontal brain regions are responsible for verbal mediation, analytic abilities, monitoring, and inhibition of prepotent responses, all of which may be directly tied to emerging emotion regulation skills (Dawson et al., 1994; Fox et al., 1996). Emotional control is a consequence of the dynamic interaction of the frontal regions (Fox, 1994). Again, however, there is good evidence that interactions with caregivers also provide children with opportunities for acquiring affect regulation skills (Calkins & Johnson, 1998; Cassidy, 1994; Thompson, 1994).

Studies Assessing Adrenocortical Activity

The most recent studies relating adrenocortical activity to such constructs as temperament and attachment are being conducted by Gunnar and colleagues (DeHaan, Gunnar, Tout, Hart, & Stansbury, 1997; Gunnar, 1998; Gunnar, Manglesdorf, Larson, & Hertsgaard, 1989; Larson, Gunnar, & Hertsgaard, 1991; Malone, Gunnar, & Fisch, 1985; Tout, DeHaan, Campbell, & Gunnar, 1998). In one such study, infant response to limb restraint was observed and plasma cortisol levels were obtained (Malone et al., 1985). No effects of the limb restraint on cortisol levels was observed, although the procedure of obtaining the cortisol did elicit behavioral distress, which was related to elevated cortisol levels. Clearly, behavioral distress is associated with increased cortisol production, although in this study limb restraint, observed to cause distress in infants (see Stifter & Fox, 1990), may not have created sufficient stress to elevate cortisol levels.

Gunnar has observed the response of the adrenocortical system in response to other elicitors that have been shown to produce distinct patterns of distress responses in many infants. She and her colleagues have observed the salivary cortisol responses of infants to maternal separations at both 9 and 13 months (Gunnar et al., 1989). Gunnar and colleagues observed significant associations between measures of emotional reactivity collected at 9 months and those collected at 13 months. In addition, there were significant associations between salivary cortisol and emotional tone; although the correlations were modest, the pattern of correlations suggests that infants who displayed more positive tone experienced less of an increase in salivary cortisol level from baseline to posttest. And significant relations were found between cortisol levels and emotional response to separation. No relations were found between cortisol levels and attachment classification. The multiple measures collected in this study provide evidence that the adrenocortical response at the end of the first year of life may reflect temperamental or trait-like tendencies toward emotional reactivity. This trait-like tendency may be influencing both physiological and emotional responses to separation at this age (Gunnar et al., 1989; Gunnar, Larson, Hertsgaard, Harris, & Broderson, 1992). Again, we see evidence that emotional responsivity in infancy is tied to dispositional tendencies that may be observed in an interactional setting, and which may trigger underlying physiological responses.

More recent work from this research group, however, presents a more complex picture of the role of the adrenocortical system in social and emotional functioning, and suggests links to more complex social behavior. First, good evidence has emerged from this work that caregiving may buffer cortisol responding. Gunnar and colleagues observed that infants in secure attachment relationships who appeared inhibited in the laboratory were less likely to display elevated cortisol levels than were inhibited insecurely attached infants. Although some children may have the behavioral profile of inhibition, the physiological response does not suggest a high level of stress (Nachmias, Gunnar, Manglesdorf, Parritz, & Buss, 1996). These data suggest that beyond the first year of life, the effects of caregiving may be potent in altering a child's physiological stress response; this may have important implications for subsequent social development.

A second factor that appears to play a role in cortisol responding is the context in which a child is tested. Gunnar and colleagues (DeHaan et al., 1997) found that measures of cortisol reactivity taken at home correlated with shyness, whereas those collected in the school setting correlated with outgoing behavior. These findings are consistent with recent work from Fox's laboratory, where fear at 14 months of age predicted shyness at 4 years of age, and shyness was correlated with morning cortisol collected at home, but not with cortisol collected in the laboratory (Schmidt, Fox, Rubin, & Sternberg, 1997). Gunnar suggests that familiar contexts are better for indexing internalizing-spectrum problems, and that shy children may have de-

veloped coping behaviors that function in the school setting and may serve to alter their experience of stress and anxiety.

A third factor that may play a role in the relations between cortisol and emotions is a child's gender. Gunnar and colleagues (Tout et al., 1998), in a recent study of the relations between cortisol and social behavior, found that for boys externalizing behavior was significantly correlated with cortisol reactivity, while internalizing behavior was significantly correlated with mean cortisol levels over the course of several days. No such relations were found for girls. Given that few sex differences are typically reported in studies of psychophysiological relations in infancy, these differences may emerge as a function of early socialization experiences. Perhaps, as parents interact with children and engage in emotion socialization, strategies acquired by boys versus girls may differentially affect the cortisol–behavior linkages that are typically seen in infancy.

One conclusion to be drawn from the studies of adrenocortical functioning and early emotional and social behavior is that complex, socially influenced regulatory processes play a role in both cortisol reactivity and behavioral responses to stressors. The reactivity of the HPA system has been shown to be quite sensitive to the effects of coping. Gunnar's work demonstrates that particular coping behaviors (such as inhibition) or environmental conditions that support coping (such as a secure attachment relationship) may moderate the relation between HPA activity and behavior (Gunnar, 1994; Gunnar et al., 1992). In such cases, children may display a particular behavioral profile indicative of arousal, but this behavior may not be accompanied by underlying physiological arousal.

CONCLUSION

In this chapter, we have adopted the position that emotion is neither a purely behavioral nor a purely physiological phenomenon. This premise, and methodological developments in the study of infancy, have led to attempts to study both behavioral and physiological manifestations of emotion in infancy. The studies we have reviewed from the past two decades have assessed heart rate, brain electrical activity, and adrenocortical activity in infancy. These studies indicate that (1) there are normative changes occurring in these response systems during the first year of life; (2) there are changes in these response systems that are functions of particular emotion or behavior elicitors; and (3) there are individual differences in the reactivity of these response systems, which may be observed in infancy. Importantly, these studies demonstrate the role that this early reactivity plays in the development of systems of behavioral regulation. Observed differences in physiological responses to particular types of elicitors suggest that what we are in fact observing is a complex interactional system involving emotions, physiology, and interactions with caretakers and others. These constructs are at the core of an infant's developing regulatory system, which serves to integrate and manage emotional and behavioral responses of an infant in addition to, or in lieu of, caretaker regulation.

This review has focused on some of the most recent programs of research collecting multiple measures of infant emotion. Such programs are just beginning to provide a picture of the complex interactions among behavioral and physiological systems that may be observed during infancy. Whereas early work in this area focused on the emotional correlates of physiological measures, more recent work has used longitudinal samples of children to explore both the underlying physiology of emotional behavior, and the contributions of both physiology and emotional behavior to later social functioning. The next decade is likely to see investigators taking aim at lingering challenges in this area, including addressing issues of sex differences, synchrony among multiple physiological systems, and predictors of early psychopathology.

ACKNOWLEDGMENTS

Support for the writing of this chapter was provided by grants from the National Institutes of Health to Nathan A. Fox (Grant No. HD 17899) and Susan D. Calkins (Grant No. MH 55584).

REFERENCES

Ax, A. F. (1953). The physiological differentiation between fear and anger in humans. *Psychosomatic Medicine, 15,* 433–442.

Berger, H. (1929). Uber das Elektrekephalogram de Menschen. *Archives für Psychiatrie und Nervenkrankheit, 87,* 527–570.

Bretherton, I. (1985). Attachment theory: Retrospect and prospect. In I. Bretherton & E. Waters (Eds.), Growing points in attachment theory and research. *Monographs of the Society for Research in Child Development, 50*(1–2, Serial No. 209), 3–38.

Buss, A. H., & Plomin, R. (1984). *Temperament: Early developing personality traits.* Hillsdale, NJ: Erlbaum.

Calkins, S. D. (1994). Origins and outcomes of individual differences in emotional regulation. In N. A. Fox (Ed.), Emotion regulation: Biological and behavioral considerations. *Monographs of the Society for Research in Child Development, 59*(2–3, Serial No. 240), 53–72.

Calkins, S. D. (1997). Cardiac vagal tone indices of temperamental reactivity and behavioral regulation in young children. *Developmental Psychobiology, 31,* 125–135.

Calkins, S. D., & Fox, N. A. (1992). The relations among infant temperament, security of attachment and behavioral inhibition at 24 months. *Child Development, 63,* 1456–1472.

Calkins, S. D., Fox, N. A., & Marshall, T. R. (1996). Behavioral and physiological antecedents of inhibition in infancy. *Child Development, 67,* 523–540.

Calkins, S. D., & Johnson, M. C. (1998). Toddler regulation of distress to frustrating events: Temperamental and maternal correlates. *Infant Behavior and Development, 21,* 379–395.

Calkins, S. D., Smith, C. L., Gill, K. & Johnson, M. C. (1998). Maternal interactive style across contexts: Relations to emotional, behavioral and physiological regulation during toddlerhood. *Social Development, 7,* 350–369.

Campos, J. J., Barret, K. C., Lamb, M., Goldsmith, H. H., & Stenberg, C. (1983). Socioemotional development. In P. H. Mussen (Series Ed.) M. Haith, & J. J. Campos, (Vol. Eds.) *Handbook of child psychology: Vol. 2. Infancy and developmental psychobiology* (4th ed., pp. 783–915). New York: Wiley.

Campos, J. J., Emde, R., Gaensbauer, T., & Henderson, C. (1975). Cardiac and behavioral interrelationships in the reactions of infants to strangers. *Developmental Psychology, 11,* 589–601.

Campos, J. J., Hiatt, S., Ramsay, D., Henderson, C., & Svejda, M. (1978). The emergence of fear of heights. In M. Lewis & L. Rosenblum (Eds.), *The development of affect* (pp. 149–182). New York: Plenum Press.

Cassidy, J. (1994). Emotion regulation: Influences of attachment relationships. In N. A. Fox (Ed.), Emotion regulation: Biological and behavioral considerations. *Monographs of the Society for Research in Child Development, 59*(2–3, Serial No. 240), 228–229.

Cicchetti, D., Ganiban, J., & Barnett, D. (1991). Contributions from the study of high-risk populations to understanding the development of emotional regulation. In J. Garber & K. A. Dodge (Eds.), *The development of emotion regulation and dysregulation* (pp. 15–48). Cambridge, England: Cambridge University Press.

Cole, P., Michel, M. K., & O'Donnell, L. (1994). The development of emotion regulation and dysregulation. In N. A. Fox (Ed.), Emotion regulation: Biological and behavioral considerations. *Monographs of the Society for Research in Child Development 59*(2–3, Serial No. 240), 73–100.

Columbo, J. & Fagan, J. (Eds.). (1990). *Individual differences in infancy.* Hillsdale, NJ: Erlbaum.

Davidson, R. J. (1984). Affect, cognition and hemispheric specialization. In C. E. Izard, J. Kagan, & R. Zajonc (Eds.), *Emotions, cognition, and behavior* (pp. 320–361). New York: Cambridge University Press.

Davidson, R. J., & Cacioppo, J. T. (1992). New developments in the scientific study of emotion. *Psychological Science, 3,* 21–22.

Davidson, R. J., Chapman, J. P., Chapman, L. J., & Henriques, J. B. (1990). Asymmetrical brain electrical activity discriminates between psychometrically-matched verbal and spatial cognitive tasks. *Psychophysiology, 27,* 528–543.

Davidson, R. J., & Fox., N. A. (1982). Asymmetrical brain activity discriminate between positive versus negative affective stimuli in human infants. *Science, 218,* 1235–1237.

Davidson, R. J., & Fox, N. A. (1989). Frontal brain asymmetry predicts infant's response to maternal separation. *Journal of Abnormal Psychology, 98,* 127–131.

Dawson, G., Hessl, D., & Frey, K. (1994). Social influences on early developing biological and behavioral systems related to affective disorder. *Development and Psychopathology, 6,* 759–779.

Dawson, G., Klinger, L. G., Panagiotides, H., Hill, D., & Spieker, S. (1992). Frontal lobe activity and affective behavior of infants of mothers with depressive symptoms. *Child Development, 63,* 725–737.

Dawson, G., Klinger, L. G., Panagiotides, H., Spieker, S., & Frey, K. (1992). Infants of mothers with depressive symptoms: Electroencephalographic and behavioral findings related to attachment status. *Development and Psychopathology, 4,* 67–80.

DeGangi, G., DiPietro, J., Greenspan, S., & Porges, S. W. (1991). Psychophysiological characteristics of the regulatory disordered infant. *Behavior and Development, 14,* 37–50.

DeHaan, M., Gunnar, M., Tout, K., Hart, J., & Stansbury, K. (1997). Familiar and novel contexts yield different associations between cortisol and behavior among two-year-old children. *Developmental Psychobiology, 33,* 93–101.

Eisenberg, N., Fabes, R., Guthrie, I., Murphy, B., Maszk, P., Holmgren, R., & Suh, K. (1996). The relations of regulation and emotionality to problem behavior in elementary school. *Development and Psychopathology, 8,* 141–162.

Ekman, P. (1984). Expression and nature of emotion. In K. R. Scherer & P. Ekman (Eds.), *Approaches to emotion* (pp. 319–344). Hillsdale, NJ: Erlbaum.

Ekman, P., Levenson, R. W., & Friesen, W. V. (1983). Autonomic nervous system activity distinguishes among emotions, *Science, 221,* 1208–1210.

Emde, R. N., Gaensbauer, T. J., & Harmon, R. J. (1976). Emotional expression in infancy: A biobehavioral study. *Psychological Issues, 10,* 1–200.

Fogel, A. (1982). Affective dynamics in early infancy: Affective tolerance. In T. Field & A. Fogel (Eds.), *Emotion and early interaction* (pp. 25–58). Hillsdale, NJ: Erlbaum.

Fox, N. A. (1989). Psychophysiological correlates of emotional reactivity during the first year of life. *Developmental Psychology, 25,* 364–372.

Fox, N. A. (1991). If it's not left, it's right: Electroencephalogram asymmetry and the development of emotion. *American Psychologist, 46,* 863–872.

Fox, N. A. (1994). Dynamic cerebral process underlying emotion regulation. In N. A. Fox (Ed.), Emotion regulation: Biological and behavioral considerations. *Monographs of the Society for Research in Child Development, 59*(2–3, Serial No. 240), 152–166.

Fox, N. A., Bell, M. A., & Jones, N. A. (1992). Individual differences in response to stress and cerebral asymmetry. *Developmental Neuropsychology, 8,* 165–184.

Fox, N. A., & Calkins, S. D. (1993). Pathways to aggression and social withdrawal: Interactions among temperament, attachment, and regulation. In K. Rubin & J. Asendorpf (Eds.), *Social withdrawal, inhibition and shyness in children* (pp. 81–100). Hillsdale, NJ: Erlbaum.

Fox, N. A., Calkins, S. D., & Bell, M. A. (1994). Development and neuroplasticity: Behavioral and cognitive outcomes. *Development and Psychopathology, 6,* 677–696.

Fox, N. A., & Davidson, R. J. (1984). Hemispheric substrates of affect: A developmental model. In N. A. Fox & R. J. Davidson (Eds.), *The psychobiology of affective development* (pp. 353–382). Hillsdale, NJ: Erlbaum.

Fox, N. A., & Davidson, R. J. (1986). Taste-elicited changes in facial signs of emotion and the asymmetry of brain electrical activity in human newborns. *Neuropsychologia, 24,* 417–422.

Fox, N. A., & Davidson, R. J. (1987). Electroencephalogram asymmetry in response to the approach of a stranger and maternal separation. *Developmental Psychology, 23,* 233–240.

Fox, N. A., & Davidson, R. J. (1988). Patterns of brain electrical activity during the expression of discrete emotions in ten-month-old infants. *Developmental Psychology, 24,* 230–236.

Fox, N. A., & Davidson, R. J. (1991). Hemispheric asymmetry and attachment behaviors: Developmental processes and individual differences in separation protest. In J. L. Gewirtz & W. M. Kurtines (Eds.), *Intersections with attachment* (pp. 147–164). Hillsdale, NJ: Erlbaum.

Fox, N. A., Schmidt, L. A., Calkins, S. D., Rubin, K. H., & Coplan, R. J. (1996). The role of frontal activation in the regulation and dysregulation of social behavior during the preschool year. *Development and Psychopathology, 8,* 89–102.

Fox, N. A., & Stifter, C. A. (1989). Biological and behavioral differences in infant reactivity. In G. A. Kohnstamm, J. E. Bates, & M. K. Rothbart (Eds.), *Temperament in childhood* (pp. 169–181). New York: Wiley.

Fracasso, M. P., Porges, S., Lamb, M., & Rosenberg, A. (1994). Cardiac activity in infancy: Reliability and stability of individual differences. *Infant Behavior and Development, 17,* 277–284.

Garcia-Coll, C., Kagan, J., & Reznick, J. S. (1984). Behavioral inhibition in young children. *Child Development, 55,* 1005–1019.

Graham, F. K., & Clifton, R. K. (1966). Heart rate changes as a component of the orienting process. *Psychological Bulletin, 65,* 305–320.

Gunnar, M. R. (1989). Studies of the human infant's adrenocortical response to potentially stressful events. In M. Lewis & J. Worobey (Eds.), *Infant stress and coping* (pp. 3–18). San Francisco: Jossey-Bass.

Gunnar, M. R. (1990). The psychobiology of infant temperament. In J. Columbo & J. Fagan (Eds.), *Individual differences in infancy* (pp. 387–409). Hillsdale, NJ: Erlbaum.

Gunnar, M. (1994). Psychoendicrine studies of temperament and stress in early childhood: Expanding current models. In J. Bates & T. Wachs (Eds.), *Temperament: Individual differences at the interface of biology and behavior* (pp. 175–198). Washington, DC: American Psychological Association.

Gunnar, M. R. (1998). Quality of early care and buffering of neuroendocrine stress reactions: Potential effects on the developing brain. *Preventive Medicine, 27,* 208–211.

Gunnar, M. R., Larson, M., Hertsgaard, L. Harris, M., & Broderson, L. (1992). The stressfulness of separation among nine-month-old infants: Effects of social context variables and infant temperament. *Child Development, 63,* 290–303.

Gunnar, M. R., Manglesdorf, S., Larson, M., & Hertsgaard, L. (1989). Attachment, temperament and adrenocortical activity in infancy: A study of psychoendocrine regulation. *Developmental Psychology, 25,* 355–363.

Gunnar, M., Porter, F., Wolf, C., Rigatuso, J., & Larson, M. (1995). Neonatal stress reactivity: Predictions to later emotional temperament. *Child Development, 66,* 1–13.

Hoffheimer, J. A., Wood, B. R., Porges, S. W., Pearson, E., & Lawson, E. (1995). Respiratory sinus arrhythmia and social interaction patterns in preterm newborns. *Infant Behavior and Development, 18,* 233–245.

Lewis, M., & Ramsay, D. S. (1995a). Developmental change in infants' response to stress. *Child Development, 66,* 657–670.

Lewis, M., & Ramsay, D. S. (1995b). Stability and change in corisol and behavioral response to stress during the first 18-months of life. *Developmental Psychobiology, 28,* 419–428.

Kagan, J. (1997). Temperament and the reactions to unfamiliarity. *Child Development, 68,* 139–143.

Kagan, J., Reznick, J. S., & Snidman, N. (1987). Physiology and psychology of behavioral inhibition. *Child Development, 58,* 1459–1473.

Kagan, J., & Snidman, N. (1991). Temperamental factors in human development. *American Psychologist, 46,* 856–862.

Kopp, C. (1982). Antecedents of self-regulation: A developmental perspective. *Developmental Psychology, 18,* 199–214.

Lacey, J., & Lacey, B. (1970). The relationship of resting autonomic activity to motor impulsivity. *Research*

Publications of the Association for Research in Nervous and Mental Disease, 36, 144–209.

Larson, M., Gunnar, M., & Hertsgaard, L. (1991). The effects of morning naps, car traps, and maternal separation on adrenocortical activity in human infants. *Child Development, 62,* 362–372.

Levenson, R. W., Ekman, P., & Friesen, W. (1990). Voluntary facial expression generates emotion-specific autonomic nervous system activity. *Psychophysiology, 27,* 363–384.

Lindsley, D. B., & Wicke, J. D. (1974). The electroencephalogram: Autonomous electrical activity in man and animals. In R. Thompson & M. N. Patterson (Eds.), *Bioelectric recording techniques* (pp. 465–479). New York: Academic Press.

Malatesta, C. Z., Culver, C., Tesman, J., & Shephard, B. (1989). The development of emotion expression during the first two years of life. *Monographs of the Society for Research in Child Development, 54*(1–2, Serial No. 219).

Malone, S., Gunnar, M. R., & Fisch, R. (1985). Adrenocortical and behavioral responses to limb restraint in human neonates. *Developmental Psychobiology, 18,* 435–446.

Matheny, A. P., & Wilson, R. S. (1981). Developmental tasks and rating scales for the laboratory assessment of infant temperament. *JSAS: Catalog of Selected Documents in Psychology, 11,* 81–82.

Nachmias, M., Gunnar, M., Manglesdorf, S., Parritz, R., & Buss, K. (1996). Behavioral inhibition and stress reactivity: Moderating role of attachment security. *Child Development, 67,* 508–522.

Porges, S. W. (1991). Vagal tone: An autonomic mediator of affect. In J. Garber & K. A. Dodge (Eds.), *The development of emotion regulation and dysregulation* (pp. 111–128). Cambridge, England: Cambridge University Press.

Porges, S. W. (1996). Physiological regulation in high-risk infants: A model for assessment and potential intervention. *Development and Psychopathology, 8,* 43–58.

Porges, S. W., & Byrne, E. A. (1992). Research methods for measurement of heart rate and respiration. *Biological Psychology, 34,* 93–130.

Porges, S. W., Doussard-Roosevelt, J., Portales, L., & Greenspan, S. I. (1996). Infant regulation of the vagal "brake" predicts child behavior problems: A psychobiological model of social behavior. *Developmental Psychobiology, 29,* 697–712.

Porges, S., Doussard-Roosevelt, J., Portales, L., & Suess, P. (1994). Cardiac vagal tone: Stability and relation to difficultness in infants and 3-year-olds. *Developmental Psychobiology, 27,* 289–300.

Richards, J. E. (1985). Respiratory sinus arrhythmia predicts heart rate and visual responses during visual attention in 14- and 20-week-old infants. *Psychophysiology, 22,* 101–109.

Richards, J. E. (1987). Infant visual sustained attention and respiratory sinus arrhythmia. *Child Development, 58,* 488–496.

Richards, J. E., & Cameron, D. (1989). Infant heart rate variability and behavioral developmental status. *Infant Behavior and Development, 12,* 45–58.

Rothbart, M. K. (1981). Measurement of temperament in infancy. *Child Development, 52,* 569–578.

Rothbart, M. K. (1989). The early development of behavioral inhibition. In S. Reznick (Ed.), *Perspectives on behavioral inhibition* (pp. 139–158) Chicago: University of Chicago Press.

Rothbart, M. K., & Derryberry, D. (1981). Development of individual differences in temperament. In M. E. Lamb & A. L. Brown (Eds.) *Advances in developmental psychology* (Vol. 1, pp. 37–86). Hillsdale, NJ: Erlbaum.

Ruff, H., & Rothbart, M. K. (1996). *Attention in early development.* New York: Oxford University Press.

Schmidt, L. S., Fox, N. A., Rubin, K., & Sternberg, E. (1997). Behavioral and neuroendocrine responses in shy children. *Developmental Psychobiology, 30,* 127–140.

Stansbury, K., & Gunnar, M. (1994) Adrenocortical activity and emotion regulation. In N. A. Fox (Ed.), Emotion regulation: Biological and behavioral considerations. *Monographs of the Society for Research in Child Development, 59*(2–3, Serial No. 240), 108–134.

Stifter, C. A., & Fox, N. A. (1990). Infant reactivity: Physiological correlates of newborn and 5-month temperament. *Developmental Psychology, 26,* 582–588.

Stifter, C. A., Fox, N. A., & Porges, S. W. (1989). Facial expressivity and vagal tone in five- and ten-month-old infants. *Infant Behavior and Development, 12,* 127–137.

Stifter, C. A., & Jain, A. (1996). Psychophysiological correlates of infant temperament: Stability of behavior and autonomic patterning from 5 to 18 months. *Developmental Psychobiology, 29,* 379–391.

Suess, P. E., Porges, S. W., & Plude, D. J. (1994). Cardiac vagal tone and sustained attention in school-age children. *Psychophysiology, 31,* 17–22.

Thompson, R. A. (1990). Emotion and self-regulation. In R. A. Thompson (Ed.), *Nebraska Symposium on Motivation: Vol. 36. Socioemotional development* (pp. 367–467). Lincoln: University of Nebraska Press.

Thompson, R. A. (1994). Emotion regulation: A theme in search of a definition. In N. A. Fox (Ed.) Emotion regulation: Biological and behavioral considerations. *Monographs of the Society for Research in Child Development, 59*(2–3, Serial No. 240), 25–52.

Tout, K., DeHaan, M., Campbell, E. K., & Gunnar, M. (1998). Social behavior correlates of cortisol activity in childcare: Gender differences and time-of-day effects. *Child Development, 69,* 1247–1265.

Tronick, E. Z. (1989). Emotions and emotional communication in infants. *American Psychologist, 44,* 112–119.

CHAPTER 14

Vocal Communication of Emotion

Tom Johnstone
Klaus R. Scherer

FROM EXPRESSION
TO COMMUNICATION

There is a growing consensus among emotion psychologists that emotion needs to be viewed as a multicomponent entity (Frijda, 1986; Lang & Cuthbert, 1984; Lazarus, 1991; Lewis & Michalson, 1983; Scherer, 1984; Smith & Ellsworth, 1985). Rather than treating subjective experience or feeling as a synonym of emotion, psychologists now generally consider it just one of several components of the total emotion construct. Two other major components are neurophysiological response patterns (in the central and autonomic nervous systems) and motor expression (in face, voice, and gesture). These three components—feeling, physiology, and expression—are often referred to as the "emotional reaction triad." Many theorists favoring a componential view include the evaluation or appraisal of the antecedent event and the action tendencies generated by the emotion, as components of the emotional process (see Frijda, 1986; Lazarus, 1991; Scherer, 1984; Smith & Ellsworth, 1985).

In considering emotion as a phylogenetically evolved, adaptive mechanism that facilitates an organism's attempt to cope with important events affecting its well-being, Scherer (1984, 1993) has proposed that changes in the respective components are integrated or synchronized within the emotion episode. This proposal is based on the assumption that all the resources of an organism need to be mobilized, and all systems coupled, in order to maximize the organism's chances to cope with an important event. Since all components interact with each other, changes in one component will produce changes in another. For example, the elevated respiration rate required for increased oxygen supply under arousal will affect facial expression (mouth shape) and vocal expression (changes in subglottal pressure) as well as a number of peripheral physiological parameters.

Ever since Darwin's (1872) pioneering work on the expression of emotions in humans and animals, expressive behaviors have been explained as consequences of other adaptational responses (as described above) or as functional responses in their own right (e.g., facial muscle movements to block odor intake or to sharpen the vision; preparatory movements for intended action; see Ekman, 1972; Ekman & Friesen, 1975; Frijda & Tcherkassof, 1997; Scherer, 1992; Smith & Scott, 1997). However, the motor expression component occupies a special role in this adaptational context: It extends the adaptational response beyond the boundary of the individual and his or her action potential, by communicating the individual's reaction to an event and intention to act in a certain way (the action tendency) to the social environment. Once expressive motor behavior starts to serve as a signal, there will be selective shaping of functionally based movements for the purpose of communication, through processes such as ritualization, formalization, or symbolization (see Chevalier-Skolnikoff, 1973; Eibl-Eibesfeldt, 1984; Leyhausen, 1967; Redican, 1982; Schneider & Dittrich, 1990; Van Hooff, 1972).

Scherer and his collaborators have suggested acknowledging the dual determinants of expressive signals by differentiating between "push effects," in which physiological processes such as respiration and muscle tone push expressions in a certain direction, and "pull effects," in which external factors such as social norms or listener expectations pull expressions in a certain direction (Scherer, Helfrich, & Scherer, 1980). In the case of push effects, internal support and action subsystems will affect the production of vocalization in an essentially nondirective manner. For example, increased muscle tension produced by ergotropic arousal can affect breathing patterns, the functioning of the vocal folds, the shape of the vocal tract, and facial expression. In addition, the behaviors resulting from a particular emotional state, such as threat postures and rapid movement, will affect vocalization (Zahavi, 1982). Thus, as muscle tone is likely to be higher in sympathetic arousal, the fundamental frequency of the voice (F_0) will also be higher. Pull effects, on the other hand, are governed by physical communication conditions (e.g., noise), social norms or conventions such as display rules, listener expectations, or other context factors. These pull effects influence the production of signs by specifying a particular motor target pattern, as opposed to mental concepts or internal physiological processes that push out expression (for detailed discussions of push and pull effects, see Scherer, 1985; Scherer & Wallbott, 1990). Of course, once a signal has been symbolized through consistent shaping by pull effects, it acquires representational status.

To describe the functions of emotional expression, Scherer (1992) has suggested using the "organon" model of Bühler (1934). In this model, an expressive behavior has three functions: as a symbol representing the component of emotion it stands for; as a symptom of the state of the expressor; and as an appeal, or signal, designed to elicit a response from the receiver(s). The vervet monkey alarm call (Marler, 1984), for example, serves all three of these functions: It functions as a symbol of different

predators, as a symptom of the fear state of the animal, and as an appeal to others to run away. Furthermore, these functions are mutually interdependent. For example, if a call refers to an air predator, both the emotional reaction and the appeal may be very different from those made in reference to a ground predator. In the first case, both emitter and receiver might seek shelter under a bush and freeze; in the second, they might become highly activated and run up a tree.

The tripartite nature of emotional expression—serving as a symptom of changes in organismic subsystems; as a communicative act; and, in its symbolized form, as a representational sign—is at the root of many of the current debates about the nature of expression. Much confusion can result from overemphasis on one of these three functions. For example, Dawkins and Krebs (1978) and Caryl (1979) have highlighted the appeal function, claiming that most if not all expressive behavior can be explained as strategic intention signaling. More recently, Fridlund (1994), opposing a "readout view" of expression, has reiterated the concept of strategic intention movements, in what he calls a new "behavioral ecology view" of expression. Such views appear to neglect the involuntary physiological changes accompanying emotional arousal—changes that affect facial and vocal expression independently of any intentional effort (e.g., the respiration changes due to stage anxiety will affect a speaker's glottal pulses and thus change voice quality, in spite of powerful intentions to keep the voice straight). Furthermore, the claim that virtually all expressive behavior is exclusively determined by strategic intentions and does not provide any reliable information about underlying states has been strongly challenged by Hinde (1981), who has shown that there are many situations in which truthful signaling is clearly advantageous to the sender. In other cases, where there is a conflict between several behavioral alternatives (e.g., fight and flight), maximum ambiguity in the meaning of the expressive display, rather than outright deceit, would seem to be the optimal strategy. Similarly, Zahavi (1982) has shown that an individual who feels superior in an agonistic encounter does not gain by deception, whereas the weaker individual actually stands to lose: Producing the deceptive signal is costly and may reduce the chances for successful flight (e.g., by depleting energy).

Zahavi concludes that the cost of the signal is what selects for its reliability.

One can argue that the sincerity attributed to a sender is directly correlated with the extremeness (and thus the cost in terms of both muscular exertion and social image) of an affect display, and that the closer a signal comes to being determined by push effects, the more trustworthy it is seen as being. Scherer (1994) has predicted that "raw" affect vocalizations will be interpreted as more spontaneous and reliable signals, as well as more truly felt, than will conventionalized, ritualized "vocal emblems," produced in a socially stereotyped way with "typical intensity" (cf. Hinde, 1981). For example, the pain experienced by a sender emitting an unarticulated roar seems more real to us than the one indicated by the use of conventionalized emblems such as "Ouch!" For the sake of credibility of the signaled state, pull effects cannot move too far away from the original push effects on which they are based (except, of course, for expressions with iconic or arbitrary coding of external referents).

Quite apart from cost aspects, the efficacy of strategic deceit clearly depends on the general reliability of the signal as an index of the emotional state that is actually present. For example, counterfeit money only works if the real money actually buys something. It is difficult to envisage an economy with only counterfeit money circulating. Similarly, if an expressive signal does not represent anything but the (potentially deceptive) intent of the signaler (and if, in addition, it is a cheap signal), it will quickly lose its value. Of course, the matter is frequently complicated by the fact that the emotional process underlying expressive signaling is often highly complex and even conflictual, with different action tendencies and behavioral intentions being activated, and pull effects (including those generated by strategic considerations) constantly changing the signal.

MULTIPLE DETERMINANTS OF THE NATURE OF AFFECT VOCALIZATION

In discussing the origins and functions served by emotional expression, we have touched in the preceding section upon how a range of push and pull factors shape the resulting speech signal. Things are further complicated

by the way in which the components of the human speech system subserve many other functions that are indirectly, or not at all, linked to emotional communication. How these multiple systems manage to fulfill their functions simultaneously is a largely unaddressed question. For example, in the case of respiration, it is unclear whether the respiratory requirements of speech have priority over, or are subservient to, the demands of the emotional response system. Perhaps there is a tradeoff between the two systems, whereby an effort is made to satisfy all needs, albeit suboptimally. In addressing such questions, we need to consider the multiple determinants, both push and pull, of vocal affect expression.

Physiology

The most fundamental determinants of vocal affect are the physiological changes that accompany emotions, which in turn produce changes in the functioning of the vocal production systems (see Scherer, 1986, for a thorough treatment). In summary, it is accepted by many emotion psychologists that emotions are accompanied by various adaptive responses in the autonomic and somatic nervous systems (Cacioppo, Berntson, Larsen, Poehlmann, & Ito, Chapter 11, this volume; Levenson, Ekman, Heider, & Friesen, 1992; Öhman, 1994; Smith, 1989; Stemmler, 1996). These responses will lead to changes in the functioning of parts of the speech production system, such as respiration, vocal fold vibration, and articulation. For example, with a highly aroused emotion such as rage, increased tension in the laryngeal musculature coupled with raised subglottal pressure will provoke a change in the production of sound at the glottis, and hence a change in voice quality. Whether or not the physiological responses (and hence the resulting vocal changes) that accompany emotions are emotion-specific is an ongoing topic of debate. Scherer (1986) has suggested, however, that it is feasible to formulate a number of concrete predictions about the physiological, and hence the vocal, reactions in response to appraisal profiles that generate specific needs for organismic adaptation.

Cognitive and Attentional Constraints

Certain emotional situations impose high demands on attention and cognition, with the result that speech planning and execution can be expected to suffer, leading to changes in speech fluency and prosody. The presence of new and unexpected information, leading to an orienting response and refocusing of attention (as in surprise), can cause speech errors and interruptions. Emotions such as anxiety, which entail sustained cognitive workload, adversely affect speech planning and execution (Tolkmitt & Scherer, 1986). In contrast, other emotions (e.g., contentment) may improve speech fluency through the minimizing of extraneous, distracting thoughts. In summary, the effect of any emotion on speech will depend on the attentional and cognitive conflict between the speaker's emotional response and the focus of speech. There is also evidence that focusing of attention and cognitive load are accompanied by physiological changes, such as different breathing styles (Boiten, 1993), which are likely to affect the voice.

Vocal Transmission Characteristics

One feature of vocal expression is that it is optimally suited to relatively indirect communication over long distances. Visual contact between speaker and listener is not necessary. Moreover, sound can be used to attract attention, as listeners almost always have their listening "turned on" and open to sounds coming from virtually any source (Scherer, 1994). In contrast, over long distances the voice is not a particularly private medium. One might predict that these characteristics of the vocal channel make it more suitable for the signaling of certain emotions than of others. This hypothesis is consistent with the fact that different emotions are expressed and perceived more or less easily in the voice. For example, fear and alarm are among the most clearly vocally expressed emotions. There is obvious adaptive benefit to being able to warn cohorts of danger by communicating such affective states over long distances. Disgust, on the other hand, has been found to be universally badly communicated in the voice, possibly because it is an emotion that, from an evolutionary perspective, needs to be communicated only over relatively short distances and can thus be expressed very well visually. (There are, however, other ways of expressing disgust vocally, which are intimately connected to the physiological reaction to disgusting stimuli. See Scherer, 1994, and the section on decoding studies, below.)

Role of Language

One of the most obvious, but possibly most complicated, examples of how a functional system quite distinct from emotion can nevertheless have an effect on emotional expression is the use of the voice as a carrier signal for language. Human speech has been grafted onto a phylogenetically older vocal call system that was mainly used for affective and social signaling. It is unclear to what extent the evolution of spoken language might have been constrained by the affective signaling system, or alternatively how spoken language in its present form constrains emotional expression. There is overwhelming evidence that the two systems can be dissociated; that is, they can function independently of one another (Gorelick & Ross, 1987; Lieberman & Michaels, 1962; Ross, 1984; Scherer, Ladd, & Silverman, 1984; Starkweather, 1956). Some research has shown less use of short term changes in fundamental frequency to express emotion in tone languages (in which short-term F_0 contours are used to carry lexical information) than in Indo-European languages (in which F_0 plays no lexical role) (Ross, Edmondson, & Seibert, 1986). Thus it seems that in some cases at least, use of a particular acoustic feature in spoken language limits its use for the communication of emotion.

It is also likely that, in parallel with the development of spoken language, more formal, prototypical ways of expressing emotions or at least emotional attitudes (e.g., contempt, sarcasm, and curiosity) have been established. These affective representations, which could be described as a type of "affective pragmatics," are partly determined by cultural norms, such as rules governing politeness and etiquette in speech; they thus probably vary across cultures and languages. They are also likely to be enlisted for strategic social aims, as discussed earlier in this chapter and in Scherer (1988). Such emotion prototypes however, have been based upon, and thus still reflect, original push factors (Scherer, 1986; Scherer, Banse, & Wallbott, 1999).

RESEARCH EVIDENCE ON THE ENCODING OF EMOTION

Until recently there was little systematic knowledge about the details of the encoding of emotion in the voice, in terms of either the externalization of underlying psychophysiological states or the realization of affective pragmatics. A growing interest in emotion psychology, coupled with progress in speech science, has led to an increasing number of studies addressing these issues. This section provides an overview of the existing literature in this area and highlights the questions that remain to be answered, as well as a number of new questions that have been brought to light.

Methodology

There is a great amount of variation in the methods that have been used to study the encoding of vocal affect (see Scherer, 1982, 1986; Wallbott & Scherer, 1986). A lack of consistency in number and type of speakers, in number and type of emotions studied, in type of stimulus materials or speech samples used, and in the nature of the context and the eliciting conditions limits the extent to which prior studies can be compared and results accumulated. In the case of choosing suitable speech materials, this reflects a lack of sophistication in designing speech experiments—a problem that can be resolved by adopting some of the standard speech material used in mainstream speech science. Speakers have ranged from university students to radio professionals, pilots, and actors, with actors being the most common. Since acted portrayals probably represent culturally shaped prototypes of affective speech, their use in encoding studies is valid; however, this needs to be supplemented by other types of affective speech occurring as a result of genuine emotions, either induced in the laboratory or observed in natural settings.

Martin (1990) provides an overview of the techniques that have been used in the induction of emotions, which include emotional stories, pictures, music, or films and mental imagery. Computer games and tasks are other possible techniques for the induction of real emotions in the laboratory and have begun to be used in various forms by researchers (Anderson & Ford, 1986; Banse, Etter, Van Reekum, & Scherer, 1996; Kaiser, Wehrle, & Edwards, 1994; Kappas, 1997; MacDowell & Mandler, 1989; Van Reekum, Johnstone, & Scherer, 1997). Computer games can be programmed to manipulate emotion-eliciting situations while controlling for extraneous factors, and are more interactive than other induction techniques. The problem with all of these methods, however, is

that ethical constraints prevent anything but the induction of low-magnitude emotions, which may not provide sufficient power for their differentiation on the basis of vocal cues. The study of "real-life" emotional speech in natural situations is difficult because of the poor acoustic recording conditions usually present. One obvious candidate for the study of fairly intense emotions is sporting events, where competitors, spectators, and commentators alike often experience a range of emotions of quite high intensity. "Real-life" and confrontational television programs are also intriguing possibilities for gathering emotional speech, although the ethics of such programs are perhaps more dubious than many laboratory studies that have been disallowed by university ethics committees.

Acoustic Measures of Emotional Speech

In principle, the encoding of emotion in the voice can be measured at any of a number of stages, from the physiological changes in various parts of the vocal production system to the perceptual judgment of vocal quality by a listener. The decision as to which stage (or stages) is most suitable depends on the specific research project and its goals. In order for researchers to be able to integrate data across both encoding and decoding studies, however, measurement of the physical (i.e., acoustic) properties of the propagating speech sound is most appropriate. Many acoustic measures of human speech and vocal sounds have fairly well-understood relationships with perceived aspects of speech. Although the relationships between the physiology of speech production and the resulting acoustic signal are less clear, there exists a large and rapidly expanding literature on the subject (see Borden & Harris, 1994, for an overview of speech production and perception). Acoustic analysis thus allows a comparison of studies of emotion encoding in speech with studies focused on the decoding or perception of expressed emotion (which will be discussed in the next section).

For the sake of our discussion here, we subdivide acoustic measures of speech into four categories: time-related measures, intensity-related measures, measures related to fundamental frequency, and more complicated time–frequency–energy measures. The first three categories are linked mainly to the perceptual dimensions of speech rate, loudness, and pitch, respectively, whereas the fourth category has more to do with perceived timbre and voice quality. Since speech is a rapidly changing, dynamic signal, most standard acoustic variables are measured over very short speech segments, over which it can be assumed that the signal is relatively stable. To obtain long-term or suprasegmental measures, the short-term acoustic variables can be aggregated over longer time frames. Since emotion is assumed to be a fairly long-lasting phenomenon, most research to date has used this approach, typically aggregating variables over single or multiple phrases or sentences. As research leads to more precise hypotheses, especially concerning affective pragmatics, it will be necessary to examine emotional speech at shorter time scales. The following discussion is a brief introduction to the four acoustic categories and their associations with speech production and perception; many texts offer a more detailed treatment of the acoustics of speech (e.g., Borden & Harris, 1994; Deller, Proakis, & Hansen, 1993).

Time-Related Measures

The speech signal consists of a temporal sequence of different types of sounds (those corresponding to vowels, consonants, and interjections) and silence, all of which can be carriers of affective information. The most conceptually simple time-related measures of speech are the rate and duration of both vocal sounds and pauses, which are expected to vary for different expressed emotions. In practice, however, there exist no clear guidelines as to which basic units of vocal sound are most appropriate for the analysis of emotional speech. Past research has been limited mostly to measures of overall phrase duration and word rate. A similar problem exists for measurements of silence. It seems necessary to distinguish between different types of silence, such as micropauses that might occur between words or phrases, and longer pauses reflecting hesitations.

Intensity-Related Measures

Although the amplitude of a speech signal is a direct measure of the sound pressure, an acoustic measure that more closely reflects both the production and perception of speech is intensity. Intensity is a measure of the amount of energy in a speech signal, and therefore re-

flects the effort required to produce the speech. It is also the case that the perceived loudness of speech depends on the intensity rather than the amplitude. The standard unit used to quantify intensity is a logarithmic transform of the intensity, called the decibel (dB).

Although it is quite easy to measure, the intensity of speech is dependent on several factors other than those that are (usually) of interest. The distance and orientation of the speaker relative to the microphone, the acoustic characteristics of the recording location, and the calibration of the recording equipment must all be carefully controlled if intensity measurements are to be free of artifacts. Despite these issues, both intensity and variability of intensity have been shown to be useful acoustic variables in the measurement of affect.

Measures Related to Fundamental Frequency

One of the most frequently used vocal cues is fundamental frequency, measured in cycles per second, or hertz (Hz). F_0 is the rate at which the vocal folds open and close across the glottis, and it strongly determines the perceived pitch of the voice. It varies continuously and often quite rapidly, as a function of both linguistic and paralinguistic aspects of speech. Over the course of a phrase or utterance, F_0 can be quantified in terms of F_0 floor (the base level of F_0 during the utterance) and F_0 range (the extent to which F_0 rises above the floor level during the utterance). Other measures derived from F_0 include F_0 variance, F_0 skewness, and jitter, which is the extent to which the time for the vocal folds to open and close fluctuates rapidly and randomly from one vocal cycle to the next. Although mean F_0 has been used in a number of studies of vocal affect, its continued use is discouraged except for comparison with previous research, as its value really reflects the combined effects of F_0 floor and F_0 range.

More complicated F_0-related acoustic variables have been proposed to examine the relative power of the fundamental frequency and the harmonics (F_1, F_2, etc.), which is determined by the manner in which the vocal folds open and close. Some of these, such as the ratio of F_1 to F_0 and the spectral slope of the glottal spectrum, have been used as indicators of voice quality (Klatt & Klatt, 1990). Unfortunately, measurement of these parameters necessitates that the frequency characteristics of the vocal fold vibration be separated from those due to the vocal tract resonance; this involves an estimation process (usually inverse filtering) that is at best highly mathematically complicated, and at worst very unreliable.

Combined Time–Frequency–Energy Measures

During speech the morphology of the vocal tract is varied by placement of the various articulators (i.e., tongue, lips, teeth) in different configurations. Each articulatory configuration produces a specific pattern of resonant frequencies, thus forming the individual sounds (phonemes) of a language. It is customary to characterize each phoneme by the amplified frequencies corresponding to that phoneme, which are called "formants." Although the formants primarily carry phonetic information, they are still affected by changes to the vocal tract that accompany different emotions, such as changes to articulator muscle tension and salivation. The amount of resonance (formant amplitude) and the range of frequencies amplified in a given formant (formant bandwidth) may change considerably with different emotional states. Unfortunately, analysis of the formants of speech is a time-consuming process riddled with methodological pitfalls, and thus it has rarely been applied to the study of affective speech.

A related measure is the "long-term average spectrum" (LTAS), which is the distribution of energy over a range of frequencies, averaged over an extended time period (at least 30 seconds). Calculated separately for the voiced and unvoiced sections of speech, the LTAS is an attempt to arrive at an estimate of the long-term resonance characteristics of the vocal tract by "averaging out" all the phoneme-dependent variation, such as that measured in formant analysis. The remaining measure should reflect both speaker-dependent characteristics and resonant characteristics attributable to fairly long-term changes in speaker state, such as emotions (Pittam, 1987; Pittam, Gallois, & Callan, 1990).

Glottal waveform analysis is a technique yielding a number of parameters that characterize the sound produced at the glottis, prior to the effects of vocal tract resonance. The aim is to quantify aspects of the glottal waveform that can be directly related to the physiology and

mechanics of the opening and closing of the vocal folds (Fant, 1993). Its close relationship to glottal physiology makes it a promising candidate for studies on affective speech.

In addition to using the various types of acoustic measures individually, researchers can obtain more complex variables by combining two of the three dimensions. For example, Scherer and Oshinsky (1977) used variations in the vocal envelope (a measure that combines the amplitude and time dimensions) in studying the attribution of emotional state. Although studies are relatively scarce, there is evidence that the temporal pattern of F_0 change—that is, the form of the intonation contour, may also play an important role in the communication of affect (Cosmides, 1983; Frick, 1985; Mozziconacci, 1995, 1998; Uldall, 1960).

Evidence on Acoustic Correlates of Emotion

Space limitations prevent us from referring in detail to the previous research on the encoding of vocal affect. For more detailed reviews, including extensive references to previous studies, the reader should consult Frick (1985), Scherer (1986), and Banse and Scherer (1996). Below we provide a brief summary of the major findings for the most commonly studied emotions.

1. *Stress.* Although stress is not a single, well-defined emotion, it is useful to start this overview with a look at research on the acoustic indicators of psychological and physiological stress, which were until recently the focus of more research in speech science than specific emotions were. Conditions of high stress or high mental workload have generally been found to lead to raised values of F_0, greater intensity, and lower utterance duration (i.e., faster speech). Stress-induced variation in the position or precision of formants has also been reported in some studies. These results are difficult to interpret, however, because changes to these parameters seem to depend on factors such as the speaker's susceptibility to and strategies for coping with stress, as well as the type of stress (i.e., cognitive or emotional; see Tolkmitt & Scherer, 1986).

2. *Anger.* In general, an increase in mean F_0 and in mean intensity has been found in angry speech. Some studies also show increases in F_0 variability and in the range of F_0 across the ut-

terances encoded. Considering that mean F_0 is not a single acoustic measure, it is not clear whether angry speech has a higher F_0 level or a wider range of F_0 or both. It is possible that those studies finding increased F_0 range and variability have measured "hot" anger or rage, whereas those studies not finding these characteristics may have measured "cold" anger or irritation, as found by Banse and Scherer (1996). F_0 contours tend to be directed downward and articulation rate tends to be generally increased for hot anger. Anger also seems to be characterized by an increase in high-frequency energy, which, together with the increase in intensity, probably reflects greater subglottal pressure leading to more energy in the higher harmonics.

3. *Fear.* Expected high arousal levels for fear are consistent with convergent evidence showing increases in intensity, mean F_0, F_0 floor, and F_0 range, although Banse and Scherer (1996) found a decrease in F_0 range. As with anger, the increased intensity of fearful speech accompanies an increase in high-frequency energy. Rate of articulation is also higher. Related emotions such as anxiety or worry also show faster articulation, but data on the other variables are less consistent. Some studies have found an increase in mean F_0, but Banse and Scherer (1996) reported a decrease in mean F_0, F_0 floor, and F_0 range. A decrease in intensity for anxious speech has also been reported.

4. *Sadness.* As with fear, the findings converge across the studies that have included sadness. Decreases in mean F_0, F_0 floor, F_0 range, and intensity are usually found (although Banse & Scherer, 1996, reported increased F_0 range), as are downward-directed F_0 contours. Corresponding to the decrease in intensity, voiced high frequency energy seems attenuated, indicating weaker higher harmonics. Rate of articulation also decreases for sadness. Most studies reported in the literature seem to have studied the quieter, more resigned forms of this emotion, rather than the more highly aroused forms such as desperation (where correlates reflecting arousal are found, such as increased intensity, increased F_0 floor, and increased high-frequency energy).

5. *Joy.* This is one of the few positive emotions frequently studied, most often in the form of elation rather than the more subdued forms, such as enjoyment or happiness. Consistent with the high arousal level that one might expect, there is a strong convergence of findings of increases in mean F_0, F_0 floor, and intensity. F_0 range and F_0 variability are also found to increase. There is also inconclusive evidence for an increase in high-frequency energy and an increase in the rate of articulation. Quieter forms of the emotion, such as contentment, seem to be characterised by relaxed vocal settings, leading to low mean F_0, low F_0 floor, lower intensity, slower articulation, and weaker higher harmonics.

6. *Disgust.* As noted by Scherer (1989), the results for disgust tend not to be consistent across the encoding studies. The few studies that have included this emotion vary in their induction procedures from having an actor simulate emotion to having subjects view unpleasant films and measuring their disgust (or possibly displeasure). The studies using the former procedure found a decrease in mean F_0, whereas those using the latter found an increase in mean F_0. Even within studies, little consistency in the acoustic characteristics of disgusted speech has been found, implying that disgust is simply not well encoded by speakers. This conclusion is echoed in the decoding literature (see below), where disgust is universally reported to be poorly recognized in speech.

7. *Boredom.* Bored speech is generally slow and monotonous, with low F_0 floor, low F_0 range and variability, and slow rate of articulation. Interested speech tends to be the opposite, with large F_0 range and increased speaking rate.

It is evident from this brief review that where there is considerable consistency in the findings, it is usually related to arousal, regardless of the specific quality of the emotion under investigation. This should not, however, be taken as evidence that discrete emotions are not differentiated by vocal cues. Indeed (as we shall see in the ensuing section on decoding studies), given the high recognition of emotions in speech, there must exist emotion-specific acoustic patterns. There are several reasons why acoustic patterns that differentiate emotions with similar arousal have not yet been consistently found.

For one thing, very few acoustic parameters have been measured in most previous studies. Furthermore, the relatively simple acoustic measures employed preclude a finer level of emotion differentiation, because they tend to be exactly those measures that are most affected by physiological arousal. Many more precise acoustic measures, some of which have been mentioned above in the category of "combined time–frequency–energy parameters," could be applied to the analysis of emotional speech. Indeed, ongoing research that makes use of formant analysis, spectral and cepstral analysis, intonation scoring, and inverse filtering of the speech signal to arrive at an estimate of the glottal waveform looks very promising (Bachorowski & Owren, 1995, 1996; Banse & Scherer, 1996; Klasmeyer, 1997).

A second factor limiting the identification of emotion-specific acoustic patterns has been the lack of precision in defining emotional states. As can be seen from the preceding overview, often two or more forms of the same basic, or modal, emotion exist. Examples are anger (rage vs. irritation), happiness (contentment vs. elation), sadness (disappointment vs. distress) and fear (anxiety vs. terror). Although in some sense semantically similar, the different forms often have quite different vocal profiles, neither of which will be discovered if both emotions are lumped together under one label.

The recent study by Banse and Scherer (1996) has shown that a greater range of acoustic parameters, coupled with a better specification of expressed emotions, can result in a sizeable increase in the discriminative power of the acoustic parameters. Further improvements should be possible through greater refinement of the acoustic parameters. For example, it remains unclear how the measures of average voiced spectrum used by Banse and Scherer relate to either vocal tract or glottal waveform characteristics. Measurement of formant frequencies, amplitudes, and bandwidths, as well as measurement of the glottal waveform, would provide better understanding of the underlying processes involved in emotion encoding and might also increase emotion discrimination.

A final word is warranted concerning the effects of individual and cultural differences on affective speech. Although there is overwhelming evidence from decoding studies (see below) that affective speech is quite similar across individuals and cultures, relatively little has been done to quantify these effects in vocal affect encoding. Most commonly the effects of the individual speaker have been factored out of the analyses as an unwanted source of variance. Very few cross-cultural or cross-language studies have been carried out on emotion encoding in the voice.

RESEARCH EVIDENCE ON THE DECODING OF PORTRAYED EMOTION

Accuracy of Decoding Discrete Emotions from Voice Samples

A large number of empirical studies have demonstrated that human listeners as judges can correctly recognize or infer speaker affect state or attitude from voice samples, regardless of the verbal content spoken. In the most common paradigm, speakers (often actors, either amateur or professional) are asked to vocally portray different emotional states through the production of standard utterances (e.g., numbers, letters of the alphabet, nonsense syllables, or standardized sentences). These voice samples are recorded on audiotape and later presented to lay judges, who are requested to identify or categorize the emotion expressed in each of the different portrayals.

Scherer (1989) reviewed about 30 of these studies and computed an average accuracy percentage of about 60% for studies that did not use pathological voice samples or filtered speech. This largely exceeds the percentage to be expected (approximately 12%) if listener judgments were based on guessing or other chance factors. This amount of recognition accuracy is all the more notable, in light of the fact that many of the earlier studies included emotions such as love, pride, or jealousy, which are not part of the set of basic or fundamental emotions (e.g., anger, joy, sadness, fear) generally studied in facial expression research.

More recent, methodologically well-controlled studies confirm Scherer's estimate on overall vocal emotion recognition accuracy. In a study of disgust, surprise, shame, interest, joy, fear, sadness, and anger, van Bezooijen (1984) found a mean accuracy of 65%. Based on another series of studies of five emotions (fear, joy, sadness, anger, and disgust) using different types of listener groups, Scherer, Banse, Wallbott, and Goldbeck (1991) reported a mean accuracy of 56%. Using the same stimulus material, Scherer et al. (1999) conducted a series of cross-cultural studies including eight European countries and one Asian country. They reported an accuracy percentage of 67% for the European countries and 52% for the Asian country (Indonesia). Finally, in the most comprehensive study to date, Banse and Scherer (1996) used a large stimulus set consisting of

14 emotions (in many cases, two members of one emotion family were included—e.g., hot and cold anger) spoken by 12 professional actors. When judgments of emotional voice samples from the same emotion family were aggregated (to render the data comparable to earlier work) the accuracy percentage amounted to 55%. In summary, the accurate recognition of emotion from standardized voice samples using actor portrayals seems to lie near 60%—about five times higher than what would be expected by chance. Although data from cross-cultural studies are still rare, there is some indication (see Frick, 1985; Scherer et al., 1999) that vocal expressions by members of one culture, for at least some emotions, are universally recognized by members of other cultures.

The evidence is similar to what has been found for the accurate recognition of facially expressed emotions (see Keltner & Ekman, Chapter 15, this volume), although the overall accuracy percentage for vocal emotion expressions is somewhat lower than that found in equivalent studies on the decoding of facial expressions (see Table 14.1, reproduced from Scherer, in press). Sadness and anger are best recognized in the voice, followed by fear. For these three emotions, the accuracy percentages are generally similar to those for facial recognition. Joy, which is very well recognized in the face, has rather mixed accuracy percentages in different studies on vocal expression, possibly due to differences with respect to whether quiet happiness or elated joy is being portrayed by the actors. Disgust is at the bottom of the scale, with the accuracy barely above chance level for the voice, although this emotion is reliably recognized in the face.

It is intriguing to speculate about the sources for these differences between emotions. As discussed in the section on the determinants of affective expression, the voice is probably more suited to the expressive and communicative needs of certain emotions than of others. For instance, there is a clear adaptive advantage to being able to warn (fear) or threaten (anger) others in a fairly indirect way over large distances—something for which vocal expression is ideally suited. The high recognition of sadness is less easily explained, although the physiological concomitants of sadness push it in a direction away from most other emotions, so that it might be recognized through its relatively unique vocal profile. In contrast, naturally occurring vocal expressions of disgust probably consist of brief affect bursts or vocal emblems (e.g., "Yuck!") rather than of long sentences spoken with a "disgust-specific" voice quality (see Scherer, 1994). Another possibility is that the variability in the vocal expression of disgust mirrors the diversity of the modalities involved—that is, nasal, oral, and/or visual, as well as moral evaluation (Rozin, Haidt, & McCauley, Chapter 40, this volume).

The patterns of results reported above underline the need to analyze the recognizability of different emotions separately. In addition, confusion matrices should be regularly reported, as errors are not randomly distributed and the patterns of misidentification provide important information on the judgment process. For example, the confusion matrix reported by Banse and Scherer (1996, Table 9, p. 633) provides interesting insights into the potential sources of the errors. Whereas disgust portrayals are generally confused with those of most negative emotions, there are more specific patterns for the other emotions. On the whole, as one might expect, there are many errors between members of the same emotion family. For example, hot anger is confused consistently only with cold anger and contempt; interest is confused more often with pride and happiness than with the other 11 emotions taken together. Rather than considering confusions as errors, one could interpret them as indicators of the vocal similari-

TABLE 14.1. Accuracy (%) of Facial and Vocal Emotion Recognition in Intercultural Studies

	Neutral	Anger	Fear	Joy	Sadness	Disgust	Surprise	Mean
Facial/Western/20		78	77	95	79	80	88	78
Vocal/Recent Western/11	74	77	61	57	71	31		
Facial/Non-Western/11		59	62	88	74	67	77	65
Vocal/Non-Western/1	70	64	38	28	58			

Note. Empty cells indicate that the respective emotions have not been studied in these conditions. Numbers following the slash in the first column indicate the number of cultures studied. From Scherer (1999). Copyright 1999 by Macmillan. Reprinted by permission.

ty or proximity between emotion categories. Banse and Scherer have proposed that the confusion patterns can be largely explained in terms of three dimensions of similarity: quality, intensity, and valence. However, as they have pointed out, if the three dimensions of similarity accounted for all errors, one would expect approximately symmetrical confusions between emotions, which is not always the case. For example, the substantial confusion of elation portrayals with portrayals of hot anger, panic fear, and despair is not mirrored by confusions of portrayals of those three categories with elation portrayals. It is possible that some emotions (e.g., hot anger) may be expressed by a very typical configuration of acoustic features (i.e., an emotion-specific vocal prototype), but that other emotions (e.g., elation) may lack such a unique acoustic profile. In the case of the prototypical expression of emotions, listeners probably use a top-down, pattern-matching recognition process (for an empirical analysis of top-down vs. bottom-up recognition for facial expression, see Wallbott & Ricci Bitti, 1993), whereas decoders confronted with a display of elation may have to analyze the acoustic pattern in a piecemeal, bottom-up fashion. Such bottom-up processing is more likely to be influenced by single prominent features such as high intensity, which in the case of elation makes the stimulus similar to hot anger or despair.

An alternative explanation for the asymmetry in confusions is that decoders have built-in response biases, which in the case of potentially ambiguous information lead to the selection of one emotion over another. Such biases might be based either upon the relative frequency of occurrence of different expressed emotions, or the relative adaptive importance of detecting different emotions in a speaker. It could be argued, for example, that detecting fear or anger (where one's well-being might be at stake) is more important than detecting happiness. These sort of response biases are particularly important to consider in the design of decoding studies. By giving decoders an explanation (either a true one or a cover story) of where the speech samples originated, researchers might unwittingly be installing specific response biases based upon the decoders' expectations of the most likely emotions to be encountered.

The methodology generally used in judgment studies has recently come under severe scrutiny with respect to a number of important issues, such as the presence of explicit or implicit baselines for judgment, the use of between- and within-judgment designs (e.g., all judges judging all stimuli vs. one judge per stimulus), the role of fixed versus open responses, the type of judges used, and so forth (Russell, 1994; but see also Ekman, 1994). Although these issues need to be taken into account, there is growing evidence that under normal circumstances, judgment data are often quite robust with respect to these factors.

Identifying the Acoustic Cues Used in Emotion Inference from Voice

Given that listeners are able to recognize vocally portrayed emotions with better than chance accuracy, one should be able to determine which acoustic cues are used by listeners to attribute specific emotions to a speaker. Even when a listener's attribution is inaccurate, it is still useful to know how the misattribution might relate to the acoustic properties of the spoken expression. Different research strategies have been used to determine the importance of various acoustic cues in judging expressed emotion.

Use of Masking or Subtractive Resynthesis

The first approach consists of commencing with realistic emotion portrayals (from real life or produced by actors) and masking particular verbal/vocal cues to see how this reduces recognition of expressed emotion. Studies by Scherer et al. (1984), Scherer, Feldstein, Bond, and Rosenthal (1985), and Friend and Farrar (1994) have applied different masking techniques (filtering, randomized splicing, playing backward, pitch inversion, and tone–silence coding), each of which removes certain acoustic cues from the speech signal. The systematic use of these techniques thus allows researchers to determine which acoustic cues carry which type of emotional information. Since intelligibility is removed by all of these masking procedures, their application permits the use of natural, "real-life" speech material without biasing listener judgments with emotional verbal content. For example, the study by Scherer et al. (1984) concluded that voice quality parameters and F_0 level covaried with the strength of the judged emotion, conveying emotion independently of the verbal context.

However, different intonation contour types were found to interact with sentence grammar in an all-or-nothing, configurational manner, and conveyed more attitudinal information.

Use of Additive Resynthesis or Synthesis

Recently the quality of speech synthesis has become good enoungh to be used to systematically manipulate different acoustic cues, starting from a neutral synthesized utterance, in an attempt to produce synthetic emotional expressions. In an early study, Lieberman and Michaels (1962) studied the effect of variations of F_0 and envelope contour on emotion inference. Scherer and Oshinsky (1977) studied the effects of several cues (amplitude variation; pitch level, contour, and variation; tempo; envelope; harmonic richness; tonality; and rhythm) on emotion attributions to sentence-like sound sequences and musical melodies. More recent work with the aim of adding emotional expressivity to text-to-speech systems (Murray & Arnott, 1993) has met with mixed success, but nevertheless shows great promise if it can be done in a systematic manner.

Resynthesis techniques make it possible to take neutral natural voices and systematically change different cues via digital manipulation of the sound waves. In a number of studies by Scherer and his collaborators, resynthesis of real utterances has been used to systematically manipulate F_0 level, contour, variability, and range, as well as intensity, duration, and accent structure (Ladd, Silverman, Tolkmitt, Bergmann, & Scherer, 1985; Tolkmitt, Bergmann, Goldbeck, & Scherer, 1988). Listener judgments of apparent speaker attitude and emotional state for each stimulus showed strong direct effects for all of the variables manipulated, with relatively few effects due to interactions between the manipulated variables. Of all variables studied, F_0 range affected the judgments the most, with narrow F_0 range being judged as signaling sadness and wide F_0 range being judged as expressing high-arousal, negative emotions such as annoyance or anger. High speech intensity was also interpreted as a sign of negative emotions or aggression. Fast speech led to inferences of joy, with slow speech judged as a mark of sadness. Only very minor effects for speaker and utterance content were found, indicating that the results are likely to generalize over different speakers and utterances.

Use of Unaltered Emotion Portrayals

It is possible to use acoustic analyses to measure the acoustic characteristics of vocal emotion portrayals (acted or natural), and then to correlate these with the listeners' judgments of the underlying emotion or attitude of the speaker. Several studies of this type have yielded information on which vocal characteristics affect the judges' inference (Scherer, Rosenthal, & Koivumaki, 1972; van Bezooijen, 1984). In one of the most recent and most thorough studies of this type, Banse and Scherer (1996) showed that a large proportion of the variance in judgments of emotion was explained by a set of about 9–10 acoustic measures, including mean F_0, standard deviation of F_0, mean energy, duration of voiced periods, proportion of energy up to 1,000 Hz, and spectral dropoff. Table 14.2 (adapted from Banse & Scherer, 1996, Table 8, p. 632) shows the direction (i.e., positive or negative) of beta coefficients resulting from regressing judges' emotion ratings on the acoustical parameters, as well as the total multiple correlation coefficients. The data indicate that quite specific patterns of acoustic parameters are used to infer different emotional states.

Comparison of Human Judges with Statistical Discrimination

Banse and Scherer (1996, Table 9, p. 633) also compared the performance of human judges to statistical algorithms such as discriminant analysis and jackknifing. Such an approach provides a test of whether the acoustic measures correlated to listener judgments do indeed discriminate the different expressed emotions. If the set of acoustic cues being analyzed is relatively similar to the set being used by listeners, one would expect statistical routines to approach human levels of discrimination. Banse and Scherer found not only that the discrimination rates were very similar, but that there was a high correspondence between the confusion matrices. The use of more sophisticated classification routines, particularly those that allow for easy interpretation of decision rules (such as decision tree algorithms), should shed more light on the way human judges infer speaker state from acoustic characteristics of speech.

Regardless of the analytic and statistical methods used in decoding studies, there is also a need to progress from simply measuring listeners' ability to discriminate between different

TABLE 14.2. Direction of Beta Weights, and Multiple Correlations, Resulting from Regressing Judges' Emotion Ratings on Acoustical Parameters

	Mean F_0	SD F_0	Mean energy	Voiced duration	HI	LFE	R
Hot anger	+	+			−		.63***
Cold anger							.16
Panic	+						.39***
Anxiety	+	−	−				.38***
Despair	+	−		+	+		.44***
Sadness			−			+	.49***
Elation	+					+	.39***
Happiness							.27*
Interest							.18
Boredom	−		+	+			.40***
Shame			−				.38***
Pride	−						.28*
Disgust						−	.17
Contempt	−	+					.36***

Note. Empty cells indicate beta weights not significantly different from zero. HI, Hammarberg index; LFE, proportion of voiced energy up to 1,000 Hz. Adapted from Banse and Scherer (1996). Copyright 1996 by the American Psychological Association. Adapted by permission.
*$p \leq .05$. ***$p \leq .001$.

expressed emotions, toward measuring the perceived quality, reality or authenticity of emotional expressions. Although a listener may be quite able to identify the intended emotion expressed in a spoken sample, this could reflect simply the use of stereotypical emotion prototypes by the speaker, rather than realistic emotion portrayal. This is obviously an important consideration when acted emotions are used in research, but it is equally important in other settings, when for a variety of reasons (e.g., task demands, social pressures) speakers may be acting to some extent. Even if one regards such acted emotional expressions as valid in their own right, it still seems important to examine how these expressions are perceived, compared with more natural affective speech.

CONCLUSIONS

This chapter has highlighted some of the many evolutionary, physiological, cognitive, social, and cultural factors that shape the way humans express and perceive emotions in speech. With such a large and seemingly disparate number of determinants, it might seem as if the topic were too messy to allow us to expect any invariance in empirical findings. Perhaps surprisingly, however, our summary of research into the production and perception of emotional speech has

revealed considerable consistency. On the production side, the evidence is starting to accumulate that humans consistently modify their speech in specific ways to express different emotions. Results of perception studies indicate that emotions expressed in speech are to a large extent successfully detected by a variety of populations, on the basis of an experimentally identifiable set of acoustic parameters. One reason for the consistency in the results is no doubt that most research to date has been limited to settings in which many of the factors described above have been eliminated or controlled for. In addition to further refinement of analysis techniques, and a focus on real as well as acted emotional speech, there is clearly a need for studies that better quantify the relative contribution of culture, language, and social strategy to the vocal comunication of emotion. To address these issues in a manner that allows results from different studies to be integrated and compared, a coordinated, interdisciplinary approach to research on the vocal communication of emotion will be required.

REFERENCES

Anderson, C. A., & Ford, C. M. (1986). Affect of the game player: Short-term effects of highly and mildly aggressive video games. *Personality and Social Psychology Bulletin, 12*(4), 390–402.

Bachorowski, J.-A., & Owren, M. J. (1995). *Vocal expression of emotion is associated with formant characteristics.* Paper presented at the 130th Meeting of the Acoustical Society of America, St. Louis, MO.

Bachorowski, J.-A., & Owren, M. J. (1996). *Vocal expression of emotion is associated with spectral properties of speech.* Paper presented at the 131st Meeting of the Acoustical Society of America, Indianapolis, IN.

Banse, R., Etter, A., Van Reekum, C., & Scherer, K. R. (1996). *Psychophysiological responses to emotion-antecedent appraisal of critical events in a computer game.* Paper presented at the 36th Annual Meeting of the Society for Psychophysiological Research, Vancouver, British Columbia, Canada.

Banse, R., & Scherer, K. R. (1996). Acoustic profiles in vocal emotion expression. *Journal of Personality and Social Psychology, 70*(3), 614–636.

Boiten, F. (1993). Component analysis of task-related respiratory patterns. *International Journal of Psychophysiology, 15*(2), 91–104.

Borden, G. J., & Harris, K. S. (1994). *Speech science primer: Physiology, acoustics and perception of speech* (3rd ed.). Baltimore: Williams & Wilkins.

Bühler, K. (1934). *Sprachtheorie.* Stuttgart: Fischer.

Caryl, P. G. (1979). Communication by antagonistic displays: What can games theory contribute to ethology? *Behaviour, 68,* 136–169.

Chevalier-Skolnikoff, S. (1973). Facial expression of emotion in nonhuman primates. In P. Ekman (Ed.), *Darwin and facial expression* (pp. 11–89). New York: Academic Press.

Cosmides, L. (1983). Invariances in the acoustic expression of emotion during speech. *Journal of Experimental Psychology: Human Perception and Performance, 9,* 864–881.

Darwin, C. (1872). *The expression of the emotions in man and animals.* London: John Murray.

Dawkins, R., & Krebs, J. R. (1978). Animal signals: Information or manipulation? In N. B. Davies & J. R. Krebs (Eds.), *Behavioural ecology* (pp. 282–309). Oxford: Blackwell.

Deller, J. R., Proakis, J. G., & Hansen, J. H. L. (1993). *Discrete-time processing of speech signals.* New York: Macmillan.

Eibl-Eibesfeldt, I. (1984). *Die Biologie des menschlichen verhaltens: Grundriss der Humanethologie.* München: Piper.

Ekman, P. (1972). Universals and cultural differences in facial expression of emotion. In J. R. Cole (Ed.), *Nebraska Symposium on Motivation* (Vol. 19, pp. 207–283). Lincoln: University of Nebraska Press.

Ekman, P. (1994). Strong evidence for universals in facial expressions: A reply to Russell's mistaken critique. *Psychological Bulletin, 115*(2), 268–287.

Ekman, P., & Friesen, W. V. (1975). *Unmasking the face: A guide to recognizing emotions from facial clues.* Englewood Cliffs, NJ: Prentice-Hall.

Fant, G. (1993). Some problems in voice source analysis. *Speech Communication, 13*(1), 7–22.

Frick, R. W. (1985). Communicating emotion: The role of prosodic features. *Psychological Bulletin, 97*(3), 412–429.

Fridlund, A. J. (1994). *Human facial expression: An evolutionary view.* New York: Academic Press.

Friend, M., & Farrar, M. J. (1994). A comparison of content-masking procedures for obtaining judgments of discrete affective states. *Journal of the Acoustical Society of America, 96*(3), 1283–1290.

Frijda, N. H. (1986). *The emotions.* Cambridge, England: Cambridge University Press.

Frijda, N. H., & Tcherkassof, A. (1997). Facial expressions as modes of action readiness. In J. A. Russell & J. M. Fernandez-Dols (Eds.), *The psychology of facial expression: Studies in emotion and social interaction* (pp. 78–102). New York: Cambridge University Press.

Gorelick, P. B., & Ross, E. D. (1987). The aprosodias: Further functional-anatomical evidence for the organization of affective language in the right hemisphere. *Journal of Neurology, Neurosurgery and Psychiatry, 50*(5), 553–560.

Hinde, R. A. (1981). Animal signals: Ethological and games-theory approaches are not incompatible. *Animal Behaviour, 29,* 535–542.

Kaiser, S., Wehrle, T., & Edwards, P. (1994). *Multimodal emotion measurement in an interactive computer game: A pilot study.* Paper presented at the 8th Conference of the International Society for Research on Emotions, Storrs, CT.

Kappas, A. (1997). *His master's voice: Acoustic analysis of spontaneous vocalizations in an ongoing active coping task.* Paper presented at the 37th Annual Meeting of the Society for Psychophysiological Research, Falmouth, MA.

Klasmeyer, G. (1997). Perceptual importance of selected voice quality parameters. *Proceedings of the IEEE International Conference on Acoustics, Speech and Signal Processing, 3,* 1615–1618.

Klatt, D. H., & Klatt, L. C. (1990). Analysis, synthesis, and perception of voice quality variations among female and male talkers. *Journal of the Acoustical Society of America, 87*(2), 820–857.

Ladd, D. R., Silverman, K. E. A., Tolkmitt, F., Bergmann, G., & Scherer, K. R. (1985). Evidence for the independent function of intonation contour type, voice quality, and F_0 range in signaling speaker affect. *Journal of the Acoustical Society of America, 78,* 435–444.

Lang, P. J., & Cuthbert, B. N. (1984). Affective information processing and the assessment of anxiety. *Journal of Behavioral Assessment, 6*(4), 369–395.

Lazarus, R. S. (1991). *Emotion and adaptation.* New York: Oxford University Press.

Levenson, R. W., Ekman, P., Heider, K., & Friesen, W. V. (1992). Emotion and autonomic nervous system activity in the Minangkabau of West Sumatra. *Journal of Personality and Social Psychology, 62*(6), 972–988.

Lewis, M., & Michalson, L. (1983). *Children's emotions and moods: Developmental theory and measurement.* New York: Plenum Press.

Leyhausen, P. (1967). Biologie von Ausdruck und Eindruck (Teil 1). *Psychologische Forschung, 31,* 113–176.

Lieberman, P., & Michaels, S. B. (1962). Some aspects of fundamental frequency and envelope amplitude as related to the emotional content of speech. *Journal of the Acoustical Society of America, 34*, 922–927.

MacDowell, K. A., & Mandler, G. (1989). Constructions of emotion: Discrepancy, arousal, and mood. *Motivation and Emotion, 13*(2), 105–124.

Marler, P. (1984). Animal communication: Affect or cognition? In K. R. Scherer & P. Ekman (Eds.), *Approaches to emotion* (pp. 345–368). Hillsdale, NJ: Erlbaum.

Martin, M. (1990). On the induction of mood. *Clinical Psychology Review, 10*, 669–697.

Mozziconacci, S. J. L. (1995). Pitch variations and emotions in speech. *Proceedings of the XIIIth International Congress of Phonetic Sciences, 1*, 179–181.

Mozziconacci, S. J. L. (1998). *Speech variability and emotion: Production and perception.* Eindhoven: Technische Universiteit Eindhoven.

Murray, I. R., & Arnott, J. L. (1993). Toward a simulation of emotion in synthetic speech: A review of the literature on human vocal emotion. *Journal of the Acoustical Society of America, 93*, 1097–1108.

Öhman, A. (1994). The psychophysiology of emotion: Evolutionary and non-conscious origins. In G. d'Ydewalle, P. Eelen, & P. Bertelson (Eds.), *International perspectives on psychological science: Vol. 2. The state of the art* (pp. 197–227). Hove, England: Erlbaum.

Pittam, J. (1987). The long-term spectral measurement of voice quality as a social and personality marker: A review. *Language and Speech, 30*, 1–12.

Pittam, J., Gallois, C., & Callan, V. (1990). The long-term spectrum and perceived emotion. *Speech Communication, 9*(3), 177–187.

Redican, W. K. (1982). Facial displays of emotion by monkeys and apes: An evolutionary perspective on human facial displays. In P. Ekman (Ed.), *Emotion in the human face* (2nd ed., pp. 212–280). New York: Cambridge University Press.

Ross, E. D. (1984). Right hemisphere's role in language, affective behavior and emotion. *Trends in Neurosciences, 7*(9), 342–346.

Ross, E. D., Edmondson, J. A., & Seibert, G. B. (1986). The effect of affect on various acoustic measures of prosody in tone and non-tone languages: A comparison based on computer analysis of voice. *Journal of Phonetics, 14*(2), 283–302.

Russell, J. A. (1994). Is there universal recognition of emotion from facial expression?: A review of the cross-cultural studies. *Psychological Bulletin, 115*(1), 102–141.

Scherer, K. R. (1982). Methods of research on vocal communication: Paradigms and parameters. In K. R. Scherer & P. Ekman (Eds.), *Handbook of methods in nonverbal behavior research* (pp. 136–198). New York: Cambridge University Press.

Scherer, K. R. (1984). On the nature and function of emotion: A component process approach. In K. R. Scherer & P. Ekman (Eds.), *Approaches to emotion* (pp. 293–318). Hillsdale, NJ: Erlbaum.

Scherer, K. R. (1985). Vocal affect signalling: A comparative approach. In J. Rosenblatt, C. Beer, M.-C. Busnel, & P. J. B. Slater (Eds.), *Advances in the study of behavior* (Vol. 15, pp. 189–244). New York: Academic Press.

Scherer, K. R. (1986). Vocal affect expression: A review and a model for future research. *Psychological Bulletin, 99*, 143–165.

Scherer, K. R. (1988). On the symbolic functions of vocal affect expression. *Journal of Language and Social Psychology, 7*, 79–100.

Scherer, K. R. (1989). Vocal correlates of emotion. In A. Manstead & H. Wagner (Eds.), *Handbook of psychophysiology: Emotion and social behavior* (pp. 165–197). Chichester, England: Wiley.

Scherer, K. R. (1992). Vocal affect expression as symptom, symbol, and appeal. In H. Papousek, U. Jürgens, & M. Papousek (Eds.), *Nonverbal vocal communication: Comparative and developmental approaches* (pp. 43–60). New York: Cambridge University Press.

Scherer, K. R. (1993). Neuroscience projections to current debates in emotion psychology. *Cognition and Emotion, 7*(1), 1–41.

Scherer, K. R. (1994). Affect bursts. In S. H. M. van Goozen, N. E. van de Poll, & J. A. Sergeant (Eds.), *Emotions: Essays on emotion theory* (pp. 161–196). Hillsdale, NJ: Erlbaum.

Scherer, K. R. (1999). Universality of emotional expression. In D. Levinson, J. J. Ponzetti, Jr., & P. F. Jorgenson (Eds.), *Encyclopedia of human emotions* (pp. 669–674). New York: Macmillan.

Scherer, K. R., Banse, R., & Wallbott, H. G. (1999). *Emotion inferences from vocal expression correlate across languages and cultures.* Manuscript submitted for publication.

Scherer, K. R., Banse, R., Wallbott, H. G., & Goldbeck, T. (1991). Vocal cues in emotion encoding and decoding. *Motivation and Emotion, 15*(2), 123–148.

Scherer, K. R., Feldstein, S., Bond, R. N., & Rosenthal, R. (1985). Vocal cues to deception: A comparative channel approach. *Journal of Psycholinguistic Research, 14*, 409–425.

Scherer, K. R., Ladd, D. R., & Silverman, K. E. A. (1984). Vocal cues to speaker affect: Testing two models. *Journal of the Acoustical Society of America, 76*, 1346–1356.

Scherer, K. R., & Oshinsky, J. (1977). Cue utilization in emotion attribution from auditory stimuli. *Motivation and Emotion, 1*, 331–346.

Scherer, K. R., Rosenthal, R., & Koivumaki, J. (1972). Mediating interpersonal expectancies via vocal cues: Differential speech intensity as a means of social influence. *European Journal of Social Psychology, 2*, 163–176.

Scherer, K. R., & Wallbott, H. G. (1990). Ausdruck von Emotionen. In K. R. Scherer (Ed.), *Enzyklopädie der Psychologie. Band C/IV/3 Psychologie der Emotion* (pp. 345–422). Göttingen, Germany: Hogrefe.

Scherer, U., Helfrich, H., & Scherer, K. R. (1980). Paralinguistic behaviour: Internal push or external pull? In H. Giles, P. Robinson, & P. Smith (Eds.), *Language: Social psychological perspectives* (pp. 279–282). Oxford: Pergamon Press.

Schneider, K., & Dittrich, W. (1990). Evolution und Funktion von Emotionen. In K. R. Scherer (Ed.), *Enzyklopädie der Psychologie: Band C/IV/3. Psychologie der Emotion* (pp. 41–114). Göttingen, Germany: Hogrefe.

Smith, C. A. (1989). Dimensions of appraisal and physiological response in emotion. *Journal of Personality and Social Psychology, 56*(3), 339–353.

Smith, C. A., & Ellsworth, P. C. (1985). Patterns of cognitive appraisal in emotion. *Journal of Personality and Social Psychology, 48*(4), 813–838.

Smith, C. A., & Scott, H. S. (1997). A componential approach to the meaning of facial expressions. In J. A. Russell & J. M. Fernandez-Dols (Eds.), *The psychology of facial expression. Studies in emotion and social interaction* (pp. 229–254). New York: Cambridge University Press.

Starkweather, J. A. (1956). Content-free speech as a source of information about the speaker. *Journal of Personality and Social Psychology, 35*, 345–350.

Stemmler, G. (1996). Psychophysiologie der Emotionen [Psychophysiology of emotions]. *Zeitschrift für Psychosomatische Medizin und Psychoanalyse, 42*(3), 235–260.

Tolkmitt, F. J., Bergmann, G., Goldbeck, T., & Scherer, K. R. (1988). Experimental studies on vocal communication. In K. R. Scherer (Ed.), *Facets of emotion: Recent research* (pp. 119–138). Hillsdale, NJ: Erlbaum.

Tolkmitt, F. J., & Scherer, K. R. (1986). Effect of experimentally induced stress on vocal parameters. *Journal of Experimental Psychology: Human Perception and Performance, 12*(3), 302–313.

Uldall, E. (1960). Attitudinal meanings conveyed by intonation contours. *Language and Speech, 3*, 223–234.

van Bezooijen, R. (1984). *The characteristics and recognizability of vocal expression of emotions.* Dordrecht, The Netherlands: Foris.

Van Hooff, J. A. R. A. M. (1972). A comparative approach to the phylogeny of laughter and smiling. In R. Hinde (Ed.), *Non-verbal communication* (pp. 209–241). Cambridge, England: Cambridge University Press.

Van Reekum, C. M., Johnstone, T., & Scherer, K. R. (1997). *Multimodal measurement of emotion induced by the manipulation of appraisals in a computer game.* Paper presented at the 3rd European Conference of Psychophysiology, Konstanz, Germany.

Wallbott, H. G., & Ricci Bitti, P. (1993). Decoders' processing of emotional facial expression: A top-down or bottom-up mechanism? *European Journal of Social Psychology, 23*(4), 427–443.

Wallbott, H. G., & Scherer, K. R. (1986). Cues and channels in emotion recognition. *Journal of Personality and Social Psychology, 51*(4), 690–699.

Zahavi, A. (1982). The pattern of vocal signals and the information they convey. *Behaviour, 80*, 1–8.

CHAPTER 15

Facial Expression of Emotion

Dacher Keltner
Paul Ekman

The study of facial expression has been central to the field of emotion since its inception, and is the continued focus of theoretical controversy and ongoing research (e.g., Ekman, 1973, 1993, 1994; Russell, 1994). Questions as diverse as the structure, biological substrates, and universality of emotion have been addressed with studies that examine facial expression. In this chapter, we address three aims. We first briefly review the history of the study of facial expression. We then review evidence relevant to three long-standing questions: Are facial expressions of emotion best viewed as discrete systems or as dimension-based entities? Are facial expressions accurate indicators of emotion? And in what ways are facial expressions of emotion universal, and in what ways are they culturally specific? Finally, we highlight a new area of investigation—individual differences in facial expression—that promises important discoveries.

HISTORY OF THE STUDY OF FACIAL EXPRESSION OF EMOTION

Research on facial expression began with Darwin's *The Expression of the Emotions in Man and Animals* (1872/1998). To substantiate his theory that expressions are universal, Darwin obtained data from informants in different countries and analyzed observers' responses to different expressions—methods that continue to guide the study of facial expression today. Floyd Allport (1924) proposed an alternative to Darwin's account of universality—species-constant learning. Other early theorists focused on the structure of facial expressions of emotion, and on the nature of the information that expressions convey. Woodworth (1938) proposed a set of six emotion categories to bring order to the variety of responses observers gave when judging the emotion shown in expressions. Schlosberg (1954) proposed three dimensions that underlie categorical judgments. In an influential review, Bruner and Tagiuri (1954) concluded that facial expression does not provide much accurate information. In the 1950s and 1960s there was not much research on facial expression, but Plutchik (1962) and Tomkins (1962, 1963) both provided influential evolutionary accounts of facial expression. Tomkins and McCarter (1964) provided the first evidence that very high agreement could be achieved by observers in the judgment of facial expression. And Tomkins directly influenced both Izard and Ekman in their separate cross-cultural research in the late 1960s. (For a comprehensive analysis of the literature on facial expression from the turn of the century until 1970, see Ekman, Friesen, & Ellsworth, 1972).

Two developments in the late 1960s and early 1970s galvanized the study of facial expression. First, the independently conducted cross-cultural studies by Ekman and his collaborators and by Izard strongly suggested universality in interpreting facial expressions of emotion (Ekman, Sorenson, & Friesen, 1969; Ekman & Friesen, 1971; Izard, 1977). These findings countered prevailing ideas of cultural relativism, and suggested that the study of facial expression is germane to central questions regarding human nature.

Second, researchers developed objective measures of facial expression (Ekman & Friesen, 1978; Izard, 1977), which some emotion researchers used to measure facial activity itself directly, rather than studying observers' judgments of the emotions they saw in an expression (see Ekman & Rosenberg, 1997, for a sample of diverse studies measuring facial activity). Whereas previously facial activity was measured via electromyography, it is far more intrusive and less precise than scoring systems measuring the changes in the appearance of the face. For example, precise measurement clarified contradictory findings on smiles (Ekman & Friesen, 1982; Ekman & Davidson, 1993). Given these conceptual and methodological advances, the study of facial expression now extends to diverse areas of emotion research.

DIMENSIONS OR DISCRETE EMOTIONS

A central question in the field of emotion is whether emotions are better thought of as discrete systems or as interrelated entities that differ along global dimensions, such as valence, activity, or approach or withdrawal (Ekman et al., 1982; Russell, 1997; Schlosberg, 1954). Most discrete-emotions theorists take an evolutionary approach; they posit that each discrete emotion has a different adaptive function that should be served by fundamentally distinct responses. A dimensional approach argues that emotions are not discrete and separate, but are better measured and conceptualized as differing only in degree on one or another dimension (usually three dimensions have been posited). The dimensional perspective is more common among those who view emotions as being socially learned and culturally variable. Four recent developments in the study of facial expression suggest that facial expressions are fruitfully thought of as discrete systems.

Categorical-Judgment Studies

Categorical-judgment studies have addressed whether the perception of facial expressions of emotion is categorical or dimension-based (e.g., Etcoff & Magee, 1992). Studies of the categorical perception of colors and sounds find that within-category distinctions are more difficult to make than between-category discriminations (reviewed in Etcoff & Magee, 1992). On the boundary of two categories, accuracy in discrimination rises. In the studies of the perception of facial expression, continua of facial expressions were computer-generated, with each continuum defined by two endpoints that were prototypical facial expressions of emotion (e.g., anger and fear). The remaining stimuli between the endpoints included facial expressions that varied by equal physical differences. For all possible pairs within a continuum, participants were presented with two target stimuli and then a third stimuli that was identical to one of the first two stimuli, and were asked to indicate which stimulus the third stimulus resembled.

If facial expressions are perceived categorically, one would expect discriminations between faces within a category to be less accurate than between pairs of faces between categories that differed by an equal physical amount (i.e., a categorical-boundary effect). Indeed, the evidence from studies using computer-generated drawings of facial expressions (Etcoff & Magee, 1992) as well as computer-morphed photographs of facial expressions of emotion (Young et al., in press) has yielded boundary effects. There appear to be discrete boundaries between the facial expressions of emotion, much as there are perceived boundaries between different hues or sounds.

Neuropsychological Evidence: Functional Magnetic Resonance Imaging, Lesion, and Disease Studies

Studies of the central nervous system correlates of facial expressions also bear upon the dimensionality versus discrete issue. Discrete-emotions theorists have argued that the experience and perception of different facial expressions of emotion involve distinct central nervous system regions (e.g., Ekman, 1992a; Izard, 1993). Dimensional theorists have proposed that valence is primary in determining the perception of facial expressions (e.g., Russell, 1997), implying that the same brain region might primarily be involved in the perception of different facial expressions of negative emotion. Two kinds of evidence suggest that distinct brain regions are activated in the process of perceiving different negative emotions.

First, one class of studies has presented photographs of facial expressions of emotion and, typically with the use of functional magnetic resonance imaging, has ascertained that the perception of different facial expressions elicits activity in different brain regions. The perception of fearful faces activates regions in the left amygdala (Morris et al., 1996), even when the presentation of the fear face is masked by the presentation of an immediately ensuing neutral expression (Whalen et al., 1998). The perception of sad faces activates the left amygdala and right temporal lobe (Blair, Morris, Frith, Perrett, & Dolan, 1998). The perception of angry faces activates the right orbito-frontal cortex and anterior cingulate cortex (Blair et al., 1998). The perception of disgusted faces activates the anterior insula and limbic coritico-striatal-thalamic region (Phillips et al., 1997). Studies that have measured event-related potentials on the scalp have found that angry, happy, and fearful faces elicit different event-related potentials in children as young as 7 months old (Nelson & de Haan, 1997; Pollack, Cicchetti, Klorman, & Brumaghim, 1997). Finally, preliminary evidence indicates that the stimulation of a specific brain region produces laughter (Fried, Wilson, MacDonald, & Behnke, 1998). It should be noted that whereas dimensional theorists have also claimed that distinctions among negative emotions follow from higher order, effortful inferences (Russell, 1997), the perception of some negative facial expressions of emotion activates the amygdala, which is associated with relatively automatic information processing (LeDoux, 1996).

Second, disease and lesion studies indicate that the perception of different emotions seems to be located in different brain regions. Specifically, lesions to the amygdala impair the ability to recognize fearful facial expressions and vocalizations, but not the ability to recognize facial expressions of sadness (Calder et al., 1996). Individuals suffering from Huntington's disease, which affects the basal ganglia, were unable to recognize disgust expressions accurately but were accurate in judging facial expressions of other negative emotions (Sprengelmeyer et al., 1996). Even carriers of Huntington's disease were unable to recognize facial expressions of disgust (Gray, Young, Barker, Curtis, & Gibson, 1997).

Whereas these previous studies have established that the perception of different facial expressions activates different brain regions, less is known about whether the display of different facial expressions activates different brain regions. Work in progress studying multiple emotions via brain imaging techniques should provide important findings relevant to this matter (Davidson, Ekman, Saron, Senulis, & Friesen, 1990; Ekman, Davidson, & Friesen, 1990).

Facial Expressions of Emotion and Autonomic Physiology

Discrete-emotions theorists have proposed that different emotions, and by implication different facial expressions, are linked to relatively distinct patterns of autonomic nervous system activity. Dimensional theorists, on the other hand, expect the major dimensions of emotion meaning, most notably valence and arousal, to organize the connections between facial expression and autonomic physiology (for relevant arguments, see Levenson, Ekman, & Friesen, 1990).

Several kinds of studies have examined the autonomic patterns associated with different facial expressions. In the "directed facial action" studies, participants were asked to follow instructions to contract specific facial muscles to produce configurations resembling prototypical facial expressions of emotion (e.g., Ekman, Levenson, & Friesen, 1983; Levenson, Ekman, & Friesen, 1990). Participants' autonomic physiology was recorded as they held the prototypical facial expressions of emotion. Although methodological problems with these studies have been noted (e.g., Cacioppo, Berntson, Larsen, Poehlmann, & Ito, Chapter 11, this volume), the studies have indicated that facial configurations of negative emotion produce distinctions in autonomic activity. Specifically, anger, fear, and sadness all produced greater heart rate acceleration than disgust, and anger produced greater finger temperature than fear, indicative of increased vasodilation and increased blood flow to peripheral muscles (Ekman et al., 1983). These autonomic distinctions among negative emotions have been replicated across populations (Levenson et al., 1990), in young and elderly participants (Levenson, Carstensen, Friesen, & Ekman, 1991), in different cultures (Levenson, Ekman, Heider, &

Friesen, 1992), and in a relived-emotion task (Levenson et al., 1991). A simple valence account has trouble explaining these autonomic distinctions among the facial expressions of different negative emotions.

Other studies have linked spontaneous facial expressions of emotion to distinct autonomic responses. The oblique eyebrows and concerned gaze of sympathy were associated with heart rate deceleration, whereas the facial display of distress was associated with increased heart rate (Eisenberg et al., 1989). The elevated heart rate and respiratory response of laughter appear to be different from the autonomic responses associated with facial expressions of other emotions (Ruch, 1993). Embarrassment, which has its own distinct display, is probably associated with the blush, which differs from the autonomic responses of other emotions (Shearn, Bergman, Hill, Abel, & Hinds, 1990).

Facial Expressions and Evoked Responses in Others

Consistent with the view that facial expressions evolved to elicit distinct behaviors in conspecifics (Darwin, 1872/1998; Hauser, 1996), recent evidence indicates that facial expressions evoke fairly specific responses in observers (for reviews, see Dimberg & Öhman, 1996; Keltner & Kring, 1998). Facial expressions of anger, even when presented below an observer's conscious awareness, evoked fear-related facial and autonomic responses that were distinct from the responses evoked by smiles (Esteves, Dimberg, & Öhman, 1994). Facial expressions of distress have been shown to evoke sympathy (Eisenberg et al., 1989), and embarrassment and shame displays evoke amusement and sympathy, respectively (Keltner, Young, & Buswell, 1997). Facial expressions of different negative emotions evoke different emotions in observers, which fits a discrete-systems approach to emotion more closely than a dimensional one.

Reconciliation of Discrete-Systems and Dimensional Perspectives

We have reviewed evidence indicating that facial expressions are perceived categorically and linked to distinct brain regions, autonomic activity, and evoked responses in others. Although this evidence lends credence to the discrete-systems accounts of emotion, we believe that dimensional approaches are useful in many ways. For example, the discrete-systems perspectives may best apply to the current, momentary experience of emotion; dimensional accounts may be most productively applied to emotional experience aggregated across time, and to the study of moods. It is also possible to reconcile these two approaches. For example, although the differences among emotions may seem to be categorical in nature, the differences within a category of emotion—say among the varieties of anger—may be productively accounted for by such dimensions as intensity and unpleasantness (Ekman, 1992a; Ekman et al., 1982).

What Are the Distinct Facial Expressions of Emotion?

The preceding review raises a more general question: What are the distinct facial expressions of emotion? The literature has almost exclusively focused on seven emotions: anger, disgust, fear, happiness, sadness, surprise, and contempt (the most contested of these expressions) (Ekman, O'Sullivan, & Matsumoto, 1991; Matsumoto, 1992; Russell, 1991a). This same list of emotions has been replicated (with slight variations) in analyses of the structure-of-emotion lexicon, both in the United States (e.g., Shaver, Schwartz, Kirson, & O'Connor, 1987) and in other cultures (Romney, Moore, & Rusch, 1997); these replications suggest that this parsing of emotions is valid across methods, and not as culturally biased as some have argued (Wierzbicka, 1990).

Researchers are now examining other facial expressions of emotion by additionally studying the temporal dynamics of expression, and attending to gaze, head, and postural activity. For example, encoding studies linking expressive behavior to emotional experience have documented distinct expressions for embarrassment and shame (Keltner, 1995; Keltner & Buswell, 1997; Keltner & Harker, 1998) and sympathy (Eisenberg et al., 1989), as well as different experiential correlates of laughter and smiling (Keltner & Bonanno, 1997). Ensuing judgment studies have found that posed displays of embarrassment, shame, amusement (laughter), and sympathy do reliably convey information about emotion, but not to the same extent as the displays of the traditionally studied emotions (Haidt & Keltner, 1999; Keltner & Buswell, 1996). Finally, research has focused on the blush (Leary, Britt, Cutlip, & Templeton, 1992; Shearn, et al., 1990) and the iconic tongue protrusion (Haidt & Keltner, 1999), both of which convey emotion.

FACIAL EXPRESSIONS AS ACCURATE INDICATORS OF EMOTION

Do facial expressions reliably convey information about emotion? This question reduces to two more specific questions that have been the subject of heated debate and contrasting opinions. First, do distinct facial expressions correspond to other indices of emotion? Second, can observers judge facial expressions of emotion accurately?

Until the late 1960s, it was widely assumed that facial expression was a noisy, unreliable system with little reliable communicative value. Authors cited myriad examples—for example, individuals smiling at the decapitation of a rat (Landis, 1924) —that challenged notions of a one-to-one correspondence between facial expression and the experience of emotion (for a review, see Ekman, 1973). Facial expression was assumed to be like the phonemes of a language: The units of communication were thought to be attached to specific events and experiences in a specific way as part of the cultural construction of emotion.

More recently, it has been claimed that facial expressions of emotion do not relate to the experience of emotion (Fernandez-Dols & Ruiz-Belda, 1997), but are instead determined by context-specific social motives (Fridlund, 1992). Although attempts to document relations between facial expression and other markers of emotion face numerous difficulties related to the elicitation, timing, and measurement of emotion (Rosenberg & Ekman, 1994), several relevant studies now exist. These studies have documented consistent and even substantial links between facial expression and other markers of emotion.

Correspondence between Facial Expressions and the Experience of Emotion

Several studies concern the relation between facial expressions and the experience of emotion as measured in self-report instruments. An early review of 11 studies with contrasting meth-

ods indicated that the effect size of the relation between facial expression and experience was small to moderate, but consistently significant across studies (Matsumoto, 1987). Studies using more precise facial coding systems have consistently found relations between facial expression and the experience of emotion. In one study, subjects' facial responses when viewing films correlated with subsequent self-reports of emotion (Ekman, Friesen, & Ancoli, 1980). "Duchenne smiles," which involve the raising of the cheeks, but not "non-Duchenne smiles," have been shown to relate to the experience of positive emotion in young and old adults (e.g., Frank, Ekman, & Friesen, 1993; Hess, Banse, & Kappas, 1995; Keltner & Bonanno, 1997; Smith, 1995). The unique facial actions of embarrassment and amusement (e.g., gaze aversion and smile controls vs. the open-mouthed smile) were found to be related in distinct ways to self-reports of those emotions (Keltner, 1995). Spontaneous laughter and smiling were found to have some distinct experiential and social correlates (Keltner & Bonanno, 1997). Reviews of the literature on humor and laughter find that the intensity of laughter or smiling correlates between .3 and .4 with self-reports of the funniness of the humorous stimuli (McGhee, 1977; Ruch, 1995). These findings are all the more impressive when one considers the logical upper limits of the strength of correlations between measures coming from such different sources. Also, certain methodological practices would increase the strength of the association between facial expression and the experience of emotion, but are used infrequently. Within-subjects designs (Ruch, 1995) and improved self-report measures yield more precise and robust associations between facial expression and the experience of emotion (Rosenberg & Ekman, 1994).

Correspondence between Facial Expression and Other Markers of Emotion

Other studies, fewer in number, have ascertained whether different facial expressions of emotion relate to other markers of emotional response. As we have seen, the production of different facial expressions relates to different markers of emotion-relevant autonomic activity (Levenson et al., 1990) and different patterns of central nervous system activity (Ekman & Davidson, 1993). Spontaneous facial expressions have been shown to relate to different autonomic responses in the case of anger (see Rosenberg et al., 1998), sympathy (Eisenberg et al., 1989), and laughter (Keltner & Bonanno, 1997). Spontaneous Duchenne and non-Duchenne smiles relate to the activation of different brain regions (e.g., Ekman et al., 1990; Davidson et al., 1990). Finally, a recent study of bereaved adults' discussions of their deceased spouses found that the adults' facial expressions of anger, sadness, Duchenne laughter, and smiling tended to co-occur with distinct, theoretically relevant semantic themes (e.g., justice and loss) coded in their spontaneous verbal discourse (Bonanno & Keltner, 2000).

Studies of Accuracy in Facial Expression Judgment

Whereas most studies in which observers made judgments of facial expression have focused on agreement among observers, or between different groups of observers, a few studies have compared observers' judgments with an independent measure of what emotion is being experienced to evaluate accuracy. Ekman, Friesen, O'Sullivan, and Scherer (1980), for example, compared observers' judgments when individuals were truthfully and dishonestly describing their emotions. Accuracy was quite high when the people being judged were being truthful and poor when the people were lying. In more recent studies (Ekman, 1992b), in which observers judged facial expressions while also hearing the words, the accuracy of most observers' judgments was at chance levels when the subjects were deliberately lying. That research did show, however, that a few people can reach high accuracy; in other words, the information is present in the face to detect lies, but most people miss it. Other recent studies have found that observers can reliably differentiate individuals' spontaneous displays of embarrassment and amusement (Keltner, 1995) and love and desire (Gonzaga, Keltner, & Smith, 2000).

UNIVERSALS IN FACIAL EXPRESSIONS OF EMOTION

The search for universals in facial expression has a long and storied history (Darwin, 1872/1998; Ekman, 1973, 1998). Whether or not people of different cultures express emotion

similarly in the face bears critically, although not definitively, upon the extent to which emotions are innate, evolved, and culturally determined (see Ekman, 1973). Consistent with his *Zeitgeist,* Darwin believed that facial expressions of emotion are universal; he distributed questionnaires to missionaries in different parts of the world, querying whether their observations led them to conclude that people in those faraway cultures expressed emotion in similar ways (Darwin, 1872/1998). A universalist view of facial expression, however, was short-lived. The 1930s, 1940s, and 1950s were dominated by social scientists—most notably Klineberg (1940), La Barre (1947), and Birdwhistell (1970)—who claimed that people in different cultures express emotions differently in the face. Their claims were based on faulty observational research, imprecise definitions of facial expressions, and failures by most to consider the role of display rules. Nevertheless, they guided an initial wave of research on the cultural specificity in the interpretation of emotion (reviewed in Ekman, 1973). Since then, numerous studies have been conducted that have more firmly established the universality and cross-cultural variation in facial expressions of emotion.

Evidence for Universality in Facial Expression

Four kinds of evidence point to universals in facial expressions of emotion. First, beginning with Ekman's initial work with the preliterate, isolated Fore of New Guinea and Izard's work with the a number of literate cultures, judgment studies have addressed whether people who speak different languages and espouse different folk beliefs about emotion interpret facial expressions of emotion in similar ways (for reviews, see Ekman, 1998; Izard, 1977; Russell, 1994). Conducted in dozens of cultures, these studies have typically presented participants with photographs of theoretically derived facial expressions of emotion, and have asked participants to label the expressions with a word from a list of emotion terms. The forced-choice, within-subjects methods of these studies have been critiqued (e.g., Fridlund, 1992; Russell, 1994; see responses of Ekman, 1994; Izard, 1994), and the meaning of the obtained levels of accuracy has been questioned (Russell, 1994). Nevertheless, the studies reveal that across cultures people judge facial expressions of emotion with levels of accuracy that exceed chance, typically achieving accuracy rates between 60% and 80% (when chance levels vary between 17% and 50%). These results have led theorists of differing theoretical persuasions to conclude that people across cultures judge facial expressions of anger, contempt, disgust, fear, sadness, and surprise in similar ways (Ekman, 1994; Russell, 1994).

Several new studies, conducted in response to the critiques of traditional studies, have continued to document accuracy in the judgments of facial expressions. For example, one widespread criticism of traditional judgment studies pertains to the forced choice methods. A recent study in the United States and rural India (Haidt & Keltner, 1999), however, found that accuracy in judging facial expressions changes little when individuals are allowed to interpret the expressions in their own words (see also Izard, 1977). Another critique of traditional judgment studies is that they used posed rather than spontaneous facial expressions of emotion as stimuli. A recent study also found that observers were quite accurate in judging the spontaneous displays of amusement (i.e., laughter), anger, disgust, embarrassment, and shame (see Study 5, Keltner, 1995). Although there are clearly cultural variations in the accuracy with which individuals judge facial expressions of emotion (see Russell, 1994), as well as context effects upon judgment (Russell, 1997), the accuracy with which individuals judge facial expressions of emotion appears to be quite robust.

Second, two studies provide suggestive evidence of some universals in the expression of emotion. Cross-cultural studies of actual emotional behavior require cross-cultural equivalence in the meaning of emotional stimuli as well as the relative absence of the influence of culturally based display rules (Ekman, 1973). The first study documented that when videotaped without awareness, Japanese and U.S. students showed remarkably similar negative facial expressions in response to viewing a stress-inducing film (Ekman, 1973). More recently, it was found that 5- and 12-month-old Japanese and U.S. infants responded with similar facial, postural, and vocal expressions of anger in response to a nonpainful arm restraint (Camras, Oster, Campos, Miyake, & Bradshaw, 1992). Ethological research, although not having safeguards against a single observer's possible bias, has shown that people in different cultures display similar facial expressions, such as

laughter, embarrassment, or anger during play, flirtation, or fighting, respectively (e.g., Eibl-Eibesfeldt, 1989).

Third, one study has examined the relations between facial expression and other markers of emotion across cultures. One study we referred to earlier asked participants in the United States and the Minangkabau, a matrilineal, Muslim culture in Indonesia, to configure their faces into the expressions of different emotions, during which time their autonomic physiology was recorded (Levenson et al., 1992). Importantly, deliberately making the same set of facial movements produced similar autonomic responses in the two cultures (see details above).

Finally, some studies have gathered people's reports of facial expressions associated with different emotions. Although self-reports of behavior are clearly subject to a variety of biases, this evidence could be used to address the universality of facial expression. For example, across cultures people are in high agreement that embarrassment is expressed in a nervous smile and gaze aversion (reviewed in Keltner & Buswell, 1997). Other studies that have systematically gathered individuals' descriptions of expressive behavior across cultures could be similarly synthesized (e.g., Scherer & Wallbott, 1994).

The universality of facial expression, it is important to note, by no means implies universality in other components of emotion. Facial expressions of emotion may be the most universal of the different facets of emotion because of their central role in meeting different social problems that have been observed in different cultures, such as forming attachments, negotiating status, or apologizing for transgressions (Ekman, 1992a; Keltner & Kring, 1998). Other facets of emotion, such as the descriptions people give to the private feelings of emotion, may demonstrate more cultural variation.

Evidence for Cultural Variation in Facial Expression

The claims about cross cultural variation in facial expression, often found in ethnographic studies, are dramatic. The Utku of the Arctic were claimed never to express anger in the face (Briggs, 1960). In many cultures laughter is pervasive at funerals (Keltner & Bonanno, 1997). A survey of the ethnographic literature would no doubt evince consistent and widespread cultural differences in facial expressions for every emotion. These claims, however, suffer from obvious methodological problems, including questions about whether participants were responding to similar stimuli, and whether observations avoided ambiguities in such terms as "smile," "frown," and "laugh." More controlled studies have documented several ways in which cultures vary in the display and perception of facial expression of emotion.

First, individuals from different cultures differ in the emotional intensity that they attribute to facial expressions of emotion (Matsumoto & Ekman, 1989). In a first study to address this issue, Japanese participants attributed more emotion than U.S. participants to all facial expressions of emotion posed by individuals of European and Asian descent, except for expressions of disgust (Matsumoto & Ekman, 1989). Interestingly, members of the two cultures differed in which facial expression they judged to be expressing the most intense emotion: for the Japanese participants, it was the disgust expression; for the U.S. participants, it was the happiness and anger expressions. In recent work, Matsumoto and colleagues have explored how culturally relevant variables, such as power distance and individualism, account for cultural differences in the intensity of emotion attributed to facial expression (e.g., Matsumoto & Kudoh, 1993).

Second, individuals from different cultures vary in the inferences they draw from facial expressions of emotion. For example, U.S. as compared to Japanese college students were more likely to infer that an individual displaying a Duchenne smile was highly sociable (Matsumoto & Kudoh, 1993), consistent with the tendency in the United States to make dispositional inferences from social behavior. One might also expect cultures that somaticize emotional experience (e.g., Russell, 1991b) to be more likely to infer somatic responses associated with facial expressions. Other such cross-cultural predictions can be derived from the literature on emotion and culture (e.g., Mesquita & Frijda, 1992; Markus & Kitayama, 1991).

Third, recent studies lend credence to ethnographic examples that strikingly different events elicit similar facial expression in different cultures. For example, in one study Japanese students indicated that it was more appropriate to show negative facial expressions to outgroup members (Matsumoto, 1990). U.S. students, in contrast, indicated that it was more appropriate to display negative emotion to ingroup members. People from India were more likely to mention affiliation in explaining photographs of a Duchenne smile, whereas people from the United States were more likely to mention individual achievement (Haidt & Keltner, 1999), consistent with claims about independent and interdependent cultures (Markus & Kitayama, 1991). Whether these cultural differences in facial expressions are observed in real social interactions remains an empirical question.

Finally, very limited evidence points to ways in which members of different cultures vary in their actual expressive behavior. Members of different cultures are likely to vary in the latency of their facial expressions of emotion: For example, U.S. infants responded with anger more quickly than Japanese infants in the study by Camras et al. (1992). Cultures may also differ in the range of expressions used to convey a particular emotion. For example, although individuals from India and the United States agreed in their interpretation of a prototypical embarrassment display, only individuals from India indicated that a tongue bite expression—a Southeast Asian display of self-conscious emotion—expressed embarrassment. Cultures may vary most in the meaning of these iconic displays of emotion (see Ekman & Friesen, 1982, for related discussion on cultural variation in emblems). And in what is still the only study to show the operation of different display rules in different cultures, Ekman (1973) showed cultural differences in the control of facial expression. When an authority figure was present, Japanese participants more than U.S. participants masked negative emotional expressions in response to watching an unpleasant film with a smile, although they had shown nearly identical facial expressions when watching such films alone.

INDIVIDUAL DIFFERENCES IN FACIAL EXPRESSIONS OF EMOTION

Notwithstanding the conceptual and methodological promises of studying individual differences in facial expression (Keltner, 1996), it is only recently that this issue has attracted the attention of empirical researchers. We trace this oversight to two historical trends. First, the early researchers of expressive behavior, such as

Wolff (1943), focused on individual differences in a variety of expressive behaviors (such as gait, signature, or posture), but they did not consider facial expression. The study of the face may have been tainted by the pitfalls and ill repute of the study of physiognomy (Ekman, 1978). Second, researchers have concentrated on universal, prototypical facial expressions, thus ignoring individual variation in such expressions. Recent studies, however, have begun to illuminate how personality traits and psychological disorders relate to facial expressions of emotion.

Personality and Facial Expressions of Emotion

Theorists have long claimed that individual differences in emotion relate to the central processes and structures of personality (Malatesta, 1993; Pervin, 1993). Consistent with this claim, studies have documented that extraversion and neuroticism relate to facial expressions of positive and negative emotion, respectively (Keltner, 1996), consistent with self-report studies (Larsen & Ketelaar, 1991; Watson & Clark, 1992). Other studies have ascertained that individuals vary in their overall emotional expressiveness (e.g., Gross & John, 1997; Keltner & Ekman, 1996; Larsen & Diener, 1987), although there is some question concerning the correspondence between self-report measures of the disposition to experience intense emotion and expressive behavior in response to discrete stimuli (Keltner & Ekman, 1996).

These findings raise five questions for future research. First, when do these individual differences in facial expression emerge? Some work has identified individual differences in facial expression as early as 7 months of age (Izard, Hembree, & Huebner, 1987), suggesting that individual differences in facial expression may contribute to the development and continuity of temperament (Malatesta, 1990). Second, what are the biological underpinnings of these individual differences in emotion (e.g., Kagan, Reznick, & Snidman, 1988)? Third, are these individual differences in emotional expression largely due to individual differences in emotion elicitation thresholds, exposure to emotional stimuli, or baseline mood (see Bolger & Schilling, 1991; Larsen & Ketelaar, 1991). Fourth, in what contexts are relations between personality and facial expression most robust?

Initial evidence indicates that these relations are most robust in familiar, ambiguous contexts (e.g., Moskowitz & Coté, 1995). Finally, how might facial expressions of emotion mediate important personality–environment relations (e.g., see Caspi & Bem, 1990)?

Psychopathology and Facial Expressions of Emotion

Early emotion theorists expressed great interest in the relations between emotions and psychological disorders (Ekman, 1984; Izard, 1971; Plutchik, 1980). Although they assumed emotions to serve important functions, they viewed emotions that are inappropriate, excessive, or insufficient to the context as potentially dysfunctional and leading to disrupted lives. Researchers have begun to attend systematically to the relations between different disorders and facial expressions of emotion (for a review, see Keltner & Kring, 1998).

Initial research has been largely descriptive in nature, ascertaining how different disorders relate to different facial expressions of emotion. For example, depressed patients exhibit limited facial expressions, particularly expressions of positive emotions (Berenbaum & Oltmanns, 1992; Ekman & Friesen, 1974; Ekman, Matsumoto, & Friesen, 1997; Jones & Pansa, 1979; Ulrich & Harms, 1985; Waxer, 1974). Schizophrenic patients have been shown to be less facially expressive than nonpatients in response to emotional films (Berenbaum & Oltmanns, 1992; Kring, Kerr, Smith, & Neale, 1993; Kring & Neale, 1996; Mattes, Schneider, Heimann, & Birbaumer, 1995), in response to cartoons (Dworkin, Clark, Amador, & Gorman, 1996), and during social interactions (Krause, Steimer, Sanger-Alt, & Wagner, 1989; Mattes et al., 1995), but they report experiencing the same or greater amount of emotion and exhibit the same amount of skin conductance reactivity (or more) as nonpatients (Kring & Neale, 1996). Adolescent males prone to aggression and delinquent behavior were shown in one study to express less embarrassment and more anger in the face than controls (Keltner, Moffitt, & Stouthamer-Loeber, 1995). This basic research pinpoints which emotions may play prominent roles in the different disorders, and dispels certain misconceptions about the emotional nature of certain disorders—for example, that individuals with schizophrenia experience flat affect.

These findings point to important lines of inquiry. First, reliance upon the known relations between emotion and autonomic and central nervous system structures can guide the discovery of physiological mechanisms that contribute to different disorders. Illustrative studies include work on depression, reduced positive affect, and resting brain asymmetries (e.g., Davidson, 1993), and work relating autism and self-conscious emotion (Capps, Yirmiya, & Sigman, 1992). Second, guided by what is known about facial expressions of emotion, research can begin to document how emotional features of psychological disorders relate to specific styles of interaction and relationships, thus producing and perpetuating the disorders (for relevant evidence and speculation, see Keltner & Kring, 1998). For example, individuals high in psychopathy show an autonomic response to facial expressions of anger but not sadness (Patrick, 1994), suggesting that they may fail to respond to others' distress in ways that usually disinhibit antisocial behavior. Finally, facial expression can be used as a measure of progress in response to treatment (e.g., Ekman et al., 1997) and trauma, such as the loss of a spouse (Bonanno & Keltner, 1997).

CONCLUSIONS

In this chapter, we have drawn upon classic and contemporary studies of facial expression to address three abiding questions: Are facial expressions of emotion best thought of as discrete systems or as entities that vary along global dimensions? Are observers accurate in judging facial expressions? And are there universal facial expressions of emotion? The answers to these three questions have proved to be affirmative, yet several questions need empirical attention. We have also examined the emergent studies of individual differences in facial expressions of emotion.

Given the breadth of issues covered in the study of facial expression, we inevitably have been unable to review important research on facial feedback (Matsumoto, 1987), the development of facial expression (Izard et al., 1987), componential accounts of facial expression (Smith & Scott, 1997), and the relation between facial temperature and the experience of emotion (Zajonc, 1985). Nor have we been able to devote significant attention to another important line of new research on facial expression:

the manner in which facial expressions of emotion systematically shape social interactions (Keltner & Kring, 1998). Finally, our discussion of methods has had to be limited, and we simply note the importance of novel methods, such as quasi-experiments, the study of spontaneous expression in social interaction (e.g., Keltner, Young, Heerey, Oemig, & Monarch, 1998; Levenson & Gottman, 1983), and automated techniques for coding facial expression (Bartlett, Hager, Ekman, & Sejnowksi, 1998; Ekman, Huang, Sejnowski, & Hager, 1993).

Once largely ignored, the study of facial expression is now at the center of the emergent field of affective science. The study of facial expression will continue to be germane to basic questions about emotion, culture, and communication. The study of facial expression will present continued opportunities for the study of emotion-relevant experience and autonomic and central nervous system physiology. Finally, the study of facial expression will continue to allow researchers to seek answers to fundamental questions about human nature.

REFERENCES

Allport, F. H. (1924). *Social psychology.* Boston: Houghton Mifflin.

Bartlett, M. S., Hager, J. C., Ekman, P., & Sejnowksi, T. J. (1998). *Measuring facial expression by computer image analysis.* Manuscript submitted for publication.

Berenbaum, H., & Oltmanns, T. F. (1992). Emotional experience and expression in schizophrenia and depression. *Journal of Abnormal Psychology, 101,* 37–44.

Birdwhistell, R. L. (1970). *Kinesics and context.* Philadelphia: University of Pennsylvania Press.

Blair, R. J. R., Morris, J. S., Frith, C. D., Perrett, D. I., & Dolan, R. J. (1998). *Differential neural responses to sad and angry faces: Involvement of the amygdala and orbitofrontal cortex.* Manuscript submitted for publication.

Bolger, N., & Schilling, E. A. (1991). Personality and the problems of everyday life: The role of Neuroticism in exposure and reactivity to daily stressors. *Journal of Personality, 59,* 355–386.

Bonanno, G. A., & Keltner, D. (1997). Facial expressions of emotion and the course of conjugal bereavement. *Journal of Abnormal Psychology, 106,* 126–137.

Bonanno, G. A., & Keltner, D. (2000). *Coherence between discrete facial expressions of emotion and core relational appraisal themes in bereavement narratives.* Manuscript submitted for publication.

Briggs, J. L. (1960). *Never in anger: Portrait of an Eskimo family.* Cambridge, MA: Harvard University Press.

Bruner, J. S., & Tagiuri, R. (1954). The perception of people. In G. Lindzey (Ed.), *Handbook of social psychology* (Vol. 2, pp. 634–654). Reading, MA: Addison-Wesley.

Calder, A. J., Young, A. W., Rowland, D., Perrett, D. I., Hodges, J. R., & Etcoff, N. L. (1996). Facial emotion recognition after bilateral amygdala damage: Differentially severe impairment of fear. *Cognitive Neuropsychology, 13,* 699–745.

Camras, L. A., Oster, H., Campos, J. J., Miyake, K., & Bradshaw, D. (1992). Japanese and American infants' responses to arm restraints. *Developmental Psychology, 28,* 578–583.

Capps, L., Yirmiya, N., & Sigman, M. (1992). Understanding of simple and complex emotions in nonretarded children with autism. *Journal of Child Psychology and Psychiatry, 33,* 1169–1182.

Caspi, A., & Bem, D. J. (1990). Personality continuity and change across the life course. In L. A. Pervin (Ed.), *Handbook of personality: Theory and research* (pp. 549–575). New York: Guilford Press.

Darwin, C. (1998). *The expression of the emotions in man and animals.* New York: Philosophical Library. (Original work published 1872)

Davidson, R. J. (1993). Parsing affective space: Perspectives from neuropsychology and psychophysiology. *Neuropsychology, 7,* 464–475.

Davidson, R. J., Ekman, P., Saron, C., Senulis, J., & Friesen, W. J. (1990). Emotional expression and brain physiology: I Approach/withdrawal and cerebral asymmetry. *Journal of Personality and Social Psychology, 58,* 330–341.

Dimberg, U., & Öhman, A. (1996). Behold the wrath: Psychophysiological responses to facial stimuli. *Motivation and Emotion, 20,* 149–182.

Dworkin, R., Clark, S. C., Amador, X. F., & Gorman, J. M. (1996). Does affective blunting in schizophrenia reflect affective deficit or neuromotor dysfunction? *Schizophrenia Research, 20,* 301–306.

Eibl-Eibesfeldt, I. (1989). *Human ethology.* New York: Aldine/de Gruyter.

Eisenberg, N., Fabes, R. A., Miller, P. A., Fultz, J., Shell, R., Mathy, R. M., & Reno, R. R. (1989). Relation of sympathy and distress to prosocial behavior: A multimethod study. *Journal of Personality and Social Psychology, 57,* 55–66.

Ekman, P. (1973). Cross-cultural studies of facial expression. In P. Ekman (Ed.), *Darwin and facial expression: A century of research in review* (pp. 169–222). New York: Academic Press.

Ekman, P. (1978). Facial signs: Facts, fantasies, and possibilities. In T. Sebeok (Ed.), *Sight, sound, and sense* (pp. 124–156). Bloomington: Indiana University Press.

Ekman, P. (1984). Expression and the nature of emotion. In K. Scherer & P. Ekman (Eds.), *Approaches to emotion* (pp. 319–344). Hillsdale, NJ: Erlbaum.

Ekman, P. (1992a). An argument for basic emotions. *Cognition and Emotion, 6,* 169–200.

Ekman, P. (1992b). *Telling lies: Clues to deceit in the marketplace, marriage, and politics* (2nd ed.). New York: W.W. Norton.

Ekman, P. (1993). Facial expression and emotion. *American Psychologist, 48,* 384–392.

Ekman, P. (1998). Introduction. In C. Darwin (1872/1998), *The expression of the emotions in man and animals.* (p. xxi–xxxvi). New York: Oxford University Press.

Ekman, P., & Davidson, R. J. (1993). Voluntary smiling changes regional brain activity. *Psychological Science, 4,* 342–345.

Ekman, P., Davidson, R. J., & Friesen, W. V. (1990). The Duchenne smile: Emotional expression and brain physiology. II. *Journal of Personality and Social Psychology, 58,* 342–353.

Ekman, P., & Friesen, W. V. (1971). Constants across cultures in the face and emotion. *Journal of Personality and Social Psychology, 17,* 124–129.

Ekman, P., & Friesen, W. V. (1974). Nonverbal behavior and psychopathology. In R. J. Friedman & M. M. Katz (Eds.), *The psychology of depression: contemporary theory and research* (pp. 203–232). New York: Wiley.

Ekman, P., & Friesen, W. V. (1978). *Facial Action Coding System: A technique for the measurement of facial movement.* Palo Alto, CA: Consulting Psychologists Press.

Ekman, P., & Friesen, W. V. (1982). Felt, false, and miserable smiles. *Journal of Nonverbal Behavior, 6*(4). 238–252.

Ekman, P., Friesen, W. V., & Ancoli, S. (1980). Facial signs of emotional experience. *Journal of Personality and Social Psychology, 39,* 1125–1134.

Ekman, P., Friesen, W. V., & Ellsworth, P. C. (1982). *Emotion in the human face.* Cambridge, England: Cambridge University Press.

Ekman, P., Friesen, W. V., O'Sullivan, M., & Scherer, K. (1980). Relative importance of face, body, and voice in judgments of personality and affect. *Journal of Personality and Social Psychology, 38,* 270–277.

Ekman, P., Huang, T. S., Sejnowski, T., & Hager, J. C. (1993). *Final report to NSF of the planning workshop on Facial Expression Understanding, July 30 to August 1, 1992.* Washington, DC: National Science Foundation.

Ekman, P., Levenson, R. W., & Friesen, W. V. (1983). Autonomic nervous system activity distinguishes among emotions. *Science, 221,* 1208–1210.

Ekman, P., Matsumoto, D., & Friesen, W. V. (1997). Facial expression in affective disorders. In P. Ekman & E. L. Rosenberg (Eds.), *What the face reveals* (pp. 331–341). New York: Oxford University Press.

Ekman, P., O'Sullivan, M., & Matsumoto, D. (1991). Contradictions in the study of contempt: What's it all about? *Motivation and Emotion, 15,* 293–296.

Ekman, P., & Rosenberg, E. L. (Eds.). (1997). *What the face reveals.* New York: Oxford University Press.

Ekman, P., Sorenson, E. R., & Friesen, W. V. (1969). Pan-cultural elements in facial displays of emotions. *Science, 164,* 86–88.

Esteves, F., Dimberg, U., & Öhman, A. (1994). Automatically elicited fear: Conditioned skin conductance responses to masked facial expressions. *Cognition and Emotion, 8,* 393–413.

Etcoff, N. L., & Magee, J. J. (1992). Categorical perception of facial expressions. *Cognition, 44,* 227–240.

Fernandez-Dols, J. M., & Ruiz-Belda, M. A. (1997). Spontaneous facial behavior during intense emotional episodes: Artistic truth and optical truth. In J.A. Russell & J. M. Fernandez-Dols (Eds.), *The psychology of facial expression* (pp. 255–294). Cambridge, England: Cambridge University Press.

Frank, M., Ekman, P., & Friesen, W. V. (1993). Behavioral markers and recognizability of the smile of enjoyment. *Journal of Personality and Social Psychology, 64,* 83–93.

Fridlund, A. J. (1992). The behavioral ecology and sociality of human faces. *Review of Personality and Social Psychology, 13,* 90–121.

Fried, I., Wilson, C. L., MacDonald, K. A., & Behnke, E. J. (1998). Electric current stimulates laughter. *Nature, 391,* 650.

Gonzaga, G., Keltner, D., & Smith, M. (2000). *Encoding and decoding evidence for distinct displays of love and desire.* Manuscript submitted for publication.

Gray, J. M., Young, A. W., Barker, W. A., Curtis, A., & Gibson, D. (1997). Impaired recognition of disgust in Huntington's disease gene carriers. *Brain, 120,* 2029–2038.

Gross, J. J., & John, O. P. (1997). Revealing feelings: Facets of emotional expressivity in self-reports, peer ratings, and behavior. *Journal of Personality and Social Psychology, 72,* 435–448.

Haidt, J., & Keltner, D. (1999). Culture and facial expression: Open ended methods find more faces and a gradient of universality . *Cognition and Emotion, 13,* 225–266.

Hauser, M. D. (1996). *The evolution of communication.* Cambridge, MA: MIT Press.

Hess, U., Banse, R., & Kappas, A. (1995). The intensity of facial expression is determined by underlying affective states and social situations. *Journal of Personality and Social Psychology, 69,* 280–288.

Izard, C. E. (1971). *The face of emotion.* New York: Appleton-Century-Crofts.

Izard, C. E. (1977). *Human emotions.* New York: Plenum Press.

Izard, C. E. (1993). Four systems of emotion activation: Cognitive and non-cognitive processes. *Psychological Review, 100,* 68–90.

Izard, C. E. (1994). Innate and universal facial expressions: Evidence from developmental and cross-cultural research. *Psychological Bulletin, 115,* 288–299.

Izard, C. E., Hembree, E. A., & Huebner, R. R. (1987). Infants' emotional expressions to acute pain: Developmental change and stability of individual differences. *Developmental Psychology, 23,* 105–113.

Jones, I. H., & Pansa, M. (1979). Some nonverbal aspects of depression and schizophrenia occurring during the interview. *Journal of Nervous and Mental Disease, 167,* 402–409.

Kagan, J., Reznick, J. S., & Snidman, N. (1988). Biological bases of childhood shyness, *Science, 240,* 167–171.

Keltner, D. (1995). The signs of appeasement: Evidence for the distinct displays of embarrassment, amusement, and shame. *Journal of Personality and Social Psychology, 68,* 441–454.

Keltner, D. (1996). Facial expressions of emotion and personality. In C. Malatesta-Magai & S. H. McFad-

den (Eds.), *Handbook of emotion, adult development, and aging* (pp. 385–401). New York: Academic Press.

Keltner, D., & Bonanno, G. A. (1997). A study of laughter and dissociation: The distinct correlates of laughter and smiling during bereavement. *Journal of Personality and Social Psychology, 73,* 687–702.

Keltner, D., & Buswell, B. N. (1996). Evidence for the distinctness of embarrassment, shame, and guilt: A study of recalled antecedents and facial expressions of emotion. *Cognition and Emotion, 10*(2), 155–171.

Keltner, D., & Buswell, B. N. (1997). Embarrassment: Its distinct form and appeasement functions. *Psychological Bulletin, 122,* 250–270.

Kelter, D., & Ekman, P. (1996). Affective intensity and emotional responses. *Cognition and Emotion, 10*(3), 323–328.

Keltner, D., & Harker, L. A. (1998). The forms and functions of the nonverbal display of shame. In P. Gilbert & B. Andrews (Eds.), *Interpersonal approaches to shame* (pp. 78–98). Oxford: Oxford University Press.

Keltner, D., & Kring, A. (1998). Emotion, social function, and psychopathology. *Review of General Psychology, 2,* 320–342.

Keltner, D., Moffitt, T., & Stouthamer-Loeber, M. (1995). Facial expressions of emotion and psychopathology in adolescent boys. *Journal of Abnormal Psychology, 104,* 644–652.

Keltner, D., Young, R., & Buswell, B. N. (1997). Appeasement in human emotion, personality, and social practice. *Aggressive Behavior, 23,* 359–374.

Keltner, D., Young, R. C., Heerey, E. A., Oemig, C., & Monarch, N. D. (1998). Teasing in hierarchical and intimate relations. *Journal of Personality and Social Psychology, 75,* 1231–1247.

Klineberg, O. (1940). *Social psychology.* New York: Henry Holt.

Krause, R., Steimer, E., Sanger-Alt, C., & Wagner, G. (1989). Facial expressions of schizophrenic patients and their interaction partners. *Psychiatry, 52,* 1–12.

Kring, A. M., Kerr, S. L, Smith, D. A., & Neale, J. M. (1993). Flat affect in schizophrenia does not reflect diminished subjective experience of emotion. *Journal of Abnormal Psychology, 102,* 507–517.

Kring, A. M., & Neale, J. M. (1996). Do schizophrenics show a disjunctive relationship among expressive, experiential, and psychophysiological components of emotion? *Journal of Abnormal Psychology 105,* 249–257.

La Barre, W. (1947). The cultural basis for emotions and gestures. *Journal of Personality, 16,* 49–68.

Landis, C. (1924). Studies of emotional reactions: II. General behavior and facial expression. *Journal of Comparative Psychology, 4,* 447–509.

Larsen, R. J., & Diener, E. (1987). Affect intensity as an individual difference characteristic: A review. *Journal of Research in Personality, 21,* 1–39.

Larsen, R. J., & Ketelaar, T. (1991). Personality and susceptibility to positive and negative emotional states. *Journal of Personality and Social Psychology, 61,* 132–140.

Leary, M. R., Britt, T. W., Cutlip, W. D., II, & Templeton, J. L. (1992). Social blushing. *Psychological Bulletin, 112,* 446–460.

LeDoux, J. E. (1996). *The emotional brain: The mysterious underpinnings of emotional life.* New York: Simon & Schuster.

Levenson, R.W., Carstensen, L. L., Friesen, W. V., & Ekman, P. (1991). Emotion, physiology, and expression in old age. *Psychology and Aging, 6,* 28–35.

Levenson, R. W., Ekman, P., & Friesen, W. V. (1990). Voluntary facial action generates emotion-specific autonomic nervous system activity. *Psychophysiology, 27,* 363–384.

Levenson, R. W., Ekman, P., Heider, K., & Friesen, W. V. (1992). Emotion and autonomic nervous system activity in the Minangkabau of West Sumatra. *Journal of Personality and Social Psychology, 62,* 972–988.

Levenson, R. W., & Gottman, J. M. (1983). Marital interaction: Physiological linkage and affective exchange. *Journal of Personality and Social Psychology, 45,* 587–597.

Malatesta, C. Z. (1990). The role of emotions in the development and organization of personality. In. R.A. Thompson (Ed.), *Nebraska Symposium on Motivation: Vol. 36. Socioemotional development* (pp. 1–56). Lincoln: University of Nebraska Press.

Markus, H. R., & Kitayama, S. (1991). Culture and the self: Implications for cognition, emotion, and motivation. *Psychological Review, 98,* 224–253.

Matsumoto, D. (1987). The role of facial response in the experience of emotion: More methodological problems and a meta-analysis. *Journal of Personality and Social Psychology, 52,* 769–774.

Matsumoto, D. (1990). Cultural similarities and differences in display rules. *Motivation and Emotion, 14,* 195–214.

Matsumoto, D. (1992). More evidence for the universality of a contempt expression. *Motivation and Emotion, 16,* 363–368.

Matsumoto, D., & Ekman, P. (1989). American–Japanese cultural differences in intensity ratings of facial expressions of emotion. *Motivation and Emotion, 13,* 143–157.

Matsumoto, D., & Kudoh, T. (1993). American–Japanese cultural differences in attributions of personality based on smiles. *Journal of Nonverbal Behavior, 17,* 231–243.

Mattes, R. M., Schneider, F., Heimann, H., & Birbaumer, N. (1995). Reduced emotional response of schizophrenic patients in remission during social interaction. *Schizophrenia Research, 17,* 249–255.

McGhee, P. E. (1977). Children's humour: A review of current research trends. In A.J. Chapman & H.C. Foot (Eds.), *It's a funny thing, humour* (pp. 199–209). Oxford: Pergamon Press.

Mesquita, B., & Frijda, N. (1992). Cultural variations in emotions: A review. *Psychological Bulletin, 112,* 179–204.

Morris, J. S., Frith, C.D., Perrett, D.I., Rowland, D., Young, A.W., Calder, A. J., & Dolan, R. J. (1996). A differential neural response in the human amygdala to fearful and happy facial expressions. *Nature, 383,* 812–815.

Moskowitz, D. S. & Coté, S. (1995). Do interpersonal traits predict affect?: A comparison of three models. *Journal of Personality and Social Psychology, 69,* 915–924.

Nelson, C. A., & de Haan, M. (1997). A neurobehavioral approach to the recognition of facial expression in infancy. In J. A. Russell & J. M. Fernandez-Dols (Eds.), *The psychology of facial expression* (pp. 176–204). Cambridge, England: Cambridge University Press.

Patrick, C. (1994). Emotion and psychopathy: Startling new insights. *Psychophysiology, 31,* 319–330.

Pervin, L. A. (1993). Affect and personality. In M. Lewis & J. M. Haviland (Eds.), *Handbook of emotions* (pp. 301–311). New York: Guilford Press.

Phillips, M. L., Young, A. W., Senior, C., Brammer, M., Andrew, C., Calder, A.J., Bullmore, E.T., Perrett, D.I., Rowland, D., Williams, S. C. R., Gray, J. A., & David, A. S. (1997). A specific neural substrate for perceiving facial expressions of disgust. *Nature, 389,* 495–498.

Plutchik, R. (1962). *The emotions: Facts, theories, and a new model.* New York: Random House.

Plutchik, R. (1980). *Emotion: A psychoevolutionary synthesis.* New York: Harper & Row.

Pollack, S. D., Cicchetti, D., Klorman, R., & Brumaghim, J. T. (1997). Cognitive brain event related potentials and emotion processing in maltreated children. *Child Development, 68,* 773–787.

Romney, A. K., Moore, C. C., & Rusch, C. D. (1997). Cultural universals: Measuring the semantic structure of emotion terms in English and Japanese. *Proceedings of the National Academy of Sciences USA, 94,* 5489–5494.

Rosenberg, E. L., & Ekman, P. (1994). Coherence between expressive and experiential systems in emotion. *Cognition and Emotion, 8,* 201–229.

Rosenberg, E. L., Ekman, P., Jiang, W., Buyback, M., Coleman, R. E., Hanson, M., O'Connor, C., Waugh, R., & Blumenthal, J. (1998). *Facial expressions of emotion predict myocardial ischemia.* Manuscript submitted for publication.

Ruch, W. (1993). Exhilaration and humor. In M. Lewis & J. M. Haviland (Eds.) *Handbook of emotions* (pp. 605–616). New York: Guilford Press.

Ruch, W. (1995). Will the real relationship between facial expression and affective experience please stand up: The case of exhilaration. *Cognition and Emotion, 9,* 33–58.

Russell, J. A. (1991a). The contempt expression and the relativity thesis. *Motivation and Emotion, 15,* 149–168.

Russell, J. A. (1991b). Culture and categorization of emotion. *Psychological Bulletin, 110* (3), 426–450.

Russell, J. A. (1994). Is there universal recognition of emotion from facial expression?: A review of cross-cultural studies. *Psychological Bulletin, 115,* 102–141.

Russell, J. A. (1997). Reading emotions from and into faces: Resurrecting a dimensional-contextual perspective. In J. A. Russell & J. M. Fernandez-Dols (Eds.), *The psychology of facial expression* (pp. 295–320). Cambridge, England: Cambridge University Press.

Scherer, K. R., & Wallbott, H. G. (1994). Evidence for universality and cultural variation of differential emotion response patterning. *Journal of Personality and Social Psychology, 66,* 310–328.

Schlosberg, H. (1954). Three dimensions of emotion. *Psychological Review, 61,* 81–88.

Shaver, P., Schwartz, J., Kirson, D., & O'Connor, C. (1987). Emotion knowledge: Further exploration of a prototype approach. *Journal of Personality and Social Psychology, 52,* 1061–1086.

Shearn, D., Bergman, E., Hill, K., Abel, A., & Hinds, L. (1990). Facial coloration and temperature responses in blushing. *Psychophysiology, 27,* 687–693.

Smith, C. A., & Scott, H. S. (1997). A componential approach to the meaning of facial expression. In J. A. Russell & J. M. Fernandez-Dols (Eds.), *The psychology of facial expression* (pp. 229–254). Cambridge, England: Cambridge University Press.

Smith, M. C. (1995). Facial expression in mild dementia of the Alzheimer type. *Behavioural Neurology, 8,* 149–156.

Sprengelmeyer, R., Young, A. W., Calder, A. J., Karnat, A., Lange, H., Homberg, V., Perrett, D. I., & Rowland, D. (1996). Loss of disgust: Perceptions of faces and emotions in Huntington's disease. *Brain, 119,* 1647–1665.

Tomkins, S. S. (1962). *Affect, imagery, consciousness: Vol. 1. The positive affects,* New York: Springer.

Tomkins, S. S. (1963). *Affect, imagery, consciousness: Vol. 2. The negative affects,* New York: Springer.

Tomkins, S. S., & McCarter, R. (1964). What and where are the primary affects? Some evidence for a theory. *Perceptual and Motor Skills, 18,* 119–158.

Ulrich, G., & Harms, K. (1985). A video analysis of the nonverbal behavior of depressed patients and their relation to anxiety and depressive disorders. *Journal of Affective Disorders, 9,* 63–67.

Watson, D., & Clark, L. A. (1992). On traits and temperament: General and specific factors of emotional experience and their relation to the five factor model. *Journal of Personality, 60,* 441–476.

Waxer, P. H. (1974). Nonverbal cues for depression. *Journal of Abnormal Psychology, 83,* 319–322.

Whalen, P. J., Rauch, S. L., Etcoff, N. L., McInerney, S. C., Lee, M. B., & Jenike, M. A. (1998). Masked presentations of emotional facial expressions modulate amygdala activity without explicit knowledge. *Journal of Neuroscience, 18,* 411–418.

Wierzbicka, A. (Ed.) (1990). The semantics of emotion [Special issue]. *Australian Journal of Linguistics, 10*(2).

Wolff, W. (1943). *The expression of personality: Experimental depth psychology.* New York: Harper.

Woodworth, R. S. (1938). *Experimental psychology.* New York: Henry Holt.

Young, A. W., Rowland, D., Calder, A. J., Etcoff, N. L., Seth, A., & Perrett, D. I. (in press). Facial expression megamix: Tests of dimensional and category accounts of emotion recognition. *Cognition.*

Zajonc, R. B. (1985). Emotion and facial efference: A theory reclaimed. *Science, 228,* 15–21.

PART III

DEVELOPMENTAL CHANGES

CHAPTER 16

Motivational, Organizational, and Regulatory Functions of Discrete Emotions

Carroll E. Izard
Brian P. Ackerman

A few discrete emotions emerge early in life, including joy, interest, sadness, anger, fear, and disgust. Another few emotions emerge later in middle childhood as a function of both maturational and social processes; these emotions include shame, guilt, shyness, and contempt. Each of these emotions has a unique adaptive function in motivating, organizing, and regulating behavior, both alone and in emotion patterns. Each emotion also plays an important role in the development of personality and individual differences in responding to environmental challenges.

In this chapter, we explore the adaptive functions of emotions from the perspective of differential-emotions theory (DET; Izard, 1977). We begin by describing the theoretical assumptions underlying our approach and locating these assumptions in historical and theoretical contexts. We then describe the motivational, organizational, and regulatory functions of some of the discrete emotions. In the final section, we discuss the implications of these assumptions for conceptualizing the development of personality.

THEORETICAL FRAMEWORK

Adaptive Functions of Emotions

Seven broad assumptions provide a theoretical frame for understanding the relations among the emotions system, behavior, and personality development.

1. The emotions system constitutes the primary *motivational* system for human behavior (Izard, 1971; Tomkins, 1962). Motivation concerns the goals of behavior. Whereas few theorists adopt the strong version of this principle, many acknowledge emotions as important factors in motivating perception, thought, and action (Frijda, 1986; Lazarus, 1991).

2. Each of the discrete emotions serves distinct functions in the way it *organizes* perception, cognition, and actions (behavior) for coping and creative endeavors, and in the way it contributes to personality and behavioral development (Ackerman, Abe, & Izard, 1998; Izard, 1977). An increasing number of studies support this basic principle (Martin, Horder, & Jones,

1992; Niedenthal & Kitayama, 1994; Renninger, Hidi, & Krapp, 1992). These investigations show that trait emotion or induced emotion guides perception, increases the selectivity of attention, and helps determine the content of working memory. Yet understanding the complex relations between specific emotions and behavior remains a significant challenge.

3. Personally significant situations typically activate a coherent pattern of interacting emotions (Izard, 1972; Izard & Youngstrom, 1996). The complexity of emotion–behavior relations results, in part, from the highly interactive nature of discrete emotions within the emotions system and in the formation of emotion patterns. Like the reciprocal interactions between discrete emotions and cognition, the reciprocal relations among the emotions in an activated pattern include interemotion *regulatory* processes. Regulation occurs in that the neural and motivational processes underlying one emotion in the pattern serve to amplify or dampen another emotion in the pattern. Although the cognitive and motor systems subserve many effective techniques of emotion regulation, some situations may require both of these systems operating with interemotion processes to achieve the adaptive level of arousal. Thus interemotion processes may always be factors in the optimal regulation of a given discrete emotion.

It is important to note, however, that though DET holds that the discrete emotions characteristically operate in a pattern of two or more emotions, each emotion retains its specific motivational properties. This position contrasts sharply with the view that emotion can be understood in terms of certain broad dimensions, such as pleasantness and arousal (cf. Watson & Tellegen, 1985). The positions converge to the extent that the causal influence of a broad dimension results from the interaction of discrete emotions. Many might agree, for instance, that interacting positive emotions could account for the pleasantness dimension.

4. Emotion–behavior relations begin to develop early and remain stable over time (Izard, 1977; Plutchik, 1980). Although the repertoire of specific responses for a given emotion changes as development proceeds, the new responses are complementary to the ones that remain and functionally similar to those that disappear. The sadness that elicits crying in the infant and toddler may produce only a sad countenance in the older child, but both forms of behavior invite nurturance or social support.

5. The capacity of emotions to motivate, organize, and sustain particular sets of behaviors contributes to the development of personality. Consistently high levels of joy or positive emotionality frequently lead to and facilitate social interactions and the emergence of the trait of extraversion (Abe & Izard, 1999).

6. Individual differences in emotion activation thresholds and in the frequency and intensity with which particular emotions are experienced and expressed are major determinants of specific traits and broad dimensions of personality.

7. Though each emotion has an inherently adaptive function (Izard, 1989; Lazarus & Smith, 1988; Leventhal, 1980; Plutchik, 1980), emotions may contribute to maladaptive behavior in response to threat or challenge. Such behavior usually reflects problems in interemotion and emotion–cognition relations and in emotion–cognition–action patterns. If the motivational component of fear, for instance, has been linked to inappropriate cognition to form maladaptive affective–cognitive structures, then activation of the emotion will result in maladaptive behavior.

Historical Context

The issue of whether emotions have two or three broad dimensions or 7 or 11 distinct units represents a fundamental question in emotion theory and has concerned scientists since the beginnings of psychology as a discipline. Early on, progenitors of the science of psychology and emotions theory articulated opposing views. Darwin (1872/1965), for example, described a dozen or so discrete emotions and argued that the expressions of some of these emotions evolved from functional systems. In his theory, the expressions that characterize certain of the discrete emotions are patterns of movement that served adaptive functions in evolution. Darwin made his arguments on this subject clear and prominent in his book on emotions, but he did not emphasize the notion that emotion expressions continue to serve adaptive functions in contemporary life. However, a careful reading of his work shows that he believed that the expressions of the emotions remain useful mechanisms. Darwin's description of the role of expressions includes what psychologists label "adaptive functions."

Darwin identified two adaptive functions of emotion expressions: social communication and the regulation of emotion experiences. Regarding the first, he said that the mother's smile of approval or frown of disapproval starts the child on the right path. Regarding the second function, he said that suppressing the expression of an emotion attenuates the experience of that emotion, and that the free and full expression of an emotion amplifies the emotion experience. In his statements about the evolution and adaptive functions of the emotions, Darwin was clearly talking about discrete emotions. He gave specific and anatomically detailed descriptions of unique and separate emotion expressions.

In contrast to Darwin, Spencer (1890) conceptualized emotions as dimensions of consciousness. Wundt (1897) extended Spencer's ideas and maintained that all emotion feelings can be explained in terms of three dimensions: pleasantness–unpleasantness, relaxation–tension, and calm–excitement. Variations of this approach were enunciated later by several highly influential investigators (Duffy, 1941; Lindsley, 1951; Schlosberg, 1941; Woodworth, 1938). Because of their efforts and a psychology that was largely controlled by behaviorism, the dimensional approach to the study of emotion was dominant in psychology until about the last third of the 20th century.

Well before discrete-emotions theories gained almost equal footing with dimensional theories, Tomkins (1962, 1963) wrote a brilliant exposition of his affect theory that identified eight separate emotions. At the same time, Plutchik (1962) published the early version of his theory, and he too described eight discrete emotions. Although he used different labels, most of his eight map directly onto those of Tomkins. Tomkins's and Plutchik's functionalist approach tied their work to the Darwinian tradition and had immediate appeal to a few psychologists who were open to the possibility that a bioevolutionary perspective might offer new insights on emotions and their role in developmental processes, personality, social relations, cognition, and actions (e.g., Ekman, 1972; Izard, 1971). It was at least 20 years after the appearance of the volumes by Tomkins and Plutchik, however, that discrete-emotions theories began having a significant impact on the field and guiding the work of a significant number of researchers.

Theoretical Context

The historical tensions between dimensional and discrete-emotions approaches frames theoretical debates today. Currently, a number of emotion researchers consider the discrete-emotions and dimensional approaches as complementary rather than as contradictory (cf. Watson & Tellegen, 1985). Indeed, even investigators who have developed discrete-emotions theories sometimes resort to a methodology that derives from the dimensional approach (e.g., Izard, 1972; Lang, 1984). A major reason for doing this is that on average it is easier to obtain reliable measures at the level of broad dimensions, such as valence (pleasantness–unpleasantness) or positive and negative emotionality, than at the level of discrete emotions. In the language of psychometrics, indices of discrete emotions are primary factors, and indices of broad dimensions are secondary factors; hence the greater stability of the latter (Izard, Libero, Putnam, & Haynes, 1993; Watson & Clark, 1992).

Nonetheless, the positions have different implications for understanding the role of emotions in motivating and organizing behavior, and in the development of personality and psychopathology. For example, negative emotionality operating as an entity and a discrete negative emotion (e.g., sadness) may influence personality development and behavior quite differently. In addition, reliable indices of discrete emotions (Izard, 1972) are useful in analyzing traits of personality and the syndromes of anxiety, depression, and hostility (Blumberg & Izard, 1985, 1986; Izard & Youngstrom, 1996; Watson & Clark, 1992).

At a pattern level, one subset or pattern of emotions (e.g., the depression pattern) may influence behavior quite differently than another (e.g., the hostility pattern), and both may have a different impact than general negative emotionality or a state characterized simply by negative valence and high arousal. These ideas suggest the utility of distinguishing between a discrete-emotions approach and a dimensional approach to emotion–behavior relations.

Another broad theoretical issue concerns the relations between the emotions system and cognition. For some theorists, cognitive processes of appraisal and attribution recruit emotions. This view privileges the cognitive system in activating emotions and in describing and understanding emotion–cognition relations. Differential-emotions theorists would agree that affective and cognitive processes are usually reciprocally interrelated. However, according to DET, an emotion may be activated by noncognitive processes, including other emotions (see Izard, 1993); emotion experiences have organizational characteristics that minimally involve cognition; and emotions recruit cognition to form both transitory and stable affective–cognitive structures. In sum, basic functions of emotion reflect inherent and privileged aspects of the emotions system per se.

The debate about emotion–cognition relations is framed in part by what is meant by the term "emotion." In DET, an emotion is a particular set of neural processes instigating efferent processes that may or may not lead to an observable expression but that always lead to a unique conscious experience. The subjective experience may or may not be accessible through cognitive processes or the language system. An emotion has three levels or aspects—neural, expressive, and experiential—and the term "emotion" refers to all three components operating as an integral system.

In infants, the efferent processes in emotion activation typically lead to expressive behavior. However, as a function of both maturation and socialization, the relations between the neural activation process and expressive behavior change with development (Izard, Hembree, & Huebner, 1987). As children gain more mastery over the somatic muscles of expression, and as socialization proceeds, children learn to regulate and modify emotion expressions and expressive styles. Eventually, observable expression in some situations may be completely inhibited or dissociated. Because feedback from expressive behavior contributes to the activation and regulation of emotion experiences (Duclos et al., 1989; Laird, 1974; Matsumoto, 1987; Strack, Martin, & Stepper, 1988; Winton, 1986), a child's learning to regulate emotion expressions is part of the process of learning to regulate emotion experiences (Darwin, 1872/ 1965; Izard, 1990; James, 1890/1990).

Emotion experience constitutes a quality of consciousness. It can be described as a feeling or motivational state that may include an action tendency or feeling of action readiness. For some negative emotions (e.g., anger, fear), the action tendency supports quite specific goals (attack, defense/protection). In positive emotion states (joy/happiness, interest), the individual experiences wider-ranging response tendencies toward more general goals such as affiliation and exploration (Izard, 1977). Emotion experience proper does not include cognition. However, emotion feeling/motivational

states contain information. They generate cues for decision and action. This can be conceived as a tendency to perceive and think in ways congruent with the information in the emotion. Although emotion feelings differ qualitatively from thought and decision processes, their cue-producing function typically recruits the cognitive system, rapidly and automatically. The integration or coordinated interaction of emotion and appropriate cognition produces adaptive behavior.

In the typical case, emotion experience recruits cognitive processes in an orderly fashion. That is, an emotion recruits cognitive and behavioral tendencies relevant to the dominant emotion in consciousness. The quality of consciousness that is joy recruits responses that are appropriate to joy as a motivational state. Similarly, the feeling/motivational state of sadness recruits cognitive and motoric responses congruent with this state, and so on for anger and the other discrete emotions (Bower, 1987; Izard, Wehmer, Livsey, & Jennings, 1965). The recruitment of cognition by an emotion feeling/motivational state and a subsequent effective action lay the groundwork for the development of an adaptive affective–cognitive structure. An "affective–cognitive structure" is an association or bond between emotion feeling and cognition. It is the most common type of mental structure, the fundamental building block of mind and memory.

Making a clean break between motivational state and cognition, and in particular between the subjective experience of emotion and the cognition that it recruits, has a number of implications for theory and empirical research (Izard, 1992). For example, it invites us to explore the possibility that unconscious motivation may be an emotion experience that is not cognitively tagged or articulated. Therefore, it is not possible to access this emotion experience through the language system. In alexithymia and certain other conditions, for example, feelings become chronically dissociated from cognition. These conditions represent extreme illustrations of the relative independence of emotion and cognition.

This clear break also facilitates conceptualization of the emergence of emotions (i.e., experience and expression) in childhood. For example, we term the basic emotions that emerge early in infancy (e.g., joy, sadness, fear, anger) "independent" emotions (see Ackerman et al., 1998), because the emergence does not require or reduce to cognitive processes (i.e., of a representational or computational nature). In contrast, emotions that fully emerge in middle childhood (i.e., shame, guilt) are "dependent" emotions, because emergence seems tied to self-processes, and to representational processes associated with both maturational influences and social experiences (cf. Lewis, 1992).

Finally, another important consequence of separating emotion feeling from cognition is that it makes it easier to formulate hypotheses about the role of cognition in emotion activation. If cognition is viewed as part of emotion experience per se, then it becomes difficult to examine cause–effect relations among cognitive and emotion processes. Heuristic advantages accrue to the position that an emotion experience consists of a motivational/feeling state that stems directly from neural processes without intervening cognitive interpretations. This allows us to conceptualize appraisal/evaluative processes as independent determinants of emotions and other cognitive processes as consequences.

THE ADAPTIVE FUNCTIONS
OF DISCRETE EMOTIONS

Despite the substantial body of evidence that testifies to the validity and usefulness of the concepts of discrete emotions, they have not been accepted universally by emotion theorists and researchers. In this section, we describe the adaptive functions of discrete emotions that provide evidence for the usefulness of the construct. We address three questions about a sample of specific emotions. First, does each discrete emotion have functions that can be readily understood as providing an adaptive advantage in evolution? Second, does this specific emotion continue to serve functions that facilitate development, adaptation, and coping? Third, does this emotion tend to co-occur with certain other emotions, so that the whole group forms a coherent set or pattern that provides an adaptive advantage? Finally, we try to show that a principal function of the emotions system is that of organizing and motivating characteristic patterns of responses or traits of personality.

The Functions of Interest

The definition of the emotion of "interest" overlaps with that of the terms "curiosity,"

"wonder," "urge to explore or discover," and "intrinsic motivation" (Deci, 1992). Healthy people in a safe and comfortable environment experience interest far more of the time than any other emotion. Its relative dominance of consciousness testifies to its significance for adaptation. Interest motivates exploration and learning, and guarantees the person's engagement in the environment. Survival and adaptation require such engagement. Interest supports creativity because it immerses one in the object or task and cues a sense of possibility. To paraphrase Tomkins (1962), interest is the only emotion that can sustain long-term constructive or creative endeavors.

Interest is the mechanism of selective attention—the mechanism that keeps attention from straying more or less randomly through the vast array of stimuli that constantly impinge on the senses. Interest not only focuses attention on a particular object, person, situation, or task; its status as an emotion provides the motivation and energy mobilization for engagement and interaction. Interest animates and enlivens the mind and body. Interest provides the motivation and resources for constructive and creative endeavor, the development of intelligence, and personal growth (cf. Deci, 1992; Tomkins, 1962).

Interest occurs in many patterns in which the emotions influence each other reciprocally. Interest may be part of the pattern of emotions in anxiety. In the anxiety pattern, interest may attenuate fear sufficiently to enable approach responses. Lorenz (1950) provides the classic example in his observation of a raven. From a high limb of a tall tree, the raven studies an object on the ground. The raven flies closer for a better look, then returns to a limb a bit closer to the object than its first perch. It flies down again and this time back up to a limb yet closer to the object. This continues until the raven lands by the object and begins actively exploring it. We can infer that interest motivates the approach responses, and that fear motivates the retreats to safe distances. Similar emotion dynamics characterize any novel situation that activates the urge to explore (interest) and imagery about possible threats from the unknown. Young people often describe their first trip abroad as a mix of interest and fear. In the cases of Lorenz's raven and the students' travel adventures, interest attenuates fear and sustains activity toward the goal. Recurring low levels of fear may serve to keep the exploration within safe bounds.

Interest most typically occurs in a pattern with joy. This pattern typifies the important developmental processes in children's play (cf. Singer, 1979). Interest sustains active engagement in the game. Happiness follows from achievement of a goal, mastery, or some incongruous event. Periodic joy provides respite from the activity driven by intense interest and serves as a reward that promotes return to the game. In a similar vein, Deci (1992) sees interest and joy as a blend that characterizes intrinsic motivation. He defines intrinsic motivation in terms of innate psychological needs—competence (White, 1959), self-actualization (Maslow, 1954), and relatedness—similar in substance to the conception of interest and joy as innate emotions characterized by motivational/feeling states.

The Functions of Joy/Happiness

The joy experience is different from sensory pleasure, but the latter often leads to the former, as when the culmination of sexual or postprandial pleasure increases intimacy and leads to enjoyable social interaction. Joy heightens an openness to experience. Such openness in social situations can contribute to affiliative behavior and the strengthening of social bonds. Social bonds and the social support they provide create a highly adaptive mechanism that can easily be conceived as an advantage in evolution and development. In species in which the young experience a long period of dependency, a strong social bond between parent and offspring is essential to survival (Hamburg, 1963; Mellen, 1981). No other emotion serves this function so effectively, providing significant benefits at little or no cost.

Joy also has recuperative powers and can serve as an antidote to stress (Tomkins, 1962). Although not specifically identifying joy, Lazarus and his colleagues have argued that positive emotions function as "breathers" in relieving stress, and that they sustain coping in taxing situations (Lazarus, Kanner, & Folkman, 1980).

The expression of joy serves another distinct function: The smile has the capacity to operate as a universally recognizable signal of readiness for friendly interaction. By the principles of contagion, empathy, and facial feedback, joy expression can contribute to the well-being of the social surround (Izard, 1990; Lelwica & Haviland, 1983; Tomkins, 1962).

Joy occurs in patterns with other emotions. We have already discussed the interest–joy pattern. Another pattern has been identified in common language as "tears of joy." This idiom and our own experiences suggest that joy and sadness co-occur. How can two emotions, more or less polar opposites, exist in consciousness together or even alternate in rapid sequence? A glance at the picture of a lost loved one can trigger memories of happy times together, as well as memories of the sad times surrounding the person's death. These memories are powerful activators of joy and sadness, respectively. The joy can serve as a reminder of the advantages that accrued from the relationship and can moderate the sadness. The sadness motivates renewal and strengthening of bonds with other loved ones. Similarly, tears and smiles may follow a victory in intellectual or athletic competition—joy from the achievement, sadness over the sacrifices endured while captivated by the goal.

The Functions of Sadness

Sadness, like joy, can also strengthen social bonds. For example, on the loss of a loved one, families and friends come together and renew emotional ties. The breaking of a tie through death is a compelling reminder of the value of family, friendships, and community. A review by Averill (1968) suggests that in the course of evolution, grief, by strengthening communal bonds, increased the probability of surviving. Although several emotions may be involved in grief, sadness is the dominant one.

A unique function of sadness is its capacity to slow the cognitive and motor systems. In one study, mothers' facial and vocal expressions of sadness during face-to-face mother–child interactions increased sadness expressions and significantly decreased exploratory play in their 9-month-old infants (Termine & Izard, 1988). Because play is the principal and virtually continuous activity of healthy infants and children, the slowing of play behavior dramatically demonstrates this function of sadness.

The sadness-induced slowing of mental and motor activity can have adaptive effects. The slowing of cognitive processes may enable a more careful look for the source of trouble and deeper reflection on a disappointing performance or a failure that instigated the sadness (see Tomkins, 1963). This slower and more deliberate scrutiny of the self and the circumstances may help the individual gain a new per-spective—one that facilitates plans for a better performance in the future. Such plans and the anticipation of another attempt may ameliorate the sadness.

Sadness also communicates to the self and to others that there is trouble (Tomkins, 1963). A sad expression, particularly on the face of a friend or loved one, is likely to generate em-pathic sadness in the observer. The sadness one feels with (or for) a friend increases the likeli-hood that one will feel sympathy and lend a helping hand (Moore, Underwood, & Rosen-han, 1984). Thus sadness may often be the key emotion in the personal distress that plays a key role in empathic, sympathetic, and altruistic be-havior (see Eisenberg & Strayer, 1987). If the sadness focuses on the other person and not on the self, and if the sadness (distress) is not too intense, it will facilitate prosocial behavior (Barnett, King, & Howard, 1979; Fabes, Eisen-berg, Karbon, Troyer, & Switzer, 1994).

Sadness occurs in several dynamically sig-nificant patterns. We have already discussed the joy–sadness pattern, "tears of joy." One other important pattern is the sadness–anger pattern that characterizes some low moods, including depression (Izard, 1971). Many clinicians and clinical investigations have shown that de-pressed people typically report elevated feel-ings of anger, along with the even more elevat-ed feelings of sadness (Rutter, Izard, & Read, 1986).

Tomkins (1963) speculated that extended and unrelieved sadness (distress) is an innate activator of anger. This notion is consistent with our idea that emotion patterns may self-orga-nize to enable interemotion relations that in-clude regulatory processes. In the depression pattern (Blumberg & Izard, 1986), the energy-mobilizing effects of anger counteract the sad-ness-induced slowing effect on mental and mo-tor processes. In turn, the sadness in the pattern helps moderate the intensity of the anger. With-out this cross-emotion regulatory process, ei-ther the sadness or the hostility could lead to personal disaster. Sadness in the extreme caus-es almost total loss of interest in the physical and social environment, and hence intense de-jection and withdrawal.

We have found that the anger in depression typically appears in what we have called the "hostility triad": anger, disgust, and contempt (Blumberg & Izard, 1985; Marshall & Izard, 1972). Even normal people report the co-occur-rence of these three emotions during imagery or recall of an anger-eliciting situation. The anger or hostility in depression is typically di-rected toward the self, and in extreme cases its interaction with sadness results in suicide. In contrast, we would predict violence if the hos-tility should dominate in the pattern and be-come directed outward toward people seen as responsible for the loss or failure that triggered the depression.

The Functions of Anger

In the colorful language of Tomkins (1991), the principal function of anger is to make bad mat-ters worse and increase the probability of an anger response. He hastened to add that this need not be an aggressive response, acknowl-edging (as do most emotion theorists) that there is no necessary connection between anger and aggression (cf. Averill, 1983).

Indeed, anger expression may prevent ag-gression. This is the case when the alpha male in a primate colony casts a hard stare at a chal-lenger (Chevalier-Skolnikoff, 1973), or when a parent does the same to inhibit a fight between two children. Furthermore, the effects of an anger expression toward another adult may even truncate the anger-related response of the angry individual. This may be the case if the anger expression elicits an immediate sad ex-pression and apology from the other person.

A unique function of the experience of anger is that of mobilizing and sustaining energy at high levels. Other emotions, even the positive emotions of interest and joy, mobilize energy and sustain goal-directed activity, but not usual-ly at the high level of intensity that can be maintained by strong anger. Anger directs in-creased blood flow away from the viscera and toward the muscles of action (Cannon, 1929). No other emotion can equal the consistency and vigor of anger in increasing and sustaining ex-tremely high levels of motor activity. It is no coincidence that some coaches in contact sports, aided greatly by the media, foster mild anger (and contempt) for opposing coaches and players.

The relation of anger to aggressive behavior illustrates the process of one emotion's regulat-ing another and complicating emotion–behav-ior relations. Many believe that anger leads to aggression, but anger leads to many other forms of behavior more frequently than to ag-gression (Averill, 1983). Other emotions often play a role in motivating aggressive behavior, either directly or through their interactions with anger. For example, a challenge to one's ego or self-esteem that increases attention to the self may activate a pattern in which shame precedes, activates, and amplifies anger. In individuals with spuriously high self-esteem, this pattern greatly increases the likelihood of aggression and violence (Baumeister, Smart, & Boden, 1996). The picture becomes even more complex with the addition of contempt—a direct cause of shame and a direct or indirect cause of aggression (Izard, 1977; cf. Baumeister et al., 1996; Lewis, 1987; Tomkins, 1963).

The Functions of Shame

The capacity for experiencing shame reflects the vulnerability of the individual to the sanctions and criticisms of parents, other adults, and peers. Persons who fail to fulfill their responsibility in the family and community may become the subjects of ridicule and contempt— strong stimuli for shame. Thus shame acts as a force for social conformity and social cohesion, and the anticipation of shame or shame avoidance motivates the individual to accept his or her share of responsibility for the welfare of the community (see Lewis, 1971; Tomkins, 1962).

No other emotion is as effective as shame in calling attention to failures and weaknesses in the functioning of the self. Consequently, it relates significantly to self-concepts and self-feeling or self-esteem. Shame results from conditions that heighten self-awareness, and shame is more likely to occur when the exposed self appears inadequate or some aspect of the self seems inept or inappropriate (for a review of the role of the self in the development and activation of shame, see Lewis, 1992). The exposure one feels during the experience of shame highlights personal inadequacies in performance and feelings of incompetence. Because of this relation between the vulnerability of the self and proneness to shame, shame anticipation and shame avoidance motivate the acquisition of skills and competence. In this way, shame plays a significant role in the development of self-adequacy (see Lewis, 1971; Lynd, 1961; Tangney, 1990; Tomkins, 1963).

Shame plays a role in several important emotion patterns. We have already noted that shame may be present in both the anxiety and depression patterns. The fear–shame pattern provides the emotion dynamics of social anxiety or so-cial phobia. In this pattern, shame directs attention toward the need to strengthen the self through the acquisition of social skills. We have described the shame–anger pattern above in the section on anger.

The Functions of Fear

The unique function of fear is to motivate escape from dangerous situations. Fear anticipation motivates avoidance behavior. Neither escape nor avoidance implies that the behavior must involve flight. Indeed, fear sometimes disengages the motor system, resulting in freezing behavior. Furthermore, the threat may be psychological as well as physical. Threats to one's self-concept, one's integrity, or one's psychological well-being can elicit fear, and such threats are rarely eliminated by physically running away. Nevertheless, whether the threat is physical or mental or both, fear performs its basic function of motivating escape and alleviating fear-eliciting conditions.

Fear provides an excellent example of the power of emotion to organize and direct perceptual and cognitive processes. Fear tends to produce "tunnel vision" by focusing attention on the source of the threat and restricting cue utilization (see Easterbrook, 1959). Keen attention to the threatening agent or situation can be adaptive in guiding self-protective behavior. Such restrictions on attentional processes in unrealistic or unwarranted fear are maladaptive.

Fear participates in several important emotion patterns. For example, it is the key emotion in the anxiety pattern. Other emotions in the anxiety pattern serve, in part, to attenuate fear. We have already described the interaction of fear and interest, particularly as they affect explorations of the unknown.

THE FUNCTIONS OF EMOTIONS IN THE DEVELOPMENT OF PERSONALITY

A major general function of the emotions and the emotions system is the organization of traits and dimensions of personality (Izard, 1991; Malatesta, 1990). That emotions affect the development of personality is a truism, but the matter of how this is accomplished is not so obvious. We sketch three mechanisms involving continuous influence, the early emergence of individual differences in activation thresholds, and the increasing stabilization of emotion patterns with development.

Principle of Continuous Influence

We have argued that emotions are motivational and that they organize and motivate cognition and action. It follows that emotions should affect an individual's characteristic way of thinking and acting—his or her personality. Many agree that personality (established emotion–cognition–action patterns) produces individual differences in response to episodes of intense emotional feelings. We propose that emotions influence personality functioning continuously, not just episodically. The principle of continuous influence follows from our assumption that some emotion at some level of intensity is continually present in consciousness (e.g., Izard, 1989). Furthermore, we have maintained that each emotion influences perception, cognition, and action in a particular way. This suggests that specific emotions help shape specific traits, and that particular patterns of emotions influence particular broad dimensions of personality. Several empirical studies support the notion that emotions have specific effects in shaping personality; more conservatively, this evidence shows significant correlations among measures of emotion expressions and emotion feelings and personality traits (Abe & Izard, 1999; Emmons & Diener, 1986; Izard et al., 1993; Jones, Cheeks, & Briggs, 1986; Keltner, 1996; Larsen & Ketelaar, 1989; Malatesta & Wilson, 1988; Watson & Clark, 1992).

Activation Thresholds

Differences in activation thresholds play a significant role in the development of personality. Common observation suggests that people differ widely in readiness or proneness to express different emotions. These differences emerge early in life, as suggested by temperament theorists (see Goldsmith et al., 1987), and they transact with caregiving experiences to influence personality development. For example, Kochanska and colleagues (see Kochanska, 1995) have found that toddler fearfulness in combination with gentle or more power-assertive socialization facilitates or inhibits internalization of social relations. Similarly, Kagan and Snidman (1991) have provided evidence for individual differences in behavioral inhibition in infants and toddlers that may derive from different thresholds for experiencing shyness or fear. Other researchers have demonstrated threshold differences between such groups as normal children and children with Down's syndrome (Cicchetti & Sroufe, 1976).

These individual differences in activation thresholds and in subsequent emotion experiences may be quite stable. For example, Izard et al. (1993) found that indices of discrete emotions remained stable in a group of women for periods of up to 3 years. In this study, indices of 11 discrete emotions showed individual stability even during the first 6 months after childbirth, when important hormonal and social changes occur (O'Hara, 1987). Even during the postpartum period, when indices of some emotion experiences showed group instability, these and all other indices continued to show individual stability. Thus each individual woman tended to retain her rank within the group. Of particular relevance to the concept of interemotion dynamics, the mean score on each emotion in a pattern of four depression-related emotions declined systematically during the period of "postpartum blues" without affecting individual rank difference.

Stability of Emotion Patterns

Two other concepts help clarify the role of emotions in the development of personality: stable patterns of emotions, and affective–cognitive structures. Not only is there stability in the frequency of experiencing a particular emotion, but some emotions co-occur with regularity, and the regularity increases with development. Such co-occurrence is probably a function of both innate and learned relationships among emotions (Izard, 1972; Tomkins, 1962). We have identified several patterns in our discussion of interemotion dynamics. Some of these patterns have a high level of stability. An example is the interaction of interest and joy in play and affiliative behavior. Another example of a stable pattern of emotions is the sadness–anger interaction that characterizes depression (Blumberg & Izard, 1985, 1986). Frequently occurring stable patterns of emotions influence cognition and actions in particular ways, and these responses and response tendencies become characteristics or traits of the individual.

An affective–cognitive structure, as defined earlier, is a bond or association between an emotion or pattern of emotions and a thought or set of thoughts (schema or script). Such affective–cognitive structures (emotion scripts) or related sets of them can motivate a related pattern of behaviors manifested as a personality trait. As indicated earlier, emotion experiences typically influence normal personality functioning through affective–cognitive structures. The important exceptions are emotion experiences that are not labeled or cognitively articulated, or emotion experiences that have become dissociated from the cognitions once associated with them. Such unlabeled or dissociated emotion experiences are conceived of as the major source of unconscious motivation.

To summarize the role of emotions in personality development, individual differences in emotion activation thresholds lead to differences in the frequency of emotion experiences. Frequent experiences of a particular emotion tend to organize particular types of cognition and action, and recurring patterns of emotion–cognition–action sequences lead to the development of a characteristic way of responding, a personality trait. For example, people with low thresholds for positive emotions are characteristically happy, and their positive emotionality tends to be stable over time. For many people, positive mood lowers the threshold for social interaction; because of this, positive emotionality in infancy and childhood increases the likelihood of the emergence of the personality dimension of extraversion. In a similar fashion, low thresholds for negative emotions set the stage for the development of the personality dimension of negative emotionality or neuroticism (Abe & Izard, 1999).

SUMMARY

This chapter is based on the assumption that the emotions system constitutes the primary motivational system for human behavior, and that each discrete emotion serves unique functions in coping and adaptation. The chief premise of the chapter is that each emotion motivates and organizes perception, cognition, and actions (behavior) in particular ways. Thus individual differences in emotion thresholds lead to individual differences in patterns of behavior that become organized as traits of personality.

The chapter presents evidence and argument for the unique organizing and motivational functions of discrete emotions. It makes explicit the principle of emotion dynamics through discussion of several emotion patterns in which one emotion influences another emotion in a pattern. Finally, the chapter proposes that recurring patterns of interacting emotions play a significant role in behavior and the development of personality.

REFERENCES

Abe, J. A., & Izard, C. E. (1999). A longitudinal study of emotion expression and personality relations in early development. *Journal of Personality and Social Psychology, 77*(3), 566–577.

Ackerman, B. P., Abe, J. A., & Izard, C. E. (1998). Differential emotions theory and emotional development: Mindful of modularity. In M. F. Mascolo & S. Griffin (Eds.), *What develops in emotional development?* (pp. 85–106). New York: Plenum Press.

Averill, J. R. (1968). Grief: Its nature and significance. *Psychological Bulletin, 70*, 721–748.

Averill, J. R. (1983). Studies on anger and aggression: Implications for theories of emotion. *American Psychologist, 38*, 1145–1162.

Barnett, M., King, L. M., & Howard, J. A. (1979). Inducing affect about self and other: Effects on generosity in children. *Developmental Psychology, 15*, 164–167.

Baumeister, R. F., Smart, L., & Boden, J. M. (1996). Relation of threatened egotism to violence and aggression: The dark side of high self-esteem. *Psychological Review, 103*, 5–33.

Blumberg, S. H., & Izard, C. E. (1985). Affective and cognitive characteristics of depression in 10- and 11-year-old children. *Journal of Personality and Social Psychology, 49*, 194–202.

Blumberg, S. H., & Izard, C. E. (1986). Discriminating patterns of emotions in 10- and 11-year-old children's anxiety and depression. *Journal of Personality and Social Psychology, 51*, 852–857.

Bower, C. H. (1987). Commentary on mood and memory. *Behaviour Research and Therapy, 25*, 443-455.

Cannon, W. B. (1929). *Bodily change in pain, hunger, fear and rage: An account of recent researches into the function of emotional excitement.* New York: Appleton-Century-Crofts.

Chevalier-Skolnikoff, S. (1973). Facial expression of emotion in nonhuman primates. In P. Ekman (Ed.), *Darwin and facial expression* (pp. 11–89). New York: Academic Press.

Cicchetti, D., & Sroufe, L. A. (1976). The relationship between affective and cognitive development in Down syndrome infants. *Child Development, 47*, 920–929.

Darwin, C. R. (1965). *The expression of the emotions in man and animals.* Chicago: University of Chicago Press. (Original work published 1872)

Deci, E. L. (1992). On the nature and functions of motivation theories. *Psychological Science, 3*, 167–171.

Duclos, S. E., Laird, J. D., Schneider, E., Sexter, M., Stern, L., & Van Lighten, O. (1989). Emotion-specific effects of facial expressions and postures on emotional experience. *Journal of Personality and Social Psychology, 57*, 100–108.

Duffy, E. (1941). An explanation of emotional phenomena without the use of the concept "emotion." *Journal of General Psychology, 25*, 283–293.

Easterbrook, J. A. (1959). The effect of emotion on cue utilization and the organization of behavior. *Psychological Bulletin, 66*, 183–201.

Eisenberg, N., & Strayer, J. (Eds.). (1987). *Empathy and its development.* New York: Cambridge University Press.

Ekman, P. (1972). Universals and cultural differences in facial expressions of emotion. In J. R. Cole (Ed.), *Nebraska Symposium on Motivation* (Vol. 19, pp. 207–283). Lincoln: University of Nebraska Press.

Emmons, R. A., & Diener, E. (1986). An interactional approach to the study of personality and emotion. *Journal of Personality, 54*, 1221–1228.

Fabes, R. A., Eisenberg, N., Karbon, M., Troyer, D., & Switzer, G. (1994). The relations of children's emotion regulation to their vicarious emotional responses and comforting behaviors. *Child Development, 65*, 1678–1693.

Frijda, N. H. (1986). *The emotions.* New York: Cambridge University Press.

Goldsmith, H. H., Buss, A., Plomin, R., Rothbart, M., Thomas, A., Chess, S., Hinde, R., & McCall, R. (1987). Roundtable: What is temperament?: Four approaches. *Child Development, 58*, 505–529.

Hamburg, D. A. (1963). Emotions in the perspective of human evolution. In P. H. Knapp (Ed.), *Expression of emotions in man* (pp. 300–317). New York: International Universities Press.

Izard, C. E. (1971). *The face of emotion.* New York: Appleton-Century-Crofts.

Izard, C. E. (1972). *Patterns of emotions: A new analysis of anxiety and depression.* New York: Academic Press.

Izard, C. E. (1977). *Human emotions.* New York: Plenum Press.

Izard, C. E. (1989). The structure and functions of emotions: Implications for cognition, motivation, and personality. In I. S. Cohen (Ed.), *The G. Stanley Hall lecture series* (Vol. 9, pp. 35–73). Washington, DC: American Psychological Association.

Izard, C. E. (1990). Facial expressions and the regulation of emotions. *Journal of Personality and Social Psychology, 58*, 487–498.

Izard, C. E. (1991). *The psychology of emotions.* New York: Plenum Press.

Izard, C. E. (1992). Basic emotions, relations among emotions, and emotion–cognition relations. *Psychological Review, 99*, 561–565.

Izard, C. E. (1993). Four systems for emotion activation: Cognitive and noncognitive processes. *Psychological Review, 100*, 68–90.

Izard, C. E., Hembree, E. A., & Huebner, R. R. (1987). Infants' emotion expressions to acute pain: Developmental change and stability of individual differences. *Developmental Psychology, 23*, 105–113.

Izard, C. E., Libero, D. Z., Putnam, P., & Haynes, O. M. (1993). Stability of emotion experiences and their relation to traits of personality. *Journal of Personality and Social Psychology, 64*, 847–860.

Izard, C. E., Wehmer, C. M., Livsey, W., & Jennings, I.

R. (1965). Affect awareness, and performance. In S. S. Tomkins & C. E. Izard (Eds.), *Affect, cognition, and personality* (pp. 2–41). New York: Springer.

Izard, C. E., & Youngstrom, E. A. (1996). The activation and regulation of fear and anxiety. In D. A. Hope (Ed.), *Nebraska Symposium on Motivation: Vol. 43. Perspectives in anxiety, panic, and fear* (pp. 2–59). Lincoln: University of Nebraska Press.

James, W. (1990). *The principles of psychology.* New York: Dover. (Original work published 1890)

Jones, W. H., Cheeks, J. M., & Briggs, S. R. (Eds.). (1986). *Shyness: Perspectives on research and treatment.* New York: Plenum Press.

Kagan, J., & Snidman, N. (1991). Infant predictors of inhibited and uninhibited profiles. *Psychological Science, 2*, 40–44.

Keltner, D. (1996). Facial expressions of emotion and personality. In C. Malatesta-Magai & S. H. McFadden (Eds.), *Handbook of emotion, aging, and the lifecourse* (pp. 385–402). New York: Academic Press.

Kochanska, G. (1995). Children's temperament, mothers' discipline, and security of attachment: Multiple pathways to emerging internalization. *Child Development, 66*, 597–615.

Laird, J. D. (1974). Self-attribution of emotion: The effects of expressive behavior on the quality of emotional experience, *Journal of Personality and Social Psychology, 29*, 475–486.

Lang, P. J. (1984). Cognition in emotion: Cognition in action. In C. E. Izard, J. Kagan, & R. B. Zajonc (Eds.), *Emotions, cognition, and behavior* (pp. 192–226). New York: Cambridge University Press.

Larsen, R. J., & Ketelaar, T. (1989). Extroversion, neuroticism, and susceptibility to positive/negative mood induction procedures. *Personality and Individual Differences, 10*, 1221–1228.

Lazarus, R. S. (1991). *Emotion and adaptation.* New York: Oxford University Press.

Lazarus, R. S., Kanner, A. D., & Folkman, S. (1980). Emotions: A cognitive-phenomenological analysis. In R. Plutchik & H. Kellerman (Eds.), *Emotion: Theory, research, and experience. Vol. 1. Theories of emotion* (pp. 189–217). New York: Academic Press.

Lazarus, R. S., & Smith, C. A. (1988). Knowledge and appraisal in the emotion–cognition relationship. *Cognition and Emotion, 2*, 281–300.

Lelwica, M., & Haviland, J. M. (1983, April). *Response or imitation: Ten-week-old infants' reactions to three emotion expressions.* Paper presented at the biennial meeting of the Society for Research in Child Development, Detroit, MI.

Leventhal, H. (1980). Toward a comprehensive theory of emotion. In L. Berkowitz (Ed.), *Advances in experimental social psychology* (Vol. 13, pp. 141–165). New York: Academic Press.

Lewis, H. (1971). *Shame and guilt in neurosis.* New York: International Universities Press.

Lewis, H. (Ed.). (1987) *The role of shame in symptom formation.* Hillsdale, NJ: Erlbaum.

Lewis, M. (1992). *Shame: The exposed self.* New York: Free Press.

Lindsley, D. B. (1951). Emotion. In S. S. Stevens (Ed.), *Handbook of experimental psychology* (pp. 473–516). New York: Wiley.

Lorenz, K. (1950). Part and parcel in animal and human societies. In K. Lorenz (Ed.), *Studies in animal and human behaviour* (Vol. 2, pp. 115–195). London: Methuen.

Lynd, H. M. (1961). *On shame and the search for identity*. New York: Science Editions.

Malatesta, C. Z. (1990). The role of emotions in the development and organization of personality. In R. A. Thompson (Ed.), *Nebraska Symposium on Motivation: Vol. 36. Socioemotional development* (pp. 1–56). Lincoln: University of Nebraska Press.

Malatesta, C. Z., & Wilson, A. (1988). Emotion cognition interaction in personality development: A discrete emotions, functionalist analysis. *British Journal of Social Psychology, 27*, 91–112.

Marshall, A. G., & Izard, C. E. (1972). Depression as a pattern of emotions and feelings: Factor-analytic investigations. In C. E. Izard (Ed.), *Patterns of emotions: A new analysis of anxiety and depression* (pp. 237–254). New York: Academic Press.

Martin, M., Horder, P., & Jones, G. V. (1992). Integral bias in naming of phobia-related words. *Cognition and Emotion, 6*, 479–486.

Maslow, A. H. (1954). *Motivation and personality*. New York: Harper & Row.

Matsumoto, D. (1987). The role of facial response in the experience of emotion: More methodological problems and a meta-analysis. *Journal of Personality and Social Psychology, 52*, 769–774.

Mellen, S. L. V. (1981). *The evolution of love*. San Francisco: Freeman.

Moore, B., Underwood, B., & Rosenhan, D. L. (1984). Emotion, self, and others. In C. E. Izard, J. Kagan, & R. B. Zajonc (Eds.), *Emotions, cognition, and behavior* (pp. 464–483). New York: Cambridge University Press.

Niedenthal, P. M., & Kitayama, S. (Eds.). (1994). *The heart's eye: Emotional influences in perception and attention*. San Diego, CA: Academic Press.

O'Hara, M. W. (1987). Postpartum "blues," depression and psychosis: A review. *Journal of Psychosomatic Obstetrics and Gynecology, 7*, 205–227.

Plutchik, R. (1962). *The emotions: Facts, theories, and a new model*. New York: Random House.

Plutchik, R. (1980). *Emotion: A psychoevolutionary synthesis*. New York: Harper & Row.

Renninger, K. A., Hidi, S., & Krapp, A. (1992). *The role of interest in learning and development*. Hillsdale, NJ: Erlbaum.

Rutter, M., Izard, C. E., & Read, P. B. (Eds.). (1986). *Depression in young people: Developmental and clinical perspectives*. New York: Guilford Press.

Schlosberg, H. S. (1941). A scale for the judgement of facial expressions. *Journal of Experimental Psychology, 29*, 497–510.

Singer, J. L. (1979). Affect and imagination in play and fantasy. In C. E. Izard (Ed.), *Emotions in personality and psychopathology* (pp. 13–34). New York: Plenum Press.

Spencer, H. (1890). *The principles of psychology* (Vol. 1). New York: Appleton.

Strack, F., Martin, L. L., & Stepper, S. (1988). Inhibiting and facilitating conditions of the human smile: A nonobtrusive test of the facial feedback hypothesis. *Journal of Personality and Social Psychology, 54*, 768–777.

Tangney, J. P. (1990). Assessing individual differences in proneness to shame and guilt: Development of the Self-Conscious Affect and Attribution Inventory. *Journal of Personality and Social Psychology, 59*, 102–111.

Termine, N. T., & Izard, C. E. (1988). Infants' responses to their mothers' expressions of joy and sadness. *Developmental Psychology, 24*, 223–229.

Tomkins, S. S. (1962). *Affect, imagery, consciousness: Vol. 1. The positive affects*. New York: Springer.

Tomkins, S. S. (1963). *Affect, imagery, consciousness: Vol. 2. The negative affects*. New York: Springer.

Tomkins, S. S. (1991). *Affect, imagery, consciousness: Vol. 3. The negative affects: Anger and fear*. New York: Springer.

Watson, D., & Clark, L. A. (1992). On traits and temperament: General and specific factors of emotional experience and their relation to the five-factor model. *Journal of Personality, 60*, 441–476.

Watson, D., & Tellegen, A. (1985). Toward a consensual structure of mood. *Psychological Bulletin, 98*, 219–235.

White, R. W. (1959). Motivation reconsidered: The concept of competence. *Psychological Review, 66*, 297–333.

Winton, W. M. (1986). The role of facial response in self-reports of emotion: A critique of Laird. *Journal of Personality and Social Psychology, 50*, 808–812.

Woodworth, R. S. (1938). *Experimental psychology*. New York: Holt.

Wundt, W. (1897). *Outlines of psychology* (C. H. Judd, Trans.). New York: C. E. Stechert.

CHAPTER 17

The Emergence of Human Emotions

Michael Lewis

Observation of newborn infants reveals a rather narrow range of emotional behavior. They cry and show distress when pained, lonely, or in need of food and attention. They look attentive and focused on objects and people in their world. They appear to listen to sounds, to look at objects, and to respond to tickle sensations. Moreover, they seem to show positive emotions, such as happiness and contentment. When fed, picked up, or changed, they show relaxed body posture, smile, and appear content. Although they show a wide range of postural and even facial expressions, the set of discrete emotions that they exhibit is rather limited. Yet, in a matter of months and indeed by the end of the third year of life, these same children display a wide range of emotions. Indeed, some have suggested that by this age, almost the full range of adult emotions can be said to exist (Lewis, 1992b). In 3 years, the display and range of human emotions goes from a few to the highly differentiated many. In order to understand this rapid development, it is necessary for us to consider the set of issues that will enable a careful articulation of their development. The first issue to be discussed, therefore, is the topic of the topology of emotional features. Embedded within this is a consideration of the development of these features. Finally, the developmental sequence over the first 3 years of life is considered.

THE TOPOLOGY OF EMOTION

In order to talk about developmental issues involved in the study of emotion, it is important that we first make clear what we mean by the term "emotion." "Emotion," like the term "cognition," refers to a class of elicitors, behaviors, states, and experiences. If we do not distinguish among these features of emotion, study of them and their development becomes difficult. For example, Zajonc (1980) argued that emotions can occur without cognitions, while Lazarus (1982) argued that emotions require cognition. As we shall see, each of them was describing a different feature of emotional life. Because of this, each could arrive at diametrically opposing positions without endangering his own argument. The reasons for this are quite simple: As we shall see, Zajonc was arguing for emotions as states, whereas Lazarus argued for emotions as experience.

Emotional Elicitors

In order for an emotion to occur, some stimulus event—what I will call the "emotional elicitor"—must trigger a change in the state of the organism. The state of the organism can be a change in an idea, or it can be a change in the physiological state of the organism. The triggering event may either be an external or internal stimulus. External elicitors may be nonsocial (e.g., loud noise) or social (e.g., separation from a loved one). Internal elicitors may range from changes in specific physiological states to complex cognitive activities. Since it is obviously much harder to identify and manipulate an internal elicitor than an external one, it is not surprising that most research deals with external stimuli—that is, with an attempt to determine precisely which features of the elicitor activate the emotion.

A major problem in defining an emotional elicitor is that not all stimuli can be characterized as emotional elicitors. For example, a blast of cold air may cause a drop in body temperature and elicit shivering, but one is reluctant to classify this occurrence as an emotional event. In general, we use our "common sense" to define an event as an emotional elicitor. Thus, for example, the approach of a stranger or experience on a visual cliff apparatus is usually the eliciting event for fear. The approach of a familiar parent is not used for fear, but is used as an elicitor to measure joy or happiness. Events that we use to elicit particular emotions grow out of our common experiences. Unfortunately, such experiences may not be correct. As we can see in studies on fear, not all children show fear at a stranger's approach (Lewis & Rosenblum, 1974).

The problem of the nature of elicitors becomes even more serious when we try to measure physiological reactions to emotional events. For example, in the presentation of a horror film and the measurement of physiological response to that horror film, one can assume that the elicitor is a fearful one. What physiologically appears is then taken as the response to fear. When subjects are questioned as to the nature of the elicitor and what emotions it produces, it is often the case that (1) they do not produce the emotion believed associated with the elicitor, or (2) they produce a diverse set of emotional reactions. Schwartz and Weinberger (1980), for example, asked subjects what emotion they had to a set of different events and found that they offered a variety of emotions for the same elicitor. A colleague and I (Lewis & Michalson, 1983) likewise asked adults to mention the emotions produced by such elicitors as going to the wedding of their child or the death of a parent. These individuals gave a variety of emotions in response to any such elicitor. Such research as this suggests that we have little information, excluding our common experi-

ence, in regard to the nature of emotional elicitors.

While from a scientific viewpoint little information about which emotions are elicited by which stimulus events is available, it appears to be the case that within a culture adult individuals seem to possess common knowledge in regard to how they should react emotionally to particular stimulus events. So, for example, at the death of a friend's parent, we know the emotion others either are likely to have or are expected to show. The script learning of appropriate emotions by stimulus conditions, whether or not these are "true" emotions or simply playacting, informs us that knowledge about emotional elicitors and appropriate emotional responses is something that is acquired. In reviews of this subject (see Harris, 1989; Lewis, 1989), data on children's acquisition of such knowledge reveal that by the age of 10 years children have a good sense of what are the appropriate emotions for appropriate stimulus elicitors. The learning of these emotional scripts appears to take place quite early. I (Lewis, 1989), for example, asked children to choose which emotional expression was likely to go with a set of stories that included receiving gifts at a birthday party, being lost from your mother in a grocery store, and falling and hurting yourself. Children as young as 3 to 5 years were already capable of responding appropriately—that is, the way adults would respond to these same emotional scripts. Learning what is appropriate vis-à-vis the culture is important for children, and they acquire such knowledge early. The acquisition of such knowledge does not necessarily imply that the situations do not produce the emotions that are commonly believed to occur under such conditions. All that needs to be pointed out is the possibility that specific stimulus events are more likely to elicit some emotions rather than others. The emotion elicitors can be a function of what a child has learned in terms of how to behave, as well as a function of some automatic process whereby specific events elicit specific emotions.

Development of Elicitors

There is a class of elicitors that has little developmental history. A loud and sudden noise causes startling, and possibly fear, in organisms throughout their lives. The looming of a visual event causes startle and attention, and perhaps fear as well. The sight of food always serves as a positive elicitor, if one is hungry. It would therefore seem possible to imagine a class of events, either biologically determined or learned in the very beginning of life, that would consistently produce a particular emotional state. Even for this class of more automatic-like elicitors, the developmental experiences of the organisms may be such as to inhibit or restrict the elicitor from operating in its natural way.

In the class of elicitors with a developmental course, the structure that supports the elicitor–response connection is likely to undergo change. Within this class are elicitors that are biologically connected to a response, as well as elicitors that are connected to a response through learned associations. For example, infants' fear of strangers may be biologically programmed; over time, stranger fear may decline because the biological structure supporting the elicitor–response connection has broken down or has been altered by experience. Learned associations between elicitors and responses may also be subject to developmental change because new structures are formed or old ones are extinguished; for instance, the formation of new structures can be predicated on cognitive changes. The data from numerous sources suggest that important cognitive factors play a role in mediating the effects of classes of events in the elicitation of fear (see, e.g., Campos & Stenberg, 1981; Feinman & Lewis, 1984). Several of these cognitive processes are considered here, and more could probably be added to the list. These capacities are regarded as critical and serve as examples of the role that cognitive development might play in mediating the development of fear elicitors. First, memory must play an important role in the elicitation of fear. Children must be able to recognize and associate past events that were noxious. The white coats of doctors may be associated with pain and thus acquire the capacity to elicit fear. In terms of cognitive expectancy, violation per se does not seem to be a fear elicitor. In fact, violation of expectancy may be arousing, and the particular emotion produced may depend on whether the organism can assimilate and control the event (Lewis & Goldberg, 1969). Some events that are uncontrollable are likely to elicit fear as well (see Gunnar, 1980).

Tracing the developmental course of elicitors is a difficult task to do. The development of other cognitive processes—categorization, classification, reasoning, and the like—is also likely to influence which elicitors produce what emotional responses; for example, failure in a task produces sadness in children prior to 24 months of age, while failure at a task after 24 months is likely to produce shame or guilt. The same elicitor produces different emotions, depending upon children's cognitive capacity. Before children can evaluate their actions against some standard, the failure to achieve a goal results in sadness. Once children are capable of this evaluation of self, the emotion as a consequence of the failure is likely to be shame or guilt (Lewis, 1992b). Such findings as these alert us to several problems concerning emotional elicitors. These include (1) that some elicitors may have an automatic biological adaptive connection to emotions, whereas others are connected through learned associations; (2) that individuals may differ in the extent to which the same elicitor produces different emotions; and (3) that the relation between emotional elicitors and emotional outcomes changes as a function of the meaning system of a particular individual.

Emotional States

Emotional states are inferred constructs. These states are defined as particular constellations of changes in somatic and/or neurophysiological activity. Emotional states can occur without organisms' being able to perceive these states. Individuals can be angry as a consequence of a particular elicitor and yet not perceive the angry state that they are in. An emotional state may involve changes in neurophysiological and hormonal responses, as well as changes in facial, bodily, and vocal behavior. Two views exist concerning emotional states. According to the first, these states are associated with specific receptors; indeed, they constitute the activation of these receptors (Izard, 1977; Tomkins, 1962, 1963). In the second, emotional states are not associated with specific receptors and do not exist as specific changes; instead, they are general response tendencies associated with specific cognitions (Mandler, 1975, 1980; Ortony, Clore, & Collins, 1988; Schachter & Singer, 1962).

In the first view, specific emotional states are postulated that have concomitant physiological components and that are expressed in specific facial and bodily behaviors. There is a one-to-one correspondence between the emotion, such as anger, fear, sadness, or happiness, and some internal specific state that matches this emotion. This view of specific emotional states has served, since Darwin's (1872/1965) initial formulation, as the basis of what we believe to be the correspondence between the specific emotions we experience and the functions of our bodies. They are inferred states. Except for bodily and facial expression, no one-to-one correspondence has been found between such inferred physiological changes and emotions. Investigators exploring brain function (Davidson & Fox, 1982; Nelson & Bosquet, 2000; Nelson & Bloom, 1977) and those looking at specific autonomic nervous system changes (Ekman, 1989) argue for some correspondence between specific internal states and specific emotions. Even so, the evidence for specific states remains lacking.

The nonstate theories, cognitive in nature, argue less for a specific correspondence between an internal state and emotions; rather, cognitive activity is seen as the determiner of specific emotions. Either general arousal models, such as Schachter and Singer's (1962) model, or cognitive theory models have as their basic tenet a denial of the existence of specific states; rather, emotions occur as a consequence of thinking (Ortony et al., 1988).

Specific states, having specific stimuli that elicit them, can be found. For example, the theory of innate releasing mechanisms (IRMs) suggests that animals will show a fear response, given a particular stimulus event. The argument made here is that there is a direct correspondence between a specific elicitor and a specific state. Watson (1919) argued that there are specific elicitors in infants; fear is produced by a falling sensation or by loud noises. Likewise, attachment theorists argued that children show joy or attachment to the objects that take care of them (Bowlby, 1969). On the other hand, it is quite clear that certain specific emotions can be produced only through cognitive processes.

For example, certain elicitors invoke cognitive processes, which in turn may elicit or produce specific emotional states. In such cases, cognition is necessary for the elicitation of a specific state, but may not be the material of that state. Consider the emotion of shame. One must have certain cognitions for shame to occur. Shame occurs when persons evaluate their behavior against some standard and find that they have failed. Moreover, they evaluate their total selves as failures (Lewis, 1992b). Such cognitions can lead to a specific emotional

state, which may have specific bodily activity. The views proposed are quite complex:

1. An emotional state can be elicited in some automatic fashion by certain stimulus events—for example, the case of fear when an animal sees a predator (IRM).

2. Emotional states are not elicited automatically through some innate "prewiring," but rather through cognitive evaluative processes. Plutchik (1980) and I (Lewis, 1992b) have argued for distinguishing between different emotional states by using the difference between prewired and cognitive evaluation.

3. There are no specific emotional states, but only general arousal, which is interpreted vis-à-vis the events surrounding the arousal (Schachter & Singer, 1962). In this model, there is an emotional state, but it is only a general one.

4. There are no emotional states at all, but only cognitive processes which lead to specific emotions. These differences have important implications for any theory of emotional development.

What is clear is even if there are specific emotional states, they may bear little correspondence to our emotional lives—either emotional expressions or our experience of emotions. So for example, it may be quite possible to have a specific emotional state but to be unaware of it, ignore it, or even deny it. Likewise, we may have a specific emotional state but choose not to express it. Thus, for example, I may be angry at my dean for not giving me a raise, but I am not likely to express that anger when I see her. Emotional states, then, are inferred, and whether they are specific, general, or nonexistent awaits further research.

If we hold to the existence of emotional states, then for the most part they must be viewed as transient patterned alterations in ongoing levels of neurophysiological and/or somatic activity. These transient, ongoing changes in our level of neurophysiological and somatic activity imply that there is a constant stream of change. It becomes difficult to imagine, therefore, being awake and not being in some emotional state or some level of arousal. However, since there need not be any correspondence between the emotional state and emotional experience and expression, there is no reason to assume that we are aware of the states that we are in. This does not mean that these states are not affecting our ongoing behavior—only that they are not apparent (Lewis, 1991).

Development of Emotional States

In a discussion of the developmental issues pertaining to emotional states, two issues need to be addressed. The first concerns the nature of the different states and how they are derived; the second pertains to the developmental course of states once they emerge. For example, if emotional states are viewed as specific, the question of how specific states develop needs to be addressed. Two general models are possible. According to one, specific emotional states are derived from developmental processes. Such processes may be purely maturational, or they may be interactive, involving the organism with its environment. The second model does not depict a role for development in the emergence of specific states; rather, discrete emotional states are assumed to be innate.

In the first model, the infant has two basic states or one bipolar state at birth: a negative or distress state and a positive or satiated state. Subsequent states emerge through the differentiation of this basic bipolar state. Differentiation theories focus on both the modulation of the bipolar state and the general arousal state. Hedonic tone and arousal may be the dimensions necessary to generate specific emotional states. This idea was proposed by Bridges (1932) and is considered a differentiation hypothesis. This theory has been adopted by others, including Spitz (1965), Sroufe (1979), and Emde, Gaensbauer, and Harmon (1976), who have added a contextual dimension to the scheme.

The way in which the interface of arousal and hedonic tone develops into specific emotional states remains speculative. It has been argued that both mother–child interaction and maturation underlie the process of differentiation (Als, 1975; Brazelton, Koslowski, & Main, 1974; Sander, 1977). The regulation of the child's state may be the mechanism leading to differentiation. Although some theorists stress that emotional differentiation is determined more by biological than by interactive factors, the combination of the two forces seems most likely. While such a theory is appealing, the derivation of specific emotional states remains without empirical support.

A much simpler developmental model concerning differentiation can be considered from a purely biological perspective. Such a biologi-cal model can be imagined in which undifferentiated emotion becomes differentiated as a function of maturation. According to such a view (see Lewis & Michalson, 1983), the rate of differentiation and the unfolding of differentiated emotion states are programmed according to some physiological timetable. The differentiation from general to specific structures is a common process in morphology; there is no reason not to consider such a possibility in emotional development. The most likely explanation of emotional development is the differentiation of emotion states which occurs as a function of maturation, socialization, and cognitive development—a topic to which I return shortly. Whatever processes underlie this differentiation, the model is developmental in nature.

An alternative model is that some discrete states are preprogrammed in some sense and need not be further differentiated (Izard, 1978). They exist at birth, even though they may not emerge until a later point in development. The view is unlike the differentiation model in that discrete emotional states do not develop from an original undifferentiated state, but are innate at birth in already differentiated form. In this "discrete-systems model," specific emotion states emerge either in some predetermined order or as needed in the life of the infant. They may co-occur with the emergence of other structures, although they are independent of them. The emotional system essentially operates according to biological directives.

These different models address the conceptual difference between experience and structure found in the arguments of Hume and Kant. In one case, experience produces a structure (Hume, 1739/1888). In the other case, experience is assimilated into innate structures (Kant, 1781/1958). In the study of emotional development, the question that one must address is whether emotional states are preformed and depend only on the development of cognitions, or whether cognitions themselves produce the emotional states or structures. Such a distinction is rather fine, but has important theoretical implications. Such a distinction can be seen in the study of fear (Lewis & Rosenblum, 1974). Is each fear state the same as other fear states, regardless of the circumstances, or do fear states differ as a function of the elicitors? For example, is the fear state produced by a loud noise the same as the fear state produced by the association of a doctor's white coat with the pain of a needle? Are emotional states independent of or dependent on particular cognitions? If emotional states are independent, they need not be created by the cognitions.

The first issue in the development of states concerns the origin of discrete emotional states. The second issue focuses on the developmental changes in emotional states once they have emerged. For example, 8-month-old children may show behaviors reflecting fear at the appearance and approach of strangers, and 2-year-old children may exhibit fear behaviors when they have broken their parents' favorite lamp. Do similar fear states underlie the fear expressions in both cases? Although the elicitors of states and the children's cognitive capacities are different in these two cases, the underlying emotional states may be similar.

Major developmental changes may occur in (1) the events that produce emotional states, (2) the behavioral responses used to reference states, and (3) the cognitive structures of children. Whether the emotional state itself changes as a function of development is difficult to determine. However, there may well be important physiological and neural changes that differentiate young and old organisms. Given that there are important physiological changes that occur over age, the physiological processes associated with emotional states may change over time. If this were the case, then the consistency of an emotion may be a function of our experience of it more than the underlying state. What is clear and what will be shown below is that the appearance of particular emotions may be dependent upon new cognitions, as well as the fact that new cognitions may allow for the development of new emotions. The former case can be seen again in the example of fear. While 1-year-old infants may be fearful of falling off a "visual cliff," they are not fearful of failing an exam or being caught cheating on their income tax. Such fears in an adult are due to elaborate social and cognitive development. An example of the latter—that is, cognitions' producing new emotions—has to do with classes of emotions called "self-conscious evaluative emotions." These emotions, such as pride and shame, cannot occur until elaborate cognitive processes have occurred (see Stipek, Recchia, & McClintic, 1992).

Emotional Expressions

Emotional expressions make reference to those potentially observable surface changes in face, voice, body, and activity level. Emotional expressions are seen by some as the manifestations of internal emotional states (Ekman & Friesen, 1974). In fact, no single measure of emotional states is more differentiating than emotional expressions. The problem with emotional expressions is that they are soon capable of being masked, dissembled, and in general controlled by the individual. Moreover, emotional expressions are subject to wide cultural and socialization experiences. Thus the relationship between expressions and states remains somewhat vague (Lewis & Michalson, 1983). The measurement of emotional expression is reviewed in detail in other chapters, so I spend little time on the definition of emotional expression except to make several points.

First, emotional expressions tend to be studied in terms of facial expression, and while body postures have been studied (see, e.g., Argyle, 1975), the study of children's emotional expressiveness in terms of body postures and activity has received little attention. Vocalizations are one of the least understood aspects of emotional expression, although they seem to be important conveyors of emotional states. Indeed, vocal expressions are extremely powerful and may have the ability to elicit similar emotional states in others. Vocalization may be much more contagious than facial or bodily expressions. For example, movies are much funnier when seen with others who laugh out loud than when seen by oneself. Because of the contagious nature of vocalization, vocal expression may be the target of early socialization efforts. Crying is a case in point. Crying behavior is quickly brought under control as parents socialize their children not to cry when distressed or in need. Locomotion may be another mode of expressing emotions. For example, running away from and running toward an object are locomotive responses associated with negative and positive emotions. Indeed, it is often infants' moving away from an unfamiliar toy or person, independent of facial expression, that is used to reference fear (Schaffer, Greenwood, & Parry, 1972).

Although there are some data on emotional expressions in each of these four modalities (facial, postural, vocal, and locomotor), the relations between them have received almost no attention. It seems reasonable to assume that sobering, crying, and running away form a coherent response that reflects the emotional state of fear. The particular modality used to express an emotion may be a function of specific rules of socialization or of a response hierarchy in which one modality has precedence over another. Such a hierarchy may be determined either by a set of biological imperatives or by a set of socialization rules. The use of one or more channels to express a particular emotion may be determined by a complex set of interactions. One issue of particular interest is the effect on some expressions when one modality is inhibited. Inhibition in a particular modality can be experimentally produced, for example, by preventing a child from moving about. For instance, if children are prevented from running away from an approaching stranger because they are restrained in a highchair, they may express their internal state more intensely through alternative means, such as changes in facial musculature. Another example of the use of differential modalities in expressing emotions occurs in the work on stress. We (Lewis, Ramsay, & Kawakami, 1993), for example, found that infants who do not express the emotion of distress when pained are more likely to show large adrenocortical responses. Suomi (1991) and Levine and Wiener (1989) have found a similar phenomenon in nonhuman primates. Monkeys that do not show loud cries of distress upon being separated from their mothers are much more likely to show higher adrenocortical responses. Thus the relationship between modalities of expression may play an important role in determining what emotional expressions are presented and the intensity of them.

Development of Emotional Expressions

The question concerning the development of emotional expressions takes many forms. It is quite clear that discrete emotional expressions can be seen in infants at very young ages. Although there is some discussion as to the number of discrete emotions that are visible (as opposed to mixtures), theories as to the development of emotional expression depend upon whether or not emotional expressions are believed to be directly connected to emotional states. Even more central to the issue of the development of emotional expressions is the particular system used to measure them. Because measurement systems for coding expressions other than facial ones are scarce, little is known about the development of other expressions.

Thus most attention has been paid to facial expressions and their development.

Another developmental problem concerns the issue of context. Emotional expressions may be connected to emotional states and to particular elicitors, and the likelihood of observing an emotional expression depends on the nature of the connections. That is, an investigator must know what is likely to make a child afraid in order to produce and measure fear expressions. Since emotional elicitors have a developmental course, as discussed above, and emotional expressions are produced by a specific situation, the study of the development of expressions is more complicated than it would seem. The failure to observe an expression in response to a particular elicitor does not constitute grounds for concluding that the expression is not present at that age, since it might appear under other circumstances.

The developmental course of emotional expressions, then, is uncharted. Nevertheless, parents have no difficulty in responding to questions designed to examine their beliefs about when children first express emotions (Pannabecker, Emde, Johnson, Stenberg, & David, 1980). Generally, parents tend to agree about when they think their children first show a particular emotion. It remains, however, to be determined whether their responses are a function of when emotions actually emerge or whether their answers reflect their own belief systems. It is likely that if such questions were asked of parents in different cultures or at different historical times, different results would be obtained. Thus, while 87% of American parents see anger in their babies within the first 3 months (Pannabecker et al., 1980), it may be the case that in cultures characterized by less aggression, parents see the emergence of anger somewhat later. The problem with the emergence of emotional expressions and their meaning is quite complicated. The face is an active set of muscles; it is likely to produce combinations that can be measured as reflecting particular emotions.

We are much more inclined to believe that particular emotional expressions reflect a specific underlying state in infants and young children when we see particular faces in particular contexts. Thus, for example, when children show wary or fearful faces at the approach of a stranger, we are more apt to credit those faces as meaning that the children are in a fear state than if the children show those same faces toward their mothers, who are sitting next to them. My associates and I (Alessandri, Sullivan, & Lewis, 1990; Lewis, Alessandri, & Sullivan, 1990) have observed children's facial responses as they learn a simple task of pulling a string in order to turn on a slide. In the course of their learning, as measured by increases in arm-pulling rate over an observed base rate, we have observed particular emotional expressions that appear appropriate for the particular phase of learning. Thus, for example, infants show interest when setting out to solve the problem, surprise and joy at the point of discovery, and disinterest and distress after they have completely mastered the task. Moreover, infants show angry faces when their instrumental responding is interfered with. These faces, expressed in the context of particular situations, lend validating meaning to the connection between facial expression and internal state. Nevertheless, the question of whether a facial expression truly reflects an emotional state cannot be answered. Indeed, except for phenomenological self-report, it cannot even be addressed in human adults. Adults often make faces that do not reflect the emotional states they report having.

Izard (1978) sees an innate connection between emotional expressions and their states. However, there is no reason to assume that this is the case. In fact, one might think of the developmental process as the connection of expressions to states. Alternatively, there may be no development; there may be, from the start, an innate connection between facial expression and some underlying internal state (Lewis & Michalson, 1985).

Emotional Experiences

Emotional experience is the interpretation and evaluation by individuals of their perceived emotional state and expression. Emotional experience requires that individuals attend to their emotional states (i.e., changes in their neurophysiological behavior), as well as the situations in which the changes occur, the behaviors of others, and their own expressions. Attending to these stimuli is neither automatic nor necessarily conscious. Emotional experience may not occur because of competing stimuli to which the organism's attention is drawn. For example, consider the following scenario: The car a woman is driving suddenly has a blowout in the front tire; the car skids

across the road, but the woman succeeds in bringing it under control and stopping the car on the shoulder. Her physiological state as well as her facial expression may indicate that while she is bringing the car under control, her predominant emotional state is fear. Because her attention is directed toward controlling the car, however, she is not aware of her internal state or of her expressions. She only experiences fear after she gets out of the car to examine the tire. Emotional experiences thus require people to attend to a select set of stimuli. Without attention, emotional experiences may not occur, even though an emotional state may exist. Many other examples are possible. From the clinical literature, a patient may be in a particular emotional state (e.g., depression), but may attend to select features of that state (e.g., fatigue), and so may only experience tiredness. Or a patient may not experience pain at the dentist when distraction is provided through the use of earphones and loud music.

The emotional experience may not necessarily be conscious, either. If one is willing to distinguish between conscious and unconscious experiences, emotional experiences may occur at different levels of consciousness. Such an analysis forms the basis of much psychoanalytic thought. For example, individuals may be in an emotional state of anger. That is, with proper measurement techniques, one would find a pattern of internal physiological responses indicative of anger. Moreover, these persons may act toward those objects that or persons who have made them angry in a way that suggests they are intentionally behaving in response to an internal state of anger. Nonetheless, the persons may deny that they feel anger or are acting in an angry fashion. Within the therapeutic situation, such people might be shown that (1) they are angry, and (2) they are responding intentionally as a consequence of that anger. The therapeutic process may further reveal that unconscious processes are operating in a fashion parallel to conscious ones. Defense mechanisms, for example, function to separate levels of awareness. Although awareness may not be at a conscious level, unconscious awareness may still exert powerful effects. Slips of the tongue, accidents, and classes of unintentional conscious behavior may all be manifesting intentional unconscious awareness (Freud, 1901/1960). Thus people may experience their internal states and expressions and be aware of this experience, or they may experience them in an unconscious mode in which the conscious perception of the experience is unavailable.

Up until this point we have assumed that there exists an internal state that is experienced. As some have argued, the experiencing of an emotion does not have to rely upon any internal state at all. In fact, no internal state may exist. For those who do not believe in the construct of a unique set of variables marking a specific state (Ortony et al., 1988), the experience of the state is nothing more than a cognitive construction, utilizing such perceptions as the nature of the experience, past history, the responses of others, and so on. Under such a view, emotional experiences are the unique and specific states themselves. From a cognitive-constructive point of view, such a view of emotions is quite reasonable. In fact, data on spinal injury patients suggest that emotional experiences can occur without specific physiological states. Thus, for example, spinal injury patients who are incapable of receiving neural messages from below the waist report sexually orgasmic experiences, even though no state information is available to them. They construct the experience from their past knowledge and not from any change in their neurophysiological state.

Emotional experiences occur through the interpretation and evaluation of states, expressions, situations, behaviors of others, and beliefs about what ought to be happening. Emotional experiences are therefore dependent on cognitive processes. Cognitive processes involving interpretation and evaluation are enormously complex and involve various perceptual, memory, and elaborating processes. Evaluation and interpretation not only involve cognitive processes that enable organisms to act on information, but are very much dependent on socialization to provide the content of the emotional experience. The particular socialization rules are little studied and not well understood (see Lewis & Michalson, 1983; Lewis & Saarni, 1985; and, more recently, Kahlbaugh & Haviland, 1994, for a discussion of some of the socialization rules).

Not all theories of emotional experience need be tied to the context, nor do all suggest that there is an underlying emotional state. However, all emotional experience does involve an evaluative interpretive process, including the interpretation of internal states, context, behavior of others, and meaning given by the culture.

Development of Emotional Experiences

The development of emotional experiences is one of the least understood aspects of emotion. Emotional experiences require that the organism possess some fundamental cognitive abilities including the ability to perceive and discriminate, recall, associate, and compare. Emotional experiences also require a particular cognitive ability—that is, the development of a concept of self. Emotional experiences take the linguistic form "I am frightened" or "I am happy." In all cases the subject and object are the same, that is, oneself. Until an organism is capable of objective self-awareness (Duval & Wicklund, 1972), the ability to experience may be lacking. Emotional experience requires both general cognitive capacities—something I touch upon below—and the specific cognitive capacity of self-referential behavior, or what I have referred to as "consciousness" (Lewis, 1991, 1992a, 1992b).

General cognitive processes necessary for organisms to perceive and discriminate elicitors of particular behaviors, whether these be internal or external to them, as well as overt emotional expressions of themselves and of others, have a developmental course. For example, infants younger than 6 months are generally unable to discriminate between facial patterns and do so on the basis of discrete features (Caron, Caron, & Myers, 1982). Schaffer (1974) demonstrated that children cannot make simultaneous comparisons prior to 7 or 8 months of age. This would suggest that infants are not capable of experiencing emotions prior to this point. Moreover, some emotional experiences may require a higher level of cognitive processing than others, and some are likely to develop earlier than others. For example, fear probably emerges earlier than shame, since the former requires less cognitive and evaluative processing than the latter (Lewis, 1992b).

If emotional experience is the consequence of an evaluation of one's bodily changes, and also of the context and the behaviors of others, then two processes are necessary for most emotional experiences: (1) the knowledge that the bodily changes are uniquely different from other changes (i.e., they are internal rather than external), and (2) the evaluation of these changes. The internal–external distinction for emotional development is important, because it addresses the differences between experience and expression. If we believe that facial expression is equivalent to an emotional state or experience, then it is possible to infer an internal event by examining its external manifestation. If, however, we do not subscribe to the view of a one-to-one correspondence between expression and experience, then all we can say is that there is an external manifestation of some unperceived internal event. Emotional experiences, by nature, are internal events. Moreover, the internal and external distinction can only be carried out by a self capable of making the distinction between the self and the other. Such evaluation may involve the process of self-awareness.

Self-awareness is an information-processing and decision-making event related to internal stimuli. It logically requires an organism to possess the notion of agency (Lewis, 1991). The term "agency" refers to that aspect of action that makes reference to the cause of the action—not only who or what is causing the stimulus to change, but who is evaluating it. The stimulus change itself may have the effect of alerting the organism and forcing it to make some type of evaluation. Emotional experience requires that the organism be capable of attending to itself. Thus the statement "I am happy" implies two things. First, it implies that I have an internal state called happiness, and second, that I perceive that internal state of myself. Until organisms are capable of this cognitive capacity, they should not be capable of emotional experiences (Lewis, 1992a, 1992b; Lewis & Brooks-Gunn, 1978, 1979; Lewis & Michalson, 1983). This does not mean that infants, prior to acquiring an objective self or consciousness of the self, do not have unique emotional states; they do. What seems reasonable to postulate is that an individual can be in a particular emotional state and yet not experience it. Just as we have seen in the example of the woman whose car slides off the road, an emotional state can exist without experience, so we can imagine an infant's having an emotional state without being able to experience it. This leads to the rather peculiar proposition that a child can be in a state of pain or can be in a state of fear, yet not experience that state, if by "experiencing it" we mean being able to make reference to the self as having that state. In a series of studies, my collaborators and I have demonstrated that the emergence of this self-conscious process does not occur prior to 15 months of age, and that it seems to emerge mostly as a function of maturation in the second half of the second year of life. It is only then that children both can be in a particular emotional state and can be said to experience that state. Moreover, the production of certain states requires self-awareness; therefore, certain emotions are unlikely to occur until this cognitive process emerges (Lewis, Sullivan, Stanger, & Weiss, 1989).

Once the basic cognitive processes that allow for objective self-awareness or consciousness occur, organisms are capable of experiencing emotions. As I have pointed out, they may be capable of experiencing existing emotional states as well as capable of experiencing emotions that have no internal state, either because internal emotional states do not exist or because the organisms are experiencing a different emotional state than that which exists. The rules that govern how we experience our emotional states or how we create emotional experiences themselves are complex and varied. Clearly, socialization rules are involved, on a cultural as well as on a familiar or individual level. For example, in cultures that do not tolerate interpersonal aggression—Japan, for example—the experiencing of anger is culturally inappropriate. It may be the case that Japanese children or adults may act in an angry way and may even have an emotional state of anger. However, since having such a state is inappropriate, they are not likely to have the emotional experience of anger. Exactly how the socialization process proceeds so as to influence, modify, alter, or accent emotional experiences is little understood. Clearly, the topic of the socialization of emotion involves the socialization of at least all four features of emotion discussed here. It affects the meaning of stimuli and what we allow events to do in terms of acting as elicitors of particular emotions. It affects the emotional expressiveness dimension of emotion, and, finally, it affects the emotional experience.

From an interpersonal and intrapersonal point of view, the socialization rules that act on the experiencing of emotion are somewhat better articulated. Freud's theory of the unconscious and of defense mechanisms addresses this point. Defense mechanisms have as their chief function preventing individuals from experiencing emotions or, alternatively, from having emotions that they do not like to have. For example, denial and repression serve the function of preventing people from having particular emotional experiences that they deem unacceptable. They prevent it by not allowing them to become conscious or self-aware. Projection, on the other hand, allows for the experiencing of the emotion—not as the self's experiencing it, however, but as the self's experiencing it in another. As we can see in each defense mechanism, the major function is to provide means for altering emotional experience.

REINTEGRATING EMOTIONAL LIFE

In the preceding discussion, I have focused upon specific features of emotional life. As I have tried to indicate, confusion among these features is apt to lead to nonproductive discussions. Thus emotions can be considered cognitive if we focus on emotional experiences and can be considered noncognitive if we focus on emotional states. Moreover, in the discussion of "emotion," I have disassembled some of the features that go into emotional life. The purpose of this discussion has been to see how the developmental process can affect each of these components. Unfortunately, the disassemblance does a disservice to the complexity of emotional life. Moreover, it does not allow us to look at developmental issues that may be related to the relationships between various components. Consider, as an example, the relationship between emotional expression and state. As we (Lewis & Michalson, 1983) have tried to demonstrate, the relationship between emotional expression and state may well undergo developmental change. It seems reasonable to assume that very early in life, emotional expressions and states may have little correspondence. At some point in development, there appears to be some coherence between emotional states and expressions. States and expressions seem to bear some one-to-one relation to one another; for instance, a child smiling at someone's joke reflects an internal state of amusement or happiness. However, we know that children very quickly learn to dissemble expression from internal states: Children as young as $2\frac{1}{2}$ years of age are quite capable of successfully lying about committing a transgression, through verbal response as well as through facial response (Lewis, Stanger, & Sullivan, 1989). With socialization and further development, the disassembling of expression from internal state takes place. Thus there is a

developmental course in the connection between expression and state. A similar analysis can be made for the coherence between internal state and experience. Earlier in the developmental process, children may have internal states which they do not experience. There may then be a period in which internal states and experiences form some coherence, only to change once again so that experiences of emotion can take place without internal states. These developmental sequences in the coherence between features of emotional life need more careful articulation.

A MODEL OF EMOTIONAL DEVELOPMENT

In what follows, I present a model of the emergence of different emotions over the first 3 years of life. I choose this period since it represents the major developmental leap of the majority of adult emotions in emotional development. This is not to say that past 3 years of age other emotions do not emerge, or that the emotions that have emerged are not elaborated more fully. I suspect that both are the case.

One problem with articulating a model of the emergence of emotional life has to do with the appropriate markers for the emotions. Are we making reference solely to emotional expressions, or are we talking about emotional states or experiences? Given the content of our inquiry—namely, the study of the emergence of emotions in the first 3 years of life—we are presented with a difficulty. The ability to do more than observe the emitted behaviors of the child is all that is possible. In order to get at emotional experiences, we need language in the form of "I am sad" or "I am ashamed." Since during this period the language of the child is quite limited, the study of emotional experience is impossible. Likewise, the study of emotional states is difficult to undertake because it is a construct that has not been demonstrated; that is, there has been little success to date in finding a unique configuration of neurophysiological events that mark unique emotions in adults, let alone children and infants.

What we are left observing are emotional expression and behavior. However, all does not appear lost, especially if we observe emotional behavior in context. This allows us, at least from the adult meaning system, to assume that the child's expression reflects something more than a surface manifestation of the emotion. Observation of fear over the approach of a stranger, or joy when a mother appears, allows us to accept that an internal state of fear or joy exists. With these limitations in mind, the following discussion and mapping of emotional development can take place.

Following Bridges (1932), as well as others, we assume that at birth the child shows a bipolar emotional life. On the one hand, there is general distress marked by crying and irritability. On the other hand, there is pleasure marked by satiation, attention, and responsivity to the environment. Attention to and interest in the environment appears from the beginning of life, and we can place this in the positive pole; or, if we choose, we can separate this, thus suggesting a tripartite division with pleasure at one end, distress at the other, and interest as a separate dimension (see Figure 17.1).

By 3 months, joy emerges. Infants start to smile and appear to show excitement/happiness when confronted with familiar events, such as faces of people they know or even unfamiliar faces. Also by 3 months, sadness emerges, especially around the withdrawal of positive stimulus events. Three-month-old children show sadness when their mothers stop interacting with them. Disgust also appears in its primitive form—a spitting out and getting rid of unpleasant-tasting objects placed in the mouth. Thus, by 3 months children are already showing interest, joy, sadness, and disgust, and exhibiting these expressions in appropriate contexts.

Anger has been reported to emerge between 4 and 6 months (Stenberg, Campos, & Emde, 1983). Anger is manifested when children are frustrated—in particular, when their hands and arms are pinned down and they are prevented from moving. However, we (Lewis et al., 1990) have shown anger in 2-month-old infants when a learned instrumental act was removed. This study demonstrates the earliest known emergence of anger. Anger is a particularly interest-

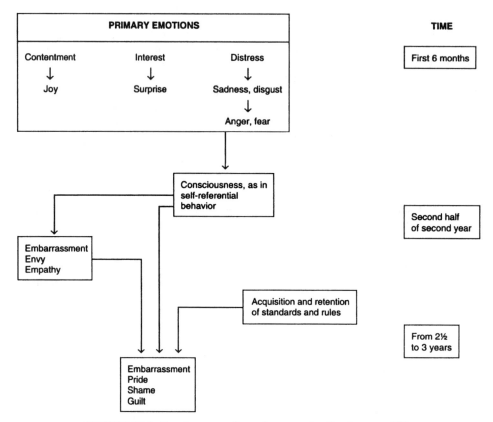

FIGURE 17.1. Development of emotions over the first 3 years of life.

ing emotion since, from Darwin (1872/1965) on, it has been associated with unique cognitive capacity. Anger is thought to be both a facial and motor/body response designed to overcome an obstacle. Notice that in this definition of anger, the organism has to have some knowledge in regard to the instrumental activity toward a goal. For anger to be said to be adaptive, it has to be a response that attempts to overcome a barrier blocking a goal. In some sense, then, means–ends knowledge has to be available, and the demonstration of anger at this early point in life reflects the child's early knowledge acquisition relative to this ability (Lewis, 1991).

Fearfulness seems to emerge still later. Again, fearfulness reflects further cognitive development. Schaffer (1974) has shown that in order for children to show fearfulness, they have to be capable of comparing the event that causes them fearfulness with some other event, either internal or external. Thus, for example, in stranger fear infants have to compare the face of a stranger to their internal representation or memory of faces. Fear occurs when the face is found to be discrepant or unfamiliar relative to all other faces that the children remember. Children's ability to show fearfulness, therefore, does not seem to emerge until this comparison ability emerges. Children begin to show this behavior at about 7 to 8 months, although it has been reported by some to occur even earlier, especially in children who seem to be precocious. In the first 8 or 9 months of life, children's emotional behavior reflects the emergence of the six early emotions, called by some "primary emotions" or "basic emotions" (see, e.g., Izard, 1978; Tomkins, 1962).

Surprise also appears in the first 6 months of life. Children show surprise when there are violations of expected events; for example, when infants see a midget (a small adult) walking toward them, they are reported to show interest and surprise rather than fear or joy (Brooks & Lewis, 1976). Surprise can be seen when there is violation of expectancy or as a response to discovery, as in an "Aha!" experience. We (Lewis, Sullivan, & Michalson, 1984) showed that when children were taught an instrumental arm-pulling response, they showed surprise at the point when they discovered that the arm pull could turn on a slide. Surprise can reflect either a violation or a confirmation of expectancy. Cognitive processes play an impor-

tant role in the emergence of these early emotions, even though the cognitive processes are limited; this is not so for the next class of emotions.

Figure 17.1 indicates that a new cognitive capacity emerges sometime in the second half of the second year of life. The emergence of consciousness or objective self-awareness (self-referential behavior) gives rise to a new class of emotions. These have been called "self-conscious emotions" and include embarrassment, empathy, and envy. Although little work exists in the development of these emotions, several studies support the emergence of embarrassment at this point in development. We (Lewis, Sullivan, et al. 1989) have shown that the emergence of embarrassment only takes place after consciousness or self-recognition occurs. In a study of children 9–24 months of age, we were able to demonstrate that embarrassment is related to the emergence of self-recognition. Empathy, too, emerges in relation to self-recognition (Halperin, 1989). While no studies on envy have been conducted, observation of children between 18 and 24 months of age reveals the appearance of envy.

Two points are to be noticed about this class of emotions. First, the observation of these emotions requires measuring not only a facial expression, but bodily and vocal behavior as well. Whereas the earlier emotions can be observed readily in specific facial configurations, these new emotions require measurement of bodily behavior. Embarrassment, for example, is best measured by nervous touching, smiling, gaze aversion, and return behaviors. The second important point related to the emergence of these emotions is that while they reflect self-consciousness, they do not require self-evaluation. The emergence of these self-conscious emotions is related uniquely to the cognitive milestone of paying attention to the self. This topic is taken up in more detail in another chapter (see Lewis, Chapter 39, this volume).

Figure 17.1 also shows a second cognitive milestone, which occurs sometime between 2 and 3 years of age. This ability is characterized by children's capacity to evaluate their behavior against a standard; the standard can either be external, as in the case of parental or teacher sanction or praise, or it can be internal, as in the case of children developing their own standards. This capacity to evaluate personal behavior relative to a standard develops in the third year of life. The ability to compare personal behavior to a standard gives rise to another set of emotions. We have called these "self-conscious evaluative emotions"; they include pride, shame, and guilt, among others. These emotions require that children have a sense of self and be capable of comparing their own behavior against standards. If children fail vis-à-vis the standard, they are likely to feel shame, guilt, or regret. If they succeed, they are likely to feel pride (Lewis, 1992a). It is important to note that pride and shame are quite different from happiness and sadness. For example, we can win a lottery and feel quite happy about winning the money; however, we would not feel pride, because we would not view the winning of the lottery as having anything to do with our behavior. The same is true for failure; we might feel sad if we were not able to do something, but if it was not our fault, then we would not feel shame or guilt. These complex social evaluative emotions make their appearance at about 3 years of age (see Lewis, 1992b; Stipek, et al., 1992).

Thus, by 3 years of age, the emotional life of a child has become highly differentiated. From the original tripartite set of emotions, the child comes within 3 years to possess an elaborate and complex emotional system. While the emotional life of the 3-year-old will continue to be elaborated and will expand, the basic structures necessary for this expansion have already been formed. New experiences, additional meaning, and more elaborate cognitive capacities will all serve to enhance and elaborate the child's emotional life. However, by 3 years of age, the child already shows those emotions that Darwin (1872/1965) characterized as unique to our species—the emotions of self-consciousness. With these, the major developmental activity has been achieved.

REFERENCES

Alessandri, S. M., Sullivan, M. W., & Lewis, M. (1990). Violation of expectancy and frustration in early infancy. *Developmental Psychology*, *26*(5), 738–744.

Als, H. (1975). *The human newborn and his mother: An ethological study of their interaction.* Unpublished doctoral dissertation, University of Pennsylvania.

Argyle, M. (1975). *Bodily communication.* New York: International Universities Press.

Bowlby, J. (1969). *Attachment and loss: Vol. 1. Attachment.* New York: Basic Books.

Brazelton, T. B., Koslowski, B., & Main, M. (1974). The origins of reciprocity: The early mother–infant interaction. In M. Lewis & L. A. Rosenblum (Eds.), *The effect of the infant on its caregiver* (pp. 49–76). New York: Wiley.

Bridges, K. M. B. (1932). Emotional development in early infancy. *Child Development*, *3*, 324–334.

Brooks, J., & Lewis, M. (1976). Infants' responses to strangers: Midget, adult and child. *Child Development*, *47*, 323–332.

Campos, J., & Stenberg, C. (1981). Perception, appraisal, and emotion: The onset of social referencing. In M. E. Lamb & L. R. Sherrod (Eds.), *Infant social cognition: Empirical and theoretical considerations* (pp. 273–314). Hillsdale, NJ: Erlbaum.

Caron, R. F., Caron, A. J., & Myers, R. S. (1982). Abstraction of invariant face expressions in infancy. *Child Development*, *53*, 1008–1015.

Darwin, C. R. (1965). *The expression of the emotions in man and animals.* Chicago: University of Chicago Press. (Original work published 1872)

Davidson, R. J., & Fox, N. A. (1982). Asymmetrical brain activity discriminates between positive versus negative affective stimuli in human infants. *Science, 218*, 1235–1237.

Duval, S., & Wicklund, R. A. (1972). *A theory of objective self-awareness.* New York: Academic Press.

Ekman, P. (1989). The argument and evidence about universals in facial expressions of emotion. In J. Wagner & A. Manstead (Eds.), *Handbook of social psychophysiology* (pp. 143–164). New York: Wiley.

Ekman, P., & Friesen, W. V. (1974). Detecting deception from the body or face. *Journal of Personality and Social Psychology*, *29*, 288–298.

Emde, R. N., Gaensbauer, T., & Harmon, R. (1976). Emotional expression in infancy: A biobehavioral study. *Psychological Issues*, *10*(1, Whole No. 37).

Feinman, S., & Lewis, M. (1984). Is there social life beyond the dyad?: A social-psychological view of social connections in infancy. In M. Lewis (Ed.), *Beyond the dyad* (pp. 13–41). New York: Plenum Press.

Freud, S. (1960). *The psychopathology of everyday life* (A. Tyson, Trans.). New York: Norton. (Original work published 1901)

Gunnar, M. R. (1980). Control, warning signals and distress in infancy. *Developmental Psychology, 16*, 281–289.

Halperin, M. (1989, April). *Empathy and self-awareness.* Paper presented at the biennial meeting of the Society for Research in Child Development, Kansas City, MO.

Harris, P. (1989). *Children and emotion: The development of psychological understanding.* Oxford: Blackwell.

Hume, D. (1888). *A treatise of human nature* (L. A. Selby-Bigge, Ed.). Oxford: Clarendon Press. (Original work published 1739)

Izard, C. E. (1977). *Human emotion.* New York: Plenum Press.

Izard, C. E. (1978). Emotions and emotion–cognition

relationships. In M. Lewis & L. A. Rosenblum (Eds.), *The development of affect* (pp. 389–413). New York: Plenum Press.

Kahlbaugh, P. E., & Haviland, J. M. (1994). Nonverbal communication between parents and adolescents: A study of approach and avoidance behaviors. *Journal of Nonverbal Behavior, 18*, 91–113.

Kant, I. (1958). *Critique of pure reason* (N. Kemp Smith, Trans.). New York: Macmillan. (Original work published 1781)

Lazarus, R. S. (1982). Thoughts on the relations between emotion and cognition. *American Psychologist, 37*, 1019–1024.

Levine, S., & Wiener, S. G. (1989). Coping with uncertainty: A paradox. In D. S. Palermo (Ed.), *Coping with uncertainty: Behavioral and developmental perspectives* (pp. 1–16). Hillsdale, NJ: Erlbaum.

Lewis, M. (1989). Cultural differences in children's knowledge of emotional scripts. In P. Harris & C. Saarni (Eds.), *Children's understanding of emotion* (pp. 350–373). New York: Cambridge University Press.

Lewis, M. (1991). Ways of knowing: Objective self-awareness or consciousness. *Developmental Review, 11*, 231–243.

Lewis, M. (1992a). The self in self-conscious emotions. A commentary. In D. Stipek, S. Recchia, & S. McClintic (Eds.), Self-evaluation in young children. *Monographs of the Society for Research in Child Development, 57*(1, Serial No. 226), 85–95.

Lewis, M. (1992b). *Shame: The exposed self.* New York: Free Press.

Lewis, M., Alessandri, S., & Sullivan, M. W. (1990). Violation of expectancy, loss of control, and anger in young infants. *Developmental Psychology, 26*, 745–751.

Lewis, M., & Brooks-Gunn, J. (1978). Self-knowledge and emotional development. In M. Lewis & L. Rosenblum (Eds.), *The development of affect* (pp. 205–226). New York: Plenum Press.

Lewis, M., & Brooks-Gunn, J. (1979). *Social cognition and the acquisition of self.* New York: Plenum Press.

Lewis, M., & Goldberg, S. (1969). Perceptual–cognitive development in infancy: A generalized expectancy model as a function of the mother–infant interaction. *Merrill–Palmer Quarterly, 15*, 81–100.

Lewis, M., & Michalson, L. (1983). *Children's emotions and moods: Developmental theory and measurement.* New York: Plenum Press.

Lewis, M., & Michalson, L. (1985). Faces as signs and symbols. In G. Zivin (Ed.), *Development of expressive behavior: Biology–environmental interaction* (pp. 153–182). New York: Academic Press.

Lewis, M., Ramsay, D. S., & Kawakami, K. (1993). Affectivity and cortisol response differences between Japanese and American infants. *Child Development, 64*, 1722–1731.

Lewis, M., & Rosenblum, L. (Eds.). (1974). *The origins of fear.* New York: Wiley.

Lewis, M., & Saarni, C. (Eds.). (1985). *The socialization of emotion.* New York: Plenum Press.

Lewis, M., Stanger, C., & Sullivan, M. W. (1989). De-

ception in 3-year-olds. *Developmental Psychology, 25*, 439–443.

Lewis, M., Sullivan, M. W., & Michalson, L. (1984). The cognitive–emotional fugue. In C. E. Izard, J. Kagan, & R. Zajonc (Eds.), *Emotions, cognition, and behavior* (pp. 264–288). New York: Cambridge University Press.

Lewis, M., Sullivan, M. W., Stanger, C., & Weiss, M. (1989). Self-development and self-conscious emotions. *Child Development, 60*, 146–156.

Mandler, G. (1975). *Mind and emotion.* New York: Wiley.

Mandler, G. (1980). The generation of emotion: A psychological theory. In R. Plutchik & H. Kellerman (Eds.), *Emotion: Theory, research, and experience. Vol. 1. Theories of emotion* (pp. 219–244). New York: Academic Press.

Nelson, C. A., & Bloom, F. E. (1997). Child development and neuroscience. *Child Development, 68*, 970–987.

Nelson, C. A., & Bosquet, H. (2000). Neurobiology of fetal and infant development: Implications for infant mental health. In C. H. Zeanah, Jr. (Ed.), *Handbook of infant mental health* (2nd ed., pp. 37–59). New York: Guilford Press.

Ortony, A., Clore, G. L., & Collins, A. (1988). *The cognitive structure of emotions.* New York: Cambridge University Press.

Pannabecker, B. J., Emde, R. N., Johnson, W., Stenberg, C., & David, M. (1980). *Maternal perceptions of infant emotions from birth to 18 months: A preliminary report.* Paper presented at the International Conference of Infant Studies, New Haven, CT.

Plutchik, R. (1980). *Emotion: A psychoevolutionary synthesis.* New York: Harper & Row.

Sander, L. W. (1977). Infant and caretaking environment: Investigation and conceptualization of adaptive behavior in a system of increasing complexity. In E. J. Anthony (Ed.), *The child psychiatrist as investigator* (pp. 170–183). New York: Plenum Press.

Schachter, S., & Singer, J. E. (1962). Cognitive, social, and physiological determinants of emotional state. *Psychological Review, 69*, 379–399.

Schaffer, H. R. (1974). Cognitive components of the infant's response to strangeness. In M. Lewis & L. A. Rosenblum (Eds.), *The origins of fear* (pp. 11–24). New York: Wiley.

Schaffer, H. R., Greenwood, A., & Parry, M. H. (1972). The onset of wariness. *Child Development, 43*, 165–175.

Schwartz, G. E., & Weinberger, D. A. (1980). Patterns of emotional responses to affective situations: Relations among happiness, sadness, anger, fear, depression, and anxiety. *Motivation & Emotion, 4*(2), 175–191.

Spitz, R. A. (1965). *The first year of life.* New York: International Universities Press.

Sroufe, L. A. (1979). Socioemotional development. In J. D. Osofsky (Ed.), *Handbook of infant development* (pp. 462–516). New York: Wiley.

Stenberg, C. R., Campos, J. J., & Emde, R. N. (1983). The facial expression of anger in seven-month-old infants. *Child Development, 54*, 178–184.

Stipek, D., Recchia, S., & McClintic, S. (1992). Self-evaluation in young children. *Monographs of the Society for Research in Child Development, 57*(1, Serial No. 226).

Suomi, S. (1991). Primate separation models of affective disorders. In J. Madden (Ed.), *Neurobiology of learning, emotion and affect* (pp. 195–213). New York: Raven Press.

Tomkins, S. D. (1962). *Affect, imagery, consciousness: Vol. 1. The positive affects.* New York: Springer.

Tomkins, S. D. (1963). *Affect, imagery, consciousness: Vol. 2. The negative affects.* New York: Springer.

Watson, J. B. (1919). *Psychology from the standpoint of a behaviorist.* Philadelphia: Lippincott.

Zajonc, R. B. (1980). Feeling and thinking: Preferences need no inferences. *American Psychologist, 35,* 151–175.

CHAPTER 18

Understanding Emotion

Paul L. Harris

AWARENESS OF EMOTION

According to both orthodox Freudian theory and contemporary neuropsychological approaches to emotion, our ability to know and report on the emotions that we feel is limited. This argument implies that a scientific study of emotion should not be restricted to those aspects of our emotional lives that are accessible to awareness. It should include emotional processes that may escape our awareness, but reveal themselves nonetheless via telltale facial expressions or various psychophysiological indices. Although the strength of this argument is undeniable, it is important to remember that human beings do have some access, however partial, to their emotional experience. We shall not fully understand human emotions unless we take that capacity for awareness and reflection seriously. Our ability to report on and anticipate our emotional state critically turns on the extent to which we are aware of, and understand, the way that we feel. Moreover, it is likely that our awareness of emotion, however partial, can change and improve. Indeed, it is part of the Freudian legacy that it is possible to develop such insight into our own emotional lives. Change and improvement is also possible with respect to our understanding of other people. At first we may rely on an immediate attunement to the way they express their emotions. However, our full understanding may depend on a less immediate and more reflective meditation on their history and their subjective appraisal of events.

In this chapter, I focus on those aspects of our awareness and understanding of emotion that are not special attainments, nurtured in the therapeutic environment, but rather ordinary and natural attainments of child development. I first describe children's ability to report on emotion, and review intriguing evidence that family conversation about emotion may promote the accuracy and completeness with which children make such reports. I then consider in more detail the way in which children's understanding of emotion changes with development. I argue that children cannot rely on a script-based conceptualization, but must attend to the relation between appraisal processes and ensuing emotion. Next, I consider the repercussions that children's understanding of emotion may have, once they move outside the family and start to build relationships with their peers. Finally, I describe recent research on children's understanding of the intertwining of emotion, thinking, and memory.

TALKING ABOUT EMOTION

Children's Reports of Emotion

Recent theories of emotion are rightly preoccupied by the continuities that Darwin (1872/1998) emphasized between human beings and nonhuman primates with respect to both the function and the communication of emotions. It is worth emphasizing, however, that human beings, unlike other primates, can put their emotions into words. Arguably, this capacity only amplifies a preexisting mode of nonverbal communication. However, my guess is that it produces a psychological revolution. It allows human beings to communicate what they feel not just about ongoing situations, but about past, future, recurrent or hypothetical situations. More succinctly, it allows humans not just to express emotion but to report on emotion, current as well as noncurrent. These reports provide an opportunity to share and explain emotional experience that is found in no other species.

To document young children's emerging ability to talk about emotion, Wellman, Harris, Banerjee, and Sinclair (1995) examined language production in a small group of children recorded in an intensive longitudinal study from 2 to 5 years of age. Wellman et al. (1995) concentrated on all those utterances in which children referred either to an emotion or, for comparison purposes, to an inner state that is not an emotion (namely, pain). The findings revealed that even 2-year-olds can talk systematically about emotion. They refer to a small set of emotional states—both positive (feeling happy or good; laughing; and feeling love or loving) and negative (feeling angry or mad; feeling frightened, scared, or afraid; and feeling sad or crying). Although children talk most often about their own feelings, they also talk about the feelings of other people. Moreover, children's attributions of emotion are not triggered simply by the recognition of animate, expressive displays, because they readily attribute various emotions to dolls, stuffed animals, and made-up characters. In sum, almost as soon as they are able to talk, children begin to report on their own feelings and on those of other people, and they project such feelings onto nonhumans.

Despite this emerging communicative capacity, it is possible to insist that when children start to put their own feelings into words, they are not engaged in any self-conscious reporting of their experience. Thus Wittgenstein (1958) suggested that early emotion utterances should be seen not as reports of emotion, but as vocal expressions of emotion, on a par with exclamations such as "Ouch!" or "Ow!" A close examination of 2-year-olds' utterances shows that this proposal is ill founded. If children's references to emotion were simply supplements to, or substitutes for, the ordinary facial and behavioral indices of emotion, we would expect them to be triggered by ongoing or current emotions. However, about half of 2-year-olds' references to emotion are concerned with past, future, and recurrent feelings, and this pattern continues among 3- and 4-year-olds.

This stable pattern shows that from their earliest emergence, we can think of children's utterances about emotion as referential reports, and not as lexical substitutes for scowls and smiles. Indeed, Wittgenstein's analysis does a poor job even with respect to children's pain utterances. Here too, children talk not only about current feelings. They also refer to pains that they might experience in the future or have experienced in the past. More generally, analysis of children's references to emotion shows that they can be mainly categorized as descriptive statements even if they are sometimes used in an instrumental fashion—to obtain sympathy, or to influence the emotional state of another person (Dunn, Brown, & Beardsall, 1991; Wellman et al., 1995). Indeed, this bias toward commentary is evident below 2 years of age. Dunn, Bretherton, and Munn (1987) found that children between 18 and 24 months old used conversation about feelings primarily to comment on their own feelings or those of another person, even though their mothers—to whom most of these comments were directed—used such conversations in a more didactic or pragmatic fashion.

To what extent are children able to offer not just a report but an accurate report of emotion? Naturalistic observation provides some encouraging evidence. Preschool children were observed in their day care centers as they engaged in free play (Fabes, Eisenberg, Nyman, & Michaelieu, 1991). When one of the children was seen to express an emotion—of happiness, sadness, distress, or anger—a child standing close by, who had witnessed the incident but not actually caused it, was approached and asked to say what had happened. Even 3-year-olds, the youngest group questioned, gave an account of what the target child was feeling and of what had provoked the emotion that corresponded with the adult observers' own observations about two-thirds of the time. Among 5-year-olds, agreement with the adult observers occurred more than three-quarters of the time. In future research, it will be interesting to investigate whether children offer more accurate reports when they are bystanders to an emotion or experiencers of an emotion. It would be reasonable to expect the latter, because children talk about their own emotions more than those of others. However, it is possible that the very experience of emotion may sometimes distort or block accurate report and analysis as it does among children dealing with a highly charged experience, such being hospitalized (Harris, 1989, Ch. 8; Harris & Lipian, 1989).

Family Discussion of Emotion

Families vary in the linguistic environment that they offer to children for the interpretation and regulation of emotion. Consider a child with a parent who frequently discusses emotion—by drawing out the child's own feelings, by calling attention to the way that his or her actions may have emotional implications for other members of the family, or by elaborating on the feelings of story characters. Consider, on the other hand, a parent who is more constrained in talking about emotion, whether with respect to the child or to other people. These two different types of conversation partners may have an impact on the extent to which a child understands how an emotion comes about, or is prepared to talk about emotion, or both.

Recent research has established that there is indeed marked variation among families in the frequency with which emotions are discussed. Thus Dunn, Brown, and Beardsall (1991) found that some children never made any mention of emotion during an hour-long home visit, whereas others made more than 25 such references; variation among the mothers was equally great. Accumulating evidence also indicates that the frequency with which preschool children engage in family discussion about emotions and their causes is correlated with their later ability to identify how someone feels. The link has been found both over a relatively short period straddling the third birthday (i.e., from 33 to 40 months; Dunn, Brown, Slomkowski, Tesla, & Youngblade, 1991), as well as over a more extended period from 3 to 6 years (Dunn, Brown, & Beardsall, 1991; Brown & Dunn, 1996).

Such correlational data are, of course, open to various interpretations. One possibility is that the correlation reflects some stable attribute of a child that manifests itself both in psychological talk and in sensitivity to emotion. For example, some children may be naturally empathic—they may seek out and engage in more conversations about emotion, and may also display a keen ability to assess how other

people feel, as measured by standard tests of emotion understanding. However, it is also plausible to suppose that the correlation reflects the didactic role that conversation can play for children. Frequent family discussion may prompt children to talk about emotion and increase their understanding and perspective taking. One piece of evidence that fits this second proposal has been reported by Garner, Carlson-Jones, Gaddy and Rennie (1997): They found that children's perspective taking is likely to be correlated with family discussion of emotion that focuses not simply on what a person feels, but rather on *why* someone feels a given emotion. Still, this line of interpretation leaves open various ways in which that didactic benefit may come about. Conversation about emotionally charged episodes may alter the format in which children encode such episodes. Alternatively, conversation about emotion, especially when it is conducted by a primary caretaker, may form part of a sensitive acknowledgment of the child's own emotional life—an acknowledgment that the child eventually comes to share. I consider these two possibilities in turn.

A Narrative Format for Emotion?

Conversation can provide children with a narrative format for organizing the episodes of everyday life, and this format is likely to embrace episodes that are emotionally charged. A coherent, causally connected, narrative representation may help children to think through the emotional implications of a given episode. The age period from 2 to 5 years is when children become increasingly proficient at recalling episodes from their past. According to Nelson (1993), this is because they begin to participate in joint recollection of past episodes with adults who prompt them to organize such episodes into coherent narratives. Eventually, children start to impose a narrative structure on ongoing events even in the absence of a conversation partner. The extent to which children do this successfully appears to depend in part on the conversational style of their parents (Reese & Fivush, 1993; Reese, Haden, & Fivush, 1993). Some parents—so-called "high-elaborative" parents—talk about past events in rich detail with their children. They use adjectives and modifiers to indicate the interest, importance, and emotional content of an event, and they situate it in its spatial and temporal context. They make efforts to develop the conversation by posing questions that include fresh information, and they offer a coherent narrative rather than citing unrelated aspects of an episode. By contrast, "low-elaborative" parents pose simple questions requiring factual responses (such as a place name or object label), provide little new information through their questions, and frequently move to a different topic with each question. If this proposal is applied to emotionally charged episodes, children who are often prompted to recall such episodes in the context of conversation with parents who adopt a high-elaborative style may end up better able to construct a coherent encoding of an ongoing episode for themselves and more likely to encode its emotional implications.

Dunn (1996) highlights two pieces of evidence consistent with this emphasis on recall and encoding. First, emotionally charged episodes are frequently the subjects of sharing and recall. Thus, when young children talk about past episodes with family members, they often focus on events that have provoked negative or positive emotion (Brown, 1993). Similarly, adolescents and adults who have undergone an emotionally charged experience are prone to share that experience repeatedly with other people; indeed, the more intense the emotion, the more the experience giving rise to it is likely to be shared, and shared over a longer interval (Rimé, 1995). Thus, throughout the lifespan, emotionally charged episodes are strong candidates for sharing, joint recall, and narrative restructuring. Second, young children are indeed better able to work out the psychological implications of an episode if they have encoded it in a coherent fashion. Three-year-olds who normally do poorly on a standard test of psychological understanding—the so-called "false-belief" task—perform better if they are prompted to structure the events leading to the false belief into a coherent narrative (Lewis, 1994).

ACCEPTING EMOTION?

The proposal above emphasizes the cognitive skills that conversation may nurture with respect to the encoding and recall of emotionally charged episodes. A different proposal has emerged in the context of attachment theory. Talk about emotion, especially on the part of the caretaker, may index a more wide-ranging acceptance of the child's own emotions, be they positive or negative—an acceptance that facilitates the child's open expression, communication, and acknowledgment of emotion. In this view, parental attitudes and conversation have their primary impact on the child's own emotional life, which has in turn a beneficial effect on the child's acknowledgment and understanding of emotion.

Recent evidence gathered in the context of attachment theory provides some support for this line of thinking. Steele, Steele, Croft, and Fonagy (1999) interviewed prospective mothers about their attachment to their own parents, using the Adult Attachment Interview (George, Kaplan, & Main, 1985). These reports were rated for their coherence, and for the extent to which interviewees provided a realistic acknowledgment of negative as well as positive feelings. Several years later, when the children subsequently born to these mothers had reached the ages of 5 and 6 years, the children were tested on their understanding of the extent to which a given situation can provoke a mixture of positive and negative feelings. An interesting relationship emerged between the parent and child measures. Specifically, the coherence and the degree of reflection with which a child's mother talked about her own attachment was a predictor of later performance by her child on the assessment of emotion understanding—over and above any contribution made by the child's age.

Given the lengthy temporal lag between the interview with the mother and the assessment of the child, and the clear independence of these two measures from one another, the relationship between them is intriguing and provocative. How should it be interpreted? In line with attachment theory, Steele et al. (1999) propose a two-step model: The mother's emotional sensitivity and coherence (as indexed by the Adult Attachment Interview during pregnancy) fosters a secure attachment with her child, and this secure attachment in turn promotes the child's acceptance and understanding of emotion.

This interpretation is plausible, and it is consistent with attachment theory. Nevertheless, it is worth emphasizing that the alternative proposal considered earlier can also explain the results. A mother who is able to produce a coherent and reflective narrative about her relationship to her own parents is likely to engage in coherent and informative discourse about a variety of emotionally charged past episodes when talking to her child. As described earlier, this elaborative style may in turn help the child to encode such episodes in a more coherent fashion. This account makes a straightforward prediction that can easily be checked with existing research tools. The way that mothers respond in the Adult Attachment Interview should be closely related to their conversational style as assessed by memory researchers. More specifically, mothers who obtain high scores for coherence in the Adult Attachment Interview should display a high-elaborative style when discussing past episodes with their children. In short, if this speculation is correct, children's understanding of emotion is promoted in a relatively direct fashion by the conversational style of their parents, especially the recall style. Although this recall style may indeed have additional and independent effects on a child's attachment status, there is no need—according to this model—to assume that the child's attachment status serves as the proximal determinant of his or her understanding of emotion.

In the next few years, we may expect to see much more research on the question of how children come to vary in their understanding of emotion, and the part that family talk may play in promoting that variation. In this regard, we can anticipate an increasing confluence of findings from research on (1) early attachment; (2) children's developing capacity for recall of past events, especially emotionally charged events; and (3) individual differences in children's understanding of mind and emotion. For the most part, these topics have been studied independently of one another, but this is likely to change. Such a confluence is likely to yield practical as well as theoretical benefits. If we know more about how children's understanding of emotion can be facilitated in the context of the family, we should be able to reproduce some of those beneficial effects through deliberate and systematic therapeutic intervention.

BEYOND SCRIPTS: DESIRES, BELIEFS, AND EMOTION

In the preceding section, I have talked in global terms about the child's ability to report on and to understand emotion. In this section, I consider in more detail the nature of this understanding and the way that it changes in the course of development. One simple and attractive proposal is that children develop an increasingly elaborate set of scripts for various emotions. Thus they identify the type of situations that elicit various emotions—fear, sadness, happiness, guilt, and so forth (Barden, Zelko, Duncan, & Masters, 1980; Harris, Olthof, Meerum Terwogt, & Hardman, 1987)—and they identify the typical actions and expressions that accompany a particular emotional state (Trabasso, Stein, & Johnson, 1981). This notion of script-based knowledge has several advantages. It assimilates children's understanding of emotion to a wider body of research on children's recall and understanding of sequentially organized events (cf. Nelson & Gruendel, 1979). It highlights the fact that an understanding of emotion calls for a causal understanding of the connections among its sequential components. It is sufficiently flexible to be of service if we look outside the Western world to children's understanding of emotion in cultures where different emotional themes are prominent; for example, Lutz (1987) has used this approach in her analysis of the emotion concepts of children on the island of Ifaluk in the Western Pacific. Finally, the notion of an emotion script fits comfortably with a possibility raised in the preceding section—that children's understanding may be elaborated not just in the context of emotionally charged encounters, but in the context of family discussions in which past episodes are rehearsed and organized into a causally coherent narrative sequence.

However, closer scrutiny of the script concept reveals a conceptual difficulty: The same situation can elicit different emotions, depending on the appraisal that the actor makes of the situation. This means that if the child attempts to store a list of scripts for emotion, it will be necessary to store different scripts for different people. An alternative and more economical solution is to define the eliciting situation in more abstract terms. For example, it is possible to define situations that provoke happiness as "situations that are judged by an actor to bring about the fulfillment of his or her goals." A move in this direction, however, tacitly acknowledges that emotions are very special kinds of scripts. They do not begin with the kind of objective event that we normally associate with scripts (e.g., the action of sitting down at a table can be seen as the first move in the dinner script). Rather, they begin with an event that is inherently psychological (namely, a person appraising a situation). A more fruitful approach to children's understanding of emotion, therefore, is to acknowledge that children may indeed construct scripts for given emotions—but that key elements of these scripts will include a diagnosis not of the objective situation that faces the actor, but rather an analysis of how the actor appraises that situation. To make the same point differently, it is not just psychologists who have to recognize the role of appraisal processes in emotion. Young children must do the same.

The limitations of the script-based approach can be highlighted in another way. Children with autism are often good at remembering recurrent sequences of events. Indeed, part of the clinical picture of autism is a disposition to become upset at an unexpected departure from a routine sequence. Their script-sensitive memory appears to serve children with autism quite well with respect to emotion. Thus, they readily judge that certain situations (getting nice things to eat, birthday parties) make people happy, whereas other situations (having to go to bed early, falling over) make people unhappy (Baron-Cohen, 1991; Tan & Harris, 1991). Using a different technique, Ozonoff, Pennington, and Rogers (1990) showed that autistic children could select the appropriate facial expression to go with various emotionally charged pictures, For example, they chose a sad face for a picture of a child looking at a broken toy, and an angry face for a picture of two children fighting. Despite this apparent familiarity with routine emotions scripts, children with autism perform poorly in comparison to nonautistic controls when a correct attribution of emotion requires then to go beyond the objective situation and consider how a protagonist's beliefs influence his or her appraisal of that objective situation (Baron-Cohen, 1991; Harris, 1991). The clear implication is that normal children do go beyond a script-based analysis and take into account the protagonist's appraisal of the situation.

If we accept this argument, we can ask in more detail how children make sense of the process of appraisal. Recent research increasingly points to a two-stage development. First, 2- and 3-year-olds appreciate the role that desires or goals play in determining a protagonist's appraisal and ensuing emotion. For example, they understand that an elephant may feel happy to be given milk if she wants milk, whereas another animal may feel upset if he prefers juice instead (Harris, Johnson, Hutton, Andrews, & Cooke, 1989; Yuill, 1984). By 4

and 5 years of age, this simple desire-based concept of emotion is elaborated to include beliefs and expectations. Children realize that it is not the match between desire and actual outcome that triggers emotion, but the match between desire and expected outcome. Suppose, for example, that the elephant wants some milk and is about to get it, so that if the match between desire and actual outcome is the only factor taken into consideration, she should feel happy. Suppose further, however, that the elephant wrongly expects to get something other than milk. In that case, 4- and 5-year-olds realize that the elephant will feel upset rather than happy (Harris et al., 1989). They appreciate that her appraisal of the situation, and her ensuing emotion, are based on the mismatch between her desire and the expected outcome, even when the expectation is ill founded.

The shift from a desire to a belief–desire conception of mind and emotion is now well established. Emotion judgment tasks, such as the one just described, are a useful source of evidence because whether children are asked to take only desires into account or beliefs and desires, they can still be asked to make the same simple binary judgment—namely, whether the animal is happy rather than sad. Another important source of evidence is children's spontaneous talk about psychological states. In the preceding section, I have described the way that children report on emotional states (Wellman et al., 1995). Using a similar database, Bartsch and Wellman (1995) have examined children's references to other mental states. Their analysis reveals that children talk systematically about desires and goals throughout most of the third year, chiefly using the term "want." Then, starting at about the third birthday, children also begin to make reference to beliefs, mainly using the terms "know" or "think." Eventually, at about the fifth birthday, talk about beliefs becomes as frequent as talk about desires.

This developmental pattern is probably universal. Tardif and Wellman (in press) report that children learning to speak Cantonese and Mandarin display a similar progression: Talk about goals and desires emerges early; talk about beliefs and expectations shows a later increment. These data help to rule out various possible interpretations of the lag between talk about desires and talk about knowledge and belief. For example, it might be argued that it arises because in English the predicate complement structure is simpler for the verb "want" than for the verbs "think" and "know." However, in Mandarin and Cantonese, the predicate complement structure is relatively simple across references to both desires and thoughts. Indeed, it is worth noting that in both Mandarin and Cantonese some polysemous mental verbs can be used to indicate either desire or thought. Yet, despite the availability of the same lexical item for both meanings, the lag between references to desire and thought still emerges. In sum, whether we focus on children's emotion judgments by using experimental tasks involving a simple binary judgment, or on children's spontaneous references to mental processes in the course of their everyday conversation (be it in English, in Mandarin, or in Cantonese), the evidence is robust that children focus initially on an agent's goals, but increasingly take into account his or her thoughts and beliefs.

How should we explain this pattern of development? Most commentators acknowledge that it reflects a developing appreciation of the way that an agent entertains an attitude to a given target—for example, an attitude of liking or fearing—and also construes that target in a particular way, whether the construal is accurate or not. To that extent, most commentators see the child as becoming increasingly sensitive to the role of various appraisal processes. Nevertheless, beyond this consensus, there is a healthy disagreement about how that increased sensitivity comes about. Some have argued that a key development is children's developing understanding of the way that the appraisal of a target comes to include a mental representation of that target (Bartsch & Wellman, 1995; Flavell, 1988; Astington & Gopnik, 1988; Perner, 1991). Others have argued that children may get better not at understanding the representational nature of appraisal processes, but rather at simulating or mimicking the appraisal that someone else may make of a target, given partial or biased information about it (Gordon, 1986; Harris, 1989). Whatever the merits of these two ideas, they both remain regrettably silent about the kind of experiences that might stimulate children to make progress. Here we can reflect once again on the role that language may play, especially sustained and intimate conversation within the family. To make this point, I need to backtrack briefly to examine the recent spate of research on the child's so-called "theory of mind."

We can often work out people's mental state without talking to them. Thus, we often infer what other people think, know, or feel by keeping track of their movements, and by taking note of what they did or did not witness. For example, knowing that two colleagues have missed a college committee meeting, I will infer their state of ignorance and duly update them about any decisions reached. The past decade of research on children's understanding of beliefs and emotions has mainly probed children's developing facility at this type of observational inference (Astington, Harris, & Olson, 1988; Flavell & Miller, 1998). However, we also often learn what other people think or feel not by tracking where they were at what time, but by listening to what they say. Indeed, it is possible to argue that children's developing appreciation of the way that people vary in their thoughts and attitudes is fueled by their increasing involvement in conversation (Harris, 1996). For example, in the course of conversation, children can realize that their conversation partners may know or believe something that they do not, and vice versa. In fact, successful conversation involves a moment-to-moment acknowledgment of such variation in information. To the extent that conversation stimulates children to reflect on the thoughts and beliefs of their conversation partners, we would expect those children with limited access to conversation to be delayed in their understanding of thoughts and beliefs.

However, conversation goes beyond the exchange of information; it involves the sharing and comparing of attitudes, especially emotional attitudes. Thus, in discussing their experience with a conversation partner, children will often learn that an episode that made them giggle or cry can provoke a very different reaction in a sibling or caretaker. Conversation is likely to highlight and clarify the way that emotional reactions vary from one person to another, depending on their appraisal of the episode in question. Arguably, the more children engage in conversation about emotion, the more they become alert to its subjectivity, particularly if the conversation provides a way to make sense of the appraisal processes that underpin it. This proposal leads to an interesting prediction. Recent research with deaf children, especially deaf children raised in nonsigning families, has shown that they perform poorly on theory-of-mind tasks (Peterson & Siegal, 1995, 1997). Until now this research has focused primarily on their understanding of belief, especially false belief. However, if the analysis above is correct, we would expect deaf children raised in nonsigning families to show parallel difficulties in the understanding of emotion–especially if the emotional reaction has to be understood not in terms of the objective situation, but rather in terms of the way that the situation is appraised.

UNDERSTANDING EMOTION AND PEER RELATIONS

Hitherto, I have discussed ways in which experiences within the family may influence children's understanding of emotion. We may now consider possible consequences of that developing understanding. In particular, we may ask whether children's understanding of emotion has an impact on their social relationships when they move outside the family and start to form relationships with peers. Three recent studies have explored this possibility. Denham, McKinley, Couchoud, and Holt (1990) tested preschoolers (mean age = 44 months) for their emotion knowledge: Children had to identify a puppet's emotion (of happiness, sadness, anger, or fear), both when it exhibited a prototypical reaction (e.g., fear during a nightmare) and an atypical reaction (e.g., sadness at going to preschool). In addition, a sociometric measure was used to assess children for their acceptance as playmates among their peers. Children with higher scores on the emotion test proved to be more popular among their peers, even when the contributions of age and gender were removed. Cassidy, Parke, Butkovsky, and Braungart (1992) obtained very similar results with first-grade children. Children's overall score in an interview about the causes, consequences, and associated expression of emotion was correlated with popularity. Finally, in a longitudinal study of 4- and 5-year-olds, Edwards, Manstead and MacDonald (1984) found that children who were accurate at identifying facial expressions of emotion proved to be more popular 1–2 years later (even when their initial popularity was taken into account). The consistency among these three studies is striking. At the same time, caution is again needed in interpreting the findings (Manstead, 1995). Acceptance by peers may increase children's opportunities for learning about emotion. Alternatively, a third variable such as intelligence or verbal ability may underpin both emotion understanding and popularity. Nevertheless, a plausible in-

terpretation is that children's understanding of emotion helps them to handle peer interaction in a more sensitive fashion, and that this makes them more popular.

However, even if we accept this conclusion for the moment, further research is needed to clarify just how that sensitivity should be construed. We may consider two possible interpretations: one framed in terms of social cognition, the other framed in terms of nonverbal discrimination. First, in line with the discussion so far, it is possible to argue that children differ primarily in the extent to which they build up a coherent understanding of key emotions—an understanding that specifies the relevant appraisal processes, experiential states, and behavioral and psychological consequences. In this view, children with greater expertise in the domain of emotion are essentially more knowledgeable, and it is this knowledge that helps them in dealing with their peers. An alternative possibility is that children differ primarily in their sensitivity to subtle nonverbal signals of emotion. For example, they may be more sensitive to the difference between a forced and a genuine smile, or between a look of fear and a look of surprise. In this view, children with greater expertise in the domain of emotion are chiefly distinguished by their more nuanced reading of the subtle indices of emotion displayed by their peers.

The obvious way to investigate this question is to dissect the concept of emotion understanding in a more analytic fashion. For example, it is possible to devise tests of understanding that bypass any presentation of non-erbal expressive cues. Conversely, it is possible to devise tests that focus directly on nonverbal discrimination, without requiring children to articulate any wider understanding of the situational antecedents or consequences of even the names of particular emotions. If the same group of children were given tests of both types, we could assess which displays a stronger relation to peer acceptance.

In carrying out such a study, it would be worth keeping in mind the following intriguing possibility. Consider briefly an apparently unrelated field, but one that has made a major contribution to our understanding of domain-specific expertise: research on chess players pioneered by De Groot (1965) in Amsterdam. He discovered, not surprisingly, that grand masters know more about chess than weaker players do. They have a huge library of remembered games that they can exploit in thinking through any particular game. In addition, however, their superior chess knowledge infuses the way that they perceive the board. If they glance for a few seconds at an incomplete game, they can accurately remember the disposition of the pieces (Chase & Simon, 1973). The implication of this research is that expertise consists not only of greater knowledge, but of more accurate and rapid encoding of meaningful patterns. To return to the domain of emotion, then, we should be prepared to find that children who perform well on tests of knowledge also do well on tests of nonverbal discrimination.

THOUGHTS, MEMORIES, AND FEELINGS

One obvious feature of our experience of emotion is that most intense emotions subside over time. If children are able to report on their experience of emotion—and, as we have seen, their early talk about emotion suggests exactly this—then we might expect them to be aware of this relationship between time and emotion. Several studies have shown that young children are quite sensitive to that relationship. Children were told about various emotionally charged episodes that befell a story character just before school started. For example, they might be told that the character had lost a fight with the school bully. Children were then asked to say how the character would feel at various points during the day, and the following morning (Harris, 1983; Harris, Guz, Lipian, & Man-Shu, 1985; Taylor & Harris, 1983). The results showed that even 4-year-olds appreciate that an intense emotional reaction will wane over time. They make that judgment whether the initial emotion is positive or negative, and they make it about their own emotional experience as well as that of story characters. Moreover, the judgment is one that children make in quite different cultures—for example, whether they are growing up in the West or in China. A plausible conclusion from these orderly data is that the waning of intense emotion is a universal experience, acknowledged and understood by young children everywhere.

However, as adults, we also acknowledge that our emotions do not always dissipate in a steady and gradual fashion. We realize that we are prey to flashbacks and reminders that override, however temporarily, the underlying pattern of dissipation. To what extent do young children understand this intrusive and regenerative influence of memory? In an initial investigation of this question, children were asked about a story character who woke up on the day after an emotionally charged experience, and either started thinking about the experience again, or alternatively had forgotten about it (Harris et al., 1985). By 6 years of age, children realized the likely impact on emotion: They claimed that the character would feel happier thinking about a positive experience than forgetting about it, but would feel happier forgetting about a negative experience than thinking about it. Four-year-olds were less systematic, but they did reach conclusions similar to the 6-year-olds' for the positive experience.

In a more extensive investigation of the same issue, Lagattuta, Wellman, and Flavell (1997) tested children ranging from 3 to 6 years of age for their understanding of the impact of reminding on felt emotion. Children listened to stories in which the protagonist experienced a sad event and later encountered a reminder. Children were told that the story character felt sad in the presence of a reminder, and were scored for the extent to which they were able to explain that the reminder made the protagonist think back to the earlier sad event. The majority of 5- and 6-year-olds were able to articulate such explanations, whereas this was rare among 4-year-olds. Nonetheless, in a follow-up study in which the cues were identical to (and not just associated with) items involved in the initial event, some 3-year-olds also provided such explanations, especially after they were explicitly asked whether the character was thinking back to the past event.

To summarize these findings, there is ample evidence that children understand the way that an emotional reaction is often dictated by the immediate situation. At the same time, young children also show some understanding that people's emotional lives are not simply a function of the current situation. An emotional reaction does not instantly cease once a person leaves the situation that gave rise to it. The emotion lingers on or recurs, albeit with a waning intensity. Young children can also increasingly articulate the contexts in which reactivation, however partial, of the original emotion can take place. They realize that a further encounter with some component of the earlier episode triggers thoughts and associated feelings about that episode. Indeed, it is possible that emotionally infused memories and thoughts are an especially salient context for children to discover important features of our mental life. Flavell, Green, and Flavell (1995) found that young children were especially alert to the likelihood that someone in an emotionally charged situation (waiting for an inoculation) would be engaged in mental activity, notably thinking; they often ignored that possibility when the person was engaged in more neutral situations (e.g., reading or talking). Rumination that is emotionally charged may be especially salient to young children (1) because it is frequently linked not to the actual situation, but to some past or future situation; and (2) because such thoughts have an involuntary, intrusive quality that is less evident for more neutral thoughts.

CONCLUSIONS

In this chapter, I have examined several interrelated aspects of children's understanding of emotion: their ability to report emotion in words; their sensitivity to key components of the appraisal processes that modulate a person's emotional response to a given situation (namely, the person's desires and beliefs); the link between emotion understanding and peer relations; and, finally, children's developing appreciation of the way that emotions are sustained or dissipated, not simply because the eliciting situation recedes in time and space, but rather because the process of rumination and recollection that an emotionally charged situation sets in motion gradually subsides.

At various points, I have touched on a larger and more complex theme that deserves more attention in future research. Arguably, children's developing understanding of emotion is simply an epiphenomenon of the underlying process of emotion. Understanding may operate at a "meta" level, sealed off from the underlying emotional process that is its subject matter. To take a concrete example, it is possible to assert that a child functions at two separate levels: On one level, there is the child's experience and display of sadness; at a separate level, there is the child's capacity for reporting on and ruminating about that experience. Increased sophistication at the latter level may have few or no repercussions for processing at the former level.

Such a stark separation between levels may simplify our scientific analysis, but it probably distorts or ignores some important features of human emotion. It predicts that a disruption or delay in the development of an understanding of emotion need have no repercussions for the basic emotional processes themselves. There are several reasons for thinking that such repercussions do exist, however. First, there is a therapeutic tradition suggesting that intense emotional experiences that are reworked in the context of communication and rumination have different sequelae from those that are not. Such reworking need not be in the context of discussion with a trained therapist; it can also occur in the context of a privately written narrative (Pennebaker, 1996). One plausible extrapolation of these findings is that the emotional lives of children who grow up in homes where there is open discussion of emotionally charged encounters will be different from those of children from homes where such discussion does not occur.

Second, this capacity for communication and rumination dramatically alters the contexts in which children can seek support and reassurance. Attachment theorists have emphasized the way that a caretaker may or may not provide reassurance at moments of distress. Typically, they have focused on those moments when the precipitating factor is fairly easy for the caretaker to discern: The child is unnerved by a stranger, or distressed by the caretaker's recent absence, or fretful about the caretaker's imminent departure. However, the emotional horizon of the older child is much larger; he or she can be distressed or fearful of events that might happen in the future or that happened in the more distant past. In such contexts, children who can report on their feelings and discuss their causes are clearly better placed to receive reassurance.

Finally, it is likely that children's ability to understand and predict their own emotions has an effect on their decision making about what course of action to take. In its turn, that chosen course of action will lead to—or enable children to avoid—certain emotional consequences. For example, recent evidence shows that the ability to anticipate guilt can serve as a brake or warning signal when a guilt-inducing transgression is contemplated (Lake, Lane, & Harris, 1995). That warning signal is sufficient to help children to inhibit the transgression and to avoid any subsequent guilt. Stated in more general terms, children's insight into their emotional lives does not simply permit the children to expect the inevitable; it allows the children to make choices about what their emotional lives should be like.

REFERENCES

Astington, J. W., & Gopnik, A. (1988). Knowing you've changed your mind: Children's understanding of representational change. In J. W. Astington, P. L. Harris, & D. R. Olson (Eds.), *Developing theories of mind* (pp. 193–206). New York: Cambridge University Press.

Astington, J., Harris, P. L., & Olson, D. (Eds.). (1988). *Developing theories of mind*. New York: Cambridge University Press.

Barden, R. C., Zelko, F. A., Duncan, S. W., & Masters, J. C. (1980). Children's consensual knowledge about the experiential determinants of emotion. *Journal of Personality and Social Psychology, 39*, 968–976.

Baron-Cohen, S. (1991). Do people with autism understand what causes emotion? *Child Development, 62*, 385–395.

Bartsch, K., & Wellman, H. M. (1995). *Children talk about the mind*. New York: Oxford University Press.

Brown, J. R. (1995). Telling "what happened": A study of children's early conversations about the past. *Dissertation Abstracts International, 54*(5-B), 2780.

Brown, J. R., & Dunn, J. (1996). Continuities in emotion understanding from three to six years. *Child Development, 67*, 789–802.

Cassidy, J., Parke, R. D., Butkovsky, L., & Braungart, J. M. (1992). Family–peer connections: The roles of emotional expressiveness within the family and children's understanding of emotions. *Child Development, 63,* 603–618.

Chase, W. G., & Simon, H. A. (1973). Perception in chess. *Cognitive Psychology, 4*, 55–81.

Darwin, C. (1998). *The expression of the emotions in man and animals* (3rd ed.). London: HarperCollins. (Original work published 1872)

De Groot, A. (1965). *Thought and choice in chess*. The Hague: Mouton.

Denham, S. A., McKinley, M., Couchoud, E. A., & Holt, R. (1990). Emotional and behavioral predictors of preschool peer ratings. *Child Development, 61,* 1145–1152.

Dunn, J. (1996). The Emanuel Miller Memorial Lecture 1995. Children's relationships: Bridging the divide between cognitive and social development. *Journal of Child Psychology and Psychiatry, 37*, 507–518.

Dunn, J., Bretherton, I., & Munn, P. (1987). Conversations about feeling states between mothers and their young children. *Developmental Psychology, 23*, 132–139.

Dunn, J., Brown, J., & Beardsall, L. (1991). Family talk about feeling states and children's later understanding of others' emotions. *Developmental Psychology, 27*, 448–455.

Dunn, J., Brown, J., Slomkowski, C., Tesla, C., & Youngblade, L. (1991). Young children's understanding of other people's feelings and beliefs: Individual differences and their antecedents. *Child Development, 62*, 1352–1366.

Edwards, R., Manstead, A. S., & MacDonald, C. J. (1984). The relationship between children's sociometric status and ability to recognize facial expressions of emotion. *European Journal of Social Psychology, 14*, 235–238.

Fabes, R. A., Eisenberg, N., Nyman, M., & Michaelieu, Q. (1991). Young children's appraisals of others' spontaneous emotional reactions. *Developmental Psychology, 27*, 858–866.

Flavell, J. H. (1988). The development of children's knowledge about the mind: From cognitive connections to mental representations. In J. W. Astington, P. L. Harris, & D. R. Olson (Eds.), *Developing theories of mind* (pp. 244–267). New York: Cambridge University Press.

Flavell, J. H., Green, F. L., & Flavell, E. R. (1995). Young children's knowledge about thinking. *Monographs of the Society for Research in Child Development, 60*(1, Serial No. 243).

Flavell, J. H., & Miller, P. (1998). Social cognition. In W. Damon (Series Ed.) & D. Kuhn & R. S. Siegler (Vol. Eds.), *Handbook of child psychology: Vol. 2. Cognition, perception, and language* (5th ed., pp. 851–898). New York: Wiley.

Garner, P. W., Carlson-Jones, D., Gaddy, G., & Rennie, K. M. (1997). Low-income mothers' conversations about emotions and their children's emotional competence. *Social Development, 6*, 37–52.

George, C., Kaplan, N., & Main, M. (1985). *The Adult Attachment Interview*. Unpublished manuscript, Department of Psychology, University of California at Berkeley.

Gordon, R. M. (1986). Folk psychology as simulation. *Mind and Language, 1*, 158–171.

Harris, P. L. (1983). Children's understanding of the link between situation and emotion. *Journal of Experimental Child Psychology, 36*, 490–509.

Harris, P. L. (1989). *Children and emotion: The development of psychological understanding*. Oxford: Blackwell.

Harris, P. L. (1991). The work of the imagination. In A. Whiten (Ed.), *Natural theories of mind* (pp. 283–304). Oxford: Blackwell.

Harris, P. L. (1996). Desires, beliefs and language. In P. Carruthers & P. Smith (Eds.), *Theories of theories of mind* (pp. 200–220). Cambridge, England: Cambridge University Press.

Harris, P. L., Guz, G. R., Lipian, M. S., & Man-Shu, Z. (1985). Insight into the time course of emotion among Western and Chinese children. *Child Development, 56*, 972–988.

Harris, P. L., Johnson, C. N., Hutton, D., Andrews, G., & Cooke, T. (1989). Young children's theory of mind and emotion. *Cognition and Emotion, 3*, 379–400.

Harris, P. L., & Lipian, M. S. (1989). Understanding emotion and experiencing emotion. In C. Saarni & P. L. Harris (Eds.) *Children's understanding of emotion* (pp. 241–258). New York: Cambridge University Press.

Harris, P. L., Olthof, T., Meerum Terwogt, M., & Hardman, C. E. (1987). Children's knowledge of situations that provoke emotion. *International Journal of Behavioral Development, 10*(3), 319–343.

Lagattuta, K. H., Wellman, H. M., & Flavell, J. H.

(1997). Preschoolers' understanding of the link between thinking and feeling: Cognitive cuing and emotional change. *Child Development, 68,* 1081–1104.

Lake, N., Lane, S., & Harris, P. L. (1995). The expectation of guilt and resistance to temptation. *Early Development and Parenting, 4,* 63–73.

Lewis, C. (1994). Episodes, events and narratives in the child's understanding of mind. In C. Lewis & P. Mitchell (Eds.), *Children's early understanding of mind: Origins and development* (pp. 457–480). Hove, England: Erlbaum.

Lutz, C. (1987). Goals, events, and understanding in Ifaluk emotion theory. In D. Holland & N. Quinn (Eds.), *Cultural models in language and thought* (pp. 290–312). Cambridge, England: Cambridge University Press.

Manstead, A. S. R. (1995). Children's understanding of emotion. In J. J. Russell, J.-M. Fernández-Dols, A. S. R. Manstead, & J. C. Wellenkamp (Eds.), *Everyday conceptions of emotion* (pp. 315–331). Dordrecht, The Netherlands: Kluwer.

Nelson, K. (1993). The psychological and social origins of autobiographical memory. *Psychological Science, 4,* 7–14.

Nelson, K., & Gruendel, J. (1979). At morning it's lunchtime: A scriptal view of children's dialogues. *Discourse Processes, 2,* 73–94.

Ozonoff, S., Pennington, B. F., & Rogers, S. J. (1990). Are there emotion perception deficits in young autistic children? *Journal of Child Psychology and Psychiatry, 31,* 343–361.

Pennebaker, J. (1996). Cognitive, emotional, and language processes in disclosure. *Cognition and Emotion, 10,* 601–626.

Perner, J. (1991). *Understanding the representational mind.* Cambridge, MA: MIT Press.

Peterson, C., & Siegal, M. (1995). Deafness, conversation and theory of mind. *Journal of Child Psychology and Psychiatry, 36,* 459–474.

Peterson, C., & Siegal, M. (1997). Psychological, biological, and physical thinking in normal, autistic, and deaf children. In W. Damon (Series Ed.) & H. M. Wellman & K. Inagaki (Vol. Eds.), *New directions for child development: Vol. 75. The emergence of core

domains of thought* (pp. 55–70). San Francisco: Jossey-Bass.

Reese, E., & Fivush, R. (1993). Parental styles of talking about the past. *Developmental Psychology, 29,* 596–606.

Reese, E., Haden, C. A., & Fivush, R. (1993). Mother–child conversations about the past: Relationships of style and memory over time. *Cognitive Development, 8,* 403–430.

Rimé, B. (1995). The social sharing of emotion as a source for the social knowledge of emotion. In J. J. Russell, J.-M. Fernández-Dols, A. S. R. Manstead, & J. C. Wellenkamp (Eds.), *Everyday conceptions of emotion* (pp. 475–489). Dordrecht, The Netherlands: Kluwer.

Steele, H., Steele, M., Croft, C., & Fonagy, P. (1999). Infant–mother attachment at one year predicts children's understanding of mixed emotions at six years. *Social Development, 8,* 161–178.

Tan, J., & Harris, P. L. (1991). Autistic children understand seeing and wanting. *Development and Psychopathology, 3,* 163–174.

Tardif, T., & Wellman, H. M. (in press). Acquisition of mental state language in Mandarin and Cantonese-speaking children. *Developmental Psychology.*

Taylor, D. A., & Harris, P. L. (1983). Knowledge of the link between emotion and memory among normal and maladjusted boys. *Developmental Psychology, 19,* 832–838.

Trabasso, T., Stein, N. L., & Johnson, L. R. (1981). Children's knowledge of events: A causal analysis of story structure. In G. Bower (Ed.), *Learning and motivation* (Vol. 15, pp. 237–282). New York: Academic Press.

Wellman, H. M., Harris, P. L., Banerjee, M., & Sinclair, A. (1995). Early understanding of emotion: Evidence from natural language. *Cognition and Emotion, 9,* 117–149.

Wittgenstein, L. (1958). *Philosophical investigations.* Oxford, England: Blackwell.

Yuill, N. (1984). Young children's coordination of motive and outcome in judgements of satisfaction and morality. *British Journal of Developmental Psychology, 2,* 73–81.

CHAPTER 19

Emotion and Identity

Jeannette M. Haviland-Jones
Patricia Kahlbaugh

According to Wundt, apperception is a voluntary act of the mind giving synthetic unity to our experience (Blumenthal, 1975). The very act of perceiving contributes an organization that goes beyond the influence of external stimuli. What are most real to any of us at any given moment are our emotions and thoughts, and when these are apperceived, they are organized into the synthetic unity of an identity. The search for identity or for the "true inner self" requires ongoing constructions of connections between emotion and self-knowledge.

Our perspective on the fusion of emotion and identity reflects an emerging concern with emotion processes in identity formation, change, and maintenance. It also reflects an interest in how social constructs such as individual and group identity create and maintain certain ideas about emotions (Hochschild, 1983; Lutz, 1988). Issues of emotion and identity necessarily inform each other and constrain interpretations of each other on a conceptual level as well as on a personal level.

In this chapter, our first goal is to present our perspective on emotion, what constitutes emotion, and how emotions relate to each other. Based on this perspective, three ways of organizing personal identity in 20th-century Western culture are described: (1) identity more rationally dichotomized through consciousness and self-evaluation ("good–bad," "I–me"); (2) identity more empirically compartmentalized

as a collection of roles, goals, and traits; and (3) identity as a dynamic, creative construct combining the dichotomous and compartmentalized aspects but providing a new and still emerging *Weltanschauung*. Within each description of an identity construction, we review (a) the place usually, and sometimes inevitably, assigned to emotion within that construction; (b) the socioideological biases imposed on that construction in connection with emotion; and (c) one or two examples of the changes in theory that have occurred in each construction as new research on emotion has become more fully integrated with that approach.

A PERSPECTIVE ON DIFFERENTIAL EMOTION

Our approach to emotion conceives of different emotions as having separable modes of expression and different functions (Haviland & Kramer, 1991; Haviland & Walker-Andrews, 1992; Malatesta, 1990). For example, in Tomkins's (1987) theory of affect and in theories related to his position, the most basic hypothesis is that different emotions are links between perceived stimuli and responses, perceived causes and effects, self and others. Emotion is a major aspect of the apperceptive process. It provides contingency between internal events and external events. The "innate scripts . . . connect stimuli and response by imprinting both with the same abstract analogic quality and thus amplify both" (Tomkins, 1987, p. 148). We extend this idea to propose that the emotional system is the value-making system in identity over the long term.

The affects provide "rules for differential resonance to every major abstract profile," according to Tomkins (1987, p. 149). This approach obviously differs from the more social-constructivist approaches in that there is at some level an unconstructed (or, as Tomkins said, "innate") set of emotions or emotion processes. However, as will become apparent, our approach differs from Tomkins's original theory in that the functions of the basic emotions may be significantly changed in interactions. As an example, mothers respond to their children with an intense gaze pattern when they are discussing sexuality. This might suggest affiliation, but coupled with the mothers' complete lack of reciprocity in turn taking (Kahlbaugh, Lefkowitz, Valdez, & Sigman, 1997; Lefkowitz, Kahlbaugh, & Sigman, 1996), their behavior is more indicative of the intrusiveness and dominance of contempt. This interaction melds an affiliative contact with a distancing contact, creating new valences and changing the balance within the interaction.

The dialectical and sometimes "chaotic" elements in processes of emotional apperception are important in providing a bridge between the discrete-emotions theories and the social-constructivist theories. If one accepts the premise that basic emotions function as systems over time, then the interaction of two or more such systems is likely to produce emerging systems with chaotic aspects (Abraham, Abraham, & Shaw, 1990), from which new and unusual stable networks or processes may emerge. It is from such processes that broad individual and cultural differences in identity, and hence in the construction of emotion, emerge.

Emotions are not merely reactive responses to designated things or events, but are the metaphoric forms that "resonate" to and unite scenes, experiences, internal cues, and thoughts. These apperceptions of events in the Wundtian sense are not imaginary or lacking in substance. Just as a narrative or drawing is an identifiable network connecting analogous elements, an emotion functions because it is an analogic process and form. Just as certain cells of the visual system respond to targeted patterns in the environment telling us that "move-

ment" or a "corner" has been detected, certain other patterns respond to sad, fearful, angry (and so forth) sensory patterns with the information that a "sad," "fearful," or "angry" analogue has been detected. The response patterns for the emotion are then adapted for the designated system. So, for "sadness," the slowed, deliberate, rhythmic, and only slowly variable motions and thoughts are usually analogous. But as numerous researchers have argued, these systems may be an intrinsic or evolution-created mechanism, and may be constructed from generalized processes or may be systems that emerge from the interaction and growth of both (e.g., Panksepp, 1998).

Emotions as intervening modes of processing information or as responses have little to do with identity or personality when they are isolated as part of neural hard-wiring or biochemistry. Responding with anger to an inoculation in infancy does not necessarily contribute to identity. However, when several "angry–medical" events become interconnected and attract other events, such as "fear–strangers" or, even more generally, "fear–unpredictability," then they contribute meaning to each other and lead to a system of interrelated emotions and events, settings, people, or ideas. Now issues related to identity arise. The emotion–identity link goes beyond the sum of external stimuli, because the apperceiving mind provides its own organization as it synthesizes emotions into the unity of an identity.

From our perspective, emotion "glues" together chunks of experience through processes of emotional magnification and resonance, and thus creates identity. Emotion functions as the "glue" for identity in two ways: (1) It attracts the self to new experiences because it seeks out and recognizes a familiar or meaningful emotional signature; and (2) it connects separate experiences that share emotional processes, providing meaning and value to experience. This view of the centrality of emotion in identity may seem to clash with a compelling argument that identity is a consciousness of one's memories—that is, one's history—in some organized pattern, often a continuous narrative. Here it seems reasonable that a narrative memory process might be the glue. In writing of such narrative memory, Lewis (1997) leads us back to our view by pointing out that personal narratives are "rewritten as often as necessary" because they are required to provide meaning to the individual. "Meaning for individuals not only speaks to how they reconstruct the past but also addresses how they are to understand how the past may or may not influence the future" (p. 67). At one level, it is indisputable that a sense of one's own identity is constructed from narrative memory as Lewis describes it. However, we believe that we are arguing about a motivational process that underlies the very construction of such memories and the motivation for their construction. If people organize their thoughts, memories, and future hopes around happy events, it would be circularly the case that they are most themselves when this organization functions well and should have a sense of not being themselves if it does not function. Moreover, happy people should use particular strategies for thought (including memory construction) that are somewhat different from those of people who feel most themselves when they are excited or exhilarated, for example.

As long ago as Baldwin (1897/1913), psychologists have argued that an infant's first imitations emerge out of awareness that people have emotions or motives. People's emotions act as a beacon to the infant, signaling that they are experiential entities, which can be imitated. These imitations form the basis of the infant's own identity and allow for the creation of inventive imitations in the future (see Kahlbaugh, 1993). Importantly, these early imitations are not of actions only, but of feelings resulting from them.

In this theory of affect, we would argue that an adaptive and recognizable adult identity should be interconnected with sets of rules that are emotionally dense and that offer usable information about life. The power a set of rules has in the total identity is determined by how much of what is necessary in one's unique life is given meaning by it. The meaningfulness is likely to be of far more importance than its reward qualities. Taking meaningful negative emotion out of the life of a person such as Virginia Woolf would hypothetically unravel her identity (Haviland, 1984). Identity constructions may include many or few sets of these information bits × emotions combinations, but affect theory requires that meaningful information about identity be emotionally magnified.

Haviland and Goldston (1992) have described two types of emotional magnification that may be useful in identity constructions. In the first type of emotional magnification, a single content issue or theme may be emotionally elaborated. The same theme is associated frequently with many different emotions. For example, affiliative and romantic behavior is emotionally elaborated by adults but not by children; events such as birthdays, and objects or activities such as video games, are more emotionally elaborated by children (see also Stapley & Haviland, 1989). However, it is not just the frequency of emotional episodes that is important, but their diversity and, most importantly, their organization. Emotionally elaborating or magnifying content is not merely decorating it, but allows us to predict that the content has particular irresistible motivational organization. That is, the content is emotionally and cognitively "hot." There is some evidence that such emotionally elaborated roles are difficult to abandon (Tomkins, 1987) and are productive of cognitive change (Haviland & Kramer, 1991).

In the second type of emotional magnification, a single emotion can be "content-elaborated," and this has a different significance. For example, if being "exhilarated" is related to death, love, life, thought, and so forth, as it was for Virginia Woolf (Haviland, 1984), then one would argue that exhilaration or qualities of excitement are content-elaborated. Perhaps one would argue that this is a working definition of a personality trait—that Woolf was a person who needed exhilaration and sought it everywhere, probably using it in part as a defense against losses, sadness, and depression. The content elaboration of an emotion produces emotion scripts in which the experience of an emotion is the primary link between different roles or scenes. This is true for mothers, who behave more affiliatively than their adolescents do across a number of diverse conversational contexts and whose emotional behavior is consistent across large periods of time (Kahlbaugh et al., 1997). This adds to the creation of a consistent parental self. Because the emotion is linked to so many contexts, it is assumed to have a large role in the individual's identity (see Magai & McFadden, 1995).

The role of emotional magnification has been considered largely as an intrapsychic phenomenon in affect theory. It is somewhat puzzling that the other major emotional process—emotional contagion or resonance—has also frequently been considered to be an intrapsychic phenomenon, although it can be used interpersonally (e.g., Hatfield, Cacioppo, & Rapson, 1992; Haviland & Lelwica, 1987;

Hoffman, 1977; Zahn-Waxler & Radke-Yarrow, 1990). The concept of resonance is most often used in affect theories to explain how primitive emotional communication operates. The forms or signs of emotions in oneself or a companion are considered sufficient information to produce or induce emotionally analogous behaviors. So smiling deliberately at oneself aids in intrapersonal resonance with happiness, just as a smile or even praise from another will have a similar interpersonal effect. However, the processes of resonance can be conceptually and experimentally expanded to include many social constructions of emotion.

Progress in the study of emotion is just beginning to lead to a comprehension of emotional processes in identity construction. Historically, emotional processes such as magnification or resonance (in their diverse forms) have only been suspected to be primary factors in identity formation. Sociologists and historians, as well as psychologists, have argued that individual identity issues are complementary to sociocultural identity issues (e.g., Simon, 1992). Even the observations and theories of individual scholars are influenced by the emotional signatures of their historical times (Tweney, 1998). Emotional processes occurring within a culture influence individual identity constructions at every level and are themselves influenced by such constructions. Acknowledging this interactive process, we discuss each construction emotion–identity construction on both the individual and socioideological levels.

IDENTITY CONSTRUCTIONS AS GESTALTS

In this section we look at identity constructions as gestalts. By "gestalt," we mean the most stable arrangement or pattern of emotion and identity elements. As the term implies, the specific emotion and identity elements provide different "spins" or dynamics. When joyous emotions enter a pattern, they may produce a different process than that for anger, for example. Or it may be that when two or more emotions form a constellation such as a happy–sad combination, certain identity patterns are likely to stabilize.

By using the idea of "gestalt," we again bring up the idea that the mind actively imposes order onto its experience. We discuss three general types of patterns that differ in the number and type of relationships that are included. What is not initially obvious from our approach is that each gestalt may be likely to construct particular interpretations of emotion, such that the view of emotion and the view of individual identity make a meaningful match. Because of this, we examine "the place of emotion" in each approach; this often involves commentary on the group or cultural identity, and we illustrate different approaches with examples.

Although the basic concept of individual identity requires that each person have a singular identity, the complexity of the singular identity and the types of elements that constitute it vary. Reflecting progressive changes in logic and mathematics, as well as in the social sciences, the study of identity has produced models that roughly fit into the three categories presented here. Although we present only three models, it is obvious that the permutations on these models and the possible additional models are multitudinous, and that different cultures or historical time periods outside our own are likely to produce greater diversity. As unique people adapt to changing circumstances, new patterns will always be evolving. One consequence of this that is seldom discussed is that developmental patterns for complex social, cognitive, and personality development may also be multitudinous. Some people may develop in stage-like patterns. Others may develop in accretional patterns. Yet others may develop in progressive–regressive patterns. (For further review, see Magai & Haviland-Jones, in press.)

Dichotomous Identity Constructions

Numerically, the simplest model is dualistic; it can be represented metaphorically by a "yin–yang" symbol. In the dichotomous models, elements stand in opposition to each other, or at the very least in contrasts such as figure–ground. Sets of dualities, such as pleasant–unpleasant, conscious–unconscious, emotional–rational, active–passive, and so forth, are the "stuff" (material) of the dichotomous model. In these models, many collections of opposites or contrasts can be contained. Jung's (1921/1971) model, one of the more complex examples, depicts the personality as composed of four sets of elements in logical opposition.

The critical aspect of the dichotomous model is that every element defined in identity requires and often attracts its opposite or contrast. Emotions can be themselves a conglomerate requiring a conglomerate opposite such as rationality, but when individual emotions are examined, they also require opposites; for example, happiness requires unhappiness. Recently one of us was playing "opposites" with a 4-year-old. The adult said "In" and the child said "Out," the adult said "Good" and the child said "Bad," and so forth. Finally the child said, "This is easy because we have two hands." It is seductive, in that dualistic thinking is a simple approach that corresponds to the clear dualities in our physical world (including our bodies), such as left–right, up–down, and so on.

The Place of Emotion

The traditional dichotomous systems have given us theories of "emotionality" in animal behavior (Hall, 1934) as well as in human behavior. In most of the studies on which these systems are based, the particular emotion is considered immaterial; the focus is on sheer emotionality. That fear is the usual emotion portrayed has not been considered significant in the animal studies. Information from one emotion is assumed to generalize to other emotions. We might also mention emotionally undifferentiated dichotomies such as Wundt's pleasant–unpleasant dimensions (Fancher, 1996); theories of bimodal emotional–rational types in personality (Jung, 1923/1971); or, in social psychology, theories of motivational approach–avoidance (Lewin, 1938).

The dichotomous approaches may also examine specific emotions as opposites of each other—for example, Schlosberg's (1952) two dimensions of emotion, or Darwin's (1872/1998) argument that some emotion displays arise in opposition. Dichotomous systems almost always have evaluative good–bad implications, because the analogy between the dichotomous evaluative approach and any other dichotomy is so compelling.

Socioideological Concerns

In the dichotomous approaches two ideas tend to emerge, usually following the good–bad evaluative trend. First, the idea that one part of the self controls the other is similar to the Platonic view of reason as master of the slave emotions (de Sousa, 1987), and is thus congruent with late-19th-century approaches to psychology as revisionist philosophy. Second, the distinction between self as unwitting experiencer and self as knowledgeable evaluator is central. On the one side, the self is at the mercy of the flow of emotion; on the other side, the self manages this flow, segmenting it into episodes to create a coherent gestalt.

Dichotomous approaches to emotion are compatible with certain ways of looking at identity, both individually and culturally. On the cultural level, historians such as Mitzman (1987) describe the efforts made by the masterful "elite" and intellectual Europeans to constrain the emotional excesses of peasants in the 17th and 18th centuries. But this idea is clearly not constrained to those centuries; examples abound. In these evaluative associations emotion of any sort is suspect, and the connectionistic goal is to harness the emotions and to construct culturally cognized versions of them, such as duty, faith, or patriotism. In this sense, basic emotions as functioning parts of identity have little value.

Dichotomous views of individual identity date from a similar historical time and were dominant at the end of the 19th century in the West. Although the culmination of this theory may well have been in G. H. Mead's (1934) work, an earlier version exists in that of William James (1890). In James's dualistic approach to identity, he drew attention to the distinction between the "I" and the "me"—the active, experiential system versus the analytic empirical system. This distinction articulates the difference between the subjective self ("I") and the objective self ("me") (see James, 1890, pp. 378–379). A similar dichotomy occurs even more strongly in Freud's work (e.g., Freud, 1923/1961), where the id is the originator of activity or the source of motivation, and the ego (with the superego) is the interpreter and evaluator of that activity. The id, then, is the emotional self, the self that experiences and motivates. It is not necessary to have different types of emotion in these identities; emotionality is quite global.

In research, the stable identity of the adult is studied in terms of its rational components, much as the history of peoples is studied in terms of elite adult leaders. In developmental approaches, the emerging self-conscious (i.e., self-recognizing) identity overtakes the self-experiencing, emotional identity. Stern (1985), for example, discusses this as the emergence of the verbal self over the nonverbal self.

Examples

The dialectic contained in the opposition of elements has an obvious potential for interactive change. Each side of the dialectic defines and influences the other. The psychodynamic vision of extreme emotional stoicism functioning as a defense against hysteria is an example of the dynamism that emerges. Such dialectic theorists have added the interpersonal duality of self–other, and they have likewise extended the self-evaluative system to visions of the self as evaluated by others and the self as evaluating others, and so forth (e.g., "good mother–bad mother"; Sullivan, 1953). However, since emotions do not always appear to have opposites, nor do they (as a group) always appear to oppose rationality, the dualistic models have presented empirical problems.

To give an example of the research that originates from these theories, we consider the modern categorization of two disorders involving negative affect, anxiety and depression. Most psychiatric classifications adhere to the concept that there are at least two classes of negative affect disorders; hence there is a compartmentalized classification. However, each negative affect disorder contains poorly differentiated negative emotions mixed with other "irrational" symptoms, thus reflecting remnants of the dichotomous approach to emotionality but producing complex syndromes. More importantly, one finds that a recommended "cure" for emotional disorders such as depression is cognitive therapy. The combinations of negative emotions are managed by balancing them with rationality.

Modern extrapolations from the dichotomized model used in research on identity have relied on global positive–negative emotional evaluation as part of their method and interpretation. For example, Ogilvie (1987) identifies dichotomous outcomes of emotional interpretation of self: the undesired self and the desired self. The undesired self represents all that we do not wish to become or continue to be—and what we in fact have concretely experienced as the worst part of the self. This definition, of course, reflects an emotional value, in that each side of the self is judged within an evaluative ethic. The emotions (negative in this instance) have a function, in that they give the undesired self the task of defining the boundaries of self—"that sort of person I will not be."

The distinction between good self and bad

self, or idealized self and actual self, in present-day personality research has its roots in the dynamic clinical work of the 20th century (Adler, 1954; Horney, 1950; Rogers, 1942). Both the modern interpretations (e.g., Ogilvie, 1987) and the early clinical visions (e.g., Horney, 1950) of the dichotomized identity acknowledge that the "good" and the "bad" sides of the self use emotion differently. In their descriptions, the undesired self is more closely related to the actual experience of emotion; it is still the emotional side, and it is largely devalued. However, when the dichotomized negative–positive emotions are expanded somewhat and used more broadly as traits, as will be seen in descriptions of the research that follows in the next section, the dichotomized models begin to merge with the compartmentalized models.

Compartmentalized Identity Constructions

The concept of compartmentalized emotions is probably the most widespread approach at present to looking at emotions, and correspondingly the most favored mode of examining identity. The compartmentalized system is exemplified by biological classification strategies, or topologies—that is, basic groupings that may exist independently of each other. In biological classification one examines evolution as a connector among the classifications. The number of compartments in the modes or the elements in the compartments is limited empirically, not logically. There are an unlimited number of basic elements that may interact with each other in interesting manners. As an example of how seemingly unlimited these categories are, one can look at the taxonomies generated by the structuralists, which produced a list of 43,000 separate sensations as a basis of all cognitive thought.

The limitation of compartmentalized approaches seems to be that there is no clear way to give each factor or element its own process or way of changing the internal processes of other "compartments." Each compartment is immutable. Each factor is assumed to operate similarly; some attention is paid to its weight, but little attention is paid to the emergence of new components or to the loss over time and circumstances of old ones. Therefore, there is no required, logical, or dynamic organization of the components, as there is in the dichotomous models. This may be a present-day limitation rather than a necessity in such models, however.

The Place of Emotion

Compartmentalized identity constructions look at identity as a set of relatively independent, interacting factors. Numerically, these constructions are more complex than the dichotomous constructions, and they tend to be based more on empirical observations and less on logical reconstructions. Thus this approach is preferred by many researchers. In this approach to identity, emotions are usually considered to be traits. In this sense, they are separated from the drive functions and the unconscious functions that flourish in the dichotomous models. This broadens the dichotomous view by providing multiple traits and opening up the domain of observable identity traits.

Compartmentalized theories are supported by a rich tradition in social psychology dating from the middle of the 20th century (e.g., Adorno, Frenkel-Brunswik, Levinson, & Sanford, 1950; Allport, 1961; Kelly, 1955; Rosenberg & Jones, 1972). According to the compartmentalized constructions, the internal parameters of an individual's identity consist of multiple roles and traits adapted to fit particular life situations. Thus identity is a fairly flexible and pragmatic affair, allowing the individual the opportunity to adapt him- or herself to different situational or person-oriented contexts that arise concurrently as well as developmentally.

Those following this tradition study identity by examining how people describe themselves in the various compartments of their lives (their activities, characteristics, reactions to situations, and relationships to other people), and by analyzing how these descriptions fall into the various groups or typologies (what roles and traits go together and in what situations). Statements such as "I am good with people," "I am excitable," "I am Italian," and "I am a father" are all examples of disparate roles or traits that contribute to identity. Identity is the sum of relationship skills, cognitive skills, feelings, physical abilities, and so forth. These traits are associated with the roles one performs, including relationship roles, work roles, and cultural roles, producing an amalgamated identity.

The compartmentalized models, with their implied view of people as autonomous, control-ling information processors, have tended to neglect the dark, irrational socioemotional combinations common in the evaluative, dichotomous approaches; instead, they give a special place to emotions that promote autonomy, separation, and control. Because of this, when emotion is specifically addressed in these constructions, pride, self-esteem or the lack thereof (shame), and hostility in the form of self-assertion tend to be emphasized (e.g., Lewis, Sullivan, Stanger, & Weiss, 1989; Schneider, 1977; Scheff, 1988). However, many approaches give no special preference to type of emotion, allowing whatever traits of emotion are offered by an individual a place. Both uses of emotion in defining identity are quite distinct from the dichotomous definitions of emotions as syndromes.

Socioideological Concerns

The compartmentalized approaches are eminently suited to Western 20th-century technoculture. Ideologically they are egalitarian and autonomous, in that all traits are created equal in the personality; none are inherently better or more powerful, although some may dominate at particular times. In that context, emotion is democratically considered to be one of a multitude of equal trait types—ones that can be used or abandoned. Emotional traits such as "happiness" or "guilt," or, equally, "unemotional," occur alongside traits such as "famous" or "ineffective" or "free-thinking" or "middle-class."

The egalitarian mode of considering emotion or personality lends itself to models of change. To change family relationships, professions, or even one's status or bad habits, one acquires new traits, reorganizes the old traits, and/or inhibits a few traits. This can be accomplished in a goal-oriented manner (Markus & Nurius, 1986), through the individual's own "self-help" plans, through mandated retraining, or through external organization of environmental demands.

In terms of larger social identities, the compartmentalized identity is closely related to politically anti-class-conscious and socially malleable ideals, as well as to pragmatic scientific beliefs. Surveys and other "empirical" assessments define political and social groups; there is no acceptance of "natural" or necessary sets. A person is a combination of the "self-made" and "environmentally responsive," but emotional processes have little explicit role in the formation, maintenance, or development of the compartmentalized identity; they are definitely not the "glue" of identity.

Examples

At first glance, the late-20th-century personality and identity theories of compartmentalist thinkers may appear to have incorporated emotion. For example, the comprehensive five-factor theory of personality (see McCrae & Costa, 1989) includes many emotional items. However, this is only superficial. The five-factor approach, like other compartmentalized theories, is a static presentation with no internal dynamic processes. Each of the factors, as well as each of the trait items composing the factors, is treated without consideration of the possibilities that the traits on one factor may organize certain features of identity in one way and that other traits or factors may have different and nonequal functions. This outcome of compartmentalized approaches leads them to be incompatible with dichotomous approaches, with their process orientation, but this may be temporary.

A developmental approach (Haviland, Davidson, Reutsch, Gebelt, & Lancelot, 1994) has combined a compartmentalized approach with differential-affect theory to provide a more dynamic approach. The research emerged from a view of identity as changing over the lifespan (Erikson, 1968; Loevinger, 1976). Erikson proposed that the optimal time to form a personal identity is not in childhood (as proposed by Freud), but in late adolescence. Erikson argued that the identification with parents and consequent suppression of negative affect are not the equivalent of attaining an adult identity, but are only limited childhood identifications. Eriksonian theory describes an adolescent identity crisis that proceeds from a very limited "foreclosed" position, in which only roles defined and acceptable in childhood are contained in the identity. This "foreclosure" is followed by trial stages or new categories of behavior, in which new roles needed for adult society and for the emerging culture of the developing person are adapted to the needs of the young person.

Using the compartmentalized model but extending it to explore interactions among compartments, Haviland et al. (1994) predicted that the connections between the clusters of roles and traits would change as more adult identities emerged. In fact, children connected many emotions to roles such as son or daughter. The son role might be associated as often with happiness as with anger, for example. But in early adolescence, only a few negative emotions were connected with childhood roles. At this point there were few connections among roles in general or between roles and emotion. There were no complex or hierarchical connecting organizations among the roles, as there had been in childhood. For most middle to late adolescents, disparate, chaotic role–trait clusters of a highly idiosyncratic nature occurred—such as "me as a dieter" or "me as a Grateful Dead follower"—with little emotional connection. In young adulthood, again the traditional roles of "son/daughter," "student," or "friend," as well as new professional and sexual roles, were intricately interconnected and elaborated by all types of emotion; this suggested a reorganization of identity after a period of relative instability.

The Haviland et al. (1994) study suggests that the affect-based approach to identity holds some promise, particularly for describing change. The emotion traits do not appear to be equal to other traits, but their inclusion or exclusion from compartments in the identity set is related to the complexity and stability of the set connections. To use the concept of emotional elaboration, identity transformation occurs when the emotional salience or power of roles changes.

General survey and diary studies designed to follow change in emotional expression and identity have found consistent developmental change in the events that are emotionally elaborated (Haviland & Goldston, 1992; Haviland & Kramer, 1991). Although the emotional elaboration of different events across development may be a commonplace notion, the connection of this with identity is a new use for old concepts and illustrates the continuing place for compartmentalized identity constructs.

Dynamic Identity Constructions

Heraclitus argued in ancient times that the essential nature of all things is fire, and that the only constant in the universe is change. With Darwin, this belief in the dynamic nature of the world was given a scientific mechanism for the transmutation of all life. Paradoxically, the *mechanism* of spontaneous variation and natural selection ensures a random, chaotic process, where prediction is limited because it is sensitive to independent movements in both genes and environments. Although Darwin's impact on many disciplines within psychology is well understood, the specific emphasis on dynamic systems is relatively new. This dynamic model is beginning to have a larger impact in psychology (see Abraham et al., 1990; Levine & Fitzgerald, 1992; van Geert, 1997), although its scientific and philosophical merits have reached beyond the scientific community into the popular press, where the shorthand term for much of the approach is "chaos" (see Gleick, 1987) or "complexity" (see Waldrop, 1992).

Dynamic systems theory is devoted to elements in motion; it is the science of process rather than state. Whereas both of the models discussed earlier posit linear, additive, or even bidirectional patterns in their total gestalt, the dynamic model emphasizes emergence of new forms and nonlinear change. In this sense, dynamic systems are similar to Pepper's (1970) hypothesis of an organismic world, in which the bidirectional opposition of two features (e.g., subject–object) creates a new quality organization or stage. Werner, Piaget, and Baldwin were influenced by Darwin, and all developed models in which new forms emerge out of the tension of opposites. Note that dynamic systems theory may incorporate some of the earlier dichotomous theory of opposites, but is less evaluative; it focuses on how the activity of opposites creates new kinds of awareness. It may also incorporate some of the compartmentalized models as well, as stable constructions around certain types of attractors, because it is not necessary to have opposition to create change.

A quintessential example of dynamic models is seen in the creative dynamic of assimilation and accommodation (habit and novelty; see Piaget, 1945/1951), which parallels Darwin's inner and outer dynamic of spontaneous variation (what we now know as genes) and natural selection (environment). In dynamic models, the addition is that new features emerge nonlinearly whenever two or more oscillating systems interact (van Geert, 1997). Such models may begin to demonstrate how different emotions can interact to produce emotional behavior that is quite different from what would be predicted for each one independently. It may also be useful for examining emotions changing in different contexts.

Interest in psychological dynamic systems has grown substantially at the end of the 20th century (e.g., Cavanaugh & McGuire, 1994; Fogel & Branco, 1997; Kelso, 1997; Lewis, 1995; Thelen, 1996; van Geert, 1997) and covers a wide range of topics, such as infant development, cognitive development, neurobiology, social psychology, family systems, and clinical disorders. Proponents of these approaches look for many processes that will be useful in psychology, such as small effects' becoming larger and vice versa, rather than effects' remaining constant. Self-organization, idiosyncratic patterns, orderly processes moving into disorder and back again—all these fall into the purview of dynamic systems. These theorists also look for the splitting (called "bifurcation" in dynamic systems) of a single system into two systems with different and even opposing properties, rather than searching only for linear, cumulative change.

The Place of Emotion

Emotions may be central organizing features in some dynamic constructions of identity. In the dynamic approach, identity is a product of intersubjective memories, present events, and emotional resonances; all of these may be systems that change over time, constantly providing new configurations as well as periodic repetitions. Emotional events as motivational systems that help make up identity are likely to have a special role in changing the larger system and in stabilizing it.

It is not necessary in dynamic approaches that emotion be a "large" effect. An emotional experience may be a periodic effect, or it may be small at the origin of the behavior being studied and still attract more and more resonating elements when it occurs. In dynamic systems theory, such small effects are called "butterfly" effects. They are not necessarily reproducible, because the contexts in which they operate may not be reproducible, but they may nevertheless be critical. This approach is compatible with certain analyses of therapeutic cases, in which nonreproducible large effects such as adult identity disorder may stem from small occurrences in distant, emotionally elaborated childhood events.

To return to our proposal at the beginning of this chapter that emotion is the "glue" of identity, a dynamic approach traces information about the "small" processes involved in emotion. A particular emotional process may set events in motion in a unique pattern. These patterns become identity constellations in which emotional elements resonate with one another and with other people's emotions, providing meaningful and memorable value to the events. The process orientation of this approach opens up a great many possibilities for crisis and change, which may be more germane for certain lives and types of identities as well as for certain historical epochs.

Research within the realm of dynamic system tends to focus on how emotions function to create attractions among identity elements or among individuals (such as empathy and understanding), as well as on splits or bifurcations, which may function in identity to create autonomy and novelty. Critical questions therefore address such issues as how emotions act as attractors to connect disparate events and systems, as well as how they set boundaries or reach points for chaotic spinoffs. Because all emotions can function in these ways, accounts are just as likely to place value on happiness and interest as on sadness, fear, and anger or even shame, pride, and contempt. That is, contempt can act as an attractor for a system at one time and as a bifurcator at another time. The value or function of an emotion is not fixed, but rather is defined by its activity in a specific context and time.

Socioideological Concerns

The *Zeitgeist* of the dynamic approach includes an expectation of change and uniqueness. It also includes an appreciation for the importance of small effects on large systems and of large effects on small systems. The third major assumption involves qualitative or state changes that may occur randomly or chaotically but within certain boundaries and which tend to self-organize once again into complex patterns. To bring the concepts into a simple current event, this is the ethos that can argue for preserving seemingly superfluous greenspace or endangered species, on the chaotic off-chance that they will be needed for future biotechnology or even for happiness.

The dynamic approach is in part a logical and mathematical outcome of the dichotomous combined with the compartmentalized approaches, but it contains chaotic and systematic state or qualitative aspects that seldom emerge within the other models. In dichotomous approaches, with their anticipation of attractive

and antagonistic sides of identity issues, there is a bit of the idea about splitting or bifurcations, and therefore about certain types of state changes—a Jekyll-and-Hyde effect. In the compartmentalized approaches, there is a bit of the idea that every empirically observed factor has the potential to enter the predictive equations for boundaries and divisions or bifurcations in essential ways. Clearly each model contains aspects of the others, but the primary assumptions differ. It is closely tied to belief systems and even moral assumptions. When popular versions of chaos theory were first discussed, it was noteworthy how many people projected personal values on the theory, as if it threatened the harmony of experience.

The importance of dynamic systems in several theoretical and research domains that are tangential to identity is growing. Historically, several of the dynamic clinical psychologies or epistemological philosophies (e.g., Foucault, 1966/1973; Piaget, 1951) have shown qualities similar to the ones described in the dynamic approach. More recently, empirical approaches to dynamic systems in general and developmental psychology (Abraham et al., 1990; Levine & Fitzgerald, 1992; Lewis, 1997; Thelen & Smith, 1995) have begun to appear.

The dynamic systems approach supports the possibility that many fewer aspects of personality are predictable from early events than we had anticipated previously. The dynamic approach can even lead to the hypothesis that the singularity and predictability of identity are illusions of sorts (e.g., Lewis, 1997). Faith in the predictability of identity is rather like faith in the predictability or stability of weather. The long-term weather reports may tell us about climate and the boundaries on predicting certain types of storms, but they are quite poor at pinpointing specific or singular weather events. Lewis (1997), who relies upon a pragmatic contextualism in his rejection of causal and linear models of human development, points out that we value our beliefs about continuity and stability so highly that we determine the goodness of interventions such as Head Start programs for disadvantaged children on the basis of their ability to change permanently the educational abilities of the children. That such programs change the educational abilities of the children during the time that they are used, but often erratically later, actually fits with any number of dynamic models—but not the static and linear causal ones.

Examples

Several lines of research that are emotion-specific have anticipated the dynamic approaches. Apparently much of emotion research requires attention to context, to developmental history, and to the qualitatively different aspects of different emotions. This research has opened the window occasionally to considering the particular emotions of cnjoyment/pleasure (Isen, 1990), anger (Dodge & Coie, 1987), and sadness (Zahn-Wexler & Radke-Yarrow, 1990), as well as the various emotions of autonomy (Lewis et al., 1989). Stern's (1985) research on the emotional and cognitive capacities of infants has emphasized the responses of infants and their mothers to each other's emotion signals during interactions. They seem to change their patterns of response both to regulate the exchange and to regulate their separate experiences. They thereby create new and qualitatively different systems of relationships, in which the old signals may take on new meanings and functions adapted for the new system. Lewis (1995) has investigated cognitive–emotion interactions to show patterns of self-organization responsible for stability and change. Here the emphasis is more on intrapsychic interaction than interpersonal interaction; in all cases of this sort, however, the research demonstrates that approaches to each emotion require consideration of social and cognitive contexts as well as moods, and that different time (developmental and linear) scales affect processes.

An example of recent research on the interaction of intrapersonal and interpersonal emotions is Kahlbaugh's work (Kahlbaugh, 1992; Kahlbaugh & Haviland, 1994; Kahlbaugh et al., 1997). Although nonverbal displays of affiliation between parents and children remain fairly consistent across the adolescent period, younger adolescents (aged 11 to 13 years) show much more hiding, covering, and self-examination (nonverbal shame behaviors) than older adolescents or children, and more than their parents. Young adolescents are presumed to be more vulnerable to shame, both because of changes in interpersonal support (which may be seen as a loss of a family that defends one) and because of changes in the intrapersonal experience of emotion (related to physical and cognitive changes). Shame and identity are linked in two ways. First, shame suggests vulnerability and uncertainty to other people; it cautions them to interact more carefully, perhaps more positively with an adolescent. The shame can be contagious, so that others experience feelings of vulnerability or self-consciousness too. Second, the feelings of shame may increase introspection, so that the individual whose identity is vulnerable focuses intellectually on identity processes, actually asking the classic question "Who am I?" The adolescent's vulnerability becomes an attractor for the interpersonal and intrapersonal system changes.

In contrast, older adolescents display more contempt than younger ones, and this display emphasizes the adolescent sense of separateness and eventually leads to a change in the dynamic of the family interaction. Again, the direction of the change is not predictable from the change itself. In one family the emerging autonomy of the child may be greeted with relief, as an indication that there is one more adult; in another family the same behavior is a blow to the power of the adults. One could argue that contempt often emerges in reaction to protect against the vulnerability of shame. Now, instead of introspective submission, adolescents offer clear displays of contemptuous autonomy. Emotions have played a primary, functional role in these interpersonal identity models.

OVERVIEW AND SUMMARY

It will have struck the reader that this chapter is compartmentalized and has many dichotomous features as well, but that the two of us have a slight preference for the dynamic model. The reasons for this may be pragmatic, in that our coming intellectual period in history may well understand itself in these terms. It also represents personal attempts to establish continuity in identity within our own historical time. Analysis of theories of personality and of personalities suggests that we all tend to resonate to theories that reflect our own interpretation of ourselves, even though we make unique adaptations within the boundaries of larger systems. Magai and Haviland-Jones (in press) show that emotional preferences in the context of the perception of the self lend themselves to intellectual preferences and create theories of self and others. These apperceptions of identity are not superficial. It is possible to have an identity that is largely understood as dichotomous or as compartmentalized in its emotional and sometimes also cognitive organization. It is also possible to have a more dynamic organization, and it is possible to move among these general types. This chapter illustrates the position that our personal identities and mass identities, and equally our theories and research on identity, are reflected in the emotional present and past and in the anticipated future.

REFERENCES

Abraham, F. D., Abraham, R. H., & Shaw, C. D. (1990). *A visual introduction to dynamical system theory for psychology*. Santa Cruz, CA: Aerial Press.

Adler, A. (1954). *Understanding human nature*. New York: Fawcett.

Adorno, T. W., Frenkel-Brunswik, E., Levinson, D. J., & Sanford, R. N. (1950). *The authoritarian personality*. New York: Harper & Row.

Allport, G. W. (1961). *Pattern and growth in personality*. New York: Holt, Rinehart & Winston.

Baldwin, J. M. (1913). *Social and ethical interpretations in mental development*. New York: Macmillan. (Original work published 1897)

Blumenthal, A. L. (1975). A reappraisal of Wilhelm Wundt. *American Psychologist, 30,* 1081–1088.

Cavanaugh, J. C., & McGuire, L. C. (1994). *Chaos theory as a framework for understanding adult lifespan learning*. Westport, CT: Greenwood Press.

Darwin, C. (1998). *The expression of the emotions in man and animals* (3rd ed.). New York: Oxford University Press. (Original work published 1872).

de Sousa, R. (1987). *The rationality of emotion*. Cambridge, MA: MIT Press.

Dodge, K. A., & Coie, J. D. (1987). Social–information processing factors in reactive and proactive aggression in children's peer groups. *Journal of Personality and Social Psychology, 53,* 1146–1158.

Erikson, E. H. (1968). *Identity: Youth and crisis*. New York: Norton.

Fancher, R. E. (1996). *Pioneers in psychology*. New York: Norton.

Fogel, A., & Branco, A. U. (1997). Metacommunication as a source of indeterminism in relationship development. In A. Fogel, M. C. Lyra, & J. Valsiner (Eds.), *Dynamics and indeterminism in developmental and social processes* (pp. 65–92). Mahwah, NJ: Erlbaum.

Foucault, M. (1973). *The order of things*. New York: Vintage Books. (Original work published 1966)

Freud, S. (1961). The ego and the id. In J. Strachey (Ed. and Trans.), *The standard edition of the complete psychological works of Sigmund Freud* (Vol. 19, pp. 3–66). London: Hogarth Press. (Original work published 1923)

Gleick, J. (1987). *Chaos: Making a new science*. New York: Viking Penguin.

Hall, C. S. (1934). Emotional behavior in the rat: 1. Defaecation and urination as measures of individual differences in emotionality. *Journal of Comparative Psychology, 18,* 385–403.

Hatfield, E., Cacioppo, J. T., & Rapson, R. (1992). The logic of emotion: Emotional contagion. In M. S.

Clark (Ed.), *Review of personality and social psychology: Vol. 14. Emotional and social behavior* (pp. 151–177). Newbury Park, CA: Sage.

Haviland, J. M. (1984). Thinking and feeling in Woolf's writing: From childhood to adulthood. In C. E. Izard, J. Kagan, & R. B. Zajonc (Eds.), *Emotions, cognition, and behavior* (pp. 515–546). Cambridge, England: Cambridge University Press.

Haviland, J. M., Davidson, R., Reutsch, C., Gebelt, J., & Lancelot, C. (1994). The place of emotion in identity. *Journal of Research on Adolescence, 4,* 503–518.

Haviland, J. M., & Goldston, R. (1992). The agony and the ecstasy: Emotion in narrative. In K. Strongman (Ed.), *International review of studies on emotion* (Vol. 2, pp. 219–247). Chichester, England: Wiley.

Haviland, J. M., & Kramer, D. A. (1991). Affect–cognition relations in an adolescent diary: 1. The case of Anne Frank. *Human Development, 34,* 143–159.

Haviland, J. M., & Lelwica, M. (1987). The induced affect response: 10-week-old infants' responses to three emotion expressions. *Developmental Psychology, 23,* 97–104.

Haviland, J. M., & Walker-Andrews, A. (1992). An ecological approach to affect theory and social development. In V. B. Hasselt & M. Hersen (Eds.), *Handbook of social development: A life-span perspective* (pp. 29–49). New York: Plenum Press.

Hochschild, A. R. (1983). *The managed heart: The commercialization of human feeling*. Berkeley: University of California Press.

Hoffman, M. L. (1977). Empathy: Its development and prosocial implications. In C. B. Keasey (Ed.), *Nebraska Symposium on Motivation* (Vol. 26, pp. 169–217). Lincoln: University of Nebraska Press.

Horney, K. (1950). *Neurosis and human growth*. New York: Norton.

Isen, A. (1990). The influence of positive and negative affect on cognitive organization: Some implications for development. In N. Stein, B. Leventhal, & T. Trabasso (Eds.), *Psychological and biological approaches to emotion* (pp. 75–94). Hillsdale, NJ: Erlbaum.

James, W. (1890). *The principles of psychology* (Vol. 1). New York: Henry Holt.

Jung, C. G. (1971). *Psychological types*. Princeton, NJ: Princeton University Press. (Original work published 1921)

Kahlbaugh, P. (1992). A study of parent–child interactions and emotional development. *Dissertation Abstracts International, 53,* 3180 B.

Kahlbaugh, P. E. (1993). James Mark Baldwin: A bridge between social and cognitive theories of development. *Journal for the Theory of Social Behavior, 23,* 79–103.

Kahlbaugh, P. E., & Haviland, J. M. (1994). Nonverbal communication between parents and adolescents: A study of approach and avoidance behaviors. *Journal of Nonverbal Behavior, 18,* 91–113.

Kahlbaugh, P., Lefkowitz, E. S., Valdez, P., & Sigman, M. (1997). Affective nature of mother–adolescent communication concerning sexuality and conflict. *Journal of Research on Adolescence, 7,* 221–239.

Kelly, G. A. (1955). *The psychology of personal constructs* (2 vols.). New York: Norton.

Kelso, J. A. (1997). *Dynamic patterns: The self-organi-

zation of brain and behavior. Cambridge, MA: MIT Press.

Lefkowitz, E. S., Kahlbaugh, P. E., & Sigman, M. (1996). Turn-taking in mother–adolescent conversations about sexuality and conflict. *Journal of Youth and Adolescence, 25,* 307–321.

Levine, R., & Fitzgerald, H. E. (Eds.). (1992). *Analysis of dynamic systems in psychology*. New York: Plenum Press.

Lewin, K. (1938). *The conceptual representation and measurement of psychological forces*. Durham, NC: Duke University Press.

Lewis, M. (1995). Cognition–emotion feedback and the self-organization of developmental paths. *Human Development, 38,* 71–102.

Lewis, M. (1997). *Altering fate: Why the past does not predict the future*. New York: Guilford Press.

Lewis, M., Sullivan, M. W., Staanger, C., & Weiss, M. (1989). Self development and self-conscious emotions. *Child Development, 60,* 146–156.

Loevinger, J. (1976). *Ego development: Conceptions and theories*. San Francisco: Jossey-Bass.

Lutz, C. (1988). *Unnatural emotions: Everyday sentiments on a Micronesian atoll and their challenge to Western theory*. Chicago: University of Chicago Press.

Magai, C., & Haviland-Jones, J. M. (in press). *The matrix of emotion and life trajectories*. New York: Cambridge University Press.

Magai, C., & McFadden, S. H. (1995). *The role of emotions in social and personality development: History, theory, and research*. New York: Plenum Press.

Malatesta, C. Z. (1990). The role of emotions in the development and organization of personality. In R. A. Thompson (Ed.), *Nebraska Symposium on Motivation: Vol. 36. Socioemotional development* (pp. 1–56). Lincoln: University of Nebraska Press.

Markus, H., & Nurius, P. (1986). Possible selves. *American Psychologist, 41,* 954–969.

McCrae, R. R., & Costa, P. T. (1989). The structure of interpersonal traits: Wiggins's circumplex and the five factor model. *Journal of Personality, 57,* 17–40.

Mead, G. H. (1934). *Mind, self and society*. Chicago: University of Chicago Press.

Mitzman, A. (1987). The civilizing offensive: Mentalities, high culture and individual psyches. *Journal of Social History, 20,* 663–688.

Ogilvie, D. M. (1987). The undesired self: A neglected variable in personality research. *Journal of Personality and Social Psychology, 52,* 379–385.

Panksepp, J. (1998) *Affective neuroscience: The founda-tions of human and animal emotions*. New York: Oxford University Press.

Pepper, S. C. (1970). *World hypotheses*. Berkeley, CA: University of California Press.

Piaget, J. (1951). *Play, dreams and imitation in childhood* (C. Gattegnot & F. M. Hodgson, Trans.). London: Routledge & Kegan Paul. (Original work published 1945)

Rogers, C. (1942). *Counseling and psychotherapy*. Cambridge, MA: Riverside Press.

Rosenberg, S., & Jones, R. A. (1972). A method for investigating and representing a person's implicit personality theory: Theodore Dreiser's view of people. *Journal of Personality and Social Psychology, 22,* 372–386.

Schlosberg, H. (1952). The description of facial expressions in terms of two dimensions. *Journal of Experimental Psychology, 44,* 229–237.

Scheff, T. (1988). Shame and conformity: The deference emotion system. *American Sociological Review, 53,* 395–406.

Schneider, C. D. (1977). *Shame, exposure and privacy*. Boston: Beacon Press.

Simon, H. A. (1992). What is an "explanation" of behavior? *Psychological Science, 3,* 150–161.

Stapley, J., & Haviland, J. M. (1989). Beyond depression: Gender differences in normal adolescents' emotional experiences. *Sex Roles, 20,* 295–308.

Stern, D. (1985). *The interpersonal world of the infant*. New York: Basic Books.

Sullivan, H. S. (1953). *The interpersonal theory of psychiatry*. New York: Norton.

Thelen, E., & Smith, L. B. (1995). *A dynamic systems approach to the development of cognition and affect*. Cambridge, MA: The MIT Press. (Original work published 1994)

Tomkins, S. S. (1987). Script theory. In J. Aronoff, A. I. Rabin, & R. A. Zucker (Eds.), *The emergence of personality* (pp. 187–216). New York: Springer.

Tweney, R. D. (1998). Toward a cognitive psychology of science: Recent research and its implications. *Current Directions in Psychological Science, 7,* 150–154.

van Geert, P. (1997). Time and theory in social psychology. *Psychological Inquiry, 8,* 143–151.

Waldrop, M. M. (1992). *Complexity: The emerging science at the edge of order and chaos*. New York: Simon and Schuster.

Zahn-Waxler, C., & Radke-Yarrow, M. (1990). The origins of empathic concern. *Motivation and Emotion, 5,* 153–166.

CHAPTER 20

The Social Context
of Emotional Development

Carolyn Saarni

An assumption in this chapter on emotional development that needs to be made explicit is that emotional experience is inextricable from the relationships we enjoy, suffer through, or simply endure. A couple of delimitations should also be made clear: I do not discuss the biological contexts of emotion, nor do I extensively review emotional development in infancy (both of these topics are covered in other chapters of this volume). Instead, I shall address emotional development relative to the social contexts primarily experienced by children and young adolescents. I begin with a theoretical examination of the role played by context in emotional development and emotional communication; I include as well a brief discussion of how a social-constructivist view of development makes use of context. Next, I consider some of the theoretical dilemmas that face a contextual perspective. I conclude with a brief review of several studies that illustrate especially well the role played by context in children's emotional functioning.

"SOCIAL CONTEXT"
AND ITS SIGNIFICANCE
FOR EMOTIONAL DEVELOPMENT

What do we mean by "social context," and why is it significant for emotional development? To concretize the implications of this question, I begin by presenting three extended descriptions of emotion learning in three cultural settings.

The first is drawn from Mel Konner's work with the Zhun/twasi !Kung bushmen in northwestern Botswana (Konner, 1972); the second gives us an interesting comparison with the socialization of anger and aggression in a South Baltimore subculture (Miller & Sperry, 1987); and the last is based on a Japanese sample (Conroy, Hess, Azuma, & Kashiwagi, 1980).[1]

!Kung Child Rearing

Konner described the !Kung child-rearing style as permissive, attentive, affectionate, and extremely rich in stimulation and opportunities for exploration. I was especially intrigued by his description of tantrums and their relation to aggression in !Kung 2- to 5-year-olds:

Unlike the passive tantrums we are familiar with, a Zhun/twa tantrum is often characterized by beating, object beating and throwing of objects, all directed at the mother, in addition to frowning, grimacing and crying. Mothers are quite serene as the tantrum progresses, often laughing and talking to other adults while they ward off the tiny blows. They do not respond with the immediate anger characteristic of Western mothers hit by their children, but usually allow the episode to run its course. . . . If aggression *is* something that can be *displaced* or *redirected*, then this difference in the acceptability of real aggression against parents may help to account for the relative lack of fighting among young children in Zhun/twa society. (p. 301; italics Konner's)

Konner also described the children as chasing and hitting animals such as dogs and cows that belonged to the village, and even killing small animals; this aggression toward animals was also acceptable, for it was viewed as appropriate imitation of adult activities that would be undertaken in hunting. Peer aggression rarely occurred, and I can imagine that this sort of amicable atmosphere among !Kung children provided the foundation for the development of amicable adult relations, which would be adaptively necessary for a nomadic society with a hunter–gatherer economy.

South Baltimore Child Rearing

In contrast to Konner's description of how aggression was channeled in !Kung society, Miller and Sperry (1987) studied a South Baltimore community made up of working-class descendants from early immigrant Polish, Irish, Italian, and Appalachian laborers, in which mothers appeared to promote interpersonal aggression among young children. Mothers used teasing provocations to elicit mock aggressive reactions from their children; they reinforced their children's retaliation toward other children for presumed injuries or threats; and they modeled in both their discourse and their behavior the significance of aggressive interaction. One mother put it quite vividly:

> "Oh, Peggy, she made me so mad one day I thought I'd take her by the neck and just strangle her, that's how mad I got with her. She kept throwin' a fit, wanted to get down [off the counter]. . . . She wants to go play the machines like those [bigger] kids do. . . . So she couldn't have her way. She couldn't get down so she threw a fit. And she almost, she scared me, she almost fell off the counter. I beat her. Oh, I was so mad. I think it, I was scared more than anything." (p. 11)

Here is another example:

> "Now she likes to wrestle with me. I'll take her upstairs and we go on the bed and start wrestling. And I'll say, 'Take your fist and hit me.' 'Cause I try to teach her in case somebody else is doin' it. 'Cause some kids do take their fist and hit you hard. [laughs] I let her punch me. Sometimes she sneaks a good one in on me." (p. 17).

Miller and Sperry's richly descriptive ethnographic study presents an intriguing contrast to the gentle !Kung: Tantrums were met with violence—and yet, as in !Kung society, aggression

toward the mothers was tolerated (even encouraged), as long as it was conducted in an apparently playful context. Needless to say, the young $2\frac{1}{2}$-year-old girls who were the objects of Miller and Sperry's investigation learned to become emotionally and socially competent in *their cultural context,* where self-defense and retaliation were necessary aspects for girls' and women's survival (physical violence toward women by men was commonplace in this community). Similarly, the !Kung children became emotionally and socially competent in *their cultural context,* but did so by learning just the opposite pattern from the South Baltimore children: They learned to get along with their peers in a friendly and cooperative fashion, and channeled their aggression toward animals as part of rehearsal for hunting.

Japanese Child Rearing

The Japanese sample of children was part of a cross-cultural comparison undertaken by Conroy et al. (1980). They questioned both U.S. and Japanese mothers of 3- to 4-year-old firstborn children about a variety of hypothetical situations that were likely to occur in the home and that reflected noncompliance on the part of preschoolers. The results of their survey indicated that Japanese mothers were more likely than U.S. mothers to appeal to *feelings* in order to gain their preschoolers' compliance. Conroy et al. gave the following example of a Japanese mother's response: "It is not Mommy alone who is shopping. Other people are also here to shop, and the store owners have neatly lined things up so that the customers will buy them. Therefore, it will be annoying to them if you behave this way." (p. 168) The U.S. mothers were more likely to grab their children firmly by an arm and order the children to stay close. Japanese mothers were also found to use gentle persuasion to elicit compliance from their children: "You drew very well. You can draw even better if you use paper instead of the wall" (p. 169). U.S. mothers were more likely to demand an immediate cessation of the drawing on the wall and to command the children to clean up the mess. In other words, overt coercion was more often used by U.S. mothers with noncompliant preschoolers, often leading to a battle of wills, whereas the Japanese mothers appealed to their children's sense of wanting to please and cooperate, leading to strong emotional connection or *amae* (see also Lewis, 1986, for an analysis of Japanese parental control as reflecting an emphasis on cooperation). The willfulness of U.S. preschoolers is congruent with U.S. socialization values of independence and self-assertion; the responsiveness to others so noticeable in Japanese preschoolers is consistent with the Japanese socialization values of sympathy and social conscientiousness (Shigaki, 1983).

Development and Context

These three comparisons of differing social contexts and concomitant emotional functioning illustrate the plasticity of emotional development as well as its embeddedness in interpersonal communication (both verbal and nonverbal), but they do not really tell us exactly how emotional development is affected by context. Does emotional development have an endpoint, suggested by trait-like concepts such as "emotional intelligence," which is expressed in the current context (Mayer & Salovey, 1997)? Or is emotional development a series of accumulated changes that reflect one's past opportunities for learning emotion-laden meaningful connections, but that only become manifest or expressed in the context of the moment? Theorists such as Lerner and Kauffman (1985) have described contextualism relative to development as a view that emphasizes successive (as opposed to progressive or endpoint-oriented) probabilistic change in the transactions between individual and environment over time. This view allows for more plasticity in development than do more constrained developmental models that focus primarily on structural change (e.g., when a cognitive-developmental approach assumes that the endpoint is the acquisition of formal operations). Contextualism may also be thought of as pragmatic and instrumental, with philosophical roots in the work of William James (1907/1975) and especially John Dewey (1925, 1934; see also Donnelly, 1993). To understand the pragmatics of a given instance of behavior, one would need to consider the interpenetration of subject and context; that is, the person acts on his or her world even as the world reciprocally acts on the person. This is also the relational-functionalist position in developmental theory, insofar as behavior is responsive to an *affordant* environment (i.e., an environment that allows for interaction) and behavior functions so as to engage instrumentally with that affordant environment (e.g., Campos, 1994).

Time and Context

Lewis (1997) has argued that a contextual view of development means that "earlier events are unlikely to have much relation to later ones." This is especially so "if the earlier events that are studied are not related to the needs and plans of the individual as they exist now or in the future" (p. 68). This is a potent idea for emotional development, for it means that emotion-laden behavior at Time 1 need not influence or be related to emotion-laden behavior at Time 2, *unless* Time 1 and Time 2 are both occasions that are defined by the same needs and plans of the individual expressing the emotion-laden behavior. But this raises a double-barreled question: How might needs and plans be continuous across time and thus recurrently elicit similar emotional responses, and exactly how much time are we talking about? One possible solution is to think in terms of how the future can be embedded in the present: Our emotional functioning is revealed in how we strive to reach our goals, or how we are faced with having to revise them, or how we may be blocked from attaining them. This process may yield consequences that prove to be relatively desirable or undesirable in the here-and-now, but we do not live only in the present. The very fact that we have goals and intentions means that the future affects our present action. Our wants and desires are the sources of our motives, and thus they orient us toward the future, providing us, so to speak, with some navigational strategies for making it through the contextual landscape presently facing us (see also the discussion by Josephs, 1998). Thus, although we may debate as to whether the only known endpoint toward which our development "progresses" is our own death, we are not devoid of a future in the shorter run. It is firmly entrenched in our goals, and from this standpoint, our present adaptive efforts are wedded to our future. How far into the future, 10 seconds or 10 years, is not known, for the dynamic flux inherent in context (especially in those circumstances not under our control) can intervene and lay waste to the best of our long-range plans. This is not to imply that contextual shifts are somehow undesirable; indeed, they can also provide unexpected opportunities for change or even release from an otherwise dreary and emotionally numbing life situation.

To complicate our thinking about emotional

development still further, Lewis (1997) also argues for the idea that a given behavior can instrumentally serve as the means to multiple goals, just as a variety of different behaviors may be useful for reaching the same goal. An example common in Western societies that illustrates the first point is crying: The tears that are shed may be in response to a loss or in response to being deeply moved (as in awe-inspiring events). Similarly, a social smile may function as a metacommunicative comment about one's own minor social gaffe, or may function as a signal to another that his or her social gaffe was noticed but excused. As a further illustration, different emotional-expressive behaviors may be recruited to reach the same general goal; for example, when children want to be accepted by their friends (the goal), they variously adopt "cool emotional fronts" (Gottman, Katz, & Hooven, 1997; Saarni & von Salisch, 1993) but can also smile engagingly and genuinely (von Salisch, 1991, 1996). Both strategies are useful for children's fostering their relationships with peers.

"Maps" and Linkages between Behaviors and Goals

I use the metaphor of a "map" for thinking about how emotion-laden behaviors and goals can link up with one another in a variety of direct or circuitous routes. The map metaphor also helps in considering why a given goal might be most directly and simply reached by employing behavior *A,* but because of some complicating contextual nuance, the goal is in fact better reached by using behavior *B,* which is a less direct route but ultimately more effective. I am reminded of old-fashioned clichés such as "The best way to a man's heart is through his stomach" when I contemplate this idea of a map (an alternative metaphor might be a "network") for how behaviors and goals are pragmatically linked, but what may also be suggested by these old clichés is that they are also *scripts* for how a given society develops expectations and beliefs about how behaviors are planfully related to goals (Abelson, 1981). It is the socialization of these scripted expectations and beliefs that provides continuity and predictable meaningfulness to the diversity of linkages among behaviors and goals, so evident in the earlier illustrations of !Kung permissiveness, South Baltimore aggressiveness, and Japanese cooperativeness.

COMMUNICATION OF EMOTION AND CONTEXT

The Role of the Message Recipient

A number of developmental theorists have asserted that emotion *communication* cannot be separated from its context (Barrett, 1993; Saarni, 1989, 1990; Trevarthen, 1984, 1993; Vandenberg, 1998a, 1998b). Certainly the meaning of a particular facial expression is qualified by the context in which it occurs, as Camras (1991) has described: Her young daughter's expression of disgust was revealed both when her face was washed and when she was merely pulled into an upright position. It is the onlooker or recipient of the communicative message who must infer what is being communicated by the sender about his or her emotional experience. Did little Justine Camras experience both face washing and being pulled upright as distressingly aversive, or were these events simply interrupting whatever she was doing at the time? Or was one aversive and the other effortful? It is the parents, upon witnessing their baby's emotional-expressive behavior in conjunction with some situation, who attribute distress, irritability, or effort to their infant. Thus emotion communication becomes more complicated, for now we must add to the context surrounding the sender's emotional-expressive message the context surrounding the recipient as he or she attributes meaningfulness to the message. As an illustration, compare the two hypothetical vignettes below involving the same child but different parents:

Barbara picked up her 5-year-old son, Matthew, from kindergarten. She noticed that he looked glum and barely responded to her question about how school went. She began to worry that maybe he had gotten in trouble with some kids or maybe he had been scolded by the teacher for something. She thought that maybe he'd lighten up and feel better if she suggested stopping to buy an ice cream cone. Matthew agreed that he'd definitely like an ice cream cone, and they did not talk further about his initial withdrawn behavior. Barbara hoped that nothing too terrible had happened to him at school that day.

Brad picked up his 5-year-old son, Matthew, from kindergarten. He noticed that he looked glum and barely responded to his question about how school went. Brad recalled from other times that Matthew sometimes dealt with changes in his routine by becoming withdrawn, so he asked the boy if the class had had a substitute teacher that day. Matthew said yes, and added that she'd be there again tomorrow. Brad reassured his son that he'd feel better about the teacher the next day when he had become more familiar with her.

The somewhat contrived example above illustrates what is commonplace in many families: The same emotional-expressive behavior in seemingly the same context on the part of a child elicits different interpretations by the parents. Children, being the clever creatures that they are, often figure out how to use these different attributions made by their parents about them to their advantage. For instance, Matthew could get an ice cream cone out of one parent and a little bit of understanding and reassurance out of the other. In short, recipients of emotional-expressive messages bring to those messages their own emotional expectancies, perhaps projecting their own learned emotion-in-context associations onto the senders' messages. There is an immediate context experienced by the sender, influencing the emotions felt, the coping efforts initiated, and the subsequent communicative behavior directed toward another; however, the sender's emotion-laden message is endowed with still additional contextual richness by the recipient, including the emotional response evoked in the recipient by the sender's message (see also Lutz, 1983; Ratner & Stettner, 1991; Steinberg & Laird, 1989).

Reciprocal Emotion Communication

Cross-cultural research on emotion socialization suggests that "emotions can be seen as both the medium and the message of socialization. Their uniqueness, and their crucial importance for understanding development, lies in this dual and encompassing role" (Lutz, 1983, p. 60). Certainly the examples of three different cultural contexts above illustrate how parents' emotional responses to their children constitute both modality and meaning in the socialization of anger and aggression. The two parental responses to Matthew in the vignette above also demonstrate how emotional responses by the child are reciprocally responded to with emotion-laden parental reactions (worry, caring). Thus, even as we may observe emotional development *in the child*, those who interact with the child are communicating their own emotions *to the child*, often elicited by their evaluation of the child's

emotional behavior. Parenthetically, infancy researchers have long noted this sort of complementary, reciprocal, and incremental "dovetailing" of responses to one another on the parts of infant and mother (e.g., Cappella, 1981; Wasserman & Lewis, 1982). In addition to parents and other family members who are engaged in this reciprocal emotion-socializing process with children, the larger world of peers, the mass media, and other adult figures such as teachers are also part of the social context. Thus children acquire both emotion-laden beliefs and emotional-expressive behaviors that reflect these different influences. At the same time, their cultural beliefs about feelings and how they have learned to express their emotions converge toward (sub)cultural norms (Doubleday, Kovaric, Dorr, Beizer-Seidner, & Lotta, 1986; Wierzbicka, 1994). In short, children become culturally predictable—a view elaborated by McNaughton (1996) on parenting practices and cultural identity, and by Tomasello, Kruger, and Ratner (1993) on the significance of intersubjectivity in cultural learning and human development.

SOCIAL CONSTRUCTIVISM AND EMOTIONAL DEVELOPMENT

Similar to a functionalist model of emotion, in which there is very great emphasis on the context in which emotion is experienced (Barrett & Campos, 1987; Campos, 1994), a social-constructivist approach also views emotional experience as embedded in the conditions that justify it; that is, we do not have emotions in a vacuum, nor can we decisively tell what we are feeling based *solely* on introspection (Armon-Jones, 1986). But this perspective also emphasizes that we learn to give meaning to our context-dependent experience via our social exposure and our cognitive-developmental capacities, with this last component permitting us to transform our context by the very fact that we interact with it (Carpendale, 1997). In this sense, a social-constructivist approach to emotion is highly individualized: Our emotional experience is contingent on specific contexts, unique social history, and current cognitive-developmental functioning. Our unique social history includes our immersion in our culture's beliefs, attitudes, and assumptions; our observation of important others (as in social referencing—e.g., Mumme, Fernald, & Herrera, 1996); and the patterns of reinforcement from those with whom we are significantly involved. All of these factors contribute to our learning what it means to feel something and then to do something about it. The concepts we assign to emotional experience are saturated with nuance and context-dependent meaning, including the social roles we occupy, such as gender and age roles.

As for our current cognitive-developmental functioning, Lewis and Michalson, in their landmark 1983 volume, *Children's Emotions and Moods,* use the metaphor of a musical fugue to describe the interweaving and inseparable processes of cognition and emotion in human development. (Think of emotional experience as a melody that loses its identity if we begin to isolate and remove its various strands or musical subthemes.) Lewis and Michalson found that 6-month-old infants showed cycles of emotional expressivity interspersed with instrumental behaviors as they learned to pull on a strap attached to their arms in order to make a picture of another infant appear on a screen in front of them, along with a recording of the *Sesame Street* theme song. Based on their close-grained analysis of the infants' learning, Lewis and Michalson concluded that the processing of information that was apparently involved in the infants' learning how to get the picture and music to "work" for them was inextricably linked with their affective responses to the stimuli. For these young infants, cognition and emotion formed an integral system that functioned motivationally and thus facilitated the infants' learning how to get the desired picture and music to play. In short, they responded emotionally to the context and subsequently were able to manipulate it (see also Feinman, 1992; Trevarthen, 1993).

With access to emotion-laden language, the cognition–emotion "fugue" of older children becomes a complex melody indeed: They are no longer dependent solely on direct exposure to immediate emotion-eliciting circumstances, or on having to perceive directly others' emotional responses, as in social referencing. They can now traverse time and space to learn about emotional experience, be it about others' emotions or in response to their own feelings. Books, the mass media, the Internet, narratives, and other family "stories" can become powerful sources of emotional influence and learning. Through direct or indirect exposure to others, children learn the emotional behaviors, norms, and symbols of their culture (or subculture) as unintended consequences of social interaction

(Gordon, 1989), and they become active creators of their own emotional experience (much like the infants described above in Lewis and Michalson's research). Gordon states that "having understood the cultural meaning of an emotion, children become able to act *toward* it— magnifying, suppressing, or simulating it in themselves, and evoking or avoiding it in other people" (1989, p. 324; italics Gordon's). Thus, Gordon firmly embeds emotional experience in relationships and emphasizes the social process aspects of emotion in ways that developmental psychologists have only more recently begun to investigate explicitly. It is also this emphasis on our own active creation of emotional experience, integrated as it is with our cognitive-developmental functioning and our social experience, that underlies my use of the term "constructivism" and differentiates it from the more commonly encountered term "social construction of emotions" (Armon-Jones, 1986). The latter is related, in that it poses that all emotions are sociocultural products, but it does not allow for the vagaries of human development or for the active transformation of context that occurs by virtue of our interaction with it.

THEORETICAL DILEMMAS REGARDING A CONTEXTUAL VIEW OF EMOTIONAL DEVELOPMENT

Among the theoretical disputes involving a contextual view of emotional development are three that I address here. The first is the issue of whether emotional development derives its primary impetus from temperament rather than context. The second is that our explanatory constructs (such as "emotion" or "context") are in themselves contextualized. The third is that defining context with some degree of precision, or even developing a taxonomy of contexts, is exceedingly difficult; this contributes to a haphazard accumulation of research results, which are long on richness of detail but short on being incisive or systematic.

Temperament versus Context

The old nature-versus-nurture debate is still prominent among the theoretical conflicts facing a contextual view of emotional development. For example, some might argue that emotional development is primarily driven by temperament—presumably a biological feature of the individual, reflecting constitutional and/or genetic differences in such response styles as "emotionality." Emotionality includes both lability and intensity of emotional response, and occasionally also the hedonic tone of the response (i.e., it is often presumed to refer to negative rather than positive emotional experience). However, this is an oversimplification of temperament's role in emotional experience, according to Goldsmith (1993). He contends that temperament and emotional development should be thought of as interrelated parts of a complex dynamic system that may manifest their respective roles in the relative consistency and variability shown when individuals must negotiate significant transitions. I understand his comments to mean that temperament presumably provides some degree of response *style* consistency over time and across situations (see also Thompson, 1994), whereas specific emotional reactions yield the variability that comes from the influence of specific contexts, specific appraisals, specific social transactions, and the unique meaning systems that are applied to make sense of emotional experience.

Rothbart and Bates (1998) make additional arguments about the complex interplay between temperament and emotion arising from interactions among different temperament patterns (e.g., emotionality interacting with impulsivity). But exactly how these complex temperament × temperament interactions manifest themselves appears to be dependent on context for elicitation. There is also a good likelihood that temperament and context also interact together in complex ways, as when an impulsive child seeks out opportunities for thrill-seeking experience. Another sort of complex interaction between temperament and context may be found in how gender interacts with temperament. Whether gender is indexing socially acquired sex role factors (namely, cultural context variables) or biological factors associated with one's sex is not usually clarified in empirical research, but "gender" appears to yield quite different outcomes when conjoined with temperament ratings of emotionality (reviewed in Rothbart & Bates, 1998).

The Contextualization of Explanatory Constructs

A caution that we must keep in mind is that when constructs such as "temperament," "emo-

tion," "intelligence," and the like are used to refer to a variety of behaviors shown by an individual in a variety of situations, the behaviors are made meaningful by whoever is doing the observing, categorizing, or dimensionalizing of these alleged temperament/emotion/intelligence-related behaviors. This very process of attributing meaning reflects cultural beliefs, and Western social scientists tend to locate "causes" of behavior inside the person—a view not necessarily shared by those who live in non-Western societies (Kitayama & Markus, 1994). In some societies it may be ancestors who require appeasement and who make their needs known through an individual's current emotional experience (Harris, 1978); in other societies it may be the individual's place in a kinship hierarchy that "determines" emotional-expressive behavior (Wu, 1996). Our ways of construing our scientific beliefs (i.e., our higher-order explanatory principles) and observations are themselves contextualized by culture; how we make sense of emotional development does not escape this cultural contextualization, regardless of how "scientific" we may believe our methods and theories to be (for parallel arguments regarding the scientific study of children in context, see Packer, 1989).

The Taxonomy of Context

In an early paper, Lewis (1978) noted how difficult the task of creating a meaningful taxonomy of situations is. One can use physical properties such as the location of a situation; or the functional activities associated with situations such as eating, playing, or working; or the social/relational aspect of situations such as being with family members or with peers. But these dimensions interact with one another as well, such as playing with peers may occur away from home more often for older children but less often for younger children. The former complex interaction of situational features in older children's play means that there will be less adult supervision, whereas for younger children there is more supervision. What then are the implications for the nature of their emotional experience in these different play settings? This kind of task—to take salient features of a context and combine them to yield research questions—is less often done than the reverse, which is to compare older and younger children's play with peers and "discover" that the context affects what they do!

Along the same lines, Brownell (1989) has noted that if we do not think about context in a careful way, then "we run the risk of trivializing the study of context by 'discovering' that development depends on everything" (p. 198). Brownell has raised a couple of additional questions that researchers of development in context should address. First, how "context" is defined affects "which aspects of context play what roles in development, and which aspects of the social context are most important for which aspects of development" (p. 198). Examples of how investigators have examined emotional development relative to different definitions of context include emphasizing the verbal/sociolinguistic environment to which the child is exposed (e.g., Denham & Auerbach, 1995; Dunn, Brown, & Beardsall, 1991; Lewis & Freedle, 1973; Miller & Sperry, 1987); studying the peer group setting as a mutually influencing context for emotional experience and/or emotion understanding (e.g., Asher & Rose, 1997; Saarni, 1988; Underwood, Hurley, Johanson, & Mosley, 1999); and examining the influence of emotional-expressive signals on emotional functioning (e.g., Cassidy, Parke, Butkovsky, & Braungart, 1992; Halberstadt, 1991; Hubbard, 1995; Lewis & Michalson, 1985; Saarni, 1992). Second, Brownell has also questioned how the features of the individual (e.g., emotion, behavior, temperament, etc.) constrain or facilitate transactions with a social context, and whether there are some aspects of development that may be more reactive or sensitive to contextual features than others.

In considering Brownell's questions relative to emotional development, I think that we have made some advances in answering them. Researchers often explicitly invoke context as a substantial part of their investigation into some emotional process. Moreover, in recent years a number of studies have been carried out in different social contexts (e.g., within the family, between peers), and others have described in detail the kinds of processes characterizing the emotion-laden transactional flow back and forth between child and context (for relevant reviews, see Saarni, 1999). Systemic approaches as well as process-oriented studies seem especially well suited to an examination of emotional development in context, but this sort of research approach is rare in investigations of emotional development. (However, see Bainum, Lounsbury, & Pollio, 1984, for a naturalistic study of smiling and laughing in young children, or Saarni, 1992, for a study of school-age children's attempts to influence the emotional state of a depressed adult; examples of naturalistic studies with adults that emphasize the social systems surrounding expressive behavior, specifically smiling, include Kraut & Johnson, 1979, and Fernandez-Dols & Ruiz-Belda, 1995.) In the next section I review several relevant studies that seem particularly illustrative of how context has been incorporated into research on emotional development.

SOME EXEMPLARY STUDIES FOR UNDERSTANDING EMOTIONAL DEVELOPMENT IN SOCIAL CONTEXT

As mentioned earlier, I do not dwell at length on infancy studies in this chapter, but I think it is worth noting that one of the more thought-provoking early studies was carried out by Lewis and Feiring (1981) on "social transitivity" as a feature of social contexts affecting both emotional and social behavior in 15-month-old toddlers. In this study, three conditions were devised: In one group of toddlers, each child observed his or her mother interacting responsively with a stranger; in a second group, each child witnessed two strangers interacting positively with one another (and the mother was in the room but was uninvolved); and in the third group, each child saw no interaction at all (the mother and a stranger merely sat reading in the same room together, with the child present). The toddlers' play behavior and social engagement with the stranger and wariness shown toward the stranger were coded. The results revealed that although the young children did not show any overt negative behavior toward the stranger, they did engage much more readily in playing with the stranger whom they had observed interacting warmly with their mothers. The children also were friendlier toward the stranger whom they had observed positively interacting with another stranger, and although they approached, they showed the greatest degree of wariness toward the stranger in the last condition, in which the adults were uninvolved with one another. Lewis and Feiring argued that for social transitivity to work, there has to be an important affiliation involved—in this case, the affiliation with the mother, whose behavior renders the social exchange meaningful for the observing child. The youngster is then prepared to respond with similarly emotionally toned behavior (in this case, friendliness) in the subsequent interaction. Thus the results of this study speak to Brownell's (1989) first question above: It is the significance of children's relations with important others that mediates the meaningfulness of social contexts and therefore makes them differentially responsive to some contexts over others. Readers are referred to additional resources reviewing research with infants and toddlers that elaborate on this issue and related topics (e.g., Fogel et al., 1992; Saarni, Mumme, & Campos, 1998; Sroufe, 1996; Thompson, 1998).

Emotion Scripts and Context

There are a great many relevant social cognition studies, the majority of them using hypothetical vignettes, in which children's and youths' understanding of emotions in social and communicative contexts are addressed. Readers are referred to Banerjee (1997), Harter (1998), Saarni (1999), and Saarni et al. (1998) for reviews. I also think that investigations using hypothetical scenarios with children will tend to elicit children's *script* knowledge about emotional functioning, and that script knowledge, by definition, will tend to be more uniform in the sense that individual differences may be minimized (e.g., Saarni, 1997). However, some studies have built contextual variations into the hypothetical vignettes (e.g., Zeman & Shipman, 1998) and have examined individual differences (such as age group or gender) relative to these contextual variations in the scripts embedded in the vignettes. Scripts entail sequential expectancies, and as such they allow us to access our beliefs about a predictable event sequence (Abelson, 1981). Abelson has also emphasized that scripts require learning: One must learn that antecedent and consequent events are meaningfully linked—indeed, "enabled," to use Abelson's term. What this means is that when one of these antecedent events occurs, an expectancy is activated to embark upon a course of action that follows the script. Typically the social cognition studies using hypothetical vignettes investigate whether children of different ages will demonstrate this sort of predictable script understanding. However, scripts are much more complex than simple habitual routines; they are fluid cognitive constructions that take into account contextual features. And as a result, children and youth sometimes surprise adults by coming up with novel expectancies about how an emotion script is expected to unfold (for a discussion of experimenter and developmental bias in emotion scripts, see Lewis, 1989).

Turning to research undertaken with older children and how their emotional experience plays out in social contexts, I limit myself to just a few studies that are observational in nature or have used intensive interviews about children's own experience. Observational research, whether the investigators are so inclined or not, is invariably confronted by the influence of context (e.g., Bates, 1976; Casey, 1993; Grolnick, Bridges, & Connell, 1996; Olthof & Engelberts-Vaske, 1997). Because of space limitations, I cannot address the rich literature on young children's acquisition of discourse strategies and narrative practices as they relate to a contextual view of emotional development (e.g., Fivush, 1991; Nelson, 1996; Oppenheim, Nir, Warren, & Emde, 1997); nor can I review here the many fascinating investigations of how young children employ language to mediate their understanding of emotions in context (e.g., Bretherton, Fritz, Zahn-Waxler, & Ridgeway, 1986; Cervantes & Callanan, 1998; Denham & Auerbach, 1995; Dunn, Bretherton, & Munn, 1987) or to manipulate others in disputes and conflicts (e.g., Dunn & Brown, 1994; Dunn et al., 1991).

Relationship Closeness and Emotional Experience

Effects of Peer Liking and Gender

As noted in regard to the Lewis and Feiring (1981) study, one of the major dimensions of social context that affects emotional functioning is the significance of relationship, particularly the closeness of the affiliation between two or more interactants. An investigation that combined the contextual features of relationship closeness with gender was undertaken by Fabes, Eisenberg, Smith, and Murphy (1996). They collected observations on children's naturally occurring anger episodes with well-liked and not-liked peers over the course of 6 months; the children ranged in age from about $4\frac{1}{2}$ to about $6\frac{1}{2}$ years old. Context proved to be a powerful determinant of how children reacted to provocation. Boys, but not girls, experienced more anger episodes with well-liked peers than with not-liked peers; Fabes et al. speculated that this was in part due to differences in the nature of boys' play, which included more struggles over dominance and competition, both being likely to elicit more conflict and subsequent anger. They also found that when the antecedents of a potentially anger-eliciting situation were ambiguous, well-liked peers were given the "benefit of the doubt," such that the children were less likely to react angrily to the provocation. For not-liked peers, this flexibility was not as readily extended. Children's anger reactions were also less intense and appeared more controlled toward their well-liked peers than toward their not-liked peers, even when the nature of the provocation was virtually the same. Not surprisingly, coping with the aftermath of an anger episode was also quite different when it occurred with a well-liked peer: Boys showed more constructive and instrumental coping, and they were less likely to react with hostile aggression or give up as though they had been intimidated. These latter behaviors were more likely to be shown toward not-liked peers. Interestingly, girls were more likely to opt for indirect social aggression, such as social exclusion, when angered.

Another powerful context factor associated with gender was that only 14% of the observed provocations involved a mixed-gender dyad. What this means is that what children learn about anger and its management comes mostly from same-sex peer interaction. This raises interesting questions as to whether teens may not be as competent in negotiating and managing anger-provoking interactions that emerge in close relationships with the opposite sex as they may be in close same sex-relationships. They may simply have less practice in doing so, although sibling relationships may provide an alternative avenue for children to learn how to negotiate with opposite-gender children and youths (albeit of younger or older ages).

Friendships

In a complementary investigation, Asher and Rose (1997) examined close friendships among school-age children (as opposed to whether the children were simply rated as "popular" or accepted by others) for the sorts of emotional tensions and conflicts that are unique to close relationships between peers. They concluded that there are five primary nodes around which children at times experience emotional dilemmas

with their friends. In the following list, I have included quotes taken from their chapter (Asher & Rose, 1997, p. 203) that illustrate these five nodes particularly well.

1. Respecting the need for equity and reciprocity: "He is my very best friend because he tells me things and I tell him things. He shows me a basketball move and I show him, too, and he never makes me sad."
2. Providing help, even when it might be inconvenient or have a cost to it: "My friend is really nice. Once my nose was bleeding about a gallon every thirty minutes and he helped me."
3. Being trustworthy and reliable, even when it might be in conflict with other desires: "Jessica has problems at home and with her religion and when something happens she always comes to me and talks about it. We've been through a lot together."
4. Managing disputes and conflicts (as opposed to terminating the friendship or escalating the conflict into aggression): "Angie is very special to me. If we get in a fight we always say we are sorry. And if she says she would play with me, she plays with me."
5. Recognizing that friendships are part of larger dynamic networks such as classrooms or neighborhoods (sometimes a friend wants to spend time with others, and sulking about it is both useless and potentially threatening to the friendship): "Tammy is really forgiving. She understands when I pick partners other than her."

As is evident from the quotes above, children relish and value their friendships, which represent rich emotional experience. They gain from friendships companionship, support, and validation; given that these interpersonal goals are highly prized, children must learn to modify their behavior, including their emotional responses, so as to maintain these interpersonal rewards. What is it, then, that children influence in one another so that they can do this?

Asher and Rose (1997) give us some ideas as to what might be going on in their research on what children do to resolve friendship conflicts. Essentially, they found that children who used compromising strategies and espoused relationship goals ("I would try to stay friends") had the least conflict in their friendships and enjoyed more friendships than those children who dealt with conflicts by retaliating or behaving in an aggressive or controlling fashion. Children with close friends appeared to be able to cope with conflict and tension, showed empathy and understanding of both their own and others' feelings, recognized that their emotional-expressive behavior had an impact on others, and desired emotional closeness. In short, friendships truly represent the dyadic "space" in which one can see the intersubjectivity of emotional experience. Readers are also referred to Parker and Herrera's (1996) study comparing abused and nonabused children's friendships for further contextual effects on close peer relationships, and to Whitesell and Harter (1996) for an investigation of young adolescents' coping with hypothetical provocation from best friends versus acquaintances. In both studies, gender played an especially significant contextual role.

Status and Provocation

Under the rubric of status and provocation, I consider two observational studies. The first of these (Underwood & Hurley, in press; Underwood et al., 1999) was carried out with a large sample of children aged 8 to 12 years; the children's sociometric status was assessed, and the researchers used a child confederate to provoke the children. The second study (Cole, Zahn-Waxler, & Smith, 1994) assessed the risk status of 5-year-olds for behavioral disorders and used the mildly interpersonally stressful "disappointing gift" paradigm (Saarni, 1984) to provoke the children.

The Provoking Confederate

Underwood and Hurley (1999; Underwood et al., 1999) were able to obtain a sample of over 300 children to participate in a rigged computer game with a child confederate who had been trained to deliver mildly insulting comments to each child subject, regardless of whether the subject child won (infrequently) or lost (frequently) the computer game. The child confederate made comments such as "You must be especially bad at computer games," "How come you keep losing? Don't you want to win that prize?", or "I'm just letting you win so you don't feel bad." The children had also completed a sociometric rating scale that, in addition to the traditional "popular" versus "rejected" categories, allowed the investigators to distinguish those children who obtained an especially high aggression-initiating nomination from their peers.

To the investigators' surprise (Underwood & Hurley, 1999), the children nominated as aggressive by their peers behaved no differently with the provoking confederate child than nonaggressive children did. The rejected children also did not differ from the popular children, except for a couple of trivial differences such as the popular children tended to maintain neutral facial expressions a bit more (but this was not a significant difference). Interestingly, the rejected children were significantly more likely than other children to ask the researchers to stop the computer game before it came to an end, and these might have been the children who would have become very upset or angry if they had been forced to "stick it out" with the insulting confederate.

As for age and gender differences in this provoking interaction, girls revealed sad facial expressions a bit more often than boys, but neither gender revealed angry expressions to any great degree. Neutral expressions increased with age, whereas sadness and the rare anger expressions decreased with age. The authors point out that this behavioral outcome contradicted a social cognition study (Underwood, 1997) in which older children claimed in response to hypothetical vignettes that they would be more likely to express their anger than younger children claimed to be. This difference in contexts—hypothetical vignettes versus a "live" encounter—is especially interesting relative to script understanding, because both situations involved being taunted by a peer. However, the live encounter was between two children who did not know one another, and the hypothetical vignettes featured the protagonist's being taunted by a classmate in front of others. Thus two important contextual differences emerge here, in addition to the very significant live-versus-hypothetical context difference: familiar relationships with others, and having an audience witness one being insulted.

We need a study that uses the same children as subjects in both a live encounter and an interview featuring hypothetical vignettes, and that examines the same contextual influences in both situations. Such a study would then allow us to isolate the effect of an actual encounter versus a hypothetical interaction on children's social emotional-expressive behavior. Ideally, the study would also elicit their beliefs about whether they would dissemble their emotional-expressive behavior in the hypothetical situation (as Underwood, 1997 did); it would also include an exit interview after the live encounter (e.g., Casey, 1993; Saarni, 1992), or even have the children subsequently watch their videotapes to find out how they construe *post hoc* their emotional reaction to the insulting confederate, regardless of their expressive display.

The Disappointing Gift

Cole et al. (1994) used the Child Behavior Checklist (Achenbach & Edelbrock, 1983) and other evaluative measures to assess 4- and 5-year-old children (51 boys and 31 girls) for their disruptive behavior. The children's risk status was then estimated, yielding high-, moderate-, and low-risk groups. Gender differences indicated that girls were more likely to show depressive and anxious symptoms, and that the high-risk group was associated with more externalizing behaviors.

After the children had become familiar with the lab, they ranked some "gifts" in order of preference and were subsequently given their least preferred choice in the presence of an experimenter who did not know their risk status. She then left each child alone for a minute, and a second experimenter returned to say it was a mistake; at that time, she also questioned the children about their feelings about the so-called gift (over 70% reported negative feelings) and whether they thought the first experimenter had been aware of how they felt about the disappointing gift (almost 80% reported they did not think she knew how they felt). The children's facial expressions and verbal behavior were coded and aggregated, and among the many results were several interesting context findings. At-risk boys generally displayed more angry and disruptive (rude) behavior when the experimenter was present, but after she had left, both low-risk and at-risk boys were similar in their negative displays when alone. Conversely, a distinguishing factor with the girls was the amount of positive behavior displayed: Low-risk girls showed the most, and the high-risk girls showed the least, when the experimenter was present immediately after having given the girls the disappointing gift. However, after she left the girls alone, low-risk girls displayed the most negative emotion over the disappointing gift (primarily indexed by brow furrowing), whereas the at-risk girls appeared not to respond to this context alteration; they showed no change in their expressive behavior, regardless of whether the experimenter was present or not.

I will not describe here Cole et al.'s lengthy interpretation of their results (which focused on the interaction of gender role with at-risk behavior in young children), but suffice it to say that the contextual feature that once again was pivotal to emotional-expressive behavior was *interpersonal* in nature. But characteristics of the children interacted with this contextual feature—namely, gender and propensity for problematic behavior. Rothbart and Bates (1998) might well look at such an outcome and conclude that once again the dynamic interplay of temperament (assuming that the at-risk children were also manifesting socially taxing temperamental characteristics as part of their problematic behavior) and gender is dependent on context for elicitation.

Influencing the Emotional State of Others

The final observational study of social context effects on children's emotional-expressive behavior to be described here was conducted by myself (Saarni, 1992). Children were faced with how to cheer up a despondent "market researcher" who previously had been very friendly. The social task to be accomplished seemed straightforward, but the children's management of their own emotions and behavior presented complex challenges in this case. Being confronted with this depressed woman could make the children sad, angered that they had glibly agreed to try to cheer her up, or challenged to try to make her happier. A total of 80 children across three age groups (7–8, 9–10, and 11–12 years) met individually on two separate occasions with a woman introduced to them as a "market researcher." The first time she was visibly in a happy emotional state and engaged the children warmly; on the second occasion, a week later, she was in a sad, depressed state. Although she maintained facial regard and eye contact with each child, she adopted a slumped posture, did not smile, and spoke little (and then in a flat monotone). After 3 minutes of such despondent interaction, she ended the session by becoming more animated and positive; this was done for ethical reasons, so that children would leave the session believing that they had been effective in cheering her up. An "assistant" accompanied the children to and from their classrooms, and prior to this second meeting had asked the children to help cheer up her "colleague," who was feeling quite "down." All agreed to do so.

The children were videotaped throughout their interaction with the market researcher while doing a task for her. This allowed for the establishment of a base rate of emotional-expressive behaviors for when the children were with the market researcher in her happy state. This base rate could then be compared to what they attempted to do when trying to cheer her up in her sad state. As a check on the manipulation, a mirror was placed behind the children in a slightly offset position, so that the video camera could also simultaneously capture the "market researcher's" expressive behavior toward the child.

Results indicated that the oldest children (11–12 years) were the most positive in their emotional-expressive behavior in both happy and sad sessions, and that the middle age group revealed a curiously flat emotional profile in response to the two emotional state variations. Among the youngest children were those who did appear to become "engulfed" by the sad researcher's demeanor and looked as though they would very nearly cry, crawl under the table, or try to leave. Interestingly, the 11- to 12-year-olds, while showing the most positive behavior toward the sad researcher, also revealed the most tension-filled expressive behavior—for example, biting their lips, touching themselves, rubbing their fingers together, and so forth. From an impressionistic standpoint, these oldest children seemed more self-contained and less influenced by the sad researcher's emotional-expressive behavior, despite the tension-laden nonverbal behaviors. The content of their conversation with her was also more often "upbeat," and they talked more than the two younger groups, who tended to "clam up" when faced with the sad woman. Few gender differences were found in this study, but older girls did smile more at the sad market researcher as a strategy to try to cheer her up. In contrast, some of the older boys appeared annoyed at the prospect of having to help cheer someone up, despite having agreed to do so (e.g., they drummed their fingers on the table, bumped around in their seats, etc.).

The interpersonal context manipulation—having to interact with either a cheerful person or a depressed one—clearly elicited different emotional-expressive behavior from the children, but the results of the exit interview, conducted by the video "assistant" as the children were walked back to their classrooms, were more mixed. The children verbally acknowl-edged that they were quite aware of the market researcher's affective state, but they were less consistent in knowing how they acted toward her. The youngest children gave proportionately the largest number of "don't know" responses; the 9- to 10-year-olds indicated that they thought they had cheered up the sad market researcher by being very task-oriented; and the oldest children were the most likely to give socially oriented rationales (e.g., "I tried to talk about pleasant things" or "I tried to be nice to her"). Moreover, 24% of the oldest children's responses explicitly addressed their own expressive behavior as a way to cheer her up—most typically "I smiled at her a lot." Twice as many girls gave this sort of response than boys, and in fact the frequency of their smiles with the depressed woman was about 50% higher than that of the boys.

This study was also unusual in that after each child left the room, the market researcher completed a short rating form on her perception of the child, as well as about her own affective reaction to the child. She rated nearly half of the youngest children as appearing very uncomfortable in her presence when she acted depressed, as compared to 26% of the middle age group and none of the oldest group. Fully half of the oldest children were rated as behaving in a relatively comfortable and relaxed fashion. As for her own affective comfort level after interacting with each child, significant differences were found relative to age group, with the market researcher feeling more often relieved when interacting with the oldest children and more often feeling guilty when working with the youngest children. These subjective reports by the market researcher dovetailed nicely with the observed emotional-expressive behavior displayed by the children; the use of experimenter subjective reports may prove to be a useful strategy for further examination of how intersubjectivity plays itself out in emotion-laden interpersonal exchanges.

This observational study raised many questions about the mutual interaction of two individuals' emotional-expressive cues, as well as the added effect on children when they are aware of being videotaped. The context manipulation, interacting with either a happy or a sad person, overlapped with other contextual features: This was a relatively unfamiliar individual, who was an adult (more powerful status relative to the children), and the larger setting was that the children were at their school. Dealing at home with depressed adults who are well known to children is a very different context, and one that has been productively explored by Zahn-Waxler and her colleagues with younger children (Zahn-Waxler, Cole, & Barrett, 1991; Zahn-Waxler, Kochanska, Krupnick, & McKnew, 1990). But in both settings, the effect of having to interact with a depressed adult is noticeably more negative for younger children. Perhaps one of the emotional tasks that young adolescents in North American society begin to learn is how, when, and with whom to "disconnect" their emotions from those of another so as to maintain their own emotional boundaries when it is adaptive for them to do so (e.g., adolescents are relatively less involved in parental conflict; Cummings, Ballard, & El-Sheikh, 1991; Cummings & Davies, 1994).

CONCLUSION

I began this chapter by stating an assumption that guides my perspective on emotional development—namely, that our emotional experience is inseparable from our relationships with others. I want to conclude the chapter by summarizing for the reader several important parameters of social context that suffuse those relationships and thus influence our emotional behavior. The first parameter that I have discussed is the closeness of relationship between interactants; the relative status or difference in dominance between two individuals is also important. Investigators of nonverbal communication have, of course, long recognized these two dimensions as significant contributors to expressive behavior (e.g., Mehrabian, 1981). A third dimension of social context that we would be wise to take into account in observational as well as social cognition studies is the degree to which emotional behavior is *exposed*—that is, how public or private emotional-expressive behavior is. Children begin to incorporate this dimension into their self-presentations with the advent of self-consciousness (e.g., Lewis, 1992), and their ability to make social comparisons between themselves and others will further affect their use of this dimension (e.g., Ruble, Boggiano, Feldman, & Loebl, 1980; Saarni & Weber, 1999). In addition to these three *dimensions*, people are motivated to construct a desired identity (which incorporates social categories such as gender) that derives its meaningfulness from others' responses to the self's

projected image (Baumeister, 1993; Harter, 1998); it is in this sense that identity itself constitutes a contextual *process* that permeates people's emotional and social experience (see, e.g., research by Harter, Waters, Whitesell, & Dastelic, 1998, on adolescents' use of personal "voice" or self-schema as an integration of socioemotional expectations). Emotional communication reflects the interaction of these identity construction processes, and they are part of what characterizes the dynamic quality of intersubjectivity.

ACKNOWLEDGMENT

Parts of this chapter have been adapted from Saarni (1999). Copyright 1999 by The Guilford Press. Adapted by permission.

NOTE

1. Given the length of time since these different datasets were collected, it may well be that these cultural contrasts would no longer be found in the increasing "homogenization" of global societies. See also the relevant discussion on cultural globalization by Hermans and Kempen (1998).

REFERENCES

Abelson, R. (1981). Psychological status of the script concept. *American Psychologist, 36*, 715–729.

Achenbach, T., & Edelbrock, C. (1983). *Manual for the Child Behavior Checklist and Child Behavior Profile.* Burlington: University of Vermont, Department of Psychiatry.

Armon-Jones, C. (1986). The thesis of constructionism. In R. Harré (Ed.), *The social construction of emotions* (pp. 32–56). Oxford: Blackwell.

Asher, S., & Rose, A. (1997). Promoting children's social-emotional adjustment with peers. In P. Salovey & D. Sluyter (Eds.), *Emotional development and emotional intelligence* (pp. 196–224). New York: Basic Books.

Bainum, C. K., Lounsbury, K., & Pollio, H. (1984). The development of laughter and smiling in nursery school children. *Child Development, 55*, 1946–1957.

Banerjee, M. (1997). Peeling the onion: A multilayered view of children's emotional development. In S. Hala (Ed.), *The development of social cognition* (pp. 241–272). Hove, England: Psychology Press.

Barrett, K. (1993). The development of nonverbal communication of emotion: A functionalist perspective. *Journal of Nonverbal Behavior, 17*, 145–169.

Barrett, K. C., & Campos, J. J. (1987). Perspectives on emotional development: II. A functionalist approach to emotions. In J. D. Osofsky (Ed.), *Handbook of infant development* (2nd ed., pp. 555–578). New York: Wiley.

Bates, J. (1976). Effects of children's nonverbal behavior upon adults. *Child Development, 47,* 1079–1088.

Baumeister, R. (1993). Self-presentation: Motivational, cognitive, and interpersonal patterns. In G. van Heck, P. Bonaiuto, I. J. Deary, & W. Nowack (Eds.), *Personality psychology in Europe* (Vol. 4, pp. 257–280). Tilburg, The Netherlands: Tilburg University Press.

Bretherton, I., Fritz, J., Zahn-Waxler, C., & Ridgeway, D. (1986). Learning to talk about emotions: A functionalist perspective. *Child Development, 57,* 529–548.

Brownell, C. A. (1989). Socially-shared cognition: The role of social context in the construction of knowledge. In L. Winegar (Ed.), *Social interaction and the development of children's understanding* (pp. 173–205). Norwood, NJ: Ablex.

Campos, J. J. (1994, Spring). The new functionalism in emotion. *SRCD Newsletter,* pp. 2, 4, 7.

Camras, L. (1991). Conceptualizing early infant affect: Emotions as fact, fiction or artifact? In K. T. Strongman (Ed.), *International review of studies on emotion* (Vol. 1, pp. 16–28). New York: Wiley.

Cappella, J. (1981). Mutual influence in expressive behavior: Adult–adult and infant–adult dyadic interaction. *Psychological Bulletin, 89,* 101–132.

Carpendale, J. (1997). An explication of Piaget's constructivism: Implications for social cognitive development. In S. Hala (Ed.), *The development of social cognition* (pp. 35–64). Hove, England: Psychology Press.

Casey, R. (1993). Children's emotional experience: Relations among expression, self-report, and understanding. *Developmental Psychology, 29,* 119–129.

Cassidy, J., Parke, R., Butkovsky, L., & Braungart, J. (1992). Family–peer connections: The roles of emotional expressiveness within the family and children's understanding of emotions. *Child Development, 63,* 603–618.

Cervantes, C., & Callanan, M. (1998). Labels and explanations in mother–child emotion talk: Age and gender differentiation. *Developmental Psychology, 34,* 88–98.

Cole, P. M., Zahn-Waxler, C., & Smith, K. D. (1994). Expressive control during a disappointment: Variations related to preschooler's behavior problems. *Developmental Psychology, 30,* 835–846.

Conroy, M., Hess, R. D., Azuma, H., & Kashiwagi, K. (1980). Maternal strategies for regulating children's behavior: Japanese and American families. *Journal of Cross-Cultural Psychology, 11,* 153–172.

Cummings, E. M., Ballard, M., & El-Sheikh, M. (1991). Responses of children and adolescents to interadult anger as a function of gender, age, and mode of expression. *Merrill–Palmer Quarterly, 37,* 543–560.

Cummings, E. M., & Davies, P. T. (1994). *Children and marital conflict: The impact of family dispute and resolution.* New York: Guilford Press.

Denham, S., & Auerbach, S. (1995, April). *Mother–child dialogue about emotions and preschoolers' emotional competence.* Paper presented at the biennial meeting of the Society for Research in Child Development, Indianapolis, IN.

Dewey, J. (1925). *Experience and nature.* La Salle, IL: Open Court Press.

Dewey, J. (1934). *Art as experience.* New York: Berkeley.

Donnelly, M. E. (Ed.). (1993). *Reinterpreting the legacy of William James.* Washington, DC: American Psychological Association.

Doubleday, C., Kovaric, P., Dorr, A., Beizer-Seidner, L., & Lotta, J. (1986, August). *Children's knowledge of cultural norms for emotional expression and behavior.* Paper presented at the American Psychological Association, Washington, DC.

Dunn, J., Bretherton, I., & Munn, P. (1987). Conversations about feeling states between mothers and their young children. *Developmental Psychology, 23,* 132–139.

Dunn, J., & Brown, J. (1994). Affect expression in the family, children's understanding of emotions, and their interactions with others. *Merrill–Palmer Quarterly, 40,* 120–137.

Dunn, J., Brown, J., & Beardsall, L. (1991). Family talk about feeling states and children's later understanding of others' emotions. *Developmental Psychology, 27,* 448–455.

Fabes, R., Eisenberg, N., Smith, M., & Murphy, B. (1996). Getting angry at peers: Associations with liking of the provocateur. *Child Development, 67,* 942–956.

Feinman, S. (Ed.). (1992). *Social referencing and the social construction of reality in infancy.* New York: Plenum Press.

Fernandez-Dols, J., & Ruiz-Belda, M. (1995). Expression of emotion versus expressions of emotions. In J. A. Russell, J. Fernandez-Dols, A. Manstead, & J. Wellenkamp (Eds.), *Everyday conceptions of emotion: An introduction to the psychology, anthropology and linguistics of emotion* (pp. 505–522). Dordrecht, The Netherlands: Kluwer.

Fivush, R. (1991). The social construction of personal narratives. *Merrill–Palmer Quarterly, 37,* 59–82.

Fogel, A., Nwokah, E., Young Dedo, J., Messinger, D., Dickson, K. L., Matusov, E., & Holt, S. (1992). Social process theory of emotion: A dynamic systems approach. *Social Development, 1,* 122–150.

Goldsmith, H. H. (1993). Temperament: Variability in developing emotion systems. In M. Lewis & J. M. Haviland (Eds.), *Handbook of emotions* (pp. 353–364). New York: Guilford Press.

Gordon, S. L. (1989). The socialization of children's emotions: Emotional culture, competence, and exposure. In C. Saarni & P. Harris (Eds.), *Children's understanding of emotion* (pp. 319–349). Cambridge, England: Cambridge University Press.

Gottman, J., Katz, L. F., & Hooven, C. (1997). *Meta-emotion.* Hillsdale, NJ: Erlbaum.

Grolnick, W., Bridges, L., & Connell, J. (1996). Emotion regulation in two-year-olds: Strategies and emotional expression in four contexts. *Child Development, 67,* 928–941.

Halberstadt, A. G. (1991). Toward an ecology of expressiveness: Family socialization in particular and a model in general. In R. S. Feldman & B. Rime (Eds.), *Fundamentals of nonverbal behavior* (pp. 106–160). New York: Cambridge University Press.

Harris, G. (1978). *Casting out anger*. Cambridge, England: Cambridge University Press.

Harter, S. (1998). The development of self-representations. In W. Damon (Series Ed.) & N. Eisenberg (Vol. Ed.), *Handbook of child psychology: Vol. 3. Social, emotional, and personality development* (5th ed., pp. 553–617). New York: Wiley.

Harter, S., Waters, P. L., Whitesell, N., & Dastelic, D. (1998). Level of voice among female and male high school students: Relational context, support, and gender orientation. *Child Development, 34*, 892–901.

Hermans, H. J., & Kempen, H. J. (1998). Moving cultures: The perilous problems of cultural dichotomies in a globalizing society. *American Psychologist, 53*, 1111–1120.

Hubbard, J. (1995). *Emotion expression, emotion awareness, and goal orientation: The role of sociometric status, aggression, and gender*. Paper presented at the the biennial meeting of the Society for Research in Child Development, Indianapolis, IN.

James, W. (1975). Pragmatism. In W. James, *Pragmatism and the meaning of truth* (F. Bowers, Ed.). Cambridge, MA: Harvard University Press. (Original work published 1907)

Josephs, I. (1998). Constructing one's self in the city of the silent: Dialogue, symbols, and the role of "as-if" in self-development. *Human Development, 41*, 180–195.

Kitayama, S., & Markus, H. (Eds.). (1994). *Emotion and culture*. Washington, DC: American Psychological Association.

Konner, M. (1972). Aspects of the developmental ethology of a foraging people. In N. Blurton-Jones (Ed.), *Ethological studies of child behavior* (pp. 285–304). Cambridge, England: Cambridge University Press.

Kraut, R., & Johnson, R. (1979). Social and emotional messages of smiling: An ethological approach. *Journal of Personality and Social Psychology, 37*, 1539–1553.

Lerner, R. M., & Kauffman, M. (1985). The concept of development in contextualism. *Developmental Review, 5*, 309–333.

Lewis, C. (1986). Children's social development in Japan: Research directions. In H. Stevenson, H. Azuma, & K. Hakuta (Eds.), *Child development and education in Japan* (pp. 186–200). New York: Freeman.

Lewis, M. (1978). Situational analysis and the study of behavioral development. In L. Pervin & M. Lewis (Eds.), *Perspectives in interactional psychology* (pp. 49–66). New York: Plenum Press.

Lewis, M. (1989). Cultural differences in children's knowledge of emotional scripts. In C. Saarni & P. Harris (Eds.), *Children's understanding of emotion* (pp. 350–374). New York: Cambridge University Press.

Lewis, M. (1992). *Shame: The exposed self*. New York: Free Press.

Lewis, M. (1997). *Altering fate: Why the past does not predict the future*. New York: Guilford Press.

Lewis, M., & Feiring, C. (1981). Direct and indirect interactions in social relationships. In L. Lipsitt & C. Rovee-Collier (Eds.), *Advances in infancy research* (Vol. 1, pp. 129–161). Norwood, NJ: Ablex.

Lewis, M., & Freedle, R. (1973). Mother–infant dyad: The cradle of meaning. In P. Pliner, L. Krames, & T. Alloway (Eds.), *Communication and affect: Language and thought* (pp. 127–155). New York: Academic Press.

Lewis, M., & Michalson, L. (1983). *Children's emotions and moods: Developmental theory and measurement*. New York: Plenum Press.

Lewis, M., & Michalson, L. (1985). Faces as signs and symbols. In G. Zivin (Ed.), *The development of expressive behavior: Biology–environment interactions* (pp. 153–182). New York: Academic Press.

Lutz, C. (1983). Parental goals, ethnopsychology, and the development of emotional meaning. *Ethos, 11*, 246–262.

Mayer, J., & Salovey, P. (1997). What is emotional intelligence? In P. Salovey & D. Sluyter (Eds.), *Emotional development and emotional intelligence* (pp. 3–31). New York: Basic Books.

McNaughton, S. (1996). Ways of parenting and cultural identity. *Culture and Psychology, 2*, 173–202.

Mehrabian, A. (1981). *Silent messages: Implicit communication of emotions and attitudes*. Blemont, CA: Wadsworth.

Miller, P., & Sperry, L. L. (1987). The socialization of anger and aggression. *Merrill–Palmer Quarterly, 33*, 1–31.

Mumme, D. L., Fernald, A., & Herrera, C. (1996). Infants' responses to facial and vocal emotional signals in a social referencing paradigm. *Child Development, 67*, 3219–3237.

Nelson, K. (1996). *Language in cognitive development: Emergence of the mediated mind*. New York: Cambridge University Press.

Olthof, T., & Engelberts-Vaske, A. (1997). Kindergarten-aged children's reactions to an emotionally charged naturalistic event: Relations between cognitions, self-reported emotions, and emotional behaviour. *Journal of Child Psychology and Psychiatry, 38*, 449–456.

Oppenheim, D., Nir, A., Warren, S., & Emde, R. (1997). Emotion regulation in mother–child narrative co-construction: Associations with children's narratives and adaptation. *Developmental Psychology, 33*, 284–294.

Packer, M. J. (1989). The development of practical social understanding in elementary school-age children. In L. T. Winegar (Ed.), *Social interaction and the development of children's understanding* (pp. 67–94). Norwood, NJ: Ablex.

Parker, J., & Herrera, C. (1996). Interpersonal processes in friendship: A comparison of abused and nonabused children's experiences. *Developmental Psychology, 32*, 1025–1038.

Ratner, H., & Stettner, L. (1991). Thinking and feeling: Putting Humpty Dumpty together again. *Merrill–Palmer Quarterly, 37*, 1–26.

Rothbart, M., & Bates, J. E. (1998). Temperament. In W. Damon (Series Ed.) & N. Eisenberg (Vol. Ed.), *Handbook of child psychology: Vol. 3. social, emotional, and personality development* (5th ed., pp. 105–176). New York: Wiley.

Ruble, D., Boggiano, A., Feldman, N., & Loebl, J. (1980). A developmental analysis of the role of social comparison in self-evaluation. *Developmental Psychology, 16*, 105–115.

Saarni, C. (1984). An observational study of children's attempts to monitor their expressive behavior. *Child Development, 55,* 1504–1513.

Saarni, C. (1988). Children's understanding of the interpersonal consequences of dissemblance of nonverbal emotional-expressive behavior. *Journal of Nonverbal Behavior, 12*(4, Pt. 2), 275–294.

Saarni, C. (1989). Children's understanding of strategic control of emotional expression in social transactions. In C. Saarni & P. Harris (Eds.), *Children's understanding of emotion* (pp. 181–208). New York: Cambridge University Press.

Saarni, C. (1990). Emotional competence: How emotions and relationships become integrated. In R. A. Thompson (Ed.), *Nebraska Symposium on Motivation: Vol. 36. Socioemotional development* (pp. 115–182). Lincoln: University of Nebraska Press.

Saarni, C. (1992). Children's emotional-expressive behaviors as regulators of others' happy and sad states. *New Directions for Child Development, 55,* 91–106.

Saarni, C. (1997). Coping with aversive feelings. *Motivation and Emotion, 21,* 45–63.

Saarni, C. (1999). *The development of emotional competence.* New York: Guilford Press.

Saarni, C., Mumme, D., & Campos, J. (1998). Emotional development: Action, communication, and understanding. In W. Damon (Series Ed.) & N. Eisenberg (Vol. Ed.), *Handbook of child psychology: Vol. 3. Social, emotional, and personality development* (5th ed., pp. 237–309). New York: Wiley.

Saarni, C., & von Salisch, M. (1993). The socialization of emotional dissemblance. In M. Lewis & C. Saarni (Eds.), *Lying and deception in everyday life* (pp. 106–125). New York: Guilford Press.

Saarni, C., & Weber, H. (1999). Emotional displays and dissemblance in childhood: Implications for self-presentation. In R. Feldman & P. Philippot (Eds.), *The social context of nonverbal behavior* (pp. 71–105). Cambridge, England: Cambridge University Press.

Shigaki, I. S. (1983). Child care practices in Japan and the United States: How do they reflect cultural values in young children? *Young Children, 38,* 13–24.

Sroufe, A. (1996). *Emotional development.* Cambridge, England: Cambridge University Press.

Steinberg, S., & Laird, J. (1989). Parent attributions of emotion to their children and the cues children use in perceiving their own emotions. *Motivation and Emotion, 13,* 179–191.

Thompson, R. A. (1994). Emotion regulation: A theme in search of definition. In N. Fox (Ed.), The development of emotion regulation: Biological and behavioral considerations. *Monographs of the Society for Research in Child Development, 59*(2–3, Serial No. 240), 25–52.

Thompson, R. A. (1998). Early sociopersonality development. In W. Damon (Series Ed.) & N. Eisenberg (Vol. Ed.), *Handbook of child psychology: Vol. 3. Social, emotional, and personality development* (5th ed., pp. 25–104). New York: Wiley.

Tomasello, M., Kruger, A. C., & Ratner, H. H. (1993). Cultural learning. *Behavioral and Brain Sciences, 16,* 495–552.

Trevarthen, C. (1984). Emotions in infancy: Regulators of contact and relationships with persons. In K. Scher-er & P. Ekman (Eds.), *Approaches to emotion* (pp. 129–157). Hillsdale, NJ: Erlbaum.

Trevarthen, C. (1993). The function of emotions in early infant communication and development. In J. Nadel & L. Cumaioni (Eds.), *New perspectives in early communicative development* (pp. 48–81). London: Routledge.

Underwood, M. K. (1997). Peer social status and children's choices about the expression and control of positive and negative emotions. *Merrill–Palmer Quarterly, 43*(4), 610–634.

Underwood, M. K., & Hurley, J. (1999). Emotion regulation and peer relationships during the middle childhood years. In C. Tamis-LeMonda & L. Balter (Eds.), *Child psychology: A handbook of contemporary issues* (pp. 237–258). Philadelphia, PA: Psychology Press/Taylor & Francis.

Underwood, M. K., Hurley, J., Johanson, C., & Mosley, J. (1999). An experimental, observational investigation of children's responses to peer provocation: Developmental and gender differences in middle childhood. *Child Development, 70,* 1428–1446.

Vandenberg, B. (1998a). Hypnosis and human development: Interpersonal influence of intrapersonal processes. *Child Development, 69,* 262–267.

Vandenberg, B. (1998b). Infant communication and the development of hypnotic responsivity. *International Journal of Clinical and Experimental Hypnosis.*

von Salisch, M. (1991, April). *Emotional expressions in peer negotiations.* Paper presented at the biennial meeting of the Society for Research in Child Development, Seattle, WA.

von Salisch, M. (1996). Relationships between children: Symmetry and asymmetry among peers, friends, and siblings. In A. E. Auhagen & M. von Salisch (Eds.), *The diversity of human relationships* (pp. 59–77). New York: Cambridge University Press.

Wasserman, G., & Lewis, M. (1982). The effects of situations and situation transitions on maternal and infant behavior. *Journal of Genetic Psychology, 140,* 19–31.

Whitesell, N., & Harter, S. (1996). The interpersonal context of emotion: Anger with close friends and classmates. *Child Development, 67,* 1345–1359.

Wierzbicka, A. (1994). Emotion, language, and cultural scripts. In S. Kitayama & H. Markus (Eds.), *Emotion and culture* (pp. 133–196). Washington, DC: American Psychological Association.

Wu, D. Y. H. (1996). Chinese childhood socialization. In M. H. Bond (Ed.), *The handbook of Chinese psychology* (pp. 143–154). New York: Oxford University Press.

Zahn-Waxler, C., Cole, P. M., & Barrett, K. C. (1991). Guilt and empathy: Sex differences and implications for the development of depression. In J. Garber & K. Dodge (Eds.), *The development of emotion regulation and dysregulation* (pp. 243–272). New York: Cambridge University Press.

Zahn-Waxler, C., Kochanska, G., Krupnick, J., & McKnew, D. (1990). Patterns of guilt in children of depressed and well mothers. *Developmental Psychology, 26,* 51–59.

Zeman, J., & Shipman, K. (1998). Influence of social context on children's affect regulation: A functionalist perspective. *Journal of Nonverbal Behavior, 22,* 141–165.

PART IV

SOCIAL/PERSONALITY ISSUES

CHAPTER 21

Subjective Emotional Well-Being

Ed Diener
Richard E. Lucas

Emotional well-being, like physical health, can be judged on a variety of dimensions. Yet, in both realms, it is difficult to say which of these dimensions are essential for overall well-being. Can a woman say that she is in good physical shape because she is free of disease, or must she also have an abundance of energy and a great deal of strength? Does a man have *emotional* well-being if he is free from depression, or must he have a positive opinion of himself and his life? Myers and Diener (1995) found that psychologists overwhelmingly focus on the negative aspects of individuals' lives. The number of psychological articles published on negative states exceeds those published on positive states by a ratio of 17:1. In response to this unbalanced treatment of psychological well-being, researchers have begun to examine the positive side of the emotional well-being spectrum. The field of "subjective well-being" (SWB), which examines such topics as happiness, life satisfaction, and morale, has flourished (see Diener, Suh, Lucas, & Smith, 1999; Kahneman, Diener, & Schwarz, 1999; Strack, Argyle, & Schwarz, 1991).

As its name implies, SWB consists of people's *own* evaluations of their lives. Although measures such as crime statistics, health indices, and indicators of wealth are surely related to quality of life, these external indicators cannot capture what it means to be happy. An activist for society's downtrodden, for example, may thrive in a high-crime, low-income neighborhood. The sense of meaning and personal satisfaction this individual gains from helping others will not be reflected in traditional social indicators. People evaluate conditions differently, depending on their expectations, values, and previous experiences. SWB researchers assign importance to this subjective element and assess individuals' thoughts and feelings about their lives.

To capture this subjective element, SWB researchers examine individuals' evaluations of their lives. These evaluations can be either cognitive (e.g., life satisfaction or satisfaction with one's job) or affective (the presence of joy) (Andrews & Withey, 1976). Although these components are separable (see, e.g., Lucas, Diener, & Suh, 1996), they often interrelate, suggesting the existence of a higher-order construct of SWB (Kozma, 1996). Methodologies used to assess SWB include national surveys, daily experience sampling, longitudinal studies, and controlled experiments.

It should be noted from the outset that the majority of people report positive affect most of the time (Diener & Diener, 1996). In a national U.S. survey, Andrews (1991) found that people from all age groups, socioeconomic groups, and ethnic groups reported satisfaction scores well above neutral. Positive reports of SWB are also found among citizens of most nations (e.g., Diener & Diener, 1993; Veenhoven, 1993). Therefore, when we discuss the correlates and possible causes for SWB, we are mainly discussing factors that make some people *more* happy than others.

DEFINING AND MEASURING SUBJECTIVE EMOTIONAL WELL-BEING

Emotions and moods are ubiquitous phenomena—they give either a pleasant or an unpleasant quality to virtually all of one's waking moments. In an experience-sampling study of emotional experience, Diener, Sandvik, and Pavot (1991) found that people reported some affect virtually all of the time. Furthermore, emotional experiences are valenced; that is, we can easily tell whether they are positive or negative (Kahneman, 1999). Given the ubiquity of emotion and its valenced nature, it is not surprising that when people evaluate their "happiness," the pleasantness of their affect appears to play a central role. Larsen (1989) found that self-report SWB scales fall at the end of the pleasantness dimension of the emotion circumplex. Emotional pleasantness is a strong predictor of reports of happiness and life satisfaction, outpredicting such factors as physical pleasure and satisfaction with specific life domains. Thus results suggest that emotional pleasantness is highly related to global reports of emotional well-being. We begin by defining the experience of subjective emotional well-being as feeling a preponderance of pleasant rather than unpleasant affect in one's life over time.

The Structure of Emotional Well-Being

When the concept of SWB is critically analyzed, a number of questions regarding the scientific usefulness of the construct arise: (1) In light of the fact that people's emotions fluctuate constantly, is there a coherent construct of stable and cross-situational emotional well-being? (2) Should discrete, specific emotions be studied rather than global pleasant and unpleasant emotions? (3) Are intense pleasant emotions or prolonged and frequent pleasant emotions more important to the experience of emotional well-being?

Momentary versus Long-Term Mood

It is clear from time-sampling and observational studies that human emotions fluctuate over time. Diener and Larsen (1984) found that people's pleasant emotions at random times in various situations correlated an average of only .10. Green, Goldman, and Salovey (1993) found that people's emotions recorded on two mornings 2 weeks apart correlated only slightly. Given this instability in mood and emotion, does it make sense to study emotional well-being differences between individuals? Should we instead be studying the situations that cause momentary emotions?

Although emotions fluctuate, they move around a mean level that varies across individuals. That is, life events produce upward and downward shifts in a person's momentary or daily affect, but when moods are averaged over several weeks or months, these shifts average out to reveal the person's mean level of emotion. Individuals differ greatly from one another on their mean level on the pleasant–unpleasant dimension of mood. It is this mean level that exhibits a degree of stability over time and across situations, and forms the core of SWB (Diener & Larsen, 1984).

The stability of well-being is not attributable to artifacts of self-report measurement. For example, individuals' SWB as reported by family members correlated .44 with that reported by their friends. This correlation rose to .70 when corrected for the unreliability of the measures (Sandvik, Diener, & Seidlitz, 1993). Furthermore, Magnus (1991) found that a person's level of reported SWB correlated .60 over a 4-year interval; and Costa and McCrae (1988) found high levels of stability in SWB, even when the measurement came from different sources (spouse reports vs. self-reports). Eid and Diener (in press) measured SWB constructs on multiple occasions and found that the influence of current mood on SWB judgments was small. Diener and Larsen (1984) found that even across different types of situations, emotional experiences were stable: An individual's mean level of pleasant affect in work situations correlated .70 with mean level of pleasant affect in recreation situations, and an individual's mean level of pleasant affect in social situations correlated .70 with the mean level of pleasant affect in solitary situations. Thus there is stability in the average emotional life of individuals that transcends the momentary fluctuations in mood. Moreover, this coherent pattern is related to other variables in interesting and theoretical ways, thus making long-term SWB an important scientific construct.

We must caution, however, that single reports

of global well-being may not measure exactly the same construct as the aggregation of multiple-moment or daily reports of well-being. Kahneman (1999), for example, reviews evidence that some people weight certain emotional information more heavily than others do when making global judgments. In a study of patients undergoing colonoscopy, Redelmeier and Kahneman (1996) found that patients weighted the peak experience and the end experience most heavily. Therefore, when the colonoscopy was extended with an unnecessary and mildly painful procedure, patients rated the overall procedure as less painful than if the colonoscopy had been stopped earlier but after a more painful part. Even though the patients were in pain for a longer period of time, they rated the overall experience as less painful when it ended with a mildly painful experience. Thus researchers must be careful not to assume that global reports reflect an accurate aggregation of individual situations.

Discrete Emotions versus Global Pleasantness

In many studies of affect, discrete emotions such as joy, anger, or anxiety are the focus. Would it be preferable in the field of SWB to study long-term levels of specific emotions, rather than a broad categorization of emotions in terms of pleasantness and unpleasantness? Although studying long-term average levels of discrete emotions is certainly worthwhile, there are also reasons for studying well-being as the global or average level of pleasant and unpleasant emotions. First, situations that produce an unpleasant emotion (such as fear) also usually produce other unpleasant emotions (such as anger or sadness; e.g., Polivy, 1981). Second, there is a tendency for individuals who often experience specific unpleasant emotions to frequently experience other unpleasant emotions as well (Diener & Emmons, 1985; Watson & Clark, 1984). Third, many of the cognitive and action tendencies that occur with specific emotions are likely to occur with other emotions of the same hedonic valence. Thus there seems to be a degree of covariation among the specific pleasant emotions and among the discrete unpleasant emotions, which justifies study at a more global level. Although the study of specific emotions is valuable, researchers should not overlook the long-term coherence found within the hedonic categories of emotions (e.g., pleas-

ant and unpleasant). There is coherence over time and across specific emotions in these categories, indicating that it is also necessary to study the processes underlying global affective phenomena.

Frequent versus Intense Emotions

If positive emotions tend to influence one's overall emotional well-being, it is useful to ask what *types* of emotional experience lead to the greatest overall well-being. Do individuals consider the frequency of their positive emotional experiences when judging their happiness, or is the intensity of these experiences weighted most heavily? Diener, Sandvik, and Pavot (1991) reported that judgments of well-being are based primarily on the frequency of pleasant affect, and less so on the intensity of affect. They argued that intense positive emotions are less important to the experience of long-term emotional well-being because such intense emotions are so rare, and also because they are often counterbalanced by costs. Individuals who experience pleasant emotions intensely also have a tendency to experience unpleasant emotions intensely as well (Larsen & Diener, 1987; Schimmack & Diener, 1997). Thus individuals appear to weight frequency of positive emotional experiences most heavily in determining overall well-being. Although there is evidence that intensity of pleasant emotions plays less of a role because those who experience them often experience intense negative emotions as well, it is not clear whether this can explain the smaller effect of intensity in overall well-being judgments.

Independence of Pleasant and Unpleasant Moods

A fourth structural concern is whether or not pleasant affect and unpleasant affect are independent dimensions or opposite poles of a single dimension. In 1969, Bradburn reported that pleasant affect and unpleasant affect are not polar opposites and that each correlates with a distinct set of personality traits. Costa and McCrae (1980) replicated this finding, showing that pleasant affect correlates moderately with extraversion but not neuroticism, whereas negative affect correlates moderately with neuroticism but not extraversion. Watson and his colleagues (e.g., Watson, Clark, & Tellegen, 1988; Watson & Tellegen, 1985) argue that pleasant and unpleasant affect are distinct and orthogonal factors. This two-factor structure has often been replicated (Diener & Emmons, 1985; Warr, Barter, & Brownbridge, 1983; Zevon & Tellegen, 1982). Furthermore, some researchers have found different physiological correlates for pleasant and unpleasant affect (e.g., Davidson, 1993).

Theorists on the other side of this debate suggest that pleasant and unpleasant affect are really two poles along a single dimension. Green, Goldman, and Salovey (1993), for example, found that when measurement error was controlled by means of structural equation modeling, the correlation between pleasant and unpleasant affect was −.85. Similarly, Russell (1980) proposed a circumplex model of affect in which emotions can be described in terms of their pleasantness–unpleasantness, and in terms of their level of arousal. According to this model, if arousal is held constant, pleasant and unpleasant affect will exhibit strong negative correlations. The debate between these two camps continues, and no resolution of the opposing interpretations is acceptable to all. Researchers should be aware that the structure of emotions depends on the content and intensity of the emotions sampled (Diener & Iran-Nejad, 1986; Watson, 1988).

Summary

There appears to be some long-term stability in the amounts of pleasant and unpleasant emotions that people experience. People experience some level of affect, with its concomitant hedonic tone, virtually all of their waking moments, but they rarely experience intense emotions. It is perhaps for this reason that the amount of time people experience pleasant versus unpleasant affect is weighted heavily when people report their happiness.

Measuring Emotional Well-Being

SWB has often been measured by means of simple one-time self-reports. These self-reports may consist of single-item or multiple-item scales that ask respondents to reflect on how happy they are. The evidence to date indicates that self-reports of happiness are valid: Most instruments show impressive internal consistency, temporal stability, and convergence with non-self-report measures of well-being. Headey and Wearing (1989), for example, reported reliabili-

ties between .5 and .6 for a 6-year interval. These values tend to be lower for single-item measures and for measures of the affective components of SWB, whereas multiple-item scales and measures of the cognitive components (e.g., life satisfaction) tend to exhibit higher reliabilities (Larsen, Diener, & Emmons, 1985). Eid and Diener (in press) found that between 74% and 83% of the variance in life satisfaction judgments was due to stable life satisfaction rather than situation-specific factors such as current mood. In a study examining the convergent validity of well-being measures, Sandvik et al. (1993) found strong convergence between self-reports of SWB and interview ratings, peer reports, the average daily ratio of pleasant to unpleasant moods, and memory for pleasant minus unpleasant events. Measures of SWB also show structural invariance across time and across cultural groups (Andrews, 1991; Balatsky & Diener, 1993; MacKinnon & Keating, 1989; Lawrence & Liang, 1988). Andrews and Withey (1976) suggested that about 65% of the variance in self-reports of well-being is valid variance; Sandvik et al. (1993) estimated this number to be between 50% and 66%.

Measures of SWB are also responsive to changing life circumstances. In a 6-year longitudinal study, Headey and Wearing (1989) found that positive and negative life events led to concomitant increases and decreases in SWB. Suh, Diener, and Fujita (1996) replicated this finding and demonstrated that although SWB scales are sensitive to the influence of life events, the effects of these events are relatively short-lived. Similar results have been found in national surveys: Reports from nations in turmoil show low well-being (e.g., Europe after World War II, Eastern Europe in 1991), suggesting that the measures are sensitive to external conditions in theoretically meaningful ways (Veenhoven, 1994).

Diener, Sandvik, Pavot, and Gallagher (1991) found that self-reports of SWB are often not contaminated by social desirability. However, a number of other biases and artifacts can potentially influence reports of emotional well-being. Schwarz, Strack, and their colleagues found that the type of response scale used, the response options, and the order and presentation of questions can all influence the levels of SWB that individuals report (see Schwarz & Strack, 1991). Furthermore, momentary mood can influence reports of global emotional well-being (e.g., Schwarz & Clore, 1983); however, Pavot and

Diener (1993) and Eid and Diener (in press) found that the influence of current mood on global well-being reports is usually small. Another influence on reports of global well-being is a positivity tendency (Diener, Napa-Scollon, Oishi, Dzokoto, & Suh, 1999), although this response style is likely to be substantive rather than artifactual.

Diener (1994) recommends that multimethod batteries be used to assess SWB. A major limitation of self-report is that it relies exclusively on persons' cognitive labels of their emotions. But emotion is recognized to be a multichannel phenomenon that includes physiological, facial, nonverbal, cognitive, behavioral, and experiential components. In order to obtain a complete picture of a person's SWB, it is desirable to include peer reports, coding of nonverbal behavior, and so forth, in order to assess the full range of emotional responses. In addition, one cannot completely rule out the effects of self-presentation or other artifacts when one compares the self-reported SWB of various groups. Thus the use of additional methods of measurement is imperative. When the measures converge, one will obtain greater confidence in the results. When the measures diverge, one will gain more complex knowledge of the emotional well-being of the groups being compared.

CORRELATES OF EMOTIONAL WELL-BEING

In 1967, Wilson reviewed the limited empirical evidence regarding the "correlates of avowed happiness." He concluded that the happy person is a "young, healthy, well-educated, well-paid, extroverted, optimistic, worry-free, religious, married person with high self-esteem, job morale, modest aspirations, of either sex, and of a wide range of intelligence" (p. 294). In the more than 30 years since Wilson's review, thousands of studies have been conducted, and we now know much more about the correlates of SWB (see Diener et al., 1999, for a more detailed review).

A number of Wilson's conclusions have stood the test of time. Most significantly, Wilson was correct about (and probably underestimated the importance of) personality. Researchers consistently find that the personality traits of extraversion, neuroticism, optimism, and self-esteem correlate with measures of SWB (Diener & Lu-

cas, 1999). However, we must caution that the pattern of relations may vary across cultures. Diener and Diener (1995) found that the size of the correlation between self-esteem and life satisfaction was greater in individualistic nations than in collectivistic nations, perhaps because the former place greater emphasis on autonomy and internal feelings. We and our colleagues (Lucas, Diener, Grob, Suh, & Shao, 1998) found that extraversion was correlated less strongly with pleasant affect in collectivistic nations than in individualistic nations (though the correlation was strong in both). In another paper (Oishi, Diener, Suh, & Lucas, 1999), we have suggested that values and goals may mediate the relations among personality traits and well-being constructs. Although the exact cause for the relations between personality and SWB is unclear, the relation itself is robust.

Wilson was also correct that income plays a role in SWB, though this relation is more complex than Wilson could have known. Studies of personal wealth, national wealth (i.e., gross national product), and studies of the very wealthy find significant correlations between wealth and SWB (for a review, see Diener et al., 1999). The relation is often larger among those at the lowest levels of income, though greater income has a small effect even beyond the subsistence level (Diener, Diener, & Diener, 1995). Nevertheless, it is noteworthy that overall rapid increases in wealth in many nations have not been accompanied by increases in SWB (Diener & Oishi, in press), suggesting that rising standards of comparison may negate the effects of societal increases in wealth on SWB.

Marriage and religion also show consistent correlations with SWB. A number of studies in the United States (e.g., Glenn, 1975; Gove & Shin, 1989) and other countries (e.g., Mastekaasa, 1995; White, 1992) support Wilson's conclusion that married individuals tend to be happier than divorced or unmarried individuals, and longitudinal work suggests that marriage may have some causal effect on SWB. Recent studies on religion show that the religious are often happier than the nonreligious. More specifically, SWB correlates with religious certainty (Ellison, 1991), strength of one's relationship with the divine (Pollner, 1989), prayer experiences (Poloma & Pendleton, 1991), and participation in religious activities (Ellison, Gay, & Glass, 1989; Gartner, Larson, & Allen, 1991). Both marriage and religiosity tend to have an effect on SWB, even after other demographic factors (such as age, income, and education) are controlled (Diener et al., 1999). Nevertheless, longitudinal studies may not support the causal role of religiosity (Levin & Taylor, 1998)

Although Wilson's description of the happy individual was accurate in a number of respects, a few of Wilson's conclusions have been overturned by subsequent research. Most significantly, SWB researchers now question the popular notion that people become more unhappy as they age. In a study that examined national probability samples from 40 nations, Diener and Suh (1998) found that although pleasant affect tended to decline with age, there were no significant trends in life satisfaction and unpleasant affect. In a meta-analytic analysis of the variability in the relation between age and SWB across the 40 nations, Lucas and Gohm (in press) found that the size and direction of the relation were very consistent across the 40 nations studied. Diener and Suh (1998) suggested that decreases in positive affect may be due to the fact that most studies measure aroused types of pleasant emotions. If less aroused emotions such as "contentment" and "affection" are examined, age declines may not be found.

Recent research also suggests that Wilson overemphasized the relation between health and SWB. Although health is positively related to well-being, this relation holds primarily for self-reported health measures (e.g., George & Landerman, 1984; Larson, 1978; Okun, Stock, Haring, & Witter, 1984). When objective health (e.g., physicians' ratings) is examined, the correlation weakens considerably or even disappears (e.g., Okun & George, 1984; Watten, Vassend, Myhrer, & Syversen, 1997). Self-reports of health reflect one's level of emotional adjustment as well as one's objective physical condition (Hooker & Siegler, 1992; Watson & Pennebaker, 1989), and the relation between health and SWB is artificially inflated by this emotional component. This problem of "Pollyanna effects" in SWB appears in other domains (e.g., job morale) and provides further evidence regarding the need for non-self-report measures.

THEORIES ON THE CAUSES OF SUBJECTIVE EMOTIONAL WELL-BEING

Much of the research summarized above answers the question "What external conditions are necessary for happiness to ensue?" Do people need to have a lot of money to be happy, or can they have a modest income? Do they need to be married, or can they be single? These questions reflect an underlying theoretical assumption in which people have universal needs, and the degree to which these needs are met by external circumstances and personal resources determines happiness (Wilson, 1967). Unfortunately, the effects of these variables are often small, leading some researchers to complain of a lack of theoretical progress in the field (e.g., Ryff, 1989; Wilson, 1967). Thus researchers have shifted their emphasis from studies of external factors and demographics to studies of psychological variables that moderate the effects of external variables. People's needs and the resources they have to meet these must be examined in the context of individual lives, goals, values, and personalities. Although no complete theoretical formulation is available, we (Diener et al., 1999) have recently suggested the components that such a theory must include.

"Bottom-Up" Situational Influences

Situational and external influences clearly have an effect on SWB (see Argyle, 1999, for a review), but even resources that many would consider to be most important for happiness have only a small effect. Resources such as income (Diener, Sandvik, Seidlitz, & Diener, 1992; Veenhoven, 1991), health (Okun & George, 1984), physical attractiveness (Diener, Wolsic, & Fujita, 1995), and intelligence (Diener, 1984; Emmons & Diener, 1985) have little effect on happiness. Furthermore, only small percentages of variance in happiness can be explained by the demographics of the individuals studied. Argyle (1999) estimated the explained variance to be about 15%.

Clearly, a theory of SWB must include more than an inventory of resources and external factors that lead to happiness. Diener and Diener (1995), for example, found that the relation between income and life satisfaction is stronger in poorer countries than in more wealthy countries. These data suggest that resources do not have universal effects on well-being; they must all be considered in the context of the lives in which they are experienced.

Dispositional Influences

One important moderator of situational effects on happiness is personality. We (Diener & Lucas, 1999) have reviewed evidence from temperament studies, heritability studies, longitudinal studies, and cross-situational consistency studies that suggests the existence of stable emotional styles of responding to events and circumstances. Although people may often respond similarly to similar events, the intensity and duration of their response is likely to be influenced by their personalities.

As with theoretical formulations of bottom-up factors, theories of the relation between personality and SWB must go beyond simply categorizing relations and strive to understand the processes underlying them. A number of studies have addressed the question of underlying processes in the relation between extraversion and positive affect. Pavot, Diener, and Fujita (1990) and Diener, Sandvik, Pavot, and Fujita (1992), for example, found that extraverts are happier than introverts even when they are alone. Furthermore, these studies show that extraverts are happier whether they live alone or with others, or whether they work in social or nonsocial jobs. We (Lucas et al., 1998) found that the relation between extraversion and pleasant affect was strong in an international sample of college students from 40 nations, suggesting that the relation is not due to cultural factors unique to the United States. Larsen and his colleagues (Larsen & Ketelaar, 1991; Rusting & Larsen, 1997) found that extraverts were more susceptible than introverts to a pleasant mood induction, and that high-neuroticism subjects were more susceptible than stable participants to an unpleasant mood induction. The propensity for greater well-being on the part of stable extraverts suggests that a broad temperament influence may be at work.

A temperament-based explanation can take many forms, and the influence of temperament on SWB has been tested in a variety of theoretical frameworks. Gray (1987), for example, suggested that the biological substrate underlying extraverts' greater sensitivity to positive stimuli is a system he calls the "behavioral activation system" (BAS). This system is sensitive to signals of reward and nonpunishment (as opposed to the "behavioral inhibition system" [BIS], which is sensitive to signals of punishment). The BAS may be responsible for the production of positive affect, and thus individual differences in the strength of this system could lead to differential levels of happiness. When exposed to the same stimuli, individuals with a strong BAS will respond differently from those with a weak BAS.

An alternate explanation of the relation between personality and SWB is that the *resting level* of emotional experience, rather than our reactions to emotion-eliciting events, is determined by personality. This "dynamic equilibrium model" formulated by Headey and Wearing (1989) suggests that personality determines one's resting level. Events can move people away from this level (and move people in similar ways), but people will eventually return to their baseline, much as the body's temperature returns to 98.6 °F after a fever.

One final theoretical model posits an indirect effect of personality on SWB: Personality may influence the events one experiences, and these events may in turn influence happiness. In longitudinal studies, Headey and Wearing (1989) and Magnus, Diener, Fujita, and Pavot (1993) found that extraverts actually experienced more positive events than did introverts. Magnus et al. (1993) suggested that extraverts may be able to wrest more rewards from their environments, and hence experience greater amounts of well-being.

The explanations of the personality–SWB relations reviewed above are not mutually exclusive. People may have different resting levels of emotion, as well as characteristic styles of responding to emotionally charged stimuli. A theory of SWB must take these dispositional influences into consideration when evaluating the effects of external influences on well-being. Although the loss of a loved one may cause sadness and grief in most individuals, the intensity, duration, and means of coping with this tragedy may all be influenced by one's personality.

Goals

A number of theoretical approaches to SWB can be grouped together as "telic theories" (Diener, 1984). These approaches posit that happiness occurs when a person arrives at some end state. The end state may be set by innate biological drives, as in some need theories (e.g., Maslow, 1954); by psychological needs or motives (Murray, 1938); or by conscious goals (Emmons, 1986). These models are similar to the dispositional explanation of well-being, in that they recognize that different events and circumstances affect individuals differently depending on the context of their lives. Because needs and goals depend on learning, life cycle, and biological factors, SWB may result from quite different telic states for different people at different times in their lives.

At their simplest, goal theories suggest that progress toward goals and attainment of goals lead to increased positive affect (e.g., Brunstein, 1993; Emmons, 1986). However, more complex theories of the relations between goals and SWB have been proposed. Emmons (1986), for example, finds evidence that certain characteristics of goals (rather than progress toward goals) affect happiness. The value that one places on goals and the degree of effort that a goal requires tend to be associated with positive affect, whereas conflict between goals and ambivalence toward goals tends to be associated with negative affect.

Many goal theories have the ability to explain the small effects of resources and other bottom-up factors: Only those factors that relate to one's goals (which can vary across individuals) should influence well-being. Cantor and Sanderson (1999), for example, argue that the importance of certain goals changes across individuals, cultures, and developmental phases. Subjective emotional well-being results, according to their theory, when an individual chooses and is able to attain goals that are valued by the individual and culture, and are appropriate to the individual's developmental phase. We (Oishi et al., 1999) found that achievement in certain domains influenced overall well-being only when those domains were related to respondents' goals. Thus goals provide an important context for the events and circumstances that individuals experience. We must understand this individual context before we can understand the impact of events.

Culture

An additional contextual factor that is related to theories of goals and SWB is the culture in which the individuals being studied are immersed. Although goals can vary among individuals within a culture, certain goals may be more prevalent in certain cultures. These differences may result in differential levels of happiness in different cultures. However, the impact of culture on individuals' well-being extends beyond the goals that they hold. Culture also affects the weighting of different sources of pleasure and pain. Thus SWB may mean different things in different places.

Suh, Diener, Oishi, and Triandis (1998), for example, examined the weighting of emotions in judgments of overall satisfaction with one's life across nations that differed along the dimension of individualism–collectivism. Individualist cultures tend to view the self as an autonomous, self-sufficient entity. Consequently, feelings and emotions are weighted heavily as determinants of behavior. Collectivist cultures, on the other hand, stress harmony with family and friends rather than stressing one's autonomy from these people. Feelings about the self are weighted less heavily in these cultures. When Suh et al. (1998) looked at the influence of emotions on overall well-being, they found that emotions were a stronger determinant of global life satisfaction in individualist cultures than they were in collectivist cultures. Similarly, Diener and Diener (1995) found that feelings about the self (i.e., self-esteem) were more highly related to life satisfaction in individualist nations than in collectivist nations. Just as individuals may have different goals across cultures, they may have different ideas of what it means to be happy.

Social Comparison

It has been hypothesized that a person's level of subjective well-being is in part determined by comparisons he or she makes with standards (Michalos, 1985). Often people's standards come from observing people around them or remembering what they themselves were like in the past. It is hypothesized that if people exceed these standards, they will be happy and satisfied, but that if they fall short of their standards, they will experience low levels of SWB (e.g., Michalos, 1985). In recent years, social comparison research has begun to acknowledge that the process of making social comparisons is more subtle than originally believed (Diener & Fujita, 1997). People do not simply look around and judge their happiness by their distance above or below their friends and neighbors on relevant domains. Instead, people choose their targets for comparison, the information to which they attend, and the uses they make of this information in complex ways.

Wood (1996) states that social comparison is simply "the process of thinking about information about one or more other people in relation to the self" (p. 520). The targets for comparison can be proximate individuals, individuals one sees on television, or even individuals that people construct in their minds (Wood, Taylor, & Lichtman, 1985). People can pay attention to similarities, dissimilarities, or both when comparing themselves to the targets. And finally, people do not always contrast themselves to the targets (i.e., they do not always feel unhappy when they are worse off, and they do not always feel happy when they are better off). Some people may find comparisons with more successful individuals motivating, while others may simply be reminded of their own lack of success. Diener and Fujita (1997) suggest that social comparison may actually be used as a coping strategy and may be influenced by personality and SWB. Thus the choice of comparison target, the type of information to which the individual attends, and the uses the individual makes of this information may be results rather than causes of emotional well-being.

Adaptation, Adjustment, and Coping

Just as certain events may affect people differently, depending on their goals and personalities, reactions to an event may be markedly different, depending on the amount of time that has progressed since the event occurred. The processes that can account for these differences constitute an important part of theories of SWB.

Events that occurred recently have a greater impact on well-being than events that happened in the past (Headey & Wearing, 1989; Suh et al., 1996). Silver (1982) found that quadriplegics and paraplegics adapt at least partially to their injuries within weeks. Similarly, Mehnert, Krauss, Nadler, and Boyd (1990) found that individuals who acquired their disabilities later in life were less satisfied with life than those who acquired their disabilities at birth or early in life. Mehnert et al. interpreted this as evidence for adaptation: Those who had their disabilities longer had more time to adapt. Winter, Lawton, Casten, and Sando (in press) found that recently widowed individuals experienced more negative affect than individuals who had lost their spouses some time in the past, and that recently married individuals experienced more positive affect than long-married individuals (see Loewenstein & Frederick, 1999, for other examples of adaptation).

Yet there is still evidence that suggests a limit to people's ability to adapt completely. In the Mehnert et al. (1990) study, individuals with disabilities were still less happy than people without disabilities, even if they did adapt. Indeed, people with disabilities acquired at birth were less happy than the nondisabled. Loewen-

stein and Frederick (1999) review additional domains in which people cannot adapt (e.g., chronic noise). A number of questions remain regarding people's ability to adapt. For example, do people adapt to worsening conditions, or only to stable conditions or one-time events? Furthermore, it is unclear whether adaptation represents a decrease in emotional response, an adjustment in goals and strategies for coping with the event, an adjustment of what is required to call oneself happy (Kahneman, 1999), or all three. A theory of SWB must more clearly explain the processes responsible for adaptation: When does adaptation occur, what processes are responsible for adaptation, and what are the limits to individuals' abilities to adapt?

CONCLUSIONS

Although the field of SWB has developed somewhat independently of the field of emotion research, a number of interesting observations about affect and emotion can increase our understanding of emotional well-being.

1. When people evaluate their well-being, the ratio of their pleasant to unpleasant emotions over time plays a pivotal role. Emotions are central to SWB for several reasons. First, people seem to feel some affect during virtually all of their waking moments, and all affect seems to have a hedonic valence (either pleasant or unpleasant). Thus affect carries a large weight in evaluating well-being, because it contributes pleasantness or unpleasantness on a continual basis. Second, affect is related to a person's evaluation of life because emotion arises from the evaluations the person makes of events as these events transpire. Thus a person who interprets his or her life as composed of desirable events will experience more pleasant than unpleasant emotions over time.

2. The emotion system is reactive to immediate events and the current physiological state of the person. Thus a person's emotions fluctuate over time. Nevertheless, there are processes that influence the intermediate- and long-term average pleasantness or unpleasantness of a person's emotional life. For example, people seem to be predisposed by their genetic temperament to experience certain emotions. In addition, personality factors may contribute to the creation of life circumstances that foster pleasant or unpleasant emotional experiences (Magnus et al., 1993).

Thus there are longer-term factors that produce coherent patterns of affect, and these are legitimate subjects for scientific inquiry.

3. Intense affect, the stock in trade of most psychologists who study emotion, is rare in the natural daily lives of most adult humans. Most emotions are felt at mild levels (Diener & Iran-Nejad, 1986; Diener, Sandvik, & Pavot, 1991). Because people feel some level of mild emotion virtually all the time, the frequency and duration of pleasant and unpleasant emotions are weighted heavily when a person evaluates his or her emotions and life satisfaction. Although intense emotional experiences are undoubtedly important, their rarity often seems to diminish their long-term impact on well-being.

4. Factors such as income, physical attractiveness, and health have only a modest influence on long-term levels of emotion. Furthermore, people adapt or habituate to events. The findings suggest that the emotion system to some extent adjusts to current circumstances, but the limits of adaptation are not known.

5. Most people report being somewhat happy. Although some theories (e.g., Brickman & Campbell, 1971; Frijda, 1988) suggest that people should be affectively neutral or unhappy most of the time, existing SWB data strongly contradict this prediction (Diener & Diener, 1996). Most people report experiencing mild pleasant affect most of the time. Thus, despite a degree of adaptation to long-term circumstances, people are able to derive pleasant emotions from daily living.

6. Theories of well-being must acknowledge that events and circumstances must be understood in the context of the lives in which they are experienced. Personality, goals, culture, and other contextual factors change the meaning of events for different people.

Future theoretical advances must clarify the relations and influences among these factors. By including the positive end of the emotional well-being spectrum in research programs, we not only increase our understanding of the good life and happiness; we also broaden our knowledge of the processes underlying emotions more generally.

ACKNOWLEDGMENT

This chapter is based on work supported by a National Science Foundation Graduate Fellowship awarded to Richard E. Lucas.

REFERENCES

Andrews, F. M. (1991). Stability and change in levels and structure of subjective well-being: USA 1972 and 1988. *Social Indicators Research, 25,* 1–30.

Andrews, F. M., & Withey, S. B. (1976). *Social indicators of well-being: America's perception of life quality.* New York: Plenum Press.

Argyle, M. (1999). Causes and correlates of happiness. In D. Kahneman, E. Diener, & N. Schwarz (Eds.), *Well-being: The foundations of hedonic psychology* (pp. 353–373). New York: Russell Sage Foundation.

Balatsky, G., & Diener, E. (1991). Subjective well-being among Russian students. *Social Indicators Research, 28,* 21–39.

Bradburn, N. M. (1969). *The structure of psychological well-being.* Chicago: Aldine.

Brickman, P., & Campbell, D. T. (1971). Hedonic relativism and planning the good society. In M. H. Appley (Ed.), *Adaptation level theory: A symposium* (pp. 287–302). New York: Academic Press.

Brunstein, J. C. (1993). Personal goals and subjective well-being: A longitudinal study. *Journal of Personality and Social Psychology, 65,* 1061–1070.

Cantor, N., & Sanderson, C. A. (1999). Life task participation and well-being: The importance of taking part in daily life. In D. Kahneman, E. Diener, & N. Schwarz (Eds.), *Well-being: The foundations of hedonic psychology* (pp. 230–243). New York: Russell Sage Foundation.

Costa, P. T., & McCrae, R. R. (1980). Influence of extraversion and neuroticism on subjective well-being: Happy and unhappy people. *Journal of Personality and Social Psychology, 38,* 668–678.

Costa, P. T., & McCrae, R. R. (1988). Personality in adulthood: A six-year longitudinal study of self-reports and spouse ratings on the NEO Personality Inventory. *Journal of Personality and Social Psychology, 54,* 853–863.

Davidson, R. J. (1993). The neuropsychology of emotion and affective style. In M. Lewis & J. M. Haviland (Eds.), *Handbook of emotions* (pp. 143–154). New York: Guilford Press.

Diener, E. (1984). Subjective well-being. *Psychological Bulletin, 95,* 542–575.

Diener, E. (1994). Assessing subjective well-being: Progress and opportunities. *Social Indicators Research, 31,* 103–157.

Diener, E., & Diener, C. (1996). Most people are happy. *Psychological Science, 7,* 181–185.

Diener, E., & Diener, M. (1995). Cross-cultural correlates of life satisfaction and self-esteem. *Journal of Personality and Social Psychology, 68,* 653–663.

Diener, E., Diener, M., & Diener, C. (1995). Factors predicting the subjective well-being of nations. *Journal of Personality and Social Psychology, 69,* 851–864.

Diener, E., & Emmons, R. A. (1985). The independence of positive and negative affect. *Journal of Personality and Social Psychology, 47,* 1105–1117.

Diener, E., & Fujita, F. (1997). Social comparisons and subjective well-being. In B. Buunk & R. Gibbons (Eds.), *Health, coping, and social comparison* (pp. 329–357). Mahwah, NJ: Erlbaum.

Diener, E., & Iran-Nejad, A. (1986). The relationship in experience between various types of affect. *Journal of Personality and Social Psychology, 50,* 1031–1038.

Diener, E., & Larsen, R. J. (1984). Temporal stability and cross-situational consistency of affective, behavioral, and cognitive responses. *Journal of Personality and Social Psychology, 47,* 871–883.

Diener, E., & Lucas, R. E. (1999). Personality and subjective well-being. In D. Kahneman, E. Diener, & N. Schwarz (Eds.), *Well-being: The foundations of hedonic psychology* (pp. 213–229). New York: Russell Sage Foundation.

Diener, E., Napa-Scollon, C., Oishi, S., Dzokoto, V., & Suh, E. M. (1999). *Individual and national differences in the construction of life satisfaction judgments: Is happiness the sum of its parts?* Manuscript in preparation, University of Illinois.

Diener, E., & Oishi, S. (in press). Money and happiness: Income and subjective well-being across nations. In E. Diener & M. Suh (Eds.), *Culture and subjective well-being.* Cambridge, MA: MIT Press.

Diener, E., Sandvik, E., & Pavot, W. (1991). Happiness is the frequency, not the intensity, of positive versus negative affect. In F. Strack, M. Argyle, & N. Schwarz (Eds.). *Subjective well-being: An inderdisciplinary perspective* (pp. 119–139). Oxford: Pergamon Press.

Diener, E., Sandvik, E., Pavot, W., & Fujita, F. (1992). Extraversion and subjective well-being in a U.S. national probability sample. *Journal of Research in Personality, 26,* 205–215.

Diener, E., Sandvik, E., Pavot, W., & Gallagher, D. (1991). Response artifacts in the measurement of subjective well-being. *Social Indicators Research, 24,* 35–56.

Diener, E., Sandvik, E., Seidlitz, L., & Diener, M. (1992). The relationship between income and subjective well-being: Relative or absolute? *Social Indicators Research, 28,* 253–281.

Diener, E., & Suh, E. M. (1998). Subjective well-being and age: An international analysis. *Annual Review of Gerontology and Geriatrics, 17,* 304–324.

Diener, E., Suh, E. M., Lucas, R. E., & Smith, H. (1999). Subjective well-being: Three decades of progress— 1967–1997. *Psychological Bulletin, 125,* 276–302.

Diener, E., Wolsic, B., & Fujita, F. (1995). Physical attractiveness and subjective well-being. *Journal of Personality and Social Psychology, 68,* 653–663.

Eid, M., & Diener, E. (in press). Global judgments of subjective well-being: Situational variability and long-term stability. *Annual Review of Quality of Life Methods.*

Ellison, C. G. (1991). Religious involvement and subjective well-being. *Journal of Health and Social Behavior, 32,* 80–99.

Ellison, C. G., Gay, D. A., & Glass, T. A. (1989). Does religious commitment contribute to individual life satisfaction? *Social Forces, 68,* 100–123.

Emmons, R. A. (1986). Personal strivings: An approach to personality and subjective well-being. *Journal of Personality and Social Psychology, 51,* 1058–1068.

Emmons, R. A., & Diener, E. (1985). Factors predicting satisfaction judgments: A comparative examination. *Social Indicators Research, 16,* 157–167.

Frijda, N. H. (1988). The laws of emotion. *American Psychologist, 53,* 349–358.

Gartner, J., Larson, D. B., & Allen, G. D. (1991). Religious commitment and mental health: A review of the empirical literature. *Journal of Psychology and Religion, 19,* 6–25.

George, L. K., & Landerman, R. (1984). Health and subjective well-being: A replicated secondary analysis. *International Journal of Aging and Human Development, 19,* 133–156.

Glenn, N. D. (1975). The contribution of marriage to the psychological well-being of males and females. *Journal of Marriage and Family Relations, 37,* 594–600.

Gove, W. R., & Shin, H. (1989). The psychological well-being of divorced and widowed men and women. *Journal of Family Issues, 10,* 122–144.

Gray, J. A. (1987). *The psychology of fear and stress.* Cambridge, England: Cambridge University Press.

Green, D. F., Goldman, S., & Salovey, P. (1993). Measurement error masks bipolarity in affect ratings. *Journal of Personality and Social Psychology, 64,* 1029–1041.

Headey, B., & Wearing, A. (1989). Personality, life events, and subjective well-being: Toward a dynamic equilibrium model. *Journal of Personality and Social Psychology, 57,* 731–739.

Hooker, K., & Siegler, I. C. (1992). Separating apples from oranges in health ratings: Perceived health includes psychological well-being. *Behavior, Health, and Aging, 2,* 81–92.

Kahneman, D. (1999). Assessments of individual well-being: A bottom-up approach. In D. Kahneman, E. Diener, & N. Schwarz (Eds.), *Well-being: The foundations of hedonic psychology* (pp. 3–25). New York: Russell Sage Foundation.

Kahneman, D., Diener, E., & Schwarz, N. (Eds.). (1999). *Well-being: The foundations of hedonic psychology.* New York: Russell Sage Foundation.

Kozma, A. (1996). *Top-down and bottom-up approaches to an understanding of subjective well-being.* Paper presented at the World Conference on Quality of Life, University of Northern British Columbia, Prince George, British Columbia, Canada.

Larsen, R. J. (1989, August). Personality as an affect dispositional system. In L. A. Clark & D. Watson (Chairs), *Emotional bases of personality.* Symposium conducted at the meeting of the American Psychological Association, New Orleans.

Larsen, R. J., & Diener, E. (1985). A multitrait–multimethod examination of affect structure: Hedonic level and emotional intensity. *Personality and Individual Differences, 6,* 631–636.

Larsen, R. J., & Diener, E. (1987). Affect intensity as an individual difference characteristic: A review. *Journal of Research in Personality, 21,* 1–39.

Larsen, R. J., Diener, E., & Emmons, R. A. (1985). An evaluation of subjective well-being measures. *Social Indicators Research, 17,* 1–18.

Larsen, R. J., & Ketelaar, T. (1991). Personality and susceptibility to positive and negative emotional states. *Journal of Personality and Social Psychology, 61,* 132–140.

Larson, R. (1978). Thirty years of research on the subjective well-being of older Americans. *Journal of Gerontology, 33,* 109–125.

Lawrence, R. H., & Liang, J. (1988). Structural integration of the Affect Balance Scale and the Life Satisfaction Index A: Race, sex, and age differences. *Psychology and Aging, 3,* 375–384.

Levin, J. S., & Taylor, R. S. (1998). Panel analyses of religious involvement and well-being in African Americans: Contemporaneous vs. longitudinal effects. *Journal for the Scientific Study of Religion, 37,* 695–709.

Loewenstein, G., & Frederick, S. (1999). Hedonic adaptation: From the bright side to the dark side. In D. Kahneman, E. Diener, & N. Schwarz (Eds.), *Well-being: The foundations of hedonic psychology.* New York: Russell Sage Foundation.

Lucas, R. E., Diener, E., Grob, A., Suh, E. M., & Shao, L. (1998). *Cross-cultural evidence for the fundamental features of extraversion: The case against sociability.* Manuscript submitted for publication.

Lucas, R. E., Diener, E., & Suh, E. M. (1996). Discriminant validity of well-being measures. *Journal of Personality and Social Psychology, 71,* 616–628.

Lucas, R. E., & Gohm, C. (in press). Age and sex differences in subjective well-being across cultures. In E. Diener & M. Suh (Eds.), *Culture and subjective well-being.* Cambridge, MA: MIT Press.

MacKinnon, N. J., & Keating, L. J. (1989). The structure of emotions: Canada–United States comparisons. *Social Psychology Quarterly, 52,* 70–83.

Magnus, K. B. (1991). *A longitudinal analysis of personality, life events, and subjective well-being.* Unpublished honors thesis, University of Illinois.

Magnus, K. B., Diener, E., Fujita, F., & Pavot, W. (1993). Extraversion and neuroticism as predictors of objective life events: A longitudinal analysis. *Journal of Personality and Social Psychology, 65,* 316–330.

Maslow, A. H. (1954). *Motivation and personality.* New York: Harper.

Mastekaasa, A. (1995). Age variations in the suicide rates and self-reported subjective well-being of married and never-married persons. *Journal of Community and Applied Social Psychology, 5,* 21–39.

Mehnert, T., Krauss, H. H., Nadler, R., & Boyd, M. (1990). Correlates of life satisfaction in those with disabling conditions. *Rehabilitation Psychology, 35,* 3–17.

Michalos, A. C. (1985). Multiple discrepancies theory (MDT). *Social Indicators Research, 16,* 347–413.

Murray, H. A. (1938). *Explorations in personality.* New York: Oxford University Press.

Myers, D. G., & Diener, E. (1995). Who is happy? *Psychological Science, 6,* 10–19.

Oishi, S., Diener, E., Suh, E. M., & Lucas, R. E. (1999). Value as a moderator in subjective well-being. *Journal of Personality, 67,* 158–184.

Okun, M. A., & George, L. K. (1984). Physician- and self-ratings of health, neuroticism and subjective well-being among men and women. *Personality and Individual Differences, 5,* 533–539.

Okun, M. A., Stock, W. A., Haring, M. J., & Witter, R. A. (1984). Health and subjective well-being: A meta-analysis. *International Journal of Aging and Human Development, 19,* 111–132.

Pavot, W., & Diener, E. (1993). Review of the Satisfaction with Life Scale. *Psychological Assessment, 5,* 164–172.

Pavot, W., Diener, E., & Fujita, F. (1990). Extraversion and happiness. *Personality and Individual Differences, 11,* 1299–1306.

Polivy, J. (1981). On the induction of emotion in the laboratory: Discrete moods or multiple affect states? *Journal of Personality and Social Psychology, 41,* 803–817.

Pollner, M. (1989). Divine relations, social relations, and well-being. *Journal of Health and Social Behavior, 30,* 92–104.

Poloma, M. M., & Pendleton, B. F. (1991). The effects of prayer and prayer experiences on measures of general well-being. *Journal of Psychology and Theology, 29,* 71–83.

Redelmeier, D., & Kahneman, D. (1996). Patients' memories of painful medical treatments: Real-time and retrospective evaluations of two minimally invasive procedures. *Pain, 116,* 3–8.

Russell, J. A. (1980). A circumplex model of affect. *Journal of Personality and Social Psychology, 39,* 1161–1178.

Rusting, C. L., & Larsen, R. J. (1997). Extraversion, neuroticism and susceptibility to positive and negative affect: A test of two theoretical models. *Personality and Individual Differences, 22,* 607–612.

Ryff, C. D. (1989). Happiness is everything, or is it?: Explorations on the meaning of psychological well-being. *Journal of Personality and Social Psychology, 57,* 1069–1081.

Sandvik, E., Diener, E., & Seidlitz, L. (1993). Subjective well-being: The convergence and stability of self-report and non-self-report measures. *Journal of Personality, 61,* 317–342.

Schimmack, U., & Diener, E. (1997). Affect intensity: Separating intensity and frequency in repeatedly measured affect. *Journal of Personality and Social Psychology, 73,* 1313–1329.

Schwarz, N., & Clore, G. L. (1983). Mood, misattribution, and judgments of well-being: Informative and directive functions of affective states. *Journal of Personality and Social Psychology, 45,* 513–523.

Schwarz, N., & Strack, F. (1991). Evaluating one's life: A judgment model of subjective well-being. In F. Strack, M. Argyle, & N. Schwarz (Eds.), *Subjective well-being: An interdisciplinary perspective* (pp. 27–48). Oxford: Pergamon Press.

Silver, R. L. (1982). *Coping with an undesirable life event: A study of early reactions to physical disability.* Unpublished doctoral dissertation, Northwestern University, Evanston, IL.

Strack, F., Argyle, M., & Schwarz, N. (Eds.). (1991). *Subjective well-being: An interdisciplinary perspective.* Oxford: Pergamon Press.

Suh, E. M., Diener, E., & Fujita, F. (1996). Events and subjective well-being: Only recent events matter. *Journal of Personality and Social Psychology, 70,* 1091–1102.

Suh, E. M., Diener, E., Oishi, S., & Triandis, H. (1998). The shifting basis of life satisfaction judgments across cultures. *Journal of Personality and Social Psychology, 70,* 1091–1102.

Veenhoven, R. (1991). Is happiness relative? *Social Indicators Research, 24,* 1–34.

Veenhoven, R. (1993). *Happiness in nations.* Rotterdam, The Netherlands: Risbo.

Veenhoven, R. (1994). *Correlates of happiness: 7836 findings from 603 studies in 69 nations: 1911–1994.* Unpublished manuscript, Erasmus University, Rotterdam, The Netherlands.

Warr, P., Barter, J., & Brownbridge, G. (1983). On the independence of positive and negative affect. *Journal of Personality and Social Psychology, 44,* 644–651.

Watson, D. (1988). The vicissitudes of mood measurement: Effects of varying descriptors, time frames, and response formats on measures of positive and negative affect. *Journal of Personality and Social Psychology, 55,* 128–141.

Watson, D., & Clark, L. A. (1984). Negative affectivity: The disposition to experience aversive emotional states. *Psychological Bulletin, 96,* 465–590.

Watson, D., Clark, L. A., & Tellegen, A. (1988). Development and validation of brief measures of positive and negative affect: The PANAS scales. *Journal of Personality and Social Psychology, 54,* 1063–1070.

Watson, D., & Pennebaker, J. W. (1989). Health complaints, stress, and distress: Exploring the central role of negative affectivity. *Psychological Review, 96,* 234–254.

Watson, D., & Tellegen, A. (1985). Towards a consensual structure of mood. *Psychological Bulletin, 98,* 219–235.

Watten, R. G., Vassend, D., Myhrer, T., & Syversen, J. L. (1997). Personality factors and somatic symptoms. *European Journal of Personality, 11,* 57–68.

White, J. M. (1992). Marital status and well-being in Canada. *Journal of Family Issues, 13,* 390–409.

Wilson, W. (1967). Correlates of avowed happiness. *Psychological Bulletin, 67,* 294–306.

Winter, L., Lawton, M. P., Casten, R. J., & Sando, R. L. (in press). The relationship between external events and affect states in older people. *International Journal of Aging and Human Development.*

Wood, J. V. (1996). What is social comparison and how should we study it? *Personality and Social Psychology Bulletin, 22,* 520–537.

Wood, J. V., Taylor, S. E., & Lichtman, R. R. (1985). Social comparison in adjustment to breast cancer. *Journal of Personality and Social Psychology, 49,* 1169–1183.

Zevon, M. A., & Tellegen, A. (1982). The structure of mood change: An idiographic/nomothetic analysis. *Journal of Personality and Social Psychology, 43,* 111–112.

CHAPTER 22

Gender, Emotion, and Expression

Leslie R. Brody
Judith A. Hall

Increasingly, research on gender and emotion has gone beyond basic questions about the existence of gender differences. Recent research explores the complexities of when and how gender differences vary as a function of participants' ages, cognitive processes, personality characteristics, motives, and cultural backgrounds, as well as task characteristics, situational circumstances, and the nature of the interpersonal processes involved.

Culture and context become particularly important when emotions are viewed as adaptive or functional for fulfilling interpersonal and intrapersonal goals. Since males and females are often socialized to have different motives and goals—depending on their ages, cultural backgrounds, and socialization histories—it is not surprising both that gender differences are widely documented, and that they are sometimes inconsistent, varying as a function of these same factors. Interpersonal goals that may differ for males and females include fulfilling culturally prescribed gender roles (e.g., the role of child caretaker vs. economic provider); social motives, such as needs for intimacy versus control; and adapting to the power and status imbalances between the two sexes, in which men typically have higher power and status than do women (see Brody, 1997). Intrapersonal processes may also differ for males and females, including the ways in which anxiety and conflict are regulated and the types of self-schemas (e.g., independence vs. interdependence) that are maintained

(Cross & Madson, 1997). Both interpersonal and intrapersonal processes may be influenced by a complex interaction or feedback loop between gender differences in underlying biological processes (such as temperament) and social and cultural responses to those differences (especially on the part of caretakers), which are in turn influenced by cultural values surrounding gender and gender roles.

In our chapter we summarize the major trends in the burgeoning research on gender and emotion, focusing on normal adult populations, and highlighting some of the contextual variations in gender differences that have important implications for both emotion and gender theorists. Our review focuses on gender differences in emotional expression, including nonverbal communication behaviors related to emotion. Because of space limitations, we do not cover the extent and nature of gender differences in aggression, withdrawal, or crying. We also refer to stereotypes about gender and emotion, as well as to gender differences in emotional experience and emotional decoding when relevant. Finally, we present a theoretical model for understanding the origins of gender differences, which integrates the immediate precursors or proximal causes that are operative in particular social situations (Hall, Carter, & Horgan, in press) with a developmental model that looks at more distal causes and incorporates biological, social, and cultural factors (Brody, 1999).

STEREOTYPES AND DISPLAY RULES

The stereotype that females are the more emotional sex tends to be pervasive across 30 diverse cultures, with only 3 exceptions among the 30 (Fischer & Manstead, in press). Among American samples, women are believed to be more emotionally skilled and expressive than men, specifically regarding sending and receiving nonverbal cues, smiling, laughing, gazing, expressing emotions overall, and expressing sadness and fear, whereas males are stereotyped to be more logical and to express more anger than females (Briton & Hall, 1995). The belief that women are more expressive of emotion appears to be stronger than the belief that women experience more intense or more frequent emotions (Johnson & Shulman, 1988).

People's estimates of gender differences in nonverbal behaviors tend to correspond to the extent of gender differences, as indicated by meta-analytic studies of these characteristics (Briton & Hall, 1995). This should be relatively unsurprising, because our most automatically encoded and retrievable memories are based on frequently occurring behaviors, which may form the basis for many stereotypes (Hasher & Zacks, 1984). On the other hand, as pointed out by Brody (1997), gender and emotion stereotypes are imprecise, overly general, and ignore the importance of the modality and manner in which an emotion is expressed, as well as the situational and cultural context within which emotional expression occurs. Because stereotypes ignore both the social context and individual differences, they often lead to the erroneous assumption that gender differences in emotional expressiveness are exclusively biological in origin.

Despite these cautions, stereotypes about gender and emotion warrant a closer analysis, because they powerfully shape the reality of gender differences in at least two ways. First, in any given interaction, gender stereotypes may generate expectancies about our same- and opposite-sex partners that influence and elicit particular behaviors and emotional expressions from them, becoming self-fulfilling prophecies (Hall & Briton, 1993). Second, stereotypes have a strong implicit prescriptive aspect, taking the form of display rules, which are cultural norms regulating how, when, and where emotions can be expressed by males and females in any particular culture. Violating stereotypic display rules can lead to negative social consequences, such as social rejection, reduced attractiveness to the opposite sex, and even occupational discrimination (see Fiske & Stevens, 1993).

The powerful effects of stereotypes should influence us to look cautiously at studies on gender differences. Researchers who rely on observations to code the emotions expressed by males and females may be biased (even unconsciously) to see their research participants' emotional behaviors in ways that conform to gender stereotypes. Furthermore, when acting as research participants, males and females may distort their reports of emotional functioning in ways that conform to gender stereotypes.

SELF-REPORT MEASURES → *problematic*

Drawing conclusions about gender differences in emotional expression from self-report measures is especially problematic, since measurement issues often obscure whether a task is assessing emotional experience or expression. This is particularly evident in masculinity–femininity scales and other self-report measures that include "emotional" in their content. To be emotional implies that emotions are both felt and expressed. With this caution in mind, we review the studies on gender differences that have used self-report measures.

Findings on General Emotional Expression

A wide variety of self-report measures have indicated that women rate themselves as more expressive than men and more intensely expressive than men (Gross & John, 1998). Gender differences showing more intense emotionality in women than men have been especially consistent on global self-report measures, such as the Affect Intensity Measure (AIM; Diener, Sandvik, & Larsen, 1985). Participants who have completed the AIM have ranged in age from 16 to 68, and have come primarily from the United States, although recent data have shown the same pattern of gender differences in participants from Asian countries (Brody, 1997).

Gross and John (1998) recently factor-analyzed six frequently used self-report measures of emotional expression and identified five factors: positive expressivity, negative expressivity, the intensity of emotional expression, expressive confidence (such as enjoying acting), and masking or emotional regulation (such as suppressing anger). Gender differences were significant for three of the five factors: Women reported moderately greater positive and negative expressiveness than men, and much higher intensity than men.

Findings on Specific Emotions

The specific positive emotions reported more intensely or more frequently by women include joy, love, affection, warmth, and feelings of well-being (see Allen & Haccoun, 1976; Brody, 1993; Fischer & Manstead, in press). Gender differences in positive emotions emerge most clearly in situations involving intimate interpersonal relationships. Females also generally report more empathy and sympathy than do males (see Lennon & Eisenberg, 1987).

Many negative emotions—including distress; sadness; disgust; feelings of vulnerability, such as fear and hurt; and feelings of dysphoric self-consciousness, such as shame and embarrassment—are also reported more by women than by men (see Brody, 1999). Sadness, depression, and dysphoria are also reported to be more intense and of longer duration by women than by men (Allen & Haccoun, 1976; Scherer, Wallbott, & Summerfield, 1986). Although gender differences in guilt have been inconsistent (Brody, 1996; Ferguson & Crowley, 1997; Harder & Zalma, 1990), Ferguson and Crowley (1997) argue that shame is a predominant emotional experience for women that organizes their defensive functioning, whereas guilt is a predominant emotional experience for men.

Although men may express more anger through vocal, facial, and behavioral modalities than women, women and men show no difference on self-report questionnaires in which they check off how frequently or intensely they get angry. Usually these questionnaires do not specify the context in which the anger occurs (see Brody, 1997). However, when situational information is provided in self-report measures, or when participants are interviewed about angry feelings, women actually express more anger and more intense anger than men do. Women also report more enduring experiences of anger than men do. Moreover, they are more likely to report hurt or disappointment in re-

sponse to anger-inducing situations than are men (Brody, 1993; Frost & Averill, 1982).

Emotions that males sometimes report expressing or are reported by others to express more frequently or intensely than females are contempt (Stapley & Haviland, 1989), loneliness (Schmitt & Kurdek, 1985), pride and confidence (Collins & Frankenhaeuser, 1978), and guilt (Brody, 1993). However, gender differences in contempt, guilt, and loneliness have been inconsistent across studies, depending on situational circumstances and the characteristics of the particular samples assessed (see Brody, 1999).

Self-Report Data: What Are They Measuring?

Women's reports of higher affective intensity on global self-report measures such as the AIM may *not* accurately reflect sex differences in affective intensity at the time emotions are initially expressed or evoked. For example, Seidlitz and Diener (1998) found that men actually reported positive events in their lives to be *more* intense than did women when using daily rating forms, but not when subsequently recalling those same events. Self-reports of emotional intensity on the AIM were not significantly related to the intensity of emotional reactions reported at the time events occurred (see also Barrett, Robin, Pietromonaco, & Eyssell, 1998). Seidlitz and Diener (1998) speculate that women may encode experiences in more detail than men, which subsequently contributes to their reports of more intense emotions relative to men on global measures such as the AIM, even in the absence of gender differences in emotional intensity at the time feelings are actually expressed. Several alternative explanations are also possible, including the idea that in the time elapsed since an event, women may cumulatively experience more emotion than men—perhaps, for example, ruminating over the event, which retriggers emotional experiences. And, as pointed out earlier, the AIM and other global self-report measures blur the distinction between emotional experience and emotional expressiveness, which may also contribute to the discrepancy between scores obtained on these measures and scores obtained on more specific measures.

It is also possible that participants complete global self-report measures by attempting to portray themselves in a socially desirable light,

conforming to gender stereotypes. Some research supports this idea. The extent to which
students endorsed gender stereotypes related to
the extent to which they themselves reported experiencing different emotions from those of the
opposite sex (Grossman & Wood, 1993). These
data suggest that stereotypes may sometimes
distort or influence responses to global self-
report measures. On the other hand, experiences
may also influence stereotypes. A man who is
himself very unemotional may conclude that
women must be very different from him; in his
case, stereotypes would follow from emotional
experiences, and not the other way around.

However, the gender differences that appear
on global self-report measures, with females reporting a wide range of both more frequent and
more intense emotions than men, are unlikely
to be solely determined by stereotypes, self-
presentation biases, or even memory-encoding
differences between males and females. Gender
differences appear on many other measures of
emotional expressiveness, including observations of interactions, the verbalization of emotion, facial expressions, and nonverbal measures, as we document below.

VERBALIZING EMOTIONS

Consistent with self-report data, women have
been found to refer to both positive and negative emotions more often in conversations with
others and in their writing samples. For example, in writing a response story to a scenario in
which they had to deal with an obstructive travel agent, females talked more about feelings
and made more emotional references than did
males (Girdler, Turner, Sherwood, & Light,
1990; see also Brody, 1999).

In both self-descriptions and observations of
marital interactions, wives are more willing to
tell their husbands when they are feeling tense;
they are more apt to disclose their feelings; and
they are more apt to try to explain their feelings
than are husbands (Burke, Weir, & Harrison,
1976). Actual observations of marriages corroborate that women express more emotions in
words—especially more negative emotions, including more distress and anger—than men do.
Men have been found to withdraw from criticism and marital conflict by "stonewalling"
more than their wives do; this involves inhibiting facial action and minimizing listening and

eye contact (Levenson, Carstensen, & Gottman,
1994).

FACIAL EXPRESSIONS AND NONVERBAL BEHAVIORS

Women are more facially expressive of most
emotions, with the possible exception of anger,
than are men in both naturalistic and posed situations. This has been found to be true in studies using electromyographic measures of facial
muscle reactivity (Dimberg & Lundquist,
1990), as well as in studies using judges' ratings (Biehl et al., 1997). Quantitative reviews
have also concluded that women are more facially and gesturally expressive than men (Hall,
1984; Hall et al., in press; LaFrance & Hecht,
in press). It is important to note, however, that
these behaviors do not always reflect emotional
states. Facial expressions can serve discourse
functions as well as emotional ones (Chovil,
1991–1992), and hand gestures are often related to the process of speech encoding (Krauss,
Chen, & Chawla, 1996). Smiling is notably ambiguous as to its "real" emotional meaning,
with some authors suggesting the possibility
that smiling for women reflects false positivity
(Bugental, Love, & Gianetto, 1971). However,
more recent research suggests that women's facial expressions are less discrepant from their
words than are men's (Halberstadt, Hayes, &
Pike, 1988), and also indicates that women produce more "authentic" smiles than men do (as
measured by whether eye muscles have been
activated; Hecht, 1995; Merton, 1997).

Men may convey anger more clearly in their
facial expressions than women. For example,
when participants were videotaped as they discussed angry, sad, and happy emotional memories, a panel of judges was subsequently able to
identify participating men's facial displays of
anger (independently of verbal content) more
accurately than women's (Coats & Feldman,
1996). Other studies have indicated that men
show more facial reactivity in response to angry stimuli than women do (Dimberg &
Lundquist, 1990).

VOCAL EXPRESSIVENESS

Research on gender differences in vocal expressiveness is quite inconsistent, with some

suggestions in the literature that men may convey emotions more clearly through their voices than women do. For example, a recent study found men to be superior at expressing fear and anger through the voice (Bonebright, Thompson, & Leger, 1996). Other studies show gender differences in specific vocal characteristics, such as men conveying more "harshness" (a rough and rasping quality associated with anger and joy) than women, as well as more laxness (a sonorous and resonant voice quality associated with shame, interest, and neutral speech) (Bezooyen, 1984). Men have also been found to speak more loudly than women in at least two studies (Hall, 1984).

However, other studies indicate no gender differences in the patterns of vocal characteristics (such as loudness, pitch level, timbre, and rate) used to express emotion, or in the clarity with which males and females convey emotional expressions (Bezooyen, 1984; Hall, 1984; Hall et al., in press).

SITUATIONAL AND RELATIONSHIP SPECIFICITY

In What Situation Is Emotion Being Expressed?

It is critical to note that gender differences in each modality of emotional expression vary a great deal, depending on the particular situation and its meaning for each sex, as appraisal theories of emotion might predict. For example, when participants recorded their emotions in response to random beeps by pagers for a 1-week period, women reported more positive affect states (happy, cheerful, and friendly, as opposed to unhappy, irritable, and angry) while at work than they did while at home. The opposite was true of men: They reported more positive affect states while at home (Larson, Richards, & Perry-Jenkins, 1994).

Studies also indicate that the meaning of a situation for the two sexes affects patterns of emotional expressiveness. Jealousy may provide one of the clearest examples of this. Women respond with higher skin conductance to imagery in which their partners are emotionally involved with another lover than they do to images of sexual infidelity. In contrast, men manifest higher skin conductance, pulse rate, and greater brow contraction to images of sexual infidelity than they do to imagining their

partners' forming deep attachments to someone else (Buss, Larsen, Westen, & Semmelroth, 1992).

To Whom Is Emotion Being Expressed?

One of the critical aspects of context affecting emotional expressiveness is who the participants in the interaction are. The intimacy of their relationship, their power and status with respect to each other, and their respective genders may each affect the types of emotions they express. For example, both men and women express more emotions to people they know intimately than to those they don't. However, women from a wide variety of cultures express emotions to a greater number of people than men, who tend to limit themselves to expressing emotions only to intimate partners (Rimé, Mesquita, Philippot, & Boca, 1991). Both sexes are also more comfortable disclosing feelings (with the possible exception of anger) to women than to men (Timmers, Fischer, & Manstead, 1998). In a meta-analysis of sex differences in self-disclosure (which includes but is not limited to the disclosure of feelings), women self-disclosed more to female partners, but not more to male partners, than males did (Dindia & Allen, 1992). Anger may be the only feeling that is verbally disclosed or directed more toward men than toward women, especially in situations in which no provocation is involved (Bettencourt & Miller, 1996).

CULTURAL SPECIFICITY

Some research using global self-report measures such as the AIM indicates that females across diverse cultures express more intense positive and negative emotions than males (see Brody, 1997). Other research indicates that across cultures, females also express more nonverbal emotional reactions, including facial reactions, vocal reactions, body movements, laughing, and smiling, when expressing joy, sadness, fear, and anger (Scherer et al., 1986; see also Fischer & Manstead, in press). Moreover, in a six-nation study using U.S. and Japanese college students as posers of facial expressions, the emotions depicted by females were more accurately judged by every cultural group (Biehl et al., 1997).

Gender of judge × gender of poser × culture

[handwritten margin note: → difference w/ individualistic + collectivist countries]

interactions have also been found to exist for at least some emotions, however (Matsumoto, 1992), and a recent study indicates that the extent of gender differences varies across different cultures and for specific emotions. Using the International Survey on Emotion Antecedents and Reactions cross-cultural database initiated by Klaus Scherer at the University of Geneva, Fischer and Manstead (in press) compared individualistic and collectivistic cultures on the extent to which gender differences were evident. Gender differences in the intensity of joy, shame, disgust, and guilt, and in the nonverbal behaviors associated with those same emotions, were greater in individualistic than in collectivistic countries. Fischer and Manstead (in press) hypothesize that males in individualistic cultures are especially likely to minimize emotional expressions, because expressing emotions might threaten the control that is critical to their status as independent males.

PHYSIOLOGICAL AROUSAL

Recent research suggests that gender differences in physiological arousal, including changes in heart rate, blood pressure, skin conductance, and levels of catecholamines (epinephrine and norepinephrine), are specific to particular physiological measures as well as to particular tasks and circumstances (see Brody, 1999). For example, in the same situations, some measures of arousal (such as neuroendocrine functioning or blood pressure) show men to be more aroused than women, while others (such as heart rate) show women to be more aroused than men (see Polefrone & Manuck, 1987).

Arousal and Negative Affect

Widely cited research has indicated that, relative to that of their wives', husbands' physiological arousal is more likely to correspond to their negative affect during marital conflict discussions (Levenson et al., 1994). In particular, there are more consistent links between the expression or suppression of anger and physiological reactivity, especially blood pressure changes, for men than for women (Burns & Katkin, 1993). However, gender differences in emotionally stimulated arousal may occur because researchers often use the same anger-inducing task for women and men, such as being harassed. The two sexes may differ in how angry they get in response to such situations. When the two sexes are exposed to treatments that they designate in advance to be anger-inducing, there are no differences in the physiological arousal they exhibit. Both sexes show higher heart rates and greater amplitudes in skin conductance, as well as increases in diastolic blood pressure under these conditions (Frodi, 1976). And, contrary to previous marital conflict studies showing that men's physiological arousal is more connected to their negative affect than women's, recent research has indicated that wives' but not husbands' physiological arousal may vary as a function of the quality of their marital interaction (Kiecolt-Glaser et al., 1996). Marital quality and stress may affect women's physiological functioning to a greater extent than previously acknowledged, especially when the stresses are related to women's changing gender roles.

Internalizers, Externalizers, and Generalizers

Previous reviews of gender differences in the patterns of relationships among physiological arousal and other modes of emotional expression (Manstead, 1991) have suggested that men are more often "internalizers" (showing physiological arousal with no overt emotional expressions), whereas women are more often "externalizers" (showing overt emotional expressions with no corresponding physiological arousal). For example, work by Buck and his colleagues (Buck, Miller, & Caul, 1974; Buck, 1977) showed a negative relationship between facial expressiveness and skin conductance responses in adult males, and a similar pattern in preschool boys. Brody's (1999) review of the current literature suggests something different. Males may indeed be internalizers, but across a wide variety of studies, women appear to be "generalizers," expressing emotions in many modalities simultaneously. When the definition of "generalizers" is broadened to include a correspondence not only between physiological arousal and facial expressiveness, but among all modalities of emotional expression, females especially conform to a generalizing pattern. Brody (1999) cites evidence for this hypothesis from studies on empathy, distress, and sympathy; stress and anxiety; and anger.

DECODING OF EXPRESSIVE CUES

In three nonoverlapping reviews of gender differences in the accuracy of decoding nonverbal cues, Hall (1978, 1984; Hall et al, in press) concluded that females are superior to males at identifying affect from nonverbal cues of face, body, and voice, with the possible exception of anger. In at least 80% of all retrieved studies, females scored higher. Notably, the gender difference was relatively invariant across the gender of the stimulus person, tasks, different ages of the subjects being tests, and cultures. The one exception to women's superior decoding cues may be when expressions of anger are concerned; here, women have sometimes been found to read facial cues less accurately than men do, especially when the encoder is male (Rotter & Rotter, 1988; Wagner, MacDonald, & Manstead, 1986).

OVERVIEW IN RELATION TO GENDER ROLES

In brief, especially in American and other individualistic cultures, females are both stereotyped to be and in fact are more intensely expressive of most positive and many negative emotions (as indicated by self-report, writing samples, the content of verbalizations, observations of social interactions, and facial expressions) than are men. Women are also superior to men at recognizing and decoding affective expressions in others from nonverbal face, body, and voice cues. In some contexts, females have been found to be relatively weaker than males in facially, behaviorally, and vocally expressing anger, as well as in recognizing anger. Males have generally been found to report more pride, contempt, and loneliness than females; fewer intropunitive affects (e.g., shame, embarrassment, and anxiety); less fear and vulnerability; and less intense positive affects. Moreover, evidence suggests that women tend to generalize their emotional expressiveness across physiological, facial, and verbal modalities, while men tend to internalize their feelings—that is, to manifest heightened physiological arousal along with no overt facial or verbal emotional expressions. We have emphasized that it is difficult to distinguish between gender differences in emotional experience versus expression, and we have also emphasized that gender differences are often situationally and culturally specific.

Situational and cultural specificity may occur because gender differences in emotion are adaptive for the differing roles that males and females play in a particular culture or even in a particular situation. Expressing different emotions is adaptive for the two sexes' gender roles (including caretaking vs. provider roles); the power and status imbalances between men and women; the gender-role-related motives the two sexes may have for intimacy versus control; and differing self-schemas, including individualism versus interdependence (see Brody, 1999; Cross & Madson, 1997). For example, the emotions that women display more than men (e.g., warmth, happiness, shame, fear, and nervousness) may be related to motives for affiliation and intimacy; to a self-schema based on interdependence; to perceived vulnerability in the face of lower power; and to their traditional gender roles (including child caretaking and social bonding, which necessitate being able to read the emotion signals of others). Greater male pride, loneliness, and contempt are consistent with the male roles of differentiating from and competing with others; with maintaining a relatively high-status position; and with a self-schema based on individualism or independence. Even patterns of physiological arousal can be seen as adaptive for gender roles. Internalization, or not expressing emotions outwardly, may enable males to maintain control; women's style of generalization may be adaptive for a more interdependent style, in which boundaries between self and others are more open.

The complex questions of why men and women differ in their emotional experience and expression are difficult to resolve. For example, although women's low status and power may explain heightened expressions of vulnerability, recent evidence indicates that status differences do not relate to gender differences in smiling (Hecht, 1995; Hall & Friedman, 1999). In our view, there are multiple, interrelated factors that span cultural, biological, societal, interpersonal, and intrapersonal levels of analysis. In the following section, we present an integration of evidence and theories to explain these differences.

THE ETIOLOGY OF GENDER DIFFERENCES

We propose two etiological models (see Hall et al., in press; Brody, in press; Brody, 1999), which encompass the proximal and distal factors that influence the emergence of gender differences both over time and in specific situations.

A Developmental Perspective

The first model includes distal factors, such as gender differences in temperament, socialization history, gender-segregated play patterns, and cultural values, all of which contribute to the nature of gender differences. An integration of these factors has been proposed by Brody (1999) and involves a feedback loop in which differing temperamental characteristics of male and female infants elicit differential responses from caretakers and peers. Differing characteristics include higher activity and arousal levels in males, higher levels of sociability in females, and faster maturation rates for self-control processes and language development in females (see Brody, 1999, and Maccoby, 1998). Along with cultural values and differential display rules, temperament contributes to gender differences in early emotional socialization by parents and peers.

The socialization of emotional expression is especially influenced by characteristics of the family system, including the parents' own temperaments, their gender role attitudes and behaviors, the quality of their marital relationships, their cultural and socioeconomic backgrounds, and the particular gender constellation of the children in their families (Brody, 1999). For example, the extent to which fathers are involved in child care has been found to relate to the emotions expressed by their daughters and sons, with involved fathers having sons who express more vulnerability (including warmth and fear) and daughters who express less fear and sadness and more competition relative to their same-sex peers (Brody, 1997). And, consistent with object relations analyses of development (Chodorow, 1978), males and females themselves may be motivated to express emotions differently in order to develop distinct gender role identities—both identifying with and imitating same-sex caretakers and peers, and de-identifying with opposite-sex caretakers and peers.

Putting Distal and Proximal Causes Together: The Example of Smiling

Hall et al. (in press) have proposed a model that integrates some of the distal factors we have discussed (such as gender differences in social roles and cultural values, social knowledge, and developmental history) with more proximal causes of gender differences in emotional expressiveness, using smiling as an illustrative case, as displayed in Figure 22.1. This model highlights the importance of affective, experiential factors in men's and women's expressive behaviors in any given situation. Although conformity to gender role norms as one possible cause of smiling is acknowledged in the model (see LaFrance & Hecht, in press), the model includes other factors that are theorized to be significant contributors to women's smiling, and by implication to gender differences in smiling (Hall et al., in press).

The factors proposed to influence women's smiling are (1) positive affect; (2) gender-based motives, roles, and values; (3) characteristics of the situation; and (4) social knowledge and learning. Obviously many of these are the products of cultural learning. Though the figure does not show it, we assume there are influences among these factors. The key feature of the model is the inclusion of intra- and interindividual feedback processes that serve to intensify women's positive affect during social interaction.

First, there is physiological and cognitive feedback from smiling itself (Strack, Martin, & Stepper, 1988): Smiling enhances positive affect through both direct physiological mechanisms and through attributional processes. If we take women's greater smiling as a starting point, facial feedback would produce more positive affect in women than in men.

Second, there is positive feedback stemming from the motives that produce greater smiling in women. For example, if women smile partly to fulfill their internalized conception of "femininity," this would reinforce their feelings of femininity and produce positive affect. Other examples of motives that vary with gender are interpersonal trust, liking for others, and capacity for intimacy. Some of these motives intrinsically imply more positive affect (such as liking others). But, in addition, acting on these motives (showing that one is trusting, that one likes others, etc.) produces positive affect because one is acting in concordance with a gender-relevant value (Wood, Christensen, Hebl, & Rothgerber, 1997).

Other examples are based on knowledge differences more than motivation. If women are more socially skilled, as is suggested by many

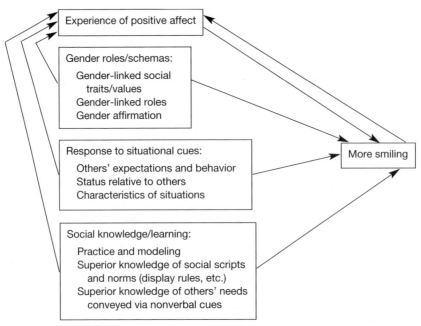

FIGURE 22.1. Affective, motivational, and cognitive factors in women's smiling. Reprinted from Hall, Carter, and Horgan (in press). Copyright Cambridge University Press. Reprinted by permission.

studies, then they may realize that smiling is socially useful in that it puts others at ease, facilitates further interaction, and so forth. So the skill may lead directly to more smiling, but there should also be positive feedback because it is reinforcing to feel socially competent and to know that one has promoted comfort and communication. Positive affect should be enhanced, which again should lead to more smiling.

A third kind of feedback is interpersonal: Other people respond favorably to women in general. Furthermore, to the extent that women fulfill others' gender role expectations by smiling, those others should reward women with favorable responses, which should enhance women's positive affect and their subsequent smiling. Furthermore, smiling itself is highly reciprocal: The more one is smiled at, the more one will smile (with attendant impact on positive affect). Finally, there is emotional contagion: Women are more likely to "catch" the emotions of others than men are (Doherty, 1997). This too should increase the intensity of women's positive affect, to the extent that people treat them more positively than they treat men.

For men, these same feedback processes are likely to be weaker because their social motives

are different, and these in turn should promote less positive responses from others, less facial feedback, and so forth. We suggest that the net effect is that women experience numerous positive feedback cycles involving their own behavior, their cognitions, their physiological processes, and others' behaviors that sum to create enhanced positive affect in immediate social interactions compared to men, which ultimately influences how much they smile relative to men. It is important to note that this model may not generalize beyond immediate social interactions, as indicated by the fact that women are more likely than men to suffer from depression.

CONCLUDING THOUGHTS

As in our chapter in the first edition of this volume (Brody & Hall, 1993), we have continued to find consistent gender differences in emotional expressiveness and decoding across several types of data. For example, gender stereotypes have frequently been borne out by data on actual patterns of behavior. We have argued that the differential expression of emotions for the two sexes is adaptive for the successful fulfillment of gender roles, and we have also emphasized that gender differences in any particular modality of emotional expression are culturally and situationally specific. We have alluded to a developmental etiological model that integrates temperament and socialization factors, and, using smiling as an example, we have shown that proximal affective experience is likely to be an important determinant of the gender difference in smiling. Motivational and cognitive factors are likely to contribute both to differential affective experiences and to smiling differences through feedback processes.

DIRECTIONS FOR FUTURE RESEARCH

Research on gender and emotion sheds new light on the nature of emotion as well as the nature of gender. What is beginning to be convincingly illuminated is that both emotional expression and gender have complex interacting biological, social, and cultural roots. For example, the capacity to experience and express pleasure and pain may be hard-wired, but the regulation and expression of emotions over the course of development are continually shaped in new directions by socialization history, which differs for the two sexes and for different cultural groups. Increasing evidence suggests that even the nature of the hard-wiring of emotions (e.g., as evidenced by electroencephalographic patterns) may be influenced by social factors (see Dawson, Frey, Panagiotides, Osterling, & Hessl, 1997). Similarly, biological gender differences may contribute to the differing environmental or social stimulation that the two sexes receive, but the nature of biological gender differences is in turn shaped by environmental inputs as development unfolds (see Katz & Shatz, 1996). Continued research that explores the interactions between biological and cultural factors in the emergence of gender differences in such processes as facial feedback, emotional contagion, and nonverbal behaviors would be invaluable.

REFERENCES

Allen, J., & Haccoun, D. (1976). Sex differences in emotionality: A multi-dimensional approach. *Human Relations, 29*, 711–720.

Barrett, L. F., Robin, L., Pietromonaco, P., & Eyssell, K. (1998). Are women the more emotional sex?: Evidence from emotional experiences in social context. *Cognition and Emotion, 12*, 555–578.

Bettencourt, B. A., & Miller, N. (1996). Gender differences in aggression as a function of provocation: A meta-analysis. *Psychological Bulletin, 119*, 422–447.

Bezooyen, R. (1984). *Characteristics of vocal expressions of emotion.* Dordrecht, The Netherlands: Foris.

Biehl, M., Matsumoto, D., Ekman, P., Hearn, V., Heider, K., Kudoh, T., & Ton, V. (1997). Matsumoto and Ekman's Japanese and Caucasian Facial Expressions of Emotion (JACFEE): Reliability data and cross-national differences. *Journal of Nonverbal Behavior, 21*, 3–21.

Bonebright, T. L., Thompson, J. L., & Leger, D. W. (1996). Gender stereotypes in the expression and perception of vocal affect. *Sex Roles, 34*, 429–445.

Briton, N., & Hall, J. (1995). Beliefs about female and male nonverbal communication. *Sex Roles, 32*, 79–90.

Brody, L. R. (1993). On understanding gender differences in the expression of emotion: Gender roles, socialization and language. In S. Ablon, D. Brown, E. Khantzian, & J. Mack (Eds.), *Human feelings: Explorations in affect development and meaning* (pp. 89–121). Hillsdale, NJ: Analytic Press.

Brody, L. R. (1996). Gender, emotional expressiveness and parent–child boundaries. In R. Kavanaugh, B. Zimmerberg-Glick, & S. Fein (Eds.), *Emotion: Interdisciplinary perspectives* (pp. 139–170). Hillsdale, NJ: Erlbaum.

Brody, L. R. (1997). Beyond stereotypes: Gender and emotion. *Journal of Social Issues, 53*, 369–393.

Brody, L. R. (1999). *Gender, emotion and the family.* Cambridge, MA: Harvard University Press.

Brody, L. R. (in press). The socialization of gender differences in emotional expression: Display rules, infant temperament, and differentiation. In A. Fischer (Ed.), *Gender and emotion.* Cambridge, England: Cambridge University Press.

Brody, L. R., & Hall, J. A. (1993). Gender and emotion. In M. Lewis & J. M. Haviland (Eds.), *Handbook of emotions* (pp. 447–460). New York: Guilford Press.

Buck, R. (1977). Nonverbal communication accuracy in preschool children: Relationships with personality and skin conductance. *Journal of Personality and Social Psychology, 33*, 225–236.

Buck, R., Miller, R., & Caul, W. (1974). Sex, personality, and physiological variables in the communication of affect via facial expression. *Journal of Personality and Social Psychology, 30*, 587–596.

Bugental, D., Love, L., & Gianetto, R. (1971). Perfidious feminine faces. *Journal of Personality and Social Psychology, 17*, 314–318.

Burke, R. J., Weir, T., & Harrison, D. (1976). Disclosure of problems and tensions experienced by marital partners. *Psychological Reports, 38*, 531–542.

Burns, J., & Katkin, E. (1993). Psychological, situational, and gender predictors of cardiovascular reactivity to stress: A multivariate approach. *Journal of Behavioral Medicine, 16*, 445–465.

Buss, D., Larsen, R., Westen, D., & Semmelroth, J. (1992). Sex differences in jealousy: Evolution, physiology and psychology. *Psychological Science, 3*, 251–255.

Chodorow, N. (1978). *The reproduction of mothering.* Berkeley: University of California Press.

Chovil, N. (1991–1992). Discourse-oriented facial displays in conversation. *Research on Language and Social Interaction, 25*, 163–194.

Coats, E., & Feldman, R. (1996). Gender differences in nonverbal correlates of social status. *Personality and Social Psychology Bulletin, 22*, 1014–1022.

Collins, A., & Frankenhaeuser, M. (1978). Stress responses in male and female engineering students. *Journal of Human Stress, 4*, 43–48.

Cross, S., & Madson, L. (1997). Models of the self: Self- construals and gender. *Psychological Bulletin, 122*, 5–37.

Dawson, G., Frey, K., Panagiotides, H., Osterling, J., & Hessl, D. (1997). Infants of depressed mothers exhibit atypical frontal brain activity: A replication and extension of previous findings. *Journal of Child Psychology and Psychiatry, 38*, 179–186.

Diener, E., Sandvik, E., & Larsen, R. (1985). Age and sex effects for emotional intensity. *Developmental Psychology, 21*, 542–546.

Dimberg, U., & Lundquist, L. (1990). Gender differences in facial reactions to facial expressions. *Biological Psychology, 30*, 151–159.

Dindia, K., & Allen, M. (1992). Sex differences in self-disclosure: A meta-analysis. *Psychological Bulletin, 112*, 106–124.

Doherty, R. W. (1997). The Emotional Contagion Scale: A measure of individual differences. *Journal of Nonverbal Behavior, 21*, 131–154.

Ferguson, T. J., & Crowley, S. (1997). Gender differences in the organization of guilt and shame. *Sex Roles, 37*, 19–44.

Fischer, A., & Manstead, A. (in press). Culture, gender and emotion. In A. Fischer (Ed.), *Gender and emotion*. Cambridge, England: Cambridge University Press.

Fiske, S., & Stevens, L. (1993). What's so special about sex?: Gender stereotyping and discrimination. In S. Oskamp & M. Costanzo (Eds.), *Gender issues in contemporary society Claremont Symposium on Applied Social Psychology: Vol. 6.* (pp. 173–196). Newbury Park, CA: Sage.

Frodi, A. (1976). Experiential and physiological processes mediating sex differences in behavioral aggression. *Goteberg Psychological Reports, 6*, 18–35.

Frost, W., & Averill, J. (1982). Differences between men and women in the everyday experience of anger. In J. Averill, *Anger and aggression: An essay on emotion* (pp. 281–316). New York: Springer-Verlag.

Girdler, S., Turner, J., Sherwood, A., & Light, K. (1990). Gender differences in blood pressure control during a variety of behavioral stressors. *Psychosomatic Medicine, 52*, 571–591.

Gross, J., & John, O. (1998). Mapping the domain of expressivity: Multimethod evidence for a hierarchical model. *Journal of Personality and Social Psychology, 74*, 170–191.

Grossman, M., & Wood, W. (1993). Sex differences in intensity of emotional experience: A social role interpretation. *Journal of Personality and Social Psychology, 65*, 1010–1022.

Halberstadt, A. G., Hayes, C. W., & Pike, K. M. (1988). Gender and gender role differences in smiling and communication consistency. *Sex Roles, 19*, 589–604.

Hall, J. A. (1978). Gender effects in decoding nonverbal cues. *Psychological Bulletin, 85*, 845–857.

Hall, J. A. (1984). *Nonverbal sex differences: Communication accuracy and expressive style.* Baltimore: Johns Hopkins University Press.

Hall, J. A., & Briton, N. (1993). Gender, nonverbal behavior, and expectations. In P. D. Blanck (Ed.), *Interpersonal expectations: Theory, research, and applications* (pp. 276–295). Cambridge, England: Cambridge University Press.

Hall, J. A., Carter, J., & Horgan, T. (in press). Gender and nonverbal behavior. In A. Fischer (Ed.), *Gender and emotion*. Cambridge, England: Cambridge University Press.

Hall, J. A., & Friedman, G. (1999). Status, gender, & nonverbal behavior: A study of structured interactions between employees of a company. *Personality and Social Psychology Bulletin, 25*, 1082–1091.

Harder, D., & Zalma, A. (1990). Two promising shame and guilt scales: A construct validity comparison. *Journal of Personality Assessment, 55*, 729–745.

Hasher, L., & Zacks, R. (1984) Automatic processing of fundamental information: The case of frequency of occurrence. *American Psychologist, 39*, 1372–1388.

Hecht, M. A. (1995). *The effect of power and gender on smiling.* Unpublished doctoral dissertation, Boston College.

Johnson, J., & Shulman, G. (1988). More alike than meets the eye: Perceived gender differences in subjective experience and its display. *Sex Roles, 19*, 67–79.

Katz, L. C., & Shatz, C. J. (1996). Synaptic activity and the construction of cortical circuits. *Science, 274*, 1133–1138.

Kiecolt-Glaser, J., Newton, T., Cacioppo, J. T., MacCallum, R. C., Glaser, R., & Malarkey, W. (1996). Marital conflict and endocrine function: Are men really more physiologically affected than women? *Journal of Consulting and Clinical Psychology, 64*, 324–332.

Krauss, R., Chen, Y., & Chawla, P. (1996). Nonverbal behavior and nonverbal communication: What do conversational hand gestures tell us? In M. P. Zanna (Ed.), *Advances in experimental social psychology* (Vol. 28, pp. 389–450). San Diego, CA: Academic Press.

LaFrance, M., & Hecht, M. A. (in press). A meta-analysis of sex differences in smiling. In A. Fischer (Ed.), *Gender and emotion*. Cambridge, England: Cambridge University Press.

Larson, R., Richards, M., & Perry-Jenkins, M. (1994). Divergent worlds: The daily emotional experience of mothers and fathers in the domestic and public spheres. *Journal of Personality and Social Psychology, 67*, 1034–1046.

Lennon, R., & Eisenberg, N. (1987). Gender and age differences in empathy and sympathy. In N. Eisenberg & J. Strayer (Eds.), *Empathy and its development* (pp. 195–217). Cambridge, England: Cambridge University Press.

Levenson, R., Carstensen, L., & Gottman, J. (1994). The influence of age and gender on affect, physiology, and their interrelations: A study of long-term marriages. *Journal of Personality and Social Psychology, 67*, 56–68.

Maccoby, E. (1998). *The two sexes*. Cambridge, MA: Harvard University Press.

Manstead, A. (1991). Expressiveness as an individual difference. In R. S. Feldman & B. S. Rime (Eds.), *Fundamentals of nonverbal behavior* (pp. 285–328). Cambridge, England: Cambridge University Press.

Matsumoto, D. (1992). American–Japanese cultural differences in the recognition of universal facial expressions. *Journal of Cross-Cultural Psychology, 23,* 72–84.

Merton, J. (1997). Facial-affective behavior, mutual gaze, and emotional experience in dyadic interactions. *Journal of Nonverbal Behavior, 21,* 179–201.

Polefrone, J., & Manuck, S. (1987). Gender differences in cardiovascular and neuroendocrine response to stressors. In R. Barnett, L. Biener, & G. Baruch (Eds.), *Gender and stress* (pp. 13–38). New York: Free Press.

Rimé, B., Mesquita, B., Philippot, P., & Boca, S. (1991). Beyond the emotional event: Six studies on the social sharing of emotion. *Cognition and Emotion, 5,* 435–465.

Rotter, N., & Rotter, G. (1988). Sex differences in the encoding and decoding of negative facial emotions. *Journal of Nonverbal Behavior, 12,* 139–148.

Scherer, K., Wallbott, H., & Summerfield, A. (1986). *Experiencing emotion: A cross-cultural study*. Cambridge, England: Cambridge University Press.

Schmitt, J., & Kurdek, L. (1985). Age and gender differences in and personality correlates of loneliness in different relationships. *Journal of Personality Assessment, 49,* 485–496.

Seidlitz, L., & Diener, E. (1998). Sex differences in the recall of affective experiences. *Journal of Personality and Social Psychology, 74,* 262–271.

Stapley, J., & Haviland, J. M. (1989). Beyond depression: Gender differences in normal adolescents' emotional experience. *Sex Roles, 20,* 295–309.

Strack, F., Martin, L., & Stepper, S. (1988). Inhibiting and facilitating conditions of the human smile: A nonobtrusive test of the facial feedback hypothesis. *Journal of Personality and Social Psychology, 54,* 768–777.

Timmers, M., Fischer, A., & Manstead, A. (1998). Gender differences in motives for regulating closeness. *Personality and Social Psychology Bulletin, 24,* 974–985.

Wagner, H., MacDonald, C., & Manstead, A. (1986). Communication of individual emotions by spontaneous facial expressions. *Journal of Personality and Social Psychology, 50,* 737—743.

Wood, W., Christensen, P., Hebl, M., & Rothgerber, H. (1997). Conformity to sex-typed norms, affect, and the self-concept. *Journal of Personality and Social Psychology, 73,* 523–535.

CHAPTER 23

The Effects of Mood on Social Judgment and Reasoning

Joseph P. Forgas
Patrick T. Vargas

MOOD AND JUDGMENTS

The original *Star Trek* TV series from the late 1960s featured an alien character who was perhaps most memorable for his ability to always think logically, unencumbered by mood or emotions. The pointy-eared Vulcan Mister Spock was consistently able to arrive at a logical conclusion to any problem. While the other members of the starship's crew were floundering about, wrestling with their situationally induced moods, Spock would calmly suggest a logical way to survive their predicaments. It is interesting that a character should be so well remembered for his ability to think logically at all times. He aroused interest because he was so unlike humans in his ability to obviate the influence of emotion and mood on his judgments (not to mention his pointy ears). Unlike Spock, however, real people are very much influenced by mood.

Mood obviously has an impact on social judgments and reasoning. Social judgments are highly constructive (Asch, 1946; Heider, 1958), and the same information may take on very different coloring, depending on the mood we are in. When we are in a bad mood, the cheery office coworker seems more like a pest than a loyal friend; the market researcher who calls during suppertime receives a particularly nasty goodbye. When we are in a good mood, even the sour office coworker can seem like a fine lunchtime companion; the charity worker on the phone may be more likely to get an encouraging donation. However, these examples oversimplify the effects of mood on social judgments and behaviors. In fact, the impact of mood on social judgments and behaviors is neither simple nor straightforward, and it has a variety of manifestations. Mood congruence and incongruence effects have both been demonstrated reliably, and at times mood seems to have no effect at all on social judgments and reasoning. The goal of this chapter is to present a comprehensive model of how mood influences social cognition, judgments, and reasoning, and to outline some of our recent empirical work inspired by the model.

The Affect Infusion Model (AIM; Forgas, 1995a) is a multiprocess framework that is designed to explain various ways in which mood can have an impact on social judgments and reasoning. We argue that different processing strategies adopted by people in response to different circumstances are the key to understanding the reasons why we sometimes observe congruence, incongruence, and no mood effects on judgments. The AIM also suggests that mood can have both informational and processing effects on cognition. Informational effects occur because mood influences the content of cognition (*what* people think). Processing effects occur because mood influences the process of cognition (*how* people think). The AIM specifies how situational and contextual variables can determine how people approach a judgmental or reasoning task, and the kind of processing strategies they adopt. Unlike many other models of social cognition, the AIM recognizes that people can select between a number of alternative processing strategies when dealing with a particular task (cf. Brewer, 1988; Petty & Cacioppo, 1986). According to the AIM, situational and contextual influences ultimately determine what kind of processing strategy is used, and thus the kind of effect that moods have on our judgments, decisions, and actions.

The main objective of the AIM is to offer a systematic framework within which the role of different processing strategies in mediating mood effects on social judgments and reasoning can be understood. By specifying the circumstances under which mood should or should not influence judgments, the AIM offers answers to a number of important questions posed in the recent literature: Why does context seem to play such a critical role in mood effects on cognition? What sorts of processing strategies are most likely to be influenced by mood? Are there particular types of targets that are more or less susceptible to mood effects on judgments? What kinds of processing strategies are most and least likely to produce mood congruence?

THE AFFECT INFUSION MODEL

"Affect infusion" is defined here as the process whereby affectively loaded information exerts an influence on and becomes incorporated into cognitive and judgmental processes, entering into a person's deliberations and eventually coloring the outcome (cf. Forgas, 1995a). The AIM predicts that affect infusion is most likely under conditions that promote elaborative, open, constructive information processing (Fiedler, 1991; Forgas, 1991a, 1991c, 1995a). In contrast, there should be less affect infusion under conditions that promote the direct or motivated retrieval of existing information without additional elaboration or processing. The AIM assumes (1) that the extent and effects of affect infusion are dependent on the kind of processing strategy used, and (2) that people seek to adopt the simplest and least effortful processing strategy that satisfies contextual requirements.

The AIM identifies four distinct processing strategies: "direct-access," "motivated," "heuristic," and "substantive" processing. According to the theory, direct-access and motivated processing involve relatively closed, predetermined, and directed information search and selection strategies that allow little scope for open, constructive elaboration. Thus there is little opportunity for affect infusion during direct-access or motivated processing. In contrast, heuristic and substantive processing are more open-ended and constructive processing styles that require more open, elaborate, and generative information search and selection strategies, and thus allow for greater affect infusion. We shall briefly review each of these four processing strategies before considering more recent research stimulated by the AIM framework (see Figure 23.1).

The direct-access processing strategy is the simplest way of producing a judgment or decision, based on the direct retrieval of a preexisting response. Most of us do have a rich source of such crystallized, preformed judgments on which we can draw, and the assumption of effort minimization suggests that this strategy should be used whenever possible. Such stored judgments and decisions are most likely to be used when the target is well known or familiar, and when there are no strong cognitive, affective, situational, or motivational cues calling for more elaborate processing. Direct-access processing precludes affect infusion, as there is little cognitive elaboration involved, and thus no opportunity for affectively primed information to be incorporated in a judgment. In fact, several studies reported an absence of affect infusion under conditions favoring the direct-access retrieval of stored judgments (Srull, 1984; Salovey & Birnbaum, 1989, Exp. 3).

The motivated processing strategy tends to be used when there are strong and specific motivational pressures for a particular outcome to be achieved. Because motivated processing involves highly selective, guided, and targeted information search strategies directed by a specific motivational objective, affect infusion is again unlikely. Indeed, motivated processing guided by objectives such as mood maintenance or mood improvement is the key mechanism for producing affect-incongruent cognitive and judgmental outcomes (Berkowitz & Troccoli, 1990; Clark & Isen, 1982; Clore, Schwarz, & Conway, 1994; Forgas, 1991b; For-

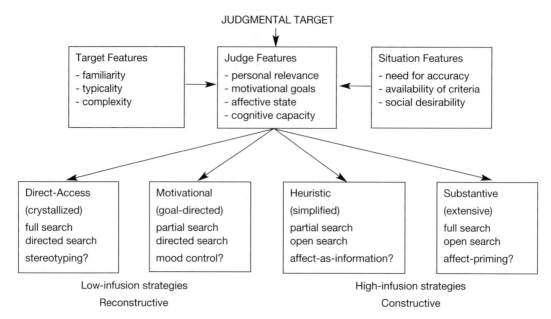

FIGURE 23.1. A schematic outline of the multiprocess Affect Infusion Model (AIM). Affect congruence in social judgments and decisions depends on which of four different information-processing strategies is adopted by a judge. Processing choices are determined by a range of judge, target, and situational characteristics.

gas & Fiedler, 1996; Isen, 1987; Sedikides, 1994). Numerous specific goals may trigger motivated processing, such as mood repair, mood maintenance, self-evaluation maintenance, ego enhancement, achievement motivation, affiliation, and ingroup favoritism (Forgas, 1991b; Forgas & Fiedler, 1996; Forgas, Bower, & Moylan, 1990). Normative pressures arising within a group interaction may also lead to motivated processing and the elimination of affect infusion (Forgas, 1990). Despite the motivated character of many judgments, the precise information search and selection strategies implied by motivated processing have rarely been documented (Forgas, 1989, 1991b).

The heuristic processing strategy is evoked when neither stored responses nor a motivational goal can guide judgments, and people seek to compute a constructive response with minimal effort. In such cases people tend to rely on limited information, to employ cognitive shortcuts or heuristics, and generally to avoid elaborative or substantive information processing. This kind of processing occurs in many areas of social cognition (Brewer, 1988; Petty & Cacioppo, 1986). In terms of the AIM, heuristic processing is likely when the target is simple or highly typical, personal relevance is low, there are no motivational objectives, there is limited cognitive capacity,

and/or the situation does not demand accuracy. Heuristic judgments may be based on superficial or irrelevant associations (Griffitt, 1970) or on erroneous inferences made from a prevailing affective state (Clore et al., 1994; Schwarz & Clore, 1988). The possibility that incidental affect may directly inform judgments was first suggested in conditioning theories (Berkowitz, 1993; Clore & Byrne, 1974), and was reformulated in the more recent affect-as-information model (Clore et al., 1994; Schwarz & Clore, 1988). Judges seeking to compute a quick and relatively effortless response may misattribute their mood state as informative about their evaluative reactions to a target. Thus heuristic processing can produce some affect infusion effects, but it does not adequately account for affective influences on judgments and reasoning under conditions involving more elaborate and generative processing.

The substantive processing strategy requires that actors select, learn, and interpret novel information and relate this information to their preexisting knowledge structures. Substantive processing is more likely when the target is complex or atypical, the judge has no specific motivation to pursue, the judge has adequate cognitive capacity, and/or there are explicit or implicit situational demands for extensive processing. In terms of the AIM, substantive processing is adopted only when simpler processing strategies prove inadequate. Affect infusion in the course of substantive processing is most parsimoniously explained in terms of affect priming. Since social cognition and judgments require constructive processing, temporary mood may selectively prime the ideas, memories, and interpretations used by a judge, influencing the way complex and often ambiguous social stimuli are perceived, learned, interpreted, and responded to. The affect-priming principle suggests that affect can indirectly inform social judgments through facilitating access to related cognitive categories (Bower, 1981, 1991). Just as the activation of a construct like "bread" facilitates the activation of concepts like "jam," "butter," "crust," and so on, the activation of mood states may facilitate the activation of other mood-linked memory structures (Bower, 1991; Forgas, 1992a, 1992c, 1995a).

The AIM also makes the counterintuitive prediction that affect infusion should be enhanced when more extensive and constructive processing is required to deal with a judgment or decision. This nonobvious prediction has received strong empirical support in recent years (Fiedler, 1991; Forgas, 1992b, 1992d, 1993, 1994a, 1994b, 1998a, 1998b, 1998c, 1999a, 1999b; Sedikides, 1995). In circumstances requiring substantive processing, affect can influence a wide variety of social judgments, including behavior interpretation (Forgas, Bower, & Krantz, 1984), person perception (Baron, 1987; Forgas & Bower, 1987), perceptions of health and illness (Salovey & Birnbaum, 1989), judgments of the self (Sedikides, 1995), and reactions to persuasion (Petty, Gleicher, & Baker, 1991). Other studies report mood effects on stereotype judgments (Forgas, 1990; Haddock, Zanna, & Esses, 1994), intergroup decisions (Forgas & Fiedler, 1996), and causal attributions (Forgas et al., 1990), as well as other judgments (Mayer, Gaschke, Braverman, & Evans, 1992) in circumstances likely to require substantive processing.

More specific evidence linking substantive processing to affect infusion comes from data on processing latency and memory (Forgas & Bower, 1987). Consistent with the affect-priming principle, people seem to process mood-congruent information selectively, and are faster in producing mood-congruent judgments (Forgas & Bower, 1987; Figure 23.2). In fact,

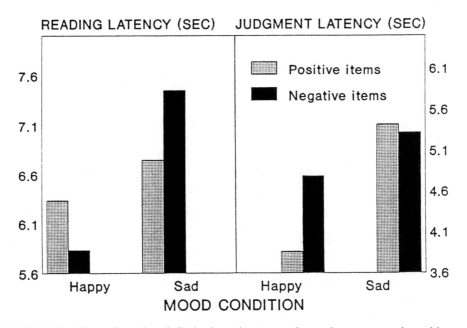

FIGURE 23.2. The effects of mood on (left) the time taken to encode mood-congruent and mood-incongruent information about a person, and (right) to produce subsequent mood-congruent or incongruent judgments. Consistent with the operation of affect-priming mechanisms, people take longer to encode mood-congruent information into a richer associative base, but are faster in producing mood-congruent judgments. From Forgas and Bower (1987). Copyright 1987 by the American Psychological Association. Reprinted by permission.

atypical, unusual, or complex targets that recruit longer and more substantive processing also produce greater affect infusion effects. Such a link between extended processing and greater affect infusion has been demonstrated in several recent studies using more or less complex and atypical people (Forgas, 1992b, 1992d), relationships (Forgas, 1993; Forgas & Moylan, 1991; Forgas, Levinger, & Moylan, 1994), and conflict episodes (Forgas, 1994a) as stimuli. These results confirm that, consistent with the AIM, processing differences indeed mediate differential levels of affect infusion. However, under what conditions are these various processing strategies employed?

VARIABLES DETERMINING PROCESSING CHOICES

The variables determining processing choices are an integral part of the AIM (see Figure 23.1). Features of the *target*, the *judge*, and the *situation* are the main variables of interest. Important target features include familiarity, complexity, and typicality. Important judge features include personal relevance, motivational goals, cognitive capacity, and affective state. Important situational features include perceived need for accuracy, social desirability expectations, and the availability of objective criteria.

In general, the more familiar a judgmental target is, the more likely it is that perceivers will use a low-affect-infusion processing strategy. Familiarity here means more than just prior exposure to a stimulus. It implies that the judge possesses a ready response to the target. Consistent with the AIM, mood has little effect on evaluations of familiar products that can be evaluated via direct-access processing; however, mood does have an impact on evaluations of unfamiliar products (Srull, 1984). Of course, judgments about even highly familiar targets, such as intimate partners, may show affect infusion when other factors (e.g., personal relevance; Forgas et al., 1994) promote more substantive processing.

Targets that are more complex, atypical, or unusual should also recruit more extensive processing, and greater affect infusion. Consistent with this prediction, several studies have found greater affect infusion when people need to take longer to process complex, atypical, or otherwise cognitively demanding targets (Forgas, 1992b, 1992d, 1994a, 1998a, 1998b). Targets of greater personal relevance tend to encourage either motivated processing or more substantive processing. There is evidence that even simple manipulations of personal relevance can have profound effects on processing strategies and subsequent affect infusion (Forgas & Fiedler, 1996; Forgas, 1991b). In particular, greater personal relevance combined with sad mood tends to recruit a motivated, mood-repairing strategy (Forgas, 1989, 1991b).

Indeed, whenever judges are influenced by a strong preexisting motivation, affect infusion tends to be reduced or eliminated. Affect itself, if consciously attended to, may have motivational properties, calling for mood maintenance or mood repair, and often producing mood-incongruent outcomes (Berkowitz & Troccoli, 1990; Sedikides, 1994). Motivated processing may also account for the more volatile affect infusion effects observed under conditions of negative, compared to positive, mood (Forgas et al., 1984; Forgas & Bower, 1987).

The ability to engage in substantive processing is also heavily dependent on the judge's cognitive capacity. Heuristic processing is more likely when cognitive capacity is low, and substantive processing is more likely when cognitive capacity is available (Mackie & Worth, 1991). Affect infusion tends to be reduced when judges must handle excessive amounts of information, are put under time pressure, are distracted, or are otherwise cognitively impaired.

A key feature of the AIM is the recognition that affect can play a dual role in judgments and decisions, influencing both the processing choices people make (how they think) and the kind of information they subsequently consider (what they think). Consistent with other models, the AIM also predicts that positive moods typically generate more superficial, more heuristic, and less effortful processing strategies, whereas negative moods trigger more vigilant, more effortful processing styles. This positive–negative processing asymmetry can be explained in terms of cognitive capacity effects (Mackie & Worth, 1991), in terms of functional evolutionary principles, or in terms of motivational accounts (Clark & Isen, 1982). The AIM does not differentiate among these explanations, but simply assumes that positive and negative affect trigger different kinds of processing styles.

The emphasis on different processing strategies is thus a key feature of the AIM. The model also suggests that the processing consequences of good or bad moods are weaker than and secondary to the processing requirements associated with target, judge, and situation variables. Several experiments now confirm that more complex, demanding, or ambiguous targets tend to elicit more extensive, substantive processing strategies and thus greater affect infusion by *both* happy and sad people (Forgas, 1992b, 1993, 1995b).

Given the complex pragmatics of social situations, the judgmental context itself can also impose processing requirements and thus influence mood effects (Forgas, 1981, 1982). Different situations call for different standards of accuracy, impose different expectations and social desirability pressures, and imply varying levels of scrutiny and publicity. Paradoxically, making people more accountable for their decisions, making judgments public, or increasing the likelihhod of scrutiny may induce more careful, elaborative processing and greater mood effects (Kaplan & Forgas, 1998).

It is important to remember that processing choices are multidetermined, and that these variables can interact with each other. Based on the available empirical evidence, the AIM seeks to link contextual variables systematically in terms of their processing implications. The processing effects of factors such as familiarity, complexity, typicality, and specific motivation are quite straightforward and relatively robust, as suggested by recent empirical results. However, several variables may recruit either heuristic or substantive processing, with affect infusion predicted under either processing strategy. For example, high personal relevance, in the absence of specific motivation, should result in substantive processing and affect-priming effects; however, low personal relevance, again in the absence of specific motivation, should result in heuristic processing and affect-as-information effects. Both routes lead to affect infusion. However, this does not make the model unfalsifiable, because heuristic and substantive processing can be empirically distinguished in terms of processing variables such as memory, processing latency, and judgmental latency.

MOOD CONGRUENCE IN JUDGMENTS: HOW THE MODEL INTEGRATES PREVIOUS WORK

The goal of the AIM is to provide a tenable and parsimonious explanation of how, when, and why mood does or does not have an influence on social judgments and reasoning. The model predicts the *absence* of affect infusion under conditions of direct access or motivated processing, and the *presence* of affect infusion during heuristic and substantive processing.

Consistent with the model, crystallized judgments that can be processed via the direct-access strategy rarely show mood effects. Given that most people have a wealth of stored judgments and reactions, the direct-access strategy is probably quite common in day-to-day life. Judgments about highly familiar consumer products (Srull, 1984) or judgments about familiar, positive health events by young, healthy people (Salovey & Birnbaum, 1989) showed no affective distortion. In contrast, affect did influence judgments about unfamiliar, negative health events (e.g., contracting an illness) (Salovey & Birnbaum, 1989, Exp. 3). In another study, mood had a significant impact on unfamiliar judgments about life satisfaction, but did not have an impact on judgments about highly familiar and specific issues, such as satisfaction with living quarters (Schwarz, Strack, Kommer, & Wagner, 1987). Similarly, mood was found to have a significant impact on judgments about global self-esteem, but it did not have an impact on more domain-specific aspects of self-esteem (Levine, Wyer, & Schwarz, 1994). Any task for which crystallized responses are available may be immune from affect infusion when no substantive processing is required.

According to the AIM, affect infusion is also unlikely when motivated processing is used. Several studies found that priming effects (including affect priming) may disappear under conditions of motivated processing. Drawing judges' attention to their mood states is often enough to elicit motivated thinking (Berkowitz & Troccoli, 1990; Clore et al., 1994). Attempts to correct effortfully for possible biases can also eliminate affect infusion (Clark & Isen, 1982). Affect itself, and negative affect in particular, may frequently trigger motivated processing (Clark & Isen, 1982) and motivated decisions (Schachter, 1959). In one series of experiments (Forgas, 1989), happy or sad subjects were asked to select a partner either for themselves or for somebody else. Motivated processing was selectively adopted by sad subjects who were also personally involved (i.e., selecting a partner for themselves). In a follow-up study, actual processing strategies and step-by-step information search patterns were also recorded. Sad subjects were found to recall more diagnostic information about rewarding partners (Forgas, 1991b, Exp. 1), and they selectively searched for and used information relevant to this motivated objective, to the exclusion of other information (Forgas, 1991b, Exps. 2 and 3). As predicted by the AIM, there was no evidence for affect infusion in any of these motivated judgments.

There are likely to be significant individual differences between people in their propensity to engage in motivated processing. One recent study (Forgas, 1998a) found that people who score highly on measures of social desirability and Machiavellianism are more motivated in tasks such as bargaining and negotiation, and show significantly less affect infusion in their judgments and behaviors, than do low scorers on these measures. Specifically, positive mood produced more optimistic judgments and more cooperative planned and actual bargaining strategies, but only among people who were less concerned with social desirability and were less Machiavellian. Presumably individuals who were highly concerned about social desirability or were high in Machiavellianism were habitually inclined to employ a motivated strategy when dealing with ambiguous social situations such as negotiation. Such a processing strategy is likely to be incompatible with affect infusion, as suggested by the AIM and as found here.

Motivated processing can often produce an opposite, mood-incongruent outcome. For example, sad subjects may be motivated to change their mood through better recall of mood-incongruent material (Erber & Erber, 1994). Similarly, people actively attending to their mood also show affect incongruence (Berkowitz & Troccoli, 1990). Similar results were found by Sedikides (1994); with the passage of time, however, self-descriptions became mood-incongruent, as subjects engaged in more motivated processing to alleviate their negative mood state. Recently, Forgas and Ciarrochi (1999) found that this ability to spontaneously reverse the negative cognitive consequences of aversive moods via motivated processing is an important feature of everyday mood management strategies. Motivated processing may also arise due to situational pressures during a group interaction. In one recent study (Forgas, 1990), there was clear evidence of affect infusion in individuals' judgments

about social stereotypes such as Catholics, Jews, doctors, or farmers. When the same judgments were discussed in a group several weeks later, happy subjects showed an increased mood-congruent bias; however, among sad subjects an opposite, mood-incongruent pattern was found. It seems that in the group, social norms and values became more salient and more motivated, targeted processing was adopted (Brown, 1965). Thus it appears that the presence of the group moderated the amount of affect infusion by inducing a motivation to process information in a more egalitarian manner. Another study showed that individual characteristics such as high trait anxiety have somewhat similar motivational consequences (Ciarrochi & Forgas, 1999a). People low in trait anxiety made more negative judgments of an outgroup when they were feeling bad, but people high in trait anxiety showed a reverse, motivated pattern, producing more lenient judgments.

These studies show that mood has little congruent impact on social judgments and reasoning under conditions that require relatively little constructive, elaborative processing. Both direct-access processing (based on preformed, crystallized judgments) and motivated processing (guided by a specific preexisting objective) involve highly targeted, selective information search strategies that tend to reduce opportunities for incidental affect infusion. There are other circumstances, however, when mood is likely to produce clear and consistent congruent effects, as the next section suggests.

AFFECT INFUSION IN HEURISTIC AND SUBSTANTIVE PROCESSING

As a general rule, in terms of the AIM, the more constructive thinking is required to compute a particular judgment, the greater the degree of affect infusion should be. Heuristic and substantive processing are the most likely mechanisms producing affect infusion. But what determines whether people use heuristic or substantive processing strategies? In order to engage in systematic, substantive information processing, people must be *both* motivated and able to do so. If either of these preconditions is absent, judges are more likely to engage in heuristic processing. Motivation to process substantively is enhanced when personal relevance is high and/or when the target is unusual or complex. However, judges must also have sufficient time and cognitive capacity to use substantive processing. The presence of time constraints or cognitive business will impede substantive processing and thus the infusion of affect into judgments. Because social perceivers often suffer from information overload (i.e., they are often cognitively busy), and prefer to expend minimal cognitive effort whenever possible (i.e., they are cognitive misers), simplified, heuristic processing is a common strategy in judgments (Brewer, 1988).

According to the AIM, affect infusion under heuristic processing occurs due to the affect-as-information mechanism (Schwarz & Clore, 1988). Judges may look to their current mood as a convenient (but often mistaken) shortcut to infer how they feel about a particular object or issue (i.e., "How do I feel about it?"). A number of studies found mood-congruent judgments in circumstances conducive to heuristic processing. For example, when judges are contacted over the telephone (Schwarz & Clore, 1988), or asked on the street (Forgas & Moylan, 1987) to make quick, off-the-cuff judgments about issues they have not thought much about before, it is quite likely that heuristic processing may be used, and that responses may be distorted by the prevailing affective state. In such situations, people are probably unwilling or unable to consider the issue carefully by substantively processing the relevant information. Instead, they may simply ask themselves, "Well, how do I feel about it?", and in doing so may misattribute their mood caused by the weather or a movie they have just seen as evidence for a positive or negative reaction. These mood effects are easily eliminated simply by making judges more aware of the correct source of their moods (Clore at al., 1994; Schwarz & Clore, 1988). According to the AIM, however, most everyday instances of affect infusion should occur when people engage in more elaborate, open-ended processing.

Affect infusion during substantive processing should occur because mood can act as a prime, opening up a host of mood-congruent associations to be used in constructive judgments. Indeed, when substantive processing is used, the more extensive the processing, the more affect is able to influence judgments (Bower, 1981; Forgas & Bower, 1987). Judgments about more complex stimuli, requiring more elaborate and substantive processing, should show greater mood effects than judg-

ments about simpler stimuli should. There are now numerous studies, covering a wide variety of mood manipulations and judgment domains, supporting this hypothesis.

The Process Dependence of Affect Infusion into Judgments

By varying the extent to which social perceivers needed to engage in substantive processing, we were able to demonstrate that longer processing is related to greater mood infusion. In one such study, participants were asked to make judgments about typical and atypical persons. Atypical targets should recruit more extensive processing and thus be more subject to the influence of mood. After watching mood-inducing films, participants read about and formed impressions of typical and atypical students (Forgas, 1992b, Exp. 1). Impressions of the atypical target showed greater affect infusion than did impressions of the typical target. Recall data offered further evidence for the affect-priming hypothesis: Recall was better about atypical than typical targets, consistent with the more extensive processing these stimuli received (Forgas, 1992d, Exp. 2). In a third study, reaction times were also recorded (Forgas, 1992b, Exp. 3). Consistent with the AIM, participants took significantly longer to make judgments about atypical compared to typical targets, and there was a correspondingly greater affect infusion into these more elaborately processed judgments (Figure 23.3).

In a conceptually similar set of studies (Forgas, 1995b), nonverbal stimuli were used to control for possible semantic priming effects. Images of well-matched or badly matched couples were used to create targets that required more or less elaborate processing. In the first of these studies, happy, neutral, or sad people judged pictures of couples designed to be either typical (well matched for physical attractiveness) or atypical (mismatched for physical attractiveness). Again, consistent with the AIM, judgments of atypical couples produced greater affect infusion. A second study showed that recall was also better about mismatched couples, suggesting that they recruited greater information-processing effort, as expected. In a third study, images of couples were created that could differ both in terms of physical attractiveness and race, allowing for three degrees of match–mismatch to be manipulated (fully

MOOD EFFECTS ON IMPRESSIONS ABOUT
TYPICAL AND ATYPICAL PERSONS

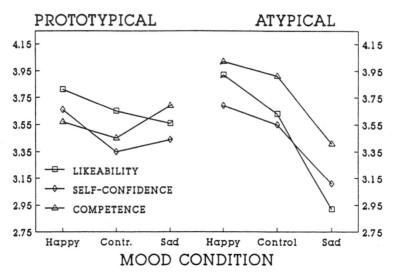

FIGURE 23.3. The effects of mood on judgments about more or less prototypical others: Mood effects are significantly greater when the targets are atypical and require more extensive processing. From Forgas (1992b). Copyright 1992 by the American Psychological Association. Reprinted by permission.

matched, partly matched, fully mismatched). As predicted by the AIM, the degree of atypicality was directly related to the size of the mood effect on judgments (Figure 23.4). In a fourth study, a mediational analysis of processing latencies confirmed that the time taken to process information about more or less well-matched couples significantly mediated the relationship between mood and judgments. That is, longer processing latencies increased, and shorter processing latencies decreased, the extent of mood congruence and affect infusion. Although consistent with the AIM, this is nevertheless a surprising and paradoxical effect, since intuitively one would expect longer and more systematic processing to reduce rather than increase affective biases in social judgments and decisions.

Interestingly, social judgments about highly familiar real-life events such as relationship conflicts show a similar affect sensitivity. In the first of three experiments (Forgas, 1994a), subjects feeling happy or sad after reading affectively laden literary passages were asked to make causal attributions for happy or conflict episodes in their current intimate relationship. Sad mood produced more internal, self-blaming attributions for conflicts, and more external

attributions for happy events, in a pattern of mood-congruent self-deprecating judgments. In contrast, happy subjects were more likely to blame external factors for conflicts, but took greater credit for happy events. Additional studies showed that these mood effects on attributions were consistently greater when more extensive, constructive processing was required to deal with more complex, serious events (Figure 23.5). The possibility that mood effects on judgments may be particularly marked when serious and personally involving issues are at stake is, of course, of considerable practical relevance to areas of clinical and relationship research. The general principle predicted by the AIM, and supported in these studies, is that the effects of mood on social judgments tend to be most robust when perceivers are encouraged to think substantively and constructively about social judgments.

In a series of studies, Sedikides (1995) further confirmed this principle in the domain of self-relevant judgments. In these experiments, people experiencing happy or sad mood were asked to think about central (well-known, familiar) and peripheral (less well-known) aspects of their self-concept. Consistent with the AIM, results showed that familiar, central as-

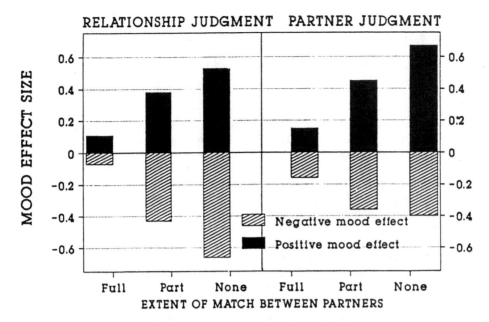

FIGURE 23.4. Mood effects on judgments about fully matched, partly matched, and mismatched couples. Mood effects are significantly greater when the partners in a couple are unusual and mismatched, and thus require more extensive processing. Data from Forgas (1995b).

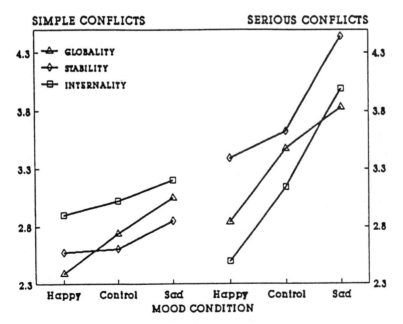

FIGURE 23.5. Mood effects on judgments about more or less serious relationship conflicts: Mood has a greater influence on inferences about serious conflicts that require more substantive processing. From Forgas (1994a). Copyright 1994 by the American Psychological Association. Reprinted by permission.

pects of the self-concept required less extensive processing and were less influenced by affect, while peripheral aspects of the self-concept required more extensive processing and showed greater affect sensitivity.

In addition to mood congruence, affective states also have processing consequences. Forgas (1998c) found recently that the kind of vigilant, systematic attention to stimulus details recruited by negative moods tends to reduce or even eliminate such common judgmental biases as the fundamental attribution error. These experiments asked happy or sad subjects to make inferences about the underlying attitudes of people who either freely chose or were coerced into writing essays on either popular (e.g., against nuclear testing) or unpopular (e.g., supporting nuclear testing) positions. Results showed that happy people were far more likely to commit the fundamental attribution error and to infer internal causation based on the unpopular-position essay, despite clear evidence that the essay was coerced. In contrast, negative mood resulted in a significant elimination of the fundamental attribution error (Figure 23.6). Some of these affect infusion effects may also have important practical implications—for ex-

ample, in the domain of marketing and consumer judgments.

The Pleasure of Possessions: Affect and Consumer Judgments

Affect may play a particularly important role in how people evaluate their personal possessions. In modern industrial societies, the ownership of objects is heavily imbued with emotional meaning. Obtaining material possessions is a major source of work motivation and satisfaction for most people. In a social environment where most relationships are superficial and are based on surface characteristics, the things we own may take on a special emotional significance in defining and displaying our claimed status and social identity to others. It is not surprising, then, that the mere act of owning an object appears to increase its value to many people. This so-called "endowment effect" has been defined as the premium people expect for giving up an object already owned. This effect is not simply due to a misestimation of the transaction costs or the real value of the object. Rather, subjective feelings about the prospect of losing a possession seem to play a dominant

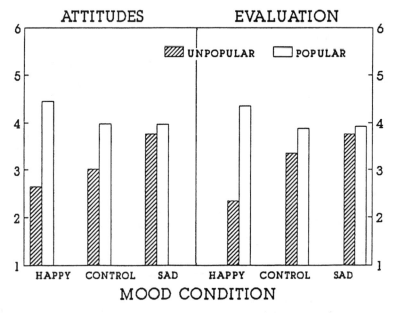

FIGURE 23.6. The effects of mood on the fundamental attribution error: Positive mood increases, and negative mood decreases, correspondent inferences based on coerced essays advocating popular and unpopular opinions. On the left: Inferences about attributed attitudes concerning forest preservation. On the right: Inferences indicating evaluative impressions about the writer. From Forgas (1998c). Copyright 1998 by the American Psychological Association. Reprinted by permission.

role in generating the endowment effect. Interestingly, the effects of mood on such judgments have not been investigated previously, even though prior work does suggest that affect can significantly influence at least some aspects of how consumer items are cognitively represented (Srull, 1984). In terms of the AIM, we may expect that when in a happy mood, people should find it easier to selectively recall positive information related to the pleasure of owning an object (Bower, 1991; Forgas & Bower, 1987), and should thus overvalue that item and be more reluctant to part with it. When in a sad mood, people should selectively access negative information related to an object, and thus should value it less. However, these mood effects may be more limited for people inclined to disregard their affective states, such as those scoring low on measures of emotionality.

In two recent experiments (Ciarrochi & Forgas, 1999b), participants who were induced to feel good or bad estimated the subjective and objective value of a number of consumer items they owned or wanted to own. Participants also completed a scale called Openness to Feelings (OF). Both experiments predicted and found a significant interaction between personality (OF) and mood on consumer evaluations. Individuals scoring high on OF showed a clear mood-congruent pattern: Positive mood increased, and negative mood decreased, their valuation of their material possessions. In contrast, people scoring low on OF showed the opposite, mood-incongruent bias. These effects were confirmed both in Experiment 1 (which used an autobiographical mood induction) and Experiment 2 (which used exposure to happy or sad films to induce moods). These results clearly illustrate not only that affect has a significant influence on consumer judgments, but also that these effects are significantly moderated by personality characteristics such as openness to feelings. Given the broad evidence for mood effects in a variety of judgments, could it be that affect infuses not only judgments, but also subsequent strategic social behaviors? This hypothesis was investigated in some recent experiments.

Affect and Intergroup Judgments

The process sensitivity of mood effects on social judgments and decisions is further illustrated by a series of experiments conducted on intergroup judgments (Forgas & Fiedler, 1996).

In these experiments, people feeling happy or sad were asked to make reward allocation decisions between members of an ingroup and an outgroup; the traditional minimal-group paradigm developed by Tajfel (cf. Tajfel & Forgas, 1981) was used. In the first study, when group membership was of little personal significance, happy people were actually more likely than sad people to allocate rewards unfairly to their ingroup. This effect occurred because positive mood promoted a more simple, heuristic processing style, leading to a greater reliance on simple group category information in performing the allocation task. By introducing a manipulation of group relevance in second and third studies, Forgas and Fiedler caused some subjects to think more substantively (high group relevance) and others to think more heuristically (low group relevance). As predicted by the AIM, sad subjects were now more likely than happy subjects to discriminate against the outgroup, but only when engaged in substantive processing. A series of regression analyses specifically supported predictions made by the AIM that the relationship between mood and these intergroup allocation decisions was significantly mediated by different processing strategies.

Affect Infusion in Behavior Planning

Social judgments and reasoning are usually performed as part of behavior planning, as an antecedent of purposive action (Heider, 1958). Given the strong evidence for affective influences on social judgment and reasoning reviewed above, it seems reasonable to assume that affect may also influence actual strategic behaviors. Generally, favorable judgments should be expected to precede approach, or friendly behaviors; unfavorable judgments should be expected to precede avoidance, or unfriendly behaviors. Forgas (1998a, 1998b, 1998c, 1999a, 1999b) recently conducted a number of studies examining the role of affect in a variety of strategic social behaviors.

One recent set of studies examined mood effects on negotiator cognition and bargaining strategies (Forgas, 1998a). Bargaining and negotiation are complex, indeterminate, and unpredictable events, and are likely to require open, constructive thinking as people prepare their approach and plan their strategies. To the extent that substantive processing is required to plan a bargaining encounter, affect was expected to significantly bias people's planned and actual negotiating strategies. In three studies, subjects received a mood induction, and then planned and participated in an interpersonal/informal and an intergroup/formal bargaining encounter. These experiments provided convergent evidence showing that positive mood resulted in more cooperative, integrative plans; more optimistic perceptions of the partner; and more constructive, cooperative bargaining behaviors (Figure 23.7). Forgas also found that positive affect influenced not only bargaining strategies, but also outcomes: Subjects who felt good were not only more cooperative, but also obtained better results. These mood effects on negotiation were a direct consequence of the prenegotiation plans and judgments formed, suggesting a close link between affect infusion into judgments on the one hand, and subsequent behaviors on the other. Interestingly, individual differences played a significant role in moderating mood effects on strategic bargaining. People who scored high on measures likely to predict a habitually motivated approach to interpersonal tasks (such as need for approval and Machiavellianism) were significantly less influenced by mood than were low scorers. This result supports our earlier argument that affect infusion tends to be reduced whenever people adopt more targeted, motivat-

ed processing because of situational or personal factors.

A further series of experiments explored affect infusion into strategic interpersonal behaviours in a field setting, using an unobtrusive procedure. Mood was manipulated by placing folders containing positively or negatively valenced images on desks in a library. Students arriving to sit at the desks and who looked through the images were subsequently approached by a confederate who made either a polite ("May I . . .") or an impolite request ("Give me . . .") for some writing paper, in what appeared an impromptu, naturalistic encounter. Impolite requests were expected to elicit more extensive information processing because of their unexpected nature, violating conventions of request politeness (Forgas, 1985; Gibbs, 1985). And as predicted by the AIM, evaluations of, recall of, and compliance with the impolite request showed greater mood congruence than did evaluations of, recall of, and compliance with polite requests. Similarly, judgments and impressions about the requester also showed greater mood congruence when the request was impolite (and thus elicited more detailed processing) than when the requester was polite. These results, obtained in an unobtrusive field study, are generally consistent with the key prediction of the AIM that affective influ-

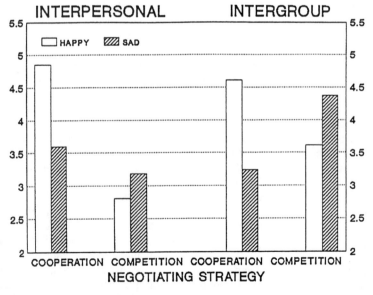

FIGURE 23.7. Mood effects on bargaining and negotiation strategies: Positive mood increases planned and actual cooperation, and negative mood increases competitive strategies. From Forgas (1998a). Copyright 1998 by the American Psychological Association. Reprinted by permission.

ences on social judgments and behaviors tend to be greater when more constructive processing is recruited by unusual, complex or otherwise problematic social situations.

Affect Infusion and Communication

Consistent with the theoretical arguments outlined above, several recent experiments also found that manipulated affective states can have a significant direct influence on people's planned and actual communication strategies (Forgas, 1998b, 1999a, 1999b). One relevant series of experiments explored the way people formulate and use verbal messages such as requests. Requesting is also an intrinsically complex behavioral task characterized by uncertainty and ambiguity. Requesters need to formulate their messages to be sufficiently direct so as to maximize compliance, yet polite enough to avoid giving offense. We expected that mood should influence request formulations, with a more confident, direct strategy adopted in a positive mood, consistent with the greater availability of positively valenced thoughts and associations. Furthermore, in terms of the AIM, these mood effects should be greater when the situation is more complex and demanding, and requires more substantive and elaborate processing.

In the first experiment, people feeling happy or sad after thinking about positive or negative personal episodes (Forgas, 1999a) selected more or less polite requests that they would use in an easy and a difficult request situation. Induced mood had a significant influence on request preferences, with happy participants preferring more direct, impolite forms, and sad persons using indirect, polite requests. Furthermore, these mood effects on requesting were significantly greater in the more difficult, demanding request situation that required more extensive, substantive processing strategies (Figure 23.8). In follow-up experiments, participants' formulation of their own open-ended requests showed very similar mood effects (Forgas, 1999a). A third experiment predicted and found that mood also had a relatively greater influence on more unusual, unconventional behaviors (such as producing an impolite, direct request) that required more substantive processing (Forgas, 1999a). These findings indicate that mood effects on behavior regulation are indeed process-dependent, with affect infusion enhanced when more constructive processing is required by a more difficult strategic task (Fiedler, 1991; Fiedler & Forgas, 1988; Forgas, 1995a).

This pattern was also obtained in an unobtrusive experiment looking at naturally produced requests (Forgas, 1999b). After an audiovisual mood induction, participants had to get a file from a neighboring office, and their words were

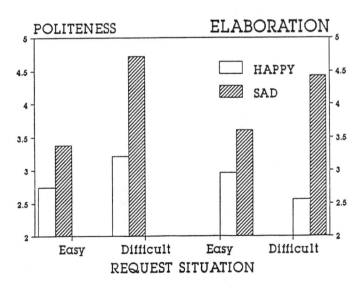

FIGURE 23.8. The effects of mood on the politeness and elaboration of requests produced in more or less difficult situations: Negative mood increases, and positive mood decreases, request politeness and elaboration, and they do so most in difficult situations that require more extensive processing. From Forgas (1999a). Copyright 1999 by the American Psychological Association. Reprinted by permission.

recorded by a concealed tape recorder. Results showed a significant mood effect on these natural, unobtrusively elicited requests. Sad people used more polite, elaborate forms, and happy people used more direct and less polite forms. Negative mood also increased the latency (delay) in posing the request, consistent with the more cautious, defensive strategies induced by bad mood. Recall data confirmed that unconventional requests were also recalled better, confirming the more elaborate, in-depth processing of these messages. These experiments show that affect infusion into the planning and execution of strategic behaviors is significantly mediated by the kind of processing strategy people employ. In particular, the production of more complex, demanding interpersonal judgments and behaviors seems to be especially affect-sensitive, as suggested by the AIM.

SUMMARY AND CONCLUSIONS

The influence of affective states on thoughts, judgments, and decisions has long been a source of interest and fascination to laypersons and philosophers alike. Psychologists were relatively late to recognize the importance of this phenomenon, most probably because of the traditional separation among affect, cognition, and conation—the three "faculties of mind"—throughout most of the history of the discipline (Hilgard, 1980). During the last two decades, considerable empirical evidence has demonstrated mood-congruent influences on learning, memory and associations (Bower, 1981, 1991). Explanations of these phenomena have evolved from earlier psychoanalytic and conditioning approaches (Berkowitz, 1993; Feshbach & Singer, 1957) to the more recent cognitive/ information-processing accounts. The affect-priming hypothesis (Bower, 1981, 1991) offers a particularly simple and parsimonious account of many mood-congruent phenomena, including judgmental effects (Forgas & Bower, 1987; Forgas et al., 1984).

This chapter has aimed to provide a timely review and integration of mood effects on social judgments and decisions. With accumulating empirical evidence, it has also become clear that mood congruity in judgments is neither necessary nor universal. In fact, in many circumstances mood either has no effect or has an incongruent effect on judgments. This chapter has sought to integrate these diverse findings in terms of a comprehensive multiprocess theory, the AIM. The literature suggests that affect infusion is absent whenever a judgmental task can be performed via a simple, well-rehearsed direct access strategy or a highly motivated strategy. In these conditions there is little need, as well as little opportunity, for incidentally primed mood-congruent information to infuse constructive information processing (Fiedler, 1991). By assuming that affect infusion is limited to circumstances involving constructive processing, the model can account for most of the empirical evidence in the literature demonstrating mood congruence or its absence. The AIM identifies four distinct information-processing strategies used by people when performing a judgment: (1) the direct access of highly cued, crystallized responses; (2) motivated processing, guided by a specific motivation, such as mood repair; (3) heuristic processing, using whatever shortcuts and heuristics are available; and (4) substantive processing, when individuals use selective, constructive processing to integrate the available information with preexisting and affectively primed knowledge structures.

Of course, affect priming is not the only mechanism likely to produce affect infusion. The affect-as-information model can also explain at least some of the mood-congruent judgmental phenomena reported in the literature (Clore et al., 1994). The kind of heuristic processing implied by the affect-as-information model is most likely when judges lack personal involvement, cognitive capacity, and/or motivation to engage in substantive processing. We believe that affect priming is the most likely mechanism likely to lead to mood congruence in most everyday judgmental tasks. The evidence reviewed here clearly supports the predictions derived from the AIM. Counterintuitive results showing that more extensive, substantive processing enhances mood congruity provide especially strong support for the AIM (Forgas, 1992b, 1992d, 1994a, 1994b, 1995b, 1998a, 1998b). Conversely, other studies have shown the disappearance of mood congruity whenever people approach a cognitive task from a motivated perspective (Forgas, 1991a, 1991b; Forgas & Fiedler, 1996; Sedikides, 1995). Indeed, the tendency to alternate between substantive and motivated processing strategies (producing affect infusion and affect control, respectively) may be thought of as part of an ongoing homeostatic strategy of controlled mood management, according to a recently developed mood management model (Forgas & Ciarrochi, 1999; Forgas, Johnson, & Ciarrochi, 1998).

Mood-congruent judgment occurs not only in the laboratory, but also in many real-life situations. Affect infusion can be an important part of organizational decisions, appraisal judgments, consumer preferences, and health-related judgments (Baron, 1987; Forgas & Moylan, 1987; Mayer et al., 1992; Salovey, O'Leary, Stretton, Fishkin, & Drake, 1991; Sedikides, 1992). Indeed, the more judges need to engage in open, constructive processing, the more likely it is that affect will infuse their responses. Even such highly involved and complex tasks as judging relationship conflicts show such mood-congruent biases (Forgas, 1994b).

To conclude, by postulating four distinct information-processing strategies, the AIM offers a parsimonious account for a variety of mood effects observed in the literature. Generally, the evidence reviewed here confirms that affect infusion into judgments and decisions is most likely in conditions requiring constructive, substantive processing. We hope that by further clarifying the characteristics and conditions conducive to affect priming in judgments and decisions, the present chapter will encourage growing interest in this important research area.

ACKNOWLEDGMENTS

This work was supported by a Special Investigator Award from the Australian Research Council, and by the Research Prize from the Alexander von Humboldt Foundation, to Joseph P. Forgas. The contribution of Stephanie Moylan and Joan Webb to this project is gratefully acknowledged.

REFERENCES

Asch, S. E. (1946). Forming impressions of personality. *Journal of Abnormal and Social Psychology, 41,* 258–290.

Baron, R. (1987). Interviewers' moods and reactions to job applicants: The influence of affective states on applied social judgments. *Journal of Applied Social Psychology, 16,* 16–28.

Berkowitz, L. (1993). Towards a general theory of anger and emotional aggression. In T. K. Srull & R. S. Wyer (Eds.), *Advances in social cognition* (Vol. 6, pp. 1–46). Hillsdale, NJ: Erlbaum.

Berkowitz, L., & Troccoli, B. T. (1990). Feelings, direc-

tion of attention, and expressed evaluations of others. *Cognition and Emotion, 4,* 305–325.

Bower, G. H. (1981). Mood and memory. *American Psychologist, 36,* 129–148.

Bower, G. H. (1991). Mood congruity of social judgments. In J. P. Forgas (Ed.), *Emotion and social judgments* (pp. 31–53). Oxford: Pergamon Press.

Brewer, M. (1988). A dual-process model of impression formation. In T. K. Srull & R. S. Wyer (Eds.), *Advances in social cognition* (Vol. 1, pp. 1–36). Hillsdale, NJ: Erlbaum.

Brown, R. (1965). *Social psychology.* New York: Freeman.

Ciarrochi, J. V., & Forgas, J. P. (1999a). On being tense yet tolerant: The paradoxical effect of trait anxiety and aversive mood on intergroup judgments. *Group Dynamics: Theory, Research and Practice, 3,* 227–238.

Ciarrochi, J. V., & Forgas, J. P. (1999b) *The pleasure of possessions: Affect and consumer judgments.* Manuscript submitted for publication.

Clark, M. S., & Isen, A. M. (1982). Towards understanding the relationship between feeling states and social behavior. In A. H. Hastorf & A. M. Isen (Eds.), *Cognitive social psychology* (pp. 73–108). New York: Elsevier/North-Holland.

Clore, G. L., & Byrne, D. (1974). The reinforcement affect model of attraction. In T. L. Huston (Ed.), *Foundations of interpersonal attraction* (pp. 143–170). New York: Academic Press.

Clore, G. L., Schwarz, N., & Conway, M. (1994). Affective causes and consequences of social information processing. In R. S. Wyer & T. K. Srull (Eds.), *Handbook of social cognition* (2nd ed., pp. 323–417). Hillsdale, NJ: Erlbaum.

Erber, R., & Erber, M. W. (1994). Beyond mood and social judgment: Mood incongruent recall and mood regulation. *European Journal of Social Psychology, 24,* 79–88.

Feshbach, S., & Singer, R. D. (1957). The effects of fear arousal and suppression of fear upon social perception. *Journal of Abnormal and Social Psychology, 55,* 283–288.

Fiedler, K. (1991). On the task, the measures and the mood in research on affect and social cognition. In J. P. Forgas (Ed.), *Emotion and social judgments* (pp. 83–104). Oxford: Pergamon Press.

Fiedler, K., & Forgas, J. P. (Eds.). (1988). *Affect, cognition, and social behavior.* Toronto: Hogrefe.

Forgas, J. P. (Ed.). (1981). *Social cognition: Perspectives on everyday understanding.* New York: Academic Press.

Forgas, J. P. (1982). Episode cognition: Internal representations of interaction routines. In L. Berkowitz (Ed.), *Advances in experimental social psychology* (Vol. 15, pp. 59–100). New York: Academic Press.

Forgas, J. P. (Ed.). (1985). *Language and social situations.* New York: Springer.

Forgas, J. P. (1989). Mood effects on decision-making strategies. *Australian Journal of Psychology, 41,* 197–214.

Forgas, J. P. (1990). Affective influences on individual and group judgments. *European Journal of Social Psychology, 20,* 441–453.

Forgas, J. P. (Ed.). (1991a). *Emotion and social judgments.* Oxford: Pergamon Press.

Forgas, J. P. (1991b). Mood effects on partner choice: Role of affect in social decisions. *Journal of Personality and Social Psychology, 61,* 708–720.

Forgas, J. P. (1991c). Affect and cognition in close relationships. In G. Fletcher & F. Fincham (Eds.), *Cognition in close relationships* (pp. 151–174). Hillsdale, NJ: Erlbaum.

Forgas, J. P. (1992a). Affect in social judgments and decisions: A multi-process model. In M. Zanna (Ed.), *Advances in experimental social psychology* (Vol. 25, pp. 227–275). New York: Academic Press.

Forgas, J. P. (1992b). On bad mood and peculiar people: Affect and person typicality in impression formation. *Journal of Personality and Social Psychology, 62,* 863–875.

Forgas, J. P. (1992c). Affect and social perceptions: Research evidence and an integrative model. In W. Stroebe & M. Hewstone (Eds.) *European review of social psychology* (Vol. 3, pp. 183–224). Chichester, England: Wiley.

Forgas, J. P. (1992d). Mood and the perception of unusual people: Affective asymmetry in memory and social judgments. *European Journal of Social Psychology, 22,* 531–547.

Forgas, J. P. (1993). On making sense of odd couples: Mood effects on the perception of mismatched relationships. *Personality and Social Psychology Bulletin, 19,* 59–71.

Forgas, J. P. (1994a). Sad and guilty?: Affective influences on the explanation of conflict episodes. *Journal of Personality and Social Psychology, 66,* 56–68.

Forgas, J. P. (1994b). The role of emotion in social judgments: An introductory review and an affect infusion model (AIM). *European Journal of Social Psychology, 24,* 1–24.

Forgas, J. P. (1995a). Mood and judgment: The affect infusion model (AIM). *Psychological Bulletin, 117*(1), 39–66.

Forgas, J. P. (1995b). Strange couples: Mood effects on judgments and memory about prototypical and atypical targets. *Personality and Social Psychology Bulletin, 21,* 747–765.

Forgas, J. P. (1998a). On feeling good and getting your way: Mood effects on negotiation strategies and outcomes. *Journal of Personality and Social Psychology, 74,* 565–577.

Forgas, J. P. (1998b). Asking nicely?: Mood effects on responding to more or less polite requests. *Personality and Social Psychology Bulletin, 24,* 173–185.

Forgas, J. P. (1998c). On being happy and mistaken: Mood effects on the fundamental attribution error. *Journal of Personality and Social Psychology, 75,* 318–331.

Forgas, J. P. (1999a). On feeling good and being rude: Affective influences on language use and request formulations. *Journal of Personality and Social Psychology, 76,* 928–939.

Forgas, J. P. (1999b). Feeling and speaking: Mood effects on verbal communication strategies. *Personality and Social Psychology Bulletin, 25,* 850–863.

Forgas, J. P., & Bower, G. H. (1987). Mood effects on person perception judgements. *Journal of Personality and Social Psychology, 53,* 53–60.

Forgas, J. P., Bower, G. H., & Krantz, S. (1984). The influence of mood on perceptions of social interactions. *Journal of Experimental Social Psychology, 20,* 497–513.

Forgas, J. P., Bower, G. H., & Moylan, S. J. (1990). Praise or blame?: Affective influences on attributions for achievement. *Journal of Personality and Social Psychology, 59,* 809–818.

Forgas, J. P. & Ciarrochi, J. (1999). *Mood congruent and incongruent thoughts over time: The role of self-esteem in mood management efficacy.* Manuscript submitted for publication.

Forgas, J. P., & Fiedler, K. (1996). Us and them: Mood effects on intergroup discrimination. *Journal of Personality and Social Psychology, 70,* 36–52.

Forgas, J. P., Johnson, R., & Ciarrochi, J. (1998). Affect control and affect infusion: A multi-process account of mood management and personal control. In M. Kofta, G. Weary, & G. Sedek (Eds.), *Personal control in action: Cognitive and motivational mechanisms* (pp. 155–196). New York: Plenum Press.

Forgas, J. P., Levinger, G., & Moylan, S. (1994). Feeling good and feeling close: Mood effects on the perception of intimate relationships. *Personal Relationships, 2,* 165–184.

Forgas, J. P., & Moylan, S. J. (1987). After the movies: The effects of transient mood states on social judgments. *Personality and Social Psychology Bulletin, 13,* 478–489.

Forgas, J. P., & Moylan, S. J. (1991). Affective influences on stereotype judgments. *Cognition and Emotion, 5,* 379–397.

Gibbs, R. (1985). Situational conventions and requests. In J. P. Forgas (Ed.), *Language and social situations* (pp. 97–113). New York: Springer.

Griffitt, W. (1970). Environmental effects on interpersonal behavior: Ambient effective temperature and attraction. *Journal of Personality and Social Psychology, 15,* 240–244.

Haddock, G., Zanna, M. P., & Esses, V. M. (1994). Mood and the expression of intergroup attitudes: The moderating role of affect intensity. *European Journal of Social Psychology, 24,* 189–206.

Heider, F. (1958). *The psychology of interpersonal relations.* New York: Wiley.

Hilgard, E. R. (1980). The trilogy of mind: Cognition, affection, and conation. *Journal of the History of the Behavioral Sciences, 16,* 107–117.

Isen, A. (1987). Positive affect, cognitive processes and social behavior. In L. Berkowitz (Ed.), *Advances in experimental social psychology* (Vol. 20, pp. 203–253). New York: Academic Press.

Kaplan, M., & Forgas, J. P. (1998). *The effects of time pressure and motivation to process on mood effects on social judgments.* Unpublished manuscript, University of New South Wales, Sydney, New South Wales, Australia.

Levine, S. R., Wyer, R. S., & Schwarz, N. (1994). Are you what you feel?: The affective and cognitive determinants of self-judgments. *European Journal of Social Psychology, 24,* 63–78.

Mackie, D., & Worth, L. (1991). Feeling good, but not thinking straight: The impact of positive mood on persuasion. In J. P. Forgas (Ed.), *Emotion and social judgments* (pp. 201–220). Oxford: Pergamon Press.

Mayer, J. D., Gaschke, Y. N., Braverman, D. L., & Evans, T. W. (1992). Mood congruent judgment is a general effect. *Journal of Personality and Social Psychology, 63,* 119–132.

Petty, R. E., & Cacioppo, J. T. (1986). *Communication and persuasion: Central and peripheral routes to attitude change.* New York: Springer-Verlag.

Petty, R. E., Gleicher, F., & Baker, S. (1991). Multiple roles for affect in persuasion. In J. P. Forgas (Ed.), *Emotion and social judgments* (pp. 181–200). Oxford: Pergamon Press.

Salovey, P., & Birnbaum, D. (1989). Influence of mood on health-related cognitions. *Journal of Personality and Social Psychology, 57,* 539–551.

Salovey, P., O'Leary, A., Stretton, M., Fishkin, S., & Drake, C. A. (1991). Influence of mood on judgments about health and illness. In J. P. Forgas (Ed.), *Emotion and social judgments* (pp. 241–262). Oxford: Pergamon Press.

Schachter, S. (1959). *The psychology of affiliation.* Stanford, CA: Stanford University Press.

Schwarz, N., & Clore, G. L. (1988). How do I feel about it?: The informative function of affective states. In K. Fiedler & J. P. Forgas (Eds.), *Affect, cognition, and social behavior* (pp. 44–62). Toronto: Hogrefe.

Schwarz, N., Strack, F., Kommer, D., & Wagner, D. (1987). Soccer, rooms and the quality of your life: Mood effects on judgments of satisfaction with life in general and with specific life domains. *European Journal of Social Psychology, 17,* 69–79.

Sedikides, C. (1992). Changes in the valence of self as a function of mood. *Review of Personality and Social Psychology, 14,* 271–311.

Sedikides, C. (1994). Incongruent effects of sad mood on self-conception valence: It's a matter of time. *European Journal of Social Psychology, 24,* 161–172.

Sedikides, C. (1995). Central and peripheral self-conceptions are differentially influenced by mood: Tests of the differential sensitivity hypothesis. *Journal of Personality and Social Psychology, 69*(4), 759–777.

Srull, T. K. (1984). The effects of subjective affective states on memory and judgment. In T. Kinnear (Ed.), *Advances in consumer research* (Vol. 11, pp. 530–533). Provo, UT: Association for Consumer Research.

Tajfel, S., & Forgas, J. P. (1981). Social categorization: Cognitions, values and groups. In J. P. Forgas (Ed.), *Social cognition: Perspectives on everyday understanding* (pp. 113–140). New York: Academic Press.

CHAPTER 24

Emotion Expression in Groups

Ursula Hess
Gilles Kirouac

OBJECTIVES

One salient aspect of our daily lives is the emotions evoked by social interactions. We get angry at a slight, are happy about an unexpected meeting, or become sad because of a separation from family and friends. Yet the same slight may lead to different reactions, depending on who did the slighting—a boss or a best friend. And we also expect that the reaction to a slight may depend on who was slighted—a man or a woman, someone from the southern part of the country or someone from the north. In other words, it seems to matter who the interaction partners are and to what group they belong.

This question is the topic of the present chapter. Specifically, we present a theoretical framework for the influences of the interaction partners' social group membership on both the *display* of emotion and the *recognition* of these displays. "Social group" in this context is defined loosely as members of a social category who share a common characteristic associated with shared beliefs or roles regarding emotionality. In the present context we focus on gender, culture, and status as examples of social groups. Later in the chapter, we present empirical evidence for the proposed framework.

SOCIAL GROUP MEMBERSHIP AND EMOTION DISPLAYS

The communication of emotions is an important aspect of everyday interactions. People have likes and dislikes, get angry or despondent when faced with obstacles, are happy or disappointed about a gift—and express these experiences via facial, vocal, or postural behaviors that can be observed and interpreted by others. Yet such emotion displays provide information not only about the feeling state of the senders, but also about their perception of the world, as well as their relationship with current interaction partners. For example, an anger display informs us that the sender feels wronged in some way and assesses this wrong as one that can be redressed. In addition, an anger display signals dominance (e.g., Knudson, 1996) and can thus be considered informative regarding the relative power of the anger-expressing individual (Coats & Feldman, 1996). Conversely, a sadness display informs us that the sender has experienced a loss that is assessed as irrevocable, and this type of display is associated with submissiveness (e.g., Knudson, 1996). Thus emotion displays are inherently informative about how a situation is perceived by the sender. Yet the perception of a given situation is likely to vary with the social group membership of the sender. That is, the sender's status (high or low), gender, and cultural background all impinge on how a given situation is experienced and reacted to.

The notion that social group membership plays a role in the expression and experience of emotions has been endorsed by researchers from very different backgrounds. Interestingly, both evolutionary accounts of emotions emphasizing the biological basis of emotions, and sociology-of-emotion accounts (see Kemper, Chapter 4, this volume), positing that emotions are socially engendered, note the importance of group membership for emotional reactions.

An argument for the importance of group membership based on the evolutionary development of emotion expressions has been advanced by Turner (1997), who asserts that emotions evolved in part to provide the means for effective sanctioning and the enforcement of moral codes within groups of hominids. His basic argument is that the communication of emotions was a necessary prerequisite for social bonding among asocial hominids. In a similar vein, Preuschoft and van Hooff (1997) present evidence that the degree to which situational determinants of the primate silent bared-teeth display (the presumed precursor of the human smile) and the relaxed open-mouth display (the presumed precursor of human laughter) overlap can be traced to the social relationships within primate groups—specifically, to the level of hierarchical structure within the group. These notions have in common that "emotion norms" in groups of early hominids depended on the specific structure of the group (i.e., differed among groups).

In a very different view—that of emotions as socially constructed—the importance of power and status relations for the elicitation and even the construction of emotions is stressed (e.g., Lutz, 1988; Burkitt, 1997; see Reddy, 1997, for a critique). Kemper (1990) raises the question regarding differences in emotional reactions between members of different groups in terms of gender, age, and social class; he suggests differences in the phenomenal indicators of power and status, as well as differences in the gain and loss of power and status, as possible sources for such differences. That is, he suggests that members of different social groups differ in their evaluation of emotion-eliciting events and their consequences, and that these differences may lead to differences in emotional reactions.

Thus the notion that social group membership can influence the experience and expression of emotion, as well as the interpretation of emotional messages, can be encountered in widely different domains. In the following section, we present a conceptual framework of social group membership influences on the encoding and decoding of emotions, based on appraisal theories of emotion. In this context we first discuss whether group membership defines rather than influences emotion displays—that is, the question regarding the biological versus cultural basis of emotion. Next we address the question what it is that emotion displays communicate—that is, the question regarding the function of emotion.

CONCEPTUAL FRAMEWORK

The Universality of Emotions

Theories of Universality versus Cultural Specificity

It has been maintained that emotions are culturally bound phenomena, and that different cultures have inherently different emotion experiences and concepts, as evidenced by differences in emotion vocabulary between different languages (see Russell, 1991; Wierzbicka, 1995). Furthermore, from a social constructivist position it is argued that emotions are defined by the discourse structures of a society or group (see Reddy, 1997, for an overview and critique). In both cases the notion of universal, biologically based emotions is viewed with skepticism or rejected. On the other hand, we find the notion that emotions are biologically based and that universal expressions exists for at least some emotions (e.g., Ekman, 1992).

However, the notion that emotions are biologically based and the notion that they are culturally informed are not incongruent. Appraisal theories of emotion make it possible to bring these two positions into accord. Specifically, we suggest that the basic emotion process is biologically grounded and universal, but that the type of events attended to, the appraisal of these events, and the relevant norms for behavior may vary as a function of culture, gender, relative power status, and the relationship between the interaction partners (see also Mesquita, Frijda, & Scherer, 1997; Frijda, Markam, Sato, & Wiers, 1995).

An Appraisal Perspective

Appraisal theories of emotion (e.g., Scherer, 1986; Frijda, 1986) posit that an individual's emotional reactions are based on evaluations of internal or external events. Although theories differ with regard to the exact number and type of the evaluations—Frijda et al. (1995) list 23 appraisal dimensions culled from different theories—these generally include novelty, pleasantness, uncertainty, presence of obstacles, controllability, an attribution of agency, and a notion of justice or fairness. It is important to note that from this perspective, emotions are intimately related to the processing of information. Whereas the specific information processed and the norms applied to the resulting behavior may differ between cultures or groups, the basic process as such may be considered the same (see Mesquita et al., 1997). Thus social group membership influences the information appraised and the outcome of some of the appraisals, as well as the resulting behavior, but not the basic appraisal process as such.

Functions of Emotions

It is important to keep in mind that emotion displays serve different functions—as, indeed, all messages do (see Bühler, 1934). From the perspective described above, emotion displays are symptoms of an underlying emotional state. But, as Darwin (1872/1965) already pointed out, emotion displays also serve as signals and inform us about the behavioral intentions of others. Finally, emotion displays also have an appeal function: They solicit reactions from the interaction partner. Thus an expression of sadness informs us about the feeling state of the sender, but also about the fact that he or she considers the situation as uncontrollable and thus is not likely to attempt to do something about it. Finally, the sadness display may solicit us to offer help or comfort. (For a more detailed discussion of this issue, see Hess, Banse, & Kappas, 1995.)

These three different functions of emotion displays deserve special consideration in the framework of the current discussion. The different functions of emotion displays in a social context depend to some degree on the real or presumed social identity of the interaction partners. For example, the appeal function of different modes of emotion display can be expected to vary with group membership, as some modes may be considered less appropriate for some groups than for others. Similarly, the signal value of a specific display may vary for members of different groups. For example, Crawford, Kippax, Onyx, Gault, and Benton (1992) suggest that women's tendency to cry when angry leads men to misinterpret the women's anger as depression or helplessness, which in turn may lead to condescending behavior, which then further increases the women's anger.

In sum, appraisal theories of emotion allow for group membership influences on the appraisal process and, through this process, on the encoding of emotion displays. In addition, a consideration of the signal and appeal functions of emotions points to the possibility of different consequences for emotion displays by members of different groups. Hence knowledge of social norms regarding the display of emotions is important for selecting appropriate responses in an emotional situation, as well as for interpreting the emotion displays of an interaction partner.

Social Group Influences on the Encoding of Emotions

Based on the theoretical framework presented above, two major sources of influence of social group membership on the experience and expression of emotions can be postulated. First, social group membership influences the encoding of emotions at the level of the appraisal process—either by influencing the *perception* of the event (i.e., by guiding attention to specific elements of the situation) or by influencing the *outcome* of the emotional appraisals. For example, members of a specific group may consider themselves to be systematically in positions of low power, and thus may appraise situations as difficult to change. In this case, we would expect a tendency to show more sadness as opposed to anger in response to emotion-eliciting events that are not goal-conducive.

Second, group membership can influence the emotional display as such; that is, emotion displays may be adopted to comply with social norms or display rules that vary as a function of social group membership. In this context, differences in appeal functions (i.e., the anticipated rewards or costs for members of different groups) may moderate the level of adherence to display rules. Thus members of social groups who anticipate few costs for violating social norms should be less motivated to adhere to display rules than should members of groups who anticipate high costs for such violations (for a more detailed discussion of display rules, see Saarni, Chapter 20, this volume).

Social Group Influences on the Decoding of Emotions

Whereas social group influences on the *encoding* of emotions follow directly from appraisal theory and the literature on display rules, the influences on the *decoding* of emotions deserve a more detailed analysis. In this context it is important to bear in mind that emotion displays not only serve several functions, but also provide several types of information to the decoder. Specifically, emotion displays both signal the internal state of the sender and provide information regarding the sender's appraisal of the situation. Thus an expression of anger, for example, implies that the sender has the power to redress the wrong. Recent research on impression formation as a function of emotional expressions confirms that individuals showing anger are perceived as more dominant, whereas individuals showing happiness are perceived as more affiliative (Knudson, 1996); these perceptions are modulated by the sex and ethnicity of the target person (Hess, Blairy, & Kleck, 1999).

Furthermore, emotion displays provide information regarding the sender's behavioral intentions. Regarding this last issue, Averill (1997) has conceptualized emotional roles as analogous to social roles, and notes that emotions entrain obligations. For instance, an angry person is expected to react to redress a wrong; otherwise, the sincerity of the anger display may be doubted. From a different perspective, Frijda, Kulpers, and ter Shure (1989) discuss states of "action readiness," defined as "the individual's readiness or unreadiness to engage in interaction with the environment" (Frijda et al., 1989, p. 213). These states of action readiness describe the behavioral intentions of individuals who experience an emotional state towards their environment.

From the discussion above, it follows that the decoding of emotions via perspective taking is likely to be informed by knowledge regarding the elements of a situation that can be expected to elicit emotions, as well as by shared emotion norms and beliefs regarding the emotional expressivity of members of different groups. Specifically, when the decoder is faced with the task of interpreting the interaction partner's emotional behavior, two sources of information are available.

First, the sender's expressions (facial, vocal, postural, etc.) can be used to draw inferences regarding the presumed emotional state of the sender, via a pattern-matching approach (e.g., Buck, 1984). For example, the presence of upturned corners of the mouth and of wrinkles around the eyes can be interpreted as signaling happiness. The second source of information—the knowledge that the receiver possesses regarding both the sender and the social situation in which the interaction takes place—can take two forms. First, if the sender and the receiver know each other well, the receiver is usually aware of the sender's personality, beliefs, preferences, and emotional style. This knowledge permits the receiver to take the perspective of the sender, and thereby helps the receiver to deduce the emotional state that the sender is most likely experiencing in a given situation. For example, a given expression of happiness in a very gregarious person may be interpreted as suggesting less happiness than would the same expression shown by a person known to be very timid. Second, even when sender and receiver are meeting for the first time, the receiver may be able to employ stereotypical information to deduce some aspects of the sender's likely beliefs, personality, emotional style, etc. using information on the sender's group membership.

To summarize, emotional facial displays are polyvalent messages whose form and meaning can be modified by the social context of the situation. The conceptual framework presented above suggests that social group membership influences the encoding of emotions by predisposing individuals to pay more attention to some events than to others, to evaluate them differently, to conform their displays to the relevant social norms, or to prefer certain behaviors because they confer more advantageous consequences. Conversely, the decoder will be guided by emotion-relevant norms and beliefs in their attention to expressive displays and in their attribution of internal states based on these. That is, given that context information is used as part of the process of understanding the other (which allows one to take the other's perspective in a given situation), the social context as well as the group membership of the interaction partners can be expected to modify the interpretation of a specific expression in a specific context. Therefore, stereotype-based knowledge regarding the social group membership of the sender may be translated into decoding rules that bias the attribution of internal states to a sender. Figure 24.1 summarizes these processes.

EMPIRICAL EVIDENCE

In this section we present some evidence from the literature regarding each of the processes described above. For this we have focused on social groups described by gender, status, and culture, as well as on ingroup–outgroup distinctions.

Emotion Antecedent Appraisals

Perception of Emotion-Eliciting Events

Whereas some emotion-eliciting situations are quite simple in structure (e.g., encountering a bear in the woods), many social situations are

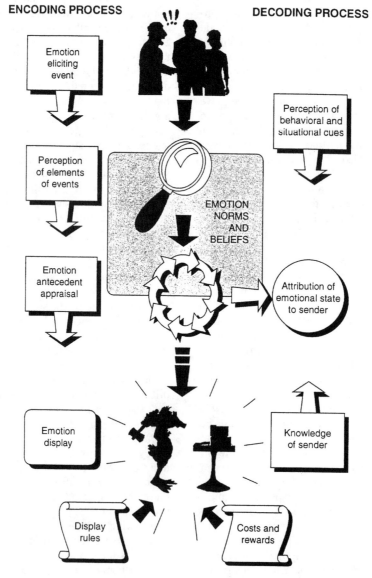

FIGURE 24.1. Summary of social group influences on the encoding and decoding of facial emotion displays.

complex and allow for the possibility that inter-actants focus on different elements of the situation both when appraising the situation and when attributing emotional states to others via perspective taking. For example, it has been noted that girls in general are more sensitive to social contexts than boys are (Meerum-Terwogt & Olthof, 1989). Similarly, Suh, Diener, Oishi, and Triandis (1998) discuss evidence that members of collectivistic cultures are more likely to attend to external, socially shared elements of an emotion stimulus, whereas members of individualistic cultures pay more attention to internal cues. They suggest that this difference in focus can lead to differences in emotional reactions and in appraisals of well-being. Thus folk theories of emotion that emphasize different aspects of a situation may lead to differences in both the encoding and decoding of emotions.

Encoding. Differences in emphasis on aspects of a situation essentially change the database for the emotional appraisal process. Thus a given situation can be considered as threatening to self-esteem when one is attending to aspects of the situation relevant to the self, but as simply tedious when attention is shifted away from the self. Hochschild (1983) describes an incident where an airline passenger threw a cup of coffee at a flight attendant, and notes the difference in perception between the airline and the flight attendant. The airline focused on the situation as an example of public contract work (and thus not a possible source of anger), whereas the flight attendant focused on the personal insult (and therefore felt angry). Kitayama, Markus, Kurokowa, and Negishi (1993, cited in Matsumoto, 1996, p. 46) report evidence that generic positive emotions (i.e., "feeling good") are associated with socially engaged feelings for Japanese students, whereas for U.S. students they are linked to socially disengaged feelings (e.g., pride). These differences may lead to differences in pleasantness appraisals, depending on whether or not social cues are present in a situation.

Decoding. Yet differences in conceptualization and attention to aspects of the situation lead to differences in emotion recognition not only with regard to self-perceptions of emotional state, but also with regard to the perception of the emotional state of others. For example, emotional displays may be interpreted as physical symptoms. Lutz (1990) describes how media reports of the emotional consequences of premenstrual syndrome lead to an interpretation of emotional reactions in line with this notion—that is, as physical symptoms rather than as emotional states. Similarly, Lillard (1998) cites evidence that members of some cultures tend to conceptualize certain types of situations (e.g., loss) in terms of illness rather than as emotion-eliciting.

In a related vein, Frijda et al. (1995) suggest that linguistic emotion categories focus the individual's attention on aspects of meaning of the environment, and thus sensitize the individual to them in line with cultural prescriptions linked to the use of these emotion words. This process may explain the finding by Matsumoto and Assar (1992) that bilingual speakers of Hindi and English decode emotional facial expressions differently when the judgments are made in Hindi as opposed to English.

Appraisal of Events

Most data on the influence of group membership on the appraisal of emotions stem from cross-cultural research focussing on the issue of the universality of emotions. Mesquita et al. (1997) suggest that cultural differences can be understood as differences in the practice of using, or propensity to use, certain appraisal dimensions. For example, Scherer (1997a, 1997b), based on data from 37 countries on different continents, concluded that although a sizable degree of similarities in appraisal profiles was found across countries, there were also some notable differences. He notes that those differences were most notable in relation to notions of agency (did the other person do this on purpose?) and justice. Frijda and Mesquita (1994) studied appraisal processes in Dutch, Turkish, and Surinamese individuals who all lived in the Netherlands. Their results point to a number of differences, including the attribution of agency. For example, Dutch subjects attributed less agency to others in anger-eliciting situations (inconsiderate behavior of others). Furthermore, Frijda et al. (1995) found strong similarities in the use of appraisal dimensions among participants from the Netherlands, Indonesia, and Japan; however, they also noted that the Japanese participants, more often than Dutch or Indonesian individuals, appraised situations as immutable and inevitable, and reported action tendencies of apathy and "desire to depend upon someone else."

Emotion Displays

Thus emotion antecedent appraisals may differ for members of different groups, and as a consequence actual emotional behavior is likely to differ. For example, we may expect that the Japanese participants in the study by Frijda et al. (1995) would also display more apathy. However, even in situations where appraisal patterns do not differ, behavioral reactions may—either because of constraints placed by display rules, or because of the anticipated consequences of emotion displays.

Display Rules

"Display rules" (Ekman & Friesen, 1969) are prescriptive and proscriptive norms for emotion displays that are pervasive and socialized early in life (see, e.g., Saarni, Chapter 20, this volume). Gallois (1994), in a recent review of emotion communication in interpersonal situations, concludes not only that interpersonal situations involving verbal and nonverbal emotional communication (such as self-disclosure or conflict) are highly rule-governed, but that the rules are perceived as normative for the interactions. Consequently, even minor violations of emotion norms can create substantial problems for the interaction process (see also Gallois, 1993, for a discussion of this issue). Three types of display rules can be distinguished.

First, normative rules exist regarding the intensity of emotion displays or the overall emotionality of a group. For example, women are generally expected to be more expressive than are men (see e.g., Brody & Hall, Chapter 22, this volume), and Asian Americans describe themselves as less emotionally expressive than other ethnic groups (Gross & John, 1995). Furthermore, it has been proposed that individuals in high power may have more latitude in their emotional expressivity (e.g., LaFrance, 1999).

Second, display rules proscribe and prescribe specific emotion displays for specific situations (e.g., solemn appearance at a funeral), as well as specific modes of expressive behavior (e.g., physically aggressive behavior in women). Finally, display rules regulate the level of emotionality for different types of social relationships. For example, Argyle (1986) investigated the relevance of each of 32 rules (e.g., "Should not use swear words in the presence of the other person") for different social relationships (e.g.,

persons living together, work colleagues, repair technician and client). Although strong similarities were found across Hong Kong, Japan, Italy, and Britain, some differences emerged. Specifically, Japanese subjects endorsed rules for restraining emotional expressiveness (e.g., "Should not show anger in front of the other person") for a larger number of relationship types than did members of Western cultures, whereas Italian subjects tended to endorse rules prescribing emotional expressiveness for a larger number of relationships. Aune, Buller, and Aune (1996) describe how rules for the expression of positive and negative emotions change over the course of the development of romantic relationships, and they note sex differences for the display of emotions as relationships progress from dating to more developed relationships.

In sum, display rules govern a large number of social interactions, and they have a pervasive influence on the intensity of the expressions shown, on what is shown to whom, and on the specific mode of emotion expression. Conversely, display rules also provide information regarding the expected emotional behavior in a given situation. This information can be used for the decoding of emotion displays and for the attribution of internal states to the sender. It is thus useful to consider display rules as rules for both the encoding and the decoding process. We briefly present some empirical evidence for the influence of display rules on both processes.

Encoding Rules. Research on cultural differences in display rules has mostly been guided by Hofstede's (1980) four dimensions of cultural variation—specifically, the individualism–collectivism dimension (see also Markus & Kitayama, 1991; Triandis, 1994). Specifically, it has been suggested that collectivistic cultures endorse emotion displays that foster group harmony (e.g., Matsumoto, 1991), whereas individualistic cultures may be more open to expressions of conflict (Triandis, Bontempo, Villareal, Asai, & Lucca, 1988).

For example, Matsumoto (1990) found that U.S. Americans (individualistic culture) considered the display of disgust and sadness toward members of the outgroup as well as of happiness in public as more appropriate than did Japanese (collectivistic culture), who in turn rated the display of anger to members of the outgroup as well as to lower-status individuals as more appropriate. Also, Stephan, Stephan, and de Vargas (1996) report evidence that participants from Costa Rica, a collectivist culture, expected to feel equally comfortable expressing emotions to both ingroup and outgroup members, whereas participants from the United States, an individualistic culture, expected to feel more comfortable expressing emotions to family members than to strangers.

Another social group characteristic that has been studied in the context of emotion norms is status. For example, the expression of anger is more permissible for high-authority individuals than for those with low authority (see e.g., Averill, 1997). Coats and Feldman (1996) found that high-status men tended to be more expressive of anger than low-status men; however, high-status women tended to be more expressive of happiness than low-status women. Conversely, based on ethological findings, smiling is a sign of appeasement (e.g., Preuschoft & van Hooff, 1997; Henley, 1977). Hence, individuals low in status may be expected to smile more. Dovidio, Brown, Heltman, Ellyson, and Keating (1988) confirmed this notion for men: They found that subordinate men smiled more, whereas no difference was found for women. Deutsch (1990) reports similar findings.

Decoding Rules. Less attention has been devoted to the influence of display rules on the decoding of emotions. However, when an observer is employing perspective taking, knowledge about the sender's expected behavior in a given situation is highly useful. This knowledge can be based on actual knowledge of the other person. For example, Colvin, Vogt, and Ickes (1997) note that individuals who know each other well may actually dispense to some degree with paying close attention to the interaction partner's actual behavior, and instead base their attributions on their knowledge of the other person. This may explain why after a certain length of acquaintance empathic accuracy, which initially increases with length of acquaintanceship, decreases again (Colvin et al., 1997). But even when sender and receiver are meeting for the first time, the receiver may be able to employ stereotypical information about the sender's group membership to deduce some aspects of the sender's likely beliefs, personality, emotional style, and so forth. In this context, Karniol's (1990) model of the process involved in predicting others' internal states is useful.

Among the important elements of this model are information about situations and the behavior they elicit, group stereotypes and the behavior of prototypical group members, and information about specific individuals. For the special case of attributions of emotions to others, stereotypical knowledge about the emotional style of members of a specific group provides relevant information. That is, knowing that the sender is male or female or is a member of a specific ethnic group may elicit knowledge regarding the display rules appropriate to the situation, as well as stereotypical knowledge regarding the emotional style of members of the relevant group.

For example, many people share the stereotype that individuals from the northern part of a given country are less emotional than those from the southern part of the country (Pennebaker, Rimé, & Blankenship, 1996). Hence, an expression of, for example, anger shown by a person with a northern accent may be considered to indicate a more intense emotional state than a similar expression by a person with a southern accent, for whom such expressions are considered more typical.

A number of studies have in fact shown that norms regarding the general emotional expressivity of a group influence the attribution of intensity of emotional states by members of this group. Hess, Blairy, and Kleck (1997) report evidence that emotional expressions are judged to express an emotion more or less intensely, depending on whether the sender is a man or a woman. This influence of rules for levels of emotionality on the decoding of emotion displays is further illustrated by a study showing that Japanese participants attribute lower intensity to emotional expressions by senders of both Japanese and European descent (Matsumoto & Ekman, 1989). Matsumoto and Ekman conclude that the dominant display rules lead the Japanese subjects to discount the intensity of emotion displays. Similar findings were reported by Ekman et al. (1987), who found that Asians rated the facial expressions of happiness, fear, and surprise shown by non-Asian stimulus persons as less intense than did non-Asian raters. Also, Pittam, Gallois, Iwawaki, and Kroonenberg (1995) found that while the same dimensional structure explained both Japanese and Australian subjects' concepts of emotion expression for eight emotions, generally, both Japanese and Australian subjects rated Japanese individuals as less emotionally expressive. Conversely, Matsumoto (1993) found that African Americans perceived greater intensity when judging emotions.

Similarly, members of cultures that proscribe the expression of anger have been found to be less efficient in decoding anger expressions. For example, MacAndrew (1986) found that Malaysian decoders required considerably longer exposure times to accurately recognize anger in tachistoscopically presented expressions than did U.S. decoders. Furthermore, Matsumoto (1992) found Japanese participants to be less accurate in recognizing anger than U.S. participants.

However, norms for restricted emotion expression need not always lead to less accurate judgments. For example, Markham and Wang (1996) note that in a society that restricts the range of acceptable behaviors, knowledge of acceptable emotion displays eliminates choices, thus facilitating the decoding of prototypical emotion expressions such as those used in emotion research. Consistent with this view, Markham and Wang (1996) found Chinese children to be better at decoding emotional expressions of six basic emotions than Australian children.

As mentioned above, people associate different personality traits with different emotion displays; for example, individuals showing anger are rated as more dominant. However, the sex and ethnicity of the sender modulate these attributions. Hess et al. (1999) found, for example, that although both men and women who showed fear were rated as less dominant than those who showed anger, the decrease in perceived dominance was less marked for women. This difference in rated dominance of men and women showing anger versus fear was even more pronounced for Japanese stimulus persons. Furthermore, studying the influence of the ethnicity of the decoder, Matsumoto and Kudoh (1993) found that whereas U.S. participants tended to rate smiling individuals as not only more sociable but also more intelligent and attractive, Japanese participants rated them as only more sociable.

In sum, norms regarding emotion displays influence both the encoding and the decoding of emotion displays. In addition, they may influence the attribution of personality traits to the sender. Such influences may have important consequences for interpersonal relationships. In this context, Brunel (1989) argues that therapists find it more difficult to be empathic to-

ward members of another group, be it another ethnic group or even just the other sex.

Consequences of Emotion Displays

The anticipated consequences of displaying certain emotions or of choosing certain modes of emotion expression can influence the degree of adherence to display rules, and the motivating influences of different rewards may be different for different social groups. The importance of the anticipated consequences of certain emotional displays for the encoding of emotions can be seen in the socialization of display norms. For example, Zeman and Garber (1996) report that children's primary reasons to control certain emotion expressions, such as (for boys especially) pain or sadness, were the anticipated negative interpersonal consequences of disclosing these emotions. Davis (1995) investigated possible reasons for the greater expression of negative affect by boys in the "disappointing gift" paradigm and found that when boys were motivated to mask negative affect by self-gain (in a game task), they reduced their expression of negative affect; however, girls were still better at masking negative affect.

Similar effects have been observed for adults. Thus Stoppard and Gruchy (1993) investigated the anticipated costs and rewards of either expressing or not expressing positive emotions in self- and other-oriented contexts. They found that women expected more costs when not expressing positive emotions in other-oriented contexts, but no differences whether they did or did not express positive emotions in self-directed contexts. Men, however, always expected more rewards when expressing positive emotions, regardless of context.

The expression of certain emotions can have quite tangible consequences. Looking at a different type of attributional consequence, Heise (1989) suggest that lively emotion displays may moderate stigmatization based on deviant conduct. Similarly, a study by LaFrance and Hecht (1995) suggests that individuals who smile are perceived as trustworthier and may thus receive more leniency when committing transgressions.

More generally, higher emotional expressiveness has been associated with more positive evaluations. For example, Riggio and Friedman (1986) found that men who scored higher on measures of nonverbal skill and extraversion showed more fluid expressive behavior and made better impressions on judges, while women who scored higher on a measure of nonverbal skill showed more facial expressiveness and created more favorable first impressions.

Also, certain expressive modes (e.g., crying when angry) are more permissible, and thus more likely to procure positive effects, for women than for men (Crawford et al., 1992; see also Shields, 1987). Deffenbacher, Oetting, Lynch, and Morris (1996) investigated both the different forms of anger expression and anger consequences; they found gender differences in the anticipation of consequences, based on the *mode* of anger expression chosen. The emphasis here is not on the notion that the expression of anger per se is proscribed, but rather on the choice of a particular type of expression.

SOCIALIZATION

Emotional styles and display rules tend to be transmitted explicitly by instructions from parents, as well as more subtly by means of differences in interactive styles. In fact, part of the process of the socialization of emotions is the acquisition of knowledge regarding which situations elicit what emotion, how different emotions are expressed in a socially acceptable manner, and how to react to the emotion displays of others (see Saarni, Chapter 20, this volume). Some display rules are taught quite explicitly—for example, when parents admonish their children to show pleasure at a gift, or to express displeasure by talking to the offending other instead of using their fists. However, other, more subtle influences are also at work. For example, Goldschmidt (1997) discusses a study by Grossmann, Fremmer-Bombik, & Rudolph (1988), who measured attachment styles in two German cities—one in the north (a region known for its restrained emotional style) and one in the south (where a more open emotional style is encouraged). Goldschmidt draws attention to the fact that only 30% of children from northern Germany showed a secure attachment style, as opposed to 58% in the south. These findings were paralleled by the adult attachment styles of the mothers. Goldschmidt suggests the difference in attachment style as a means of socializing the "cultural tone" differences between the two regions. As regards the socialization of gender differences, there is evidence that parents' emotion language differs as a function of children's gender. In general, parents and siblings talk more about emotions (Dunn, Bretherton, & Munn, 1987) and more about certain types of emotions (e.g., sadness) with girls than with boys (e.g., Adams, Kuebli, Boyle, & Fivush, 1995).

SUMMARY AND CONCLUSIONS

Social group membership influences the expression of emotions on different levels. First, shared beliefs about the nature of emotion-eliciting events can attract attention to certain elements of a social situation rather than others, and thus can influence the database for emotion antecedent appraisals. Second, social group membership may influence the outcome of appraisal processes. Third, shared display rules modulate the expression of certain emotions as well as the mode of emotion expression. Finally, anticipated consequences may modulate adherence to display rules. Emotion expressions also influence person perception processes, and hence some emotional displays may be rewarded by entraining a more positive evaluation of the sender.

Social group membership further influences the decoding of emotion displays—that is, the attribution of internal states to the sender. Thus cultural norms and gender-specific emotion norms bias the recognition of specific emotions in specific contexts or by members of a specific group. Such biases influence the accuracy with which certain emotions are decoded in contexts where these expressions are proscribed. Furthermore, these norms have been shown to bias the *intensity* of the underlying state that is attributed to a certain emotion display. Emotion norms may lead members of a culture to ascribe less intensity to displays of culturally disapproved emotion displays, as well as to ascribe different levels of intensity to similar emotion displays shown by men and women. This bias may also lead to failures to recognize certain displays correctly, especially those of medium to low intensity.

On one hand, the failure to recognize proscribed emotion displays may have positive effects on everyday interactions. As Ickes and Simpson (1997) note with regard to empathic accuracy in couples, it is not always a good idea for one partner to know exactly what the other feels, especially when the feeling is based on difficult-to-reconcile differences in outlook.

However, in other contexts the failure to recognize an emotional state or the misjudgment of its intensity may entrain negative consequences for future interactions.

One should note that most research on the encoding and decoding of emotional states as a function of social group membership has been conducted on "pure" emotions and has used intense prototypical expressions. This has specific implications for culture-based group differences, as it has been argued that subordinate levels of emotion, characterized by differences in intensity, are more likely to be culture-specific. For example, different levels of fear, such as alarm, anxiety, and dread, may be more likely to reflect cultural differences (e.g., Shaver, Wu, & Schwarz, 1992; see Izard, 1994). This is of growing importance in today's increasingly multicultural environment. Moreover, gender- and status-based differences tend to interact with cultural differences such that, for example, gender-based display rules may be more salient in some cultures than others. Given that emotion rules can be transmitted in quite subtle ways, it may not be always easy for members of different cultures to know the types of rules that underlie the emotional behavior of others.

Future research on these issues should address two questions in particular. First, does the influence of emotion-relevant stereotypes for members of particular groups extend from encounters with strangers to situations where the interaction partners know each other? Findings by Gaelick, Bodenhausen, and Wyer (1985) regarding the different interpretation of neutral facial expressions by husbands and wives suggest that it may. Also, Karniol's (1990) model posits that generalized knowledge about situations is always relevant. Specifically, she suggests that when specific knowledge about a person is available, observers make predictions based on both generalized and specific knowledge and have to find an intersection between the two types of knowledge. However, most studies on emotion recognition in interaction with close others have focused on conflictual relationships, and more extensive research looking at a wider range of expressions in relationships not characterized by marital distress is clearly needed.

Second, the question arises whether the observed differences in the perceived intensity of emotion expression as well as in decoding accuracy across social groups translate into quali-tative differences in the attribution of emotional states (e.g., displeasure vs. irritation vs. animosity vs. anger) and, more importantly, into differences in the attribution of intentions to the sender.

In conclusion, we have presented a framework for the integration of social group influences on the display and recognition of emotions into current thinking about emotion processes. This framework is based on appraisal theories of emotion, which distinguish between the treatment of information by emotion antecedent appraisal processes on the one hand, and the expressive component of emotional states as well as behavioral intentions on the other hand. Socially shared emotion norms and beliefs within a group can (1) filter information before appraisal, (2) bias appraisal processes, (3) proscribe and prescribe specific expressive modes, and (4) differentially reward adherence to display norms. Conversely, these shared norms and beliefs also influence the decoding process in a parallel fashion, either by filtering the situational information that is considered for emotion attributions or by facilitating attributions in concordance with expected displays.

This framework may help to structure future research in this field—research that in a global context demanding increased interactions between different groups is of increasing importance.

ACKNOWLEDGMENT

Preparation of this chapter was supported in part by a grant from the Conseil de Recherche en Science Humaine to Ursula Hess and Gilles Kirouac.

REFERENCES

Adams, S., Kuebli, J., Boyle, P. A., & Fivush, R. (1995). Gender differences in parent–child conversations about past emotions: A longitudinal investigation. *Sex Roles, 33,* 309–323.

Argyle, M. (1986). Rules for social relationships in four cultures. *Australian Journal of Psychology, 38,* 309–318.

Aune, K. S., Buller, D. B., & Aune, R. K. (1996). Display rule development in romantic relationships: Emotion management and perceived appropriateness of emotions across relationship stages. *Human Communication Research, 23,* 115–145.

Averill, J. R. (1997). The emotions: An integrative approach. In R. Hogan, J. A. Johnson, & S. R. Briggs (Eds.), *Handbook of personality psychology* (pp. 513–541). San Diego, CA: Academic Press.

Brunel, M. L. (1989). L'empathie en counseling interculturel. *Santé Mentale au Québec, 14,* 81–94.

Buck, R. (1984). *The communication of emotion.* New York: Guilford Press.

Bühler, K. (1934). *Sprachtheorie.* Jena, Germany: Fischer.

Burkitt, I. (1997). Social relationships and emotions. *Sociology, 31,* 37–55.

Coats, E. J., & Feldman, R. S. (1996). Gender differences in nonverbal correlates of social status. *Personality and Social Psychology Bulletin, 22,* 1014–1022.

Colvin, C. R., Vogt, D., & Ickes, W. (1997). Why do friends understand each other better than strangers do? In W. Ickes (Ed.), *Empathic accuracy* (pp. 169–193). New York: Guilford Press.

Crawford, J., Kippax, S., Onyx, J., Gault, U., & Benton, P. (1992). *Emotion and gender: Constructing meaning from memory.* London: Sage.

Darwin, C. (1965). *The expression of the emotions in man and animals.* Chicago: University of Chicago Press. (Original work published, 1872)

Davis, T. L. (1995). Gender differences in masking negative emotions: Ability or motivation? *Developmental Psychology, 31,* 660–667.

Deffenbacher, J. L., Oetting, E. R., Lynch, R. S., & Morris, C. D. (1996). The expression of anger and its consequences. *Behaviour Research and Therapy, 34,* 575–590.

Deutsch, F. M. (1990). Status, sex, and smiling: The effect of role on smiling in men and women. *Personality and Social Psychology Bulletin, 16,* 531–540.

Dovidio, J. F., Brown, C. E., Heltman, K., Ellyson, S. L., & Keating, C. F. (1988). Power displays between women and men in discussion of gender-linked tasks: A multichannel study. *Journal of Personality and Social Psychology, 55,* 580–587.

Dunn, J., Bretherton, I., & Munn, P. (1987). Conversations about feeling states between mothers and their children. *Developmental Psychology, 23,* 132–139.

Ekman, P. (1992). An argument for basic emotions. *Cognition and Emotion, 6,* 169–200.

Ekman, P., & Friesen, W. V. (1969). The repertoire of nonverbal behavior: Categories, origins, usage, and coding. *Semiotics, 1,* 49–98.

Ekman, P., Friesen, W. V., O'Sullivan, M., Chan, A., Diacoyanni-Tarlatzis, I., Heider, K., Krause, R., LeCompte, W. A., Pitcairn, T., Ricci-Bitti, P. E., Scherer, K., Tomita, M., & Tzavaras, A. (1987). Universals and cultural differences in the judgements of facial expressions of emotion. *Journal of Personality and Social Psychology, 53,* 712–717.

Frijda, N. (1986). *The emotions.* Cambridge, England: Cambridge University Press.

Frijda, N. H., Kuipers, P., & ter Shure, E. (1989). Relations among emotion appraisal and emotional action readiness. *Journal of Personality and Social Psychology, 57,* 212–228.

Frijda, N., Markam, S., Sato, K., & Wiers, R. (1995). Emotions and emotion words. In J. A. Russell, J.-H. Fernández-Dols, A. S. R. Manstead, & J. C.

Wellenkamp (Eds.), *Everyday conceptions of emotion* (pp. 121–143). Dordrecht, The Netherlands: Kluwer.

Frijda, N. H., & Mesquita, B. (1994). The social roles and functions of emotions. In S. Kitayama & H. R. Markus (Eds.), *Emotion and culture: Empirical studies of mutual influence* (pp. 51–87). Washington, DC: American Psychological Association.

Gaelick, L., Bodenhausen, G. V., & Wyer, R. S. (1985). Emotional communication in close relationships. *Journal of Personality and Social Psychology, 49,* 1246–1265.

Gallois, C. (1993). The language and communication of emotion. *American Behavioral Scientist, 36,* 309–338.

Gallois, C. (1994). Group membership, social rules, and power: A social psychological perspective on emotional communication. *Journal of Pragmatics, 22,* 301–324.

Goldschmidt, W. (1997). *Nonverbal communication and culture.* In U. Segerståle & P. Molnár (Eds.), Nonverbal communication: Where nature meets culture (pp. 229–244). Mahwah, NJ: Erlbaum.

Gross, J. J., & John, O. P. (1995). Facets of emotional expressivity: Three self-report factors and their correlates. *Personality and Individual Differences, 19,* 555–568.

Grossmann, K., Fremmer-Bombik, E., & Rudolph, J. (1988). Maternal attachment representations as related to patterns of infant–mother attachment and maternal acre during the first year. In R. A. Hinde & J. Stevenson-Hinde (Eds.), *Relationships within families: Mutual influences* (pp. 241–260). Oxford: Clarendon Press.

Heise, D. R. (1989). Effect of emotion display on social identification. *Social Psychology Quarterly, 52,* 10–21.

Heise, D. R., & Calhan, C. (1995). Emotion norms in interpersonal events. *Social Psychology Quarterly, 58,* 223–240.

Henley, N. M. (1977). *Body politics: Power, sex and nonverbal communication.* Newark, NJ: Prentice-Hall.

Hess, U., Banse, R., & Kappas, A. (1995). The intensity of facial expression is determined by underlying affective state and social situation. *Journal of Personality and Social Psychology, 69,* 280–288.

Hess, U., Blairy, S., & Kleck, R. E. (1997). The relationship between the intensity of emotional facial expressions and observers' decoding. *Journal of Nonverbal Behavior, 21,* 241–257.

Hess, U., Blairy, S., & Kleck, R. E. (1998). *The influence of expression intensity, gender, and ethnicity on judgments of dominance and affiliation.* Manuscript submitted for publication.

Hochschild, A. (1983). *The managed heart.* Berkeley: University of California Press.

Hofstede, G. (1980). *Culture's consequences: International differences in work-related values.* Beverly Hills, CA: Sage.

Ickes, W., & Simpson, J. A. (1997). Managing empathic accuracy in close relationships. In W. Ickes (Ed.), *Empathic accuracy* (pp. 218–250). New York: Guilford Press.

Izard, C. E. (1994). Innate and universal facial expressions: Evidence from developmental and cross-cultural research. *Psychological Bulletin, 115,* 288–299.

Karniol, R. (1990). Reading people's minds: A transformation rule model for predicting others' thoughts and feelings. In M. P. Zanna (Ed.), *Advances in experimental social psychology* (Vol. 23, pp. 211–247). San Diego, CA: Academic Press.

Kemper, T. D. (1990). Social relations and emotions: A structural approach. In T. D. Kemper (Ed.), *Research agendas in the sociology of emotion* (pp. 207–237). Albany: State University of New York Press.

Knudson, B. (1996). Facial expressions of emotion influence interpersonal trait inferences. *Journal of Nonverbal Behavior, 20,* 165–182.

LaFrance, M. (1999). Obligated to smile: The effects of power and gender on facial expression. In P. Philippot, R. Feldman, & E. Coats (Eds.), *The social context of nonverbal behavior* (pp. 45–70). Cambridge, England: Cambridge University Press.

LaFrance, M., & Hecht, M. A. (1995). Why smiles generate leniency. *Personality and Social Psychology Bulletin, 21,* 207–214.

Lillard, A. (1998). Ethnopsychologies: Cultural variations in theories of mind. *Psychological Bulletin, 123,* 3–32.

Lutz, C. (1988). *Unnatural emotions: Everyday sentiments on a Micronesian atoll and their challenge to Western theory.* Chicago: University of Chicago Press.

Lutz, C. A. (1990). Engendered emotion: Gender, power, and the rhetoric of emotional control in American discourse. In C. A. Lutz & L. Abu-Lughod (Eds.), *Language and the politics of emotion. Studies in emotion and social interaction* (pp. 69–91). Cambridge, England: Cambridge University Press.

MacAndrew, F. T. (1986). A cross-cultural study of recognition thresholds for facial expressions of emotion. *Journal of Cross-Cultural Psychology, 17,* 211–224.

Markham, R., & Wang, L. (1996). Recognition of emotion by Chinese and Australian children. *Journal of Cross-Cultural Psychology, 27,* 616–643.

Markus, H. R., & Kitayama, S. (1991). Culture and the self: Implications for cognition, emotion, and motivation. *Psychological Review, 98,* 224–253.

Matsumoto, D. (1990). Cultural similarities and differences in display rules. *Motivation and Emotion, 14,* 195–214.

Matsumoto, D. (1991). Cultural influences on facial expressions of emotions. *Southern Communication Journal, 56,* 128–137.

Matsumoto, D. (1992). American–Japanese differences in the recognition of universal facial expressions. *Journal of Cross-Cultural Psychology, 23,* 72–84.

Matsumoto, D. (1993). Ethnic differences in affect intensity, emotion judgments, display rule attitudes, and self-reported emotional expression in an American sample. *Motivation and Emotion, 17,* 107–123.

Matsumoto, D. (1996). *Culture and psychology.* Pacific Grove, CA: Brooksdale.

Matsumoto, D., & Assar, M. (1992). The effects of language on judgments of universal facial expressions of emotion. *Journal of Nonverbal Behavior, 16,* 85–99.

Matsumoto, D., & Ekman, P. (1989). American–Japanese differences in intensity ratings of facial expressions of emotion. *Motivation and Emotion, 13,* 143–157.

Matsumoto, D., & Kudoh, T. (1993). American–Japanese cultural differences in attribution of personality based on smiles. *Journal of Nonverbal Behavior, 17,* 231–243.

Meerum-Terwogt, M., & Olthof, T. (1989). Awareness and self-regulation of emotion in young children. In C. Saarni & P. L. Harris (Eds.), *Children's understanding of emotion* (pp. 209–237). New York: Cambridge University Press.

Mesquita, B., Frijda, N. H., & Scherer, K. R. (1997). Culture and emotion. In J. W. Berry (Ed.), *Handbook of cross-cultural psychology: Vol. 2. Basic processes and human development* (pp. 254–297). Boston: Allyn & Bacon.

Pennebaker, J. W., Rimé, B., & Blankenship, V. E. (1996). Stereotypes of emotional expressiveness of northerners and southerners: A cross-cultural test of Montesquieu's hypothesis. Journal of Personality and Social Psychology, 70, 372–380.

Pittam, J., Gallois, C., Iwawaki, S., & Kroonenberg, P. (1995). Australian and Japanese concepts of expressive behavior. *Journal of Cross-Cultural Psychology, 26,* 451–473.

Preuschoft, S., & van Hooff, J. A. R. A. M. (1997). The social function of "smile" and "laughter": Variations across primate species and societies. In U. Segerståle & P. Molnár (Eds.), *Nonverbal communication: Where nature meets culture* (pp. 171–190). Mahwah, NJ: Erlbaum.

Reddy, W. M. (1997). Against constructionism: The historical ethnography of emotions. *Current Anthropology, 38,* 327–351.

Riggio, R. E., & Friedman, H. S. (1986). Impression formation: The role of expressive behavior. *Journal of Personality and Social Psychology, 50,* 421–427.

Russell, J. A. (1991). Culture and the organization of emotions. *Psychological Bulletin, 110,* 426–450.

Scherer, K. R. (1986). Vocal affect expression: A review and a model for future research. *Psychological Bulletin, 99,* 143–165.

Scherer, K. R. (1997a). Profiles of emotion-antecedent appraisal: Testing theoretical predictions across cultures. *Cognition and Emotion, 11,* 113–150.

Scherer, K. R. (1997b). The role of culture in emotion-antecedent appraisal. *Journal of Personality and Social Psychology, 73,* 902–922.

Shaver, P. R., Wu, S., & Schwarz, J. C. (1992). Cross-cultural similarities and differences in emotion and its representation: A prototype approach. In M. S. Clark (Ed.), *Review of personality and social psychology: Vol. 13. Emotion* (pp. 175–212). Newbury Park, CA: Sage.

Shields, S. A. (1987). Women, men, and the dilemma of emotion. In P. Shaver & C. Kendrick (Eds.), *Sex and gender* (pp. 229–250). Newbury Park, CA: Sage.

Stephan, W. G., Stephan, C. W., & de Vargas, M. C. (1996). Emotional expression in Costa Rica and the United States. *Journal of Cross-Cultural Psychology, 27,* 147–160.

Stoppard, J. M., & Gruchy, C. D. (1993). Gender, context, and expression of positive emotion. *Personality and Social Psychology Bulletin, 19,* 143–150.

Suh, E., Diener, E., Oishi, S., & Triandis, H. C. (1998). The shifting basis of life satisfaction judgments across cultures: Emotions versus norms. *Journal of Personality and Social Psychology, 74,* 482–493.

Triandis, H. C. (1994). Cultural syndromes and emotion. In S. Kitayama & H. R. Markus (Eds.), *Emotion and culture: Empirical studies of mutual influence* (pp. 285–306). Washington, DC: American Psychological Association.

Triandis, H. C., Bontempo, R., Villareal, M. J., Asai, M., & Lucca, N. (1988). Individualism and collectivism: Cross-cultural perspectives on self–ingroup relationships. *Journal of Personality and Social Psychology, 54,* 323–338.

Turner, J. H. (1997). The evolution of emotions: The nonverbal basis of human social organization. In U. Segerstråle & P. Molár (Eds.), *Nonverbal communication: Where nature meets culture* (pp. 211–223). Mahwah, NJ: Erlbaum.

Wierzbicka, A. (1995). The relevance of language to the study of emotions. *Psychological Inquiry, 6,* 248–252.

Zeman, J., & Garber, J. (1996). Display rules for anger, sadness, and pain: It depends on who is watching. *Child Development, 67,* 957–973

CHAPTER 25

Temperament as an Emotion Construct: Theoretical and Practical Issues

John E. Bates

This chapter discusses the construct of temperament. Individual differences in emotional phenomena are the essence of temperament and personality concepts. Emotions, emotion regulation, and their development are the main focus in temperament research, as highlighted well by Goldsmith (1993) in the chapter on temperament in the first edition of the *Handbook* (Lewis & Haviland, 1993). The present chapter focuses on temperament concepts in developmental research, as did Goldsmith's still authoritative chapter, but it puts greater emphasis on emotion and temperament concepts most relevant to clinical developmental psychology. This chapter asks: What are emotion and temperament, how do they help explain children's individual differences in adjustment, and what hints do they give for practical problem solving?

CONCEPTS OF EMOTION AND TEMPERAMENT

Emotion

The concept of "emotion" in this chapter, based on recent definitions, centers on emotional events at multiple levels, including brief events, extended moods, and stable predispositions to particular emotional states. Descriptions of emotional states represent every level of theory, from biochemical process to social system (Cole, Michel, & Teti, 1994; Eisenberg, 1998; Goldsmith, 1993; Lazarus, 1991; Lewis, 1993; Saarni, Mumme, & Campos, 1998). The most frequently encountered view of emotion in the developmental psychology literature ultimately focuses upon the social, adaptive functions of emotion. This multilevel, functionalist view of emotion, highly compatible with the present chapter's view of temperament, is consistent with the long-standing conceptual links between emotion and temperament (e.g., Lewis & Michalson, 1983).

Emotion events have a complex set of properties. Properties often mentioned include, first, basic motivational conditions that interact with environmental incentives to produce emotional events. These conditions are basic in the sense that they can occur without verbal or self-conscious ability, as can be seen in studies of very young humans (Goldsmith, 1993) and rats (Blass, 1992). These are such things as an impulse to dominate, the anger one feels at being thwarted, the gravitation toward other people, or the distress of separation. A second property of emotion is that emotions are events happening in the material reality of the brain—bound by all the known and unknown laws of material reality, including neural firings in particular locations and times, neurochemicals interacting with brain tissue, genes unfolding in actions with and upon the systems of the body, and genes responding to both bodily and environmental changes. All these events occur not only in moments of time, but also in a developmental process.

A third property is that these events happen at a cognitive level—a meaningful pattern of neural events that in a way transcends the neural events. This transcendence is not only in the form of information, but also in the form of action directed back upon the emotions, their regulation, and the reactions from the environment. Emotional events can be cognitive without being consciously verbalized. A fourth property, however, is that emotions are often perceived in terms of verbally coded meanings. There are many words for emotion events, indicating that humans are intensely interested in emotion distinctions. Artistic and psychological observers depict many variations in the ways emotions arise, are experienced, and are resolved (Lazarus, 1991).

A fifth property is that emotions are transactional. Emotional events usually happen as part of social transactions, even if those transactions are happening in symbolic space. Society and culture are often seen as reflecting and shaping people's emotional characteristics, by providing opportunities and threats and by teaching meanings of environmental stimuli. Developmentally oriented clinicians are especially interested in the shaping that may occur. One family, for example, may teach that insults call for aggressive retaliation, while another may teach that verbal insults should be ignored. Families and peers are thought to influence values and provide models for expression and regulation of emotions (e.g., Katz & Gottman, 1997; Mize & Pettit, 1997).

A sixth and final aspect of emotion is that people are often active agents in constructing their effective environment—in selecting the emotion stimuli with which they interact. They make these choices through very basic, nonreflective motivational and attentional processes (Patterson & Newman, 1992; Rothbart & Bates, 1998), as well as through conscious choices (Maslow, 1968). Clinicians know people who habitually amplify stress responses by intensely focusing on thoughts that elicit negative emotions and by ignoring positive elements of a situation (Kramer, 1993). There are many

traditional methods of promoting and inhibiting emotions (e.g., admonitions, adventure seeking, alcohol, appeals to God, and art, merely to start the list). Choices also occur at a societal level: For example, society considers how and whether to modulate the roots of certain styles of adjustment, especially maladaptive patterns of aggression and depression—two especially important forces of human nature. Individual choice is a challenge to scientific research, because it is often hard to explain even post hoc and even harder to predict a priori. In actuality, however, despite many possibilities for change, research on personality and adjustment shows substantial degrees of continuity (e.g., Caspi, 1998). On the other hand, again, however, environments do sometimes change, and so apparently do people's motivations and self-regulatory approaches. Continuity and change are essentially two ways of looking at the same topic.

How do continuities in personality occur? Findings of continuity may reflect continuity in biological, cultural, and social factors, as well as psychological factors. In many instances one can point to the adaptive value of the styles of behavior, whether adaptation occurs through assimilation of the environment or accommodation to it. Behaviors that succeed are likely to be kept. Just as in culture itself (Fischer, 1989; see especially p. 896), continuity in a child's personality or adjustment is not really a stasis, but rather reflects many things happening (Caspi, 1998). Cultures and subcultures and family systems directly shape ways of emotional interpretation and expression, and they intentionally moderate individual traits. Genotypic characteristics of the child, such as negative affectivity, can elicit feelings from others (e.g., reciprocal negativity) that in turn fully exercise the child's predisposition. Likewise, children can select environments that are consistent with their adaptive characteristics, as in the case of the highly active and physically fearless person who selects vigorous, dangerous activities.

Discontinuities in personality are perhaps less frequent than continuities, but they are nevertheless quite interesting. They can theoretically come from many sources. Some may reflect purposeful change. For example, an explorative child may learn to modulate approach impulses for the sake of social success. Nontraditional methods, such as clinical interventions, are also increasingly available. Interventions can be based on increasingly precise notions of neural systems and of the particular motivational and self-regulatory characteristics associated with diagnostic categories (e.g., Julien, 1995). In addition to biological interventions, there are also empirically supported psychosocial interventions directed at the regulatory systems in both the environment and in the child, via verbal/cognitive instruction as well as via reward, nonreward, and punishment of behavior (e.g., Fleischman, Horne, & Arthur, 1983; Hembree-Kigin & McNeil, 1995). These treatments do not deny temperament, but they do not focus on it. Psychosocial interventions that do focus on measures of emotion patterns, emotion regulation patterns, and temperament are still at an experimental stage. They are discussed after further discussion of emotion and temperament and their role in development.

In thinking further about the general construct of emotion, it may be useful to consider the obvious fact that emotion research deals in hypothetical constructs. Emotion constructs attempt to capture a measurable sense of very complex events, and ultimately, let us hope, to evolve toward an artful science. The generic construct of "emotion" is an umbrella term. Specific emotions do have conceptual qualities linking them together in the class of emotion, but the most important scientific and practical work happens at the level of more specific emotion concepts. These points are true of temperament too (Bates, 1989b; Rothbart & Bates, 1998).

Lists of primary emotions usually include positive emotions classified as contentment and joy, and negative emotions classed as distress, disgust, anger, fear, and sadness (Lewis, 1993). Also primary, but perhaps conceptually separable from both positive and negative groupings, are interest and surprise. The primary emotions appear, with neural and cognitive development, over the first 8 months of infancy; the negative emotions further differentiate over the next few years, with continued neural and cognitive development, into self-conscious emotions of shame, pride, and guilt (Lewis, 1993; Nelson, 1994). The primary emotions can be linked in complex ways to particular neural structures, including systems for detecting and approaching reward stimuli, for social bonding, for responding with fight or flight to unconditioned pain and frustration stimuli, for detecting conditioned signals of danger or nonreward and inhibiting behavior, and for regulating the automatic and executive focusing of attention (Rothbart, Derryberry, & Posner, 1994; Rothbart & Bates, 1998). Individual differences in these same systems are the neural bases for temperament. And individual differences in emotional behavior patterns are intimately involved in the process of adjustment.

Temperament

The most basic definition of "temperament" is that it is a set of biologically rooted, early-appearing, and relatively stable individual differences in reactivity to stimuli and self-regulation of that reactivity (Rothbart & Bates, 1998). As pointed out by Goldsmith (1993), the emotions most relevant to the construct of temperament are the more "basic" kinds of emotional reactions (such as the families of emotions classed as fear, joy, or anger), as opposed to the more "advanced" emotions (such as guilt). Emotions' intensity, sensitivity to environmental triggers, and ease of resolution are also aspects of temperament. Emotion characteristics, based partly in temperament, are major components of the construct of "personality." The most frequently cited distinction between temperament and personality is that personality includes dispositions toward more developmentally advanced and complex states such as aesthetic emotions (Lazarus, 1991), as well as cognitive/verbal modes of emotion regulation, such as goals, values, and learned responses. Despite this established definition, there is evidence that differences in rate of early development of advanced emotions can build at least partially on the foundation of a basic-emotion trait. Lewis and Ramsay (1997) showed that infants with high levels of distress to an inoculation at age 6 months were by 18 months more likely to show self-recognition—one requirement for self-conscious emotions such as shame.

One definitional debate has concerned the point in development at which a temperamental trait must appear in order to qualify for status as temperament. Some have argued that the traits must be present at birth, so as to avoid the conceptual messiness of possible environmental influences. However, since environmental influences are probably present before birth, and since biological influences can appear at later stages of development, there seems no great value to putting under the temperament rubric only traits that appear in early infancy. Traits may appear relatively late in development but may still meet other criteria for fitting under the temperament rubric, such as having implications for emotional functioning, being relatively stable, and having strong biological roots. Goldsmith (1993) argues that temperament should only be strongly stable between epochs of biobehavioral developmental shifts. One can think of temperament itself developing, as new control systems are constructed and as temperament interacts with environment (Rothbart & Bates, 1998). Traits that most theorists would consider to be temperament would concern relatively basic emotion and emotion regulation traits. There is some evidence that the basic emotions and traits of anger, fear, disgust, self-controlled attention, joy, and perhaps love make early appearances, over the first 6 months, although some regulatory traits take longer to appear (Nelson, 1994; Rothbart & Bates, 1998).

Another debate has been on how stable a trait that is to be called temperament should be. This is at least partly resolved by considering the level at which one is conceiving of temperament (Bates, 1989b; Goldsmith, 1993; Rothbart & Bates, 1998). At the surface level of behavioral traits—such as the tendency to be inhibited in novel situations—there surely must be change, as species-typical unfolding of one's potential, but also as products of life experience. At the neural level, small changes occur constantly. Substantial neural changes may occur, but presumably at a slower rate than changes in the behavioral phenotype, which can be achieved by changes in any of a number of neural/cognitive systems. And finally, at the genetic level, again changes may occur (Gottlieb, 1992), but they are presumably even less frequent (Bates, 1989b; Rothbart & Bates, 1998). Levels of continuity found to date in the behavioral phenotypes of temperament and personality have been moderate. This is found not only with measures of self- and other-perceptions, but also with laboratory and other objective measures of style of adaptation (Caspi, 1998; Goldsmith, 1993; Kagan, 1998; Rothbart & Bates, 1998). Evidence on the organization and stability of the supposedly underlying neural patterns is not sufficient for conclusions at this time (Fahrenberg, 1991).

CONSIDERING TEMPERAMENT AS AN EMOTION CONSTRUCT

Emotions can be thought of as conceptually summarizing many facets of human life. Emotions are reciprocally causal or at least correlated with (1) interactions in the world; (2) regulatory processes, both within the individual and in the form of social scaffolding; and (3) motivations, both verbally mediated and nonverbal. These conceptual correlates of emotion are undoubtedly themselves interconnected. For the sake of simplification, Figure 25.1 represents a chosen order in conceptual closeness of the constructs.

Emotions play a pivotal role in mental and motor actions. Motivations, which are particular needs and goals, influence emotional events and are probably influenced by the events themselves. Motivation qualities may also influence actions in a direct way, too, such as in relatively instinctual actions or highly abstract cognitive actions in pursuit of goals in the absence of distinct emotional responses. However, emotional events seem likely to mediate many if not most of the motivational conditions. Rusting and Larsen (1998), for example, suggest that associative networks may be differentially rich in accord with one's basic personality. They showed that the personality trait of extraversion was more closely related to performance on word completion, reaction time, and recall tasks when stimuli had a positive valence, whereas neuroticism was more closely related to performance when the stimuli were negative. Regulation qualities, whether conscious or not, may similarly influence emotion events, as well as directly influence mental or motor actions. Regulation qualities include not only basic neural and cognitive processes such as attentional orienting, but also more advanced neural and cognitive processes such as executive control of attention (Rothbart et al., 1994), as well as more complex, verbally mediated events such as a conscious reminder to oneself to consider alternative responses (as we sometimes teach impulsive children). Another example of verbal regulation is regulation by means of the verbal conception one holds of one's goal—such as the distinction Higgins (1997) draws between a "promotion focus," which is the goal of gaining something, and a "prevention focus," which is avoiding something—a distinction that affects task performance.

Figure 25.1 omits a path of influence between the motivation and regulation constructs, because it seems likely that the relations between them are most often mediated by emotional events. Nevertheless, there may actually be some direct connections—in fact, particular

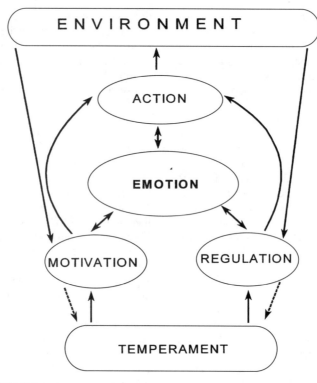

FIGURE 25.1. A conceptual diagram of temperament as an emotion construct.

regulatory orientations may themselves constitute motivation, as in Higgins's (1997) notion of promotion focus versus prevention focus. Environmental influences probably are most direct in affecting motivational and regulatory events, which then influence emotions and actions. For example, goal attainment can have the effect of reducing some immediate aspects of motivation for that goal and at the same time can increase the likelihood of regulatory processes (such as cognitive-behavioral strategies) that augment future efforts toward the goal.

Temperament can fit into the emotion picture as follows: Temperamental dispositions, such as the tendency to be fearful in novel situations, to be easily distressed, or to be strongly attracted to potential mastery experiences, constitute the basis of individual differences in motivation and regulation constructs. Those differences are expressed by individual differences in the emotions, and ultimately in cognitive and behavioral actions. To portray temperament's part in emotional differences more adequately, an advanced version of Figure 25.1 would ideally depict specific emotions grouped by positive and

negative valences, as well as developmentally basic and advanced specific emotions. Temperamental predispositions and motivation and regulation traits would also ideally be represented in a differentiated way, corresponding to the differentiation in emotional constructs. At this point there is some convergence in personality research on a "Big Three" or "Big Five" conceptual grid of individual-difference dimensions. Such a grid always includes dimensions representing positive emotionality and approach; negative, anxious emotionality; and major aspects of self-regulation (Zuckerman, Kuhlman, Joireman, Teta, & Kraft, 1993). These qualities of functioning have been related to underlying neural systems, such as Gray's (1993) behavioral approach system (BAS) and behavioral inhibition system (BIS), and the anterior attentional system for executive control of attention (Rothbart et al., 1994). Caspi (1998) provides one thoughtful diagram of theoretical connections between temperament dimensions and the Big Five, with, for example, extraversion developing largely from activity/ energy level and positive emotionality, and agreeableness developing from positive emo tionality and attentional persistence. Also in the ideal diagram, the multiple levels of the temperament and emotion constructs, from genetic to social, would be represented.

Genetic Levels of Temperament

At their deepest levels, temperamental predispositions involve genetic inheritance. Research has convincingly demonstrated that relatives' personality resemblance to one another is more a function of shared genes than it is a function of shared environment; however, some traits regarded as temperament may also receive influences from shared environmental qualities, especially positive emotionality traits, such as the tendency to be joyful (Goldsmith, Buss, & Lemery, 1997). A portion of many personality traits is also likely to consist of nonshared environmental influences, such as differential treatment by parents or different peer groups (Caspi, 1998). Genes code for particular proteins, which influence likelihoods of neural structures and processes (Plomin & Saudino, 1994; Rothbart & Bates, 1998). Relatively little is known about processes translating the genetic code into particular neural events and into personality, but there are exciting openings to such knowledge. There appears to be, for example, evidence of a particular gene for a kind of dopamine receptor involved in individual differences in P3 orienting responses in the electroencephalogram (EEG) (Boomsma, Anokhin, & de Geus, 1997), as well as of a gene for another kind of dopamine receptor associated with novelty seeking and drug abuse (Hamer, 1997; Rose, 1995).

Neural Levels of Temperament

Theoretically, configurations of neural structures—the synaptic densities, the amounts of various types of neurotransmitter-creating cells—influence the characteristic responses of an individual. The responses are in amounts of neurotransmitters produced; neural synapses and impulses in particular places and at particular frequencies; and the likelihood of particular end states in motivations, emotions, cognitions, self-regulatory actions, and behavior (Dahl, 1996; Fox, 1994; Schore, 1996). For example, children whose brains show asymmetrically more activation in the right versus the left frontal lobe tend to express high levels of negative emotions and inhibition, while those who show the reverse asymmetry (more left-hemisphere activation) are inclined toward more positive and approaching emotions and actions (Fox, 1994). There are other neural systems in dynamic balance in shaping adaptation to the world, especially the BAS and BIS (Gray, 1993) and the sympathetic and parasympathetic branches of the autonomic nervous system (Schore, 1996; for summaries of other neural systems in relation to particular temperament dimensions, see Bates and Wachs, 1994, and Rothbart & Bates, 1998).

Phenotypic Levels of Temperament

At the level of observable behavior patterns, temperamental phenotypes must reflect not only motivational and regulatory genotypes, but also the opportunities and perils of the environment, as well as developmental shaping of reactivity and self-regulation. The intricate dances in emotions and their regulatory systems serve adaptive functions in social relations. Most people have been blessed with moderate assets for social adaptation. To remain in their groups, they need to respond to social needs and keep their affective displays within sustainable limits—neither too high nor too low in intensity or frequency, and congruent with social process. They show positive affect and assert some power, but when approach behaviors get to be too risky, they also rein in assertive power with the aid of negative feelings such as anxiety or conscious control of behavior. The particular balance that an individual strikes, as influenced by temperament and the particular pressures of the environment, shapes the sustainability of social roles and thus the individual's adjustment.

TEMPERAMENT, EMOTION, AND ADJUSTMENT

This chapter emphasizes a concept called "adjustment style" (Bates, in press), which reflects an interest in not only adjustment on a single dimension at a fixed point in time, but configurations of social adaptations, their patterns of stability over development, and their predictable changes. The major examples are internalizing problems, such as anxiety disorders and social withdrawal, and externalizing problems, such as aggressiveness and conflict with authority. Internalizing and externalizing problems are conceptually and, to a moderate degree, empirically distinct. Whether arrayed in dimensions or sorted into a diagnosis, individuals' adjustment characteristics often show genetic heritability and appreciable consistency over time (Caspi, 1998), as if there is a basic personality at work in the shaping of an individual's life course. Of course, in actuality there are multiple personalities at work—those of family members, other caregivers, and peers. And adjustment itself only has meaning as a relational concept.

In the face of the relational meaning of adjustment, is it meaningful to think of adjustment style, based in personality, as an individual concept too? One might say no, pointing to the numerous cases of qualitatively different adjustments in different settings—such as home and school, as indicated by the generally modest degrees of agreement between parent and teacher reports (Achenbach, 1991). However, one might also say yes, if one expects moderate overall consistency and allows for behavioral distinctions due to situational constraints as well as to individual differences in self-regulatory capacities. There is mounting evidence that temperament traits measured in early childhood do, to some degree, predict adjustment in later years (Bates, 1989a; Caspi, 1998; Rothbart & Bates, 1998; Shaw, Owens, Vondra, Keenan, & Winslow, 1996). Moreover, consistent with the notion of adjustment styles, particular dimensions of temperament tend to predict particular dimensions of adjustment. General negative emotionality predicts both internalizing and externalizing problems, but fear of novelty tends to predict internalizing problems more than externalizing ones, and early resistance to control or deficient inhibitory control tends to predict externalizing problems more than internalizing ones (Bates, 1989a; Caspi, 1998; Kagan, 1998; Kochanska, Murray, & Coy, 1997; Rothbart & Bates, 1998). Despite this progress, there is much variance in adjustment that is not accounted for by temperamental differences, and the phenomenon of different adjustment in different settings is a challenge that temperament researchers are just beginning to address (Wachs, 1992) .

One answer to the challenge of different adjustment in different settings is to suggest that the temperamental basis of adjustment style could be expressed differently in different places, but there should be a logic to the different expressions. Consider, for example, the case of one boy who resembles several cases I have worked with:

Michael's adjustment pattern around his parents was, since his infancy, a more or less continuous effort to dominate people in various ways, with frequent efforts to thwart their basically well-intentioned efforts to dominate him. However, at school his pattern was adequately (but not exceptionally) compliant with adults, and rather distant from peers. What was a plausible temperamental underpinning? One thread consisted of strong dominance and reward-seeking tendencies, which could be also characterized as mastery motivation or behavioral approach. This was shown in many home and sports situations. Associated with the approach motivation, there were also difficulties in changing motivational sets in response to environmental feedback. A second thread was a high level of general arousal, which amplified motivations, perhaps explaining the boy's tendencies to quick and intense anger when approach actions were blocked. Third was a pattern of anxious discomfort in the face of new adaptive demands, also amplified by general arousability. The latter created problems, but also hinted that Michael had some ability to respond anxiously to social punishment. Fourth, although least well-observed clinically, there appeared to be a lower-than-normal tendency to form affectionate bonds. His family had loved him, indulged him, and despite numerous discipline efforts, essentially allowed him to dominate in coercive and other ways for many years. However, he was not often genuinely affectionate or considerate to his family, and was often disagreeable. As would be expected, he strongly resisted his parents' increasing efforts to require cooperative behavior, but he often responded to positive incentives such as a new video game. In school, however, where he had been handled with more impartial firmness along with positive responsiveness, his behavior was not a large problem. He had difficulty in reading, but his competitive nature was eventually turned toward efforts to improve his skills. He was seen by his teachers as more immature than aggressive. They met his rare outbursts and his frequent, milder forms of resistance with a calm strength. His outbursts appeared to have been met with social punishment and nonreward from his peers.

The foregoing clinical observations are consistent with theoretical formulations of the interactions between temperament and socializing environment (Bates et al., 1994). However, such a detailed adjustment style profile has not yet been verified in longitudinal, empirical research. Clinical notes can be a starting point for research, but only that. It is possible to construct a number of other temperament–environment transactional processes for the wide variety of adjustment styles. Some children are relatively well adjusted at home and not at school; some parents are stress-inducing, and some are inconsistent and irritable; some peer groups are flexible and forgiving, whereas others are rigid and rejecting. Do children who show different trajectories in adjustment across years of development differ systematically in other empirical details of their social environments and their personalities? Although many children are relatively stable in their adjustment, quite a few children improve, especially across middle childhood, and some children's behavior becomes worse with age. According to recent findings from one moderately large, multisite study, significant but small portions of the changes are associated with measurable qualities such as gender and parenting (McFadyen-Ketchum, Bates, Dodge, & Pettit, 1996), neighborhood characteristics (Beyers, Bates, Dodge, & Pettit, 1999; Pettit, Bates, Dodge, & Meece, 1999), and ethnic group status (Keiley, Bates, Dodge, & Pettit, in press). More to the point, however, is this question: What are the temperament and emotion components in adjustment style?

TEMPERAMENT AND EMOTION IN DEVELOPMENTAL PROCESS

Emotion and emotion regulation can be thought of as part of our interface with the world—an integral part of our guidance system. Theoretically, this guidance system is a major part of the very complex construct of individual adjustment. Cole et al. (1994) argue that "all forms of psychopathology have concomitant symptoms of emotion dysregulation" (p. 99). Empirically, there is some evidence for the operation of emotion and emotion regulation traits and environmental qualities in individual differences in adjustment.

First, as stated previously in the argument for the notion of adjustment style, temperamental qualities do in fact predict adjustment style. The findings suggest a pattern of roughly homologous linkages between adjustment dimensions and corresponding temperamental predis-positions toward negative emotionality, positive emotionality, and manageability (Bates, 1989a; Caspi, 1998; Rothbart & Bates, 1998). Adaptation may also be affected by temperament dispositions toward seeking social warmth, which are theoretically crucial in the effectiveness of socialization practices (Rothbart & Bates, 1998). The linkages found so far do explain a part of the variability in adjustment outcomes, both within and across sources of information about child traits, and over shorter and longer time intervals; however, they account for only moderate amounts of variance in outcome. One way to explain more of the variance might be to consider temperament's environmental context. From a clinician's perspective, as pointed out by Thomas, Chess, and Birch (1968) and others, temperament traits are meaningful only in transactions with the environment.

Many research studies have focused on direct effects of environment. One key environment is the family, especially the parents. Parent–child relationship differences, which can be arrayed on dimensions of positive involvement and power/control, imply differences in the incentive conditions for the different emotions. For example, angrily restrictive parenting elicits more negative affect than inductive parenting. What specific environmental factors might have direct effects on emotions, regulation, and adjustment?

Warmly responsive parenting is especially salient in infancy, and may play a role throughout children's development (Rothbaum & Weisz, 1994; Steinberg, Lamborn, Darling, Mounts, & Dornbusch, 1994). Kopp (1982) and Thompson (1998) have pointed out how early stages in the development of self-regulation of emotion and behavior require active parental participation. An infant with a responsive caregiver has less opportunity to be overwhelmed with distress, as shown by the finding that infants subjected to the stress of separation from their mothers but given warmly responsive substitute caregivers showed relatively low cortisol responses, compared to infants with passive caregivers (Gunnar, 1994; Nachmias et al., 1996). Moreover, an infant with a responsive caregiver also has a greater opportunity to develop verbal/cognitive means of self-regulation than an infant with an unresponsive caregiver (Olson, Bates, & Bayles, 1984). Finally, Ainsworth, Blehar, Waters, and Wall (1978) found that positively responsive mothers end up with more securely attached infants. Supporting evidence comes not only from naturalistic, correlational studies (e.g., Bates et al., 1985), but also from quasi-experimental clinical research (van den Boom, 1994). Securely attached children have been found to be emotionally better modulated than anxiously attached children (Sroufe, 1983) and better equipped to work and have fun with their caregivers in solving difficult problems (Matas, Arend, & Sroufe, 1978; Frankel & Bates, 1990). Indicators of early positive parent–child involvement do predict better adjustment in later childhood (Pettit & Bates, 1989; Pettit et al., 1997). Intriguingly, however, evidence on the predictiveness of attachment security itself is mixed, as explained well by Thompson (1998).

In considering the nonconverging literature on attachment–adjustment relations, Greenberg, Speltz, and DeKlyen (1993) have suggested that family stress may moderate the longer-term effects of attachment security. If stresses are high, attachment security may play a more crucial role in the balance of adaptation than if they are low. It seems likely that family stress may increase odds of unresponsive and perhaps episodically harsh parenting (e.g., see Hetherington & Clingempeel, 1992; Patterson, Reid, & Dishion, 1992). In such circumstances, it seems likely that key issues in emotion regulation—for instance, the shame + relationship repair cycle (Schore, 1996)—may be poorly resolved. The shame cycle may be important in the development of children's ability to read emotional cues from others, such as approval versus irritation; this ability should serve as a vitally important regulatory tool (Saarni et al., 1998).

In one other type of environmental effect on emotional development, a recent EEG study suggests that experience of abusive treatment biases a child to encode negative social stimuli as meaningful more readily than positive ones (Pollack, Cicchetti, Klorman, & Brumaghim, 1997). Children who had been abused showed stronger cognitive event-related P3 potentials when detecting an angry face target than when detecting a happy face target; nonabused children did not show this difference. Other studies have shown that measures of physically and otherwise punitive, harsh, and ineffectual parenting are themselves associated with both externalizing and internalizing problems (Dumas & LaFreniere, 1993; Rothbaum & Weisz, 1994; Patterson et al., 1992; Dobkin, Tremblay, & Sacchitelle, 1997; Haapasalo & Tremblay, 1994; Weiss, Dodge, Bates, & Pettit, 1992).

The studies just mentioned are a very few of the many studies showing direct links between environmental characteristics and children's emotional and behavioral adjustments. The relations have been typically of modest to moderate size. This encourages the search for interactive effects (Wachs, 1992).

Relatively solid, empirical findings of interactions between temperament and environment measures have begun to shed light on how the relations between attachment and adjustment depend on other variables in the system. First, there are findings of interactions between temperament and attachment in predicting social development. When preschool children were relatively fearless in unfamiliar and novel situations, and when they were also securely attached to their mothers (i.e., in a positive partnership), they tended to show more signs of conscience than similarly outgoing children who were insecurely attached (Kochanska, 1991, 1995, 1997).

There have also been studies of interactions between child temperament and parental control in accounting for child adjustment. Again, it appears likely that the effects of parenting interact with the temperament of the child in the development of behavioral adjustment. And Kochanska's (1997) research is again relevant: Preschoolers who were fearful in a novel situation showed more signs of conscience when their mothers were gentle in their control than when they were harsh. Colder, Lochman, and Wells (1997) obtained a similar result in older children. Arcus and Gardner (1993), and Park, Belsky, Putnam, and Crnic (1997) provide another relevant set of studies. These studies suggest (with varied methods) that highly stress-reactive infants with stern parents are less likely to develop behavioral inhibition in toddlerhood than stress-reactive infants with parents who are not stern.

Also relevant here is this finding (Bates et al., 1998): Young children's temperamental resistance to control directly predicted their externalizing behavior problems across middle childhood, but this effect was stronger in dyads where the mothers were observed to be low in control of the children during home visits than in dyads where the mothers were observed to be high in control. This pattern was seen in two separate samples and for outcomes as reported by teachers and mothers. Scatterplots of the relations suggested that the difference between the relations could be seen at both ends of the continuum. Resistant children with mothers who responded relatively often to their actual and potential misbehaviors were not as likely to develop externalizing behaviors as resistant children with less controlling mothers; at the same time, nonresistant children with highly controlling mothers showed higher levels of behavior problems than nonresistant children with less controlling mothers. This pattern may reflect a complex set of temperament–environment transactional processes (detailed in Bates et al., 1998). As one example, resistant but maternally controlled children may eventually learn to modulate unruly stimulation seeking. This happens perhaps with the aid of shame + repair cycles, as envisioned by Schore (1996). As another example, nonresistant but still maternally controlled children may be trained to express frustration as a means of gaining some autonomy.

Another topic relevant to the interaction of child and environmental characteristics is the stress response. Lewis and Ramsay (1997) noted that cortisol-indexed responses to inoculation after age 6 months predicted whether children would show recognition of a blemish on themselves in the second year. The onset of self-recognition is theoretically and empirically related to the emergence of shame emotions. Schore (1996) argues that shame experiences produce cortisol responses, but that qualities of a securely attached mother–child relationship facilitate the resolution of the shame experience, which leads to socialization of impulses. In a further step, according to Kochanska's (1997) research, it appears that a child who is prone to distress in a novel situation is more likely to develop signs of conscience when the mother is gentle rather than harsh in her control, whereas the bold child's conscience development is more sensitive to secure attachment between mother and child (as indexed by the Q-sort measure of attachment), as mentioned earlier. Thus several studies describe variants on an interaction between child temperamental stress responsivity and environmental pressures.

Interactions between one temperamental trait and another within a child may also be important, as Lewis and Michalson (1983) pointed out in considering individuals' profiles of emotion characteristics. One theoretically plausible model has inhibitory tendencies stemming from a capacity for anxiety, which helps to brake aggressive, impulsive tendencies (Fowles, 1994). The case described earlier in this chapter gives one example. There is also

some empirical support: In a 1-year follow-up analysis, children who showed acting-out tendencies were slightly more likely to decline in externalizing behavior when they were initially also showing anxiety symptoms (Bates, Pettit, & Dodge, 1995); in another study, Tremblay (1992) showed such moderation over a longer span of development (see also Kerr, Tremblay, Pagani, & Vitaro, 1997). Or, to consider a somewhat different pair of temperamental traits, Fox, Schmidt, Calkins, Rubin, and Coplan (1996) reported that outgoing children who had EEG asymmetries associated with negative emotionality were more likely to show externalizing behavior problems (such as fighting) than similarly outgoing children who were more prone to positive emotions. There are other important lines of theory and empirical data showing similar things. Especially interesting is the widespread work on a variety of self-regulation qualities based ultimately in both neural systems, such as adaptive attentional shifting or focusing attention, and learning experiences (Rothbart & Bates, 1998; Moffitt, 1993; Newman & Wallace, 1993). As one example, Eisenberg et al. (1997) have shown that regulation qualities' correlations with adjustment are moderated by the general level of emotional intensity. That general emotional intensity represents a separate system beyond the specific emotion tendencies is argued by Dawson's (1994) observation of generalized frontal EEG activity associated with both positive and negative emotional expressions. Executive control qualities, like the ability to slow one's motor responses or to systematically search an array of comparison stimuli, have been shown to predict social adjustment (Kochanska et al., 1997). In brief, temperamentally based anxious inhibition and executive functioning traits can brake tendencies toward impulsive reward-seeking behavior and thus influence social adaptations.

PRACTICAL IMPLICATIONS

The research on temperament and emotion in developmental psychopathology suggests some possible future applications. First, early temperament qualities of negative emotionality, novelty fear, and self-regulatory tendency have in several studies been found to predict homologous components of adjustment style in later childhood, adolescence, and adulthood. Second, studies suggest modest linkages between environmental variables of parental warmth and power and child adjustment, and between abusive discipline and neurally based cognitive conditioning of orientation to threat. Third, temperament–environment interactions have been suggested by recent research. The available evidence does not suggest extremely powerful interaction effects; however, if we consider the still narrow portions of the system empirically encompassed so far, as well as the only moderate amounts of variance accounted for by temperament and environment separately, the evidence is quite encouraging. Caregivers' warmth and responsiveness, and associated secure attachment, appear to be of particular importance for children who are relatively fearless. This may be partly due to the socializing effects of more positive resolutions of the shame caregivers induce when they rein in children's impulses. Whether a caregiver uses mild rather than power assertive responses to a child's misbehavior may be of particular importance for a child with a fearful temperament. Mild control seems likely to help the fearful child explore and understand social control contingencies better than either overprotective or harsh control, which may activate anxiety and narrow the perceptual/cognitive field. Finally, let us consider temperament–temperament interactions. Children with stronger self-regulatory tendencies may be more likely than less self-regulated children to short-circuit the development of negative temperament traits into negative adjustment traits. The specific examples here are only a few of those that should be considered ultimately, but they do provide some possible practical implications.

It should be possible to develop assessments of temperament–environment process, or descriptions of the child's temperament in relation to the environment. These assessments might allow more precise targeting and adaptations of standard medical or psychosocial interventions keyed to child and family development profiles. As one example of a psychological intervention informed by temperament concepts, in a clinic dealing with acting-out problems in young children, a therapist might consider a child's resistance to control in relation to the control style of the chief socialization agents. A mismatch pattern, such as high resistance in a child along with low control in a parent, could cue a therapist to emphasize effective control techniques in a parent training intervention, or to find solutions to the parent's unwillingness to try to con-

trol. Or a fearless child with a firm but cool parent might cue a therapeutic emphasis on building a warm, responsive partnership. In contrast, a temperamentally low-resistance child and a highly controlling parent, or a fearful child and a harsh parent, might cue an emphasis on gentle persuasion and nonarousing forms of parental control. Clinically, I have observed temperament–parenting combinations in which oppositional children have varying levels of positive and negative emotionality in general and of anxiety and resistance to control in particular, and in which parental behaviors vary on dimensions of warmth/responsiveness and control. I have also observed differences in children's regulation abilities—sometimes apparently based in temperament, other times due to chronic stress, such as cumulative sleep deprivation in a busy or chaotic family (Bates, Viken, Alexander, Beyers, & Stockton, 1995). Empirical work is needed on standardizing assessments of such profiles and evaluation of the value of matching treatment emphases.

A number of clinicians use temperament concepts, but the appropriate, controlled efficacy studies, such as the one designed by Mc-Clowry (1998), are just beginning (Bates et al., 1994). Aside from the empirical challenges of assessing the temperament and environmental types and validating them, there will also be the clinical challenge of developing effective interventions. It is one thing to say that a cool parent would become more effective with a fearless child by becoming warmer and more fun, but it is another thing to find a way to help such a parent actually become warmer and more fun. Standard parent behavioral training modules focus on such skills, but are not always sufficient. In most treatments, whether based in the family, the school, or both, time and cooperative resources are strictly limited. It is to be hoped that temperament–environment profiles may guide prioritizing and efficient resource allocations. Such targeting is likely to be especially important in secondary prevention work (e.g., Conduct Problems Prevention Research Group, 1992; Yoshikawa, 1994) with families identified as high-risk, but not initially seeking treatment.

CONCLUSION

Temperament is a construct that is especially useful in exploring personality aspects of emotion. Personality aspects of emotion are rooted in basic genetic and neural processes, but are highly relevant to behavioral patterns of social adaptation over time and development. Fairly stable individual differences in emotion and emotion regulation are central in the dimensions of temperament. Temperament, especially when conceived at the level of behavioral phenotype, can change. However, if the notion of temperament has merit, there should often be some logical pattern to changes. The phenotype of temperament should theoretically depend not only on biologically based predispositions, but also on environmental conditions, both as elicitors of emotional responses and as shapers of emotional and regulatory responses. There may also be transactional shaping and choosing of environments in accord with, or even counter to, temperament. However, at the deepest levels of emotional and regulatory predisposition, the influences of environment will presumably manifest themselves only in instances of extreme or very long-lasting environments.

There is beginning to be evidence of how temperamental and parental control traits interact to moderate the future trajectories of children's adjustment styles, but it seems likely that these temperament–environment and temperament–temperament interactions and how they describe or shape adjustment style are very complex. Knowledge growth in this area is accelerating. It is possible that formulations of temperament and environment will allow more practical, successful solutions to adaptational problems.

Most current empirically validated child therapies have multiple modules, directed at multiple facets of the problems. For at least some families, increased focus may allow increased chances of achieving a core change. Parents of young children seem, in clinical impression, to use temperamental interpretations more readily than do parents of older children. If this turns out to be empirically true, interventions designed with the aid of the temperament–environment formulations may be especially helpful with younger children and their caregivers.

Two particular formulations suggest directions for developing assessments and targeted interventions. First, it seems possible that the emphasis in treating the negatively reactive young child, who is at risk for inhibition and anxiety problems, should be on firm but not harsh or arousing parental control. For the fearless and outgoing child, in contrast, the emphasis should plausibly be on the building of a warm, responsive partnership between child and parent. Second, for a young child who is hard to manage, who does not quickly inhibit reward-seeking behavior when told to do so, and who is thereby at special risk for aggression problems, the emphasis perhaps should be on firm control, whereas for the manageable child the emphasis may need to be more on the respectful building of child autonomy. These possibilities are speculative; however, it does seem likely that they could form the basis of some productive research. Temperament and emotion constructs may prove to give not only a theoretical window into the development of individual differences in personality and adjustment, but ultimately a set of practical tools for the prevention and treatment of adjustment problems.

REFERENCES

Achenbach, T. M. (1991). *Manual for the Child Behavior Checklist/4–18 and 1991 Profile.* Burlington: University of Vermont, Department of Psychiatry.

Ainsworth, M. D. S., Blehar, M. C., Waters, E., & Wall, S. (1978). *Patterns of attachment: A psychological study of the Strange Situation.* Hillsdale, NJ: Erlbaum.

Arcus, D., & Gardner, S. (1993, March). *When biology is not destiny.* Paper presented at the biennial meeting of the Society for Research in Child Development, New Orleans, LA.

Bates, J. E. (1989a). Applications of temperament concepts. In G. A. Kohnstamm, J. E. Bates, & M. K. Rothbart (Eds.), *Temperament in childhood* (pp. 321–355). Chichester, England: Wiley.

Bates, J. E. (1989b). Concepts and measures of temperament. In G. A. Kohnstamm, J. E. Bates, & M. K. Rothbart (Eds.), *Temperament in childhood* (pp. 3–26). Chichester, England: Wiley.

Bates, J. E. (in press). Adjustment style in childhood as product of parenting and temperament. In T. D. Wachs & G. A. Kohnstamm (Eds.), *Temperament in context.* Hillsdale, NJ: Erlbaum.

Bates, J. E., Maslin, C. A., & Frankel, K. A. (1985). Attachment security, mother–child interaction, and temperament as predictors of behavior problem ratings at age three years. In I. Bretherton & E. Waters (Eds.), Growing points in attachment theory and research (pp. 167–193). *Monographs of the Society for Research in Child Development, 50*(1–2, Serial No. 209).

Bates, J. E., Pettit, G. S., & Dodge, K. A. (1995). Family and child factors in stability and change in children's aggressiveness in elementary school. In J. McCord (Ed.), *Coercion and punishment in long-term per-*

spectives (pp. 124–137). New York: Cambridge University Press.

Bates, J. E., Pettit, G. S., Dodge, K. A., & Ridge, B. (1998). The interaction of temperamental resistance to control and restrictive parenting in the development of externalizing behavior. *Developmental Psychology, 34,* 982–995.

Bates, J. E., Viken, R. J., Alexander, D., Beyers, J., & Stockton, L. (1995, March). *Sleep and adjustment in preschool children.* Paper presented at the biennial meeting of the Society for Research in Child Development, Indianapolis, IN.

Bates, J. E., & Wachs, T. D. (Eds.). (1994). *Temperament: Individual differences at the interface of biology and behavior.* Washington, DC: American Psychological Association Press.

Bates, J. E., Wachs, T. D., & Emde, R. N. (1994). Toward practical uses for biological concepts of temperament. In J. E. Bates & T. D. Wachs (Eds.), *Temperament: Individual differences at the interface of biology and behavior* (pp. 275–306). Washington, DC: American Psychological Association.

Beyers, J., Bates, J. E., Dodge, K. A., & Pettit, G. S. (1999). *Neighborhood, family, and individual characteristics and the development of children's externalizing behaviors.* Unpublished manuscript, Indiana University.

Blass, E. M. (1992). The ontogeny of motivation: Opioid bases of energy conservation and lasting affective change in rat and human infants. *Current Directions in Psychological Science, 1,* 116–120.

Boomsma, D., Anokhin, A., & de Geus, E. (1997). Genetics of electrophysiology: Linking genes, brain, and behavior. *Current Directions in Psychological Science, 6,* 106–110.

Caspi, A. (1998). Personality development across the life course. In W. Damon (Series Ed.) & N. Eisenberg (Vol. Ed.), *Handbook of child psychology: Vol. 3. Social, emotional, and personality development* (5th ed., pp. 311–388). New York: Wiley.

Colder, C. R., Lochman, J. E., & Wells, K. C. (1997). The moderating effects of children's fear and activity level on relations between parenting practices and child symptomatology. *Journal of Abnormal Child Psychology, 25,* 251–263.

Cole, P. M., Michel, M. K., & Teti, L. O. (1994). The development of emotion regulation and dysregulation: A clinical perspective. In N. A. Fox (Ed.), The development of emotion regulation: Biological and behavioral considerations. *Monographs of the Society for Research in Child Development, 59*(2–3, Serial No. 240), 73–100.

Conduct Problems Prevention Research Group. (1992). A developmental and clinical model for the prevention of conduct disorders: The FAST Track Program. *Development and Psychopathology, 4,* 509–527.

Dahl, R. E. (1996). The regulation of sleep and arousal: Development and psychopathology. *Development and Psychopathology, 8,* 3–27.

Dawson, G. (1994). Frontal electroencephalographic correlates of individual differences in emotion expression in infants: A brain systems perspective on emotion. In N. A. Fox (Ed.), The development of emotion regulation: Biological and behavioral considerations. *Monographs of the Society for Research in Child Development, 59*(2–3, Serial No. 240), 135–151.

Dobkin, P. L., Tremblay, R. E., & Sacchitelle, C. (1997). Predicting boys' early-onset substance abuse from father's alcoholism, son's disruptiveness, and mother's parenting behavior. *Journal of Consulting and Clinical Psychology, 65,* 86–92.

Dumas, J. E., & LaFreniere, P. J. (1993). Mother–child relationships as sources of support or stress: A comparison of competent, average, aggressive, and anxious dyads. *Child Development, 64,* 1732–1754.

Eisenberg, N. (1998). Introduction. In W. Damon (Series Ed.) & N. Eisenberg (Vol. Ed.), *Handbook of child psychology: Vol. 3. Social, emotional, and personality development* (5th ed., pp. 1–24). New York: Wiley.

Eisenberg, N., Fabes, R. A., Shepard, S. A., Murphy, B., Guthrie, I., Jones, S., Friedman, J., Poulin, R., & Maszk, P. (1997). Contemporary and longitudinal prediction of children's social functioning from regulation and emotionality. *Child Development, 68,* 642–664.

Fahrenberg, J. (1991). Differential psychophysiology and the diagnosis of temperament. In J. Strelau & A. Angleitner (Eds.), *Explorations in temperament: International perspectives on theory and measurement* (pp. 317–333). New York: Plenum.

Fischer, D. H. (1989). *Albion's seed: Four British folkways in America.* New York: Oxford University Press.

Fleischman, M. J., Horne, A. M., & Arthur, J. L. (1983). *Troubled families: A treatment approach.* Champaign, IL: Research Press.

Fowles, D. (1994). A motivational theory of psychopathology. In W. Spaulding (Ed.), *Nebraska Symposium on Motivation: Vol. 41. Integrated views of motivation and emotion* (pp. 181–238). Lincoln: University of Nebraska Press.

Fox, N. A. (1994). Dynamic cerebral processes underlying emotion regulation. In N. A. Fox (Ed.), The development of emotion regulation: Biological and behavioral considerations. (pp. 152–166). *Monographs of the Society for Research in Child Development, 59* (2–3, Serial No. 240).

Fox, N. A., Schmidt, L. A., Calkins, S. D., Rubin, K. H., & Coplan, R. J. (1996). The role of frontal activation in the regulation and dysregulation of social behavior during the preschool years. *Development and Psychopathology, 8,* 89–102.

Frankel, K. A., & Bates, J. E. (1990). Mother–toddler problem solving: Antecedents in attachment, home behavior, and temperament. *Child Development, 61,* 810–819.

Goldsmith, H. H. (1993). Temperament: Variability in developing emotion systems. In M. Lewis & J. M. Haviland (Eds.), *Handbook of emotions* (pp. 353–364). New York: Guilford Press.

Goldsmith, H. H., Buss, K. A., & Lemery, K. S. (1997). Toddler and childhood temperament: Expanded content, stronger genetic evidence, new evidence for the importance of environment. *Developmental Psychology, 33,* 891–905.

Gottlieb, G. (1992). *Individual development and evolu-*

tion: The genesis of novel behavior. New York: Oxford University Press.

Gray, J. A. (1993). The neuropsychology of temperament. In J. Strelau & A. Angleitner (Eds.), *Explorations in temperament: International perspectives on theory and measurement* (pp. 105–128). New York: Plenum.

Greenberg, M. T., Speltz, M. L., & DeKlyen, M. (1993). The role of attachment in the early development of disruptive behavior problems. *Development and Psychopathology, 5,* 191–213.

Gunnar, M. R. (1994). Psychoendocrine studies of temperament and stress in early childhood: Expanding current models. In J. E. Bates & T. D. Wachs (Eds.), *Temperament: Individual differences at the interface of biology and behavior* (pp. 175–198). Washington, DC: American Psychological Association.

Haapasalo, J., & Tremblay, R. E. (1994). Physically aggressive boys from ages 6 to 12: Family background, parenting behavior, and prediction of delinquency. *Journal of Consulting and Clinical Psychology, 62,* 1044–1052.

Hamer, D. (1997). The search for personality genes: Adventures of a molecular biologist. *Current Directions in Psychological Science, 6,* 111–114.

Hembree-Kigin, T. L., & McNeil, C. B. (1995). *Parent–child interaction therapy.* New York: Plenum Press.

Hetherington, E. M., & Clingempeel, W. G. (1992). Coping with marital transitions. *Monographs of the Society for Research in Child Development, 57*(2–3, Serial No. 227).

Higgins, E. T. (1997). Beyond pleasure and pain. *American Psychologist, 52,* 1280–1300.

Julien, R. M. (1995). *A primer of drug action* (7th ed.). New York: Freeman.

Kagan, J. (1998). Biology and the child. In W. Damon (Series Ed.) & N. Eisenberg (Vol. Ed.), *Handbook of child psychology: Vol. 3. Social, emotional, and personality development* (5th ed., pp. 177–235). New York: Wiley.

Katz, L. F., & Gottman, J. M. (1997). Buffering children from marital conflict and dissolution. *Journal of Clinical Child Psychology, 26,* 157–171.

Keiley, M. K., Bates, J. E., Dodge, K. A., & Pettit, G. S. (in press). A cross-domain growth analysis: Externalizing and internalizing behaviors during 8 years of childhood. *Journal of Abnormal Child Psychology.*

Kerr, M., Tremblay, R. E., Pagani, L., & Vitaro, F. (1997). Boys' behavioral inhibition and the risk of later delinquency. *Archives of General Psychiatry, 54,* 809–816.

Kochanska, G. (1991). Socialization and temperament in the development of guilt and conscience. *Child Development, 62,* 1379–1392.

Kochanska, G. (1995). Children's temperament, mothers' discipline, and security of attachment: Multiple pathways to emerging internalization. *Child Development, 66,* 597–615.

Kochanska, G. (1997). Multiple pathways to conscience for children with different temperaments: From toddlerhood to age 5. *Developmental Psychology, 33,* 228–240.

Kochanska, G., Murray, K., & Coy, K. C. (1997). In-hibitory control as a contributor to conscience in childhood: From toddler to early school age. *Child Development, 68,* 263–277.

Kopp, C. B. (1982). Antecedents of self-regulation: A developmental perspective. *Developmental Psychology, 18,* 199–214.

Kramer, P. D. (1993). *Listening to Prozac.* New York: Viking.

Lazarus, R. S. (1991). *Emotion and adaptation.* New York: Oxford University Press.

Lewis, M. (1993). The emergence of human emotions. In M. Lewis & J. M. Haviland (Eds.), *Handbook of emotions* (pp. 223–235). New York: Guilford Press.

Lewis, M., & Haviland, J. M. (Eds.). (1993). *Handbook of emotions.* New York: Guilford Press.

Lewis, M., & Michalson, L. (1983). *Children's emotions and moods: Developmental theory and measurement.* New York: Plenum Press.

Lewis, M., & Ramsay, D. S. (1997). Stress reactivity and self-recognition. *Child Development, 68,* 621–629.

Maslow, A. H. (1968). *Toward a psychology of being* (2nd ed.). Princeton, NJ: Van Nostrand.

Matas, L., Arend, R. A., & Sroufe, L. A. (1978). The continuity of adaptation in the second year: Relationship between quality of attachment and later competence. *Child Development, 49,* 547–556.

McClowry, S. G. (1998). The science and art of using temperament as the basis for intervention. *School Psychology Review, 27,* 551–563.

McFadyen-Ketchum, S. A., Bates, J. E., Dodge, K. A., & Pettit, G. S. (1996). Patterns of change in early childhood aggressive–disruptive behavior: Gender differences in predictions from early coercive and affectionate mother–child interactions. *Child Development, 67,* 2417–2433.

Mize, J., & Pettit, G. S. (1997). Mothers' social coaching, mother–child relationship style, and children's peer competence: Is the medium the message? *Child Development, 68,* 291–311.

Moffitt, T. E. (1993). The neuropsychology of conduct disorder. *Development and Psychopathology, 5,* 135–151.

Nachmias, M., Gunnar, M., Mangelsdorf, S., Parritz, R. H., & Buss, K. (1996). Behavioral inhibition and stress reactivity: The moderating role of attachment security. *Child Development, 67,* 508–522.

Nelson, C. A. (1994). Neural bases of infant temperament. In J. E. Bates & T. D. Wachs (Eds.), *Temperament: Individual differences at the interface of biology and behavior* (pp. 47–82). Washington, DC: American Psychological Association.

Newman, J. P., & Wallace, J. F. (1993). Diverse pathways to deficient self-regulation: Implications for disinhibitory psychopathology in children. *Clinical Psychology Review, 13,* 699–720.

Olson, S. L., Bates, J. E., & Bayles, K. (1984). Mother–infant interaction and the development of individual differences in children's cognitive competence. *Developmental Psychology, 20,* 166–179.

Park, S. -Y., Belsky, J., Putnam, S., & Crnic, K. (1997). Infant emotionality, parenting, and 3-year inhibition: Exploring stability and lawful discontinuity in a male sample. *Developmental Psychology, 33,* 218–227.

Patterson, C. M., & Newman, J. P. (1993). Reflectivity and learning from aversive events: Toward a psychological mechanism for the syndromes of disinhibition. *Psychological Review, 100,* 716–736.

Patterson, G. R., Reid, J. B., & Dishion, T. J. (1992). *Antisocial boys.* Eugene, OR: Castalia.

Pettit, G. S., & Bates, J. E. (1989). Family interaction patterns and children's behavior problems from infancy to age 4 years. *Developmental Psychology, 25,* 413–420.

Pettit, G. S., Bates, J. E., & Dodge, K. A. (1997). Supportive parenting, ecological context, and children's adjustment: A seven-year longitudinal study. *Child Development, 68,* 908–923.

Pettit, G. S., Bates, J. E., Dodge, K. A., & Meece, D. W. (1999). The impact of after-school peer contact on early adolescent externalizing problems is moderated by parental monitoring, perceived neighborhood safety, and prior adjustment. *Child Development, 70,* 768–778.

Plomin, R., & Saudino, K. J. (1994). Quantitative genetics and molecular genetics. In J. E. Bates & T. D. Wachs (Eds.), *Temperament: Individual differences at the interface of biology and behavior* (pp. 143–171). Washington, DC: American Psychological Association.

Pollack, S. D., Cicchetti, D., Klorman, R., & Brumaghim, J. T. (1997). Cognitive brain event-related potentials and emotion processing in maltreated children. *Child Development, 68,* 773–787.

Rose, R. J. (1995). Genes and human behavior. *Annual Review of Psychology, 46,* 625–654.

Rothbart, M. K., & Bates, J. E. (1998). Temperament. In W. Damon (Series Ed.) & N. Eisenberg (Vol. Ed.), *Handbook of child psychology: Vol. 3. Social, emotional, and personality development* (5th ed., pp. 105–176). New York: Wiley.

Rothbart, M. K., Derryberry, D., & Posner, M. (1994). A psychobiological approach to the development of temperament. In J. E. Bates & T. D. Wachs (Eds.), *Temperament: Individual differences at the interface of biology and behavior* (pp. 83–116). Washington, DC: American Psychological Association.

Rothbaum, F., & Weisz, J. R. (1994). Parental caregiving and child externalizing behavior: A meta-analysis. *Psychological Bulletin, 116,* 55–74.

Rusting, C. L., & Larsen, R. J. (1998). Personality and cognitive processing of affective information. *Personality and Social Psychology Bulletin, 24,* 200–213.

Saarni, C., Mumme, D. L., & Campos, J. J. (1998). Emotional development: Action, communication, and understanding. In W. Damon (Series Ed.) & N. Eisenberg (Vol. Ed.), *Handbook of child psychology: Vol. 3. Social, emotional, and personality development* (5th ed., pp. 237–309). New York: Wiley.

Schore, A. N. (1996). The experience-dependent maturation of a regulatory system in the orbital prefrontal cortex and the origin of developmental psychopathology. *Development and Psychopathology, 8,* 59–87.

Shaw, D. S., Owens, E. B., Vondra, J. I., Keenan, K., & Winslow, E. (1996). Early risk factors and pathways in the development of disruptive behavior problems. *Development and Psychopathology, 8,* 679–699.

Sroufe, L. A. (1983). Infant–caregiver attachment and patterns of adaptation in preschool: The roots of maladaptation and competence. In M. Perlmutter (Ed.), *Development and policy concerning children with special needs. Minnesota Symposia on Child Psychology* (Vol. 16, pp. 41–83). Hillsdale, NJ: Erlbaum.

Steinberg, L., Lamborn, S. D., Darling, N., Mounts, N. S., & Dornbusch, S. M. (1994). Over-time changes in adjustment and competence among adolescents from authoritative, authoritarian, indulgent, and neglectful families. *Child Development, 65,* 754–770.

Thomas, A., Chess, S., & Birch, H. G. (1968). *Temperament and behavior disorders in children.* New York: New York University Press.

Thompson, R. A. (1998). Early sociopersonality development. In W. Damon (Series Ed.) & N. Eisenberg (Vol. Ed.), *Handbook of child psychology: Vol. 3. Social, emotional, and personality development* (5th ed., pp. 25–104). New York: Wiley.

Tremblay, R. (1992). The prediction of delinquent behavior from childhood behavior: Personality theory revisited. In J. McCord (Ed.), *Advances in criminological theory: Vol. 3. Facts, frameworks, and forecasts* (pp. 193–230). New Brunswick, NJ: Transaction.

van den Boom, D. C. (1994). The influence of temperament and mothering on attachment and exploration: An experimental manipulation of sensitive responsiveness among lower-class mothers with irritable infants. *Child Development, 65,* 1457–1477.

Wachs, T. D. (1992). *The nature of nurture.* Newbury Park, CA: Sage.

Weiss, B., Dodge, K. A., Bates, J. E., & Pettit, G. S. (1992). Some consequences of early harsh discipline: Child aggression and a maladaptive social information processing style. *Child Development, 63,* 1321–1335.

Yoshikawa, H. (1994). Prevention as cumulative protection: Effects of early family support and education on chronic delinquency and its risks. *Psychological Bulletin, 115,* 28–54.

Zuckerman, M., Kuhlman, D. M., Joireman, J., Teta, P., & Kraft, M. (1993). A comparison of three structural models for personality: The Big Three, the Big Five, and the Alternative Five. *Journal of Personality and Social Psychology, 65,* 757–768.

CHAPTER 26

The Cultural Psychology of the Emotions: Ancient and New

Richard A. Shweder
Jonathan Haidt

Great, deep, wide and unbounded, the ocean is nevertheless drunk by underwater fires; in the same way, Sorrow is drunk by Anger. (Translation of an unidentified Sanskrit stanza from India in the early Middle Ages; Gnoli, 1956, p. 35)

This chapter recapitulates and expands a description of the cultural psychology of the emotions that appeared in the first edition of the *Handbook*. A cultural/symbolic/meaning-centered approach to the study of the emotions is defined and illustrated, using some sources that are quite ancient (e.g., a 3rd century Sanskrit text, the "Rasādhyāya" of the *Nātyaśāstra* and others that are quite new. The chapter then examines the moral context of emotional functioning. It is suggested that the character and meaning of particular emotions are systematically related to the kind of ethic (autonomy, community, or divinity) prevalent in a cultural community (Shweder, 1990b; Shweder, Much, Mahapatra, & Park, 1997; Haidt, Koller, & Dias, 1993; Jensen, 1995).

In recent years there have been several major reviews of contemporary research on similarities and differences in emotional meanings across cultural groups (Good & Kleinman, 1984; Kleinman & Good, 1985; Kitayama & Markus, 1994; Lutz & White, 1986; Marsella, 1980; Mesquita & Frijda, 1992; Russell, 1991; Scherer, Wallbott, & Summerfield, 1986; Shweder & LeVine, 1984; Shweder, 1991,

1993, 1994; White & Kirkpatrick, 1985). There have also been several books and essays defining the character of a new interdisciplinary field for cross-cultural research on the emotions, which has come to be known as "cultural psychology" (e.g., Bruner, 1990; Cole, 1988, 1990, 1996; D'Andrade, 1995; Goddard, 1997; Howard, 1985; LeVine, 1990; Lutz, 1985a; Markus & Kitayama, 1991, 1992; Markus, Kitayama, & Heiman, 1996; Much, 1995; Peacock, 1984; Shweder, 1990, 1991, 1999a, 1999b; Shweder et al., 1998; Shweder & Sullivan, 1990, 1993; Stigler, Shweder, & Herdt, 1990; Wierzbicka, 1993, 1997; Yang, 1997. For a discussion of the historical antecedents of cultural psychology, see Jahoda (1992). In anthropology, the two most notable forums for research on the cultural psychology of the emotions are the journals *Ethos: Journal of the Society for Psychological Anthropology*, and *Culture, Medicine and Psychiatry*.

The major goals of cultural psychology are to spell out the implicit meanings that give shape to psychological processes, to examine the distribution of those meanings across ethnic groups and temporal–spatial regions of the world, and to identify the manner of their social acquisition. Related goals are to reassess the principle of psychic unity or uniformity, and to develop a credible theory of psychological diversity or pluralism. The emphasis in cultural psychology is upon the way the human mind can be transformed and made functional in a number of different ways, which are not equally distributed across ethnic and cultural communities around the world. Hence the slogan popular among cultural psychologists, "One mind, but many mentalities: universalism without the uniformity," which is meant to express that pluralistic emphasis (see Shweder, 1991, 1996, 1998; Shweder et al., 1998).

One hallmark of cultural psychology is a conception of "culture" that is symbolic and behavioral at the same time. Culture, so conceived, can be defined as ideas about what is true, good, beautiful, and efficient that are made manifest in the speech, laws and customary practices of a self-regulating group (Goodnow, Miller, & Kessel, 1995; Shweder et al., 1998; Shweder, 1999a, 1999b). In research on cultural psychology, "culture" thus consists of meanings, conceptions, and interpretive schemes that are activated, constructed or brought "online" through participation in normative social institutions and routine practices (including linguistic practices) (see e.g., D'Andrade, 1984; Geertz, 1973; LeVine, 1984; Miller, Potts, Fung, Hoogstra, & Mintz, 1990; Shweder, 1991, 1999a,b). According to this view, a culture is that subset of possible or available meanings which, by virtue of enculturation (informal or formal, implicit or explicit, unintended or intended), has become active in giving shape to the psychological processes of the individuals in a group.

A second hallmark of cultural psychology is the idea that interpretation, conceptualization, and other "acts of meaning" can take place rapidly, automatically, and un-self-consciously. Indeed it is assumed that "acts of meaning" (e.g., the judgment that the human body may become polluted or desanctified because it is a temple for the soul; or that illness is a means of empowerment because it unburdens a person of accumulated spiritual debts; or that shyness, shame, modesty, and embarrassment are good emotions because they are forms of civility) can take place so rapidly, automatically, and un-self-consciously that from the point of view of an individual person they are indistinguishable from "raw" experience or "naked" consciousness itself (see, e.g., Geertz, 1984, on "experience-near" concepts; Kirsh 1991, on "thought in action"; and Nisbett & Wilson, 1977, on the unconscious "knowing more than we can tell"; see also Fish, 1980). According to this view, many rapid, automatic, and un-self-conscious psychological processes are best understood not as "pure," "fundamental," or "intrinsic" processes, but rather as content-laden processes, which are contingent on the implicit meanings, conceptual schemes, and interpretations that give them life (Markus, et al., 1996; Nisbett & Cohen, 1995; Shweder, 1990a; Stigler, 1984; Stigler, Chalip, & Miller, 1986; Stigler, Nusbaum & Chalip, 1988).

In the context of the study of the emotions, the intellectual agenda of cultural psychology can be defined by four questions:

1. What is the generic shape of the meaning system that defines an experience as an emotional experience (e.g., anger, sadness, or shame) rather than as an experience of some other kind (e.g., muscle tension, fatigue, or emptiness? (see, e.g., Harré, 1986a, 1986b; Lakoff, 1987; Levy, 1984a, 1984b; Shweder, 1994; Smedslund, 1991; Solomon, 1976, 1984; Stein & Levine, 1987; Wierzbicka, 1986, 1992, 1999).

2. What particular emotional meanings (e.g., Pintupi *watjilpa,* Balinese *lek,* Newar *lajja,* Ifaluk *fago,* American "happiness") are constructed or brought "online" in different ethnic groups and in different temporal–spatial regions of the world)? (see, e.g., Abu-Lughod, 1985, 1986; Appadurai, 1985; Briggs, 1970; Gerber, 1985; Geertz, 1959; Lutz, 1982, 1988; Miller & Sperry, 1987; Myers 1979a, 1979b; Parish, 1991; Rosaldo, 1980, 1983, 1984; Schieffelin, 1976, 1983, 1985a, 1985b; Stearns & Stearns, 1988; Swartz, 1988; Wierzbicka, 1986, 1990, 1997, 1999; Wikan, 1984, 1989.)

3. To what extent is the experience of various states of the world (e.g., "loss," "goal blockage," "status degradation," "taboo violation") "emotionalized" (e.g., as sadness, anger, fear, or guilt) rather than "somatized" (e.g., as tiredness, chest pain, or appetite loss) in different ethnic groups and in different temporal–spatial regions of the world? (see, e.g., Angel & Guarnaccia, 1989; Angel & Idler, 1992; Angel & Thoits, 1987; Kleinman, 1986; Levy, 1984a, 1984b; Shweder, 1988.)

4. Precisely how are emotionalized and somatized meanings brought "online," socialized,

enculturated, or otherwise acquired? More specifically, what is the role of everyday discourse and social interpretation in the activation of emotionalized and somatized meanings? (See, e.g., Bruner, 1990; Garvey, 1992; Miller & Sperry, 1987; Miller et al. 1990; Miller, Mintz, Hoogstra, Fung, & Potts, 1992; Miller & Hoogstra, 1992; Ochs & Schieffelin, 1984; Schieffelin & Ochs, 1986; Shweder et al., 1998; Shweder & Much, 1987).

Any comprehensive review of answers to these questions would have to address hundreds of years of theoretical arguments, empirical sightings, and philosophical reflections in the literatures of several different civilizations (see Dimock, 1974; Harré, 1986b; Kakar, 1982; Kleinman, 1986; Rorty, 1980; Shixie, 1989; Solomon, 1976; Veith, 1978). In this chapter our aim is simply to formulate the first two of those questions in ways that seem promising, provocative, and productive for future interdisciplinary research.

We start the discussion, however, in the 3rd century A.D. in India with a relatively detailed examination of a Sanskrit text (the "Rasādhyāya" of the *Nāṭyaśāstra* that was written relatively close to the beginning of the historical record of systematic human self-consciousness about the emotions. It is through an analysis of this venerable text—an ancient example of a cultural psychology—that we address contemporary concerns. The "Rasādhyāya" is a useful intellectual pole star on which to concentrate a discussion of the cultural psychology of the emotions, for three reasons: (1) The text, although ancient, compares favorably with any contemporary treatise on the symbolic character of emotional experience; (2) the text, although famous among Sanskritists and scholars of South Asian civilization, is hardly known at all by emotion researchers in anthropology and psychology; and (3) the text provides the opportunity for an object lesson about the universally appealing yet culturally revealing character of all accounts about what is "basic" to the emotional nature of human beings.

THE BASIC EMOTIONS OF THE "RASĀDHĀYA"

In Sanskrit the word for "existence" and the word for "mental state" (*bhāva*) are the same, and mental states are said to "bring into exis-

tence the essence of poetry" (Gnoli, 1956, p. 63). So one should not be surprised to discover that between the 3rd and 11th centuries A.D., Hindu philosophers of poetics and drama, interested in human emotions as objects of aesthetic pleasure, posited the existence of eight or nine basic emotions (*sthāyi-bhāva*)—four of which they viewed as primary—and developed a relatively detailed account of the symbolic structures that give them shape and meaning.

There is no standard English translation of the Sanskrit terms for the postulated basic emotions. Indeed, there is no agreement about whether they should be translated as "emotions" or as "mental states" or as "feelings," or about whether they should be translated as "basic" or "dominant" or "permanent" or "universal" or "natural" or "principal" emotions (or mental states or feelings). The eight basic (or dominant) emotions (or mental states or feelings) are variously translated as follows: (1) sexual passion, love, or delight (*rati*); (2) amusement, laughter, humor, or mirth (*hāsa*); (3) sorrow (*śoka*); (4) anger (*krodha*); (5) fear or terror (*bhaya*); (6) perseverance, energy, dynamic energy, or heroism (*utsāha*); (7) disgust or disillusion (*jugupsā*); and (8) amusement, wonder, astonishment, or amazement (*vismaya*). Some early medieval commentators mention an additional basic (or dominant) emotion (or mental state or feeling), (9) serenity or calm (*sama*). To simplify our exegesis, we refer to the eight (or nine) as "basic emotions," and we label them "sexual passion," "amusement," "sorrow," "anger," "fear," "perseverance," "disgust," "wonder," and "serenity." Of the basic emotions, four are privileged as primary basic emotions: sexual passion, anger, perseverance, and disgust (with serenity sometimes substituted or linked to disgust as a primary basic emotion).

The canonical Sanskrit text on the "emotions," attributed to Bharata, is the sixth chapter, the "Rasādhyāya," of the *Nāṭyaśāstra*, which is a book about drama. Ancient and medieval Hindu thought specialized in "psychological" topics concerned with the nature of consciousness. Much of Sanskrit philosophy elevated the human mind and body to the status of sacramental objects, and was disinclined to draw sharp oppositions among the material, the sensate, the conscious, the poetic, and the divine. In Sanskrit drama the primary aim of the aesthetic experience was psychological as well; indeed, it was the symbolic representation of emotional states per se that set the stage for aesthetic and revelatory experience (see Dimock, 1974). The famous sixth chapter of the *Nāṭyaśāstra* is about the narrative structure (the causes, consequences, and concomitants) of eight basic emotional states and the most effective means (via facial expression, voice, posture, setting, character, action, and physiological response) of their representation in the theatre.

The *Nāṭyaśāstra* was probably written some time between the 3rd and 5th centuries A.D. The most famous explication and commentary on the text, itself a critique of earlier explications and commentaries and the source of our knowledge of the earlier commentaries, derives from the 10th and 11th century Kashmiri Brahman philosopher Abhinavagupta (partial translations and contemporary commentaries can be found in Masson & Patwardhan, 1970, and Gnoli, 1956; see also Dimock, 1974, and Keith, 1924).

One major concern of the text and commentaries is to define the nature and significance (both aesthetic and theological) of an elusive metaemotion called *rasa*. *Rasa* means "to taste," "to savor," or "to sample," but when the term is used to refer to the grand metaemotion of Hindu aesthetic experience it is usually translated as aesthetic "pleasure," "enjoyment," or "rapture." It is a pleasure that lasts only as long as the dramatic illusion that makes *rasa* a reality. Because it is possible for members of the audience who witness a drama (the *rasiki*) to experience enjoyment or pleasure (*rasa*) even from the apprehension of negative emotional states (disgust, fear, anger, sorrow), which in other circumstances one might want to avoid or repress, Abhinavagupta and others reasoned that *rasa* must be an autonomous metaemotion, a *sui generis* form of consciousness.

A second major concern of the text and commentaries is to differentiate eight (or nine) varieties, colors, or flavors of *rasa,* each related to one of the basic emotions. There is no standard English translation of the Sanskrit terms for the eight (or nine) *rasa.* They are variously translated as (1) the erotic or love (*sṛṅgara*, the *rasa* of sexual passion); (2) the comic (*hāsya*, the *rasa* of amusement); (3) the compassionate or pathetic (*karuna*, the *rasa* of sorrow); (4) the furious or fury (*raudra*, the *rasa* of anger); (5) the heroic (*vīra*, the *rasa* of perseverance); (6) the terrifying or terror (*bhayānaka,* the *rasa* of fear); (7) horror, the loathsome, the odious or the disgusting (*bībhatsa*, the *rasa* of disgust); (8) the marvelous, the awesome, admiration, or

wonder (*adbhuta,* the *rasa* of wonder); and (9) the quietistic or calm (*śānta*, the *rasa* of serenity). When viewed from the perspective of their relationship to the eight (or nine) basic emotions of everyday life, the eight (or nine) flavors of *rasa* (the pleasure of the terrifying, the delight of horror, etc.) are sometimes translated as the eight (or nine) "sentiments" or "moods" of the theater.

A third major concern of the text and commentaries is to give an account of the precise relationship between the *rasa* and the basic emotions (*sthāyi-bhāva*) to which they are said to correspond. In general, when the actor on stage effectively portrays a particular *bhāva,* the appreciative audience experiences the corresponding *rasa.* But is the relationship one of identity, such that the audience's experience of the *rasa* of fear is itself a real everyday experience of fear? Or is the experience of the *rasa* of fear a mere simulation, imitation, or pretense of everyday fear? Or is it perhaps an intensification or amplification of the basic emotion? Ultimately, the idea is advanced that the experience of the *rasa* of a basic emotion is something entirely different from the experience of the basic emotion itself.

Instead, the relationship of the eight (or nine) *rasa* to the eight (or nine) basic emotions is akin to the relationship of an intentional state to its intentional object. To experience *rasa* is to experience the pleasure or enjoyment (an intentional state) that results from the dramatically induced perception of the hidden or unconscious generic symbolic structures (the intentional objects) that lend shape and meaning to the basic emotions in everyday life. To paraphrase Bharata, in drama the basic emotions are brought to a state of *rasa*. This happens to the very extent that their implicit symbolic codes are revealed and savored (or tasted) as objects of pleasure and as a means of self-consciousness and transcendence.

According to this line of reasoning then, what "flavors" or "colors" the *rasa* and distinguishes them from each other is that each has a different intentional object, one of the eight (or nine) "basic" emotions, which are thought to be possessed by all human beings at birth. Nevertheless there is still something common to all the flavors of *rasa*. It is the pleasure, enjoyment, delight, or rapture that comes from being artfully transported out of time, place, and the immediacies of personal emotional experiences—beyond "the thick pall of mental stupor which cloaks one's own consciousness" (Gnoli, 1956, p. 53)—into the hidden depths of the soul, where one perceives, tastes, and savors the transcendental or impersonal narrative forms that are immanent or implicit in the most deeply rooted modes of human experience.

Thus, viewed generically, all *rasa* possess that quality of pleasure or enjoyment that comes from the tasting of a transcendent form that had previously been hidden from the consciousness it had organized. It is this *sui generis* experience of delight, viewed as an intentional state aimed at the basic emotions as its intentional object, which explains how even disgust, anger, fear, and sorrow can be objects of pleasure when they present themselves as objects of aesthetic encounter. Thus viewed, what is common to the *rasa* is a metaemotion, the feeling of delight that comes from the clear apprehension of the symbolic forms implicit in ordinary emotional experience. This line of reasoning is suggestive of a parallel type of analysis of "empathy." Empathy may be viewed as a metaemotion motivated by its own characteristic source of enjoyment or pleasure, which makes it possible to be responsive to another person's negative emotional states such as sorrow or guilt. By this analysis, empathic sorrow or empathic guilt is not the same as the direct or secondary experience of sorrow or guilt. Instead, empathy is a dignifying experience precisely because, as a witness to someone else's emotional experience, one is transported out of oneself. It is as if empathy is also a metaemotion, but of a middle scale. It is less detached than the experience of *rasa*, which comes from witnessing the generic symbolic structure that lends shape and meaning to a basic emotion; yet it is more detached than the experience of a basic emotion itself, which is the unwitnessed and all too immediate experience of everyday personal life. (For an account of the psychology of empathy, see Hoffman, 1990.)

Having summarized, however incompletely, a few key elements of the "Rasādhyāya" and subsequent commentaries, we would now like to ask two questions about the text. (1) What can the "Rasādhyāya" tell us about the symbolic structure of emotional experience? (2) What does it reveal about itself as a cultured (hence parochial or local) account of what is "basic" to human emotional experience? We treat the second question first.

THE WONDER OF THE SANSKRIT EMOTIONS: A CULTURAL ACCOUNT

Contemporary emotion researchers are likely to find the account of the basic emotions in the "Rasādhyāya" both familiar and strange. If we compare the Sanskrit list of nine (eight plus one) basic emotions (sexual passion, amusement, sorrow, anger, fear, perseverance, disgust, wonder, and sometimes serenity) with Paul Ekman's well-known contemporary list of nine (six plus three) basic emotions (anger, fear, sadness, happiness, surprise, and disgust, plus interest, shame, and contempt), which he derives from the analysis of everyday facial expressions (Ekman, 1980, 1984), the two lists are not closely coordinated, although they are not totally disjoint either.

Richard Schechner (1988, pp. 267–289), in his volume *Performance Theory*, presents a series of photographs of facial expressions that he claims are iconic representations of the nine *rasa* of the *Nāṭyaśāstra*. This, of course, is a rather risky thing to do. The *Nāṭyaśāstra* never abstracts out facial expressions as the key markers of the basic emotions, but rather treats them as one element in an array of constituents; and there is every reason to believe that in Hindu drama facial expressions unfold dynamically in a sequence of movements, which are not easily frozen into a single frame. Nevertheless, Schechner posits direct analogies between six of his facial expressions for the *rasa* and the six facial expressions from Ekman's primary scheme—equating, for example, Ekman's representation of the face of surprise with the face for the *rasa* of wonder (*adbhuta*) and Ekman's representation of the face of happiness with the face for the *rasa* of sexual passion (*sṛṅgara*). Schechner thinks he sees a universal pattern reflected in the two schemes. He states, "Humankind has countless gods, but I would be very surprised if there were not some agreement concerning the basic emotions" (1988, p. 266).

In our view, several of Schechner's equations are dubious. For example, in Ekman's photo of the face of surprise, the mouth is wide open; it is not similar to the mouth of the *rasa* of wonder, which is closed and faintly suggestive of a smile. (The mouth is closed in all of the facial expressions of the *rasa*, which may be related to a cultural evaluation concerning the vulgarity of an open mouth.) And in Ekman's photo of the face of happiness, the eyes are directly frontal; they are not similar to the eyes of the *rasa* of sexual passion, where the gaze is conspicuously averted to one side, perhaps suggestive of secrecy or conspiracy. More importantly, because Schechner's equation of North American "happiness" with Sanskrit "sexual passion" seems peculiar from the start, it should also be noted that Ekman's photo of the face of happiness, bears no resemblance whatsoever to the face of the *rasa* of amusement (*hāsya*), which is the *rasa* one might have intuitively expected to be connected to the Western conception of "happiness."

We strongly doubt that most North Americans could spontaneously generate accurate descriptions for the majority of the nine facial icons of the *rasa* displayed in Schechner's book. (Curiously, one of the faces that U.S. graduate students seem to identify without much difficulty is the Sanskrit face of serenity, which as far as we know is not a basic emotion on any Western list. In informal experiments conducted in classes at the University of Chicago, they also converge in their responses to faces of fear, disgust, and sorrow, but not to the others.) Indeed, we believe one can plausibly argue that happiness, surprise, and most of the basic emotions on Ekman's list do not have close analogues among the basic emotions of the "Rasādhyāya," and any sense of easy familiarity with the Sanskrit list is more apparent than real.

As we read the "Rasādhyāya" and commentaries, three of the nine basic emotions (anger, fear, and sorrow) are genuinely familiar, in the sense of possessing an equivalent shape and meaning for medieval Hindus and contemporary North Americans. Of course, to acknowledge those three points of dense similarity is not to suggest that those three emotional meanings must be cross-cultural universals. Wierzbicka (1992; see also 1990, 1997, 1999), an anthropological linguist and polyglot who specializes in the study of semantic universals and the language of the emotions, has brought to a halt facile claims about translation equivalence, by arguing that "sadness" as understood in European and North American conceptions of the emotions is not an empirical universal and is neither lexicalized, important, nor salient in most of the languages of the world. She claims that from the point of view of the study of the linguistic semantics of emotion terms

around the world, there are no basic or universal emotions.

Nevertheless, anger, fear, and sorrow are easy to recognize in the "Rasādhyāya." Sorrow, for example, is said to arise from misfortune, calamity, and destruction, and from "separation from those who are dear, [their] downfall, loss of wealth, death and imprisonment." "It should be acted out by tears, laments, drying up of the mouth, change of color, languor in the limbs, sighs, loss of memory, etc." (Masson & Patwardhan, 1970, p. 52). Sorrow is said to be accompanied by other mental states, including world-weariness, physical weariness, lifelessness, tears, confusion, dejection, and worry.

Anger and fear are also easy to recognize in the text. Anger, for example, is said to arise from provocative actions, insult, lies, assault, harsh words, oppression, and envy. The actions accompanying it include beating, splitting open, crushing, breaking, hitting, and drawing blood. "It should be acted out by red eyes, furrowing of the brows, biting one's lips and grinding one's teeth, puffing the cheeks, wringing the hands, and similar gestures." It is accompanied by other mental states, including an increase in determination or energy, rashness, violence, sweat, trembling, pride, panic, resentment, and stuttering (see Masson & Patwardhan, 1970, pp. 52–53).

For three of the nine basic emotions described in the "Rasādhyāya," it is easy to recognize the underlying script, to see the self in the other, and to arrive at a cross-cultural and transhistorical agreement about what is basic in emotional functioning (at least for them and us). Yet as one moves beyond sorrow, anger and fear to disgust, amusement, wonder, perseverance, sexual passion, and serenity, the way in which consciousness is partitioned or hierarchically structured into basic and nonbasic states in the "Rasādhyāya" seems less and less familiar, despite any initial appearances to the contrary. This decline in familiarity is similar to the "gradient of recognition" that Haidt and Keltner (1999) found when studying facial expressions in India and the United States: Some expressions are very well recognized across cultures, some are less well recognized, and there is no clear or bounded set of "universal" facial expressions.

Thus it becomes clear upon examination of the relevant Sanskrit texts and commentaries that medieval Hindu "disgust" differs from modern North American disgust. Medieval

Hindu disgust is partitioned into two subtypes: The first includes aspects of horror and disillusionment, as well as world-weariness associated with the quest for detachment, transcendence, and salvation. The second includes horror at the sight of blood. Medieval Hindu disgust is, as the anthropologist McKim Marriott has suggested to us, more like a domain of the loathsome, and it gathers together within its territory a broad range of human responses to the ugly, the nasty, and the odious. Rozin, Haidt, and McCauley (Chapter 40, this volume) argue that contemporary North American disgust has a similarly broad and heterogeneous domain of elicitors, but that moral and interpersonal disgust are highly variable across cultures.

It also becomes clear upon examination that medieval Hindu "wonder" is not contemporary North American "surprise," but rather a state of mind closer to admiration than to startle or shock. For Hindu wonder has less to do with a sudden violation of expectations and more to do with one's reactions to the opportunity to witness divine, heavenly, or exalted feats, events, or beings (including, e.g., the feats of a juggler). It is even possible to do such witnessing with one's mouth closed, as long as the eyes are wide open!

Similarly it becomes clear upon examination that medieval Hindu "amusement" (which includes contemptuous, indignant, or derisive laughter at the faults and inferior status of others) is not contemporary North American "happiness," which has celebratory implications. Indeed, happiness, shame, indignation, arrogance, and some contempt-like emotions are explicitly mentioned in the "Rasādhyāya" for inclusion among 33 nonbasic ("accompanying") mental states. Thus it seems reasonable to assert that the basic emotion designated by medieval Hindu philosophers as "amusement" is not adequately translated as "happiness" or as "contempt." (It should be noted that while the text provides little basis for determining equivalence of meaning for the terms used to translate the 33 nonbasic mental states, there is good reason to doubt that "shame" and "happiness" have the same implications and associations, or play the same psychological role, in India as they do in contemporary North America. (See Shweder, 1994, on the positive qualities of shame in India, where it is a virtue associated with civility, modesty, and an ability to rein in one's destructive powers in support of

the social order rather than with the diminishment of the ego; see also Parish, 1991, and below.)

It also becomes clear upon examination of the text that medieval Hindu "perseverance" is not contemporary North American "interest," but is rather deeply connected to heroic determination and a willingness to engage in acts requiring endurance and self-sacrifice. In the context of the early medieval Hindu scriptures, when the Hindu goddess Durga (or Kali) endured trials and tribulations yet persisted in a seemingly hopeless battle against uncountable demons in an effort to save the world, her efforts are said to have displayed the heroic *rasa* of perseverance. Mere interest had very little to do with it; she would probably rather have been doing something else (see below).

In sum, the two lists of nine basic human emotions truly overlap at only three points. All the other apparent points of similarity (amusement as happiness, their disgust as our disgust, wonder as surprise, perseverance as interest) turn out to be merely apparent; and for several of the emotions (sexual passion, serenity, shame, contempt), there is not even an illusion of transcultural equivalence. In the end, most of the items cannot be easily mapped across the two lists.

There are other ways in which the "Rasādhyāya" presents us with a somewhat unfamiliar portrait of the way consciousness is organized. One has to do with the way the text divides the basic emotions into *primary* basic emotions and *secondary* basic emotions. According to the text and commentaries, the four primary basic emotions are sexual passion, anger, perseverance, and disgust. The four secondary basic emotions are amusement, sorrow, wonder, and fear. The ninth basic emotion, serenity, is sometimes viewed as a primary basic emotion and either substituted for disgust or associated with disgust (through a causal sequence that begins with horror and revulsion over attachments in the world and ends with the serenity of ego alienation, detachment, and salvation).

In commenting on this scheme, it is perhaps worth noting in passing that Sigmund Freud might find much of value in a conception that treats sexual passion and anger (and perseverance and disgust) as the deepest aspects of human experience. One wonders whether Freud would have interpreted perseverance and disgust as analogues to the life and death instincts.

More notable, however, is the fact that the primary basic emotions are primary primarily because they are the "emotions" associated in classical and folk Hindu thought with the four worthy ends or goals of life. One of these goals of life—pleasure (*kāma*)—is linked to sexual passion. A second goal—control, autonomy, and power (*artha*)—is linked to anger. A third goal—social duty and moral virtue (*dharma*)—is linked to perseverance. The fourth and perhaps highest goal—salvation or the attainment of divinity (*moksha*)—is linked to disgust and/or serenity. In other words, presupposed by this famous formulation about the organization of human emotions are a special theory of morality and human motivation, and a specific way of life. Thus it is hardly surprising that this particular medieval South Asian conception of the hierarchical structuring of consciousness into basics versus nonbasics and primary basics versus secondary basics should seem somewhat strange to emotion researchers in North America, and vice versa.

There is yet another way in which the "Rasādhyāya" presents us with an unfamiliar portrait of the organization of consciousness. For the eight or nine items on the Sanskrit list are bound to seem like a disparate and anomalous collection, at least from the point of view of North American folk and academic conceptions about how to partition consciousness into kinds of mental states (see D'Andrade 1987). Indeed, one might expect North American emotion researchers to recoil at the very suggestion that the Sanskrit list is really a list of basic "emotions" at all. North American folk and academic psychology do not really classify serenity, wonder, sexual passion, amusement, or perseverance as definitive or clear examples of "emotions" (see Shaver, Schwartz, Kirson, & O'Connor, 1987). Sexual passion would probably be classified as a motive or, alternatively, as a nonemotional feeling. Serenity might be classified as a nonemotional feeling or a state of mind, although not a motive. Perseverance would probably be classified as a quality of will or agency, or perhaps a formal property of motivation. Amusement and wonder seem to be none of the above. Indeed after reading the text and commentaries and the various nonequivalent translations of *bhāva* and *rasa* (are they mental states, emotions, feelings, moods, sentiments, or what?), one might begin to suspect that in the "Rasādhyāya" one is faced with a somewhat different conception of how to parti-

tion a person into parts and how to divide consciousness into kinds.

It is of course possible (indeed, likely) that in some ways the "Rasādhyāya" presupposes a partitioning of the person into parts that is not coordinate with our own conception of the person, and that is why it is so hard to settle on any single translation equivalent for the Sanskrit *bhāva* and *rasa*. This is a familiar kind of translation problem, and it is encountered even across European languages and subcultures. Wierzbicka (1989), for example, has analyzed in detail the many distortions of meaning that occur when the Russian word *duša* is translated into English. *Duša* is a lexical item signifying a key Russian cultural concept that has to do with the partitioning of a person into parts. It is typically translated into English as "soul," or alternatively as "mind" or "heart" or "spirit." None of these lexical mappings is adequate, because none of these English words signifies the full and equivalent set of meanings associated with *duša*. For example, Wierzbicka (1989, p. 52) notes that it is one of two parts of the person; that one cannot see it; that because of this part, things can happen in a person that cannot happen in anything other than a person; that these things can be good or bad; that because of this part, a person can feel things that nothing other than a person can feel; that other people can't know what these things are if the person doesn't say it; that a person would want someone to know what these things are; and that because of this part, a person can be a good person and feel something good toward other people.

Similar issues concerning variations in the organization of consciousness arise in connection with the research of Steven Parish (1991) on conceptions of the mental life among the South Asian Hindu Newars of Nepal (see also Appadurai, 1990; Brenneis, 1990). For the Newars, mental states such as memory, desire, feeling, thought, and emotion, which we would spatially differentiate between the head and the heart (and perhaps the gut and the skin), are all thought to be located together in the heart; this heart of the mental life is thought to be animated by a god, who makes perception and experience possible. Consequently, for the Newars "the efforts of individuals to monitor their inner life often draw on the sense of a divine agency," and it is believed that "a person sees because the god sees through his or her eyes" (Parish, 1991, p. 316). So it would be surprising indeed if the set of meanings associated with the Sanskrit terms *rasa* and *bhāva* could be easily mapped onto the set of meanings associated with any single English term or phrase, such as "emotion," "feeling," "mood," "sentiment," "mental state," or "consciousness." We look forward to the day when Sanskritists do for the concept signified by the term *bhāva* what Wierzbicka has done for the concept signified by the Russian word *duša*

For the time being, however, we are not going to try to solve the very deepest of questions about the partitioning of the person into parts and the division of consciousness into kinds. Instead, we are going to argue that it is helpful enough to know what the text tells us. What the "Rasādhyāya" tells us is that in drama the *sthāyi-bhāva* (we'll keep calling them "basic emotions") are brought to a state of *rasa*. More importantly, however, what the text tells us is that the *rasa* are nothing more than the union of three script-like or narrative components:

1. The determinants, causes, or eliciting conditions (*vi-bhāva*), which includes all the background information, settings, events, and action tendencies that might make manifest some state of the world and one's relationship to it (e.g., forced separation from something one cherishes; finding oneself powerless in the face of danger).

2. The consequences (*anu-bhāva*), which includes eight types of involuntary somatic responses (sweating, fainting, weeping, etc.), and various action tendencies (abusing the body, brandishing weapons) and expressive modes (bodily movement, voice tone, facial expression)—for example, wailing and tears.

3. The "accompanying" mental states (*vyabhicari-bhāva*), which are something like a 33-item symptom list of secondary side effects, including emotions, feelings, and cognitive states; some of these effects are weariness, reminiscence, panic, envy, dreaming, confusion, sickness, shame, and even death.

In other words, in the "Rasādhyāya" one finds a relatively elaborate account of the symbolic structures that give shape and meaning to a selected subset of mental experiences, which because they have been privileged for symbolic elaboration have become transformed into "basic" mental experiences for that culturally constituted world. That is, in the "Rasādhyāya" one finds an ancient yet sophisticated text in the cultural psychology of the emotions.

THE SYMBOLIC STRUCTURE OF THE EMOTIONS

The strategy adopted in the "Rasādhyāya" is to define a basic emotion by the implicit symbolic structure that gives shape and meaning to that emotion (its *rasa*—the intentional object of aesthetic pleasure in the theatre) and then to define that symbolic structure by resolving it into its determinants, consequences, and accompanying side effects. This strategy is directly parallel to various contemporary approaches to the cultural psychology of the emotions.

One aspect of this symbolic (or, as some would call it, "cognitive") approach is the view that kinds of emotions are not kinds of things like plants or animals. Instead they are (*rasa*-like) interpretive schemes of a particular script-like, story-like, or narrative kind that give shape and meaning to the human experience of those conditions of the world that have a bearing on self-esteem (see Shweder, 1994). The elements that are proposed as slots in the story may vary slightly from scholar to scholar, although most of the slots in use today can be found in the "Rasādhyāya."

Mesquita and Frijda (1992; also see Ellsworth, 1991; Frijda, 1986; Lazarus, 1991; Lewis, Sullivan, & Michalson, 1984; Lewis, 1989; Lutz, 1985b; Russell, 1991; Stein & Levine, 1987), for example, parse each emotion script into a series of slots including "antecedent events," "event coding" (type of condition of the world), "appraisal" (judged implications for self-esteem and well-being), "physiological reaction patterns," "action readiness," "emotional behavior," and "regulation." Shweder (1994) suggests a parsing of emotion scripts into slots such as "self-involving conditions of the world" (e.g., loss and gain, protection and threat), "somatic feelings" (e.g., muscle tension, pain, dizziness, nausea, fatigue, breathlessness), "affective feelings" (e.g., agitation, emptiness, expansiveness), "expressive modes" (e.g., face, posture, voice), and "plans for self-management" (e.g., to flee, to retaliate, to celebrate, to invest). (See also Shweder, 1991, where a slot is provided in the emotion narrative for variations in "social regulation" or the normative appropriateness of certain emotions' being experienced or expressed.)

The primary assumption of the symbolic approach is the same as the approach of the "Rasādhyāya"—namely, that the "emotion" (e.g., sadness, fear, or love) is not something independent of or separable from the conditions that justify it, from the somatic and affective events that are ways of feeling or being touched by it, from the actions it demands, or the like. The "emotion" is the whole story: a kind of somatic event (fatigue, chest pain, goose flesh) and/or affective event (panic, emptiness, expansiveness) experienced as a perception of some antecedent conditions (death of a friend, acceptance of a book manuscript for publication, a proposition to go out to dinner) and their implications for the self (e.g., as loss, gain, threat, possibility), and experienced as well as a social judgment (e.g., of vice or virtue, sickness or health) and as a kind of plan for action to preserve one's self-esteem (attack, withdraw, confess, hide, explore). The "emotion" is the entire script. It is the simultaneous experience of all the components, or, perhaps more accurately, the unitary experience of the whole package deal.

A second aspect of the symbolic approach is the view that for the sake of comparison and translation, any "emotion" is decomposable into its narrative slots. From this point of view, to ask whether people are alike or different in their emotional functioning (or whether emotion words in different languages are alike or different in their significations) is really to ask several more specific questions:

1. Are they alike or different in their somatic experiences (e.g., muscle tension, headaches, etc.)? (the somatic phenomenology question)

2. Are they alike or different in their affective experiences (e.g., emptiness, calm, pleasantness)? (the affective phenomenology question)

3. Are they alike or different in the antecedent conditions of those somatic and affective experiences (e.g., infertility, job loss, winning the lottery)? (the environmental determinants question)

4. Are they alike or different in the perceived implications of those antecedent conditions for self-esteem (e.g., irreversible loss, fame and recognition)? (the self-appraisal question)

5. Are they alike or different in the extent to which showing or displaying that state of consciousness has been socially baptized as a vice or virtue or as a sign of sickness or health? (the social appraisal question)

6. Are they alike or different in the plans for

the self-management of self-esteem that get activated as part of the emotion script (e.g., celebration, attack, withdrawal from social contacts)? (the self-management question)

7. Are they alike or different in the iconic and symbolic vehicles used for giving expression to the whole package deal (e.g., facial expressions, voice, posture, and action)? (the communication question)

Given this type of decomposition of the definition of an emotion to its constituent narrative slots, the issue of translation equivalence becomes a matter of pattern matching, as one tries to determine whether the variables in each of those slots are linked in similar ways across cultures.

BITE YOUR TONGUE: THE CASE OF HINDU *LAJJA*

For example, the contemporary Hindu conception of *lajja* (or *lajya*) has recently been explicated for two communities in South Asia, the Newars of Bhaktapur in Nepal (Parish, 1991) and the Oriyas of Bhubaneswar in Orissa, India (Menon & Shweder, 1994, 1998; Shweder & Menon, in press)—and, as spelled out below, there is even more to be said about *lajja* than can be found in those two accounts. *Lajja* is often translated by bilingual informants and dictionaries as "shame," "embarrassment," "shyness," or "modesty"; yet, as should become obvious from the following bit of cultural exegesis, every one of these translations is problematic or fatally flawed.

For starters *lajja* is something one deliberately shows or puts on display the way we might show our "gratitude," "loyalty," or "respect." It is a state of consciousness that has been baptized in South Asia as a supreme virtue, especially for women, and it is routinely exhibited in everyday life (e.g., every time a married woman covers her face or ducks out of a room to avoid direct affiliation with those members of her family she is supposed to avoid). Parish (1991, p. 324) describes it as both an emotion and a moral state. It is by means of their *lajja* that those who are civilized uphold the social order—by showing perseverance in the pursuit of their own social role obligations; by displaying respect for the hierarchical arrangement of social privileges and responsibilities; by acting shy, modest, or deferential and not encroaching on the prerogatives of others; by covering one's face, remaining silent, or lowering one's eyes in the presence of superiors. Like gratitude, loyalty, or respect, *lajja,* which is a way of showing one's civility and commitment to the maintenance of social harmony, is judged in South Asia to be a very good thing.

While *lajja* may be experienced by both men and women, it is an emotion and a virtue associated with a certain feminine ideal. It is talked about as a lovely ornament worn by women. *Lajja* is the linguistic stem for the name of a local creeper plant (a "touch-me-not"), which is so coy that upon the slightest contact it closes its petals and withdraws into itself. To say of a woman that she is full of *lajja* is a very positive recommendation. Here is one reason why.

Perhaps the most important collective representation of *lajja* in various regions of eastern India is the tantric icon portraying the mother goddess Kali, brandishing weapons and a decapitated head in her 10 arms, eyes bulging and tongue out, with her foot stepping on the chest of her husband, the god Siva, who is lying on the ground beneath her. Based on interviews with 92 informants in Orissa, India, Menon and Shweder (1994, 1998; Shweder & Menon, in press) have been examining the meaning of this icon and its significance for our understanding of *lajja.*

The gist of the story, as it is narrated by local experts, is that once upon a time the male gods gave a boon to a minor demon, Mahisasura, to the effect that he could only be killed at the hands of a naked female. They thereby turned Mahisasura into a major demon who was able unimpeded to terrorize all the male gods. In order to destroy the demon, the male gods pooled all their energy and powers and created the goddess Durga, and armed her with their own weapons. On their behalf they sent Durga into battle against Mahisasura, but they neglected to tell her about the boon. She fought bravely but could not kill the demon; he was too strong and clever. In desperation Durga appealed for guidance from an auspicious goddess, who let her in on the secret. As one informant narrated the story:

> So Durga did as she was advised to [she stripped], and within seconds after Mahisasura saw her [naked], his strength waned and he died under her sword. After killing him a terrible rage entered Durga's mind, and she asked herself, "What kinds of gods are these that give to demons such boons, and apart from that what kind of gods are these that they do not have the honesty to tell me the truth before sending me into battle?"

Durga felt humiliated by her nakedness and by the deceit. She decided that such a world with such gods did not deserve to survive; she therefore took on the form of Kali and went on a mad rampage, devouring every living creature that came in her way. The gods then called on Siva, Kali's husband, to do something to save the world from destruction at the hands of the mother goddess. Siva lay in her path as she came tramping along, enraged. Absorbed in her wild dance of destruction, Kali accidentally stepped on Siva and placed her foot on her husband's chest, an unspeakable act of disrespect. When she looked down and saw what she had done, she came back to her senses—in particular to her sense of *lajja,* which she expressed by biting her tongue between her teeth. She reined in her anger and became calm and still. To this day in Orissa, India, "Bite your tongue" is an idiomatic expression for *lajja,* and the biting of the tongue is the facial expression used by women as an iconic apology when they realize, or are confronted with the fact, that they have failed to uphold social norms.

One moral of the story is that men are incapable of running the world by themselves, even though they are socially dominant. They rely on women to make the world go round. Yet in a patriarchal society, men humiliate women by the way they exploit female power, strength, and perseverance. This leads to anger and rage in women, which is highly destructive of everything of value and must be brought under control, for the sake of the social order. *Lajja* is a salient ideal in South Asia because it preserves social harmony by helping women to swallow their rage.

If we decompose *lajja* into its constituent narrative slots, it becomes apparent just how hazardous it can be to assume that one can render the emotional meanings of others with terms from our received English lexicon for mental states. (See Geertz, 1984, p. 130, on the difficulties of translating the Balinese term *lek.* Balinese *lek* seems much like Hindu *lajja.* Geertz notes that *lek* has been variably translated and mistranslated and that "'shame' is the most common attempt." He tries to render it as "stage fright.") Hindu *lajja* does not map well onto words like "shame," "embarrassment," "shyness," "modesty," or "stage fright." An analysis of the constituents of *lajja* helps us see why.

From the perspective of social appraisal and self-appraisal, for example, to be full of *lajja* is to be in possession of the virtue of behaving in a civilized manner and in such a way that the social order and its norms are upheld. It is not a neurosis, and it does not connote a reduction in the strength of the ego. Indeed, *lajja* promotes self-esteem. Of course, to be perceived or labeled as someone without *lajja*—as someone who encroaches on the station of others, or fails to live up to the requirements of his or her own station—is unpleasant and arousing. Parish notes that to feel *lajja* is sometimes associated with blushing, sweating, and altered pulse (1991, p. 324), but we suspect that such a somatic phenomenology is a feature of the anxiety provoked by the social perception of the absence of *lajja* and is not definitive of *lajja* itself. For to experience *lajja* is to experience that sense of virtuous, courteous, well-mannered restraint that led Kali to rein in her rage.

The environmental determinants of *lajja* as a sense of one's own virtue and civility are as varied as the set of actions that are dutiful and responsible, given one's station in life in a world in which all people are highly self-conscious about their social designation (see Geertz, 1984, for a brilliant attempt to capture the dramatic qualities of such a world). They include events that we would find familiar (not being seen naked by the wrong person in the wrong context) as well as many events that might seem alien or strange (never talking directly to one's husband's elder brother or to one's father-in-law; never being in the same room with both one's husband and another male to whom he must defer).

From the perspective of self-management, South Asian *lajja* may appear at first glance to be similar to North American shame or embarrassment. It activates a habit or routine that sometimes results in hiding, covering up, and withdrawing from the scene. Yet what is really being activated by *lajja* is a general habit of respect for social hierarchy and a consciousness of one's social and public responsibilities, which in the context of South Asian norms may call for avoidance, silence, withdrawal, or other deferential, protective, or nonaggressive gestures and actions.

Finally, consider the semantic structure of "shame" and *lajja* in the minds of informants.

When middle-class Euro-American college students are presented with the triad of terms "shame–happiness–anger" and asked, "Which is most different from the other two?," they are most likely to respond that either "happiness" or "shame" is most different from the other two, perhaps on the grounds that "shame" and "anger" go together because they are both unpleasant feelings, or that "happiness" and "anger" go together because they are both ego-expanding emotions. Neither response is typical of responses in the South Asian community where Menon and Shweder (1994) have worked, where *lajja* (shame?) and *suka* (happiness?) are thought to go together in the triad test, and *raga* (anger?), perceived as destructive of society, is the odd emotion out. Here something seems to be amiss in the translation process. Something may well have been amiss in most past attempts to equate emotions across languages and across local cultural worlds (see Wierzbicka, 1992).

THE SOCIAL AND MORAL CONTEXT OF EMOTIONAL EXPERIENCE

The case of *lajja* illustrates the dependence of emotional experience on its social and moral context. To understand *lajja,* one must understand the moral goods that Oriyas strive to achieve. This strategy of viewing emotions against the background of their associated moral goods can be extended to other emotions using a framework that has proved useful in recent cultural-psychological work. Shweder et al. (1997; see also Shweder, 1990b; Haidt et al., 1993; Jensen, 1995) suggest that moral goods do not vary randomly from culture to culture, but rather tend to cluster into three sets of related goods or three ethics, known as the ethics of autonomy, the ethics of community, and the ethics of divinity. Cultures rely upon the three ethics to varying degrees. The relative weights of the three ethics within a culture appear to affect the experience and expression of emotion, as well as the way emotions are conceptualized by both local folk and local experts.

In cultures that emphasize an ethics of autonomy, the central object of value is the individual. Within that type of cultural world, the most salient moral goods are those that promote the autonomy, freedom, and well-being of the individual, with the result that nothing can be condemned that does not demonstrably harm others, restrict their freedom, or impinge on their rights. Haidt et al. (1993), for example, found that U.S. college students (a population steeped in the ethics of autonomy) responded to stories about violations of food and sexual taboos (e.g., eating one's already dead pet dog) with disgust. Nevertheless, these students felt compelled by the logic of their ethical stance to separate their feelings of disgust from their moral judgments. As a result they held firmly to the view that their personal emotional reactions did not imply that the actions were wrong. They spoke exclusively in the language of the ethics of autonomy, pointing out that nobody was hurt, and that the people involved had a right to do as they pleased in a private setting. Disgust plays an ambiguous role in such an autonomy-based cultural world (see Rozin et al., Chapter 40, this volume). In such a cultural world, the moral domain is constructed so that it is limited to issues of harm, rights, and justice (Turiel, 1983), and the emotions that are experienced as moral emotions (e.g., anger, sympathy, and guilt) are those that respond to a rather narrow class of ethical goods (e.g., justice, freedom, and the avoidance of harm). In such a cultural world, the focus of ordinary folk and social scientists alike is upon individuals' striving to maximize their personal utility (e.g., Lazarus, 1991; Plutchik, 1980; Stein, Trabasso, & Liwag, Chapter 28, this volume). Happiness, sadness, pride, and shame are viewed as responses to individual gains and losses, successes and failures. Other moral goods (such as loyalty, duty, and respect for status) that might be linked to the emotions are either lost or undertheorized.

Nevertheless, in many parts of the world the moral domain has been constructed in such a way that it is broader than, or at least different from, an ethics of autonomy. In cultures that emphasize an ethics of community, ontological priority is given to collective entities (the family, guild, clan, community, corporation, or nation), and the central moral goods are those that protect these entities against challenges from without and decay from within (e.g., goods such as loyalty, duty, honor, respectfulness, chastity, modesty, and self-control). In such a world, individual choices (what to wear, whom to marry, how to address others) take on a moral significance and an ethical importance (Shweder, Mahapatra, & Miller, 1987), and the

successful pursuit of individual goals may even be a cause for embarrassment or shame. Haidt et al. (1993), for example, found that outside of college samples, people of lower socioeconomic status generally thought it was morally wrong to eat one's already dead pet dog or to clean one's toilet with the national flag. Even when these actions were judged to be harmless, they were still seen as objectively disgusting or disrespectful and hence as morally wrong. In a cultural world based on an ethics of community, emotions may exist that are not fully felt by those whose morality is based on an ethics of autonomy. *Lajja* is a clear example, since it is not the type of emotion that will be experienced in a world that sees hierarchy and the exclusive prerogatives of others as unjust or as a form of oppression, rather than as a powerful and legitimate object of admiration and/or respect (Menon & Shweder, 1998). To select another example, *song*, the righteous indignation of the Ifaluk (Lutz, 1988), may require a sense of close, valued, and inescapable community. Whereas North American "anger" is triggered by a violation of rights and leads to a desire for revenge, Ifaluk *song* appears to be triggered by violations of relationships, and it leads to a socially shared emotion that brings the violator back into voluntary conformity (Lutz, 1988).

Similarly, emotions related to honor and heroism may require a strong attachment and dedication to a collectivity or group, for whom the hero lays down his or her life. The *Nāṭyaśāstra*'s otherwise puzzling inclusion of perseverance or heroism as a basic emotion, equal to anger and fear, seems more intelligible against the backdrop of the ethics of community. A James Bond-type hero may display perseverance as he battles to save the "free world," yet we do not think he inspires the same *rasa* in a North American audience that an Indian audience savors when a Hindi film hero battles to avenge the death of his father. Many older classic North American films raised themes of family honor, but such themes have become less common in recent decades, as the ethics of autonomy has pushed back the ethics of community. Unlike Hindi films, modern North American films rarely embed the hero in the thick traditions and obligations of family history. It is a rare movie indeed when we meet the hero's parents.

The third ethic, the ethic of divinity, may have a similar differential activation and enabling effect on the emotional life. In the ethic of divinity, people (and sometimes animals) are seen as containing a bit of God (or a god) within them, and the central moral goods are those that protect and dignify the person's inherent divinity. The body is experienced as a temple, so matters that seem to be personal choices within the ethics of autonomy (e.g., food and sexual choices, personal hygiene) become moral and spiritual issues associated with such goods as sanctity, purity, and pollution.

Within the terms of a cultural world focused on an ethics of divinity, even love and hate may lose their simple positive versus negative hedonic valences. A modern spiritual guide (Yatiswarananda, 1979, p. 187) says that hatred and attachment are both fetters that "degrade the human being, preventing him from rising to his true stature. Both must be renounced." Hindu scriptures are full of stories such as that of Pingala, a greedy courtesan who sought incessantly for wealth. One day she was deeply disappointed that nobody came to give her gifts. "Her countenance sank and she was very much down in spirits. Then as a result of this brooding an utter disgust came over her that made her happy" (Yatiswarananda, 1979, p. 160, referring to Bhagavatam 11.8.27). While secularized Westerners can easily recognize these feelings of greed, attachment, and self-disgust, the story points to feelings about attachment and renunciation that may not be readily available to those who lack an ethic of divinity. Secularized Western folk may feel pride upon giving up an attachment to cigarettes, or even to money; however, if this renunciation is set within a script of personal accomplishment and health concerns, it is a different emotion (according to the present account) than if it is a component of a script about the purification and advancement of the soul toward reunion with God.

Of course, the very idea of an emotion connected with renunciation seems paradoxical, since spiritual progress in many Eastern religions is measured by the degree to which one moves beyond the experience of emotions. Only once this paradox is grasped does the mysterious ninth emotion of the *Nāṭyaśāstra* make sense. Serenity or calmness is an important part of Hindu emotional life and emotional discourse precisely because of the centrality of an ethics of divinity in everyday Hindu life. Not surprisingly, it is on no Western lists of basic emotions.

CONCLUSION: THE CULTURAL PSYCHOLOGY OF THE EMOTIONS ANEW

As we enter a new era of collaborative research among anthropologists, psychologists, and physiologists, concerned with similarities and differences in emotional functioning on a worldwide scale, a major goal for the cultural psychology of the emotions will be to decompose the emotions (and the languages of the emotions) into constituent narrative slots. It is to be hoped that by means of the decomposition of the symbolic structure of the emotions, it will be possible to render the meaning of other people's mental states without assimilating them in misleading ways to an a priori set of lexical items available in the language of the researcher (e.g., rendering Hindu *lajja* as English "shame").

It is one of the great marvels of life that across languages, cultures, and history, it is possible, with sufficient knowledge, effort, and insight, to truly understand the meanings of other people's emotions and mental states. Yet one must also marvel at one of the great ironies of life—namely, that the process of understanding the consciousness of others can deceptively appear to be far easier than it really is, thereby making it even more difficult to achieve a genuine understanding of "otherness." Thus, in the end, this discussion of the cultural psychology of the emotions and meditation on the venerable "Rasādhyāya" of the *Nāṭyaśāstra* are really pleas for a decomposition of emotional states into their constituent narrative slots (environmental determinants, somatic phenomenology, affective phenomenology, self-appraisal, social appraisal, self-management strategy, and communication codes). Unless we take that step, we will continue to be prone to the bias that the emotional life of human beings is "basically" the same around the world. The truth may well be that when it comes to "basic" emotions we (medieval Hindus and contemporary North Americans, Pintupis and Russians, Inuit and Balinese, etc.) are not only basically alike in some ways, but are basically different from each other as well.

REFERENCES

Abu-Lughod, L. (1985). Honor and the sentiments of loss in a Bedouin society. *American Ethnologist, 12,* 245–261.

Abu-Lughod, L. (1986). *Veiled sentiments: Honor and poetry in a Bedouin society*. Berkeley: University of California Press.

Angel, R., & Guarnaccia, P. (1989). Mind, body and culture: Somatization among Hispanics. *Social Science and Medicine, 12*(28), 1229–1238.

Angel, R., & Idler, E. L. (1992). Somatization and hypochondriasis: Sociocultural factors in subjective experience. *Research in Community and Mental Health, 7,* 71–93.

Angel, R., & Thoits, P. (1987). The impact of culture on the cognitive structure of illness. *Culture, Medicine and Psychiatry 11,* 465–494.

Appadurai, A. (1985). Gratitude as a social mode in South India. *Ethos, 13,* 236–245.

Appadurai, A. (1990). Topographies of the self: Praise and emotion in Hindu India. In C. Lutz & L. Abu-Lughod (Eds.), *Language and the politics of emotion* (pp. 92–112). New York: Cambridge University Press.

Brenneis, D. (1990). Shared and solitary sentiments: The discourse of friendship, play and anger in Bhatgaon. In C. Lutz & L. Abu-Lughod (Eds.), *Language and the politics of emotion* (pp. 113–125). New York: Cambridge University Press.

Briggs, J. L. (1970). *Never in anger: Portrait of an Eskimo family*. Cambridge, MA: Harvard University Press.

Bruner, J. S. (1990). *Acts of meaning*. Cambridge, MA: Harvard University Press.

Cole, M. (1988). "Cross-cultural research in the sociohistorical tradition. *Human Development, 31,* 137–157.

Cole, M. (1990). Cultural psychology: A once and future discipline? In J. J. Berman (Ed.), *Nebraska Symposium on Motivation: 1989, Vol. 37. Cross-cultural perspectives*. Lincoln: University of Nebraska Press.

Cole, M. (1996). *Cultural psychology: A once and future discipline*. Cambridge, MA: Harvard University Press.

D'Andrade, R. G. (1984). Cultural meaning systems. In R. A. Shweder & R. A. LeVine (Eds.), *Culture theory: Essays on mind, self, and emotion* (pp. 88–119). Cambridge, England: Cambridge University Press.

D'Andrade, R. G. (1987). A folk model of the mind. In D. Holland & N. Quinn (Eds.), *Cultural models in language and thought*. Cambridge, England: Cambridge University Press.

D'Andrade, R. G. (1995). *The development of cognitive anthropology*. New York: Cambridge University Press.

Dimock, E. C. (1974). *Literatures of India: An introduction*. Chicago: University of Chicago Press.

Ekman, P. (1980). Biological and cultural contributions to body and facial movement in the expression of emotions. In A. Rorty (Ed.), *Explaining emotions* (pp. 73–101). Berkeley: University of California Press.

Ekman, P. (1984). Expression and the nature of emotion. In K. Scherer & P. Ekman (Eds.), *Approaches to emotion* (pp. 319–343). Hillsdale, NJ: Erlbaum.

Ellsworth, P. (1991). Some implications of cognitive appraisal theories of emotion. *International Review of Studies of Emotion, 1,* 143–161.

Fish, S. (1980). *Is there a textbook in this class?: On the authority of interpretive communities*. Cambridge, MA: Harvard University Press.

Frijda, N. (1986). *The emotions*. Cambridge, England: Cambridge University Press.

Garvey, C. (1992). Introduction: Talk in the study of socialization and development. *Merrill–Palmer Quarterly, 38*(1), iii–viii.

Geertz, C. (1973). *The interpretation of culture*. New York: Basic Books.

Geertz, C. (1984). From the nature point of view. In R. A. Shweder & R. A. Levine (Eds.), *Culture theory: Essays on mind, self, and emotion* (pp. 123–136). Cambridge, England: Cambridge University Press.

Geertz, H. (1959). The vocabulary of emotion: A study of Javanese socialization processes. *Psychiatry, 22,* 225–236.

Gerber, E. R. (1985). Rage and obligation: Samoan emotions in conflict. In G. M. White & J. Kirkpatrick (Eds.), *Person, self and experience: Exploring Pacific ethnopsychologies* (pp. 121–167). Berkeley: University of California Press.

Gnoli, R. (1956). *The aesthetic experience according to Abhinavagupta*. Rome: Istituto Italiano per Il Medio ed Estremo Oriente.

Goddard, C. (1997). Constrastive semantics and cultural psychology: 'Surprise' in Malay and English. *Culture and Psychology, 2,* 153–181.

Good, B. J., & Kleinman, A. M. (1984). Culture and anxiety: Cross-cultural evidence for the patterning of anxiety disorders. In A. H. Tuma & J. D. Maser (Eds.), *Anxiety and the anxiety disorders* (pp. 297–324). Hillsdale, NJ: Erlbaum.

Goodnow, J., Miller, P., & Kessel, F. (Eds.). (1995). *New directions for child development: Vol. 67. Cultural practices as contexts for development*. San Francisco: Jossey-Bass.

Haidt, J., & Keltner, D. (1999). Culture and facial expression: Open-ended methods find more faces and a gradient of recognition. *Cognition and Emotion, 13,* 225–266.

Haidt, J., Koller, S., & Dias, M. (1993). Affect, culture, and morality, or is it wrong to eat your dog? *Journal of Personality and Social Psychology, 65,* 613–628.

Harré, R. (1986a). An outline of the social constructionist viewpoint. In R. Harré (Ed.), *The social construction of emotions* (pp. 2–14). Oxford: Blackwell.

Harré, R. (Ed.) (1986b). *The social construction of emotions*. Oxford: Blackwell.

Hoffman, M. L. (1990). Empathy and justice motivation. *Motivation and Emotion, 14*(2), 151–172.

Howard, A. (1985). Ethnopsychology and the prospects for a cultural psychology. In G. M. White & J. Kirkpatrick (Eds.), *Person, self and experience: Exploring Pacific ethnopsychologies* (pp. 401–420). Berkeley: University of California Press.

Jahoda, G. (1992). *Crossroads between culture and mind: Continuities and change in theories of human nature*. Cambridge, MA: Harvard University Press.

Jensen, L. A. (1995). Habits of the heart revisited: Autonomy, community, divinity in adults' moral language. *Qualitative Sociology, 18,* 71–86.

Kakar, S. (1982). *Shamans, mystics and doctors: A psychological inquiry into India and its healing traditions*. New York: Knopf.

Keith, A. B. (1924). *The Sanskrit drama*. London: Oxford University Press.

Kirsh, D. (1991). Today the earwig, tomorrow man? *Artificial Intelligence, 47,* 161–184.

Kitayama, S., & Markus, H. R. (1994). *Emotion and culture: Empirical studies of mutual influence*. Washington, DC: American Psychological Association.

Kleinman, A. (1986). *The social origins of distress and disease*. New Haven, CT: Yale University Press.

Kleinman, A., & Good, B. (1985). (Eds.). *Culture and depression: Studies in the anthropology and cross-cultural psychiatry of affect and disorder*. Berkeley: University of California Press.

Lakoff, G. (1987). *Women, fire and dangerous things: What categories reveal about the mind*. Chicago: University of Chicago Press.

Lazarus, R. S. (1991). Progress on a cognitive–motivational–relational theory of emotion. *American Psychologist, 46,* 819–834.

LeVine, R. A. (1984). Properties of culture: An ethnographic view. In R. A. Shweder & R. A. LeVine (Eds.), *Culture theory: Essays on mind, self, and emotion* (pp. 67–87). Cambridge, England: Cambridge University Press.

LeVine, R. A. (1990). Infant environments in psychoanalysis: A cross-cultural view. In J. Stigler, R. Shweder, & G. Herdt (Eds.), *Cultural psychology: Essays on comparative human development* (pp. 454–476). New York: Cambridge University Press.

Levy, R. I. (1984a). Emotion, knowing and culture. In R. A. Shweder & R. A. LeVine (Eds.), *Culture theory: Essays on mind, self, and emotion* (pp. 214–237). Cambridge, England: Cambridge University Press.

Levy, R. I. (1984b). The emotions in comparative perspective. In K. R. Scherer & P. Ekman (Eds.), *Approaches to emotion* (pp. 397–412). Hillsdale, NJ: Erlbaum.

Lewis, M. (1989). Cultural differences in children's knowledge of emotional scripts. In P. Harris & C. Saarni (Eds.), *Children's understanding of emotion* (pp. 350–374). New York: Cambridge University Press.

Lewis, M., Sullivan, M., & Michalson, L. (1984). The cognitive–emotional fugue. In C. E. Izard, J. Kagan, & R. Zajonc (Eds.), *Emotions, cognition, and behavior* (pp. 264–288). New York: Cambridge University Press.

Lutz, C. (1982). The domain of emotion words on Ifaluk. *American Ethnologist, 9,* 113–128.

Lutz, C. (1985a). Ethnopsychology compared to what?: Explaining behavior and consciousness among the Ifaluk. In J. White & J. Kirkpatrick (Eds.), *Person, self and experience: Exploring Pacific ethnopsychologies,* (pp. 35–79). Berkeley: University of California Press.

Lutz, C. (1985b). Depression and the translation of emotional worlds. In A. Kleinman & B. Good (Eds.), *Culture and depression: Studies in the anthropology and cross-cultural psychiatry of affect and disorder* (pp. 63–100). Berkeley: University of California Press.

Lutz, C. (1988). *Unnatural emotions: Everyday sentiments on a Micronesian atoll and their challenge to Western theory*. Chicago: University of Chicago Press.

Lutz, C., & White, G. (1986). The anthropology of emotions. *Annual Review of Anthropology 15,* 405–436.

Markus, H. R., & Kitayama, S. (1991). Culture and the self: Implications for cognition, emotion and motivation. *Psychological Review, 98,* 224–253.

Markus, H. R., & Kitayama, S. (1992). The what, why and how of cultural psychology: A review of Shweder's *Thinking through cultures. Psychological Inquiry, 3*(4).

Markus, H. R., Kitayama, S., & Heiman, R. (1996). Culture and "basic" psychological principles. In E. T. Higgins & A. W. Kruglanski (Eds.), *Social psychology: Handbook of basic principles*. New York: Guilford Press.

Marsella, A. J. (1980). Depressive experience and disorder across cultures: A review of the literature. In H. Triandis & J. Draguns (Eds.), *Handbook of cross-cultural psychology* (Vol. 6, pp. 237–289). Boston: Allyn & Bacon.

Masson, J. L., & Patwardhan, M. V. (1970). *Aesthetic rapture: The Rasādhyāya of the Nāṭyaśāstra*. Poona, India: Deccan College.

Menon, U., & Shweder, R. A. (1994). Kali's tongue: Cultural psychology and the power of "shame" in Orissa, India. In S. Kitayama & H. Markus (Eds.), *Emotion and culture* (pp. 241–284). Washington, DC: American Psychological Association.

Menon, U., & Shweder, R. A. (1998). The return of the 'white man's burden': The encounter between the moral discourse of anthropology and the domestic life of Hindu women. In R. A. Shweder (Ed.), *Welcome to middle age! (and other cultural fictions)* (pp. 139–188). Chicago: University of Chicago Press.

Mesquita, B., & Frijda, N. (1992). Cultural variations in emotions: A review. *Psychological Bulletin, 112,* 179–204.

Miller, P., & Hoogstra, L. (1992). Language as tool in the socialization and apprehension of cultural meanings. In T. Schwartz, G. M. White, & C. A. Lutz (Eds.), *The social life of psyche: Debates and directions in psychological anthropology*. Cambridge, England: Cambridge University Press.

Miller, P., Mintz, J., Hoogstra, L., Fung, H., & Potts, R. (1992). The narrated self: Young children's construction of self in relation to others in conversational stories of personal experience. *Merrill–Palmer Quarterly, 38*(1), 45–67.

Miller, P., Potts, R., Fung, H., Hoogstra, L., & Mintz, J. (1990). Narrative practices and the social construction of self in childhood. *American Ethnologist, 17,* 292–311.

Miller, P., & Sperry, L. (1987). Young children's verbal resources for communicating anger. *Merrill–Palmer Quarterly, 33,* 1–31.

Much, N. C. (1995). Cultural psychology. In J. Smith, R. Harré, & L. van Langenhove (Eds.), *Rethinking psychology*. London: Sage.

Myers, F. R. (1979a). Emotions and the self: A theory of personhood and political order among Pintupi aborigines. *Ethos 7,* 343–370.

Myers, F. R. (1979b). The logic and meaning of anger among Pintupi aborigines. *Man, 23,* 589–610.

Nisbett, R. E., & Cohen, D. (1995). *The culture of hon-*

or: The psychology of violence in the South. Boulder, CO: Westview Press.

Nisbett, R. E., & Wilson, T. D. (1977). Telling more than we can know: Verbal reports on mental processes. *Psychological Review, 84*(3) 231–259.

Ochs, E., & Schieffelin, B. (1984). Language acquisition and socialization: Three developmental stories. In R. A. Shweder & R. A. LeVine (Eds.), *Culture theory: Essays on mind, self and emotion* (pp. 276–320). Cambridge, England: Cambridge University Press.

Parish, S. (1991). The sacred mind: Newar cultural representations of mental life and the production of moral consciousness. *Ethos 19*(3), 313–351.

Peacock, J. L. (1984). Religion and life history: An exploration in cultural psychology. In E. M. Bruner (Ed.), *Text, play and story: The construction and reconstruction of self and society* (pp. 94–116). Washington, DC: American Ethnological Society.

Plutchik, R. (1980). *Emotion: A psychoevolutionary synthesis*. New York: Harper & Row.

Rorty, A. (Ed.). (1980). *Explaining emotions*. Berkeley: University of California Press.

Rosaldo, M. Z. (1980). *Knowledge and passion: Ilongot notions of self and social life*. Cambridge, England: Cambridge University Press.

Rosaldo, M. Z. (1983). The shame of headhunters and the autonomy of self. *Ethos, 11,* 135–151.

Rosaldo, M. Z. (1984). Toward an anthropology of self and feeling. In R. A. Shweder & R. A. LeVine (Eds.), *Culture theory: Essays on mind, self, and emotion* (pp. 137–157). Cambridge, England: Cambridge University Press.

Russell, J. A. (1991). Culture and the categorization of emotions. *Psychological Bulletin, 110*(3), 426–450.

Schechner, R. (1988). *Performance theory*. London: Routledge.

Scherer, K. R., Wallbott, H. G., & Summerfield, A. B. (Eds.). (1986). *Experiencing emotion: A cross-cultural study*. Cambridge, England: Cambridge University Press.

Schieffelin, B., & Ochs, E. (Eds.). (1986). *Language socialization across cultures*. New York: Cambridge University Press.

Schieffelin, E. L. (1976). *The sorrow of the lonely and the burning of the dancers*. New York: St. Martin's Press.

Schieffelin, E. L. (1983). Anger and shame in the tropical forest: On affect as a cultural system in Papua, New Guinea. *Ethos, 11,*181–191.

Schieffelin, E. L. (1985a). The cultural analysis of depressive affect: An example from New Guinea. In A. Kleinman & B. Good (Eds.), *Culture and depression: Studies in the anthropology and cross-cultural psychiatry of affect and disorder* (pp. 101–133). Berkeley: University of California Press.

Schieffelin, E. L. (1985b). Anger, grief and shame: Toward a Kaluli ethnopsychology. In G. M. White & J. Kirkpatrick (Eds.), *Person, self and experience: Exploring Pacific ethnopsychologies* (pp. 168–182). Berkeley: University of California Press.

Shaver, P., Schwartz, J., Kirson, D., & O'Connor, C. (1987). Emotion knowledge: Further exploration of a prototype approach. *Journal of Personality and Social Psychology 52*(6), 1061–1086.

Shixie, L. (1989). Neurasthenia in China: Modern and traditional criteria for its diagnosis. *Culture, Medicine and Psychiatry 13,* 163–186.

Shweder, R. A. (1988). Suffering in style [Review *of Social origins of disease and distress* by A. Kleinman]. *Culture, Medicine and Psychiatry, 12,* 479–497.

Shweder, R. A. (1990a). Cultural psychology: What is it? In J. Stigler, R. Shweder, & G. Herdt (Eds.), *Cultural psychology: Essays on comparative human development* (pp. 1–43). New York: Cambridge University Press.

Shweder, R. A. (1990b). In defense of moral realism. *Child Development, 61,* 2060–2068.

Shweder, R. A. (1991). *Thinking through cultures: Expeditions in cultural psychology*. Cambridge, MA: Harvard University Press.

Shweder, R. A. (1993). Everything you ever wanted to know about cognitive appraisal theory without being conscious of it: A review of Richard S. Lazarus' *Emotion and adaptation*. *Psychological Inquiry 4,* 322–326.

Shweder, R. A. (1994). "You're not sick, you're just in love": Emotion as an interpretive system. In P. Ekman & R. Davidson (Eds.), *The nature of emotions: Fundamental questions* (pp. 32–44). New York: Oxford University Press.

Shweder, R. A. (1996). True ethnography: The lore, the law and the lure. In R. Jessor, A. Colby, & R. A. Shweder (Eds.), *Ethnography and human development: Context and meaning in social inquiry* (pp. 15–52). Chicago: University of Chicago Press.

Shweder, R. A. (Ed.). (1998). *Welcome to middle age! (and other cultural fictions)*. Chicago: University of Chicago Press.

Shweder, R. A. (1999a). Cultural psychology. In R. A. Wilson & F. Keil (Eds.), *MIT encyclopedia of cognitive sciences* (pp. 211–213). Cambridge, MA: MIT Press.

Shweder, R. A. (1999b). Why cultural psychology? *Ethos, 27,* 62–73.

Shweder, R. A., Goodnow, J., Hatano, G., LeVine, R.A., Markus, H. R., & Miller, P. (1998). The cultural psychology of development: One mind, many mentalities. In W. Damon (Series Ed.) & R. Lerner (Vol. Ed.), *Handbook of child psychology: Vol. 1.Theoretical models of human development* (5th ed., pp. 865–937). New York: Wiley.

Shweder, R. A., & LeVine, R. A. (Eds.). (1984). *Culture theory: Essays on mind, self, and emotion*. Cambridge, England: Cambridge University Press.

Shweder, R. A., Mahapatra, M., & Miller, J. G. (1987). Culture and moral development. In J. Kagan & S. Lamb (Eds.), *The emergence of morality in young children* (pp. 1–83). Chicago: University of Chicago Press.

Shweder, R. A., & Menon, U. (in press). Dominating Kali: Hindu family values and tantric power. In J. Kripal & R. McDermott (Eds.), *Encountering Kali: Cultural understanding at the extremes*. Under review.

Shweder, R. A., & Much, N. C. (1987). Determinations of meaning: Discourse and moral socialization. In W. Kurtines, & J. Gewirtz (Eds.), *Social interaction and socio-moral development* (pp. 197–244). New York: Wiley.

Shweder, R. A., & Much, N. C., Mahapatra, M., & Park, L. (1997). The "big three" of morality (autonomy, community, divinity) and the "big three" explanations of suffering. In A. M. Brandt & P. Rozin (Eds.), *Morality and health* (pp. 119–169). New York: Routledge.

Shweder, R. A., & Sullivan, M. (1990). The semiotic subject of cultural psychology. In L. A. Pervin (Ed.), *Handbook of personality: Theory and research* (pp. 399–416). New York: Guilford Press.

Shweder, R. A., & Sullivan, M. A. (1993). Cultural psychology: Who needs it? *Annual Review of Psychology, 44,* 497–523.

Smedslund, J. (1991). The pseudoempirical in psychology and the case for psychologic. *Psychological Inquiry, 2*(4), 325–338.

Solomon, R. C. (1976). *The passions.* New York: Doubleday/Anchor.

Solomon, R. C. (1984). Getting angry: The Jamesian theory of emotion in anthropology. In R. A. Shweder & R. A. LeVine (Eds.), *Culture theory: Essays on mind, self and emotion* (pp. 238–254). Cambridge, England: Cambridge University Press.

Stearns, C. Z., & Stearns, P. N. (Eds.). (1988). *Emotion and social change: Toward a new psychohistory.* New York: Holmes & Meier.

Stein, N., & Levine, L. J. (1987). Thinking about feelings: The development and organization of emotional knowledge. In R. E. Snow & M. J. Farr (Eds.), *Aptitude, learning and instruction.* Hillsdale, NJ: Erlbaum.

Stigler, J. (1984). "Mental abacus": The effect of abacus training on Chinese children's mental calculation. *Cognitive Psychology, 16,* 145–176.

Stigler, J., Chalip, L., & Miller, K. (1986). Culture and mathematics learning. *Review of Research in Education, 15,* 253–306.

Stigler, J., Nusbaum, H. & Chalip, L. (1988). Developmental changes in speed of processing: Central limiting mechanisms on shell transfer. *Child Development, 59,* 1144–1153.

Stigler, J., Shweder, R., & Herdt, G. (Eds.). (1990). *Cultural psychology: Essays on comparative human development.* New York: Cambridge University Press.

Swartz, M. J. (1988). Shame, culture, and status among the Swahili of Mombasa. *Ethos, 16,* 21–51.

Turiel, E. (1983). *The development of social knowledge: Morality and convention.* Cambridge, England: Cambridge University Press.

Veith, I. (1978). Psychiatric foundations in the Far East. *Psychiatric Annals, 8*(6) 12–41.

White, G. M., & Kirkpatrick, J. (Eds.). (1985). *Person, self and experience: Exploring Pacific ethnopsychologies.* Berkeley: University of California Press.

Wierzbicka, A. (1986). Human emotions: Universal or culture-specific? *American Anthropologist, 88,* 584–594.

Wierzbicka, A. (1989). Soul and mind: Linguistic evidence for ethnopsychology and cultural history. *American Anthropologist, 91*(1), 41–58.

Wierzbicka, A. (Ed.). (1990). The semantics of the emotions [Special issue]. *Australian Journal of Linguistics, 10*(2).

Wierzbicka, A. (1992). Talk about emotions: Semantics, culture and cognition. *Cognition and Emotion, 6*(3–4), 285–319.

Wierzbicka, A. (1993). A conceptual basis for cultural psychology. *Ethos, 21,* 205–231.

Wierzbicka, A. (1997). *Understanding cultures through their key words: English, Russian, Polish, German and Japanese.* New York: Oxford University Press.

Wierzbicka, A. (1999). *Emotions across languages and cultures: Diversity and universals.* New York: Cambridge University Press.

Wikan, U. (1984). Shame and honour: A contestable pair. *Man, 19,* 635–652.

Wikan, U. (1989). Illness from fright or soul loss: A North Balinese culture-bound syndrome? *Culture, Medicine and Psychiatry, 13,* 25–50.

Yang, K. S. (1997). Indigenizing Westernized Chinese psychology. In M. Bond (Ed.), *Working at the interface of culture: Twenty lives in social science* (pp. 62–76). London: Routledge.

Yatiswarananda, S. (1979). *Meditation and spiritual life.* Bangalore, India: Sri Ramakrishna Ashrama.

PART V
COGNITIVE FACTORS

CHAPTER 27

Positive Affect and Decision Making

Alice M. Isen

Most people seem to have a sense that affect (feelings, emotion) can influence their decisions and thought processes, at least under certain circumstances. However, it is usually assumed that such influence is something irregular or unusual; that only strong and infrequent feelings would have such effects; and that most often only negative feelings such as anger, sadness, or fear would have an impact on thinking processes. Furthermore, most people assume that when affect plays a role in their decision processes, such influences are disruptive and tend to make their decisions "irrational" and less appropriate than otherwise.

Interestingly, however, a growing body of research indicates that even mild, and even positive, affective states can markedly influence everyday thought processes, and do so regularly. For example, the presence of positive feelings has been found to cue positive material in memory, making access to such thoughts easier, and thus making it more likely that positive material will "come to mind" (e.g., Isen, Shalker, Clark, & Karp, 1978; Nasby & Yando, 1982; Teasdale & Fogarty, 1979). This reflects the fact that material in mind is organized and accessible in terms of its positive affective tone, and that people spontaneously use positive affect as a way to organize their thoughts (Isen, 1987). Thus the evidence indicates that, far from being an infrequent influence on thought processes, common positive feelings are funda-

mentally involved in cognitive organization and processing.

Positive affect has also been found to promote creativity and flexibility in problem solving and negotiation, as well as both efficiency and thoroughness in decision making, and other indicators of improved thinking (e.g., Carnevale & Isen, 1986; Estrada, Isen, & Young, 1997; Estrada, Isen, & Young, 1994; Greene & Noice, 1988; Hirt, Melton, McDonald, & Harackiewicz, 1996; Isen, Daubman, & Nowicki, 1987; Isen, Johnson, Mertz, & Robinson, 1985; Isen & Means, 1983; Isen, Rosenzweig, & Young, 1991; Lee & Sternthal, 1999). These effects have been found in a wide range of settings and populations, ranging from young adolescents (e.g., Greene & Noice, 1988) to practicing physicians engaging in diagnostic reasoning (Estrada et al., 1994, 1997), and in the literatures on consumer behavior (e.g., Lee & Sternthal, 1999) and on behavior in organizations (e.g., George & Brief, 1996; Staw & Barsade, 1993; Staw, Sutton, & Pelled, 1994). Furthermore, recent studies in the coping literature are finding that even when people must cope with adverse events, positive affect is helpful, facilitating effective coping and reducing defensiveness (e.g., Aspinwall, 1998; Aspinwall & Taylor, 1997; Taylor & Aspinwall, 1996; Trope & Neter, 1994; Trope & Pomerantz, 1998).

Therefore, under many circumstances the influence of mild positive feelings on thinking and decision making has been found to be not only substantial, but facilitative, leading to improved decision making and problem solving. How can these two views—people's intuitions and the findings of such studies—be reconciled?

First, it is likely that, typically, when we think about feelings influencing thought, we tend not to pay a lot of attention to mild affect and therefore are less likely to attribute influence to it. Second, we may be especially unlikely to pay attention to common, mild *positive* feelings. Consequently, if people are asked to think about the possible impact of feeling or emotion on thought processes, they are most likely to answer at first in terms of strong affect and probably negative affect. People may not realize immediately that positive feelings, including those mild positive states that they experience frequently, do influence thought processes.

Furthermore, the influence of positive affect is usually facilitative, but we often take positive outcomes of everyday processes more or less for granted, not searching for causes or connections unless things go wrong or performance is impaired (e.g., Weiner, 1985). Thus we may not notice facilitative effects of positive feelings, but may pay more attention when we have reason to think that happy feelings have impaired people's judgment or problem solving.

All of these phenomena most likely contribute to people's underestimation of positive affect as a facilitating factor in decision making and problem solving. In addition, results of some studies have also indicated that there are times when positive affect actually does at least appear to impair or interfere with problem solving or thinking (e.g., Bless, Bohner, Schwarz, & Strack, 1990; Bodenhausen, Kramer, & Susser, 1994; Mackie & Worth, 1989; Melton, 1995). However, most studies reporting such effects find specific conditions under which impairment is observed, rather than general impairment. In addition, most of the studies addressing positive affect's influence on thinking do not find impaired performance, but rather report more flexibility and generally enhanced thinking and problem solving. Thus one important task will be to try to understand what factors play a role in determining the influence of positive affect on performance.

This chapter presents some of the findings regarding the impact of mild positive affect on thinking and decision making, and explores the processes underlying them and the circumstances under which they are likely to be observed. The focus is on decision making and problem solving, but in order to understand affect's influence on decisions, it will be helpful to consider its impact on cognitive organization (i.e., the way material is thought about and related to other material) and on motivation. This is because organization or context, and motivation (including the person's goals), play crucial roles in decision making (e.g., Bransford, 1979; Simonson, 1989, 1990; Tversky & Kahneman, 1981). In fact, some of the reasons for the discrepancy among the studies mentioned above may lie in these other effects of positive feelings, including some that are now being discovered relating to expectancy motivation and intrinsic motivation. Finally, the chapter briefly mentions a recently proposed theoretical account, at the neurological level, that may help shed light on some of these phenomena (Ashby, Isen, & Turken, 1999).

To address all of these topics in this single chapter, consideration of each must be brief. I hope that the chapter will serve as a springboard for thought, even though it cannot be exhaustive or provide a detailed review of all of the literature in this rapidly growing field. I begin, then, by considering the influence of positive affect on cognitive organization.

POSITIVE AFFECT, FLEXIBILITY, AND COGNITIVE ORGANIZATION

A growing body of literature indicates that positive affect influences the way in which stimuli are thought about or related to other ideas in mind. For example, studies have shown that people in whom positive affect has been induced, in any of a variety of simple ways, (e.g., watching 5 minutes of a comedy film, receiving a small bag of candy, or giving word associations to positive words) have a broader range of associates, and more diverse associates, to neutral material (Isen et al., 1985). Similarly, people in such conditions are able to categorize material more flexibly, seeing ways in which nontypical members of categories can fit or be viewed as members of the category (Isen & Daubman, 1984; Kahn & Isen, 1993; Isen, Niedenthal, & Cantor, 1992). This has been found for items in natural categories such as those used by Rosch (1975; Isen & Daubman, 1984); for products in the mildly pleasant class of snack foods (Kahn & Isen, 1993); and for person types in positive, but not in negative, person categories (Isen et al., 1992). Thus positive affect enables people to see more similarities among items.

It has also been found that if people are specifically asked to focus on differences and find ways in which items differ from one another, positive affect can result in more perceived *difference* as well (Isen, 1987, p. 234; Murray, Sujan, Hirt, & Sujan, 1990). Together, these studies can be interpreted as indicating that positive affect promotes cognitive flexibility: People who are feeling happy become more able to make associations among ideas and to see more different, multiple relations (similarities *or* differences) among stimuli than do people in a neutral feeling state.

It is important to note that the impact of positive feelings on thought processes, and especially on the results of assigned tasks (such as judgments, ratings, sortings, categorizations, etc.), depends on particulars of the task and the situation. Nonetheless, the effect is regular, predictable, and understandable. If asked to judge similarity among items, people in positive-affect conditions indicate greater similarity than do control subjects; if asked to find differences among the same items, they may indicate more difference. As will be explained next, this may not be as irrational as it sounds; nor is it the result of simple response bias.

The process that underlies these effects, as suggested by the word association findings reported above (Isen et al., 1985), may be that people experiencing positive affect may engage in greater elaboration about the material. Thus they see more aspects of the items and have more, and more diverse, associations to the items, as those studies reported. Then, as explained by Tversky and Gati (1978) for knowledge about material in general (i.e., not affective material or induced affect specifically), the context supplied by the task (searching for differences vs. searching for similarities) will determine whether this greater elaboration (greater knowledge, in the work by Tversky & Gati) results in a judgment of greater similarity or of greater difference. Those authors found that people rated pairs of items about which they knew more (e.g., the United States and the Soviet Union) as more similar to each other than pairs about which they knew less (e.g., Bo-

livia and Ceylon) when the task required a similarity judgment, but that people also rated the pairs about which they knew more as more *different* from each other when the task focused attention on differences. Thus, to return to the affect situation, if people in positive-affect conditions have more information (elaboration) about material, or more associations to it, then, relative to controls, they would be expected to indicate more perceived similarity or difference among the items, depending on the context created by the question posed.

Nature of the Materials

Another aspect of the context that is critically important in determining the impact that positive affect will have is the nature, including the valence, of the materials being considered. Thus one cannot expect positive affect to influence the categorization of, or increase the perceived similarity (or difference) of, *all* stimuli, automatically.

To illustrate this point, let us examine the results of one study that extended the work on affect's impact on categorization to the area of person categorization (Isen et al., 1992). In that study, subjects were asked to rate the degree to which nonprototypic examples of positive or negative categories of people (e.g., "bartender" as a member of the category "nurturant people," or "genius" as a member of the negative category "unstable people") fit as members of the category. Compared with control subjects, positive-affect subjects rated the weakly related members of the positive categories as fitting better in the category, but this was not observed for the negative person categories. That is, people in the positive-affect condition rated "bartender" as a better exemplar of the category "nurturant people" than did control subjects, but they did not rate "genius" as a better exemplar of the category "unstable people." In accord with results of studies showing that positive affect cues positive material in memory and enables more ready access to such material and to a broader range of such associates (e.g., Isen et al., 1985; Isen et al., 1978; Teasdale & Fogarty, 1979), people in the positive-affect condition could presumably see more positive aspects of the relatively neutral type "bartender"; however, nothing in their affective state would be expected to prompt their seeing the person type "genius" as better fitting a negative superordinate category, in that situation.

This interaction illustrates the importance of the type of material with which the subject is asked to work, in determining the effects of feelings. Although an underlying process (increased elaboration) is postulated to occur, this process is expected to be different for different kinds of material in the situation described (and also different for different situations, such as dangerous vs. safe situations). Since positive affect cues positive material, the elaborative process would be expected to occur with positive material (for all subjects) or for positive-affect subjects working with neutral material (see Isen et al., 1985).

Additionally, presentation of negatively valenced material, if negative enough, may also result in people's not dealing with the material; and this tendency may be more notable among people in whom positive affect has been induced, who may be seeking to maintain that positive state (e.g., Isen & Simmonds, 1978). This will probably depend on the degree of negativity in the materials, the importance of the task, and so forth. It should also be pointed out that if the negative materials are bad enough, they may go so far as actually to overturn the affect induction itself.

However (as will be discussed more fully later, in the section on decision making), in a negative frame, where the task requires people to focus on possible meaningful loss or cope with difficult situations, there is evidence that people in a positive-affect state face the situation directly and deal with it. For example, in a loss-framed situation, those in a state of positive affect have been found to have more thoughts about losing than do controls (e.g., Isen & Geva, 1987), and behave conservatively so as to protect themselves from the loss (Isen & Geva, 1987; Isen, Nygren, & Ashby, 1988; Isen & Simmonds, 1978; Nygren, Isen, Taylor, & Dulin, 1996). This is also compatible with data showing that positive affect promotes effective coping in negative or stressful situations that have to be dealt with (e.g., Aspinwall & Taylor, 1997) and reduces "defensiveness" (e.g., Trope & Pomerantz, 1998). In the study under discussion here (Isen et al., 1992), however, there was no negative frame (loss or danger) to the task; therefore, such motivational and methodological additional complications were probably not in evidence, and the effect of positive affect simply did not extend to the negative material, as it often does not. The point illustrated is that use of negative material in studies of the influ-

ence of positive affect can make for complexity in formulating predictions.

A methodological point is worth noting here as well. The interaction observed in the person categorization study (Isen et al., 1992), between induced affect and the valence of the materials, also indicates that the impact of affect on categorization is not an artifact or indicator of processes such as response bias, nonsystematic thinking, generally "loosened associations" (e.g., Schwarz & Bless, 1991), or reduction in cognitive capacity. This is because the interaction between affect and category valence shows that positive affect, in comparison with the control group, influences the categorization of one type of material (positive), but does not change the way the other material (negative) is organized; by contrast, the alternative interpretation—global effects, such as carelessness, nonsystematic processing, loosened associations, or reduced cognitive capacity—should result in all categories' or stimulus materials' being affected equally.

Similarly, a study of the impact of positive affect on job perceptions and satisfaction also found that people in whom positive affect had been induced perceived an interesting task that they had been assigned, but not a meaningless one, as richer and more satisfying (Kraiger, Billings, & Isen, 1989). Again, this can be seen as reflecting an ability on the part of the positive-affect subjects to see additional associations and aspects of interesting things. At the same time, the interaction with type of task again indicates that a substantive process related to elaboration and thinking, rather than an artifact such as response bias, "seeing things through rose-colored glasses," or nonsystematic processing, is responsible for the observed effects.

Creative Problem Solving

Another series of studies reflecting affect's influence on cognitive organization indicates, as would be expected from the kinds of findings described above, that positive affect promotes creative or innovative responding (e.g., Isen et al., 1987; see Isen, 1999, for a fuller review). Such responding can be seen as involving cognitive flexibility or the ability to put ideas together in new ways, and has been measured by tasks such as the "candle problem" (Duncker, 1945) and the Remote Associates Test (Mednick, Mednick, & Mednick, 1964), in addition to word associations and flexible classifications as described above.

These studies also confirm that positive affect is distinct from negative affect and from affectless "arousal" in increasing cognitive flexibility and creativity. For example, in studies that examined the influence of negative affect, where the affect was induced by having subjects view a few minutes of the film *Night and Fog* (a French documentary of the World War II German death camps), people in this condition did not perform better than controls on the Remote Associates Test items. Similarly, where affectless "arousal" was induced by having subjects step up and down on a cinderblock for 2 minutes, so that their heart rates were increased by 66%, participants did not perform better than controls on the Remote Associates Test.

Theoretically, arousal should not be expected to increase creativity, since it is thought to facilitate the *dominant* response in a person's response repertoire rather than an innovative one (e.g., Berlyne, 1967; Easterbrook, 1959; Matlin & Zajonc, 1968). Nonetheless, its effect was investigated because people sometimes have the hunch that it is "arousal," rather than or as a component of positive affect, that is responsible for the facilitative effect of positive feelings. However, the data from these studies do not support this hunch (see Isen et al., 1987; Isen, 1990; and Isen & Daubman, 1984, for discussion). Moreover, reconceptualizations of the "arousal" concept have suggested that it may not be a unitary construct and may need to be investigated differently from the way it has been addressed in the past (e.g., Lacey, 1967, 1975; Neiss, 1990; Venables, 1984).

More recently, tests of these effects of positive feelings on creative problem solving have been extended to include investigation of performance on routine tasks, in order to examine whether there is evidence for an alternative interpretation having to do with effort, global motivation, or simple activation (in other words, whether positive-affect participants are simply trying harder). In order to address this alternative interpretation, in some studies we examined positive affect's influence on the performance of two types of routine tasks—circling the letter *a* every time it appeared in pages of randomly ordered letters, and long division—while also examining affect's influence on creative problem solving, represented

by two tasks (the Remote Associates Test and a logical problem-solving task, meant to represent something like scientific creativity). These studies indicated a facilitative influence of positive affect on the Remote Associates Test and the logical problem-solving task, but not on either of the routine tasks, on which performance of the positive-affect and control subjects did not differ (Isen, Berg, & Chen, 1993). This suggests that it is not just an increase in overall motivation that is responsible for the positive-affect subjects' improved performance on creative tasks.

Another study has reported that positive affect can facilitate the process of negotiation and result in improved outcomes in an integrative bargaining situation (Carnevale & Isen, 1986). An integrative-bargaining task is one in which, in order to reach the optimal agreement, people must make tradeoffs on different issues, of differing value to them, about which they are bargaining. Reaching agreement on such a task requires seeing possibilities, thinking innovatively, and reasoning flexibly about how tradeoffs might be made. Obvious compromises or simple yielding will not result in satisfactory outcomes (for greater detail, see, e.g., Pruitt, 1983).

In this study, people in the positive-affect condition who bargained face to face were significantly less likely to break off negotiation, and more likely to reach agreement, and to reach the optimal agreement possible in the situation, than were face-to-face bargainers in the control condition. They were also less likely to engage in aggressive tactics during the negotiation, and reported more enjoyment of the session (Carnevale & Isen, 1986). And they were better able than controls to figure out the other person's payoff matrix (rate of profit for each component of the agreement), which differed for the two bargainers. These results support the suggestion that positive affect facilitates a problem-solving approach and improves people's ability to integrate ideas and see ways of relating aspects of situations to each other, in order to come up with a good solution to a problem. It may also indicate a greater tendency or ability on the part of people in a state of positive affect to see things from another person's perspective, an ability that may relate to the "dopamine hypothesis" described later.

Thus, in summary of this section, positive affect appears to influence the way in which cognitive material is organized—how ideas are related to one another in mind. In particular, it has been found, in most situations, to give rise to greater elaboration in response to neutral or positive stimulus material (but not negative material) and a richer context, which in turn promotes flexibility in thinking. (It should be noted that, depending on the task, with positive *material*, although the elaboration effect is occurring, the difference between positive-affect and control subjects may not be apparent: The material itself induces positive affect, and this produces the effect even in the "control" condition. See Isen et al., 1985.)

This means that in a task (that deals with material of neutral-to-positive valence) undertaken while a person is feeling happy, one should expect unusual and innovative, though reasonable and logical, thoughts and responses. It is a mistake to assume that people in whom positive affect has been induced will think only those arguments and thoughts about the experimental materials that are provided by the experimenters. From the research reviewed here, we should expect people in the positive-affect condition to think about the materials in a more elaborated, extensive, flexible, responsible, and positive way—provided that the materials are not negative or boring.

In the case of negative material, it is more difficult to predict the behavior of people in a state of positive affect. If there is not a clear reason to focus on the negative material, we would expect people in a positive-affect condition not to elaborate the negative material more than controls. In some tasks (e.g., categorization, word association), this will result in their responses' not differing from those of control subjects (e.g., Isen et al., 1985, 1992). On other tasks, we would expect positive-affect participants actively to avoid, or show caution with, the materials, if possible in the situation. This might mean they would appear to be impaired in ability to perform the task, or slower on the task, compared with controls. However, in situations where the person needed to deal with the negative material, or where it would be to the person's longer-term benefit to do so, the research indicates that people in positive affect will show greater elaboration and enhanced coping even with negative materials or problematic situations (e.g., Aspinwall & Taylor, 1997; Isen & Geva, 1987; Trope & Pomerantz, 1998). Issues related to these distinctions are discussed in the next two sections.

POSITIVE AFFECT AND MOTIVATION

All of the work described thus far indicating that positive affect promotes enjoyment and enrichment of potentially enjoyable, though work-related, tasks (e.g., Carnevale & Isen, 1986; Kraiger et al., 1989) suggests that positive affect may influence task motivation (because richer tasks are also more motivating). I have already mentioned two kinds of possible effects of feelings on motivation: one on global motivation or trying harder, and one on a specific motivation or direction of effort (the tendency to behave so as to maintain the positive state).

Regarding global motivation, recall that there is no evidence as yet to suggest that positive affect simply raises effort on all tasks (e.g., Isen et al., 1993). In addition, other studies, such as those investigating the influence of affect on creativity, have reported effects of positive feelings that differ from those resulting from mere "arousal" (e.g., Isen et al., 1987). Therefore, it seems more promising to investigate specific aspects of tasks and task motivations that are facilitated by positive feelings.

With regard to the possibility that positive affect may introduce a motive to maintain the positive state, several studies suggest that this is likely (e.g., Isen & Simmonds, 1978; see also Isen, 1987, for discussion). One early study showed, for example, that people in whom positive affect had been induced were *less* likely than controls to help a stranger, when the helping task was one that was portrayed as virtually certain to make them feel depressed (Isen & Simmonds, 1978). This is in contrast with the often-obtained finding that in general, people who are feeling happy are more likely than controls to help, in any of a variety of ways (e.g., Cunningham, 1979; Isen, 1970; Isen & Levin, 1972). Thus the results of the study by Isen and Simmonds (1978) were interpreted as indicating that positive affect engenders a motive to avoid loss of the positive state. Such a motive may also be related to positive-affect subjects' relative risk aversion, which has been observed under certain circumstances (e.g., Isen & Geva, 1987; Isen et al., 1988; Isen & Patrick, 1983; Nygren et al., 1996) and which is discussed below in the section on decision making.

As a result of this preference to avoid loss of the positive state, people feeling happy may tend to leave more negative topics for another time, or at least to consider doing so, when that is possible. Consequently, positive affect may influence responses, performance, or latency of responding, differently, on tasks involving negative material.

The results of studies from a growing number of domains, however, suggest that the motive to maintain positive affect should not be expected to be automatic or absolute in its effects, nor to result in blind, irrational bias, nor in distortion of negative stimuli or tasks (e.g., Isen et al., 1985; Isen & Shalker, 1982; Schiffenbauer, 1974). Furthermore, evidence is accumulating that positive affect, far from leading people to ignore or "defend against" needed negative information, enables effective coping and reduces "defensiveness" in problematic situations that must be dealt with (e.g., Aspinwall, 1998; Aspinwall & Taylor, 1997; Trope & Neter, 1994; Trope & Pomerantz, 1998). Thus it seems likely that positive affect promotes effective thinking about even negative material, if doing so is useful or necessary, even though it also leads people to sidestep unnecessary consideration of undesirable material. This is yet another way in which positive affect promotes flexible problem solving.

Even though I have noted that positive affect does not simply raise general motivation or effort on all tasks through something akin to general "arousal" or activation, recent work suggests that it may influence the cognitive processes that relate to expectancy motivation. In this way, positive affect may increase at least some aspects of motivation (see Kanfer, 1990, & Vroom, 1964, for detailed discussions of expectancy motivation). Two recent studies addressing the influence of positive affect on components of expectancy motivation found that positive affect (1) could increase the expectation that effort would lead to improved performance on the task at hand; and (2) could increase the perceived value of an outcome, whether the outcome was winning a lottery (Study 1) or obtaining a job (Study 2). Positive affect also increased perceived "instrumentality" of behavior (i.e., the perceived link between performance and outcome) in the context of succeeding at getting a job, but not in the context of winning a lottery (Erez, Isen, & Purdy, 1999). This makes sense, since the probability of winning a lottery cannot readily be influenced by effort or performance.

Several other studies from additional areas of investigation also report findings compatible with those just described. These studies find that positive affect leads to increased enjoyment or pleasure from relatively positive material and situations (e.g., Kraiger et al., 1989), and point to two other kinds of motives that appear to be fostered by positive affect: (1) intrinsic motivation, and (2) variety seeking (stimulation seeking) among safe, enjoyable alternatives.

For example, one series of studies suggests that positive affect promotes variety seeking among safe and pleasant products (Kahn & Isen, 1993). Three studies reported that people in whom positive affect had been induced, when given the opportunity to make several choices in a food category (such as soup or snacks), showed more switching among alternatives than controls and included a broader range of items in their choice sets, as long as the circumstances did not make unpleasant or negative potential features of the items salient. In contrast, when a negative but not risky feature, (e.g., the possibility that a low-salt product would taste less good than the regular) was salient, there was no difference between the positive-affect and control groups in variety seeking. Thus there is evidence that positive affect promotes stimulation seeking—that is, enjoyment of variety and of a wider range of possibilities—but only when the situation does not prompt the person to think of unpleasant outcomes.

Another interesting possibility regarding the impact of affect on motivation, suggested by the results of three studies, is that positive affect may promote intrinsic motivation (Estrada et al., 1994; Isen & Reeve, 1992). In one study, people in whom positive affect had been induced by receipt of a small bag of candy spent more time, relative to controls, working on a task that promised to be interesting (a puzzle) than a task on which they could earn money but that promised to be boring and involved time pressure (finding particular combinations of numbers in three pages of randomly ordered numbers during a limited time period). Thus people in the positive-affect condition appeared relatively less influenced by the extrinsic motivator (money) and more influenced by the intrinsic motivator (interest in the task) than people in the control condition. They also reported more liking for the puzzle task after working on it than did controls, which is another indicator of intrinsic motivation. In this study, subjects were free to choose whichever task they preferred to work on. A follow-up study conceptually replicated this finding, but also showed that when positive-affect subjects knew that the more boring task had to be completed (not for money this time), they were as likely as controls to work on it (Isen & Reeve, 1992).

These findings directly support the observation made earlier that positive affect promotes enjoyment (in particular, enjoyment of tasks in which the subject is interested) and increases the likelihood of engaging in activities that are enjoyable or expected to be fun. They are also compatible with the findings indicating that positive affect increased the perception of task enrichment and satisfaction in regard to interesting jobs (Kraiger et al., 1989). At the same time, they show that people in positive-affect conditions will not avoid work tasks, or more boring, unpleasant, or difficult tasks, if it is clear that those tasks need to be done or if there is some potential benefit in doing them. People who feel good prefer pleasant things and enjoy them more when they do them; however, relative to control subjects, they do not shirk, irrationally "defend against," or irresponsibly refuse to engage in, less pleasant tasks.

not better economy, but better world

Another series of studies, investigating the influence of positive affect on physicians' decision making, suggests that positive affect may influence the relative strength of intrinsic (humanistic) as opposed to extrinsic (money and status) sources of practice satisfaction among physicians (Estrada et al., 1994). That is, relative to a control group, physicians in whom positive affect had been induced attributed greater importance to humanistic than to extrinsic sources of satisfaction, on a questionnaire asking about the sources of their satisfaction from practicing medicine.

It should also be mentioned, in the context of motivations induced by positive affect, that a large body of evidence indicates that under normal circumstances positive affect promotes helpfulness, generosity/responsibility, and friendliness/sociability (see Isen, 1987, for a review and discussion). Of course, as we have seen, this tendency can be overridden by such factors as the potential affective consequences of the helping task (e.g., Isen & Simmonds, 1978), or by other factors, such as dislike of the person or organization in need, that might cause the person not to want to help (e.g., Forest, Clark, Mills, & Isen, 1979). These findings may also indicate that people who are happy may feel more free to behave as they want to behave. Moreover, these latter effects may

themselves depend on such factors as the amount of harm that might come to the person in need if the potential helper did not help, and so on (see Isen, 1987, for discussion). The point here is that positive affect in general promotes not selfishness, but a tendency to be kind to both self and others, social connectedness, responsibility, and the ability to see situations from another person's perspective.

Thus, in sum, positive affect appears to produce a variety of behaviors that may be seen as resulting not only from the cognitive effects that have been discussed (such as increased elaboration and access to positive material, increased integration of concepts and ability to see connections among ideas, etc.), but also from apparent motivational changes. Some of these motivational changes are themselves cognitively mediated via components of expectancy motivation, such as expectation that additional effort will lead to improved performance, liking for a desirable outcome, and the perceived link between performance and obtaining the outcome. On the basis of the data presented here, it seems reasonable to propose that positive affect gives rise to two broad classes of motives: (1) enjoyment, interest, exploration, and graciousness in neutral-to-positive situations (or in situations where negatives or uninteresting things can be ignored safely); and (2) self-protection and conservativenesss in clearly negative situations in which the person must, for some reason, respond to the negative material. The relevance of these two kinds of findings for decision making is considered in the next section.

POSITIVE AFFECT AND DECISION MAKING

At the outset, it should be noted that consideration of the influence of affect on decision making involves recognition of the interacting roles of affect, the valence or interestingness of the task, the framing of the situation, the importance or utility of the task, and other aspects of the situation. Moreover, the processes described are not postulated to be automatic, but rather are seen as depending on people's interpretations of the situation. This suggests that processes such as decision making and problem solving may be hierarchically organized rather than monolithic—that before the problem is actually addressed, some command or executive decisions (attention deployment decisions) or evaluations may be made regarding how important the task is, what its utility may be, how dangerous or safe the situation is, or whether the person has any control over its eventual outcome, as well as what its hedonic consequences may be, how disruptive of ongoing feelings it might prove to be, and so on. These decisions may influence the way in which the problem is framed or addressed. Furthermore, it may also be that the person goes back and re-evaluates such decisions while solving the task problem.

To state this a bit differently, perhaps the person makes a series of decisions in deciding or solving a problem, and perhaps an early one in the series relates to the domain of the task, with regard to both valence and importance. A helpful way of viewing this first level of decision may be in terms of the framing or scope of the problem. That is, the person may derive a sense of whether this is a situation that offers the opportunity for enjoyment (gaining something, sharing, etc.), or is a situation that includes the potential for harm (the possibility of losing what the person already has or needs), as well as a sense of what his or her options are.

A conceptualization in terms of the framing of the situation has been useful in the decision-making and risk-taking literature, where differences have been found in people's decisions according to whether the problem was framed as a potential gain or as a potential loss (e.g., Kahneman & Tversky, 1979; Tversky & Kahneman, 1981). The parallel to Kahneman and Tversky's work is not exact, because in the well-known "Asian disease" problem, for example, the situation still involves danger, whether negatively or positively framed. However, framing as studied previously in the decision-making literature may nonetheless bear some relevance to the two types of motives and actions (exploration vs. self-protection) resulting from positive affect that are under discussion here. Issues related to the framing of the experimental situation, and to the possibility of a kind of hierarchical evaluation or decision process (especially as this interacts with affect), need to be explored more fully.

Risk

One kind of decision that has been studied as a function of positive affect is risk preference (e.g., Arkes, Herren, & Isen, 1988; Isen & Geva, 1987; Isen et al., 1988; Isen & Patrick, 1983; Isen, Pratkanis, Slovic, & Slovic, 1984; Nygren et al., 1996). In these studies, people in whom positive affect had been induced were more risk-averse than people in control conditions, when the risk situation about which they were reasoning was a realistic one that made them focus on the probability of a real, meaningful loss (e.g., Arkes et al., 1988; Isen & Patrick, 1983; Isen & Geva, 1987). Otherwise, they appeared more risk-prone than controls (Arkes et al., 1988; Isen & Patrick, 1983).

For example, when betting chips representing subjects' credit for participating in the study, those in whom positive affect had been induced bet fewer (Isen & Patrick, 1983), and required a higher probability of winning before agreeing to a substantial bet (Isen & Geva, 1987), compared with people in control conditions. They also showed more thoughts about losing in a thought-listing task following this assessment (Isen & Geva, 1987). Interestingly, when asked just to indicate their likelihood of taking a risk on a hypothetical task (such as starting up a business in an unstable foreign land), without having to wager anything of value to themselves, people in the positive-affect conditions indicated greater riskiness, less caution (Isen & Patrick, 1983). Similarly, when people were asked, without an affect induction, to estimate what effect they *thought* positive affect would have on their risk preference, they intuited that it would increase their riskiness (Isen et al., 1984).

The relative risk aversion observed among positive-affect subjects considering real risks may relate to affect maintenance: People who are feeling happy risk losing that state, as well as any tangible stake, if they lose a gamble. Therefore, perhaps because they have more to lose, they are more risk-averse than controls. This interpretation is supported by results of a study that examined the utility associated with various outcomes, and found that people in whom positive affect had been induced displayed a greater negative utility for a given loss than did controls (Isen et al., 1988). These results, showing that a loss seems worse to people who are feeling happy, fit with the suggestion that positive affect may result in a tendency or motive to protect the induced positive state in situations of potential loss.

The results just described indicate that positive affect increases the negative utility of a real, meaningful potential loss. At the same time, positive affect has been found to increase expectation or probability of success in situations of risk/gamble assessment (e.g., Johnson & Tversky, 1983; Nygren et al., 1996). Thus it seems that the two components of risk assessment, probability and utility, are influenced in functionally opposite ways by positive affect. Although the subjective probability of winning is increased by positive affect, the negative utility or perceived danger of the potential loss is also increased. Moreover, the resultant behavior—relative risk avoidance by positive-affect people—suggests that the utility information (or the information relevant to potential loss) is more salient and influential in positive-affect subjects' decisions than the probability information (or information relevant to potential gains). In fact, a recent series of studies suggests that this is the case (Nygren et al., 1996). These findings, then, together with the rest of the findings regarding positive affect and risk preference, illustrate (as noted in other contexts) that the influence of positive affect on risk perception does not appear to be simple, but interacts with task and setting characteristics in the situation.

Complex Decision Making

Another type of decision making that has been studied as a function of positive affect is what might be called "complex decision making," in which people are asked to choose the best item from among several alternatives (e.g., to choose a car for purchase) or to solve a complex problem (e.g., to make a medical diagnosis). Results of two studies suggest that people in whom positive affect has been induced are more efficient in decision making, but at the same time may also be more thorough, if the task lends itself to increased effort or care (Isen & Means, 1983; Isen et al., 1991).

In the first study, in which the decision task was to choose a hypothetical car for purchase from among six alternatives differing along nine dimensions (fuel economy, purchase price, etc.), the affect and control groups did not differ in their choices, but people in the positive-affect condition were more efficient in deciding. That is, they took significantly less time than those in the control condition, displayed significantly less redundancy in their search, and eliminated unimportant dimensions from consideration (Isen & Means, 1983).

The second study (Isen et al., 1991) used materials patterned on those of the car-choice experiment, but different in topic. In this study, the subjects were medical students who had completed their third (a clinical) year of medical training, and the task was to choose, from among six descriptions of patients varying with regard to each of nine health-relevant factors (cough, chest X-ray, etc.), the patient most likely to have lung cancer. The results of this study were compatible with those of the car-choice study, but particular measures produced different results because of the contextual differences. As had been found in the earlier study, people in the positive-affect condition reached the same answer (a correct one) to the assigned question as did controls, but they did so significantly earlier in their protocols. In this study, however, they then went on to do more than the assigned task—for example, suggesting diagnoses for the other patients, and in some cases thinking about treatments. Although participants in the positive-affect condition were more efficient than controls, particular measures (total amount of time working with the materials, amount of redundancy in the search process, etc.) were not good indicators of this group's efficiency, as they had been in the car-choice study, because in the present case the positive-affect group went beyond the assigned task and continued to work on the materials after reaching that decision. The different specific results in these two studies illustrate the importance of attention to the specifics of the situation in anticipating the impact of positive affect on particular measures. These findings also show that understanding the situation from the perspective of the participant, rather than that of the experimenter, is important.

The results of the medical diagnosis study suggest another possible influence of positive affect on decision making: greater integration of cognitive material. Subjects in the positive-affect condition in the medical diagnosis study showed significantly less confusion and a significantly greater tendency to integrate material with which they were working. Thus, as has been discussed earlier regarding the cognitive impact of positive affect, it appears that under conditions of positive affect, people integrate material used in decision processes. This enables them to be less overwhelmed by the task, to show less confusion, and to work faster. Then they can either finish sooner, as in the car-choice task, or turn their attention to other details or tasks within the materials, as in the medical diagnosis situation.

Another recent study, examining physicians' diagnostic processes, reported that doctors in whom positive affect had been induced (this time by receipt of a small bag of candy) identified the domain of the medical problem significantly earlier in their protocols than control physicians did; they were also more open to information, being significantly less likely than the physicians in the control group to distort or ignore information that did not fit with a diagnostic hypothesis they were considering (Estrada at al., 1997). This study confirms that positive affect does facilitate integration of information for decision making, and that it also fosters openness to information. At the same time, this study found no evidence that positive affect promotes premature closure in decision making, superficial processing, jumping to conclusions without sufficient evidence, or any indication of any impairment in thinking.

The findings of the medical decision-making studies suggest that positive affect may promote not only more efficiency but also more thoroughness, as well as openness to information, in a person's approach to a decision task. It should also be noted, however, that such an effect may be observed only where the materials allow for this possibility. Moreover, compatibly with similar points made earlier in this chapter, this may be true only for material that positive-affect people *want* or need to think about, or in which they are interested. A similar point has been made by Forgas (1991), who also found that positive affect increased the efficiency of decision making under some, but not all, circumstances. Results of the medical decision-making studies indicate, notably, that such material includes tasks requiring complex consideration of serious topics of interest to the subjects, and is not be limited to stereotypically "positive" or fun topics.

Heuristics

Several studies have addressed the issue of whether positive affect, rather than facilitating careful thinking and performance, takes up cognitive capacity (e.g., Mackie & Worth, 1989, 1991) and/or undermines motivation to think carefully (e.g., Bless et al., 1990; Schwarz & Bless, 1991; Schwarz, Bless, & Bohner, 1991), and thus results in the use of heuristics as contrasted with systematic cognitive processing. These studies were intended to show

that positive affect leads to careless, less systematic, or impaired processing.

One approach uses an attitude change paradigm and infers nonsystematic processing from the patterns of arguments that are successful in bringing about attitude change. For example, attitude change in response to relatively weak (though not irrational) arguments is taken as indication of nonsystematic processing; therefore, if positive-affect participants show as much attitude change when weak arguments are presented as they do when strong arguments are presented, these studies conclude that positive affect interferes with systematic processing (e.g., Mackie & Worth 1989).

As I suggested in the first edition of this chapter (Isen, 1993), one problem with this inference is that this kind of evidence is indirect. For example, attitude change may be reported for reasons unrelated to processing of the message: People in positive affect may want to be more agreeable (which is known from the social psychology literature to be associated with positive affect). Or they may think of additional good arguments of their own, and this may lead positive-affect subjects to display more change in attitude, independent of the strength of the arguments presented by the researchers. Alternative interpretations like these are supported by the fact that positive-affect participants did not differ from other participants in their recognition that the "weak" arguments were weaker than the "strong" arguments, or in ability to recall the message content, when these factors were measured directly (Bless et al., 1990; Mackie & Worth, 1989). In addition, in some instances the materials used in the studies focused on negative, upsetting topics, and the situation did not provide much justification for working on the task (see Isen, 1993, for fuller discussion of this issue). Consequently, people in a state of positive affect may have been less likely to engage the task. Thus it remains unclear from such studies that inability or lack of motivation to "think straight" is what causes any difference between groups in reported attitude change.

In another approach that has been taken, authors have reasoned that use of stereotypes may reflect heuristic or nonsystematic processing, and positive affect has been investigated as a determinant of stereotype use (e.g., Bodenhausen et al., 1994). The paper by Bodenhausen et al. (1994) illustrates the complexity of the findings in that area: Whereas three of four studies reported in that paper indicated that positive affect did result in increased use of a stereotype, the fourth study showed that this difference disappeared if participants were given a reason to pay more attention to the task (e.g., if they were to be accountable for their decisions). Again, any evidence that there might be from these studies for the suggestion that positive affect interferes with systematic processing would be indirect and open to alternative interpretation. Furthermore, the fact that the effect disappeared when the importance of the task was increased undermines the suggestion that, as a rule, positive affect leads to use of stereotypes and to nonsystematic processing generally.

In addition, as regards stereotyping in particular, recent work by Dovidio, Gaertner, and their colleagues suggests ways in which positive affect may reduce intergroup hostility and discrimination, which are often taken as related to stereotyping. This work found that positive affect led people to make note of shared commonalities in otherwise differentiated and hostile social groups (e.g., Colgate Democrats and Colgate Republicans). Furthermore, people in a state of positive affect were more likely to categorize the groups together and treat members of the other group as members of their own, enlarged in-group, rather than as outgroup members, because of these shared identities (Dovidio, Gaertner, Isen, & Lowrance, 1995). This, too, is not compatible with the idea that positive affect leads to stereotyping, with all of the implications that this usually carries.

In another approach to the question of whether positive affect impairs systematic processing, some studies have reported impaired reasoning performance among people in whom positive affect was induced (e.g., Melton, 1995). As noted above, in the context of the attitude change studies, it is possible that findings of seemingly impaired processing may result from the materials and context of the particular experiments that report the findings. This may be the case in the reasoning studies as well. A recent preliminary study has found, in fact, that materials like those used by Melton (1995) actually are relatively tedious and annoying to experimental participants, and that use of this kind of material can depress performance (Isen & Christianson, 1999). This most recent study specifically compared positive-affect subjects' performance on equivalent syllogistic reasoning tasks that used neutral mater-

ial versus boring, annoying material, and found that positive affect facilitated performance on the neutral syllogistic reasoning task but not on the annoying reasoning task (Isen & Christianson, 1999). It should also be mentioned that the neutral task was concrete, while the annoying version was abstract, but the two did not differ in difficulty.

Thus the evidence that positive affect per se disrupts systematic processing per se is not as clear as is often assumed. In cases where it appears to do so, this may be the result of a lack of motivation *for the task presented*; however, this kind of motivational effect is different from one that postulates general interference with motivation overall, or with motivation to process systematically. In fact, a recent study found, to the contrary, that positive affect increased people's preference for thinking carefully as measured by Cacioppo, Petty, and Kao's (1984) Need for Cognition scale (Isen & Aaker, 1997).

Finally, Schwarz and his colleagues—long proponents of the view that positive affect interferes with systematic processing because of undermining the motivation to think carefully—have recently reported results incompatible with that view (Bless et al., 1996). Acknowledging that "the evidence that heuristic processing is due to the hypothesized motivational or capacity deficits is less conclusive than is often assumed" (p. 665), they report results of three studies showing that although people in positive affect demonstrated a greater tendency, relative to controls, to use a script to organize their learning and memory of a story, they also performed better than controls on a secondary task that had to be performed simultaneously. In the words of Bless et al. (1996), this finding "is incompatible with the assumption that happy moods decrease either cognitive capacity or processing motivation in general, which would predict impaired secondary-task performance" (p. 665).

Bless et al.'s (1996) finding also supports the suggestion made in the first edition of this *Handbook* chapter (Isen, 1993) that heuristic and systematic cognitive processes may not necessarily be alternatives to one another, but may occur together. That is, "chunking," integration, or some other method of simplifying a complex set of data may actually free up capacity or resources for use on other tasks (Isen, 1984, 1987; Isen et al., 1991). This view is also compatible with the two-part process involving both elaboration and integration that was identified in the cognitive-style literature as "integrative complexity" by Harvey, Hunt, and Schroeder (1961) and others; according to this concept, processing that appears "simplified" actually results from more elaborated, differentiated processing and from better understanding of the issues (Isen, 1993). Thus integration, or even use of simplifying strategies, does not necessarily imply nonsystematic processing.

Bless et al. (1996) now propose that positive affect fosters reliance on existing habits and general knowledge structures, but acknowledge that this says nothing about systematic processing and that such reliance on existing habits and general knowledge structures may even free up capacity and enable enhanced overall performance. However, still reasoning, as they did previously, in terms of presumed evolved adaptive functioning that favors negative affect as more conducive to learning and careful attention to data, they contrast the process of using general knowledge structures with that of relying on data and engaging in learning, as if these two processes will not occur together. Their revised position, which now allows for systematic, effective processing among people who are feeling happy, is somewhat more compatible with the findings showing that positive affect results in improved performance on a wide variety of tasks requiring systematic processing. However, it still seems at variance with the wide range of findings showing that positive affect increases the innovativeness of people's responses and thinking, their openness and flexibility in thinking, and even their variety seeking among safe and enjoyable alternatives (e.g., Estrada et al., 1997; Isen et al., 1985; Kahn & Isen, 1993; see Isen, 1999, for a review). These findings certainly do not fit with the notion that positive affect promotes only, or even primarily, utilization of established general knowledge structures and old or habitual ways of looking at things. Perhaps, again, the problem arises in assuming that if habitual knowledge structures are used, then new learning, attention to the data at hand, and an open-minded cognitive stance will not occur or be used simultaneously.

In sum, the evidence that, as a rule, mild positive affect disrupts systematic processing is actually not compelling. This is because the studies attempting to show this are difficult to interpret—either because several levels of inference are required in order to reach that conclusion (as, e.g., in the studies using an attitude change paradigm); because they did not include an affect control group (positive and negative affect were contrasted); or because they used materials allowing for alternative interpretation, such as ones involving tedious tasks, negative topics or matters over which subjects had no control. (See Schwarz et al., 1991, for a review of these studies and a contrasting view.)

In fact, the evidence suggests that positive affect fosters integration of material, or efficient processing, while still enabling people to work systematically on problems (e.g., Estrada et al., 1997; Isen et al., 1991). Moreover, processes such as "chunking," integration, or cognitively organizing may indeed free up cognitive resources for additional processing. For almost a decade now, studies have been confirming that positive affect enables improved performance, even where simplifying devices are also used (e.g., Bless et al., 1996; Isen et al., 1991; Lee & Sternthal, 1999). That is, for people in a state of positive affect, heuristics and systematic processing seem to be able to be used together, rendering processing both more efficient and more thorough (see Isen, 1987, 1993, for discussion and Fredrickson, 1998, for a related view). In addition, however, the evidence shows that positive affect promotes creativity, innovation, openness to ideas and to new ways of looking at things, diversity in thinking, and exploration and trying new things (as long as the situation is not dangerous). Even where the situation is problematic, however, positive affect will foster many of these innovative, open processes (though not risk taking), thus facilitating coping as well. These findings suggest, in contrast with the position recently advanced by Bless et al. (1996), that positive affect will foster learning new ideas and strategies, and attention to data, at the same time that it promotes making use of existing knowledge structures.

This is not to say that positive affect, no matter how intense and no matter what the circumstances, cannot interfere with cognitive processing. Certainly it may be true that intense positive feelings or captivating good news may sometimes interfere with performance (or may do so for at least certain kinds of tasks). For example, news of winning an important prize or victory may distract us and interfere with performance of a more mundane task. But the reason may be just that the new topic distracts us from the other task, or changes what we want to think about—not that positive affect itself necessarily drains our capacity or signals us not to process systematically. In other words, in this regard, positive affect may be no different from any other interesting topic that causes us to refocus attention.

A NEUROPSYCHOLOGICAL THEORY OF POSITIVE AFFECT'S INFLUENCE ON COGNITION

Recently, a neuropsychological theory of the influence of positive affect on cognitive processing has been proposed that may help extend our understanding of affect and its influence on thought and behavior (Ashby et al., 1999). This theory focuses on the role of the neurotransmitter dopamine and proposes that many of the observed effects of positive affect on cognition may result from increased levels of dopamine in certain brain regions. Noting that dopamine is known to be associated with reward, this theory proposes that it is also present at increased levels during positive-affect situations. Although other neurotransmitters no doubt play a role as well, and may even act in concert with dopamine to determine specific nuances of behavior, the evidence is strong that brain levels of dopamine may well mediate many of the cognitive effects of positive affect that have been observed.

For example, because dopamine release into portions of the anterior cingulate region of the brain is thought to be involved in flexible selection of cognitive perspective and switching among alternative perspectives (see Ashby et al., 1999, for a review of this literature), it is likely that release of dopamine in these areas mediates the increased flexibility observed under conditions of positive affect. This, then, would implicate dopamine in many of the effects of positive feelings that have been observed: creativity; openness to information; exploration; integration of ideas; effective problem solving; focus on important negative information, when that is needed; ability to keep others' perspectives as well as one's own in mind seemingly simultaneously (and therefore possibly also many of the social effects of positive affect that have been established over the years, such as cooperativeness, friendliness, social responsibility, improved negotiation skills, and generosity to both self and others)—just to name a few that come to mind most readily.

In addition, because there are many excitatory dopamine receptors in frontal brain areas, the prefrontal cortex, and the olfactory bulb and cortex, this theory also predicts that positive affect will facilitate processes influenced by those areas of the brain, such as attention deployment (the "executive" function), working memory, memory consolidation, and olfactory processing. On the other hand, it also suggests some processes that should not be enhanced, because dopamine receptors are not concentrated in some areas; visual and auditory perception, for example, should not be influenced by positive affect. As an aside, it might also be noted that this kind of analysis could also offer a possible mechanism for carrying out the preliminary dichotomous assignment of situations to the realm of "danger" (negative frame) versus "safety" (positive frame), as proposed earlier in this chapter. Damasio (1994), for example, has proposed that via activity in the amygdala, every experience is "tagged" with a positive or negative valence in an early stage of processing. Clearly, much remains to be explored relating to the dopamine hypothesis, but these kinds of predictions provide more specific targets than we have had in the past, and ideally this theoretical approach will contribute to our understanding.

This neurological theory adds to our tools for studying the impact of affect; however, it cannot replace studies conducted on the cognitive and behavioral levels. Rather than viewing these levels of analysis (e.g., neurological vs. behavioral) as opposing one another as ways to advance understanding, it is possible instead to attempt to bring them together and integrate work from these multiple levels of analysis. That is, understandings from the neurological level can help to inform and guide our search for behavioral and cognitive (as well as other neurological) effects and determinants of feelings, as we seek to deepen our understanding of affect itself and of the cognitive processes and range of behaviors that will be influenced. Similarly, research on the behavioral and cognitive level can point to neurological processes that may be critical. Indeed, it was studies on the behavioral and cognitive levels of analysis that led to our understanding that positive affect promotes flexibility and creativity, and thus to the present hypothesis that dopamine may mediate at least some of the cognitive and behavioral effects of positive affect.

Similarly, discovery of the role of neurological processes in these relationships should not cause us to assume that the effects are genetic or immutable, or to lose sight of the fact of continual learning and plasticity in human behavior and cognitive processes. When neurological mechanisms mediating behavior are identified, it is sometimes tempting to attribute them (and the behavior or cognitive processes they mediate) to genetic or innate factors, to see them as the products of very early learning, or to view them as somehow immutable or very difficult to change. Yet there is no need to assume that all neurological structures and/or processes are innate; in fact, there is growing evidence that neurological changes also result from learning and experience. For one example, elaborated at length in this chapter, the evidence is overwhelming that small, everyday positive-affect-inducing events can give rise to these remarkable cognitive and behavioral (and possibly neurological) effects.

Likewise, one need not assume that these effects and processes are automatic, even if a neurological process is identified. In fact, as has been emphasized throughout this chapter, the evidence underscores the role of people's plans, goals, understandings, and expectations in determining their reactions to the situations in which they find themselves. Events may not generate positive affect, or cause dopamine release, unless they are interpreted and integrated by people's purposive understanding and behavior. Moreover, even after dopamine is released, the specific reactions may still depend on aspects of contexts and people's plans and goals (possibly governing uptake and release of neuotransmitters). If dopamine in the anterior cingulate associated with positive affect helps to increase flexibility and alternative perspective taking, for example, the particular way in which this added potential for flexibility is implemented (or not implemented) still depends on people's resolution of the possibilities, constraints, contingencies, and so forth that they understand (e.g., Isen, 1993; Martin, Ward, Achee, & Wyer, 1993; Smith & Shaffer, 1991; Wegener, Petty, & Smith, 1995). This, as we know from the many studies now showing interactions between affect and situational aspects of the task (e.g., Bodenhausen et al., 1994; Forgas, 1991; Isen & Christianson, 1999; Isen et al., 1985, 1992; Martin et al., 1993; Wegener et al., 1995; and many others), depends upon other factors in the situations, as well as on the affect and the dopamine themselves.

Thus the ultimate cognitive and behavioral effects of dopamine in the anterior cingulate region are nonetheless mediated by factors in the situation influencing people's plans, goals, and purposes. Dozens of studies point to the importance of these purposive factors.

CONCLUSION

In summary of the work presented in this chapter, it seems appropriate to emphasize once again that the influence of affect depends on what it makes the person think about, and that this is determined not by the affective state alone, but by the affect in conjunction with several aspects of the situation that together influence the person's goals, judgments, and expectations. Brain regions activated by neurotransmitters (particularly dopamine) associated with positive affect play a role in the effects of feelings, but this is only one of several influences that together determine resultant cognitive processes and behavior.

Despite the complex interaction of factors that determines affect's ultimate impact on thought processes and behavior, a few general conclusions can be offered: All else being equal, positive affect tends to promote exploration and enjoyment of new ideas and possibilities, and new ways of looking at things—especially in enjoyable or "safe" situations. Therefore, people who are feeling good may be alert to possibilities, may explore and play, and may solve problems both more efficiently and more thoroughly than controls. However, in "dangerous" situations or situations of potential loss rather than gain, people who are feeling good respond cautiously. They should be expected to avoid unpleasant material or situations where possible. But in situations in which they must think about possible losses or difficulties, they may be expected to consider the negative possibilities thoroughly and effectively.

A general statement regarding positive affect's influence on systematic thinking may be the following: If people who are happy can be expected to want to think about the topic or task that is presented to them (and this will include tasks involving serious topics in which they are competent and interested), then, compared with controls, they will elaborate on the task more and deal with it effectively and efficiently. In contrast, if people in whom positive affect has been induced can be expected to prefer not to focus on the materials or topic (for whatever reason), and there is nothing in the situation that requires, recommends, or alerts them that they should attend to the boring or negative task, then the person in a positive feeling state may not perform that task, may do so with as little effort as possible, or may be slower to engage in it. This should not be taken as evidence that positive feelings disrupt systematic thinking as a rule by taking up cognitive capacity or by reducing the motivation to process carefully, or that positive-affect subjects *cannot* perform the task. Rather, it only reflects the sensible behavior of people who are feeling free to do what they prefer. For if there is a reason for positive-affect subjects to work on a less preferred task, evidence suggests that they will also do that.

Thus, generally, common positive feelings seem to promote activities that foster enjoyment and maintenance of those feelings, but in rational, responsible, adaptive ways. In addition, they provide many benefits (apart from the happiness inherent in them). They enhance flexibility and can facilitate creative problem solving, enabling people to come up with solutions to difficult problems that others find extremely hard to solve (while at the same time not detracting from performance on routine tasks), and in some instances enabling mutually satisfying negotiated solutions to interpersonal disputes. Positive affect has been found to give rise to elaboration and a wide range of cognitive associations in response to neutral stimulus material (while not reducing association to negatively toned words). It increases preference for variety and acceptance of a broader range of options in people's choice sets, when the choice is among safe, enjoyable alternatives, but does not promote risk taking in situations of genuine risk. Happy feeling can lead to efficient and thorough decision making; it stimulates enjoyment of enjoyable tasks and perception of interesting tasks as even more enriched (but not at the cost of working on less interesting things if they need to be done). When less interesting or slightly negative tasks are presented, those things may be deferred if that is an option, but will be addressed effectively if not. Socially, of course, positive affect is known to promote the very important processes of generosity, helpfulness, and responsibility, under most circumstances.

This chapter has examined some of the evidence regarding ways in which positive affect influences decision making. Clearly, however, more work is needed to explore these relationships, the circumstances under which they occur, and the processes that are involved in producing them. The new neurological proposal focusing on dopamine levels in certain brain regions provides some additional hypotheses and extends our understanding of some of the processes already identified; still, much remains to be understood about this proposal itself and how it can be integrated with behavioral and cognitive work that is being done. Given the importance of positive feelings in our lives, and the great advantages to social behavior and problem solving that result from people's feeling happy, positive affect seems a worthwhile topic for continued investigation.

REFERENCES

Arkes, H. R., Herren, L. T., & Isen, A. M. (1988). Role of possible loss in the influence of positive affect on risk preference. *Organizational Behavior and Human Decision Processes, 42*, 181–193.

Ashby, F. G., Isen, A. M., & Turken, A. U. (1999). A neuropsychological theory of positive affect and its influence on cognition. *Psychological Review, 106*, 529–550.

Aspinwall, L. G. (1998). Rethinking the role of positive affect and self-regulation. *Motivation and Emotion, 22*(1), 1–32.

Aspinwall, L. G. & Taylor, S. E. (1997). A stitch in time: Self-regulation and proactive coping. *Psychological Bulletin, 121*, 417–436.

Berlyne, D. E. (1967). Arousal and reinforcement. In *Nebraska Symposium on Motivation* (Vol. 15, pp. 1–110). Lincoln: University of Nebraska Press.

Bless, H., Bohner, G., Schwarz, N., & Strack, F. (1990). Mood and persuasion: A cognitive response analysis. *Personality and Social Psychology Bulletin, 16*, 331–345.

Bless, H., Schwarz, N., Clore, G. L., Golisano, V., Rabe, C. & Wolk, M. (1996). Mood and the use of scripts: Does a happy mood really lead to mindlessness? *Journal of Personality and Social Psychology, 71*(4), 665–679.

Bodenhausen, G. V., Kramer, G. P., & Susser, K. (1994). Happiness and stereotypic thinking in social judgment. *Journal of Personality and Social Psychology, 66*, 621–632.

Bransford, J. D. (1979). *Human cognition.* Belmont, CA: Wadsworth.

Cacioppo, J., Petty, R., & Kao, C. F. (1984). The efficient assessment of need for cognition. *Journal of Personality Assessment, 48*, 306–307.

Carnevale, P. J. D., & Isen, A. M. (1986). The influence of positive affect and visual access on the discovery of integrative solutions in bilateral negotiation. *Organizational Behavior and Human Decision Processes, 37*, 1–13.

Cunningham, M. R. (1979). Weather, mood, and helping behavior: Quasi-experiments in the sunshine Samaritan. *Journal of Personality and Social Psychology, 37*, 1947–1956.

Damasio, A. R. (1994). *Descartes' error.* New York: Putnam.

Dovidio, J. F., Gaertner, S.L., Isen, A. M., & Lowrance, R. (1995). Group representations and intergroup bias: Positive affect, similarity, and group size. *Personality and Social Psychology Bulletin, 21*, 856–865.

Duncker, K. (1945). On problem-solving. *Psychological Monographs, 58*(Whole No. 5).

Easterbrook, J. A. (1959). The effect of emotion on cue utilization and the organization of behavior. *Psychological Review, 66*, 183–201.

Erez, A., Isen, A. M., & Purdy, C. (1999). *The influence of positive affect on components of expectancy motivation.* Unpublished manuscript, University of Florida.

Estrada, C., Isen, A. M., & Young, M. J. (1994). Positive affect influences creative problem solving and reported source of practice satisfaction in physicians. *Motivation and Emotion, 18*, 285–299.

Estrada, C. A., Isen, A. M., & Young, M. J. (1997). Positive affect facilitates integration of information and decreases anchoring in reasoning among physicians. *Organizational Behavioral and Human Decision Processes, 72*, 117–135.

Forest, D., Clark, M., Mills, J. & Isen, A. M. (1979). Helping as a function of feeling state and nature of the helping behavior. *Motivation and Emotion, 3*(2), 161–169.

Forgas, J. P. (1991). Affective influences on partner choice: Role of mood in social decisions. *Journal of Personality and Social Psychology, 61*, 708–720.

Fredrickson, B. L. (1998). What good are positive emotions? *Review of General Psychology, 2*, 300–319.

George, J. M., & Brief, A. P. (1996). Motivational agendas in the workplace: The effects of feelings on focus of attention and work motivation. In L. L. Cummings & B. M. Staw (Eds.), *Research in organizational behavior* (Vol. 18, pp. 75–109). Greenwich, CT: JAI Press.

Greene, T. R., & Noice, H. (1988). Influence of positive affect upon creative thinking and problem solving in children. *Psychological Reports, 63*, 895–898.

Harvey, O. J., Hunt, D. E., & Schroeder, H. M. (1961). *Conceptual systems and personality organization.* New York: Wiley.

Hirt, E. R., Melton, R. J., McDonald, H. E., & Harackiewicz, J. M. (1996). Processing goals, task interest, and the mood-performance relationship: A mediational analysis. *Journal of Personality and Social Psychology, 71*, 245–261.

Isen, A. M. (1970). Success, failure, attention, and reactions to others: The warm glow of success. *Journal of Personality and Social Psychology, 15*, 294–301.

Isen, A. M. (1984). Toward understanding the role of affect in cognition. In R. Wyer & T. Srull (Eds.), *Handbook of social cognition* (Vol. 3, pp. 179–236). Hillsdale, NJ: Erlbaum.

Isen, A. M. (1987). Positive affect, cognitive processes, and social behavior. In L. Berkowitz (Ed.), *Advances in experimental social psychology* (Vol. 20, pp. 203–253). New York: Academic Press.

Isen, A. M. (1990). The influence of positive and negative affect on cognitive organization: Some implications for development. In N. Stein, B. Leventhal, & T. Trabasso (Eds.), *Psychological and biological approaches to emotion* (pp. 75–94). Hillsdale, NJ: Erlbaum.

Isen, A. M. (1993). Positive affect and decision making. In M. Lewis & J. Haviland (Eds.), *Handbook of emotions* (pp. 261–277). New York: Guilford Press.

Isen, A. M. (1999). Positive affect and creativity. In S. Russ (Ed.), *Affect, creative experience, and psychological adjustment* (pp. 3–17). Philadelphia: Brunner/Mazel.

Isen, A. M., & Aaker, J. (1997). *The influence of positive affect on preference for systematic cognitive processes.* Unpublished manuscript, Cornell University.

Isen, A. M., Berg, J. W., & Chen, M. (1993). *The influence of affect on creative vs. routine tasks.* Unpublished manuscript, Cornell University.

Isen, A. M., & Christianson, M. (1999). *Positive affect facilitates performance on an interesting reasoning task but not on a tedious one.* Unpublished manuscript. Cornell University.

Isen, A. M., & Daubman, K. A. (1984). The influence of affect on categorization. *Journal of Personality and Social Psychology, 47*, 1206–1217.

Isen, A. M., Daubman, K. A., & Nowicki, G. P. (1987). Positive affect facilitates creative problem solving. *Journal of Personality and Social Psychology, 52*, 1122–1131.

Isen, A. M., & Geva, N. (1987). The influence of positive affect on acceptable level of risk: The person with a large canoe has a large worry. *Organizational Behavior and Human Decision Processes, 39*, 145–154.

Isen, A. M., Johnson, M. M. S., Mertz, E., & Robinson, G. F. (1985). The influence of positive affect on the unusualness of word associations. *Journal of Personality and Social Psychology, 48*, 1413–1426.

Isen, A. M., & Levin, P. F. (1972). Effect of feeling good on helping: Cookies and kindness. *Journal of Personality and Social Psychology, 21*, 384–388.

Isen, A. M., & Means, B. (1983). The influence of positive affect on decision-making strategy. *Social Cognition, 2*, 18–31.

Isen, A. M., Niedenthal, P., & Cantor, N. (1992). An influence of positive affect on social categorization. *Motivation and Emotion, 16*, 65–78.

Isen, A. M., Nygren, T. E., & Ashby, F. G. (1988). The influence of positive affect on the subjective utility of gains and losses: It is just not worth the risk. *Journal of Personality and Social Psychology, 55*, 710–717.

Isen, A. M., & Patrick, R. (1983). The effect of positive feelings on risk-taking: When the chips are down. *Organizational Behavior and Human Performance, 31*, 194–202.

Isen, A. M., Pratkanis, A. R., Slovic, P., & Slovic, L. M. (1984). *An influence of affect on risk preference.* Paper presented at the meeting of the American Psychological Association, Washington, DC.

Isen, A. M., & Reeve, J. M. (1992). *The influence of*

positive affect on intrinsic motivation. Unpublished manuscript. Cornell University.

Isen, A. M., Rosenzweig, A. S., & Young, M. J. (1991). The influence of positive affect on clinical problem solving. *Medical Decision Making, 11* (3), 221–227.

Isen, A. M., & Shalker, T. E. (1982). Do you "accentuate the positive, eliminate the negative" when you are in a good mood? *Social Psychology Quarterly, 45,* 58–63.

Isen, A. M., Shalker, T., Clark, M. S., & Karp, L. (1978). Affect, accessibility of material and behavior: A cognitive loop? *Journal of Personality and Social Psychology, 36,* 1–12.

Isen, A. M., & Simmonds, S. F. (1978). The effect of feeling good on a helping task that is incompatible with good mood. *Social Psychology Quarterly, 41,* 345–349.

Johnson, E., & Tversky, A. (1983). Affect, generalization and the perception of risk. *Journal of Personality and Social Psychology, 45,* 20–31.

Kahn, B. E., & Isen, A. M. (1993). The influence of positive affect on variety-seeking among safe, enjoyable products. *Journal of Consumer Research, 20,* 257–270.

Kahneman, D., & Tversky, A. (1979). Prospect theory: An analysis of decisions under risk. *Econometrica, 47,* 263–291.

Kanfer, R. (1990). Motivation theory and industrial and organizational psychology. In M. D. Dunnette & L. M. Hough (Eds.), *Handbook of industrial and organizational psychology* (Vol. 1, pp. 75–170). Palo Alto, CA: Consulting Psychologists Press.

Kraiger, K., Billings, R. S., & Isen, A. M. (1989). The influence of positive affective states on task perceptions and satisfaction. *Organizational Behavior and Human Decision Processes, 44,* 12–25.

Lacey, J. I. (1967). Somatic response patterning and stress: Some revisions of activation theory. In M.H. Appley & R. Trumball (Eds.), *Psychological stress: Issues in research* (pp. 14–44). New York: Appleton-Century-Crofts.

Lacey, J. I. (1975). Psychophysiology of the autonomic nervous system. In J.R. Nazarrow (Ed.), *Master lectures on physiological psychology* (Audiotape). Washington, DC: American Psychological Association.

Lee, A., & Sternthal, B. (1999). The effects of positive mood on memory *Journal of Consumer Research, 26,* 115–127.

Mackie, D. M., & Worth, L. T. (1989). Processing deficits and the mediation of positive affect in persuasion. *Journal of Personality and Social Psychology, 57,* 27–40.

Mackie, D. M., & Worth, L. T. (1991). Feeling good but not thinking straight: The impact of positive mood on persuasion. In J. P. Forgas (Ed.), *Emotion and social judgment* (pp. 201–220). Oxford: Pergamon Press.

Martin, L. M., Ward, D. W., Achee, J. W., & Wyer, R. A. (1993). Mood as input: People have to interpret the motivational implications of their moods. *Journal of Personality and Social Psychology, 64,* 317–326.

Matlin, M. W., & Zajonc, R. B. (1968). Social facilitation of word associations. *Journal of Personality and Social Psychology, 10,* 455–460.

Mednick, M. T., Mednick, S. A., & Mednick, E. V. (1964). Incubation of creative performance and specific associative priming. *Journal of Abnormal and Social Psychology, 69,* 84–88.

Melton, R. J. (1995). The role of positive affect in syllogism performance. *Personality and Social Psychology Bulletin, 21,* 788–794.

Murray, N., Sujan, H., Hirt, E. R., & Sujan, M. (1990). The influence of mood on categorization: A cognitive flexibility interpretation. *Journal of Personality and Social Psychology, 59,* 411–425.

Nasby, W., & Yando, R. (1982). Selective encoding and retrieval of affectively valenced information. *Journal of Personality and Social Psychology, 43,* 1244–1255.

Neiss, R. (1990). Ending arousal's reign of error: A reply to Anderson. *Psychological Bulletin, 107,* 101–105.

Nygren, T. E., Isen, A. M., Taylor, P. J., & Dulin, J. (1996). The influence of positive affect on the decision rule in risk situations: Focus on outcome (and especially avoidance of loss) rather than probability. *Organizational Behavior and Human Decision Processes, 66*(1), 59–72.

Pruitt, D. G. (1983). Strategic choice in negotiation. *American Behavioral Scientist, 27,* 167–194.

Rosch, E. (1975). Cognitive representations of semantic categories. *Journal of Experimental Psychology: General, 104*(3), 192–233.

Schiffenbauer, A. (1974). Effects of observer's emotional state on judgments of the emotional state of others. *Journal of Personality and Social Psychology, 30*(1), 31–36.

Schwarz, N., & Bless, H. (1991). Happy and mindless, but sad and smart?: The impact of affective states on analytic reasoning. In J.P. Forgas (Ed.), *Emotion and social judgment* (p. 55–71). Oxford, England: Pergamon.

Schwarz, N., Bless, H., & Bohner, G. (1991). Mood and persuasion: Affective states influence the processing of persuasive communications. In M. Zanna (Ed.), *Advances in experimental social psychology* (Vol. 24, pp. 161–199). New York: Academic Press.

Simonson, I. (1989). Choice based on reasons: The case of attraction and compromise effects. *Journal of Consumer Research, 16,* 158–174.

Simonson, I. (1990). The effect of purchase quantity and timing on variety-seeking behavior. *Journal of Marketing Research, 27,* 150–162.

Smith, S. M., & Shaffer, D. R. (1991). The effects of good moods on systematic processing: "Willing but not able, or able but not willing?" *Motivation and Emotion, 15,* 243–279.

Staw, B. M., & Barsade, S. G. (1993). Affect and managerial performance: A test of the sadder-but-wiser vs. happier-and-smarter hypotheses. *Administrative Science Quarterly, 38,* 304–331.

Staw, B. M., Sutton, R. I., & Pelled, L. H. (1994). Employee positive emotion and favorable outcomes at the workplace. *Organizational Science, 5,* 51–71.

Taylor, S. E., & Aspinwall, L. G. (1996). Mediating and moderating processes in psychosocial stress: Appraisal, coping, resistance and vulnerability. In H.B. Kaplan (Ed.), *Psychosocial stress: Perspectives on structure, theory, life-course, and methods* (pp. 71–110). San Diego, CA: Academic Press.

Teasdale, J. D., & Fogarty, S. J. (1979). Differential effects of induced mood on retrieval of pleasant and unpleasant events from episodic memory. *Journal of Abnormal Psychology, 88*, 248–257.

Trope, Y., & Neter, E. (1994). Reconciling competing motives in self-evaluation: The role of self-control in feedback seeking. *Journal of Personality and Social Psychology, 66*, 646–657.

Trope, Y., & Pomerantz, E. M. (1998). Resolving conflicts among self-evaluative motives: Positive experiences as a resource for overcoming defensiveness. *Motivation and Emotion, 22*, 53–72.

Tversky, A., & Gati, I. (1978). Studies of similarity. In E. Rosch & B. B. Lloyd (Eds.), *Cognition and categorization* (pp. 79–98). Hillsdale, NJ: Erlbaum.

Tversky, A., & Kahneman, D. (1981). The framing of decisions. *Science, 211*, 453–458.

Venables, P. H. (1984). Arousal: An examination of its status as a concept. In M. G. H. Coles, J. R. Jennings, & J. A. Stern (Eds.), *Psychophysiological perspectives: Festschrift for Beatrice and John Lacey* (pp. 134–142). New York: Van Nostrand Reinhold.

Vroom, V. H. (1964). *Work and motivation.* New York: Wiley.

Wegener, D. T., Petty, R. E., & Smith, S. E. (1995). Positive mood can increase or decrease message scrutiny: The hedonic contingency view of mood and message processing. *Journal of Personality and Social Psychology, 69*, 5–15.

Weiner, B. (1985). "Spontaneous" causal thinking. *Psychological Bulletin, 97*, 74–84.

CHAPTER 28

A Goal Appraisal Theory of Emotional Understanding: Implications for Development and Learning

Nancy L. Stein
Tom Trabasso
Maria D. Liwag

How are emotional events understood and re-membered? Are emotional situations different from other situations that occur in everyday interaction? Are young children between 2½ and 5 years of age able to understand, remember, and act upon events that affect them emotionally? Can they talk about their feelings, beliefs, preferences, goals, and plans? Are they aware that other people have the same types of knowledge and feeling states as they do? Most importantly, how does children's understanding compare to that of adults? Do children use similar mental structures to interpret emotional events, or does their understanding change qualitatively, as a function of development and experience?

To answer these questions, we present a model of goal appraisal processes (Stein, Trabasso, & Liwag, 1993) that describes the thinking and evaluation carried out during acts of remembering and talking about emotional events. We show how our model elucidates the roles that knowledge and goal-directed understanding play in determining social awareness and

action in young children. We use as evidence data from our studies on memories for real-life emotional and conflictual events.

Throughout this chapter, we argue that children use conscious and unconscious appraisal processes to understand, evaluate, and respond to events that provoke emotion. From the very beginning, emotional understanding is goal-based, expressive, and action-oriented. Experiencing emotion involves continual monitoring of personally relevant goals; relies on both causally and categorically based inferences; and involves a constant appraisal of the value and worth of events, people, objects, activities, ideas, internal states, and anything that impinges on the psychological and physical well-being of the person involved. Thus, even in toddlerhood (at least from the age of 2 years on), children understand events in an organized and systematic way, much as adults do. The basis of their understanding is dependent upon a continual evaluation and appraisal of incoming information, especially as this information is related to the attainment of personally meaningful goals.

To show how appraisals guide and regulate emotional understanding, we summarize a series of empirical studies on preschool children's memory for real-life emotional events. We show how children's memories can be analyzed in terms of goal appraisal processes and how these appraisals give rise to the causal and narrative structuring of emotional experience.[1] We compare our theoretical and empirical orientations to those of Fivush (1991, 1996; Fivush & Hudson, 1990) and to those of Wellman and his collaborators (Bartsch & Wellman, 1995; Wellman, Harris, Banerjee, & Sinclair, 1995). We also compare our theories to those of Lazarus and Smith (Lazarus, 1991; Smith & Lazarus, 1993).

We point out that a serious problem with other approaches is a failure to describe broadly the content and context of children's and adults' thinking and reasoning processes. As a result, several researchers (Bartsch & Wellman, 1995; Fivush, 1996; Fivush & Hayden, 1997; Howe, Courage, & Petersen, 1996) believe that development is better characterized by the unfolding and emergence of *qualitatively* different mental operations that become available to children as they grow older. Results from some of their studies promote the hypothesis that children are fundamentally different types of thinkers than adults (see Carey & Gelman, 1991, for an extended discussion of this hypothesis).

For example, children are thought to undergo qualitative changes in their ability to make inferences about other people's desires and beliefs (Bartsch & Wellman, 1995). Young children are thought to be different because they do not "appear" to have access to the same senses of self that adults have (Fivush, 1996; Howe et al., 1996), such as a "narrative" self or a self that intentionally remembers and compares itself to other people. Younger children are also more likely to express incomplete knowledge about a specific situation (Brown & Dunn, 1996; Stein & Albro, 1997), and do not express linguistically many of the causal complexities about emotion that older children and adults do. These omissions from naturalistic talk about emotion often result in researchers' concluding that young children, especially those below the age of 4 years, have a qualitatively different understanding of themselves and others when compared to older children and adults.

Results from many empirical studies question these assertions. Mental structures used to encode and represent intentional action are present very early in infancy. Investigators studying infants' development of perception and action describe very young children as being engaged in intentional goal-directed thinking in almost every situation and context considered (Gergely, Nadasdy, Csibra, & Biro, 1995; Haith, 1994; Alessandri, Sullivan, & Lewis, 1990; Stenberg & Campos, 1990; von Hofsten, 1994; Willatts, 1990; Woodward, 1998). These goal-directed mental processes are similar to those described by Bartlett (1932), Miller, Galanter, and Pribram (1960), and Newell and Simon (1972), and subsequently by researchers studying the development of narrative understanding (Mandler & Johnson, 1977; Rumelhart, 1975, 1977; Schank, 1982; Schank & Abelson, 1977; Stein & Glenn, 1979; Stein & Goldman, 1981; Stein & Trabasso, 1982) and by those using artificial intelligence as an approach to studying intentional action (Lehnert, 1985; Sacerdoti, 1975; Suchman, 1987; Wilensky, 1978).

These goal-directed processes regulate and guide the understanding and expression of emotion and action-oriented behavior. To respond emotionally, people must be able to activate stable mental representations that encode expectations about the nature, content, and causal structure of an event. Furthermore, they must be able to recognize when their expectations are violated, and they must be able to determine how these violations have affected personally meaningful goals. Otherwise, emotional reactions would not be experienced.[2] These types of appraisals are thought to be carried out by children as young as 4 months of age (Stenberg & Campos, 1990). Infancy researchers (Haith, 1994; Roberts & Ondrejko, 1994; von Hofsten, 1994) have adopted different sets of behavioral criteria to show how very young children develop and respond to the same types of expectations that adults do.

The facts that infants develop expectations; that they show evidence of tracing and responding to the causes of an event (Haith, 1994; von Hofsten, 1994; Woodward, 1998); that they remember the location of events, people, and objects; and that they change and revise their subsequent actions in the face of failure and violation of expectation (Alessandri et al., 1990; Lewis, Alessandri, & Sullivan, 1990) all strongly support the hypothesis that goal appraisal processes operate in the very earliest phases of infancy. Certainly these processes are involved in understanding and interpreting experience well before the onset of language. The interactive routines that parents and children carry out by the age of 8 months (Duncan & Farley, 1990) reflect infants' rich knowledge about the nature of family interaction. Infants are able to respond to rules that permit and prohibit forms of action, and they are sensitive to rules for communicating their internal states to others (Quasthoff, 1991, 1992; Snow, 1990; Stern, 1992).

Much of what infants learn during these interactions is nonverbal and stored in visual, auditory, tactile, or motoric representations. Children know how other people sound, smell, move, act, and talk. They know what makes other people angry; they know how to provoke anger in other people; and they operate on this knowledge far before the age of 2 years. Much of this knowledge is conceptual and can be directly accessed by young children, as evidenced in their solutions to everyday problems, in their memories for everyday routines, and in their fantasy talk and play. As children progress from infancy through toddlerhood and into the preschool years, both nonverbal and verbal knowledge structures become more detailed and elaborated. The mental processes and structures that they use, however, do not necessarily change.

The study of emotional understanding and goal-directed action allows us to describe the contents of children's beliefs, emotions, goals, and plans of action reported during the experience of an emotion. We present examples of preschool children's evaluations and explicit talk about themselves and other people during the retrieval of an emotional memory. Children talk about their beliefs and goals in reference to themselves and to other people; they talk about events, objects, and actions during problem solving; and they talk about those things that have a direct impact directly on their ability to maintain personal goals and states of well-being.

Analyzing memories for emotional and conflictual events is a good starting point for describing young children's abilities to engage in complex thinking processes. Emotional situations, in contrast to those that rely more on routine script knowledge, always involve the reporting of some aspect of novelty and violation of expectation (Mandler, 1984; Stein & Levine, 1987, 1990; Stein et al., 1993). The report of novelty is typically focused on an unexpected precipitating event that challenges or violates prior beliefs and that requires conscious processing of the precipitating event (Mandler, 1984; Stein & Levine, 1987, 1990). Children as well as adults activate knowledge about what *should* have occurred in comparison to what *did* occur. Depending upon the situation, their current goals, and their willingness to disclose what they know, children may or may not choose to report their knowledge, feelings, and evaluations of an event.

When children are not under threat, they easily access and talk about the reasoning, thinking, and planning they carried out during an emotional episode. Their answers to "Why" questions that focus on explanation, or to predictive questions that focus on "What will happen if . . . ," "Pretend that . . . ," "Suppose that . . . ," almost always elaborate and clarify their understanding of the specifics of a situation. We suggest that fundamental differences in development are not associated with the emergence of different mental operations. Rather, the major differences lie in the specific content knowledge children and adults access, the preferences they develop for specific goals, and shifts in the importance of one goal over another as children develop and gain more experience.

A GOAL APPRAISAL PROCESS MODEL OF EMOTIONAL UNDERSTANDING AND MEMORY

Our theory of goal appraisal processes focuses on describing the mental processes and behaviors associated with goal-directed action. We focus on the content of specific beliefs (knowledge) activated and/or challenged during emotional experience, the content of positive and negative appraisals made about an emotional event, inferences carried out with respect to the antecedents and consequences of an emotional event, wishes and plans devised to cope with the effects of an emotional event, and actions carried out to maintain significant personal goals. We assess the contents of these processes by analyzing children's spontaneous and probed recall about their emotional experiences.

Our theoretical approach is based upon Stein and Levine's theory of emotion understanding

(Stein & Levine, 1987, 1989, 1990); Stein and Trabasso's theory of goal appraisal processes (Stein & Trabasso, 1992; Stein et al., 1993; Stein, Trabasso, & Liwag, 1994; Trabasso & Stein, 1994); and Stein, Folkman, and Trabasso's theory of goal appraisal processes related to states of psychological well-being (Folkman & Stein, 1997; Lazarus & Folkman, 1984; Stein, Folkman, Trabasso, & Richards, 1997). For us, emotional understanding describes and focuses on the personal significance and meaning of events experienced in everyday interaction. People continually monitor and appraise the state of their world in an effort to detect changes in the status of personally significant goals. Changes are perceived when goals are blocked, attained, or threatened (Stein & Levine, 1987, 1990; Stein et al., 1993), and perceiving changes in goal states induces immediate changes in emotional states and general states of well-being.

In analyzing emotional memories, we show how children and adults talk about changes in personally meaningful goals. This type of talk is generally narrative in form and is directly linked to the evaluation of *anything* that affects the status of an important goal. We refer to this talk as the "language of goal appraisals" because the talk reveals the sequence of causal thinking, evaluation, goal setting, goal planning, and goal-directed action that is carried out as a function of perceiving changes in the status of valued goals. We use our model to show how emotional experience has been encoded and how people make sense of incoming information in an "online" manner (Stein & Levine, 1990; Stein et al., 1993, 1994; Trabasso & Stein, 1994, 1997). We also describe how people use beliefs about the past and future to devise plans for maintaining states of well-being in the present.

One of our core assumptions is that memory for an emotional event is a function of how the event was understood as it occurred. Understanding involves perceptual analysis, evaluation, and inference making. Therefore, memory is never an exact replica of the original experience, even if people rehearsed and updated their memory as the event was experienced. Memory is constrained and influenced by personal knowledge, current motivational states, and the focus of attention during the processing of an event (see Bartlett, 1932; for reviews of current approaches to memory for everyday events, see Kihlstrom, 1996, 1998; Ross, 1989,

1997; and Stein, Wade, & Liwag, 1997). Although emotional memories can be accurate, they do not encompass or encode an entire situation (Ornstein, Shapiro, Clubb, & Follmer, 1997; Ross, 1989; 1997; Stein et al., 1993; 1994; Stein, Wade, & Liwag, 1997). All memories are "biased" and reflect the operating goals and attentional stance of the person involved.

The assertion that memory is constrained by personal preferences, desires, and values is not new. Bartlett (1932) made the same claim in his seminal work on everyday memory. He believed that current attitudes, desires, and prior knowledge guided and organized all memory. The problem for Bartlett was, as it is for all of us who study memory in everyday contexts, was how to characterize and describe event representation. The task is difficult because it entails using models of complex network representations to describe and analyze how people appraise and understand an event (see Mandler, 1984; Stein & Levine, 1987; Stein et al., 1993; and Trabasso & Stein, 1994, for descriptions of the processes involved in remembering emotional events). Despite the difficulty, however, the structure and contents of goal-directed thought and action can be described quite systematically. The appraisals generated during an emotion-provoking situation are constrained both by people's motivations and by the organization of goal-directed knowledge and action.

A pivotal constraint that operates during emotional understanding is that people prefer to be in states of goal success, satisfaction, and pleasure rather than in states of goal failure, loss, and pain (Folkman & Stein, 1997; Stein & Levine, 1987, 1990; Stein & Trabasso, 1992; Stein et al., 1993). When people succeed in attaining desired goal states, or when they succeed in avoiding or escaping from undesired goal states, they experience positive emotions and pleasurable states of well-being. When they fail to attain or maintain desired goal states, or when they cannot prevent undesired goal states from occurring or continuing, they experience negative emotions and negative psychological states.

Another constraint that influences emotional understanding is that only six different combinations of goal outcomes are possible when people engage in goal-directed action. Given that a goal is considered desirable, people may want something and be able to attain it; they may want it, but not be able to attain it; or they may want it, but be uncertain of its attainment.

Given that a goal is undesirable, people may not want the goal state to occur, but fail in preventing its occurrence; they may not want the goal state to occur, and may succeed in preventing its occurrence; or they may not want the goal state to occur, but be uncertain as to whether it will occur.

As we have noted in past studies (Stein & Levine, 1987, 1990; Stein & Trabasso, 1989, 1992; Stein et al., 1993, 1994), specific combinations of goal outcome states then map onto specific emotions. Happiness is associated with two goal outcome states: wanting something and attaining it, and not wanting something and not attaining it (i.e., avoiding it). Fear is associated with two outcome states: not wanting something but being uncertain that the state can be avoided, and wanting something but being uncertain that the goal can be attained. Anger and sadness are associated with two goal outcome states: wanting something but not attaining it, or not wanting something but having it.

For a specific emotion to be elicited, however, more than a change in the status of goal outcome states must be perceived and evaluated. Beliefs about the probability of attaining, maintaining, avoiding, or preventing a goal state must also be activated. "Beliefs" are organized forms of knowledge that carry an expectation about the state of some aspect of the world. Beliefs often carry a value judgment (e.g., good or bad) or a preference (e.g., liking or disliking) for the aspect under consideration. Beliefs reflect what people think is, was, or could be true about their world (Folkman & Stein, 1997; Stein & Liwag, 1997; Stein & Levine, 1987, 1990; Stein et al., 1993, 1994). When people understand the significance of an event, they activate organized belief systems to evaluate the personal impact of the event. In doing so, they generate precise inferences about how an event has already affected them and how it will affect them in the future.

The ways in which these goal appraisal processes operate during emotional understanding and remembering can be understood by using a series of five questions: (1) "What happened?" (2) "How do I feel about it?" (3) "What can I do about it?" (4) "What did I do about it?" and (5) "What were the consequences of carrying out a plan of action?" Each question reflects a class of inferences made in relation to evaluating the status of goals affected by a precipitating event. We use these questions as a pedagogical device to organize our data presentation on goal appraisal processes. The questions correspond to the temporal and causal unfolding of an emotional episode, and allow us to specify the *exact* nature of goal appraisal processes involved in understanding and remembering emotional events.

PARENTS' AND CHILDREN'S NARRATIVE MEMORIES OF EMOTIONAL EVENTS

In the remainder of this chapter, we focus on parents' and preschool children's memories of emotional events where children were observed to experience different emotional reactions. The subjects of this study were 77 children, 42 boys and 35 girls. Younger preschoolers ranging in age from 2.3 to 4.0 years ($M = 3.3$ years) composed approximately half of the sample (43%); the remaining half consisted of older preschoolers, aged 4.1 to 6.6 years ($M = 5.0$ years). Although the ethnic background of the sample varied (it included children of African, Asian, and Hispanic descent), the majority of the children (73%) were of European descent.

Nominations of emotional events were generated by first asking parents to talk about the most recent instances where they observed their children actually expressing happiness, anger, sadness, and fear. In a subsequent interview, children were given a brief synopsis of their parents' nominations of the emotion-precipitating events and asked the following series of questions: (1) *Recognition of precipitating event*: "Do you remember this event happening?" (2) *Recall of emotion*: "How did you feel when this happened?" (3) *Recall of emotion episode*: "Can you tell me exactly what happened? What did you think about? What did you do?"

After completing their initial recollection, children were asked the following series of probe questions: (1) *Reasons*: "Why did [event] make you feel [emotion]?"[3] (2) *Wishes/plans*: "What did you wish you could do?" (3) *Actions*: "What did you do?" Before any probe questions were asked, children were given instructions to try to remember everything possible about a specific emotional experience, without being given any information about what their parents reported except for the emotion-precipitating event itself. The data from children's spontaneous narratives and their answers to all probe questions were parsed into clausal units and categorized according to the basic functional categories of an emotion episode (e.g., precipitating event, feelings, reasons for feelings, thoughts/beliefs, goals, plans, actions, outcomes, and goal revision strategies). A fuller description of the criteria used to categorize clauses into functional categories, and a more detailed set of results from our parent–child emotion studies can be found in the following sources: Folkman and Stein (1997), Liwag (1995), Liwag and Stein (1995), Stein and Liwag (1997), and Stein et al. (1993, 1994).

The important point for the purposes of this chapter is that clauses in children's narratives and their answers to probe questions were first scored according to each functional category of an episode without being summed into a total score. It is imperative to explore how young children understand each dimension of an emotion episode. The function of each category of an emotion episode differs with respect to the types of information it contains. Children may include some categories more frequently than others, and these inclusions may be important in determining the exact nature of emotional understanding.

"What Happened?"

Memories of "What happened?" refer to three specific dimensions: (1) a precipitating event, or the particular event that precipitated an emotional reaction; (2) goal outcome appraisals, or appraisals about which goals had been affected, their value to the child, and whether the goal(s) were attained, threatened, or blocked; and (3) beliefs, or organized evaluations and appraisals of precipitating events and various aspects of such events.

Precipitating Events

Identifying the precipitating event that precedes an emotion is critical to understanding emotional experience. Precipitating events are used as markers to signal what initiated the changes in the status of valued goals. The precipitating event is often cited as the reason for an emotional response, without including any mention of the changes that have been perceived with respect to the status of important goals. For example, when asked why he was so angry at a little girl he had just met, one of our 3-year-old boys yelled, "*She broke my gun*!!" at the experi-

menter and at the video camera. Further conversation with this little boy revealed that he had indeed made goal-based appraisals about the changes in his goals, including the fact that he could no longer play with the gun and that this "new" gun was very valuable. He also stated specific beliefs about what friends were and were not allowed to do with another person's possessions, and what could and should be done to the little girl who broke his new gun.

This little boy, however, was quite perplexed about why he should have to be more explicit about his thinking and reasoning, given that he had just "told" the experimenter "why" he was so angry. By referring to the precipitating event that began the causal flow of his thinking and narration, in conjunction with using the appropriate prosodic emphasis and nonverbal communicative cues about the disastrous nature of the event, he thought he was quite clear in conveying the central meaning and significance of the precipitating event. His belief about his informativeness was especially clear when the little boy was yelling at the experimenter, exclaiming disbelief that another child destroyed his new toy gun.[4]

Grice (1989), in his theory of conversational interaction, devised a list of axioms that regulate conversations. Two of these axioms are informativeness and relevance. Grice asserted that all parties to a conversation assume that each person will be as informative as possible and will focus on the relevant information that reflects the speaker's intended meaning. Since the events of everyday interaction are complex, speakers have the obligation to select what they consider to be the most informative and relevant. They assume that correct inferences will be made by their listeners if they adhere to these principles.

Our data suggest that even the very youngest children use rules of informativeness and relevance in reporting their personal experiences. Children expect their listeners to infer the appropriate meaning of an event, especially when the children use the expressive systems of the face, hands, and voice as additional cues. Indeed, specific emotion states, goals, and beliefs are often communicated through the voice and the face. If children believe they have answered probe questions through enactment and indirect speech acts, they will not repeat themselves or be redundant in answering further questions. Many children become extremely irritated at an experimenter who persistently probes for additional information when they have just indicated that they have already made everything "explicit."

The absence of explicit reference to the thoughts or beliefs of other people or the self does not necessarily speak to the lack of understanding on the part of a child, as Wellman and his colleagues (Bartsch & Wellman, 1995; Wellman et al., 1995) imply. These omissions more often reflect the assumptions children have made about the ease that a listener should have in making correct inferences about their intended meaning during a conversational interaction. Because rules of conversation apply to children as well as to adults, conclusions about memory, beliefs, and appraisal processes on the basis of linguistic data alone, especially those gathered in "naturalistic interaction" with only an audiotape available, need convergent validity procedures that assess children's understanding more explicitly. Thus, in our studies, both spontaneous narration and probed narration were used.

In our first set of analyses, we examined the types of precipitating events parents and children associated with each of four emotions. A content taxonomy of 22 event categories was constructed and based on all parental nominations of precipitating events. Using frequency as the criterion, we then determined which of these 22 events were prototypic for each emotion for parents and then for children. Table 28.1 contains the prototypic events that parents and children identified as causing children's happiness, sadness, anger, and fear. The "% of parents' recall" column presents the prototypic events parents nominated for each emotion. The "% of children's recall" column indicates the events children actually said elicited each of the four emotions.

The number of prototypic events nominated by parents and children for each emotion differed. An event was defined as prototypic if it had a high rate of mention and if its frequency of mention stood apart from the frequency of other events nominated for each specific emotion. As an example, for the emotion of anger, parents nominated four events with approximately an equal rate of mention, and the frequencies associated with these events were sig-

TABLE 28.1. Prototypic Precipitating Events for Four Different Emotions

Prototypic events	% of parents' recall	% of children's recall
Angry		
Child is punished	0	22
Child's goals are in conflict with another's	15	0
Child's possessions are taken away/destroyed	14	0
Child is forced to do something	14	0
Child is intruded upon	12	0
Sad		
Child is separated from significant others	32	10
Child is punished	0	20
Child is denied desirable objects	0	10
Child is unable to engage in desirable activities	0	10
Afraid		
Child perceives a threat to self or others	23	40
Child experiences undesirable sensory stimuli	22	0
Child's emotions are elicited by real or imaginary animate beings	14	20
Child has nightmares/bad dreams	0	13
Happy		
Child engages in/masters desirable activities	22	21
Child gets desirable objects	18	19
Child participates in family activities	14	0
Child plays	0	18

nificantly higher than the frequencies associated with all other events parents nominated for anger. Children, on the other hand, nominated only one event frequently enough for it to be considered prototypic. Its high frequency separated it from the frequency of all other events children identified as causing their anger. The percentages listed for the prototypic events in each emotion category do not add up to 100 because only the most prototypic events are included in the table.

Two conclusions can be reached from the precipitating-event analysis for parents. First, parents nominated categorically distinct events for positive versus negative emotions. Events that provoked happiness did not overlap with those that provoked sadness, anger, or fear. Second, although events nominated for each negative emotion overlapped with events nominated for the other two negative emotions, different prototypic events were nominated for each negative emotion. Threats to children's safety and well-being, events that overloaded children's sensory capacities (e.g., a loud noise or fast movement), and situations that exposed children to real or imaginary animate beings (e.g., ghosts, monsters, witches) were reported to cause fear. Situations where children were forced to do something against their will, instances where they had their toys taken away or destroyed, and times when they were physically intruded upon or perceived their goals to be in conflict with another person's goals (usually a parent's) elicited *anger*. Being separated from significant others, such as parents, grandparents, and best friends elicited sadness.

Children also identified distinct prototypic events that elicited happiness and fear. Engaging in and mastering a valued activity and getting desired objects were the prototypes for happiness, while being physically threatened and enduring specific types of sensory stimulation were the prototypes for fear. Furthermore, children's responses for these two emotions were in strong agreement with their parents' nominations.

Children, however, did not identify distinct prototypic events for anger and sadness. Being punished generated both anger and sadness in equal amounts. According to Stein and Levine (1987, 1990), however, the expression of anger and sadness to the same event is to be expected. Anger and sadness both occur as a result of loss or as the result of experiencing an aversive state. Children and adults frequently express both emotions in response to loss and aversion. Anger is expressed with respect to the agent who caused the loss or aversive state; sadness is expressed in response to the perceived consequences of losing something or being put into an unpleasant state.

Unlike the degree of parent–child agreement about events that elicited happiness and fear in children, major disagreements occurred in parents' and children's appraisals of events that evoked children's anger and sadness. Parents nominated a wider array of events that caused children's anger than children accepted. According to parents, the prototypic events that caused children's anger were having their possessions taken away, having their goals conflict with those of another person, being forced to do something, and being intruded upon. Not one child remembered expressing anger to these events. Rather, children focused solely on punishment as being responsible for their angry responses.

In nominating events that caused sadness for their children, one event was prototypic for parents: being separated from people who were significant in a child's life. Some children did agree with their parents' assessment of events that caused sadness, but they also recalled feeling sad in response to many more events than their parents nominated as causing sadness. The event that caused the most sadness for children was that of being punished—the same event that caused the most anger in children.

Goal Outcome Appraisals

How did children appraise the impact of these precipitating events on their personal goals? They gave "goal outcome appraisals" in response to both "What happened" and "Why" questions for each emotion. A goal outcome appraisal involved explicit recall of (1) what was desired ("I really wanted to go shopping with my mom") and (2) what actually happened ("but she wouldn't let me"). According to our analysis of emotional understanding (Stein & Levine, 1987, 1989; Stein et al., 1993), goal outcomes that explain or cause a particular emotion do not overlap with those for other emotions, except for anger and sadness.

Children's appraisals of their goals were classified into one of five goal outcome combinations: (1) wanting something and getting it; (2) not wanting something and not getting it; (3) wanting something and not getting it; (4) not wanting something but getting it; and (5) not wanting something but being uncertain about its attainment. The outcome of wanting something but not being certain of attaining it was never mentioned by the children.

The children's explicit goal outcome appraisals largely conformed to our expectations. Goal outcome appraisals for explaining reasons for happiness had little overlap (9%) with those that explained their negative emotions. Three-quarters (74%) of the children associated happiness with attaining something they wanted (e.g., a desired toy or favorite food, a special treat, etc.). An additional 15% expressed happiness as the outcome of not attaining something that they did not want.

Anger and sadness explanations were focused on failure and being put into aversive states. Approximately 62% of sad goal outcome appraisals and 43% of angry goal outcome appraisals focused on wanting something but not attaining it. When children explained their emotions for not wanting something but having to do it anyway, the respective percentages associated with sadness and anger were reversed: Approximately 29% of these goal outcome appraisals were linked to sadness, and 57% were linked to anger. Thus, although sadness and anger were linked to both types of goal outcome appraisals, aversive states of attaining unwanted goals were associated more with anger than with sadness. Conversely, loss was more frequently associated with sadness than with anger.[5]

These results replicate the empirical findings of Stein and Levine (1989) and Levine (1995). These researchers found that children and adults were more likely to express anger than sadness in response to aversive states. Similarly, they found that loss states evoked more sadness in children than anger. Adults and children responded similarly to loss states. Adults, however, were more sensitive to who or what caused a particular loss. If a physical event caused the loss, most adults responded with sadness. If an animate agent caused the loss state, adults expressed anger more frequently than sadness. The importance of responsibility, especially when an agent intentionally caused a loss for another person, was the dimension that differentiated adults' conception of anger from that of the preschool children. The presence of intentional harm was not sufficient to elicit anger in young children, even when children fully recognized that the loss was intentionally caused by another person. Children more often felt sad when one person intentionally harmed another. Thus agency is not a prerequisite for the experience of anger in children.

The adult prototype of anger apparently includes a focus on harmful intentional action (Shaver, Schwartz, O'Connor, & Kirson, 1987). However, what becomes a prototypic event is influenced by experience and cultural prescriptives. Adults may have learned that there are conditions under which anger is sanctioned and can be expressed appropriately, with or without agents (Stein & Levine, 1989).

To return to our goal outcome analysis, when fear was expressed, it occurred most frequently (71%) as a result of not wanting something but being uncertain about the outcome. Our theory assumes that fear involves uncertainty about whether an undesired outcome or the loss of a desired state will occur. Essentially, fear is an emotion that occurs in response to threat. In talking about fear, children as young as 3 years of age explicitly recognized the presence of uncertainty and talked about future goal outcomes that were not desirable but that could occur. The future tense (e.g., "He's going to hit me") or the perfect conditional (e.g., "He was going to hit me") was used to signal states that had not yet occurred.

Although we did not anticipate fear reactions to existing aversive states, 29% of the children responded with fear reactions. The children's narratives reveal why fear occurred in response to the presence of aversive states. Children focused first on the *event* that caused a change in the status of a goal. Then they used this event to signal that a desired outcome state was implicitly uncertain. For example, many children talked about supernatural beings like monsters and ghosts by saying, "Well, I was afraid because there was a monster in my room," signaling the presence of a being that the children did not desire. The presence of the monster implied that the monster might harm them, but its occurrence was uncertain. The detailed probing and analysis of children's implications uncovered these meanings in regard to aversive states.

Beliefs

Beliefs are expressed in the form of evaluations and appraisals of emotional events, as well as of people, places, objects, feelings, and just about anything that occurs in an emotional event. Most beliefs carry a positive or negative valence that is easily identifiable. We identified and coded each evaluative belief in each narrative.

Two sets of beliefs were identified. In the first set, the primary foci were on appraisals of harms, benefits, and obligations; relationships; abilities; ownership; and states of the world. The eight specific categories in the first set were: (1) *physical harm* (e.g., "I thought about maybe when I touched the light bulb, maybe it would be hot, or maybe it would, if I touched it, and it burn me"); (2) *benefits or gains* (e.g., "I felt, I thought to myself, now I get a chance to be here when Amy comes"); (3) *losses or denials* (e.g., "I felt that it, I thought it [cable TV] would never come back"); (4) *obligations or appropriate behavior* (e.g., "And I thought that I had to play baseball"); (5) *abilities* (e.g., "'Cause I tried swimming before and I could do it"); (6) *qualities of relationships* (e.g., "Becky's not my friend, but Zuri is"); (7) *ownership* (e.g., "It was my key, not daddy's key, or not Mommy's key—only Aaron's key"); and (8) *the nature of or states of the world* (e.g., "It's the Sea Witch. The, the Sea Witch, uh, had turned his daddy into a, it's a kind of wave shape, but it isn't a wave. It's really, really, really, really, a monster").

Fifty-five beliefs from this first set were reported in happy narratives. Of these, 47% focused on gains or benefits. Abilities accounted for 11% while losses or denials accounted for 9%. The remaining categories each accounted for about 2% of the happy beliefs. Of interest is the fact that negatively valenced beliefs occurred in happy narratives and did so primarily at the beginning of the report. As children began their narratives about happy feelings, most focused first on the lack states that motivated them to action. They then reported their dislike of these lack states and their reasons for wanting to change these states. When children began to focus on plans of action with respect to existing lack states, they switched their stances from negative to positive evaluations. They often related how valuable the goal under consideration was and the number of other goals that could be attained if the primary goal was accomplished. When children reported that they succeeded in accomplishing their goals, they focused on the unexpected benefits of goal success, and they generated evaluations about the people who helped them attain their goals.

There were 35 beliefs expressed for fear. The modal belief was harm (52%), followed by beliefs about the state of the world (29%), losses or denials (11%), and gains or benefits (3%). For sadness (for which 64 beliefs were expressed), the modal belief was about losses or denials (37%), followed by gains or benefits (27%) and harm (14%). The remaining 19% of sad beliefs were evenly distributed over the other five categories of beliefs. For anger (for which 15 beliefs were expressed), the modal belief was about gains or benefits (34%), followed by appraisals of relationships (27%), obligations or appropriateness of behavior (13%), and ownership (7%).

Narratives about negative emotional experiences included both positive and negative beliefs. In angry, sad, and fearful narratives, positive beliefs/appraisals were often generated at the beginning of the narrative and indicated how valuable a goal was or how satisfied the narrator was before the state of the world changed in response to loss or an impending loss. The value of the lost or blocked goal was also stated, especially in terms of the positive moral evaluations children associated with the attainment of desired goals. Once a goal was blocked, however, negative beliefs about other people and the state of the world were then expressed. Thus, in narratives about negative emotional experiences, negative beliefs were generated primarily *after* an undesired change of state occurred. These shifts in valence during the episode reflect changes in appraisals of real-life emotional experiences.

For each of the four emotions, children focused on expectations about harms or benefits that should have occurred, did occur, or would occur. For fear, the primary focus was on beliefs about the harm that could have occurred. For happiness, the primary focus was on the expected benefits that did occur. For anger and sadness, the primary focus was on the expected benefits that should have occurred but did not.

Each type of emotion narrative also contained beliefs that were prototypic and distinct to a particular emotion. In angry narratives, children expressed their beliefs about the moral obligations of others who broke their promises, and they also talked about not being sure whether they could ever trust these people again. Furthermore, beliefs about the possibility of terminating relationships were expressed primarily in angry narratives. In sad narratives, the focus was primarily on beliefs about further losses that were experienced or that would occur, given that a goal was blocked. In fearful narratives, the focus was on the uncertain nature of the world, given that either harm had occurred or was thought to be soon on the way. Finally, happy narratives were those in which children expressed their beliefs about their emerging positive abilities and other goals that could be accomplished because of the success of the focal goal.

Although state-of-the-world beliefs focused primarily on what children believed to be true about their world, some children focused on what they thought other people believed to be true about the state of the world. For example, one child who was yelled at by her mother explained how her mother had mistakenly thought that she had dropped a cup: "She thought that I was making the noise. And that that's what she thought. I was dropping the cup. That's why she yelled at me . . ." (girl, 5.2 years old). This young girl also recalled how she corrected her mother's false belief by telling her mother that it was her little brother who had made the noise.

Children also expressed awareness of what others might think and do in response to their own actions: "My mama says she gonna get me a costume, and when I go under the water, boy, everybody, they think, it's the killer whale, a real one. 'Cause I'm gonna have sharp teeth" (boy, 3.8 years old); "Well, I was just very quiet when my mom was driving home in the back, and she thought I was asleep" (boy, 6.0 years old).

The most interesting set of appraisals, with respect to children's understanding of other people's beliefs, were generated during children's reports about obligations they had to uphold. Children most often talked about these obligations in terms of conversations with one of their parents. For example, in relating why she had to go school, one little girl (4.0 years old) reported: "One day my mom was just saying, 'But, darling, you *have to* go to school.'" A little boy (3.4 years old) reported: "I haven't saw him, and mamma said I gotta stay here and go to school." Another 3-year-old boy reported: "My mom said I don't hafta play with him." All of these children stated their evaluations about their parents' beliefs in the form of obligatory conversational statements made by their parents. When interviewers probed these children further and asked, for example, "Did your mom think you should go to school?" the answer was always "Yes."

Approximately 22% of state-of-the-world

beliefs were challenges to or violations of what children expected to happen. Belief violations occurred most often in angry episodes (38%) and least often in happy episodes (15%). They were expressed as contrasts between what a child thought or expected and what really took place: "Well, I thought that my mom would get me another pillow, but she was just laying there on the couch" (boy, 6.0 years old); "I was thinking about him [Dad] would spank me, but he didn't" (boy, 3.7 years old).

The second set of beliefs that we identified focused on *personal* evaluations. These beliefs were both positive and negative, and were classified into the following categories: (1) preferences ("I really like T-shirt so much" vs. "I hate worms"); (2) personal dispositions ("She's nice and she's pretty" vs. "Carly was, was mean"); (3) habitual behaviors ("I did funny stuff. Um . . . made funny faces at them" vs. "Not good for me coming home"); (4) mental states ("My mom knew that I was supposed to go to Joshy's house to sleep over" vs. "She didn't remember if she put it in the basket"); and (5) qualities of objects or events ("'Cause it is a comfortable pillow" vs. "It went real loud. That very much thunder from the storm. Very loud").

Across all emotion episodes, 28% of personal evaluations were focused on the self while 72% were focused on other people, objects, or events. Liking or disliking was by far the most common type of judgment expressed toward people, objects, or events (46% across all emotions). Evaluations of specific and habitual behaviors of people were also relatively frequent (about 30% across the four emotions). This is not surprising. Livesley and Bromley (1973) reported that children appraise people in concrete dispositions and behavioral terms. What is noteworthy about our data, however, is that preschoolers also evaluated people's mental or knowledge states (an average of 12%) as well as their personality traits (an average of 5%).

The respective numbers of personal evaluations for anger, sadness, fear, and happiness were 24, 98, 31, and 95. Statements of preferences predominated (50%, 37%, 26%, and 37%, respectively), followed by habitual behaviors (29%, 29%, 30%, and 26%, respectively). Qualities of objects or events led most frequently to fear (32%), followed by happiness (20%), sadness (17%), and anger (4%). Of interest, mental states were nearly equally given as reasons for anger, sadness, fear, and happiness (13%, 13%, 6%, and 11%, respectively). Personality traits or enduring attributes of persons were the least frequent personal evaluations (4%, 4%, 6%, and 6%, respectively).

Fear episodes were focused more on nonhumans (e.g., supernatural creatures, animals) and environmental states of the world (e.g., thunder or darkness). Thus a slightly different pattern of evaluation emerged. The qualities of these events were appraised more often (32%) than similar events in other emotion narratives. Fear narratives also included appraisals of the potentially dangerous habitual behaviors of nonhuman agents (30%). Children were less concerned about expressing their preferences while expressing fear, and more oriented toward expressing their beliefs about the probability that harm would occur. To children reporting fearful emotions, the fact that they talked about potential negative consequences might again indicate the importance of implied conversational postulates. Disliking monsters or ghosts might be so obvious that the dislike did not have to be stated.

Narrative Functions of Beliefs. When children talked about beliefs in the context of an emotion episode, what functions did these evaluative statements serve? We found that explanation was the most common function of these appraisals. About 50% of the time, children expressed a belief or a judgment in order to explain or justify their own emotions (e.g., "I was sad because I thought I was staying at my cousin's forever"), desires (e.g., "I want to go to the circus because circuses are fun"), and behaviors (e.g., "My mother . . . um, I woke her up because I thought she'd probably go on back up to sleep"). Children also used other people's beliefs to provide explanations for a person's goals and actions (e.g., "And actually, see, 'cause, um, my mom got in my way 'cause she thought I was going to go under [the water]. And I said stop, 'cause I wasn't going to go under").

Approximately 25% of beliefs focused on negative or positive consequences of outcomes that had occurred. In many instances, evaluations of outcomes also served as reasons for the subsequent goals and plans that were activated. Thus children were clearly sensitive and felt it necessary to use evaluations both as explanations for events and as devices to assess the impact of events.

"How Do I Feel about It?"

Parent–Child Discrepancies in Reports of Emotions

If we were using only parental reports to understand children's emotional experience, we might assume that parents had little difficulty correctly identifying their children's emotions. Parents were quite accurate in identifying when their children were happy, with 80% of the children agreeing with their parents' assessments. Lesser degrees of agreement between parents and children, however, were found for the negative emotions—anger (22%), fear (49%), and sadness (72%). When parents thought that their children were feeling anger, many children reported sadness (39%), happiness (22%), or neutral feelings (17%). When parents reported that their children were afraid, some children reported neutral feelings (23%), sadness (19%), or anger or happiness (5% each). Finally, when parents reported that the children were sad, some children reported happiness (19%), neutral feelings (7%), or anger (2%).

Thus disagreements between parents and children were most often found in parents' appraisals of children's anger and fear. In particular, children reported feeling sadness far more often than the anger that parents attributed to them. Similarly, only half of the children agreed with their parents assessment of their fear. Although children agreed with the majority of their parents' assessments of sadness, children reported sadness more often than parents reported sadness, and children expressed sadness in response to events that parents did not consider: when they were punished, when they could not obtain desirable objects, and when they could not engage in desirable activities. Parents appraised these events as eliciting their children's anger.

The discrepancies between children's and parents' reports of emotional reactions underscore the fact that having parents recall memories of events that precipitated a specific emotion in their children does not guarantee that the parents have appraised the children's emotions accurately. Events, as our data indicate, are *always* interpreted through some frame of reference. For most parents in our study, the frame was observational, with parents purporting to use expressive indicators of specific emotional reactions. Despite the parents' care in choosing situations where they had behavioral and conversational evidence to support their nominated event, children did not always agree with their parents' emotion attributions.

An analysis of both children's and parents' narratives (Levine, Stein, & Liwag, 1999) revealed that one reason for parents' inaccuracies, according to their children, was that parents often misconstrued the value and meaning of a particular activity for their children. Parents often failed to assess accurately children's assessment of the impact of a loss, denial, or prohibition. To parents, once an activity or object was denied, the incident was over and no longer carried any great significance for their children. According to children's reports, however, the effects of these denials, prohibitions, and punishments lasted far longer than the immediate surround of the emotion episode.

The lack of congruence between parents' and children's judgments of the value of a particular object or activity, as well as parental misconceptions about the consequences of loss and punishment, were often due to information that was *not* revealed to parents. Children often used privileged information as a basis for their feelings. For example, one mother reported that she took her youngest son to the grocery store every week, so that he would be happy and have a chance to spend some time with her alone. When asked how he felt about going to the grocery store every week with his mother, the little boy said he felt sad and really terrible. According to him, every time he went to the grocery store with his mother, his older brother got into his room and played with his favorite toys. Thus, to the little boy, going to the supermarket with his mother—despite the fact that he got a chance to pick out his favorite treats in addition to being with his mother—was not enough to make him happy, given what was going on at home every time he left his room.

The discrepancies between children's and parents' feelings and knowledge about an event that both experienced are of central interest to researchers who study theories of mind, perspective taking, and conflict resolution. Although the current trend is to believe that young children are incapable of knowing what other people believe, in many of our parental reports of children's emotional feelings and beliefs, *parents* could not accurately identify exactly how their children appraised an event or what their children believed about an event. What parents could do well was to identify the goals

of their children. What they could not do well was to judge how important a goal was to their child, the impact of a loss on their child, and their child's *future* thinking and behavior.

Recent studies on perspective taking during adult conversation also illustrate that adults can be quite erroneous in specifying the contents of others' belief system, especially when they do not have access to privileged information (Horton & Keysar, 1996; Stein, 1996). Furthermore, even husbands and wives consistently make errors in their appraisals of their spouses' beliefs. Television programs such as *The Dating Game* or *The Newlywed Game* have relied on such lack of knowledge to create general embarrassment for a newly introduced or married couple. In many instances, husbands and wives fail to predict correctly the beliefs that their spouses reportedly hold (Ross, 1989).

Another reason for the discordance in parents' and children's emotion attributions stemmed from the differences in the time frames used to recall an event. Upon analysis of the time lines of both the parents' and children's reports, we (Levine et al., 1997) discovered that children often reported sadness to anger-provoking events because they reported subsequent episodes and attempts to resolve their goal failure. Similarly, when children reported that they felt happy about those events that parents nominated as causing anger, children included subsequent episodes where they did manage to succeed at attaining their goals.

The ways in which children talk about their emotional responses to a precipitating event may be regulated by their final goal resolution rather than by their initial response to the precipitating event. Children often deleted the initial segments of the event sequence in order to make their report coherent in terms of the final resolution. If probed for information about initial emotional responses, however, even our very youngest children easily provided critical information about their initial emotional responses. We found that 60% of children who initially disagreed with their parents' assessments of their expression of anger did admit to experiencing anger in addition to the emotion they initially reported. They were also quite skilled at giving plausible reasons for why they experienced anger in addition to the emotion they first reported. However, their interchanges with our experimenters clearly showed that the emotion they initially selected was the one that organized the memory representation.

Reasons for Emotions

According to our theory, emotions are provoked when a conjoint set of conditions occurs: An event is perceived to change the status of a goal *in conjunction with* the goal's being either desired or undesired. Both components are necessary conditions for the evocation of emotion. Children tend to explicate these two dimensions by focusing on one of four different explanations: (1) the antecedent conditions that affected the changes in goals; (2) violations of their expectations about the change in the status of a goal; (3) the consequences of the precipitating event in terms of new changes that would now regulate achieving other important goals; and (4) the blockage, threat, or success of the specific goal under consideration, along with its value (Stein & Liwag, 1997).

The reasons children gave for each emotion are included in Table 28.2. Children often generated more than one explanation for each emotion. As a result, we focused on whether or not each type of reason was stated at least once in each emotion narrative. Therefore, the percentages of reasons for a given emotion do not add up to 100. They are independent of the percentages of reasons in other categories.

The reasons for anger, sadness, and happiness were focused primarily on specific goals that changed in status. Approximately 50% of the children included references to explicit goals to explain why they felt angry, sad, or happy (e.g., "I was happy because I really wanted that toy"; "I was sad because I really wanted a puppy"). Much of the time, children simply stated the goal that they desired (e.g., "I really wanted that game"), without stating explicitly whether their desired goal was attained or denied (e.g., "But I didn't get it"). The only times children did not include frequent mention of

their desired goals was in fear narratives. When talking about fearful events, children focused more on future consequences as reasons for their fear (e.g., "I was afraid because I could get hurt").

Consequences were frequent explanations for fear (92%), happiness (37%), and sadness (34%), but not for anger (0%). Antecedent or precipitating events occurred most often for anger (25%), followed by sadness (17%), happiness (11%), and fear (8%). Violations of expectations occurred uniformly across the four emotions and averaged 11%.

A subsequent analysis was carried out on the nature of the antecedent conditions mentioned in children's emotion narratives. Agents were cited in 45% of all references to antecedent conditions. Specifying an agent as the cause of a precipitating event, however, occurred most frequently in explanations for anger (70%). In most anger narratives, parents were identified as the agents who prohibited children from doing something they wanted, punished them, or forced them to do something against their will. When causes were given as explanations for fear and sadness, agents were referenced 50% of the time. In fear narratives, most agents were nonhuman imaginary creatures (e.g., monsters, the title character from the movie *Beetlejuice,* a shark that appeared in a dream) or animals (including an ant, a dog, and a pelican) who had threatened the children's physical safety or psychological security. Approximately 35% of the happy explanations that focused on precipitating events included references to parental agents who had facilitated their children's goal success.

In sum, children's explanations for emotions focused primarily on references to the goals that had changed in status, with an implied reference to the fact that the goal was either

TABLE 28.2. **Percentages of Children Citing Each Type of Reason at Least Once for Each Emotion**

	Emotion			
Reasons	Angry	Sad	Afraid	Happy
Antecedent conditions				
Precipitating events	25	17	8	11
Violations of expected outcomes	13	10	8	13
Consequences/outcomes	0	34	92	37
Goals/preferences	63	54	17	57
Others	13	10	17	11

blocked or facilitated. Future-oriented conditions, in the form of consequences, were also generated as explanations for emotions, especially in the cases of fear. Frightened children were preoccupied with the harm, injury, or pain they believed was about to be inflicted on them. In contrast, angry children never stated future-oriented conditions. They were preoccupied with blocked goals, and with the agents, events, and violations that created obstacles to these goals.

"What Can I Do about It?"

Our theory (Stein & Levine, 1987, 1990; Stein et al., 1993) specifies that goal reinstatement is the primary wish associated with conditions of goal failure, regardless of both the emotion experienced or the realistic possibility of reinstating a goal. Wishes signify the value of a goal, independent of whether or not the goal can be actualized. Wishes also function to facilitate the coping process by providing specific guidelines as to what is liked and preferred. By comparing what is desired to what is possible, people can then generate plans of action that create connections between old preferences and achievable goal states. Without desires that determine which goals should be valued and which should be achieved, people would not be able to create or substitute new goals in the face of failure.

The types of wishes that children generated in response to feeling one of four different emotions were analyzed. Ninety-five percent of the wishes that accompanied expressions of happiness did not overlap with those for any other emotion. For happiness, the children

wished to maintain their original goal (63%), to attain a new goal (32%), or to prevent an undesirable state (5%). Wishes associated with fear were highly distinct from those associated with anger and sadness. Ninety-two percent of those who experienced fear wished they could prevent an undesirable state from occurring, and the remaining 8% wished to reinstate the original goal. Thus, for wishes, happiness and fear were clearly separable from one another, and they were also distinct with respect to the emotions of anger and sadness.

The greatest amount of overlap in wishes occurred when angry and sad wishes were analyzed. For anger and sadness, children primarily wished to reinstate the original goal (40% and 36%, respectively) or substitute a new goal (20% and 46%, respectively). Anger resulted in one unique wish: a desire to seek revenge (40%). Sadness was associated less frequently with wishes of goal abandonment (2%), revenge (8%), and prevention of an undesirable state (8%).

"What Did I Do about It?"

We also examined plans of action that children carried out as a result of the emotional event. We did so by first describing the actions children reported carrying out, and then comparing the actions to the wishes they wanted to carry out. The relationships between wishes and plans of action are summarized in Table 28.3.

The relationship between what children wanted to do and what they did was quite high for prevention, maintenance, revenge, and attainment. Less successful wishes were goal

TABLE 28.3. Percentages of Goal-Directed Actions Carried Out in Relation to Wishes Expressed

Action (what child did)	Wish (what child wanted to do)					
	Maintain	Attain	Reinstate	Substitute	Revenge	Prevent
Maintain	<u>71</u>	22				
Attain	29	<u>56</u>				7
Reinstate			<u>38</u>	25		
Substitute			25	<u>25</u>	33	
Abandon			31	25		
Revenge			6		<u>67</u>	
Prevent				8		<u>93</u>
Express emotion		22		17		

Note. Percentages indicating matches between children's wishes and actions are underscored.

substitution and goal reinstatement. When children said they wanted to reinstate their original goal, only 38% actually did so. When they said they wanted to substitute a new goal, only 25% did that.

In recalling anger episodes, children often reported that little hope existed for reinstating their original goals, even though they initially believed that their goals could and should be reinstated. Thus children recognized that existing circumstances permitted only goal substitution, abandonment, or revenge, despite their desire for reinstatement. Angry children who desired reinstatement were most likely to substitute a new goal and to seek revenge. Sad children were also most likely to substitute a new goal, but they abandoned their original goal at a much higher rate than did angry children.

"What Were the Consequences of Carrying Out a Plan of Action?"

In order to examine children's recall about the certainty of goal resolutions reached at the end of the emotion episodes, narratives were coded in terms of the specific final outcomes generated. We distinguished outcomes focusing on goals that succeeded and failed from outcomes focusing on goals that were still unresolved or awaiting resolution with respect to attainment. A clear majority of negative emotion episodes were resolved in a specific certain fashion (69% for sadness, 78% for fear, and 94% for anger). However, only 46% of happy memories contained a definite resolution. A lower rate of resolved goals may have occurred in reporting happy experiences because children tended to generate more long-range goals than were possible, rather than goals they had already attained (e.g., "When I grow up, I wanna be a Ninja Turtle"). They also expressed more fanciful or whimsical desires (e.g., "I wish I could have a million more Legos"; "Pretty soon, I'm going to Ireland and catch a leprechaun").

For the narratives that included definitely resolved goals, the type of goal resolution varied significantly across emotion. Sad episodes ended in goal failure significantly more often (76%) than either angry (33%), fearful (30%), or happy (2%) episodes. No matter how optimistic children were at the beginning of a sad narrative, they reported that their efforts had been carried out in vain. In fearful and angry episodes, despite initial or impending goal failures, children reported that they managed to escape from or avoid aversive situations through their own efforts or through the intervention of other people. When children decided to seek revenge, most of them succeeded.

CONCLUSIONS

Throughout this chapter, we have demonstrated that young preschool children have acquired a rich array of knowledge about situations, emotions, other people, and themselves. Emotional memories serve as one of the richest sources of evaluations made about the self with respect to events and goals of personal significance. As such, these memories are excellent indicators of what children value, how they think about their goals, the conditions they perceive to facilitate or block their goals, and plans of action they create to cope with maintaining their goals and positive states of psychological well-being.

In all of our studies, we found that preschool children had distinctly different types of memories and appraisals of those events that made them happy, sad, angry, and afraid. Children clearly distinguished between those events that made them happy and those that made them sad, angry, and afraid. Happy memories were associated with goal success and continued goal attainment, whereas memories for the negative emotions were associated with threats to valued goals or goal failures that actually occurred. Memories for fearful events were clearly distinguished from memories for angry and sad events. Remembering fearful events entailed a focus on threats to physical harm, beliefs about the insecure nature of the world, efforts to prevent harm, and plans of action that actually succeeded in stopping the harm.

Angry and sad memories, although distinct from fearful memories, contained more similarities to one another. Both anger and sad memories focused on goal failure, the desire to reinstate a valued goal, and the impossibility of doing so in many instances. Angry memories, however, differed from sad memories in important ways. Angry memories carried almost an exclusive focus on the *cause* of goal failure. Furthermore, the desire for revenge was expressed almost exclusively as a part of an angry reaction. Sad memories, in contrast, focused primarily on the *consequences* of goal failure, and the predominant way of coping with sadness, in addition to goal substitution, was to abandon the goal altogether.

Our data and those from a series of studies by other researchers (see Stein, Wade, & Liwag, 1997, and Stein, 1996, for reviews of current literature on emotional understanding) suggest that children as young as 2½ to 3 years of age have acquired substantial knowledge of the basic "stuff" of mental processes, including beliefs, preferences, goals, mental states, personal dispositions, and emotions. Given that emotional memories are full of appraisals of the current, past, and future states of children's worlds, the collection of more systematic data on each component of appraisal processing seems warranted.

To date, the clear majority of existing studies on children's theory of mind have not focused on children's emotional memories to describe what children know about themselves and other people. Flavell, Flavell, Green, and Moses (1990), however, carried out one of the few studies that examined beliefs children acquired about other people across a variety of domains. Their results indicated that young children did in fact understand and appraise other people's preferences and goals quite accurately. In their study, however, children experienced difficulty in predicting what other people knew and believed about specific *factual information* (e.g., when moving the location of a piece of candy from one spot to another, without a second person's seeing the move, children often became confused and chose the second location as the place a second individual would look for the candy). The results from other studies on theory of mind (see Chandler, Fritz, & Hala, 1989, and Clements & Perner, 1994, for examples) show that if specific methodologies are used and include nonverbal indicators of children's knowledge, even very young children understand quite a bit about the factual beliefs of other people.

An advance in studying children's developing theory of mind would result if researchers focused on an explanatory framework that illustrates how children acquire knowledge in specific domains and situations and the conditions under which they choose to communicate about their appraisals and beliefs. As of now, most theory-of-mind investigators (see Leslie, 1991; Roth & Leslie, 1989; Wellman et al., 1995) do not advocate a serious study of situations or the processes that result in understanding. As an example, Wellman et al. (1995) have analyzed naturalistic tapes of children's lan-

guage about "emotion," without having access to the nature of children's goals and motivations and without varying the nature of the situation with respect to the necessity and wisdom of communicating beliefs and appraisals of the situation. Furthermore, Wellman et al. have no theory of how emotion episodes are represented, no description of the understanding process, and no explanation for how appraisals of emotion situations interact with and determine the acquisition of knowledge and what is represented in memory.[6]

The results of our studies of emotional memory clearly indicate that children make appraisals and evaluations about other people, situations, and themselves throughout their attempts to encode and remember emotion-provoking situations (see Trabasso & Stein, 1997, for an encoding study with 3-year-old children, and Stein & Boyce, 1995, for a fire alarm encoding study that details the online appraisal process carried out during emotional reactions). The differences between our studies and many of those that describe children's theory of mind is that our studies are motivated by a model that is knowledge-based and focused on the importance of specific situations in determining what inferences get carried out and what knowledge gets activated. Rather than assume that children's thinking is governed by qualitative developmental differences in understanding, our theory posits that children, even in infancy, continually make appraisals of themselves and other people, especially in regard to personally significant goals.

Our theory is based on the study of narrative comprehension and is sensitive to the constraints, inference processes, and meaning analyses that get carried out in everyday interaction and conversation. One implication of using a narrative approach to study emotional understanding and memory is that we focus on the *process* of building a meaning representation. Thus we emphasize the types of thinking that get carried out as understanding progresses and unfolds over time. Causal inferences made during understanding predict the quality and accuracy of the memory representation, especially in emotional situations (Stein, 1996; Stein & Glenn, 1979; Stein & Levine, 1989; Trabasso & Stein, 1997; Trabasso, Stein, & Johnson, 1981). Although we did not have access to the situations that parents described as provoking emotion in their young children, we did have access to parents' detailed analysis of these situations, and we analyzed both the content and organizational structure of children's narratives (Liwag & Stein, 1995; Stein & Liwag, 1997; Stein et al., 1994).

Over 90% of all children recalled emotional episodes in a causally structured manner (Liwag & Stein, 1995), such that even their minimal recall corresponded to a well-formed episode. Answers to probe questions posed by the experimenters provided additional evidence that young children made detailed causal inferences about both antecedents and consequences of emotions. Furthermore, the analysis of four different emotions showed that the types and directions of causal inferences were significantly influenced by the type of emotion experienced. Anger clearly biased children's attention to antecedent conditions, while fear clearly biased attention toward a focus on outcomes that had not yet occurred. Happy and sad narratives showed that children focused on both antecedents and consequences of an event.

These data, taken together with our results from past studies (Trabasso et al., 1981; Trabasso & Stein, 1997), indicate that children are able to form coherent and meaningful representations of events, especially those that are personally meaningful and those that elicit an emotional response. Although Fivush and Hayden (1997) show significant developmental differences in the coherence structure of children's autobiographical narratives, we did not find any developmental differences in either the complexity or the coherence of children's emotion narratives (Liwag & Stein, 1995; Levine et al., 1999).

The difference between our results and those of Fivush and Hayden (1997) can be explained primarily in terms of the types of events and situations that were being recalled. Our situations were appraised as highly emotional by both children and their parents. Fivush and Hayden's subjects talked about many different events, some of which were emotional and some of which were not. They also talked about new experiences, such as excursions to a science center. Although their narratives were fairly well structured, they lacked the causal force of narratives focusing on one event that affected personal states of well-being and had definite consequences that required plans of action. Thus, in concluding what children know and don't know about events and what they are capable of

remembering, we need to keep in mind the specific situations that are being studied, especially if we are to advance a knowledge-based theory of memory and comprehension.

The results from the present study also speak to the necessity of collecting data on older children and adults, as well as on children between the ages of 2 and 5 years. As we have indicated throughout this chapter, adults experience many of the same difficulties that theory-of-mind researchers contend are found only in young children. Ross (1989) and Horton and Keysar (1996) have both demonstrated that adults are quite biased in terms of their knowledge of other people. Horton and Keysar have shown that adults often lack access to privileged information that other people have, and therefore they make serious errors in predicting the content of other people's beliefs. Thus it would seem appropriate for us to determine what our subjects know and what they do not know before we measure their understanding of other people. This approach requires that an analysis of the content knowledge of a situation become more important than is now the case.

Finally, the importance of understanding the rules of conversation and complex language communication needs to be considered. To date, the primary criteria used by theory-of-mind researchers to determine whether children understand others' beliefs are narrowly focused on the use of internal-state language (such as "think," "know," "remember," "believe," etc.). Our analysis of narrative data in the domain of emotional memories and memory for conflictual interaction suggests that both children and adults use a much broader array of language to signal their understanding of other people's knowledge and beliefs.

As we have demonstrated, one technique used by both children and adults (see Stein, Folkman, Trabasso, & Richards, 1997, for an analysis of adult narratives) to signal what another believes is to report "exactly" what the other has said in conversation. Thus we would contend that most references to other people's beliefs are *not* expressed by using the language of mental states. In fact, if attempts are made to focus blame and responsibility on others, statements of actions are always better as evidence than the thoughts of other people. Therefore, better criteria for defining and identifying beliefs need to be developed.

NOTES

1. See Bakhtin (1981), Labov and Waletsky (1967), Stein and Liwag (1997), Trabasso and Özyürek (1997), and Wertsch (1990) for similar stances on evaluation processes.
2. See Stein and Levine (1990) for the differences between general affective responses that do not encode a violation of expectation, and emotional responses that always encode a violation of expectation and a plan of action.
3. Children were asked "Why" questions twice: once to elicit the reason for the emotional reaction, and again to elicit the cause of the reason for the explanation given for an emotional reaction. The procedure went as follows: "E: Why did you feel angry? C:'Cause she broke my gun. E: What about breaking your gun made you angry? C: She's not supposed to do that. It's a new gun."
4. Siegel (1991) and Grice (1989) have described the importance of understanding indirect speech acts and the implicit axioms to which children and adults adhere as they converse with one another. It is almost impossible to interpret a conversation correctly without visual access to the original situation. The prosody in the voice, the facial expressions, and the gestures are as critical to a meaning analysis as the expressive language. Without access to children's nonverbal displays during narration and answers to probe questions with respect to children's goal and belief inferences, we would have concluded that our children did not have very well-developed beliefs about other people and that they did not understand well the complexity of their own goal-directed actions.
5. Anger was not a consequence of any of the remaining goal outcome combinations; 2% of the sadness responses were explained by wanting something that was attained or by not wanting something that was uncertain as to attainment. Only 1% of the sadness responses were not explained by explicit goal outcomes.
6. Wellman et al. (1995) and Bartsch and Wellman (1995) rely heavily upon Dennett's (1987) intentional-stance theory, which speaks to the relationship between beliefs and desires. This theory, however, is missing two core elements necessary for describing emotional understanding. The theory does not speak to the structure and importance of value judgments, nor does it describe the dynamic inference processes that occur during appraisal and understanding.

ACKNOWLEDGMENTS

This study was supported in part by a grant from the Smart Foundation to Nancy L. Stein, by Grant No. HD 25742 from the National Institute of Child Health and Human Development to Tom Trabasso and Nancy L. Stein, and by a Spencer Foundation Grant to Tom Trabasso. Maria D. Liwag was supported by an Irving B. Harris Fellowship from the Harris Center for Developmental Studies and the Harris Foundation.

REFERENCES

Alessandri, S. M., Sullivan, M. W., & Lewis, M. (1990). Violation of expectancy and frustration in early infancy. Developmental Psychology, 26(5), 738–744.

Bartlett, F. C. (1932). Remembering. Cambridge, England: Cambridge University Press.

Bakhtin, M. M. (1981). The Dialogic imagination. (C. Emerson & M. Holquist, Eds. & Trans.). Austin, TX: University of Texas Press.

Bartsch, K., & Wellman, H. (1995). Children talk about the mind. Oxford: Oxford University Press.

Brown, J. R., & Dunn, J. (1996). Continuities in emotion understanding from three to six years. Child Development, 67, 789–802.

Carey, S., & Gelman, R. (1991). The epigenesis of mind. Hillsdale, NJ: Erlbaum.

Chandler, M., Fritz, A. S., & Hala, S. (1989). Small scale deceit: Deception as a marker of 2-, 3-, and 4-year olds' early theories of mind. Child Development, 60(6), 1263–1277.

Clements, W.A., & Perner, J. (1994). Implicit understanding of beliefs. Cognitive Development, 9(4), 425–454.

Dennett, D. (1987). The intentional stance. Cambridge, MA: MIT Press.

Duncan, S., & Farley, A. (1990). Achieving parent–child co-ordination through convention: Fixed- and variable-sequence conventions. Child Development, 61, 742–753.

Fivush, R. (1991). The social construction of personal narratives. Merrill–Palmer Quarterly, 37, 59–82.

Fivush, R. (1996). Are young children's memories constructed through discourse? In K. Pezdek & W. P. Banks (Eds.), The recovered memory/false memory debate (pp. 151–168). San Diego, CA. Academic Press.

Fivush, R., & Hayden, C. A. (1997). Narrating and representing experience: Preschoolers' developing autobiographical accounts. In P. W. van den Broek, P. J. Bauer, & T. Bourg (Eds.), Developmental spans in event comprehension and representation (pp.169–198). Mahwah, NJ: Erlbaum.

Fivush, R., & Hudson, J. (Eds.). (1990). Knowing and remembering in young children. Cambridge, England: Cambridge University Press.

Flavell, J. H., Flavell, E. R., Green, F. L., & Moses, L. (1990). Young children's understanding of fact beliefs versus value beliefs. Child Development, 61, 915–928.

Folkman, S., & Stein, N. L. (1997). Adaptive goal processes in stressful events. In N. L. Stein, P. A. Ornstein, B. Tversky, & C. J. Brainerd (Eds.), Memory for everyday and emotional events (pp. 113–138). Hillsdale, NJ: Erlbaum.

Gergely, G., Nadasdy, Z., Csibra, G., & Biro, S. (1995). Taking the intentional stance at 12 months of age. Cognition, 56, 165–193.

Grice, P. (1989). *Studies in the way of words*. Cambridge, MA: Harvard University Press.

Haith, M. (1994). Visual expectations as the first step toward the development of future-oriented processes. In M. Haith, J. Benson, R. Roberts, & B. Pennington (Eds.), *The development of future-oriented processes* (pp. 11–38) Chicago: University of Chicago Press.

Horton, W. S., & Keysar, B. (1996). When do speakers take into account common ground? *Cognition, 59*(1), 91–117.

Howe, M. L., Courage, M. L., & Petersen, C. (1996). How can I remember when "I" wasn't there?: Long term retention of traumatic experiences and the emergence of the cognitive self. In K. Pezdek & W. P. Banks (Eds.), *The recovered memory/false memory debate*. (pp. 121–150). San Diego, CA: Academic Press.

Kihlstrom, J. (1996). Trauma and memory. In K. Pezdek & W. P. Banks (Eds.), *The recovered memory/false memory debate* (pp. 297–312). San Diego, CA: Academic Press.

Kihlstrom, J. F. (1998). Exhumed memory. In S. J. Lynn & K. M. McConkey (Eds.), *Truth in memory* (pp. 3–31). New York: Guilford Press.

Labov, W., & Waletsky, J. (1967). Narrative analysis: Oral versions of personal experience. In J. Helan (Ed.), *Essays on the verbal and visual arts* (pp. 12–44). Seattle: University of Washington Press.

Lazarus, R. S. (1991). *Emotion and adaptation*. New York: Oxford University Press.

Lazarus, R. S., & Folkman, S. (1984). *Stress, appraisal, and coping*. New York: Springer-Verlag.

Lehnert, W. (1985). *A theory of questioning*. Hillsdale, NJ: Erlbaum.

Leslie, A. (1991). *Information processing and conceptual knowledge: The theory of TOMM*. Paper presented at the biennial meeting of the Society for Research on Child Development, Seattle, WA.

Levine, L. (1995). Young children's understanding of the causes of anger and sadness. *Child Development, 66*, 697–709.

Levine, L. J., Stein, N. L., & Liwag, M. (1999). Remembering children's emotions: Sources of concordant and discordant accounts between parents and children. *Developmental Psychology, 35*(3), 210–230.

Lewis, M., Alessandri, S. M., & Sullivan, M. W. (1990). Violation of expectancy, loss of control, and anger expressions in young infants. *Developmental Psychology, 26*(5), 745–751.

Livesley, W. J., & Bromley, D. B. (1973). *Person perception in childhood and adolescence*. Chichester, England: Wiley.

Liwag, M. D. (1995). *Preschoolers' understanding of emotional experience: A goal based appraisal analysis*. Unpublished doctoral dissertation, University of Chicago.

Liwag, M. D., & Stein, N. L. (1995). Children's memory for emotion episodes: The importance of emotion enactment cues. *Journal of Experimental Child Psychology, 60*, 2–31.

Mandler, G. (1984). *Mind and body: Psychology of emotion and stress*. New York: Norton.

Mandler, J. M., & Johnson, N. S. (1977). Remembrance of things parsed: Story structure and recall. *Cognitive Psychology, 9*, 111–151.

Miller, G. A., Galanter, E., & Pribram, K. H. (1960). *Plans and the structure of behavior*. New York: Holt, Rinehart & Winston.

Newell, A., & Simon, H. A. (1972). *Human problem solving*. Englewood Cliffs, NJ: Prentice-Hall.

Ornstein, P. A., Shapiro, L. R., Clubb, P. A., & Follmer, A. (1997). The influence of prior knowledge on children's memory for salient medical experiences. In N. L. Stein, P. A. Ornstein, B. Tversky, & C. J. Brainerd (Eds.), *Memory for everyday and emotional events* (pp. 83–112). Hillsdale, NJ.: Erlbaum.

Quasthoff, U. (1991, July). *Mechanisms of narrative development: An interactive approach*. Paper presented at the Eleventh International Conference of the International Society for the Study of Behavioral Development, Minneapolis, MN.

Quasthoff, U. (1992). On the ontogenesis of doing personal reference: Syntactic, semantic, and interactional aspects. *Folia Linguistica, 503–538.*

Roberts, R. J., & Ondrejko, M. (1994). Perception, action, and skill: Looking ahead to meet the future. In M. Haith, J. Benson, R. Roberts, & B. Pennington (Eds.), *The development of future-oriented processes* (pp. 87–118). Chicago: University of Chicago Press.

Ross, M. (1989). Relation of implicit theories to the construction of personal histories. *Psychological Review, 96*(2), 341–357.

Ross, M. (1997). Validating memories. In N. L. Stein, P. A. Ornstein, B. Tversky, & C. J. Brainerd (Eds.), *Memory for everyday and emotional events* (pp. 49–82). Hillsdale, NJ.: Erlbaum.

Roth, D., & Leslie, A. M. (1989). The recognition of attitude conveyed by utterance. A study of preschool and autistic children. In G. E. Butterfield, P. L. Harris, A. M. Leslie, & H. M. Wellman (Eds.), *Perspectives on the child's theory of mind* (pp. 315–330). Oxford: British Psychological Society/Oxford Science.

Rumelhart, D. E. (1975). Notes on a schema for stories. In D. G. Bobrow & A. Collins (Eds.), *Representation and understanding* (pp. 211– 236). New York: Academic Press.

Rumelhart, D. E. (1977). Understanding and summarizing brief stories. In D. LaBerge & J. Samuels (Eds.), *Basic processes in reading: Perception and comprehension*. Hillsdale, NJ: Erlbaum.

Sacerdoti, E. D. (1975). *A structure for plans and behavior* (Technical Report No. 109). Stanford Research Institute Artificial Intelligence Center.

Schank, R. C. (1982). *Dynamic memory*. New York: Cambridge University Press.

Schank, R. C., & Abelson, R. P. (1977). *Scripts, plans, goals and understanding*. Hillsdale, NJ: Erlbaum.

Shaver, P., Schwartz, J., O'Connor, C., & Kirson, D. (1987). Emotion knowledge: Further explorations of a prototype approach. *Journal of Personality and Social Psychology, 52*, 1016–1086.

Siegel, M. (1991). *Knowing children: Experiments in conversation and cognition*. Hove, England: Erlbaum.

Smith, C., & Lazarus, R. (1993). Appraisal components, core relational themes, and the emotions. *Cognition and Emotion, 7*(3–4), 233–269.

Snow, C. E. (1990). Building memories: The ontogeny of autobiography. In D. Cicchetti & M. Beeghley (Eds.), *The self in transition: Infancy to childhood* (pp. 213–242). Chicago: University of Chicago Press.

Stein, N. L. (1995, July). *The language of compromising, winning, and losing: An analysis of men's and women's negotiations.* Paper presented at the Conversational Symposium, Linguistic Society of America, Albuquerque, NM.

Stein, N. L. (1996). Children's memory for emotional events: Implications for testimony. In K. Pezdek & W. P. Banks (Eds.), *The recovered memory/false memory debate* (pp. 169–196). San Diego, CA: Academic Press.

Stein, N. L., & Albro, E. R. (1997). Building complexity and coherence: Children's use of goal-structured knowledge in telling stories. In M. Bamberg (Ed.), *Narrative development: Six approaches* (pp. 5–44). Mahwah, NJ: Erlbaum.

Stein, N. L., & Boyce, W. T. (1995). *The role of physiological reactivity in attending to, remembering, and responding to an emotional event.* Paper presented at the biennial meeting of the Society for Research on Child Development, Indianapolis, IN.

Stein, N. L., Folkman, S., Trabasso, T., & Richards, T. A. (1997). Appraisal and goal processes as predictors of psychological well-being in bereaved caregivers. *Journal of Personality and Social Psychology, 72*(4), 872–884.

Stein, N. L., & Glenn, C. G. (1979). An analysis of story comprehension in elementary children. In R. D. Freedle (Ed.), *New directions in discourse processing* (Vol. 2, pp. 53–119). Norwood, NJ: Ablex.

Stein, N. L., & Goldman, S. (1981). Children's knowledge about social situations: From causes to consequences. In S. Asher & J. Gottman (Eds.), *The development of friendship* (pp. 297–321). New York: Cambridge University Press.

Stein, N. L., & Levine, L. (1987). Thinking about feelings: The development and organization of emotional knowledge. In R. Snow & M. Farr (Eds.), *Aptitude, learning and instruction* (Vol. 3, pp. 165–197). Hillsdale, NJ: Erlbaum.

Stein, N. L., & Levine, L. (1989). The causal organization of emotional knowledge: A developmental study. *Cognition and Emotion, 3*(4), 343–378.

Stein, N. L., & Levine, L. (1990). Making sense out of emotion: The representation and use of goal structured knowledge. In N. L. Stein, B. Leventhal, & T. Trabasso (Eds.), *Psychological and biological approaches to emotion* (pp. 45–73). Hillsdale, NJ: Erlbaum.

Stein, N. L., & Liwag, M. D. (1997). A goal-appraisal process approach to understanding and remembering emotional events. In P. van den Broek, P. Bauer, & T. Bourg (Eds.), *Developmental spans in event comprehension and representation* (pp. 199–236). Hillsdale, NJ: Erlbaum.

Stein, N. L., & Trabasso, T. (1982). Children's understanding of stories: A basis for moral judgment and dilemma resolution. In C. J. Brainerd & M. Pressley (Eds.), *Verbal processes in children: Progress in cognitive development research* (pp. 161–188). New York: Springer-Verlag.

Stein, N. L., & Trabasso, T. (1989). Children's understanding of changing emotional states. In C. Saarni & P. L. Harris (Eds.), *Children's understanding of emotion* (pp. 50–77). Cambridge, England: Cambridge University Press.

Stein, N. L., & Trabasso, T. (1992). The organization of emotional experience: Creating links among emotion, thinking and intentional action. *Cognition and Emotion, 6*(3–4), 225–244.

Stein, N. L., Trabasso, T., & Liwag, M. D. (1993). The representation and organization of emotional experience: Unfolding the emotion episode. In M. Lewis & J. M. Haviland (Eds.), *Handbook of emotions* (pp. 279–300). New York: Guilford Press.

Stein, N. L., Trabasso, T., & Liwag, M. D. (1994). The Rashomon phenomenon: Personal frames and future-oriented appraisals in memory for emotional events. In M. Haith, J. Benson, R. Roberts, & B. Pennington (Eds.), *The development of future-oriented processes* (pp. 409–436). Chicago: University of Chicago Press.

Stein, N. L., Wade, E., & Liwag, M. D. (1997). A theoretical approach to understanding and remembering harmful events. In N. L. Stein, P. A. Ornstein, B. Tversky, & C. J. Brainerd (Eds.), *Memory for everyday and emotional events* (pp. 15–48). Hillsdale, NJ: Erlbaum.

Stenberg, C. R., & Campos, J. J. (1990). The development of anger expressions in infancy. In N. L. Stein, B. Leventhal, & T. Trabasso (Eds.), *Psychological and biological approaches to emotion* (pp. 247–282). Hillsdale, NJ: Erlbaum.

Stern, D. (1992). *Diary of a baby.* New York: Basic Books.

Suchman, L.A. (1987). *Plans and situated actions: The problem of human–machine communication.* New York: Cambridge University Press.

Trabasso, T., & Özyürek, A. (1997). Communicating evaluation in narrative understanding. In T. Givon (Ed.), *Conversation: Cognitive, communicative, and social perspectives* (pp. 269–302). Amsterdam: Benjamins.

Trabasso, T., & Stein, N. L. (1994). Using goal-plan knowledge to merge the past with the present and the future in narrating events on-line. In M. Haith, J. Benson, R. Roberts, & B. Pennington (Eds.), *The development of future-oriented processes* (pp. 323–349). Chicago: University of Chicago Press.

Trabasso, T., & Stein, N. L. (1997). Narrating, representing, and remembering event sequences. In P. van den Broek, P. Bauer, & T. Bourg (Eds.), *Developmental spans in event comprehension and representation* (pp. 237–270). Hillsdale, NJ: Erlbaum.

Trabasso, T., Stein, N. L., & Johnson, L. (1981). Children's knowledge of events: A causal analysis of story structure. In G. Bower (Ed.), *The psychology of learning and motivation* (Vol. 15, pp. 237–281). New York: Academic Press.

von Hofsten, C. (1994). Planning and perceiving what is going to happen next. In M. Haith, J. Benson, R. Roberts, & B. Pennington (Eds.), *The development of future-oriented processes* (pp. 63–86). Chicago: University of Chicago Press.

Wellman, H. M., Harris, P., Banerjee, M., & Sinclair, A. (1995). Early understanding of emotion: Evidence from natural language. *Cognition and Emotion, 9*(2–3), 117–149.

Wertsch, J. (1990). The voice of rationality in a sociocultural approach to mind. In L. C. Moll (Ed.), *Instructional implications and applications of sociohistorical psychology.* New York: Cambridge University Press.

Wilensky, R. (1978). *Understanding goal-based stories.* Unpublished doctoral dissertation, Yale University.

Willatts, P. (1990). The development of problem-solving strategies in infancy. In D. Bjorklund (Ed.), *Children's strategies: Contemporary views of cognitive development* (pp. 23–66). Hillsdale, NJ: Erlbaum.

Woodward, A. (1998). Infants selectively encode the goal object of an actor's reach. *Cognition, 69*(1), 1–34.

CHAPTER 29

Cognitive and Social Construction in Emotions

P. N. Johnson-Laird
Keith Oatley

In a recent instance of road rage, Jack Nichol-son got angry with a driver who had cut him off. At a red light, the movie star got out of his car and attacked the offending driver's Mercedes with a golf club (Mizell, 1997). This is an excellent example of an emotion and the behavior it engenders. Nearly all of us are capable of feeling violent anger, and some of us *in extremis* may allow it to take over our behavior. In a contrasting pacific mood, most of us are able to fall in love. Here is a case reported in a newspaper:

> On Monday Cpl. Floyd Johnson, 23, and the then Ellen Skinner, 19, total strangers, boarded a train at San Francisco and sat down across the aisle from each other. Johnson didn't cross the aisle until Wednesday, but his bride said, "I'd already made up my mind to say yes if he asked me to marry him." "We did most of the talking with our eyes," Johnson explained. Thursday the couple got off the train in Omaha with plans to be married. Because they would need to have the consent of the bride's parents if they were married in Nebraska, they crossed the river to Council Bluffs, Iowa, where they were married Friday. (Cited by Burgess & Wallin, 1953, p. 151)

What is newsworthy about this case is how closely it conforms to our Western cultural ideal. Over a third of Americans in a sample taken by Averill (1985) reported having had experiences conforming to the ideal embodied in this newspaper story. An equal number reported that their experiences of love did not conform to this ideal, but they based their responses on any single departure from the ideal and a generally unfavorable attitude toward it—hence also showing that they were influenced by it.

These instances of anger and love seem particularly Western. But, to what extent are emotions cognitive and social constructions—feelings and behaviors acquired from interactions with other people? Our goal in this chapter is to answer this question. One thesis is that emotional life is entirely a social construction, and so the emotions that you experience are very different from those of, say, an Utka, a member of a group of Inuit, because your respective social lives differ. Like Jack Nicholson, you can feel anger; but perhaps, as we discuss later, the Utka people cannot. You and they live in different cultures, different environments, and different mental worlds. The antithesis is that appearances are deceptive; that human emotions are natural and inborn; and that continuities exist between adults and children, and between humans and animals. Emotions are based on genetically determined neural and hormonal programs, which include involuntary physiological processes, facial expressions, distinctive qualities in speaking, and urges to act.

In the past, these two approaches have been in competition: Emotions have been viewed as either socially constructed or biological. Solomon (1984, p. 240), for instance, wrote: "My thesis is that emotions are to be construed as cultural acquisitions, determined by the circumstances and concepts of a particular culture as well as, or rather much more than, by the functions of biology and, more specifically, neurology." Likewise, Geertz (1980) remarked that the passions are as cultural as political institutions—to which Leach (1981) responded, "complete rubbish," and went on to assert, "I can make no sense of a line of thought which claims that 'passions' are culturally defined." He evidently subscribed to the view that emotions are biological events, the same the world over (Lindzey, 1954). The argument has been messy—based on different definitions of emotion, ambiguous observations, and selection of evidence. Our plan is to describe the approaches, then to propose a synthesis based on a current line of theorizing about emotions, and finally to show how this theory makes sense of the evidence. The outcome, we hope, is an answer to our question about the ways in which emotions depend on social interactions with others.

SOCIAL CONSTRUCTION OR EVOLUTION, OR BOTH?

To answer our question, which is a special case of the nature–nurture puzzle, we need to formulate a rough account of emotion so that the opposing parties are at least arguing about the same thing, and to articulate the two theoretical positions.

In its broadest sense, an emotion brings together cognitions, evaluations, neurophysiological processes, somatic changes, subjective feelings, facial expressions, and behaviors. You perceive that someone has cut you off in traffic (a cognition); you evaluate the event as a threat to your autonomy (an evaluation); various changes occur in your brain (neurophysiological processes); they prompt your heart to pump faster and hormones to be released into your bloodstream, which prepare you for action (somatic changes); you feel anger mounting within you (a feeling); you grimace in anger (a facial expression), and you honk your horn (an action). Theorists differ about which components

of this typical vignette, the term "anger" refers to, and they differ still more about the causal relations among its different components. Some restrict emotion only to the subjective feelings; others—behaviorists, perhaps—restrict it to the bodily changes and behaviors; still others restrict it to the neurophysiological processes in the brain. There is no right answer; science does not proceed by a priori definition. What matters is the particular theory of emotion, which may concern only a subset of the components above, and its supporting evidence. Hence we will bear in mind the different components, and the fact that different theories deal with different subsets of them.

Examples of the Two Types of Theories

There are varieties of both social construction theories and biological theories. We cannot review them all, and so we consider just some paradigmatic examples in order to state their contrasts as starkly as possible.

Armon-Jones (1986) distinguishes between two forms of social constructionism. The weak thesis "concedes to the naturalist the existence of a limited range of natural emotion responses" (Armon-Jones, 1986, p. 38). The task of the psychologist is then to determine the extent to which emotions, even those that are natural, are socially constructed.

The strong thesis rests on three principal tenets. The first is that emotions are preeminently complexes of feelings and attitudes. The second is that emotions, like other experiences and behaviors, are social products. They are based on beliefs, shaped by language, and derived from culture. They are not modifications of natural states. They are not fixed, but protean. Reality seems solid and seamless, but it is a construction from social interactions. Ideas and experiences that people take to be fundamental, such as those of self, accordingly differ in different cultures. In the West the self is individualistic, autonomous, the source of action. In many Eastern societies the self is, as Markus and Kitayama (1991) have said "interdependent," derived from belonging to a group. From such differences grow differences in emotions (Shweder, 1991). North Americans may experience anger when they perceive a threat to their autonomy—even in driving an automobile. For many Asians such threats do not occur, since they neither believe in nor depend on any such concept—but threats to their sense of social relatedness may make them anxious. The third tenet is that emotions depend on social experience and the cultivation of an individual's sensibilities. Not everyone is capable of experiencing each emotion. Indeed, there are epochs and cultures that are devoid of certain emotions, because they did not develop then or there.

Averill (1985), a defender of social construction—though not perhaps of the strong thesis—argues that the first person to formulate such an account was H. Finck, a music critic for the *New York Evening Post*. For Finck (1887), a paradigm case of a socially constructed emotion is love. Love, he argued, is a complex of feelings, attitudes, and sentiments. They include an aesthetic appreciation of human form in the person of the loved one, together with impulses of sympathy, solicitude, and self-sacrifice. Likewise, not everyone has the talent for love. Like a passion for music, it must be cultivated. Moreover, love as we know it in the West is of a rather recent origin. Finck dated it to 1274, when Dante fell in love with Beatrice.

Finck had started by assuming that love is part of human nature, and his most original idea, he thought, was to give up this assumption in favor of the invention of love in the Renaissance. He later said that he was overjoyed when he discovered a truth that had escaped previous scholars: In classical texts written in ancient Greek, Latin, and Hebrew, love as a refined and altruistic sentiment was unknown; and in anthropological accounts of other cultures, it was also unknown. Averill (1985) recounts how William James was among those to review Finck's book. He did so unfavorably. James argued what has become the standard naturalist case: Culture may contribute to damping or inflaming emotions, but it scarcely creates them. In response to such reviews and to his own critique that he had not presented all the evidence, Finck published a second book of 800 pages, with an abundance of evidence. Averill judges that although James's influence has been greater, Finck's argument was the better. Culture does not just, as James claimed, affect the intensity of emotions. It gives rise to qualitatively different emotions. In classical times, no one experienced modern love; since the rebirth of humanism, it is a possibility for those of us who live in the West. Proponents of the strong thesis accordingly consider each element in the story of Floyd Johnson and Ellen Skinner and

point out how it differs from other cultures. They conclude that such differences are profound, and that apparent similarities to courtship practices in remote peoples are superficial. Likewise, they deny that a human emotion has any connection with states in animals, since it depends on cultural beliefs, which animals cannot have.

The strong thesis is not just a 19th century speculation. Some modern theorists defend it. For instance, Harré (1986) reviews the evidence from evolutionary theories and writes: "Psychologists have always had to struggle against a persistent illusion that in such studies as those of the emotions there is something there, the emotion, of which the emotion word is a mere representation" (p. 4). The strong thesis is attractively radical and fun to defend.

The antithesis of these views is to be found amongst the proponents of evolutionary psychology (e.g., Pinker, 1997). The intellectual godfather of the movement is of course Charles Darwin, who in 1872 reported on his survey of expressions in aboriginal populations in different parts of the world, some remote from European influence. He summarized the results thus: "The same state of mind is expressed throughout the world with remarkable uniformity; and this fact is in itself interesting as evidence of the close similarity in bodily structure and mental disposition of all the races of mankind" (Darwin, 1872/1965, pp. 15–17). He bolstered his account by a simple experiment, typical of Darwin:

> I put my face close to the thick glass-plate in front of a puff-adder in the Zoological Gardens, with the firm determination of not starting back if the snake struck at me; but, as soon as the blow was struck, my resolution went for nothing, and I jumped a yard or two backwards with astonishing rapidity. My will and reason were powerless against the imagination of a danger which had never been experienced. (Darwin, 1872/1965, p. 38)

In this example, an emotion and its effect were like a reflex. Darwin saw such processes as reactions triggered by specific circumstances and dependent on the automatic operation of neural mechanisms. Darwin found that neither his will nor his ability to reason could alter the operations of the mechanism; its origins were in evolution and in individual development.

Modern evolutionary psychologists go further (Tooby & Cosmides, 1990; see also Cosmides & Tooby, Chapter 7, this volume). They have no doubt that emotions—and many cognitive abilities—have their origins in the adaptations of our forebears to meet the exigencies of their lives; individuals who developed emotions had a greater chance to survive and to reproduce. As Pinker (1997, p. 380) writes, "emotions are adaptations, well-engineered software modules that work in harmony with the intellect and are indispensable to the functioning of the whole mind." But are all emotions based on adaptations? With ingenuity, it seems possible to account for any emotion in this way. What, for example, is the adaptive value of the pleasure one feels at natural beauty? Pinker (1997, p. 386) cites various behavioral ecologists to support the case for an innate predisposition for the landscape of savannahs, the homelands of our hunter–gatherer ancestors. One factor in the development of agriculture some 10,000 years ago, according to the archeologist Steven Mithen (1996, p. 224), was modern humans' mental ability to develop "social relationships" with plants and animals, like those with people. Agriculture arose because people treated plants and animals as social beings. He quotes Humphrey (1984, p. 27): "Many of mankind's most prized technological discoveries, from agriculture to chemistry, may have had their origin . . . in the fortunate misapplication of social intelligence."

Yet psychologists cannot go back to the Stone Age to test natural selection at work in shaping the mind. The best they can do is to use ethological and paleontological evidence to speculate about what was adaptive for our ancestors. The strength of the approach is that it explains success where a task taps into a hypothesized adaptation and failure where it does not. But what do evolutionary psychologists do if they fail to corroborate a postulated adaptation? They can argue, like Pinker, that not all mental processes are adaptations, or they can rewrite their "just so" story to fit the facts (Simon, 1991). So it is hard to see how any empirical result could refute evolutionary psychology. It is a useful heuristic for generating hypotheses, rather than a refutable theory.

In sum, at one extreme, emotions are mental constructions based on social life: Different society, different emotions. At the other extreme, emotions are innate reactions that evolved as adaptations in our evolutionary ancestors: Different society, same emotions. As so often in nature–nurture controversies, the evidence suggests that neither party is quite right, and so we turn from thesis and antithesis to a potential synthesis.

A POTENTIAL SYNTHESIS

To resolve the debate between social and innate accounts of emotions, we need to determine the purposes of emotions. Some authors have regarded them as essentially purposeless; others have treated them as worse than useless, as impediments to the rational governance of life—a notion that runs from Plato to Freud, along with the doctrine that unbridled emotions lead to self-destruction (Ellis, 1994). Yet all social mammals appear to have an emotional life, which is a strong hint that emotions do have functions (see, e.g., Minsky, 1985; Nesse, 1991).

How then can we bring together the innate, social, and purposeful components of emotion? One answer is that emotions are communications, both within the brain and externally among conspecifics. In formulating such a theory, we have argued that emotions are central to cognitive processing: "They are part of a management system to co-ordinate each individual's multiple plans and goals under constraints of time and other limited resources" (Oatley & Johnson-Laird, 1987, p. 31; see Oatley & Johnson-Laird, 1996, for a later formulation). Hence emotions are a more flexible control system than the innate fixed action patterns characteristic of insect-like invertebrates, and more computationally efficient—in time and in demands on working memory—than deliberative reasoning. Our theory distinguishes among basic, object-oriented, and complex emotions.

Basic emotions are innate and common to all human societies. They consist of happiness and sadness, and anger and fear; they correspond to the internal nonsymbolic signals that can propagate from one processing module in the brain to another. For the propagation of emotion, these modules are quasi-autonomous and have some of the properties of parallel distributed processors. Normally an emotion depends on a cognitive evaluation that sets some processing modules into a particular emotional mode. This evaluation need not be conscious. If the emotional signal but not the content of the cognition impinges on consciousness, then the individual will feel happy, sad, angry, or frightened, for no apparent reason. Normally, however, cognitions are conscious and culture-dependent. The existence of two separate channels of communication for fear—one emotional and rapid, and the other cognitive and slower—has been corroborated in a series of studies carried out by LeDoux (1996).

Object-oriented emotions are necessarily related to a known object: attachment, parental care, sexual desire, disgust, and personal rejection. Perhaps, as Nico Frijda (personal communication, 1996) has suggested, these five object-oriented emotions can be reduced to two—an emotion of attraction (including attachment, parental care, and sexual desire) and one of repulsion (including disgust and personal rejection). They too appear to occur in all cultures. Their propagation in the brain depends on linking an emotion mode to a representation of the object of the emotion, and so they cannot be consciously experienced without an awareness of the object of the emotion.

Complex emotions are elaborations of the basic and object-oriented emotions, but they depend as well on conscious evaluations that are social and that make reference to mental models of the self or others. They therefore cannot be experienced for no apparent reason, and they include such emotions as remorse, indignation, pride, embarrassment, and romantic love (in the Western sense). For example, you may feel remorse—sadness about an action—because you judge yourself to have acted against the moral code embodied in your idealized mental model of your self. Thus complex emotions integrate a nonsemantic emotional signal and a conscious cognitive evaluation. Romantic love, as we think of it now in the West, is a complex emotion. Its innate components are sexual desire and happiness. Its cognitive components include altruism, idealized models of the loved one and the self, and, when apart, a longing for the other. The components exist separately in different societies, but their integration into a recognizable complex is a cultural accomplishment. What you see when you fall in love, what you imagine in such circumstances, what you resonate to when you read a love story, is a complex that includes sexual desire, aesthetic attraction to the other, and the altruism that Finck stressed. The story of Floyd Johnson and Ellen Skinner would have no point if they merely met on a train and later had sexual intercourse. Any sense of what the event might have meant to them, any altruistic impulses that each had for the other, any re-

arrangements of long-term personal plans that they made, would be inexplicable. The social construction of emotions accordingly concerns the acquisition from social interactions of cognitive evaluations and their corresponding emotions.

In sum, basic emotions are founded on biological mechanisms; they can be objectless, but they can include culturally derived semantic content. Object-oriented emotions are likewise founded on such mechanisms; they necessarily include a conscious cognition of their objects. Complex emotions always include conscious cognitive evaluations. The cognitions underlying some instances of basic emotions (such as Jack Nicholson's road rage) and all object-oriented and complex emotions, as we will argue, can vary from society to society and from individual to individual. They reflect norms and conventions of your society, especially your model of your self, acquired in childhood from parents or caregivers (Bowlby, 1988).

Other cognitive theories postulate the existence of basic emotions (e.g., Ekman, 1992; Stein, Trabasso, & Liwag, 1993; Power & Dalgleish, 1997). Some critics reject them, arguing instead that emotions are made up of components that cannot stand alone as emotions, such as autonomic responses and cognitive appraisals (Ortony, Clore, & Collins, 1988; Ortony & Turner, 1990), prototypes (Russell, 1991), or tendencies toward certain global actions (Frijda, 1986). Yet anger can be perfectly well understood in an assertion such as this: "For no good reason, Joseph K. woke up feeling angry." Here is no prototypical sequence, and K.'s mental state may not be accompanied by any somatic or bodily or behavioral components. The referent of the word "anger" can be grasped only if you have experienced anger, and it cannot be analyzed into any smaller components. People know about prototypical sequences—an insult angers someone, who responds aggressively. Yet anger, as the example shows, is part of the sequence, not the sequence itself.

Construction can be well understood, we argue, in terms of three postulates of our communicative theory. First, emotions should be guides to life, and so should interact with the human capacity for reasoning and planning. Second, there should be distinctions between basic emotions that can occur without cultural content, and complex emotions that always have culture-dependent objects and causes.

Third, complex emotions in particular should offer good examples of social construction that differ from one society to another. We examine each of these issues. We take a different direction from that of many articles and books on social construction: For social construction to occur, there must be cognitive construction, so here we introduce this element into the discussion.

EMOTION AND COGNITION AS GUIDES TO LIFE

Most people cope satisfactorily with the problems of daily life, but make egregious errors in tests of reasoning. This discrepancy is the fundamental paradox of rationality. Its resolution illuminates the interrelations between emotion and reason. In fact, it is impossible to deduce rational solutions to all of life's problems, or even of many of them, if only because deduction is not a tractable process. As the number of premises increases, any system of reasoning eventually runs out of time and memory before it reaches a conclusion. Unless the brain somehow bypasses computational constraints, reasoning is therefore bounded (Simon, 1982). The paradox is that perfect rationality is for the angels.

One solution to the paradox, proposed by evolutionary psychologists, is to abandon general deductive competence in favor of specialized inferential modules. An example would be a module for "checking for cheaters," which is supposed to have evolved because it conferred selective advantage on our hunter–gatherer ancestors (Cosmides, 1989). There are two problems with this solution: Evidence in its favor is open to alternative explanation, and it offers no account of abstract logical competence, which is a human ability (Johnson-Laird, 1999).

Another solution to the paradox is that the mind contains two separate mechanisms for reasoning: one for abstract deductive competence, which depends on rule-governed processes, and another for the informal, tacit reasoning of daily life, which depends on associative processes (see, e.g., Sloman, 1996; Evans & Over, 1996). The problem with this hypothesis is that there is little evidence for two systems of reasoning—no disputed cases, no interactions between them, no data other than the paradox itself that calls for two systems. The resolution of the paradox, we suggest,

does depend on two systems—but one for reasoning and one for emotions. People do demonstrate a modicum of rational competence in the laboratory (see Evans, Newstead, & Byrne, 1993, for a review). A modicum of rationality is important to achieving the goals of everyday life, and crucial for a technical grasp of logic, the probability calculus, and decision theory. But it is only a modicum; it explains why people make mistakes in reasoning, particularly in the laboratory, but sometimes in life. And it explains why tests of reasoning predict academic success, and how it was possible for humanity to have invented logic and the other calculi. Reasoning is costly, but emotions can yield rapid intuitive assessments of what to do to cope with daily life. They depend on heuristics rather than exhaustive rational inference.

If emotions guide our lives, then they should interact with thinking. On the one hand, they should influence our inferences. On the other hand, our thinking should influence our emotions. We examine the causal effects in both directions.

Emotions Influence Thinking

A clear case of emotions' governing thinking occurs in decision making. Economists long ago formulated a normative account based on "subjective expected utility" (i.e., the product of the utility of an outcome with the subjective probability of the outcome's occurrence). There are various ways to axiomatize rationality so that a rational decision maximizes subjective expected utility. Amos Tversky and his colleague Danny Kahneman showed that people systematically violate these principles. Ask yourself, for example, which of the following options you would prefer:

A sure gain of $900, or a 90% chance of $1,000.

Like most people, you would probably settle for the sure gain, though the expected values of the two outcomes are the same. Now ask yourself which of the following options you would prefer:

A sure loss of $900, or a 90% chance of a loss of $1,000.

Again, like most people, you would probably opt for the possible loss of $1,000, though again the expected values of the two outcomes are the same. Kahneman and Tversky's (1979) account of the phenomena in "prospect theory" reflects this asymmetry in the emotional effects of losses and gains. People assess them in relation to a reference point (typically the status quo), and they tend to take risks in a domain of losses, but not in a domain of gains.

Is this aspect of decision making universal or affected by cultural considerations? Geertz (1972/1973), in his classic study of Balinese cockfights, reports a different conception of gambling from that of the West. The protagonists in a cockfight—the owners of the cocks and their allies—make large gambles on the outcome with equal odds. The more equally matched the birds, the vaster the amount wagered, and the greater the emotion engendered by the fight. Geertz considers such gambles "deep play," an expression that Bentham coined to refer to bets in which the stakes are so high that it is irrational to make them—one is in over one's head. "But for the Balinese," Geertz writes (1972/1973, p. 432), ". . . the explanation lies in the fact that in such play, money is less a measure of utility, had or expected, than it is a symbol of moral import, perceived or imposed." In other words, individuals are putting their lives on the line for something that they believe in: their honor, respect, and status. Only the side bets made by individual pairs of spectators reflect the likely outcome of the fights with odds adjusted accordingly.

In general, there are marked cultural differences, and differences from one epoch to another, in probabilistic thinking. Hacking (1975) remarks that anyone who played dice in Roman times armed with the probability calculus would soon have won the whole of Gaul. Wright and Phillips (1980) report that the British make finer differentiations and more accurate estimates of probabilities than their Asian counterparts. Asians have a greater tendency to be overconfident and to assert that they are 100% sure of events when in fact they are wrong. These differences, Wright and Phillips suspect, arise from contrasting child-rearing practices in Asia and the West. Risk itself is a cultural concept (Bontempo, Bottom, & Weber, 1997).

One effect of emotion on thinking bears out folk wisdom on the topic: A happy state of mind can improve performance. Isen, Daubman, and Nowicki (1987), for instance, examined Duncker's "candle problem," in which a subject is given only a candle and a box of tacks and must fix the candle to a wall. The problem can be solved only if the subject realizes that the box of tacks should itself be emptied and pinned to the wall as a support for the candle. One group of subjects was shown a humorous movie clip to induce happiness, and significantly more of them solved the problem than those of groups shown a sad clip, an emotionally neutral clip, or no clip at all. But emotions can preoccupy people and thereby impair their thinking. In a study of complex reasoning, Oaksford, Morris, Grainger, and Williams (1995) also showed snippets of movies to different groups of subjects to make them happy or sad. The task was to determine what information was relevant to testing the truth or falsity of a conditional rule (i.e., Wason's "selection task"). Neither group performed as well as those who were shown an emotionally neutral film or no film at all. This result fits Ellis and Ashbrook's (1988) theory of depression, which postulates that it leads to rumination on one's own depressed state instead of the allocation of resources to the task in hand. It also fits the deleterious effects of stress on cognitive failure (Reason, 1988).

One pertinent factor is the appropriateness of the emotion to the task in hand. If you feel happy because you have just been amused by a clip from a comedy, then your emotion is irrelevant to testing the truth or falsity of a conditional rule—unless it is about the movie. But, emotions can be an index of progress toward a goal: happiness as you progress toward it, frustration as it is eluding you, and melancholic rumination when it is irretrievable (Carver & Scheier, 1990; Martin & Tesser, 1996). If your emotion is relevant to your goals, then its effects are predictable (Oatley & Johnson-Laird, 1987). Anxiety leads to vigilance when stimuli compete for attention, but depression does not (Broadbent & Broadbent, 1988; Mathews, Mackintosh, & Fulcher, 1997). Conversely, depression leads to a better recall of sad events or words, whereas anxiety does not affect the recall of threatening words (Teasdale, 1988).

Studies of thinking have revealed analogous effects. When people assessed the probability of risk to themselves from future negative events, those who were anxious assigned a higher risk than did those who were not anxious (Johnson & Tversky, 1983). And when mildly depressed individuals estimated their control over outcomes in which they lost or gained small sums of money, they were sadder and wiser—more accurate, in short—than control subjects (Alloy & Abramson, 1979, 1988).

Suppose you have 10 seconds to answer the following question:

"I am worse than my boss.

My boss is worse than my colleagues.

Who is worst?"

If you are in a normal frame of mind, or anxious, then as Power and Wykes (1996) have shown, you are more likely to err with this sort of problem than with one about happiness. If you are depressed, however, then you are used to ruminating about negative states of affairs, and your performance is not adversely affected. Your emotional reactions also have a qualitative effect on how you reason. In a study carried out by Oatley, Nundy, and Larocque (see Oatley, 1996), the subjects read a short story by Russell Banks, "Sarah Cole: A Type of Love Story," in which a heartless man breaks off a love affair with great cruelty. Its effect was to make some subjects sad and others angry. Those who were saddened tended to reason backward to antecedent events in the story; sadness is indeed an emotion of loss, in which one ruminates about past events to try to make sense of them. Those who were angered, however, tended to reason forwards to prospective goals; anger leads to plans for revenge, as Aristotle wrote, or to alternative plans to reach the goal that has been frustrated.

Imagine that you drive to the airport to catch a plane, and that on the way you stop for a drink. You reach the airport 5 minutes late and miss your flight. You are disappointed. Your emotions are liable to lead you to think to yourself: "If only I hadn't stopped to have a drink, then I wouldn't have missed my flight." This conditional thought is counterfactual, and it expresses a causal relation (Miller & Johnson-Laird, 1976, Sec. 6.3.5). It conveys two states of affairs. First, it presents the facts of the matter: "I stopped to have a drink. I missed my flight." Second, it conveys an alternative possibility to what actually happened, and in this counterfactual world, "I didn't stop to have a drink. I didn't miss my flight." As Ruth Byrne (1997) and her colleagues have shown, counterfactual conditionals make certain inferences easier because they spell out these two possibilities. One reason why people entertain such counterfactuals is to learn from their mistakes—to correct plans that did not work. Hence, when things go badly, you often think about counterfactual possibilities (Landman, 1993). You may imagine certain changes to the world (Kahneman & Tversky, 1982; Kahne-

man, 1995), especially those events that depend on intentional actions, such as stopping to have a drink (Girotto, Legrenzi, & Rizzo, 1991; Legrenzi, 1998). Thus a negative outcome can lead to a dysphoric emotion and to counterfactual thinking. Indeed, Roese and his colleagues showed in an unpublished study (see Roese, 1997) that people saddened by watching the film *Bambi* and seeing the death of Bambi's mother were faster than control subjects to complete a counterfactual prompt about their earlier performance in a separate anagram test. Sadness elicits counterfactual thinking.

Thinking Influences Emotions

Emotions prompt inferences, but do inferences cause emotions? Zajonc (1980) argued that preferences do not depend on inferences, but Lazarus (1982) retorted that they do not depend on conscious inferences. Indeed, such cognitive evaluations are often rapid and rudimentary. A striking feature of works of art and fiction is that they can create genuine emotions. You have real feelings for imaginary events, which— even as you laugh or weep—you know to be fictitious. Music is still more mysterious, since it can move you even though it refers to nothing. The oddity of real emotions to unreal events appears to be universal to all epochs and cultures. Its most plausible interpretation is that the cognitive evaluations that engender emotions are sufficiently crude that they contain no reality check.

The rudimentary nature of cognitive appraisals is borne out by studies of the cues to action and to attitudes. Bargh (1992) has shown that participants who solved sentence anagrams about old people walked away from the experiment more slowly than those who unscrambled sentences about other topics. Thus emotions and stereotyped attitudes are automatically elicited without our awareness. What matters, Bargh argues, is not that we are unaware of the prompting stimulus, but that we are unaware of how we have interpreted it. We do not question our implicit biases, because we do not realize that they are biases.

The rudimentary nature of evaluations for basic emotions is borne out by LeDoux (1996; see also LeDoux & Phelps, Chapter 10, this volume). He has traced the neural pathways underlying fear, from the perceptual input to the somatic and behavioral responses. The amygdala, a region beneath the cortex to which it is richly interconnected, activates a panoply of responses—the release of stress hormones, suppression of pain, autonomic responses, and various behaviors (Tranel, 1997). LeDoux has identified two routes for information to the amygdala. The slow route goes from the sensory thalamus (a way station for perceptual information) to the amygdala by way of the cortex. The fast route, however, goes directly from the sensory thalamus to the amygdala. Because it bypasses the cortex, the signal depends on only a crude analysis. It is purely emotional: One feels fearful without knowing why. Only the cortical route allows one access to a full representation of what caused the response.

Conscious inferences also cause emotions. By "conscious" inferences, we mean those that people are aware of making, though they too depend on many unconscious processes. The obvious cases in daily life are those in which people infer that a situation exists, which in turn triggers an emotion. For instance, you park your car in the street. When you return, it is missing. You infer that it has been stolen, and you are shocked and annoyed. Likewise, as we will see, the outcomes of decisions can affect our emotions.

RELATIONS BETWEEN BASIC AND COMPLEX EMOTIONS

We (Oatley & Johnson-Laird, 1987) have proposed a fundamental relation between basic and complex emotions as a model of how individually and culturally constructed complex emotions are built on basic emotions. We have argued that the emotions we call "complex" always involve at least one basic emotion, together with an evaluation of the self in a social situation. Hence every complex emotion will be dependent on an individual and cultural construction of self. Embarrassment in the West, for example, is founded on fear plus an evaluation of the self as an unwanted object of others' attention. Lewis (1992) has shown that embarrassment and shame do not occur in development until after the emergence of the cognitive sense of self.

A striking example of the dependence of a complex emotion on cultural mores is provided by the case of jealousy, as described by Hupka (1991). Although in the West jealousy is an emotion that arouses fear and anger when an interloper trespasses upon an exclusive sexual re-

lationship, among the Todas of India this is not so. For the Todas, the self is not strongly dependent on sexual exclusivity. Recreational sex is common, and a man is not jealous of his wife's taking part in it within their social group. On the other hand, his sense of self is highly invested in his first son, and he does experience symptoms of jealousy if his second son gets married before the first one. As with embarrassment and shame, the complex emotion is based on something biological, but the form it takes and the circumstances in which it is elicited depend on constructions that are culturally specific.

Recent neurological evidence for the distinction between basic and complex emotions comes from the study of brain-damaged individuals. Damasio (1994) has argued that basic emotions (his term is "primary" emotions) depend on the amygdala, because damage to the amygdala impairs basic emotions in humans, monkeys, and rats. He also argues that damage to the ventromedial area of the human prefrontal lobes leads to an incapacity to feel complex emotions (his term for them is "secondary" emotions), and in consequence to a decline in the ability to make sensible decisions in daily life. Patients with damage to this area of the brain lose the capacity to feel complex emotions, and they are also unable to make plans, to choose courses of action, or to cope with everyday life. The classic case is that of Phineas Gage who, by mistake, in tamping down an explosive with a metal bar, set off a spark that fired the bar through his prefrontal lobes. He survived, but thereafter was unable to lead a normal life.

Damasio describes a similar modern case: "Elliot" was successful in business and a good husband and father until he developed a brain tumor. The surgeons removed it, but were forced to take out some tissue from the ventromedial part of his prefrontal cortices. On his recovery from surgery, his personality had undergone an astonishing change. He remained highly intelligent, but was unable to plan effectively even for a few hours ahead. He was dismissed from a series of jobs; he had several marriages and divorces; and he went bankrupt. In short, as Damasio (1994, p. 38) writes, "he could no longer be an effective social being." In most respects Elliot seemed normal, even passing memory tests that usually reflect damage to the prefrontal lobes. Like other such patients, he did have basic emotions—a propensity that yields an initial impression that these patients lead a normal emotional life. He would show fear, for example, if someone were to scream unexpectedly behind him. Damasio summarizes the relations between basic (primary) emotions and complex (secondary) emotions in the following terms: "The prefrontal, acquired dispositional representations needed for secondary emotions are a separate lot from the innate dispositional representations needed for primary emotions. But . . . the former need the latter in order to express themselves" (1994, p. 137).

The lack of complex emotions impairs the ability to cope with everyday problems. Damasio argues that emotions depend on "somatic markers" either of good outcomes to encourage you to persevere or of bad outcomes to warn you of impending danger. These markers, essentially "gut reactions," enable you to respond immediately without the need for rational analysis. Damasio writes: "There is still room for using a cost/benefit analysis and proper deductive competence, but only after the automated step drastically reduces the number of options" (1994, p. 173). Thus, unlike normal individuals, patients with prefrontal damage do not exhibit the standard galvanic skin response (GSR) to pictures of shocking scenes or other emotionally disturbing material. Most strikingly, they fail in decision-making tasks designed to mimic certain aspects of daily life.

In one study (Bechara, Damasio, Damasio, & Anderson, 1994), the participants were given $2,000 in dummy money at the start of a gambling game. They then turned over cards in one of four decks labeled A, B, C, and D. Cards in decks A and B usually yielded a reward of $100, but occasionally a big loss of up to $1,250. Cards in decks C and D usually yielded a reward of only $50, but occasionally a small loss of less than $100. Most normal individuals soon learned to turn only cards in decks C and D. The prefrontal patients, including Elliot, did not learn to switch to these two decks; in consequence, they went "bankrupt" in the game (as in life). One interesting manipulation was that if the regimen of the game was switched so that usually the player suffered small losses, and just occasionally (for decks A and B) there was a big win, then the performance of the prefrontal patients was indistinguishable from that of the control subjects. Hence the patients were sensitive to losses, but only in the short term. This conjecture was borne out by a replication in which the participants' GSRs were measured

during the game. The normal participants developed standard GSRs in anticipation of bad outcomes, but the prefrontal patients did not.

A corollary to Damasio's account is that emotions underlie the decisions of normal individuals, and that a plausible theory of human decision making should take emotions into account. Decision theorists have indeed been moving in this direction (Frank, 1988; Mellers, Schwartz, & Cooke, 1998). The outcomes of decisions have emotional effects that are independent of their expected utilities. You are more pleased by a surprising win than by an expected win; likewise, you are more disappointed by a surprising loss than by an expected loss (Mellers et al., 1998). When you make a choice, you can anticipate your emotional reactions to its outcomes, and use your anticipations to help you to make your choice—a hypothesis for which there is increasing evidence (e.g., Bar-Hillel & Neter, 1996; Mellers et al., 1998). Would you, for example, have your child vaccinated against whooping cough when there was a minute chance that the vaccination would have a fatal side effect? Many people refuse. They anticipate the regret of causing their children's death, even though the children are more at risk from dying from whooping cough (Baron, 1994). Likewise, when you consider what happened after a choice, your thinking, as we have seen, is often counterfactual: You compare what happened with what might have happened, and in this way you can ameliorate bad outcomes and amplify small gains (Bolles & Messick, 1995). You make a decision that subsequently you come to regret. Which is more regrettable—a choice that led to action, or one that led to failure to act? The evidence is unclear (cf. Gilovich & Medvec, 1995; Kahneman, 1995).

THE SOCIAL CONSTRUCTION OF EMOTIONS

Roughly speaking, "culture" is a system of concepts by which human beings communicate and develop their knowledge about attitudes toward life (Geertz, 1973, p. 89). It is passed from parents to children, and from one member of a society to another. Its effects on socializing emotions occur in three ways in a hierarchy of increasing importance. First, it determines what emotions will be expressed and what behaviors are acceptable as expressions of emotions. Second, it influences which situations lead to particular emotions. Third, it regulates the existence and experience of complex emotions. We examine each of these in turn.

Social Constraints and Prescriptions

The most superficial effects of culture are on which emotions are appropriate to express in a particular situation, and on the acceptable ways in which to express them. These prescriptions take effect from the process of socializing infants and children, and from explicit training regimens designed to shape emotions (Oatley & Jenkins, 1996). The prescriptions may reflect folk theories of emotion and mental health, as well as moral and religious systems. Thus, for many philosophies and religions, emotions as a whole are to be eschewed; Buddhists, the Stoics, and Gurdjieff and his followers have all inveighed against them. Other prescriptions have been aimed at particular emotions. All such constraints embody the belief that emotions can be modified by social practices—that emotions are constructions that depend on beliefs, and that are controllable by proper interpretations and correct thinking.

One of the most compelling results from this standpoint is that many forms of psychotherapy have successful outcomes. On average, both behavioral and psychoanalytically based therapies successfully decrease measures of anxiety (Smith, Glass, & Miller, 1980). For depression, which has flourished in 20th-century Western cultures, cognitive therapy is based on the Stoic principle of thinking "properly" about events liable to provoke depressive moods. It rests on the assumption that depressed individuals err in their reasoning—overgeneralizing, jumping to conclusions, and inferring that their depressed mood is a consequence of wrongdoing (see Beck, Rush, Shaw, & Emery, 1979). The therapy has effects that are as large as, and sometimes larger than, those of antidepressant drugs (Robinson, Berman, & Neimeyer, 1990).

Emotional behavior can also be shaped by teaching. Hochschild (1983) studied this process in the training of Delta Air Lines stewardesses. They were taught to give a kind of emotional performance, just as in the theater (cf. Sartre's [1943] censure of waiters guilty of bad faith in "performing" the role of waiters). The stewardesses had to project emotions of pleasurable welcome by using memories of instances of personal hospitality, as Stanislavski

recommended (Hochschild, 1983, p. 105). The aim was to induce a certain emotional tone in the passengers.

Work that calls for individuals to conjure up emotions in themselves in order to induce them in others is quite widespread. Hochschild discusses jobs at the interface between a company and the customers; debt collection, for instance, is a kind of inverse of being a flight attendant. "Create alarm" was the instruction of one debt-collecting company's boss (Hochschild, 1983, p. 146). Ellis (1991) discusses a person who worked as an erotic dancer in a strip bar, and who similarly was called on to play an emotional role. Over a third of all paid jobs in the United States in 1970 called for substantial amounts of emotional labor, and within these jobs, women were twice as numerous as men (Hochschild, 1983).

The creation of emotions at work serves social purposes—to sell more airline tickets, to persuade the customer, to provide pleasant support for a (usually male) boss. Such constructions need merely have behavioral verisimilitude. The individual's own feelings may not be socially constructed at all, but merely evoked by the situation, its threats, its contradictions, and its longueurs. The role is acted. It contrasts with the real social roles that we must all take on. Goffman (1961) argued that our very individuality and our emotions derive from a full engagement in these social roles—not just at work or in games, but as friends, as parents, as lovers. To foster a self apart from engagement in these roles is a maneuver that some people try; however, its effects are not to maintain individuality, but to be disengaged and alienated, suffering a sense of emptiness and pointlessness.

A subtler form of socialization is described by Briggs (1970) in her account of the 17 months she spent living with an Inuit family belonging to a group called the Utka (Utkuhikhalingmiut). These people cope with the vicissitudes of Arctic life with calm acceptance and humor. As adults they do not express anger, nor do they use anger in child rearing. According to Solomon (1984, p. 244), Briggs's account shows that the Utka "do not, as her title *Never in Anger* indicates, get angry. Not only do they not express anger; they do not 'feel' angry, and . . . they do not talk about it. They do not get angry in circumstances that would surely incite us to outrage, and they do not get angry in other circumstances either." Anger may be rare or nonexistent among adult Utka (1) because they do not interpret their many physical hardships as frustrations, and (2) because they do not see themselves as autonomously separate from other members of their community, and hence as thwarted or let down by others.

Granted that anger is a basic emotion, another interpretation of Utka society is possible. Stearns and Stearns (1985, p. 814) write that "Briggs described how the Utka Eskimo tribe disapproves of anger and seeks to suppress it through socialization. . . . But the study does not prove that the Utka are a people without anger. They regularly sulk when challenged (anger turned inward?), and . . . routinely beat and otherwise abuse dogs." Even Solomon (1984) mentions that Briggs herself describes them as getting "heated up," that is, they feel annoyed, even hostile, though they do not lose their tempers. It seems that anger occurs in the Utka as a basic emotion, but perhaps it underlies few if any complex emotions. The Utka do not get angry in arguments.

One much-cited explanation is in terms of what Ekman (1972) calls "display rules" that allow or disallow expression of emotions when an underlying affect program is activated. According to this idea, the Utka do become angry, but socially derived display rules forbid expression of their anger. The empirical basis of display rules, however, as Fridlund (1994) has pointed out, is a single study that was never published in full, and that is open to plausible alternative interpretations.

We prefer the explanation in terms of our (Oatley & Johnson-Laird, 1996) theory, described above in relation to how embarrassment is based on fear plus an evaluation of self. Not only do innate basic emotions have an inchoate quality, but when they occur in social life (as compared, for instance, with Darwin's reaction to a striking snake) they depend on how events are appraised within a society, and on individuals' habits of mind (consider Jack Nicholson's road rage). According to us, therefore, an emotion such as anger occurs when there is an evaluation of an event relevant to an important goal, or to the sense of self, of the person concerned. Where social goals in one culture differ from those of another, or where the constructions of certain kinds of events in one culture differ from those of another, then the emotions expected in one society do not occur in the other, or do not occur in the same ways.

Anger is managed in many societies. The Tahitians, according to Levy (1984), have cultural devices for dealing with it, though it is a rare occurrence. Unlike most peoples, the Philippine Ilongots can be paid for their anger, which then dissolves: they forget about it because they fear it will lead to violence (Rosaldo, 1984). In the West, according to Averill (1982), anger is a temporary social role that is entered in order to adjust social relationships. This pattern, Averill argues, is embodied in the law, which has operationalized certain rules about anger. In extreme cases of anger, one individual may kill another, but British and North American law—like Greek and Roman law—treats some homicides as more reprehensible than others. The key factor is the perpetrator's state of mind. When a killing is planned or occurs in the course of another crime, to kill is to murder. By contrast, to kill unintentionally is manslaughter. It includes killings that occur because the perpetrator is angry. But the defense of manslaughter can succeed only if the emotion conforms to societal rules: The provocation must have been sufficient to arouse an ordinary person to anger; the killing must have occurred as a result of the anger and in the "heat of passion," rather than "in cold blood"; and it must have been done within a limited time after the provocation, so that the anger did not have time to cool.

From diaries of cases of less extreme instances of anger, Averill determined that most episodes concerned a person whom the angry participant knew and liked, and that the most common motive (for 63% of incidents) was to assert authority or independence, or to improve the participant's self-image. Despite most people's finding the anger subjectively unpleasant, 62% of people who had become angry, and 70% of the targets of anger, rated the anger as ultimately beneficial. In the West, anger can accordingly serve a social purpose. It is potentially destructive, but it can function to readjust a long-term relationship. One person fails to fulfill an obligation or expectation, and so another becomes angry. The anger provokes the other person, and a quarrel occurs. The resolution of the episode often includes a change in the relationship, a better understanding between the two parties, and more realistic expectations about their mutual behaviors.

Culture and Cognitive Evaluations

A more profound influence of culture is on the cognitive evaluations leading to particular emotions. Once individuals have been socialized in this way, their reactions are difficult for them to control. For us, for instance, a baby crawling on all fours is charming. For the Balinese, however, it is animal-like and a matter of revulsion (Geertz, 1972/1973). Eating for the Balinese is also disgusting, and thus it is an activity—as in one of the director Luis Bunuel's telling movie fantasies—to be carried out in private. Disgust and aversions to food indeed constitute an excellent case of culturally determined emotional reactions. Disgust depends on an innate response of food avoidance (a clear evolutionary adaptation to potential toxicity), but many cognitions that now elicit it depend on culture. Rozin (1996) has demonstrated that disgust obeys the classical laws of "magical thinking": the law of contagion (bad things are conveyed by contact) and the law of similarity (like things produce like consequences). Brand-new and unused bottles for urine samples are "contagious" backward in time; people do not like to drink from them. A mixture of peanut butter and cheese in the shape of dog turds is cheerfully eaten by toddlers, to the horror of their parents. One man's meat is indeed another man's disgust. Darwin (1872/1965) recounted an incident when he was eating his lunch of preserved meat in Tierra del Fuego in front of a group of fascinated natives. One of them pushed his finger into the meat and was evidently disgusted by its moist softness. Darwin was equally disgusted, but for a different reason—someone had touched his food. What one culture eats, another shuns with disgust. Buddhists don't eat meat; Hindus don't eat beef; Jews and Muslims don't eat pork; and so on *ad vomitorium*.

Just as emotion-inducting cognitions are shaped by culture, so too are the conventional gestures that convey emotional attitudes, and the language for describing and expressing emotions. In North America, a common insulting gesture is to raise the middle finger with the back of the hand turned toward the person to be insulted. The gesture may be recognized elsewhere, but in England, the comparable gesture is to raise the forefinger and middle finger in a "V" shape and to wave them with the back of the hand turned toward the person to be insulted. Churchill, in his "Victory" sign, took pains to turn the front of his hand toward the spectators in order to avoid any chance of misinterpretation. If you make the "V" sign to a Londoner, he or she is likely to be incensed, whereas an inhabitant of San Francisco is more

likely to be puzzled. These simple differences have their more grandiloquent analogies in the differences between cultures in the modes of linguistic, artistic, and musical expression.

The variety of emotional vocabularies can be viewed by what Heelas (1986) calls a "Cook's Tour" of cultures. The Chewong, a small group of aboriginal Malaysians, seem to have just eight words for emotions; Howell (1981) writes, "They rarely use gestures of any kind, and their faces register little change as they speak" (pp. 134–135). By contrast, in the West, lack of emotional expression during speech would be socially awkward. We have found nearly 600 words in English for referring to emotions (Johnson-Laird & Oatley, 1989). There may be an analogy with color terminology, which similarly varies from one culture to another (Berlin & Kay, 1969), and yet all normal members of these cultures are able to see and to discriminate the basic colors. We surmise that they are also all able to experience the basic and object-oriented emotions. Just as color terminology may reflect the relative importance of distinctions in color, so too emotional vocabularies may reflect their relative importance. Heelas (1986) argues that in some societies certain kinds of emotion are much discussed, with fine distinctions drawn among them. They act as centers around which significant cultural institutions revolve. Following Levy (1984), he describes these emotions as "hypercognized." In the West, love and guilt are examples. In other societies, other emotions are hypercognized—for example, fear and shyness among the Chewong, and gentleness among the Tasaday (Nance, 1975). There may also be a corresponding lack of discourse about certain emotions, which can be described as "hypocognized." Depression, for instance, is commonly discussed in the West, but is not well represented in non-Western experience or vocabularies (Marsella, 1980).

Culture and Complex Emotions

Complex emotions, as we have argued, depend on conscious evaluations. They are regulated by social norms, and so their experience depends on social constructions. They also depend on underlying basic and object-oriented emotions. An example of the determining role of culture is in the life of the Ik, a mountain people in Africa who had been banned from hunting, part of their ancestral way of life. Turnbull (1972) described how they came to live on the brink of starvation, and how they scavenged and competed for food. The effects over three generations were a progressive dehumanization, the breakdown of social and familial relations in selfish competition, and the loss of much of emotional life, with the exception of *Schadenfreude* when other people made mistakes. Turnbull's description is compatible with the maintenance of basic emotions. Complex emotions, such as love, remorse, and sorrow, however, seemed absent from the life of the Ik.

Certain complex emotions are specific to particular cultures. The Tahitians experience an "uncanny" emotion when they sense a ghost, which, according to Levy (1984), is felt and interpreted as something different from fear. The Javanese experience *sungkan*, a feeling of respectful politeness and restraint before superiors or unfamiliar people (Geertz, 1959). The Japanese have *amae*, a feeling of passive love, helplessness, and merging with the other (Morsbach & Tyler, 1986). The Gururumba, who live in the highlands of New Guinea, refer to a certain emotional episode as "being a wild pig" (Averill, 1980), by analogy to the occasional misbehavior of their domesticated pigs. In this state of mind, people become violently aggressive, engage in petty thieving, and run off into the forest. They rarely do real damage and usually return to normal village life, apparently with no memory for the episode, which is never referred to again by anyone. It occurs when a person becomes socially bankrupt as a result of too many obligations. The Gururumba attribute this loss of social control to a bite from the ghost of a recently dead person.

These snapshots fail to do justice to other cultures. What is needed is a "thick description," to use Geertz's (1973) term for a rich account of how a culture works. One person who has succeeded in formulating such a description is Lutz (1988), who has written about emotional life on Ifaluk, a tiny Micronesian atoll. What she has done is not to become an Ifaluk person, which is impossible for an adult North American, but to pay careful attention to her own socialization into Ifaluk society and to the occasions when her North American assumptions and those of the Ifaluk people did not mesh. Such occasions are the culture shocks of ordinary tourists. They can give rise to embarrassment or worse, but they can also be invaluable pointers to tacit assumptions of both the host culture and that of the guest. Lutz describes, for instance, how she smiled as she watched a 5-year-old girl dance and make silly faces. A woman sitting with Lutz said, "Don't smile at her—she'll think you are not *song* [justifiably angry]" (p. 167). To show off and be *ker* (happy/excited), as the little girl was being, is to be too pleased with oneself and not to attend to the concerns of others. It calls for social disapproval by a display of *song*, which is not anger in a Western individualistic sense, but disapproval, which one is obliged to display if a social rule is broken. For the Ifaluk, children of 6 are socially intelligent. They should be able to behave with respect for the feelings of others— mutual concern is the prevailing tone of Ifaluk society. Happiness is not valued as in North America, but disapproved of because it can cause one to disregard others. The woman was explaining to Lutz that the girl was becoming old enough to understand such matters.

On Ifaluk, as in the West, people are interested in emotions, but they regard them as aspects of relationships rather than as signs of individuality. Many salient emotions on Ifaluk are made from parts that can be described in English. Thus Lutz translates the Ifaluk *ker* as "happiness/excitement," and *fago* as "compassion/ love/sadness." *Fago* is a complex emotion, akin to love, but it refers to the idea that everyone with whom one is close should be together, that anyone in need should be helped, and that the absence of a loved one is a cause of sadness. Absence is likely to cause a person to feel in need because of being away from loved ones, and it is likely to give rise to this somewhat sad and affectionate emotion.

CONCLUSIONS

When Jack Nicholson lost his temper and attacked a fellow driver's Mercedes, his emotion had an innate basis. The capacity for anger is innate and is by no means unique to human beings. What differ from one culture to another, and from one individual to another within a culture, are the occasions that provoke anger. Not everyone succumbs to "road rage"; it occurs only in certain automobile-centered cultures, and only to some people within them. Other emotions, however, may be common to all societies: The death of a person to whom one is attached, for example, elicits sadness universally. But social and cultural norms influence the expression of the emotion, the methods of mourn-

ing, and its associated rituals. More importantly, they also create some situations that stimulate an emotion in the first place. The hypothesis that emotions are social constructions has
been defended in various guises—as a redress
to an overemphasis on biological or evolutionary underpinnings to emotion, or as a full-
fledged theory of emotion (e.g., Averill, 1982;
Hochschild, 1983). It offers views below the
surface of our emotional interactions; suggests
purposes for emotions that biological accounts
might overlook; shows that emotions are not
just feelings of isolated individuals, but part of
the substance of social interactions; and offers
answers to the persistently fascinating question
of which emotions are appropriate to which circumstances.

To those who suppose that emotion is nothing but innate reactions, we say this: Consider
the cultural variety in the causes of emotions
and the variety of complex emotions from one
society to another. And to those who suppose
that emotion is nothing but social construction,
we say this: Consider the existence of emotions
in social mammals, the universality of certain
modes of emotional responses, and the known
neurophysiology of emotional responses. The
case for at least some innate component in
emotions is overwhelming. There is probably a
core of basic and object-oriented emotions
common to humanity. Something is "there" in
an emotion, over and above talk and social
practices—something that transcends culture,
that precedes language, and that is not infinite-
ly malleable. At the same time, basic emotions
are inchoate; by adulthood they have been giv-
en substance and expression by culture.

From Darwin's image of recoiling from a
striking snake with his "will and reason powerless . . ." we easily summon up the idea of a natural emotion of fear operating now in modern
humans, as it has done for millions of years in
our animal ancestors. Equally, we see the role
of social construction in the story of Floyd
Johnson and Ellen Skinner. Two young people
in North American culture meet by chance, fall
in love, and elope. In our view, emotions are
like natural language. There is an innate basis
for language in human beings, but each language has its own vocabulary and syntax. Com-
parably, there is an innate basis for emotions in
human beings, but each culture has its own cognitive evaluations that call forth emotions and
its own complex emotions that mesh with its
social practices.

REFERENCES

Alloy, L. B., & Abramson, L. Y. (1979). Judgement of
contingency in depressed and non-depressed students: Sadder but wiser? *Journal of Experimental
Psychology, 108*, 441–485.

Alloy, L. B., & Abramson, L. Y. (1988). Depressive realism: Four theoretical perspectives. In L. B. Alloy
(Ed.) *Cognitive processes in depression* (pp.
223–265). New York: Guilford Press.

Armon-Jones, C. (1986). The thesis of constructionism.
In R. Harré (Ed.), *The social construction of emotions*
(pp. 32–56). Oxford: Blackwell.

Averill, J. R. (1980) Emotion and anxiety: Sociocultur-
al, biological, and psychological determinants. In A.
O. Rorty (Ed.), *Explaining emotions* (pp. 37–72).
Berkeley: University of California Press.

Averill, J. R. (1982). *Anger and aggression. An essay on
emotion.* New York: Springer.

Averill, J. R. (1985). The social construction of emotion: With special reference to love. In K. J. Gergen &
K. E. Davis (Eds.), *The social construction of the person* (pp. 89–109). New York: Springer-Verlag.

Bargh, J. A. (1992). Does subliminality matter to social
psychology?: Awareness of the stimulus versus
awareness of its influence. In R. F. Bornstein & T. S.
Pittman (Eds.) *Perception without awareness: Cognitive, clinical, and social perspectives* (pp. 236–255).
New York: Guilford Press.

Bar-Hillel, M., & Neter, E. (1996). Why are people reluctant to exchange lottery tickets? *Journal of Personality and Social Psychology, 70*, 17–27.

Baron, J. (1994). Nonconsequentialist decisions. *Behavioral and Brain Sciences, 17*, 1–42.

Bechara, A., Damasio, A. R., Damasio, H., & Anderson,
S. (1994). Insensitivity to future consequences following damage to human prefrontal cortex. *Cognition, 50*, 7–12.

Beck, A. T., Rush, A. J., Shaw, B. F., & Emery, G.
(1979) *Cognitive therapy of depression.* New York:
Guilford Press.

Berlin, B., & Kay, P. (1969). *Basic color terms: Their
universality and evolution.* Berkeley: University of
California Press.

Bolles, T. L., & Messick, D. M. (1995). A reverse outcome bias: The influence of multiple reference points
on the evaluation of outcomes and decisions. *Organizational Behavior and Human Decision Processes,
61*, 262–275.

Bontempo, R. N., Bottom, W. P., & Weber, E. U. (1997).
Cross-cultural differences in risk perception: a mod-
el-based approach. *Risk Analysis, 17*, 479–488.

Bowlby, J. (1988). *A secure base: Clinical applications
of attachment theory.* London: Routledge.

Briggs, J. L. (1970). *Never in anger: Portrait of an Eskimo family.* Cambridge, MA: Harvard University
Press.

Broadbent, D. E., & Broadbent, M. (1988). Anxiety and
attentional bias: State and trait. *Cognition and Emotion, 2*, 165–183.

Burgess, E. W., & Wallin, P. (1953). *Engagement and
marriage.* Philadelphia: Lippincott.

Byrne, R. M. J. (1997). Cognitive processes in counterfactual thinking about what might have been. In D. L. Medin (Ed.), *The psychology of learning and motivation* (Vol. 37, pp. 105–154). San Diego, CA: Academic Press.

Carver, C. S., & Scheier, M. F. (1990). Origins and functions of positive and negative affect: A control process view. *Psychological Review, 97,* 19–35.

Cosmides, L. (1989). The logic of social exchange: Has natural selection shaped how humans reason? Studies with the Wason selection task. *Cognition, 31,* 187–276.

Damasio, A. R. (1994). *Descartes' error: Emotion, reason, and the human brain.* New York: Putnam.

Darwin, C. (1965). *The expression of the emotions in man and animals.* Chicago: University of Chicago Press. (Original work published 1872)

Ekman, P. (1972). Universals and cultural differences in facial expressions of emotion. In J. Cole (Ed.), *Nebraska Symposium on Motivation* (Vol. 19, pp. 207–283). Lincoln: University of Nebraska Press.

Ekman, P. (1992). An argument for basic emotions. *Cognition and Emotion, 6,* 169–200.

Ellis, A. (1994). *Reason and emotion in psychotherapy.* New York: Birch Lane Press.

Ellis, C. (1991). Emotional sociology. In N. Denzin (Ed.), *Studies in social interaction* (pp. 123–145). Greenwich, CT: JAI Press.

Ellis, H. C., & Ashbrook, P. W. (1988). Resource allocation model of the effects of depressed mood states. In K. Fiedler & J. Forgas (Eds.), *Affect, cognition and social behaviour.* Toronto: Hogrefe.

Evans, J. St. B. T, Newstead, S. E., & Byrne, R. M. J. (1993). *Human reasoning: The psychology of deduction.* Hillsdale, NJ: Erlbaum.

Evans, J. St. B. T., & Over, D. E. (1996). *Rationality and reasoning.* Hove, England: Psychology Press.

Finck, H. T. (1887). *Romantic love and personal beauty.* London: Macmillan.

Frank, R. H. (1988). *Passions within reason: The strategic role of the emotions.* New York: Norton.

Fridlund, A. J. (1994). *Human facial expression: An evolutionary view.* San Diego: Academic Press.

Frijda, N. H. (1986). *The emotions.* Cambridge, England: Cambridge University Press.

Geertz, C. (1973) Deep play: Notes on the Balinese cockfight. In C. Geertz, *The interpretation of cultures: Selected essays* (pp. 412–453). New York: Basic Books. (Original work published 1972)

Geertz, C. (1973). *The interpretation of cultures: Selected essays.* New York: Basic Books.

Geertz, C. (1980). *Negara: The theatre state in nineteenth-century Bali.* Princeton, NJ: Princeton University Press.

Geertz, H. (1959). The vocabulary of emotion. *Psychiatry, 22,* 225–237.

Gilovich, T., & Medvec, V. H. (1995). The experience of regret: What, why, and when. *Psychological Review, 102,* 379–395.

Girotto, V., Legrenzi, P., & Rizzo, A. (1991). Event controllability in counterfactual thinking. *Acta Psychologica, 78,* 111–133.

Goffman, E. (1961). *Encounters: Two studies in the sociology of interaction.* Indianapolis, IN: Bobbs-Merrill.

Hacking, I. (1975). *The emergence of probability.* Cambridge, England: Cambridge University Press.

Harré, R. (1986). The social constructionist viewpoint. In R. Harré (Ed.), *The social construction of emotions* (pp. 2–14). Oxford: Blackwell.

Heelas, P. (1986). Emotion talk across cultures. In R. Harré (Ed.), *The social construction of emotions* (pp. 234–266). Oxford: Blackwell.

Hochschild, A. R. (1983). *The managed heart: Commercialization of human feeling.* Berkeley: University of California Press.

Howell, S. (1981). Rules not words. In P. Heelas & A. Lock (Eds.), *Indigenous psychologies: The anthropology of the self* (pp. 133–143). London: Academic Press.

Humphrey, N. (1984). *Consciousness regained.* Cambridge, England: Cambridge University Press.

Hupka, R. B. (1991). The motive for the arousal of romantic jealousy: Its cultural origin. In P. Salovey (Ed.) *The psychology of jealousy and envy* (pp. 252–270). New York: Guilford Press.

Isen, A. M., Daubman, K. A., & Nowicki, G. P. (1987) Positive affect facilitates creative problem solving. *Journal of Personality and Social Psychology, 52,* 1122–1131.

Johnson, E. J., & Tversky, A. (1983). Affect, generalization, and the perception of risk. *Journal of Personality and Social Psychology, 45,* 20–31.

Johnson-Laird, P. N. (1999). Deductive reasoning. *Annual Review of Psychology, 50,* 109–135.

Johnson-Laird, P. N., & Oatley, K. (1989). The language of emotions: An analysis of a semantic field. *Cognition and Emotion, 3,* 81–123.

Kahneman, D. (1995). Varieties of counterfactual thinking. In N. J. Roese & J. M. Olson (Eds.), *What might have been: The social psychology of counterfactual thinking* (pp. 375–396). Hillsdale, NJ: Erlbaum.

Kahneman, D., & Tversky, A. (1979). Prospect theory: An analysis of decision under risk. *Econometrica, 47,* 263–291.

Kahneman, D., & Tversky, A. (1982). The simulation heuristic. In D. Kahneman, P. Slovic, & A. Tversky (Eds.), *Judgment under uncertainty: Heuristics and biases* (pp. 201–208). New York: Cambridge University Press.

Landman, J. (1993). *Regret: The persistence of the possible.* New York: Oxford University Press.

Lazarus, R. S. (1982). Thoughts on the relationship between emotion and cognition. *American Psychologist, 37,* 1019–1024.

Leach, E. (1981, April 4). A poetics of power [Review of C. Geertz's *Negara*]. *New Republic,* p. 14.

LeDoux, J. (1996). *The emotional brain: The mysterious underpinnings of emotional life.* New York: Simon & Schuster.

Legrenzi, P. (1998). *La felicità.* Bologna, Italy: Il Mulino.

Levy, R. I. (1984) Emotion, knowing, and culture. In R. A. Shweder & R. A. LeVine (Eds.), *Culture theory: Essays on mind, self, and emotion* (pp. 214–237). Cambridge, England: Cambridge University Press.

Lewis, M. (1992). *Shame: The exposed self.* New York: Free Press.

Lindzey, G. (1954). *Psychology.* Cleveland, OH: Worth.

Lutz, C. A. (1988). *Unnatural emotions: Everyday sentiments on a Micronesian atoll and their challenge to Western theory.* Chicago: University of Chicago Press.

Markus, H. R., & Kitayama, S. (1991). Culture and the self: Implications for cognition, emotion and motivation. *Psychological Review, 98,* 224–253.

Marsella, A. J. (1980). Depressive disorder and experience across cultures. In H. C. Triandis & J. Draguns (Eds.), *Handbook of cross-cultural psychology* (Vol. 6, pp. 237–289). Boston: Allyn & Bacon.

Martin, L. L., & Tesser, A. (1996). Ruminative thoughts. In R. S. Wyer, Jr. (Ed.), *Advances in social cognition* (Vol. 9, pp. 1–47). Hillsdale, NJ: Erlbaum.

Mathews, A., Mackintosh, B., & Fulcher, E. P. (1997). Cognitive biases in anxiety and attention to threat. *Trends in Cognitive Science, 1,* 340–345.

Mellers, B. A., Schwartz, A., & Cooke, A. D. J. (1998). Judgment and decision making. *Annual Review of Psychology, 49,* 447–477.

Miller, G. A., & Johnson-Laird, P. N. (1976). *Language and perception.* Cambridge, MA: Harvard University Press.

Minsky, M. (1985). *The society of mind.* New York: Simon & Schuster.

Mithen, S. (1996). *The prehistory of the mind: The cognitive origins of art, religion and science.* London: Thames & Hudson.

Mizell, L. (1997). *Aggressive driving: Three studies.* Washington, DC: AAA Foundation for Traffic Safety.

Morsbach, H., & Tyler, W. J. (1986) A Japanese emotion: Amae. In R. Harré (Ed.), *The social construction of emotions* (pp. 289–307). Oxford: Blackwell.

Nance, J. (1975). *The gentle Tasaday.* New York: Harcourt Brace Jovanovich.

Nesse, R. M. (1991, November–December). What good is feeling bad? *The Sciences,* pp. 30–37.

Oaksford, M., Morris, F., Grainger, B., & Williams, J. M. G. (1995). *Mood, reasoning and central executive processes.* Unpublished manuscript, Department of Psychology, University of Warwick, Warwick, England.

Oatley, K. (1996). Emotions, rationality, and informal reasoning. In J. Oakhill & A. Garnham (Eds.) *Mental models in cognitive science* (pp. 175–196). Hove, England: Psychology Press.

Oatley, K., & Jenkins, J. M. (1996). *Understanding emotions.* Oxford: Blackwell.

Oatley, K., & Johnson-Laird, P. N. (1987). Towards a cognitive theory of emotions. *Cognition and Emotion, 1,* 29–50.

Oatley, K., & Johnson-Laird, P. N. (1996). The communicative theory of emotions: Empirical tests, mental models, and implications for social interaction. In L. L. Martin & A. Tesser (Eds.), *Striving and feeling: Interactions among goals, affect, and self-regulation* (pp. 363–393). Hillsdale, NJ: Erlbaum.

Ortony, A., Clore, G. L., & Collins, A. (1988). *The cognitive structure of emotions.* New York: Cambridge University Press.

Ortony, A., & Turner, T. J. (1990). What's basic about basic emotions? *Psychological Review, 74,* 431–461.

Pinker, S. (1997). *How the mind thinks.* New York: Norton.

Power, M., & Dalgleish, T. (1997). *Cognition and emotion: From order to disorder.* Hove, England: Psychology Press.

Power, M., & Wykes, T. (1996) The mental health of mental models and the mental models of mental health. In J. Oakhill & A. Garnham (Eds.), *Mental models in cognitive science* (pp. 197–222). Hove, England: Psychology Press.

Reason, J. T. (1988). Stress and cognitive failure. In S. Fisher & J. T. Reason (Eds.), *Handbook of life stress, cognition and health.* Chichester, England: Wiley.

Robinson, L. A., Berman, J. S., & Neimeyer, R. A. (1990). Psychotherapy for the treatment of depression: A comprehensive review of controlled outcome studies. *Psychological Bulletin, 108,* 30–49.

Roese, N. J. (1997). Counterfactual thinking. *Psychological Bulletin, 121,* 133–148.

Rosaldo, M. Z. (1984). Toward an anthropology of self and feeling. In R. A. Shweder & R. A. LeVine (Eds.), *Culture theory: Essays on mind, self, and emotion* (pp. 137–157). Cambridge, England: Cambridge University Press.

Rozin, P. (1996). Towards a psychology of food and eating: From motivation to module to model to marker, morality, meaning, and metaphor. *Current Directions in Psychological Science, 5,* 18–24.

Russell, J. A. (1991). In defense of a prototype approach to emotion concepts. *Journal of Personality and Social Psychology, 60,* 37–47.

Sartre, J.-P. (1943). *Being and nothingness.* New York: Philosophical Library.

Shweder, R. A. (1991). *Thinking through cultures: Expeditions in cultural psychology.* Cambridge, MA: Harvard University Press.

Simon, H. A. (1982). *Models of bounded rationality* (2 vols.). Cambridge, MA: MIT Press.

Simon, H. A. (1991). Cognitive architectures and rational analysis: Comment. In K. VanLehn (Ed.), *Architectures for intelligence: The 22nd Carnegie-Mellon Symposium on Cognition.* Hillsdale, NJ: Erlbaum.

Sloman, S. A. (1996). The empirical case for two systems of reasoning. *Psychological Bulletin, 119,* 3–22.

Smith, M. L., Glass, G. V., & Miller, T. I. (1980). *The benefits of psychotherapy.* Baltimore: Johns Hopkins University Press.

Solomon, R. C. (1984). Getting angry: The Jamesian theory of emotion in anthropology. In R. A. Shweder & R. A. LeVine (Eds.), *Culture theory: Essays on mind, self, and emotion* (pp. 238–254). Cambridge, England: Cambridge University Press.

Stearns, P. N., & Stearns, C. Z. (1985). Emotionology: Clarifying the history of emotions and emotional standards. *American Historical Review, 90,* 813–886.

Stein, N. L., Trabasso, T., & Liwag, M. (1993). The representation and organization of emotional experience: Unfolding the emotion episode. In M. Lewis & J. M. Haviland (Eds.), *Handbook of emotions* (pp. 279–300). New York: Guilford Press.

Teasdale, J. D. (1988). Cognitive vulnerability to persistent depression. *Cognition and Emotion, 2,* 247–274.

Tooby, J., & Cosmides, L. (1990). The past explains the present: Emotional adaptations and the structure of ancestral environments. *Ethology and Sociobiology, 11,* 375–424.

Tranel, D. (1997). Emotional processing and the human amygdala. *Trends in Cognitive Science, 1,* 46–47.

Turnbull, C. M. (1972). *The mountain people.* New York: Simon & Schuster.

Wright, G. N., & Phillips, L. D. (1980). Cultural variation in probabilistic thinking: Alternative ways of dealing with uncertainty. *International Journal of Psychology, 15,* 239–257.

Zajonc, R. B. (1980). Feeling and thinking: Preferences need no inferences. *American Psychologist, 35,* 151–175.

CHAPTER 30

Emotion and Memory

W. Gerrod Parrott
Matthew P. Spackman

Just as moods and emotions modify behavior and expression, so too do they modify thinking. Of the many types of thinking that may be modified, long-term memory has probably received the most attention. Memory is important not only as a phenomenon in itself, but also as a component of virtually all thinking: Perception, social judgment, and problem solving all rely on the recall of stored information. Many tasks that might appear largely independent of memory, such as reports of life satisfaction or perceptions of self-esteem, may in fact be performed via memory-based strategies, such as the availability heuristic. Thus, if moods and emotions bias memory, they also bias the recall of stored information more generally and thereby affect an enormous variety of mental operations.

Moods and emotions are known to affect memory in a number of ways. This chapter provides an overview of the known effects and of the most important explanations of them. The explanations traditionally offered by cognitive psychologists have been associational and mechanistic, but such explanations are presently being supplemented or supplanted by motivational and contextual theories. In this chapter we argue in support of these trends, focusing on a recently discovered phenomenon known as "mood-incongruent recall" and its implications for the theory of emotion and memory. This phenomenon is but one of many effects of emo-

tion on memory, and it is not necessarily the most frequent or representative; yet we believe that its existence forcefully demonstrates why motivational and contextual theories are necessary to explain the effect of emotion on memory. Contemporary theories of emotion and memory tend to be too mechanical and static, and at the end of this chapter we outline ways in which theory can better account for the important effects of meaning, of context, and of motivation.

Before beginning, we must point out that several definitions of "emotion" are found in the literature on emotion and memory. Some researchers conceive of emotion in an undifferentiated manner, investigating the effects of overall arousal, excitement, agitation, or drive without distinguishing among different types of emotional states. Others treat emotional states as varying along two or more continuous dimensions, such as arousal and valence. The third and most common approach to emotional states treats them as discrete categories, distinguishing sad, irritable, anxious, and cheerful moods and contrasting their effects on memory. Although these differences in definition are not crucial for all purposes, they are for some, so we note them in our review.

A distinction between moods and emotions has not been made consistently in any of these traditions. The term "mood" usually seems the most apt to us, given our emphasis on how emotional states alter cognition unrelated to the original object of the emotion (see Frijda, Chapter 5, this volume). We use the terms "emotional state" and "mood" interchangeably to refer to these states, and use the terms "emotional material" and "emotional content" to refer to thoughts and memories that have a non-neutral emotional tone.

AN OVERVIEW OF THE BASIC PHENOMENA

The focus of this chapter is on the ways in which emotional states and content influence the formation, recollection, and forgetting of long-term memories. It should be noted that research has also addressed the related topics of the mental representation and organization of material stored in long-term memory, and, increasingly, the neuropsychology of memory. These topics also relate to emotion and memory, but are covered elsewhere in this volume (see Stein, Trabasso, & Liwag, Chapter 28; Russell & Lemay, Chapter 31; LeDoux & Phelps, Chapter 10, this volume). Even when we limit our subject matter to emotion's effects on memory formation and recollection, the number of ways in which emotions might affect memory is quite large. One of the more valuable services a good overview can provide, therefore, is a tractable scheme with which to think about these effects. We hope to set out such a scheme below.

The Emotion-and-Memory Triangle

The field of emotion and memory can be thought of as addressing two fundamental ways in which emotion can be a factor in memory: Emotion can be a characteristic of the material that is remembered, and it can be a characteristic of the psychological state of the remember-er. In the case of emotional material, emotion is ascribed to the information that is held in memory; for example, it may be that a word has favorable connotations or that a life experience was painful. In the case of emotional psychological states, a careful distinction must be made between two times when emotional states may affect memory: when memories are being formed (known as "encoding") and when memories are being recalled (known as "retrieval"). (A third time—the intermediate peri-

od between encoding and retrieval, known as "storage"—has been studied more from the point of view of mental representation than from that of recall and forgetting.) In summary, there are three principal ways in which emotion can affect memory: by being a quality of the material being remembered, by being a quality of a person's mental state when encoding information, and by being a quality of a person's mental state when recalling information. These three do not exhaust the ways in which emotion and memory may be related (e.g., one might investigate how remembering emotional episodes thereupon changes the emotional state of the rememberer), but they do sum up the ways in which emotion bears upon memory itself.

At the risk of stating the obvious, these three aspects of memory—content, encoding, and re-call—must all be present in any act of remembering. One could not, for example, study recall without there having been prior encoding or without there being content to be recalled. Therefore, if research were to study the effect of emotion on only one of these aspects of memory, it would have to vary emotion in that aspect while "holding emotion constant" in some sense for the other two aspects of memory. Numerous methodological and conceptual issues arise with the manipulation or selection of emotional states and with the notions of "holding emotion constant" or of inducing a "neutral mood." These issues are addressed in most treatments of research methods in cognition and emotion (e.g., Parrott & Hertel, 1999).

The relations among these three potentially emotional aspects of memory are depicted pictorially in Figure 30.1, where the three aspects appear as the corners of a triangle. The entire triangle should be thought of as being present in any instance of recall, even if some or all of the corners signify the absence of emotion for that aspect of memory.

Some research has indeed addressed these aspects in isolation. For example, research on memory content suggests that emotional stimuli tend to be better remembered than unemotional stimuli, be they events, pictures, or words (see reviews by Rapaport, 1950; Revelle & Loftus, 1990). Research on emotion at the time of encoding has shown that intense emotion improves memory for central details while undermining memory for background details, probably because emotion biases attention and

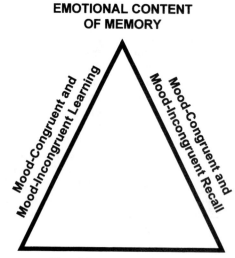

FIGURE 30.1. The emotion-and-memory triangle. The corners represent the three principal ways that emotion can influence memory. The sides represent the three pairwise interactions between these aspects of memory, and constitute the main topics of research on emotion and memory.

subsequent rehearsal (Heuer & Reisberg, 1992).

Yet research addressing only a single corner of the emotion-and-memory triangle does not characterize most of the research that has been conducted. Because the effects of emotion on one of these aspects often interact in important ways with the effects of emotion on another, it has proven useful to investigate the pairwise interactions between these three aspects of memory. These interactions have been the topics of much research, and they are represented as the sides of the triangle presented in Figure 30.1.

At the time of encoding, the emotional state of the person forming a memory may interact with the emotional content of the material being encoded to determine how well the material is learned; this interaction provides a more complete account of the effect of emotion on learning than does either aspect alone. Its effects, independent of any emotional state existing during retrieval, are known as "mood-congruent learning" when material with emotional content matching the learner's emotional state is learned better than material with contrasting emotional content, and as "mood-incongruent learning" when the reverse occurs.

As our triangular figure makes clear, at the

time of retrieval there are two distinguishable effects. The first of these involves the interaction between the emotional state existing at the time of encoding and the emotional state existing at the time of retrieval. The effects of this interaction, independent of any emotional content of the memory itself, are known as "mood-dependent recall." The second effect present at the time of retrieval involves the interaction between the emotional state existing at retrieval and the emotional content of the memories that are recalled. The effects of this interaction, independent of any emotional state existing during encoding, are known as "mood-congruent recall" when memories with emotional content matching the rememberer's mood are better recalled, and as "mood-incongruent recall" when memories with emotional content contrasting with the rememberer's mood are better recalled. Each of these three effects has been the topic of considerable empirical research, and we now address each in turn.

Mood and Learning

In research on mood and learning, research participants are typically induced into one of several moods and then exposed to material that is itself expressive of various moods. At a later time, in a neutral mood, the participants are tested for their memory of the material. In a classic example of such research, Bower, Gilligan, and Monteiro (1981) studied memory for a brief story about two college students, one doing well and the other doing poorly. Prior to reading the story, participants in the experiment were hypnotized to feel either happy or sad. A memory test given the next day when participants were in neutral moods showed that participants remembered more facts about the character whose mood agreed with their own than they did about the other character. This result demonstrates "mood-congruent learning." Subsequent research has generally found support for mood-congruent learning, although its occurrence has been found to depend on factors such as whether the material being learned is thought of as referring to the self (Nasby, 1994).

A more dramatic qualification has been found to be based on the intensity of emotional content of the material being learned. Rinck, Glowalla, and Schneider (1992) induced a happy or sad mood in participants who were then asked to rate the emotional valence of words. Mood-congruent learning occurred for words having intensely positive or negative valence, but mood-incongruent learning occurred for words having only mildly positive or negative valence. Rinck et al. produced persuasive evidence that the task of rating words for their emotional valence played a role in this result. This task is simple for words having intense valence, but is more difficult for words having only a mild valence, because it is necessary to spend more time thinking about their meanings. Such extra thought is, of course, well known to lead to richer encoding and superior subsequent retrieval. Mood-incongruent learning has also been observed in schoolchildren (Forgas, Burnham, & Trimboli, 1988), and under certain conditions can result in subsequent mood-incongruent recall (Clark, Teasdale, Broadbent, & Martin, 1983).

Mood-Dependent Recall

One way that mood at the time of retrieval can influence memory is by being similar to, or different from, the mood that was present at the time of encoding (regardless of the emotional content of the memory). In everyday life it is somewhat difficult for pure mood-dependent recall to occur, because it is so common for the emotional tone of an event to be related to the emotional state present at time of encoding. For example, at the time one is encoding one's memory for winning the lottery, it is likely that there is a happy emotional state as well as happy emotional content. For this reason, research on mood-dependent recall must ensure non-emotionality of memory content, in addition to manipulating emotional state during encoding and retrieval.

Despite all the experimental control employed in carrying out such research, mood-dependent recall is notorious for being the most unreliable of the emotion-and-memory phenomena. The literature is replete with accounts of failures to find any effect or to replicate effects that were once found (Bower & Mayer, 1991). Nevertheless, meta-analysis suggests that congruence between moods at encoding and retrieval does improve memory independently of memory content (Ucros, 1989). Furthermore, recent research suggests a number of factors that improve the chances of observing mood-dependent memory. Memory for internally generated events, such as reasoning or imagined events, seems more sensitive to mood-dependent influence than does memory for external events (Beck & McBee, 1995; Eich & Metcalfe, 1989). Strong, stable moods also appear to enhance the effect (Eich, 1995b). Thus, mood-dependent recall appears to be a real phenomenon, but one that occurs only under certain conditions.

Mood-Congruent and Mood-Incongruent Recall

The emotional state present at the time of retrieval can also interact with emotion via the emotional content of the material remembered. Mood-congruent recall has been reported in dozens of articles (Blaney, 1986; Singer & Salovey, 1988; Matt, Vazquez, & Campbell, 1992). To cite a classic example, Snyder and White (1982) induced happy or sad moods in participants by asking them to imagine a series of very happy or very sad feelings and thoughts. Participants were then asked to recall autobiographical memories from the previous week of their lives. Mood-congruent recall was obtained: Happy participants recalled more happy memories than did sad participants, and sad participants recalled more sad memories than did happy participants. Because autobiographical memories were retrieved, there is no guarantee that it was not the mood state present at time of encoding rather than the emotional content of the memories that produced the effect. That is, the data do not rule out the possibility that mood-dependent recall rather than mood-congruent recall occurred. Most researchers, however, believe that this alternative interpretation is unlikely. Mood-dependent recall appears to occur only in certain contexts, whereas mood-congruent recall occurs under a much wider range of contexts (Blaney, 1986). Furthermore, although mood-congruent recall has most commonly been obtained with autobiographical memories, other types of memory tasks that are much less likely to generate congruent moods at time of encoding have also yielded the effect (e.g., pleasant and unpleasant personality trait words; Clark & Teasdale, 1985). Thus there seems to be evidence that mood-congruent recall occurs independently of mood-dependent recall, and that mood-congruent recall is the more robust of the two effects.

As research on mood-congruent recall progressed, however, it became clear that accounting for this effect would not be a simple task. It has been widely observed that there is some tendency for mood-congruent recall to be more reliably observed with happy moods than with sad moods (Blaney, 1986; Isen, 1987; Singer & Salovey, 1988). The effect appears even more difficult to detect with anxious moods (Mathews & MacLeod, 1994).

There have been reports of mood-incongruent recall as well. In one series of four experiments, mood-incongruent recall was consistently obtained on the first autobiographical memory recalled (Parrott & Sabini, 1990). The nature of the mood induction influenced whether recall was incongruent to emotional state: Incongruent recall was obtained when natural moods were studied outside the laboratory (induced by receiving a grade on an examination in one experiment or by being exposed to sunny or cloudy weather in another) or when moods were induced in the laboratory with participants unaware that mood alteration was the intention of the procedure (happy or gloomy music was played, ostensibly for an auditory judgment task). In contrast, when participants in a fifth experiment were told that the purpose was to study the effects of moods, and were asked to alter their moods while listening to music, the opposite pattern of results was obtained: Mood-congruent recall was observed,

just as in numerous previous studies. Parrott (1994) repeated one of these experiments with the inclusion of a neutral-mood control condition and showed that mood-incongruent recall occurred in both the happy and sad conditions.

INTERPRETATIONS: MECHANISMS, MOTIVES, AND MEANINGS

Historically, the first effects that researchers discovered all involved congruence: congruence between emotional states in mood-dependent recall, and congruence between emotional state and emotional content of memory in mood-congruent recall and mood-congruent learning. For this reason, mood-congruent effects underlay the original reasons why psychologists became excited by these findings and the original theories they advanced to explain them. If emotions influence memory in these congruent ways, psychologists reasoned that these effects might have vast explanatory powers. The biased memories, poor self-image, and pessimism associated with clinical depression might be explained by a cycle of sad moods' biasing memory, which might then bias thinking and thereby further depress mood (Beck, 1976; Clark & Teasdale, 1982). Seemingly forgotten aspects of traumatic events might be remembered if the original emotional state were to be reinstated (Bower, 1981). In fact, once the centrality of memory to thought is appreciated, mood-congruent memory biases can be seen to play a role in self-perception; in judgments of other people; in the effect of persuasive communications; and in evaluations of political candidates, consumer products, or just about anything else (Bower, 1991).

Associative Mechanisms

The first and most influential explanation of these mood-congruent phenomena was the associative-network theory, first suggested by Isen, Shalker, Clark, and Karp (1978) and set out in a more detailed and widely known form by Bower (1981). According to associative-network theory, human memory can be modeled as a network of concepts that are linked together to describe an event. The concepts are represented as "nodes" in the network, and the associations between the concepts are represented as "links" between the nodes. If a person is consciously aware of a certain thought or concept, the corresponding nodes are said to be "activated" above a certain threshold. Activation is said to "spread" throughout the network, weakening as a function of associative distance. If one adds to these assumptions the idea that emotions are represented in the network and are linked to emotional events and concepts, the theory predicts mood-congruent encoding, mood-congruent recall, and mood-dependent recall (Bower, 1981).

Two decades have passed since the associative-network theory was proposed, and it is now widely accepted that the theory cannot account for what is known about emotion and memory, at least not without radical reformulation. Some of the effects that it predicts do not seem to occur, at least not reliably. These include not only mood-dependent recall (discussed previously), but also difficulties in distinguishing unemotional thoughts about emotion from emotional thoughts; in accounting for why spreading activation would not be diluted to ineffectiveness by the thousands of links over which it must surely be spread (the so-called "fan-out effect"); and in explaining why memory effects are observed more readily in some moods (e.g., happiness) than in others (e.g., anxiety) (Isen, 1987; Singer & Salovey, 1993; Teasdale & Barnard, 1993; Williams, Watts, MacLeod, & Mathews, 1997). Furthermore, some reliable effects of emotion on memory are not predicted by associative-network theory, most notably effects that are incongruent with mood.

These limitations of associative-network theory raise two possibilities: that mood-congruent effects are artifacts of research methods, or that the theory must be modified or replaced. The first possibility is raised by research suggesting that laboratory mood inductions may encourage mood-congruent recall more than would be the case in everyday life (Blaney, 1986; Eich, 1995a; Parrott & Sabini, 1990; Perrig & Perrig, 1988).

Several recent experiments have strongly suggested that mood-congruent recall is not simply an artifact of research procedures. Subject compliance does not entirely explain mood-congruent recall in laboratory settings (Berkowitz & Tróccoli, 1986; Parrott, 1991; Parrott & Hertel, 1999). Furthermore, mood-congruent recall has now been found in much less artifact-prone settings, such as naturally produced and drug-induced moods. Mayer, Mc-

Cormick, and Strong (1995) found evidence of mood-congruent recall simply by correlating self-reported everyday moods with the results of a category retrieval test. Researchers have also found mood-congruent recall while investigating the effects of the mood-depressing drug haloperidol (Kumari, Hemsley, Cotter, Checkley, & Gray, 1998).

In summary, there is good reason to believe that mood-congruent recall indeed occurs naturally in everyday life under some conditions. Yet, as we will see, there is equally good reason to believe that mood-incongruent recall sometimes occurs as well. It therefore seems essential to explore alternatives to associative-network theory, and two alternatives have been widely considered. The first posits that memory may be subject to motivational influences as well as to associative influences. The second conceives of memory as constructive and context-sensitive rather than as associative. We consider each in turn.

From this point onward, we limit our consideration to mood-congruent and mood-incongruent recall, because the other two effects of emotion on memory have not lent themselves to either of these new directions. The phenomenon of mood-dependent recall was the centerpiece of Bower's (1981) statement of the associative-network theory, and its main contribution has been to demonstrate the limited applicability of that theory rather than to suggest new directions for theory. The effects of emotion on learning have been found to yield counterintuitive mood-incongruent results under some conditions, but, as we have seen, these results can be reconciled with an associative approach to memory without too much difficulty. We therefore focus on the consequences of the discovery of mood-incongruent recall.

Motivational Theories of Emotion and Memory

As is implied by their name, motivational theories hold that persons' motives are of paramount importance to the sorts of memories they recall. Advocates of these theories point to a growing body of research that contradicts results predicted by the associative-network theory (Isen, 1984, 1987; Singer & Salovey, 1988, 1993, 1996). In motivational theories, memories are viewed as aspects of a dynamic and developing individual rather than as static nodes in an associative network (McAdams, 1988). Memories can be actively recruited to maintain, alter, or reinforce a person's mood, goals, and plans (Singer & Salovey, 1996). Emotion is not viewed solely for its associational value, but more for its motivational value.

Motivational approaches to memory typically employ a narrative perspective, positing that persons understand and organize their lives around stories (Bruner, 1986; Gillespie, 1992; McAdams, 1996). Singer has suggested that repetition of certain emotionally laden and personally meaningful memories, called "self-defining memories," creates a core understanding of the self around which a personal narrative is constructed (Moffitt & Singer, 1994; Singer & Salovey, 1993). Such self-defining memories constitute the main character in the drama of an individual's life (Gillespie, 1992). In such a drama, the main character's motivation to maintain or protect his or her self-concept is likely to result in attempts to maintain or alter the current emotional state through recall of appropriate emotional events.

On the basis of a motivational theory, Singer hypothesized that persons' emotional reactions to important memories would reflect the relationship of those memories to the achievement of desired goals (Singer, 1990; Singer & Moffitt, 1991–1992). This hypothesis was tested in a series of studies that solicited autobiographical memories and life goals. It was found that the emotional tone that persons attributed to their recollections depended on the relevance of these events to the achievement of goals. Memories with either pleasant or unpleasant emotional content could be selected for the same motivational effect. For example, while training for an athletic event, a person might provide self-encouragement by recalling either the exhilaration of past victories or the agony of past defeats (Singer & Salovey, 1996).

There are many ways in which motivation can influence the relation between emotion and memory. Painful or ego-threatening memories may be repressed; self-verifying or anger-justifying memories may be sought (Singer & Salovey, 1993). One motive for the recall of emotional events that has received much attention is the self-regulation of one's current emotional state. The original impetus for this line of research came from recognition of the limitations of associative-network theory. On the basis of this theory, it was difficult to explain why a never-ending positive feedback loop did not oc-

cur, with mood-congruent recall biasing memory and thought, which further amplified the current emotional state, which further biased memory and thought, and so on (Blaney, 1986; Bower, 1981; Clark & Isen, 1982; Ingram, 1984; Singer & Salovey, 1988). Some additional mode of operation had to be posited, and motivated emotional self-regulation was hypothesized to influence memory beyond the effects of automatic association. Thus one motive for mood-congruent recall might be to sustain or intensify one's presently experienced mood, and one motive for mood-incongruent recall might be to alter one's present emotional state—either to decrease its intensity or to induce a different emotional state in its place. In the past decade, researchers have begun to investigate the ways in which memory may be related to emotional self-regulation.

Some research has addressed the question of efficacy: Is it true that recalling an emotional memory will alter one's emotional state? One reason to suspect an affirmative answer is that researchers have successfully used recall of autobiographical memories as one means of inducing moods in the laboratory. Manipulation checks in such research suggest that the technique works (Parrott & Hertel, 1999). To find whether it is effective even when a strong emotional state already exists, one might consider the results of an experiment in which the technique was used twice—once to induce either a happy or a sad mood, and then a second time to induce whichever mood was not induced the first time. Results showed that even a brief description of a mood-incongruent event succeeded in removing prior happy and sad moods, and that a vivid, detailed description succeeded in inducing a different mood (Erber & Erber, 1994, Study 1).

Given that memory may be used to regulate emotional state, questions arise as to when people will be motivated to do so, and whether they do so when the motive exists. These questions have been addressed in two ways: in terms of the situations that will motivate emotional self-regulation, and in terms of the personality traits associated with emotional self-regulation. We consider each of these approaches.

Situational Determinants of
Emotional Self-Regulation

The most commonly held assumption about emotional self-regulation is that of simple hedonism: People want to feel good. In particular, people in good moods want to stay that way, and people in bad moods want to feel less bad. These two motives are often termed "positive mood maintenance" and "negative mood repair," respectively (e.g., Carlson & Miller, 1987; Clark & Isen, 1982), and most of the literature on memory and emotion considers self-regulation only in these terms. It is often asserted, for example, that the existence of these two motives explains why mood-congruent recall is more readily observed in happy moods than in sad moods (e.g., Singer & Salovey, 1993). It is also often asserted that although emotional self-regulation may explain why mood-incongruent recall occurred for sad participants in Parrott and Sabini's (1990) experiments, it cannot explain mood-incongruent recall for those who were happy (e.g., Clore, Schwarz, & Conway, 1994).

It can be argued, however, that such an hedonic approach to emotional self-regulation is doubly misguided: It incorrectly suggests that the most important aspect of emotional states is their hedonic quality, and it incorrectly suggests that there are no motives to inhibit good moods or to maintain bad ones (Parrott, 1993). A more accurate set of assumptions would emphasize how moods and emotions can convey information about a person's well-being and about the extent to which current plans and goals are being achieved (Oatley & Johnson-Laird, 1987; Schwarz, 1990). Good moods signal that things are going well, so they therefore often motivate people to worry less about making mistakes, to accept risks, and to be creative and integrative. Anxious or irritable moods, in contrast, can signal that problems and threats exist, so they often motivate people to focus on the source of threat, to become careful and analytical, and to try hard to solve the problem at hand (Isen, 1987; Schwarz & Bless, 1991). For these reasons, bad moods are sometimes useful and good moods sometimes counterproductive. Anxiety or irritability can be very useful in a situation that requires focused, analytical problem solving, or when one must motivate oneself to work hard and forgo relaxation and play. Emotions such as anger can be useful for communicating one's displeasure to another (something hard to do when one is feeling jovial). Although people surely do like to avoid pain and to experience pleasure, immediate gratification is not always the best path to long-term success. Happiness and contentment may undercut the motivation to work hard and to concentrate on small details. Socially, the appearance of happiness may not always be appropriate or desirable either. Thus, because of the various mental and social aspects of moods and emotions, there should be occasions when people's motivations for emotional self-regulation tend away from happiness and toward one of the less pleasurable emotional states. (For a more detailed discussion of these motives, see Parrott, 1993.)

Accordingly, there are numerous situations in which mood-incongruent recall might be expected to occur in the service of emotional self-regulation. Only a few have been investigated to date. For example, when students are in class, both positive or negative emotions may be distracting, and displays of strong emotion may be inappropriate. One of the experiments reported by Parrott and Sabini (1990) was conducted in a classroom setting shortly after the beginning of class. The observed mood-incongruent memories may have been motivated by students finding themselves needing to reduce the intensity of their moods, both good and bad. This finding has been replicated by Erber and Erber (1994, Study 2). They induced happy or sad moods by asking students to recall either a happy or a sad autobiographical memory. They then asked students to recall one additional memory of their own choosing. On some occasions they made this request at the beginning of class, whereas on others they made it at the end of class. Interestingly, these researchers obtained mood-incongruent recall at the beginning of class but mood-congruent recall at the end of class. They interpreted this finding in motivational terms: At the beginning of class students would perceive their moods as interfering with their classwork, whereas at the end of class they would not. It is interesting to consider that the second situation producing mood-incongruent recall in Parrott and Sabini's (1990) studies was the sunniness or cloudiness of the weather students experienced just prior to entering a university library. Although the research was not planned to test situational influences on self-regulatory motives, in retrospect it seems noteworthy that this situation was one in which students might have been motivated to moderate their emotional states in preparation for study. Such a finding has now been obtained with a nonautobiographical memory task. Mayer, Gayle, Meehan, and Haarman (1990) induced happy and sad moods by asking participants to listen to music following one of five sets of instructions, only one of which permitted participants to alter their induced moods during the task. In this condition only, the saddest participants showed mood-incongruent recall in their memory of positive and negative words, extending the effect to this type of memory task.

In summary, there is now evidence that people will recall mood-incongruent material in situations where a happy or sad mood is distracting or inappropriate. To date, only a few other situations in which memory might be employed for emotional self-regulation have been explored. There is now substantial evidence that mood-incongruent recall may be obtained in laboratory settings in which participants are unaware of the relevance of their emotions to the purposes of the research, but it is still unclear what aspects of the laboratory setting influence motives to self-regulate. It is also unclear why mood-incongruent recall has not been observed in some experiments that appear to meet these criteria (e.g., Ehrlichman & Halpern, 1988; Kumari et al., 1998). One hypothesis about how different laboratory situations influence self-regulatory motives focuses on motives related to social interaction (Parrott, 1993). These motives have not been systematically studied with respect to memory, but an experiment on selective self-exposure to information is suggestive. In two studies, Erber, Wegner, and Therriault (1996) induced happy and sad moods by playing music but not informing the participants that mood alteration was the goal of the music. All participants believed that they would first read and rate a selection of newspaper stories; half believed that they would then perform another solitary task, whereas the other half believed that they would then work on a task with another person. The participants were next asked to select a subset of stories they would like to rate from a list of newspaper headlines ranging from cheerful to depressing. Participants expecting to work with a stranger on an upcoming task tended to choose headlines that were incongruent with their moods, whereas those expecting to work alone did not differ in their selections as a function of their moods. These findings suggest that expectations of social interaction may motivate people to dampen or eradicate their moods. Whether the presence or absence of such expectations accounts for why some experiments obtain mood-incongruent recall and others do not cannot be discerned from published reports,

but this hypothesis seems worth pursuing in future research.

Personality Determinants of Emotional Self-Regulation

The other method of investigating whether retrieval of memories is moderated by motivation to regulate emotions is to examine individual differences on relevant personality traits. Four traits have been investigated in this connection.

One trait very straightforwardly associated with emotional self-regulation is the general tendency to engage in self-control. In one study, participants were exposed to sad or neutral music and asked to recall an autobiographical memory (Parrott & Sabini, 1989). Participants who were below the median in self-control, as assessed with the Self-Control Schedule (Rosenbaum, 1980), tended to recall memories congruent with their moods, but those above the median in self-control recalled memories that did not differ from those of the neutral control condition.

Research using a different measure of self-control has replicated these findings. Smith and Petty (1995, Experiment 2) used the Negative Mood Regulation Scale (Catanzaro & Mearns, 1990) to measure dispositions toward self-control. Their research compared participants scoring high and low on this scale when made sad by viewing a film clip or when slightly happy after viewing a neutral film clip. The participants low in negative mood regulation exhibited mood-congruent recall after the sad clip compared to the neutral control clip, but the recall of those high in negative mood regulation was no different after the sad and neutral films.

In both of these studies, there was no tendency for mood-incongruent recall overall or even in highly self-controlling participants. It is therefore interesting to consider an experiment in which there was an overall tendency to recall mood-incongruent memories for the first of the three memories recalled. The mood-incongruent effect occurred with equal magnitude for participants high and low in self-control. In contrast, for the third memory recalled, for which there was no overall effect of mood on memory, individual differences in self-control had a strong effect: Participants who heard sad music and were high in self-control tended to recall mood-incongruent memories, whereas those low in self-control tended to recall mood-congruent memories (Parrott, 1994).

One explanation for this pattern of results is that when situational determinants of mood-incongruent recall are strong, individual differences in self-regulation do not exert much additional effect. Rather, it is when there is not a strong situational determinant of mood on memory that individual differences will exert their most noticeable effects. These measures of self-control did not predict the memories of participants who heard happy music, perhaps because the items in the various individual-difference scales only address unpleasant states. Whether the tendency to regulate pleasant states is moderated by individual differences that are separate from the tendency to regulate unpleasant states is a question awaiting further investigation.

Another individual difference posited to affect mood regulation is depression, which is associated with impairments in the ability to repair moods (Teasdale & Barnard, 1993). In one experiment sad moods were induced by showing participants a melancholy segment from a movie, and participants were then asked to recall two strongly emotional memories (Josephson, Singer, & Salovey, 1996). In this experiment participants tended to recall a memory congruent with their mood at first (when compared to a neutral control), but the type of memory recalled next depended on participants' tendencies to feel depressed. Participants with low depression scores tended to recall a more positive second memory, whereas those with high depression scores tended to recall another negative memory. Interestingly, of the participants recalling first a sad and then a happy memory, two-thirds cited a desire to improve their mood when asked why they recalled a happy memory.

The third individual difference that has been studied is self-esteem. Smith and Petty (1995) compared individuals high and low in self-esteem for the types of memories they recalled when in neutral or sad moods. One experiment tested autobiographical memories, and a second tested incidental recall of newspaper headlines varying in pleasantness. In both experiments the memories of participants low in self-esteem were mood-congruent, whereas those of participants high in self-esteem were not affected by sad mood.

Finally, it has been argued that a prerequisite of emotional self-regulation is emotional awareness, and therefore that individual differences in the tendency to openly acknowledge one's emotional states may moderate mood-incongruent recall. A pair of experiments by McFarland and Buehler (1997) lends support to this hypothesis. Negative and neutral moods were induced by providing false performance feedback in one study and by producing expectations of a stressful or unstressful test in another. Emotion acknowledgment was assessed either by a measure of repression–sensitization (Epstein & Fenz, 1967) or by a measure of metamood experience (derived from Mayer & Gaschke, 1988). In both experiments the average memory of the participants who scored above the median on the measure of emotion acknowledgment was mood-incongruent. There was a tendency for participants scoring below the median on emotion acknowledgment to recall memories congruent with their mood.

Implications for Associative-Network Theory

In summary, there is now abundant evidence that mood-incongruent recall is a robust and reliable effect, and that its occurrence is predicted by situations and by personal dispositions related to emotional self-regulation. Associative-network theory in no way predicts these effects, so the question becomes how this theory should be adjusted. The possibilities range between two extremes: retaining associative-network theory but supplementing it by positing additional influences that can modify its predictions, or, at the other extreme, abandoning the theory altogether. Let us begin with the first of these extremes and work our way toward the other.

If the assumptions of associative-network theory are to be retained, the theory must be combined with additional assumptions to form a composite model of emotion and memory. The addition most commonly considered has been that there can be motivational influences of emotions on memory in addition to associative influences (Singer & Salovey, 1993). Forgas's (1995) affect infusion model is a good example of a multiprocess approach that combines both associative and motivated elements into a composite theory. It posits four separate strategies altogether and delineates the conditions that help determine their use.

Other theories modify associative-network theory rather than simply supplementing it. Good examples of this approach are the proposals for multilevel cognitive architectures, such as Teasdale and Barnard's (1993) theory of interacting cognitive subsystems, or Johnson and Multhaup's (1992) theory of multiple-entry, modular memory. The former theory, for example, proposes multiple representational subsystems and two levels of meaning. It incorporates motivation by allowing for mood repair and other redirections of thinking based on previous learning history.

These recent theories mark an important trend toward rejecting the idea that emotional states influence memory in a straightforward or invariant manner. Other strategies attempt this goal by moving even farther from the assumptions of associative-network theory. We address two possibilities of this type next.

Constructivist and Contextualist Theories of Emotion and Memory

Constructivist and contextualist accounts maintain that emotion is not simply a static retrieval cue attached to a memory unit. Rather, emotion is an aspect of the whole of the context in which an event is experienced or recalled, and as such it helps define the encoded or remembered event. For example, imagine that John, a graduate student struggling to support himself financially while trying to complete his dissertation, misses the bus to school one day. He thinks to himself, "I'll never make it through this program. I never have enough time to study or to do my research. I can't even make my bus on time. I'll never finish this dissertation." In this example, a negative mood leads to interpreting a simple event as the "last straw." Emotion at the time of retrieval may serve to redefine this event. When John finally completes his dissertation and is filled with happiness at his graduation ceremony, he looks back at the time when he missed the bus and thinks to himself, "I always knew I could do it. Things looked bleak there for a while, but I never doubted I'd be here today."

Such an example brings to mind the constructive approach to memory pioneered by Bartlett (1932). In Bartlett's well-known research on memory for verbal accounts, he found that persons' recollections were never quite accurate. The remembered accounts were always somehow slightly different from the original and were reflective of each person's beliefs and preoccupations at the time of retrieval. For example, Bartlett pointed out that his famous experiment on memory for the folk tale

"The War of the Ghosts" was conducted at the end of World War I, a time when separation from one's family was a salient concern for his subjects. In one group of subjects, despite the fact that many of the details of a particular account were forgotten, 18 persons out of 20 remembered that a particular character had stated he could not join the ghosts' war party because his relatives did not know where he was. Bartlett suggested that one's "active organisation of past reactions, or of past experiences" constructs a "schema" for a remembered event (p. 201). Such schemas are not static, unchanging scripts, but are flexible, and they lead to construction of memories on the basis of one's context. Emotional states may have their effects partly by influencing the construction of schemas.

This constructive approach to memory continues today (for reviews, see Gillespie, 1992; Isen, 1984, 1987; Lewis, 1997). Researchers such as Bransford and Franks (1971) demonstrated that people construct meanings from sentences not merely on the basis of serial combination of words, but on the basis of context, background knowledge, and relations among the parts of the sentence that may change the interpretation of the sentence as a whole. Ross (1989) showed how implicit theories of the stability or changeableness of personal attributes leads to biased episodic memories of such things as past characteristics and attitudes, membership in political parties, experiences of pain, and fondness for dating partners. Lewis (1997) reviews a variety of studies suggesting that one's current psychological state is a stronger predictor of the quality of childhood memories than is the actual nature of the event being remembered. On the basis of such work, memory for events has come to be viewed not simply as a process of recalling individually encoded items, but rather as a constructive process that relies on the whole of the context at the time both of encoding and of retrieval, including emotional aspects of those contexts.

Contextualist theories vary in how much they depart from associative-network theory in explaining the role of context in memory. Some maintain that memories are still encoded into some sort of associative network, albeit one amenable to dynamic change according to contextual interpretations (e.g., Isen, 1984). Others, however, make a more radical break. Gillespie (1992), for example, asserts that there is no storage of memory units at all; we immediately have all of our past experience at the present. This radical contextual theory of memory posits that memories are not things that are stored in some sort of network and recalled with accompanying emotional content, but rather that the present is a constitution of the past, an idea that owes much to the writings of Martin Heidegger (who stated that a "Da-Sein [being there] is its past," 1927/1996, p. 17). The past is already in the present as it is constituted on the basis of a present unity of the whole of one's experience. In this way, there is no need for the suggestion of some network; rather, there is only lived experience. Lewis (1997) is similarly radical in contending that present experience readily alters memory and influences present behavior more than does the actual past.

For a radical contextualist, the associations and nodes of modern memory theory have no more explanatory power than did the concept of "aether" in the physics of Isaac Newton's day. In an essay on this topic, Williams (1995) points out that the corpuscular metaphysics of that time required that there be some contact between bodies to cause the observed movements of planets. Newton posited aether to supply this contact, but the formulation of the concept of aether (or of "force," for that matter) required explanation just as much as did the original phenomenon of action at a distance (as Newton himself eventually decided). Likewise, Williams (1995) argues, modern psychologists feel a need to postulate mental structures in attempting to explain how past events can affect present events (e.g., how the emotional tone with which an event is encoded can affect the manner or circumstances in which it is recalled). As with the Newtonians' concepts of aether and force, however, the suggestion of the existence of such structures—be they physiological or informational—does not truly explain the phenomena in question, because the hypothesis of the existence of such structures itself requires explanation.

It may be seen, then, that the basic point of contention between constructionist or contextualist theories and more traditional associative-network or motivational theories is that of whether memories are static, encoded units or dynamic constructions. For the most part, findings in the field to date may be explained by either type of theory. Where the two points of view seem to diverge most plainly is not in their abilities to serve as explanatory frameworks, but at the level of phenomenological experience. Whereas a static, associative-network model of memory has served well in beginning to outline the ways in which persons' minds may work, this metaphor begins to break down when one contrasts the imagery associated with the concept of retrieval of one's fixed memories with the phenomenological experience of comprehension or understanding of one's past (see Winograd & Flores, 1986, for further discussion of the weaknesses of associative or computer metaphors of cognition).

CONCLUSION

What seems to us most problematic about traditional theories of emotion and memory, such as associative-network theory or basic-emotion theory (Bower, 1991; Oatley & Johnson-Laird, 1987), is their tendency to describe emotions as "mechanisms"—as preprogrammed routines that are executed invariably whenever they are triggered. As has been shown, the desirability of different emotional states will change, depending on circumstances such as the task at hand and the social context. The significance or meaning of emotional states is affected by a variety of personal and cultural factors (Parrott, 1993). An interesting empirical investigation of such ideas was carried out by Martin, Abend, Sedikides, and Green (1997), although they were measuring judgment rather than memory per se. They found that participants' judgments favored a happy story when the participants were in a happy mood, but favored a sad story when they were in a sad mood. That is, moods produced no general evaluative or motivational bias to like or dislike stimuli. Rather, the effect of moods was to produce a preference for stories that were supposed to produce that sort of mood; people liked the story that was supposed to produce the mood that they were then feeling.

We have reviewed the range of explanations for such context-specific effects. Adherents to constructivist or contextualist theories would argue that memories are constructions and that the effect of emotions depends on their significance in the current context; some would also deny that fixed associations exist. Less extreme departures from associative-network theory might concede that it is the formation of retrieval cues rather than the structure of associations that accounts for many of the effects of emotion on memory. In either case, the result will be a theory denying that emotional states invariably generate certain effects independently of context. In the face of the complexities of context sensitivity, it becomes clear that in drawing conclusions regarding the effects of emotion on memory, the best psychologists can aspire to is a sense of what meanings and motives commonly arise in various emotional states and how these possibilities can affect memory. It is impossible to specify fixed, context-free rules about the effects of happiness, sadness, or anxiety on cognitive activity. Meaning and motivation both play important parts, and neither fits the mechanistic model.

Although associational theorists have also identified motivational and contextual effects, there has been a strong tendency to concentrate on the associational models and their predictions. Why? Perhaps it is because these models are viewed as making straightforward, empirical predictions, relatively free of the complexities of individual interpretations and motivations. For example, Bartlett's (1932) theory is often criticized as being too complex and vague to be testable (e.g., Baddeley, 1976). Because mechanistic theories have been so successful in the physical sciences, there may be a tendency for mechanistic and context-free explanations to be equated with scientific explanations (Toulmin, 1990). But surely it is the subject matter that should dictate the form of scientific theory and research! The findings from research on emotion and memory that we have reviewed suggest that greater emphasis on motivation and interpretation, and less on automatic association, is desirable and necessary.

The present state of research on emotion and memory seems similar to the state of research on memory earlier in this century, when Bartlett (1932) was doing his work. Just as Bartlett criticized Ebbinghaus's approach for being too stimulus-bound, so do we believe that much contemporary theorizing about emotion is too "mechanism-bound," attempting to understand basic emotions as fixed, predetermined reactions that always influence behavior, motivation, and thinking in the same manner. Just as Bartlett criticized Ebbinghaus's work on memory on the grounds that it attempted to avoid meaning, so do we believe that contemporary research needs to consider the meaning of emotions in context and how this meaning shapes emotions' effects. Bartlett characterized memory as "effort after meaning"; research on

emotion and memory needs to explore how emotional states influence that effort.

REFERENCES

Baddeley, A. D. (1976). *The psychology of memory* . New York: Basic Books.

Bartlett, F. C. (1932). *Remembering: A study in experimental and social psychology* Cambridge, England: Cambridge University Press.

Beck, A. T. (1976). *Cognitive therapy and the emotional disorders.* New York: International Universities Press.

Beck, R. C., & McBee, W. (1995). Mood-dependent memory for generated and repeated words: Replication and extension. *Cognition and Emotion, 9,* 289–307.

Berkowitz, L., & Tróccoli, T. (1986). An examination of the assumption in the demand characteristics thesis: With special reference to the Velten mood induction procedure. *Motivation and Emotion, 10,* 337–349.

Blaney, P. H. (1986). Affect and memory: A review. *Psychological Bulletin, 99,* 229–246.

Bower, G. H. (1981). Mood and memory. *American Psychologist, 36,* 129–148.

Bower, G. H. (1991). Mood congruity of social judgments. In J. P. Forgas (Ed.), *Emotion and social judgments* (pp. 31–53). Oxford: Pergamon Press.

Bower, G. H., Gilligan, S. G., & Monteiro, K. P. (1981). Selectivity of learning caused by affective states. *Journal of Experimental Psychology: General, 110,* 451–473.

Bower, G. H., & Mayer, J. D. (1991). In search of mood-dependent retrieval. In D. Kuiken (Ed.), *Mood and memory: Theory, research and applications* (pp. 133–168). Newbury Park, CA: Sage.

Bransford, J. D., & Franks, J. J. (1971). The abstraction of linguistic ideas. *Cognitive Psychology, 2,* 331–350.

Bruner, J. (1986). *Actual minds, possible worlds.* Cambridge, MA: Harvard University Press.

Carlson, M., & Miller, N. (1987). Explanation of the relation between negative mood and helping. *Psychological Bulletin, 102,* 91–108.

Catanzaro, S. J., & Mearns, J. (1990). Measuring generalized expectancies for negative mood regulation: Initial scale development and implications. *Journal of Personality Assessment, 54,* 546–563.

Clark, D. M., & Teasdale, J. D. (1982). Diurnal variation in clinical depression and accessibility of memories of positive and negative experiences. *Journal of Abnormal Psychology, 91,* 87–95.

Clark, D. M., & Teasdale, J. D. (1985). Constraints on the effects of mood on memory. *Journal of Personality and Social Psychology, 48,* 1595–1608.

Clark, D. M., Teasdale, J. D., Broadbent, D. E., & Martin, M. (1983). Effect of mood on lexical decisions. *Bulletin of the Psychonomic Society, 21,* 175–178.

Clark, M. S., & Isen, A. M. (1982). Toward understanding the relationship between feeling states and social behavior. In A. H. Hastorf & A. M. Isen (Eds.), *Cognitive social psychology* (pp. 73–108). New York: Elsevier.

Clore, G. L., Schwarz, N., & Conway, M. (1994). Affective causes and consequences of social information processing. In R. S. Wyer & T. K. Srull (Eds.), *Handbook of social cognition* (2nd ed., Vol. 1, pp. 323–418). Hillsdale, NJ: Erlbaum.

Ehrlichman, H., & Halpern, J. N. (1988). Affect and memory: Effects of pleasant and unpleasant odors on retrieval of happy and unhappy memories. *Journal of Personality and Social Psychology, 47,* 1105–1117.

Eich, E. (1995a). Mood as a mediator of place dependent memory. *Journal of Experimental Psychology: General, 124,* 293–308.

Eich, E. (1995b). Searching for mood dependent memory. *Psychological Science, 6,* 67–75.

Eich, E., & Metcalfe, J. (1989). Mood dependent memory for internal versus external events. *Journal of Experimental Psychology: Learning, Memory, and Cognition, 15,* 443–455.

Epstein, S., & Fenz, W. D. (1967). The detection of areas of emotional stress through variations in perceptual threshold and physiological arousal. *Journal of Experimental Research in Personality, 2,* 191–199.

Erber, R., & Erber, M. W. (1994). Beyond mood and social judgment: Mood incongruent recall and mood regulation. *European Journal of Social Psychology, 24,* 79–88.

Erber, R., Wegner, D. M., & Therriault, N. (1996). On being cool and collected: Mood regulation in anticipation of social interaction. *Journal of Personality and Social Psychology, 70,* 757–766.

Forgas, J. P. (1995). Mood and judgment: The affect infusion model (AIM). *Psychological Bulletin, 117,* 39–66.

Forgas, J. P., Burnham, D. K., & Trimboli, C. (1988). Mood, memory, and social judgments in children. *Journal of Personality and Social Psychology, 54,* 697–703.

Gillespie, D. (1992). *The mind's we: Contextualism in cognitive psychology.* Carbondale: Southern Illinois University Press.

Heidegger, M. (1996). *Being and time* (J. Stambaugh Trans.). Albany: State University of New York Press.(Original work published 1927)

Heuer, F., & Reisberg, D. (1992). Emotion, arousal, and memory for detail. In S.-Å. Christianson (Ed.), *The handbook of emotion and memory: Research and theory* (pp. 151–180). Hillsdale, NJ: Erlbaum.

Ingram, R. E. (1984). Toward an information-processing analysis of depression. *Cognitive Therapy and Research, 8,* 443–478.

Isen, A. M. (1984). Toward understanding the role of affect and cognition. In R. Wyer & T. Srull (Eds.), *Handbook of social cognition* (Vol. 3, pp. 179–236). Hillsdale, NJ: Erlbaum.

Isen, A. M. (1987). Positive affect, cognitive processes, and social behavior. In L. Berkowitz (Ed.), *Advances in experimental social psychology* (Vol. 20, pp. 203–253). New York: Academic Press.

Isen, A. M., Shalker, T. E., Clark, M., & Karp, L. (1978). Affect, accessibility of material in memory, and behavior: A cognitive loop? *Journal of Personality and Social Psychology, 36,* 1–12.

Johnson, M. K., & Multhaup, K. S. (1992). Emotion and MEM. In S.-Å. Christianson (Ed.), *The handbook of emotion and memory: Research and theory* (pp. 33–66). Hillsdale, NJ: Erlbaum.

Josephson, B. R., Singer, J. A., & Salovey, P. (1996). Mood regulation and memory: Repairing sad moods with happy memories. *Cognition and Emotion, 10,* 437–444.

Kumari, V., Hemsley, D. R., Cotter, P. A., Checkley, S. A., & Gray, J. A. (1998). Haloperidol-induced mood and retrieval of happy and unhappy memories. *Cognition and Emotion, 12,* 495–506.

Lewis, M. (1997). *Altering fate: Why the past does not predict the future.* New York: Guilford Press.

Martin, L. L., Abend, T., Sedikides, C., & Green, J. D. (1997). How would I feel if. . .? Mood as input to a role fulfillment evaluation process. *Journal of Personality and Social Psychology, 73,* 242–253.

Mathews, A. M., & MacLeod, C. (1994). Cognitive approaches to emotion and emotional disorders. *Annual Review of Psychology, 45,* 25–50.

Matt, G. E., Vazquez, C. & Campbell, W. K. (1992). Mood-congruent recall of affectively toned stimuli: A meta-analytic review. *Clinical Psychology Review, 12,* 227–255.

Mayer, J. D., & Gaschke, Y. (1988). The experience and meta-experience of mood. *Journal of Personality and Social Psychology, 55,* 102–111.

Mayer, J. D., Gayle, M., Meehan, M. E., & Haarman, A.-K. (1990). Toward better specification of the mood-congruency effect in recall. *Journal of Experimental Social Psychology, 26,* 465–480.

Mayer, J. D., McCormick, L. J., & Strong, S. E. (1995). Mood-congruent memory and natural mood: New evidence. *Personality and Social Psychology Bulletin, 21,* 726–746.

McAdams, D. P. (1988). *Power, intimacy, and the life story: Personological inquiries into identity.* New York: Guilford Press.

McAdams, D. P. (1996). Alternative futures for the study of human individuality. *Journal of Research in Personality, 30,* 374–488.

McFarland, C., & Buehler, R. (1997). Negative affective states and the motivated retrieval of positive life events: The role of affect acknowledgment. *Journal of Personality and Social Psychology, 73,* 200–214.

Moffitt, K. H., & Singer, J. A. (1994). Continuity in the life story: Self-defining memories, affect, and approach/avoidance personal strivings. *Journal of Personality, 62,* 21–43.

Nasby, W. (1994). Moderators of mood-congruent encoding: Self-/other-reference and affirmative/nonaffirmative judgement. *Cognition and Emotion, 8,* 259–278.

Oatley, K., & Johnson-Laird, P. N. (1987). Towards a cognitive theory of emotions. *Cognition and Emotion, 1,* 29–50.

Parrott, W. G. (1991). Mood induction and instructions to sustain moods: A test of the subject compliance hypothesis of mood congruent memory. *Cognition and Emotion, 5,* 41–52.

Parrott, W. G. (1993). Beyond hedonism: Motives for inhibiting good moods and for maintaining bad moods. In D. M. Wegner & J. W. Pennebaker (Eds.), *Handbook of mental control* (pp. 278–305). Englewood Cliffs, NJ: Prentice-Hall.

Parrott, W. G. (1994). An association between emotional self-control and mood-incongruent recall. In N. H. Frijda (Ed.), *Proceedings of the VIIIth Conference of the International Society for Research on Emotions* (pp. 313–317). Storrs, CT: International Society for Research on Emotions.

Parrott, W. G., & Hertel, P. (1999). Research methods in cognition and emotion. In T. Dalgleish & M. Power (Eds.), *The handbook of cognition and emotion* (pp. 61–81). Chichester, England: Wiley.

Parrott, W. G., & Sabini, J. (1989, August). Mood, self-control, and the recall of autobiographical memories. Paper presented at the 97th Annual Convention of the American Psychological Association, New Orleans, LA.

Parrott, W. G., & Sabini, J. (1990). Mood and memory under natural conditions: Evidence for mood incongruent recall. *Journal of Personality and Social Psychology, 59,* 321–336.

Perrig, W. J., & Perrig, P. (1988). Mood and memory: Mood-congruity effects in absence of mood. *Memory and Cognition, 16,* 102–109.

Rapaport, D. (1950). *Emotions and memory.* New York: International Universities Press.

Revelle, W., & Loftus, D. A. (1990). Individual differences and arousal: Implications for the study of mood and memory. *Cognition and Emotion, 4,* 209–237.

Rinck, M., Glowalla, U., & Schneider, K. (1992). Mood-congruent and mood-incongruent learning. *Memory and Cognition, 20,* 29–39.

Rosenbaum, M. (1980). A schedule for assessing self-control behaviors: Preliminary findings. *Behavior Therapy, 11,* 109–121.

Ross, M. (1989). Relation of implicit theories to the construction of personal histories. *Psychological Review, 96,* 341–357.

Schwarz, N. (1990). Feelings as information: Informational and motivational functions of affective states. In E. T. Higgins & R. M. Sorrentino (Eds.), *Handbook of motivation and cognition: Foundations of social behavior* (Vol. 2, pp. 527–561). New York: Guilford Press.

Schwarz, N., & Bless, H. (1991). Happy and mindless, but sad and smart?: The impact of affective states on analytic reasoning. In J. Forgas (Ed.), *Emotion and social judgment* (pp. 55–71). Oxford: Pergamon Press.

Singer, J. A. (1990). Affective responses to autobiographical memories and their relationship to long-term goals. *Journal of Personality, 58,* 535–563.

Singer, J. A., & Moffitt, K. H. (1991–1992). An experimental investigation of specificity and generality in memory narratives. *Imagination, Cognition, and Personality, 11,* 233–257.

Singer, J. A., & Salovey, P. (1988). Mood and memory: Evaluating the network theory of affect. *Clinical Psychology Review, 8,* 211–251.

Singer, J. A., & Salovey, P. (1993). *The remembered self: Emotion and memory in personality.* New York: Free Press.

Singer, J. A., & Salovey, P. (1996). Motivated memory: Self-defining memories, goals, and affect regulation. In L. Martin & A. Tesser (Eds.), *Striving and feeling: Interactions among goals, affect, and self-regulation* (pp. 229–250). Hillsdale, NJ: Erlbaum.

Smith, S. M., & Petty, R. E. (1995). Personality moderators of mood congruency effects on cognition: The role of self-esteem and negative mood regulation. *Journal of Personality and Social Psychology, 68,* 1092–1107.

Snyder, M., & White, P. (1982). Moods and memories: Elation, depression, and the remembering of the events of one's life. *Journal of Personality, 50,* 149–167.

Teasdale, J. D., & Barnard, P. J. (1993). Affect, cognition, and change: Re-modelling depressive thought. Hove, England: Erlbaum.

Toulmin, S. (1990). *Cosmopolis: The hidden agenda of modernity.* New York: Free Press.

Ucros, C. G. (1989). Mood state-dependent memory: A meta-analysis. *Cognition and Emotion, 3,* 139–167.

Williams, J. M. G., Watts, F. N., MacLeod, C., & Mathews, A. (1997). *Cognitive psychology and emotional disorders* (2nd ed.). Chichester, England: Wiley

Williams, R. N. (1995). Temporality and psychological action at a distance. *Journal of Mind and Behavior, 16,* 63–76.

Winograd, T., & Flores, F. (1986). *Understanding computers and cognition: A new foundation for design.* Norwood, NJ: Ablex.

CHAPTER 31

Emotion Concepts

James A. Russell
Ghyslaine Lemay

Imagine that while you are reading this chapter, you are sitting at a sidewalk café and observing the passers-by. You see a couple in love, a worried lawyer, and an angry teenager. You notice that the weather is very pleasant. You notice that you yourself have a pleasant, relaxed feeling.

Between all such observations and the raw data on which they are based intervene certain filters—processes by which the raw data are grouped, ordered, and interpreted. These processes include the concepts[1] expressed by the words *in love, worried, angry, pleasant,* and *relaxed.* Concepts play an identical role in more formal observations, including self-reports gathered on psychometric instruments and ratings by trained observers in a laboratory. These same concepts appear in formal scientific theories of the events they are concepts of.

There is much more to the study of emotion than the study of concepts. Nevertheless, a focus on concepts provides a revealing vantage point from which to view the scientific study of emotion. In that study, concepts play two key roles. First, cognitive science demonstrates the role of concepts in everyday understanding, including understanding of emotion; second, the philosophy of science demonstrates the role of concepts in the beginnings of, the everyday work of, and the final products of science. In this chapter, we examine emotion concepts in both of these roles.

TWO TASKS IN THE PSYCHOLOGY OF EMOTION

Within the subject matter of psychology happen to fall two fascinating topics sometimes confused with one another. One is human emotion, a perennial mystery. The second topic is the human understanding of emotion. This second topic is sometimes thought to be merely a surrogate for the first. In our view, the second topic is fully as profound and mysterious as the first, and fully as worthy of study.

A related distinction, also sometimes overlooked in writings on emotion, is that between concepts of emotion and the events they are concepts of. Admittedly, the two are related. As science progresses, the concepts come to be the best representation available of the events. Still, sometimes even the best scientific theories are overthrown, and history suggests that our current folk theories and even current scientific theories of emotion will probably someday come to be seen as amateur efforts. This possibility underscores the need to study both emotion concepts and emotion events, but separately.

With these two distinctions in mind, we can see that concepts present the psychology of emotion with two great tasks. One task is descriptive: to provide an account of the folk-psychological concepts actually used by children and adults (of various cultures, speaking

various languages) in their everyday understanding of emotion. What is the nature of the
concepts ordinary people use in their observations of the emotions, moods, and feelings they
experience or witness? Specific questions to be
studied concern the properties of emotion concepts, children's acquisition of those concepts,
and cultural and individual differences and similarities in those concepts. Answers to these
questions do not tell us directly about emotion
events.

The other task is prescriptive: to develop a
set of scientifically valid concepts that provide
an account of emotion events, by which we
mean those phenomena now called *love, anxiety, anger, shame, serenity,* and the like. By
what concepts can the heterogeneous class of
emotion events be described and understood?
What role, if any, should everyday concepts
play as scientific tools? Need they be tidied up
and redefined?

These two tasks must not be confused with
one another, although they are complementary
and highly interrelated. Everyday conceptualizations suggest scientific hypotheses, and the
lay public often adopts scientific concepts.
Everyday concepts may influence emotions
(e.g., interpreting himself as unduly afraid,
Johnny becomes embarrassed), and emotions
are the subject matter for everyday concepts of
emotion. Indeed, a theme developed in this
chapter is the strong relation between these two
uses of concepts. In both cases, concepts are
parts of theories. Theory is not just a quaint
metaphor. Fritz Heider, George Kelly, and
many others have suggested an analogy between psychological processes and scientific
processes. Wellman (1993) has developed the
notion that children are young theorists, and
that emotion is one of the topics about which
they theorize. Human beings are amateur scientists; scientists are human beings. Here we suggest a deep continuity from a child's cognitive
development to the folk psychology of everyday thinking to the working models and successful theories of advanced science.

WHAT ARE CONCEPTS AND WHY DO WE NEED THEM?

We begin with what seems a paradox. . . . Were we to
utilize fully our capacity for registering the differences in
things and to respond to each event encountered as unique,
we would soon be overwhelmed by the complexity of our
environment. (Bruner, Goodnow, & Austin, 1956, p. 1)

The external world provides an infinite number
of different patterns of stimulation happening
in different contexts, and a human being is capable of perceiving and registering very small
differences. If we were to perceive each stimulus pattern as unique, we would have no basis
for an appropriate response. Cognitive, perceptual, mnemonic, and reasoning processes are
known to be limited, and it is impossible for us
to handle more than a fraction of what we experience. The question is how we make sense of
such a variety of events.

The solution is to order and to group those
events so that they can be responded to on the
basis of their similarity to each other rather
than their uniqueness. Concepts are procedures
that do so. Concepts are mental processes that
transform the raw data of experience into manageable units (grouping them into categories
and ordering them along dimensions). Concepts thus serve cognitive economy and are involved in perception, memory, thinking, solving problems, and any other psychological
process. Concepts are tools, primitive versions
of which can be found in infants, and sophisticated versions of which are part of advanced
science. Concepts can also be thought of as
parts of a larger network of assumptions and
other cognitive skills. Thus any concept is
"theory-laden."

Figure 31.1 shows an assumption often implicit in writing on emotion. The same concept,
such as *anger,* underlies a variety of phenomena, including the use of words, the perception
of emotion in self and in others, and thinking
about emotion. For a psychologist to conclude
that an infant (or an adult, for that matter) has a
concept such as *anger* is thus to make a number
of different and strong claims.

Many who study emotion have assumed
what is called the classical view of concepts,
and some continue to do so. In the last several
decades, new views of concepts have
emerged—probabilistic and theory-based accounts. We examine each in turn.

The Classical View

The "classical" view dates at least to Aristotle.
The two main assumptions of the classical view
are the following:

1. A concept is a summary description of a
set of events. This summary description is the
result of the abstraction of the defining proper-

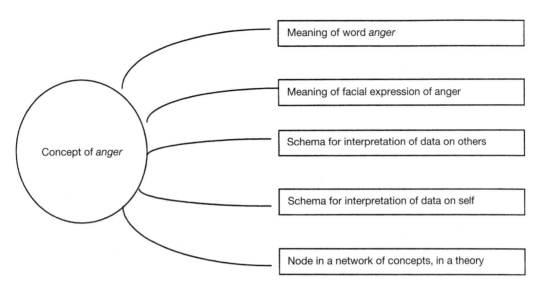

FIGURE 31.1. The concept of *anger*.

ties of that set. For example, the concept *square* is a list of four properties: closed figure, four sides, sides equal in length, equal angles.

2. The properties are each necessary and together sufficient to define the concept. For example, for a geometric figure to be a square, it must have all of these properties. Any geometric figure having these four properties is a square.

The classical view captures what scientists aim at, and, as in the case of geometry, achieve. However, a major discovery of cognitive science has been that the classical view cannot handle most everyday concepts (Estes, 1994; Medin, 1989; Smith & Medin, 1981; Wittgenstein, 1953). Over the years, various problems have surfaced for the classical view (see Smith & Medin, 1981, for an extended review). Here we review three main criticisms.

The first criticism concerns a failure to specify defining properties for most concepts. Consider the concept of *furniture*. What are the necessary properties of furniture? Can you sit on it? It would be difficult to sit on a bookshelf. What is it made of? Furniture can be made of metal, plastic, fabrics, and so on. Is it found indoors? Picnic tables are usually found outdoors. It would be very difficult to find any property common to all furniture, and if there are some, they would not be unique to this concept. For example, if we say that furniture is useful, we can think of hundreds of useful objects that are

not furniture. (And some furniture is pretty useless.) If we say that furniture is whatever is used to furnish, then we have to define the concept *to furnish*. For a psychologist, the important question is whether people who know the meaning of the concept *furniture* know a list of necessary and sufficient properties. The same is true for *emotion, anger, love,* and the like. It is difficult to prove the nonexistence of such definitions, but so far none has appeared.

A second criticism formulated against the classical view is the existence of unclear cases. To return to our example of *furniture,* everyone would agree that a kitchen table is a piece of furniture. But what about light fixtures and carpeting? Would you consider them to be furniture as well? According to the classical view, determining whether an instance is a member of a category is very simple: You check whether the candidate possesses the defining properties of the category. It's a matter of all or nothing. But if a concept lacks defining properties, or if you are not aware of all the defining properties, then some cases are difficult to categorize. Conversely, failure to categorize consensually and reliably indicates that no such list exists. For *emotion,* everyone agrees that love is an emotion and a chair is not, but even the experts disagree on whether surprise, guilt, and respect are emotions.

The third criticism is a surprising empirical finding known as the "goodness-of-example" or "typicality" effect. According to the classical view, instances of a category all possess the defining properties of that category, and therefore should be equally good as exemplars of the category. However, a large body of empirical evidence has shown that some instances are judged to be better, and are generally processed faster (e.g., in a categorization task) and with higher accuracy (see Chang, 1986, and Smith & Medin, 1981, for partial reviews). A chair would be categorized faster and more accurately than a lamp as *furniture*. The classical view has no principled means to account for such effects.

The Probabilistic View

One alternative to the classical view is the probabilistic view, according to which the properties defining a concept are not essential nor sufficient (Reed, 1972; Rosch, 1975; Rosch & Mervis, 1975). Instead, the properties of each instance of a category have a probability of occurrence within the category. For example, properties of the concept *bird* include "have feathers," "have wings," and "can fly." These properties are true for most birds. However, some birds, such as penguins or ostriches, can't fly. A plucked robin without wings remains a bird. Each property has a probability of being associated with the concept of *bird*. In this case, according to the probabilistic view, "can fly" has a smaller probability of being associated with a particular instance than does "have feathers." The higher the probability is, the more salient the property is in the representation of the concept. A concept is thus formed of a set of properties that are characteristic of category membership (properties with a high probability of occurrence) but are not necessary.

An immediate consequence of probabilistic rather than defining properties is that the categories are ill defined and have fuzzy boundaries (Reed, 1972; Rosch, 1973). Category membership is graded rather than all or none. Rosch (1973) proposed that the category has an internal structure: The most typical instances are located at the center of the category, and the least typical at the periphery. That is, the more characteristic properties an instance has, the more typical it is, and the more likely it is to be included in the category. In contrast, instances sharing fewer properties with the other instances of the category (and more with instances of other categories) fall at the periphery

of the category. For example, chickens have feathers, wings, and beaks, and lay eggs, but they don't fly. When asked to rate the typicality of birds, people generally judge chickens as being less typical than robins.

Typicality has proved to have an influence on the encoding of new instances and on the processing of old ones. First, typical instances are categorized faster (Rips, Shoben, & Smith, 1973; Rosch, 1973; Fehr, Russell, & Ward, 1982). Also, the typical members of a category are the first to be learned by children (Mervis, 1980; Rosch, 1973) and are more likely to be named first when participants are asked to recall all members of a category (Mervis, Catlin, & Rosch, 1976). In verification tasks where participants are asked to verify whether an instance is a member of a category, the fastest "yes" responses are achieved with the most typical instances (Rips et al., 1973; Rosch, 1973). In tasks where participants are asked to discriminate between two stimuli ("same–different" response format), the presentation of a prime facilitates the "same" response when the two stimuli are typical, but it inhibits the "same" response when the two stimuli are not typical (Rosch, 1973, 1975). Lemay (1997) obtained similar results with facial expressions of emotion.

There is now a healthy competition among different probabilistic models. Although these different models share the two assumptions presented above, they differ in other ways. At one extreme is the prototype or schema view, according to which a concept is a single abstract summary representation that has all characteristic properties of the category. In this sense, the schema view is similar to the classical view in considering a concept abstract. The prototype is an ideal exemplar of the category. At the other extreme is the exemplar view, according to which a concept is represented by a collection of specific cases with no abstract summary (Reed, 1972; Medin & Schaffer, 1978; Estes, 1986; Nosofsky, 1986; see Ashby, 1992, for a review of several exemplar-based models). In its extreme form, the exemplar view rejects the possibility of the abstraction of any summary information (e.g., Reed, 1972).

The exemplar view has received a great deal of empirical support (see Nosofsky, 1992, for a review of several studies). Even though most studies have involved simple artificial categories, there is some evidence that children encode specific examples when learning a new concept. Kossan (1981) observed that second-graders were more likely to encode specific examples when learning a new concept and were more likely to use specific examples when asked to categorize new instances. Kossan also found that fifth-graders were more likely to use exemplars when they had to categorize complex stimuli. She concluded that young children's conceptual strategy relies mainly on specific exemplars rather than on abstracting a general rule when learning a new concept.

There is some evidence that emotion concepts are represented by exemplars as well. Conway (1990) compared the types of images elicited when people were presented with abstract concepts, objects, activities, and feelings. Feelings mainly elicited "autobiographical memories," whereas abstract concepts elicited images that were not based on specific experience. He concluded that emotion concepts are primarily represented in terms of memories of emotional experiences.

The Theory-Based View

Medin (1989) and Murphy and Medin (1985) argued that similarity alone is insufficient to explain conceptual coherence. According to these authors, there are not enough constraints put on similarity in the probabilistic models. In order to solve that problem, they proposed the theory-based view. According to this view, as we experience the world, we observe correlations between the properties of objects or events. We develop and use theories to explain those correlations and to structure the concept.

What is appealing in the theory-based view is that it provides a basis for deciding which properties are relevant in defining a category. Some properties are prominent in our concepts because of their importance in our knowledge of the world, and others are excluded because they are irrelevant in our theories (Medin, 1989). Theories allow us to achieve coherence when there is no obvious similarity between the instances of a category. For example, consider chicken, lobster, carrot, almond, and pineapple. All these instances have different compositions (animal, vegetable) and look very different (different colors, shapes, and textures). So, in terms of similarity based on their observable properties, all these instances are different. However, they have this in common: They are edible for humans, and therefore included in the category *food*. Presumably, the concept *food*

is embedded in a naive theory of the biology of nutrition.

Psychology and allied disciplines have provided several models of concept formation and structure. The old notion that a concept is a set of necessary and sufficient properties is gone, but the exact replacement is not clear. The precise details of structure and process of a given emotion concept has yet to be worked out, but this revolution in thinking about concepts has revealed new properties of emotion concepts, to which we now turn.

A DESCRIPTION OF EVERYDAY EMOTION CONCEPTS

This section concerns emotion concepts as they are used in everyday life. Everyday emotion concepts are part of the cognitive processes not just of university-educated North American students, but of our primitive ancestors, our present-day cousins living in hunter–gatherer societies, and very young children. In all such cases, we need to portray the concepts as they actually exist, flaws and all. (A later section considers how they can be tidied up, improved, and otherwise made more useful for scientific work.)

The concepts used for emotion are a heterogeneous lot. Some are more general (*emotion, mood, feeling, temperament*), whereas others are more specific (*pride, guilt, outrage*). Some imply an object (whatever it is that one is afraid of, in love with, or angry at), whereas others do not (one can be tense, anxious, relaxed, happy, or depressed without knowing why). Some seem to form natural bipolar pairs (*happy–sad, tense–relaxed, elated–depressed*), whereas others do not, or at least not as clearly (*tension, outrage, terror,* and *agitation* all seem without an exact opposite, or perhaps to share the same opposite of *calmness*).

Available research leads us to conclude that all eight of the following properties are required to give a complete portrait of how emotions are conceptualized. Any one of these eight properties, considered alone, provides only a partial picture and—like any partial truth—can be misleading.

1. *Fuzzy boundaries.* The concepts expressed by the words *emotion, anger, love,* and the like have fuzzy boundaries (Fehr & Russell, 1984; Russell & Fehr, 1994); similar evidence

exists for comparable terms in other languages (Smith & Tkel-Sbal, 1995; Turk Smith & Smith, 1995). Speakers who know the meanings of these words are uncertain whether some subcategories or some actual instances are or are not members of the categories denoted. It appears that individuals have no sure means to decide questions of membership unequivocally, and therefore sometimes do not know whether what they are experiencing or witnessing is really an emotion, really love, and so on.

2. *Dimensions.* As we have said, some pairs of concepts (those 180° apart in Figure 31.2; see below) specify bipolar continua, such as *tense–calm, elated–depressed,* and *happy–sad.* We refer to these concepts as "dimensions." Such dimensions have two interesting properties. First, the clearest cases, such as those just mentioned, do not imply an object that the feeling is about (one can be anywhere on the dimension of *happy–sad* without knowing why). Second, some dimensions appear to exist in all languages and in young children (Lutz, 1982; Russell, 1991; Russell & Bullock, 1985; Wierzbicka, 1995). Osgood, May, and Miron's (1975) semantic differential research found bipolar affective dimensions in every language examined.

Watson and Tellegen's (1985) claim of the independence of positive and negative affect seemed to challenge the bipolarity of these pairs. New evidence and analyses, however, have found support for bipolarity (Russell & Carroll, 1999), and Watson and Tellegen (1999) agree that the evidence supports bipolarity.

3. *Relativity of categories.* Some concepts specify groups of events that seem to differ qualitatively from another group. We refer to these concepts as "categories." *Love, shame, fear, anger, embarrassment,* and *pride* are examples. Emotion categories are in some ways similar but in some ways different across historical periods, sociocultural variation, and even age. Lists of categories have been compiled since the Chinese encyclopedia *Li Chi* of the 1st century B.C. The list varies with historical period; for example, Harré and Finlay-Jones (1986) described a category of emotion, *accidie,* named in English during the Middle Ages, but now all but forgotten. And the list varies with language. For example, whereas the number of categories named in English has been estimated between 500 and 2,000, the number in Chewong was estimated at 7 (Howell, 1981). Categories that seem "basic" to speakers of

English may be missing in other languages; *sadness,* for example, is missing in Tahitian (Levy, 1973), and *anxiety* is missing in various languages (Russell, 1991).

4. *Typicality.* Membership in each emotion category is a matter of degree rather than all or none. Gradedness of membership has been found for subcategories, for personal experiences of emotion, and for facial expressions of emotion (Russell & Fehr, 1994).

5. *Inter-category structure.* Emotion categories and dimensions are related to each other in a systematic manner. "Structures of emotion" attempt to represent these relations (see Diener, 1999; Russell & Feldman Barrett, 1999). For example, both multidimensional scaling and factor analyses of emotion-related words, faces, and situations converge on placing categories within a two-dimensional space such as that shown in Figure 31.2. Note that prototypical emotion categories fall in only certain regions of the full space. One implication of any such structure is that a particular instance is not typically a member of only one category (in which case the categories would be mutually exclusive), but of several categories, albeit to varying degrees (Russell & Fehr, 1994; Russell & Bullock, 1986).

If so, why does it seem that a given event is often a member of exactly one category? Can't one be afraid, and nothing else? Fear usually presupposes values on dimensions; when afraid, one is typically more unhappy than happy, more aroused than calm. In such cases, however, only one category name comes readily to mind, presumably because that one category name summarizes other properties, and no other category name is nearly as relevant. Those cases that seem like just one category are probably close to the prototypes (idealized exemplars) for that category.

6. *Scripts.* Emotion categories are understood in terms of a "script," which is a prototypical sequence of causally connected and temporally ordered subevents (Fehr & Russell, 1984). For example, the category *anger* begins with some offense, which produces bodily activation, a rush of thoughts and a feeling of displeasure, followed by a desire for revenge. Lakoff (1987) calls the script a cognitive model, and Medin (1989) calls it a theory. Ortony, Clore, and Collins (1988) provide an analysis of emotion concepts as consisting of either pleasure or displeasure plus the (cognitive representation of) the eliciting situation. Doré and

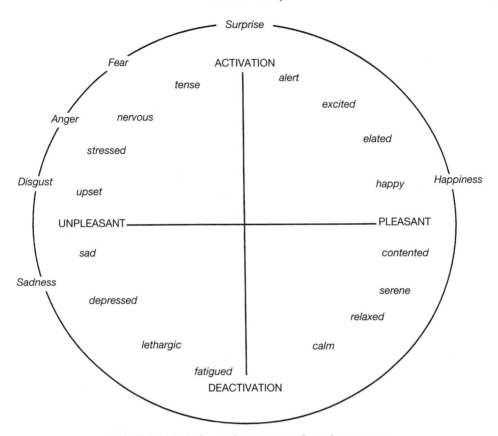

FIGURE 31.2. A circumplex structure of emotion concepts.

Kirouac (1985, 1986) provide evidence that emotion categories are defined by the eliciting situation.

7. *Hierarchy.* Emotion categories are embedded in a fuzzy hierarchy (Russell & Fehr, 1994). That emotion categories form a hierarchy has long been supposed (e.g., in the use of hierarchical cluster analysis or in schematic a priori hierarchies), but attempts to portray that hierarchy have not been successful. At the topmost level (most general) are such general concepts as *emotion, mood,* and *affect.* In a middle level are the kinds of categories that come first to mind: *love, anger, elation, shame, grief, jealousy, contentment,* and so on. At the lowest level are subordinate categories: *puppy love, parental love, patriotic love,* and so on.

The problem is that emotion categories do not form a classical hierarchy in which subcategories are logical subsets of more superordinate categories. Instead, emotion categories vary in two properties. The first is breadth: Some, such as *unhappy,* are quite broad (and hence appear in the upper regions of the hierarchy), whereas others, such as *outrage,* are quite narrow (and hence appear in the lower regions). The second property is degree of overlap: Most but perhaps not all instances of *outrage* are also instances of *anger;* most but perhaps not all instances of *anger* in turn are instances of *unhappiness.*

8. *Theory-embeddedness.* Emotion categories are embedded in a broader theory of mind. Human beings explain others in terms of beliefs, desires, and other intentional states (Harris, 1989; Russell, Fernández-Dols, Manstead, & Wellencamp, 1995; Wellman, 1993).

Summary. These eight properties are not competing accounts. Rather, they are highly interrelated (e.g., variations along the dimensions of property 2 yield the circumplex of property 5). Historically, however, psychologists have searched for one property that is *the* way to describe emotion concepts—hence controversies about categories versus dimensions, cluster analysis versus multidimensional scaling, and fuzzy categories versus the circumplex. We have stated the eight properties starkly, but some have received much more attention than others.

THE DEVELOPMENT OF EMOTION CONCEPTS

These eight properties are endpoints of a developmental course. A full understanding of emotion concepts requires an account of their origin and development. Let us begin with the question of nature versus nurture. On this topic, the full range of possibilities is available.

At one end of that range are the many psychologists who assume that even infants understand the emotions of their caregivers (from vocal and facial expressions) in terms of adult-like categories appropriately labeled *anger, happiness,* and the like (Izard, 1994). This assumption presupposes (often implicitly) something like innate primitive emotion categories (*anger, fear, sadness,* etc.), which, from this perspective, are pancultural natural kinds. What children must acquire through experience are the names for these categories, information about them, and the rules about what emotions are socially appropriate in what circumstances.

At the other end of the range is the position is that the child must learn from the culture or construct from experience every aspect of a conceptual scheme for emotions (Harré & Finlay-Jones, 1986). Estes's (1986) exemplar model of concepts presupposes just such an environmental account, in that an adult concept is a set of experienced exemplars.

We suggest a position that lies midway between these traditional extremes. *Anger, fear,* and so on are not pancultural. Still, there are great similarities in emotion concepts across cultures. We therefore suggest that emotion concepts are end products of a developmental process, albeit a highly constrained one. A child begins with general constraints on how to interpret the emotion world, and then is guided by experience, by observation, and by the folk theory of the surrounding culture.

One important initial (and universal, we hypothesize) constraint is property 2, the bipolar dimensions of pleasure–displeasure and degree of arousal. A variety of events in the child's world are given meaning in these terms: A subjective experience may be felt as pleasant-and-aroused; the word *fear* is initially interpreted as

meaning unpleasant-and-aroused; the caregiver's sad demeanor appears unpleasant-and-unaroused. Thus, from a very early age, children have their own way of interpreting what they experience and witness. Very young children discriminate different emotions, but the basis of discrimination is pleasure and arousal dimensions, rather than adult-like categories appropriately labeled *anger, fear,* and the like—which develop only after exposure to emotion events and the surrounding culture, and which only slowly approach their adult form. The interplay and unfolding of these influences result in both the similarities and differences in the specific emotion concepts seen across different languages and cultures (property 3, relativity of categories).

The child's initial interpretation of any emotional event is relatively "undifferentiated" (relatively high in the fuzzy hierarchy; property 7). The child's developmental task is to differentiate within this global interpretation to reach the adult taxonomy for emotional states used by the child's community (Bridges, 1932). Consider a case that an adult would label *jealousy*: A teenage boy shouts and glares when his girlfriend walks off with another boy. Our hypothesis is that a very young child does not interpret this scene as jealousy per se, but perceives the teenager as in a state of displeasure-and-high-arousal (Russell & Paris, 1994). Although lacking the concept of *jealousy,* the young child still makes sense of the scene witnessed. Bullock and Russell (1986) have proposed a sequence of six steps that highlights the possible interplay between initial universal ways of conceptualizing emotion and accumulating environmental influence. The child only slowly moves from the global interpretation to the particular one. And this movement is brought about in part by the child's acquiring a script (property 6)—in this example, about *jealousy.* Questions about the development of emotional understanding can thus be focused on the question of how the child acquires an emotion script.

There are at least two general, not mutually exclusive answers to this question. The first answer is that the properties that make up an emotion script are likely to be correlated. Personal experience and observation of others will encounter these correlations. When the child observes someone with wide-open eyes and raised eyebrows, that person is probably facing something unexpected. If the situation is also threatening, the person is also likely to withdraw.

When the child observes another person, this time with glaring eyes and clenched fists, that person is more likely to be faced with frustration and injustice. The second person is also more likely to make threats and to act aggressively. Thus two episodes initially interpreted as unpleasant-and-aroused can come to be differentiated into fear and anger.

The second answer to the question of how scripts develop is that the surrounding culture provides information about specific emotions. Parents and others label and interpret the young child's own emotions, as well as the emotions of others (Dunn, Brown, & Beardsall, 1991). Children acquire the culture's emotion terms for, its rules about, and its accumulated knowledge of—its theory of—emotion (Manstead, 1995).

Whatever the fate of the specific developmental account sketched here, we want to emphasize the usefulness of a developmental perspective in understanding emotion concepts, and vice versa. Some hypotheses about adult concepts, such as exemplar views versus innate views, concern origins. A developmental perspective suggests that it is probably naive to suppose that different societies, or even two different people, have identical concepts (although they must be similar enough to allow communication). Similarly, the properties of emotion concepts delimited in the study of adults raise questions and suggest answers about the development of those properties.

PRESCRIPTION FOR A SCIENCE OF EMOTION

We now turn to a brief discussion of theoretical psychology. Our aim is not to advance a theory, but to raise some neglected questions.

The preceding section has concerned the folk concepts implicit in the everyday understanding of emotion, and yet much of the research on this topic is presented either as direct evidence on the nature of emotion events or at least as providing a scientific conceptualization of emotion. An essential but neglected question is just how suited the everyday conceptualization of emotion is for scientific work. Not all of the properties of the everyday conceptual system per se are desirable from a scientific point of view. Vague boundaries, an unspecified number of overlapping categories, and graded membership work against the precision and rigor aimed at in science. Just as folk physics provided an

initial hypothesis for scientific physics rather than a valid theory, the folk psychology of emotion is the beginning rather than the end of scientific psychology.

To illustrate, consider the question of the boundary to the domain of study: Which events must be accounted for by any theory of emotion (and therefore potentially count as evidence for or against a given theory), and which fall outside the domain and are therefore irrelevant? The usual solution to this problem is to rely on the everyday concept of *emotion*. This solution is often implicit; indeed, so far in this chapter, we have been writing as if all relevant concepts were limited to emotion and its subcategories, and we have written of theories of *emotion*. Sometimes this solution is explicit. Ortony (1987), for example, criticized taxonomies including concepts that are not clear subcategories of *emotion*, such as feelings of *sleepiness, surprise,* and *guilt*. Unfortunately, however, the concept of *emotion* has blurry boundaries, so that while some events clearly are emotions and some are not, the border between them is ambiguous (*relaxation, respect, friendliness, surprise, pride,* and *guilt* seem to straddle the fence between emotions and nonemotions). Furthermore, the concept of *emotion* is itself an everyday folk concept, which does not appear in all languages (Russell, 1991). Finally, we can find no justification for assuming that the concept of *emotion* defines nature's own boundary. To limit the domain of interest here to *emotion* would be like excluding *black* and *white* from the domain of *color* because, when one is buying film, the word *color* contrasts with the term *black and white*.

Rather than restrict the domain of interest a priori to whatever is covered by the everyday concept of *emotion* found in the English language, we suggest a more empirical solution. The domain of study consists of the closely interconnected set of events or states. The relevant concepts are those empirically needed to describe those events. For example, although *calmness* is not a subcategory of *emotion,* it is needed because it is part of the same descriptive network, expressing the bipolar opposite of *tension, stress, anger,* and *fear.* Our rationale is the same as that for including the categories of *black* and *white* in the domain of *color.*

Another widespread assumption is that the English language concepts of *happiness, fear, anger,* and *sadness* (plus from two to six more) provide the basic scientific units for a psychology of emotion. Of course, great clarity would be achieved if hundreds of different emotion categories could be reduced to some small but fixed number of "basic" emotions. This was the goal of categorical accounts proposed by Tomkins (1962, 1963) and those he inspired, such as Izard (1971) and Ekman (1972). Because emotional episodes are complex, there are various ways to divide them into "basic" categories. Here are five possibilities.

1. One system could classify emotional episodes according to the facial expression involved (if facial expressions are in fact involved). Ekman (1984) proposed that all emotions produce facial expressions, and that the natural boundaries between types of emotion can be determined by differences in facial expressions. He subsequently abandoned the idea (Ekman, 1994), apparently for two reasons: (a) categories of emotion for which no facial signal exists (he listed *awe, guilt,* and *shame* as potentially lacking a facial signal), and (b) different categories that share the same signal (different categories of positive emotions all share the smile).

2. Emotional episodes could be classified according to the pattern of autonomic nervous system activity involved, and Ekman, Levenson and Friesen (1983) argued that such patterns yield a set of "basic emotions" similar—although not identical—to that yielded by the study of facial expressions. Research has yet to establish patterns associated with specific emotions (Zajonc & McIntosh, 1992; Cacioppo, Berntson, Larsen, Poehlmann, & Ito, Chapter 11, this volume).

3. Emotional episodes could be classified by the cognitive processes involved. Roseman, Spindel, and Jose (1990), Frijda (1986), Scherer (1984), and Smith and Ellsworth (1985) have developed such systems for the appraisal of the antecedent situation, and the convergence across authors is great. Ortony et al. (1988) proposed a classification based on the combination of pleasure–displeasure and cognitive presuppositions. Weiner (1985) similarly classified emotions based on the attributions involved. All such cognitive taxonomies postulate many more basic emotions than do schemes based on facial expressions or autonomic activity.

4. Emotional episodes could be classified by the action involved (Frijda, 1986; Plutchik, 1980). Such proposals remain rudimentary, and

have been more speculative than empirical. They also face the obvious difficulty that angry persons do not always act aggressively, frightened persons do not always flee, and there seems to be no particular behavior unique to happiness.

5. Finally, emotional episodes could be classified by the brain structures and neurotransmitters that underlie them (Panksepp, 1989; Johnson-Laird & Oatley, 1989.)

These five lines of research do not seem to be converging on the same set of "basic" categories (Turner & Ortony, 1992). In pointing to this problem, we do not mean to question the importance of the instances of fear, anger, happiness, and so on (the so-called "basic" emotions), nor do we mean to question the search for basic concepts—those elemental units out of which all else can be built. That search is highly important. We do, however, suggest that the everyday concepts of *fear, anger,* and the like are too complex to be those sought-after elements.

In their search for the elemental building blocks of an emotion, Johnson-Laird and Oatley (1989) focused on a key question: What can one feel without knowing why? Now most emotion categories presuppose an object—something that one is angry about, afraid of, in love with, and so on. If so, such emotions are complex and therefore cannot serve as elemental building blocks. In the search for elemental building blocks, dimensions such as *happy–sad* have the advantage of not being about something and thus appear simpler.

Emotion categories, thought of as scripts, can be decomposed into subevents. One theoretical question is raised by this decomposition: Do we need to postulate a mechanism that generates the subevents or a mechanism that generates the pattern among them (their coherence)? Imagine a deck of 52 playing cards. You deal out various poker hands of 5 cards each. You could categorize the resulting hands: flush, straight, straight flush, full house, three of a kind, and so forth. Nevertheless, it would be incorrect to suppose that one needs to postulate some generative mechanism for the patterns (e.g., the straight flush mechanism). Thus decomposition of emotion raises the possibility that mechanisms might exist for the generation of the constituents, but no additional mechanism for the generation of the resultant pattern that defines the emotion category. The poker example suggests that the key fact here is the degree of association among the constituents. If certain packages of constituents nearly always co-occur, then some generating mechanism might be needed. But if the packages represent little more than the occasional co-occurence of the constituents, no such mechanism would be needed. Again, the point is to set aside a priori assumptions and seek more empirically answerable questions. Here the question might be about the empirical degree of association among subevents that together form emotion categories.

CONCLUSION

Concepts are everywhere in the psychology of emotion. They are part of the subject matter of the discipline, and they are used as scientific tools. Indeed, in the study of emotion, we can do little without relying on everyday concepts directly or indirectly. For instance, to assess emotion, whether in a highly structured protocol or simply on the spot, we rely on someone's (perhaps even a psychologist's) description of that emotion, or on an instrument that was validated against lay descriptions. Thus, in the study of mood, we ask our patients, clients, or participants in experiments to describe how they feel. Or we may use a biological index that had previously been shown to correlate with such reports.

The concepts expressed by the words *emotion, anger, love,* and hundreds of others are filters that transform raw data into the perception that, for example, someone is acting emotional, is being angry, or has fallen in love. These filters are needed to make sense of the raw data but are often invisible, as though observation were a direct registration of an event. But observation is not direct, and an examination of the mental filtering of raw data is necessary to understand the observations on which the science of emotion depends. Concepts simplify the complex world; they are used to group together different events. Simplifying is both their benefit and their problem. We have no guarantee that our current concepts group events together in the right way.

Studies of the semantics of emotion language and of how children's concepts of emotion change with development reveal a heterogeneous array of concepts. It is small wonder that psychologists have argued about dimen-

sions versus categories, about what counts as an emotion, and about the nature of emotion. Everyday concepts are fuzzy enough to support a variety of seemingly contradictory opinions. This is not to say that the events that these are concepts of are in some sense fuzzy. Nothing about the fuzziness of our current everyday concepts precludes the refinement and honing of these concepts into scientifically useful tools.

The psychology of emotion addresses two quite different topics: emotion and the understanding of emotion. In both arenas, concepts are central, but in completely different ways. In the science of emotion per se, we seek to mold concepts to scientific standards. In our view, emotion researchers have been highly conservative in the concepts proposed, rarely straying far from the everyday concepts inherited from our ancestors.

The second topic, human understanding of emotion, requires a completely different attitude toward concepts. Here concepts are part of the subject matter. The goal is therefore to describe them as accurately as possible, including both their desirable and undesirable properties. The recent revolution in understanding concepts in general promises rapid progress on this second topic.

NOTE

1. Many authors use "concept" and "category" interchangeably. Others use "concepts" to refer to the mental representation, or intention, and "category" to refer to sets of objects in the real world, or extension. We use both "concept" and "category" to refer to mental representations. Later, we develop the idea that categories and dimensions are different types of concepts. Because we believe that the crucial distinction is between mental representations and the events represented, we use italics to indicate when a word such as *anger* refers to the concept, and roman type when it refers to the event.

REFERENCES

Ashby, F. G. (1992). Multidimensional models of categorization. In F. G. Ashby (Ed.), *Multidimensional models of perception and cognition* (pp. 449–484). Hillsdale, NJ: Erlbaum.

Bridges, K. M. B. (1932). Emotional development in early infancy. *Child Development, 3,* 324–334.

Bruner, J. S., Goodnow, J., & Austin, G. A. (1956). *A study of thinking.* New York: Wiley.

Bullock, M., & Russell, J. A. (1986). Concepts of emotion in developmental psychology. In C. E. Izard & P. B. Read (Eds.), *Measuring emotions in infants and children* (Vol. 2, pp. 203–237). Cambridge, England: Cambridge University Press.

Chang, T. M. (1986). Semantic memory: Facts and models. *Psychological Bulletin, 99,* 199–220.

Conway, M. A. (1990). Conceptual representation of emotions: The role of autobiographical memories. In K. J. Gilhooly, M. T. G. Keane, R. H. Logie, & G. Erdos (Eds.), *Lines of thinking: Reflections on the psychology of thought* (Vol. 2, pp.133–143). Chichester, England: Wiley.

Diener, E. (1999). Introduction to special section on the structure of emotion. *Journal of Personality and Social Psychology, 76,* 803–804.

Doré, F. Y., & Kirouac, G. (1985). Identifying the eliciting situations of six fundamental emotions. *Journal of Psychology, 119,* 423–440.

Doré, F. Y., & Kirouac, G. (1986). Reliability of accuracy and intensity judgments of eliciting situations of emotions. *Canadian Journal of Behavioural Science, 18,* 92–103.

Dunn, J., Brown, J., & Beardsall, L. (1991). Family talk about feeling states and children's later understanding of others' emotions. *Developmental Psychology, 27,* 448–455.

Ekman, P. (1972). Universal and cultural differences in facial expressions of emotions. In J. Cole (Ed.), *Nebraska Symposium on Motivation,* (Vol. 19, pp. 207–283). Lincoln: University of Nebraska Press.

Ekman, P. (1984). Expression and the nature of emotion. In K. S. Scherer and P. Ekman (Eds.), *Approaches to emotion* (pp. 319–344). Hillsdale, NJ: Erlbaum.

Ekman, P. (1994). Strong evidence for universal in facial expressions: A reply to Russell's mistaken critique. *Psychological Bulletin, 115,* 268–287.

Ekman, P., Levenson, R. W., & Friesen, W. V. (1983). Autonomic nervous system activity distinguishes among emotions. *Science, 221,* 1208–1210.

Estes, W. K. (1986). Array model of category learning. *Cognitive Psychology, 18,* 500–549.

Estes, W. K. (1994). *Classification and cognition.* New York: Oxford University Press.

Fehr, B., & Russell, J. A. (1984). Concept of emotion viewed from a prototype perspective. *Journal of Experimental Psychology: General, 113,* 464–486.

Fehr, B., Russell, J. A., & Ward, L. (1982). Prototypicality of emotions: A reaction time study. *Bulletin of the Psychonomic Society, 20,* 253–254.

Frijda, N. H. (1986). *The emotions.* Cambridge, England: Cambridge University Press.

Harré, R., & Finlay-Jones, R. (1986). Emotion talk across time. In R. Harré (Ed.), *The social construction of emotions* (pp. 220–233). Oxford: Basil Blackwell.

Harris, P. L. (1989). *Children and emotion: The development of psychological understanding.* Oxford: Basil Blackwell.

Howell, S. (1981). Rules not words. In P. Heelas & A. Lock (Eds.), *Indigenous psychologies: The anthropology of the self* (pp. 133–143). London: Academic Press.

Izard, C. E. (1971). *The face of emotion.* New York: Appleton-Century-Crofts.

Izard, C. E. (1994). Innate and universal facial expressions: Evidence from developmental and cross-cultural research. *Psychological Bulletin, 2,* 288–299.

Johnson-Laird, P. N., & Oatley, K. (1989). The language of emotion: An analysis of a semantic field. *Cognition and Emotion, 3,* 81–123.

Kossan, N. E. (1981). Developmental differences in concept acquisition strategies. *Child Development, 52,* 290–298.

Lakoff, G. (1987). Cognitive model and prototype theory. In U. Neisser (Ed.), *Concepts and conceptual development: Ecological and intellectual factors in categorization* (pp. 63–100). Cambridge, England: Cambridge University Press.

Lemay, G. (1997). *La catégorisation des expressions faciales émotionnelles: une étude dimensionnelle.* Unpublished doctoral dissertation, Université Laval, Québec, Québec, Canada.

Levy, R. I. (1973). *Tahitians.* Chicago: University of Chicago Press.

Lutz, C. (1982). The domain of emotion words in Ifaluk. *American Ethnologist, 9,* 113–128.

Manstead, A. S. R. (1995). Children's understanding of emotion. In J. A. Russell, J. M. Fernández-Dols, A. S. R. Manstead, & J. C. Wellencamp (Eds.), *Everyday conceptions of emotion: An introduction to the psychology, anthropology and linguistics of emotion* (pp. 315–332). Dordrecht, The Netherlands: Kluwer.

Medin, D. L. (1989). Concepts and conceptual structure. *American Psychologist, 44,* 1469–1481.

Medin, D. L., & Schaffer, M. M. (1978). Context theory of classification learning. *Psychological Review, 85,* 207–238.

Mervis, C. B. (1980). Category structure and the development of categorization. In R. Spiro, B. C. Bruce, & W. F. Brewer (Eds.), *Theoretical issues in reading comprehension* (pp. 279–307). Hillsdale, NJ: Erlbaum.

Mervis, C. B., Catlin, J., & Rosch, E. (1976). Relationships among goodness-of-example, category norms, and word frequency. *Bulletin of the Psychonomic Society, 7,* 283–284.

Murphy, G. L., & Medin, D. L. (1985). The role of theories in conceptual coherence. *Psychological Review, 92,* 289–316.

Nosofsky, R. M. (1986). Attention, similarity, and the identification–categorization relationship. *Journal of Experimental Psychology: General, 115,* 39–57.

Nosofsky, R. M. (1992). Similarity scaling and cognitive process models. *Annual Review of Psychology, 43,* 25–53.

Ortony, A. (1987). Is guilt an emotion? *Cognition and Emotion, 1,* 289–298.

Ortony, A., Clore, G. L., & Collins, A. (1988). *The cognitive structure of emotions.* Cambridge, England: Cambridge University Press.

Osgood, C. E., May, W. H., & Miron, M. S. (1975). *Cross-cultural universals of affective meaning.* Urbana: University of Illinois Press.

Panksepp, J. (1989). The neurobiology of emotions: Of animal brains and human feelings. In H. Wagner & A. Manstead (Eds.), *Handbook of social psychophysiology* (pp. 5–26). Chichester, England: Wiley.

Plutchik, R. (1980). *Emotion: A psychoevolutionary synthesis.* New York: Harper & Row.

Reed, S. K. (1972). Pattern recognition and categorization. *Cognitive Psychology, 3,* 382–407.

Rips, L. J., Shoben, E. J., & Smith, E. E. (1973). Semantic distance and the verification of semantic relations. *Journal of Verbal Learning and Verbal Behavior, 12,* 1–20.

Rosch, E. H. (1973). Natural categories. *Cognitive Psychology, 4,* 328–350.

Rosch, E. H. (1975). Cognitive representations of semantic categories. *Journal of Experimental Psychology: General, 104,* 192–233.

Rosch, E. H., & Mervis, C. B. (1975). Family resemblances: Studies in the internal structure of categories. *Cognitive Psychology, 7,* 573–605.

Roseman, I. J., Spindel, M. S., & Jose, P. E. (1990). Appraisal of emotion-eliciting events: Testing a theory of discrete emotions. *Journal of Personality and Social Psychology, 59,* 899–915.

Russell, J. A. (1991). Culture and the categorization of emotions. *Psychological Bulletin, 110,* 426–450.

Russell, J. A., & Bullock, M. (1985). Multidimensional scaling of emotional facial expressions: Similarity from preschoolers to adults. *Journal of Personality and Social Psychology, 48,* 1290–1298.

Russell, J. A., & Bullock, M. (1986). Fuzzy concepts and the perception of emotion in facial expressions. *Social Cognition, 4,* 309–341.

Russell, J. A., & Carroll, J. M. (1999). On the bipolarity of positive and negative affect. *Psychological Bulletin, 125,* 3–30.

Russell, J. A., & Fehr, B. (1994). Fuzzy concepts in a fuzzy hierarchy: Varieties of anger. *Journal of Personality and Social Psychology, 67,* 186–205.

Russell, J. A., & Feldman Barrett, L. (1999). Core affect, prototypical emotional episodes and other things called *emotion*: Dissecting the elephant. *Journal of Personality and Social Psychology, 76,* 805–819.

Russell, J. A., Fernández-Dols, J. M., Manstead, A. S. R., & Wellencamp, J. C. (Eds.). (1995). *Everyday conceptions of emotion: An introduction to the psychology, anthropology and linguistics of emotion.* Dordrecht, The Netherlands: Kluwer.

Russell, J. A., & Paris, F. A. (1994). Do children acquire concepts for emotions abruptly? *International Journal of Behavioral Development, 17,* 349–365.

Scherer, K. R. (1984). On the nature and function of emotion: A component process approach. In K. R. Scherer & P. Ekman (Eds.), *Approaches to emotion* (pp. 293–318). Hillsdale, NJ: Erlbaum.

Smith, C. A., & Ellsworth, P. C. (1985). Patterns of cognitive appraisal in emotion. *Journal of Personality and Social Psychology, 48,* 813–838.

Smith, E. E., & Medin, D. L. (1981). *Categories and concepts.* Cambridge, MA: Harvard University Press.

Smith, K. D., & Tkel-Sbal, D. (1995). Prototype analysis of emotion terms in Palau, Micronesia. In J. A. Russell, J. M. Fernández-Dols, A. S. R. Manstead, & J. C. Wellencamp (Eds.), *Everyday conceptions of emotion: An introduction to the psychology, anthropology and linguistics of emotion* (pp. 85–102). Dordrecht, The Netherlands: Kluwer.

Tomkins, S. S. (1962). *Affect, imagery, and consciousness: Vol. 1. The positive affects.* New York: Springer.

Tomkins, S. S. (1963). *Affect, imagery and consciousness: Vol. 2. The negative affects.* New York: Springer.

Turk Smith, S., & Smith, K. D. (1995). Turkish emotion concepts: A prototype analysis. In J. A. Russell, J. M. Fernández-Dols, A. S. R. Manstead, & J. C. Wellencamp (Eds.), *Everyday conceptions of emotion: An introduction to the psychology, anthropology and linguistics of emotion* (pp. 103–120). Dordrecht, The Netherlands: Kluwer.

Turner, T. J., & Ortony, A. (1992). Basic emotions: Can conflicting criteria converge? *Psychological Review, 99,* 566–571.

Watson, D., & Tellegen, A. (1985). Toward a consensual structure of mood. *Psychological Bulletin, 98,* 219–235.

Watson, D., & Tellegen, A. (1999). Issues in the dimensional structure of affect: Effects of descriptors, measurement error, and response formats. *Psychological Bulletin, 125,* 601–610.

Weiner, B. (1985). An attributional theory of achievement motivation and emotion. *Psychological Review, 92,* 548–573.

Wellman, H. M. (1993). Early understanding of mind: The normal case. In S. Baron-Cohen, H. Tager-Flusberg, & D. J. Cohen (Eds.), *Understanding other minds: Perspectives from autism* (pp. 10–39). Oxford: Oxford University Press.

Wierzbicka, A. (1995). Everyday conceptions of emotion: A semantic perspective. In J. A. Russell, J. M. Fernández-Dols, A. S. R. Manstead, & J. C. Wellencamp (Eds.), *Everyday conceptions of emotion: An introduction to the psychology, anthropology and linguistics of emotion* (pp. 17–47). Dordrecht, The Netherlands: Kluwer.

Wittgenstein, L. (1953). *Philosophical investigations.* New York: Macmillan.

Zajonc, R. B., & McIntosh, D. N. (1992). Emotions research: Some promising questions and some questionable promises. *Psychological Science, 3,* 70–74.

CHAPTER 32

Current Directions in Emotional Intelligence Research

Peter Salovey
Brian T. Bedell
Jerusha B. Detweiler
John D. Mayer

Basic research in emotion has proliferated over the past few decades, and although there is still a great deal to be learned, a consistent view of emotion has begun to emerge from this work. Affective phenomena constitute a unique source of information for individuals about their surrounding environment and prospects, and this information informs their thoughts, actions, and subsequent feelings. The essential assumption in our work has been that individuals differ in how skilled they are at perceiving, understanding, and utilizing this emotional information, and that a person's level of "emotional intelligence" contributes substantially to his or her intellectual and emotional well-being and growth. In this chapter, we review our model of emotional intelligence and the competencies it highlights, including a brief discussion of measurement issues. We then describe how emotional intelligence influences self-regulatory coping and goal setting.

Personality psychology most often emphasizes differences in the way people typically think, feel, and act. However, as Mischel (1990) has pointed out, people relate to the world in a manner that is much more flexible than the terms "dispositions" and "styles" might alone suggest. According to Mischel, cognitive psychology's essential lesson for personality psychologists is that individuals selectively construct their experiences of reality and that the result of this process depends heavily on their "construction competencies" (i.e., information-processing abilities that determine the range of potential thoughts, feelings, and behaviors the individual can enlist within and across situations). To understand the person, we must augment our study of dispositions with an appreciation for these competencies. The investigation of such competencies, aside from general intelligence, has focused largely on social problem-solving skills and other practical abilities and has been referred to as "social intelligence," among other labels (Cantor & Kihlstrom, 1985, 1987; Gardner, 1983; Sternberg, 1985, 1988; Sternberg & Smith, 1985; Thorndike, 1920; Thorndike & Stein, 1937; Wagner & Sternberg, 1985).

We believe that emotional competencies are fundamental to social intelligence (Salovey & Mayer, 1990). This is because social problems and situations are laden with affective information. Moreover, emotional competencies apply not only to social experiences but to experiences within the individual. Indeed, some investigators have argued that self-knowledge and the individual's inner life are characterized most saliently by emotional experiences (e.g., Showers & Kling, 1996). Thus emotional intelligence is more focused than social intelligence, in that it pertains specifically to emotional phenomena and yet can be applied directly to a broad range of emotional problems embedded in both interpersonal *and* intrapersonal experience (Epstein, 1998; Mayer & Salovey, 1997; Saarni, 1990, 1997; Salovey & Mayer, 1990). It is this efficient, parsimonious nature of the emotional intelligence framework that we find so compelling. Indeed, we find it puzzling that psychology has taken so long to recognize the importance of emotional competencies.

EMOTION: History
FROM DISINFORMATION
TO INFORMATION

Emotion, historically, has taken a back seat to cognition. Philosophers and scientists (psychologists included) have relied on and glorified analytic intelligence throughout much of Western history. Aristotle (384–322 B.C.), for example, argued that the human intellect is "the highest thing in us, and the objects that it apprehends are the highest things that can be known" (1976, p. 328; see also Aristotle, 1947). At the same time, emotion has been regarded as an inferior, often disruptive element of human nature. The passions are fallible guides for action. Anger often leads to unjust acts of violence; fear often leads to debilitating cowardice. This sentiment toward feeling was the impetus for Malebranche's unequivocal prescription: "Impose silence on your senses, your imagination, and your passions, and you will hear the pure voice of inner truth" (quoted in James, 1890/1950, p. 10).

As a result of the historic mistrust of emotion, many psychologists have taken the position that the intellect and passions are at cross purposes (e.g., Schaffer, Gilmer, & Schoen, 1940; Woodworth, 1940). From this perspective, the intellect provides accurate information, while emotion clouds our minds with disinformation. Young (1936) even went so far as to say that emotions have no conscious purpose and cause "a complete loss of cerebral control" (pp. 457–458). It is quite understandable, then, that early conceptions of intelligence in the field of psychology were decidedly rational. According to Terman, "An individual is intelligent in proportion as he is able to carry on abstract thinking" (1921, p. 128). Being emotional was not seen as being smart.

Contemporary psychology has moved away from this view that reason is superior to emotion, and toward an emphasis on the functionality of emotions. This shift originated in the philosophy of David Hume and the ethological observations of Charles Darwin. Hume (1739/1948), an early 18th century empiricist philosopher, argued that emotional impulses motivate all action. He believed that reason does nothing more than consider facts and generate inferences about the world relevant to achieving and prioritizing the agendas set by the passions. Freud (1923/1962) held a somewhat similar position. He emphasized the primacy of the id, the seat of the self's emotionality and psychic energy, and maintained that the other aspects of the self are derivative. Freud, much as Hume did, put reason in the service of emotion.

Although Hume challenged the position that reason is superior to emotion, it was not until Darwin published *The Expression of the Emotions in Man and Animals* (1872/1965) that the functional purpose of emotion was established. Through his intensive ethological observations of animal life, Darwin revealed that emotions serve at least two highly advantageous functions. First, emotion energizes adaptive behaviors such as flight (fear) and procreation (love or lust). Second, emotion gives rise to a signaling and communication system that confers a significant survival advantage on entire species as well as individual organisms (e.g., a single deer's fear response upon seeing a predator quickly informs other deer of the threat). By attributing these functions to emotion, Darwin brought attention to the adaptive, seemingly intelligent nature of emotional expression.

Today great emphasis is placed on the psychological importance of emotion, and it is generally accepted that emotions augment rather than interfere with other cognitive capacities. Emotions certainly have the signaling function identified by Darwin (e.g., Ekman, 1984). Moreover, there is wide agreement that emotions are the primary source of motivation—they arouse, sustain, and direct human action (e.g., Izard, 1971; Leeper, 1948; Tomkins, 1962). Finally, many emotion researchers have adopted a broad affect-as-information view, according to which internal emotional experiences provide individuals with important information about their environment and situation. This information shapes the individuals' judgments, decisions, priorities, and actions (e.g., Schwarz, 1990; Schwarz & Clore, 1983).

EMOTIONAL INTELLIGENCE: A FRAMEWORK

When we first began developing the concept of "emotional intelligence" (e.g., Salovey & Mayer, 1990), our intention was to draw closer attention to the cooperative relationship between emotion and reason. Humans are not, in any practical sense, predominantly rational beings, nor are they predominantly emotional beings. They are both. Thus a person's ability to adapt and cope in life depends on the integrated functioning of emotional and rational capacities. As Tomkins has said, "Out of the marriage of reason with affect there issues clarity with passion. Reason without affect would be impotent, affect without reason would be blind" (1962, p. 112). Success in life depends on one's ability to reason about emotional experiences and other affect-laden information, and to respond in emotionally adaptive ways to the inferences drawn by reason about one's situation, prospects, and past.

Generally, we have described emotional intelligence as the ability to perceive and express emotions, to understand and use them, and to manage emotions so as to foster personal growth (Mayer & Salovey, 1997; Salovey & Mayer, 1990). More formally, however, we define emotional intelligence by the specific competencies it encompasses, including the ability to perceive, appraise, and express emotion accurately; the ability to access and generate feelings when they facilitate cognition; the ability to understand affect-laden information and make use of emotional knowledge; and the ability to regulate emotions to promote emotional and intellectual growth and well-being. Our model of emotional intelligence is presented in Table 32.1. The model is composed of four branches, each of which represents a class of skills, ordered hierarchically according to their complexity. The subskills of each branch are further organized according to their complexity, such that the more sophisticated sub-

skills of each branch increasingly depend on skills from the other branches of the model.

Perception, Appraisal, and Expression of Emotion

Individuals can be more or less skilled at attending to, appraising, and expressing their own emotional states. These competencies are basic information-processing skills in which the relevant information consists of feelings and mood states. For example, some individuals, called "alexithymic," are unable to express their emotions verbally, presumably because they have difficulty identifying their feelings (Apfel & Sifneos, 1979). These basic emotional competencies are important, because those who can quickly and accurately appraise and express their emotions are better able to respond to their environment and to others. There is some evidence, for instance, that individuals who can communicate their emotions skillfully are more empathic and less depressed than those who are unable to do so (Mayer, DiPaolo, & Salovey, 1990; Notarius & Levenson, 1979; Prkachin, Craig, Papageorgis, & Reith, 1977).

Individuals must also appraise the emotions of others. Again, there are individual differences in people's ability to perceive accurately, understand, and empathize with others' emotions (reviewed in Buck, 1984), and individuals who are best able to do so may be better able to respond to their social environment and build a supportive social network (Salovey, Bedell, Detweiler, & Mayer, 1999).

Emotional Facilitation of Thinking

Emotional states and their effects can be harnessed by individuals toward a number of ends. For example, positive moods make positive outcomes appear more likely, whereas negative moods make negative outcomes appear more likely (Johnson & Tversky, 1983; Mayer, Gaschke, Braverman, & Evans, 1992). Addressing a problem while in different moods may enable individuals to consider a wider range of possible actions and outcomes (Mayer & Hanson, 1995). Likewise, a number of investigators (e.g., Isen, 1987; Palfai & Salovey, 1993; Schwarz, 1990) have argued that emotions create different mental sets that are more or less adaptive for solving certain kinds of problems. That is, different emotions create different information-processing styles. Happy

TABLE 32.1. The Emotional Intelligence Framework

Perception, appraisal, and expression of emotion

- Ability to identify emotion in one's physical and psychological states.
- Ability to identify emotion in other people and objects.
- Ability to express emotions accurately, and to express needs related to those feelings.
- Ability to discriminate between accurate and inaccurate, or honest and dishonest, expressions of feelings.

Emotional facilitation of thinking

- Ability to redirect and prioritize one's thinking based on the feelings associated with objects, events, and other people.
- Ability to generate or emulate vivid emotions to facilitate judgments and memories concerning feelings.
- Ability to capitalize on mood swings to take multiple points of view; ability to integrate these mood-induced perspectives.
- Ability to use emotional states to facilitate problem solving and creativity.

Understanding and analyzing emotional information; employing emotional knowledge

- Ability to understand how different emotions are related.
- Ability to perceive the causes and consequences of feelings.
- Ability to interpret complex feelings, such as emotional blends and contradictory feeling states.
- Ability to understand and predict likely transitions between emotions.

Regulation of emotion

- Ability to be open to feelings, both those that are pleasant and those that are unpleasant.
- Ability to monitor and reflect on emotions.
- Ability to engage, prolong, or detach from an emotional state, depending upon its judged informativeness or utility.
- Ability to manage emotion in oneself and others.

Note. Adapted from Mayer and Salovey (1997). Copyright 1997 by Peter Salovey and David Sluyter. Adapted by permission of Basic Books, a member of Perseus Books, L.L.C.

moods facilitate a mental set that is useful for creative tasks in which one must think intuitively or expansively in order to make novel associations (e.g., Isen, Daubman, & Nowicki, 1987; see also Isen, Chapter 27, this volume). Sad moods generate a mental set in which problems are solved more slowly with particular attention to detail, using more focused and deliberate strategies. Palfai and Salovey (1993) have argued that these two different information-processing styles (i.e., intuitive and expansive vs. focused and deliberate) should be effective for two different kinds of problem-solving tasks: inductive problems such as analogical reasoning, and deductive logical tasks, respectively.

Emotionally intelligent individuals may also be able to harness the motivational qualities of emotion. For example, a student may focus purposefully on the negative consequences of failing to submit a term paper on time, in order to self-induce a state of fear that will spur him to get an early start on the paper. Another student may remind herself of all her successes before sitting down to write the paper. The self-induced positive mood that results bolsters her confidence in writing the paper, and she may be more likely to persevere when faced with a particularly challenging section of it.

Understanding and Analyzing Emotional Information; Employing Emotional Knowledge

A third branch of emotional intelligence concerns essential knowledge about the emotional system. The most fundamental competency at this level concerns the ability to label emotions with words and to recognize the relationships among exemplars of the affective lexicon. The emotionally intelligent individual is able to recognize that the terms used to describe emotions are arranged into families, and that groups of emotion terms form fuzzy sets (see Ortony, Clore, & Collins, 1988). For instance, individuals learn that words such as "rage," "irritation," and "annoyance" can be grouped together as terms associated with anger. Perhaps more importantly, the relations among these terms are deduced—that annoyance and irritation can lead to rage if the provocative stimulus is not eliminated; or that envy is often experienced in contexts that evoke jealousy, but jealousy is less likely to be part of envy-provoking situations (Salovey & Rodin, 1986, 1989).

To understand the emotions, individuals must learn what emotions convey about relationships. Lazarus (1991), for example, describes how "core relational themes"—the central harm or benefit in adaptational encounters that underlies each emotion—are associated with different kinds of feelings. Anger results from a demeaning offense against the self, guilt from transgressing a moral imperative, and hope from facing the worst but yearning for better (see Lazarus, 1991, Table 3.4, p. 122).

Increased complexity in this domain of emotional intelligence is represented by knowledge that emotions can combine in interesting and subtle ways. At a high school reunion, nostalgic conversation can give rise to wistful feelings, a blend of both joy and sorrow. Startled surprise at the wonders of the universe, combined with fear about one's insignificant place in it, may give rise to awe.

Finally, understanding and analyzing emotions includes the ability to recognize transitions among emotions. For example, Tangney and her colleagues have written extensively about how shame but not guilt can turn quickly to rage. Individuals can literally be shamed into anger (Tangney, Wagner, Fletcher, & Gramzow, 1992).

Regulation of Emotion

Emotional knowledge also contributes to the fourth component of emotional intelligence, emotion regulation. However, individuals must develop further competencies in order to put their knowledge into action. They must first be open to the experience of mood and emotion, and must then practice and become adept at engaging in behaviors that bring about desired feelings. These emotion-regulating skills enable individuals to engage in mood maintenance and mood repair strategies, such as avoiding unpleasant activities or seeking out activities that they typically find rewarding. Individuals who are unable to manage their emo-

tions are more likely to experience negative affect and remain in poor spirits (Erber, 1996).

Through the self-reflective experience of emotion, individuals acquire knowledge of the correlates and causes of their emotional experiences. Knowledge of emotion thus enables individuals to form theories of how and why emotions are elicited by different situations. This ability to understand and analyze emotional experiences translates into the ability to understand oneself and one's relation to the environment better, which may foster effective emotion regulation and greater well-being. In the psychotherapy literature, this has been termed "emotional literacy" (Steiner & Perry, 1997).

Although our work has focused primarily on reflective metamood abilities (i.e., thoughts about moods; see Mayer & Gaschke, 1988), it is worth noting that emotional intelligence may manifest itself in a second way. Individuals often react emotionally toward their direct experiences of emotion, and these metaemotional experiences can either facilitate or impede functioning (Gottman, 1997). For example, a person can feel ashamed for having felt or expressed anger toward a loved one. The metaemotion in this case is shame, which takes as its object the individual's direct experience of anger, and it may motivate the individual to inhibit anger or at least to suppress angry behavior in the future. This type of learned emotional restraint can be highly advantageous to parents and children, between lovers, and in most other social relationships. To date, there have been very few investigations of metaemotion (although see Gottman, 1997), in part because studying emotional responses to direct emotional experiences is a complex affair. However, metaemotion is a fascinating instance of how humans take themselves and their experiences as objects and respond to these objects in a higher-order manner.

The ability to help others enhance or repair their moods is also an important skill. Individuals often rely on their social networks to provide not just a practical but an emotional buffer against negative life events (for a review, see Stroebe & Stroebe, 1996). Moreover, individuals appear to derive a sense of efficacy and social worth from helping others feel better and from contributing to the joy of their loved ones. The ability to manage others' emotional experiences also plays a significant role in impression management and persuasion. Although this skill is sometimes employed unscrupulously by sociopaths, cult leaders, and some advertisers, impression management and persuasion are often employed prosocially as well. Thus, individuals who are able to regulate the emotions of others effectively are better able to act prosocially and to build and maintain solid social networks.

One might ask this: What skills, beyond emotional knowledge, undergird competence at emotion regulation? We cannot answer this question definitively, because very little research has explored the distinction between emotional knowledge and emotion regulation. However, this distinction can be illustrated quite easily. Consider the embarrassment many of us experience while dancing. Those of us who enjoy dancing are able to lose ourselves in the music and motion of dance. Unfortunately, this delightful state is elusive when we are anxious about being evaluated by others. The reality, however, is that few others typically care how we dance. Other dancers are either too engrossed or, ironically, too embarrassed to notice us, and spectators pass over those of us whose dancing is at worst a little boring and are attracted instead to those whose dancing is marked by skill and elegance. Interestingly, those of us who find dancing embarrassing are often aware that no one else is paying attention to our dancing. We even understand that our fear of being evaluated is itself our greatest impediment on the dance floor. This is metaemotional knowledge. However enlightening this knowledge is, it enables only a few of us to actually overcome our embarrassment. This is because emotion regulation is distinct from the metaemotional knowledge it presupposes. That is, regulatory skills are needed in order to put metaemotional knowledge into action.

Summary

Much remains to be learned about each of the components of emotional intelligence. As a result, our conception of emotional intelligence is still evolving. Nonetheless, our understanding of emotional intelligence already has translated into some productive research. We next turn to measures of emotional intelligence, after which we discuss some of the findings and implications that have stemmed from the use of these measures and the theory more generally.

MEASURING EMOTIONAL INTELLIGENCE

The concept of emotional intelligence has had immediate intuitive and popular appeal (e.g., Goleman, 1995a; Segal, 1997), and it has been possible to organize much past and contemporary research using the notion of emotional competencies. Attempts to operationalize and directly measure this construct were inevitable. Guided by the original framework of emotional intelligence, Mayer and Salovey initially examined the meta-, or reflective, experience of mood (e.g., Mayer & Gaschke, 1988; Salovey, Mayer, Goldman, Turvey, & Palfai, 1995). Two self-report scales to assess metamood cognitions have been employed: a trait scale (Salovey et al., 1995) and a state scale (Mayer & Stevens, 1994). The former is the 30-item Trait Meta-Mood Scale (TMMS), which taps into people's beliefs about their propensity to attend with clarity to their own mood states and to engage in mood-repair. The items of this measure are straightforward—for example, "I pay a lot of attention to how I feel" (Attention), "I can never tell how I feel" (Clarity, reverse-scored), and "I try to think good thoughts no matter how badly I feel" (Repair). The psychometric properties of this scale are quite good, and some empirical findings have been generated from its use (Goldman, Kraemer, & Salovey, 1996; Salovey et al., 1995). Nevertheless, the TMMS has its limitations. First, its factor structure consists of only three dimensions (i.e., Attention, Clarity, and Repair), representing only a few of the emotional competencies outlined in our framework. Moreover, the TMMS, like other self-report measures (see, e.g., Bar-On, 1997), essentially asks individuals whether or not they are emotionally intelligent; it does not require individuals to demonstrate their emotional competencies. We believe that a more valid measure of core emotional intelligence requires a test that relies on tasks and exercises rather than on self-report.

More recent task-based attempts to measure emotional intelligence have focused on comprehensive aptitude-type tests that rely on the assessment of relevant skills. The Multifactor Emotional Intelligence Scale (MEIS and its successor, the MSCEIT) can be administered with pencil and paper or on computer (Mayer, Caruso, & Salovey, 1998; Mayer, Salovey, & Caruso, 1997). It is organized into four main branches, reflecting our current framework for understanding emotional intelligence—Identifying Emotions, Using Emotions, Understanding Emotions, and Managing Emotions. Within each of these four branches, a series of subtests has been designed to assess various competencies, as illustrated in Table 32.2.

Some of the tasks included on the computerized version of the MEIS involve identifying the consensual feelings suggested by colors, abstract artistic designs, and pieces of music. In a study done some years ago, the ability to identify the emotions suggested by colors and artistic designs correlated with traditional ratings of empathy (Mayer et al., 1990). Measures of emotional intelligence have since been revised, with these revisions emphasizing such issues as reporting styles of emotions, alternative methods of assessing correct responses, and new tasks to measure emotional intelligence (Mayer & Geher, 1996). The MEIS and the MSCEIT represent the culmination of this work (Mayer et al., 1998), and the MEIS has now been administered to a normative sample of 503 adults ranging in age from 17 to 70 years. Scale scores for the four main branches appear to be internally consistent, with Cronbach alphas of .84, .86, .89, and .81, respectively (Mayer, Caruso, & Salovey, 1999).

Although the construct of emotional intelligence has generated considerable interest, the measurement of it is emerging rather slowly, and validity data are especially scarce. There is a converging sense among researchers of what

TABLE 32.2. The Subtests of the Multifactor Emotional Intelligence Scales (MEIS)

I. Identifying Emotions
• In Faces
• In Designs
• In Stories
• In Music (computerized version only)

II. Using Emotions
• Synesthesia
• Feeling Biases

III. Understanding Emotions
• Complex Blends
• Progressions
• Transitions
• Perspectives

IV. Managing Emotions
• Self-Help
• Helping Others

emotional intelligence is (a set of competencies concerning the appraisal and expression of feelings, the use of emotions to facilitate cognitive activities, knowledge about emotions, and the regulation of emotion) and what emotional intelligence is not (good character, optimism, delay of gratification, or persistence) (see Mayer, Salovey, & Caruso, in press, for a comparison of our model of emotional intelligence to those popularized by others). Yet there is considerably less consensus on how best to measure emotional intelligence. Although we have argued for the advantages of task-based and behavioral assessment (Mayer et al., 1990; Mayer, Salovey, & Caruso, in press), various self-assessments have also appeared that may measure important aspects of individuals' perceptions of their competencies in this domain (Bar-On, 1997; Schutte et al., 1998). Other self-tests that have been repackaged under the rubric of emotional intelligence appear to have little to do with this construct (e.g., Simmons & Simmons, 1997).

Some validity work has been carried out. For example, Bar-On (1996) reported that his measure, the Emotional Quotient Inventory, differentiated U.S. Naval Academy students who felt personally successful from those who did not, Latina immigrants scoring high versus low on an acculturation scale, prisoners from nonprisoners, and the like. Although this kind of concurrent validation is helpful, the predictive validity of measures of emotional intelligence remains an open question. In very recent work, we measured the association of subscales of the MEIS to Verbal test performance on the Scholastic Aptitude Test (SAT) and found that the Synesthesia and Complex Blends subscales accounted for significant variance in SAT Verbal scores, even after baseline verbal intelligence (as estimated via a vocabulary test) was controlled for. Findings such as these suggest that while verbal intelligence is the best predictor of verbal aptitude as measured by the SAT Verbal test, there is a component of test performance that is accounted for by aspects of emotional intelligence. We suspect that at a minimum, individuals with emotional competencies may be better able to cope with the stress of the testing situation, producing some "value added" to their SAT scores.

Despite what has been learned about the measurement of emotional intelligence over the past few years, research on the psychometric properties in general, and the validity in particular, of most emotional intelligence tests is still in its adolescence. Thus Boring's (1923) suggestion that "intelligence is what the tests test" (p. 35) is especially misleading in this area of study. As we settle on a clear conceptual understanding of emotional intelligence, we will continue to refine and expand measures of emotional intelligence to reflect this understanding. With this in mind, we now turn our attention toward some early but promising findings pertaining to emotional intelligence and what these findings suggest with respect to particularly relevant domains—coping with stressors and other aspects of self-regulation.

EMOTIONALLY INTELLIGENT SELF-REGULATION: COPING AND GOAL SETTING

We believe, with others (e.g., Izard, 1971; Tomkins, 1962), that emotion is the wellspring of human motivation, the "primary provider of blueprints for cognition, decision and action" (Tomkins, 1962, p. 22). This view implies that emotional intelligence amounts to motivational or self-regulatory intelligence. To the extent that one has highly developed emotional knowledge and competencies, successful and efficient self-regulation toward desired ends should be facilitated. In the following sections, we explore two related forms of self-regulation—coping and goal setting—and we suggest ways in which emotional competencies might influence these processes.

Coping with the Past: The Emotional Benefits of Cognitive Housecleaning

Because past events cannot be changed, coping with a previous traumatic experience is a matter of understanding the event and reinterpreting it in a more meaningful way. The importance of emotional competencies is perhaps most evident in these cases, in that individuals are forced to respond to the powerful emotions elicited by memories of past events. Elsewhere, we have argued that successful coping depends on the integrated operation of many emotional competencies, and we have suggested that deficiencies in basic emotional competencies such as emotion perception and expression will interfere with the development and implementation of more complex coping skills such as emotion regulation (Salovey et al., 1999). The

relevance of the emotional intelligence framework to two specific methods of coping—rumination and disclosure—is reviewed below.

"Rumination" is defined as "passively and repetitively focusing on one's symptoms of distress and the circumstances surrounding those symptoms" (Nolen-Hoeksema, McBride, & Larson, 1997, p. 855). Nolen-Hoeksema (1991), who has investigated rumination extensively, regards it as a particular style of responding to stressful events that tends to intensify and lengthen periods of depressed mood. Following the 1989 Loma Prieta earthquake in California, for example, Nolen-Hoeksema and Morrow (1991) found that people who had a more ruminative response style before the earthquake exhibited higher levels of depression 10 days after the event. Similarly, newly bereaved men identified as ruminators prior to their loss experienced longer and more severe periods of depression after their partners' death (Nolen-Hoeksema et al., 1997). The deleterious effects of ruminative coping have been corroborated in a number of laboratory studies as well (e.g., Nolen-Hoeksema & Morrow, 1993).

Although ruminating about a negative experience exacerbates one's negative mood, Pennebaker has demonstrated that disclosing emotional traumas in writing, even anonymously, has numerous beneficial effects (see Pennebaker, 1997, for a review). These benefits, which can be achieved by writing about a traumatic experience from just once to a few times over several weeks, include fewer health center visits and improved grades among college students; enhanced immune system functioning (see Booth & Pennebaker, Chapter 35, this volume); and in some cases fewer self-reports of physical symptoms, distress, and depression (Cameron & Nicholls, 1998; Greenberg & Stone, 1992; Pennebaker, Colder, & Sharp, 1990; Pennebaker, Kiecolt-Glaser, & Glaser, 1988). These impressive findings have been replicated among such diverse populations as maximum-security prisoners and recently unemployed professionals (see Smyth, 1998, for a meta-analysis).

Pennebaker's findings serve as the perfect complement to the research on rumination. The outward linguistic expression of traumatic experiences facilitates the coping process, whereas internally ruminating over a negative event only makes things worse. Pennebaker's (1997) model of cognitive changes nicely captures the critical difference between rumination and emotional disclosure. The model suggests that repeated disclosures help organize a person's thoughts and feelings about a traumatic experience. In effect, emotional disclosure is like cognitive housecleaning: The disclosure process restructures disturbing experiences, giving them a coherent, meaningful place in the person's life. In contrast, it would seem that individuals who ruminate are unable to find meaning in negative experiences. The excessive attention they pay to their negative feelings may indicate that they have become stuck in their attempt to make sense of their feelings. This view is supported by compelling evidence that effective emotional disclosures are characterized by specific cognitive changes. Examining the written emotional disclosures of their subjects, Pennebaker and his colleagues found that the thinking of those who benefited most from emotional disclosure grew more insightful and causal over time, and that their writing displayed a balanced use of negative emotion words along with more frequent use of positive emotion words (Pennebaker, Mayne, & Francis, 1997; Pennebaker & Francis, 1996).

From the perspective of emotional intelligence, it seems plausible that individuals may differ in their ability to bring about the cognitive changes that characterize effective emotional disclosures. A pair of studies lends direct support to this hypothesis. The first found that individuals who consistently monitor their moods generate a greater number of ruminative responses following questions asking them to list some of the specific strategies that they use to cheer themselves up (Swinkels & Giuliano, 1995). This underscores the notion that simply paying too much attention to one's emotions may be maladaptive. In a second study, this finding was extended (Salovey et al., 1995). Specifically, whereas depressed affect was positively correlated with attention to emotions, it was negatively correlated with clarity in discriminating feelings. In this study, participants watched a 12-minute segment of a documentary on drinking and driving that contained graphic footage of serious automobile accidents and the traumas experienced by the victims. The film had a powerful impact, lowering participants' moods substantially. Subsequently, participants performed a thought-sampling task under the pretext of a second study. Recovery of positive mood after this task was best predicted by the Clarity subscale of the TMMS. That is, those individuals who reported that they were usually very clear about their feelings were more likely to rebound from the induced negative mood. Analyses of the thought samplings indicated that individuals who experienced their moods clearly showed a reduction in their negative thoughts over time, whereas those who were less clear about their feelings continued to ruminate. Together, these two studies suggest that excessive attention to negative moods leads to rumination, but that clarity in labeling one's feelings facilitates resolving one's thoughts about a past trauma.

In general, we believe that individuals who can identify how they are feeling, understand the implications of these feelings, and effectively regulate their emotional experiences will cope more successfully with negative experiences than will less emotionally intelligent individuals. At a basic level, those who are unable to perceive and appraise their own emotional states accurately may fail to recognize the origin of their troubles. If so, the coping process will stall, precluding effective emotional disclosure. In previous work from our own lab, individuals open to emotional experience (even when negative) report lower levels of depression than those who claim to "fight the feeling" or claim that "everything is OK" (Mayer, Salovey, Gomberg-Kaufman, & Blainey, 1991).

In addition, emotionally intelligent individuals should be able to recognize and pursue the most effective means of coping. For instance, Nolen-Hoeksema and colleagues have argued that one of the most effective approaches for disengaging from a ruminative coping cycle is distraction (Morrow & Nolen-Hoeksema, 1990; Nolen-Hoeksema & Morrow, 1993). When people use pleasant activities to relieve their moods, they show better problem-solving skills and fewer negative thoughts (Lyubomirsky & Nolen-Hoeksema, 1995). One of the most advanced skills within the reflective regulation of emotion is the ability to ameliorate negative emotions and promote pleasant emotions (Mayer & Salovey, 1997). Thus we would argue that individuals who are skilled at regulating emotions should be better able to move to repair their emotional states by using pleasant activities as a distraction from negative affect.

Engaging in distraction is different, however, from avoiding negative affect altogether. Wegner's work on ironic processes (e.g., Wegner, Erber, & Zanakos, 1993) has demonstrated that attempts to avoid negative thoughts and feelings altogether are doomed to fail. The failure of sheer mental willpower occurs because the suppressed thoughts and feelings are maintained as markers of how successfully the person has avoided them. This work is consistent with the model of cognitive changes, suggesting that a negative experience will continue to challenge one's thoughts and feelings until it is resolved and is thus no longer something that needs to be avoided. A further component of reflective regulation is the ability to understand emotions without exaggerating or minimizing their importance (Mayer & Salovey, 1997). As a result, emotionally intelligent individuals should be able to strike a healthy balance between pleasant distractions and coming to terms with their feelings. Some types of distractions may even facilitate active coping. For instance, we would expect emotionally intelligent individuals to seek out the company of others in an effort to be reminded by them that life is good. Individuals naturally turn to others in order to discuss and make sense of negative life events (Pennebaker & Harber, 1993), and the availability of high-quality social support may prevent individuals from ruminating (Nolen-Hoeksema, 1991).

Finally, emotionally intelligent individuals should disclose their emotional experiences more often because they are more apt to recognize that sharing is an efficient means of organizing and thus regulating one's emotions. Moreover, the linguistic features characterizing effective emotional disclosure (i.e., insight, causal thinking, and a balance of emotion) reflect one's ability to understand, analyze, and actively regulate emotion. Thus individuals with strong emotional competencies should be able to (1) recognize their emotional responses to a trauma as natural, (2) see the trauma and their emotions in the broader context of their lives, and (3) make positive attributions about the trauma and their emotions.

The "take-home point" is that emotional intelligence fosters effective coping. For example, Goldman, Kraemer, and Salovey (1996) surveyed students three times over the course of a semester: at the start of the semester, during midterm examinations, and during final examinations. They found that when stress was high, students who said they were able to regulate their moods (as measured with the TMMS) visited the health center less frequently than students who felt they could not regulate their feelings. In times of low stress, the ability to repair moods did not predict health center visits.

Thus there is some evidence that emotionally intelligent individuals do in fact cope better when stressful experiences arise.

Coping with the Future: Setting and Accomplishing Goals

As humans, we also possess the ability to self-regulate toward desired goals far in the future. As a result, day-to-day goals are typically embedded in long-term pursuits. Unfortunately, striving to accomplish distant goals can be stressful. Long-term goals, although they may be more meaningful than proximal goals, are often more complex and less manageable (Little, 1989). A great deal of work has investigated the tradeoff between proximal goals and distal goals, and has explored strategies that help individuals strike an effective balance between their need for immediate, concrete direction and their need for overarching, meaningful strivings (Bandura & Cervone, 1983). These investigations typically compare self-regulatory strategies or individual dispositions facilitating or, alternatively, impeding goal attainment. In an effort to extend this work, we would like to draw attention to competencies that should facilitate the adoption of effective self-regulatory strategies. In this section, we review some work that has investigated the relative structuring of proximal versus distal goals, and we suggest ways in which consideration of emotional intelligence may inform this work.

Recently, Taylor, Pham, Rivkin, and Armor (1998) have investigated the role of mental simulation in self-regulatory goal setting. The premise of this work is that people can use mental simulations to envision future possibilities and to develop and rehearse plans that will help them realize desirable outcomes. Not all mental simulations are equally effective, however. On the one hand, there are process simulations, which emphasize in detail the steps one must take in order to achieve a goal. For instance, a student mentally simulating what it would take to earn a good grade on an upcoming test might imagine performing, in sequence, the tasks comprising successful progress toward and achievement of a good grade (e.g., reviewing lecture notes, reading texts, discussing course material with fellow students, reviewing difficult material one last time the morning before the test, and carefully answering each question during the testing session). This type of mental simulation is extremely effective. Process simulations capitalize on the imagination's ability to make future events seem real, enabling individuals to "experience" the problems and emotions that will arise as they pursue a goal. As a result, individuals can rehearse means of solving these problems and of managing unwanted emotions, and they can make use of anticipated positive feelings to motivate themselves further.

Another form of mental simulation is outcome simulation, in which the person simply imagines the desired outcome, such as earning a good grade on the exam. Unlike process simulations, outcome simulations are not effective and may even be counterproductive. Outcome simulations make people feel wonderful about themselves. It is almost as if they have already accomplished their goals. Unfortunately, this is precisely why these simulations fail to be constructive. Those who simulate outcomes alone may do nothing to bring those outcomes about because they are satisfied with their imagined successes. Interestingly, popular self-help books almost exclusively tout outcome simulations as a means of achieving one's goals (e.g., Fanning, 1994; Peale, 1982). Making people feel good about themselves appears to be the key to selling books, regardless of whether immediate gratification actually promotes successful self-regulation.

In a convincing demonstration of how these types of mental simulation differ, Pham and Taylor (1999) assigned students preparing for an introductory psychology midterm exam to either a process simulation condition, an outcome simulation condition, or a control condition. Students in the process simulation condition were asked to visualize in detail studying for the exam, and they were given examples of study situations to help make their visualizations more concrete. In contrast, students in the outcome simulation condition were asked to vividly imagine having earned a high grade on the exam. Finally, students in the control condition were asked simply to monitor their studying prior to the exam. All students received a hint sheet outlining the study skills mentioned in the simulation conditions, in order to hold constant the amount of study information given across the conditions. The results of this study showed that students who mentally simulated the process leading to a good grade studied more and actually received higher grades than did students who merely imagined receiving a high grade. The performance of students in the control condition fell in between the performance of the two simulation conditions. Process simulation appeared to improve performance by decreasing exam anxiety and increasing planning and problem solving. Process simulations prepare individuals both emotionally and cognitively for the steps they must take to achieve a goal, and this preparation effectively facilitates goal attainment.

Although Taylor and her colleagues have manipulated the type of mental simulations used by participants in their experiments, people undoubtedly utilize mental simulations on their own, either spontaneously or in response to the advice of others or popular wisdom. We believe that emotional intelligence may play an important role in determining the type (i.e., process or outcome) and quality of the mental simulations that a person employs. Individuals who are emotionally intelligent better understand the tradeoff between feeling good now (outcome simulation) and finding satisfaction in pursuing challenging, less immediate goals (process simulation). This knowledge, combined with an ability to manage their feelings in order to delay gratification, enables emotionally intelligent individuals to enlist process simulations rather than outcome simulations. Moreover, effective mental simulations enable people to anticipate and prepare to manage the emotions they will experience as they pursue their goals. Emotional intelligence facilitates this aspect of simulation in at least three respects. First, a solid understanding of the causes and consequences of emotion will make a process simulation more vivid and realistic. In addition, the ability to generate or emulate emotional states further enhances the realism of the visualization process. Finally, the capacity for effective emotion regulation provides a concrete means of managing the feelings anticipated by a mental simulation. Emotional intelligence thus provides a skills-based foundation for adopting and most effectively engaging in process simulations—the type of mental simulation most likely to lead to goal attainment.

Focusing on Goal Pursuit Rather Than Attainment

The investigation of mental simulation seems to place a premium on goal attainment, but we should not let the directedness of self-regulation—the seemingly tireless pursuit of ends—

Flow

obscure a much more fundamental point about it. Taylor's focus on process simulations should remind us that truly satisfying experiences consist of *doing*, not just *having*. What fills life with happiness is the process of accomplishing, not simply accomplishments. No psychologist has more persuasively championed this theme than Csikszentmihalyi (1990), whose remarkable study of "flow" has yielded a model of optimal human experience that is both descriptive and prescriptive. "Flow" refers to states of experience in which individuals become totally engrossed in what they are doing—so much so that they forget about their daily concerns, lose track of time, and act as if nothing but the present activity matters. Csikszentmihalyi originally observed this immensely rewarding state among artists, surgeons, rock climbers, and others who often seem to lose themselves in their work and hobbies, but his subsequent investigations found that flow can and does happen to everyone.

Much of Csikszentmihalyi's work describes the essential components of flow and suggests how this state can be incorporated into our daily lives. As Csikszentmihalyi observes, "There are two main strategies we can adopt to improve the quality of life. The first is to try making external conditions match our goals. The second is to change how we experience external conditions to make them fit our goals better" (1990, p. 43). Although both of these strategies are important, controlling consciousness and our experience of external conditions is a much more enduring means of achieving happiness than always expecting the world to meet our expectations. The key to controlling consciousness is to weave enjoyment into the fabric of our daily lives, making each activity we pursue an end in itself. To do this, we must set challenging goals for ourselves that lead us to unexpected, novel accomplishments. However, we must make certain that these goals are neither impossible nor onerous. We can do this by ensuring that our goals are clear and provide immediate feedback. If we challenge ourselves in this way, we will reap the rewards of feeling in control, and we will grow through our day-to-day, moment-to-moment accomplishments: "When experience is intrinsically rewarding, life is justified in the present, instead of being held hostage to a hypothetical future gain" (Csikszentmihalyi, 1990, p. 69).

The recipe for bringing flow into one's life is not as easy to follow as it seems. As Csikszent-

mihalyi points out, "Control over consciousness is not simply a cognitive skill. At least as much as intelligence, it requires the commitment of emotions and will" (1990, p. 21). Csikszentmihalyi asserts that analytical intelligence is insufficient to achieve flow. It is not enough for individuals to understand that vague goals must be restructured into more manageable, immediately rewarding steps. In addition, individuals must at least (1) have an understanding of how it would feel to pursue activities that offer a greater sense of control and more immediate feedback; (2) be able to generate the positive feelings associated with such activities anticipatorily, in order to bolster their motivation; and (3) be able to manage, almost to the point of exclusion, negative feelings such as anxiety, frustration, or impatience that accompany thoughts about accomplishing more distal goals, especially when consideration of distal goals fails to inform one's immediate actions. These prerequisites draw heavily on the most sophisticated aspects of emotional intelligence, especially emotion regulation; without them, the consistent incorporation of flow experiences into one's life would seem impossible.

The concept of flow involves structuring our activities and how we think about them in ways that lead naturally to satisfying experiences. But sometimes our best-laid plans go astray, and these failures threaten to "block the flow" of experience. How do people respond when their goals are blocked? Obviously, failing to attain a goal is unpleasant. Even moving more slowly than expected toward a goal can be aversive (Carver & Scheier, 1990; Hsee & Abelson, 1991). However, not everyone reacts similarly when a goal is blocked. Some people are able to disengage gracefully when they realize a goal is out of reach. Others react more negatively, ruminating about their failure and its broader implications.

McIntosh (1996) has proposed a model explaining why certain individuals react strongly to goal nonattainment. The model begins with the observation that goals are structured hierarchically, which restates the notion that proximal, day-to-day goals (such as going for a run) are instrumental in achieving more general, distal strivings (such as being healthy or slim). Occasionally a particular lower-order goal must be achieved in order to reach a higher-order goal, but typically there are a number of ways to accomplish goals higher up the goal hierarchy (e.g., eating properly also promotes health and weight control). Nonetheless, some individuals tend to view particular lower-order goals as necessary even when they are not. McIntosh refers to these individuals as "linkers," because they interpret failure to attain lower-order goals as failure to attain their more distal goals. Linkers believe more firmly than others that their happiness depends on the accomplishment of goals, both big and small, proximal and distal. When a proximal goal is linked to an intermediate goal in the hierarchy, the person may become distressed if the initial goal is blocked. For instance, not running today may be taken as evidence that one will never exercise routinely, which may be disheartening. More dramatically, the proximal goal may be linked to a goal at the very top of the hierarchy. Not running today may be taken as evidence that one will never be healthy, slim, attractive, happy, or a good person. In this way, a minor failure can lead to a depressed or even hopeless state.

In support of the linking model, McIntosh has shown that linkers are more likely than non-linkers to ruminate about a current, unrealized goal (Martin, Tesser, & McIntosh, 1993), and that linkers report less happiness and more negative feelings as a result of their propensity to ruminate (McIntosh, 1996). In a short-term prospective study, McIntosh, Harlow, and Martin (1995) asked college students to complete measures of linking, stress, rumination, depression, and physical symptoms at an initial session and then again after a 2-week interval. Students who tended to link the attainment of lower-order goals to the attainment of higher-order goals reported more rumination, depression, and physical symptoms overall than their nonlinking peers. Moreover, linkers who reported experiencing stressful events at the time of the first session were the most likely to report depression and physical symptoms at the second session. In contrast, high stress at the first session failed to predict later depression and physical symptoms among nonlinkers. This parallels Nolen-Hoeksema's (e.g., Nolen-Hoeksema & Morrow, 1991, 1993) finding that ruminators report elevated levels of depression after experiencing stress, whereas individuals who do not ruminate are more resilient. Indeed, McIntosh's studies may explain in part why some people ruminate whereas others do not. People who link lower-order goals to higher-order goals appear to ruminate more when they experience stress or failure, and rumination mediates the influence of goal linking on subsequent dissatisfaction and negative affect.

Emotional intelligence makes it easier to take stock of various goals; it enables the individual to sense the personal importance of each goal and to use this information in reasoning about competing goals as well as alternate means of achieving long-term pursuits. This analysis enables emotionally intelligent individuals to invest themselves wisely in specific activities. If a setback or failure occurs, these individuals experience a loss, but the loss is well defined and assessable with respect to other means of moving forward. This stabilizes self-regulation in much the same way that effective emotional disclosures facilitate coping: by clarifying the individual's situation and averting ruminative thinking and paralysis.

FINAL THOUGHTS ON EMOTIONAL INTELLIGENCE

Most constructs in personality and social psychology mature for decades before they find a popular audience. The fate of emotional intelligence, however, has been quite different. Some time after our initial work on the subject was published (e.g., Mayer et al., 1990; Mayer & Salovey, 1993; Salovey & Mayer, 1990), a popular book on emotional intelligence appeared and skyrocketed up the best-seller list (Goleman, 1995a). With this book, emotional competencies went almost overnight from a set of abilities worthy of further study (our view) to a wealth of personal assets capable of determining a person's character, life achievements, and health (Goleman's view). Truly extraordinary claims on behalf of emotional intelligence are now commonplace—for example, "Having great intellectual abilities may make you a superb fiscal analyst or legal scholar, but a highly developed emotional intelligence will make you a candidate for CEO or a brilliant lawyer" (Goleman, 1995b, p. 76). It would seem that in proposing the framework of emotional intelligence, we stumbled upon a panacea for individuals and society alike without even knowing it!

Despite the recent popularization of the construct, empirical research on emotional intelligence is still in its infancy. The problematic issues in this area of work are not surprising, given the relative immaturity of this research domain. For one, the term "emotional intelligence" is used to represent various aspects of the human condition. We prefer to focus narrowly on specific abilities and competencies concerned with appraising, understanding, and regulating emotions, and with using them to facilitate cognitive activities. However, others have defined emotional intelligence in terms of motivation (persistence, zeal), cognitive strategies (delay of gratification), and even character (being a good person). Emotional intelligence may contribute to persistence, delay, and character, but they are not one and the same thing. The con artist may be especially skilled at reading and regulating the emotions of other people, but may have little of what is commonly thought to be good character. Second, this area of research will not prove to be productive unless the abilities that make up emotional intelligence can be measured reliably and unless these abilities are related to important, real-world outcomes. We think less attention should be focused on the issue of whether a monolithic "emotional quotient" has utility, or on gathering together various measures of social competence and calling them "emotional intelligence," and more on the development of tasks that can be used to assess actual emotion-related skills. We are not confident that self-reported abilities in this domain will prove any more useful than they have in the measurement of traditional, analytic intelligence. Finally, we urge educators and business managers to maintain their present interest in emotional intelligence, but to be skeptical of quick-fix programs served up by glib consultants— emotional intelligence "in a box." Although emotional intelligence research may challenge us to reconsider our notions of what it means to be smart (and what it means to be in touch with feelings), it will not, at the end of the day, be the key to reducing international conflict, fighting the war on drugs, or terminating the global plague of AIDS. Grandiose claims to the contrary serve only as palliatives to the public and as suppressors of scientific inquiry.

ACKNOWLEDGMENTS

Preparation of this chapter was facilitated by grants from the American Cancer Society (RPG-93-028-05-PB), the National Cancer Institute (R01-CA68427), the National Institute of Mental Health (P01-MH/DA56826), and the Andrew W. Mellon Foundation to Peter Salovey. This work was also supported by a National Science Foundation Graduate Fellowship to Brian T. Bedell.

REFERENCES

Apfel, R. J., & Sifneos, P. E. (1979). Alexithymia: Concept and measurement. *Psychotherapy and Psychosomatics, 3,* 180–190.

Aristotle. (1947). On the soul (J. A. Smith, Trans.). In R. McKeon (Ed.), *Introduction to Aristotle* (pp. 145–235). New York: Random House.

Aristotle. (1976). *Ethics* (J. A. K. Thomson, Trans.). London: Penguin Books.

Bandura, A., & Cervone, D. (1983). Self-evaluative and self-efficacy mechanisms governing the motivational effects of goal systems. *Journal of Personality and Social Psychology, 45,* 1017–1028.

Bar-On, R. (1996, August). *The era of the EQ: Defining and assessing emotional intelligence.* Paper presented at the 104th Annual Convention of the American Psychological Association, Toronto.

Bar-On, R. (1997). *EQ-I: Bar-On Emotional Quotient Inventory.* Toronto: Multi-Health Systems.

Boring, E. G. (1923, June 6). Intelligence as the tests test it. *New Republic,* pp. 35–37.

Buck, R. (1984). *The communication of emotion.* New York: Guilford Press.

Cameron, L. D., & Nicholls, G. (1998). Expression of stressful experiences through writing: Effects of a self-regulation manipulation for pessimists and optimists. *Health Psychology, 17,* 84–92.

Cantor, N., & Kihlstrom, J. F. (1985). Social intelligence: The cognitive basis of personality. In P. Shaver (Ed.), *Review of personality and social psychology* (Vol. 6, pp. 15–33). Beverly Hills, CA: Sage.

Cantor, N., & Kihlstrom, J. F. (1987). Personality and social intelligence. Englewood Cliffs, NJ: Prentice-Hall.

Carver, C. S., & Scheier, M. F. (1990). Origins and functions of positive and negative affect: A control-process view. *Psychological Review, 97,* 19–35.

Csikszentmihalyi, M. (1990). *Flow: The psychology of optimal experience.* New York: Harper & Row.

Darwin, C. (1965). *The expression of the emotions in man and animals.* Chicago: University of Chicago Press. (Original work published 1872)

Ekman, P. (1984). Expression and the nature of emotion. In K. Scherer & P. Ekman (Eds.), *Approaches to emotion* (pp. 319–344). Hillsdale, NJ: Erlbaum.

Epstein, S. (1998). *Constructive thinking: The key to emotional intelligence.* New York: Praeger.

Erber, R. (1996). The self-regulation of moods. In L. L. Martin & A. Tesser (Eds.), *Striving and feeling: Interactions among goals, affect, and self-regulation* (pp. 251–275). Hillsdale, NJ: Erlbaum.

Fanning, P. (1994). *Visualization for change* (2nd ed.). Oakland, CA: New Harbinger.

Freud, S. (1962). *The ego and the id.* (J. Strachey, Ed.; J. Riviere, Trans.). New York: Norton. (Original work published 1923)

Gardner, H. (1983). *Frames of mind: The theory of multiple intelligences.* New York: Basic Books.

Goldman, S. L., Kraemer, D. T., & Salovey, P. (1996). Beliefs about mood moderate the relationship of stress to illness and symptom reporting. *Journal of Psychosomatic Research, 41,* 115–128.

Goleman, D. (1995a). *Emotional intelligence.* New York: Bantam.

Goleman, D. (1995b). EQ: What's your emotional intelligence quotient? *The Utne Reader, 72,* 74–76.

Gottman, J. M. (1997). *Meta-emotion: How families communicate emotionally.* Mahwah, NJ: Erlbaum.

Greenberg, M. A., & Stone, A. A. (1992). Emotional disclosure about traumas and its relation to health: Effects of previous disclosure and trauma severity. *Journal of Personality and Social Psychology, 63,* 75–84.

Hsee, C. K., & Abelson, R. P. (1991). Velocity relation: Satisfaction as a function of the first derivative of outcome over time. *Journal of Personality and Social Psychology, 41,* 1–15.

Hume, D. (1948). A treatise of human nature. In H. D. Aiken (Ed.), *Hume: Moral and political philosophy* (pp. 1–169). New York: Hafner Press. (Original work published 1739)

Isen, A. M. (1987). Positive affect, cognitive processes, and social behavior. In L. Berkowitz (Ed.), *Advances in experimental social psychology* (Vol. 20, pp. 203–253). New York: Academic Press.

Isen, A. M., Daubman, K. A., & Nowicki, G. P. (1987). Positive affect facilitates creative problem solving. *Journal of Personality and Social Psychology, 52,* 1122–1131.

Izard, C. E. (1971). *The face of emotion.* New York: Appleton-Century-Crofts.

James, W. (1950). *The principles of psychology* (Vol. 2). New York: Dover. (Original work published 1890)

Johnson, E. J., & Tversky, A. (1983). Affect, generalization, and the perception of risk. *Journal of Personality and Social Psychology, 15,* 294–301.

Lazarus, R. S. (1991). *Emotion and adaptation.* New York: Oxford University Press.

Leeper, R. W. (1948). A motivational theory of emotions to replace "emotions as disorganized response." *Psychological Review, 55,* 5–21.

Little, B. R. (1989). Personal projects analysis: Trivial pursuits, magnificent obsessions, and the search for coherence. In D. M. Buss & N. Cantor (Eds.), *Personality psychology: Recent trends and emerging directions* (pp. 15–31). New York: Springer-Verlag.

Lyubomirsky, S., & Nolen-Hoeksema, S. (1995). Effects of self-focused rumination on negative thinking and interpersonal problem solving. *Journal of Personality and Social Psychology, 69,* 176–190.

Martin, L. L., Tesser, A., & McIntosh, W. D. (1993). Wanting but not having: The effects of unattained goals on thoughts and feelings. In D. M. Wegner & J. W. Pennebaker (Eds.), *The handbook of mental control* (pp. 552–572). New York: Prentice-Hall.

Mayer, J. D., Caruso, D., & Salovey, P. (1998). *The Multifactor Emotional Intelligence Scale: MEIS.* (Available from J. D. Mayer, Department of Psychology, University of New Hampshire, Conant Hall, Durham, NH 03824).

Mayer, J. D., Caruso, D., & Salovey, P. (1999). Emotion-

al intelligence meets traditional standards for an intelligence. *Intelligence, 27,* 267–298.

Mayer, J. D., DiPaolo, M., & Salovey, P. (1990). Perceiving the affective content in ambiguous visual stimuli: A component of emotional intelligence. *Journal of Personality Assessment, 54,* 772–781.

Mayer, J. D., & Gaschke, Y. N. (1988). The experience and meta-experience of mood. *Journal of Personality and Social Psychology, 55,* 102–111.

Mayer, J. D., Gaschke, Y. N., Braverman, D. L., & Evans, T. W. (1992). Mood-congruent judgment is a general effect. *Journal of Personality and Social Psychology, 63,* 119–132.

Mayer, J. D., & Geher, G. (1996). Emotional intelligence and the identification of emotion. *Intelligence, 22,* 89–113.

Mayer, J. D., & Hanson, E. (1995). Mood-congruent judgment over time. *Personality and Social Psychology Bulletin, 21,* 237–244.

Mayer, J. D., & Salovey, P. (1993). The intelligence of emotional intelligence. *Intelligence, 17,* 433–442.

Mayer, J. D., & Salovey, P. (1997). What is emotional intelligence? In P. Salovey & D. J. Sluyter (Eds.), *Emotional development and emotional intelligence* (pp. 3–31). New York: Basic Books.

Mayer, J. D., Salovey, P., & Caruso, D. (1997). *Emotional IQ test* [CD-ROM version]. Needham, MA: Virtual Knowledge.

Mayer, J. D., Salovey, P., & Caruso, D. (in press). Competing models of emotional intelligence. In R.J. Sternberg (Ed.), *Handbook of human intelligence* (2nd ed.). New York: Cambridge University Press.

Mayer, J. D., Salovey, P., Gomberg-Kaufman, S., & Blainey, K. (1991). A broader conception of mood experience. *Journal of Personality and Social Psychology, 60,* 100–111.

Mayer, J. D., & Stevens, A. (1994). An emerging understanding of the reflective (meta-) experience of mood. *Journal of Research in Personality, 28,* 351–373.

McIntosh, W. D. (1996). When does goal nonattainment lead to negative emotional reactions, and when doesn't it?: The role of linking and rumination. In L. L. Martin & A. Tesser (Eds.), *Striving and feeling: Interactions among goals, affect, and self-regulation* (pp. 53–77). Hillsdale, NJ: Erlbaum.

McIntosh, W. D., Harlow, T. F., & Martin, L. L. (1995). Linkers and nonlinkers: Goal beliefs as a moderator of the effects of everyday hassles on rumination, depression, and physical complaints. *Journal of Applied Social Psychology, 25,* 1231–1244.

Mischel, W. (1990). Personality dispositions revisited and revised: A view after three decades. In L. A. Pervin (Ed.), *Handbook of personality: Theory and research* (pp. 111–134). New York: Guilford Press.

Morrow, J., & Nolen-Hoeksema, S. (1990). Effects of responses to depression on the remediation of depressive affect. *Journal of Personality and Social Psychology, 58,* 519–527.

Nolen-Hoeksema, S. (1991). Responses to depression and their effects on the duration of depressive episodes. *Journal of Abnormal Psychology, 100,* 569–582.

Nolen-Hoeksema, S., McBride, A., & Larson, J. (1997).

Rumination and psychological distress among bereaved partners. *Journal of Personality and Social Psychology, 72,* 855–862.

Nolen-Hoeksema, S., & Morrow, J. (1991). A prospective study of depression and posttraumatic stress symptoms after a natural disaster: The 1989 Loma Prieta earthquake. *Journal of Personality and Social Psychology, 61,* 115–121.

Nolen-Hoeksema, S., & Morrow, J. (1993). Effects of rumination and distraction on naturally occurring depressed mood. *Cognition and Emotion, 7,* 561–570.

Notarius, C. I., & Levenson, R. W. (1979). Expressive tendencies and physiological response to stress. *Journal of Personality and Social Psychology, 37,* 1201–1204.

Ortony, A., Clore, G. L., & Collins, A. (1988). *The cognitive structure of emotions.* Cambridge, England: Cambridge University Press.

Palfai, T. P., & Salovey, P. (1993). The influence of depressed and elated mood on deductive and inductive reasoning. *Imagination, Cognition, and Personality, 13,* 57–71.

Peale, N. V. (1982). *Positive imaging: The powerful way to change your life.* New York: Fawcett Crest.

Pennebaker, J. W. (1997). Writing about emotional experiences as a therapeutic process. *Psychological Science, 8,* 162–166.

Pennebaker, J. W., Colder, M., & Sharp, L. K. (1990). Accelerating the coping process. *Journal of Personality and Social Psychology, 58,* 528–537.

Pennebaker, J. W., & Francis, M. E. (1996). Cognitive, emotional, and language processes in disclosure. *Cognition and Emotion, 10,* 601–626.

Pennebaker, J. W., & Harber, K. D. (1993). A social stage model of collective coping: The Loma Prieta earthquake and the Persian Gulf War. *Journal of Social Issues, 49,* 125–145.

Pennebaker, J. W., Kiecolt-Glaser, J. K., & Glaser, R. (1988). Disclosures of traumas and immune functioning: Health implications of psychotherapy. *Journal of Consulting and Clinical Psychology, 56,* 239–245.

Pennebaker, J. W., Mayne, T. J., & Francis, M. E. (1997). Linguistic predictors of adaptive bereavement. *Journal of Personality and Social Psychology, 72,* 863–871.

Pham, L. B., & Taylor, S. E. (1999). From thought to action: Effects of process- versus outcome-based mental simulations on performance. *Personality and Social Psychology Bulletin, 25,* 250–260.

Prkachin, K. N., Craig, K. B., Papageorgis, D., & Reith, G. (1977). Nonverbal communication deficits and response to performance feedback in depression. *Journal of Abnormal Psychology, 86,* 224–234.

Saarni, C. (1990). Emotional competence: How emotions and relationships become integrated. In R. A. Thompson (Ed.), *Nebraska Symposium on Motivation: Vol. 36. Socioemotional development* (pp. 115–182). Lincoln: University of Nebraska Press.

Saarni, C. (1997). Emotional competence and self-regulation in childhood. In P. Salovey & D. J. Sluyter (Eds.), *Emotional development and emotional intelligence: Educational implications* (pp. 35–66). New York: Basic Books.

Salovey, P., Bedell, B. T., Detweiler, J. B., & Mayer, J. D. (1999). Coping intelligently: Emotional intelligence and the coping process. In C.R. Snyder (Ed.), *Coping: The psychology of what works* (pp. 141–164). New York: Oxford University Press.

Salovey P., & Mayer, J. D. (1990). Emotional intelligence. *Imagination, Cognition and Personality, 9,* 185–211.

Salovey, P., Mayer, J. D., Goldman, S. L., Turvey, C., & Palfai, T. P. (1995). Emotional attention, clarity, and repair: Exploring emotional intelligence using the Trait Meta-Mood Scale. In J. W. Pennebaker (Ed.), *Emotion, disclosure, and health* (pp. 125–154). Washington, DC: American Psychological Association.

Salovey, P., & Rodin, J. (1986). Differentiation of social-comparison jealousy and romantic jealousy. *Journal of Personality and Social Psychology, 50,* 1100–1112.

Salovey, P., & Rodin, J. (1989). Envy and jealousy in close relationships. In C. Hendrick (Ed.), *Review of personality and social psychology* (Vol. 10, pp. 221–246). Beverly Hills, CA: Sage.

Schaffer, L. F., Gilmer, B., & Schoen, M. (1940). *Psychology.* New York: Harper.

Schutte, N. S., Malouff, J. M., Hall, L. E., Haggerty, D., Cooper, J. T., Golden, C. J., & Dornheim, L. (1998). Development and validation of a measure of emotional intelligence. *Personality and Individual Differences, 25,* 167–177.

Schwarz, N. (1990). Feelings as information: Informational and motivational functions of affective states. In E. T. Higgins & E. M. Sorrentino (Eds.), *Handbook of motivation and cognition: Foundations of social behavior* (Vol. 2, pp. 527–561). New York: Guilford Press.

Schwarz, N., & Clore, G. L. (1983). Mood, misattribution, and judgments of well-being: Informative and directive functions of affective states. *Journal of Personality and Social Psychology, 45,* 513–523.

Segal, J. (1997). *Raising your emotional intelligence: A practical guide.* New York: Holt.

Showers, C. J., & Kling, K. C. (1996). The organization of self-knowledge: Implications for mood regulation. In L.L. Martin & A. Tesser (Eds.), *Striving and feeling: Interactions among goals, affect, and self-regulation* (pp. 151–173). Hillsdale, NJ: Lawrence Erlbaum.

Simmons, S., & Simmons, J.C. (1997). *Measuring emotional intelligence.* Arlington, TX: Summit.

Smyth, J. M. (1998). Written emotional expression: Effect sizes, outcome types, and moderating variables. *Journal of Consulting and Clinical Psychology, 66,* 174–184.

Steiner, C., & Perry, P. (1997). *Achieving emotional literacy: A personal program to increase your emotional intelligence.* New York: Avon.

Sternberg, R. J. (1985). *Beyond IQ: A triarchic theory of human intelligence.* Cambridge, England: Cambridge University Press.

Sternberg, R. J. (1988). *The triarchic mind: A new theory of human intelligence.* New York: Viking.

Sternberg, R. J., & Smith, C. A. (1985). Social intelligence and decoding skills in nonverbal communication. *Social Cognition, 3,* 168–192.

Stroebe, W., & Stroebe, M. (1996). The social psychology of social support. In E. T. Higgins & A. W. Kruglanski (Eds.), *Social psychology: Handbook of basic principles* (pp. 597–621). New York: Guilford Press.

Swinkels, A., & Giuliano, T. A. (1995). The measurement and conceptualization of mood awareness: Monitoring and labeling one's mood states. *Personality and Social Psychology Bulletin, 21,* 934–949.

Tangney, J. P., Wagner, P. E., Fletcher, C., & Gramzow, R. (1992). Shamed into anger?: The relation of shame and guilt to anger and self-reported aggression. *Journal of Personality and Social Psychology, 62,* 669–675.

Taylor, S. E., Pham, L. B., Rivkin, I. D., & Armor, D. A. (1998). Harnessing the imagination: Mental simulation, self-regulation, and coping. *American Psychologist, 53,* 429–439.

Terman, L. M. (1921). Second contribution to "Intelli-gence and its measurement: A symposium." *Journal of Educational Psychology, 12,* 127–133.

Thorndike, E. L. (1920). Intelligence and its uses. *Harper's Magazine, 140,* 227–235.

Thorndike, R. L., & Stein, S. (1937). An evaluation of the attempts to measure social intelligence. *Psychological Bulletin, 34,* 275–284.

Tomkins, S. S. (1962). *Affect, imagery, and consciousness: Vol. 1. The positive affects.* New York: Springer.

Wagner, R. K., & Sternberg, R. J. (1985). Practical intelligence in real-world pursuits: The role of tacit knowledge. *Journal of Personality and Social Psychology, 50,* 737–743.

Wegner, D. M., Erber, R., & Zanakos, S. (1993). Ironic processes in the mental control of mood and mood-related thought. *Journal of Personality and Social Psychology, 65,* 1093–1104.

Woodworth, R. S. (1940). *Psychology* (4th ed.). New York: Holt.

Young, P. T. (1936). *Motivation of behavior.* New York: Wiley.

PART VI

HEALTH AND EMOTIONS

CHAPTER 33

Emotions and Physical Illness: Causes and Indicators of Vulnerability

Howard Leventhal
Linda Patrick-Miller

WHY CHAPTERS ON EMOTION AND HEALTH?

Our contribution to the first edition of this *Handbook* opened by pointing to the "large and ever-growing body of epidemiological data [that] links health outcomes such as cardiovascular disease, cancer, and autoimmune disease to psychosocial variables" (Leventhal & Patrick-Miller, 1993, p. 365). Because emotional processes have repeatedly been identified as possible mediators of these associations, we suggested that the connection between emotional processes and illness can provide basic insights into the structure and function of emotional systems. This perspective on emotional processes generated comments on the following four questions:

1. Are emotions best represented as dimensions (Russell, 1980) or as discrete (i.e., differential) categories (e.g., see Ekman, 1992; Ekman, Friesen, & Ellsworth, 1972; Izard, 1991)?
2. Is social communication the primary function of emotion (Fridlund, 1991)?

3. Are emotions a product of a hierarchically structured processing system (Leventhal, 1984; Leventhal & Scherer, 1987)?
4. Are emotions multicomponent structures (Ortony & Turner, 1990) that are organized by associative processes?

Our assumption that emotional expression and awareness function as sources of information for interpersonal and intrapersonal communication has added a new perspective to our analysis of the connection between affect and illness (Leventhal, Patrick-Miller, Leventhal, & Burns, 1997). The major goal of this chapter is to introduce this perspective and to delineate its implications for understanding how emotions and illness are interconnected.

A PERSPECTIVE ON THE FUNCTION OF EMOTION IN DISEASE PROCESSES

The growing body of data on the relationship of psychological and emotional factors to physical health appears to focus upon two views of the relationships of emotional experience to physical illness: (1) a *causal* perspective (i.e., emotions as mediators and/or causes of illness), and (2) an *outcome* perspective (i.e., emotions as products of illness). In our view, these seemingly distinct perspectives are two sides of the same coin. Illness and emotion are linked by complex, bidirectional processes (Leventhal & Patrick-Miller, 1993; Leventhal et al., 1997). Emotions can have an impact on illness via direct and indirect pathways, and illness can act upon emotion through many if not all of the same pathways. We propose an additional view of the relationships among emotions and illness: an *indicator* perspective (i.e., emotions as indicators of systemic vulnerability to disease, neither active in nor causal to this vulnerability).

The Causal/Mediational Perspective

The causal perspective posits that emotional processes can function as antecedent determinants of illness. The connection can be direct or indirect. The relationship of emotional activation to cardiovascular disease appears to fit the direct pattern. Complex cognitive processes (e.g., interpretations of the social environment as competitive, hostile, and threatening; Lazarus, 1991; Scherer, 1984) and expressive behaviors provoking hostile and/or competitive responses from others, which are characteristic of individuals expressing Type A behavior (Friedman & Rosenman, 1974) and chronic hostility (Smith, 1992), are assumed to sustain emotionally mediated neuroendocrinological reactions; these reactions increase cardiovascular reactivity (CVR), elevate blood pressure and heart rate, and produce progressive arterial damage and atherosclerosis (Manuck, 1994). These psychologically induced physiological changes lead in turn to the development of essential hypertension, which further damages arterial walls and increases vulnerability to acute cardiovascular events, such as myocardial infarction (MI) or stroke. Such acute disease episodes are precipitated by exposure to major negative life events such as earthquakes (Leor, Poole, & Kloner, 1996), which activate and stress a now compromised cardiovascular system (Kamarck & Jennings, 1991).

The connection can also be indirect, such that the activation of emotional processes leads to behavioral changes that induce disease. Depression, for example, can lead to a variety of self-medicative, self-stimulative, and risk-taking behaviors, such as excessive alcohol consumption in men and cigarette smoking in women (Lerman et al., 1997). These behaviorally introduced pathogens can produce physiological changes leading to serious chronic illness, such as hepatic necrosis and pulmonary DNA alterations preceding liver cirrhosis and lung cancer. The disease risk from these pathogens will vary by individual. It is not known whether the individuals most at risk for a specific linkage (e.g., a genetic susceptibility to lung cancer from smoking) are the same individuals most at risk for the pathogenic behavior (e.g., the genetic predisposition to experience cigarette smoking as a means of ameliorating depression). These indirect pathways are the most clear and probably the most potent contributors to the causal development of illness.

The Outcome Perspective

The outcome perspective, the inverse of the causal pathway, contends that disease is the casual antecedent to emotion. Like the causal pathway, the connection could presumably involve direct physiological links or indirect, cognitively and behaviorally mediated changes. The outcome pathway has been of importance for at least three reasons. First, it is a potential confound in studies designed to detect direct causal effects of emotion on disease development. To eliminate this confound in longitudinal studies, individuals must be recruited well before disease onset to eliminate the possibility that "predisease" emotions are consequences of preclinical disease physiology (see the review by Friedman & Booth-Kewley, 1987).

A second focus of the outcome perspective has been on research examining the factors mediating emotional adjustment to illness. These investigations assess how coping procedures influence the impact of disease on functioning and the consequences of these processes for emotional status and quality of life (Maes, Leventhal, & DeRidder, 1995). Typical of these studies are findings showing that physical illness leads to functional decline and disruption of activities of daily living, which then increase depressed mood (Berkman et al., 1986; Zeiss, Lewinsohn, Rohde, & Seeley, 1996). The topics and diseases covered in this literature range from social comparison as a means of regulating mood and self-esteem among patients facing cancer (Wood & Van der Zee, 1997), coronary bypass surgery (Kulik & Mahler, 1987, 1997), and arthritis-related functional impairments (Park, 1994; Fifield, Tennen, Reisine, & McQuillan, 1998), to the processes involved in the interpretation and control of the symptoms and distress caused by common illness (Suls, Martin, & Leventhal, 1997).

Finally, more and more studies are examining the direct pathways through which disease processes, particularly immunological, have impacts on the neuroendocrine system, producing behavioral, cognitive, and affective/mood effects (Gibertini, Newton, Klein, & Friedman, 1995; Hart, 1988; Smith, Tyrrell, Coyle, & Higgins, 1988). Studies examining the connections between disease and affects in this "reverse" direction not only demonstrate that the connections among emotion and disease are bidirectional; they provide the clearest available pictures of these paths.

The Indicator (Vulnerability/Resource) View

The indicator perspective proposes that conscious affective processes are indicators of somatic resources (Leventhal et al., 1997). Reports of negative and of positive affects are largely independent and respond to different underlying mechanisms. Reports of high levels of energy appear to indicate availability of resources, and reports of negative affect seem to indicate reduced resources, for combating physiological challenges (Benyamini, Leventhal, & Leventhal, in press). As indicators, emotions have no causal significance. Being depressed or fatigued can mean that one is susceptible to attack, and being happy or energetic can mean that one is able to fend off attack, but it need not mean that depression or fatigue is actively causing depletion, or that depletion is a consequence of a psychological disorder or a comorbid physical disease.

It is important to recognize that emotion measures and the processes they reflect (e.g., depression, fear, and anger) are sensitive to a wide range of stimuli (e.g., environmental events), and that they are consequently not specific to illness (David, Green, Martin, & Suls, 1997).

THE COMMUNICATIVE FUNCTION AND STRUCTURE OF EMOTION

Viewing emotions as causes, as outcomes, or as vulnerability indicators does not necessarily mean that these are separate or discrete classifications. An emotional reaction can serve any one or any combination of these functions. For example, anger and hostility may be intensified by the occurrence of disease; that is, the symptoms and distress of disease may create a sense of victimization and anger, which may activate physiological processes that increase the risk of coronary events. In many instances, however, emotions are simply indicators of depletion of somatic resources by age-related, economic, environmental, and/or interpersonal stressors, and the depletion predicts increased likelihood of serious disease following exposure to pathogens. Hostility may play such a role, indicating increased vulnerability to a coronary episode in response to sudden and severe life stress. It may also play a "causal" role, creating highly threatening, interpersonal situations.

Emotions can make an active contribution to behavior even when serving as indicators of vulnerability and making no direct contribution to disease processes. Chronic depressed affect may be an indicator of reduced resources to combat infectious disease, and can also result in social isolation; chronic hostility may be an indicator of risk of cardiovascular events in response to severe and unexpected environmental demands, and can also result in counteraggression and job loss. In neither case, however, need the physiology accompanying either the depression or the hostility make a direct contribution to disease processes. These relationships of emotion to disease are made possible by the structure of the underlying emotional mechanisms.

The Multicomponent, Hierarchical Structure of Emotion Mechanisms

Emotion theorists have made a strong case for the multicomponent, hierarchical structure of emotion mechanisms and the role of emotion in both interpersonal (Fridlund, 1991; Lang, 1979; Lang, Kozak, Miller, Levin, & McLean, 1980; Leventhal, 1979) and intrapersonal (Leventhal & Mosbach, 1983) communication. These features of emotional processes are important because they help us understand the bidirectional nature of the emotion–illness link, and why and how emotions can have indicator functions with respect to disease processes.

Hierarchical Structure

Physiological and psychological analyses agree that emotional processes are complex and hierarchically arranged (Johnson & Multhaup, 1992). Many investigators conflate hierarchy with reductionism, arguing that social, psychological, and physiological analyses form a hierarchical system. We reject that position. We believe instead that physiological and psychological analyses are two perspectives or languages for describing the same phenomena, each providing a view of emotional processes.

Hierarchical systems are well represented in psychological models of emotion. Our early proposals were of a three-level, hierarchical processing system. The base, or sensory–motor, level was thought to consist of primitive emotion "seeds" defining the "raw, experiential feel" of primary emotions, such as fear, anger, disgust, and joy (Leventhal, 1984; see also Izard, 1971, and Tomkins, 1962). The middle level was thought to consist of emotion schemas, constructed by associative processes that connect and expand the range of stimuli and responses linked to the primary emotions (Bower & Cohen, 1982). Perceptual sensitivity to rapid motion, constraints on physical movements, and so forth favor some stimuli over others in the associative process (Mandler, 1992). The resulting emotion schemas can be prototypic, summarizing the content and organization of lifelong emotional experience, or episode-specific, reflecting the content and organization of highly salient affective experiences. Situations processed at this level result in most everyday emotional experiences. The third, most abstract conceptual level was thought to serve as a higher-order executive mechanism for verbalizing and regulating emotional experiences and their situational elicitors. (For more details about this model see Johnson & Multhaup, 1992.)

Dissociation and the Emotion–Disease Link

If a degree of parallelism is assumed between physiological function and structure on the one hand and psychological function and structure on the other, it is reasonable to expect that patterned central nervous system (CNS) activity is the basis for conscious emotional experience, and that peripheral autonomic activity contributes less (Panksepp, 1993, 1998). The cessation of patterned CNS activity also ends its correlated emotional experience, although the "residual" peripheral activity may amplify subsequent emotional and evaluative reactions (Zillmann, 1978). Sustained peripheral activity can also promote physiological processes that damage organ structure and increase susceptibility to disease (Smith, 1992). The separation of the neural mechanisms involved in the formation of associative, declarative, or conceptual content of emotional situations (LaBar, LeDoux, Spencer, & Phelps, 1995; Phelps, LaBar, & Spencer, 1997) also allows us to talk about emotional events without "becoming emotional."

Dissociation of conceptual or executive processes from schematic, associative processes is common in a hierarchical emotional system, as verbalizations need not activate the schematic or expressive–motor level. Dissociation can also result from active processes, as specific mental procedures designed to control emotional experience may uncouple the schematic CNS activity that generates emotional experience from its peripheral physiological processes. For example, individuals characterized as "repressors" (low in trait anxiety and high in social desirability) use positive imagery to suppress negative emotions activated by threatening films. The use of positive imagery appears automatic or nondeliberate (Boden & Baumeister, 1997). Although positive imagery may control the schemas producing emotional experience, it may have less impact on the peripheral autonomic accompaniments of the initial activation of negative affect. Similar dissociative processes can occur in nonrepressors if environmental stimuli directs their attention away from events that are eliciting negative affects. Declines in feedback control (e.g., weakening parasympathetic inhibition of sympathetic activation) render dissociation more likely as one ages (Leventhal et al., 1997). Dissociative processes will play an important role in the analysis of the causal and indicator functions of emotion.

MODELS FOR DIRECT CAUSATION

Much of the research addressing the relationships among emotion and disease has focused upon the causal (i.e., emotion-to-disease) pathway. It is unclear, however, how well the data support this outlook. To evaluate this view, we consider some of the major findings in the emotion–disease literature. Next, we consider how the indicator framework (i.e., emotions as signs of vulnerability to disease) accounts for the findings. We propose that the primary function of emotional processes in emotion–disease links is as indicators of activity within the system, and that this indicator function or property is a product of the bidirectional nature of the system.

Criteria for Direct Causal Models

Three basic criteria appear necessary (if not necessarily sufficient) to support a direct relationship between emotion and disease: (1) a specific emotion–disease linkage, (2) the exclusion of potentially causal "third factors," and (3) a mechanism consistent with the known pathophysiology of the disease. Long-term longitudinal studies predicting longevity from measures of emotional distress during adolescence and early adulthood (Friedman & Booth-Kewley, 1987) are often believed to provide the strongest evidence for a causal role of emotion in the generation of disease. The implication drawn from these findings is that the physiological processes associated with emotional maladjustment and distress either are the direct causes of later disease, or are responsible for undermining somatic defenses, resulting in the same outcome.

The perceived strength of these studies lies in the substantial temporal gap between personality assessment and mortality. The gap is presumed to rule out an important "third-factor" artifact—namely, that the measure of distress and/or maladjustment reflects the presence of preclinical disease. This strength, however, is coupled with an important deficit: In virtually all of these studies, the emotional maladjustment predicts all-cause mortality. Given the enormous differences between the etiological mechanisms and developmental histories of the most prevalent fatal diseases (e.g., the cardiovascular and malignant diseases), as well as the differences within the cardiovascular and malignant categories, the failure to identify specific emotion–disease links makes it difficult to propose a physiological mechanism mediating these outcomes. The value of specificity can be seen when the physiological mediators connect-

ing emotional factors with coronary heart disease (CHD) and cancer are examined.

Models for Coronary Heart Disease

The connection of the Type A behavior pattern and/or hostility to cardiovascular disease (Friedman & Rosenman, 1974; Smith, 1992) provides what many regard as the strongest evidence for a direct link of a specific emotional pattern to a specific disease (Contrada, Leventhal, & O'Leary, 1990; Dembroski & Costa, 1987; Matthews, 1988). The behavioral patterns identified with chronic hostility initiate a hierarchy of physiological processes, beginning with activation of the sympathetic adrenal–medullary (SAM) system (Henry, 1983). SAM activation increases CVR, including heart rate and blood pressure, which through a variety of mechanical, cellular, and molecular processes can lead to the development of CHD (Manuck, 1994). Elevations in blood pressure (1) cause shear stresses that damage coronary artery walls; (2) activate genes that promote lymphocyte penetration of arterial walls; and (3) increase blood lipids and platelet activity, leading to plaque deposition on arterial walls. These atherogenic processes reduce diameter and decrease arterial wall flexibility, restricting blood flow and inducing chronic hypertension (Hajjar & Nicholson, 1995). Atherosclerosis increases vulnerability to MI and stroke (Matthews, 1988; Smith & Pope, 1990; Smith, 1992). Indeed, acute emotional episodes can trigger acute cardiac events in individuals with compromised cardiovascular systems (Kamarck et al., 1991; Verrier & Mittleman, 1996). Epidemiological studies show increases in sudden cardiac death during major life traumas such as the Los Angeles earthquake (Leor et al., 1996), and following acute anger episodes (Mittleman et al., 1995). These data strengthen the inferred direct link between distress and MI, as there is no concurrent increase in noncardiac mortality.

The findings are impressive because they provide a plausible picture correlating psychological to physiological processes for both the development of the disease conditions that compromise the system (atherosclerosis and hypertension), and the events initiating critical disease episodes (stroke and MI). There are weaknesses, however, with respect to the role of emotion in the development of the atherosclerotic changes that form the basis for later vulnerability. The original data on Type A behavior described a generic behavior pattern. Although it suggested that the intense demands and competitive environment of modern life are cardiopathological (Friedman & Rosenman, 1974), it fell short of connecting a specific emotion to the CHD process. Later evidence extracted hostility and anger as the components of Type A behavior associated with the physiological changes leading to cardiovascular disease, and evidence linking hostility to a lifelong pattern of CVR has further strengthened the inference of a causal connection (Matthews, Woodall, & Allen, 1993; Matthews & Woodall, 1988).

The causal model requires persuasive connections between the psychological hierarchy associated with hostility and Type A behavior and the physiological hierarchy associated with CHD. Hostility and Type A behavior pattern are presumed products of cognitive factors involved in the interpretation of the social and work environments: Hostile individuals perceive others as competing for scarce resources and themselves as having to work harder and faster to obtain deserved rewards. These higher-level cognitions manifest themselves in instrumental and expressive behaviors (e.g., the characteristic rapid and emphatic speech) that elicit competitive and hostile reactions from others (Scherwitz, Berton, & Leventhal, 1978). Exposure to achievement challenges and hostile behavior, and to the anger these induce, increases CVR (Diamond et al., 1984; Engebretson, Matthews, & Scheier, 1989; Hokanson, 1970; Smith, Allred, Morrison, & Carlson, 1989; Smith, Gallo, Goble, Ngu, & Stark, 1998; Uchino, Cacioppo, & Kiecolt-Glaser, 1996). These changes, as well as activation of the SAM response, are examples of levels in the physiological hierarchy that are connected to levels in the psychological hierarchy.

The psychophysiological pathways underlying these psychophysiological relationships are complex, however, leaving abundant room for "third factors" to account for associations between the psychological hierarchy defining hostility and/or Type A behavior and the physiological hierarchy associated with CHD. For example, a gene that promotes the migration of arterial-wall-damaging blood cells, and that also creates the conditions for the behavioral expression of hostility, could be a "third factor" responsible for the association of hostility and the development of CHD. A hypothesis of this sort is quite reasonable from an evolutionary perspective. Natural selection would have favored those aggressive and/or hostile individuals whose concurrent adrenergic activation also stimulated their immune defenses, enhancing their recovery from injuries incurred during interpersonal combat.

The strongest version of this genetic hypothesis—that genetic factors cause both hostility and atherosclerosis, without any causal relation between hostility and atherosclerosis—seems unlikely. However, the genetic factor that helps to shape the pathogenic physiological response pattern, adrenergic hyperreactivity, may be involved in the diathesis of the hostile behavior pattern. Years of activation of a genetically programmed vigorous and angry response to challenging situations may develop hostility as a trait. Such responses to interpersonal challenge elicit complementary reactions from others, generating self-fulfilling life situations (Plomin, 1998). Thus, the operation of a third factor is not inconsistent with the causal hypothesis. The genetic factor can cause both behavioral and physiological reactions (a correlative relationship), with the lifelong activation of distress strengthening the linkage (a causal relationship). If there were no causal component, emotional distress would function solely as a vulnerability indicator. If both the third-factor and causal hypotheses are true, anger and/or hostility indices would serve both as indicators of vulnerability and as markers of active contribution to the disease process.

The nature and duration of anger and hostility pose an additional challenge to the causal role for emotion in the development of CHD. The physiological reactions accompanying anger possess the requisites for producing cardiac pathology, but however pathognomonic they may be, they are typically not of sufficient duration to evoke the long-term alterations in cardiovascular function and structure necessary for the development of CHD. The chronicity of hostility, on the other hand, is consistent with the assumption that it plays a causal role (Smith, 1992). But is hostility an emotion? If we differentiate anger from hostility, identifying the former as an affect and the latter as a response style—a distinction consistent with the subjective experience of hostile persons, who are unlikely to see themselves as angry—then a question can be raised as to whether emotion per se is playing the causal role in the development of disease. The hostile behavior pattern may reflect, however, a schematic structure created by the repeated elicitation of anger in association with competitive, hostile thoughts and actions. Once these associative schemas are formed, the physiology of anger will be evoked whenever hostile and competitive thoughts and expressions are engaged, even in the absence of angry emotion. Angry emotion will be a factor in this diathesis, even though the hostile response style sustaining pathognomonic peripheral changes is not experienced as anger by the hostile individual. The classical conditioning of anger physiology to hostile thoughts and expressive behaviors is consistent with a hierarchical model.

Although it may seem that distinguishing between emotional episodes (which are typically conscious and reportable) and response styles (which are neither conscious nor reportable) is introducing one too many slices in the conceptual pie, these differentiations will be important for changing behavior to lower the risk of cardiovascular disease. Differences in the schemas underlying the hostility and anger that reflect the individual's belief that his ire is justified in response to a perceived personal affront, and in the hostile individual's conceptual framing of the world as chronically competitive and unforgiving, may require different approaches to change. The value of such interventions is seen in studies demonstrating that reductions in behavioral and emotional components of the Type A construct decrease biological risk factors of CHD, as well as risk of reinfarction and rate of mortality in post-MI patients (Frasure-Smith & Prince, 1985, 1989; Linden, Stossel, & Maurice, 1996; Mendes de Leon, Powell, & Kaplan, 1991).

Models for Cancer

As a thorough treatment of the relationships between emotion and neoplastic disease can be found in this volume (see Miller & Schnoll, Chapter 34), we make only the following critical points. Cancers, like CHD, are etiologically multifactorial and developmentally multiphasic, only considerably more so. This disease complexity has rendered investigation of direct causal linkages between emotions and cancer vulnerable to many of the same challenges: the difficulty of making specific connections between the emotional hierarchy and the physiological hierarchy, as well as "third-factor" interpretations. What renders the study of emotion

and cancer different from that of CHD, however, is the degree of involvement of the immune system, and the window that this affords to view the bidirectionality of the processes: emotion to disease and disease to emotion.

THE INDICATOR FUNCTION OF EMOTION IN A BIDIRECTIONAL SYSTEM

The difficulty in demonstrating distress/emotions as causal antecedents of illness contrasts with the ease with which we can see the effects of illness on behavior. When we become acutely ill with an infectious disease, we become febrile and shiver; lose our appetites for food, water, and sex; and curl up and sleep (Hart, 1988). These changes are part of our systemic defense against the pathogen, and as such are critical for our survival. The physiological changes, such as resetting the thermoregulatory set point and replicating and mobilizing T and B lymphocytes, are highly energy-consumptive processes. Maintaining just one 1° of fever, a shift that reduces microbial replication and potentiates the immune response, requires a 13% increase in the metabolic rate in adults (Kluger & Vaughn, 1978). The accompanying behavioral changes, which are orchestrated by the immune response and mediated by its chemical messengers, the cytokines, function to conserve the energy necessary to sustain the host's defense against the infectious agent (Hart, 1988; Maier & Watkins, 1998). Thus the immune system not only creates an environment inimical to the pathogen, but also eliminates the behavioral system's competition for somatic resources by making us "sick" (i.e., suppressing overt behavior, motivation, and mood, while facilitating recovery).

Illness-induced moods are typically characterized by fatigue, depression, or distress and are reported in association with the full spectrum of illness severity, from mild to life-threatening. The sensitivity of conscious mood reports to even minor stimulation of immune activity was illustrated in a recent study in which preventive immunizations against influenza and tetanus given to healthy elderly subjects first suppressed and then stimulated fatigued mood, in concordance with the neuroendocrine changes associated with immune activation. Measures of depression and anxiety, however, failed to detect these changes

(Patrick-Miller, 1998). The findings of this and other studies of this pathway are also consistent with the indicator model of emotion. The post-immunization affective changes were more pronounced among individuals whose ability to respond to the stress of the immunological challenge might be compromised. The stress susceptibility factor with the greatest effect on immune-related affective change was trait negative affect. Following the active immune stimulation, as compared to placebo, subjects highest in trait negative affect reported the greatest changes in fatigue (Patrick-Miller, 1998).

Studies of the relationship of affect and more severe, life-threatening illnesses are also consistent with the indicator function of affect. Early investigators of the relationship between psychological factors and neoplastic disease described the cancer-prone Type C personality (Morris & Greer, 1980; Temoshok & Fox, 1984) and the association of its "helplessness" and "passive acceptance" with poorer prognosis in patients with breast cancer or malignant melanoma (Greer, Morris, & Pettingale, 1979; Pettingale, 1984; Pettingale, Morris, Greer, & Haybittle, 1985; Temoshok, 1987). Animal models provide the most convincing support for such a causal link. Animals exposed to uncontrollable stressors develop deficits in motivation, contingent learning, and coping (Weiss, 1972), and consequently a "depressive" state that includes decreased activity, eating, and grooming (Seligman, 1975), as well as increased growth of implanted malignant tumor cells (Sklar & Anisman, 1979; Riley, Fitzmaurice, & Spackman, 1981). Likewise, mice selectively bred for socially inhibited behavior exhibit chronically low natural killer cell activity, which has been associated with decreased defense against tumor initiation and metastasis (Herberman & Ortaldo, 1981). They are also more than twice as likely to develop tumors after carcinogen exposure than either socially aggressive or normal mice (Petitto et al, 1993; Petitto, Lysle, Gariepy, & Lewis, 1994). Although there appears to be a parallel between the behavior patterns of these uncontrollably stressed and socially inhibited animals and those of the Type C personality, the casual linkages among these factors remain unproven (Petitto et al. 1993). The data are, however, consistent with an indicator function of emotion.

Immune activity (the migration and proliferation of cells, the manufacture of proteins for the production of cytokines and antibodies, etc.) is energy-consumptive. It must therefore draw upon the host's resources to meet its energy demands, which reduces the resources available for other efforts (Leventhal et al., 1997). And like other perturbations of life, both large and small, immune stimuli are stressors (Dunn, 1993; Harbuz, Rees, & Lightman, 1993); as such, the responses they generate include central depletion of the neurotransmitter norepinephrine (NE) (Besedovsky et al., 1983; Dunn, Powell, Meitin, & Small, 1989; Terao, Oikawa, & Saito, 1994; Zalcman, Shanks, & Anisman, 1991)—the physiological underpinning of the psychomotor fatigue (Weiss, Glazer, Pohorecky, & Miller, 1975) and of the "learned helplessness" (Seligman, 1975) exhibited by animals exposed to uncontrollable stressors. Thus mood and emotional experience appear to be the domain for the conscious representation of the physiological processes involved in somatic energy level, distribution, and use. Such mood effects are indicators, therefore, of the availability of resources for combating disease processes, and they can predict specific disease outcomes. The disease outcomes they predict and how well they do so depend upon a variety of contextual factors, primarily the presence of a specific compromised organ system.

Depression, for example, is associated with increased risk of all-cause mortality in epidemiological studies (Wulsin, Vaillant, & Wells, 1999), and depressed affect is associated with higher frequency of restenosis following coronary artery angioplasty and the higher risk of mortality following MI (Frasure-Smith, Lespérance, Juneau, Talajic, & Bourassa, 1999) and coronary bypass surgery (Frasure-Smith, Lespérance, & Talajic, 1993; Lespérance, Frasure-Smith, & Talajic, 1996). The findings in some studies that only depression of recent onset increases the risk of acute cardiovascular episodes and its associated mortality (Penninx et. al., 1998), and that fatigue or vital exhaustion is the component of depression that predicts both acute cardiac events (Appels et al., 1994) and their outcomes (Frasure-Smith et al., 1999; Frasure-Smith, Lespérance, & Talajic, 1995), suggest that depressed mood/exhaustion may serve as an indicator of a lack of resources to sustain or rehabilitate a patient's compromised cardiovascular system, rather than playing a causal role in restenosis or death. That the subjective sense of "exhaustion" appears to be the marker of vulnerability, predicting systemic loss of vitality and resistance to disease, emphasizes the value of identifying critical components within each affect domain and relating them to a specific physiological disease stage. Causal questions aside, both depression/exhaustion and hostility/anger can serve as indicators of vulnerability to risk of CHD and cardiac death.

NEW DIRECTIONS: INFECTIOUS DISEASES AND WOUND HEALING

Much of the difficulty that has emerged in examining the causal relationship between emotion and disease can be linked to two factors: (1) the prolonged and multiphasic developmental disease course, and (2) the difficulty of adequately controlling causal agents. Two recent areas of study, infectious disease and wound healing, hold great promise in elucidating emotion-to-disease causal relationships because of their inherently shorter time course and their opportunity to control exposure.

Studies examining the relationship between life stress and the development of infectious disease provide some of the strongest evidence to date of a link between emotion and disease. Studies by Kiecolt-Glaser and colleagues investigating examination stress in medical students (Kiecolt-Glaser et al., 1984; Glaser et al., 1993), marital strain in spousal pairs (Kiecolt-Glaser et al., 1987), and depression in caregivers of persons with Alzheimer's dementia (Kiecolt-Glaser, Dura, Speicher, Trask, & Glaser, 1991) have demonstrated effects on a variety of infectious illness outcomes. In addition, there is convincing evidence that stress decreases resistance to the common cold (Cohen, Tyrrell, & Smith, 1991, 1993). The critical element in Cohen and colleagues' paradigm is experimental control of exposure to the pathogen. Subjects are randomly assigned to double-blind viral exposure conditions and sequestered throughout the study. Stress is measured, but not manipulated. The data show that measures of respiratory infection (viral shedding) and its clinical manifestations (mucus secretions and symptom reports) correlate positively with the degree of psychological stress reported, even when various health behaviors are controlled for (Cohen et al., 1991).

Similarly, using a wound-healing model, Kiecolt-Glaser and colleagues (Kiecolt-Glaser, Marucha, Malarkey, Mercado, & Glaser, 1995; Marucha, Kiecolt-Glaser, & Favagehi, 1998)

demonstrated that measures of stress correspond to prolonged healing time of experimentally produced puncture wounds in dental students and caregivers of persons with Alzheimer's dementia. In both the infectious disease and healing models, as in the cancer model, the proposed direct casual mediator of the outcome relationship between stress/emotion and illness is suppressed or dysregulated immunological function (Kiecolt-Glaser & Glaser, 1995; Kiecolt-Glaser, Page, Marucha, MacCullum, & Glaser, 1998; Padgett, Marucha, & Sheridan, 1998).

These studies are impressive in their degree of experimental control and specificity of disease outcome. Thus close attention must be paid to other questions they raise, such as the strength of the causal relationship and the implications of their findings. First, the effects of stress on infection are of modest size, even though the level of pathogen exposure is high and uniform across all participants (Cohen et al., 1991, 1993, 1998). Far smaller effects of stress might be expected in real-world settings, where both the level of exposure and the proportion of the population exposed are far less extreme. In contrast, the size of the effects in wound healing has been rather impressive (Kiecolt-Glaser et al., 1998). This difference may reflect the very different disease outcomes measured: the rate of infection (disease onset) in the viral studies, as compared to the rate of healing (repair of a compromised system) in the wound-healing studies. As in the studies of stress/emotion and cardiovascular disease, the clearer and stronger impacts of stress are seen on compromised systems.

Second, it appears than even in disease states with a short developmental course, stress duration can be significant. Although both long-term (Kiecolt-Glaser et al., 1995) and short-term (Marucha et al., 1998; Padgett et al., 1998) stressors are correlated with prolonged wound healing, stress of at least 1 month is necessary to increase the risk of developing a cold (Cohen et al., 1998).

Cohen and Herbert (1996) have suggested that there is little support for the hypothesis that stress-enhanced vulnerability to viral pathogens is directly causal, or that the mediator of the effect is dysregulated neuroendocrine or immune function. However, rates of both viral infection and development of fulminant illness differ significantly between participants who do and do not have virus-specific antibody protection prior to pathogen exposure (Cohen et al., 1998; Alper et al., 1998), suggesting that the ability to develop pathogen-specific immune protection is relevant to the causal question. Likewise, studies of wound healing have shown strong correlations among measures of neuroendocrine and immunological factors that are known to be affected by stress, and duration of wound healing. In a tightly controlled study, mice subjected to restraint stress showed significant increases in corticosterone (which correspond to prolonged wound healing). Blockade of glucocorticoids (which suppress immunological factors important to wound healing, such as interleukin-1 and tumor necrosis factor; Hubner et al., 1996) returned wound-healing parameters to those of the controls, suggesting a plausible mediator in neuroendocrine/immune dysregulation (Padgett et al., 1998). Although unable to prove causality, this study provides some of the most sophisticated correlational evidence to date of the role of stress in immune-mediated disease outcomes.

Unlike the CHD and cancer studies, the data from these infectious disease and healing studies have generally related measures of stress, rather than measures of emotion, to disease acquisition or outcome. Although this raises the question of the role of emotion per se in causal models, it is not inconsistent with the indicator perspective. Rather than inducing disease vulnerability through immunosuppression, emotion may serve to communicate to self and others the depletion of somatic resources by life event management or normal aging processes (Meites, 1990).

GENES AS "THIRD FACTORS" IN INDIRECT CAUSATION

In our evaluation of causal models, we have often appealed to genetic variables as "third factors" that might account for the presumed direct pathways from emotion to illness. For example, a gene might be responsible for the association of hostility and atherosclerosis by promoting both the migration of arterial-wall-damaging cells and the creation of hostility-evoking social conditions. Such hypotheses are not wild speculations. It has long been known, for example, that depressed individuals are likely to be heavy users of tobacco (Pomerleau, Collins, Shiffman, & Pomerleau, 1993). This indirect causal path would greatly increase risk

of cardiovascular disease and various cancers (e.g., lung, bladder, etc.) for depressed individuals. Recent studies have identified genetic variables that may underlie this association (Lerman et al., 1998). One variant of the dopamine D4 receptor gene (DRD4S alleles) encourages depressed individuals to smoke for reduction of negative affect. This allele is associated with effective dopamine receptor function in brain reward centers. Thus depressed individuals whose genetic makeup provides a rich array of these receptors may be more likely to "medicate" their depressed mood by smoking.

Similarly, genes have been identified that affect the efficiency of dopamine reuptake. Individuals with faulty reuptake mechanisms have more dopamine in their reward centers and are less likely to use smoking to activate these centers (Pomerleau & Kardia, 1999). Individuals with these alleles (SLC6A3-9 and DRD2-A2) are less likely ever to smoke, are older at smoking onset, and are more successful at quitting smoking than others (Lerman et al., 1999). These effects appear robust, holding across age and ethnic groups. Investigators suggest that the quitting ease associated with SLC6A3 is mediated by novelty seeking (Sabol et al., 1999).

These data clearly demonstrate that genetic variables can be important "third factors," contributing to the relationship between emotion and disease through their effects on risk behaviors. They are, however, only first steps in exploring the way genetic factors may contribute to the relationship of psychological variables (both personality factors and emotional states) to health outcomes. Two points about these data are worth noting. First, the genetic factors identified account for but a small percentage of the variance in the outcome studies, typically 2%. Secondly, investigators in this area assert—incorrectly, in our judgment—that psychological factors mediate the relationship of genetic variables to illness and behavioral outcomes. The use of the term "mediate" in the statistical sense is correct; that is, the psychological measures account for the relationship of the genetic factors to disease or behavioral outcomes when entered into a regression equation. That psychological measures can account for more variance than a genetic factor is to be expected if several gene loci are involved in the disease and/or behavior studied. It is the "causal" implication of the term "mediate" with which we take issue. Unless the psychological factor is actively involved in the disease and/or behavioral process—for example, a stimulation-seeking trait (Sabol et al., 1999) or an affect (Lerman et al., 1999) generating behaviors that make experimenting with cigarettes more likely, or has some other specific biological effect on the disease process—the psychological factor is a noncontributing indicator or marker for a process. Indicators can be extremely valuable as predictors of outcomes, identifiers of underlying processes, and contributors to behavioral processes not directly material to the emotion–disease link. Excitement seeking, for example, may neither contribute to nor mediate the connection of genes to smoking, though it may have important consequences for social behavior and exposure to opportunities for use of illegal substances.

In the extreme case, psychological indicators—personality factors and state and trait emotions—are analogous to warning flags posted to slow traffic at work sites. The flags neither directly participate in nor necessarily identify the underlying activity (e.g., sewer construction or road resurfacing), but they slow traffic, cause gaping, and may result in accidents. It would be premature and inappropriate, however, to assume that personality factors and emotions are only indicators and do not contribute either directly or indirectly to disease outcomes. A gene in combination with environmental factors sought and created by psychological variables (e.g., selecting risk-seeking friends) may create a complex diathesis for the promotion of disease.

CONCLUSION: EMOTION AS COMMUNICATION AND THE EMOTION–DISEASE LINK

Evolutionarily, emotional processes emerged in social animals to facilitate interpersonal communication and regulate group behavior. They were built upon basic neurobiological systems that distribute somatic resources for the performance of survival behaviors. For humans, emotions are also important in intrapersonal communication, telling us about the state of our somatic behavioral systems (i.e., whether we are ready to fight, to flee, to rest and recuperate, to engage in sexual behavior, etc.). Thus we regard emotions as real and, when carefully assessed, valid indicators of the state of our social–behavioral systems. But this does not mean that emotions will or should predict disease outcomes. Experientially elaborated, multilevel emotion systems respond to a wide variety of external and internal events and their meanings. Their validity as predictors of specific disease outcomes, cognitive activities, and social behaviors depends upon the person and context. Fatigue/depression following MI may predict mortality, but may have no relationship to mortality in healthy elderly individuals. Indeed, negative affect in elderly women, reflecting social involvement and responsibilities, predicts survival (Benyamini et al., in press; Idler & Leventhal, 2000). In both cases negative affect may nonetheless adversely affect quality of life and interpersonal behaviors.

The search for direct effects, and the idea that controlling our thoughts, feelings, and actions can help us reduce the risk of disease, can mislead by encouraging false hopes. It can also inform through research on the bidirectional connections between emotion and illness, linking biological and psychological theory. Our focus on indicators is designed to identify the important roles that psychological factors can play in this investigation, and also to discourage a single-causality model that obscures the roles of emotion in the multifactorial models of the onset, development, and outcome of the most prevalent life-threatening diseases.

REFERENCES

Alper, C. M., Doyle, W. J., Skoner, D. P., Buchman, C. A., Cohen, S., & Gwaltney, J. M. (1998). Prechallenge antibodies moderate disease expression in adults experimentally exposed to rhinovirus strain hanks. *Clinical Infectious Diseases, 27,* 119–128.

Appels, A., Kop, W., Meesters, C., Markusse, R., Golombeck, B., & Falger, P. (1994). Vital exhaustion and the acute coronary syndromes. In S. Meas, H. Leventhal, & M. Johnson (Eds.), *International review of health psychology* (pp. 65–95). New York: Wiley.

Benyamini, Y., Leventhal, H., & Leventhal, E. (in press). Gender differences in processing information for making self-assessments of health. *Psychosomatic Medicine.*

Berkman, L. F., Berkman, C. S., Kasl, S., Freeman, D. H., Leo, L., Ostfeld, A. M., Cornoni-Huntley, J., & Brody, J. A. (1986). Depressive symptoms in relation to physical health and functioning in the elderly. *American Journal of Epidemiology, 124,* 372–388.

Besedovsky, H., del Ray, A., Sorkin, E., Da Prada, M., Burri, R., & Honegger, C. (1983). The immune response evokes changes in brain noradrenergic neurons. *Science, 221,* 15–64.

Boden, J. M., & Baumeister, R. F. (1997). Repressive

coping: Distraction using pleasant thoughts and memories. *Journal of Personality and Social Psychology, 73,* 45–62.

Bower, G. H., & Cohen, P. R. (1982). Emotional influences on learning and cognition. *Affect and cognition* (pp. 263–289). Hillsdale, NJ: Erlbaum.

Cohen, S., Frank, E., Doyle, W., Skoner, D. P., Rabin, B. S., & Gwaltney, J. M. (1998). Types of stressors that increase susceptibility to the common cold in healthy adults. *Health Psychology, 17,* 214–223.

Cohen, S., & Herbert, T. B. (1996). Health psychology: Psychological factors and physical disease from the perspective of human psychoneuroimmunology. *Annual Review of Psychology, 47,* 113–142.

Cohen, S., Tyrrell, D. A. J., & Smith, A. P. (1991). Psychological stress and susceptibility to the common cold. *New England Journal of Medicine, 325,* 606–612.

Cohen, S., Tyrrell, D. A. J., & Smith, A. P. (1993). Negative life events, perceived stress, negative affect and susceptibility to the common cold. *Journal of Personality and Social Psychology, 64,* 131–140.

Contrada, R. J., Leventhal, H., & O'Leary, A. (1990). Personality and health. In L. A. Pervin (Ed.), *Handbook of personality: Theory and research* (pp. 638–669). New York: Guilford Press.

David, J., Green, P., Martin, R., & Suls, J. (1997). Differential roles of neuroticism, extroversion, and event desirability for mood in daily life: An integrative model of top-down and bottom-up influences. *Journal of Personality and Social Psychology, 73,* 149–159.

Dembroski, T. M., & Costa, P. T. (1987). Coronary-prone behavior: Components of the Type A pattern and hostility. *Journal of Personality, 55,* 211–235.

Diamond, E. L., Schneiderman, N., Schwartz, D., Smith, J. C., Vorn, R., & Pasin, R. D. (1984). Harassment, hostility, and Type A determinants of cardiovascular reactivity during competition. *Journal of Behavioral Medicine, 7,* 171–189.

Dunn, A. J. (1993). Infection as a stressor: A cytokine-mediated activation of the hypothalamo-pituitary-adrenal axis? *CIBA Foundation Symposium, 172,* 226–239.

Dunn, A. J., Powell, M. L., Meitin, C., & Small, P. A. (1989). Virus injection as a stressor: Influenza virus elevates plasma corticosterone and brain concentrations of MHPG and tryptophan. *Physiology and Behavior, 145,* 591–594.

Ekman, P. (1992). Are there basic emotions? *Psychological Review, 99,* 550–553.

Ekman, P., Friesen, W. V., & Ellsworth, P. (1972). *Emotion in the human face.* New York: Pergamon Press.

Engebretson, T. O., Matthews, K. A., & Scheier, M. F. (1989). Relations between anger expression and cardiovascular reactivity: Reconciling inconsistent findings through a matching hypothesis. *Journal of Personality and Social Psychology, 57,* 513–521.

Fifield, J., Tennen, H., Reisine, S., & McQuillan, J. (1998). Depression and the long-term risk of pain, fatigue, and disability in patients with rheumatoid arthritis. *Arthritis and Rheumatism, 41,* 1851–1857.

Frasure-Smith, N., Lespérance, F., Juneau, M., Talajic,

M., & Bourassa, M. G. (1999). Gender, depression, and one year prognosis after myocardial infarction. *Psychosomatic Medicine, 61,* 26–37.

Frasure-Smith, N., Lespérance, F., & Talajic, M. (1993). Depression following myocardial infarction: Impact on 6-month survival. *Journal of the American Medical Association, 270,* 1819–1825.

Frasure-Smith, N., Lespérance, F., & Talajic, M. (1995). The impact of negative emotions on prognosis following myocardial infarction: Is it more than depression? *Health Psychology, 14,* 388–398.

Frasure-Smith, N., & Prince, R. (1985). The ischemic heart disease life stress monitoring program: Impact on mortality. *Psychosomatic Medicine, 47,* 431–445.

Frasure-Smith, N., & Prince, R. (1989). Long-term follow-up of the ischemic heart disease life stress monitoring program. *Psychosomatic Medicine, 51,* 485–513.

Fridlund, A. J. (1991). Evolution and facial action in reflex, social motive, and paralanguage. *Biological Psychology, 32,* 3–100.

Friedman, H. S., & Booth-Kewley, S. (1987). The "disease-prone personality": A meta-analytic view of the construct. *American Psychologist, 42,* 539–555.

Friedman, M., & Rosenman, R. H. (1974). *Type A behavior and your heart.* New York: Knop.

Gibertini, M., Newton, C., Klein, T. W., & Friedman, H. (1995). *Legionella pneumophilia*-induced visual learning impairment reversed by anti-interleukin-1*B. Proceedings of the Society for Experimental Biology and Medicine, 210,* 7–11.

Glaser, R., Pearson, G. R., Bonneau, R. H., Esterling, B. A., Atkinson, C., & Kiecolt-Glaser, J. K. (1993). Stress and the memory T-cell response to the Epstein–Barr virus in healthy medical students. *Health Psychology, 12,* 435–442.

Greer, S., Morris, T., & Pettingale, K. W. (1979). Psychological response to breast cancer: Effect on outcome. *Lancet, ii,* 785–787.

Hajjar, D. P., & Nicholson, A. C. (1995). Atherosclerosis: An understanding of the cellular and molecular basis of the disease promises new approaches for its treatment in the near future. *American Scientist, 83,* 460–467.

Harbuz, M. S., Rees, R. G., & Lightman, S. L. (1993). HPA axis responses to acute stress and adrenalectomy during adjuvant-induced arthritis in the rat. *American Journal of Physiology, 264,* R179–R185.

Hart, B. L. (1988). Biological basis of the behavior of sick animals. *Neuroscience and Biobehavioral Reviews, 12,* 123–137.

Henry, J. P. (1983). Coronary heart disease and arousal of the adrenal cortical axis. In T. M. Dembroski, T. H. Schmidt, & G. Blumchern (Eds.), *Biobehavioral bases of coronary heart disease* (pp. 365–381). Basel: Karger.

Herberman, R. B., & Ortaldo, J. R. (1981). Natural killer cells: Their role in defenses against disease. *Science, 214,* 24–30.

Hokanson, J. E. (1970). Psychophysiological evaluation of catharsis hypothesis. In E. L. Megargee & J. E. Hokanson (Eds.), *The dynamics of aggression* (pp. 74–86). New York: Harper & Row.

Hubner, G., Brauchle, M., Smola, H., Madlener, M.,

Fassler, R., & Werner, S. (1996). Differential regulation of pro-inflammatory cytokines during wound healing in normal and glucocorticoid-treated mice. *Cytokine, 8,* 548–556.

Idler, E. L., & Leventhal, H. (2000). *Gender differences in self-rated health, well-being and survival in the NHANES I epidemiological follow-up study, 1992.* Manuscript submitted for publication.

Izard, C. E. (1971). *The face of emotion.* New York: Appleton-Century-Crofts.

Izard, C. E. (1991). *The psychology of emotions.* New York: Plenum Press.

Johnson, M. K., & Multhaup, K. S. (1992). Emotion and MEM. In A. Christianson (Ed.), *The handbook of emotion and memory: Current research and theory* (pp. 33–66). Hillsdale, NJ: Erlbaum.

Kamarck, T., & Jennings, J. R. (1991). Biobehavioral factors in sudden cardiac death. *Psychological Bulletin, 109,* 42–75.

Kiecolt-Glaser, J. K., Dura, J., Speicher, C., Trask, O. J., & Glaser, R. (1991). Spousal care givers of dementia victims: Longitudinal changes in immunity and health. *Psychosomatic Medicine, 53,* 345–362.

Kiecolt-Glaser, J. K., Fisher, L. D., Ogrocki, P., Stout, J. C., Speicher, C. E., & Glaser, R. (1987). Marital quality, marital disruption, and immune function. *Psychosomatic Medicine, 49,* 13–34.

Kiecolt-Glaser, J. K., & Glaser, R. (1995). Psychoneuroimmunology and health consequences: Data and shared mechanisms. *Psychosomatic Medicine, 57,* 269–274.

Kiecolt-Glaser, J. K., Glaser, R., Strain, E. C., Stout, J., Tarr, K. L., Holliday, J. E., & Speicher, C. E. (1986). Modulation of cellular immunity in medical students. *Journal of Behavioral Medicine, 9,* 5–21.

Kiecolt-Glaser, J. K., Marucha, P. T., Malarkey, W. B., Mercado, A. M., & Glaser, R. (1995). Slowing of wound healing by psychological stress. *Lancet, 346,* 1194–1196.

Kiecolt-Glaser, J. K., Page, G. G., Marucha, P. T., MacCullum, R. C., & Glaser, R. (1998). Psychological influences on surgical recovery: Perspectives from psychoneuroimmunology. *American Psychologist, 53,* 1209–1218.

Kluger, M. J., & Vaughn, L. K. (1978). Fever and survival in rabbits infected with *Pasteurella multocida. Journal of Physiology, 282,* 243–251.

Kulik, J. A., & Mahler, H. I. M. (1987). The effects of preoperative roommate assignment on preoperative anxiety and postoperative recovery from bypass surgery. *Health Psychology, 6,* 525–543.

Kulik, J., & Mahler, H. I. M. (1997). Social comparison, affiliation, and coping with acute medical threats. In B. P. Buunk & F. X. Gibbons (Eds.), *Health, coping, and well-being: Perspectives from social comparison theory* (pp. 227–263). Mahwah, NJ: Erlbaum.

LaBar, K. S., LeDoux, J. E., Spencer, D. D., & Phelps, E. A. (1995). Impaired fear conditioning following unilateral temporal lobectomy in humans. *Journal of Neuroscience, 15,* 6846–6855.

Lang, P. J. (1979). A bio-informational theory of emotional imagery: Presidential address, 1978. *Psychophysiology, 16,* 495–512.

Lang, P. J., Kozak, M. J., Miller, G. A., Levin, D. N., &

McLean, A. (1980). Emotional imagery: Conceptual structure and pattern of somato-visceral response. *Psychophysiology, 17,* 179–192.

Lazarus, R. S. (1991). Cognition and motivation in emotion. *American Psychologist, 48,* 352–367.

Leor, J., Poole, W. K., & Kloner, R. A. (1996). Sudden cardiac death triggered by an earthquake. *New England Journal of Medicine, 334,* 413–419.

Lerman, C., Caporaso, N. E., Audrain, J., Main, D., Bowman, E. D., Ockshin, B., Boyd, N. R., & Shields, P. G. (1999). Evidence suggesting the role of specific genetic factors in cigarette smoking. *Health Psychology, 18,* 14–20.

Lerman, C., Caporaso, N., Main, D., Audrain, J., Boyd, N. R., Bowman, E. D., & Shields, P. G. (1998). Depression and self-medication with nicotine: The modifying influence of the dopamine D4 receptor gene. *Health Psychology, 17,* 56–62.

Lerman, C., Gold, K., Audrain, J., Ting Hsiang, L., Boyd, N. R., Orleans, C. T., Wilfond, B., Louben, G., & Caporaso, N. (1997). Incorporating biomarkers of exposure and genetic susceptibility into smoking cessation treatment: Effects on smoking-related cognitions, emotions, and behavior. *Health Psychology, 16,* 87–99.

Lespérance, F., Frasure-Smith, N., & Talajic, M. (1996). Major depression before and after myocardial infarction: Its nature and consequences. *Psychosomatic Medicine, 58,* 99–110.

Leventhal, H. (1979). A perceptual–motor processing model of emotion. In P. Pliner, K. Blankstein, & I. M. Spigel (Eds.), *Advances in the study of communication and affect: Perception of emotion in self and others* (pp. 1–46). New York: Plenum Press.

Leventhal, H. (1984). A perceptual–motor theory of emotion. In L. Berkowitz (Ed.), *Advances in experimental social psychology* (Vol. 17, pp. 117–182). New York: Academic Press.

Leventhal, H., & Mosbach, P. A. (1983). The perceptual–motor theory of emotion. In J. Cacioppo & R. Petty (Eds.), *Social psychophysiology* (pp. 353–388). New York: Guilford Press.

Leventhal, H., & Patrick-Miller, L. (1993). Emotion and illness: The mind is in the body. In M. Lewis & J. M. Haviland (Eds.), *Handbook of emotions* (pp. 365–379). New York: Guilford Press.

Leventhal, H., Patrick-Miller, L., Leventhal, E. A., & Burns, E. A. (1997). Does stress-emotion cause illness in elderly people? *Annual Review of Gerontology and Geriatrics, 17,* 138–184.

Leventhal, H., & Scherer, K. R. (1987). The relationship of emotion to cognition: A functional approach to semantic controversy. *Cognition and Emotion, 1,* 3–28.

Linden, W., Stossel, C., & Maurice, J. (1996). Psychosocial interventions for patients with coronary artery disease: A meta-analysis. *Archives of Internal Medicine, 156,* 745–752.

Maes, S., Leventhal, H., & DeRidder, D. T. D. (1995). Coping with chronic illness. In M. Zeidner & N. Endler (Eds.), *Handbook of coping: Theory, research, application* (pp. 221–251). New York: Wiley.

Maier, S. F., & Watkins, L. R. (1998). Cytokines for psychologists: Implications of bidirectional immune-to-brain communication for understanding behavior, mood, and cognition. *Psychological Review, 105,* 83–107.

Mandler, J. M. (1992). How to build a baby: II. Conceptual primitives. *Psychological Review, 99,* 587–604.

Manuck, S. B. (1994). Cardiovascular reactivity in cardiovascular disease: "Once more unto the breach." *International Journal of Behavioral Medicine, 1,* 4–31.

Marucha, P. T., Kiecolt-Glaser, J. K., & Favagehi, M. (1998). Mucosal wound healing is impaired by examination stress. *Psychosomatic Medicine, 60,* 362–365.

Matthews, K. A. (1988). Coronary heart disease and Type A behavior: Update on an alternative to the Booth–Kewley and Friedman quantitative review. *Psychological Bulletin, 104,* 373–380.

Matthews, K. A., & Woodall, K. L. (1988). Childhood origins of overt Type A behaviors and cardiovascular reactivity to behavioral stressors. *Annals of Behavioral Medicine, 10,* 71–77.

Matthews, K. A., Woodall, K. L., & Allen, M. T. (1993). Cardiovascular reactivity to the cold pressor test as a predictor of hypertension. *Hypertension, 67,* 479–485.

Meites, J. (1990). Alterations in hypothalamic–pituitary function with age. In H. J. Armbrecht, R. M. Coe, & N. Wongsurawat (Eds.), *Endocrine function and aging* (pp. 1–12). New York: Springer-Verlag.

Mendes de Leon, C. F., Powell, L. H., & Kaplan, B. H. (1991). Change in coronary-prone behaviors in the recurrent coronary prevention project. *Psychosomatic Medicine, 53,* 407–419.

Mittleman, M. A., Maclure, M., Sherwood, J. B., Mulry, R. P., Tofler, G. H., Jacobs, S. C., Friedman, R., Benson, H., & Muller, J. E. (1995). Triggering of acute myocardial infarction onset by episodes of anger: Determinants of myocardial infarction onset study. *Circulation, 92,* 1720–1725.

Morris, T., & Greer, S. (1980). A "Type C" for cancer? [Abstract]. *Cancer Detection and Prevention, 3,* 102.

Ortony, A., & Turner, T. J. (1990). What's basic about basic emotions? *Psychological Review, 9,* 315–331.

Padgett, D. A., Marucha, P. T., & Sheridan, J. F. (1998). Restraint stress slows cutaneous wound healing in mice. *Brain, Behavior, and Immunity, 12,* 64–73.

Panksepp, J. (1993). Neurochemical control of moods and emotions: Amino acids to neuropeptides. In M. Lewis & J. M. Haviland (Eds.), *Handbook of emotions* (pp. 87–107). New York: Guilford Press.

Panksepp, J. (1998). *Affective neuroscience: The foundations of human and animal emotions.* New York: Oxford University Press.

Park, D. C. (1994). Self-regulation and control of rheumatic disorders. In S. Maes & H. Leventhal (Eds.), *International review of health psychology* (pp. 189–217). Chichester, England: Wiley.

Patrick-Miller, L. J. (1998). The relationships amongst affect and immune responses following in vivo immunological challenge. *Dissertation Abstracts International, 60,* 355.

Penninx, B. W., Guralnik, J. M., Mendes de Leon, C. F., Pahor, M., Visser, M., Corti, M. C., & Wallace, R. B. (1998). Cardiovascular events and mortality in newly and chronically depressed persons >70 years of age. *American Journal of Cardiology, 81,* 988–994.

Petitto, J. M., Lysle, D. T., Gariepy, J. L., Clubb, P. H.,

Cairns, R. B., & Lewis, M. H. (1993). Genetic differences in social behavior: Relation to natural killer cell function and susceptibility to tumor development. *Neuropsychopharmacology, 8,* 35–43.

Petitto, J. M., Lysle, D. T., Gariepy, J. L., & Lewis, M. H. (1994). Association of genetic differences in social behavior and cellular immune responsiveness: Effects of social experience. *Brain, Behavior, and Immunity, 8,* 111–122.

Pettingale, K. W. (1984). Coping and cancer prognosis. *Journal of Psychosomatic Research, 28,* 363–364.

Pettingale, K. W., Morris, T., Greer, S., & Haybittle, J. (1985). Mental attitudes toward cancer: An additional prognostic factor. *Lancet, i,* 750.

Phelps, E. A., LaBar, K. S., & Spencer, D. D. (1997). Memory for emotional words following unilateral temporal lobectomy. *Brain and Cognition, 35,* 85–109.

Plomin, R. (1998). Using DNA in health psychology. *Health Psychology, 17,* 53–55.

Pomerleau, O. F., Collins, A. C., Shiffman, S., & Pomerleau, C. S. (1993). Why some people smoke and others do not: New perspectives. *Journal of Consulting and Clinical Psychology, 61,* 723–731.

Pomerleau, O. F., & Kardia, S. L. (1999). Introduction to the featured section: Genetic research on smoking. *Health Psychology, 18,* 3–6.

Riley, V., Fitzmaurice, M. A., & Spackman, D. H. (1981). Psychoneuroimmunologic factors in neoplasia: Studies in animals. In R. Ader (Ed.), *Psychoneuroimmunology* (pp. 31–93). New York: Academic Press.

Russell, J. A. (1980). A circumplex model of affect. *Journal of Personality and Social Psychology, 39,* 1161–1178.

Sabol, S. Z., Nelson, L., Fisher, C., Gunzerath, L., Brody, C. L., Hu, S., Sirota, L. A., Marcus, S. E., Greenberg, B. D., Lucas, F. R., Benjamin, J., Murphy, D. L., & Hamer, D. H. (1999). A genetic association for cigarette smoking behavior. *Health Psychology, 18,* 7–13.

Scherer, K. R. (1984). Emotion as a multicomponent process: A model and some cross-cultural data. In P. Shaver (Ed.), *Review of personality and social psychology: Vol. 5: Emotions, relationships and health* (pp. 37–63). Beverly Hills, CA: Sage.

Scherwitz, L., Berton, K. E., & Leventhal, H. (1978). Type A behavior, self-involvement and cardiovascular response. *Psychosomatic Medicine, 40,* 593–609.

Seligman, M. E. P. (1975). *Helplessness: On depression, development, and death.* San Francisco: Freeman.

Sklar, L. S., & Anisman, H. (1979). Stress and coping factors influence tumor growth. *Science, 205,* 513–515.

Smith, A., Tyrrell, D., Coyle, K., & Higgins, P. (1988). Effects of interferon alpha on performance in man: A preliminary report. *Psychopharmacology, 96,* 414–416.

Smith, T. W. (1992). Hostility and health: Current status of a psychosomatic hypothesis. *Health Psychology, 11,* 139–150.

Smith, T. W., Allred, K. D., Morrison, C. A., & Carlson,

S. D. (1989). Cardiovascular reactivity and interpersonal influence: Active coping in a social context. *Journal of Personality and Social Psychology, 56,* 209–218.

Smith, T. W., Gallo, L. C., Goble, L., Ngu, L. Q., & Stark, K. A. (1998). Agency, communion, and cardiovascular reactivity during marital interaction. *Health Psychology, 17,* 537–545.

Smith, T. W., & Pope, M. K. (1990). Cynical hostility as a health risk: Current status and future directions. *Journal of Social Behavior and Personality, 5,* 77–88.

Suls, J., Martin, R., & Leventhal, H. (1997). Social comparison, lay referral, and the decision to seek medical care. In B. P. Buunk & F. X. Gibbons (Eds.), *Health, coping, and well-being: Perspectives from social comparison theory* (pp. 195–226). Mahwah, NJ: Erlbaum.

Temoshok, L. (1987). Personality, coping style, emotion, and cancer: Towards an integrative model. *Cancer Surveys, 6,* 545–567.

Temoshok, L., & Fox, B. H. (1984). Coping styles and other psychosocial factors related to medical status and to prognosis in patients with cutaneous malignant melanoma. In B. H. Fox & B. H. Newberry (Eds.), *Impact of psychoendocrine systems in cancer and immunity* (pp. 258–287). Lewistown, NY: Hogrefe.

Terao, A., Oikawa, M., & Saito, M. (1994). Tissue-specific increase in norepinephrine turnover by central interleukin-1, but not by interleukin-6, in rats. *American Journal of Physiology, 266,* R400–R404.

Tomkins, S. S. (1962). *Affect, imagery, consciousness: Vol. 1. The positive affects.* New York: Springer.

Uchino, B. N., Cacioppo, J. R., & Kiecolt-Glaser, J. K. (1996). The relationship between social support and physiological processes: A review with emphasis on underlying mechanisms and implications for health. *Psychological Bulletin, 119,* 488–531.

Verrier, R. L., & Mittleman, M. A. (1996). Life-threatening cardiovascular consequences of anger in patients with coronary heart disease. *Cardiology Clinics, 14,* 289–307.

Weiss, J. M. (1972). Psychological factors in stress and disease. *Scientific American, 226,* 104–113.

Weiss, J. M., Glazer, H. I., Pohorecky, L. A., & Miller, N. E. (1975). Effects of chronic exposure to stressors on avoidance-escape behavior and on brain norepinephrine. *Psychosomatic Medicine, 37,* 522–534.

Wood, J. & Van der Zee, K. (1997). Social comparison among cancer patients: Under what conditions are comparisons upward and downward? In B. P. Buunk & F. X. Gibbons (Eds.), *Health, coping and well-being: Perspectives from social comparison* (pp. 299–328). Mahwah, NJ: Erlbaum.

Wulsin, L. R., Vaillant, G. E., & Wells, V. E. (1999). A systematic review of the mortality of depression. *Psychosomatic Medicine, 61,* 6–17.

Zalcman, S., Shanks, N., & Anisman, H. (1991). Time-dependent variations of central norepinephrine and dopamine following antigen administration. *Brain Research, 557,* 69–76.

Zeiss, A. M., Lewinsohn, P. M., Rohde, P., & Seeley, J. R. (1996). Relationship of physical disease and functional impairment to depression in older people. *Psychology and Aging, 11,* 572–581.

Zillmann, D. (1978). Attribution and misattribution of excitatory reactions. In J. H. Harvey, W. J. Ickes, & R. F. Kidd (Eds.), *New directions in attribution research* (Vol. 2, pp. 335–368). Hillsdale, NJ: Erlbaum.

CHAPTER 34

When Seeing Is Feeling: A Cognitive–Emotional Approach to Coping with Health Stress

Suzanne M. Miller
Robert A. Schnoll

In the last decade, there has been an explosion of research in the field of health psychology, spurred by the successes in applying basic psychological concepts and findings to understanding individuals' patterns of dealing with diverse life challenges and stressors (e.g., Baum & Singer, 1987; Lazarus, 1991; Taylor, 1990). The topics encompassed by this rapidly growing field range from prevention of disease to its early detection and long-term management, with respect to individual differences in selecting and processing health-relevant risks, information, and feedback, and the accompanying emotional consequences. Although the core topics and implicit goals within health psychology seem coherent and clear, different investigators typically adopt divergent conceptual frameworks and models to guide their research (S. M. Miller, Shoda, & Hurley, 1996; S. M. Miller, Mischel, O'Leary, & Mills, 1996).

Under close examination, however, these models tend to show considerable conceptual (and methodological) overlap, often differing more in nuances of terminology than in essential themes. Moreover, most available current models in psychology address only partial aspects or components of individual differences

in the total health-relevant emotional coping process, focusing on the particular researcher's favorite construct or variable in his or her own research program. Finally, the concepts that guide much of this research, while often rooted in earlier theorizing and findings in related areas, tend to be applied without explicit linkages to existing theory and findings. Inevitably, this disciplinary provincialism undermines the development of a genuinely cumulative theory and science; it risks conceptual overlap and confusion, rather than facilitating progressive refinement and precision (Miller & Diefenbach, 1998).

The purpose of this chapter is to apply to health psychology a potentially comprehensive theoretical conception, the "cognitive–emotional approach" to individual differences (e.g., Mischel, 1973, 1990, 1993). Increasingly strengthened by cumulative research and theorizing from several investigators over many years (e.g., Bandura, 1986; Kelly, 1955; Rotter, 1954), this approach has been stimulating a unified conceptual analysis of basic issues and topics in neighboring areas of emotion, personality, social, developmental, and clinical psychology for more than two decades (e.g., Carver & Scheier, 1981; Dodge, 1986; Dweck, 1990; Foa & Kozak, 1986; Sarason, 1979; Singer & Salovey, 1991). Rather than reflecting the ideas of any single theorist, it is a cumulative approach based on the contributions of diverse theorists and researchers. It has evolved into a distinctive general perspective for understanding individual differences in diverse domains of behavior, the processes that generate them, and their impact on how people respond—both cognitively and emotionally—to new information and to attempts to influence them (S. M. Miller, Shoda, et al., 1996; S. M. Miller, Mischel et al., 1996).

Although it has not been systematically applied to health psychology, our thesis is that a cognitive–emotional theory, broadly construed and defined, meets the theoretical and empirical challenges of this area especially well. In this chapter, we first provide an overview of the cognitive–emotional framework and its application to cancer. We then describe two prototypic profiles for responding to health threats—monitoring versus blunting—and highlight the cognitive–emotional correlates and consequences of each profile. We believe that such a unifying, comprehensive conceptual framework is useful at this juncture in the area's development, and can help health psychology evolve beyond the excitement and promise of practical, applied, health-relevant contributions to become a more genuinely cumulative science.

COGNITIVE–EMOTIONAL MODEL OF HEALTH INFORMATION PROCESSING

In cognitive social theory (S. M. Miller, Shoda, et al., 1996; S. M. Miller, Mischel, et al., 1996), the differences in adaptation to health threats reflect the difference in the interaction of three main sets of person variables, which are the units for characterizing individual differences. These include (1) the emotional/affective responses that are activated by the health threat; (2) the cognitive responses that are primed, in terms of how individuals categorize, construe, and encode information about their own health and affective states; and (3) the individuals' self-regulatory coping strategies and competencies for dealing with the emotions that arise in response to health challenges.

Emotional/Affective Responses to Health Threats

At the affective level, emotional distress primed by cancer threats generally takes the form of heightened levels of disease-related worry, intrusive ideation, depression, and anxiety (see Greer, 1994; Holland, 1998; Kornblith, 1998; Moyer & Salovey, 1996). For purposes of exposition, the cancer experience can be divided into three primary challenges: cancer risk feedback, cancer diagnosis, and survivorship. Each phase has been found to elicit clinically significant levels of emotional distress among one-quarter to one-third of individuals (Greer, 1994; Holland, 1998; Moyer & Salovey, 1996). The initial phase of a cancer diagnosis, in particular, tends to elicit high levels of psychological distress (Loscalzo & Brintzenhofeszoc, 1998; Stanton & Snider, 1993).

Negative emotional responding not only has an impact on psychological well-being and quality of life (Holland, 1998; Moyer & Salovey, 1996); it has also been shown to have an adverse impact on health status by undermining adherence to health-protective regimens (e.g., cancer screening; Miller, Fang, Manne, Engstrom, & Daly, 1999) and medical treatment recommendations (e.g., chemotherapy; Ayers et al., 1994; Kash & Lerman, 1998; Lerman et al., 1993; Richardson & Sanchez, 1998). Furthermore, accumulating evidence suggests that heightened emotional distress can have a direct impact on health status through biological pathways, notably through the suppression of immune function (Bovbjerg & Valdimarsdottir, 1998; Cohen & Herbert, 1996; Kiecolt-Glaser, Page, Marucha, MacCallum, & Glaser, 1998; Miller & O'Leary, 1993; O'Leary & Miller, 1991; O'Leary, Savard, & Miller, 1996).

Affective responding may reflect inherent characteristics of the individual, including temperamental, dispositional features such as trait anxiety (Cameron, Leventhal, & Love, 1998; Fallowfield, Hall, Maguire, & Baum, 1990) and level of physiological toughness (see Dienstbier, 1989), including pain tolerance (Breitbart & Payne, 1998). However, affective responding also appears to be critically influenced by the types of construals, beliefs, and expectancies individuals generate about the stressor, as well as the self-regulatory coping strategies they employ (S. M. Miller, Shoda, et al., 1996; S. M. Miller, Mischel, et al., 1996). Moreover, affect is likely to interact with cognition and self-regulatory behaviors in a reciprocal cycle, in which particular emotions are triggered by particular cognitions and self-regulatory strategies, and vice versa (Folkman, 1984; Rudolph, Dennig, & Weisz, 1995).

For instance, when an already anxious individual encounters a health stressor, activating such emotions as "I'm feeling terrified about my possible cancer risk," it will result in specific negative construals and beliefs (e.g., "I think my disease is very serious") and self-regulatory behaviors (e.g., "I need to run away from this"). Conversely, if an individual with a low level of premorbid distress encounters a health stressor, high levels of subsequent emotional distress are nonetheless likely to ensue if the encounter activates a pattern of threatening construals, beliefs, and expectancies (e.g., "I can't handle this") and maladaptive self-regulatory behaviors (e.g., "I need to run away from this"). The focus of this chapter is on the impact of cognition and behavior on affect, rather than the reverse; this focus is consistent with the available literature. However, it is important to bear in mind that most of this research is correlational and cross-sectional in nature. Furthermore, there is some direct indication that emotional states can cause cognitions and behaviors.

One notable study addressed the issue of reverse causality with a sample of breast cancer patients, exploring the relationship between self-regulatory coping behaviors and emotional distress (Carver et al., 1993). Initial analyses in this study showed that avoidant self-regulatory behaviors prospectively predicted emotional distress. Distress, assessed prior to breast surgery, was then used to predict postsurgery coping reactions; base-level use of the same coping responses was statistically controlled for. Presurgery levels of distress were found to influence the use of specific coping responses 6 months after surgery. Specifically, higher levels of presurgical emotional distress prospectively predicted higher levels of avoidant self-regulatory coping responses and lower levels of planning. Distress measured immediately following surgery also predicted higher levels of avoidant coping at the 6-month follow-up. These results suggest that a reciprocal relationship exists between coping behavior and emotional distress reactions among breast cancer patients. The general failure to take this approach into account constitutes a rich area for future research.

Cognitive Responses to Health Threats

The cognitive units that mediate distress reactions to medical stressors—health-relevant self-construals, beliefs, and expectancies—have to do with an individual's encoding patterns and beliefs for appraising personal health risk and disease information.

Self-Construals/Encodings

Individuals differ greatly in their encoding. That is, they categorize the same events in different ways, as evident in the differences among individuals in personal constructs (e.g., Argyle & Little, 1972; Higgins, 1990; Kelly, 1955) and in the type of information to which they attend (e.g., Cioffi, 1991; Miller, 1995). The "stimulus as coded"—not necessarily the stimulus the health psychologist has in mind—constitutes the stimulus to which a person responds. People actively transform stimuli, focusing on selected aspects cognitively, and their selective attention and interpretation of events alter the meaning and impact of information (Miller, Fang, Diefenbach, & Bales, in press; Shoda et al., 1998). In the last two decades, research on individual differences in encoding and personal constructs has become voluminous (e.g., Cantor, 1990; Markus, 1977). In the health context, a prime example of the use of the encoding concept is seen in how individuals mentally represent and interpret their illness states and physical symptoms (Leventhal, Diefenbach, & Leventhal, 1992; Miller & Diefenbach, 1998).

Individuals seem to differ reliably in the constructs and beliefs that are particularly stable or "chronic" for them over time (e.g., Higgins, King, & Mavin, 1982). A person's chronic constructs are those that are most easily and readily accessed, often with minimal cues. When primed, either by internal processes or external cues, these cognitions activate other person variables, such as the individual's affective experiences and intentions. Their interactions with each other and with new information influence the person's actions regarding health-relevant behaviors, such as whether or not to visit the physician, to undergo a follow-up diagnostic test, or to engage in healthy behaviors. For example, individuals who encode themselves with self-constructs such as "I am a healthy, hardy person and intrinsically immune" may fail to become sufficiently anxious to seek risk information (e.g., to attend to the need to be screened for cancer), and may perceive screening as personally irrelevant. People who readily encode information in terms of personal health relevance, and who easily perceive threats to their health, will respond more anxiously and attentively to messages about cancer screening (Turk & Salovey, 1985; Weinstein, 1989). In contrast, those who see themselves as not only vulnerable but helpless may become highly anxious, thereby failing to attend to risk-relevant information and seek it spontaneously (S. M. Miller, Shoda, et al., 1996; S. M. Miller, Mischel, et al., 1996).

Individual differences in the type and accessibility of chronic constructs thus have an impact on the types of health-relevant risk data a person will perceive as personally relevant (or irrelevant); guide attention and avoidance strategically; and influence how risk information is selected, processed, stored, and retrieved. Across the cancer spectrum, these differences in perceived vulnerability have been linked to the degree of emotional distress experienced. In the context of cancer risk feedback, unaffected individuals tend either to overestimate or to underestimate their risk for disease (Lerman & Schwartz, 1993). In one recent study of close to 2,000 women in a primary care facility, 31% of women overestimated their risk (as determined by the discrepancy between subjective risk perceptions and objective indices of their risk), and 26% underestimated their risk (Skinner, Kreuter, Kobrin, & Strecher, 1998).

The findings have consistently shown that higher levels of perceived vulnerability to disease are associated with heightened anxiety and depression, as well as with impaired mood and daily functioning (see Lerman & Schwartz, 1993). For instance, in two studies of female first-degree relatives of cancer patients, high perceived risk for developing ovarian cancer was related to greater intrusive ideation (Schwartz, Lerman, Miller, Daly, & Masny, 1995) and greater cancer-specific worry (Wardle, 1995). Likewise, among women undergoing diagnostic follow up for suspicious abnormal mammograms, greater perceptions of risk were associated with higher levels of diagnostic-assessment-related anxiety and breast cancer worries, which interfered with daily mood and functioning (Lerman et al., 1991). More recently, heightened perceived risk of developing breast/ovarian cancer reported by women seeking genetic testing was found to be associated with symptoms of anxiety and depression (Audrain et al., 1997).

These cross-sectional findings have been replicated in a longitudinal study of the relationship between risk perceptions and levels of psychological distress. Zakowski et al. (1997) examined perceived risk as a predictor of intrusive thoughts and avoidant ideation among women who underwent mammography screening (and had normal results). Perceived risk, assessed prior to mammography, was a significant predictor of intrusive thoughts and avoidant ideation, assessed 4 months following mammography. Further replication of the effect of risk perceptions on affect comes from a study that exposed patients at risk for cancer to either a physician who expressed a high level of worry about the patients' condition, thereby raising the patients' risk perceptions, or a physician who did not convey worry about the patients' condition (Shapiro, Boggs, Melamed, & Graham-Pole, 1992). Patients receiving mammogram results from a worried physician reported significantly higher levels of anxiety, and had higher pulse rates, than did patients receiving results from a nonworried physician. These results also suggest that the expression of worry may have a "contagion" effect.

In the context of cancer diagnosis, the few available studies addressing the link between construals and psychological adjustment have focused on the influence of perceptions of disease severity on indicators of emotional responding. The findings indicate that patients who manifest greater perceptions of disease severity also tend to report higher levels of psychological distress. Early studies documented a significant relationship between elevated perceptions of disease severity and greater emotional distress among newly diagnosed cancer patients (Marks, Richardson, Graham, & Levine, 1986) and among patients who had completed medical treatment (Weisman, 1989). Likewise, in more recent studies, greater perceived seriousness of the cancer has been related to higher levels of self-reported anxiety and depression among cancer patients (see Andrykowski & Brady, 1994; Compas et al., 1994).

Among survivors, concerns about vulnerability to disease recurrence have been found in 42–89% of breast cancer survivors (Meyer & Aspegren, 1989; Polinsky, 1994; Sneeuw et al., 1992) and 39–76% of bone marrow transplant survivors (Belec, 1992; Bush, Haberman, Donaldson, & Sullivan, 1995), and have been associated with adverse affective responses in several correlational, cross-sectional studies (Kornblith, 1998). For example, concerns about disease recurrence have been associated with greater psychological distress among survivors of adult acute leukemia, as measured by two measures of global psychological adjustment that include symptoms of anxiety and depression (Greenberg et al., 1995). Among breast cancer survivors, fear of recurrence was associated with symptoms of anxiety and depression, even several years after completion of treatment (Kornblith, 1998).

Beliefs and Expectancies

People differ greatly in their health-relevant beliefs (i.e., perceptions of control and self-efficacy) and expectancies (i.e., perceptions of optimism vs. pessimism). Obviously, expectancies are themselves both cognitive and affective in nature. One woman may have realistic expectancies about her health risks, and may believe that carefully attending to her own health as much as possible can lead to early intervention if needed and preserve her life. She believes that she can increase her survival odds by following all the best medical wisdom and taking as much control as is possible. She feels competent to do what needs to be done for her health, and expects that efforts such as breast cancer screening will make a difference to her life. In contrast, another woman may believe that her body is "so full of lumps I cannot bring myself to deal with them," and may expect that screening will simply bring her "bad news that cannot be changed anyway." Moreover, she has little faith in her own ability to make important decisions about cancer screening, even if she forced herself to try.

As these examples imply, a cognitive–emotional theory is necessary when we move from constructs to the actual choice and performance of health-protective behaviors in particular situations, and their affective consequences. Efforts to predict an individual's affects and behaviors in particular situations require attention to the specific subjective expectancies about the probable consequences of different behavioral possibilities in that situation (e.g., Mischel, 1966; Rotter, 1954). People's "If ___, then ___" outcome expectancies influence their choice of behaviors from among the alternatives that can be construed and selected within any situation.

In the context of cancer, individuals can choose among several options (such as seeing a physician for yearly screening; performing monthly cancer screening at home; or watching their diet, exercising regularly, and hoping for the best), guided by their outcome expectancies and beliefs (Cameron, Leventhal, & Leventhal, 1993).

A recent study showed that women with benign breast problems who reported high levels of perceived control over their prognosis also reported lower rates of breast cancer worry (Cunningham et al., 1998). Among women seeking testing for the *BRCA1* genetic mutation, greater perceptions of control over developing breast cancer were associated with lower rates of anxiety, depression, and intrusive and avoidant ideation (Audrain et al., 1997). In addition, greater levels of perceived control over personal prognosis and recovery have been associated with better affective responses among breast cancer patients (Lowery, Jacobsen, & DuCette, 1993; Penman et al., 1987; Taylor, Lichtman, & Wood, 1984) and among heterogeneous samples of cancer patients (Ell, Mantell, Hamovitch, & Nishimoto, 1989; Newsom, Knapp, & Schulz, 1996; Taylor, Helgeson, Reed, & Skokan, 1991; Thompson, Sobolew-Shubin, Galbraith, Schwankovsky, & Cruzen, 1993). For instance, Marks et al. (1986) and Andrykowski and Brady (1994) found that newly diagnosed cancer patients who reported greater levels of perceived control concerning their prognosis and recovery also reported lower levels of depression and anxiety. Finally, in the context of survivorship, Dirksen (1989) found that greater perceptions of control regarding personal prognosis and recovery were associated with greater satisfaction with life among melanoma survivors. Similarly, Grassi and Rosti (1996) and Blood, Dineen, Kauffman, Raimondi, and Simpson (1993) reported that greater levels of perceptions of control with regard to personal prognosis and recovery were associated with lower cancer-related stress in samples of heterogeneous and laryngeal cancer survivors, respectively.

When there is no distinctive new information about the behavior–outcome relations probable in any situation, choices will depend on relevant "generalized" expectancies that have been formed in situations encoded as similar (S. M. Miller, Shoda, et al., 1996; S. M. Miller, Mischel, et al., 1996). In the cancer risk context, several studies—although correlational and cross-sectional—have shown a relationship between higher levels of optimistic (vs. pessimistic) outcome expectancies and more positive affective responding. Stoddard (1995) found that higher levels of optimism were associated with lower levels of psychological distress among women at risk for cervical cancer. Likewise, among women seeking testing for the *BRCA1* genetic mutation, a higher level of optimism was associated with lower rates of anxiety, depression, and intrusive and avoidant ideation (Audrain et al., 1997). Similarly, women with familial risk for ovarian cancer who reported higher levels of optimism expressed lower rates of cancer-related worry and general psychological distress, compared to women who reported low levels of optimism (Wardle, 1995). Furthermore, among women undergoing a biopsy for breast cancer, higher levels of optimism were correlated with lower levels of self-reported anxiety and depression (Stanton & Snider, 1993). A study of women undergoing clinical breast examination showed that those who reported high levels of optimism also exhibited low levels of anxiety (Lauver & Tak, 1995).

This pattern has been documented among samples of recently diagnosed cancer patients as well (for a review, see Spencer, Carver, & Price, 1998). Studies with breast cancer patients (Pinder, Ramirez, Richards, & Gregory, 1994), with heterogeneous samples of cancer patients (D. L. Miller, Manne, Taylor, & Keates, 1996; Thompson & Pitts, 1993), and with patients about to undergo bone marrow transplantation (Baker, Marcellus, Zabora, Polland, & Jodrey, 1997) have shown that greater dispositional optimism is related to lower levels of anxiety and depression. One study examined optimism as a predictor of emotional responding following breast cancer surgery (Carver et al., 1993). The findings confirmed correlational results, demonstrating that optimism (assessed prior to surgery) was a significant predictor of emotional distress 1 year following surgery, even after base levels of emotional distress were controlled for. Finally, a study of breast cancer survivors found that pessimism regarding the future effects of the disease on a patient's interpersonal relationships was related to a negative body image and a sense of isolation (Gluhoski, Siegel, & Gorey, 1997).

A major problem for theories of adherence to health-protective behavior, and for individuals who attempt to practice those behaviors, is the peculiar nature of the "rewards" they provide. Adherence to behaviors such as screening is risky, in the sense that such behaviors are designed to detect—rather than to prevent—cancer. When individuals engage in a screening regimen, it increases the immediate likelihood of finding an abnormality. With core constructs about the survival of the self thus threatened, individuals may choose not to perform the behavior in order to avoid the short-term increase in anxiety generated by the possibility of detecting a lump or other symptom, even though paradoxically they may put themselves more at risk in the long term if undetected disease is allowed to progress (S. M. Miller, Shoda, et al., 1996; S. M. Miller, Mischel, et al., 1996). Although physicians and health care personnel typically focus on the benefits of cancer screening, the very act of having one's body examined in a clinical manner primes a cognitive focus on what these behaviors could lead one to find and on the disease itself. This type of attention, in turn, may increase (rather than decrease) one's sense of vulnerability and therefore may trigger intense affect and denial behaviors.

The cognitive–emotional analysis suggests that to predict a person's tendency to adhere to screening regimens, it is necessary to understand the person's specific construals, beliefs, and expectancies, and the affects these prime. If individuals perceive cancer screening as a way to discover that they are doomed, they are unlikely to be adherent. "Self-efficacy," a person's belief that he or she can execute the behavior required by a particular situation, is especially germane for difficult health-relevant behaviors (Bandura, 1986). Self-efficacy expectations, assessed by asking individuals to indicate their degree of confidence that they can do a particular task (which is described in detail), appear to be important in guiding and directing behavior. High self-efficacy expectations often predict effective performance, particularly when the potential outcome is extremely significant to the individual and emotionally salient (Lau, Hartman, & Ware, 1986). It is commonly assumed that most people place a high value on their health and are willing to enact behaviors in the service of minimizing negative medical outcomes or maximizing positive medical outcomes, but only if they feel confident to enact those behaviors.

In the context of cervical cancer screening, a strong inverse relationship between self-efficacy and anxiety has been reported, such that higher levels of self-efficacy regarding cancer screening are associated with lower levels of distress (Lobell, Bay, Rhoads, & Keske, 1994). Among samples of cancer patients undergoing treatment, patients who reported higher self-efficacy beliefs with regard to caring for themselves and promoting their own health manifested lower perceived stress and depression (Lev & Owen, 1996). Likewise, Cunningham, Lackwood, and Cunningham (1991) reported that newly diagnosed cancer patients who believed more strongly in their abilities to cope with specific treatment-related difficulties (e.g., hair loss) reported lower levels of anxiety, depression, and anger. Similarly, a study of newly diagnosed cancer patients found that self-efficacy beliefs were associated with lower depression, even after demographic and disease variables were controlled for (Beckham, Burker, Lytle, Feldman, & Costakis, 1997). Furthermore, a study by Baldwin and Courneya (1997) showed that increased efficacy beliefs with respect to exercise competency were correlated with improved self-esteem among breast cancer survivors, suggesting that greater self-efficacy is associated with more positive affective responding.

Self-Regulatory Coping Strategies and Competencies

Even if individuals have resolved to perform health-protective behaviors and believe that this will be helpful, they may still fail to execute these behaviors because they focus their feelings on fears of finding a malignant tumor, or fears about the difficulty of coping with their concerns. Other individuals, objectively at equal risk and equally resolved to be health-protective, may attend to progress step by step, reinforce themselves strategically during the process, and calmly remind themselves of what they must do and its value. These examples illustrate that the cognitive–emotional theory draws a distinction between the intentions, decisions, and choices people make about attempting health-protective behaviors on the one hand, and whether or not they actually take the subsequent steps of initiating and regularly practicing those behaviors on the other (see Rakowski et al., 1992; Rakowski, Fulton, & Feldman, 1993), given the affective consequences. This dilemma calls attention to individuals' ability to move beyond good intentions and wise decisions to perform and maintain the

health regimens to which they are trying to adhere, in the face of emotional challenges.

Successful adherence to such regimens calls for what William James (1890) saw as the essence of the "will," or what the layperson considers a basic trait, "willpower." These concepts refer to the ability to resist distractions, to remind oneself of what needs to be done, and to forgo more immediately appealing activities and temptations in order to adhere to one's long-term goals, even if one has to make oneself endure affectively aversive experiences and frustrations along the route (e.g., Mischel, Shoda, & Rodriguez, 1989). In the cognitive–emotional model, to understand this crucial quality requires analyzing the self-regulatory processes that underlie it and that are the mental "preliminaries" enabling willpower (James, 1890). These processes are especially important for adherence to long-term, "difficult" health regimens.

Cognitive–emotional theory focuses on the system of self-regulatory competencies with which individuals can guide, plan, organize, and sustain or self-control their future-oriented behavior across situations and over time, particularly in the face of barriers and frustrations that potentially distract, overwhelm, and undermine their efforts. These self-regulatory skills —or coping behaviors—include individuals' ability to remind themselves to cue the behavior and to defer other, more tempting distractions. They must instruct themselves in what needs to be done, monitor and reinforce their own performance, and carry out each step of the behavior by focusing on the procedure's enactment, without becoming anxious and overwhelmed with interfering ideation. Additional needed skills include the person's cognitive/attentional strategies for selecting, encoding, storing, and accessing information about potential health-relevant risks, stressors, and options (e.g., Miller, 1995).

Attempts to adhere to a health-protective procedure can easily become anxiety arousing and demanding, entailing a high level of uncertainty. To maintain such behavior effectively once it is attempted requires individuals to utilize a complex array of self-regulatory skills and covert symbolic activities purposefully and strategically. Individuals must instruct themselves to engage in the behavior and actually perform it, monitor their proficiency against a clear standard that is accurate and that they believe they can meet, and reinforce themselves covertly and overtly for adherence, while refraining from distractions and interfering anxiety-inducing ideation (e.g., Bandura, 1986; Meichenbaum, 1977, 1992; Sarason, Sarason, Keefe, Hayes, & Shearin, 1986). The self-statements they make during this process will affect their efforts in predictable ways. For example, if individuals have anxious thoughts that undermine their efficacy (e.g., "I can't tolerate the anxiety that this causes"), they will soon cease even trying, whereas task-relevant thoughts (e.g., "Good, now I have to check this problem") provide the needed guidance to sustain the required behavior (Dweck & Leggett, 1988; Sarason et al., 1986).

The task of self-managing to perform and maintain a health-protective program is intrinsically difficult, because it demands that individuals overcome diverse barriers (Janz & Becker, 1984). On the one hand, these impediments to adherence may stem primarily from simple forgetting, due to interference from other activities and more proximal goals, and/or due to lack of cues to prime or reinforce adherence behaviors (S. M. Miller & Diefenbach, 1998). On the other hand, adherence may be compromised by "forgetting" that is more deeply motivated to avoid the anxieties and perceived threat activated with the procedure, as well as thoughts about vulnerability and performance efficacy (Miller, 1996). Thus adherence requires individuals to do more than simply remind themselves of the task; the key is to prime self-instructions and ideation that will enable them to adhere. If individuals' thoughts about adherence are too emotionally "hot" or threatening, the task will become extremely aversive and will be avoided. If the thoughts are too "cool" or nonthreatening, the goal loses its salience and incentive value.

Laboratory studies of the ability to purposefully delay gratification show that self-regulation is enhanced by a focus on the cool, abstract, cognitive representation of the necessary activity, with cues and reminders that are task-oriented ("This is what I need to do when"), while simultaneously avoiding excessively arousing and distressing ruminations. In the process, the person needs to balance occasional "back-of-the-mind" cool representations of why it is a good idea to maintain the behavior, while paying attention to the specific steps of the task itself (e.g., Mischel, 1974; Mischel et al., 1989). These conclusions from laboratory experiments are remarkably consistent with

health research on the types of spontaneous self-regulatory coping strategies that appear to be adaptive for dealing with cancer, such as those discussed as "cooling," "abstracting," and "reframing" (Miller & Green, 1985). In particular, distancing-type strategies, which enable the individual to engage and confront the stress effectively by cognitively transforming it and mentally representing it as less stressful, appear to be emotionally adaptive in dealing with cancer threats (Dunkel-Schetter, Feinstein, Taylor, & Falke, 1992).

Among women undergoing a biopsy for a suspicious lesion detected by mammography, those whose self-regulatory style was characterized as "engagement" (i.e., actively confronting the possibility of illness) were more likely to report positive affective responses as measured by a scale of general psychological well-being, compared to women whose coping responses were characterized as "avoidance" (i.e., actively avoiding information and discussion about the illness) (Chen et al., 1996). Furthermore, in a sample of women with precancerous cervical dysplasia, high levels of both avoidant ideation and active denial/disengagement with respect to their medical condition were correlated with greater levels of depression (S. M. Miller, Rodoletz, Schroeder, Mangan, & Sedlacek, 1996). In the context of breast cancer family risk assessment, confrontive coping strategies (e.g., pursuing early detection behaviors) were associated with lower levels of anxiety and fear, whereas evasive or fatalistic strategies were associated with higher levels of distress (Lancaster, 1992). In another study, an avoidant coping approach was associated with higher levels of anxiety and depression among women undergoing breast/ovarian cancer genetic testing (DudokdeWit et al., 1998).

Research with newly diagnosed cancer patients and with those currently receiving treatment has shown an association between lower levels of anxiety and depression and greater use of "stimulus-focused" self-regulatory coping strategies, characterized as follows: attention, care, and tackling (Baider & Kaplan De-Nour, 1988; Burgess, Morris, & Pettingale, 1988; Ell et al., 1989; Heim, 1991); confrontation (Burgess et al., 1988; Weisman, 1976); suppressing competing events (to focus on managing cancer demands) (Carver et al., 1993; Wagner, Armstrong, & Laughlin, 1995); active coping (Carver et al., 1993); and a fighting spirit (Ferrero, Barreto, & Toledo, 1994;

Friedman et al., 1992; Nelson, Friedman, Baer, Lane, & Smith, 1994; Schnoll, MacKinnon, Stolbach, & Lorman, 1995; Schnoll, Harlow, Stolbach, & Brandt, 1998). A prospective study, which followed women for 4 months immediately after a mastectomy, found that patients who were assessed 1 week after surgery as using a greater number of tackling self-regulatory behaviors (e.g., active engagement of issues concerning their diagnosis and breast surgery) and fewer avoidant self-regulatory behaviors (e.g., mental evasion of the meaning of their illness or a fatalistic acquiescence to it) were less anxious and emotionally distressed 4 months following their surgery (Penman, 1982).

"Response-focused" self-regulatory behaviors (e.g., positive reinterpretation and growth) have been shown to be commonly used by cancer patients and associated with positive emotional responses (e.g., lower anxiety), particularly during uncontrollable or extremely stressful cancer-related experiences, such as medical treatment or terminal illness (Rowland & Holland, 1989). A descriptive study found that over two-thirds of a sample of breast cancer patients used response-focused self-regulatory strategies (e.g., positive reappraisal) to manage illness demands (Jarrett, Ramirez, Richards, & Weinman, 1992). Furthermore, self-regulatory coping responses characterized as acceptance (Burgess et al., 1988), threat minimization (Filipp, Klauer, Freudenberg, & Ferring, 1990; Quinn, Fontana, & Reznikoff, 1986), positive reappraisal (Dunkel-Schetter et al., 1992), finding meaning (Lewis, Haberman, & Wallhagen, 1986; O'Connor, Wicker, & Germino, 1990), communicating feelings (Orr, 1986), and relying on religion or spirituality (Jenkins & Pargament, 1995) have been associated with lower levels of anxiety and depression.

Two studies have shown response-focused self-regulatory strategies to be predictive of psychological distress among breast cancer patients. One study (Stanton & Snider, 1993) followed women from before their breast biopsy to after their breast surgery. Higher levels of response-focused self-regulatory strategies (i.e., maintaining a positive focus, utilization of social support), measured prior to biopsy, were predictive of fewer symptoms of anxiety and depression following the biopsy. The second study (Carver et al., 1993), in which breast cancer patients were followed from the time they were diagnosed until 12 months following their surgery, reported that a higher level of presurgical acceptance of the illness was a significant prospective predictor of lower levels of postsurgical emotional distress (i.e., anxiety, depression).

"Avoidance-focused" self-regulatory coping strategies, characterized as denial, behavioral disengagement, and cognitive disengagement, have been associated with mood impairment, anxiety, and depression among samples of breast, lung, and heterogeneous cancer patients (Billings & Moos, 1981; Burgess et al., 1988; Dunkel-Schetter et al., 1992; Friedman et al., 1992; Orr, 1986; Quinn et al., 1986; Rodrigue, Behen, & Tumlin, 1994; Watson et al., 1988). For example, the relationship between higher levels of avoidance-focused coping, measured by overt denial or active attempts to mentally shunt the experience aside, and greater symptoms of anxiety and depression have been demonstrated prospectively in samples of breast cancer patients (Carver et al., 1993; Penman, 1982; Stanton & Snider, 1993).

The pattern of findings appears to be the reverse in the context of cancer survivorship. In one study, confrontive self-regulatory coping behaviors (e.g., utilization of instrumental social support, adopting a positive outlook) and use of spirituality were associated with lower levels of cancer-related psychological distress among survivors (Halstead & Fernsler, 1994). In another study, stimulus-focused coping (i.e., suppression of competing events) and response-focused coping (i.e., acceptance) were inversely related to worries about health problems and mortality (Somerfield, Curbow, Wingard, Baker, & Fogarty, 1996). Moreover, in contrast to findings in the context of disease risk, diagnosis, and treatment (see Spencer et al., 1998), avoidance-focused self-regulatory coping has been found to be associated with *fewer* symptoms of depression and anxiety (Bauld, Anderson, & Arnold, 1998; Cella & Tross, 1986; Ferrero et al., 1994). In a study by Heim, Valach, and Schaffner (1997), avoidance-focused and mental diversion coping responses were reported by those with *lower*, rather than higher, levels of anxiety. In addition, Bauld et al. (1998) reported that cancer survivors who reported greater use of avoidance-focused coping tended to be less anxious. These findings, albeit preliminary, suggest that once individuals progress to the phase of survivorship, avoidant-focused self-regulatory strategies may become adaptive (i.e., predictive of lower emotional distress). In this sense, survivors who are using avoidance strategies may be "putting the experience behind them," rather than ruminating and dwelling on the memories of the life threat. This type of distancing in turn may result in better psychological adjustment.

Dynamic Interactions among the Mediating Units

The cognitive–emotional processing of health risk information continues over time and includes feedback from performance. Thus the self-regulatory process also interacts with, and feeds back dynamically to, the network of cognitions and affects that generated the original health behavior decisions. This feedback loop can lead a person to maintain or revise the behavior over the course of time. For example, if intense anxiety becomes activated during cancer screening, it may in turn feed back to change construals of one's health risk and one's efficacy beliefs with regard to health-protective behaviors. In this way, performance outcomes can feed back to revise initial intentions and decisions (Miller et al., in press; Shoda et al., 1998). Finally, cognitive–emotional processing occurs at many levels of the system in parallel, and not necessarily within either the person's control or awareness. Once an individual has successfully incorporated a screening regimen into his or her everyday routine, for example, the behavior pattern may become a habit, requiring little more than a cue or reminder to perform it. Hence, behavioral patterns can become characterized by a certain automaticity of health-relevant information processing and responding, thereby circumventing the activation of anxiety and related distress (S. M. Miller, Shoda, et al., 1996).

PROTOTYPIC COGNITIVE–EMOTIONAL RESPONSE PROFILES

Cognitive–Emotional Processing Signatures: Monitoring versus Blunting

A basic premise of the cognitive–emotional approach is that individuals are characterized by distinctive processing styles in how they select, encode, and manage threatening health information, and how they react to it affectively. First, individuals differ stably in how they typi-

cally or chronically access and activate health relevant cognitions, self-regulatory strategies, and affects in response to threatening information and feedback. One individual may have chronically higher levels of perceived vulnerability to cancer, easily accessing thoughts that he or she may develop cancer, while another person may typically feel less vulnerable. One individual may tend to activate positive outcome expectations, while another is readily pessimistic about his or her prospects. When contemplating a cancer screening or treatment regimen, one person may be more likely to experience anxious feelings and the other positive feelings. Second, individuals differ in the patterning of the interactions among the relevant cognitions and affects, as well as the interactions of these with health-relevant information. In our own research, we have focused on two prototypic examples of processing types, characterized by radically different organizations in the structure of their self-construals, outcome and efficacy expectations, and affects with regard to cancer and relevant health-protective behaviors.

In particular, we have explored two signature response styles: those of "monitors," who scan for and magnify threatening cues, and "blunters," who distract from and downgrade threatening information (Miller, 1995). The two profiles are characterized by distinctive patterns of reactions to a variety of medical and nonmedical stressors, at the affective, cognitive, and self-regulatory levels (Miller, 1995, 1996; S. M. Miller, Rodoletz, et al., 1996). The Monitor–Blunter Style Scale (MBSS; Miller, 1987, 1995) was developed to identify these attentional styles, and has been used in several medical contexts, with a broad range of populations (Miller, 1995, 1996). The MBSS is a self-report measure that describes four hypothetical, threat-evoking scenarios (e.g., "Imagine you are afraid of flying and have to go somewhere by plane"). Individuals are asked to indicate which of eight ways of coping (four monitoring and four blunting) they would engage in. The psychometric properties of the MBSS—including its reliability; it convergent, discriminative, and construct validity; and its cross-cultural consistency—have been well documented (Gard, Edwards, Harris, & McCormack, 1988; Heszen-Niejodek, 1997; Ludwick-Rosenthal & Neufeld, 1993; Miller, 1996; Miró, 1997; Ross & Maguire, 1995; van Zuuren, 1996). We now briefly review evidence for differing cognitive–emotional response profiles between monitors and blunters.

Monitoring versus Blunting in Emotional/Affective Responding

In response to threatening health information, monitors have consistently been shown to exhibit higher levels of distress than blunters (Miller, 1995). This effect has been observed with respect to such stressors as dental procedures (Muris, Meesters, & Merckelbach, 1996), cardiac catheterization (Davis, Maguire, Haraphongse, & Schaumberger, 1994), colposcopy examination (Miller & Mangan, 1983; Miller, Roussi, Altman, Helm, & Steinberg, 1994; Miller, Buzaglo, Simms, Green, & Bales, 1999), ovarian cancer screening (Schwartz et al., 1995; Wardle, 1995), and cancer treatments (Lerman et al., 1990).

For example, in the context of disease risk, when monitors are given threatening cholesterol feedback, they exhibit higher levels of depression and anxiety than blunters who receive similar information (Croyle, Sun, & Louie, 1993). Among individuals undergoing HIV risk assessment, monitoring is positively associated with higher levels of depression (Warburton, Fishman, & Perry, 1997). Among women with a family history of ovarian cancer, high levels of monitoring are related to higher levels of intrusive thoughts, depression, and anxiety (Schwartz et al., 1995). Monitoring is also related to higher rates of anxiety and depression before and after risk counseling for breast/ovarian cancer (Audrain et al., 1997; Lerman, Daly, Masny, & Balshem, 1994; Lerman et al., 1996). In a sample of women at increased risk for cervical cancer, high levels of monitoring were related to higher levels of intrusive ideation (S. M. Miller, Rodoletz, et al., 1996).

Attentional style has also been shown to influence emotional responses to recommended diagnostic and treatment regimens. Compared to blunters, monitors have been found to report higher levels of anxiety and depression during medical procedures such as amniocentesis (Phipps & Zinn, 1986; van Zuuren, 1993), hemodialysis (Christensen, Moran, Lawton, Stallman, & Voigts, 1997), and cardiac catheterization (Davis et al., 1994). In the context of a follow-up diagnostic exam for cervical cancer (colposcopy), physicians who were unaware of patients' attentional styles rated monitors to be more agitated than blunters, as indexed by muscular tension and tightness in the vaginal area (Miller & Mangan, 1983). Likewise, monitors undergoing colposcopy were more likely than blunters to anticipate and worry about experiencing pain, discomfort, and embarrassment during the procedure, and manifest symptoms of emotional distress during the exam (Miller et al., 1994); monitors were also likely to experience more pain and discomfort in the days following the procedure (Miller & Mangan, 1983).

Similarly, in the context of cancer treatment, patients undergoing chemotherapy who were characterized as monitors were more likely than blunters to report greater anxiety prior to treatment, higher levels of depression during the administration of chemotherapy, and greater and more prolonged symptoms of nausea (Gard et al., 1988; Lerman et al., 1990). Studies with pediatric cancer patients undergoing medical treatment showed that monitors reported lower levels of depressive symptoms than blunters (Phipps & Srivastava, 1997; Phipps, Fairclough, & Mulhern, 1995). Cancer survivors characterized as monitors may also be at greater risk for long-term affective difficulties. Studies of long-term emotional responding among individuals treated for phobias indicate that despite treatment efficacy (i.e., extinction of the phobia), monitors are at greater risk for continued negative emotional responding than blunters (Muris, de Jongh, van Zuuren, & Schoenmakers, 1996; Muris, Merckelbach, & de Jongh, 1995). Future research is needed to systematically assess the relationship between the monitoring–blunting dimension and affective responding among cancer survivors.

Determinants of Individual Differences in Emotional/Affective Responding

In summary, monitors experience greater distress than blunters. At the subjective level, this distress is characterized by high levels of anxiety about, rumination about, and the rehearsal of "bad news," as well as intrusive, repetitive reliving of the threatening experience (Muris, de Jongh, van Zuuren, & ter Horst, 1994; van Zuuren & Muris, 1993). At the physiological level, adverse affective responding by monitors is manifested in the form of increased muscle tension, stiffness, cardiovascular responsiveness, skin conductance, and pain reactivity (Bruehl, Carlson, Wilson, & Norton, 1996; Delitto, Strube, Shulman, & Minor, 1992; Schuck, 1998; Sparks & Spirek, 1988). It is possible that the heightened distress and arousal among monitors are linked to greater levels of trait anxiety, depression, and negative affectivity. However, monitors do not generally differ from blunters in terms of dispositional, trait-like variables (Miller, 1996).

Furthermore, the emotional correlates and consequences of monitoring and blunting become evident under high-threat conditions, but not when the threat is low or absent (Miller, 1996). For example, among at-risk pregnant women, monitors manifest greater anxiety and depression than blunters in response to amniocentesis (Phipps & Zinn, 1989). However, no differences in emotional responding emerge during pregnancy between monitors and blunters who are not at risk (see also van Zuuren, 1993). Similarly, in the laboratory, monitors display greater increases in psychophysiological arousal to high-stress segments of a frightening film, but not to low-stress and moderate-stress segments (Sparks & Spirek, 1988).

Monitors also manifest sustained higher arousal and less habituation over time in response to physical stressors (e.g., pain stimuli) than blunters do (Efran, Chorney, Arden, & Lukens, 1989; Miller, 1987). A similar pattern emerges for the response to diagnostic and treatment regimens. For example, among high-risk women participating in a surveillance program to detect early familial ovarian cancer, monitors and blunters showed equivalent levels of anxiety and cancer-specific worries and concern prior to screening (Wardle et al., 1993, 1994; Wardle, 1995). However, monitors were more emotionally adversely affected by positive (i.e., abnormal) test results. In particular, monitors who received abnormal screening feedback reported elevated levels of anxiety and concern, compared with blunters who received abnormal test results. These effects persisted at a 1-year follow-up, despite the fact that none of the women were ultimately diagnosed with cancer.

This pattern of results suggest that there are particular "psychologically diagnostic" conditions for observing the prototypic effects of individual differences in monitoring–blunting styles. Specifically, the emotional consequences of monitoring appear to be activated in response to threats that are more psychological-ly salient (i.e., more intense, severe, and prolonged). Under extreme stressors, levels of distress appear to be higher, more persistent, and less easily tolerated among monitors because of their cognitive and behavioral signatures for interpreting and managing threatening feedback and cues, as discussed next (S. M. Miller, Rodoletz, et al., 1996).

Cognitive Correlates of Monitoring

Since monitors actively seek out, amplify, and focus on threatening aspects of risk information (Miller, 1996; Miller, Combs, & Kruus, 1993; Miller, Combs, & Stoddard, 1989), they are more likely to develop threat-laden encodings when dealing with stressful situations. In the medical setting, this tendency is manifested in terms of a heightened sense of their own vulnerability and risk (Muris et al., 1995). In the cancer context, for example, monitors with a family history of ovarian cancer perceive themselves to be more likely to develop the disease than blunters do, regardless of their true level of risk. Furthermore, increased perceptions of risk among monitors are associated with greater intrusive ideation and mood disturbance (Schwartz et al., 1995). Hence the tendency of monitors to exaggerate their vulnerability is linked to greater, and often unnecessary, emotional distress.

Monitors and blunters are also characterized by divergent beliefs and expectancies about the nature and outcomes of health threats. Compared to blunters, monitors report greater negative expectations about the severity, causes, and consequences of medical threats (Gattuso, Litt, & Fitzgerald, 1992; Lerman et al., 1994; Miller, Leinbach, & Brody, 1989; Miller et al., 1994; Miller, Brody, & Summerton, 1988; Muris et al., 1994). A study of individuals seeking care for acute medical conditions (e.g., influenza, gastrointestinal problems) showed that monitors were judged to have less severe medical problems than blunters (Miller et al., 1988). Nonetheless, they reported equivalent levels of perceived severity and higher levels of physical discomfort, dysfunction, and distress, in comparison with their blunting counterparts. Among patients undergoing a gastrointestinal endoscopy (Gattuso et al., 1992), monitors were characterized by poorer self-efficacy about their ability to cope with the procedure (e.g., swallowing the tube and sitting still). In response to dental procedures or dental surgery, monitors exhibited lower levels of perceived self-efficacy and control and less positive expectations than blunters (Muris, de Jongh, et al., 1996). In particular, monitors felt that they were less able to control their pessimistic thoughts and negative thinking about the impending medical procedure (Muris et al., 1994; Muris, de Jongh, et al., 1996).

In the oncological context, women contemplating undergoing genetic risk feedback for breast/ovarian cancer who were classified as monitors believed that they would experience greater adverse emotional outcomes (such as depression, anxiety, and guilt), compared to women classified as blunters (Lerman et al., 1994). Furthermore, although monitors undergoing diagnostic follow-up for abnormal Pap smears were more likely to exhibit a sense of responsibility for the course of the disease than blunters, they were less convinced that effective solutions to their condition were available, and they exhibited greater psychological distress and worries about it (Miller et al., 1994). The low sense of self-efficacy and perceived control among monitors thus appears to activate and sustain distress, which can interfere with adaptive health care behaviors (S. M. Miller, Rodoletz, et al., 1996).

Self-Regulatory/Coping Correlates of Monitoring

The ability to successfully execute self-regulatory behaviors when faced with threats has been shown to vary as a function of attentional style (Miller, 1996). Since monitors are more alert for and attentive to threatening cues, they are more inclined to use confrontive, approach-type coping strategies. The emotional consequences and behavioral adaptiveness of this orientation depend on situational features, including the nature of the stressor and the type of informational feedback. Under low health threats or routine medical conditions, monitors are able to scan for health messages (e.g., the need to be screened) without becoming overly anxious and depressed. Hence, under these conditions, monitors are more inclined to adopt problem-focused coping strategies that facilitate adherence to medical recommendations (e.g., scheduling and undertaking routine screening; Basen-Engquist, 1997; Muris et al., 1994; Steptoe & O'Sullivan, 1986), particularly when reassuring messages are provided that include plans and cues for action (Miller et al., 1999).

As the level of threat rises, monitors tend to react with heightened levels of depression and anxiety, and—most notably—to experience cognitive interference due to high levels of intrusive and invasive threat ideation and low perceived self-efficacy (Christensen et al., 1997; Miller et al., 1994; S. M. Miller, Rodoletz, et al., 1996). Distress can be minimized for monitors under these conditions if they receive voluminous information that reduces the uncertainty and unpredictability of the situation and increases their sense of perceived control (Miller, 1995, 1996). So, for example, monitors facing aversive diagnostic procedures fare better both emotionally and behaviorally when detailed procedural and sensory information is available (Gattuso et al., 1992; Miller & Mangan, 1983; Watkins, Weaver, & Odegaard, 1986). However, when confronted with more chronic, ambiguous, and severe health stressors (e.g., high genetic risk for cancer), the distress response of monitors can escalate to more paralyzing levels (Lerman et al., 1996; S. M. Miller, Rodoletz, et al., 1996; Schwartz et al., 1995).

Furthermore, the information conveyed to patients in the latter tends to be more ambiguous and complex (e.g., "You have a __% lifetime chance of developing cancer"), and therefore less reassuring and anxiety-reducing (Miller et al., 1999). In an effort to escape from and short-circuit unbearable intrusive thinking, monitors may begin to engage in more defensive avoidant and denial-like strategies in an (unsuccessful) effort to remove themselves psychologically from intense anxiety (S. M. Miller, Rodoletz, et al., 1996). This cycle of extreme distress and avoidance ultimately undermines adherence and prevents cognitive processing of threat (Miller, 1996).

Monitoring Subtypes: Permeable versus Impermeable Self-Constructs

Individuals differ not only in the categories they use to encode, interpret, and manage information, but also in the ease with which they tend to preempt versus assimilate data that threaten to disconfirm those constructs. This "impermeable" versus "permeable" or "elastic" dimension of personal constructs (e.g., Kelly, 1955) refers to how readily an individual can incorporate new and potentially threatening (disconfirming) data into a given personal construct while still retaining it. Important stable or "chronic" constructs (Higgins, 1987) tend to be difficult to modify when the person faces data that disconfirm them sharply. Indeed, this was George Kelly's (1955) definition of "threat." The perceived discrepancy between a basic construct and the disconfirming data can generate painful cognitive conflicts and mental–emotional tension (e.g., Festinger, 1957), and such a discrepancy has been shown to underlie the development of posttraumatic symptomatology in response to extreme stress (Foa, Steketee, & Rothbaum, 1989)

Being genetically at risk for breast cancer, for example, may be interpreted by some monitors (e.g., pessimistic monitors) as confirming their worst fears that the world is a terrible and dangerous place and that they themselves are extremely vulnerable to such trauma (Audrain et al., 1997). Moreover, stress effects can occur for monitors not only when there is a "match" between core self-construals and experience ("I am vulnerable, and this diagnosis proves that the world is a terrible place"), but also when there is a "mismatch" or disconfirmation of basic self-construals ("I thought I was invulnerable, and now my world is shattered"). When monitors who have previously felt in control of their health experience a traumatic stressor, such as testing positive for a breast cancer gene mutation, it can shatter their sense of relative invulnerability to the vagaries of the body (Miller et al., in press; Shoda et al., 1998). This in turn can lead to a process of "overaccommodation," whereby existing schemas (e.g., "My body is healthy because I am getting screened" are radically altered (e.g., "My body will soon be riddled with disease") to incorporate new assumptions (e.g., "I have been told that I have a strong family history of disease")

The permeability of a construct enables it to be retained but adapted progressively to deal with data that potentially generate cognitive dissonance and might otherwise have to be avoided, denied, or distorted. The ease with which potentially disconfirming information can be assimilated into a core construct about the self depends on the degree of threat it creates. These considerations lead to the prediction, borne out in the literature (Miller, 1995), that whereas moderately challenging information to core self-constructs may be dealt with by monitors without excessive defenses, extreme perceived threat may precipitate denial and avoidance or distortion of the information that simply cannot be incorporated (Miller, 1996).

CONCLUSIONS

In this chapter, we have proposed a comprehensive framework for conceptualizing and understanding the response to health stressors. From this perspective, a person's cognitive processing and self-regulatory management of health threats reciprocally influence (and are influenced by) his or her emotional reactions. Furthermore, there are signature individual differences in the cognitive and behavioral determinants of emotional distress, particularly in the tendency to monitor or blunt threatening information. The monitoring–blunting dimension is not a "static," trait-like variable, but a highly interactive coping disposition. Its emotional consequences vary considerably as a function of situational demands, ongoing feedback over time, and monitoring–blunting subtypes. The challenge for future research is to delineate more clearly the coherences in the cognitive–emotional expression of these styles, as well as their momentary variability and situational specificity in response to health stressors.

ACKNOWLEDGMENTS

Preparation of this chapter was supported in part by American Cancer Society Grant No. PBP-89318; Department of Defense Grant Nos. BC971638 and OC970004; National Institutes of Health Grant Nos. CA58999, CA61280, CA06927, and HG01766; and appropriations from the Commonwealth of Pennsylvania. We are indebted to Lisa Brower, James Knowles, Leeann Speechley, and Calvin James for their technical assistance.

REFERENCES

Andrykowski, M. A., & Brady, M. J. (1994). Health locus of control and psychological distress in cancer patients: Interactive effects of context. *Journal of Behavioral Medicine, 17,* 439–458.

Argyle, M., & Little, B. R. (1972). Do personality traits apply to social behaviour? *Journal for the Theory of Social Behaviour, 2,* 1–35.

Audrain, J., Schwartz, M. D., Lerman, C., Hughes, C., Peshkin, B. N., & Biescecker, B. (1997). Psychological distress in women seeking counseling for breast–ovarian cancer risk: The combinations of personality and appraisal. *Annals of Behavioral Medicine, 19,* 370–377.

Ayers, A., Hoon, P. W., Franzoni, J. B., Matheny, K. B., Cotanch, P. H., & Takanyanagi, S. (1994). Influence of mood and adjustment to cancer on compliance with chemotherapy among breast cancer patients. *Journal of Psychosomatic Research, 38,* 393–402.

Baider, L. A., & Kaplan De-Nour, A. (1988). Breast cancer—a family affair. In C. L. Cooper (Ed.), *Stress and breast cancer* (pp. 58–73). Chichester, England: Wiley.

Baker, F., Marcellus, D., Zabora, J., Polland, A., & Jodrey, D. (1997). Psychological distress among adult patients being evaluated for bone marrow transplantation. *Psychosomatics, 38,* 10–19.

Baldwin, M. K., & Courneya, K.S. (1997). Exercise and self-esteem in breast cancer survivors: An application of the exercise and self-esteem model. *Journal of Sport and Exercise Psychology, 19,* 347–358.

Bandura, A. (1986). *Social foundations of thought and action: A social cognitive theory.* Englewood Cliffs, NJ: Prentice-Hall.

Basen-Engquist, K. (1997). Ovarian cancer screening and psychosocial issues: Relevance to clinical practice. *Gynecological Oncology, 65,* 195–196.

Bauld, C., Anderson, V., & Arnold, J. (1998). Psychosocial aspects of adolescent cancer survival. *Journal of Pediatric Child Health, 34,* 120–126.

Baum, A., & Singer, J. (Eds.). (1987). *Handbook of psychology and health* (Vol. 5). Hillsdale, NJ: Erlbaum.

Beckham, J., Burker, E., Lytle, B., Feldman, M., & Costakis, M. J. (1997). Self-efficacy and adjustment in cancer patients: A preliminary report. *Behavioral Medicine, 23,* 138–142.

Belec, R. H. (1992). Quality of life: Perceptions of long-term survivors of bone marrow transplantation. *Oncology Nursing Forum, 19,* 31–37.

Billings, A. G., & Moos, R. H. (1981). The role of coping responses and social resources in attenuating the stress of life events. *Journal of Behavioral Medicine, 4,* 139–157.

Blood, G. W., Dineen, M., Kauffman, S. M., Raimondi, S. C., & Simpson, K. C. (1993). Perceived control, adjustment, and communication problems in laryngeal cancer survivors. *Perceptual and Motor Skills, 77,* 764–766.

Bovbjerg, D. & Valdimarsdottir, H. (1998). Psychoneuroimmunology: Implications for psycho-oncology. In J. C. Holland (Ed.), *Psycho-oncology* (pp. 125–134). New York: Oxford University Press.

Breitbart, W., & Payne, D. K. (1998). Pain. In J. C. Holland (Ed.), *Psycho-oncology* (pp. 450–467). New York: Oxford University Press.

Bruehl, S., Carlson, C. R., Wilson, J. F., & Norton, J. A. (1996). Psychological coping with acute pain: An examination of the endogenous opioid mechanisms. *Journal of Behavioral Medicine, 19,* 129–142.

Burgess, C., Morris, T., & Pettingale, K. W. (1988). Psychological responses to cancer diagnosis: II. Evidence for coping styles (coping styles and cancer diagnosis). *Journal of Psychosomatic Research, 32,* 263–272.

Bush, N. E., Haberman, M., Donaldson, G., & Sullivan, K. M. (1995). Quality of life of 125 adults surviving 6–18 years after bone marrow transplantation. *Social Science and Medicine, 40,* 479–490.

Cameron, L. D., Leventhal, E. A., & Leventhal, H. (1993). Symptom representations and affect as determinants of care seeking in a community-dwelling, adult sample population. *Health Psychology, 12,* 171–179.

Cameron, L. D., Leventhal, H., & Love, R. R. (1998). Trait anxiety, symptom perceptions, and illness-related responses among women with breast cancer in remission during a tamoxifen clinical trial. *Health Psychology, 17,* 459–469.

Cantor, N. (1990). From thought to behavior: "Having" and "doing" in the study of personality and cognition. *American Psychologist, 45,* 735–750.

Carver, C. S., Pozo, C., Harris, S.D., Noriega, V., Scheier, M.F., Robinson, D. S., Ketcham, A. S., Moffat, F. L., & Clark, K. C. (1993). How coping mediates the effect of optimism on distress: A study of women with early stage breast cancer. *Journal of Personality and Social Psychology, 65,* 375–390.

Carver, C. S., & Scheier, M. (1981). *Attention and self-regulation: A control theory approach to human behavior.* New York: Springer-Verlag.

Cella, D. F., & Tross, S. (1986). Psychological adjustment to survival from Hodgkin's disease. *Journal of Consulting and Clinical Psychology, 54,* 616–622.

Chen, C. C., David, A., Thompson, K., Smith, C., Lea, S., & Fahy, T. (1996). Coping strategies and psychiatric morbidity in women attending breast assessment clinics. *Journal of Psychosomatic Medicine, 40,* 265–270.

Christensen, A. J., Moran, P. J., Lawton, W. J., Stallman, D., & Voigts, A. (1997). Monitoring attentional style and medical regimen adherence in hemodialysis patients. *Health Psychology, 16,* 256–262.

Cioffi, D. (1991). Beyond attentional strategies: A cognitive–perceptual model of somatic interpretation. *Psychological Bulletin, 109,* 25–41.

Cohen, S., & Herbert, T. B. (1996). Health psychology: Psychological factors and physical disease from the perspective of human psychoneuroimmunology. *Annual Review of Psychology, 47,* 113–142.

Compas, B. E., Worsham, N. L., Epping-Jordan, J. E., Grant, K. E., Mireault, G., Howell, D. C., & Malcarne, V. L. (1994). When Mom or Dad has cancer: Markers of psychological distress in cancer patients, spouses, and children. *Health Psychology, 13,* 507–515.

Croyle, R. T., Sun, Y., & Louie, D. H. (1993). Psychological minimization of cholesterol test results: Moderators of appraisal in college students and community residents. *Health Psychology, 12,* 503–507.

Cunningham, A. J., Lackwood, G. A., & Cunningham, J. A. (1991). A relationship between perceived self-efficacy and quality of life in cancer patients. *Patient Education and Counseling, 17,* 71–78.

Cunningham, L. L., Andrykowski, M. A., Wilson, J. F., McGrath, P. C., Sloan, D. A., & Kenady, D. E. (1998). Physical symptoms, distress, and breast cancer risk perceptions in women with benign breast problems. *Health Psychology, 17,* 371–375.

Davis, T. M. A., Maguire, T. O., Haraphongse, M., & Schaumberger, M. R. (1994). Preparing adult patients for cardiac catherization: Informational treatment and coping style interactions. *Heart and Lung, 23,* 130–139.

Delitto, A., Strube, M. J., Shulman, A. D., & Minor, S.

D. (1992). A study of discomfort with electrical stimulation. *Physical Therapy, 72,* 11–25.

Dienstbier, R. A. (1989). Arousal and physiological toughness: Implications for mental and physical health. *Psychological Reviews, 96,* 84–100.

Dirksen, S. R. (1989). Perceived well-being in malignant melanoma survivors. *Oncology Nursing Forum, 16,* 353–358.

Dodge, K. (1986). A social information processing model of social competence in children: Cognitive perspectives on children's social behavioral development. In *Minnesota Symposium on Child Psychology* (Vol. 18, pp. 77–125). Hillsdale, NJ: Erlbaum.

DudokdeWit, A. C., Tibben, A., Duivenvoorden, H. J., Niermeijer, M. F., Passchier, J., & Trijsburg, R. W. (1998). Distress in individuals facing predictive DNA testing for autosomal dominant late-onset disorders: Comparing questionnaire results with in depth interviews. American Journal of Medical Genetics, 75, 62–74.

Dunkel-Schetter, C., Feinstein, L. G., Taylor, S. E., & Falke, R. L. (1992). Patterns of coping with cancer. *Health Psychology, 11,* 79–87.

Dweck, C. (1990). Self-theories and goals: Their role in motivation, personality, and development. In R. A. Dienstbier (Ed.), *Nebraska Symposium on Motivation* (Vol. 38, pp. 199–235). Lincoln: University of Nebraska Press.

Dweck, C., & Leggett, E. (1988). A social-cognitive approach to personality and Motivation. *Psychological Review, 95,* 256–273.

Efran, J., Chorney, R. L., Arden, L. M., & Lukens, M. D. (1989). Coping styles, paradox, and the clod pressing task. *Journal of Behavioral Medicine, 12,* 91–103.

Ell, K.O., Mantell, J. E., Hamovitch, M. B., & Nishimoto, R. H. (1989). Social support, sense of control, and coping among patients with breast, lung, or colorectal cancer. *Journal of Psychosocial Oncology, 7,* 63–89.

Fallowfield, L. J., Hall, A., Maguire, G. P., & Baum, M. (1990). Psychological outcomes of different treatment policies in women with early breast cancer outside of a clinical trial. *British Medical Journal, 301,* 575–580.

Ferrero, J., Barreto, M. P., & Toledo, M. (1994). Mental adjustment to cancer and quality of life in breast cancer: An exploratory study. *Psycho-Oncology, 3,* 223–232.

Festinger, L. (1957). A theory of cognitive dissonance. Stanford, CA: Stanford University Press.

Filipp, S.-H., Klauer, T., Freudenberg, E., & Ferring, D. (1990). The regulation of subjective well-being in cancer patients: An analysis of coping effectiveness. *Psychology and Health, 4,* 305–317.

Foa, E., & Kozak, M. (1986). Emotional processing of fear: Exposure to corrective information. *Psychological Bulletin, 99,* 20–35.

Foa, E., Steketee, G., & Rothbaum, B. (1989). Behavioral/cognitive conceptualizations of post-traumatic stress disorder. *Behavior Therapy, 20,* 155–176.

Folkman, S. (1984). Person control and stress and coping processes: a theoretical analysis. *Journal of Personality and Social Psychology, 46,* 839–852.

Friedman, L. C., Nelson, D. V., Baer, P. E., Lane, M.,

Smith, F. E., & Dworkin, R. J. (1992). The relationship of dispositional optimism, daily life stress, and domestic environment to coping methods used by cancer patients. *Journal of Behavioral Medicine, 15,* 127–141.

Gard, D., Edwards, P. W., Harris, J., & McCormack, G. (1988). The sensitizing effects of pretreatment measures on cancer chemotherapy nausea and vomiting. *Journal of Consulting and Clinical Psychology, 56,* 80–84.

Gattuso, S. M., Litt, M. D., & Fitzgerald, T. E. (1992). Coping with gastrointestinal endoscopy: Self-efficacy enhancement and coping style. *Journal of Consulting and Clinical Psychology, 60,* 133–139.

Gluhoski, V. L., Siegel, K., & Gorey, E. (1997). Unique stressors experienced by unmarried women with breast cancer. *Journal of Psychosocial Oncology, 15,* 173–183.

Grassi, L., & Rosti, G. (1996). Psychosocial morbidity and adjustment to illness among long term cancer survivors: A six year follow up study. *Psychosomatics, 37,* 523–532.

Greenberg, D. B., Kornblith, A. B., Herndon, J. E., Zuckerman, E., Schiffer, C. A., Weiss, R. B., Mayer, R. J., Wolchok, S. M., & Holland, J. C. (1997). Quality of life for adult leukemia survivors treated on clinical trials of cancer and leukemia group B during the period 1971–1988: Predictors of later psychologic distress. *Cancer, 80,* 1936–1944.

Greer, S. (1994). Psycho-oncology: Its aims, achievements and future tasks. *Psycho-Oncology, 3,* 87–101.

Halstead, M. T., & Fernsler, J. I. (1994). Coping strategies of long term cancer survivors. *Cancer Nursing, 17,* 94–100.

Heim, E. (1991). Coping and adaptation in cancer. In C. L. Cooper & M. Watson (Eds.), *Cancer and stress: Psychological, biological, and coping studies* (pp.163–186). Chichester, England: Wiley.

Heim, E., Valach, L., & Schaffner, L. (1997). Coping and psychosocial adaptation: Longitudinal effects over time and stages in breast cancer. *Psychosomatic Medicine, 59,* 408–418.

Heszen-Niejodek, I. (1997). Coping style and its role in coping with stressful encounters. *European Psychologist, 2,* 342–351.

Higgins, E. T. (1987). Self-discrepancy: A theory relating self and affect. *Psychological Review, 94,* 319–340.

Higgins, E. T., King, G. A., & Mavin, G. H. (1982). Individual construct accessibility and subjective impressions and recall. *Journal of Personality and Social Psychology, 43,* 35–47.

Higgins, P. M. (1990). Temporary Munchausen syndrome. *British Journal of Psychiatry, 157,* 613–616.

Holland, J. C. (Ed.). (1998). *Psycho-oncology.* New York: Oxford University Press.

James, W. (1890). *Principles of psychology.* New York: Holt.

Janz, N., & Becker, M. (1984). The health belief model: A decade later. *Health Education Quarterly, 11,* 1–47.

Jarrett, S. R., Ramirez, A. J., Richards, M. A., & Weinman, J. (1992). Measuring coping in breast cancer. *Journal of Psychosomatic Research, 36,* 593–602.

Jenkins, R. A., & Pargament, K. I. (1995). Religion and spirituality as resources for coping with cancer. *Journal of Psychosocial Oncology, 13,* 51–74.

Kash, K. M., & Lerman, C. (1998). Psychological, social, and ethical issues in gene testing. In J. C. Holland (Ed.), *Psycho-oncology* (pp. 196–207.) New York: Oxford University Press.

Kelly, G. (1955). *The psychology of personal constructs.* New York: Basic Books.

Kiecolt-Glaser, J. K., Page, G. G., Marucha, P. T., MacCallum, R. C., & Glaser, R. (1998). Psychological influences on surgical recovery: Perspectives from psychoneuroimmunology. *American Psychologist, 53,* 1209–1218.

Kornblith, A. B. (1998). Psychosocial adaptation of cancer survivors. In J. C. Holland (Ed.), *Psycho-oncology* (pp. 223–241). New York: Oxford University Press.

Lancaster, D. (1992). Coping with appraised threat of breast cancer: Primary prevention coping behaviors utilized by women at increased risk. *Dissertation Abstracts International, 53,* 202B.

Lau, R., Hartman, K., & Ware, J. (1986). Health as a value: Methodological and theoretical considerations. *Health Psychology, 5,* 25–43.

Lauver, D., & Tak, Y. (1995). Optimism and coping with a breast symptom. *Nursing Residence, 44,* 202–207.

Lazarus, R. (1991). *Emotion and adaptation.* New York: Oxford University Press.

Lerman, C., Daly, M., Masny, A., & Balshem, A. (1994). Attitudes about genetic testing for breast-ovarian cancer susceptibility. *Journal of Clinical Oncology, 12,* 843–850.

Lerman, C., Daly, M., Sands, C., Balshem, A., Lustbader, E., Heggan, T., Goldstein, L., James, J., & Engstrom, P. (1993). Mammography adherence and psychological distress among women at risk for breast cancer. *Journal of the National Cancer Institute, 85,* 1074–1080.

Lerman, C., Narod, S., Schulman, K., Hughes, C., Gomez-Caminero, A., Bonney, G., Gold, K., Trock, B., Main, D., Lynch, J., Fulmore, C., Snyder, C., Lemon, S. J., Conway, T., Tonin, P., Lenoir, G., & Lynch, H. (1996). BRCA1 testing in families with hereditary breast–ovarian cancer: A prospective study of patient decision making and outcomes. Journal of the American Medical Association, 275, 1885–1892.

Lerman, C., Rimer, B., Blumberg, B., Cristinzio, S., Engstrom, P. F., MacElwee, N., O'Connor, K., & Seay, J. (1990). Effects of coping style and relaxation on cancer chemotherapy side effects and emotional responses. *Cancer Nursing, 13,* 308–315.

Lerman, C., & Schwartz, M. (1993). Adherence and psychological adjustment among women at high risk for breast cancer. *Breast Cancer Research and Treatment, 28,* 145–155.

Lerman, C., Trock, B., Rimer, B., Jepson, C., Brody, D., & Boyce, A. (1991). Psychological side effects of breast cancer screening. *Health Psychology, 10,* 259–267.

Lev, E. L., & Owen, S. V. (1996). A measure of self-care self-efficacy. *Research in Nursing and Health, 19,* 421–429.

Leventhal, H., Diefenbach, M., & Leventhal, E. (1992). Illness cognition: Using common sense to understand treatment adherence and affect cognition interaction. *Cognitive Therapy and Research, 16,* 143–163.

Lewis, F. M., Haberman, M. R., & Wallhagen, M. I. (1986). How adults with late-stage cancer experience personal control. *Journal of Psychosocial Oncology, 4,* 27–42.

Lobell, M., Bay, C., Rhoads, K., & Keske, B. (1994). Barriers to cancer screening in Hispanic women. *Proceedings of the American Society of Clinical Oncology, 13,* A466.

Loscalzo, M., & Brintzenhofeszoc, K. (1998). Brief crisis counseling. In J. C. Holland (Ed.), *Psycho-oncology* (pp. 662–675). New York: Oxford University Press.

Lowery, B. J., Jacobsen, B. S., & DuCette, J. (1993). Causal attributions, control, and adjustment to breast cancer. Journal of Psychosocial Oncology, 10, 37–53.

Ludwick-Rosenthal, R., & Neufeld, R. W. (1993). Preparation for undergoing an invasive medical procedure: Interacting effects of information and coping style. *Journal of Consulting and Clinical Psychology, 61,* 156–164.

Marks, G., Richardson, J. L., Graham, J. W., & Levine, A. (1986). Role of health locus of control beliefs and expectations of treatment efficacy in adjustment to cancer. *Journal of Personality and Social Psychology, 51,* 443–450.

Markus, H. (1977). Self-schemata and processing information about the self. *Journal of Personality and Social Psychology, 35,* 63–78.

Meichenbaum, D. (1977). *Cognitive-behavior modification: An integrative approach.* New York: Plenum Press.

Meichenbaum, D. (1993). Stress inoculation training: A 20-year update. In P. M. Lehrer & R. L. Woolfolk (Eds.), *Principles and practice of stress management* (2nd ed., pp. 373–406). New York: Guilford Press.

Meyer, L., & Aspegren, K. (1989). Long-term psychological sequelae of mastectomy and breast conserving treatment for breast cancer. *Acta Oncologica, 28,* 13–18.

Miller, D., & Green, J. (1985). Psychological support and counseling for patients with acquired immune deficiency syndrome (AIDS). *Genitourinary Medicine, 61,* 273–278.

Miller, D. L., Manne, S. L., Taylor, K., & Keates, J. (1996). Psychological distress and well being in advanced cancer: The effects of optimism and coping. *Journal of Clinical Psychology in Medical Settings, 3,* 115–130.

Miller, S. M. (1987). Monitoring and blunting: Validation of a questionnaire to assess styles of information seeking under threat. *Journal of Personality and Social Psychology, 52,* 345–353.

Miller, S. M. (1995). Monitoring versus blunting styles of coping influence the information patients want and need about cancer: Implications for cancer screening and management. *Cancer, 76,* 167–177.

Miller, S. M. (1996). Monitoring and blunting of threatening information: Cognitive interference and facilitation in the coping process. In I. G. Sarason, G. R.

Pierce, & B. R. Sarason (Eds.), *Cognitive interference: Theories, methods, and findings*(pp. 175–190). Hillsdale, NJ: Erlbaum.

Miller, S. M., Brody, D. S., & Summerton, J. (1988). Styles of coping with threat: Implications for health. *Journal of Personality and Social Psychology, 54,* 142–148.

Miller, S. M., Buzaglo, J. S., Simms, S. L., Green, V., & Bales, C. (1999). Monitoring styles in women at risk for cervical cancer: Implications for the framing of health-relevant messages. *Annals of Behavioral Medicine, 211,* 91–99.

Miller, S. M., Combs, C., & Kruus, L. (1993). Turing in and turning out: Confronting the effects of confrontation. In H. W. Krohne (Ed.), Attention and avoidance: Strategies in coping with aversiveness(pp. 51–69). Seattle: Hogrefe & Huber.

Miller, S. M., Combs, C., & Stoddard, E. (1989). Information, coping and control in patients undergoing surgery and stressful medical procedures. In A. Steptoe & A. Appels (Eds.), *Stress, personal control and health* (pp. 107–130). New York: Wiley.

Miller, S. M., & Diefenbach, M. A. (1998). The cognitive–social health information-processing (C-SHIP) model: A theoretical framework for research in behavioral oncology. In D. S. Krantz & A. Baum (Eds.), *Technology and methods in behavioral medicine* (pp. 219–244). Hillsdale, NJ: Erlbaum.

Miller, S. M., Fang, C.Y., Diefenbach, M. A., & Bales, C. B. (in press). Tailoring psychosocial interventions to the individual's health information processing style: The influence of monitoring versus blunting in cancer risk and disease. In A. Baum & B. Anderson (Eds.), *Psychosocial interventions and cancer*. Washington, DC: American Psychological Association.

Miller, S. M., Fang, C. Y., Manne, S. C., Engstrom, P. F., & Daly, M. B. (1999). Decision making about prophylactic oophorectomy among at-risk women: Psychological influences and implications. *Gynecologic Oncology, 75,* 406–412.

Miller, S. M., Leinbach, A., & Brody, D. S. (1989). Coping style in hypertensive patients: Nature and consequences. *Journal of Consulting and Clinical Psychology, 57,* 333–337.

Miller, S. M., & Mangan, C. E. (1983). Interacting effects of information and coping style in adapting to gynecologic stress: Should the doctor tell all? *Journal of Personality and Social Psychology, 45,* 223–236.

Miller, S. M., Mischel, W., O'Leary, A., & Mills, M. (1996). From human papilloma virus (HPV) to cervical cancer: Psychosocial processes in infection, detection, and control. *Annals of Behavioral Medicine, 18,* 219–228.

Miller, S. M., & O'Leary, A. (1993). Cognition, stress, and health. In P. C. Kendall & K. Dobson (Eds.), *Psychopathology and cognition* (pp. 159–189). New York: Academic Press.

Miller, S. M., Rodoletz, M., Schroeder, C., Mangan, C. E., & Sedlacek, T. V. (1996). Applications of the monitoring process model to coping with severe long-term medical threats. *Health Psychology, 15,* 216–225.

Miller, S. M., Roussi, P., Altman, D., Helm, W., & Steinberg, A. (1994). Effects of coping style on psycholog-ical reactions of low-income, minority women to colposcopy. *Journal of Reproductive Medicine, 39,* 711–718.

Miller, S. M., Shoda, Y., & Hurley, K. (1996). Applying cognitive–social theory to health-protective behavior: Breast self-examination in cancer screening. *Psychological Bulletin, 119,* 70–94.

Miró, J. (1997). Translation, validation, and adaptation of an instrument to assess the information-seeking style of coping with stress: The Spanish version of the Miller Behavioral Style Scale. *Personality and Individual Differences, 23,* 909–912.

Mischel, W. (1966). Theory and research on the antecedents of self-imposed delay of reward. *Progress in Experimental and Personality Research, 3,* 85–132.

Mischel, W. (1973). Toward a cognitive social learning reconceptualization of personality. *Psychological Review, 80,* 252–283.

Mischel, W. (1974). Processes in delay of gratification. In L. Berkowitz (Ed.), *Advances in experimental social psychology* (Vol. 7, pp. 249–292). New York: Academic Press.

Mischel, W. (1990). Personality dispositions revisited and revised: A view after three decades. In L. A. Pervin (Ed.), *Handbook of personality: Theory and research* (pp. 111–134). New York: Guilford Press.

Mischel, W. (1993). *Introduction to personality.* New York: Harcourt Brace Jovanovich.

Mischel, W., Shoda, Y., & Rodriguez, M. (1989). Delay of gratification in children. *Science, 244,* 933–938.

Moyer, A., & Salovey, P. (1996). Psychosocial sequelae of breast cancer and its treatment. *Annals of Behavioral Medicine, 18,* 110–125.

Muris, P., de Jongh, A., van Zuuren, F. J., & Schoenmakers, N. (1996). Monitoring blunting coping styles and cognitive symptoms of dental fear. *European Journal of Personality, 10,* 35–44.

Muris, P., de Jongh, A., van Zuuren, F., & ter Horst, G. (1994). Coping style, anxiety, cognitions, and cognitive control in dental phobia. *Personality and Individual Differences, 17,* 143–145.

Muris, P., Meesters, C., & Merckelbach, H. (1996). Monitoring and fearfulness in children. *Personality and Individual Differences, 21,* 1059–1061.

Muris, P., Merckelbach, H., & de Jongh, P. (1995). Exposure *Behaviour Research and Therapy, 33,* 461–464.

Nelson, D. V., Friedman, L. C., Baer, P. E., Lane, M., & Smith, F. E. (1994). Subtypes of psychosocial adjustment to breast cancer. *Journal of Behavioral Medicine, 17,* 127–141.

Newsom, J. T., Knapp, J. E., & Schulz, R. (1996). Longitudinal analysis of specific domains of internal control and depressive symptoms in patients with recurrent cancer. *Health Psychology, 15,* 323–331.

O'Connor, A. P., Wicker, C. A., & Germino, B. B. (1990). Understanding the cancer patient's search for meaning. *Cancer Nursing, 13,* 167–175.

O'Leary, A., & Miller, S. M. (1991). Stress, immune function, and health: Early settlement of a new frontier. *Clinical Immunology Newsletter, 11,* 177–180.

O'Leary, A., Savard, J., & Miller, S. M. (1996). Psyychoneuroimmunology: Elucidating the process. *Current Opinion in Psychiatry, 9,* 427–432.

Orr, E. (1986). Open communications as an effective stress management method for breast cancer patients. *Journal of Human Stress, 12,* 175–185.

Penman, D. T. (1982). Coping strategies in adaptation to mastectomy. *Psychosomatic Medicine, 44,* 117–125.

Penman, D. T., Bloom, J. R., Fotopoulos, S., Cook, M. R., Holland, J. C., Gates, C., Flamer, D., Murawski, B., Ross, R., Brandt, U., Muenz, L.R., & Pee, D. (1987). The impact of mastectomy on self-concept and social function: A combined cross-sectional and longitudinal study with comparison groups. *Women and Health, 11,* 101–130.

Phipps, S., Fairclough, D., & Mulhern, R.K. (1995). Avoidant coping in children with cancer. *Journal of Pediatric Psychology, 20,* 217–232.

Phipps, S., & Srivastava, D.K. (1997). Repressive adaptation in children with cancer. *Health Psychology, 16,* 521–528.

Phipps, S., & Zinn, A. B. (1986). Psychological response to amniocentesis: Effects of coping style. *American Journal of Medical Genetics, 25,* 143–148.

Pinder, K., Ramirez, A. J., Richards, M. A., & Gregory, W. M. (1994). Cognitive responses and psychiatric disorder in women with operable breast cancer. *Psycho-Oncology, 3,* 129–137.

Polinsky, M. L. (1994). Functional status of long-term breast cancer survivors: Determining chronicity. *Health and Social Work, 19,* 165–173.

Quinn, M. E., Fontana, A. F., & Reznikoff, M. (1986). Psychological distress in reaction to lung cancer as a function of spousal support and coping strategy. *Journal of Psychosocial Oncology, 9,* 79–89.

Rakowski, W., Dube, C. E., Marcus, B. H., Prochaska, J. O., Velker, W. F., & Abrams, D. B. (1992). Assessing elements of women's decisions about mammography. *Health Psychology, 11,* 111–118.

Rakowski, W., Fulton, J. P., & Feldman, J. P. (1993 Women's decision making about mammography: A replication of the relationship between stages of adoption and decisional balance. *Health Psychology, 12,* 209–214.

Richardson, J. L., & Sanchez, K. (1998). Compliance with cancer treatment. In J.C. Holland (Ed.), *Psychooncology* (pp. 67–77). New York: Oxford University Press.

Rodrigue, J. R., Behen, J. M., & Tumlin, T. (1994). Multidimensional determinants of psychological adjustment to cancer. *Psycho-Oncology, 3,* 205–214.

Ross, C. J. M., & Maguire, T.O. (1995). Informational coping styles: A validity study. *Journal of Nursing Measurement, 3,* 145–158.

Rotter, J. (1954). *Social learning and clinical psychology.* Englewood Cliffs, NJ: Prentice Hall.

Rowland, J. H., & Holland, J. C. (1989). Breast cancer. In J. C. Holland & J. H. Rowland (Eds.), *Handbook of psychooncology: Psychological care of the patient with cancer* (pp. 323–340). New York: Oxford University Press.

Rudolph, K. D., Dennig, M. D., & Weisz, J. R. (1995). Determinants and consequences of children's coping in the medical setting: Conceptualization, review, and critique. *Psychological Bulletin, 118,* 328–357.

Sarason, I. (1979). Three lacunae of cognitive therapy. *Cognitive Therapy and Research, 3,* 223–235.

Sarason, I., Sarason, B., Keefe, D., Hayes, B., & Shearin, E. (1986). Cognitive interference: Situational determinants and traitlike characteristics. *Journal of Personality and Social Psychology, 51,* 215–226.

Schnoll, R. A., Harlow, L. L., Stolbach, L. L., & Brandt, U. (1998). A structural model of the relationships among stage of disease, age, coping, and psychological adjustment in women with breast cancer. *Psycho-Oncology, 7,* 69–77.

Schnoll, R. A., MacKinnon, J. R., Stolbach, L. L., & Lorman, C. (1995). The relationship between emotional adjustment and two factor structures of the Mental Adjustment to Cancer (MAC) scale. *Psycho-Oncology, 4,* 265–272.

Schuck, P. (1998). Glycated hemoglobin as a physiological measure of stress and its relation to some psychological stress indicators. *Behavioral Medicine, 24,* 89–94.

Schwartz, M. D., Lerman, C., Miller, S. M., Daly, M., & Masny, A. (1995). Coping disposition, perceived risk, and psychological distress among women at increased risk for ovarian cancer. *Health Psychology, 14,* 232–235.

Shapiro, D. E., Boggs, S. R., Melamed, B. G., & Graham-Pole, J. (1992). The effect of varied physician affect on recall, anxiety, and perceptions in women at risk for breast cancer: An analogue study. *Health Psychology, 11,* 61–66.

Shoda, Y., Mischel, W., Miller, S. M., Diefenbach, M., Daly, M. B., & Engstrom, P. (1998). Psychological interventions and genetic testing: Facilitating informed decisions about BRCA1/2 cancer susceptibility. *Journal of Clinical Psychology in Medical Settings, 5,* 3–17.

Singer, J., & Salovey, P. (1991). Organized knowledge structures and personality: Person schemas, self-schemas, prototypes, and scripts. In M. J. Horowitz (Ed.), *Person schemas and maladaptive interpersonal patterns* (pp. 33–79). Chicago: University of Chicago Press.

Skinner, C. S., Kreuter, M. W., Kobrin, S., & Strecher, V. J. (1998). Perceived and actual breast cancer risk: Optimistic and pessimistic biases. *Journal of Health Psychology, 3,* 181–193.

Sneeuw, K. C. A., Aaaronson, N. K., Yarnold, J. R., Broderick, M., Regan, J., Ross, G., & Goddard, A. (1992). Cosmetic and functional outcomes of breast conserving treatment for early stage breast cancer: 2. Relationship with psychosocial functioning. *Radiotherapy and Oncology, 25,* 160–166.

Somerfield, M. R., Curbow, B., Wingard, J. R., Baker, F., & Fogarty, L. A. (1996). Coping with the physical and psychosocial sequelae of bone marrow transplantation among long term survivors. *Journal of Behavioral Medicine, 19,* 163–184.

Sparks, G. G., & Spirek, M. M. (1988). Individual differences in coping with stressful mass media: An activation–arousal view. *Human Communications Research, 15,* 191–216.

Spencer, S. M., Carver, C. S., & Price, A. A. (1998). Psychological and social factors in adaptation. In J. C. Holland (Ed.), *Psycho-oncology* (pp. 211–221). New York: Oxford University Press.

Stanton, A. L., & Snider, P. R. (1993). Coping with

breast cancer diagnosis: A prospective study. *Health Psychology, 12,* 16–23.

Steptoe, A., & O'Sullivan, J. (1986). Monitoring and blunting coping styles in women prior to surgery. *British Journal of Clinical Psychology, 25,* 143–144.

Stoddard, E. D. (1995). Optimism and coping as predictors of distress in women at risk for cervical cancer. *Dissertation Abstracts International, 56,* 2343B.

Taylor, S. E. (1990). Health psychology: The science and the field. *American Psychologist, 45,* 40–50.

Taylor, S. E., Helgeson, V. S., Reed, G. M., & Skokan, L. A. (1991). Self-generated feeling of control and adjustment to physical illness. *Journal of Social Issues, 47,* 91–109.

Taylor, S. E., Lichtman, R. R., & Wood, J. V. (1984). Attributions, beliefs about control, and adjustment to breast cancer. *Journal of Personality and Social Psychology, 46,* 489–502.

Thompson, B., & Pitts, M. C. (1993). Factors relating to a person's ability to find meaning after a diagnosis of cancer. *Journal of Psychosocial Oncology, 11,* 1–21.

Thompson, S. C., Sobolew-Shubin, A., Galbraith, M. E., Schwankovsky, L., & Cruzen, D. (1993). Maintaining perceptions of control: Finding perceived control in low-control circumstances. *Journal of Personality and Social Psychology, 64,* 293–304.

Turk, D. C., & Salovey, P. (1985). Cognitive structures, cognitive processes, and cognitive-behavior modification: I. Client issues. *Cognitive Therapy and Research, 9,* 1–17.

van Zuuren, F. J. (1993). Coping style and anxiety during prenatal diagnosis. *Journal of Reproductive and Infant Psychology, 11,* 57–59.

van Zuuren, F. J. (1996). Cognitive confrontation and avoidance in medical settings: An evaluation of the Dutch Threatening Medical Situation Inventory (TMSI). *Gedag und Gezondheid: Tijdschrift voor Psychologie und Gezondheid, 24,* 39–46.

van Zuuren, F. J., & Muris, P. (1993). Coping under experimental threat: Observable and cognitive correlates of dispositional monitoring and blunting. *European Journal of Personality, 7,* 245–253.

Wagner, M. K., Armstrong, D., & Laughlin, J. E. (1995). Cognitive determinants of quality of life after onset of cancer. *Psychological Reports, 77,* 147–154.

Warburton, L. A., Fishman, B., & Perry, S. W. (1997). Coping with the possibility of testing HIV positive. *Personality and Individual Differences, 22,* 459–464.

Wardle, F. J. (1995). Women at risk of ovarian cancer. *Monographs of the National Cancer Institute, 17,* 81–85.

Wardle, F. J., Collins, W., Pernet, A. L., Whitehead, M. I., Bourne, T. H., & Campbell, S. (1993). Psychological impact of screening for familial ovarian cancer. *Journal of the National Cancer Institute, 85,* 653–657.

Wardle, F. J., Pernet, A. L., Collins, W., & Bourne, T. H. (1994). False positive results in ovarian cancer screening: One year follow-up of psychological status. *Psychology and Health, 10,* 33–40.

Watkins, L. O., Weaver, L., & Odegaard, V. (1986). Preparation for cardiac catheterization: Tailoring the content of instruction to coping style. *Heart and Lung, 15,* 382–389.

Watson, M., Greer, S., Young, J., Inayat, Q., Burgess, C., & Robertson, A. (1988). Development of a questionnaire measure of adjustment to cancer. *Psychological Medicine, 18,* 203–209.

Weinstein, N. (1989). Effects of personal experience on self-protective behavior. *Psychological Bulletin, 105,* 31–50.

Weisman, A. D. (1976). Early diagnosis of vulnerability in cancer patients. *American Journal of the Medical Sciences, 271,* 187–196.

Weisman, A. (1989). Vulnerability and the psychological disturbances of cancer patients. *Psychosomatics, 30,* 80–85.

Zakowski, S. G., Valdimarsdottir, H. B., Bovbjerg, D. H., Borgen, P., Holland, J., Kash, K., Miller, D., Mitnick, J., Osborne, M., & Van Dee, K. (1997). Predictors of intrusive thoughts and avoidance in women with family histories of breast cancer. *Annals of Behavioral Medicine, 19,* 362–369.

CHAPTER 35

Emotions and Immunity

Roger J. Booth
James W. Pennebaker

When we consider the relationship between emotions and immunity, we endeavor to draw links between a domain of explanation about how we humans feel (the psychosocial realm in which emotions lie) and a domain of biochemical operation within the human body (the physiological network of cells and molecules that make up the lymphoid system). In the most rudimentary sense, "e-motions" are labels that we give to our dispositions to act in particular ways under a variety of circumstances. They are our descriptions of how we feel about ourselves and the world about us. Consequently, they open up to us a constellation of ways of being or acting in relation to the world. In a similar metaphorical vein, the notion of an "immune system" encompasses an aspect of what we observe as the body's relationship with the outside world in a purely physical sense. Although we often talk about the immune system as a defense or protection against potentially pathogenic or destructive organisms' impinging on us, the system is perhaps more broadly viewed as something maintaining an acceptable relationship between the structures that constitute physical self and those that are nonself.

Both emotions and immunity are instrumental in constructing and maintaining relationships between individuals and the situations in which they live. From such a perspective, various questions can be posed: How and when do emotional changes affect immune system be-

havior, and vice versa? What are the nature of the relationships among emotions, immunity, and illness? Before addressing these questions, we briefly discuss the nature of the immune system and how it might be evaluated in relation to emotions or emotional changes.

THE IMMUNE SYSTEM AS A TOPOLOGICAL SENSORY SYSTEM

In medicine, the concept of an "immune system" arose originally out of observations that people who had recovered from certain infectious illnesses often had subsequent resistance or at least altered susceptibility to those illnesses. This phenomenon later came to be termed "immunological memory" in order to signify a change or adaptation within the immune system of an organism specifically related to a particular infectious agent. Increasingly the immune system came to be synonymous with defensive or protective aspects of the body. The physiological mechanisms associated with immune processes center on the activities of white blood cells, or "lymphocytes." Lymphocytes rely on cell surface receptors to recognize and respond to specific uniquely shaped foreign agents (termed "antigens"). Various classes of lymphocytes are found in high concentrations in certain organs of the body (lymphoid organs, such as the spleen, lymph nodes, bone marrow, and thymus). They are also highly mobile cells that can circulate through the body via the bloodstream and the network of lymphatic vessels permeating the body. Various activities are associated with immune system activity—antibody production, cytotoxicity (killing of cells by specialized lymphocytes), natural killer (NK) activity, phagocytosis (ingestion and digestion of material by cells such as neutrophils of the blood), and inflammation. These are regulated by a complex network of cellular and molecular interactions in which lymphocytes and immune regulatory hormones (called "cytokines") play crucial roles. As has been revealed by research in neuroimmunology over the last few decades, the immune regulatory network appreciably overlaps and intercalates with nervous system activities (Felten, Felten, Bellinger, & Madden, 1993; Khansari, Murgo, & Faith, 1990; Sternberg, 1997; Watkins, 1994).

In short, the immune system is a dynamic system; it is a complex network of cells and molecules with access to virtually every part of the body; and it functions by sensing and responding to molecular shapes (antigens) in ways that endeavor to maintain the integrity of the body. In doing this, the immune system appears to respond effectively to foreign shapes (e.g., those of viruses or bacteria) in ways that allow it to neutralize, inactivate, remove, or assimilate this foreignness. In contrast, the immune system does not appear to behave in a similar way toward shapes that are present on the normal tissue components of the body in which it resides. This means that built into the immune system's operation are a capacity to discriminate between "self" and "nonself" antigens, and a capacity for the system as a whole to appear "self-tolerant." Such discrimination is not absolute, however. Indeed, there are illnesses (classed as "autoimmune conditions") in which immunological reactivity against self components is manifested pathologically.

We often talk about the immune system as something that *responds* to a stimulus (e.g., the antigens produced by an infectious process). In doing so, we generate a picture of a system armed and ready to repel potentially damaging invasions. Yet from the perspective of the immune system operating within the physiology of an individual's body, there is no stimulus and no immune response—only changes that trigger various other changes in order to maintain a set of relationships. Furthermore, effective recognition of and response to nonself antigens by the immune system implies that there must be some knowledge or appreciation of self in order to distinguish that which is nonself. In fact, the manner in which the components of the immune network are generated is such that self–nonself discrimination is not preprogrammed genetically; rather, it is something the immune system learns, particularly during embryonic development, but also to a degree throughout the life of an individual. Given the degree of interconnectedness between the immune and nervous systems, we must consider how much of the self–nonself learning by the immune system is affected by the psychosocial aspects of a person. We return to this a little later.

PROBLEMS IN ASSESSING IMMUNE SYSTEM ACTIVITY

It should be apparent that immune processes are many and varied, and that they are intimately interwoven with processes of the nervous system. What we observe as an immune response to a particular substance is part of the continuous self-evaluating and self-defining process of immune adaptation. How, then, can we assess the relationships between immune activity and psychosocial factors in a useful way? If we restrict ourselves to humans, we are limited in what immune material we can sample. As research in the general area of psychoneuroimmunology (PNI) has advanced, we are now appreciating that all the measures have limitations. Components of blood such as lymphocyte populations, antibodies, and cytokines are obvious and well-used sources of immune material. We must realize, however, that the lymphocyte population in the circulating blood constitutes fewer than 10% of the lymphocytes in the body; that the distribution and activities of blood lymphocytes are not necessarily representative of the total lymphoid pool; and that lymphocyte mobilization into and out of the peripheral circulation can be quite rapid and significantly affected by relatively trivial things (e.g., mild exercise or anxiety about venipuncture).

Concentrations of a class of antibodies in saliva (salivary immunoglobulin A, or sIgA) are relatively easy to measure and represent a specific compartment of the mucosal-associated lymphoid system. Despite the appeal of salivary measures, they are subject to variations affected by nonimmune factors such as salivary secretion rates. Skin tests for reactivity to allergens (immediate hypersensitivity) or antigens against which an individual has been previously immunized (delayed-type hypersensitivity) are useful functional immune parameters, but they are limited to people who have allergic sensitivities (typically only about 10–20% of the population) or who have been previously exposed to the antigen in question. In short, every immune parameter taps a different dimension of immune action and comes with its own set of advantages and drawbacks.

THE PSYCHOMETRIC PROPERTIES OF THE IMMUNE SYSTEM

The immune system was not designed by an expert in psychometrics. Psychologists, when first learning about PNI, tend to think of the "immune system" as a coherent construct like "intelligence," "negative affectivity," or "need for achievement." Psychological measures of these constructs are generally created in a deductive manner. Each item that measures the construct is assumed to correlate—however modestly—with other items that also tap the overarching construct. The immune system, and by extension immune function, is not a deductively determined process. Some immune measures, for example, are highly correlated, and others are independent. The degree to which a person is resistant to, say, a particular cold virus may be completely uncorrelated with the person's ability to ward off hepatitis. In other words, there is no representative measure of human immune behavior, partly because of the limited access to immune components in humans, but more especially because the notion of a representative measure of the immune system is essentially meaningless.

Although it is commonplace to talk about factors that enhance or suppress the immune system, these are often highly suspect attributions. When the immune system is assumed to be operating essentially as a defense system, the notion of "more means better" is readily adopted, and a fall in an immune measure is correspondingly interpreted as "immunosuppression." Yet the immune system undergoes continual change, and immunity is not a unidimensional variable. The experience of a particular stressor associated with a decrease in the number of helper T lymphocytes in the blood has too often been interpreted as an example of "stress suppressing the immune system." This is a little like claiming that the quality of a symphony diminishes when the violas play more softly. We have to be careful not to overinterpret observed immune changes as evidence of suppression or enhancement, but instead to view them as an indication of a psychoimmune relationship. It then becomes important to ask whether that relationship also correlates with any observable health changes.

EMOTIONS AS DISPOSITIONS FOR ACTION

Just as there are potential problems with some ways of understanding the immune system, so there can be confusion in appreciating what constitutes an "emotion." To us, emotions describe how we humans are disposed to act in particular situations. Any action or constellation of related actions requires a certain physiological capacity, and this necessarily involves a physical body. Therefore our ability to act is always constrained by our physiological makeup, and as our physiology changes, so we are able to act differently. When our physiology is such that we become disposed to a particular domain of actions, we label that domain an emotion. For example, under the emotion of "love," the structure of our physiology endows us with the capacity to act in ways that are different from when our emotion is "anger." Moreover, just as our emotions alter as our physiology changes, so our physiology alters as our emotions change. Thus emotions are the labels that we give to our dispositions to act in characteristic ways. Furthermore, we can distinguish emotions from "feelings" and "thoughts." Feelings and thoughts arise in the linguistic domain through which we coordinate our actions with those of other people—the domain of language. Feelings are commentaries that we generate in language to account for, or make sense of, the emotions we experience in particular contexts. Thoughts, on the other hand, are commentaries that we generate when we observe ourselves as distinct living entities and reflect upon some aspect of that existence. Accordingly, feelings are more directly linked to emotions than thoughts need be, inasmuch as feelings are the linguistic manner in which we individually interpret or express the emotional flow of our lives.

IMMUNE EFFECTS ON EMOTIONS AND ILLNESS

The large body of research in PNI into aspects of stress and immune responsiveness tells us that how we interpret and understand events in our lives has an impact on the way our immune systems function (Booth, 1998). The degree to which we perceive situations and events in our lives to be stressful is conditioned by both our emotional relationship to those situations and our general emotional disposition. It is relevant, therefore, to ask whether emotions, emotional disposition, and immune system activity are linked. We know from personal experiences that during infectious illnesses, behavior and perceptions are changed. If we monitor immune variables during such a process, we notice that certain immunological hormones (cytokines) are active. Moreover, during fever, for example, cytokines such as interleukin-1 can be detected in the brain and have been shown in animal studies to exert sedative behavioral effects, to be somnogenic, and to induce slow-wave sleep (Maier & Watkins, 1998). It is probable, then, that altered emotions during infectious illnesses are at least in part induced by changes in activity within the immune system. This relationship also holds for other illnesses as well.

Major depression and dysthymia have been associated with increased perception of day-to-day stressors, greater reliance on emotion-focused coping efforts, and reduced perception of uplifting events. Recent evidence suggests that these may be related to immune activity. Ravindran, Griffiths, Merali, and Anisman (1996a) found that dysthymia was also associated with elevated levels of circulating NK cells, but presumably not as a result of hypothalamic–pituitary–adrenocortical (HPA) axis activation, because neither plasma cortisol, adrenocorticotropic hormone (ACTH), nor norepinephrine levels were increased in the dysthymic subjects. Interestingly, in control subjects circulating NK cells were inversely related to the severity of daily hassles recently encountered, while in dysthymic patients stress and coping factors were unrelated to NK cell numbers (Ravindran, Griffiths, Merali, & Anisman,

1996b). Given the effects of inflammatory cytokines (such as interleukin-1) on sleep patterns, Bauer et al. (1995) sought to test whether induction of such cytokines in patients with depressive disorders would have any beneficial emotional effects. After a single injection of an inflammatory bacterial product (endotoxin), there was increased synthesis for several hours of the cytokines tumor necrosis factor, interleukin-1, and interleukin-6, as well as elevated body temperature. There were also transient behavioral and emotional changes. Over the subsequent 24 hours, sleep patterns altered, and all patients were in a significantly improved mood.

Cytokines are not the only immune factors to be implicated in emotion and mood disorders, however. For example, using tests for immunoglobulin E antibody reactivity to a variety of common airborne allergens, Dabkowska and Rybakowski (1997) found higher than normal reactivity in groups of patients with mood disorders and schizophrenia. Less clear at this point is the degree to which stable individual differences in mood state, such as negative affectivity or optimism, are chronically related to antibody reactivity.

Autoimmune illnesses constitute a varied group of conditions in which there is chronically altered immune activity. Certain laboratory strains of mice develop autoimmune conditions early in life, and these have been used to investigate whether there is a link between immune and emotional changes in autoimmunity. When an autoimmune mouse strain (MRL-lpr) was compared with a similar but nonautoimmune strain on a battery of tests presumed to be reflective of emotional reactivity, the autoimmune MRL-lpr strain showed increased timidity and altered emotional reactivity. In addition, high titers of serum antinuclear antibodies in MRL-lpr mice were associated with impaired emotional/behavioral tests, indicating that perhaps disturbed emotional reactivity reflects the effect of autoimmunity on the HPA axis (Sakic et al., 1994).

In a study of patients with rheumatoid arthritis, Harrington et al. (1993) reported evidence that psychoimmune processes may be implicated in short-term changes in disease activity. Fourteen patients were studied on each of six occasions, 2 weeks apart. The measures used included daily ratings of mood disturbance, undesirable events, and joint pain; clinical examination of joint swelling; and blood levels of soluble interleukin-2 receptor (an immune marker known to correlate with joint inflammation). Changes in mood disturbance were unrelated to changes in joint inflammation, but increases in mood disturbance were linked with decreased soluble interleukin-2 receptor levels and increased reported joint pain.

EMOTION EFFECTS ON IMMUNE ACTIVITY

In a number of studies, neuroticism, depression, and stress have been reported to be positively correlated with each other and with serum cortisol concentration, and inversely related to various immune measures (Black, 1994a, 1994b; Cacioppo, 1994; Gilbert, Stunkard, Jensen, Detwiler, & Martinko, 1996; Sternberg, 1997; Watkins, 1995). For example, social fear was induced in a laboratory setting in healthy subjects by having them prepare and give an oral presentation in front of an audience; this fear evoked elevated feelings of tenseness and negative bodily sensations, enhanced cardiovascular activity, elevated plasma hormone (cortisol, prolactin, and β-endorphin) levels, and changes in immunological parameters (numbers of NK and T helper cells) (Gerritsen, Heijnen, Wiegant, Bermond, & Frijda, 1996).

Negative mood (e.g., emotional distress) is known to affect immune function, but little research has addressed effects of positive mood or possible interactions between negative and positive mood factors. Stone, Marco, Cruise, Cox, and Neale (1996) assessed relationships among mood, stresses, and immune changes (assessed by salivary antibody response to an oral antigen) by having a group of 72 men over a 12-week period complete end-of-day diaries in which they rated their mood for that day and the desirability of the day's events. Regression analyses indicated that negative mood partially mediated the immunological response to both undesirable and desirable events. Undesirable events lowered antibody levels primarily by increasing negative mood; desirable events increased antibody levels by decreasing negative mood, but there was little evidence for mediation by positive mood beyond that found for negative mood (Stone et al., 1996). In another study of a group of 48 healthy women, those reporting some negative mood (about half of

them) had lower levels of NK activity than those who had no negative mood, while those with higher levels of positive mood had higher NK activity. In this study too, a significant interaction between positive and negative mood indicated that the relation between positive mood and NK activity depended on the women's experience of negative mood. Higher levels of positive mood were related to higher NK levels only among the women who reported having some negative mood over the day, raising the possibility that positive mood may moderate or buffer the effects of negative mood on immune function (Valdimarsdottir & Bovbjerg, 1997).

How people cope with event- or situation-related emotions is also a determining factor in immune effects. Using 25 healthy medical students seropositive for antibodies against Epstein–Barr virus (EBV), Glaser et al. (1993) studied memory T-cell proliferative response to several EBV antigens 1 month before a block of examinations and again on the last day of the exam series. The proliferative response to the viral antigens significantly decreased during examinations. Moreover, subjects who were high in seeking support had lower proliferative response and higher levels of antibody to viral antigens (consistent with poorer immune control of virus growth), indicating that coping mechanisms can modulate the psychological stress-related effects on these immune measures.

Problem-solving behaviors have also been associated with changes in immune function. In a study of 90 newlywed couples over a 24-hour period, those who exhibited more negative or hostile behaviors during a 30-minute discussion of marital problems showed greater decrements in functional immunological assays (NK activity and proliferative responses of T lymphocytes in culture), as well as larger increases in the numbers of circulating helper T lymphocytes. Highly negative subjects also had higher antibody titers to latent EBV than low-negativity subjects. Under the conditions, women were more likely to show negative immunological changes than men, and positive or supportive problem-solving behaviors were not related to immunological changes (Kiecolt-Glaser et al., 1993). Consistent with the neuroimmune relationship, hostile behavior was also associated with decreased serum levels of prolactin and increases in epinephrine, norepinephrine, ACTH, and growth hormone, but not cortisol (Malarkey, Kiecolt-Glaser, Pearl, & Glaser, 1994).

Significantly, the profile of neuroendocrine changes, especially the lack of involvement of cortisol, in these sorts of studies is different from that in the more directly stress-related research. In other studies, marital conflict in an experimental setting in distressed couples has been also found to affect emotions, blood pressure, and immune measures. During a conflict period, women responded with significantly greater increases in depression and hostility, and with significantly greater increases in systolic blood pressure, than those of men. Women also responded with slight decreases in T-cell proliferative response, while men displayed an increase, and change in this immune measure was associated with change in hostility and blood pressure (Mayne, Oleary, McCrady, Contrada, & Labouvie, 1997). These findings highlight the likelihood of there being different spectra of neuroimmune alteration, depending on not only the nature of events and the associated emotions, but also their significance in the overall framework of an individual's life.

The role of the context of a stressor is particularly evident when we consider the relationship between the emotional impact of serious illness in a spouse or partner and immune changes. For example, Futterman, Wellisch, Zighelboim, Lunaraines, and Weiner (1996) evaluated the effects on psychological and immunological status (percentages of total, CD4, and CD8 T cells; percentages of B cells and NK cells; and NK cytotoxicity) of having a spouse or partner undergoing a bone marrow transplant. The greatest abnormality in immune variables was detected during the waiting period before transplantation—a time when subjects also had the highest scores on negative affect, escape/avoidance coping, and psychological symptoms. Significant correlations were found among trait anxiety, escape/avoidance coping, and percentage of CD4 (helper) cells. The most significant and consistent psychological variable in predicting immune changes was escape/avoidance coping, which was inversely correlated with the immune measures (Futterman et al., 1996). In a similar vein, Kemeny et al. (1995) reported that the death of an intimate partner in HIV-positive men was associated with immune changes relevant to HIV progression.

Of particular importance is that the quality of interpersonal relationships may serve to attenuate adverse immunological changes associated with psychologically distressing emotions, and may have consequences for disease susceptibility and health. In a 5-year study of men infected with HIV, Theorell et al. (1995) found that low scores on a measure of social support at the outset was associated with a significantly more rapid progressive deterioration in CD4 count during subsequent years. Similarly, Cohen, Tyrrell, and Smith (1991, 1993) studied psychological variables associated with incidence and severity of upper respiratory tract infection following exposure to measured quantities of rhinoviruses and adenoviruses. They found not only that perceived stress and negative affectivity at the time of exposure to the virus cocktail correlated with incidence and severity of infection, but that active participation in social networks ameliorated this effect (Cohen, Doyle, Skoner, Rabin, & Gwaltney, 1997).

In summary, a growing body of evidence is indicating that negative emotions can adversely affect immune markers that, directly or indirectly, can contribute to poorer health. Of course, it is difficult to distinguish negative emotions from the factors that may be eliciting them in the first place. For example, loss-of-control experiences, adverse changes in social networks, and other known psychosocial stressors may be influencing both mood and biological state. Fortunately, some recent laboratory studies are beginning to clarify the mood–immune relationships.

EFFECTS OF INDUCED EMOTIONS ON IMMUNE VARIABLES

If our emotional experiences can be influenced by what is happening in our immune systems, and if emotional changes are associated with measurable changes in some immune variables, can we deliberately induce particular emotionality and observe corresponding immune effects? Studies conducted in this area fall into three categories: viewing emotional films or videos, deliberately inciting particular emotions, or recalling emotionally rich experiences.

In research using sIgA as an immune variable, concentrations did not change significantly after experimental participants viewed a didactic videotape, but increased significantly after subjects viewed a humorous videotape. This effect was moderated by the routine use of humor as a coping skill (Dillon, Minchoff, & Baker, 1985). Expressing emotions through laughing or crying in response to viewing humorous or sad videos can also be influential. The humorous stimulus resulted in higher sIgA concentrations, regardless of whether or not overt laughter was expressed; in contrast, overt crying was associated with decreased sIgA. Interestingly, the inhibition of weeping in the context of the same sad stimulus was not linked to lower sIgA levels (Labott, Ahleman, Wolever, & Martin, 1990; Martin, Guthrie, & Pitts, 1993).

Wittling and Pfluger (1990) examined whether the cerebral hemispheres differ in their ability to regulate cortisol secretion during emotion-related situations. Approximately 120 adults were shown either an emotionally aversive or a neutral film in the left or right hemisphere by means of a technique for lateralizing visual input. Right-hemispheric viewing of the emotionally aversive film resulted in a significantly higher increase of salivary cortisol secretion than did left-hemispheric viewing of the same film. No differences were observed with respect to the neutral film. Moreover, only the right hemisphere was able to respond neuroendocrinologically in a different manner to the emotionally aversive and the neutral film, suggesting that cortical regulation of cortisol secretion in emotion-related situations is under primary control of the right hemisphere. In another study, healthy men viewed a gruesome surgery film and were then asked to recall details of the film twice during a 30-minute period. Compared with a control group, mitogen-induced T-cell proliferative responses decreased during and after exposure to the film. This decrease was more pronounced in subjects exhibiting greater blood pressure reactivity while viewing the film (Zakowski, McAllister, Deal, & Baum, 1992).

Deliberately acting particular emotional states has been reported to affect functional and enumerative immunological parameters. Futterman, Kemeny, Shapiro, Polonsky, and Fahey (1992) examined the effects of short sessions of experimentally induced positive (happiness) and negative (anxiety, depression) affective states and a neutral state in healthy actors. Compared with a neutral condition, all mood states affected several immune parameters, regardless of the arousal level of the mood in-

duced. Furthermore, among the affective states, anxiety induced the most immunological variability and depression the least. Mitogen-induced T-cell proliferative responses were differentially sensitive to positive and negative mood states, increasing after positive moods and decreasing after negative moods. Heart rate, physical activity, and cortisol concentrations also had an impact on mood effects for the immune parameters investigated (Futterman, Kemeny, Shapiro, & Fahey, 1994). In a study of the relationship between induced mood and cytokine concentrations, an increase in secretion of cytokines associated with T-cell proliferation (e.g. interleukin-2) but not those associated with inflammation (e.g. interleukin-1 and interleukin-6) was observed in response to mild induced negative emotional changes. In contrast, the reverse of this (i.e., increased inflammatory but not T-cell proliferative cytokines) was found following positive mood changes (Mittwoch-Jaffe, Shalit, Srendi, & Yehuda, 1995).

Immunological processes are also sensitive to influences of emotions aroused by recalling or reliving emotionally rich experiences. In the research of Knapp et al. (1992), healthy volunteers recalled maximally disturbing and maximally pleasurable emotional experiences. While recalling the events, participants displayed significant cardiovascular activation, particularly during the disturbing recall condition. Emotion associated with recall of disturbing experiences promoted transient declines in mitogen-induced T-cell proliferation and small changes in NK activity, followed by a return to preemotion levels.

Intense emotional experiences have also be elicited while participants were hypnotized. For example, hypnotically induced emotional states have been reported to affect monocyte chemotaxis (Zachariae et al., 1991) and skin responses to histamine (Laidlaw, Booth, & Large, 1996). When subjects in a deep hypnotic trance were given suggestions to reexperience earlier life experiences involving intense anger and depression in random order, there were significant differences in monocyte chemotactic activity (the ability of monocyte cells to move toward a chemical attractant) between the angry and the depressed emotional states. After the happy, relaxed emotional state, chemotactic activity also significantly increased compared with activity both before hypnosis and after induction of the angry and depressed states. In contrast, no significant differences were detected for serum cortisol and catecholamine levels among emotional states (Zachariae et al., 1991). In the work of Laidlaw et al. (1996), subjects were guided to decrease skin reactivity to histamine in a cognitive–hypnotic intervention involving imagination and visualization. Mood and emotional factors contributed to skin test variance and predicted change in skin reactivity. A state of peacefulness was associated with generally low skin reactivity to histamine, while feelings of irritability and tension were associated with diminished ability to reduce reactivity during the intervention.

EMOTIONAL DISCLOSURE AND IMMUNITY

There is abundant evidence that traumatic experiences adversely affect mental and physical health. A prevalent thread in psychosomatics assumes that inhibiting or holding back one's thoughts, feelings, and behaviors is associated with long-term stress and disease, whereas actively confronting upsetting experiences through writing or talking reduces the negative effects of inhibition. In support of this model, childhood traumatic experiences, particularly those never discussed, are highly correlated with current health problems (Pennebaker & Susman, 1988). Moreover, evidence is accumulating that talking or writing about such events in general can be beneficial. Laboratory-induced verbal expression of emotion is known to be associated with immediate reductions in autonomic nervous system activity (Pennebaker, 1997a, 1997b). These physiological changes are prevalent among individuals most likely to disclose deeply upsetting events, suggesting that when people actively inhibit emotional expression, they are at increased risk for a variety of health problems. By contrast, expressing traumatic experiences by writing or talking improves physical health and is associated with fewer medical visits (Pennebaker, 1993; Pennebaker, Barger, & Tiebout, 1989; Pennebaker, Colder, & Sharp, 1990; Watson & Pennebaker, 1989). Moreover, subjects who disclose more severe traumas report fewer physical symptoms over subsequent months than do low-severity trauma subjects, and health benefits occur when severe traumas are disclosed, regardless of previous disclosure (Greenberg & Stone, 1992).

Repeatedly addressing traumatic issues by either writing or talking over a period of time is also beneficial. When subjects wrote or talked about interpersonal traumatic events for a short time on four consecutive days, there was an upsurge in negative emotion after each session (either vocal or written expression), but the painfulness of the topic decreased steadily over the time. At the end, subjects felt better about their topics and themselves and also reported positive cognitive changes (Murray & Segal, 1994).

Given the relationships between emotions and immune system behavior, the question arises as to whether the physiological and health effects resulting from writing or talking about traumatic events are also associated with immune effects. In the first published study to explore the immune effects of emotional disclosure, Pennebaker, Kiecolt-Glaser, and Glaser (1988) assigned 50 healthy undergraduates to write about either traumatic experiences or superficial topics during sessions on 4 consecutive days. After the intervention, lymphocytes from participants in the traumatic disclosure group gave significantly higher mitogen-induced proliferative responses than those from participants in the control group. As in previous studies, participants in the experimental group evidenced greater increases in negative emotion after writing than those in the control group. Interestingly, there was no significant correlation between increases in negative emotion and immune response measures. These findings hint that the context in which negative emotions are aroused may be more important in understanding relationships between emotions and immune responses than are negative emotions per se.

On the basis of this result, Esterling, Antoni, Kumar, and Schneiderman (1990) at the University of Miami hypothesized that subjects who abstained from disclosing emotional material would have poorer control of latent EBV, and that repressive interpersonal styles would correlate with the poorest control. They tested this by collecting blood from undergraduate volunteers immediately after each person had written a 30-minute essay about a stressful event that happened in his or her life. The degree of disclosure (as measured by the proportion of emotional words written) was associated with impaired control of latent EBV (i.e., high anti-EBV antibody titers), and emotional repression was also correlated with high antibody titers.

In a subsequent study, these researchers compared individuals who engaged in written and spoken emotional expression with individuals who wrote about superficial topics. Individuals in both oral and written trauma expression groups had significantly lower EBV antibody titers after the intervention than those in the control group. Although there were some differences between the written and oral groups in positive and negative emotional word use, content analysis indicated that the oral group achieved the greatest improvements in cognitive change, self-esteem, and adaptive coping strategies (Esterling, Antoni, Fletcher, Margulies, & Schneiderman, 1994). Moreover, individual differences in subjects' ability to involve themselves in the disclosure process and to abandon their avoidance of the stressful topic during the course of the study were predictive of lower anti-EBV antibody titers, and these associations were more pronounced for individuals who disclosed older and more troublesome events (Lutgendorf, Antoni, Kumar, & Schneiderman, 1994). In other research in which subjects verbally disclosed personal information regarding a traumatic or stressful experience, significant increases in NK activity were observed in these subjects compared with nondisclosure controls (Christensen et al., 1996). Furthermore, the effect of self-disclosure on NK activity was moderated by an individual's level of hostility, with high-hostility subjects exhibiting a significantly greater increase than low-hostility subjects.

The Miami group has also explored the effects of emotional disclosure in relation to notification of HIV status in men at risk of AIDS. Their results highlight the importance of cognitively processing stressful or emotional material for immune functioning in HIV-positive individuals. In the weeks following HIV serostatus notification, increased avoidance significantly predicted poorer mitogen-induced T-cell proliferative responses as well as trends toward lower circulating CD4 (helper) T-cell percentages (Lutgendorf et al., 1997).

We (Petrie, Booth, Pennebaker, Davison, & Thomas, 1995) assessed whether the health benefits of emotional disclosure would extend to effects on the immune response to an administered viral vaccine. Forty medical students who tested negative for hepatitis B antibodies were randomly assigned to write emotionally about personal traumatic events or to write descriptively about mundane topics during sessions on 4 consecutive days. On the day after the writing, all subjects were immunized with hepatitis B vaccine and monitored for specific antibody development. Compared with the control group, participants in the emotional expression group developed significantly higher antibody levels against hepatitis B antigens over the following 6 months. In this study and in subsequent research comparing written emotional disclosure groups with descriptive writing groups, there were reproducible significant between-group differences in circulating T-cell (CD4 and CD8) numbers and total circulating lymphocyte numbers, but not in CD4-to-CD8 ratios. Interestingly, although circulating lymphocyte numbers in the control group fluctuated over the time course of these studies, they stayed relatively constant in the emotional writing group, suggesting that the between-groups difference was due to a transient elevation in postwriting blood lymphocyte numbers in the descriptive writing group. This result suggests the possibility that buffering of temporal immune variation may be influential in the health-promoting effects of emotional disclosure (Booth, Petrie, & Pennebaker, 1997). A recent randomized, controlled trial bears this out (Smyth, Stone, Hurewitz, & Kaell, 1999). In it, 58 patients with asthma and 49 patients with rheumatoid arthritis were assigned to write for 3 consecutive days either about the most stressful event of their lives or about emotionally neutral topics. Over the following 4 months, patients who wrote about stressful life experiences had clinically relevant improvements in health status compared with those in the control group. The improvements in the health of these patients with immunologically related chronic conditions were beyond those attributable to the standard medical care that all participants were receiving.

Finally, a recent meta-analysis of disclosure studies involving writing reports that across studies, males appear to benefit more than females from writing (Smyth, 1998). Furthermore, the written disclosure paradigm reliably brings about improvements in participants' self-reported health, objective markers of health (e.g., physician visits), and immune changes, compared to those of people who write about nonemotional topics. In addition, emotional writing does not bring about health changes due to changes in health-related behaviors (e.g., changes in exercise, smoking, or diet).

CONCLUSIONS

In order to make sense of the findings on the relationship between emotions and immunity, it is necessary to look beyond a purely biological or physical construction of the immune system and to link its self-generative characteristics and capacity for distinguishing self from non-self to psychological, social, and cultural processes. The model of teleological coherence (harmony of purpose) (Booth & Ashbridge, 1992, 1993) proposes that the immune system, engaged in a broader process of self-determina-tion, shares with the neurological and psycho-logical domains the common goal of establishing and maintaining self-identity. Furthermore, the nature of the relationships is governed by the requirement for coherent coordination among all these self-defining aspects of an individual.

From the perspective of living beings, this means that the framework in which immune recognition occurs cannot be considered only as the context in which cells, molecules, antigens, and receptors operate, but as all the domains of life in which individuals define themselves. As a result, the personal meaning of events surrounding an antigenic stimulus (e.g., exposure to a viral or bacterial infection) is likely to condition the features (nature, specificity, magnitude, duration, etc.) of any observed immune response. Conversely, the behavior of the immune system toward self and nonself antigens can influence self-perceptions and relational perceptions within psychosocio-cultural domains. We experience this in a transient way when we contract a mild respiratory tract infection (e.g., a cold) and see the world and our relationship to it differently. Physiologically, these effects can be described through mechanisms of cross-talk between the immune and nervous systems (neuroendocrine hormones, neurotransmitters, cytokines, etc.), but such descriptions tell us little about the events in the context of coherent self-generation of a meaningful life.

It is a mistake to assume that there is a one-to-one correspondence between particular emotions and specific immune changes. Similarly, we should not expect particular types of events to have particular immune effects, because the meaning of the events in the context of individuals' lives may be a crucial determining factor. We think of certain events as stressful, and therefore expect them to have a negative impact

on immunity. That this is a gross oversimplification is exemplified by some recently published research. Air traffic control is often considered to be a rather stressful occupation because of the intensity, unpredictability, and responsibility of the workload. However, when Zeier, Brauchli, and Joller Jemelka (1996) assessed psychophysiological stress reactions in air traffic controllers before and after each of two working sessions, the working sessions caused a marked increase in the concentration and secretion rate of sIgA and cortisol, in contrast to the expected immunosuppressive effects. The cortisol response was correlated with the amount of actual or perceived workload, but the sIgA increase was not. Therefore, positive emotional engagement rather than a negative stress effect may have been responsible for the observed sIgA increase. Similarly, in a study of people who experienced life disruption from the 1994 Northridge earthquake in California, appropriateness of psychological reaction to the realistic degree of life stress was found to be least disruptive of immune system activity (Solomon, Segerstrom, Grohr, Kemeny, & Fahey, 1997).

When individuals are asked to write or talk about personally upsetting experiences, significant improvements in physical health accrue. Analyses of subjects' writing about traumas indicate that those whose health improves most tend to use a relatively high rate of positive emotion words and a moderate level of negative emotion words. Independent of verbal emotion expression, the increasing use of insight, causal, and associated cognitive words over several days of writing is linked to health improvement (Pennebaker, Mayne, & Francis, 1997). That is, the construction of a coherent story works together with the expression of both positive and negative emotions in therapeutic writing. Understanding immune behavior in terms of harmony of purpose among the different self-defining domains of an individual means that we begin to see immunity much more in terms of coherence of self-expression. The immune system functions less as a soldier and more as a gardener—more like a Neighborhood Watch group than a posse. The meaning of events in a psychosocial context may have implications for the meaning of self in an immunological context. Just as our world view is altered during immune-related illness, altering the meaning of potent events in our lives (e.g., by emotional expression or by cognitive changes) may be expected to affect immune activity as well (Booth, 1996, 1999).

ACKNOWLEDGMENTS

Work on this chapter was funded by a University of Auckland Research Committee Grant to Roger J. Booth and a National Institutes of Health grant (No. MH52391) to James W. Pennebaker.

REFERENCES

Bauer, J., Hohagen, F., Gimmel, E., Bruns, F., Lis, S., Krieger, S., Ambach, W., Guthmann, A., Grunze, H., Fritschmontero, R., Weissbach, A., Ganter, U., Frommberger, U., Riemann, D., & Berger, M. (1995). Induction of cytokine synthesis and fever suppresses REM sleep and improves mood in patients with major depression. *Biological Psychiatry, 38*(9), 611–621.

Black, P. H. (1994a). Central nervous system–immune system interactions: Psychoneuroendocrinology of stress and its immune consequences. *Antimicrobial Agents and Chemotherapy, 38*(1), 1–6.

Black, P. H. (1994b). Immune system–central nervous system interactions: Effect and immunomodulatory consequences of immune system mediators on the brain. *Antimicrobial Agents and Chemotherapy, 38*(1), 7–12.

Booth, R. J. (1996). Contrary to Lloyd, the animating idea of psychoneuroimmunology has not lost its heuristic value. *Advances in Mind–Body Medicine, 12*(1), 12–16.

Booth, R. J. (1998). Stress and the immune system. In I. M. Roitt & P. J. Delves (Eds.), *Encyclopedia of immunology* (2nd ed., pp. 2220–2228). London: Academic Press.

Booth, R. J. (1999). Language, self, meaning, and health. *Advances in Mind–Body Medicine, 15*(3), 171–175.

Booth, R. J., & Ashbridge, K. R. (1992). Teleological coherence: Exploring the dimensions of the immune system. *Scandinavian Journal of Immunology, 36*(6), 751–759.

Booth, R. J., & Ashbridge, K. R. (1993). A fresh look at the relationship between the psyche and immune system: Teleological coherence and harmony of purpose. *Advances in Mind–Body Medicine, 9*(2), 4–23.

Booth, R. J., Petrie, K. J., & Pennebaker, J. W. (1997). Changes in circulating lymphocyte numbers following emotional disclosure: Evidence of buffering. *Stress Medicine, 13*(1), 23–29.

Cacioppo, J. T. (1994). Social neuroscience: Autonomic, neuroendocrine, and immune responses to stress. *Psychophysiology, 31*(2), 113–128.

Christensen, A. J., Edwards, D. L., Wiebe, J. S., Benotsch, E. G., McKelvey, L., Andrews, M., & Lubaroff, D. M. (1996). Effect of verbal self-disclosure on natural killer cell activity: Moderating influence of cynical hostility. *Psychosomatic Medicine, 58*(2), 150–155.

Cohen, S., Doyle, W. J., Skoner, D. P., Rabin, B. S., & Gwaltney, J. M. (1997). Social ties and susceptibility to the common cold. *Journal of the American Medical Association, 277*(24), 1940–1944.

Cohen, S., Tyrrell, D. A., & Smith, A. P. (1991). Psychological stress and susceptibility to the common cold. *New England Journal of Medicine, 325*(9), 606–612.

Cohen, S., Tyrrell, D. A., & Smith, A. P. (1993). Negative life events, perceived stress, negative affect, and susceptibility to the common cold. *Journal of Personality and Social Psychology, 64*(1), 131–140.

Dabkowska, M., & Rybakowski, J. K. (1997). Increased allergic reactivity of atopic type in mood disorders and schizophrenia. *European Psychiatry, 12*(5), 249–254.

Dillon, K. M., Minchoff, B., & Baker, K. H. (1985). Positive emotional states and enhancement of the immune system. *International Journal of Psychiatric Medicine, 15*(1), 13–18.

Esterling, B. A., Antoni, M. H., Fletcher, M. A., Margulies, S., & Schneiderman, N. (1994). Emotional disclosure through writing or speaking modulates latent Epstein–Barr virus antibody titers. *Journal of Consulting and Clinical Psychology, 62*(1), 130–140.

Esterling, B. A., Antoni, M. H., Kumar, M., & Schneiderman, N. (1990). Emotional repression, stress disclosure responses, and Epstein–Barr viral capsid antigen titers. *Psychosomatic Medicine, 52*(4), 397–410.

Felten, D. L., Felten, S. Y., Bellinger, D. L., & Madden, K. S. (1993). Fundamental aspects of neural–immune signaling. *Psychotherapy and Psychosomatics, 60*(1), 46–56.

Futterman, A. D., Kemeny, M. E., Shapiro, D., & Fahey, J. L. (1994). Immunological and physiological changes associated with induced positive and negative mood. *Psychosomatic Medicine, 56*(6), 499–511.

Futterman, A. D., Kemeny, M. E., Shapiro, D., Polonsky, W., & Fahey, J. L. (1992). Immunological variability associated with experimentally-induced positive and negative affective states. *Psychological Medicine, 22*(1), 231–238.

Futterman, A. D., Wellisch, D. K., Zighelboim, J., Lunaraines, M., & Weiner, H. (1996). Psychological and immunological reactions of family members to patients undergoing bone marrow transplantation. *Psychosomatic Medicine, 58*(5), 472–480.

Gerritsen, W., Heijnen, C. J., Wiegant, V. M., Bermond, B., & Frijda, N. H. (1996). Experimental social fear: Immunological, hormonal, and autonomic concomitants. *Psychosomatic Medicine, 58*(3), 273–286.

Gilbert, D. G., Stunkard, M. E., Jensen, R. A., Detwiler, F. R. J., & Martinko, J. M. (1996). Effects of exam stress on mood, cortisol, and immune functioning: Influences of neuroticism and smoker–non-smoker status. *Personality and Individual Differences, 21*(2), 235–246.

Glaser, R., Pearson, G. R., Bonneau, R. H., Esterling, B. A., Atkinson, C., & Kiecolt–Glaser, J. K. (1993). Stress and the memory T-cell response to the Epstein–Barr virus in healthy medical students. *Health Psychology, 12*(6), 435–442.

Greenberg, M. A., & Stone, A. A. (1992). Emotional disclosure about traumas and its relation to health: Effects of previous disclosure and trauma severity.

Journal of Personality and Social Psychology, 63(1), 75–84.

Harrington, L., Affleck, G., Urrows, S., Tennen, H., Higgins, P., Zautra, A., & Hoffman, S. (1993). Temporal covariation of soluble interleukin-2 receptor levels, daily stress, and disease activity in rheumatoid arthritis. *Arthritis and Rheumatism, 36*(2), 199–203.

Kemeny, M. E., Weiner, H., Duran, R., Taylor, S. E., Visscher, B., & Fahey, J. L. (1995). Immune system changes after the death of a partner in HIV-positive gay men. *Psychosomatic Medicine, 57*(6), 547–554.

Khansari, D. N., Murgo, A. J., & Faith, R. E. (1990). Effects of stress on the immune system. *Immunology Today, 11*(5), 170–175.

Kiecolt-Glaser, J. K., Malarkey, W. B., Chee, M., Newton, T., Cacioppo, J. T., Mao, H. Y., & Glaser, R. (1993). Negative behavior during marital conflict is associated with immunological down-regulation. *Psychosomatic Medicine, 55*(5), 395–409.

Knapp, P. H., Levy, E. M., Giorgi, R. G., Black, P. H., Fox, B. H., & Heeren, T. C. (1992). Short-term immunological effects of induced emotion. *Psychosomatic Medicine, 54*(2), 133–148.

Labott, S. M., Ahleman, S., Wolever, M. E., & Martin, R. B. (1990). The physiological and psychological effects of the expression and inhibition of emotion. *Behavioral Medicine, 16*(4), 182–189.

Laidlaw, T. M., Booth, R. J., & Large, R. G. (1996). Reduction in skin reactions to histamine after a hypnotic procedure. *Psychosomatic Medicine, 58*(3), 242–248.

Lutgendorf, S. K., Antoni, M. H., Ironson, G., Klimas, N., Fletcher, M. A., & Schneiderman, N. (1997). Cognitive processing style, mood, and immune function following HIV seropositivity notification. *Cognitive Therapy and Research, 21*(2), 157–184.

Lutgendorf, S. K., Antoni, M. H., Kumar, M., & Schneiderman, N. (1994). Changes in cognitive coping strategies predict EBV-antibody titer change following a stressor disclosure induction. *Journal of Psychosomatic Research, 38*(1), 63–78.

Maier, S. F., & Watkins, L. R. (1998). Cytokines for psychologists: Implications of bidirectional immune-to-brain communication for understanding behavior, mood, and cognition. *Psychological Review, 105*(1), 83–107.

Malarkey, W. B., Kiecolt-Glaser, J. K., Pearl, D., & Glaser, R. (1994). Hostile behavior during marital conflict alters pituitary and adrenal hormones. *Psychosomatic Medicine, 56*(1), 41–51.

Martin, R. B., Guthrie, C. A., & Pitts, C. G. (1993). Emotional crying, depressed mood, and secretory immunoglobulin A. *Behavioral Medicine, 19*(3), 111–114.

Mayne, T. J., Oleary, A., McCrady, B., Contrada, R., & Labouvie, E. (1997). The differential effects of acute marital distress on emotional, physiological and immune functions in maritally distressed men and women. *Psychology and Health, 12*(2), 277–288.

Mittwoch-Jaffe, T., Shalit, F., Srendi, B., & Yehuda, S. (1995). Modification of cytokine secretion following mild emotional stimuli. *Neuroreport, 6*(5), 789–792.

Murray, E. J., & Segal, D. L. (1994). Emotional processing in vocal and written expression of feelings about traumatic experiences. *Journal of Trauma and Stress, 7*(3), 391–405.

Pennebaker, J. W. (1993). Putting stress into words: Health, linguistic, and therapeutic implications. *Behaviour Research and Therapy, 31*(6), 539–548.

Pennebaker, J. W. (1997a). *Opening up: The healing power of expressing emotions* (Rev. ed.). New York: Guilford Press.

Pennebaker, J. W. (1997b). Writing about emotional experiences as a therapeutic process. *Psychological Science, 8*, 162–166.

Pennebaker, J. W., Barger, S. D., & Tiebout, J. (1989). Disclosure of traumas and health among Holocaust survivors. *Psychosomatic Medicine, 51*(5), 577–589.

Pennebaker, J. W., Colder, M., & Sharp, L. K. (1990). Accelerating the coping process. *Journal of Personality and Social Psychology, 58*(3), 528–537.

Pennebaker, J. W., Kiecolt-Glaser, J. K., & Glaser, R. (1988). Disclosure of traumas and immune function: Health implications for psychotherapy. *Journal of Consulting and Clinical Psychology, 56*(2), 239–245.

Pennebaker, J. W., Mayne, T. J., & Francis, M. E. (1997). Linguistic predictors of adaptive bereavement. *Journal of Personality and Social Psychology, 72*(4), 863–871.

Pennebaker, J. W., & Susman, J. R. (1988). Disclosure of traumas and psychosomatic processes. *Social Science and Medicine, 26*(3), 327–332.

Petrie, K. J., Booth, R. J., Pennebaker, J. W., Davison, K. P., & Thomas, M. G. (1995). Disclosure of trauma and immune response to a hepatitis B vaccination program. *Journal of Consulting and Clinical Psychology, 63*(5), 787–792.

Ravindran, A. V., Griffiths, J., Merali, Z., & Anisman, H. (1996a). Primary dysthymia: A study of several psychosocial, endocrine and immune correlates. *Journal of Affective Disorders, 40*(1–2), 73–84.

Ravindran, A. V., Griffiths, J., Merali, Z., & Anisman, H. (1996b). Variations of lymphocyte subsets associated with stress in depressive populations. *Psychoneuroendocrinology, 21*(8), 659–671.

Sakic, B., Szechtman, H., Talangbayan, H., Denburg, S. D., Carbotte, R. M., & Denburg, J. A. (1994). Disturbed emotionality in autoimmune MRL-lpr mice. *Physiology and Behavior, 56*(3), 609–617.

Smyth, J. M. (1998). Written emotional expression: Effect sizes, outcome types, and moderating variables. *Journal of Consulting and Clinical Psychology, 66*, 174–184.

Smyth, J. M., Stone, A. A., Hurewitz, A., & Kaell, A. (1999). Effects of writing about stressful experience on symptom reduction in patients with asthma or rheumatoid arthritis: A randomized trial. *Journal of the American Medical Association, 281*(14), 1304–1309.

Solomon, G. F., Segerstrom, S. C., Grohr, P., Kemeny, M., & Fahey, J. (1997). Shaking up immunity: Psychological and immunologic changes after a natural disaster. *Psychosomatic Medicine, 59*(1), 114–127.

Sternberg, E. M. (1997). Emotions and disease: From balance of humors to balance of molecules. *Nature Medicine, 3*(3), 264–267.

Stone, A. A., Marco, C. A., Cruise, C. E., Cox, D. S., & Neale, J. M. (1996). Are stress-induced immunological changes mediated by mood?: A closer look at how both desirable and undesirable daily events influence SigA antibody. *International Journal of Behavioral Medicine, 3*(1), 1–13.

Theorell, T., Blomkvist, V., Jonsson, H., Schulman, S., Berntorp, E., & Stigendal, L. (1995). Social support and the development of immune function in human immunodeficiency virus infection. *Psychosomatic Medicine, 57*(1), 32–36.

Valdimarsdottir, H. B., & Bovbjerg, D. H. (1997). Positive and negative mood: Association with natural killer cell activity. *Psychology and Health, 12*(3), 319–327.

Watkins, A. D. (1994). Hierarchical cortical control of neuroimmunomodulatory pathways. *Neuropathology and Applied Neurobiology, 20*(5), 423–431.

Watkins, A. D. (1995). Perceptions, emotions and immunity: An integrated homeostatic network. *Quarterly Journal of Medicine, 88*(4), 283–294.

Watson, D., & Pennebaker, J. W. (1989). Health complaints, stress, and distress: Exploring the central role of negative affectivity. *Psychological Review, 96*(2), 234–254.

Wittling, W., & Pfluger, M. (1990). Neuroendocrine hemisphere asymmetries: Salivary cortisol secretion during lateralized viewing of emotion-related and neutral films. *Brain and Cognition, 14*(2), 243–265.

Zachariae, R., Bjerring, P., Zachariae, C., Arendt Nielsen, L., Nielsen, T., Eldrup, E., Larsen, C. S., & Gotliebsen, K. (1991). Monocyte chemotactic activity in sera after hypnotically-induced emotional states. *Scandinavian Journal of Immunology, 34*(1), 71–79.

Zakowski, S. G., McAllister, C. G., Deal, M., & Baum, A. (1992). Stress, reactivity, and immune function in healthy men. *Health Psychology, 11*(4), 223–232.

Zeier, H., Brauchli, P., & Joller Jemelka, H. I. (1996). Effects of work demands on immunoglobulin A and cortisol in air traffic controllers. *Biological Psychology, 42*(3), 413–423.

PART VII

SELECT EMOTIONS

CHAPTER 36

Fear and Anxiety: Evolutionary, Cognitive, and Clinical Perspectives

Arne Öhman

Very softly down the glade runs a waiting, watching shade,
And the whisper spreads and widens far and near;
And the sweat is on thy brow, for he passes even now—
He is Fear, O Little Hunter, he is Fear!

On thy knees and draw the bow; bid the shrilling arrow go;
In the empty, mocking thicket plunge the spear;
But thy hands are loosed and weak, and the blood has left thy cheek—
It is Fear, O Little Hunter, it is Fear!

Now the spates are banked and deep; now the footless boulders leap—
Now the lightning shows each littlest leaf-rib clear—
But thy throat is shut and dried, and thy heart against thy side
Hammers: Fear, O Little Hunter—this is Fear!
(Kipling, 1895/1983, pp. 176–177)

Fear and anxiety provide recurrent themes for humans pondering their existential predicament. For example, in a theological version, anxiety has been interpreted as resulting from "divine disconnection"—the experience of being separated from God's grace. In existential philosophy, on the other hand, the distress of anxiety is seen as something positive—as the mark of a person exercising his or her freedom and responsibility to choose an authentic life. In a clinical context, the vicissitude of anxiety has been understood as the key to the dynamics of psychopathology, whether it is conceptualized in terms of a learnable drive supporting escape and avoidance, or as the target of psychologically distorting defense mechanisms.

The ubiquity and controversial status of anxiety have made it a central topic for research and reflection. Thus there is a truly voluminous literature on the psychology of anxiety (see, e.g., Barlow, 1988; Rapee, 1996; Tuma & Maser, 1985), only a tiny fraction of which can be represented in this chapter. Its point of departure is that fear and anxiety are emotional phenomena, the elucidation of which has much to gain from being informed by the psychology of emotion. Conversely, empirical data on the clinical phenomena of fear and anxiety provide a rich testing ground for theories of emotion. My first purpose is to describe the emotional phenomena of fear and anxiety from a clinical perspective. The second part of the chapter is devoted to a discussion of the theoretical structures that are needed to understand the phenomena of anxiety. The concluding section discusses some of the implications of this theoretical perspective.

THE PHENOMENA OF ANXIETY AND FEAR

The Basic Components of Anxiety and Fear

Describing accurately the experiential side of emotion is a privilege of poets. From a clinical perspective, it has been described as "an ineffable and unpleasant feeling of foreboding" (Lader & Marks, 1973) ("Very softly down the glade runs a waiting, watching shade" in the Kipling poem), and it is associated with bodily changes including both somatic ("thy hands are loosed and weak") and autonomic ("thy throat is shut and dried, and thy heart against thy side/Hammers") manifestations. The relevant behavioral dimensions are escape and avoidance (e.g., Lang, 1984; Lang, Bradley, & Cuthbert, 1997). These three aspects of fear and anxiety—subjective experience as reflected in verbal reports, physiological responses, and avoidance behavior—should not be taken as alternative indicators of an inferred unitary state of anxiety, presumably isomorphic with experience, but as dissociable components of a loosely coupled anxiety response (Lang, 1968, 1978).

Distinguishing Fear and Anxiety

According to the glossary of the *Diagnostic and Statistical Manual of Mental Disorders,* fourth edition (DSM-IV; American Psychiatric Association [APA], 1994), the term "anxiety" denotes "apprehensive anticipation of future danger or misfortune accompanied by a feeling of dysphoria or somatic symptoms of tension" (p. 764). Fear differs from anxiety primarily in having an identifiable eliciting stimulus. An important difference between the two concepts, therefore, is that anxiety is often "prestimulus" (i.e., anticipatory to [more or less real] threatening stimuli), whereas fear is "poststimulus" (i.e., elicited by a defined fear stimulus). How-

ever, as eloquently argued by Epstein (1972), external stimuli are insufficient to distinguish fear and anxiety. He concluded that fear is related to coping behavior, particularly escape and avoidance. However, when coping attempts fail (e.g., because the situation is uncontrollable), fear is turned into anxiety. In Epstein's view, then, *"fear* is an avoidance motive. If there were no restraints, internal or external, fear would support the action of flight. *Anxiety* can be defined as unresolved fear, or, alternatively, as a state of undirected arousal following the perception of threat" (Epstein, 1972, p. 311). This is the distinction between fear and anxiety that I adhere to in this chapter, when a distinction is needed.

Varieties of Fear/Anxiety

Fear/anxiety may be focused on external sources, as in phobias, or it may be situationally unfocused, as in free-floating anxiety. Furthermore, as originally argued by Klein (1981) in an influential reconceptualization of anxiety, fear/anxiety may come in episodic panic attacks (i.e., as sudden emotional surges dominated by physical symptoms, sometimes with and sometimes without clear precipitants), or it may be a constant mental preoccupation with more or less reasonable threats and dangers. Even though the distinct nature of these two forms of anxiety has been called into question (e.g., Margraf, Ehlers, & Roth, 1986a, 1986b), the notion of two basic forms of anxiety has had an important impact on research, diagnosis, and treatment of anxiety.

As these descriptions imply, fear/anxiety may be regarded both as an emotional state, evoked in a particular context and having a limited duration, and as a personality trait, characterizing an individual across time and situations (e.g., Spielberger, 1972; Rapee, 1991). The differences between clinical and normal fear/anxiety include that the former is more recurrent and persistent; that its intensity is far above what is reasonable, given the objective danger or threat; that it tends to paralyze individuals and make them helpless and unable to cope; and that it results in impeded psychosocial or physiological functioning (e.g., Lader & Marks, 1973).

Factor-analytic work on both observed and self-reported symptoms of fear/anxiety agree in suggesting a division between "somatic overreactivity" (as manifested in, e.g., sweating, flushing, shallow breathing, and reports of heart palpitations, intestinal discomforts, and aches and pains) and "cognitive or psychic anxiety" (including, e.g., intrusive and unwanted thoughts, worrying, ruminations, restlessness, and sometimes feelings of muscle tension) (e.g., Buss, 1962; Fenz & Epstein, 1965; Schalling, Cronholm, & Åsberg, 1975).

THE SITUATIONAL CONTEXT OF FEAR AND ANXIETY

Traumatic Situations

Extreme danger jeopardizing one's life (or the lives of close kin) elicits intense fright and may have long-lasting consequences in the form of posttraumatic stress disorder (PTSD). Trauma may also involve natural catastrophes, such as floods or hurricanes destroying one's home or community; or it may involve seeing others being seriously injured or killed as a result of an accident or physical violence. One may be exposed to the trauma alone, as in a rape or an assault, or in a group, as in military combat. If the trauma results in PTSD, the traumatic event is persistently reexperienced (e.g., in the form of "flashbacks"); stimuli or events associated with the trauma are avoided; and the person feels generally numbed with regard to emotions. Common anxiety symptoms experienced by persons suffering from PTSD include sleep and concentration difficulties, irritability or anger outbursts, hypervigilance, and exaggerated startle. Some events, such as torture, frequently result in PTSD, whereas others, such as natural disasters or car accidents, only occasionally result in the disorder (APA, 1994).

Commonly Feared and Potentially Phobic Situations

Survival considerations, either contemporary or in an evolutionary perspective, are relevant for most situational dimensions of human fears. Arrindell, Pickersgill, Merckelbach, Ardon, and Cornet (1991) provided an extensive review of studies factor-analyzing questionnaire data on self-reported fear. After applying strict methodological criteria, they accepted 25 out of 38 published studies for their own analysis. They found that the 194 factors and components identified in these studies could be classified into a structure involving four factors. The first factor was "fears about interpersonal events or situations." It included fears of criticism and social interaction, rejection, conflicts, and evaluation, but also interpersonal aggression and display of sexual and aggressive scenes. The second factor was "fears related to death, injuries, illness, blood, and surgical procedures." This factor had a quite heterogeneous content, incorporating fears of illness, diseases, and disabilities; complaints about physical and mental problems; fears of suicide, homosexuality, and sexual inadequacy; and fears of losing control. Finally, it incorporated fears of contamination, syncope, or other threats to physical health. The third factor, "fear of animals," included common domestic animals; other small, often harmless animals; and creeping and crawling animals such as insects and reptiles. Finally, "agoraphobic fears" was the fourth factor. It involved fear of entering public places (such as stores or shopping malls) and crowds, but also fear of closed spaces (such as elevators, tunnels, theaters, or churches). Furthermore, it involved fears of traveling alone in trains or buses, crossing bridges, and entering open spaces.

All these four factors represent situations of relevance for human evolution (see Seligman, 1971). Human history is replete with examples of how social conflicts that have escalated out of control provide a potentially deadly danger, not to speak of the social threat in terms of the defeat and humiliation they may involve (Öhman, 1986). Thus it comes as no surprise that social interactions are sometimes feared. For fear of death and illness, and associated bodily conditions, there is no need to elaborate the potential survival threat. Although many animals are friendly and sought as companions, there is no question that animals as predators have provided recurrent threats in the evolution of humankind, and it is reasonable to give reptiles a privileged position as the prototypical predators (Öhman, 1986; Öhman, Dimberg, & Öst, 1985). Finally, agoraphobic fears center on the lack of security inherent in separation from safe bases and kin, and the avoidance of places associated with panic and feelings of discomfort.

It is immediately seen that the factors isolated by Arrindell et al. (1991) correspond to four prominent types of phobia: social phobia, blood phobia, animal phobia, and agoraphobia. Furthermore, the second factor incorporates fears often encountered in panic disorder, such as fears or syncope, and in obsessive–compulsive disorder, such as contamination.

Departing from a preparedness perspective on phobias (Seligman, 1971), my colleagues and I (Öhman et al., 1985) have argued that these fear factors may be taken to reflect basic behavioral systems, which have been adaptively shaped by evolution. In particular, we have suggested that social fears resulted from a dominance–submissiveness system, the adaptive function of which was to promote social order by means of facilitating the establishment of dominance hierarchies. Animal fears, on the other hand, are attributed to a predatory defense system, originating in the fear of reptiles by early mammals, and prompting rapid escape from potential predators.

These basically adaptive systems are held to be compromised into producing social and animal phobias when the fear response they engender becomes conditioned to stimuli that actually are harmless in the ecology of modern humans. The basic argument is that evolution has equipped humans with a propensity to associate fear with situations that threatened the survival of their ancestors (Seligman, 1971). The propensity must be based in the genes, and thus genetically based variation in phobias can be expected. This is supported by data from behavioral genetics, which suggest that animal phobias result from the interaction between a genetic component common to all phobias and specific environmental influences (Kendler, Neale, Kessler, Heath, & Eaves, 1992). Hence, although humans in general are prepared to acquire some fears (e.g., snake fears) easily, some individuals must be more prepared than others. Furthermore, whether a phobia is developed or not depends on environmental exposure. We have tested these ideas (see reviews by Dimberg & Öhman, 1996; McNally, 1987; Öhman, 1993) in autonomic conditioning experiments primarily comparing acquisition and resistance to extinction of skin conductance conditioning to potentially phobic (e.g., snakes, spiders, angry faces) and neutral (e.g., flowers, mushrooms, neutral faces, or friendly faces) stimuli. The general, but not invariable, finding has been that responses conditioned to potentially phobic stimuli show enhanced resistance to extinction, compared to responses conditioned to neutral stimuli (Dimberg & Öhman, 1996; McNally, 1987; Öhman, 1993). Examples of data on skin conductance responses from a single cue conditioning paradigm are given in Figure 36.1.

Panic Stimuli

Biologically oriented theorists of panic (e.g., Klein, 1981; Sheehan, 1982) have suggested that panic attacks are spontaneous or endogenously originated. Thus such theorists have held the lack of an eliciting stimulus to be one of the essential characteristics of panic. However, when prospectively assessed, naturally occurring panic attacks typically appear to have precipitants, such as arguments with family members or problems at work (Freedman, Ianni, Ettedgui, & Puthezhath, 1985) or ideations of threat and fear (Hibbert, 1984). The stimuli that elicit panic may be primarily internal—for example, changes in heart rate (Pauli et al., 1991) or other bodily symptoms. Persons suffering from panic disorder, furthermore, appear both to be more sensitive to such stimuli, and to rate them as more dangerous, than controls (Ehlers, 1993). Bodily stimuli, however, are insufficient to produce panic. According to an influential formulation by Clark (1986, 1988), it is only when the bodily stimulation is combined with a catastrophic cognitive interpretation (e.g., an impending heart attack or suffoca-

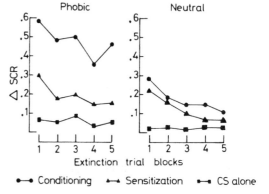

FIGURE 36.1. Extinction of skin conductance responses (SCRs) in subjects who were conditioned to potentially phobic stimuli (pictures of snakes; left panel) or neutral stimuli (pictures of houses; right panel) by receiving them paired with electric shock (unconditioned stimulus). Control subjects had the pictures and the shocks unpaired ("Sensitization") or were only exposed to pictures ("CS alone"). It is obvious that potentially phobic conditioned stimuli resulted in much larger resistance to extinction than did neutral conditioned stimuli. Data from Öhman, Eriksson, and Olofsson (1975).

tion) that panic is elicited. Thus cognitive interpretations may create a vicious circle: The catastrophic interpretation results in more intensely perceived threat and more apprehension; further bodily sensations feed further catastrophic interpretations; and so on (see Pauli et al., 1991; Rapee, 1993). If the symptoms are not given a catastrophic interpretation, however, they may not be associated with fear but with interpretations in terms of bodily problems, as in "panic without fear" (Kushner & Beitman, 1990). In agreement with the cognitive perspective, studies show that the most consistent symptomatic differences between patients with panic disorder and patients with other anxiety disorders pertain not to symptoms but to interpretation of symptoms, such as fears of dying, going crazy, or losing control (Barlow et al., 1985; Borden & Turner, 1989; Rapee, Sanderson, McCauley, & Di Nardo, 1992).

This review suggests that the phasic responses of increased state anxiety seen in phobia, PTSD, and panic typically have identifiable eliciting stimuli. Indeed, panic, phobic fear, and the intense anxiety exhibited by PTSD patients reminded of their trauma appear to result from the activation of one and the same underlying anxiety response. This anxiety response may profitably be viewed as an

> adaptation that evolved to facilitate flight from life-threatening danger. The sudden increase in the rate and strength of cardiac contractions sends extra blood to the muscles, while the gut feels empty and the skin blanches and becomes cool as blood is shunted elsewhere. Rapid and deep breathing increases blood oxygen content. Cooling sweat is secreted, muscles tighten and tremble, and the endocrine system prepares for catabolism (Nesse, Cameron, Curtis, McCann, & Huber-Smith, 1984; Mason, 1968). Intense mental activity is focused on planning escape. When the overwhelming urge to flee is translated into action, all effort is concentrated on escape. The direction of flight is towards home and trusted kin, a behavioral pattern typical of animals that rely on homes and kins for protection. (Nesse, 1987, p. 77S)

Viewed from this evolutionary perspective, it is not the fear/anxiety response in itself that is malfunctional and maladaptive, but the fact that it is triggered in a malfunctional context, as in phobias (see Öhman et al., 1985), or that it may have a dysfunctionally low threshold, as in panic (Klein, 1981, 1993; Nesse, 1987). Furthermore, the full response may be more or less complete-

ly triggered in different situations, depending upon the situational context and the overt defense responses it affords (in terms of, e.g., flight, attack, or submission). For example, active escape may be much more functional in animal phobia than in social phobia, which may account for some of the differences between these two types of disorders (Öhman et al., 1985).

THEORETICAL PERSPECTIVE: THE ROLE OF UNCONSCIOUS PROCESSES IN ANXIETY AND FEAR

According to this review, fear/anxiety is rooted in defense responses, which have evolved because they were functional devices to keep people away from potentially deadly contexts. Furthermore, these defenses have been tied to situations involving survival threats, either directly or indirectly, through evolutionary considerations. This evolutionarily inspired stimulus–response analysis, however, is by necessity incomplete, because it does not specify the mechanisms whereby a fear stimulus evokes a response.

A Functional Perspective on Anxiety

Evolved defense responses are of little use unless they are appropriately elicited. To function adequately, they require a perceptual system that can effectively locate threat. Clearly, false negatives (i.e., failing to elicit defense to a potentially hazardous stimulus) are more evolutionarily costly than false positives (i.e., eliciting the response to a stimulus that is in effect harmless). Whereas the former are potentially lethal, the latter, even though distressing to the individual, merely represent wasted energy. In an evolutionary perspective, therefore, it is likely that perceptual systems are biased toward discovering threat. Indeed, this provides an evolutionary reason for why there are anxiety disorders. To guarantee effective defense when life is at stake, the system "plays it safe" by sometimes evoking defense in what turn out to be nonthreatening contexts. Responses of the latter type, of course, seem unnecessary and unreasonable, and may be understood as "irrational anxiety" by both observers and the person. Hence, if anxiety is not (as claimed by existential philosophers) the price for the freedom to choose an authentic life, in an evolutionary perspective it may have been a price paid for continued evolution.

Effective defense must be quickly activated. Consequently, there is a premium for early detection of threat. Furthermore, threat stimuli must be detected wherever they occur in the perceptual field, independently of the current direction of attention. Coupled with the bias toward false positives, these factors mean that discovery of threat is better based on a quick, superficial analysis of potential threat stimuli wherever they are than on an effortful, detailed, and complete extraction of the meaning of one particular stimulus. The functional, evolutionary perspective, therefore, suggests that the burden of threat discovery should be placed on early, parallel-processing perceptual mechanisms, which define threat on the basis of relatively simple stimulus features.

The neuroarchitecture of such a system has been described by LeDoux (1990b, 1996) in an impressive series of studies of the neural control of auditorily elicited conditioned emotional responses in the rat. He and his coworkers have demonstrated a direct neural link from auditory nuclei (medial geniculate body) in the thalamus to the "significance evaluator" and "fear effector system" in the lateral and central amygdala, respectively. This monosynaptic link provides immediate information to the amygdala of gross features of emotionally relevant auditory stimuli. It bypasses the traditionally emphasized thalamo-cortical pathway, which gives full meaning to the stimulus, and the cortico-amygdala link, which is presumed to activate emotion. It is described as a "quick and dirty" transmission route: It "probably does not tell the amygdala much about the stimulus, certainly not much about Gestalt or object properties of the stimulus, but it at least informs the amygdala that the sensory receptors of a given modality have been activated and that a significant stimulus may be present" (LeDoux, 1990a, p. 172), so that the amygdala can start early activation of defense responses. This system is explicitly postulated to be adaptively biased toward false positives rather than false negatives. This is because it is less costly to abort falsely initialized defense responses than to fail to elicit defense when the threat is real. This system provides a neural basis for Zajonc's (1980) somewhat startling slogan that "affect precedes inference" in the generation of emotion (LeDoux, 1989).

Automatic Information-Processing Routines to Discover Threat

Elsewhere (Öhman, 1986, 1992; 1996; Öhman, Flykt, & Lundqvist, 2000), I have developed a theoretical perspective on the generation of emotion that is consistent with the functional scenario discussed above. Originating in a model of orienting response activation (Öhman, 1979), the perspective rests heavily on a distinction between "automatic" and "controlled" or "strategic" information processing (e.g., Posner, 1978; Schneider, Dumais, & Shiffrin, 1984; Shiffrin & Schneider, 1977) to argue that many perceptual channels can be automatically and simultaneously monitored for potential threat. When stimulus events implying threat are located by the automatic system, attention is drawn to the stimulus, as the control for its further analysis is transferred to the strategic level of information processing. The switch of control from automatic to strategic information processing is associated with activation of physiological responses, particularly the orienting response (Öhman, 1979).

Automatic processing can thus work in parallel across many different sensory channels without loss in efficiency. It is involuntary, in the sense that it is hard to suppress consciously once it is initiated; it does not interfere with focal attention; it is not easily distracted by attended activities; and it is typically not available for conscious introspection (Schneider et al., 1984). Controlled or strategic information processing, on the other hand, is governed by intentions. It is resource- or capacity-limited, in the sense that interference is marked between strategically controlled tasks; it works sequentially rather than in parallel; it requires effort; and it is more readily available to consciousness (Schneider et al., 1984).

This conceptualization suggests that the automatic sensory monitoring processes have a capacity for sensory events vastly exceeding that of the controlled or strategic processes. Thus they can keep track of a large number of channels, only one of which can be selected for strategic processing. Sensory messages have to compete for access to the strategic processing channel for complete sensory analysis. Given the survival contingencies implied by potential threats in the external and internal environment, it is a natural assumption that stimuli implying some degree of threat should have selection priority for strategic processing. This theoretical analysis suggests that anxiety and fear may be activated as a correlate to recruitment of defense responses after merely unconscious analyses of stimuli. As a result of these analyses, threatening stimuli are selected for further conscious, controlled processing. Because they are located by automatic perceptual mechanisms, the person is not necessarily aware of the eliciting stimuli, which may result in episodes of anxiety. Thus what appear from the inside to be "spontaneous" episodes of anxiety may in fact be the results of unconscious stimulation.

Experimental Test of the Model: Unconscious Activation of Phobias

Backward Masking

The central theoretical tenet of this model is that responses of anxiety and fear can be elicited after only a preliminary, unconscious analysis of the stimulus. Its empirical examination, therefore, requires a means of presenting fear stimuli outside of the subject's awareness. Such a means is provided by backward masking. Seminal work by Marcel (1983) demonstrated that subjects appeared to process backwardly masked target stimuli for semantic meaning, even though the intervals between targets and masks were selected to preclude conscious perception of the targets. Backward masking has been regarded as the potentially most fruitful avenue to unconscious perception (Holender, 1986; Öhman, 1999). Thus if backwardly masked fear stimuli were presented to fearful subjects, and still elicited physiological responses suggesting activation of fear/anxiety even though conscious recognition could be ruled out, the theoretical notions advanced here would receive experimental support.

Unconscious Phobic Responses

A colleague and I reported an experiment designed to test this basic assertion (Öhman & Soares, 1994). We selected research participants who feared (above the 95th percentile in the distribution) snakes but not spiders (below the 50th percentile), or vice versa. Participants in the control group feared neither stimulus. In the experiment, participants were exposed to series of pictures of snakes and spiders, with pictures of flowers and mushrooms serving as controls, while skin conductance responses were measured. In the first series, presentations

were effectively masked (see Öhman & Soares, 1993) by similar pictures that had been randomly cut to pieces, randomly reassembled, and rephotographed. Thus they were grossly similar to the target stimuli in colors and texture, but they lacked any recognizable central object. A pilot experiment using a forced-choice recognition procedure ascertained that both fearful and nonfearful participants consistently failed to identify the target with the masking parameters used. The masks interrupted presentation of the target stimuli after 30 milliseconds of exposure and remained on for 100 milliseconds during the masked presentation series. In the following series of presentations, the stimuli were presented unmasked. After these series, the participants rated the stimuli for arousal, valence, and control/dominance during separately presented masked and nonmasked rating series.

The upper panels of Figure 36.2 show skin conductance responses to masked (a) and nonmasked (b) presentations of the stimuli. It is evident that the fearful participants responded specifically to their feared stimulus, but did not differ from controls for the other stimulus categories, independently of masking. This enhanced responding to the feared stimulus cannot be attributed to conscious perception. Nevertheless, parallel data were obtained for all three rating dimensions, which suggests that some aspect of the masked stimulation became indirectly available to the conscious system (maybe through bodily feedback?). Thus the fearful participants rated themselves as more disliking, more aroused, and less in control when exposed to masked presentations of their feared stimulus.

The lower panels of Figure 36.2 show data from spontaneous skin conductance responses, a measure closely related to generalized anxiety (e.g., Lader, 1967). Again, the results show enhanced responding in the fearful groups compared to the control group, independently of masking. Thus unconscious exposure to the feared stimuli had effects on anxiety outlasting the specific responses to the stimuli. In other words, it is suggested that nonaware exposure to the feared stimulus resulted in generalized anxiety among fearful subjects.

Conditioning of Unconscious Effects

The data presented in Figure 36.2 provide strong support for the notion of anxiety as elicitable after only preliminary, preattentive, auto-

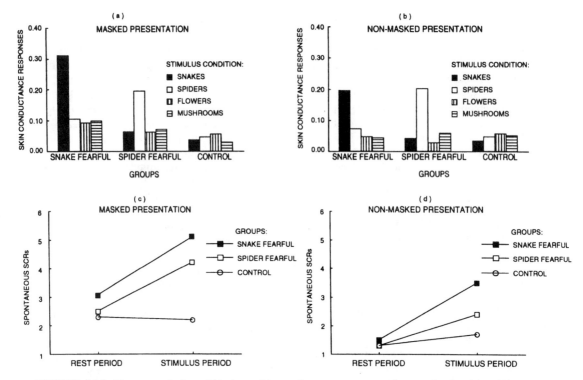

FIGURE 36.2. Upper panels (a and b) show skin conductance responses from snake-fearful, spider-fearful, and nonfearful controls to effectively masked (a) and nonmasked (b) presentations of pictures of snakes, spiders, flowers, and mushrooms. Fearful subjects showed elevated responding to their feared stimulus even if it was prevented from entering conscious perception by backward masking (a). Lower panels (c and d) show spontaneous skin conductance responses (SCRs) in the intervals between stimulation. Whereas controls did not change from rest during stimulation, the fearful subjects showed enhanced spontaneous responding, suggesting that they became anxious after both masked (c) and nonmasked (d) presentations of feared stimuli. Data from Öhman and Soares (1994).

matic, and unconscious analyses of the stimulus. One question raised by these findings concerns the origin of this effect: What is the mechanism whereby fearful subjects acquire these preattentively controlled responses to feared stimuli? Addressing this question, we (Öhman & Soares, 1993; Soares & Öhman, 1993a, 1993b) demonstrated that Pavlovian conditioning to unmasked presentations of fear-relevant stimuli (snakes and spiders) in nonfearful individuals resulted in conditioned skin conductance responses that survived backward masking. Conditioning to fear-irrelevant stimuli (flowers and mushrooms), on the other hand, resulted in more elusive responses that were abolished by masking. Similar data were obtained for another class of fear-relevant stimuli, angry faces, which were masked by neutral faces (Esteves, Dimberg, & Öhman, 1994; Parra, Esteves, Flykt, & Öhman, 1997). Furthermore, we (Esteves, Dimberg, Parra, & Öhman, 1994) reported that skin conductance responses could be conditioned to masked fear-relevant, but not to masked fear-irrelevant, stimuli. That is, after conditioning to masked angry or happy faces, subjects showed enhanced responding to subsequent nonmasked presentations of angry but not happy faces. Similarly, we (Öhman & Soares, 1998) demonstrated unconscious conditioning to masked snakes or spiders, but not to masked flowers or mushrooms. Thus not only could emotional responses be elicited to masked stimuli, but they could also be learned to such stimuli, provided that they were evolutionarily fear-relevant.

I have concluded (Öhman, 1992) that these types of preattentive effects are best interpreted in terms of the ability of biologically fear-relevant stimuli to directly activate physiological responses when such a stimulus automatically captures attention. Thus, consistent with LeDoux's (1990b) findings, the results can more plausibly be attributed to some gross and relatively simple features of the stimuli than to a complete analysis of their meaning. In further agreements with LeDoux's (1996) findings, we (Morris, Öhman, & Dolan, 1998), using brain imaging techniques, were able to demonstrate specific activation of the amygdala by masked conditioned angry faces in human subjects. Moreover, in further confirmation of LeDoux's (1996) tenets, we (Morris, Öhman, & Dolan, 1999) showed that nonconscious activation of the amygdala did not require cortical processing of the eliciting stimulus.

The theory, with its supporting database (Öhman & Soares, 1993, 1994, 1998; Soares & Öhman, 1993a, 1993b), provides a good account of animal phobias, which may be extended to social phobias (Dimberg & Öhman, 1996; Esteves, Dimberg, & Öhman, 1994; Esteves, Dimberg, Parra, & Öhman, 1994; Morris et al., 1998, 1999; Parra et al., 1997). Because phobic stimuli have direct, automatic access to the physiological arousal system, individuals with phobias perceive their bodies in full-swing responding when they consciously locate a phobic stimulus in the surroundings. Consequently, the fear is experienced as inevitable and uncontrollable. This account therefore provides a viable explanation for the "irrationality of phobias"—that is, the dissociation between conscious considerations and fear that is typical of phobias (APA, 1994).

Processing Biases in Anxiety

There is a large literature (see reviews by Mathews & MacLeod, 1994; Mogg & Bradley, 1998) on cognitive functions in anxiety, which documents that anxiety is associated with an attentional bias for focusing on threatening information in the surroundings. As Mathews (1990) has put it, "anxiety and worry are associated with an automatic processing bias, initiated prior to awareness, but serving to attract attention to environmental threat cues, and thus facilitating the acquisition of threatening information" (p. 462). This view is consistent with the functional perspective on anxiety presented above.

Selective Attention Bias in High-Anxiety Persons

To test this theory, Mathews and MacLeod (1986) had patients with generalized anxiety disorder and controls verbally "shadow" (read aloud) stories presented to one ear (the attended

channel), while series of unconnected words were presented to the other ear (the rejected channel). At the same time, they were required to respond to visually presented probes by pressing a key. Some series of the words presented to the rejected channel involved threat (e.g., "injury," "disaster," "disease," "accident"), whereas others served as emotionally neutral controls, matched for word length and frequency of occurrence in the language. When questioned after the experiment, the subjects typically remained unaware that words had been presented in the rejected channel, and they did not perform above chance levels in forced-choice recognition tests on threat and control words. Nevertheless, anxious subjects slowed their reaction times to the probes when they occurred with threat as compared to nonthreat words in the rejected channel, whereas the controls did not discriminate these conditions. Similar data were reported by MacLeod, Mathews, and Tata (1986), using a dot probe task in which reaction time probes replaced threatening and nonthreatening words at different locations on a computer screen. According to their results, patients with generalized anxiety disorder showed faster reaction times when the probes replaced a threat word than when they replaced a neutral word (indicating attention to the former), whereas the opposite pattern was shown by the controls.

This basic result was replicated by MacLeod and Mathews (1988) for medical students high and low in trait anxiety. They were tested twice, in periods with or without examination stress, to examine the relative contributions of trait and state anxiety to the previously demonstrated attentional biases. Trait anxiety was related to the bias effect, but it also interacted with state anxiety. As examination time approached and state anxiety increased, high-trait-anxious subjects showed an increased bias to respond faster to examination-relevant threat words, whereas low-trait-anxious subjects showed an increased bias away from these words. Thus trait anxiety was associated with a general attentional bias in the direction of discovering threat, and with rising state anxiety this bias became more specifically geared toward threats associated with the anticipated stressful events. Low-trait-anxious subjects, on the other hand, in general showed a bias away from threat, and as their state anxiety rose before examination, this avoidance bias came to center on threat associated with the impending stress.

To examine the potential preattentive locus of the bias, MacLeod and Rutherford (1992) used a masked version of the Stroop color–word interference task. The latency of color naming of words was examined in participants high and low in trait anxiety, and on half of the trials, the words were masked by letter fragments of the same color. High-trait-anxious participants under examination stress were slower to color-name masked threatening words than were low-trait-anxious participants. On nonmasked trials, on the other hand, both groups showed a tendency specifically to avoid exam-relevant threat words. In other words, stressed highly anxious subjects showed a preattentive generalized bias toward threat, whereas at the conscious, strategic level, they tended specifically to avoid threat related to the source of stress (i.e., the examination). These results have been confirmed by Mogg, Bradley, Williams, and Mathews (1993) and Bradley, Mogg, Millar, and White (1995), using the masked Stroop paradigm, and by Mogg, Bradley, and Williams (1995), using the dot probe task of Mathews et al. (1986). These latter studies, however, examined patients with generalized anxiety disorder and reported an anxiety-driven bias for threat with both masked and nonmasked stimuli, which stand in contrast to the masked generalized bias for, and unmasked specific avoidance of, threatening words reported with highly anxious students by MacLeod and Rutherford (1992). Thus patients with generalized anxiety disorder may show both automatic and strategic vigilance for threat, whereas high-trait-anxious students, even though automatically biased for threat, may be able to cope with anxiety by strategic avoidance of threat stimuli once they become aware of the threatening word content.

Consistent with the data on psychophysiological responding to masked stimuli, this set of data indicates that mildly threatening stimuli capture attention, independently of its current focus. As attention is then automatically switched to the threat, there is competition for processing resources, which is manifested as impeded performance in ongoing, resource-demanding tasks. We (Öhman, Flykt, & Esteves, 1999) combined the two approaches by examining attentional selectivity for pictorial stimuli in a visual search paradigm. The task of the participants was to decide whether a discrepant category was present in a visual display composed of many pictures. Nonfearful participants were faster to locate a discrepant snake or spider among distractors of flowers and mushrooms than vice versa. Furthermore, finding the snake or spider was independent of its location in the display and the number of distractors, which suggests that they were automatically located. This was not true for finding flowers or mushrooms against backgrounds of snakes or spiders. The efficiency in searching for fear-relevant stimuli was further enhanced in subjects selected to be fearful of snakes or spiders. Thus the type of stimuli previously shown to automatically elicit psychophysiological responses also automatically captured attentional in a visual search task, and the attentional bias was enhanced when the target stimulus actually elicited fear.

The Role of Expectancy and Controlled Processing in Anxiety

So far, all the explanatory burden in the discussion of mechanisms of anxiety has been put on early, automatic, and preattentive processing. However, it is clear that these mechanisms are as insufficient to account for anxiety as they are to account for any emotional phenomenon. Theories of emotion have traditionally stressed the role of controlled processing in the generation of emotion (e.g., Lazarus, Kanner, & Folkman, 1980; Mandler, 1975, 1984; Schachter & Singer, 1962). With regard to anxiety, for example, it was noted in the discussion of the stimulus conditions for panic that bodily cues did not elicit attacks unless they were coupled with catastrophic interpretations (e.g., Clark, 1986, 1988). Thus, to approach a complete mechanism-oriented account of anxiety, it is necessary to consider controlled or strategic information processing.

No Panic with Explanation of Symptoms

Anecdotal data reported by Rapee (1986) illustrate the role of cognitions in panic. Although 80% of his patients with panic disorder reported a marked similarity between panic and the symptoms they experienced after hyperventilation, none of them panicked. When questioned, they attributed the lack of panic attacks to the fact that they knew what was causing the symptoms, and that they were in a safe place in case they should panic. Rapee, Mattick, and Murrell (1986) formally tested the hypothesis that a readily available explanation for bodily symptoms would save such patients from panic attacks. They compared patients with panic disorder and social phobia who were given an explanation or no explanation for the physiological effects of CO_2 inhalation. The groups did not differ in reported symptoms, regardless of the explanation given. However, patients with panic disorder who were given no explanation reported more intense symptoms, more intense panic, and more similarity to a "natural" panic attack. In addition, they reported a higher frequency of catastrophic thoughts (e.g., "I am going to die"). The explanation given had no effect on the patients with social phobia, who experienced little panic in any of the explanation conditions. Thus these results show that patients with panic disorder are more vulnerable to anxiety attacks than patients with social phobia when given CO_2 inhalation, and that a readily available explanation of the symptoms can abort the panic attacks. Relating to one of the classical issues in the study of emotion (see Schachter & Singer, 1962), the findings of Rapee et al. (1986) show that unexplained arousal is particularly effective in prompting negatively valenced emotional experience (see Marshall & Zimbardo, 1979; Maslach, 1979).

Effects of Expectations of Control over Symptoms

The role of cognitions in aborting panic was further elucidated by Sanderson, Rapee, and Barlow (1989). Again, CO_2 inhalation was used to induce panic in patients with panic disorder. All patients were instructed that they might experience a range of physical sensations, and a range of emotional states "from relaxation to anxiety," as a result of CO_2 administration. Furthermore, they were all informed that they would be able to adjust the CO_2 mixture by manipulating a dial *if* (and only if) a designated light was illuminated. However, they were urged to stay with the experimenter-selected mixture, because that would facilitate assessment. In effect, the dial could not affect the CO_2 mixture, and none of the subjects tried to use it. The light was illuminated for half of the subjects, who thus were given an illusion of control. Subjects in this group reported a much stronger belief in control over CO_2 symptoms than did those in the no-illusion group. Ten subjects panicked during inhalation, 8 of whom were in the no-illusion group. Subjects in this group also reported more symptoms, higher intensity of symptoms, more catastrophic cognitions, and larger similarity of their response to naturally occurring panic attacks than the subjects in the illusion-of-control group. The quite dramatic effect of perceived control over symptoms reported in this study is in accordance with

the prominent place of "fear of losing control" in the symptomatology of panic attacks (Barlow et al., 1985; Borden & Turner, 1989; Rapee et al., 1992). Furthermore, it highlights the importance of cognitions in the elicitation of panic.

The Role of Physiological Feedback in Panic

The data reviewed so far have primarily dealt with the panic-inhibitory effects of correct attribution of bodily symptoms to a more or less controllable external source. However, if misattribution of physiological symptoms to uncontrollable sources is focal for panic, then false beliefs about physiological activation should also prompt panic, regardless of the actual physiological changes (Valins, 1972). This hypothesis was tested by Ehlers, Margraf, Roth, Taylor, and Birbaumer (1988). They gave patients with panic disorder and controls feedback about their heart rate by having each heartbeat trigger a tone pip. After a baseline period without feedback, there was a true-feedback period during which the actual heart rate was fed back to the subjects. However, unknown to the participants, at the end of the true-feedback period, control of the feedback was transferred to the experimenter, who produced a 50-beat increase in heart rate over a 30-second period, mimicking the heart rate of an intense panic attack (Cohen, Barlow, & Blanchard, 1985; Lader & Mathews, 1970). When participants who realized that the feedback was false were excluded, the alleged increase in heart rate produced large increases in rated anxiety and excitement, as well as in skin conductance level, in patients but not in controls. Furthermore, whereas the controls showed a significant decrease in heart rate and blood pressure from true to false feedback, the patients showed increases. Thus, in support of the hypothesis, it appeared that the false feedback of a heart rate increase was sufficient to induce an anxiety attack in the patients, whereas the controls appeared more or less unaffected by this manipulation.

Bodily Sensations and Expectancy of Anxiety in Nonfearful Individuals

It appears from the data considered in this section that patients with anxiety disorders have a bias not only to attend to threat in the environment, but also a bias to expect some types of stimuli to signal impending doom. In accordance with this expectation, they appear to react with anxiety and panic to these cues. Because all the studies reviewed so far have used patients with panic disorder as subjects, one may wonder whether the effects reported are specific to them, or whether, with appropriate expectancy inductions, nonfearful individuals could be made to respond like these patients.

This possibility was examined by van der Molen, van den Hout, Vroemen, Lousberg, and Griez (1986). They exposed normal volunteers to lactate infusion or placebo in balanced order. Lactate infusion is a well-established method for experimentally inducing anxiety, and has been specifically related to panic (see Margraf et al., 1986b, and van den Hout, 1988, for reviews). Half of the participants were instructed that "the infusions might cause unpleasant bodily sensations similar to those experienced during periods of anxiety" and that "they might experience anxious effects" (van der Molen et al., 1986, p. 678). The other half of the participants were told that the infusion would evoke feelings of "pleasant tension, such as those experienced during sports, watching an exciting movie, etc." (van der Molen et al., 1986, p. 678). The participants rated their emotional state from −100 (very anxious tension) to +100 (very pleasant excitement). The instructions had no effect in the placebo condition, which resulted in neutral emotional ratings. With lactate infusion, however, participants instructed to expect aversive symptoms and anxiety rated their state as quite negative (−64.3), whereas the participants expecting positive affect showed variable ratings averaging out as emotionally neutral. Thus the results demonstrated that the interaction between bodily cues as induced by lactate infusion, and expectancy of aversive effects, was critical in inducing anxiety. Neither infusion nor instruction per se was sufficient to induce anxiety. This result provides persuasive support for the argument that expectations of negative affect and catastrophic consequences are critical determinants of anxiety and panic attacks, as claimed by cognitive theorists (e.g., Clark, 1986, 1988).

THEORETICAL INTEGRATION

To sum up, I have argued that anxiety originates in biologically evolved defense systems, which are responsible both for acute anxiety attacks (i.e., state anxiety) and, perhaps more indirectly, for more enduring and stable levels of anxiety (i.e., trait anxiety). These defenses are served by information-processing mechanisms centered on the determination of threat and operating at several loci of information processing. In this section, a somewhat speculative integration of the information-processing mechanisms is presented. It is pictorially represented in Figure 36.3.

Feature Detectors

Stimulus information (1 in Figure 36.3) reaches feature detectors, which provide a preliminary segregation of the stimulus before the information is passed on (2) to the significance evaluation system. The important part of this system for alarm/anxiety/fear is that some stimulus features may be directly connected to the arousal system. Thus it is assumed that the alarm reaction, which may eventually surface as an anxiety response, begins to be recruited immediately when the perceptual system encounters a sign of a survival-relevant stimulus.

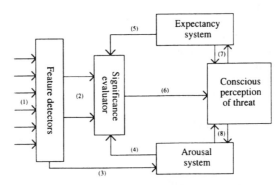

FIGURE 36.3. An information-processing model of the generation of anxiety. See text for explanations.

The feature detectors under discussion here are assumed to operate primarily on physical input. That is, they do not yet interact with memory to provide meaning to the stimulus; rather, they help in the preliminary segregation of the stimulus inflow and the direction of attention toward potentially relevant areas (e.g., Posner, 1980). Primary examples of stimulus features that may directly trigger the arousal system include high intensity and rapid rise times, provoking startle.

In attentional terms, this system may be set to discover potential threat in the environment by a filtering mechanism, giving priority to biologically important stimuli (see Öhman, 1992, for documentation of this point). Such stimuli, then, have the dual effect of immediately activating the arousal system (3) and being selected for preferential treatment by the significance evaluation system (2), which passes information directly on to the conscious perception system (6). The former of these routes may be strongly automatic, in the sense that a particular feature reflexively elicits autonomic responses. The route from feature detectors to the significance evaluator, however, may be subject to competition between stimulus features, which, as emphasized by Mathews and Mackintosh (1998), is an assumption that appears necessitated by the data on attentional bias in anxiety.

There are good data available to suggest that a direct link between features and autonomic responding is operating in phobias (Öhman & Soares, 1994) and that it may result from conditioning (Öhman & Soares, 1993; Esteves, Dimberg, & Öhman, 1994). It may also be speculated that this mechanism is operating in panic attacks. Barlow et al. (1985) reported clinical impressions suggesting that panic attacks are "usually associated with mild exercise, sexual relations, sudden temperature changes, stress, or other cues that alter physiological functioning in some discernible way, albeit outside the patient's awareness" (p. 327). If we accept Klein's (1993) argument that panic reflects the activation of an alarm system evolved to respond to suffocation hazard and prompting rapid escape from potentially deadly locations, it appears reasonable to presume that critical cues for this system would activate feature detectors that are sensitive to specific bodily stimuli. These stimuli either would result in unconditioned activation (e.g., increased CO_2 concentration in the inhaled air, lack of oxygen)

or would reflect conditioned activation of alarm (e.g., heart rate increases). In both cases, however, the process would rapidly and automatically trigger the arousal system, independently of the person's awareness of the threat stimulus. A similar argument can perhaps be made for PTSD, where the eliciting event is so threatening that it provides traumatic conditioning to associated cues, which in this way may acquire power to activate the arousal system automatically. Few data are available to support the conditioning scenario postulated here for panic disorder or PTSD; however, it is clear that a severely traumatic event (such as a failure to get air) is an extremely efficient unconditioned stimulus for persistent conditioned fear responses (Sanderson, Laverty, & Campbell, 1963).

The Significance Evaluator

The significance evaluator automatically assesses stimuli for relevance. In contrast to the feature detectors, which are selective for input in terms of a stimulus set or a filtering mechanism, this system operates by a response set or a pigeonholing mechanism (Broadbent, 1970). That is to say, its selection is "top-down" or schema-driven, in the sense that it is set by the expectancy system (5) to look for particular categories of input. This implies that its operation is predicated on a full-meaning analysis of the stimuli. This is the locus of the bias to discover threat among persons high in anxiety (e.g., Mathews, 1990; Mogg & Bradley, 1998; see review above). Thus, as part of interrelated memory systems, memorial representations of moods (Bower, 1981) or emotional responses (Lang, 1984) may prime memory areas focused on threat; as a result, the expectancy system sets the significance evaluator to respond to threat words, for example. When threat words are discovered, the conscious perception system (6) is called, and this call may result in competition with other ongoing tasks, such as responding to visual probes (MacLeod et al., 1986; Mathews & MacLeod, 1986). Such competition implies that the significance evaluator requires cognitive resources, and thus that it is at least partly a controlled processing system. Nevertheless, it operates preattentively, without any necessary conscious access (Öhman, 1992; see also Spinks & Kramer, 1991). Thus it is assumed that there is controlled processing that is not consciously available.

The significance evaluator has been viewed as central to the elicitation of orienting responses (Bernstein & Taylor, 1979; Öhman, 1979). As the significance evaluator activates the conscious perception channel (through 6) so that the eliciting stimulus (e.g., the threat) is consciously perceived, an orienting response is elicited through activation of the arousal system (8). It should perhaps be explicitly noted that the view presented here, associating the orienting response with conscious perception (Öhman, 1992), represents a change from my previous view (Öhman, 1979), which assumed that orienting responses are activated by a direct link from the significance evaluator to the arousal system. The basic argument for this change is that backward masking, which blocks the target stimulus from entering conscious perception (i.e., path 6), also blocks skin conductance responses to conditioned stimuli, unless they are biologically fear-relevant. Biologically fear-relevant conditioned stimuli, on the other hand, are presumed to activate the arousal system through path 3, and thus skin conductance responses to such stimuli survive masking (see Öhman, 1992). The important implication for anxiety is that nonconscious discovery of potential threat through the significance evaluator does not result in activation of the arousal system unless it results in conscious perception of threat. Thus the enhanced skin conductance responses to relevant threat words presented in the rejected channel of a shadowing task for subjects with obsessive–compulsive disorder (Foa & McNally, 1986) should be attributed to switches of attention between channels (Dawson & Schell, 1982; Trandel & McNally, 1987). Similarly, enhanced skin conductance responses to relevant threat words presented against a noisy background to veterans with PTSD should be attributed to conscious perception (McNally et al., 1987).

The Arousal System

Although the significance evaluator is assumed to have no effect, or only a weak effect, on the arousal system, this latter system is assumed to be able to "tune up" the significance evaluator (4). Thus increased arousal is assumed to enhance the biases of the significance evaluator, perhaps in a way analogous to the multiplicative relation between drive and habit in Hullian learning theory. This assumption explains the effect of state anxiety on attentional bias (e.g.,

MacLeod & Mathews, 1988; MacLeod & Rutherford, 1992).

The arousal system also provides critical input to the conscious perception system, which has been taken as the distinctive feature of emotional experience (Mandler, 1975). For example, the studies by Ehlers et al. (1988) and Pauli et al. (1991) demonstrated the power of such perceived input to generate anxiety in anxiety-prone individuals. However, it is important to note that the relationship between the arousal system and the conscious perception system is bidirectional. Thus, as threat and danger are consciously perceived, the arousal system is recruited to provide metabolic support for the more or less vigorous coping actions that may become necessary.

Although the arousal system is presented as a unitary system here, this is of course a gross oversimplification. The core of the system is Cannon's (1929) emergency reaction—that is, a sympatho-adrenal mobilization of bodily resources for vigorous action—but the character of the resulting physiological response is modulated by stimulus factors, available action alternatives, and the particular action chosen, as well as by characteristics of the individual (see Öhman, Hamm, & Hugdahl, 2000).

The Expectancy System

The expectancy system relies on the organization of emotion in memory. Following Lang (1984), it is assumed that memory for emotional episodes can be represented by interconnected nodes comprising stimulus, response, and meaning information. Such networks can be activated by matching input information, but because nodes are assumed to coactivate one another within the network, a partial match involving only a few nodes is sufficient to put the system into an activated state. However, the more complete the match, the stronger the activation (Lang, 1984). When activated, the system can be viewed as biasing the significance evaluator to respond to information matching active memory nodes (5). Furthermore, such matching provides information for the conscious perception system, which in turn keeps the memory foundation of the expectancy system in continual activation—maintaining, as it were, the bias to discover threat. In agreement with Mathews (1990), it is assumed that this biasing of the significance evaluator occurs at a nonconscious level of information processing.

However, the expectancy system has a dual role in generating fear and anxiety. Not only does it bias the processing of incoming information, but it also provides the context for the interpretation of inputs to the conscious perception system (see Mandler, 1975, 1984). At this level, the influence of the expectancy system occurs at a consciously reportable level, where it is more appropriate to use the term "expectancy" than in the case of biasing the significance evaluator. Thus interpretation of input from the significance evaluator (5) and the arousal system (8) by the conscious perception system occurs in continuous interaction with the expectancy system and its associated memory. This is the basis for the effects of expectancies on panic that have been discussed previously.

Perceived Threat and Coping

The conscious perception system is merely an aspect of a much broader system, whether we call it the "mind" elucidated as the "cognitive–interpretive system" (Mandler, 1975), "consciousness" (Posner, 1978), "control processing" (Schneider et al., 1984), or the "central capacity-limited channel" (Öhman, 1979). For present purposes this system has two central functions: (1) to integrate information input from the arousal system, the significance evaluator, and the expectancy system; and (2) to select an action alternative to cope with the perceived threat. When Epstein's (1972) distinction between anxiety and fear is adhered to, the latter function becomes critical for deciding the emotional effect of the perceived threat. If its nature is such that avoidance or escape provides successful coping with the threat, the result is fear. If there is no such possibility, or if attempted escape is interfered with, the result is anxiety (Epstein, 1972).

CONCLUDING DISCUSSION

To recapitulate, it has been argued that responses of fear and anxiety originate in an alarm system shaped by evolution to protect creatures from impending danger. This system is biased to discover threat, and it results in a sympathetically dominated response as a support of potential flight or fight. This response system can be triggered from three different levels of information processing, the first two of which are inaccessible to introspection. The first level concerns a direct link to an arousal system from elementary feature detectors geared to respond to biologically relevant threats. Thus the arousal system becomes collaterally and automatically activated with the activation of further information-processing stages, whose functioning may be influenced by the arousal. The second level concerns a schema-driven nonconscious bias to discover threat in the environment, which delivers information to conscious perception, but has no effect or only a weak effect on physiological arousal. The third level concerns the direct effect of expectancy and physiological arousal on the cognitive–interpretive activity resulting in perceived threat. In this concluding section of the chapter, some implications of this view of anxiety are discussed.

The Nature of the Unconscious Effects

Freud (e.g., 1900/1953), of course, believed that anxiety has an unconscious origin, residing in the interaction between bodily and instinctual energies on the one hand, and various psychological defense mechanisms on the other. Similarly, according to the present scheme, unconscious activation of bodily systems in interaction with an interpretive conscious system plays a pivotal role in the generation of anxiety. Indeed, the correspondence with classic psychodynamic notions can be pushed a step further by noting that the present scheme, in a way, does not operate with one but with two different types of unconscious. Freud distinguished between what might be termed a "drive unconscious" and a "repressed unconscious" (see Power & Brewin, 1991), which in some respects would correspond to the unconscious effects of the feature detectors and the significance evaluator, respectively, in the present model. Furthermore, in some other respects the former would correspond to the "collective unconscious" postulated by Jung (1953) to encompass the cumulative experience of the human species. In the model (Figure 36.3), this role is played by feature detectors, which have been shaped to respond particularly strongly to features associated with recurrent threats to well-being in the evolution of humankind. Elsewhere (Öhman, 1986), I have suggested that reptiles provided an archaic prototype for threats emanating from predation pressure, and that this may explain the human tendency to equip the embodiments of evil with bestial features. Thus Jung's notion of "archetypes" can in fact be reinterpreted in terms of biological preparedness (e.g., Seligman, 1971).

The other mechanism of nonconscious bias for responding to threat, residing in the significance evaluator and the expectancy system, suggests some of the Freudian notions of the unconscious. Because this bias represents schema-driven effects dependent on memorial organization (e.g., Lang, 1984), it will reflect the individual's unique personal experience. Depending on the history of the individual, he or she may respond to some potential threat cues rather than others. Furthermore, what is extremely threatening to one individual may be completely innocuous to another, because the corresponding memorial node may not be connected to nodes in memory structures related to threat. Thus effects similar to those of the classical Freudian defenses may be interpretable in these terms. Furthermore, one may even argue that the schema-driven unconscious threat-biasing system may sometimes be pitted against the feature-driven detection system in a way strongly reminiscent of the interactions between defenses and drives in psychoanalytic theory. For example, if bodily cues activate the arousal system, but the significance evaluator is biased against responding to these cues in terms of threat, then something similar to the phenomenon seen in patients with "panic without fear" (Kushner & Beitman, 1990) should result. However, whether this should be viewed as anxiety counteracted by defenses, or simply as lack of anxiety, appears a moot point. The important insight here is rather that phenomena similar to those described by psychoanalysts are readily interpretable in terms of the current model (see Power & Brewin, 1991, for further discussion of the communality between traditional psychoanalytic theories and contemporary cognitive science theories). These interpretations, furthermore, are preferable to the psychoanalytic ones because they are backed up by a scientific literature based on rigorous theorizing and controlled data, rather than based on anecdotal observations from uncontrolled case studies (see Grünbaum, 1984).

The Relationship between Fear and Anxiety

The model depicted in Figure 36.3 implies that there are in effect two types of anxiety, which both differ from fear. Following Lang (1984),

emotions can be viewed as action sets—as readinesses to respond in particular ways. Fear, then, is viewed as an emotional response related to avoidance and escape. Although such responses may be primed by the feature detectors and the significance evaluator, which may recruit metabolic support for vigorous action, the eventual overt responses are taken to occur after conscious perception of the threat. When such responses are blocked, fear is changed into anxiety (Epstein, 1972). However, if anxiety is construed as "unresolved fear" or "undirected arousal" related to perceived threat (Epstein, 1972), then the model implies that there is a more basic type of anxiety than the one resulting when avoidance motives become frustrated. This type of anxiety results from the unconscious input to the conscious perception system from the significance evaluator and the arousal system. Because the source of this input is not necessarily available to consciousness, the resulting state of undirected arousal is experienced as anxiety, or perhaps more precisely as "undirected alarm." The person knows that something is wrong, but cannot pinpoint any clear reason for it. Anxiety in this sense, then, is entirely dependent on the unconscious mechanisms, whereas the anxiety resulting from interference with avoidance is more readily appraised at the conscious level as originating in the external world or in personal shortcomings.

The "alarm" or "primary" anxiety may be channeled or "resolved" into fear, if escape is selected as the action option after a complete conscious and controlled processing of the stimulus situation. Normally, of course, the eliciting stimulus is consciously perceived simultaneously with the arousal of anxiety, as attention is directed to the preattentively located threat. It is only when the attention shift fails to locate the stimulus that preattentively elicited unconscious anxiety is left in the system without any apparent stimulus for its explanation. This may occur when the stimulus is very faint and thus fails to be perceived; when the preattentive mechanisms falsely locate a threat that is not confirmed by controlled processing; or when several more or less simultaneous stimuli (e.g., emanating from the body) mask one another. In any of these cases, an emotional state perhaps best characterized as "anxious alarm" should be the experienced result, and this state should be clearly different from anxiety generated by failed escape or avoidance.

Implications for Anxiety Disorders

The model depicted in Figure 36.3 permits the various anxiety disorders to be viewed as resulting from different emphases within the same information-processing structures.

As already noted, phobias and panic disorder are taken as resulting from the automatic activation of the arousal system by specific features located by the feature detectors. This activation provides a surge of physiological arousal, cues from which become available to the conscious perception system. Therefore, these two types of disorders should be similar in the sense that they both reflect increases in sympathetically mediated arousal. However, whereas the information reaching the conscious perception system from the arousal system is quite similar in phobias and panic disorder, the information arriving via the significance evaluator is radically different. In the case of a phobia, the source of the physiological arousal is attributed to some factor in the external world; in the case of panic, the arousal is attributed to an enemy from within. As everyone who has considered security management knows, the former case is much easier to handle than the latter. An external enemy can be met with barricades, attack, or defensive withdrawal, depending on situational factors and the relative balance of power between the threatened and the threatener. In phobias, this balance is typically interpreted as supporting flight. However, an enemy within has crossed the defensive barricades, which makes the impending danger acute. Flight is not an option, and the risks of being overwhelmed and of capitulation become acute. Therefore, catastrophic interpretations of the situation are readily invited. In this way, both the similarities and the differences in symptomatology between phobias and panic disorder can be accounted for.

If Klein's (1993) interpretation of panic as the result of an alarm system responding to suffocation threat is accepted, then a route to the understanding of agoraphobia is opened. In agoraphobia the suffocation alarm may be conditioned to environmental cues, which then become avoided. However, if the alarm response rather is conditioned to bodily cues (such as heart rate increases), then the person may end up with apparently spontaneous panic attacks, without obvious situational triggers.

In PTSD, there is an original trauma that totally recruits the individual's defense responses, often for quite protracted periods of time and at overwhelming intensities (e.g., in combat). As a result, cues may be conditioned to recruit the arousal system automatically, as in phobia and panic. In PTSD, however, the subsequent stage—cognitive preoccupation with the trauma, partly mediated through the expectancy system and the significance evaluator—appears to take on a more prominent role than in phobias and panic disorder, leading to physiological activation not only automatically but also through conscious mediation (via worries and ruminations).

Generalized anxiety disorder, finally, appears to lack arousal activation via the feature detectors; it seems to be primarily driven by the expectancy system and the bias to discover threats (Rapee, 1991). The physiological effects that are needed to turn the worry into anxiety (Mathews, 1990) are likely to be recruited through activation of the arousal system from the cognitive perception system. Thus in this disorder the expectancy–significance–perception loop appears to play the primary role and the nonconscious activation of arousal a secondary role in the problem.

The perspective provided here views phobias and panic disorders as physiologically driven, and generalized anxiety disorder as cognitively driven, with PTSD at a somewhat intermediate position between the two groups. Thus, within a unitary theoretical frame, it is possible to deal quite effectively with important aspects of the different anxiety disorders. However, whereas this account appears quite successful in dealing with the symptomatology of the disorders, it is relatively silent on the issue of etiology. Conditioning is given a role in several disorders— and, elaborated as biologically prepared learning, it may be decisive for phobias (Öhman et al., 1985)—but there is at present no information in the model to suggest why some persons develop panic disorder and others generalized anxiety disorder. In particular, the origin of the cognitively driven ruminations in generalized anxiety disorder remains a mystery.

Anxiety, Emotion, and Cognition

If the interaction between physiological cues and cognitive–interpretive activity is taken as the hallmark of emotional phenomena (e.g., James, 1884; Mandler, 1975), then fear and anxiety as described in this chapter are prima facie emotional phenomena. It has been documented that bodily cues provide some of the most important experienced symptoms in fear and anxiety, and that measurable physiological responses are prominent correlates of fear and anxiety both in the laboratory and when ambulatorily monitored in everyday life. There are good data suggesting that perceived bodily changes are critical to anxiety attacks (e.g., Pauli et al., 1991), but it is equally clear that such bodily changes are neither necessary nor sufficient for anxiety to be experienced. The anxiety is typically evoked in particular types of situations, the nature of which is such that an evolutionary origin appears a quite straightforward interpretation of their potency.

With regard to theory, an interactional perspective stresses the inextricable interplay among physiological activation, cognitive processes, and emotional responding from the very moment an effective stimulus makes contact with the relevant sensory organ. Thus it is clear that some emotional effects occur immediately upon presentation of an effective stimulus (LeDoux, 1990b, 1996; Öhman & Soares, 1994), providing some justification for the claim that "affects precedes inference" (Zajonc, 1980). However, it is equally clear that cognitions stemming from nonconscious biases play pervasive roles in the interpretation of threats (e.g., Mathews, 1990), in the volitional appraisal of the stimulus, and in deliberations about potential response alternatives. Thus, as a final point, the literature reviewed in this chapter is taken to suggest that it is hardly meaningful to ask oneself whether cognition is necessary for emotion. We appear to have reached a stage in the knowledge of fear and anxiety at which the meaningful question is how the interaction between emotion and cognition occurs, and some tentative answers to this fundamental question may already be at hand.

ACKNOWLEDGMENT

Preparation of this chapter was supported by grants from the Swedish Council for Research in the Humanities and Social Sciences.

REFERENCES

American Psychiatric Association (APA). (1994). *Diagnostic and statistical manual of mental disorders* (4th ed.). Washington, DC: Author.

Arrindell, W. A., Pickersgill, M. J., Merckelbach, H.,

Ardon, M. A., & Cornet, F. C. (1991). Phobic dimensions: III. Factor analytic approaches to the study of common phobic fears: An updated review of findings obtained with adult subjects. *Advances in Behaviour Research and Therapy, 13*, 73–130.

Barlow, D. H. (1988). *Anxiety and its disorders: The nature and treatment of anxiety and panic.* New York: Guilford Press.

Barlow, D. H., Vermilyea, J., Blanchard, E. B., Vermilyea, B. B., Di Nardo, P. A., & Cerny, J. A. (1985). The phenomenon of panic. *Journal of Abnormal Psychology, 94*, 320–328.

Bernstein, A. S., & Taylor, K. W. (1979). The interaction of stimulus information with potential stimulus significance in eliciting the skin conductance orienting response. In H. D. Kimmel, E. H. van Olst, & J. F. Orlebeke (Eds.), *The orienting reflex in humans.* Hillsdale, NJ: Erlbaum.

Borden, J. W., & Turner, S. M. (1989). Is panic a unique emotional experience? *Behaviour Research and Therapy, 27*, 263–268.

Bower, G. H. (1981). Mood and memory. *American Psychologist, 36*, 129–148.

Bradley, B. P., Mogg, K., Millar, N., & White, J. (1995). Selective processing of negative information: Effects of clinical anxiety, concurrent depression, and awareness. *Journal of Abnormal Psychology, 104*, 532–536.

Broadbent, D. E. (1970). Stimulus set and response set: Two kinds of selective attention. In D. M. Mostofsky (Ed.), *Attention: Contemporary theory and analysis.* New York: Appleton-Century-Crofts.

Buss, A. H. (1962). Two anxiety factors in psychiatric patients. *Journal of Abnormal and Social Psychology, 65*, 426–427.

Cannon, W. B. (1929). *Bodily changes in pain, hunger, fear, and rage.* New York: Appleton-Century-Crofts.

Clark, D. M. (1986). A cognitive approach to panic. *Behaviour Research and Therapy, 24*, 461–470.

Clark, D. M. (1988). A cognitive model of panic attacks. In S. Rachman & J. D. Maser (Eds.), *Panic: Psychological perspectives.* Hillsdale, NJ: Erlbaum.

Cohen, A. S., Barlow, D. H., & Blanchard, E. B. (1985). Psychophysiology of relaxation-associated panic attacks. *Journal of Abnormal Psychology, 94*, 96–101.

Dawson, M. E., & Schell, A. M. (1982). Electrodermal responses to attended and nonattended significant stimuli during dichotic listening. *Journal of Experimental Psychology: Human Perception and Performance, 8*, 315–324.

Dimberg, U., & Öhman, A. (1996). Behold the wrath: Psychophysiological responses to facial stimuli. *Motivation and Emotion, 20*, 149–182.

Ehlers, A. (1993). Interoception and panic disorder. *Advances in Behaviour Research and Therapy, 15*, 3–21.

Ehlers, A., Margraf, J., Roth, W. T., Taylor, C. B., & Birbaumer, N. (1988). Anxiety induced by false heart rate feedback in patients with panic disorder. *Behaviour Research and Therapy, 26*, 1–11.

Epstein, S. (1972). The nature of anxiety with emphasis upon its relationship to expectancy. In C. D. Spielberger (Ed.), *Anxiety: Current trends in theory and research* (Vol. 2). New York: Academic Press.

Esteves, F., Dimberg, U., & Öhman, A. (1994). Automatically elicited fear: Conditioned skin conductance responses to masked facial expressions. *Cognition and Emotion, 8*, 393–413.

Esteves, F., Dimberg, U., Parra, C., & Öhman, A. (1994). Nonconscious associative learning: Pavlovian conditioning of skin conductance responses to masked fear-relevant facial stimuli. *Psychophysiology, 31*, 375–385.

Fenz, W. D., & Epstein, S. (1965). Manifest anxiety: Unifactorial or multifactorial composition. *Perceptual and Motor Skills, 20*, 773–780.

Foa, E. B., & McNally, R. J. (1986). Sensitivity to feared stimuli in obsessive–compulsives: A dichotic listening analysis. *Cognitive Therapy and Research, 10*, 477–485.

Freedman, R. R., Ianni, P., Ettedgui, E., & Puthezhath, N. (1985). Ambulatory monitoring of panic disorder. *Archives of General Psychiatry, 42*, 244–255.

Freud, S. (1953). The interpretation of dreams. In J. Strachey (Ed. & Trans.) *The standard edition of the complete psychological works of Sigmund Freud* (Vols. 4 and 5). London: Hogarth Press. (Original work published 1900)

Grünbaum, A. (1984). *The foundation of psychoanalysis: A philosophical critique*. Berkeley: University of California Press.

Hibbert, G. A. (1984). Ideational components of anxiety: Their origin and content. *British Journal of Psychiatry, 144*, 618–624.

Holender, D. (1986). Semantic activation without conscious identification in dichotic listening, parafoveal vision, and visual masking: A survey and appraisal. *Behavioral and Brain Sciences, 9*, 1–66.

James, W. (1884). What is an emotion? *Mind, 9*, 188–205.

Jung, C. G. (1953). Two essays on analytical psychology. In C. G. Jung, *Collected works* (Vol. 7). New York: Pantheon.

Kendler, K. S., Neale, M. C., Kessler, R. C., Heath, A. C., & Eaves, L. J. (1992). The genetic epidemiology of phobias in women: The interrelationship of agoraphobia, social phobia, situational phobia and simple phobia. *Archives of General Psychiatry, 49*, 273–281.

Kipling, R. (1983). *The second jungle book*. London: Macmillan. (Original work published 1895)

Klein, D. F. (1981). Anxiety reconceptualized. In D. F. Klein & J. Rabkin (Eds.), *Anxiety: New research and changing concepts*. New York: Raven Press.

Klein, D. F. (1993). False suffocation alarms, spontaneous panics, and related conditions. *Archives of General Psychiatry, 50*, 306–317.

Kushner, M. G., & Beitman, B. D. (1990). Panic attacks without fear: An overview. *Behaviour Research and Therapy, 28*, 469–479.

Lader, M. H. (1967). Palmar skin conductance measures in anxiety and phobic states. *Journal of Psychosomatic Research, 11*, 271–281.

Lader, M., & Marks, I. (1973). *Clinical anxiety*. London: Heinemann.

Lader, M., & Mathews, A. (1970). Physiological changes during spontaneous panic attacks. *Journal of Psychosomatic Research, 14*, 377–382.

Lang, P. J. (1968). Fear reduction and fear behavior: Problems in treating a construct. In J. M. Shlien (Ed.), *Research in psychotherapy* (Vol. 3). Washington, DC: American Psychological Association.

Lang, P. J. (1978). Anxiety: Toward a psychophysiological definition. In H. S. Akiskal & W. L. Webb (Eds.), *Psychiatric diagnosis: Explorations of biological predictors*. New York: Spectrum.

Lang, P. J. (1984). Cognition in emotion: Concept and action. In C. E. Izard, J. Kagan, & R. B. Zajonc (Eds.), *Emotions, cognition, and behavior*. New York: Cambridge University Press.

Lang, P. J., Bradley, M. M., & Cuthbert, B. N. (1997). Motivated attention: Affect, activation, and action. In P. J. Lang, R. F. Simons, & M. T. Balaban (Eds.), *Attention and orienting: Sensory and motivational processes*. Mahwah, NJ: Erlbaum.

Lazarus, R. S., Kanner, A. D., & Folkman, S. (1980). Emotions: A cognitive–phenomenological analysis. In R. Plutchik & H. Kellerman (Eds.), *Emotion: Theory, research, and experience. Vol. 1. Theories of emotion*. New York: Academic Press.

LeDoux, J. E. (1989). Cognitive–emotional interactions in the brain. *Cognition and Emotion, 3*, 267–289.

LeDoux, J. E. (1990a). Fear pathways in the brain: Implications for a theory of the emotional brain. In P. F. Brain, S. Parmigiani, R. J. Blanchard, & D. Mainardi (Eds.), *Fear and defence*. London: Harwood.

LeDoux, J. E. (1990b). Information flow from sensation to emotion: Plasticity in the neural computation of stimulus value. In M. Gabriel & J. Moore (Eds.), *Learning and computational neuroscience: Foundations of adaptive networks*. Cambridge, MA: MIT Press.

LeDoux, J. E. (1996). *The emotional brain*. New York: Simon & Schuster.

MacLeod, C., & Mathews, A. (1988). Anxiety and the allocation of attention to threat. *Quarterly Journal of Experimental Psychology, 40A*, 653–670.

MacLeod, C., Mathews, A., & Tata, P. (1986). Attentional bias in emotional disorders. *Journal of Abnormal Psychology, 95*, 15–20.

MacLeod, C., & Rutherford, E. M. (1992). Anxiety and the selective processing of emotional information: Mediating roles of awareness, trait and state variables, and personal relevance of stimulus materials. *Behaviour Research and Therapy, 30*, 479–491.

Mandler, G. (1975). *Mind and emotion*. New York: Wiley.

Mandler, G. (1984). *Mind and body: Psychology of emotion and stress*. New York: Norton.

Marcel, A. (1983). Conscious and unconscious perception: An approach to the relations between phenomenal experience and perceptual processes. *Cognitive Psychology, 15*, 238–300.

Margraf, J., Ehlers, A., & Roth, W. T. (1986a). Biological models of panic disorder and agoraphobia: A review. *Behaviour Research and Therapy, 24*, 553–567.

Margraf, J., Ehlers, A., & Roth, W. T. (1986b). Sodium lactate infusions and panic attacks: A review and critique. *Psychosomatic Medicine, 48*, 23–51.

Marshall, G. D., & Zimbardo, P. G. (1979). Affective consequences of inadequately explained physiological arousal. *Journal of Personality and Social Psychology, 37*, 970–988.

Maslach, C. (1979). Negative emotional biasing of unexplained arousal. *Journal of Personality and Social Psychology, 37*, 953–969.

Mason, J. W. (1968). Overall hormonal balance as a key to endocrine functions. *Psychosomatic Medicine, 30*, 791–808.

Mathews, A. (1990). Why worry?: The cognitive function of anxiety. *Behaviour Research and Therapy, 28*, 455–468.

Mathews, A., & Mackintosh, B. (1998). A cognitive model of selective processing in anxiety. *Cognitive Therapy and Research, 22*, 539–560.

Mathews, A., & MacLeod, C. (1986). Discrimination of threat cues without awareness in anxiety states. *Journal of Abnormal Psychology, 95*, 131–138.

Mathews, A., & MacLeod, C. (1994). Cognitive approaches to emotion and emotional disorders. *Annual Review of Psychology, 45*, 25–50.

McNally, R. J. (1987). Preparedness and phobias: A review. *Psychological Bulletin, 101*, 283–303.

McNally, R. J., Luedke, D. L., Besyner, J. K., Peterson, R., Bohm, K., & Lips, O. J. (1987). Sensitivity to stress-relevant stimuli in posttraumatic stress disorder. *Journal of Anxiety Disorders, 1*, 105–116.

Mogg, K., & Bradley, B. P. (1998). A cognitive–motivational analysis of anxiety. *Behaviour Research and Therapy, 36*, 809–848.

Mogg, K., Bradley, B. P., & Williams, R. (1995). Attentional bias in anxiety and depression: The role of awareness. *British Journal of Clinical Psychology, 34*, 17–36.

Mogg, K., Bradley, B. P., Williams, R., & Mathews, A. (1993). Subliminal processing of emotional information in anxiety and depression. *Journal of Abnormal Psychology, 102*, 304–311.

Morris, J. S., Öhman, A., & Dolan, R. J. (1998). Conscious and unconscious emotional learning in the human amygdala. *Nature, 393*, 467–470.

Morris, J. S., Öhman, A., & Dolan, R. J. (1999). A subcortical pathway to the right amygdala mediating "unseen" fear. *Proceedings of the National Academy of Sciences, 96*, 1680–1685.

Nesse, R. M. (1987). An evolutionary perspective on panic disorder and agoraphobia. *Ethology and Sociobiology, 8*, 73S–83S.

Nesse, R. M., Cameron, O. G., Curtis, G. C., McCann, D. S., & Huber-Smith, M. J. (1984). Adrenergic function in panic anxiety patients. *Archives of General Psychiatry, 41*, 320–332.

Öhman, A. (1979). The orienting response, attention, and learning: An information processing perspective. In H. D. Kimmel, E. H. van Olst, & J. F. Orlebeke (Eds.), *The orienting reflex in humans*. Hillsdale, NJ: Erlbaum.

Öhman, A. (1986). Face the beast and fear the face: Animal and social fears as prototypes for evolutionary analyses of emotion. *Psychophysiology, 23*, 123–145.

Öhman, A. (1992). Orienting and attention: Preferred preattentive processing of potentially phobic stimuli. In B. A. Campbell, H. Haynes, & R. Richardson (Eds.), *Attention and information processing in infants and adults: Perspectives from human and animal research*. Hillsdale, NJ: Erlbaum.

Öhman, A. (1993). Stimulus prepotency and fear: Data

and theory. In N. Birbaumer & A. Öhman (Eds.), *The organization of emotion: Cognitive, clinical and psychophysiological perspectives*. Toronto: Hogrefe.

Öhman, A. (1996). Preferential preattentive processing of threat in anxiety: Preparedness and attentional biases. In R. M. Rapee (Ed.), *Current controversies in the anxiety disorders*. New York: Guilford Press.

Öhman, A. (1999). Distinguishing unconscious from conscious emotional processes: Methodological considerations and theoretical implications. In T. Dalgleish & M. Power (Eds.), *Handbook of cognition and emotion*. Chichester, England: Wiley.

Öhman, A., Dimberg, U., & Öst, L.-G. (1985). Animal and social phobias: Biological constraints on learned fear responses. In S. Reiss & R. R. Bootzin (Eds.), *Theoretical issues in behavior therapy*. New York: Academic Press.

Öhman, A., Eriksson, A., & Olofsson, C. (1975). One-trial learning and superior resistance to extinction of autonomic responses conditioned to potentially phobic stimuli. *Journal of Comparative and Physiological Psychology, 88*, 619–627.

Öhman, A., Flykt, A., & Esteves, F. (1999). *Emotion drives attention: Beware! There are snakes in the grass!* Manuscript submitted for publication.

Öhman, A., Flykt, A., & Lundqvist, D. (2000). Unconscious emotion: Evolutionary perspectives, psychophysiological data, and neuropsychological mechanisms. In R. Lane & L. Nadel (Eds.), *The cognitive neuroscience of emotion* (pp. 296–327). New York: Oxford University Press.

Öhman, A., Hamm, A. O., & Hugdahl, K. (2000). Cognition and the autonomic nervous system: Orienting, anticipation, and conditioning. In J. T. Cacioppo, L. G. Tassinary, & G. G. Berntson (Eds.), *Handbook of psychophysiology* (pp. 533–575). New York: Cambridge University Press.

Öhman, A., & Soares, J. J. F. (1993). On the automaticity of phobic fear: Conditioned skin conductance responses to masked fear-relevant stimuli. *Journal of Abnormal Psychology, 102*, 121–132.

Öhman, A., & Soares, J. J. F. (1994). "Unconscious anxiety": Phobic responses to masked stimuli. *Journal of Abnormal Psychology, 103*, 231–240.

Öhman, A., & Soares, J. J. F. (1998). Emotional conditioning to masked stimuli: Expectancies for aversive outcomes following nonrecognized fear-relevant stimuli. *Journal of Experimental Psychology: General, 127*, 69–82.

Parra, C., Esteves, F., Flykt, A., & Öhman, A. (1997). Pavlovian conditioning to social stimuli: Backward masking and the dissociation of implicit and explicit cognitive processes. *European Psychologist, 2*, 106–117.

Pauli, P., Marquardt, C., Hartl, L., Nutzinger, D. O., H"lzl, R., & Strian, F. (1991). Anxiety induced by cardiac perceptions in patients with panic attacks: A field study. *Behaviour Research and Therapy, 29*, 137–145.

Posner, M. I. (1978). *Chronometric explorations of mind*. Hillsdale, NJ: Erlbaum.

Posner, M. I. (1980). Orienting and attention. *Quarterly Journal of Experimental Psychology, 32*, 3–25.

Power, M., & Brewin, C. R. (1991). From Freud to cognitive science: A contemporary account of the unconscious. *British Journal of Clinical Psychology, 30*, 289–310.

Rapee, R. M. (1986). Differential response to hyperventilation in panic disorder and generalized anxiety disorder. *Journal of Abnormal Psychology, 95*, 24–28

Rapee, R. M. (1991). Generalized anxiety disorder: A review of clinical features and theoretical concepts. *Clinical Psychology Review, 11*, 419–440.

Rapee, R. M. (1993). Psychological factors in panic disorder. *Advances in Behaviour Research and Therapy, 15*, 85–102.

Rapee, R. M. (Ed.). (1996). *Current controversies in the anxiety disorders.* New York: Guilford Press.

Rapee, R. M., Mattick, R., & Murrell, E. (1986). Cognitive mediation in the affective component of spontaneous panic attacks. *Journal of Behavior Therapy and Experimental Psychiatry, 17*, 245–253.

Rapee, R. M., Sanderson, W. C., McCauley, P. A., & Di Nardo, P. A. (1992). Differences in reported symptom profile between panic disorder and other DSM-III-R anxiety disorders. *Behaviour Research and Therapy, 30*, 45–52.

Sanderson, R. S., Laverty, R. S., & Campbell, D. (1963). Traumatic conditioned responses acquired during respiratory paralysis. *Nature, 196*, 1235–1236.

Sanderson, W. C., Rapee, R. M., & Barlow, D. H. (1989). The influence of an illusion of control on panic attacks induced via inhalation of 5. 5% carbon dioxide-enriched air. *Archives of General Psychiatry, 46*, 157–162.

Schachter, S., & Singer, J. (1962). Cognitive, social, and physiological determinants of emotional state. *Psychological Review, 69*, 379–399.

Schalling, D., Cronholm, B., & Åsberg. M. (1975). Components of state and trait anxiety as related to personality and arousal. In L. Levi (Ed.), *Emotions: Their parameters and measurement.* New York: Raven Press.

Schneider, W., Dumais, S. T., & Shiffrin, R. M. (1984). Automatic and control processing and attention. In R. Parasuraman & D. R. Davies (Eds.), *Varieties of attention.* Orlando, FL: Academic Press.

Seligman, M. E. P. (1971). Phobias and preparedness. *Behavior Therapy, 2*, 307–320.

Sheehan, D. V. (1982). Panic attacks and phobias. *New England Journal of Medicine, 307*, 156–158.

Shiffrin, R. M., & Schneider, W. (1977). Controlled and automatic human information processing: II. Perceptual learning, automatic attending, and a general theory. *Psychological Review, 84*, 127–190.

Soares, J. J. F., & Öhman, A. (1993a). Backward masking and skin conductance responses after conditioning to non-feared but fear-relevant stimuli in fearful subjects. *Psychophysiology, 30*, 460–466.

Soares, J. J. F., & Öhman, A. (1993b). Preattentive processing, preparedness, and phobias: Effects of instruction on conditioned electrodermal responses to masked and non-masked fear-relevant stimuli. *Behaviour Research and Therapy, 31*, 87–95.

Spielberger, C. D. (1972). Anxiety as an emotional state. In C. D. Spielberger (Ed.), *Anxiety: Current trends in theory and research* (Vol. 1). New York: Academic Press.

Spinks, J., & Kramer, A. (1991). Capacity views of human information processing: Autonomic measures. In J. R. Jennings & M. G. H. Coles (Eds.), *Handbook of cognitive psychophysiology: Central and autonomic nervous system approaches.* Chichester, England: Wiley.

Trandel, D. V., & McNally, R. J. (1987). Perception of threat cues in post-traumatic stress disorder: Semantic processing without awareness? *Behaviour Research and Therapy, 25*, 469–476.

Tuma, A. H., & Maser, J. D. (Eds.). (1995). *Anxiety and the anxiety disorders.* Hillsdale, NJ: Erlbaum.

Valins, S. (1972). The perception and labelling of bodily changes as determinants of emotional behavior. In P. Black (Ed.), *Physiological correlates of emotion.* New York: Academic Press.

van den Hout, M. A. (1988). The explanation of experimental panic. In S. Rachman & J. D. Maser (Eds.), *Panic: Psychological perspectives.* Hillsdale, NJ: Erlbaum.

van der Molen, G. M., van den Hout, M. A., Vroemen, J., Lousberg, H., & Griez, E. (1986). Cognitive determinants of lactate-induced anxiety. *Behaviour Research and Therapy, 24*, 677–680.

Zajonc, R. B. (1980). Feeling and thinking: Preferences need no inferences. *American Psychologist, 35*, 151–175.

CHAPTER 37

The Development of Anger and Hostile Interactions

Elizabeth A. Lemerise
Kenneth A. Dodge

Since the publication of the first edition of this volume (Lewis & Haviland, 1993), research on emotions in general and on anger in particular has burgeoned. In this chapter, we trace what has been learned about the development of anger in infants and children. A focus of this chapter is on how anger develops and comes to be regulated in the context of a child's transactions with the social environment (e.g., Parke, 1994). Moreover, developmental changes and individual differences in abilities and capacities contribute to this transaction, as well as shedding light on important processes (Bridges & Grolnick, 1995; Campos, Kermoian, & Witherington, 1996). The literature reviewed includes studies on infants' and children's expression of anger; their reactions to and appraisal of anger; their regulation of and/or coping with anger in themselves and others; and their understanding of anger, including display rules. We also consider socialization processes relevant to anger, and both adaptive and maladaptive aspects of anger and angry interactions.

THE FUNCTIONAL SIGNIFICANCE OF ANGER

Although emotion theorists do not agree about whether anger is a primary human emotion (e.g., Izard, 1991) or whether anger can be differentiated from a more generalized distress state (e.g., Camras, 1992), researchers from different theoretical backgrounds do agree that anger serves a variety of adaptive functions. Anger organizes and regulates internal physiological and psychological processes related to self-defense and mastery, as well as regulating social and interpersonal behaviors (e.g., Izard & Kobak, 1991; Lewis, Sullivan, Ramsay, & Alessandri, 1992). Oatley and Jenkins (1996) offer the interesting perspective that given the limitations of humans' cognitive and information-processing capacities, emotions, such as anger, provide "ready repertoires of action. Although not perfect, emotions are better than doing nothing, or than acting randomly, or becoming lost in thought" (p. 285). Thus anger signals something important about the individual's relationship to the environment (often the social environment), and it influences the individual's response to the situation—a response that may be more or less adaptive in the short term or the long term.

Anger regulates interpersonal behaviors and comes to be regulated in an interpersonal context through socialization by caregivers, peers, and the larger social context (Oatley & Jenkins, 1996). Cultures have "display rules" wherein individuals learn when, to whom, and how to express anger (and other emotions) in culturally acceptable ways. Socialization of these display rules for anger and other emotions can be observed quite early in infancy (e.g., Malatesta & Haviland, 1982), albeit indirectly. Problems in the regulation and appropriate expression of anger have implications for individuals' social interactions and relationships. For example, preschoolers who have difficulty managing their anger constructively are less liked by peers and are seen as less socially skilled by teachers and parents (e.g., Eisenberg, Fabes, Nyman, Bernzweig, & Pinuelas, 1994). By elementary school, poorer social functioning and problem behaviors can be predicted from early intense negative emotionality and poor emotion regulation. Across the lifespan, difficulties in managing anger have been linked to the development of psychopathology (Casey & Schlosser, 1994) and disease (Barefoot, Dodge, Peterson, Dahlstrom, & Williams, 1989). On the other hand, expressing anger in socially constructive ways is associated with more favorable outcomes in preschool and elementary school children.

THE DEVELOPMENTAL COURSE OF ANGER AND ITS REGULATION

Anger in Infants and Toddlers

Validity of Infant Anger

The question of whether young infants display discrete negative emotions (including anger), as opposed to a more generalized distress reaction, has been the topic of an intense theoretical and methodological debate (e.g., Camras, Sullivan, & Michel, 1993; Izard et al., 1995; Oster, Hegley, & Nagel, 1992). It has been argued that objective methods for coding discrete negative emotions, such as the Maximally Discriminative Facial Movement Coding System (MAX; Izard, 1983) and the System for Identifying Affect Expressions by Holistic Judgments (AFFEX; Izard, Dougherty, & Hembree, 1983), lack social validity: When shown exemplars based on MAX coding, naive observers could not discriminate discrete negative emotions reliably (Oster et al., 1992).

In response, Izard et al. (1995) presented data from a series of studies speaking to the issue of whether there are discrete emotions in young infants and whether it is possible to demonstrate social validity for MAX/AFFEX

coding. They presented longitudinal data on infants aged from 2.5 months to 9.5 months, which were coded with MAX and AFFEX. These data showed very little developmental change in the frequency of discrete emotions, contrary to what would be expected if negative emotions proceed from undifferentiated distress to become more discrete with age.

Izard et al. (1995) also examined the effects of task demands on naive observers' judgments of infant and adult facial expressions. Naive raters' emotion judgments for infant and adult emotion exemplars were compared under two conditions. Observers were randomly assigned to make forced choices from a list that contained either discrete-emotion labels only or a list that contained the discrete-emotion labels plus the term "distress." Accuracy for negative emotions was better in the "discrete-only" condition than in the "discrete-plus-distress" condition. Izard et al. argued that inaccuracies in naive observers' decoding of infant facial expressions arise from two sources: individual differences and "noise" in the infant signals themselves (i.e., they are less clear than adult signals), and the ambiguity of language labels (e.g., "distress"), which add additional "noise" to the process. Moreover, there is some indication that naive raters may not consider infants "mature" enough to experience emotions like anger (see Camras et al., 1997) and thus may find global terms like "distress" as fitting better with their hypotheses about infant expressivity. Izard et al. (1995) also suggested the need for an integration of their coding systems with one developed by Oster and colleagues.

Reliable and valid measurement of emotion is essential for progress in understanding the development of anger (and other emotions). Unfortunately, this debate has had an inhibiting effect on research on infant anger. For example, because of the methodological debate, some studies of infant emotions have used more global categories of negative emotions (e.g., Camras, Oster, Campos, Miyake, & Bradshaw, 1992), have used observer judgments rather than objective scoring systems (e.g., Camras et al., 1993), and in one case actually blacked out infants' faces from the video records (e.g., Camras et al., 1997). In the remainder of this section, we summarize studies examining anger in the first year of life. As a group, these studies used the MAX/AFFEX coding schemes, which yield discrete rather than global codes for negative emotions.

Early Development of Anger

In our chapter in the first edition of this volume (Lemerise & Dodge, 1993), we reviewed work by Stenberg and Campos (1990) and Izard, Hembree, and Huebner (1987) suggesting that the first clear expressions of anger emerge at about 4 months and that anger expressions are targeted to a social figure by 7 months. These expressions were observed (and coded with MAX/AFFEX) in response to arm restraint (Stenberg & Campos, 1990) and inoculations (Izard et al., 1987). Pickens and Field (1993) have since reported observing anger expressions (coded with AFFEX) in 3-month-old infants during face-to-face interactions with mothers. Infants of depressed mothers showed more angry (and sad) facial expressions than did infants of nondepressed mothers. Nondepressed mothers' facial expressions were less negative than those of depressed mothers. Pickens and Field's results also suggest that individual differences in expressivity may be indirectly socialized, as reported in the work of Malatesta and Haviland (1982).

The adaptive significance of anger is revealed in a series of studies on contingency learning in normal infants (Lewis, Alessandri, & Sullivan, 1990; Lewis et al., 1992). Lewis and colleagues found that infants who displayed anger during extinction showed the highest levels of joy, interest, and a required arm pull operant when the learning portion of the task was reinstated. They then studied the emotions and adaptive behavior of infants exposed to cocaine *in utero* (Alessandri, Sullivan, Imaizumi, & Lewis, 1993) and found that 4-, 6-, and 8-month-old cocaine-exposed infants showed less interest and joy during learning and less anger and sadness during extinction than did matched controls. When the contingency was restored, cocaine-exposed infants did not increase the rate of the arm pull operant. The results suggest that cocaine-exposed infants' reduced emotional expressivity may make them less effective in dealing with the environment.

A recent study by Buss and Goldsmith (1998) also underscores the adaptive significance of anger and of infants' attempts to regulate their anger with behavioral strategies. Infants were studied at 6, 12, and 18 months of age. In separate sessions, infants were exposed to two anger-eliciting stimuli (a barrier problem and arm restraint) and two fear-eliciting stimuli. Infants' affect was scored with AFFEX, and the occurrences of behaviors considered to be regulatory were coded. The anger and fear tasks elicited the predicted emotions, and anger and fear were distinct and not significantly related to one another, as might be expected if they were really "distress." Moreover, infants used different regulatory strategies for anger and fear, and regulatory behaviors on the part of infants reduced their anger expressions but not their fear expressions. In other words, anger energized and organized behaviors that "worked" in the sense that they reduced anger, but the same was not true of fear. Buss and Goldsmith concluded that the emotion regulation literature's almost exclusive focus on negative emotion as a global construct has obscured important between-emotion differences in infants' regulatory strategies and their success.

Factors Affecting the Development of Anger

This body of work suggests that anger is associated with infants' attempts to master the physical environment, and that anger elicits behavioral strategies from infants that serve regulatory functions and contribute to problem solving. An infant's anger can also serve as a social signal, mobilizing a reaction from the caregiver that assists the infant in modulating his or her distress. At the same time, however, caregivers' socialization goals are to encourage positive and neutral emotions and to minimize negative emotions. Differential responding to positive and negative emotions on the part of caregivers is associated with the increasing frequency of positive and neutral expressions over time. Thus infants and caregivers mutually influence each other, and their relationship can be described as transactional.

Campos and colleagues suggested that infants' evolving abilities alter transactions with their social environments (Campos, Kermoian, & Zumbahlen, 1992; Campos et al., 1996). They hypothesized that the emergence of locomotion reorganizes infants' relationships with parents and the physical environment, resulting in "changes in the quality and intensity of the expression of affect by both the parent and the infant" (Campos et al., 1992, p. 25). For example, locomoting infants can damage objects, which can elicit parental anger, and locomoting infants' goals may be thwarted more often, which elicits infant anger. To test these hypotheses, Campos et al. (1992) interviewed parents of 8-month-old infants with (1) no loco-motor experience, (2) 5 or more weeks of loco-motor experience, and (3) at least 4 weeks of walker experience. Compared to parents of prelocomoting infants, parents of locomoting infants reported feeling angry at their infants more often, seeing them as more responsible/autonomous, increasing the use of the voice in discipline, and being more likely to use physical punishment (a "tap" on the hand). Locomoting infants, compared to prelocomoting infants, were seen by their parents as showing increased attention to distal objects, expressing more anger (especially intense anger), but also expressing more positive affect (especially connected with mastery). Aspects of the parent–child relationship also differed; locomoting infants showed more signs of attachment and intense forms of affection. The results support the idea that the emergence of developmental milestones such as locomotion reorganizes infants' transactions with the physical and social environment.

Campos and colleagues' work suggests that a parent's seeing an infant as autonomous and responsible is linked to more direct socialization strategies and less permissiveness on the part of the parent (Campos et al., 1992). The child's increasing autonomy makes it more likely that the caregiver and the child will find themselves at cross-purposes. In Goodenough's (1931) classic monograph, for children younger than 3 years, most angry outbursts were directed at caregivers during routine caregiving or other interactions. As children moved from infancy to toddlerhood, parents became less permissive of this kind of angry behavior and used a variety of strategies to discourage it. For example, with children younger than 2 to 3 years, mothers reported using coaxing, diversion of attention, ignoring, and physical restraint in response to angry outbursts. With increasing age, ignoring continued to be used for girls, whereas boys received more attention for their anger in the form of power-assertive measures such as threats, spankings, and deprivation of privileges (Goodenough, 1931). More recently, Radke-Yarrow and Kochanska (1990) reported similar sex differences in how mothers handled anger. Girls were more likely to be ignored or told to stop, whereas boys were more likely to be rewarded by receiving attention for their anger. Radke-Yarrow and Kochanska saw these differences as being consistent with culturally based gender stereotypes for the expression of anger.

Although more direct socialization methods are increasingly used as children get older, caregivers do not abandon indirect socialization methods. Denham (1993) found that mothers and their 2-year-olds responded contingently to each other's emotion displays, and that mothers seemed to have agendas similar to those reported by Malatesta and Haviland (1982)—that is, maximizing positive and neutral emotions, while minimizing negative emotions. Individual differences in social competence were associated with differences in how mothers responded to toddlers' negative emotions. For example, mothers who responded to toddlers' anger with calm neutrality or cheerful displays had toddlers who showed interest in the environment, positive emotions, and positive responses to strangers in the mothers' absence. Denham (1993) concluded that "mothers' responsiveness which worked to attenuate their children's concurrent negative affect had far-reaching contributions to social-emotional competence" (p. 725). On the other hand, as Crockenberg (1985) demonstrated, angry maternal responding to toddlers' difficult behaviors was associated with toddlers' persisting in angry, noncompliant behavior and being less likely to respond empathically to others. Thus socialization practices that act to modulate toddlers' negative arousal may make more competent and empathic behavior possible.

Another mechanism of indirect socialization involves exposure to interadult anger. Infants as young as 3 months respond differentially to mothers' natural (multimodal) displays of emotion, including anger (e.g., Haviland & Lelwica, 1987), and 5-month-old infants respond differentially to positively and negatively toned infant-directed vocalizations in their own and unfamiliar languages (Fernald, 1993). According to maternal diaries of naturally occurring emotions, children as young as 12 months may stare or "freeze," look concerned or frown, or show distress by whimpering when witnessing others' angry interactions. Slightly older children begin to use social referencing (Walden & Ogan, 1988) with their mothers (Radke-Yarrow & Kochanska, 1990). Beginning at about 16 to 18 months, toddlers use more direct strategies to deal with angry situations, such as covering their ears, leaving the room, intervening verbally and/or physically (Cummings, Zahn-Waxler, & Radke-Yarrow, 1981; Radke-Yarrow & Kochanska, 1990), or behaving aggressively.

Jenkins, Franco, Dolins, and Sewell (1995)

tested whether exposure to emotionally arous-ing situations resulted in the formation of ex-pectancies concerning adults' interactions. Tod-dlers witnessed both an emotional (sad or angry) and a neutral interaction between two female strangers. Toddlers who saw the emo-tional interaction first showed carryover ef-fects, in that their play also was disrupted when the female actors returned and behaved neutral-ly. Jenkins et al. suggested that exposure to anger (and sadness of equal intensity) influ-ences how children build models of relation-ships, which they use to interpret future interac-tions (see also Dodge, Bates, & Pettit, 1990; Schwartz, Dodge, Pettit, & Bates, 1997).

In summary, the emergence of anger in in-fants remains a topic of theoretical and method-ological debate. An answer to this question awaits the resolution of the thorny issue of how to measure infants' emotions reliably and valid-ly. Naive observers' judgments concerning in-fant anger may be biased by beliefs that infants are not capable of such emotions. However, the perception of infants as autonomous and re-sponsible coincident with the emergence of lo-comotion is associated with parental reports of infant anger. It may be that locomoting infants' goals are clearer to adult observers, and that such infants' responses to goal blockage are thus easier to interpret as anger. Research from a variety of investigators suggests that anger is an important energizer of infants' adaptive be-havior. However, the onset of locomotion often places infants' goals at odds with those of care-givers, increasing the incidence of anger be-tween them. Parents become less permissive of angry outbursts, and socialization of anger be-comes more direct. Toddlers' social-emotional competence has been linked to maternal social-ization practices that modulate strong negative emotions and encourage positive and neutral ones.

Anger and Its Regulation in Preschool-Age Children

In the preschool period, children continue to learn to coordinate their goals with those of others and are expected to show increasing con-trol of their anger. Peers emerge as important new socializers of anger in this period. Lan-guage affords children a new way to express emotions, and gives parents a powerful tool in socializing emotion. However, preschool-age children still have relatively poor control over their displays of emotion. An important devel-opmental task for preschoolers involves learn-ing to manage their arousal in the service of goals for play and affiliation with peers (Parker & Gottman, 1989). Emotion socialization processes in the family contribute to children's social and emotional competence with peers and at preschool (e.g., Denham, Mitchell-Copeland, Strandberg, Auerbach, & Blair, 1997; Dunn & Brown, 1994).

The Expression and Socialization of Anger in the Family Context

Parke (1994) has suggested three ways in which parents (and other socialization agents) can so-cialize emotion expressivity, understanding, and regulation. Parents can indirectly influence children's expressivity and emotional develop-ment through their contingent emotion displays during dyadic interaction. Also, with the advent of language, parents can more easily teach or coach their children about emotion. Finally, parents influence children's opportunities to learn about emotion by regulating their access to peers, stimulating games, and/or television programs, and by protecting versus exposing them to emotional displays/arguments (e.g, in-teradult anger; Cummings, 1994).

Because preschoolers generally have poorer control of their emotion displays than do older children, observational methods in the home and in the laboratory are often used to study anger and other emotions at this age. Across home and laboratory settings, evidence indi-cates that negative affect (especially anger) in the context of parent–child interaction, particu-larly if it is intense, reciprocated, and/or more frequent than for most children and parents, is associated with poorer child outcomes (e.g., Carson & Parke, 1996; Denham et al., 1997). Denham and colleagues found that high levels of parental anger during interactions with chil-dren were associated with distress, avoidant in-teraction styles, less prosocial behavior toward parents and peers, and poorer understanding of emotion in children. In contrast, "emotion coaching" (combining low anger with verbal strategies) was positively correlated with social competence (Denham et al., 1997; see also Dunn & Brown, 1994).

Whether parents are able to marshal their re-sources to engage in this optimal socialization pattern may depend upon their children's characteristics. Eisenberg and Fabes (1994) reported that maternal reactions to children's negative emotions are influenced by the children's temperament. In particular, mothers who perceive their children as having intense negative emotions and being poorer at regulating their emotions also report experiencing more distress and anger and using more punitive and less supportive practices. An important question concerns whether maternal socialization practices still contribute to the prediction of children's coping with anger after the variance associated with children's temperamental characteristics is controlled for. Eisenberg and Fabes (1994) reported that several socialization practices (maternal distress, problem-focused socialization, emotion-focused socialization) still contributed to the prediction of children's anger reactions at school when child temperament was controlled for.

Parents also socialize children's anger by regulating their exposure to angry situations, either intentionally or unintentionally. Children of all ages find adults' anger stressful and emotionally arousing; exposure to interadult anger may sensitize children toward anger and make them more likely to be aggressive (Cummings, 1994; Schwartz et al., 1997). Moreover, children's own negative emotionality may exacerbate the effects of witnessed anger (Davies & Cummings, 1995). Children older than 6 years show increasing sensitivity to whether conflicts are resolved, but even 4- and 5-year-olds are somewhat sensitive to this information (Shifflett-Simpson & Cummings, 1996). Conflicts are less emotionally upsetting for children when they are resolved (El-Sheikh & Cummings, 1995).

The Expression and Socialization of Anger in the Peer Context

Preschool children's emotion regulation skills equip them, for better or worse, for interactions with peers. Peers themselves, however, can also act as elicitors and socializers of children's anger. A number of theorists have argued that peer interactions provide a unique context for becoming more socially competent; learning to manage one's emotions, particularly when in conflict with peers (e.g., Putallaz & Sheppard, 1992); and developing prosocial and moral motives (Arsenio & Lover, 1995). Arsenio and colleagues conducted an interesting series of studies of preschool children's affect during and

outside of conflicts, including aggression. Arsenio and Killen (1996) videotaped, and coded with AFFEX, triads of preschoolers during table play. Conflict initiators displayed significantly more positive affect during conflicts, whereas recipients expressed more anger and sadness. In the postconflict period, the initiators, who were previously happy, became more negative in their emotion displays. The recipients' negative emotional reactions may have influenced the initiators' emotions. Children who initiated more conflicts were significantly more likely also to be targets of conflict. Interestingly, children who were "happy initiators" were more likely to be angry and surprised when they were targets of conflict. Recipients of conflict who exhibited higher levels of negative emotions (anger and sadness) were more at risk for both initiating and being the target of conflicts. Similar findings were reported for conflict and aggression observed during free play (Arsenio & Lover, 1997). In addition, anger expressed outside of conflict situations predicted both initiation of aggression and anger during aggression.

Another approach to studying anger in preschoolers is to present them with hypothetical situations. An advantage of this methodology is that standard anger-eliciting situations can be presented to all children. When researchers are studying naturally occurring conflicts and anger, not all children may exhibit the behaviors of interest, and the circumstances surrounding conflict events may vary widely and nonrandomly across participants (Murphy & Eisenberg, 1997). Denham, Bouril, and Belouad (1994) presented preschoolers with hypothetical provocation and peer entry situations and asked them how they would feel and what they would do in these situations. In addition, they did naturalistic observations of children's emotional expressivity in the classroom, obtained teacher ratings of social skills, obtained peer ratings of likability, and assessed children's emotion knowledge. Children who said that they would be angry in response to the hypothetical situations were more likely to pick aggression and less likely to pick a prosocial behavior as their responses to the situations. In the classroom, these children were less expressive, and teachers were more likely to rate them as miserable/fearful. Thus negative emotionality, including anger, was associated with aggressive solutions to these situations.

Eisenberg, Fabes, Minore, et al. (1994) used

a puppet paradigm in which preschoolers acted out their responses to hypothetical conflict situations. They reported that children's enactments with puppets related well to their observed anger reactions at preschool, as well as to reports from mothers and teachers concerning how the children handled conflict. High levels of emotionality in children were associated with higher levels of enacted aggression and less friendliness enacted with puppets. Murphy and Eisenberg (1997) found that boys' enacted friendly responses to hypothetical peer provocateurs were related to socializers' reports of high self-regulation and low emotional intensity. A general picture emerges across research methods that negative emotionality, especially anger, is associated with aggressive responding in preschoolers.

Finally, emotion-eliciting hypothetical situations were used to study cross-cultural differences in U.S. and Japanese preschoolers' emotions and coping behaviors (Zahn-Waxler, Friedman, Cole, Mizuta, & Hiruma, 1996). Children from the United States more often said that they would feel angry, and enacted more anger and aggression, than did Japanese children. U.S. mothers were more likely to say that they encouraged expression of emotions than were Japanese mothers.

Knowledge about Anger in Preschool-Age Children: Display Rules

Preschool children exhibit increasing understanding of the situational determinants of emotion and rules guiding the display of various emotions (Levine, 1995). Using hypothetical-situation methodology, Zeman, Penza, Shipman, and Young (1997) investigated the effects of audience (mother, father, friend) on 4-year-olds' use of display rules and their expectancies concerning managing emotion displays. The hypothetical situations involved eating an unappetizing meal, receiving a disappointing present, and being in a boring place. Children most often reported that they would feel angry in these situations, and that they would regulate emotion more with mothers and friends than with fathers. Children expected mothers and fathers to be more receptive than friends to displays of emotion; they were more likely to report that they would express their negative emotions when they expected to receive support or assistance. Thus children as young as 4 years both demonstrated an aware-

ness of display rules and a sensitivity to the role of context in their use.

In summary, the preschool period is a time when greater demands are placed on children by family and peers to regulate their emotions and to express them in socially constructive ways. Children make great strides in controlling their emotion displays and in understanding the situational determinants of emotion and display rules. Some children, however, begin to show signs of difficulty in managing their emotions (especially their anger), and these difficulties predict poorer social functioning and problem behaviors.

Anger and Its Regulation in School-Age Children

A number of factors converge to make the peer context a salient one for school-age children. With school entry, children spend more time with peers, and they are exposed to a greater number and variety of peers. School-age children acquire information about their own competence in various areas by comparing themselves to peers, and across the elementary school years, children increase in their use of social comparison (e.g., Stipek & MacIver, 1989). Children show increasing sensitivity to their position relative to peers, and being accepted by peers and having friends assume great importance (Parker & Gottman, 1989), making peer group norms for emotion regulation especially significant to these children. Parker and Gottman contend that school-age children learn a great deal about display rules from the reactions of peers to their own and others' emotion displays. Moreover, the peer norm during middle childhood is to avoid emotionality and give the impression of "being 'cool'—calm, unruffled, and always under emotional control" (Parker & Gottman, 1989, p. 116).

Research on elementary school children's use and understanding of display rules tends to support Parker and Gottman's (1989) view. Children expect more negative reactions from peers than from parents for expressing anger and sadness, and they report using display rules more with friends than with parents (Zeman & Garber, 1996; Zeman & Shipman, 1998). Elementary school children expect little support for expressing anger (Zeman & Shipman, 1996) and report more masking of anger than of other emotions (Underwood, 1997). However, at the same time, they see anger as hard to control and report lower self-efficacy for controlling anger than sadness (Zeman & Shipman, 1997). Interestingly, Underwood (1997) found no peer status differences in knowledge about emotion display rules, which indicates that these peer group norms are quite salient for children of this age. Finally, the importance of the peer context in promoting management of children's emotions is revealed by findings that children endorse more goals for regulating affect with peers than they do with parents (Zeman & Shipman, 1997).

Given the peer group norms for controlling one's emotions, it follows that during middle childhood, indices of peer group acceptance will be related to children's skills at reading and managing emotions, including anger (Hubbard & Coie, 1994). Cassidy, Parke, Butkovsky, and Braungart (1992) found that kindergartners' and first-graders' understanding of emotions was positively related to peer acceptance. Popular elementary school children are viewed by classmates as perceiving and understanding emotions better than rejected children (Vosk, Forehand, & Figueroa, 1983), and as more likely to use a calm versus an angry/retaliatory or avoidant approach to conflict resolution (Bryant, 1992). In contrast, rejected and controversial children are viewed by peers as being especially likely to use angry/retaliatory approaches to conflict.

Both laboratory simulations to elicit anger and hypothetical situation methodology have been used to study anger in school-age children. Graham, Hudley, and Williams (1992) presented aggressive and nonaggressive Latino and African American middle school students with hypothetical provocation situations that varied in the intent portrayed. Aggressive children reported feeling angrier and more often preferred hostile responses. In contrast, nonaggressive children's evaluations of intent influenced their anger ratings and response selection. When the provocation was perceived as unintentional, nonaggressive children felt less angry and were less likely to retaliate. The results suggest that for aggressive children, feelings of anger may "short-circuit" evaluations of intent, leading to aggressive responding (see also Dodge & Somberg, 1987).

Crick and Dodge (1994) suggested that emotional arousal may influence children's goals for social situations, and that these goals then bias children's evaluation and selection of possible responses to a provocation. To test this hypothesis, Lemerise, Harper, Caverly, and Hobgood (1998) examined the effects of angry, happy, and neutral mood induction on 480 first-through third-graders' goals and outcome expectancies for provocation situations. Children were more likely to focus on instrumental goals than on social-relational goals when an angry mood was induced than when a neutral mood was induced. Children with primarily instrumental goals had less positive expectancies for the social-relational and instrumental consequences of nonhostile responses to provocation, and higher self-efficacy for hostile responses. Aggressive/less accepted children had significantly more instrumental goals in the angry mood induction condition and significantly fewer in the happy mood induction condition, whereas highly competent children showed no effects of mood on number of instrumental goals. Overall, these results suggest that anger makes children focus on instrumental goals and makes them less concerned about whether peers like them. Moreover, less accepted/highly aggressive children seem to be more vulnerable to effects of angry mood and may be less able to self-regulate their moods.

Hypothetical-situation methodology has the advantage of presenting standard stimuli to all participants, but it may not always reveal how children actually behave when involved in emotionally arousing events. Naturalistic observations of school-age children are often not practical, because children this age have so little free-play and/or unstructured time at school compared to preschoolers. Therefore, investigators have begun to develop laboratory methods in which children can be exposed to carefully controlled, anger-eliciting stimuli (e.g., Hubbard & Coie, 2000; Underwood & Galen, 1997). Hubbard and colleagues have developed a paradigm in which children are videotaped playing a board game in which they lose to a confederate who cheats in an obvious fashion. After the simulation, children are interviewed concerning their goals, display rules, and emotions. Hubbard and Coie (2000) reported that rejected African American second-graders expressed more anger and happiness across the facial, verbal, and nonverbal modes than nonrejected peers did. Rejected children's angry facial expressions were of higher intensity and longer duration, and they were more likely to endorse the instrumental goal of winning the game than the social-relational goal of having the peer like them. Ramsden and Hubbard (1998) found no status differences in knowledge about how one should act, but popular children knew more strategies for using display rules, and rejected children reported wanting to display their anger more. Parker and Hubbard (1998) reported that aggressive children showed differences between their responses in laboratory and hypothetical contexts: They showed less knowledge and use of display rules following the laboratory simulation than following the hypothetical situations. These results suggest that the more emotionally arousing laboratory simulation may interfere with aggressive children's ability to access and use display rules.

Underwood and colleagues have also developed a laboratory simulation to study anger. Children play a computer game with a confederate who wins and makes provoking comments. In this situation, there is some indication that older children mask their emotions more than younger children. Moreover, rejected children in one study (Underwood & Hurley, 1999) exhibited more negatively toned nonverbal behavior (e.g., faking punches, banging the keyboard, etc.) and made more attempts to change the situation by pleading with or bribing the confederate. Rejected children also were more likely to stop the play session early, suggesting that they found this situation stressful and/or they lacked constructive strategies with which to cope, compared to average and popular children (Underwood & Hurley, 1999).

Because competitive games may be more appealing and salient to boys than to girls, Underwood and Galen (1997) have developed a laboratory simulation to elicit more social forms of aggression, which are known to be displayed by girls (e.g., Crick, Bigbee, & Howes, 1996). Two friends and a confederate join in the laboratory to play the game of Pictionary. The confederate is trained to be a difficult play partner who brags about her abilities, criticizes the other girls, is bossy, and plays the game badly. In one study employing this simulation, ratings of videotapes yielded higher anger ratings from girls than from boys and from elementary school children than from middle school children (Galen & Underwood, 1997).

Together, the research reported on school-age children suggests that there are individual differences in children's ability to deal with anger and provocative situations. Rejected and/or aggressive children appear to have difficulty regulating their anger in provocative situations, and this difficulty seems to contribute to goals and responses that are less socially competent and constructive. Research conducted by Eisenberg and her colleagues suggests that individual differences in negative emotionality and regulation may contribute to peer status differences in emotion-related skills and social competence. For example, Eisenberg et al. (1997) followed children from preschool to middle childhood and found a relation between a composite measure of social functioning (which included assessments of popularity and social competence) and children's temperament. Children who were high in regulatory skills and low in negative emotionality, general emotional intensity, and nonconstructive coping showed high-quality social functioning, both concurrently and longitudinally. In another study, Murphy and Eisenberg (1996) examined how 7- to 11-year-old children reported dealing with peers' anger. They found that boys who were considered by camp counselors to be low in emotional intensity and high in self-regulation reported more constructive social goals that reflected concern for the peer. The general picture emerging is that having good self-regulation skills in combination with low-intensity emotions predicts better social functioning.

The finding that individual differences in emotionality, regulation, and coping with anger observed during the preschool period show stability through middle childhood (e.g., Eisenberg et al., 1997) suggests that children may be developing characteristic ways of dealing with the social environment. The pattern of poor self-regulation and intensely negative emotionality can be described as "emotionally dysregulated" (e.g., Cole, Michel, & Teti, 1994; Dodge & Garber, 1991). Cole and colleagues have argued that such dysregulation makes for less flexible responding and is a risk factor for psychopathology (see also Magai, 1996, for an interesting discussion of the development of a personality organized around anger). Indeed, Eisenberg et al. (1996) showed that negative emotionality and low regulation were associated with a high risk for problem behaviors in a nonclinical population of elementary school children. Consistent with these findings, children with diagnosed externalizing disorders exhibit deficits in expression, appraisal, and regulation of emotion (Casey & Schlosser, 1994).

These findings are intriguing and suggest the need for further study of the effects of anger and self-regulation on children's capacity to respond in socially constructive versus maladaptive ways.

SUMMARY AND CONCLUSIONS

An examination of the developmental course of anger and its regulation reveals that the role and meaning of anger in a child's repertoire change developmentally. For infants, the expression of anger is often associated with being effective. When someone is restraining an infant's movement, or a barrier is placed between the infant and a desirable object, anger energizes and organizes behaviors (e.g., struggling, pushing away the barrier) that "work" in the sense that they reduce anger and promote obtaining goals. Infants' angry signals to others can also be very effective in producing responses to the infants that reduce their anger and increase their sense of efficacy. However, the onset of locomotion appears to change parents' views of infants; they see infants as autonomous, responsible, and angry. Moreover, parents are more likely to report getting angry with their infants after this developmental milestone. Thus the "rules" appear to change at this point, and parents begin more actively to socialize the expression of anger. Although children begin to learn that anger doesn't *always* work, they still find that it is effective in obtaining instrumental goals (Patterson, Littman, & Bricker, 1967).

The process of socializing anger is complex, and we are just beginning to understand it. The role of children's temperament in this process appears to be important, but we know much less about how parents' temperamental qualities contribute to how they respond to their children. Clearly some children experience emotions more intensely and have more difficulty regulating their emotions—facts that have long-term implications for their social functioning. An important question for future research concerns the extent to which socialization practices exacerbate or mitigate this pattern. A number of researchers have demonstrated that socialization techniques that minimize negative emotions, combined with emotion coaching, facilitate empathy and prosocial responding; that is, they promote emotional and social competence. However, it is less clear whether these techniques work equally well with children who vary in emotional intensity and self-regulation skills.

As children move from infancy to early childhood, their social circle widens, and peers become important elicitors and socializers of anger. In this more complex social world, children must learn to coordinate their goals with those of others who are much less indulgent than parents. Affiliative goals play a crucial role in motivating children to control arousal to sustain the exciting and enjoyable activity of play with peers and to maintain friendship. Children's temperamental profiles and/or their socialization experiences in the family may more or less prepare them to function effectively with peers. Difficulties with peers may further reduce children's opportunities and motivation to learn to manage anger in ways that preserve relationships.

By elementary school, children with deficits in anger regulation are at risk for problem behaviors (Eisenberg et al., 1996), and children who have been diagnosed with externalizing disorders show deficits in the expression, appraisal, and regulation of emotions, particularly anger (Casey & Schlosser, 1994). These findings underscore the importance of continuing to study how anger and other emotions regulate and come to be regulated in the context of social interactions. At present, we know somewhat more about this process for parents and children than we do about the peer context.

In conclusion, considerable progress has been made in the study of anger and its development. The results reviewed here have considerable applied significance for those working with children who have difficulties with peers as well as more serious problems. Continued progress depends on resolving methodological debates and developing new techniques to study anger.

ACKNOWLEDGMENT

Elizabeth A. Lemerise was supported by a Western Kentucky University Summer Research Fellowship during the preparation of this chapter.

REFERENCES

Alessandri, S. M., Sullivan, M. W., Imaizumi, S., & Lewis, M. (1993). Learning and emotional expressivity in cocaine-exposed infants. *Developmental Psychology, 29,* 989–997.

Arsenio, W., & Killen, M. (1996). Conflict-related emotions during peer disputes. *Early Education and Development, 7,* 43–57.

Arsenio, W., & Lover, A. (1995). Children's conceptions of sociomoral affect: Happy victimizers, mixed emotions, and other expectancies. In M. Killen & D. Hart (Eds.), *Morality in everyday life: Developmental perspectives* (pp. 87–128). Cambridge, England: Cambridge University Press.

Arsenio, W., & Lover, A. (1997). Emotions, conflicts and aggression during preschoolers' free play. *British Journal of Developmental Psychology, 15,* 531–542.

Barefoot, J. C., Dodge, K. A., Peterson, B. L., Dahlstrom, W. G., & Williams, X. B. (1989). The Cook–Medley Hostility Scale: Item content and ability to predict survival. *Psychosomatic Medicine, 51,* 46–57.

Bridges, L. J., & Grolnick, W. S. (1995). The development of emotional self-regulation in infancy and early childhood. In N. Eisenberg (Ed.), *Review of personality and social psychology: Vol. 15. Social development* (pp. 185–211). Thousand Oaks, CA: Sage.

Bryant, B. K. (1992). Conflict resolution strategies in relation to children's peer relations. *Journal of Applied Developmental Psychology, 13,* 35–50.

Buss, K. A., & Goldsmith, H. H. (1998). Fear and anger regulation in infancy: Effects on the temporal dynamics of affective expression. *Child Development, 69,* 359–374.

Campos, J. J., Kermoian, R., & Witherington, D. (1996). An epigenetic perspective on emotional development. In R. D. Kavanaugh, B. Zimmerberg, & S. Fein (Eds.), *Emotion: Interdisciplinary perspectives* (pp. 119–138). Hillsdale, NJ: Erlbaum.

Campos, J. J., Kermoian, R., & Zumbahlen, M. R. (1992). Socioemotional transformations in the family system following infant crawling onset. In N. Eisenberg & R. Fabes (Eds.), *New directions for child development: Vol. 55. Emotion and its regulation in early development* (pp. 25–40). San Francisco: Jossey-Bass.

Camras, L. A. (1992). Expressive development and basic emotions. *Cognition and Emotion, 6,* 269–283.

Camras, L. A., Oster, H., Campos, J. J., Campos, R., Ujiie, T., Miyake, K., Lei, W., & Zhaolan, M. (1997). Observer judgments of emotion in American, Japanese, and Chinese infants. In K. C. Barrett (Ed.), *New directions for child development: Vol. 77. The communication of emotion: Current research from diverse perspectives* (pp. 89–105). San Francisco: Jossey-Bass.

Camras, L. A., Oster, H., Campos, J. J., Miyake, K., & Bradshaw, D. (1992). Japanese and American infants' responses to arm restraint. *Developmental Psychology, 28,* 578–583.

Camras, L. A., Sullivan, J., & Michel, G. (1993). Do infants express discrete emotions?: Adult judgments of facial, vocal, and body actions. *Journal of Nonverbal Behavior, 17,* 171–186.

Carson, J. L, & Parke, R. D. (1996). Reciprocal negative affect in parent–child interactions and children's peer competence. *Child Development, 67,* 2217–2226.

Casey, R. J., & Schlosser, S. (1994). Emotional responses to peer praise in children with and without a diagnosed externalizing disorder. *Merrill–Palmer Quarterly, 40,* 60–81.

Cassidy, J., Parke, R. D., Butkovsky, L., & Braungart, J. M. (1992). Family–peer connections: The roles of emotional expressiveness within the family and children's understanding of emotions. *Child Development, 63,* 603–618.

Cole, P. M., Michel, M. K., & Teti, L. O. (1994). The development of emotion regulation and dysregulation: A clinical perspective. In N. A. Fox (Ed.), The development of emotion regulation: Behavioral and biological considerations. *Monographs of the Society for Research in Child Development, 59*(2–3, Serial No. 240), 73–100.

Crick, N, R., Bigbee, M. A., & Howes, C. (1996). Gender differences in children's normative beliefs about aggression: How do I hurt thee? Let me count the ways. *Child Development, 67,* 1003–1014.

Crick, N. R., & Dodge, K. A. (1994). A review and reformulation of social–information-processing mechanisms of children's social adjustment. *Psychological Bulletin, 115,* 74–101.

Crockenberg, S. (1985). Toddlers' reactions to maternal anger. *Merrill–Palmer Quarterly, 31,* 361–373.

Cummings, E. M. (1994). Marital conflict and children's functioning. *Social Development, 3,* 16–36.

Cummings, E. M., Zahn-Waxler, C., & Radke-Yarrow, M. (1981). Young children's responses to expressions of anger and affection by others in the family. *Child Development, 52,* 1274–1282.

Davies, P. T., & Cummings, E. M. (1995). Children's emotions as organizers of their reactions to interadult anger: A functionalist perspective. *Developmental Psychology, 31,* 677–684.

Denham, S. A. (1993). Maternal emotional responsiveness and toddlers' social-emotional competence. *Journal of Child Psychology and Psychiatry, 34,* 715–728.

Denham, S. A., Bouril, B., & Belouad, F. (1994). Preschoolers' affect and cognition about challenging peer situations. *Child Study Journal, 24,* 1–21.

Denham, S. A., Mitchell-Copeland, J., Strandberg, K., Auerbach, S., & Blair, K. (1997). Parental contributions to preschoolers' emotional competence: Direct and indirect effects. *Motivation and Emotion, 27,* 65–86.

Dodge, K. A., Bates, J. E., & Pettit, G. S. (1990). Mechanisms in the cycle of violence. *Science, 250,* 1678–1683.

Dodge, K. A., & Garber, J. (1991). Domains of emotion regulation. In J. Garber & K. A. Dodge (Eds.), *The development of emotion regulation and dysregulation* (pp. 3–11). New York: Cambridge University Press.

Dodge, K. A., & Somberg, D. R. (1987). Hostile attributional biases among aggressive boys are exacerbated under conditions of threat to the self. *Child Development, 58,* 213–224.

Dunn, J., & Brown, J. (1994). Affect expression in the family, children's understanding of emotion, and their interaction with others. *Merrill–Palmer Quarterly, 40,* 120–137.

Eisenberg, N., & Fabes, R. A. (1994). Mothers' reactions to children's negative emotions: Relations to children's temperament and anger behavior. *Merrill–Palmer Quarterly, 40*, 138–156.

Eisenberg, N., Fabes, R. A., Guthrie, I. K., Murphy, B. C., Maszk, P., Holmgren, R., & Suh, K. (1996). The relations of regulation and emotionality to problem behavior in elementary school children. *Development and Psychopathology, 8*, 141–162.

Eisenberg, N., Fabes, R. A., Minore, D., Mathy, R., Hanish, L., & Brown, T. (1994). Children's enacted interpersonal strategies: Their relations to social behavior and negative emotionality. *Merrill–Palmer Quarterly, 40*, 212–232.

Eisenberg, N., Fabes, R. A., Nyman, M., Bernzweig, J., & Pinuelas, A. (1994). The relations of emotionality and regulation to children's anger-related reactions. *Child Development, 65*, 109–128.

Eisenberg, N., Fabes, R. A., Shepard, S. A., Murphy, B. C., Guthrie, I. K., Jones, S., Friedman, J., Poulin, R., & Maszk, P. (1997). Contemporaneous and longitudinal prediction of children's social functioning from regulation and emotionality. *Child Development, 68*, 642–664.

El-Sheikh, M., & Cummings, E. M. (1995). Children's responses to angry adult behavior as a function of experimentally manipulated exposure to resolved and unresolved conflict. *Social Development, 4*, 75–91.

Fernald, A. (1993). Approval and disapproval: Infant responsiveness to vocal affect in familiar and unfamiliar languages. *Child Development, 64*, 657–674.

Galen, B. R., & Underwood, M. K. (1997). A developmental investigation of social aggression among children. *Developmental Psychology, 33*, 589–600.

Goodenough, F. L. (1931). *Anger in young children.* Minneapolis: University of Minnesota Press.

Graham, S., Hudley, C., & Williams, E. (1992). Attributional and emotional determinants of aggression among African-American and Latino young adolescents. *Developmental Psychology, 28*, 731–740.

Haviland, J. M., & Lelwica, M. (1987). The induced affect response: 10-week-old infants' responses to three emotion expressions. *Developmental Psychology, 23*, 97–104.

Hubbard, J. A., & Coie, J. D. (1994). Emotional correlates of social competence in children's peer relationships. *Merrill–Palmer Quarterly, 40*, 1–20.

Hubbard, J. A., & Coie, J. D. (2000). *Emotion expression processes in children's peer interaction: The role of peer rejection, gender, and aggression.* Manuscript submitted for publication.

Izard, C. E. (1983). *The Maximally Discriminative Facial Movement Coding System (MAX)* (rev. ed.). Newark: Instructional Resources Center, University of Delaware.

Izard, C. E. (1991). *The psychology of emotions.* New York: Plenum Press.

Izard, C. E., Dougherty, L., & Hembree, E. A. (1983). *A System for Identifying Affect Expressions by Holistic Judgments (AFFEX)* (rev. ed). Newark: Computer Network Services and University Media Services, University of Delaware.

Izard, C. E., Fantauzzo, C. A., Castle, J. M., Haynes, O. M., Rayias, M. F., & Putnam, P. H. (1995). The ontogeny and significance of infants' facial expressions in the first nine months of life. *Developmental Psychology, 31*, 997–1013.

Izard, C. E., Hembree, E. A., & Huebner, R. R. (1987). Infants' emotion expressions to acute pain: Developmental change and stability of individual differences. *Developmental Psychology, 23*, 105–113.

Izard, C. E., & Kobak, R. R. (1991). Emotions system functioning and emotion regulation. In J. Garber & K. A. Dodge (Eds.), *The development of emotion regulation and dysregulation* (pp. 303–321). New York: Cambridge University Press.

Jenkins, J. M., Franco, F., Dolins, F., & Sewell, A. (1995). Toddlers' reactions to negative emotion displays: Forming models of relationships. *Infant Behavior and Development, 18*, 273–281.

Lemerise, E. A., & Dodge, K. A. (1993). The development of anger and hostile interactions. In M. Lewis & J. M. Haviland (Eds.), *Handbook of emotions* (pp. 537–546). New York: Guilford Press.

Lemerise, E. A., Harper, B. D., Caverly, S., & Hobgood, C. (1998, March). *Mood, social goals, and children's outcome expectations.* Poster presented at Conference on Human Development, Mobile, AL.

Levine, L. J. (1995). Young children's understanding of the causes of anger and sadness. *Child Development, 66*, 697–709.

Lewis, M., Alessandri, S. M., & Sullivan, M. W. (1990). Violation of expectancy, loss of control, and anger expressions in young infants. *Developmental Psychology, 26*, 745–751.

Lewis, M., & Haviland, J. M. (Eds.). (1993). *Handbook of emotions.* New York: Guilford Press.

Lewis, M., Sullivan, M. W., Ramsay, D., & Alessandri, S. M. (1992). Individual differences in anger and sad expressions during extinction: Antecedents and consequences. *Infant Behavior and Development, 15*, 443–452.

Magai, C. (1996). Personality theory: Birth, death, and transfiguration. In R. D. Kavanaugh, B. Zimmerberg, & S. Fein (Eds.), *Emotion: Interdisciplinary perspectives* (pp. 172–201). Hillsdale, NJ: Erlbaum.

Malatesta, C., & Haviland, J. M. (1982). Learning display rules: The socialization of emotion expression in infancy. *Child Development, 53*, 991–1003.

Murphy, B. C., & Eisenberg, N. (1996). Provoked by a peer: Children's anger-related responses and their relations to social functioning. *Merrill–Palmer Quarterly, 42*, 103–124.

Murphy, B. C., & Eisenberg, N. (1997). Young children's emotionality: Regulation and social functioning and their responses when they are targets of a peer's anger. *Social Development, 6*, 18–36.

Oatley, K., & Jenkins, J. M. (1996). *Understanding emotions.* Oxford: Blackwell.

Oster, H., Hegley, D., & Nagel, L. (1992). Adult judgments and fine-grained analysis of infant facial expressions: Testing the validity of a priori coding formulas. *Developmental Psychology, 28*, 1115–1131.

Parke, R. D. (1994). Progress, paradigms, and unresolved problems: A commentary on recent advances in our understanding of children's emotions. *Merrill–Palmer Quarterly, 40*, 157–169.

Parker, E. H., & Hubbard, J. A. (1998, March). *Children's understanding of emotion following hypotheti-*

cal vignettes versus real-life peer interaction. Paper presented at Conference on Human Development, Mobile, AL.

Parker, J. G., & Gottman, J. M. (1989). Social and emotional development in a relational context: Friendship interaction from early childhood to adolescence. In T. J. Berndt & G. W. Ladd (Eds.), *Peer relationships in child development* (pp. 95–131). New York: Wiley.

Patterson, G. R., Littman, R. A., & Bricker, W. (1967). Assertive behavior in children: A step toward a theory of aggression. *Monographs of the Society for Research in Child Development, 32*(5, Serial No. 113).

Pickens, J., & Field, T. (1993). Facial expressivity in infants of depressed mothers. *Developmental Psychology, 29,* 986–988.

Putallaz, M., & Sheppard, B. H. (1992). Conflict management and social competence. In C. U. Shantz & W. W. Hartup (Eds.), *Conflict in child and adolescent development* (pp. 330–355). New York: Cambridge University Press.

Radke-Yarrow, M., & Kochanska, G. (1990). Anger in young children. In N. L. Stein, B. Leventhal, & T. Trabasso (Eds.), *Psychological and biological approaches to emotion* (pp. 297–310). Hillsdale, NJ: Erlbaum.

Ramsden, S. R., & Hubbard, J. A. (1998, March). *The role of sociometric status and gender in children's knowledge of display rules for anger.* Paper presented at Conference on Human Development, Mobile, AL.

Schwartz, D., Dodge, K. A., Pettit, G. S., & Bates, J. E. (1997). The early socialization of aggressive victims of bullying. *Child Development, 68,* 665–675.

Shifflett-Simpson, K., & Cummings, E. M. (1996). Mixed message resolution and children's responses to interadult conflict. *Child Development, 67,* 437–448.

Stenberg, C. R., & Campos, J. J. (1990). The development of anger expressions in infancy. In N. L. Stein, B. Leventhal, & T. Trabasso (Eds.), *Psychological and biological approaches to emotion* (pp. 297–310). Hillsdale: NJ: Erlbaum.

Stipek, D., & MacIver, D. (1989). Developmental changes in children's assessment of intellectual competence. *Developmental Psychology, 60,* 521–538.

Underwood, M. K. (1997). Peer social status and children's understanding of the expression and control of positive and negative emotions. *Merrill–Palmer Quarterly, 43,* 610–634.

Underwood, M. K., & Galen, B. R. (1997, April). Laboratory methods for investigating anger and aggression in peer interactions. In M. K. Underwood (Chair, *Creating naturalistic methods to observe peer relations and emotional expression.* Symposium conducted at the biennial meeting of the Society for Research in Child Development, Washington, DC.

Underwood, M. K., & Hurley, J. C. (1999). Emotion regulation in peer relationships during middle childhood. In L. Balter & C. Tamis-LeMonda (Eds.), *Child psychology: A handbook of contemporary issues* (pp. 58–87). Hamden, CT: Garland Press.

Vosk, B. N., Forehand, R., & Figueroa, R. (1983). Perceptions of emotions by accepted and rejected children. *Journal of Behavioral Assessment, 5,* 151–160.

Walden, T. A., & Ogan, T. A. (1988). The development of social referencing. *Child Development, 59,* 1230–1240.

Zahn-Waxler, C., Friedman, R. J., Cole, P. M., Mizuta, I., & Hiruma, N. (1996). Japanese and United States preschool children's responses to conflict and distress. *Child Development, 67,* 2462–2477.

Zeman, J., & Garber, J. (1996). Display rules for anger, sadness, and pain: It depends on who is watching. *Child Development, 67,* 957–973.

Zeman, J., Penza, S., Shipman, K., & Young, G. (1997). Preschoolers as functionalists: The impact of social context on emotion regulation. *Child Study Journal, 27,* 41–67.

Zeman, J., & Shipman, K. (1996). Children's expression of negative affect: Reasons and methods. *Developmental Psychology, 32,* 842–849.

Zeman, J., & Shipman, K. (1997). Social-contextual influences on expectancies for managing anger and sadness: The transition from middle childhood to adolescence. *Developmental Psychology, 33,* 917–924.

Zeman, J., & Shipman, K. (1998). Influence of social context on children's affect regulation: A functionalist perspective. *Journal of Nonverbal Behavior, 22*(3), 141–165.

CHAPTER 38

"Sadness"—Is There Such a Thing?

Carol Barr-Zisowitz

Sadness has not been well studied. Whereas other so-called "basic" emotions (such as anger and shame) have received book-length investigation by scholars, and even emotions no one calls "basic" (such as jealousy) have merited the same, sadness remains, so to speak, sadly neglected. The reader may object that there is a vast literature on depression and also on grief; however, though these are both cousins of sadness, they are not sadness. The brilliant synthetic effort *Culture and Depression* (Kleinman & Good, 1985) has raised the question of the relationship between sadness and depression, but for the most part the book deals with the latter. Although there is controversy over whether and to what extent depression is a universal biological disorder, and to what extent it is a culturally determined state or set of behaviors, most of the authors agree (implicitly or explicitly) that depression is an ongoing dysphoric state; that it is regarded as an illness or at least as deviant; and that it precludes the experience of positive emotions for long periods of time. However, the upsurge of interest in the study of emotion in the last decade centers on the normal and functional aspects of emotion, not on psychopathology; thus the study of sadness, a transient, normal emotion, is no more to be subsumed under depression than the study of happiness would be under mania.

Similarly, there is a huge literature on grief, largely influenced by John Bowlby's three-vol-

ume work *Attachment and Loss* (see especially Bowlby, 1980), and the seminal book by Peter Marris, *Loss and Change* (1974); however, for three reasons, studying grieving is not the same as studying sadness. First, the grief literature tends to assume rather than to investigate the relationship between situations and emotions. Grieving is conceptualized as following upon loss. My task here, on the contrary, is to focus on the emotion itself rather than on a single one of its causes. Second, the grief literature recognizes that emotions other than sadness, such as anger, come with grieving. Finally, the grief literature focuses on mechanisms and rituals for dealing with loss. The behaviors in these mechanisms interest students of emotion, but for most of us emotion implies an inner state as well as a set of behaviors, so that the study of sadness must be related to but more than the study of grief mechanisms.

PSYCHOLOGICAL APPROACHES

Although there is no major synthetic work on sadness, a number of disciplines offer work that is germane to the subject. I start with psychology, which grapples in the most straightforward way with emotions. A promising approach to understanding sadness comes from those psychologists who think, in Darwinian terms, of the function of emotion as enabling and motivating us to respond adaptively. Heavily influenced by the work of Silvan Tomkins and Paul Ekman, many psychologists have attempted to delineate differences among negative emotions by studying situations or cognitions that lead us, consciously or unconsciously, to choose a specific emotion. In addition, psychologists have assumed that by learning which emotion is appropriate to which appraisal of a situation, more can be concluded about the differing "functions" of each emotion (Folkman, Lazarus, Dunkel-Schetter, DeLongis, & Gruen, 1986). These studies have usually asked subjects to describe events that would lead to a list of "basic" emotions, including sadness, named by the investigators. However, more sophisticated studies have described types of situations or appraisals as independent variables, and then asked the subjects to describe emotions they would feel in each case (Ellsworth & Smith, 1988). Other studies have approached the question of function directly by asking subjects what they do when they experience various emotions.

What have these studies concluded about sadness? All concur in seeing sadness as an emotion experienced in the face of an event described as unpleasant; characteristically, sadness is seen as a response to a goal lost or not attained (Ellsworth & Smith, 1988; Camras & Allison, 1989; Shaver, Schwartz, Kirson, & O'Connor, 1987). After agreeing that sadness is negative, the studies attempt to distinguish it from other negative emotions. For the most part, there is a consensus that sadness is distinguished from fear by being a response to an event that has already taken place, whereas fear anticipates an event to come. There is some indication that what distinguishes sadness from guilt is the judgment that the self is not responsible for the problem. Anger is seen as the emotion chosen if another person is responsible, whereas sadness arises when nobody is at fault. The studies show, however, that the negative emotions of anger, guilt, and sadness are often felt together, and that a judgment about agency cannot always explain the choice of sadness versus anger or guilt, or why some individuals tend to pick one emotion and some another. Particularly in distinguishing anger from sadness, there is some murkiness as to which emotion is chosen when someone else is responsible for a misfortune, but it is someone over whom the subject has no control. Similarly, it is not clear that anger is seen as a legitimate emotion when someone else is responsible for a

problem if that person has done nothing considered unjust or wrong. In such cases, some subjects may feel anger while others feel sadness, so that it remains mysterious why and in what circumstances people need to recognize an injustice in order to feel angry. And of course there are subjects who admit to anger in the sense of frustration, even when it is clear to them that there is no person responsible for their problem. The psychologists have demonstrated, then, that a judgment about agency is important in our choice of the particular emotion of sadness, but have by no means thoroughly explained that choice. Their work also shows that in late 20th-century North American discourse, "sadness" and "anger" are related.

Some psychologists are less convinced that a determination about agency is the crucial appraisal that governs sadness. Roseman (1991) argues that the degree of surprise that an outcome was not better is what causes anger as opposed to sadness. Ellsworth and Smith (1988) also take account of expectations in distinguishing resignation from sadness. Resignation is seen as a response when the bad outcome is perceived as having been inevitable, whereas sadness comes when the situation might have been reversible. Stein and Levine (1990) relatedly see the difference as a plan for action: An angry person thinks he or she can replace a lost goal, while a sad one accepts the loss. Distinctions about degrees of disappointment or plans of action, however, do not explain unequivocally the differences between the negative emotions, nor do they allow us to predict which emotion will be picked by which subject in which cases. Psychologists have made a promising start, then, in attempting to understand the difference between sadness and other negative emotions, but have been unable to answer all their own questions.

Apart from the issue of distinguishing sadness from other emotions, psychologists, in their effort to clarify the "function" of sadness, have been interested in whether it is an emotion correlated with an increase or a decrease in attention. The bulk of the work seems to indicate that sadness impairs attention to tasks (Potts, Camp, & Coyne, 1989). Ellsworth and Smith (1988) have seen sadness as associated with a lowering of attention, because the emotion is seen as not being caused by another agent, and so attention is focused inward. However, they also note that sadness is sometimes named as an emotion experienced when one would want to attend closely, and they offer no clear explanation of the discrepancy. They imply that there also may be some self-protectiveness in the low-attention sadnesses, which may function to shut out an unpleasant situation. Psychologists are unable to tell us definitively, then, that the function of sadness is either to lower or to raise attention levels toward the outside world.

There seems to be more agreement, however, that sadness focuses the person on him- or herself. Hochschild (1983) and Stein and Jewett (1986) characterize it as a "me" emotion rather than an "it" emotion; they reason that the focus is on the consequences to the self of not achieving its goals, as opposed to say, anger, where the focus is on the external cause or frustration. The function of self-focus in sadness is seen as providing the individual with feedback on how well things are going, probably in order to allow the person to pay more effective attention to the pursuit of his or her goals (Stein & Jewett, 1986; Pyszczynski & Greenberg, 1987). Decreased attention to the outside conserves energy, so that the person may focus on solving the problem (Cunningham, 1988). For those who see sadness this way, there is a tendency to minimize the avoidant behaviors or self-gratifying behaviors that ensue from sadness. For example, despite the fact that his subjects named listening to music as the second most likely thing they would do if sad, and taking a nap as the fourth, Cunningham (1988) still sees sadness as having the function of fostering constructive self-examination.

Intricately connected to the question of whether the function of sadness is to focus a person inward so that he or she can solve problems is the possibility that a function of sadness may be to cue others that the individual needs help. Cunningham's (1988) evidence does not support this; his subjects chose to be alone when sad. Ellsworth and Smith (1988) do see sadness's function as a call for help, but admit that there is a problem in their inability to explain how often sadness leads to withdrawal from social situations. They also raise the problem that too much sadness may become a drain on others, and thus dysfunctional. Some psychologists solve this problem of distinguishing between cueing help and triggering rejection by calling emotions that elicit help "normal sadness," but those that elicit rejection "depression" (Swallow & Kuiper, 1987). There may well be some scientific objection to such a teleological solution.

There are several reasons for the limitations of the dominant psychological approach to sadness. First, the studies flow from the assumption that there are discrete, basic emotions, each of which has a function. This works when subjects are forced in experimentation to describe situations in which they would feel one discrete emotion named by the investigators; yet, when subjects are allowed to name their own feelings, they almost always come up with a blend of emotions. Second, since there is the assumption of universality of emotional response in the functional approach, there is no mechanism in these experiments to account for differences among individuals, though the results show that individuals vary widely in their choice both of the emotion of sadness and of the behavior that follows from the emotion. Third, although these studies attempt to elucidate the function of emotion, they tell us only half the story, since they study the individual who feels the emotion rather than how observers respond to his or her feeling. There is no way, for example, that we can determine whether the function of sadness is to elicit help simply by asking people what they do when they feel sad. We need to be looking at how others respond to sadness if we are to determine its social function; however, none of the experiments discussed above has done this even in a laboratory, and certainly not in natural settings. Fourth, since the studies are based on the subjects' descriptions of themselves, they may really be telling us more about emotion rules in our own culture than about the inner experience of basic emotion. Since the studies focus almost entirely on North American college students, they are unacceptably culture-bound. The possibility that sadness may be different in other contexts is not considered, so that the opportunity for understanding North American assumptions more clearly by investigating them from other perspectives is lost.

ANTHROPOLOGICAL AND HISTORICAL APPROACHES

Perhaps the least questioned hypothesis of North American psychologists has been that sadness is a negative emotion, characterized as being as far from pleasure as possible on dimensional scales (Russell, 1997). Several anthropological and historical studies challenge that view. Lester Little (1998) found sadness and patience praised as virtues in response to injustice in medieval monasticism. My own work on sadness in premodern England and North America discovered a highly valued sadness. Seventeenth-century English diaries revealed subjects faced with difficulty who regarded patience and wisdom as solutions, and were proud of their sadness. To be doleful was sometimes seen as the opposite of being sinful, so that one diarist even suggested that God "allowed of no joy nor pleasure, but of a kind of melancholy demeanor and austerity" (quoted in Stearns, 1988, p. 51). Melancholia as a subject of admiration fascinated many intellectuals in this period (MacDonald, 1981, p. 150 ff.; Stearns, 1988). How totally negative could such virtuous emotions feel?

Catherine Lutz (1988b) has studied the Ifaluk, a society of some 430 people who live on an island in the Pacific. In observing their emotion words, although she finds none that is the exact equivalent of our "sadness," she notes their interest in *fago*—an emotion most often felt in the face of distress of another person, which Lutz approximates as translating "compassion/love/sadness." It is plain that feeling *fago* can be painful, but it is also clear that people take pride in their ability to feel *fago*, which implies that they are calm and gentle. *Fago* is linked with generosity and maturity, and the people noted to feel it most are often those such as chiefs or benevolent spirits, who are especially respected. Capacity to feel *fago*, then, implies power. Thus to assert one's *fago* is to claim to be a good person (Lutz, 1985, 1988b), and is clearly not experienced as an entirely negative emotion.

Similarly, Kleinman and Good (1985) have noted that in many Asian societies, sadness is highly valued and associated with a step in the direction of salvation. In Iran and Sri Lanka, the ability to experience it marks a person's depth (Good, Good, & Moradi, 1985; Obeyesekere, 1985). We modern North Americans, of course, have our own pleasurable sadness in the mixed emotion of nostalgia. It appears, then, that sadness is not always an unalloyedly negative emotion.

A second hypothesis of the psychologists is that the single most important factor differentiating sadness from other emotions is a judgment about agency. If another person is considered the cause, then the response is anger; if it's someone's own fault, the response is guilt or shame. Stephen White (1998), however, in em-

phasizing how many different words were used for our "sadness" and "anger" in early medieval literature, has argued that the appropriate choice was defined by cultural norms rather than by judgments about agency. Let us look at the sadness–anger differentiation. Two kinds of situations would argue against the hypothesis that agency is the distinguishing factor: those in which a person causes the problem but the response is sadness, and those in which no person causes the problem but the response is anger. Both situations arise clearly in the evidence from outside modern North America. Jean Briggs (1970), found that the Utku, a small Inuit (Eskimo) society, have no word for sadness; the closest equivalent is *hujuujaq*, which most often implies loneliness. She tells us, however, that the Utku use the same word to describe their response to another person's lying or stealing, and that in that sense it connotes hostility. She feels they label such responses *hujuujaq* rather than words that connote primarily anger, however, because overt anger is so strictly forbidden in their society. Hence we find a recognition that another person causes the problem, with a response that resembles sadness.

My study of early Anglo-American reactions to disappointment similarly reveals that most diarists called responses to problems created by others sadness, not anger (Stearns, 1988). Mistreatment by an employer, theft, victimization by gossip, familial quarrels—in each of these cases, the diarist labeled his or her response as grief or sadness.

Other studies reveal cultures in which, although no human agency is clearly responsible for a misfortune, responses resemble what we call "angry." Michelle Rosaldo (1980), in her study of the head-hunting practices of the Ilongot, a Philippine warrior society, notes that the murders were sometimes seen clearly as avenging specific wrongs. However, when asked their motives, her subjects would speak of *uget*—it is unclear whether she wants to translate this as "bad feeling" or "grief," but at any rate it implies a weight or burden to be borne until one finds a victim (by no means necessarily the agent of the wrong) and slashes off his or her head. She is explicit that killing comes not just when one must seek vengeance, but also when people feel the need to cast off heavy weights from their hearts. Edward Schieffelin (1976, 1985b) has described similar reactions among the Kaluli of New Guinea, who sometime deal with loss by becoming angry and displaying this in a cathartic ceremony in which dancers who sing and wail about loss are then burned in anger by the observers. The loss can be through death or departure of a loved one; it does not have to have been caused by a person in order to evoke this response. A wrong or a loss may lead to furious stamping, yelling, and a wish for redress (Schieffelin, 1985a), even if it is not clear that some individual is responsible.

Catherine Lutz's Ifaluk have a word, *nguch,* for frustration not caused by another person. Someone may feel *nguch,* say, after getting tired of grating coconut for 3 hours (Lutz, 1985). Relatedly, one may feel *tang,* which implies frustration in the face of a personal misfortune one cannot redress (Lutz, 1988b). Lutz feels these words cluster closer to *song,* which is like anger, than to *fago,* which is more like sadness. Thus it seems that what the Ifaluk feel when disappointed, even though it is nobody's fault, is more like anger than sadness.

Another complex case arises in the Bedouin community of Awlad 'Ali, studied by Lila Abu-Lughod (1986). Here children are socialized to attribute misfortunes to misdeeds of others, so that mothers usually respond to crying children by asking "Who did it?" rather than "What's the matter?" People are trained to respond in a hostile mode even to entirely inevitable losses, so that, for instance, a woman losing her hair might say something equivalent to "God willing, it won't return" or "Good riddance." Thus there is abundant anger even when misfortune's cause is clearly not another person. However, Abu-Lughod informs us that the Bedouin express a sad reaction to the very same events in their poetry, in which grieving is acknowledged not only for inevitable disappointments but also for those engendered by others. A deserted spouse, for example, will use words and metaphors for sad emotions in his or her poetry. Thus the anthropologist finds here that the differentiation between the two emotions is not at all a question of deciding what caused the problem, but rather of knowing when, to what audience, and in what sort of language it is appropriate to feel one or the other. The cross-cultural evidence, then, does not support the notion that what universally differentiates sadness from other emotions is a cognition about agency.

A third issue with which North American psychologists have grappled, in the effort to determine a function for sadness, is the seeming contradiction between the sad person's tendency to turn inward in order to find solace or solve problems, and the tendency to turn outward, cueing others that he or she needs help. Clearly, sadness in North America causes both behaviors. Looking at other cultures may help us understand why. Let us start with sadness as a motivator to seek help. There has been some puzzlement that a sad individual does not always get the help he or she needs, and may even repel others. In societies less individualistic than ours, one often see a more unalloyed expectation that a sad person will receive compassion and aid. One philosopher argues that Buddhists, who eschew emotion, feel compassion itself as an allowed and valued experience (Kupperman, 1995). In the face of death or a loss of important possessions because of natural disasters, the Ifaluk speak in terms of recognition of a general vulnerability, and emphasize a collective sadness and a helpful response (Lutz, 1988b). *Tang lanal,* which means literally "cry inside," is what a person who deserves help but does not get it may feel; this is somewhat akin to *"song,"* or justifiable anger. In other words, a person who is sad can expect that others should help (Lutz, 1985). As noted earlier, Briggs's (1970) Inuit subsume most sadness under the word *hujuujaq,* which they define as "loneliness." Thus when one is distressed for no apparent reason, or even when one is cold, wet, or mosquito-bitten, one may be described as *hujuujaq.* That a word meaning "lonely" is used in these cases does seem to imply that the fundamental problem in sadness is that one needs something from others. The most common cure for such feelings is to seek out company. Logically, the Inuit expect a compassionate and protective response to the sadness of others, and have a word for that response in *naklik,* which is akin to the *fago* or compassionate response expected in Ifaluk. Schieffelin (1985a), likewise, notes that among the Kaluli sadness has an assertive sense, in that it demands a helpful response from observers.

Many grief theorists have commented on the ritualized ceremonies some societies employ to enable the group to join with and help the individual who is bereft. The discourse in these comments is frequently employed to critique modernized societies, which do not help the individual with loss. What is not noted, on the other hand, is that the former societies often demarcate quite sharply the situations in which sadness is acknowledged at all. Robert Levy (1973) has observed that the Tahitians have no word equivalent to our "sadness." They have a vocabulary for grief and lamentation, but not for a generalized sadness. Lutz (1988b) also finds the Ifaluk to be without a word that connotes our sadness in the sense of global loss or hopelessness. Her explanation is that through the word *fago*, the Ifaluk take a general responsibility to help one another, whereas with "sadness" we blame the individual or chastise the victim. Another way to think of this, however, is that communal societies do not acknowledge diffuse sadness, in part because there is an expectation that the group should aid the individual with problems. Losses for which the group has scripts, such as death, illness, loss of love, loss by natural disaster, and loneliness, are acknowledged. However, losses for which there are no scripts, such as a generalized sense of meaninglessness or loss of self-esteem, are simply not recognized. Lutz (1986) does not tell us what happens when someone feels *niyefiyef*, or regret or anger at the self—an emotion not seen by the Ifaluk as resembling sadness. Her Ifaluk will *fago* a person who is transiently embarrassed or even drunk, but a person who has drawn his difficulties on him- or herself may also be the object of anger or laughter. It is not clear what their response would be to unhappiness that has no clear cause, nor does Lutz explicitly discuss this, but we have no reason to feel from the anthropological studies that help would always be forthcoming.

In some societies, then, individuals may be socialized to minimize pain for which there are no scripted solutions. Thus Briggs's (1970) Inuit are embarrassed to be the object of too much concern, or *naklik*, which is for children, not adults. A woman explained to Briggs that she didn't tell the anthropologist of her son's death, lest she make her sad, which would in turn make the woman "sadder still and sorry for myself" (p. 325). We see here the sense that sadness demands a sad response, but also that one should suppress sadness—in part lest one be too demanding, which is unacceptable. Unfortunately, Briggs does not tell us the word in which this woman expresses "sorry for myself," but in her glossary there seems to be no such single word; this fits with Levy's (1973) observation that what we call "sadness" may be hypocognized in some societies. Briggs also found that the Inuit became quite angry and rejecting with her when she suffered a kind of diffuse sadness or depression for which they had no scripted response. Abu-Lughod's (1986)

Bedouin lend support to the notion that societies develop mechanisms to limit demands on their help, much as we tell people to "Buck up!" She feels that anger rather than sadness is often a response to loss, because a sad person may ask for help, which is considered a weakness in an adult; children, not adults, are allowed to display vulnerability. Sadness may be expressed as long as it is indirect and to some extent depersonalized and intellectualized in poetry. Writing the poetry is used to soothe the self, and does not necessarily demand a response from the listener. However, listeners often do show and express empathic concern. This seems to be possible in part because that response is not demanded directly.

Two historical studies have demonstrated a transition in the West from a more traditional position, in which scripted sadnesses are clearly acknowledged and expected to elicit help, to a more modern stance, in which the sadness of others is usually seen as an annoyance. In a book on the history of tears in France, Vincent-Buffault (1991) has described a transition from the 18th century, in which collective tears were enjoyable and there was heavy emphasis on the virtue of compassion, to the 19th century, in which tears showed an absence of self-mastery and were better suppressed. Anger at the crying person was expressed in the belief that there was something not genuine about those who cried too readily. A dignified and respected sadness would be self-contained, and quite clearly would not demand solace from others. One social dictionary she quotes defined tears as "water too often ill-employed, for it remedies nothing. Resources which women have in their command to hide an infidelity or demand a cashmere shawl . . . weapons which they employ" (cited in Vincent-Buffault, 1991, p.148). We see in this quotation the modern assumption that individuals should help themselves, as well as anger at the help seeker, whose cries were described as false "weapons." My own work on the increasing distaste for sadness in 17th- and 18th-century England and North America (Stearns, 1988) illustrates a similar change. In the earlier period, much sadness was expressed, and there were many frank tears. The crier, a private diarist, was not looking to others for aid, but in every case he or she did expect some succor from God. It was all right to be sad because help was available, even if it was not help from another person. The later effort to maintain good cheer seems to have coincided with the notion that one had to take care of one's own difficulties rather than lean on external help, even the help of the Almighty. Many historians have described a modernizing process in which there was increasing anger at and unwillingness to aid the unfortunate (MacFarlane, 1970; Lindemann, 1990). This has been associated with growing distaste for charity and condemnation of the poor, but it may also explain changing attitudes about sadness.

It appears, then, that how societies think about sadness has something to do with how they think about help. In societies more collective than our own, sadnesses are often viewed as deserving a response, but such societies limit their obligation by the absence of vocabulary for or recognition of sadnesses for which a collective response should not be expected. In societies that have other mechanisms for limiting the demands of the sad individual on the group, such as the shaming mechanisms by which the Bedouin contain complaint, or the guilt mechanism through which modern North Americans tell individuals to take care of themselves, there may be more possibility of speaking about different kinds of sadness. In all cases, the discourse about sadness is also a discourse about the demarcation between the individual's responsibility and the group's. The puzzlement of North American functionalists about whether the "purpose" of sadness is to elicit help, and their difficulty in the face of evidence that sadness in our culture often leads to rejection, are themselves expressions of that discourse. Labeling a person who requires too much help as "deviant" or "ill" assuages our own guilt in not wishing to help the needy, allowing us to marginalize the person out of the mainstream and into the medical system. The distinction between "sad" and "depressed" often draws the line between situations when we are or are not willing to offer succor.

A fourth question North American psychologists have explored and found puzzling is how sadness works to turn the individual inward. We find it functional if people are motivated by sadness to solve their problems, but are troubled by those who withdraw too far from social contacts, and those who, refusing to solve their problems, either find soothing avoidant behaviors or become apathetic. Like modern North Americans, most cultures have great fears regarding passivity, and many solutions exist.

Communally oriented societies that tolerate high levels of aggression often transform sadness into anger; those less tolerant of aggression seem to minimize sadness and emphasize goal substitution; and both may ritualize sadness through ceremony, patterned weeping, or artistic expression (Feld, 1982). Individualistic societies are likely to minimize sadness by goading individuals to solve their problems. Societies in which hierarchy is important frequently relegate "anger" to those on top, using the passivity of sadness to keep those on the bottom from advancing (Stearns, 1988).

Rosaldo's (1980) Ilongot exemplify the transformation of sadness into anger for a communal group. They describe symptoms akin to what we would label "depression" among those who are upset but inactive. Rosaldo tells us that among the Ilongot "affliction in these instances leave one ill, distressed, or helpless, humiliated but unable to redress imbalance, sick but too weak to cast off a disease . . . the . . . heart is . . . distracted. . . . Impotent to act, it dwells on its deficiencies . . . fails to find a reasonable course of action" (p. 48). She also speaks of the "'weight', grief or dizziness . . . and sickness" (p. 48) that are associated with withdrawal and passivity. All this the Ilongot see as unfocused energy, which is cured by the activity of head hunting. Happiness is the opposite of feeling weighted down; Rosaldo says that it suggests activity and sociality, and "has little to do with quietness, tranquillity, or peace" (pp. 52–53). Schieffelin's (1985a) Kaluli are similarly anxious about the dangers of passivity, which may lead to isolations from the group. They have no word for passive sadness; the two words for grief imply either compassion, or an active grief for a misfortune requiring a ritualized response.

Abu-Lughod's (1986) Bedouin use metaphors of death, illness, drowning, and apathy for describing sadness. There is a sense of danger to the self in sadness, of self-dissolution; a weeping man may be counseled, "Pull yourself together." Sadness implies weakness and vulnerability, and is associated with being a child or female. Men respond angrily to losses, even to death, in part to avoid the danger that is seen in the sad stance. The anthropologist tells of a man so upset by being deserted by his wife that he moped around and begged her to come back. The general response of his peers was that he was an idiot and would have been better off had he beaten her. To allow himself to be sad and vulnerable was to relinquish control. People would no longer fear him. Anger, not sadness, maintains selfhood. Sadness should be relegated to poetry.

Although it is true that sadness may be eschewed via anger, no society can tolerate unalloyed aggression. Even the Kaluli and the Bedouin use art forms to solve this problem. The former express grief through songs that mimic birds or stories relating sadness to a species of birds that make melodically descending sounds (Feld, 1982). The latter use ritualized poetry (Abu-Lughod, 1986).

In cultures less tolerant of aggression, sadness is also seen as a danger because of its association with passivity. Levy (1973, 1984) found his Tahitian subjects eager to seal off grief quickly, for it was associated with fatigue, lack of drive, feeling heavy, or feeling subdued. He explains that they do not have a word equivalent to our "sadness"; in part this is because sadness is not seen as an emotion, in that it is not felt by the self, but rather is the result of an outside difficulty that subdues the self. Tahitians, he believes, depend on a sense of drive and energy to get the work of the world done, and are worried about flagging enthusiasm and apathy. Although they do not condone aggression, they feel it is important to do something about bad feelings rather than to withdraw. They advise mistreated parties to talk to those who have wronged them, because anger held in can lead to weakness, loss of drive: "It's as if your head isn't right; your hair may turn gray" (Levy, 1973, p. 285). All these problems can be cured by taking an active, social stance and confronting the wrongdoer—not to do him or her violence, but to settle the situation with words.

Like the Tahitians, the Inuit studied by Briggs (1970) lack a word equivalent to our "sadness." Briggs observed behavior, particularly in her Inuit adoptive father, that seemed to be the equivalent of a kind of fatigued, aloof withdrawal, but tells us that this sort of behavior is largely ignored rather than discussed or labeled. *Qiquq*, a word meaning "clogged up," is applied sometimes to such behaviors, but not freely used for those who are respected. It may be used to describe clogged holes or nipples, but also silent withdrawal, with a sense of imminent tears. It is considered childish to behave this way. A person distressed by the bad behavior of someone else may admit to feeling *hujuujaq*, but since this word implies loneliness, it propels the person who feels it into a social stance and away from the social withdrawal condemned in *qiquq*. Like the Tahitians, the Inuit try not to let themselves get too sad about problems for which there is no solution. The acceptable feeling is *ayuqnaq,* which implies resignation, calm, and a refusal to get too upset. The Indonesian Toraja studied by Jane Wellenkamp (1988) also fear the illness or passivity of sadness. Marina Roseman's (1990) Senoi Temiar—who think that internalized sadness and anger cause a physically dangerous compaction of the head and heart called "soul loss," yet find these emotions dangerous when expressed—ritualualize them through structured harangues.

Another solution for cultures which reject anger as well as sadness is to offer prestige to those who suppress both. Among the Faeroe Islanders, taunting is used to differentiate between those who can and cannot restrain the emotions. Ritual mockery is a means to control anger by making a game of it (Gaffin, 1995). In such a situation, the sadness that might be caused by the taunting is defended against by humor or is expected to be suppressed. People who express anger are viewed as ridiculous.

Levy (1984) has raised the question of why cultures hyper- or hypocognize emotions. Emotions that are considered problems may be labeled and dealt with through suppression, or unlabeled and dealt with through repression or other unconscious mechanisms, such as denial or conversion. In the cultures thus far discussed, diffuse sadness seems to be viewed as a problem, in that it withdraws the person from society and undermines activity. In those cultures such as the Kaluli, Ilongot, and Bedouin, which are fairly tolerant of aggression, there seems to be more explicit recognition of the problem of sadness, because the problem can be treated by a not entirely unconscious transformation of the sadness into anger. For those cultures less accepting of anger, such as the Inuit and the Tahitians, there is some sense of the potential for illness in too much bad feeling. Therefore, people are counseled to get over their sadness quickly, and there seems to be some effort to deny that intense sadness exists.

There are some cultures that embrace a passive rather than an active stance, and these seem more accepting of sadness than those described above. Often these find anger a more dangerous possibility than sadness. This was certainly true of the 17th-century diarists I studied (Stearns, 1988): They were proud of their sadness, because it implied patience and humility. In the face of adversity, a sad demeanor enabled them to renounce anger and to turn to God to right their wrongs. To be angry was considered unacceptable, because it implied pride, which was ungodly. However, passivity was not seen as problematic, as it is by the Inuit or Tahitians. I have discussed elsewhere (Stearns, 1988) the utility of dignifying the passive position in a highly stratified complex society in which the vast majority of people must be socialized to be obedient and to suppress initiative. In such hierarchical situations, those on top may be urged to transform sadness to anger (White, 1998). White quotes a European medieval tale mandating a transformation of emotions for a nobleman: "Stop weeping . . . if you have grief from his death, avenge it . . . [turn their joy] into grief" (p. 141). In the 11th and 12th centuries, in relatively stable situations in Europe, anger was increasingly seen as a necessary privilege of the powerful, while it was deemed inappropriate and ridiculous in the powerless (White, 1998; Freedman, 1998; Buhrer-Thierry, 1998). Historically in Europe, then, sadness could be either active or passive, depending on one's social class.

Although anthropological and historical investigations suggest that there are as many unique emotion schematizations and "sadnesses" as there are cultures, it would seem fair to conclude that reasons to "choose" sadness are always connected to views about anger, individualism versus communalism, passivity versus activity, and hierarchy versus equality. The choice of emotions, then, is not mainly determined by a judgment about agency, as the attributionists have argued. Attribution of agency is in fact culturally determined. Attribution, then, is the dependent variable, while the independent variables are deeply held cultural assumptions about what sorts of personalities and behaviors are valuable or dangerous (Hofstede, 1984). This view can be used to explain otherwise inexplicable North American data. For instance, Stein and Jewett's (1986) failure to separate anger and sadness definitively along the criterion of whether the person who did the harm is judged to have done it intentionally is clearer when we look at the particular situations that made the children they studied feel each emotion. In four cases in which a person deliberately interfered with a child's wish, differing proportions of children expressed anger and sadness, but much more sadness was expressed

when the interferer was someone over whom the child could have little control (his teacher) and much more anger when it was a peer (pp. 253–255). The authors fail to note this, because they think of agency of harm as a generalizable attribute. However, it should be clear by now that the distinction between sadness and anger has something to do with a sense of when aggressive responses are or are not acceptable, and this is probably true in North America as well as elsewhere.

Unlike many of the societies discussed above, North Americans do not always make a conscious clear association of "sad" and "passive," at least for adults. Here, an active sadness may be envisioned that in some sense asserts the self. The sad person is counseled to figure out what is troubling him or her, and to do something about it. Perhaps this is possible for us because we look to the individual, not the group, to solve problems. Since we do not tolerate aggression as do the Kaluli, Ilongot, or Bedouin, we describe some situations they would see as cause for anger, as cause for sadness. For instance, in the face of death or loss of love, we do not justify violence as a solution. Unlike the Tahitians or Inuit, however, we are able to label and recognize diffuse sadness—perhaps because, knowing that we can stigmatize and marginalize it, we are less concerned with an individual's social withdrawal. Claiming an egalitarian democracy, we cannot suggest that sadness is a good response for those on the lower end of the socioeconomic scale. We think that "healthy" individuals should find their own solutions, which for us, ever the optimists, always exist. Nobody need be passive. Even for us, though, some sense remains of the lurking dangers of passivity. This appears in the very way in which North American psychologists analyze data about the behaviors flowing from sadness. It is notable that Shaver et al. (1987), in looking for a basic sadness, do not notice the cultural meaning of the fact that their subjects differentiate what they do when sad (namely, become active) from what they claim others do (namely, sink into apathy). They explain this difference as resulting from cognitive distortion. They do not explain the logic behind the distortion, which is that we project the "bad" passive response onto others and claim the "good" active response for ourselves; unlike early North Americans and Europeans, who valued passivity, we cannot afford to socialize the majority of our population to lack initiative, or to depend on higher forces for succor.

The anthropological and historical literature addresses many of the issues raised by North American psychologists, and refines them considerably. We learn from this literature that sadness is not always an unalloyedly negative emotion. We learn also that the extent to which a society recognizes and values sadness is related to the society's culture and social structure. We learn that sadness has no universal function, and that the discourse of contemporary psychologists on this subject flows from particular values and an intellectual tradition that probably overemphasizes categorization and unwarrantedly assumes that there is a "cause" for every phenomenon.

BIOLOGICAL APPROACHES

The complexities introduced by the evidence from other cultures does return us to our early question of whether, indeed, it is reasonable to assume that there is some basic and universal emotion represented by our word "sadness." On a superficial level, the classic studies of Paul Ekman and his followers on the universal recognition of facial expressions across cultures would seem to indicate that there is a universal sadness. However, there are problems in this conclusion. For one, Ekman's studies rely on words researchers and subjects use in describing emotions (Ekman, Friesen, & Ellsworth, 1972). Since he glosses over the whole problem of translation discussed by later anthropologists (Heelas, 1986), one cannot be certain what "sadness" means to Ekman's subjects, but it is fairly clear that the English-speaking translators have chosen words implying resignation rather than fighting. The faces identified, then, do not necessarily convey an internal universal response to situations, but rather convey a plan for action or behavior. In the sense that emotion means an appraisal of a situation leading to a particular behavior, Ekman's work does show some universal cross-cultural recognition of what behaviors may be predicted by observing faces. It does not show, however, that there is a universal basic and discrete feeling of sadness.

Wierzbicka (1995), Lutz (1988a), Shweder & Haidt, Chapter 26, this volume, and others have demonstrated that when researchers ask subjects to identify faces by emotion, they come up with the identifications expected only if they are given a very limited list of our "basic" emotions, which force them to choose words that may mean little to them. Church, Katigbak, Reyes, and Jensen (1998) attempt to rescue Ekman from the problems of cross-cultural incompetence, but unfortunately do this by delimiting the translation of Filipino words into a much more confined group of English ones. A study that has tried to correct the translation problem by having subjects speak their own language to identify faces, and using native interpreters to translate this language into English, shows that Greek uses five words and Japanese four for our "sadness," while "anger" needs six Japanese and three Greek words (Russell, Suzuki, & Ishida, 1993). Cliff Goddard has argued that this problem cannot be solved by saying "a kind of anger," for he sees profound implications for the differences among the "anger" words of the peoples of the Australian Western Desert (Goddard, 1991), and has also found words for many refined meanings of both "sadness" and "anger" in a Malay culture (Goddard, 1996). Russell (1997), by listing all faces and emotions on two dimensional scales (pleasure vs. displeasure and arousal vs. sleep), has claimed to solve the problem of universal sadness by locating it on this grid; however, this can hardly account for the many complexities we have noted, such as pleasurable sadness. I am struck by the illustrations in Little (1998, pp. 15–24), in which patience—a medieval cousin of sadness and supposedly the opposite of anger—shows the same furrowed brow and grimly set mouth as its opponent, rather than the downcast eyes, lack of eye contact, and turned-down lips Ekman posits for sadness. If there are universal emotions, how are we to understand a "patient" man with an "angry" face?

The linguist Anna Wierzbicka (1992) studied a group of Australian aborigines in which she found five different words to describe something like sadness/homesickness, as well as several more for disappointment, resigned sadness, and sadness without reason. She concludes that our emotion words are simply cultural artifacts of the English language; that not all languages have words for our so-called basic emotions; and that emotion words can never be neatly translated across different languages, not to mention cultures. Ekman, she argues, shows us faces that tend to reflect that something good or something bad happened, or perhaps what a subject plans in response, but they show nothing more.

Another type of evidence that has been used to argue for a basic affect of sadness is the crying of infants. If newborns display distinct affective states, it is difficult to think of these as anything but basic. However, although there is certainly evidence that infants make distinctly different kind of cries (Demos, 1986) and that mothers respond to them differently (Huebner & Izard, 1988), it is not clear that sadness is clearly differentiated in an infant's cry in the early months (Emde, 1984), or that the different kinds of cries correspond neatly to the difference that adults understand between sadness and anger (Tomkins, 1991, p. 113). In fact, since Ekman himself thinks of distress as more fundamental than sadness, and has stated that the face of sadness is more muted than a crying face (Ekman & Friesen, 1975), it would be difficult to say that there is a face/cry of an infant which corresponds to Ekman's basic sad face, and that supports the notion of an innate sadness as distinct from anger. As they do with infants, North American researchers try to find "basic emotions" such as sadness in other mammal species, but of course we name their emotions according to our own prior beliefs (Panksepp, 1996).

Can the psychologists' point of view be salvaged by neuroscience? Biological evidence of a particular set of neural processes is one of Izard's and Ackerman's (Chapter 16, this volume) criteria for an emotion. Although Izard and Ackerman describe anger as a mode for intensifying energy and activity, and sadness as adaptive for slowing down responses, they cannot demonstrate a particular set of neural processes. Silvan Tomkins, one of the fathers of the idea of discrete affects, was himself unable to differentiate a qualitative difference between the neuronal firings of sadness and anger, only concluding that anger is a more intense form of sadness (Tomkins, 1984, p. 173 ff.).

Is there modern evidence for different neural pathways for anger and sadness? A long-used method of neurobiologists is to consider the results of ablation of areas of the brain. Research on temporal lobe tumors on the dominant side shows that these lesions may lead to depression, but also to irritability (Paulson & Bolwig, 1992). The ablation of the rostral cingulate cor-

tex in saimuri monkeys seems to eliminate spontaneous cries of separation, yet the same part of the brain is also involved in emotions of defeat and triumph, which are surely related to anger (MacLean, 1992).

Are distinct hormones or neurotransmitters implicated? Temporal lobe seizure in rhesus monkeys, which are associated with an increase of cortisol releasing hormone (CRH), provoke the monkeys to show a pattern similar to the despondent phase of separation reactions. However, CRH also leads to depression combined with irritability (Post et al., 1992; Panksepp, 1996). Interestingly, antiseizure medications—particularly carbamazepine and valproic acid, which are used as augmentation drugs to combat depression—also work to calm those who suffer from extreme attacks of explosive anger.

Some of the episodes and disorders defined by the American Psychiatric Association's (1994) *Diagnostic and Statistical Manual of Mental Disorders,* fourth edition (DSM-IV), describe blends of the two emotions. In mixed mood episodes, there is irritability as well as depression, and in borderline personality disorder (seen by many psychiatrists as biological in origin), there are also intense variants of the two emotions. Consideration of the effects of substances of abuse may lead us to the same conclusion. Alcohol, which leads to exuberance in the early stages of use, later produces depression and inappropriate aggression. Amphetamines can cause affective blunting as well as anger. The same is true of cocaine. Sedative-hypnotics enable angry responses, but also may cause temporary depression. Since theses substances work through alteration of neurotransmitters or cell membranes, their effects on both emotions simultaneously cast doubt on a theory that they are biologically distinct.

In work contradicting the assumption of many psychologists that brain precedes mind in providing the equipment for "basic emotions," some biologists argue that all experienced "emotions" are created in some sense by external stimuli, and that these stimuli in turn are processed by a brain that has already been socialized (Halgren, 1992; MacLean, 1992).

It would seem, then, that there is no clear biological evidence so far for discrete negative emotions of sadness and anger, and that tentatively, at least, the concept of "distress" can be used to apply to both, with even biologists endorsing the possibility that the appearance of one or the other is mediated by social scripts.

Why, then, do we have words for a variety of negative emotions? This can be explained best if we keep in mind Tomkins's (1962) general argument that the function of emotion is to allow us a certain plasticity and adaptability in adjusting to our world. When adults are distressed, there are several things they can do. They can fight; they can seek help from others or attempt to rectify the situation themselves; or they can withdraw into inactivity. Clearly, the choice of what action to take will affect the biological response. There is evidence that what we call "sad" in modern North America is associated with a kind of slowing of the body, a feeling of inactivity, and a sense of sluggishness or weakness, similar to that expressed by many of the other societies discussed above, and that indeed it is hard to continue to feel "sad" when moving (Schwartz, Weinberger, & Singer, 1981; Shields, 1984; Averill, 1969; Shaver et al., 1987). This corresponds with work showing that the vocalizations of sadness are considered smaller, softer, and slower than those of anger (Scherer, 1982), and with Tomkins's (1991) notion that patterns of movement cause as well as respond to affect. It is also a way of thinking about affect that may unify the distinction Stern (1985) makes between "categorical" and "vitality" affects. Using the idea of vitality affect, we can think of sadness as slowness, sluggishness, passivity, softness, and drawing in, compared to the loud explosiveness of anger. The distinction, then, involves a distinction not of appraisal, but of activity (Frijda, 1987; Althoff, 1998; White, 1998). The choice to withdraw in the face of difficulty does seem to be in the universal repertory of biological response; it is evident in early life in some animal species (Averill, 1968), and though not apparent in the human neonate, it is certainly universal in humans at later ages.

DISCUSSION

All functioning societies must offer individuals a variety of solutions to deal with goal blockage and goal loss. We use the word "sadness" most characteristically to describe the slow, sluggish type of response, although we sometimes also use it to describe the help-seeking response.

Other societies, depending on the parameters described above (views of aggression, individualism vs. collectivism, activity vs. passivity, hierarchy vs. equality), may use different words. The words that are used and the distinctions that are made, as well as those that are glossed over, tell us about a society's values as it considers the advantages and disadvantages of the many different sorts of responses people may make when they don't get what they want (Lutz, 1988a).

We who study emotions must heed the warnings of the neostructuralists that words are only means of categorizing and that they do not represent "real" entities. Some of the questions raised in the first flurry of interest in emotion and in the earlier edition of this book ignored this wisdom, but we no longer can afford to do so. I, starting with the task of exploring "sadness," plead guilty for my earlier assumption that there is such a "thing"

Since I am now arguing that what is biologically basic is distress, not sadness, is there a way to explain the function of distress? Grief and loss theorists (Bowlby, 1980; Marris, 1974; Mahler, 1961; Averill, 1968) have felt that distress functions to help people become more aware of what they value, in part to motivate them to conserve what is important, and more particularly to maintain attachment to others. Tomkins (1963) also had such an explanation for the problem of human suffering. I am skeptical that it would be possible to operationalize such a hypothesis, though certainly it seems intuitively appealing. What I wish to emphasize, here, though, is that this notion is a notion about distress and grief, which encompass both sadness and anger, and perhaps guilt and shame.

Difficulties with "basic-affect" theories revive the possibility that the psychoanalytic concept of "drive" may have some utility in explaining emotions. Sadness, for us, appears closely related to anger, and the choice of how and when to express one or the other expresses attitudes toward aggressive impulses (Cohen, 1990; Freud, 1972). Sadness is also related to frustration of the drive for attachment (Bowlby, 1980), and the choice of how and when to express it reflects defenses relating to dependency needs. In Kohutian terms, sadness may follow upon a threat to the image of the self, the drive to maintain that image being fundamental (Kohut, 1971). Defenses against sadness, like those against other affects, are influenced both by cultural training and by the idiosyncrasies of the individual. They range over a wide gamut from entirely unconscious to explicitly understood and elaborated. Affect theorists, coming from a tradition in rebellion against psychoanalysis, may have been too quick to ignore the utility of the psychoanalytic concepts of drive, the unconscious, conflict and defense in explaining emotion.

Although fashionable anthropologists and extreme neoconstructionists are often uncomfortable with postulating that we may know more about people or cultures than they do about themselves, it seems foolish to ignore the evidence accumulated by so many disciplines, including anthropology, that the individual may feel in conflict with the group and that the group's ideals may make it difficult to deal with certain feelings. Is it not a mistake to ignore, as Abu-Lughod and Lutz (1990) have done, the nonverbal evidence for affect, and with it the indications of psychodynamic conflict (Gerber, 1985; Levy & Wellenkamp, 1989; Rosenwein, 1998: Hyams, 1998; Solomon, 1995)?

Several questions remain unanswered. Are there variants in the amount of distress felt in different societies? In societies that stress angry responses, is there less sadness than in contemporary North America? In societies that stress goal substitution or that offer comfort to the individual by meeting his or her dependency needs, is there less withdrawn sadness than here, or is there a sadness that is simply ignored? These questions are part of the larger question as to whether the sluggish, withdrawn response we label "sadness" is indeed "basic." It is notable that North Americans, like some of the Asians described above, feel "choked up" when sad (Shields, 1984), and that Tomkins (1984) noted a decrease in vocalization as an indication of "backed-up" affect (i.e., affect constrained by socialization). Indeed, Tomkins felt that all societies must limit the expression of the full cries of distress and anger. There is evidence of a sad, withdrawn response in other animals (Averill, 1968); however, for aggressive humans, who enter the world with loud tears, one wonders whether sadness in the sense of choked-up withdrawal is basic biologically, or is basic only in the sense of being a socially necessary universal—one of civilization's discontents. Evidence that sad people are physiologically activated, and yet hold still and behave sluggishly (Averill, 1969; Schwartz et al.,

1981), leads one to suspect that there may be something puzzling or even "unnatural" about sadness. This in turn raises the question of the relationship between sadness and depression. The latter is often viewed as an inability to feel emotion, and depressed people often cry less, not more than others, because affect is suppressed. To the extent that sadness implies withdrawal rather than crying to get help, is a sad response most common in societies also most prone to depression? Is there less sadness and depression in societies more tolerant of affect expression? What sorts of conditions create such societies?

Only with collaboration between disciplines can such complex questions find answers. Future studies of sadness or other emotions (and it is less clear now what "emotions" are than when the first edition of this *Handbook* was published) will find that biologists, psychologists, psychoanalysts, anthropologists, linguists, and (as Feld, 1982, has proven) even jazz musicians and birdwatchers can all tell us something helpful. We must make an effort to observe our own discourse as an artifact, rather than to reify it. But no more on my own doleful subject. Let us celebrate instead the study of emotions, which helps us to understand each other across disciplines, culture, and time.

REFERENCES

Abu-Lughod, L. (1986). *Veiled sentiments*. Berkeley: University of California Press.

Abu-Lughod, L., & Lutz, C. A. (1990). Introduction: Emotion, discourse, and the politics of everyday life. In L. Abu-Lughod & C. A. Lutz (Eds.), *Language and the politics of emotion* (pp. 1–23). Cambridge, England: Cambridge University Press.

Althoff, G. (1998). "Ira regis": Prolegomena to a history of royal anger. In B. Rosenwein (Ed.), *Anger's past* (pp. 59–74). Ithaca, NY: Cornell University Press.

American Psychiatric Association. (1994). *Diagnostic and statistical manual of mental disorders* (4th ed.). Washington, DC: Author.

Averill, J. R. (1968). Grief: Its nature and significance. *Psychological Bulletin, 70*(6), 721–748.

Averill, J. R. (1969). Autonomic response patterns during sadness and mirth. *Psychophysiology, 5*(4), 399–414.

Bowlby, J. (1980). *Attachment and loss: Vol. 3. Loss: Sadness and depression*. New York: Basic Books.

Briggs, J. L. (1970). *Never in anger*. Cambridge, MA: Harvard University Press.

Buhrer-Thierry, G. (1998). "Just anger" or "vengeful anger"?: The punishment of blinding in the early medieval West. In B. Rosenwein (Ed.), *Anger's past* (pp. 75–91). Ithaca, NY: Cornell University Press.

Camras, L. A., & Allison, K. (1989). Children's and adults' beliefs about emotion elicitation. *Motivation and Emotion, 13*(1), 53–70.

Church, A. T., Katigbak, M. S., Reyes, J. A. S., & Jensen, S. M. (1998). Language and organisation of Filipino emotion concepts: Comparing emotion concepts and dimensions across cultures. *Cognition and Emotion, 12*(1), 63–92.

Cohen, D. J. (1990). Enduring sadness: Early loss, vulnerability, and the shaping of character. *Psychoanalytic Study of the Child, 45,* 157–178.

Cunningham, M. R. (1988). What do you do when you're happy or blue?: Mood, expectancies, and behavioral interest. *Motivation and Emotion, 12*(4), 309–331.

Demos, V. (1986). Crying in early infancy: An illustration of the motivational function of affect. In T. B. Brazelton & M. W. Yogman (Eds.), *Affective development in infancy* (pp. 39–73). Norwood: Ablex.

Ekman, P., & Friesen, W. V. (1975). *Unmasking the face.* Englewood Cliffs, NJ: Prentice-Hall.

Ekman, P., Friesen, W. V., & Ellsworth, P. C. (1972). *Emotion in the human face.* New York: Pergamon Press.

Ellsworth, P. C., & Smith, C. A. (1988). From appraisal to emotion: Differences among unpleasant feelings. *Motivation and Emotion, 12*(3), 271–302.

Emde, R. N. (1984). Levels of meaning for infant emotions: A biosocial view. In K. R. Scherer & P. Ekman (Eds.), *Approaches to emotion* (pp. 77–107). Hillsdale, NJ: Erlbaum.

Feld, S. (1982). *Sound and sentiment* Philadelphia: University of Pennsylvania Press.

Folkman, S., Lazarus, R. S., Dunkel-Schetter, A., DeLongis, A., & Gruen, R. J. (1986). Dynamics of a stressful encounter: Cognitive appraisal, coping, and encounter outcomes. *Journal of Personality and Social Psychology, 50*(5), 992–1003.

Freedman, P. (1998). Peasant anger in the late Middle Ages. In B. Rosenwein (Ed.), *Anger's past* (pp. 171–190). Ithaca, NY: Cornell University Press.

Freud, A. (1972). Comments on aggression. In A. Freud, *The writings of Anna Freud* (Vol. 8, pp. 151–175). New York: International Universities Press.

Frijda, N. H. (1987). Emotion, cognitive structure, and action tendency. *Cognition and Emotion, 1*(2), 115–143.

Gaffin, D. (1995). The production of emotion and social control: Taunting, anger, and the Rukka in the Faeroe Islands. *Ethos, 23*(1), 149–172.

Gerber, E. R. (1985). Rage and obligation: Samoan emotion in conflict. In G. M. White & J. Kirkpatrick (Eds.), *Person, self, and experience: Exploring Pacific ethnopsychologies* (pp. 121–167). Berkeley: University of California Press.

Goddard, C. (1991). Anger in the Western Desert: A case-study in the cross-cultural semantics of emotion. *Man, 26*(2), 265–279.

Goddard, C. (1996). The "social emotions" of Malay (Bahasa Melayu). *Ethos, 24*(3), 426–464.

Good, B. J., Good, M. D. & Moradi, R. (1985). The interpretation of Iranian depressive illness and dysphoric affect. In A. Kleinman & B. Good (Eds.), *Culture and depression* (pp. 369–428). Berkeley: University of California Press.

Halgren, E. (1992). Emotional neurophysiology of the amygdala within the context of human cognition. In J. P. Aggleton (Ed.), *The amygdala: Neurobiological aspects of emotion, memory, and mental dysfunction* (pp. 191–228). New York: Wiley–Liss.

Heelas, P. (1986). Emotion talk across cultures. In R. Harré (Ed.), *The social construction of emotions* (pp. 234–266). Oxford: Blackwell.

Hochschild, A. R. (1983). *The managed heart.* Berkeley: University of California Press.

Hofstede, G. (1984). *Culture's consequences: International differences in work related values.* Beverly Hills, CA: Sage.

Huebner, R., & Izard, C. E. (1988). Mothers' responses to infants' facial expressions of sadness, anger, and physical distress. *Motivation and Emotion, 12*(2), 185–195.

Hyams, P. (1998). What did Henry III of England think in bed and in French about kingship and anger? In B. Rosenwein (Ed.), *Anger's past* (pp. 92–126). Ithaca, NY: Cornell University Press.

Kleinman, A., & Good, B. (Eds.). (1985). *Culture and depression.* Berkeley: University of California Press.

Kohut, H. (1971). *The analysis of the self.* New York: International Universities Press.

Kupperman, J. J. (1995). The emotions of altruism, East and West. In J. Marks & R. Ames (Eds.), *Emotion in Asian thought* (pp. 123–138). Albany: State University of New York Press.

Levy, R. I. (1973). *Tahitians: Mind and experience in the Society Islands.* Chicago: University of Chicago Press.

Levy, R. I. (1984). The emotions in comparative perspective. In K. R. Scherer & P. Ekman (Eds.), *Approaches to emotion* (pp. 397–412). Hillsdale, NJ: Erlbaum.

Levy, R. I., & Wellenkamp, J. C. (1989). Methodology in the anthropological study of emotion. In R. Plutchik & H. Kellerman (Eds.), *Emotion: Theory, research, and experience. Vol. 4. Measurement of emotion* (pp. 205–232). San Diego, CA: Academic Press.

Lindemann, M. (1990). *Patients and paupers: Hamburg 1700–1830.* New York: Oxford University Press.

Little, L. (1998). Anger in monastic curses. In B. Rosenwein (Ed.), *Anger's past* (pp. 9–35). Ithaca, NY: Cornell University Press.

Lutz, C. (1985). Depression and the translation of emotional worlds. In A. Kleinman & B. Good (Eds.), *Culture and depression* (pp. 63–100). Berkeley: University of California Press.

Lutz, C. (1986). The domain of emotion words on Ifaluk. In R. Harré (Ed.) *The social construction of emotions* (pp. 267–288). Oxford: Blackwell.

Lutz, C. (1988a). Ethnographic perspectives on the emotion lexicon. In V. Hamilton, G. H. Bower, & N. H. Frijda (Eds.), *Cognitive perspectives on emotion and motivation* (pp. 399–419). Dordrecht, The Netherlands: Kluwer.

Lutz, C. (1988b). *Unnatural emotions.* Chicago: University of Chicago Press.

MacDonald, M. (1981). *Mystical Bedlam.* Cambridge, England: Cambridge University Press.

MacFarlane, A. (1970). *Witchcraft in Tudor and Stuart England: A regional and comparative study.* New York: Harper & Row.

MacLean, P. D. (1992). The limbic system concept. In M. R. Trimble & T. G. Bolwig (Eds.), *The temporal lobes and the limbic system* (pp. 1–14). Petersfield, England: Wrightson.

Mahler, M. S. (1961). On sadness and grief in infancy and childhood. *Psychoanalytic Study of the Child, 16,* 332–349.

Marris, P. (1974). *Loss and change.* New York: Pantheon.

Obeyesekere, G. (1985). Depression, Buddhism, and the work of culture in Sri Lanka. In A. Kleinman & B. Good (Eds.), *Culture and depression* (pp. 134–152). Berkeley: University of California Press.

Panksepp, J. (1996). Affective neuroscience: A paradigm to study the animate circuits for human emotions. In R. Kavanaugh, B. Zimmerberg, & S. Fein (Eds.), *Emotion: Interdisciplinary perspectives* (pp. 29–60). Mahwah, NJ: Erlbaum.

Paulson, O. B., & Bolwig, T. G. (1992). Cerebrovascular diseases and tumours in the limbic system. In M. R. Trimble & T. G. Bolwig (Eds.), *The temporal lobes and the limbic system* (pp. 189–198) Petersfield, England: Wrightson.

Post, R. M., Weiss, S. R. B., Ketter, T. A., George, M. S., Clark, M., & Rosen, J. (1992). The temporal lobes and affective disorders. In M. R. Trimble & T. G. Bolwig (Eds.), *The temporal lobes and the limbic system* (pp. 247–265). Petersfield, England: Wrightson.

Potts, R., Camp, C., & Coyne, C. (1989). The relationship between naturally occurring dysphoric moods, elaborative encoding, and recall performance. *Cognition and Emotion, 3*(3), 197–205.

Pyszczynski, T., & Greenberg, J. (1987). Self-regulatory perseveration and the depressive self-focusing style: A self-awareness theory of reactive depression. *Psychological Bulletin, 102*(1), 122–138.

Rosaldo, M. Z. (1980). *Knowledge and passion: Ilongot notions of self and social life.* Cambridge, England: Cambridge University Press.

Roseman, I. J. (1991). Appraisal determinants of discrete emotions. *Cognition and Emotion, 5*(3), 161–200.

Roseman, M. (1990). Head, heart, odor, and shadow: The structure of the self, the emotional world and ritual performance among Senoi Temiar. *Ethos, 18,* 227–250.

Rosenwein, B. H., (1998). Controlling paradigms. In B. Rosenwein (Ed.), *Anger's past* (pp. 233–247). Ithaca, NY: Cornell University Press.

Russell, J. A. (1997). Reading emotions from and into faces: Resurrecting a dimensional–contextual perspective. In J. A. Russell & J.-M. Fernandez-Dols (Eds.), *The psychology of facial expression* (pp. 295–320). Cambridge, England: Cambridge University Press.

Russell, J. A., Suzuki, N., & Ishida, N. (1993). Canadian, Greek, and Japanese freely produced emotion labels for facial expressions. *Motivation & Emotion, 17*(4), 337–351.

Scherer, K. R. (1982). The assessment of vocal expression in infants and children. In C. E. Izard (Ed.), *Measuring emotions in infants and children* (pp. 127–163). Cambridge, England: Cambridge University Press.

Schieffelin, E. L. (1976). *The sorrow of the lonely and the burning of the dancers.* New York: St. Martin's Press.

Schieffelin, E. L. (1985a). Anger, grief, and shame: Toward a Kaluli ethnopsychology. In G. M. White & J. Kirkpatrick (Eds.), *Person, self, and experience: Exploring Pacific ethnopsychologies* (pp. 168–182). Berkeley: University of California Press.

Schieffelin, E. L. (1985b). The cultural analysis of depressive affect: An example from New Guinea. In A. Kleinman & B. Good (Eds.), *Culture and depression* (pp. 101–133). Berkeley: University of California Press.

Schwartz, G. E., Weinberger, D. A., & Singer, J. A. (1981). Cardiovascular differentiation of happiness, sadness, anger and fear—following imagery and exercise. *Psychosomatic Medicine, 43*(4), 343–364.

Shaver, P., Schwartz, J., Kirson, D., & O'Connor, C. (1987). Emotion knowledge: Further exploration of a prototype approach. *Journal of Personality and Social Psychology, 52*(6), 1060–1086.

Shields, S. A. (1984). Reports of bodily change in anxiety, sadness, and anger. *Motivation and Emotion, 8*(1), 1–21.

Solomon, R. C. (1995). The cross-cultural comparison of emotion. In J. Marks & R. Ames (Eds.), *Emotions in Asian thought* (pp. 253–294). Albany: State University of New York Press.

Stearns, C. Z. (1988). "Lord help me walk humbly": Anger and sadness in England and America, 1570–1750. In C. Z. Stearns & P. N. Stearns (Eds.), *Emotion and social change* (pp. 39–68). New York: Holmes & Meier.

Stein, N. L., & Jewett, J. L. (1986). A conceptual analysis of the meaning of negative emotions: Implications for a theory of development. In C. Izard & P. B. Read (Eds.), *Measuring emotions in infants and children* (Vol. 2, pp. 238–267). Cambridge, Cambridge University Press.

Stein, N. L. & Levine, L. J. (1990). Making sense out of emotion. In N. L. Stein, B. Leventhal, & T. Trabasso (Eds.), *Psychological and biological approaches to emotion* (pp. 45–73). Hillsdale, NJ: Erlbaum.

Stern, D. N. (1985). *The interpersonal world of the infant.* New York: Basic Books.

Swallow, S. R., & Kuiper, N. A. (1987). The effects of depression and cognitive vulnerability to depression on judgments of similarity between self and other. *Motivation and Emotion, 11*(2), 157–167.

Tomkins, S. A. (1962). *Affect, imagery, and consciousness: Vol. 1. The positive affects.* New York: Springer.

Tomkins, S. A. (1963). *Affect, imagery, and consciousness: Vol. 2. The negative affects.* New York: Springer.

Tomkins, S. A. (1984). Affect theory. In K. R. Scherer & P. Ekman (Eds.), *Approaches to emotion* (pp. 163–195). Hillsdale, NJ: Erlbaum.

Tomkins, S. A. (1991). *Affect, imagery, and consciousness: Vol. 3. The negative affects: Anger and fear.* New York: Springer.

Vincent-Buffault, A. (1991). *The history of tears: Sensibility and sentimentality in France* (T. Bridgeman, Trans.). New York: St. Martin's Press.

Wellenkamp, J. (1988). Notions of grief and catharsis among the Toraja. *American Ethnologist, 15,* 486–500.

White, S. D. (1998). The politics of anger. In B. Rosenwein (Ed.), *Anger's past* (pp. 127–152). Ithaca, NY: Cornell University Press.

Wierzbicka, A. (1992). Cross-cultural pragmatics: Talking about emotion. *Cognition and Emotions, 6*(3–4), 285–319.

Wierzbicka, A. (1995). The relevance of language to the study of emotions. *Psychological Inquiry, 6*(3), 248–252.

CHAPTER 39

Self-Conscious Emotions: Embarrassment, Pride, Shame, and Guilt

Michael Lewis

In Chapter 17, I have suggested a model for the emergence of emotional life in the first 3 to 4 years of life. Here, I focus on a unique set of emotions that emerge late and that require certain cognitive abilities for their elicitation. Whereas the emotions that appear early, such as joy, sadness, fear, and anger, have received considerable attention, this set of later-appearing emotions has received relatively little attention. There are likely to be many reasons for this. One reason is that these self-conscious emotions cannot be described solely by examining a particular set of facial movements; they necessitate the observation of bodily action more than facial cues (Darwin, 1872/1965).

A second reason for their neglect is the realization that there are no clear, specific elicitors of these particular emotions. Whereas happiness can be elicited by seeing a significant other, and fear can be elicited by the approach of a stranger, there are few specific situations that will elicit shame, pride, guilt, or embarrassment. These self-conscious emotions are likely to require classes of events that can only be identified by the individuals themselves. Consider pride. What kinds of elicitors are necessary for pride to take place? Pride requires a large number of factors, all having to do with cognitions related to the self. Pride occurs when one makes a comparison or evaluates one's behavior vis-à-vis

some standard, rule, or goal (SRG) and finds that one has succeeded. Shame or guilt, on the other hand, occurs when such an evaluation leads to the conclusion that one has failed.

The elicitation of self-conscious emotions involves elaborate cognitive processes that have, at their heart, the notion of self. Although some theories—psychoanalysis, for example (see Freud, 1936/1963 and Erikson, 1950)—have argued for some universal elicitors of shame, such as failure at toilet training or exposure of the backside, the idea of an automatic, noncognitive elicitor of these emotions does not make much sense. Cognitive processes must be the elicitors of these complex emotions (Lewis, 1992a). It is the way we think or what we think about that becomes the elicitor of pride, shame, guilt, or embarrassment. There may be a one-to-one correspondence between thinking certain thoughts and the occurrence of a particular emotion; however, in the case of this class of emotions, the elicitor is a cognitive event. This does not mean that the earlier emotions, those called "primary" or "basic," are elicited by noncognitive events. Cognitive factors may play a role in the elicitation of any emotion; however, the nature of the cognitive events are much less articulated and differentiated in the earlier ones (Plutchik, 1980).

In order to explore these self-conscious emotions, we need first to articulate the role of self in their elicitation. Following this, an attempt at a working definition through a cognitive–attributional model is presented. The chapter focuses on shame, pride, guilt, and embarrassment, although other self-conscious emotions could be included—for example, jealousy, empathy, and envy.

THE ROLE OF SELF

Elsewhere, I have attempted to clarify those specific aspects of self that are involved in self-conscious emotions—in particular, the self-conscious *evaluative* emotions (Lewis, 1992b). Self-conscious evaluative emotions first involve a set of standards, rules, or goals (SRGs). These SRGs are inventions of the culture that are transmitted to children and involve their learning of, and willingness to consider, these SRGs as their own. This process of incorporating the SRGs has been discussed by Stipek, Recchia, and McClintic (1992). What is apparent from the work of Stipek et al. is that the process of incorporation starts quite early in life. Standards, rules, and goals imply self-evaluation, for it would make little sense if we had SRGs but had no evaluation of our action in regard to them.

Having self-evaluative capacity allows for two distinct outcomes: We can evaluate our behavior and hold ourselves responsible for the action being evaluated, or we can hold ourselves not responsible. In the attribution literature, this distinction has been called either an internal or an external attribution, respectively (Weiner, 1986).

If we conclude that we are not responsible, then evaluation of our behavior ceases. However, if we evaluate ourselves as responsible, then we can evaluate our behavior as successful or unsuccessful vis-à-vis the SRGs. The determination of success and failure resides within the individual and is based on the nature of the standard that is set. For example, if a student believes that only receiving an A in an exam constitutes success, then receiving a B represents a failure for that student. On the other hand, a B may be considered a success by another.

Still another cognition related to the self has to do with the evaluation of one's self in terms of specific or global attributions. "Global self-attributions" refer to the whole self, while "specific self-attributions" refer to specific features or actions of the self (see Dweck & Leggett,

1988; Lewis, 1992b; Weiner, 1986). In almost every one of these processes, a concept of the self needs to be considered.

The need for cognitive elicitors having to do with the self was known to Darwin (1872/1965). Darwin not only described the basic, primary, or early emotions, but also dealt with the self-conscious emotions. Darwin saw these latter emotions as involving the self, although he was not able to distinguish between the various types (see also Tomkins, 1963, and Izard, 1977, for similar problems). For example, Darwin believed that blushing, which could be a sign of either shyness, embarrassment, or shame and guilt, was caused by how we appear to others; as he put it, "the thinking about others, thinking of us . . . excites a blush" (Darwin, 1872/1965, p. 325). His observation in regard to blushing indicates his concern with two issues: the issue of appearance and the issue of consciousness. He repeatedly made the point that these emotions depend on sensitivity to the opinion of others, whether good or bad. Thus the distinction between emotions that require opinion or thought of others and emotions that do not suggests that two different kinds of cognitive processes are involved.

The distinction between self-conscious emotions and primary or basic emotions remains of concern. The idea that there is a basic set of emotions grows out of the idea of human instincts or propensities. If they are basic, prewired, or genetically given, they have to be limited in number. Although we recognize an enormous variety of emotions, the existence of each one as a unique and discrete "wiring" is too burdensome a characterization of the nervous system. Instead of positing this complex set of emotions, many have argued that there is only a select number of basic, primary, or pure emotions (see Oatley & Johnson-Laird, 1987, and Ortony, Clore, & Collins, 1988, for a contrary view). In order to resolve this problem in regard to self-conscious emotions, we might instead make the distinction between emotions that involve few or simple cognitive processes and emotions that involve complex cognitive processes (Darwin, 1872/1965; Plutchik, 1980).

TOWARD A WORKING DEFINITION

A most difficult task is to try to distinguish among the different types of self-conscious emotions (e.g., embarrassment, shyness, shame, and guilt). As Darwin's analysis makes clear, all of these emotions are likely to produce blushing. Since Darwin viewed blushing as a human species-specific behavior, he also viewed these emotions as unique to humans as well. However, blushing occurs with any one of these emotions, so it is clear that blushing will do us little good in distinguishing between them.

One can turn to the psychoanalytic literature; however, its focus on guilt rather than shame (see Broucek, 1991, and Morrison, 1989, for exceptions) makes this literature suspect. For example, Freud (1905/1953) discussed the function of guilt but said little about shame. For Freud, the superego—the mechanism by which the standards of the parents are incorporated into the self, specifically via the child's fear that the parents will respond to transgression by withdrawal of love or even by punishment—is the initial source of the feeling of guilt. Freud's discussion of guilt in relationship to the superego is similar to his discussion of guilt in relation to the instinctual drives and their expression. For Freud, anxiety or fear is translatable directly into guilt. The two stages in the development of the sense of guilt related to the superego are (1) the fear of authority and (2) the fear of the superego itself, once the authority standards are incorporated. In the well-developed superego, the sense of guilt arises not only when a violation is committed, but even when a violation is being anticipated.

The guilt that Freud focuses on is not a guilt related to the whole self, but rather a guilt related to one's action (see Lewis, 1992a, for this distinction). For Freud, guilt is a specific and focused response to a transgression that can be rectified by abstinence and penance. Freud's focus on guilt, not shame, can also be found in his discussion of psychopathology. It is to be found in the overdeveloped sense of guilt resulting from an overdeveloped ego. Within normal functioning, the superego condemns the ego; this condemnation in turn gives rise to normal guilt. When Freud did mention shame, he usually did so in the context of drives and impulses that require restriction. So, for example, in discussing the impulses having to do with the erogenous zones, he stated that these impulses

would seem in themselves to be perverse—that is, to arise from erogenic zones, and to derive their activity from instincts which, in view of the direction of the subjects' development, can arouse only unpleasant feelings. They [the impulses] consequently evoke opposing mental forces [reacting impulses] which, in order to suppress this displeasure affectively, build up the mental dams of . . . disgust, shame and morality. (Freud, 1905/1953, p. 178)

Erikson, in discussing shame, had no more success in distinguishing between shame and guilt than the earlier psychoanalysts. Erikson turned more to the Darwinian view when he suggested that shame arises when "one is completely exposed and conscious of being looked at, in a word, self-conscious" (1950, pp. 223–224). Again, this self-consciousness is an undifferentiated state of being—that is, shame, shyness, embarrassment, and guilt. Erikson tried to differentiate these terms but was not completely successful. For example, he discussed "visual shame" versus "auditory guilt," but did not develop this concept. I imagine that the reference to visual shame is based on Darwin's theory that shame derives from being looked at, and that in feeling shame, one wishes to hide one's face and to disappear. Although Erikson held to a more interactional view, one involving self and self-consciousness, he also indicated that the conditions necessary for feeling shame include being in an upright and exposed position. As he stated, "Clinical observation leads me to believe that shame has much to do with a consciousness of having a front and a back, especially a 'behind'" (Erikson, 1950, pp. 223–224). Erikson believed that shame is related to specific body acts, in particular toilet functions. Erikson's familiar theory of ego challenges offers the clearest differentiation between shame and guilt, their place in human life, and events likely to elicit them. Erikson's second challenge is autonomy versus shame and doubt. Autonomy is the attempt of the child to achieve, to do for him- or herself—an attempt that is related to a developing sense of the self. Achieving muscular control, including control of the elimination of body waste, is the socialization and the developmental challenge at this life stage. Shame and doubt arise during this stage as the counterpoints to autonomy, the successful achievement. In other words, shame and doubt arise from the child's inability to fully control bodily functions. It is only after this basic ego task that the third ego task, initiative versus guilt, becomes significant. Here Erikson suggested that guilt has a reparative function.

Erikson's developmental sequence indicates a recognition that shame and guilt are different emotions—that shame precedes guilt, and that they are associated in counterpoint with different ego tasks.

There is very little agreement as to the specific elicitors of shame, guilt, and embarrassment. Many events are capable of eliciting any one of them. No particular stimulus event has been identified as the trigger for shame and guilt. It would be easier to understand these self-conscious emotions if we could specify the class of external events likely to elicit them. If it were true that shame and guilt are similar to anxiety and that they reflect the subject's fear of uncontrollable impulses, then we could consider the causes of shame to be sexual or aggressive impulses. Alternatively, if we could prove that situations having to do with toilet or genital functions are likely to elicit shame, or if we could prove that the way we appear physically or how we behave in front of others may automatically elicit embarrassment, we could then specify situations that would help us to define these self-conscious emotions and increase our understanding of what causes them. There is no such clear cause-and-effect pattern, no event that can be used consistently as an elicitor of each of these self-conscious emotions.

Alternative theories having to do with self psychology are necessary. To anticipate the argument, let me state a few broad requirements. Success or failure vis-à-vis our SRGs is likely to produce a signal to the self that results in self-reflection (see Mandler, 1975, for a discussion of events likely to cause self-reflection). This cognitive reflective process gives rise to self-attribution and to the specific emotions that accompany the different types of self-attribution. The importance of such a view resides in three important factors. First, the model does not attempt to specify what constitutes success or failure, or how the person goes about evaluating success or failure. Second, the model does not specify any particular SRG. In other words, it is not clear whether there are any specific stimuli that uniquely contribute to any of the self-conscious emotions. Third, the model assumes that self-attributions leading to specific emotions are internal events that reside in people themselves, although the SRGs are taught by others.

Although this model is based on a phenomenological and cognitive–attributional model, I do not mean to suggest that the self-conscious emotions are epiphenomenological or deserve "lower status" than the cognitive–attributional processes themselves. These self-conscious emotions may have discrete and specific locations, as well as specific processes that are themselves "bodily" in nature. The cognitions associated with these emotions may serve simply as elicitors of specific emotions in the same way as do other stimuli, such as the social behavior of others, loud noises, or sudden and uncontrolled events. The important point here is that specific emotions can be elicited through a variety of attributions. The idea that cognitions can lead to emotions has been poorly received by some, who believe that this idea implies that cognitions have real status while emotions are epiphenomenological (Schachter & Singer, 1962). I mean to give emotions the same status as cognitions. Just as cognitions can lead to emotions, emotions can lead to cognitions. The theory implies no status difference.

A COGNITIVE–ATTRIBUTIONAL THEORY

Figure 39.1 presents a structural model for defining various self-conscious emotions. In the figure, A, B, and C represent cognitive processes that serve as stimuli for these emotions.

Standards, Rules, and Goals

The first feature of the model has to do with the SRGs that govern our behavior. All of us have beliefs about what is acceptable for others and for ourselves in regard to standards having to do with actions, thoughts, and feelings. This set of beliefs, or SRGs, constitutes the information

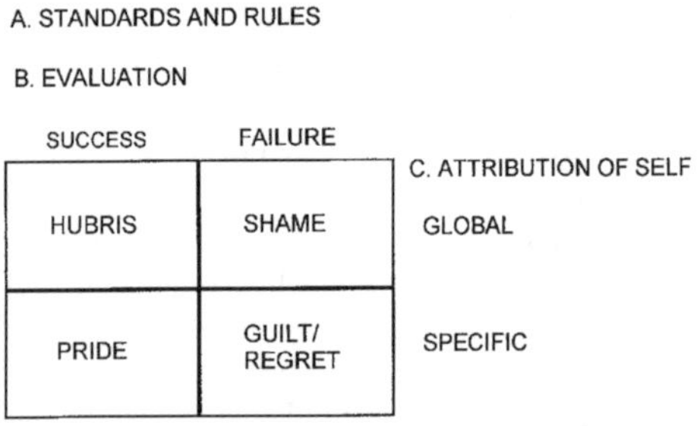

A. STANDARDS AND RULES

B. EVALUATION

	SUCCESS	FAILURE	C. ATTRIBUTION OF SELF
	HUBRIS	SHAME	GLOBAL
	PRIDE	GUILT/ REGRET	SPECIFIC

FIGURE 39.1. Structural model for the elicitation of self-conscious evaluative emotions. From Lewis (1992a). Copyright 1992 by Michael Lewis. Reprinted by permission.

one acquires through culturalization in a particular society. SRGs differ across different societies, across groups within societies, across different time epochs, and among individuals of different ages. The standards of our culture are varied and complex, yet each of us knows at least some of them. Moreover, each of us has a unique set. To become a member of any group requires that we learn them. I can think of no group that does not have SRGs, or in which violation of SRGs does not lead to negative sanctions. These SRGs are acquired through a variety of processes. They always are associated with human behavior, including thinking, action, and feeling. They are prescribed by the culture, including the culture at large, as well as by the influences of specific groups, such as clan, peers, and family.

It is safe to claim that by the age of 1 year, children are beginning to learn the appropriate action patterns reflecting the SRGs of the culture. By the second year of life, children show some understanding about appropriate and inappropriate behavior (Heckhausen, 1984; Kagan, 1981). The acquisition of these SRGs continues across the lifespan; however, some emerge early.

Evaluation

The evaluation of one's actions, thoughts, and feelings in terms of SRGs is the second cognitive–evaluative process that serves as a stimulus for self-conscious emotions. Two major aspects of this process are considered; the first has to do with the internal and external aspects of evaluation. For the model to work in describing the process of eliciting emotions, internal evaluation, as opposed to either no evaluation or external evaluation, is necessary. Individuals differ in their characteristic evaluative response. Moreover, situations differ in the likelihood that they will cause a particular evaluative response. The second consideration has to do with how individuals make a determination about success or failure in regard to any specific standard. Recent work seems to indicate that by the beginning of the third year of life children already have SRGs and seem to show distress when they violate them (Heckhausen, 1984; Lewis, Alessandri, & Sullivan, 1992; Stipek, 1983).

Internal versus External Evaluation

Within the field of attributional studies, the problem of internal versus external attribution

has received attention (Weiner, 1986). People violate SRGs but often do not attribute the failure to themselves. They may explain their failure in terms of chance or the actions of others (Seligman, 1975; Seligman et al., 1984). Internal and external evaluations are functions both of situational factors and of individual characteristics. There are people who are likely to blame themselves no matter what happens. Dweck and Leggett (1988), in studying causes of success and failure within academic fields, found that many children blamed their success or failure on external forces, although there were as many who were likely to evaluate success and failure in terms of their own actions. Interestingly, strong sex differences emerged: In academic achievement, boys were more apt to hold themselves responsible for their success and others for their failure, whereas girls were apt to blame others for their success and themselves for their failure.

Success or Failure

Another feature of the self-evaluation process has to do with the socialization of what constitutes success or failure. Once one has assumed responsibility (internal evaluation), exactly how one comes to evaluate an action, thought, or feeling as a success or a failure is not well understood. This aspect of self-evaluation is particularly important because, as we can see from Figure 39.1, the same SRGs can result in radically different feelings, depending upon whether success or failure is attributed to oneself.

Many factors are involved in producing inaccurate or unique evaluations of success or failure. These include early failures in the self system leading to narcissistic disorders (see Morrison, 1989), harsh socialization experiences, and high levels of reward for success or punishment for failure (see Alessandri & Lewis, 1996; Lewis, 1992a). The evaluation of one's behavior in terms of success and failure is a very important aspect of the organization of plans and the determination of new goals and new plans.

Attribution about Self

Another attribution in regard to the self has to do with "global" or "specific" self-attribution (Beck, 1967, 1979; Seligman, 1975). "Global" attribution refers to an individual's propensity to focus on the total self. Thus, for any particular behavior violation, some individuals, some of the time, are likely to focus on the totality of the self; they use such self-evaluative phrases as "Because I did this, I am bad (or good)." Janoff-Bulman's (1979) distinction between "characterological" and "behavioral" self-blame is particularly relevant here.

On such occasions, the focus is upon the self, both as object and as subject. The self becomes embroiled in the self. It becomes embroiled because the evaluation of the self by the self is total. There is no way out. The focus is not upon the individual's behavior, but upon the total self. There is little wonder that in using such global attribution one can think of nothing else, and one becomes confused and speechless (H. B. Lewis, 1971). We tend to focus upon ourselves, not upon our action. Because of this, we are unable to act and are driven from the field of action into hiding or disappearing.

"Specific" attribution refers to individuals' propensity in some situations, some of the time, to focus on specific actions of the self. That is, their self-evaluation is not global, but specific. It is not the total self that has done something wrong or good; instead, particular specific behaviors are judged. At such times as these, individuals will use such evaluative phrases as "What I did was wrong, and I mustn't do it again." Notice that for such occurrences, an individual's focus is not on the totality of the self, but on the specific behavior of the self in a specific situation. The focus here is on the behavior of the self in interaction with objects or persons. Here attention is on the actions of the self or the effect on other selves.

Global versus specific self-focus may be a personality style. Global attributions for negative events are generally uncorrelated with global attributions for positive events. It is only when positive or negative events are taken into account that relatively stable and consistent attributional patterns are observed. Some individuals are likely to be stable in their global and specific evaluations; under most conditions of success or failure, these subjects are likely to maintain a global or specific posture in regard to self-attribution. In the attribution literature, such dispositional factors have important consequences upon a variety of fixed "personality patterns." So, for example, depressed individuals are likely to make stable global attributions, whereas nondepressed individuals are less like-

ly to be stable in their global attributions (Beck, 1979).

In addition to the dispositional factors relating to specific or global attributions (Kochanska, 1991, 1997), there are likely to be situational constraints as well. Some have called these "prototypic situations." That is, although there are dispositional factors, not all people all the time are involved in either global or specific attributions. Unfortunately, these situational factors have not been well studied. It seems reasonable that certain classes of situations should be more likely than others to elicit a particular focus, but exactly what classes of stimuli are likely to elicit global or specific attributions remain unknown (see Lewis, 1992a).

MAKING SENSE OF THE MODEL

Given these three sets of activities—(1) the establishment of one's SRGs, (2) the evaluation of success or failure of one's action in regard to these, and (3) the attribution of the self—it is now possible to see how these factors bear on some self-conscious emotional states. It is important to point out that this model is symmetrical in relation to positive and negative self-conscious emotions. Because of this, it focuses not only upon shame and guilt but upon the other side of the axis, hubris and pride. It is the cognitive–evaluative process of the organism itself that elicits these states. The immediate elicitors of these self-conscious emotions are cognitive in nature.

The model distinguishes among four emotional states. Notice that shame is a consequence of a failure evaluation relative to the SRGs when the person makes a global evaluation of the self. Guilt is also the consequence of a failure; however, the focus is on the self's specific action. A parallel exists as a consequence of success. When success is evaluated and the person makes a global attribution, hubris (pridefulness)[1] is the resulting emotion; when success is evaluated and the person makes a specific attribution, pride is the resulting emotion. With these definitions, I move to a discussion of shame, guilt, hubris, and pride. In addition, embarrassment and shyness are discussed.

Shame

Shame is the product of a complex set of cognitive activities: individuals' evaluation of their actions in regard to their SRGs and their global evaluation of the self. The phenomenological experience of the person having shame is that of a wish to hide, disappear, or die (H. B. Lewis, 1971; Lewis, 1992a). It is a highly negative and painful state that also results in the disruption of ongoing behavior, confusion in thought, and an inability to speak. The physical action accompanying shame is a shrinking of the body, as though to disappear from the eye of the self or the other. Because of the intensity of this emotional state, the global attack on the self-system, all that individuals can do when presented with such a state is to attempt to rid themselves of it. However, since it is a global attack on the self, people have great difficulty in dissipating this emotion. There are specific actions individuals employ when shamed in efforts to undo the shame state (see Lewis, 1992a, for examples, such as reinterpretation, self-splitting [multiple personalities], or forgetting [repression]) .

Shame is not produced by any specific situation, but rather by the individual's interpretation of the event. Even more important is that shame is not related necessarily to the event's being public or private. Although many hold that shame is a public failure, this need not be so. Failure, attributed to the whole self, can be either public or private. Shame may be public, but it is as likely to be private. Each of us can think of private events when we say to ourselves, "I'm ashamed of having done that." Shame can center around moral action as well. Thus, when persons violate some moral SRG, they are ashamed.

Guilt

The emotional state of guilt or regret is produced when individuals evaluate their behavior as failure but focus on the specific features or actions of the self that led to the failure. Unlike the focus in shame on the global self, the focus in guilt is on the self's actions and behaviors that are likely to repair the failure. From a phenomenological point of view, individuals are pained by their failure, but this pained feeling is directed to the cause of the failure or the object of harm. Because the cognitive–attributional process focuses on the action of the self rather than on the totality of self, the feeling that is produced—guilt—is not as intensely negative as shame and does not lead to confusion and to the loss of action. In fact, the emotion of guilt always has associated with it a corrective action that the individual can take (but does not necessarily take) to repair the failure. Rectification of the failure and preventing it from occurring again are the two possible corrective paths. Whereas in shame we see the body hunched over itself in an attempt to hide and disappear, in guilt we see individuals moving in space as if trying to repair their action (see Barrett & Zahn-Waxler, 1987). The marked postural differences that accompany guilt and shame are helpful both in distinguishing these emotions and in measuring individual differences. We might point to blushing as a measure also distinguishing guilt from shame; however, because of the variability in the likelihood of individuals to blush, the use of blushing is not an accurate index.

Because in guilt the focus is on the specific, individuals are capable of ridding themselves of this emotional state through action. The corrective action can be directed toward the self as well as toward the other; thus, unlike shame, which is a melding of the self as subject and object, in guilt the self is differentiated from the object. As such, the emotion is less intense and more capable of dissipation.

There are levels of this negative state, having to do with the ease or availability of corrective action. In some cases, corrective action may not be as readily available as in others. In all cases, however, there is an attempt at corrective action. Should the corrective action not be forthcoming, either in thought, feeling, or deed, it is possible that a guilt experience can be converted into one of shame (H. B. Lewis, 1971). Here, then, is another difference between shame and guilt. We can be ashamed of our guilty action, but we cannot be guilty over being ashamed, suggesting a levels difference and a directional difference in the experiencing of these emotions. The emotion of guilt lacks the negative intensity of shame. It is not self-destroying, and as such can be viewed as a more useful emotion in motivating specific and corrective action. However, because it is less intense, it may not convey the motivation necessary for change or correction.

Hubris

Hubris is defined as exaggerated pride or self-confidence often resulting in retribution. It is an example of pridefulness, something dislikeable and to be avoided. Hubris is a consequence of an evaluation of success in regard to one's SRGs where the focus is on the global self. In this emotion, the individual focuses on the total self as successful. Hubris is associated with such descriptions as "puffed up." In extreme cases, it is associated with grandiosity or with narcissism (Morrison, 1989). Recently, Mueller and Dweck (1998) have shown that too much praise of children may result in negative performance; the assumed mechanism may be in the enhancement of hubris in the children so treated. In fact, "hubristic" is defined as "insolent or contemptuous." Because of the global nature of this emotion, it is likely to be transient, and in order to be able to maintain this state, the individual must either alter standards or reevaluate what constitutes success. Unlike shame, it is highly positive and emotionally rewarding; that is, the person feels good about the self.

Hubris is, however, an emotion difficult to sustain, since there is no specific action that precipitates the feeling. Because such feelings are addictive, people prone to hubris derive little satisfaction from the emotion. Consequently, they seek out and invent situations likely to repeat this emotional state. They can do this either by altering their SRGs or by reevaluating what constitutes success in their actions, thoughts, or feelings.

From the outside, other people observe the individual having hubris with some disdain. Hubristic people have difficulty in their interpersonal relations, since their own hubris is likely to interfere with the wishes, needs, and desires of others, in which case there is likely to be an interpersonal conflict. Moreover, given the contemptuousness associated with hubris, the other persons are likely to be shamed by the nature of the actions of the persons having this emotion. The three problems associated with hubris, therefore, are that (1) it is a transient but addictive emotion; (2) it is not related to a specific action, and thus requires altering patterns of goal setting or evaluation of what constitutes success; and (3) it interferes with interpersonal relationships because of its contemptuous and insolent nature.

Pride

The emotion I have labeled "pride" is the consequence of a successful evaluation of a specific action. The phenomenological experience is joy over an action, thought, or feeling well done. Here, the focus of pleasure is specific

and related to a particular behavior. In pride, the self and object are separated, as in guilt. Unlike shame and hubris, where subject and object are fused, pride focuses the organism on its action; the organism is engrossed in the specific action that gives it pride. Some investigators have likened this state to achievement motivation (see, e.g., Heckhausen, 1984; Stipek et al., 1992)—an association that seems particularly apt. Because this positive state is associated with a particular action, individuals have available to themselves the means by which they can reproduce the state. Notice that, unlike hubris, pride's specific focus allows for action. Because of the general use of the term "pride" to refer to "hubris," "efficacy," and "satisfaction" (see Note 1), the study of pride as hubris has received relatively little attention. Dweck and Leggett (1988) similarly have approached this problem through the use of individuals' implicit theories about the self, which are cognitive attributions that serve as the stimuli for the elicitation of the self-conscious emotion of mastery.

Embarrassment and Shyness

In the discussion to this point, it is clear that one can differentiate, from a behavioral as well as a phenomenological point of view, shame and guilt. There are, however, two further emotions that tend to be confused with these two—embarrassment and shyness.

Shyness

Izard and Tyson (1986) consider shyness to be sheepishness, bashfulness, a feeling of uneasiness or psychological discomfort in social situations, and oscillation between fear and interest or between avoidance and approach. In this description, shyness is related to fear and is a nonevaluative emotion centered around the individual's discomfort response to others. Such a description fits Buss's (1980) notion of shyness as an emotional response which is elicited by experiences of novelty or conspicuousness. For Buss, shyness and fear are closely related and represent a fearfulness toward others. A way of distinguishing shyness from shame is that it appears much earlier than either shame or guilt.

Such an approach to shyness seems reasonable because it fits with other notions relating the self to others, or what we might call the "social self." Eysenck (1954) has characterized people as social and asocial by genetic disposition, and Kagan, Reznick, and Snidman (1988) have pointed out the physiological responses of children they call "inhibited." These inhibited or shy children are withdrawn, are uncomfortable in social situations, and appear fearful. Shyness may be a dispositional factor not related to self-evaluation (DiBiase & Lewis, 1997; Lewis & Ramsay, 1997). Rather, it may simply be the discomfort of being in the company of other social objects—in other words, the opposite of sociability (Lewis & Feiring, 1989).

Embarrassment

For some, embarrassment is closely linked to shame (Izard, 1979; Tomkins, 1963). The most notable difference between embarrassment and shame is the intensity level. While shame appears to be an intense and disruptive emotion, embarrassment is clearly less intense and does not involve the disruption of thought and language that shame does. Second, in terms of body posture, people who are embarrassed do not assume the posture of one wishing to hide, disappear, or die. In fact, their bodies reflect an ambivalent approach and avoidance posture. Repeated looking and then looking away, accompanied by smiling behavior, seem to index embarrassment (see Edelman, 1987; Geppert, 1986; Lewis, Stanger, & Sullivan, 1989). Rarely in a shame situation do we see gaze aversion accompanied by smiling behavior. Thus, from a behavioral point of view, these two emotions appear to be different.

Phenomenologically, embarrassment is less clearly differentiated from shame than from guilt. People often report that embarrassment is "a less intense experience of shame." Similar situations that invoke shame are found to invoke embarrassment, although, as I have mentioned, its intensity, duration, and disruptive quality are not the same. It is important to differentiate two types of embarrassed behavior, since this may help us distinguish embarrassment from shame: (1) embarrassment as exposure and (2) embarrassment as less intense shame (see Lewis, 1995).

Embarrassment as Exposure. In certain situations of exposure, people become embarrassed. It is not related to negative evaluation, as is shame. Perhaps the best example is the case of being complimented. One phenomenological experience of those who appear before audiences is that of embarrassment caused by the positive comments of the introduction. Consider the moment when the speaker is introduced: The person introducing the speaker extols his or her virtues. Surprisingly, praise, rather than displeasure or negative evaluation, elicits embarrassment!

Another example of this type of embarrassment can be seen in our reactions to public display. When people observe someone looking at them, they are apt to become self-conscious, look away, and touch or adjust their bodies. When the observed person is a woman, she will often adjust or touch her hair; men are less likely to touch their hair, but may adjust their clothes or change their body posture. In few cases do the observed people look sad. If anything, they appear pleased by the attention. This combination—gaze turned away briefly, no frown, and nervous touching—looks like this first type of embarrassment.

A third example of embarrassment as exposure can be seen in the following experiment: When I wish to demonstrate that embarrassment can be elicited just by exposure, I announce that I am going to point randomly to a student. I repeatedly mention that my pointing is random and that it does not reflect a judgment about the person. I close my eyes and point. My pointing invariably elicits embarrassment in the student pointed to.

In each of these examples, there is no negative evaluation of the self in regard to SRGs. In these situations, it is difficult to imagine embarrassment as a less intense form of shame. Since praise cannot readily lead to an evaluation of failure, it is likely that embarrassment resulting from compliments, from being looked at, and from being pointed to has more to do with the exposure of the self than with evaluation. Situations other than praise come to mind, in which a negative evaluation can be inferred, although it may not be the case. Take, for example, walking into a room before the speaker has started to talk. It is possible to arrive *on time* only to find people already seated. When you are walking into the room, eyes turn toward you, and you may experience embarrassment. One could say that there is a negative self-evaluation: "I should have been earlier; I should not have made noise (I did not make noise)." I believe, however, that the experience of embarrassment in this case may not be elicited by negative self-evaluation, but simply by public exposure.

Embarrassment as Less Intense Shame.
The second class of embarrassment, which I
call "embarrassment as less intense shame,"
seems to me to be related to a negative self-
evaluation. The difference in intensity can
probably be attributed to the nature of the failed
SRG. Some SRGs are more or less associated
with the core of self; for me, failure at driving a
car is less important than is failure at helping a
student. Failures associated with less important
and central SRGs result in embarrassment
rather than shame. If this analysis is correct,
then it is possible that each of the four self-conscious emotions has a less intense form.

It may well be that embarrassment may not
be the same as shame. From a phenomenological stance, they appear very different. On the
other hand, there is the possibility that embarrassment and shame are in fact related and that
they vary only in intensity. It is safe to say that,
as a working definition, there appear to be at
least two different types of embarrassment.

SHAME AND PSYCHOPATHOLOGY

Recently my colleagues and I have extended
our interest in the development of shame to
study its relation to psychopathology. Specifically, we are concerned with how traumatic
events impact on shame and how shame then
impacts on psychosocial adjustment.

Figure 39.2 presents our general model. On
the far left side of the model is the traumatic
event. I shall be talking about studies of both
sexual abuse and maltreatment as trauma. Trauma leads to shame through the mediation of
cognitive attributions about the abuse (a), and
shame (b) in turn leads to poor adjustment (d).
The model also allows for the trauma to directly influence shame (c) and adjustment (e), although our central hypothesis is that the outcomes of trauma are mediated by how the child
thinks about the event(s). The support for this

model comes from research suggesting that individuals who are shame-prone are more likely
to evidence poor self-esteem, depression, and
dissociation (Lewis, 1992a; Ross, 1989;
Tangney, Wagner, & Gramzow, 1990). Consequently, an internal, stable, global attribution
style for negative events constitutes a risk factor for shame and subsequent poor adjustment.

Sexual Abuse and Shame

The experience of shame as a consequence of
sexual abuse is a central mechanism related to
subsequent behavior problems (Lewis, 1992a).
Little work has been done exploring this problem. The number of studies on the relation between type of abuse and the likelihood of subsequent behavior problems is small, mostly
retrospective, and inconsistent (see Browne &
Finkelhor, 1986, and Kendall-Tackett, Williams, & Finkelhor, 1993, for reviews). However, none of the studies make a direct link between shame and subsequent behavior
problems. We do know that more serious forms
of sexual contact are related to greater trauma
in children (Bagley & Ramsey, 1985; Elwell &
Ephross, 1987; Friedrich, Urquiza, & Beilke,
1986; Kendall-Tackett et al., 1993; Russell,
1986; Seidner & Calhoun, 1984; Tufts New
England Medical Center, 1984); thus, given the
nature of the trauma, shame is likely to be involved.

Our work is particularly relevant because it is
directly concerned with attributions as they are
related to self-conscious emotions, and attributions are likely to be made concerning the causes of abuse. If the abuse is attributed to an internal, global cause, the resulting emotion is
shame; therefore, how the victim evaluates the
sexual abuse event(s) is important. It is likely to
mediate subsequent long-lasting effects of the
abuse (Conte, 1985; Gold, 1986; Janoff-Bulman & Frieze, 1983; Wyatt & Mickey, 1988).
Given that making internal, stable, global attri-

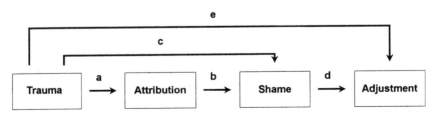

FIGURE 39.2. A model of trauma and adjustment as they relate to shame.

butions for negative events is related to poor adjustment, low self-esteem, helplessness, psychological distress, and depression (Kaslow, Rehm, Pollack, & Siegel, 1988; Lewis, 1992a; Metalsky, Abramson, Seligman, Semmel, & Peterson, 1982; Peterson & Seligman, 1983; Tangney et al.,1990), shame as the intervening cause of symptoms following sexual abuse is likely.

The work available on the relation between attribution style and sexual abuse in adults who were victimized in childhood supports the idea that attribution style mediates the long-term outcome of sexual abuse (Gold, 1986; Wyatt & Mickey, 1988). One study compared the current functioning of women who had been sexually abused as children to that of women who did not report being abused (Gold, 1986). There was a strong relation between a victim's attribution style and her adult functioning. Women who were sexually victimized in childhood, and who reported psychological distress and low self-esteem, were more likely to have an attribution style characterized by internal, stable, global attributions for negative events. Another study of women who reported being sexually abused as children found that a self-blaming attribution style was related to not having disclosed the abuse and to more severe forms of abuse (Wyatt & Mickey, 1988). These findings suggest that self-blaming attributions may be related to more shame, and hence to more unwillingness to disclose the event. One study of adolescent victims found that internal attributions for the sexual abuse, compared to external ones, were related to lower self-esteem and higher depression scores (Morrow, 1991). Adolescent victims who felt "I did something wrong and I am being punished for it" showed poorer adjustment than those who viewed the perpetrator as at fault (e.g., "because he was drinking").

Recently, we have been able to show the relations between sexual abuse, shame, and adjustment. In a longitudinal study of children aged 8 to 15 years who were known to have been sexually abused, we examined the relations of the severity of sexual abuse, shame, and attribution to adjustment (in this case, depression), using risk and protective factors as covariants.

Figure 39.3 presents these data. Our findings indicate that within 6 months of the reported abuse (left side of the figure), severity of abuse and shame were both related to depression. However, by 1 year after the reported abuse (right side of the figure), only amount of shame was related to depression. Perhaps more importantly, children whose shame decreased over the year showed decreases in depression, while children whose shame stayed the same or increased actually showed increases in depression.

Maltreatment and Shame

The same model underlying psychopathology in sexually abused children should be evident for maltreated children. While the literature on maltreatment in children (i.e., physical abuse and neglect) is extensive, there has been relatively little work on the relation between maltreatment and shame. We (Alessandri & Lewis, 1996), for example, have looked at this relation and found that shame and pride in regard to failure and success in learning achievement-like tasks are influenced by shame. Specifically, maltreatment should result in more shame and less pride relative to nonmaltreatment. The results of this study and of more recent work indicate that maltreated children show less pride

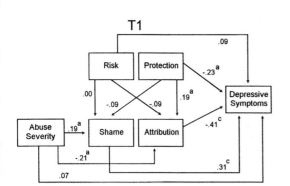
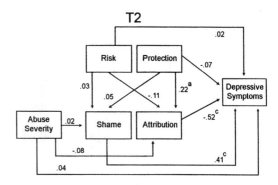

FIGURE 39.3. Depression and shame in sexually abused children. $^a p < .05$; $^b p < .01$; $^c p < .001$.

when they succeed and more shame when they fail, relative to children from the same background who have not been maltreated (see Figure 39.4).

Moreover, important sex differences appear. Maltreated girls show more shame when they fail a task and less pride when they succeed than do nonmaltreated girls. Boys on the other hand, show a suppression of both shame and pride. These sex difference findings are particularly important, since for girls trauma may result in depression (little pride and much shame), while for boys trauma may result in a suppression of emotion in general and therefore an increase in the likelihood of aggression, since they are not constrained by feelings of shame, guilt, or regret. Observations of these boys indicate higher amounts of such behaviors as throwing the test materials away, verbally aggressive statements, and (although not common) angry faces. In our most recent work (Sullivan & Lewis, 1999), we have measured these behaviors more carefully and found significant differences for maltreated and nonmaltreated boys' aggressive laboratory behavior. If these findings persist, the sex differences in response to traumas like maltreatment may explain why girls and women show high likelihood of depression while boys and men show high likelihood of aggressive behavior as a consequence of similar traumas. The extension of the investigation of the self-conscious emotions into the origins of psychopathology is likely to be of great importance, as it will link trauma, emotional reactions, and subsequent pathology.

CONCLUSION

The study of self-conscious emotions has only recently begun. The structural model outlined here (see Figure 39.1) offers an opportunity to consider and to define carefully some of the self-conscious emotions. Unless we develop a more accurate taxonomy, we will be unable to proceed in our study of these emotions. Given the renewed interest in emotional life, it is now appropriate to consider these more complex emotions, rather than the more "primary" or "basic" ones. Moreover, as others have pointed out and as we are now discovering, these self-conscious emotions are intimately connected with other emotions, such as anger and sadness (see, e.g., H. B. Lewis, 1971; Lewis, 1992a; Morrison, 1989). Finally, given the place of self-evaluation in adult life, it seems clear that the self-conscious evaluative emotions are likely to stand in the center of our emotional life (Dweck & Leggett, 1988; Heckhausen, 1984).

NOTE

1. I use here the Greek term "hubris" to differentiate it from "pride" because of the general confusion in the use of the term "pride." As I have warned before, the

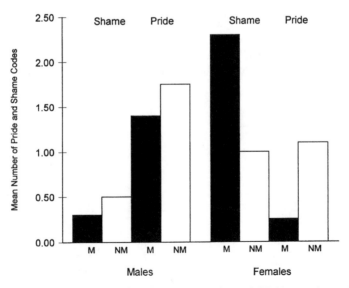

FIGURE 39.4. Shame and pride in maltreated children. M, maltreated; NM, nonmaltreated.

usage issues associated with these emotions render careful analysis most difficult. Not only do we have the problems of differentiating shame from guilt, embarrassment, and shyness, but we also have the difficulty of distinguishing between different kinds of pride. We can think of two uses of the term "pride." On the one hand, we can think of pride in one's accomplishment—the pride one feels in being successful in fulfilling a particular goal and activity. I recognize this in the discussions of achievement motivation and how children learn to feel proud about their achievements in terms of a particular SRG. On the other hand, we can also use the term "pride" to indicate a negative emotional state. One speaks of the "proud man" or the "proud woman" with some disdain. The Bible speaks of pride going before a fall, and throughout the Old and New Testaments we have examples of false pride bringing down a man. The story of Job is but one example of pride and the Lord's abhorrence of it. It is clear that the term "pride" carries a surplus of meaning, and that if we are to understand the term at all, we need to distinguish between specific pride and global pride. I have done so here by the use of the term "hubris" to represent global pride and "pride" to represent specific achievement.

REFERENCES

Alessandri, S. M., & Lewis, M. (1996). Differences in pride and shame in maltreated and nonmaltreated preschoolers. *Child Development, 67*, 1857–1869.

Bagley, C., & Ramsey, R. (1985, February). *Disrupted childhood and vulnerability to sexual assault: Long-term sequels with implications for counselling.* Paper presented at the Conference on Counseling the Sexual Abuse Survivor, Winnipeg, Manitoba, Canada.

Barrett, K. C., & Zahn-Waxler, C. (1987, April). *Do toddlers express guilt?* Poster presented at the biennial meeting of the Society for Research in Child Development, Toronto.

Beck, A. T. (1967). *Depression: Clinical, experimental, and theoretical aspects.* New York: Harper & Row.

Beck, A. T. (1979). *Cognitive therapy and emotional disorders.* New York: Times Mirror.

Broucek, F. J. (1991). *Shame and the self.* New York: Guilford Press.

Browne, A., & Finkelhor, D. (1986). Impact of child sexual abuse: A review of the research. *Psychological Bulletin, 99*, 66–77.

Buss, A. H. (1980). *Self-consciousness and social anxiety.* San Francisco: Freeman.

Conte, J. (1985). The effects of sexual abuse on children: A critique and suggestions for future research. *Victimology: An International Journal, 10*, 110–130.

Darwin, C. R. (1965). *The expression of the emotions in man and animals.* Chicago: University of Chicago Press. (Original work published 1872)

DiBiase, R., & Lewis, M. (1997). The relation between temperament and embarrassment. *Cognition and Emotion, 11*, 259–271.

Dweck, C. S., & Leggett, E. L. (1988). A social-cognitive approach to motivation and personality. *Psychological Review, 95*, 256–273.

Edelman, R. J. (1987). *The psychology of embarrassment.* Chichester, England: Wiley.

Elwell, M. E., & Ephross, P. H. (1987). Initial reactions of sexually abused children. *Social Casework, 68*, 109–116.

Erikson, E. H. (1950). *Childhood and society.* New York: Norton.

Eysenck, H. J. (1954). *The psychology of politics.* London: Routledge & Kegan Paul.

Freud, S. (1953). Three essays on the theory of sexuality. In J. Strachey (Ed. & Trans.), *The standard edition of the complete psychological works of Sigmund Freud* (Vol. 7, pp. 123–231). London: Hogarth Press. (Original work published 1905)

Freud, S. (1963). *The problem of anxiety* (H. A. Bunker, Trans.). New York: Norton. (Original work published 1936)

Friedrich, W. N., Urquiza, A. J., & Beilke, R. (1986). Behavior problems in sexually abused young children. *Journal of Pediatric Psychology, 11*, 47–57.

Geppert, U. (1986). *A coding system for analyzing behavioral expressions of self-evaluative emotions.* Munich: Max-Planck-Institute for Psychological Research.

Gold, E. R. (1986). Long-term effects of sexual victimization in childhood: An attributional approach. *Journal of Consulting and Clinical Psychology, 54*, 471–475.

Heckhausen, H. (1984). Emergent achievement behavior: Some early developments. In J. Nicholls (Eds.), *The development of achievement motivation* (pp. 1–32). Greenwich, CT: JAI Press.

Izard, C. E. (1977). *Human emotions.* New York: Plenum Press.

Izard, C. E. (1979). *The Maximally Discriminative Facial Movement Coding System (MAX).* Newark: Instructional Resources Center, University of Delaware.

Izard, C. E., & Tyson, M. C. (1986). Shyness as a discrete emotion. In W. H. Jones, J. M. Cheek, & S. R. Briggs (Eds.), *Shyness: Perspectives on research and treatment* (pp. 147–160). New York: Plenum Press.

Janoff-Bulman, R. (1979). Characterological versus behavioral self-blame: Inquiries into depression and rape. *Journal of Personality and Social Psychology, 37*, 1798–1809.

Janoff-Bulman, R., & Frieze, I. (1983). A theoretical perspective for understanding reactions to victimization. *Journal of Social Issues, 39*, 1–17.

Kagan, J. (1981). *The second year.* Cambridge, MA: Harvard University Press.

Kagan, J., Reznick, J. S., & Snidman, N. (1988). Biological bases of childhood shyness. *Science, 240*, 167–171.

Kaslow, N. J., Rehm, L. P., Pollack, S. L., & Siegel, A. W. (1988). Attributional style and self-control behavior in depressed and non-depressed children and their parents. *Journal of Abnormal Child Psychology, 16*, 163–175.

Kendall-Tackett, K. A., Williams, L. M., & Finkelhor, D. (1993). Impact of sexual abuse on children: A review and synthesis of recent empirical studies. *Psychological Bulletin, 113*, 164–180.

Kochanska, G. (1991). Socialization and temperament in the development of guilt and conscience. *Child Development, 62,* 1379–1392.

Kochanska, G. (1997). Multiple pathways to conscience for children with different temperaments: From toddlerhood to age 5. *Developmental Psychology, 33,* 597–615.

Lewis, H. B. (1971). *Shame and guilt in neurosis.* New York: International Universities Press.

Lewis, M. (1992a). *Shame: The exposed self.* New York: Free Press.

Lewis, M. (1992b). The self in self-conscious emotions. In D. Stipek, S. Recchia, & S. McClintic, Self-evaluation in young children. *Monographs of the Society for Research in Child Development, 57*(1, Serial No. 226), 85–95.

Lewis, M. (1995). Embarrassment: The emotion of self-exposure and evaluation. In J. P. Tangney & K. W. Fischer (Eds.), *Self-conscious emotions: The psychology of shame, guilt, embarrassment, and pride* (pp. 198–218). New York: Guilford Press.

Lewis, M., Alessandri, S. M., & Sullivan, M. W. (1992). Differences in shame and pride as a function of children's gender and task difficulty. *Child Development, 63,* 630–638.

Lewis, M., & Feiring, C. (1989). Infant, mother, and mother–infant interaction behavior and subsequent attachment. *Child Development, 60,* 146–156.

Lewis, M., & Ramsay, D. S. (1997). Stress reactivity and self-recognition. *Child Development, 68,* 621–629.

Lewis, M., Stanger, C., & Sullivan, M. W. (1989). Deception in three-year-olds. *Developmental Psychology, 25,* 439–443.

Mandler, G. (1975). *Mind and emotion.* New York: Wiley.

Metalsky, G. J., Abramson, L. Y., Seligman, M. E. P., Semmel, A., & Peterson, C. (1982). Attributional styles and life events in the classroom: Vulnerability and invulnerability to depressive mood reactions. *Journal of Personality and Social Psychology, 43,* 612–617.

Morrison, A. P. (1989). *Shame: The underside of narcissism.* Hillsdale, NJ: Analytic Press.

Morrow, K. B. (1991). Attributions of female adolescent incest victims regarding their molestation. *Child Abuse and Neglect, 15,* 477–483.

Mueller, C. M., & Dweck, C. S. (1998). Praise for intelligence can undermine children's motivation and performance. *Journal of Personality and Social Psychology, 75,* 33–52.

Oatley, K., & Johnson-Laird, P. N. (1987). Toward a cognitive theory of emotions. *Cognition and Emotion, 1,* 29–50.

Ortony, A., Clore, G. L., & Collins, A. (1988). *The cognitive structure of emotions.* New York: Cambridge University Press.

Peterson, C., & Seligman, M. E. P. (1983). Learned helplessness and victimization. *Journal of Social Issues, 39,* 105–118.

Plutchik, R. (1980). A general psychoevolutionary theory of emotion. In R. Plutchik & H. Kellerman (Eds.), *Emotion: Theory, research, and experience. Vol. 1. Theories of emotion* (pp. 3–33). New York: Academic Press.

Ross, C. A. (1989). *Multiple personality disorder: Diagnosis, clinical features, and treatment.* New York: Wiley.

Russell, D. E. H. (1986). *The secret trauma: Incest in the lives of girls and women.* New York: Basic Books.

Schachter, S., & Singer, J. E. (1962). Cognitive, social, and physiological determinants of emotional state. *Psychological Review, 69,* 379–399.

Seidner, A., & Calhoun, K. S. (1984, August). *Childhood sexual abuse: Factors related to differential adult adjustment.* Paper presented at the Second National Conference for Family Violence Researchers, Durham, NC.

Seligman, M. E. P. (1975). *Helplessness: On depression, development, and death.* San Francisco: Freeman.

Seligman, M. E. P., Peterson, C., Kaslow, N., Tanenbaum, R., Alloy, L., & Abramson, L. (1984). Attributional style and depressive symptoms among children. *Journal of Abnormal Psychology, 39,* 235–238.

Stipek, D. J. (1983). A developmental analysis of pride and shame. *Human Development, 25,* 42–54.

Stipek, D. J., Recchia, S., & McClintic, S. (1992). Self-evaluation in young children. *Monographs of the Society for Research in Child Development, 57*(1, Serial No. 226).

Sullivan, M. W., & Lewis, M. (1999, April). *The emotions of maltreated children in response to success and failure.* Paper presented at the biennial meeting of the Society for Research in Child Development, Albuquerque, NM.

Tangney, J. P., Wagner, P., & Gramzow, R. (1990, June). *Shame-proneness, but not guilt-proneness, is linked to psychological maladjustment.* Poster presented at the meeting of the American Psychological Society, Dallas, TX.

Tomkins, S. S. (1963). *Affect, imagery, and consciousness: Vol. 2. The negative affects.* New York: Springer.

Tufts New England Medical Center, Division of Child Psychiatry. (1984). *Sexually exploited children: Service and research project* (Final report for the Office of Juvenile Justice and Delinquency Prevention). Washington, DC: U.S. Department of Justice.

Weiner, B. (1986). *An attributional theory of motivation and emotion.* New York: Springer-Verlag.

Wyatt, G. E., & Mickey, M.R. (1988). The support of parents and others as it mediates the effects of child sexual abuse: An exploratory study. In G. E. Wyatt & G. J. Powell (Eds.), *Lasting effects of child sexual abuse* (pp. 211–226). Newbury Park, CA: Sage.

CHAPTER 40

Disgust

Paul Rozin
Jonathan Haidt
Clark R. McCauley

For North Americans, elicitors of disgust come from nine domains: food, body products, animals, sexual behaviors, contact with death or corpses, violations of the exterior envelope of the body (including gore and deformity), poor hygiene, interpersonal contamination (contact with unsavory human beings), and certain moral offenses (Haidt, McCauley, & Rozin, 1994; Rozin, Haidt, McCauley, & Imada, 1997). What unites these disparate domains? Although all involve negative or unpleasant events, there are many kinds of negative events, such as pain, confrontations, and frightening interactions, that are not disgusting. The goal of this chapter is to make sense of this varied set of elicitors—that is, to describe the meaning of disgust within both developmental and cultural contexts. We argue for a path of development in individuals and cultures that extends from the presumed origin of disgust as a rejection response to bad tastes, in the service of protecting the body, to the full range of elicitors listed above, more appropriately described as in the service of protecting the soul.

DEFINING DISGUST

There are two classic papers describing disgust, published some 70 years apart. The first, a chapter in Darwin's *The Expression of the Emo-* *tions in Man and Animals* (1872/1965), defined disgust as referring to "something revolting, primarily in relation to the sense of taste, as actually perceived or vividly imagined; and secondarily to anything which causes a similar feeling, through the sense of smell, touch and even of eyesight" (p. 253). Darwin related disgust not only to the experience of revulsion but to a characteristic facial expression. The second paper, by psychoanalyst Andras Angyal (1941), held that "disgust is a specific reaction towards the waste products of the human and animal body" (p. 395). Angyal related the strength of disgust to the degree of intimacy of contact, with the mouth as the most sensitive focus.

Tomkins's (1963) description of disgust expanded on Angyal's idea that disgust is a reaction to unwanted intimacy. According to Tomkins, disgust is "recruited to defend the self against psychic incorporation or any increase in intimacy with a repellent object" (p. 233). Our own definition of disgust, or what we call "core disgust" in this chapter, derives from those of Darwin, Angyal, and Tomkins: "Revulsion at the prospect of (oral) incorporation of an offensive object. The offensive objects are contaminants; that is, if they even briefly contact an acceptable food, they tend to render that food unacceptable" (Rozin & Fallon, 1987, p. 23).

All of these definitions, and many others, focus on the mouth and real or imagined ingestion. Tomkins (1963, 1982) held that of all the emotions, disgust has the clearest linkage to a specific motivation (hunger), and functions to oppose this motive. Ekman and Friesen (1975) see disgust as an aversion that centers on oral rejection. Wierzbicka (1986) defines disgust as feeling bad about another person's action. This feeling is "similar to what one feels when one has something in one's mouth that tastes bad and when one wants to cause it to come to be out of one's mouth" (p. 590).

Some have proposed sources other than ingestion as the origin of disgust. Freud (1905/1953) predictably linked it to sex, and others (e.g., Renner, 1944; Plutchik, 1980) see its origin as a defense against infection, with the skin playing a central role.

Miller (1997), in his broad review of disgust in the context of Western culture and history, disputes the claim that disgust originated as a food-related emotion. He argues that touch and smell are the senses most closely related to disgust, and that taste became associated with disgust more recently. Although we agree with Miller's characterization of disgust in its current form as largely a social and moral emotion, we believe that the arguments for a food origin are very convincing (Rozin & Fallon, 1987). The facial expression of disgust can be seen as functional in rejecting unwanted foods and odors, and the most distinct physiological concomitant of disgust—nausea—is a food-related sensation that inhibits ingestion.

Another conception of the core of disgust, framed in terms of the concept of pollution, comes from Mary Douglas's (1966) classic anthropological work, *Purity and Danger*. She relates dirt and pollution to a sense of violation of accepted categories, sometimes described as "matter out of place." This captures the "uncanniness" of disgust, and no doubt is a significant part of the meaning of disgust. However, there is no substantial argument for this as the origin of disgust.

In keeping with our supposition that disgust originated as a food rejection is Darwin's (1872/1965) claim that it is the phylogenetic residue of a voluntary vomiting system. Darwin designates the gape as the primary facial indicant of disgust; gapes have been described for a number of species, and indeed function to promote egress of substances from the mouth. Darwin (1872/1965) claims that disgust has food origins, holding that "The term 'disgust,' in its simplest sense, means something offen-sive to the taste" (p. 256). We presume that disgust, in its origin, is related to the general animal function of food rejection, but note that "Contrary to Darwin's expectations, no counterpart to human disgust has been distinguished in monkeys" (Chevalier-Skolnikoff, 1973, p. 82).

DISGUST AS A BASIC EMOTION

Disgust is on almost every list of basic emotions that has at least four emotions in it, from Darwin's onwards (see, e.g., Ortony, Clore, & Collins, 1988, p. 27). Disgust emerges as a basic emotion whether the primary criterion is facial (Darwin, 1872/1965; Ekman & Friesen, 1975), semantic (Johnson-Laird & Oatley, 1989), or eclectic (Izard, 1977; Scherer, 1986, 1997). Disgust stands out among the basic emotions in that it is specifically related to a particular motivational system (hunger) and to a particular part of the body (mouth). Disgust is also important for social and developmental psychology in that, along with fear, it is a primary means for socialization.

Paul Ekman (1992) has provided the clearest articulation of the characteristics of a basic emotion, and disgust meets all nine of his criteria. We consider here four of the most critical properties thought to be essential to any basic emotion.

Behavioral Component

Disgust is manifested as a distancing from some object, event, or situation, and can be characterized as a rejection.

Physiological Component

Two types of physiological changes have been associated with disgust. One distinguishes disgust from other emotions: Only disgust is associated with a *specific* physiological state. This physiological state, nausea, is typically measured by self-report. Although nausea is neither a necessary nor a sufficient condition for the experience of disgust, it is correlated with disgust. Another specific physiological aspect of disgust has been suggested by Angyal (1941), who pointed to increased salivation (itself associated with nausea and as a response to bad tastes) as a concomitant of disgust.

In spite of a large literature devoted to the

search for physiological signatures of different emotions, we know of no experimental studies of the relation of disgust to nausea or salivation. Rather, the study of the physiological side of disgust has been limited to the standard set of autonomic responses explored by psychophysiologists. In this limited arena, it appears that disgust is associated with either minimal or a predominantly parasympathetic response, whereas fear and anger are associated with a predominantly sympathetic response (Levenson, Ekman, & Friesen, 1990; Levenson, 1992).

Expressive Component

The expressive component of disgust has been studied almost entirely with reference to the face. The characteristics of the "disgust face" have received particular attention from Darwin (1872/1965), Izard (1971), Ekman (1972; Ekman & Friesen, 1975), and Rozin, Lowery, and Ebert (1994). Scholars are not in complete agreement about a prototypical disgust face. Darwin emphasized the gape (in the Facial Action Coding System [FACS; Ekman & Friesen, 1978], the gape is Action Unit [AU] 25 or 26), but he also referred to retraction of the upper lip (AU 10) and, to some extent, the nose wrinkle (AU 9), dropping of the mouth corners (AU 15), and a few other movements. Izard (1971) also emphasizes the gape and the upper lip retraction, with some associated movements. Ekman and Friesen (1975) focus on lip retraction (AU 10) and nose wrinkle (AU 9), along with a raising of the lower lip (AU 17). Finally, Rozin et al. (1994) suggest that the precise facial configuration may relate to the nature of the elicitor. It is clear from all of these accounts that activity centers around the mouth and nose, and that the movements tend either to discourage entry into the body (e.g., nose wrinkle, lower lip raise) or to encourage discharge (gape with or without tongue extension).

The *Nāṭyaśāstra* (Masson & Patwardhan, 1970), an ancient Hindu treatise on drama (see Shweder & Haidt, Chapter 26, this volume), treats disgust as one of eight basic emotions. As described by Hejmadi (2000), the multiple portrayals of disgust designated in this document are dynamic (as opposed to the standard "frozen face" used in almost all Western research) and involve actions of the whole body, especially the hands. North American subjects, as well as Indians, are able to identify these dis-

gust expressions (in both free report and forced choice among 11 emotion words) remarkably well (Hejmadi, Davidson, & Rozin, in press).

There is also an auditory expressive component to disgust, associated with an increase in fundamental frequency in speech (Scherer, 1986).

Qualia

Qualia, the mental or feeling component of emotion, may be at once the most central component of disgust and the most difficult to study. The *qualia* of disgust is often described as revulsion. In comparison to other basic emotions, the experience of disgust appears to be rather short in duration (Scherer & Wallbott, 1994). Disgust is often invoked in humor, and laughter is a common response (as opposed to the disgust face) in some disgust-eliciting situations.

CORE DISGUST

We have argued above that disgust began its evolutionary life as a distaste response, focused on the mouth. However a major theme of this chapter is that the elicitors and meaning of disgust have expanded far beyond distaste, such that there is now a qualitative difference between the two, and hence that distaste and disgust now constitute distinct psychological categories. In this and subsequent sections we chronicle the expansion of disgust from core disgust, through animal-nature disgust, interpersonal disgust, and moral disgust.

Disgust as a Category of Food Rejection

Disgust has been described as one of four categories of food rejection, the others being distaste (rejection motivated by bad sensory properties), danger (rejection motivated by fear of harm to the body), and inappropriateness (rejection of a food culturally classified as not edible) (Fallon & Rozin, 1983; Rozin & Fallon, 1987). Disgust is differentiated from danger and distaste in that the basis for rejection is ideational (knowledge of the nature or origin of an elicitor). Disgust differs from the category of inappropriateness (e.g., paper, marigolds, and sand) in that disgusting potential foods are thought to be offensive and contaminating.

Properties of Core Disgust

By the definition we have offered for core disgust, three components are required for the occurrence of the emotion: (1) a sense of oral incorporation (and hence a linkage with food or eating); (2) a sense of offensiveness; and (3) contamination potency.

Oral Incorporation

Rozin and Fallon (1987) have noted that the mouth is the principal route of entry of material things into the body, and hence can be thought of as the gateway to the body. Since putting external things into the body can be thought of as a highly personal and risky act, the special emotion associated with ingestion is understandable. The aversion response to an offensive entity in the mouth is usually stronger than response to the same entity on the body surface near but not inside the mouth, or inside the stomach (Rozin, Nemeroff, Gordon, Horowitz, & Voet, 1995).

The threat of oral incorporation is framed by a widespread belief that one takes on the properties of the food one eats ("You are what you eat"). This belief has been thought to be characteristic primarily of members of traditional cultures. Frazer (1890/1922), in *The Golden Bough*, noted: "The savage commonly believes that by eating the flesh of an animal or man, he acquires not only the physical but even the moral and intellectual qualities which are characteristic of that animal or man" (p. 573). This idea is consistent with common sense, since it is a general experience that when two things combine (in this case, a food and a person), the product has resemblances to both. Nemeroff and Rozin (1989) have found, using indirect methods (the Asch impressions technique), that even U.S. college students attribute boar-like qualities to boar eaters, and turtle-like qualities to turtle eaters.

Offensive Entities: Animals and Their Products

Angyal (1941) held that the center of disgust is animal (including human) waste products, which he saw as debasing. It is hard to avoid the conclusion that waste products have a special role in disgust. Body products are usually a focus of disgust, and are central to the related anthropological concept of pollution (Douglas,

1966; Meigs, 1978, 1984). There is widespread historical and cultural evidence for aversion to virtually all body products, including feces, vomit, urine, and blood (especially menstrual blood). For example, blood pollution at birth was a central aspect of ancient Greek religion (Parker, 1983).

In accord with Angyal's (1941) suggestion of an animal focus for disgust, Rozin and Fallon (1987) have proposed that the elicitor category for core disgust is all animals and their products as potential foods. Soler (1973/1979) argues that animal food prohibitions, such as those of the ancient Hebrews, should be seen as the rule, and that ingestion of a few animals or of specific animal parts is the exception. Thus Adam and Eve began as vegetarians, and it was only after the flood that animals were allowed by God into the human diet.

Almost all cultures eat a very small subset of potential animal foods. In North American culture, we consume only a small number of the hundreds of thousands of potentially edible animal species, and we tend to avoid the viscera, head, and a number of other parts of the few mammals that we do consume. Furthermore, as Angyal (1941) pointed out, in many cultures some care is taken to disguise the animal origin of animal food by cutting, chopping, and other culinary preparations, as well as by having names for animal foods (e.g., "pork," "beef," in English) that are distinct from the corresponding animal names.

Animals and their products seem cross-culturally to be the most favored of foods, and at the same time the most tabooed. In short, animal foods are emotionally charged (Tambiah, 1969) and tend to give rise to ambivalent responses. Many animal taboos involve disgust. Some animals are disgusting because they bear some resemblance to body products such as mucus (e.g., slugs), or because they are commonly in contact with rotting animal flesh, feces, or other human wastes (e.g., flies, cockroaches, rats, vultures, and other scavengers). Carnivorous land animals eat raw, often decaying animal flesh, and produce putrid feces. They are therefore disgusting at both ends. Herbivores are much less likely to be prohibited cross-culturally. Even the hunter–gatherer !Kung bushmen, who eat a much wider variety of species than we do, reject rodents, carnivores, and most insects (Howell, 1986).

Two other categories of animal food prohibitions deserve mention. Animals that are in some sense close to humans, either in appearance (e.g., other primates) or by virtue of a relationship with humans as pets, are rarely eaten. And finally, there is a group of anomalous animals that seem to produce a mixture of fear (danger) and disgust (e.g., spiders and snakes). These animals are feared, though they are rarely harmful to humans. Davey and his colleagues (Davey, 1993; Matchett & Davey, 1991; Ware, Jain, Burgess, & Davey, 1994; Webb & Davey, 1993) offer evidence that the aversion to these animals is based more on a motivation of disgust than fear.

Contamination

The contamination response (e.g., the rejection of a potential food if it even briefly contacted a disgusting entity) appears to be powerful and universal among adults. North American college students reject liked beverages after they have briefly contacted a sterilized cockroach (Rozin, Millman, & Nemeroff, 1986), and virtually all North Americans reject foods that have been handled or bitten by either unsavory or disliked persons (Rozin, Nemeroff, Wane, & Sherrod, 1989). Although this aversion is typically justified as an avoidance of disease, removal of this possibility (e.g., by sterilizing the offending dead cockroach) typically has only a small effect. The contamination property of disgust was commented upon, in passing, by both Darwin (1872/1965) and Angyal (1941) in their classic works.

Rozin and his colleagues have suggested that contagion effects may be instances of the sympathetic magical law of contagion (Tylor, 1871/1974; Frazer, 1890/1922; Mauss, 1902/1972), which essentially holds that "once in contact, always in contact" (Rozin & Fallon, 1987; Rozin & Nemeroff, 1990).

The law of contagion as applied to disgust is potentially crippling; everything we might eat or touch is potentially contaminated. We deal with this problem in a number of ways. First, contamination rules are developed in some cultures, such as the explicit rules establishing a threshold for contamination in the Hebrew dietary system (Grunfeld, 1982). These rules provide ritualistic relief but not necessarily psychological relief of a sense of contamination (Nemeroff & Rozin, 1992).

Most often, framing is the strategy that keeps potential contamination out of consideration—as when we do not think of the people in the kitchen who prepare our food in a restaurant, or the animal that was the source of our meat, or the fact that our bodies contain a host of disgusting substances. Indeed, as Allport (1955) noted and as a recent study has confirmed (Rozin, Haidt, McCauley, Dunlop, & Ashmore, 1999), we are disgusted by our own saliva as soon as it leaves our bodies, as when we reject drinking a glass of water that we have just spit into. The framing solution fails when the source of contamination/disgust is too salient. Thus, although we normally handle money without thinking of who touched it before us, this strategy might not protect us in the unusual case of a dollar handed over by a vagrant.

A second law of sympathetic magic, the law of similarity, accounts for some other aspects of disgust. The law of similarity, also dating from Tylor, Frazer, and Mauss (see Rozin & Nemeroff, 1990, and Nemeroff & Rozin, in press, for reviews), holds in one form that if things are superficially similar, then they resemble each other in a deep sense as well. In other words, appearance is reality. It accounts for the frequent observation that objects that look like something disgusting, but are known not to be, are often treated as disgusting. Thus we find that many North American college students are reluctant to consume imitation dog feces that they know are made out of chocolate fudge (Rozin, Millman, & Nemeroff, 1986). A combination of the laws of contagion and similarity causes many North Americans to say that they would be reluctant to consume a favorite beverage stirred by a brand-new comb or contaminated with a plastic replica of an insect (Rozin et al., 1989).

ANIMAL-NATURE DISGUST

Our discussion of disgust up to this point has focused on issues surrounding food and eating. We have presented core disgust as an oral defense in relation to potential foods, body products, and some animals. However when we asked North American and Japanese respondents to list the things they thought were disgusting, fewer than 25% of listed examples came from the three core disgust domains (Haidt, Rozin, McCauley, & Imada, 1997). Many of the other exemplars could be classified into four additional domains: inappropriate sexual acts, poor hygiene, death, and violations of the ideal body "envelope" or exterior form (e.g., gore, deformity, obesity). In the four additional domains, the focus of threat spread from oral incorporation to contact with the body in general, and even offensive sights. This spread is captured in a psychoanalytic treatment of disgust: "In summary, any modality that represents a means of entry into the self or body—the mouth, the nose, the skin, the eyes—seems to play a part in the disgust experience" (Miller, 1986, p. 300).

Death and Disgust

Contact with death and corpses is a particularly potent elicitor of disgust. Two of the items in our 32-item Disgust Scale (discussed in more detail later) that correlate most highly with the total scale score fall into the death category: "Your friend's pet cat dies, and you have to pick up the dead body with your bare hands" and "It would bother me tremendously to touch a dead body." Furthermore, individuals who score high on disgust sensitivity also score high on a fear-of-death scale (Haidt et al., 1994).

The prototypical odor of disgust is the odor of decay, which is the odor of death. The centrality of death in disgust suggests a more general construal of disgust within a modified psychoanalytic framework. Rather than as a defense against coprophilia or sexuality, disgust can be understood as a defense against a universal fear of death. Becker (1973) has argued that the most important threat to the psyche is not sexuality and aggression, but the certainty of death. Only human animals know they are to die, and only humans need to repress this threat. In this framework, Becker's "denial of death" is served by disgust, which helps to suppress thoughts or experiences that suggest human mortality.

A Theory of Disgust: Avoidance of Reminders of Our Animal Nature

These speculations about death lead naturally to an overarching description of disgust elicitors: Anything that reminds us that we are animals elicits disgust (Rozin & Fallon, 1987). An examination of the seven domains of disgust elicitors we have identified thus far suggests that disgust serves to "humanize" our animal bodies. Humans must eat, excrete, and have sex, just like animals. Each culture prescribes the proper way to perform these actions—by, for example, placing most animals off limits as

potential foods, and all animals and most people off limits as potential sexual partners. People who ignore these prescriptions are reviled as disgusting and animal-like. Furthermore, we humans are like animals in having fragile body envelopes that, when breached, reveal blood and soft viscera that display our commonalities with animals. Human bodies, like animal bodies, die. Envelope violations and death are disgusting because they are uncomfortable reminders of our animal vulnerability. Finally, hygienic rules govern the proper use and maintenance of the human body, and the failure to meet these culturally defined standards places a person below the level of humans. Animals are (often inappropriately) seen as dirty and inattentive to hygiene. Insofar as humans behave like animals, the distinction between humans and animals is blurred, and we see ourselves as lowered, debased, and (perhaps most critically) mortal.

Elias (1939/1978), in *The History of Manners*, concludes that "people, in the course of the civilizing process, seek to suppress in themselves every characteristic that they feel to be 'animal'" (p. 120). Tambiah (1969) emphasizes the importance of this distinction for humans, and points to the paradox of human fascination for and aversion to animals. Ortner (1973) notes that the one body product that does not reliably elicit disgust is tears, and these are seen as uniquely human. And Leach (1964) has pointed out that animal words are used as insults in many cultures. In general, the ethnographic literature is filled with references to the fact that humans consider themselves better than animals, and they work to maintain a clear animal–human boundary. Violations of that boundary—for example, treating an animal as a person in a pet relationship—are rather rare cross-culturally.

Miller's (1997) broad, historically based conception of disgust comes to a conclusion like ours: ". . . ultimately the basis for all disgust is *us*—that we live and die and that the process is a messy one emitting substances and odors that make us doubt ourselves and fear our neighbors" (p. xiv).

INTERPERSONAL DISGUST

The fact that direct or indirect contact with other people can elicit disgust was noted by Darwin (1872/1965). Furthermore, Angyal (1941) noted that other persons, as receptacles for waste products, are potentially disgusting.

We have found widespread evidence in the United States for aversion to contact with possessions, silverware, clothing, cars, and rooms used by strange or otherwise undesirable persons (Rozin et al., 1989; Rozin, Markwith, & McCauley, 1994). We have analyzed this interpersonal aversion into four separately identifiable components: strangeness, disease, misfortune, and moral taint (Rozin, Markwith, & McCauley, 1994). Thus a sweater worn once by a healthy stranger and then laundered is less desirable than an unworn sweater for most of the North American students we have surveyed (aversion to strangeness). This negativity is substantially enhanced if the stranger has had a misfortune (e.g., an amputated leg), a disease (e.g., tuberculosis), or a moral taint (e.g., a conviction for murder). These types of contacts seem to be both offensive and contaminating; thus they seem to be instances of disgust.

Contact with other people does open us to contact with their body products: their sweat, their saliva, their mucus, and traces of their urine and feces. But laundering or even sterilizing things used by others reduces the contamination effect only very slightly in our studies, and this fact makes it more difficult to understand interpersonal contamination simply in terms of potential contact with body products, and hence avoidance of our animal nature. Thus we currently consider interpersonal disgust, almost always mediated by contamination, as an independent category of disgust elicitors. This form of disgust clearly discourages contact with other human beings who are not intimates, and can serve the purpose of maintaining social distinctiveness and social hierarchies. In Hindu India, interpersonal contagion, mediated in part by contacts with food, is a major feature of society and a major basis for the maintenance of the caste system (Appadurai, 1981; Marriott, 1968).

MORAL DISGUST

In an extensive recent cross-cultural study of emotional responses in 37 different cultures, Scherer (1997) reports on the sequence of appraisals that his theory of emotion proposes. Surprisingly, disgust shows the highest score on immorality of all seven emotions surveyed (including anger and shame). In a related study,

disgust-producing events ranked a close second to anger-producing events in a cross-national study of "unfairness" in emotion-eliciting situations (Mikula, Scherer, & Athenstaedt, 1998).

When we elicited lists of disgusting things from North American and Japanese informants, we found that the *majority* of instances referred to moral offenses (Haidt et al., 1997). Some of these items involved some sexuality or gore (e.g., being sexually molested, reading reports of Serbian atrocities), and are thus easily assimilable to the animal-nature view of disgust. However, the word "disgusting" is often used as a synonym for "immoral" in situations that do not seem to be reminders of our animal nature. Thus our subjects have told us that racists, child abusers, hypocrites, Republicans, and liberals are all disgusting. It is our guess that moral offenses involving some reminder of our animal nature (e.g., sex and gore) are more likely to be labeled "disgusting" than are offenses that don't involve bodily issues (e.g., fraud). A lawyer who chases ambulances might be described by English speakers as "disgusting," but this could simply be a casual usage or metaphorical extension of the word.

Yet if the broad expansion of the word "disgusting" into the sociomoral domain is a quirk of the English language, it is also a quirk of almost every language we have looked at. French *dégoût*, German *Ekel*, Russian *otvraschenie*, Spanish *asco*, Hebrew *go-al*, Japanese *ken-o*, Chinese *aw-shin*, and Bengali *ghenna* all have a semantic domain covering concerns about the body, as well as concerns about other people's social behavior (Haidt et al., 1997). People of diverse cultures and languages apparently feel some similarity in their emotional reactions to sleazy politicians and to feces.

These moral offenses on the outer limits of disgust's expansion show not just the property of offensiveness, but also the property of contamination. Indirect contact with people who have committed moral offenses (such as murders) is highly aversive, to about the same extent as similar contact with someone with a serious contagious illness (Rozin, Markwith, & McCauley, 1994). In our research on contamination, one of the most potent stimuli we have discovered is Adolf Hitler's sweater. We speculate that what unites the domain of morally disgusting actions is that they reveal a lack of normal human social motivation. People who betray friends or family, or who kill in cold blood, are seen as inhuman and revolting; criminal acts with "normal" human motivations, such as robbing banks, are seen as immoral but not disgusting. This kind of disgust may represent a more abstract set of concerns about the human–animal distinction, focusing not so much on the human body as on the human body-politic—that is, the human as a member of a cooperating social entity.

Shweder, Much, Mahapatra, and Park (1997) offer a theory of moral judgment that may help clarify the moral significance of disgust, contempt, and anger (the three other-condemning moral emotions; Izard's [1977] "hostility triad"). The theory proposes that three codes of ethics underlie the morality of most cultures. One code, called the "ethics of community," focuses on issues of duty, hierarchy, and the proper fulfillment of one's social roles. Violations of this code seem to elicit the emotion of contempt. A second code, the "ethics of autonomy," encompasses issues of rights and justice. This is the most fully elaborated code in Western societies, where violations of this code are usually associated with anger. A third code, called the "ethics of divinity," focuses on the self as a spiritual entity and seeks to protect that entity from degrading or polluting acts. We propose disgust as the emotion that guards the sanctity of the soul as well as the purity of the body. Hence we see a rough match between Shweder et al.'s three moral codes and the three other-directed moral emotions. We call this the "CAD triad hypothesis" (community–contempt, autonomy–anger, divinity–disgust) (Rozin, Lowery, Imada, & Haidt, 1999).

We have tested these predictions in a study of Japanese and U.S. college students, in which they were presented with situations in which one or the other of the moral codes were violated (Rozin, Lowery, et al., 1999). Subjects were asked to select either the relevant face (from a set of contempt, anger, and disgust faces) or the relevant word ("contempt," "anger," "disgust," or their Japanese translations). In both cultures, there was a substantial though far from perfect match between the Shweder et al. code and the emotion predicted.

The disgust–morality linkage may have developed in two directions. On the one hand, events that are widely considered to be disgusting (such as eating dog meat) may be treated as moral in some cultural contexts, such as those cultures in which the divinity code is operative. On the other hand, rather than assimilating moral violations to what is already disgusting,

there seems to be some extension of the sense of disgust to a wide range of moral violations that have no obvious relation to the traditional disgust elicitors.

Disgust plays a special role in the moral domain as a means of socialization. Insofar as entities viewed as immoral are also disgusting, there is no temptation to have traffic with these entities. For example, as cigarette smoking has moved from being a preference to a negative moral value in the United States, there is an accompanying increase in disgust responses to cigarettes, cigarette smoke, cigarette residues (e.g., ashes), and cigarette smokers (Rozin & Singh, 1999). This process of conversion of an entity from a preference into a value has been called "moralization" (Rozin, 1997). It is often associated with the recruitment of a disgust response to the entity or activity in question. In the case of vegetarians, a disgust response to meat is more common in moral vegetarians than in health vegetarians (Rozin, Markwith, & Stoess, 1997).

PREADAPTATION AND THE CULTURAL EVOLUTION OF DISGUST

We believe that the "output" side of disgust (physiology, behavior, expression) has remained relatively constant in cultural evolution, and still bears noticeable similarities to its animal precursors. However, the elicitors and meaning of disgust have been transformed and greatly expanded in cultural evolution.

We have suggested a course of biological and cultural evolution of disgust, summarized in Table 40.1 (Rozin, Haidt, & McCauley, 1993; Rozin, Haidt, et al. 1997). The proposed origin is the rejection response to bad-tasting foods, even though taste in the mouth ultimately has little to do with the emotion of disgust. However, oral rejection remains an organizing principle of disgust reactions, in what we have called "core disgust." Core disgust can be thought of as a guardian of the mouth, and therefore as a guardian of the physical body. Food and its potential contaminants (body products and some animals) are the elicitors for core disgust.

Disgust then expanded further to become a guardian of the temple of the body, responding to any evidence that our bodies are really no different from animal bodies (i.e., animal-nature disgust in the domains of sexuality, body

TABLE 40.1 Proposed Pathway of Expansion of Disgust and Disgust Elicitors

	Disgust stage				
	0. Distaste	1. Core	2. Animal-nature	3. Interpersonal	4. Moral
Function	Protect body from poison	Protect body from disease/infection	Protect body and soul, denial of mortality	Protect body, soul, and social order	Protect social order
Elicitors	Bad tastes	Food/eating, body products, animals	Sex, death, hygiene, envelope violations	Direct and indirect contact with strangers or undesirables	Certain moral offenses

envelope violations, death, and hygiene). Driving this desire to distinguish ourselves from animals may be our fear of animal mortality.

The next two steps in the expansion of disgust are problematic for the "avoidance of the reminders of animal nature" view. Interpersonal contamination and moral offenses may become disgusting for reasons independent of the prior focus of disgust, but may access the already present rejection system of disgust.

This model suggests what might be called an opportunistic accretion of new domains of elicitors, and new motivations, to a rejection system that is already in place. A parallel to this model in evolutionary biology is the concept of preadaptation (Mayr, 1960). Mayr suggests that the major source of evolutionary "novelties" is the coopting of an existing system for a new function. Preadaptation can operate either to replace an original function or to accrete new functions to an existing system. A particularly appropriate example is the human mouth, whose teeth and tongue clearly evolved for food handling. However, by a process of preadaptation, they have come to be shared by the language expression system. Teeth and tongue are critical in pronunciation, but they did not evolve for that purpose. We suggest that in both cultural evolution and individual development, a process like preadaptation occurs; in development it can be described as the accessing of previously inaccessible systems for a wider range of activities, functions, or elicitors (Rozin, 1976).

We have described the cultural evolution of disgust as a sequence of stages that takes disgust further and further away from its mouth-and-food origins, through a process of preadaptation. But it has not really expanded that far beyond food, because by a parallel process of preadaptation, food itself has come to serve many functions—aesthetic, social, and moral—

besides its original nutritive function. In parallel, the food vocabulary has taken on other, metaphorical functions, again by a process of preadaptation. Thus, the very words "taste" and "distaste" come to indicate general aesthetic judgments. In Hindu India, food and eating are quintessentially social and moral activities (Appadurai, 1981).

Kass (1994) eloquently traces the history of food from nutritive to more elaborated values. He notes that "As host feeds guest, *essen* replaces *fressen*; eating supplants feeding" (p. 107); that at the table, we face each other, not the food; that when we eat we exploit an animal necessity, as a "ballerina exploits gravity" (p. 158); and that "'Nobility' is not so much a transcendence of animality as it is the turning of animality into its peculiarly human and regulated form" (pp. 158–159). Ultimately, in the important moral role of food in many religions, most notably Judaism and Hinduism, we see food elevated into a moral entity.

DEVELOPMENT OF DISGUST

Of the four categories of food rejection, it appears that the only category that is visible in infancy is distaste (e.g., bitterness). In parallel with the results from rats and other animals, there appears to be an innate and present-at-birth rejection of bitter substances in humans, accompanied by a gape (Peiper, 1963; Steiner, 1979). The danger category emerges in the first few years of life, and disgust breaks off from distaste at some later point, perhaps between 4 and 8 years, for U.S. children (Rozin, Hammer, Oster, Horowitz, & Marmara, 1986; Rozin, Fallon, & Augustoni-Ziskind, 1986). Thus, although 3-year-olds typically reject feces as food, it is not clear that this rejection has contaminating or offensive features, and it may be no different from a distaste, or a distaste combined with danger. So far as we know, there is no sense of offensiveness or rejection outside of the sensory realm in either infants or nonhumans, and hence no gape elicitors other than certain negative tastes. Disgust seems to require enculturation—a supposition confirmed by Malson's (1964/1972) review of some 50 feral humans, none of whom showed any sign of disgust.

Origins of Disgust: Feces and Decay

For adults, feces seems to be a universal disgust substance (Angyal, 1941; Rozin & Fallon, 1987), with the odor of decay as perhaps the most potent sensory attribute associated with disgust. It is also conceivable that vomit is a primary substance for disgust. Since feces, vomit, and decay are probably associated with disease vectors, it would be reasonable to suppose that there would be an innate rejection of such things. However, none seems to be reliably present in nonhuman animals, and children do not show rejection of feces early in life. Rather, it appears that the infant may be attracted to feces, and that disgust is a powerful cultural force that turns this attraction into aversion (Freud, 1910/1957; Jones, 1912/1948). The preponderance of evidence suggests that there are no innately negative nonirritant odors, and that a rejection of decay odors (without a referent object present) appears somewhere between 3 and 7 years of age (Engen & Corbit, 1970; Petó, 1936; Schmidt & Beauchamp, 1988; Stein, Ottenberg, & Roulet, 1958; but see Steiner, 1979).

Toilet Training

Given the centrality of toilet training in psychoanalytic theory, and the fact that toilet training is one of the earliest arenas for socialization, it is surprising how little is known about the process. Although children do not seem to have an aversion to feces before toilet training (Rozin, Hammer, et al., 1986), it is not clear whether the feces avoidance that appears subsequently should be characterized as disgust, as opposed to avoidance or distaste. In the period following toilet training, feces does not seem to have contaminating properties (Fallon, Rozin, & Pliner, 1984), but children do develop an aversion for substances resembling feces (e.g., mud, dirt, and mushy substances) and some-

times a marked concern for cleanliness (Senn & Solnit, 1968; Ferenczi, 1914/1952). There may be a latency period between completion of toilet training and the emergence of feces as a particularly negative disgust substance some years later. It seems likely that toilet training, with all of the attendant negative affect toward feces from significant others, plays an important role in the development of disgust.

Processes Accounting for the Spread of Response from Feces in Young Children

We believe that there is a spread of rejection responses following toilet training and the rejection of feces, but little is known about the mechanisms and events that account for this spread. Rozin and Fallon (1987) categorize these processes as "primary" (meaning that a new rejection is learned from the reactions of others or from some new information) and "secondary" (meaning that the acquisition is related to an existing disgust substance). Primary disgusts are probably frequently induced by the display of disgust in others (Tomkins, 1963), by a process that is not well understood.

Secondary disgusts may occur by two pathways (Rozin & Fallon, 1987). One is generalization, based on similarity, from existing disgust substances such as feces (Ferenczi, 1914/1952; Tomkins, 1963; Darwin, 1872/ 1965). Another pathway is evaluative conditioning (Martin & Levey, 1978; Baeyens, Crombez, Van den Bergh, & Eelen, 1988; Rozin & Zellner, 1985), a form of Pavlovian conditioning in which a valenced entity (an unconditioned stimulus—e.g., an already disgusting entity) is paired with a previously neutral entity, with the result that the neutral entity (the conditioned stimulus) changes in valence in the direction of the unconditioned stimulus.

Contamination Sensitivity

The idea of contamination is quite sophisticated in requiring a separation of appearance and reality. There is no sensory residue of past contamination in a contaminated entity; it is the history of contact that is critical (Rozin & Nemeroff, 1990; Nemeroff & Rozin, in press). Furthermore, contamination implies some conception of invisible entities (e.g., traces of cockroach) that are the vehicle of contamination. The notion of invisible entities and the notion that appearance is distinct from reality are cognitive achievements of considerable abstraction, and both seem to be absent in young children (Piaget & Inhelder, 1941/1974; Flavell, 1986). This cognitive limitation may be the principal barrier to a full childhood acquisition of disgust. The cognitive sophistication of disgust puts it in the company of other uniquely human emotions such as pride, shame, and guilt, which also do not assume an adult-like form until the age of 7 or 8 (Harris, 1989).

Rozin and his colleagues have found that a clear contamination response to disgusting contacts with a favored beverage (e.g., dog feces or a grasshopper as contaminants in milk or juice) does not appear until about 7 years of age in North American children (Fallon et al., 1984; Rozin, Fallon, & Augstoni-Ziskind, 1985, 1986). However, Siegal (1988), using more sensitive procedures, has reported contamination responses in Australian children by 4 years of age.

Parent–Child Transmission of Disgust Sensitivity

One study of disgust transmission across generations predated the development of our more comprehensive Disgust Scale (described below) and used an unvalidated scale of contamination sensitivity (focusing on disgust in a contagion context) developed by Rozin, Fallon, and Mandell (1984). The Contamination Scale (24 items) was given to University of Pennsylvania students and their parents, and the mid-parent–child correlations was $r = .52$ (Rozin et al., 1984). This relationship was confirmed in a study in Britain ($r = .33$; Davey, Forster, & Mayhew, 1991). These substantial correlations are much higher than correlations for food preferences (ranging between 0 and .30) from the same U.S. sample that generated the .52 correlation for disgust/contamination. That is, the family resemblance pattern for disgust/contamination sensitivity was more in line with correlations obtained for values (e.g., attitudes to abortion) than with those for preferences (Rozin, 1991).

It seems reasonable to attribute the parent–child resemblance in disgust sensitivity to social transmission in childhood. This presumption is supported by evidence for minimal heritability in a twin study using a short (5-item) version of the Contamination Scale used by Rozin et al. (1984): Monozygotic twins

showed a correlation of .29 on this scale, while dizygotic twins showed a correlation of .24 (Rozin & Millman, 1987).

We do not know how disgust is transmitted, but children have ample opportunities to observe and be informed about their parents' attitudes and responses in disgust situations, including toilet training.

DISGUST ACROSS CULTURES

Almost the entire literature on disgust comes from the approximately 6% of the world in which English is the native language. Consistent with our claim that the cultural evolution of disgust has involved a conservative output system and a flexible and expanding input/evaluative (elicitor/meaning) system, we hold that the principal cultural differences in disgust have to do with the input/evaluative system. Cultures may differ in the particular elicitors of disgust within one of the domains we have described. Thus, while most cultures value decayed/fermented food of a special sort, that special sort is different for different cultures (e.g., cheese for Europeans, meat for Inuit, fish for Southeast Asians in their fermented fish sauce). Each of these desirable exceptions in a particular culture is viewed by those in most other cultures as disgusting. Furthermore, the act of kissing, which involves an intimate exchange of body fluid, varies from being considered disgusting in all cases in some cultures to being considered highly desirable with certain intimates in other cultures. Similarly, cultures differ about whether dogs are best friends or dirty scavengers, or about whether or not corpses should be touched during mourning. In spite of these differences, it appears that core disgust and animal-nature disgust look relatively similar across cultures, and there seems to be a "preparedness" (Seligman, 1971) to attach disgust to certain sorts of things (e.g., food), and not others (e.g., flowers, machines).

It is primarily in the last two steps of the expansion of disgust that cultural differences seem to become most important. Interpersonal disgust appears to be most highly elaborated in India. Moral disgust in the United States is triggered most strongly by acts of brutality, or acts in which someone strips others of their dignity (e.g., racism). In Japan, participants applied the word *ken-o* more to situations in which there had been a failure to achieve a good fit in their social relationships, such as when somebody else ignored them or unfairly criticized them. We believe that U.S. disgust may be guarding against threats to an individualist, rights-based social order, whereas Japanese *ken-o* may be guarding against threats to a more collectivist, interdependent social order (Haidt et al., 1997).

An additional cultural difference is found in the moral significance attached to the kinds of biological activities that disgust regulates. Some cultures have highly elaborated the ethics of divinity (Shweder et al., 1997), and therefore see issues of purity and pollution as central to morality. Middle-class North Americans, on the other hand, see little connection between morality (justice and rights) and matters of personal hygiene. Cultures should therefore differ in the degree to which disgust is related to moral judgment. Haidt, Koller, and Dias (1993) asked North Americans and Brazilians of higher and lower socioeconomic status about a number of actions that were disgusting yet harmless, including incestuous kissing, eating one's dead pets, and eating a chicken one has just had sex with. They found that North Americans of higher socioeconomic status separated their emotional reactions from their moral judgments, while other groups were more likely to condemn disgusting actions, even when they were harmless. Miller (1997) suggests that many Westerners may be uncomfortable using disgust as a moral emotion because it is often at odds with an egalitarian ethos: Disgust puts people down, and it is easily used to condemn people whose only "crime" is that they are obese, are deformed, or have sexual preferences at odds with those of the majority.

INDIVIDUAL DIFFERENCES IN DISGUST SENSITIVITY

Based on the first seven domains of disgust elicitors, together with the fundamental role of contagion in all of these categories, we constructed a paper-and-pencil scale to measure individual differences in disgust in the United States and in Japan (Haidt et al., 1994). The 32-item Disgust Scale includes two true–false and two disgust-rating items for each of the seven disgust domains, and four similar items tapping sympathetic magical thinking. In addition to revealing wide variation in disgust sensitivity, the Disgust Scale has demonstrated positive intercorrelations of disgust sensitivities across the

different domains of elicitors—that is, evidence that the domains converge on a common dimension of sensitivity to disgust. Recent additional validation emerged from a series of "hands-on" laboratory experiences in which the Disgust Scale predicted the degree to which subjects would actually engage in a wide range of disgust activities ($r = -.42$; Rozin, Haidt, et al., 1999).

Correlations with other scales have begun to locate disgust sensitivity in relation to other individual difference measures (Haidt et al., 1994). The Disgust Scale showed a moderate positive correlation (.39) with a scale measuring fear of death (Boyar, 1964), and a moderate negative correlation (–.46) with a scale measuring sensation seeking. In our initial Disgust Scale research (Haidt et al., 1994), women were substantially more sensitive to disgust than men; the mean difference amounted to more than half a standard deviation. There are hints, however, that sensitivity to disgust declines after the teen years, and declines more for women than for men. Druschel and Sherman (1994), and Quigley, Sherman, and Sherman (1996) found that Disgust Scale scores were lower for older than for younger undergraduates. Similarly, Doctoroff and McCauley (1996) found only a small and nonsignificant tendency for higher female scores when the Disgust Scale was completed by respondents (mean age 57) to a survey mailed to suburban residents from a commercial mailing list. Convergent evidence for the increased disgust sensitivity of females, as well as additional validation for the Disgust Scale, is provided by Oppliger and Zillmann (1997). They found that disgust sensitivity is negatively related to the enjoyment of disgust humor, and that male college students show more amusement than females in both ratings of and facial reactions to disgust humor.

Besides gender, the demographic variable most correlated with Disgust Scale scores is social class. Blue-collar workers in our initial studies were more disgust-sensitive than were students and middle-class managers (Haidt et al, 1994). This result was confirmed by Doctoroff and McCauley (1996), who found education to be negatively correlated with Disgust Scale scores ($r = -.32$). Recently, another scale of disgust sensitivity has been introduced, consisting of ratings of the disgustingness of 30 stimuli/events. This scale (Disgust Experience Scale) has more items related to blood, injection, and injury than the Disgust Scale, and surprisingly correlates only .31 with the Disgust Scale (Kleinknecht, Kleinknecht, & Thorndike, 1997).

There are abundant possible linkages between disgust and psychopathology. In an early study of individual differences in disgust sensitivity, Templer, King, Brooner, and Corgiat (1984) constructed a 26-item scale to measure attitudes toward body products and body elimination (e.g., "The smell of other persons' bowel movements bothers me"). They found that scores were higher (attitudes were more negative) among an inpatient psychiatric population than among a sample of the general population. Even among the latter, high scorers also scored higher on various measures of psychopathology (including neuroticism and obsessiveness), suggesting a link between anxiety and disgust sensitivity.

Quigley et al. (1996) reported that among undergraduates, the Disgust Scale is positively correlated with obsessive–compulsive personality type and with dependent personality type. There are conceptual links between cleaning obsessions or compulsions and both disgust and contagion sensitivity, and recent research indicates a deficit in disgust facial expression detection among patients with obsessive–compulsive disorder (OCD; Sprengelmeyer, Young, Pundt et al., 1997; see "Disgust and the Brain" below). Summarizing a set of studies that suggest a qualitative difference between two forms of OCD, Power and Dalgleish (1997) suggest that when contamination (cleaning) is salient, disgust is the principal motivator, whereas when checking is salient, anxiety is the principal motivator. Altogether, the disgust–OCD linkage is very promising.

Another clinical connection is suggested by the work on animal phobias by Davey and his colleagues. These authors argue that phobias involving predatory animals (sharks or lions) invoke fear, whereas phobias involving animals that do not threaten significant physical harm (rats, spiders, snakes, slugs, maggots) are motivated primarily by disgust (Davey, 1993; Matchett & Davey, 1991; Webb & Davey, 1993; Ware et al., 1994). This distinction is buttressed by a number of experimental and psychometric findings. Nonpredatory animal phobias are correlated with disgust sensitivity, but predatory animal phobias are not (Matchett & Davey, 1991; Ware et al., 1994). The two types of animal phobias are almost uncorrelated. Priming

experiences consisting of threatening visual exposure to violent materials increased fear responses only to predatory animals, whereas priming with disgust materials increased fear only to nonpredatory animals (Webb & Davey, 1993). A particularly clear link between disgust and phobias has recently been demonstrated with respect to blood-injection-injury phobias, using both disgust sensitivity measures and emotion-specific ratings of blood-injection-injury images by phobic patients (Tolin, Lohr, Sawchuk, & Lee, 1997).

A detailed discussion of the pathologies of disgust has been provided by Power and Dalgleish (1997), who propose a major role for disgust (self-disgust) in problems of depression. A plausible linkage between disgust and eating disorders has also been proposed (Quigley et al., 1996). There is recent evidence supporting such a link: Enhanced disgust sensitivity to food and related stimuli has been found in females with eating disorders (Davey, Buckland, Tantow, & Dallos, 1998).

Very low activation of basic emotions can also have pathological consequences, though very low fear or anger does not align with any important categories of psychopathology. On the other hand, one might imagine that very low disgust might generate a highly antisocial person, since disgust is in many respects the emotion of civilization.

DISGUST AND THE BRAIN

There is universal agreement that disgust is fundamentally a negative emotion, and it should not be surprising that disgust experiences are associated with brain activation in the right frontal area (Davidson, 1992). Recently, Sprengelmeyer, Young, Calder, and their colleagues (Sprengelmeyer et al., 1996; Sprengelmeyer, Young, Sprengelmeyer, et al., 1997) reported that people with Huntington's disease, caused by late-onset degeneration of the basal ganglia, show a remarkably specific deficit in identifying disgust facial (and vocal) expressions. To this date, there is no information on deficits in production of emotional expressions. The same disgust recognition deficit is seen in people who are carriers of the Huntington's gene, but are still too young to show any of the classical symptoms. Magnetic resonance imaging evidence from normal subjects also suggests activation of basal ganglia structures, among others, when subjects view disgust faces (Phillips et al., 1997).

Reasoning from the common basal ganglia involvement in Huntington's disease and OCD (Rapoport, 1989), Sprengelmeyer, Young, Pundt, et al. (1997) also examined recognition of disgust expressions by people with OCD, and discovered the same specific and severe disgust recognition deficit. This work shows a surprisingly high degree of emotion-specific brain localization, and also provides an important tool for the study of disgust by identifying people who fail to perceive its expression.

CONCLUSION

Darwin and Angyal presented insightful and prescient analyses of the emotion of disgust many decades ago. In spite of its frequent occurrence and general classification as a basic emotion, there has been surprisingly little empirical investigation of disgust until the last 15 years. As a result, there are many unanswered questions. We know very little about the history of disgust. It is absent in nonhuman primates, yet extremely frequent and probably universal in contemporary humans. We do not know much about the sequence of events that introduced and expanded disgust over historical time (but see Miller, 1997, for the most thorough analysis of this expansion for Western cultures). We do not know whether the acceptance of the theory of evolution, and hence of human continuity with animals, played a role in the development or expression of animal-nature disgust. We do not know how disgust originates in development, nor what the principal causes of differences in disgust sensitivity are, nor why it is a focus of humor (especially in children). Many of the fundamental questions posed by Darwin's and Angyal's analyses remain unanswered.

Our analysis suggests a cultural evolution of disgust that brings it to the heart of what it means to be human. We have suggested that disgust originated as a rejection response to bad tastes, and then evolved into a much more abstract and ideational emotion. In this evolution the function of disgust shifted: A mechanism for avoiding harm to the body became a mechanism for avoiding harm to the soul. The elicitors of disgust may have expanded to the point that they have in common only the fact that decent people want nothing to do with them. At

this level, disgust becomes a moral emotion and a powerful form of negative socialization. We have presented a skeleton of evidence in support of this analysis, but there are many alternatives and points of difficulty. The complexity of disgust reflects the complexity of a species that is both animal and human.

ACKNOWLEDGMENTS

We thank the Whitehall Foundation for supporting some of the research reported in this chapter and the preparation of the original (Rozin et al., 1993) version of this chapter, and the Edmund J. and Louise W. Kahn Chair for Faculty Excellence Fund for supporting the preparation of the revision.

REFERENCES

Allport, G. W. (1955). *Becoming: Basic considerations for a psychology of personality.* New Haven, CT: Yale University Press.

Angyal, A. (1941). Disgust and related aversions. *Journal of Abnormal and Social Psychology, 36,* 393–412.

Appadurai, A. (1981). Gastro-politics in Hindu South Asia. *American Ethnologist, 8,* 494–511.

Baeyens, F., Crombez, G., Van den Bergh, O., & Eelen, P. (1988). Once in contact always in contact: Evaluative conditioning is resistant to extinction. *Advances in Behavior Research and Therapy, 10,* 179–199.

Becker, E. (1973). *The denial of death.* New York: Free Press.

Boyar, J. (1964). *The construction and partial validation of a scale for the measurement of the fear of death.* Ann Arbor, MI: UMI Dissertation Information Service.

Chevalier-Skolnikoff, S. (1973). Facial expression of emotion in nonhuman primates. In P. Ekman (Ed.), *Darwin and facial expression: A century of research in review* (pp. 11–90). New York: Academic Press.

Darwin, C. R. (1965). *The expression of the emotions in man and animals.* Chicago: University of Chicago Press. (Original work published 1872)

Davey, G. C. L. (1993). Factors infuencing self-rated fear to a novel animal. *Cognition and Emotion, 7,* 461–471.

Davey, G. C. L., Buckland, G., Tantow, B., & Dallos, R. (1998). Disgust and eating disorders. *European Eating Disorders Review, 6,* 201–211.

Davey, G. C. L., Forster, L., & Mayhew, G. (1991). Familial resemblance in disgust sensitivity and animal phobias. *Behaviour Research and Therapy, 31,* 41–50.

Davidson, R. J. (1992). Emotion and affective style: Hemispheric substrates. *Psychological Science, 3,* 39–43.

Doctoroff, G., & McCauley, C. (1996, March). *Demographic differences in sensitivity to disgust.* Poster presented at the annual meeting of the Eastern Psychological Association, Philadelphia.

Douglas, M. (1966). *Purity and danger*. London: Routledge & Kegan Paul.

Druschel, B. & Sherman, M.F. (1994, March). *Disgust sensitivity as a function of personality characteristics and gender*. Poster presented at the annual meeting of the Eastern Psychological Association, Providence, RI.

Ekman, P. (1972). Universals and cultural differences in facial expressions of emotion. In J. K. Cole (Ed.), *Nebraska Symposium on Motivation* (Vol. 19, pp. 207–283). Lincoln: University of Nebraska Press.

Ekman, P. (1992). An argument for basic emotions. *Cognition and Emotion, 6,* 169–200.

Ekman, P., & Friesen, W. V. (1975). *Unmasking the face*. Englewood Cliffs, NJ: Prentice-Hall.

Ekman, P., & Friesen, W. V. (1978). *Facial Action Coding System: A technique for the measurement of facial movement*. Palo Alto, CA: Consulting Psychologists Press.

Elias, N. (1978). *The history of manners: Vol. 1. The civilizing process* (E. Jephcott, Trans.). New York: Pantheon Books. (Original work published 1939)

Engen, T., & Corbit, T. E. (1970). *Feasibility of olfactory coding of noxious substances to assure aversive responses in young children* (Final Report, Contract No. PH 86–68–162, ICRL-RR–69–6). Washington, DC: U.S. Department of Health, Education and Welfare.

Fallon, A. E., & Rozin, P. (1983). The psychological bases of food rejections by humans. *Ecology of Food and Nutrition, 13,* 15–26.

Fallon, A. E., Rozin, P., & Pliner, P. (1984). The child's conception of food: The development of food rejections with special reference to disgust and contamination sensitivity. *Child Development, 55,* 566–575.

Ferenczi, S. (1952). The ontogenesis of the interest in money. In S. Ferenczi (Ed.), *First contributions to psychoanalysis* (E. Jones, Trans.) (pp. 319–331). London: Hogarth Press. (Original work published 1914)

Flavell, J. (1986). The development of children's knowledge of the appearance–reality distinction. *American Psychologist, 41,* 418–425.

Frazer, J. G. (1922). *The golden bough: A study in magic and religion* (abridged ed., T. H. Gaster, Ed.). New York: Macmillan. (Original work published 1890)

Freud, S. (1953). Three essays on the theory of sexuality. In J. Strachey (Ed. and Trans.), *The standard edition of the complete psychological works of Sigmund Freud* (Vol. 7, pp. 123–231). London: Hogarth Press. (Original work published 1905)

Freud, S. (1957). Five lectures on psycho-analysis. In J. Strachey (Ed. and Trans.), *The standard edition of the complete psychological works of Sigmund Freud* (Vol. 11, pp. 3–56). London: Hogarth Press. (Original work published 1910)

Grunfeld, D. I. (1982). *The Jewish dietary laws: Vol. 1. Dietary laws regarding forbidden and permitted foods, with particular reference to meat and meat products* (3rd ed.). London: Soncino Press.

Haidt, J., Koller, S., & Dias, M. (1993). Affect, culture, and morality, or is it wrong to eat your dog? *Journal of Personality and Social Psychology, 65,* 613–628.

Haidt, J., McCauley, C. R., & Rozin, P. (1994). A scale to measure disgust sensitivity. *Personality and Individual Differences, 16,* 701–713.

Haidt, J., Rozin, P., McCauley, C. R., & Imada, S. (1997). Body, psyche, and culture: The relationship between disgust and morality. *Psychology and Developing Societies, 9,* 107–131.

Harris, P. (1989). *Children and emotion*. Oxford: Basil Blackwell.

Hejmadi, A. (2000). *Rasa or aesthetic emotion: An ancient Hindu perspective*. Unpublished manuscript.

Hejmadi, A., Davidson, R., & Rozin, P. (in press). Exploring Hindu Indian emotion expressions: Evidence for accurate recognition by Americans and Indians. *Psychological Science*.

Howell, N. (1986). Feedbacks and buffers in relation to scarcity and abundance: Studies of hunter–gatherer populations. In R. Scofield (Ed.), *Beyond Malthus* (pp. 156–187). Cambridge, England: Cambridge University Press.

Izard, C. E. (1971). *The face of emotion*. New York: Appleton-century-Crofts.

Izard, C. E. (1977). *Human emotions*. New York: Plenum Press.

Johnson-Laird, P. N., & Oatley, K. (1989). The language of emotions: An analysis of a semantic field. *Cognition and Emotion, 3,* 81–123.

Jones, E. (1948). Anal-erotic character traits. In E. Jones, *Papers on psychoanalysis* (pp. 413–437). Boston: Beacon Press. (Original work published 1912)

Kass, L. (1994). *The hungry soul*. New York: Free Press.

Kleinknecht, R. A., Kleinknecht, E. E., & Thorndike, R. M. (1997). The role of disgust and fear in blood and injection-related fainting symptoms: A structural equation model. *Behavior Research and Therapy, 35,* 1075–1087.

Leach, E. (1964). Anthropological aspects of language: Animal categories and verbal abuse. In E. Lenneberg (Ed.), *New directions in the study of language* (pp. 23–64). Cambridge, MA: MIT Press.

Levenson, R. W. (1992). Autonomic nervous system differences among emotions. *Psychological Science, 3,* 23–27.

Levenson, R. W., Ekman, P., & Friesen, W. V. (1990). Voluntary facial action generates emotion-specific autonomic nervous system activity. *Psychophysiology, 27,* 363–384.

Malson, L. (1972). *Wolf children* (E. Fawcett, P. Ayrton, & J. White, Trans.). New York: Monthly Review Press. (Original work published 1964)

Marriott, M. (1968). Caste ranking and food transactions: A matrix analysis. In M. Singer & B. S. Cohn (Eds.), *Structure and change in Indian society* (pp. 133–171). Chicago: Aldine.

Martin, I., & Levey, A. B. (1978). Evaluative conditioning. *Advances in Behavior Research and Therapy, 1,* 57–102.

Masson, J. L., & Patwardhan, M. V. (1970). *Aesthetic rapture: The Rāsadhyāya of the Nāṭyaśāstra*. Poona, India: Deccan College.

Matchett, G., & Davey, G. C. L. (1991). A test of a disease-avoidance model of animal phobias. *Behaviour Research and Therapy*, *29*, 91–94.

Mauss, M. (1972). *A general theory of magic* (R. Brain, Trans.). New York: Norton. (Original work published 1902)

Mayr, E. (1960). The emergence of evolutionary novelties. In S. Tax (Ed.), *Evolution after Darwin: Vol. 1. The evolution of life* (pp. 349–380). Chicago: University of Chicago Press.

Meigs, A. S. (1978). A Papuan perspective on pollution. *Man*, *13*, 304–318.

Meigs, A. S. (1984). *Food, sex, and pollution: A New Guinea religion*. New Brunswick, NJ: Rutgers University Press.

Mikula, G., Scherer, K. R., & Athenstaedt, U. (1998). The role of injustice in the elicitation of differential emotional reactions. *Personality and Social Psychology Bulletin*, *24*, 769–783.

Miller, S. B. (1986). Disgust: Conceptualization, development, and dynamics. *International Review of Psychoanalysis*, *13*, 295–307.

Miller, W. I. (1997). *The anatomy of disgust*. Cambridge, MA: Harvard University Press.

Nemeroff, C., & Rozin, P. (1989). "You are what you eat": Applying the demand-free "impressions" technique to an unacknowledged belief. *Ethos: The Journal of Psychological Anthropology*, *17*, 50–69.

Nemeroff, C., & Rozin, P. (1992). Sympathetic magical beliefs and kosher dietary practice: The interaction of rules and feelings. *Ethos: The Journal of Psychological Anthropology*, *20*, 96–115.

Nemeroff, C., & Rozin, P. (in press). The makings of the magical mind. In K. Rosengren, C. Johnson, & P. Harris (Eds.), *Imagining the impossible: Magical, scientific, and religious thinking in children*. New York: Cambridge University Press.

Oppliger, P. A., & Zillmann, D. (1997). Disgust in humor: Its appeal to adolescents. *Humor: International Journal of Humor Research*, *10*, 421–437.

Ortner, S. B. (1973). Sherpa purity. *American Anthropologist*, *75*, 49–63.

Ortony, A., Clore, G. L., & Collins, A. (1988). *The cognitive structure of emotions*. Cambridge, England: Cambridge University Press.

Parker, R. (1983). *Miasma: Pollution and purification in early Greek religion*. Oxford: Clarendon Press.

Peiper, A. (1963). *Cerebral functions in infancy and childhood*. New York: Consultants Bureau.

Petó, E. (1936). Contribution to the development of smell feeling. *British Journal of Medical Psychology*, *15*, 314–320.

Phillips, M. L., Young, A. W., Senior, C., Brammer, M., Andrew, C., Williams, S. C. R., Gray, J., & David, A. S. (1997). A specific neural substrate for perceiving facial expressions of disgust. *Nature*, *389*, 495–498.

Piaget, J., & Inhelder, B. (1974). From conservation to atomism. In J. Piaget & B. Inhelder, *The child's construction of quantities* (pp. 67–116). London: Routledge & Kegan Paul. (Original work published 1941)

Plutchik, R. (1980). *Emotion: A psychoevolutionary synthesis*. New York: Harper & Row.

Power, M., & Dalgleish, T. (1997). *Cognition and emotion: From order to disorder*. East Sussex, England: Psychology Press.

Quigley, J.F., Sherman, M., & Sherman, N. (1996, March). *Personality disorder symptoms, gender, and age as predictors of adolescent disgust sensitivity.* Poster presented at the annual meeting of the Eastern Psychological Association, Philadelphia.

Rapoport, J. L. (1989). The biology of obsessive compulsive disorder. *Journal of the American Medical Association*, *260*, 2888–2890.

Renner, H. D. (1944). *The origin of food habits*. London: Faber & Faber.

Rozin, P. (1976). The evolution of intelligence and access to the cognitive unconscious. In J. A. Sprague & A.N. Epstein (Eds.), *Progress in psychobiology and physiological psychology* (Vol. 6, pp. 245–280). New York: Academic Press.

Rozin, P. (1991). Family resemblance in food and other domains: The family paradox and the role of parental congruence. *Appetite*, *16*, 93–102.

Rozin, P. (1997). Moralization. In A. Brandt & P. Rozin (Eds.), *Morality and health* (pp. 379–401) New York: Routledge.

Rozin, P., & Fallon, A. E. (1987). A perspective on disgust. *Psychological Review*, *94*(1), 23–41.

Rozin, P., Fallon, A. E., & Augustoni-Ziskind, M. (1985). The child's conception of food: The development of contamination sensitivity to "disgusting" substances. *Developmental Psychology*, *21*, 1075–1079.

Rozin, P., Fallon, A. E., & Augustoni-Ziskind, M. (1986). The child's conception of food: Development of categories of accepted and rejected substances. *Journal of Nutrition Education*, *18*, 75–81.

Rozin, P., Fallon, A. E., & Mandell, R. (1984). Family resemblance in attitudes to food. *Developmental Psychology*, *20*, 309–314.

Rozin, P., Haidt, J., & McCauley, C. R. (1993). Disgust. In M. Lewis & J. M. Haviland (Eds.), *Handbook of emotions* (pp. 575–594). New York: Guilford Press.

Rozin, P., Haidt, J., McCauley, C. R., Dunlop, L., & Ashmore, M. (1999). Individual differences in disgust sensitivity: Comparisons and evaluations of paper-and-pencil versus behavioral measures. *Journal of Research in Personality*, *33*, 330–351.

Rozin, P., Haidt, J., McCauley, C. R., & Imada, S. (1997). The cultural evolution of disgust. In H. M. Macbeth (Ed.), *Food preferences and taste: Continuity and change* (pp. 65–82). Oxford: Berghahn.

Rozin, P., Hammer, L., Oster, H., Horowitz, T., & Marmara, V. (1986). The child's conception of food: Differentiation of categories of rejected substances in the 1.4 to 5 year age range. *Appetite*, *7*, 141–151.

Rozin, P., Lowery, L., & Ebert, R. (1994). Varieties of disgust faces and the structure of disgust. *Journal of Personality and Social Psychology*, *66*, 870–881.

Rozin, P., Lowery, L., Imada, S., & Haidt, J. (1999). The CAD triad hypothesis: A mapping between three other-directed moral emotions (contempt, anger, disgust) and three moral ethics (community, autonomy, divinity). *Journal of Personality and Social Psychology, 76,* 574–586.

Rozin, P., Markwith, M., & McCauley, C. R. (1994). The nature of aversion to indirect contact with other persons: AIDS aversion as a composite of aversion to strangers, infection, moral taint and misfortune. *Journal of Abnormal Psychology*, *103*, 495–504.

Rozin, P., Markwith, M., & Stoess, C. (1997). Moralization: Becoming a vegetarian, the conversion of preferences into values and the recruitment of disgust. *Psychological Science, 8*, 67–73.

Rozin, P., & Millman, L. (1987). Family environment, not heredity, accounts for family resemblance in food preferences and attitudes. *Appetite, 8*, 125–134.

Rozin, P., Millman, L., & Nemeroff, C. (1986). Operation of the laws of sympathetic magic in disgust and other domains. *Journal of Personality and Social Psychology, 50*, 703–712.

Rozin, P., & Nemeroff, C. J. (1990). The laws of sympathetic magic: A psychological analysis of similarity and contagion. In J. Stigler, G. Herdt, & R. A. Shweder (Eds.), *Cultural psychology: Essays on comparative human development* (pp. 205–232). Cambridge, England: Cambridge University Press.

Rozin, P., Nemeroff, C., Horowitz, M., Gordon, B., & Voet, W. (1995). The borders of the self: Contamination sensitivity and potency of the mouth, other apertures and body parts. *Journal of Research in Personality, 29*, 318–340.

Rozin, P., Nemeroff, C., Wane, M., & Sherrod, A. (1989). Operation of the sympathetic magical law of contagion in interpersonal attitudes among Americans. *Bulletin of the Psychonomic Society, 27*, 367–370.

Rozin, P., & Singh, L. (1999). The moralization of cigarette smoking in America. *Journal of Consumer Behavior, 8*, 321–337.

Rozin, P., & Zellner, D. A. (1985). The role of Pavlovian conditioning in the acquisition of food likes and dislikes. *Annals of the New York Academy of Sciences, 443*, 189–202.

Scherer, K. R. (1986). Vocal affect expression: A review and a model for future research. *Psychological Bulletin, 99*, 143–165.

Scherer, K. R. (1997). The role of culture in emotion-antecedent appraisal. *Journal of Personality and Social Psychology, 73*, 902–922.

Scherer, K. R., & Wallbott, H. G. (1994). Evidence for universality and cultural variation of differential emotion response patterning. *Journal of Personality and Social Psychology, 66*, 310–328.

Schmidt, H., & Beauchamp, G. (1988). Adult-like odor preferences and aversions in three-year-old children. *Child Development, 59*, 1136–1143.

Seligman, M. E. P. (1971). Phobias and preparedness. *Behavior Therapy, 2*, 307–320.

Senn, M. J. E., & Solnit, A. J. (1968). *Problems in child behavior and development.* Philadelphia: Lea & Febiger.

Shweder, R. A., Much, N. C., Mahapatra, M., & Park, L. (1997). The "big three" of morality (autonomy, community, divinity), and the "big three" explanations of suffering. In A. Brandt & P. Rozin (Eds.), *Morality and health* (pp. 119–169). New York: Routledge.

Siegal, M. (1988). Children's knowledge of contagion and contamination as causes of illness. *Child Development, 59*, 1353–1359.

Soler, J. (1979). The semiotics of food in the Bible. In R. Forster & O. Ranum (Eds.), *Food and drinking history* (E. Forster & P. M. Ranum, Trans.). (pp. 126–138). Baltimore: Johns Hopkins University Press. (Original work published 1973)

Sprengelmeyer, R., Sprengelmeyer, R., Young, A. W., Calder, A. W., Karnat, A., Lange, H., Hömberg, V., Perrett, D. I., & Rowland, D. (1996). Loss of disgust: Perception of faces and emotions in Huntington's disease. *Brain, 119*, 1647–1665.

Sprengelmeyer, R., Young, A. W., Pundt, I., Sprengelmeyer, A., Calder, A. J., Berrios, G., Winkel, R., Vollmoeller, W., Kuhn, W., Sartory, G., & Przuntek, H. (1997). Disgust implicated in obsessive–compulsive disorder. *Proceedings of the Royal Society: Biological Sciences, B264,* 1767–1773.

Sprengelmeyer, R., Young, A. W., Sprengelmeyer, A., Calder, A. J., Rowland, D., Perrett, D. I., Homberg, V., & Lange, H. (1997). Recognition of facial expressions: Selective impairment of specific emotions in Huntington's disease. *Cognitive Neuropsychology, 14,* 839–879.

Stein, M., Ottenberg, P., & Roulet, N. (1958). A study of the development of olfactory preferences. *Archives of Neurology and Psychiatry, 80*, 264–266.

Steiner, J. E. (1979). Human facial expressions in response to taste and smell stimulation. In H. W. Reese & L. P. Lipsitt (Eds.), *Advances in child development and behavior* (Vol. 13, pp. 257–295). New York: Academic Press.

Tambiah, S. J. (1969). Animals are good to think and good to prohibit. *Ethnology, 8*, 423–459.

Templer, D. I., King, F. L., Brooner, R. K., & Corgiat, M. (1984). Assessment of body elimination attitude. *Journal of Clinical Psychology, 40*, 754–759.

Tolin, D. F., Lohr, J. M., Sawchuk, C. N., & Lee, T. C. (1997). Disgust and disgust sensitivity in blood-injection-injury and spider phobia. *Behaviour Research and Therapy, 35,* 949–953.

Tomkins, S. S. (1963). *Affect, imagery, consciousness: Vol. 2. The negative affects.* New York: Springer.

Tomkins, S. S. (1982). Affect theory. In P. Ekman (Ed.), *Emotion in the human face* (2nd ed., pp. 353–395). Cambridge, England: Cambridge University Press.

Tylor, E. B. (1974). *Primitive culture: Researches into the development of mythology, philosophy, religion, art and custom.* New York: Gordon Press. (Original work published 1871)

Ware, J., Jain, K., Burgess, L., & Davey, G. C. L. (1994). Disease-avoidance model: Factor analysis of common animal fears. *Behaviour Research and Therapy, 32*, 57–63.

Webb, K., & Davey, G. C. L. (1993). Disgust sensitivity and fear of animals: Effect of exposure to violent or repulsive material. *Anxiety, Coping, and Stress, 5*, 329–335.

Wierzbicka, A. (1986). Emotions: Universal or culture-specific? *American Anthropologist, 88*, 584–594.

CHAPTER 41

Love and Attachment Processes

Elaine Hatfield
Richard L. Rapson

On March 30, 1981, less than 2 hours before John W. Hinckley, Jr. shot President Ronald Reagan, he scrawled a final plea to Jodie Foster, the actress with whom he was obsessed:

Dear Jodie,

There is a definite possibility that I will be killed in my attempt to get Reagan. It is for this very reason I am writing you this letter now.

As you well know by now I love you very much. Over the past seven months I've left you dozens of poems, letters and love messages in the faint hope that you could develop an interest in me. . . .

Jodie, I would abandon this idea of getting Reagan in a second if I could only win your heart and live out the rest of my life with you. . . .

I will admit to you that the reason I'm going ahead with this attempt now is because I just cannot wait any longer to impress you. I've got to do something now to make you understand, in no uncertain terms, that I am doing all of this for your sake! By sacrificing my freedom and possibly my life, I hope to change your mind about me. This letter is being written only an hour before I leave for the Hilton Hotel. Jodie, I'm asking to please look into your heart and at least give me the chance, with this historical deed, to gain your respect and love.

I love you forever,

John Hinckley

(quoted in Caplan, 1984, pp. 46–48)

In FBI questioning after the attempted assassination, Foster denied that she had ever met or spoken to John Hinckley (Caplan, 1984, p. 48).

Passionate love rarely leads to murderous fantasies. Yet the power of love has sparked social psychologists' and emotions researchers' interest in passionate and companionate love and the attachment processes that shape them.

DEFINITIONS

Most scientists distinguish between two forms of love—"passionate love" and "companionate love." Passionate love (sometimes called "obsessive love," "infatuation," "lovesickness," or "being in love") is an intense emotion. One typical definition is the following:

A state of intense longing for union with another. Passionate love is a complex functional whole including appraisals or appreciations, subjective feelings, expressions, patterned physiological processes, action tendencies, and instrumental behaviors. Reciprocated love (union with the other) is associated with fulfillment and ecstasy. Unrequited love (separation) is associated with emptiness, anxiety, or despair. (Hatfield & Rapson, 1993, p. 5)

The Passionate Love Scale was designed to assess the cognitive, physiological, and behavioral indicants of such a "longing for union" (Hatfield & Sprecher, 1986).

Shaver, Wu, and Schwartz (1991) interviewed young people in the United States, Italy, and the People's Republic of China about their emotional experiences. In all cultures, men and women identified the same emotions as basic or prototypic: joy/happiness, love/attraction, fear, anger/hate, and sadness/depression. Men and women also agreed as to whether the various emotions should be labeled as positive experiences (such as joy) or negative ones (such as fear, anger, or sadness). They agreed completely, that is, except about one emotion—love. The U.S. and Italian subjects tended to equate love with happiness; both passionate and companionate love were assumed to be intensely positive experiences. Chinese students, however, had a darker view of love. In China there are few "happy love" ideographs. Passionate love tended to be associated with such ideographs as "infatuation," "unrequited love," "nostalgia," and "sorrow love." Students from the East and West never did come to an agreement as to the nature of love. They continued to regard each other's visions of love as "unrealistic."

Companionate love (sometimes called "true love" or "conjugal love") is a far less intense emotion. It combines feelings of deep attachment, commitment, and intimacy. Psychologists have used a variety of scales to measure companionate love. For example, Berscheid and Hatfield (1978) focused on subjects' subjective appraisals (attitudes). Sternberg (1988) assumed that companionate relationships possess little passion but a great deal of commitment and intimacy; thus he assessed companionate love by measuring commitment and intimacy. Berscheid (1983) focused on assessing how "entwined" or linked couples' organized action sequences were.

Researchers have proposed that both passionate and companionate love can be understood, in part, by examining the mother–child attachment experiences on which they are based. Researchers interested in passionate love have tended to focus on *infants'* attachments as the prototype of later passionate attachments; researchers interested in companionate love have tended to focus on *parental* attachments as the prototype of companionate love. Of course, love relationships can involve both passionate and companionate love.

PASSIONATE LOVE

The Evolutionary Soil of Passionate Love: The Triune Brain

In the 1940s, MacLean (1986) proposed that in the course of evolution, humans have ended up with a brain that possesses a "triune structure." The brain is thought to consist of three different types of brains, layered one upon the other. The oldest brain is basically reptilian. It is primarily concerned with the preservation of the self and the species. The second brain, the neomammalian brain or limbic system, is inherited from the early mammals and evolved to facilitate mother–child relationships. Such emotions as desire, affection, ecstasy, fear, anger, and sadness all derive from activities in the limbic system. The third brain, the late mammalian/early primate brain or neocortex, is inherited from the late mammals and early primates. Not until the neocortex evolved did symbolic or verbal information become important in shaping emotional experience and expression.

Love in Primates

Rosenblum and Plimpton (1981) point out that even primates may experience a primitive form of passionate love. In some species, infant primates must possess a "desire for union" if they are to survive. Separation often means death. Thus infants are prewired to cling to their mothers. Should a brief separation occur, infants quickly become frantic and begin searching for their mothers. If they return, the infants are joyous—they cling to them and/or bound about in excitement. If the mothers do not return, the infants eventually abandon all hope of contact, despair, and die. The experience Rosenblum and Plimpton describe, with its alternating lows and highs, certainly sounds much like passionate love's "desire for union."

Love in Children

Ainsworth (1989) and Bowlby (1969, 1973, 1980) carried out extensive studies into the process of attachment, separation, and loss in children. They found that infants and toddlers react to separation in the same way as do their primate ancestors.

There is some evidence that children experience passionate love very early. Bell (1902) interviewed 1,700 Indiana teachers and observed 800 children; he concluded that children could experience "sex-love" as early as 3½ years of age. Easton and Hatfield (cited in Hatfield, Schmitz, Cornelius, & Rapson, 1988) developed the Childhood Love Scale, a children's version of the Passionate Love Scale. They interviewed more than 200 boys and girls, ranging in age from 4 to 18, about their romantic feelings. Their results made it clear that Bell was right—even the youngest of children were capable of passionate love. Subsequent research (Hatfield, Brinton, & Cornelius, 1989) has made it clear that when children are anxious or fearful, they are especially vulnerable to passionate love.

Of course, passionate love becomes very powerful when children enter puberty. Perhaps this is because teenagers experience the return of old separation anxieties during the period; perhaps they are under unusual stress as they go through the agonies of adolescence. Neurophysiologists also remind us that passionate love may also be fueled by pubescent sexual and hormonal changes (Gadpaille, 1975; Money, 1980). In any case, puberty and sexual maturity may well bring a new depth to passion.

Love in Adults

Shaver and Hazan (1988) proposed that romantic love should be conceived of as a form of attachment. Children's early patterns of attachment should influence their adult attachments. For example, children are likely to become securely attached to their mothers if they are allowed to be both affectionate *and* independent. Such children should mature into secure adults who are comfortable with intimacy and are able to trust and depend on those they care for. Children may become anxious/ambivalent if they have learned to be clingy and dependent, or fearful of being smothered and restrained, or both. Such children should become anxious/ambivalent adults who fall in love easily, who seek extreme levels of closeness, and who are terrified that they will be abandoned. Their love affairs are likely to be short-lived. The avoidant child (who has been emotionally abandoned early on) may well become an avoidant adult who is uncomfortable getting too close and has difficulty depending on others. The authors have amassed considerable support in favor of this formulation.

Recently, there has been some debate as to whether or not childhood attachment experiences have a powerful impact on adult attachment styles (Waters, Treboux, Crowell, Merrick, & Albersheim, 1995; Zimmermann, Fremmer-Bombik, Sprangler, & Grossmann, 1997). In one study, for example, Lewis, Feiring, and Rosenthal (in press) followed children as they progressed from infancy to late adolescence. They found *no* consistency in attachment classification!

In any case, social psychologists have been interested in the impact that cognitive schemas, however derived, have on people's cognitions, emotions, and behaviors. ("Schemas" have been conceptualized as cognitive plans, structures, or programs that serve as guides for interpreting information and guiding action; Fiske & Taylor, 1984.) Theorists have argued that people may possess very different love schemas—that is, different cognitive models of what it is appropriate to expect from themselves, from those they love, and from their love relationships. In an elaboration of the Shaver and Hazan (1988) model, we (Hatfield & Rapson, 1996) have proposed that people's love schemas depend on (1) how comfortable they are with closeness and/or independence, and (2) how eager they are to be involved in romantic relationships. Those who are interested in romantic relationships are said to fall into one of four types: the "secure" (who are comfortable with both closeness and independence); the "clingy" (who are comfortable with closeness but fearful of too much independence); the "skittish" (who are fearful of too much closeness but comfortable with independence); and the "fickle" (who are uneasy with either closeness or independence). Of course, there are some people who are uninterested in relationships—for example, the "casual" (who are interested in relationships only if they are almost problem-free) and the "uninterested" (who are not at all interested in relationships, problem-free or not).

We (Hatfield & Rapson, 1996) have pointed out that people's love schemas may have multiple determinants. In part (as attachment theorists have proposed), they are shaped by children's early experiences and thus are relatively permanent. To some extent, love schemas change as people progress through the various developmental stages. As adolescents mature, for example, they normally become more secure in their ability to integrate closeness and independence (Erikson, 1982). In part, love schemas change with experience. Depending on their romantic experiences, people may become better (or less) able to deal with the stresses of love relationships. Finally, of course, people may react differently in different kinds of relationships. The same person, for example, may cling to a cool and aloof mate but become skittish with a smothering one (Napier, 1977).

The Love Schema Scale has been designed to identify people who possess each of the various love schemas (Hatfield & Rapson, 1996). Social psychologists have amassed considerable evidence in support of the contention that love schemas have a powerful impact on the formation, maintenance, and ending of romantic and sexual relationships (see Hatfield & Rapson, 1996, for a review of this research).

The Antecedents of Passionate Love

If passionate love is rooted in childhood attachments, certain types of people, caught up in certain types of situations, should be especially vulnerable to passion. Anything that makes adults feel as helpless and dependent as they were as children—anything that makes them fear separation and loss—should increase their passionate craving to merge with others. There is some evidence to support these speculations.

Low Self-Esteem

Reik (1949) was one of the first to propose that when self-esteem is threatened, individuals are more likely to fall prey to passionate love. Hatfield (1965) conducted an experiment to test the hypothesis that when self-esteem has been bruised, subjects should be unusually receptive to the love and affection offered by others. As predicted, women whose self-esteem was threatened *were* most attracted to potential romantic partners. (Other theorists have also found a link between low self-esteem and passionate love. See Bartholomew & Horowitz, 1991; Jacobs, Berscheid, & Hatfield, 1971.)

Dependency and Insecurity

A number of theorists have observed that people who are dependent and insecure (or who are caught up in affairs that promote such feelings) are especially vulnerable to passionate love. Berscheid and her associates (Fei & Berscheid, 1977) have argued that passionate love, dependency, and insecurity are tightly linked. When people are passionately in love, they are painfully aware of how dependent they are on those they love; dependency naturally breeds insecurity. In an ingenious experiment, Berscheid, Graziano, Monson, and Dermer (1976) found clear evidence in support of these contentions.

Anxiety

Numerous theorists, beginning with Freud (1910/1953), have proposed that passionate love is fueled by anxiety and fear (see also Hatfield, 1971; Hatfield & Rapson, 1987; Carlson & Hatfield, 1992.) This makes sense; passionate love and anxiety are closely related, both neuroanatomically and chemically (Kaplan, 1979; Liebowitz, 1983). Researchers have demonstrated that anxious individuals are especially prone to seek passionate love relationships (Solomon & Corbit, 1974; Peele, 1975). In a series of studies, Hatfield et al. (1989), for example, found that adolescents of European, Chinese, Japanese, Korean, and mixed ancestry who were either momentarily or habitually anxious were especially vulnerable to passionate love.

Neediness

Social psychologists have found that acute deprivation does seem to set the stage for passionate love. Stephan, Berscheid, and Hatfield (1971) tested the simple hypothesis that when people are sexually aroused, their minds wander, and soon their dazzling fantasies lend sparkle to drab reality. They proposed that when men are sexually aroused, they should have a greater tendency to see women as sex objects. Hence they should tend to exaggerate two of their dates' traits: their sexual desirability and their sexual receptivity. They found that they were right. As predicted, the more aroused the men, the more beautiful they thought their dates. In addition, the more aroused they were, the more likely they were to assume that their dates would be sexually receptive. Unaroused men judged their dates-to-be as a fairly "nice" women. Aroused men suspected that they were probably "amorous," "immoral," "promiscuous," "willing," "unwholesome," and "uninhibited."

The Consequences of Passionate Love

The previous sections, dealing with the *roots* of passionate love, have painted a somewhat dismal picture. We have focused on the bruised self-esteem, the dependency, and the insecurity that make people hunger for love. Here we would normally point out that when people attain love (or imagine that they might), they experience intense happiness and excitement. Why would people long for love unless they enjoyed receiving it?

The Rewards of Passionate Love

Surprisingly, we have been able to find little survey or experimental research documenting the delights of passionate love; nonetheless, interviews with lovers and insights derived from works of fiction suggest that lovers may experience at least six kinds of rewards:

1. *Moments of exultation.* When love is realized, lovers may experience moments of passionate bliss. Fehr (1993) asked young men and women in Australia and the United States to list the characteristics they associated with love. People usually listed such positive characteristics as euphoria, excitement, laughing, and contentment. (Similar results were obtained by Davis & Todd, 1982; Fitness & Fletcher, 1993; and Marston, Hecht, & Robers, 1987.)

2. *Feeling understood and accepted.* When men and women are loved, they sometimes feel fully understood, loved, and accepted.

3. *Sharing a sense of union.* Lovers may feel a sense of union with their beloved.

4. *Feeling secure and safe.* Lovers may feel safe and secure when they are with someone they love.

5. *Transcendence.* When people fall in love, they are sometimes able to transcend their former limitations.

6. *Beneficial effects on the immune system.* Smith and Hoklund (1988) suspected that love is good for people. They interviewed Danish college students. Were they in love? Were their feelings reciprocated? How happy were they? How healthy? When students were in love and knew they were loved in return, they were at their best. They were self-confident, relaxed and happy, and unusually healthy, with no sore throats or colds. When technicians drew blood samples and assayed natural killer (NK) cell activity, they found that lovers' NK cell activity was unusually low. The lovers' immune systems were at full strength. On the other hand, when students were suffering the stresses of unrequited love, they were literally at risk. They reported feeling tense and depressed, and they were especially prone to sore throats and colds. Many of them had been drinking (at least they displayed the telltale signs of a hangover). More ominously, their NK cell activity was elevated—a sign that their immune systems were trying to fight off disease.

The Costs of Passionate Love

Of course, love has its costs too. When hopes are dashed or relationships fall apart, people's self-esteem is often shattered; they feel lonely and miserable (Means, 1991; Perlman & Peplau, 1981); and they may experience intense anger and jealousy (Berscheid & Fei, 1977; Clanton & Smith, 1987). Couples who have broken up or divorced are unusually vulnerable to a host of stress-induced mental and physical diseases (Bloom, White, & Asher, 1979; Stroebe & Stroebe, 1987). Should a love affair or marriage end in death, the bereaved partner generally grieves for a very long time (Beach, Sandeen, & O'Leary, 1990; Solsberry & Krupnick, 1984; Stroebe & Stroebe, 1987).

Why Is Passion So Passionate?

There are probably two main reasons why passionate love is often such an overpowering experience. First, passionate love is a basic emotion; for our ancestors, union was a life-and-death matter. Second, passionate feelings are mixed with other intense emotional experiences—joy, jealousy, loneliness, sadness, fear, and anger.

Passionate lovers generally experience a roller-coaster rush of feelings—euphoria, happiness, vulnerability, anxiety, panic, and despair. Tennov (1979) interviewed more than 500 lovers. Almost all of them reported that passionate love (which Tennov labeled "limerence") was a bittersweet experience. Researchers have found that such emotional mixtures often produce explosive reactions (see Carlson & Hatfield, 1992). Although most of us assume that we love the people we do *in spite* of the suffering they cause us, it may be that, in part, we love them *because* of the pain they cause.

COMPANIONATE LOVE

Theorists who have tried to explain the origins of any emotion such as love have generally taken an evolutionary approach. Plutchik (1980), for one, argues that emotional "packages" are inherited, adaptive patterns of emotional experience, physiological reaction, and behavior. At every phylogenetic level, organisms face the same problems: If they are to survive and reproduce, they must find food, avoid being killed, and take advantage of reproductive opportunities. Many theorists believe that companionate love is built on the ancient circuitry evolved to ensure that mammals and primates mate, reproduce, and care for the young. In the last two decades, neuroscientists, anthropologists, and developmentalists have begun to learn more about companionate love. They have begun to study the subjective feelings, expressions, patterned physiological processes, and action tendencies associated with this form of love's ancient heritage.

The Chemistry of Companionate Love

Neuroscientists still know very little about the biological bases of companionate love and tenderness. However, neuroscientists have identified a hormone, oxytocin, which seems to promote affectionate, close, intimate bonds (Caldwell, Jirikowski, Greer, & Pedersen, 1989) and sexual and reproductive behavior (Pedersen, Caldwell, Jirikowski, & Insel, 1991). Carter, a zoologist (quoted in Angier, 1991), observes: "It [oxytocin] facilitates tactile contact between animals, and that's an early step in the development of social attachment" (p. B8). Oxytocin also promotes more intense bonds between mothers and infants; it increases mothers' eagerness to nurture their young. Finally, oxytocin appears to increase contact between same-sex pairs as well (Angier, 1991, p. B8).

The Look, Posture, Sounds, and Behaviors of Companionate Love

Some theorists have argued that love's ancient beginnings can be read today in the looks, pos-

tures, sounds, and behaviors of companionate love.

The Look of Love

Emotions researchers have found that the universal emotions—joy, love, sadness, fear, and anger—are associated with certain characteristic facial expressions. In some research, scientists have tried to pinpoint the facial expressions associated with joy and love. For example, Hatfield, Costello, Schalekamp, Hsee, and Denney (cited in Hatfield, Cacioppo, & Rapson, 1994) found that people were able to distinguish facial expressions of love from expressions of joy, sadness, fear, and anger. Exactly how the subjects did this is not yet known. The authors have speculated that perhaps when men and women are experiencing companionate love, they take on the expression mothers often instinctively display when they are happily, tenderly gazing at their young infants: They gaze downward (at the infants), their faces soften, and a slight, tender smile plays about their lips. (Bloch, Orthous, & Santibañez-H., 1987, have proposed the same hypothesis; they provide some suggestive evidence in support of this contention.)

The Posture of Love

Morris (1971) observes:

> These, then, are our first real experiences of life—floating in a warm fluid, curling inside a total embrace, swaying to the undulations of the moving body and hearing the beat of the pulsing heart. Our prolonged exposure to these sensations in the absence of other, competing stimuli leaves a lasting impression on our brains, an impression that spells security, comfort and passivity (p. 12)

After birth, Morris contends, mothers instinctively try to recreate the security of the womb. Mothers kiss, caress, fondle, and embrace their infants; they cradle them in their arms. In the womb, neonates hear the steady drumbeat of their mothers' hearts beating at 72 beats per minute. After birth, mothers instinctively hold their babies with their heads pressed against their left breasts, closest to their hearts. When their infants fret, mothers unconsciously rock them at a rate of between 60 and 70 rocks per minute, the rate that is most calming to infants. Morris points out: "It appears as if this rhythm, whether heard or felt, is the vital comforter, reminding the baby vividly of the lost paradise of the womb" (1971, p. 14). Of course, in adulthood, these same kisses, tender caresses, and embraces continue to provide security for men and women—who are unconscious of the early origins of these behaviors.

The Sounds of Love

French psychophysiologist Bloch and her colleagues (1987) argue that not just joy, but passionate love ("eroticism") and companionate love ("tenderness"), are associated with different breathing patterns and sounds. Mothers often coo or croon softly with their mouths held near their infants' heads. Bloch et al. have speculated that such tender maternal sounds become the forerunners of the breathing patterns and sounds associated with love. They studied the basic emotions and discovered that the breathing patterns associated with eroticism and tenderness were somewhat different:

> In *eroticism*, the principal feature of sexual activation is an even breathing pattern which increases in frequency and amplitude depending on the intensity of the emotional engagement; inspiration occurs through a relaxed open mouth. The face muscles are relaxed, and the eyes are closed or semi-closed. In the female version of the erotic pattern, the head is tilted backwards, and the neck is exposed. (p. 6)

On the other hand, in tenderness,

> The breathing pattern is of low frequency with an even and regular rhythm; the mouth is semi-closed, the relaxed lips forming a slight smile. Facial and antigravitational muscles are very relaxed, eyes are open and relaxed, and the head is slightly tilted to the side. The postural attitude is one of approach. Vocalization includes a humming type lullaby sound. (p. 6)

Behavioral Indicators of Love

Finally, anthropologist Eibl-Eibesfeldt (1971), in *Love and Hate,* observes that primate mothers and infants reveal their close bonds in certain characteristic behaviors. In infancy, human mothers and their infants express their feelings for one another in much the same way. And in adulthood, men and women in all cultures cannot help showing their companionate love in the same ways they did as infants. For instance, newborn infants rhythmically rotate their heads from side to side as they root for their mothers' nipples. An adult, playfully nuzzling a loved one, often finds him- or herself using motions, gestures, and rhythms from the distant past— holding the loved one's head in his or her hands, or rubbing his or her lips against the loved one's cheek with a sideways movement of the head. Eibl-Eibesfeldt graphically illustrates the kissing, mutual feeding, and embracing that bond people together.

Parent–Child Coordination

Mothers and fathers differ in how well attuned they are to their infants' rhythms. Usually both mother and child are in control of their interaction. The baby's needs must shape the general structure in which the interaction occurs; the mother then has the opportunity to regulate the tempo of the interaction. If she speeds up, she will reduce the baby's level of communication; if she slows down, she can expect a higher level of communication and engagement (Stern, 1974).

Sometimes parents are not able to shape themselves to their infants' needs. When an infant turns his or her head, needing to cut down the level of stimulation that it is receiving, a young mother may panic: "The child doesn't like me. What did I do wrong?" She may intrusively force herself on the baby, looking for reassurance, but overwhelming the infant still further. A father, in an effort to play, may frighten a child with too much noise and movement. Or the parents may give the infant too little attention. They may be bored, uninterested, or distracted. They both may be exhausted from trying to keep house and from their careers outside the home. Generally, infants respond to such lack of interest by trying to rouse their caretakers. If that proves to be impossible, they eventually withdraw completely. We might expect such parental intrusion or indifference to have a profound impact upon children's strategies for dealing with their subsequent love relationships. Such experiences may well shape their eagerness and willingness to get close to others, as well as their ability to balance closeness and distance, intimacy and independence.

CONCLUSIONS

In sum, then, researchers have proposed that both passionate and companionate love can be understood, in part, by examining the mother–child attachment experiences on which they are based. Researchers interested in passionate love have tended to focus on infants' attachments to their mothers as the prototype of later passionate attachments; researchers interested in companionate love have tended to focus on parental attachments to their infants as the prototype of companionate attachments. Of course, love relationships can involve both passionate and companionate love. In this chapter, we have reviewed research in support of these contentions.

REFERENCES

Ainsworth, M. D. S. (1989). Attachments beyond infancy. *American Psychologist, 44,* 709–716.

Angier, N. (1991, January 22). A potent peptide prompts an urge to cuddle. *The New York Times*, pp. B5–B8.

Bartholomew, K., & Horowitz, L. M. (1991). Attachment styles among young adults: A test of a four-category model. *Journal of Personality and Social Psychology, 61,* 226–244.

Beach, S. R. H., Sandeen, E. E., & O'Leary, K. D. (1990). *Depression in marriage.* New York: Guilford Press.

Bell, S. (1902). A preliminary study of the emotion of love between the sexes. *American Journal of Psychology, 13,* 325–354.

Berscheid, E. (1983). Emotion. In H. H. Kelley, E. Berscheid, A. Christensen, J. H. Harvey, T. L. Huston, G. Levinger, E. McClintock, L. A. Peplau, & D. R. Peterson (Eds.), *Close relationships* (pp. 110–168). New York: Freeman.

Berscheid, E., & Fei, J. (1977). Romantic love and sexual jealousy. In G. Clanton & L. G. Smith (Eds.), *Jealousy* (pp. 101–114). Englewood Cliffs, NJ: Prentice-Hall.

Berscheid, E., Graziano, W., Monson, T., & Dermer, M. (1976). Outcome dependency: Attention, attribution, and attraction. *Journal of Personality and Social Psychology, 34,* 978–989.

Berscheid, E., & Hatfield, E. (1978). *Interpersonal attraction* (2nd ed.). Reading, MA: Addison-Wesley.

Bloch, S., Orthous, P., & Santibañez-H., G. (1987). Effector patterns of basic emotions: A psychophysiological method for training actors. *Journal of Social and Biological Structures, 10,* 1–19.

Bloom, B. L., White, S. W., & Asher, S. J. (1979). Marital disruption as a stressful life event. In G. Levinger & O. C. Moles (Eds.), *Divorce and separation* (pp. 184–200). New York: Basic Books.

Bowlby, J. (1969). *Attachment and loss: Vol. 1. Attachment.* New York: Basic Books.

Bowlby, J. (1973). Affectional bonds: Their nature and origin. In R. Weiss (Ed.), *Loneliness: The experience of emotional and social isolation* (pp. 38–52). Cambridge, MA: MIT Press.

Bowlby, J. (1980). *Attachment and loss: Vol. 3. Loss: Sadness and depression.* New York: Basic Books.

Caldwell, J. D., Jirikowski, G. F., Greer, E. R., & Pedersen, C. A. (1989). Medial preoptic area oxytocin and female sexual receptivity. *Behavioral Neuroscience, 103,* 655–662.

Caplan, L. (1984, July 2). Annals of law: The insanity defense. *The New Yorker,* pp. 45–78.

Carlson, J. G., & Hatfield, E. (1992). *Psychology of emotion.* Fort Worth, TX: Harcourt Brace Jovanovich.

Clanton, G., & Smith, L. G. (Eds.). (1987). *Jealousy.* Lanham, MA: University Press of America.

Davis, K. E., & Todd, M. J. (1982). Friendship and love relationships. In K. E. Davis (Ed.), *Advances in descriptive psychology* (Vol. 2, pp. 79–122). Greenwich, CT: JAI Press.

Eibl-Eibesfeldt, I. (1971). *Love and hate.* New York: Holt, Rinehart & Winston.

Erikson, E. (1982). *The life cycle completed: A review.* New York: Norton.

Fehr, B. (1993). How do I love thee?: Let me consult my prototype. In S. Duck (Ed.), *Understanding relationship processes: Vol 1. Individuals in relationships* (pp. 87–120). Newbury Park, CA: Sage.

Fei, J., & Berscheid, E. (1977). *Perceived dependency, insecurity, and love in heterosexual relationships: The eternal triangle.* Unpublished manuscript, University of Minnesota.

Fiske, S. T., & Taylor, S. E. (1984). *Social cognition.* Reading, MA: Addison-Wesley.

Fitness, J., & Fletcher, G. J. O. (1993). Love, hate, anger, and jealousy in close relationships: A prototype and cognitive appraisal analysis. *Journal of Personality and Social Psychology, 65,* 942–958.

Freud, S. (1953). Contributions to the psychology of love: A special type of choice of objects made by men (J. Riviere, Trans.). In E. Jones (Ed.), *Sigmund Freud: Collected papers* (Vol. 4, pp. 192–202). New York: Basic Books. (Original work published 1910)

Gadpaille, W. (1975). *The cycles of sex.* New York: Scribner's.

Hatfield, E. (1965). The effect of self-esteem on romantic liking. *Journal of Experimental Social Psychology, 1,* 184–197.

Hatfield, E. (1971). Passionate love. In B. I. Murstein (Ed.), *Theories of attraction and love* (pp. 85–99). New York: Springer.

Hatfield, E., Brinton, C., & Cornelius, J. (1989). Passionate love and anxiety in young adolescents. *Motivation and Emotions, 13,* 271–289.

Hatfield, E., Caccioppo, J., & Rapson, R. (1994). *Emotional contagion.* New York: Cambridge University Press.

Hatfield, E., & Rapson, R. L. (1987). Passionate love/sexual desire: Can the same paradigm explain both? *Archives of Sexual Behavior, 16,* 259–278.

Hatfield, E., & Rapson, R. L. (1993). *Love, sex, and intimacy: Their psychology, biology, and history.* New York: HarperCollins.

Hatfield, E., & Rapson, R. L. (1996). *Love and sex: Cross-cultural perspectives.* Needham Heights, MA: Allyn & Bacon.

Hatfield, E., Schmitz, E., Cornelius, J., & Rapson, R. L. (1988). Passionate love: How early does it begin?

Journal of Psychology and Human Sexuality, 1, 35–52.

Hatfield, E., & Sprecher, S. (1986). Measuring passionate love in intimate relations. *Journal of Adolescence, 9,* 383–410.

Jacobs, L., Berscheid, E., & Hatfield, E. (1971). Self-esteem and attraction. *Journal of Personality and Social Psychology, 17,* 84–91.

Kaplan, H. S. (1979). *Disorders of sexual desire.* New York: Simon & Schuster.

Lewis, M., Feiring, C., & Rosenthal, S. (in press). Attachment over time. *Child Development.*

Liebowitz, M. R. (1983). *The chemistry of love.* Boston: Little, Brown.

MacLean, P. D. (1986). Ictal symptoms relating to the nature of affects and their cerebral substrate. In R. Plutchik & H. Kellerman (Eds.), *Emotion: Theory, research, and experience. Vol. 3. Biological foundations of emotion* (pp. 61–90). New York: Academic Press.

Marston, P. J., Hecht, M. L., & Robers, T. (1987). "True love ways": The subjective experience and communication of romantic love. *Journal of Social and Personal Relationships, 4,* 387–407.

Means, J. (1991). Coping with a breakup: Negative mood regulation expectancies and depression following the end of a romantic relationship. *Journal of Personality and Social Psychology, 60,* 327–334.

Money, J. (1980) *Love and love sickness.* Baltimore: Johns Hopkins University Press.

Morris, D. (1971). *Intimate behaviour.* London: Triad/Grafton Books.

Napier, A. Y. (1977). *The rejection-intrusion pattern: A central family dynamic.* Unpublished manuscript, University of Wisconsin.

Pedersen, C. A., Caldwell, J. D., Jirikowski, G., & Insel, T. R. (1991, May 19–22). *Oxytocin in maternal, sexual and social behaviors.* Paper presented at the meeting of the New York Academy of Sciences. Arlington, VA.

Peele, S. (1975). *Love and addiction.* New York: Taplinger.

Perlman, D., & Peplau, L. A. (1981). Toward a social psychology of loneliness. In S. Duck & R. Gilmour (Eds.), *Personal relationships: Vol. 3. Personal relationships in disorder* (pp. 31–56). London: Academic Press.

Plutchik, R. (1980). *Emotion: A psychoevolutionary synthesis.* New York: Harper & Row.

Reik, T. (1949). *Of love and lust.* New York: Farrar, Straus.

Rosenblum, L. A., & Plimpton, L. A. (1981). The infant's effort to cope with separation. In M. Lewis & L. Rosenblum (Eds.), *The uncommon child* (pp. 225–257). New York: Plenum Press.

Shaver, P. R., & Hazan, C. (1988). A biased overview of the study of love. *Journal of Social and Personal Relationships, 5,* 474–501.

Shaver, P. R., Wu, S., & Schwartz, J. C. (1991). Cross-cultural similarities and differences in emotion and its representation: A prototype approach. In M. S. Clark (Ed.), *Review of personality and social psychology* (Vol. 13, pp. 175–212). Newbury Park, CA: Sage.

Smith, D. F., & Hokland, M. (1988). Love and salutogenesis in late adolescence: A preliminary investigation. *Psychology: A Journal of Human Behavior, 25,* 44–49.

Solomon, R. L., & Corbit, J. D. (1974). An opponent process theory of motivation: I. The temporal dynamics of affect. *Psychological Review, 81,* 119–145.

Solsberry, V., & Krupnick, J. (1984). Adults' reactions to bereavement. In M. Osterweis, F. Solomon, & M. Green (Eds.), *Bereavement: Reactions, consequences, and care* (pp. 47–68). Washington, DC: National Academy Press.

Stephan, W., Berscheid, E., & Hatfield, E. (1971). Sexual arousal and heterosexual perception. *Journal of Personality and Social Psychology, 20,* 93–101.

Stern, D. N. (1974). Mother and infant at play: The dyadic interaction involving facial, vocal, and gaze behavior. In M. Lewis & L. A. Rosenblum (Eds.), *The effect of the infant on its caregiver* (pp. 105–121). New York: Wiley.

Sternberg, R. J. (1988). Triangulating love. In R. J. Sternberg & M. L. Barnes (Eds.), *The psychology of love* (pp. 119–138). New Haven, CT: Yale University Press.

Stroebe, W., & Stroebe, M. S. (1987). *Bereavement and health: The psychological and physical consequences of partner loss.* New York: Cambridge University Press.

Tennov, D. (1979) *Love and limerence.* New York: Stein & Day.

Waters, E., Treboux, D., Crowell, J., Merrick, S., & Albersheim, L. (1995, April). *From the Strange Situation to the Adult Attachment Interview: A 20–year longitudinal study of attachment security in infancy and early adulthood.* Poster presented at the biennial meeting of the Society for Research in Child Development, Indianapolis, IN.

Zimmermann, P., Fremmer-Bombik, E., Sprangler, G., & Grossmann, K. E. (1997). Attachment in adolescence: A longitudinal perspective. In W. Kopps, J. B. Hoeksema, & D. C. van den Boom (Eds.), *Development of interaction and attachment: Traditional and non-traditional approaches* (pp. 281–291). Amsterdam, The Netherlands: North Holland.

CHAPTER 42

Happiness

James R. Averill
Thomas A. More

When asked to give representative examples of emotion, people typically place happiness at or near the top of the list (Averill, 1975; Fehr & Russell, 1984; Shaver, Schwartz, Kirson, & O'Connor, 1987). And when asked which they would rather have for themselves or their children—wealth, fame, or happiness—most people choose happiness. An emotion of such import, it might be expected, would receive considerable attention from psychologists. But that is not the case: Happiness is among the least, rather than most, discussed of the emotions. One reason for this apparent neglect is a lack of agreement on what it means to be happy. To some people, happiness is a highly aroused state like joy or elation; to others, it connotes contentment, tranquility, or peace of mind. Still other people are happiest when engrossed in an activity, unmindful of their emotional state. And for a benighted few, happiness implies an equanimity of spirit that even misfortune cannot disturb.

Conceptions of happiness can be arranged along two dimensions, level of activation and degree of objectivity, as depicted in Table 42.1. With regard to the former, happiness can range from states of low activation (e.g., contentment, tranquility, peacefulness) to states of high activation (e.g., joy, elation, ecstasy).

Degree of objectivity refers to the extent that an emotional state can be identified on the basis of internal (subjective) or external (objec-

tive) criteria. For example, although contentment and joy differ in level of activation, both have an ineluctable subjective component; self-reports are among their most reliable indices. In order to introduce the objective end of this dimension, it is helpful to begin with a more obvious example than happiness—namely, guilt. A person need not feel guilty in order to be guilty; conversely, a person may feel guilty without being guilty. Guilt may be extreme in this respect, but it is not unusual; similar considerations apply in varying degrees to other emotions (Averill, 1994). For example, the person who is in love, jealous, angry, or the like, need not be aware of the fact at the moment; indeed, this person may the be last rather than the first to recognize his or her emotional state. And so it is with happiness. Under some conditions (hypomania), feeling happy may even be symptomatic of its opposite—depression.

A thought experiment proposed by Nozick (1989) further illustrates the distinction between subjective and objective conceptions of happiness. Imagine an "experience machine" that can, by activating relevant neural circuits, produce any set of feelings you might desire. You want pleasure? Friendship? Success? Just dial them on the machine. Anything you might want, you can experience—not just momentarily, but for as long as, and in whatever variety, you wish. Assuming that all your physiological needs were also met, so that you remain in per-

TABLE 42.1. Four Concepts of Happiness

Level of arousal	Degree of objectivity	
	Subjective (feeling good)	Objective (doing well)
	Joy	Eudaemonia
High	Rejoice ye in that day and leap for joy. (*New Testament,* Luke, vi, 23)	If we are right in our view and happiness is assumed to be acting well, the active life will be the best. (Aristotle, 1984b, *Politics,* Bk. VII, 1325b14)
	Contentment	Equanimity
Low	What is the happy life? It is peace of mind, and lasting tranquility. (Seneca, 1962, *Ad Lucillium,* Epis. XCII)	"Marvel at nothing"—that is perhaps the only thing, Numicius, that can make a man happy and keep him so. (Horace, 1966, Epistle VI)

fect health, would you choose to spend the rest of your life attached to such a machine? Most people say no, believing there is more to happiness than feeling good.

In recent years, considerable research has been devoted to "subjective well-being" and its relation to various social and demographic variables. Measures of subjective well-being typically include avowed (self-reported) happiness, as well as measures of satisfaction and morale (Andrews & Robinson, 1991). Although we touch upon that research in the discussion that follows (see Diener & Lucas, Chapter 21, this volume, for a detailed review), the present chapter is devoted to happiness in a more objective sense—namely, the emotional state associated with full engagement or optimal performance in meaningful activity.

Other than the word "happiness" itself, we do not have a good term for optimal states of full engagement. Csikszentmihalyi's (1991) concept of "flow," in which a person's abilities match the demands of a task, comes close. So, too, does Maslow's (1962) notion of "peak experience." But flow and peak experiences are subjective phenomena, and they are too focused on the moment to count as happiness. "Eudaemonia," the term used by ancient Greek philosophers, has the relevant connotation (see Vlastos, 1985), and we have used it to label the appropriate cell in Table 42.1.

Which of the four cells in Table 42.1 represents *true* happiness? As the epigrams in the table suggest, there is ample precedent for each concept. Nevertheless, we would argue that do-

ing well (objectivity) is more fundamental than feeling good (subjectivity), and that being fully engaged in life's activities (high activation) is more fundamental than disengagement (low activation), even though the latter may sometimes be more pleasant.

For the purposes of this chapter, then, we conceive of happiness in the sense of eudaemonia. Happiness so conceived (and hereafter we drop the qualifying phrase "in the sense of eudaemonia") is an episodic state. Like love and grief, episodes of happiness may last for days, months, or even years. However, unlike these other emotions, happiness is not focused on a specific object or event, nor is it manifested in a specific kind of behavior. Rather, happiness is compatible with engagement in a wide variety of meaningful activities, even if (as is often the case) temporary hardships must also be endured.

APPROACHES TO UNDERSTANDING HAPPINESS

Research on happiness can be divided into three general categories: namely, happiness in relation to (1) systems of behavior, (2) mediating mechanisms, and (3) personality characteristics. By "systems of behavior," we mean coordinated patterns of responses "designed" to achieve some goal or fulfill some function; by "mediating mechanisms," we mean the inner workings that allow a system to fulfill its functions; and by "personality characteristics," we mean traits and abilities assessed without regard to function or inner workings (Averill, 1992).

Most recent research relevant to happiness has focused on mediating mechanisms and personality characteristics. Theoretically, however, systems of behavior have precedence: Without such systems, there would be no mediating mechanisms or personality characteristics of which to speak. Historically, too, systems of behavior have been the traditional focus of discussions of happiness.

HAPPINESS IN RELATION TO SYSTEMS OF BEHAVIOR

Meaningful behavior consists not of random acts, but of responses organized with respect to some goal or end state. Following Lorenz (1971), Bowlby (1982), and others, we refer to such organized patterns of response as "systems of behavior," or "behavioral systems" for short. We do, however, expand that notion beyond its customary use in the ethological literature (Averill, 1990).

To say that a system of behavior is organized with respect to a goal or end state implies principles of organization. These principles may be biological, social, or psychological, and almost always they are a combination of all three. Biological principles are genetically encoded; social principles are found in norms, symbols, and other cultural artifacts; and psychological principles are cognitive schemas or knowledge structures. Biological and social principles represent distal causes of behavior; psychological principles are the product of both biological and social determinants, as well as the unique experiences and present circumstances of the individual.

Systems of behavior are hierarchically organized, as illustrated by the pyramids in Figure 42.1. Consider biological systems, the leftmost pyramid in the figure. Biological systems at a high level of organization or complexity ("instincts," such as attachment, reproduction, and aggression) contribute more or less directly to the survival of the species. At lower levels in the hierarchy, biological systems can be divided into "part instincts" and elementary responses, such as fixed action patterns. Similar considerations apply to social and psychological systems of behavior.

Figure 42.1 also illustrates the heterarchical organization of behavioral systems. That is, biological, social, and psychological systems interact horizontally (at the same level of complexity) as well as vertically (at different levels of complexity) to produce the behavior that is actually exhibited. Finally, it should go without saying that the system hierarchies depicted in Figure 42.1 are abstractions; like the concave and convex sides of an arc, they can be distinguished in theory, not in practice.

One of the best ways to illustrate the relation of happiness to systems of behavior is through historical example, and particularly through

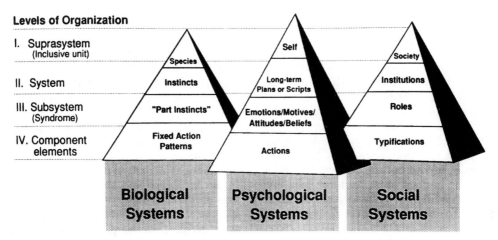

FIGURE 42.1. Three systems hierarchies organized according to biological, social, and psychological principles. Adapted by permission from Averill (1990, p. 389).

Aristotle's (ca. 330 B.C./1984a) analysis of eudaemonia. Consider the following quotation:

Each animal is thought to have a proper pleasure, as it has a proper function; viz. that which corresponds to its activity. If we survey them species by species, too, this will be evident; horse, dog, and man have different pleasures, as Heracleitus says, "asses would prefer sweepings to gold"; for food is pleasanter than gold to asses. (*Nicomachean Ethics*, 1176a3)

Put in our own terms, different species have unique systems of behavior that, when functioning properly, contribute to the survival of the animal and ultimately of the species. Elementary responses that contribute to survival are typically experienced as pleasurable—for example, the sweet taste of ripe fruit, the pleasure of sexual orgasm. Elementary responses combine to form more complex systems of behavior, as depicted in Figure 42.1. When such systems are functioning properly, the animal may be said to be happy. (See Novak & Suomi, 1988, for an application of this principle to the well-being of nonhuman primates.)

Properly functioning biological systems contribute to, but are not sufficient for, happiness in human beings. We are social animals that cannot survive outside of society. Happiness among humans must therefore take into account social as well as biological systems of behavior. To quote Aristotle once more:

Any chance person—even a slave—can enjoy the bodily pleasures no less than the best man; but no one assigns to a slave a share in happiness—unless he assigns to him also a share in human life. For happiness does not lie in such occupations, but . . . in excellent activities. (*Nicomachean Ethics*, 1177a7)

"Excellent" here means "virtuous": Excellent activities are those that properly further the goals of society; and (metaphorically speaking) the ultimate "goal" of a society—like that of a species—is preservation. The preservation of society is achieved through many subsidiary goals, which vary from one society to another. The important point is that a society defines as virtuous those behaviors vital to its survival, and condemns as vices those that are detrimental. Thus a well-socialized individual, one who has internalized the goals and values of society, associates happiness with virtuous activity. In the extreme, *true* happiness has been equated

with virtue; that is, a happy life and a virtuous life are considered identical, for both are, from a social perspective, the best life possible.

Aristotle ridiculed this "identity thesis" (equating happiness with virtue) with an obvious retort: "Those who say that the victim on the rack or the man who falls into great misfortune is happy if he is good, are . . . talking nonsense" (*Nicomachean Ethics*, 1153b19). Nevertheless, as we have just seen, Aristotle did postulate virtue as a necessary if not a sufficient condition for happiness. Bertrand Russell (1945, 1950), for one, scorned even this more modest proposal. Making virtue a necessary condition for happiness, Russell asserted, "appeals to the respectable middle-aged, and has been used by them . . . to repress the ardours and enthusiasms of the young" (1945, p. 173). Russell would link happiness primarily to psychological systems of behavior.

Psychological systems are patterns of behavior that help preserve and enhance a person's self (as opposed to the species or society). The self is here conceived of as a set of concepts or propositions about who one is as an individual and one's relation to the world. Although the roots of the self are to be found in our biological and social heritage, promotion of the self often comes into conflict with biological and social needs. Thus the martyr may sacrifice health and even life to preserve a sense of self, and the rebel may reject social values in favor of self-determined norms. Given the appropriate circumstances, we are all martyrs or rebels to some degree, for neither biological constraints nor social practices fully determine our behavior.

Five Perennial Issues

The above observations on the relation of happiness to systems of behavior allow us to address five issues that have been traditional subjects of debate (cf. Strasser, 1977; Tatarkiewicz, 1976).

First, is happiness an end in itself or a characteristic of behavior pursued for other ends? For example, do people engage in activities in order to be happy, or are people happy because they engage in activities that successfully lead to goals other than happiness (fame, fortune, or whatever)? In a classic paper, Duncker (1941) explored both sides of this issue in great detail, at least for elementary pleasures. Our own position follows from the proposition that happiness is associated with properly functioning behavioral systems. People do seek happiness, but not necessarily for its own sake. From a systems point of view, happiness is a characteristic of meaningful activities well performed. These activities differ from one species to another, from one society to another, and from one individual to another; however, if the proper goal or function of an activity is eliminated, the associated happiness soon becomes vacuous.

Second, does happiness consists of the sum of momentary pleasures (a bottom-up approach), or do pleasures contribute to happiness only when informed by higher-order principles (a top-down approach)? From a systems perspective, this is a pseudoissue, for both bottom-up and top-down approaches are legitimate and necessary when analysis involves a hierarchy. To proceed from the bottom up, happiness at the most elementary level is related to responses typically associated with simple sensory pleasures, such as smiling and laughing. (We ignore for the moment the possibility that happiness may include unpleasurable as well as pleasurable activities.) At a slightly more complex level, we may speak of particular but relatively short-term joys and contentments (associated, for example, with reading a good book). These, in turn, may be integrated into more enduring states of happiness (e.g., with respect to work or family). A life without its share of elementary pleasures could hardly be regarded as happy. But, conversely, to constitute happiness, responses that yield momentary pleasures must be subsumed within broader systems of behavior. That is, an adequate analysis of happiness must also proceed from the top down. A similar point has been made by Skinner (1986), albeit not with reference to happiness, per se, but to the role of positive reinforcement in the acquisition and maintenance of behavior. Divorced from meaningful behavior, many reinforcers are now used for the pleasures they afford; however, like junk food, they titillate the senses without providing real nourishment.

Third, is happiness necessarily related to values? As described earlier, happiness is centrally related to social systems of behavior and the values embodied in those systems. But biological systems and their associated strivings also contribute to happiness, as do psychological systems. The relative importance of biological, social, and psychological principles may vary, depending on the person and situation. For the hedonist, biological principles may predominate; for the saint or patriot, social principles; and for an individualist, psychological

principles. In general, however, social principles are the most fundamental. Human beings are born relatively "world-open," with few highly developed biological instincts. Society provides a second nature that, in actuality, becomes our first (Averill, 1980, 1997). The individualist pursuing self-fulfillment may reject some of society's values in favor of others, but only sociopaths subordinate all social values to their own biological and psychological needs. Indeed, individualism is itself a value, encouraged by some societies more than others.

In his book *Happy People*, Freedman (1978) recounts the difficulty his research assistant had when interviewing people with respect to happiness. When interviewed in groups, people joked and trivialized the topic; when interviewed in private, they grew serious but stopped talking. The research assistant concluded that it would be easier to ask people about the intimate details of their sex lives than about what makes them happy. Why might this be so? The answer, we believe, lies in the fact that happiness touches upon our deepest strivings, our goals, our ideals, and our competencies. These are not easy to articulate, and even if they were, most people would not feel comfortable discussing them with a stranger.

Fourth, does happiness consists of equanimity, or does it necessarily involve some conflict and struggle? Earlier, we have distinguished happiness in the sense of eudaemonia from happiness in the sense of equanimity (see Table 42.1). The relation of happiness to behavioral systems helps clarify this distinction. Optimizing one system of behavior (biological, social, or psychological) typically involves sacrificing others. Society restricts our biological propensities, and what is most fulfilling from an individual (psychological) perspective may be counter to the common good, whether biological or social. Even within a system hierarchy (the psychological, say), conflict is often unavoidable; a person cannot, for example, pursue two incompatible goals at once. Ultimately, happiness requires compromise among competing demands and hence cannot be equated with equanimity, which connotes a state of minimal desires. Optimal functioning, by contrast, implies an active and often conflictive engagement in the world. To paraphrase H. L. Mencken (1930), if we take equanimity as an ideal, then a hog is happier than a human, and a bacillus is happier than a hog.

Finally, are there absolute standards for hap-

piness, or is happiness relative to the person and situation? A slave could not be happy, Aristotle maintained, for a slave could never achieve his or her potentials as a rational, fully functioning human being; neither, presumably, could a person who is physically or mentally handicapped. There are good reasons for rejecting Aristotle's absolute standard (see Kraut, 1979). Unfortunately, most current investigators go to the opposite extreme, allowing each person to define happiness in his or her own terms. If people say they are happy, the reasoning goes, then presumably they are happy, whatever that might mean. As Grichting (1983) put it, "We are not prepared to second-guess our subjects as to what they mean by happiness" (p. 247). From a systems perspective, happiness can be relative, but relativity does not necessarily imply subjectivity, as the quotation by Grichting might suggest. Individuals differ in their capacities, and environmental constraints limit accomplishments. Therefore, when we speak of the proper or optimal functioning of behavioral systems, we mean in relation to a person's capacities and situation, which provide an objective context for evaluating happiness. What is optimal for one person, and hence conducive to happiness, need not be optimal for another.

Further Observations on Systems Approaches to Happiness

To summarize briefly, we may define happiness (eudaemonia) in terms of the proper or optimal functioning of behavioral systems, relative to a person's capacities and situation. In this definition, the term "optimal" requires qualification. Due to limited cognitive capacities and an overabundance of potentially relevant information, optimal functioning is a theoretical ideal that can seldom be achieved in practice. Happiness, like rationality, is necessarily "bounded" (cf. Simon, 1990).

A definition of happiness in terms of optimal functioning does not exclude subjective feelings as one manifestation. However, we question the almost exclusive reliance of current research on measures of subjective experience. To a certain extent, such reliance reflects what Natsoulas (1991) has called a "preference for scientific action at the expense of scientific thought" (p. 342). By permitting participants in a study to define happiness in their own terms, the investigator can get on with the business of

research—for example, exploring the psychological and social correlates of avowed happiness. Theoretical questions concerning the nature of happiness per se are thus set aside, or even dismissed as meaningless.

We do not deny the importance of avowed (subjective) happiness, both as a phenomenon in its own right and as a potential indicator of objective happiness. Ultimately, however, happiness can only be understood within a broader theoretical framework, such as the systems approach presented here. This is not to imply that the present division of behavioral systems according to biological, social, and psychological principles of organization is the only one possible (see Power & Dalgleish, 1997, for a more cognitively oriented approach). But all system approaches have certain features in common: namely, a definition of behavior (including cognitive activity) in terms of goals or outcomes; a recognition that behavior is both hierarchically and heterarchically organized; and a conception of happiness in terms of optimal functioning.

HAPPINESS IN RELATION TO MEDIATING MECHANISMS

A major point we wish to make in this chapter is the importance of distinguishing between systems of behavior and mediating mechanisms. A systems approach to happiness concerns the origins and functions of behavior; a mechanistic approach, by contrast, concerns the inner workings that make behavior possible. Any one system of behavior may involve a variety of mediating mechanisms and, conversely, any one mediating mechanism, may enter into a variety of behavioral systems.

In one sense, analyses in terms of behavioral systems and mediating mechanisms represent little more than a convenient division of labor. Both approaches are important and necessary (Averill, 1992). However, simply to leave the matter at that risks blurring an important fact: Current theory and research are heavily biased in favor of mechanistic explanations.

An emphasis on mechanism over function began with the Scientific Revolution of the 16th and 17th centuries. If Aristotle promoted the earlier "nonscientific" view, the British empiricist Locke presaged the modern "scientific" approach, at least as far as happiness is concerned. For Locke, happiness can be reduced to a mechanical combination of pleasures, and maximal happiness is the greatest quantity of pleasure a person is capable of experiencing over time. Gone is the Aristotelian emphasis on happiness in relation to "proper function," and on behavior interpreted in terms of ends (*telos*).

Mediating mechanisms, like behavioral systems, can be analyzed from biological, social, and psychological perspectives, and we continue our analysis along those lines. In addition, mechanisms can be either intrinsic or extrinsic. "Intrinsic" mechanisms are activated as part of a prevailing system of behavior; "extrinsic" mechanisms are activated regardless of their relation to ongoing behavior.

Biological Mechanisms

Biological mediating mechanisms consist of physiological and cognitive processes, to the extent that their operation is under genetic influence. The biological mechanisms for happiness include, among other things, pleasure centers of the brain; specialized circuitry in the left frontal lobes (which appear to be involved in positive emotional experiences); endorphins and other naturally occurring opioids; and the like. Such physiological mechanisms are discussed in detail in Section II of this handbook (especially Chapters 9–11). We do not consider them further here, except to reiterate a point made earlier: To produce happiness and not just momentary pleasures, the activation of physiological mechanisms must be associated with meaningful patterns of response (systems of behavior). When activated extrinsically (e.g., by means of drugs), the net result is often a vague sense of dissatisfaction, no matter how pleasurable the immediate experience.

Social Mechanisms

Analogous to biological mechanisms, we could define social mechanisms as physiological and cognitive processes, to the extent that they are influenced by socialization. For our present purposes, however, it is more convenient to shift focus from processes internal to the individual to processes that exist "out there" in society. Specifically, we define social mediating mechanisms as the organizations—public and private, formal and informal—that help make a society "run." Intrinsic social mechanisms foster engagement in systems of behavior

(whether biological, psychological, or social); extrinsic social mechanisms provide goods and services independently of a person's behavior.

In the United States, a small body of law has grown up around the notion, written into the Declaration of Independence and adopted by some state constitutions, that the pursuit of happiness is an "unalienable right" (Jones, 1953). Not everyone agrees with this sentiment. C. S. Lewis, in an article published in *The Saturday Evening Post* (1963/1982), asserted that "a right to happiness doesn't, for me, make much more sense than a right to be six feet tall, or to have a millionaire for your father, or to get good weather whenever you might want to have a picnic" (p. 42). Lewis was particularly concerned about the way licentiousness, greed, and selfishness are sometimes justified in the name of happiness. By contrast, Murray (1988) argues that the primary purpose of government is in fact to enable its citizens to pursue happiness.

In part, the difference between Lewis and Murray is based on their conceptions of happiness, and particularly on the subjective–objective dimension discussed earlier (see Table 42.1). For Lewis, happiness is little more than feeling good, to which no one has an unalienable right. For Murray, happiness is an objective state, the highest good; and anyone who confuses licentiousness, say, with the highest good simply does not know the meaning of happiness. But the difference between Lewis and Murray also has to do with the kinds of social mechanisms they oppose or advocate. The kinds of mechanisms mentioned by Lewis (e.g., having a millionaire for a father) are primarily extrinsic; the kinds favored by Murray are primarily intrinsic.

Adopting an explicitly Aristotelian stance, Murray (1988) argues that social policy should nurture associations ("little platoons") among individuals. The most vital of these little platoons center around the family, neighborhood, and workplace. Even the least talented among us can be a good parent, neighbor, and worker. And, as ample empirical research attests, it is primarily with respect to family, friends, and work that happiness is in fact achieved (Argyle, 1987; Bradburn, 1969; Campbell, Converse, & Rodgers, 1978; Veenhoven, 1984). The catch, according to Murray, is that to afford happiness, group endeavors must be meaningful; they must require some effort; and group members must feel responsible for their own success and failures. If government eliminates any of these requirements (e.g., through the establishment of an impersonal bureaucracy), opportunities for happiness are correspondingly diminished.

Murray's "little platoons" can be considered intrinsic social mechanisms, in that they facilitate systems of behavior as defined earlier in this chapter. Extrinsic social mechanisms, by contrast, provide goods and services without regard to an individual's own performance. State-supported lotteries provide a good example of an almost purely extrinsic social mechanism. Contrary to what might be expected, winning a large amount of money in a lottery has little enduring influence on self-reported happiness (Brickman, Coates, & Janoff-Bulman, 1978). This should come as no surprise. Unless winners use their newfound wealth to pursue activities that are intrinsically more rewarding than prior activities, there should be no long-term increase in happiness.

Similar considerations apply to other governmental programs (e.g., welfare, unemployment compensation) in which recipients are unable to take credit for the benefits they receive. Most such programs are designed as short-term measures to alleviate temporary hardships over which an individual has little control. Like winning a lottery, they cannot provide long-term happiness. From an economic standpoint, unemployment—even more than loss of income—appears to be the primary source of unhappiness (Oswald, 1997). This is entirely consistent with our perspective. Unemployment signals a person that his or her work no longer has meaning. Unemployment may also preclude participation in other meaningful activities, and it may force dependence on the kinds of extrinsic social mechanisms described above.

More permanent extrinsic mechanisms can be found in most societies, such as inherited wealth, aristocracies, and caste systems. Questions of fairness aside, these can create as many problems as they solve, because of the unfavorable social comparisons they may produce. Moreover, with the exception of the extremes of poverty and privation, socioeconomic variables such as income, housing, and the like, show little relationship to avowed happiness (Myers & Diener, 1996). As long as we deal with extrinsic social mechanisms, the pursuit of happiness may be, as Brickman and

Campbell (1971) suggest, a task to rival that of Sisyphus.

Most social organizations can be either intrinsic or extrinsic, depending on the circumstances and the attitudes of the individuals involved. This is perhaps most evident with respect to work. For many people, work occupies such a central position in their lives that it is critical to their happiness. To the extent that a job is intrinsically rewarding, it facilitates happiness. But many jobs are undertaken primarily for the money they provide—an extrinsic reward. To make matters worse, we sometimes label certain jobs as "dead-end," thus implying that they have no intrinsic value. But as Csikszentmihalyi (1991) has documented, some people have the ability to turn even the most routine tasks into challenging occupations, thus deriving intrinsic rewards from their efforts.

When work is unfulfilling, for whatever reason, many people look to leisure to find opportunities for self-expression. In addition to government organizations, such as public parks, libraries, and museums, a multibillion-dollar industry has arisen in the private sector to meet the needs for leisure: hobby shops, gambling casinos, movie theaters, amusement parks, and private hunting clubs are only a few examples. Like the workplace, organizations that facilitate leisure activities can be either intrinsic or extrinsic, depending on the type of behavior they encourage. For example, organizations that support hobbies are intrinsic, to the extent that they offer challenges that contribute to individual growth. By contrast, much of the entertainment industry can be classified as extrinsic: Passively watching television, for example, often fails to engage the individual in meaningful thought or activity, no matter how enjoyable the immediate experience.

Volunteer and philanthropic organizations also deserve brief comment. These can be distinguished from work in that they are "not for profit," and from leisure in that they are "not for fun." Previously, we have argued that the exercise of moral values is a key component of social systems of behavior and hence of happiness. For many people, volunteer organizations provide the main opportunity for virtuous expression. Visiting hospitals, aiding the poor, leading youth groups, serving on boards and advisory committees, donating time and expertise to charitable and civic organizations, participating in food co-ops—such activities contribute to happiness in significant ways, for they allow people to be good, not just look (or feel) good.

Psychological Mechanisms

From a logical analysis of the concept of happiness, Kekes (1982) has concluded that "a man is extremely unlikely to have a happy life without having a more or less clearly formed view about what his life should be" (p. 361). In line with Kekes' analysis, we define intrinsic psychological mechanisms as those processes that facilitate a person's long-range goals, and extrinsic mechanisms as those processes that are irrelevant to a person's goals or that subserve "ulterior" motives.

The three most important intrinsic mechanisms for happiness are (1) the setting of challenging but realistic goals, (2) belief in one's ability to achieve desired goals, and (3) adequate feedback about progress. Each of these has been the object of considerable research (Locke & Latham, 1990; Bandura, 1997), but only the first two have been directly related to happiness. (The relevance of the third, appropriate feedback, is intuitively obvious.)

With regard to goal setting, ample psychological research supports the notion that purpose and direction are fundamental to happiness (e.g., Emmons, 1996; Lazarus, 1991; Ryff, 1989). This is true even of young children, whose goals tend to be relatively simple, like playing with a new toy (Stein, Trabasso, & Liwag, Chapter 28, this volume). Goal-setting strategies are also important components of many happiness enhancement programs (e.g., Fordyce, 1981). One commonly advised strategy is to lower aspirations and to focus on short-term rather than on long-term goals. For many people, the advice is not unreasonable, for they are so fixated on grandiose future goals that they are unable to enjoy the present. However, the strategy has obvious limitations: Lowered aspirations and short-range goals can lead to an impoverished sense of what life should be. Pleasure without purpose is no prescription for happiness.

With regard to self-efficacy beliefs, people who lack confidence in their ability to achieve goals are unlikely to undertake challenging activities. Not surprisingly, therefore, both a belief in personal control over outcomes and the degree of perceived choice in one's life are positively related to both physical and psychological well-being (e.g., Abbey & Andrews, 1986; Deci & Ryan, 1985; Thompson, Armstrong, & Thomas, 1998).

Most recent research on happiness has concerned extrinsic rather than intrinsic psychological mechanisms (although, as stated earlier, the dividing line between intrinsic and extrinsic mechanisms is not absolute, but depends on the context). We refer in particular to the set of mechanisms encompassed by "gap theories" (e.g., Michalos, 1986; Parducci, 1995; Smith, Diener, & Wedell, 1989; Wills, 1981). According to gap theories, people judge their own happiness by comparing their actual condition or performance against some standard. If the comparison is favorable, happiness is facilitated; if it is unfavorable, happiness is impaired. Such mechanisms are "extrinsic" when the comparison is made for reasons unrelated to the behavior being evaluated (as when a person does not judge his or her performance on its merits, but simply compares it to the performance of another in order to look good).

Michalos (1985, 1986) has described six different gap theories, which address the discrepancies between (1) what one wants and what one has, (2) actual conditions and best past conditions, (3) what one has and what others have, (4) actual and ideal conditions, (5) actual conditions and expectations, and (6) a personal attribute and an environmental attribute. In one study, Michalos found that the first three of these gap-theoretic variables accounted for 38% of the variance in self-reported happiness with life as a whole. Sociodemographic variables (age, sex, housing, health, etc.) had little explanatory power over and beyond these three variables. After reviewing 41 other studies that tested gap-theoretic hypotheses, 90% of which were successful, Michalos (1986) concluded that "even a cautious reading of the evidence indicates that we are on the right track with such theories" (p. 72).

There are, however, three main problems with gap-theoretic explanations of happiness. First, gap-theoretic variables, by themselves, have little explanatory power. Downward social comparison offers an example: Why should personal satisfaction be increased by a favorable contrast between oneself and others who are less fortunate? The following are only three possibilities: (1) The comparison may focus attention on one's own good fortune; (2) the comparison may mitigate negative emotions, such as envy, anger, and frustration; and (3) to the extent that the discrepancy is perceived as deserved, the comparison may increase self-esteem. In short, on further analysis, gap-theoretic variables may be reduced to non-gap mechanisms.

Second, as the number of relevant gaps increases (cf. the six mentioned by Michalos), the possible combinations and interactions among them become unmanageable. To take only one possible interaction as an example, the gap between what one wants and what one has may be either exacerbated or mitigated by the gap between what one has and what others have. If progress is to be made, it seems that reduction to more fundamental mechanisms is not only desirable but necessary.

Third, gap-theoretic variables represent only one class of mechanism that might account for differences in happiness. Simple sensory pleasures, for example, do not always presume the existence of some prior discrepancy. The same is true of more complex constituents of happiness—for example, enjoying the company of others, taking pride in a job well done, and so forth. These reflect mechanisms that are intrinsic to the proper functioning of systems of behavior.

In short, gap theories tend to focus attention away from intrinsic sources of happiness and onto extrinsic mechanisms. Despite Michalos's (1986) optimism, a broader theoretical base than that provided by gap theories is necessary for an understanding of happiness.

Further Observations on Mediating Mechanisms

We have distinguished among biological, social, and psychological mediating mechanisms primarily as a way to organize discussion. Of greater importance from a theoretical perspective is the distinction between intrinsic and extrinsic mechanisms. This distinction is not absolute, but is relative to systems of behavior; nevertheless, if it is ignored, any relation between happiness and presumed mediators will necessarily be weak.

HAPPINESS IN RELATION TO PERSONALITY CHARACTERISTICS

People differ in their capacities for happiness. This brings us to a third major body of research—namely, the relation of happiness to personality characteristics. But before we get to that, a point needs clarification: Happiness itself is sometimes treated as a personality trait (i.e., as a stable predisposition to feel good about oneself and one's place in the world). Moreover, studies on fraternal and identical twins suggest that genetic factors may account for 80% of the variance in this predisposition (Lykken & Tellegen, 1996). Does this mean that some people—the majority, in fact—are destined to be happy regardless of circumstances, whereas others are condemned to a life of gloom? That would be an inappropriate conclusion. For one thing, the 80% heritability figure refers to a *stable* predisposition rather than to episodic states, such as joy and eudaemonia. The latter are determined by situational as well as personal factors. For another thing, it is important to keep in mind the distinction between subjective and objective conceptions of happiness (e.g., joy vs. eudaemonia). There is wisdom to the ancient adage "Count no man happy until he is dead," for only then can a life's fortunes be assessed objectively and in their totality.

Be that as it may, a predisposition to feel good is a rather specific trait. Can happiness be related to more broadly defined characteristics, that is, to traits that do not themselves refer specifically to happiness or subjective well-being?

Recent research suggests that five broad traits are sufficient to characterize much of personality: introversion–extraversion, emotional stability (typically referred to in terms of its opposite pole, neuroticism), openness to experience, agreeableness, and conscientiousness (Digman, 1990; McCrae, 1992; Wiggens & Trapnell, 1997). People who score high on extraversion and emotional stability tend to report greater happiness (Costa & McCrae, 1980; David, Green, Martin, & Suls, 1997; Emmons & Diener, 1985; Larsen & Ketelaar, 1989). Openness to experience, the third of the "Big Five" traits, seems related to the intensity of emotional reactions, both positive and negative, and is relatively independent of avowed happiness (Costa & McCrae, 1984; McCrae & Costa, 1991). Agreeableness (the fourth dimension) and conscientiousness (the fifth dimension) also make independent contributions to self-reported happiness, over and above the contributions made by the other three dimensions. Among 429 adults, McCrae and Costa (1991) found that the five factors together accounted for 19% to 25% of the variance in self-reported happiness, depending on whether the personality ratings were made by the subjects themselves or by their spouses.

The relation between personality and happiness depends in part on how happiness is assessed (DeNeve & Cooper, 1998). For example, happiness as measured by life-satisfaction scales is more closely related to conscientiousness and associated characteristics (e.g., ambition, resourcefulness, perseverance, orderliness), whereas happiness as measured by the amount of positive affect experienced, such as joy, is more closely related to extraversion and associated characteristics (e.g., sociability, enthusiasm, daring, sensation seeking).

Earlier, we have distinguished among four concepts of happiness: eudaemonia, joy, contentment, and equanimity. There is some conceptual and empirical overlap between these concepts and four of the Big Five personality traits (conscientiousness, extraversion, agreeableness, and emotional stability). The overlap is most evident in the case of eudaemonia and conscientiousness. Conscientious people tend to set high goals for themselves, and they strive to achieve those goals (Barrick, Mount, & Strauss, 1993). Eudaemonia, conceived as the proper (optimal) functioning of behavioral systems, also implies high achievement and the satisfaction that comes with it. As noted above, conscientiousness is more closely related to reports of life satisfaction than to other measures of happiness.

Of the other three concepts of happiness, joy is both conceptually and empirically related to extraversion (DeNeve & Cooper, 1998). At the present time, however, the rationale for the proposed relations between contentment and agreeableness, and between equanimity and emotional stability, is almost entirely conceptual. Agreeable persons are characterized as good-natured, tolerant, warm-hearted, and forgiving; hence they should also lead more contented lives. Similarly, people who are emotionally stable (hardy, clear-thinking, secure, composed under stress) should be better able to face life's vicissitudes with equanimity. In empirical research, unfortunately, contentment and equanimity have seldom been assessed independently from each other, or from joy and eudaemonia.

Before we leave this topic, two points deserve brief emphasis. First, the patterns of relations described above are relative, not absolute. For example, extraversion is related to eudaemonia as well as to joy, but to a lesser degree than is conscientiousness (DeNeve & Cooper, 1998). Second, regardless of how happiness is conceived, the Big Five personality factors together account for less than 25% of the variance in self-reported happiness (McCrae & Costa, 1991). This leaves considerable variance to be accounted for.

Of course, happiness has been related to personality characteristics other than the Big Five, but simply adding traits to the equation does little to solve the problem. (For detailed reviews of relevant research, see Argyle, 1987; DeNeve & Cooper, 1998; Diener, 1984; Veenhoven, 1984). Rather, we must approach the issue from a different perspective: namely, by examining the ways by which a personality trait—any trait—might be related to happiness. Two general approaches are possible, one in terms of mediating mechanisms and the other in terms of behavioral systems.

With regard to the first approach, the same or similar mechanisms may mediate both a particular personality characteristic and happiness, thus accounting for the relation between the two. For example, extraverts may be inherently less sensitive to punishment or aversive stimulation (a biological mechanism); they may be more engaged in convivial activities (a social mechanism); or they may be more prone to make favorable comparisons between themselves and others (a psychological mechanism). These examples are hypothetical, although not without empirical support (see David et al., 1997; Emmons & Diener, 1986; Headey & Wearing, 1989; Hotard, McFatter, McWhirter, & Stegall, 1989; Larsen & Ketelaar, 1989). At the present time, however, the actual mechanisms that help mediate the observed relation between extraversion (or any other personality trait) and happiness are little understood, and indeed may differ depending on how happiness is conceived—for example, as joy or eudaemonia.

The second general approach to understanding the relation between personality and happiness focuses on systems of behavior, as opposed to mediating mechanisms. This approach is most relevant to happiness conceived as eudaemonia.

A score on a personality test reflects the frequency with which a person engages in certain types of behavior (cf. Buss & Craik, 1984). Behavioral systems, too, comprise component responses (see Figure 42.1). Hence, one way of interpreting a personality trait is in terms of the behavioral systems and component responses that are most representative of the trait. Eudaemonia, we have suggested, is associated with the proper functioning of behavioral systems. Therefore, we would expect a relation between a personality trait and happiness to the extent that the behaviors representative of the trait are given optimal expression. We would also expect that behaviors optimal for one individual may not be optimal for another, depending on their respective traits.

The above considerations may be phrased somewhat differently. A personality trait represents the ability or capacity of a person to engage in certain kinds of behavior (Wallace, 1966; Willerman, Turner, & Peterson, 1976). For example, extraverts are typically more adroit in social situations than are introverts, whereas introverts have a greater capacity for solitary activities than do extraverts. To the extent that individuals differ in their capacities to act in characteristic ways, it makes little sense to ask whether extraverts, say, are happier than introverts in an absolute sense, and if so, by what mechanism. The more relevant question is this: What behavioral systems are most characteristic of extraversion, and under what conditions do they find proper expression? Similar considerations apply to the other personality traits, such as conscientiousness, agreeableness, and emotional stability, each of which reflects a different combination of strengths and weaknesses, and hence a different way of achieving happiness (cf. Schmutte & Ryff, 1997).

In short, there may be no set or absolute connection between broadly defined personality characteristics and happiness. This does not mean that personality research is irrelevant to an understanding of happiness. On the contrary, such research is necessary if we are to temper the presumed relation between happiness and behavioral systems to fit the individual case.

CONCLUDING OBSERVATIONS

Discussing happiness in a brief chapter is a formidable task, for no other topic has been the subject of more debate and controversy over the centuries. We have reduced the task by focusing primarily on one concept of happiness—namely, eudaemonia. We have also outlined three approaches to the study of happiness (systems of behavior, mediating

mechanisms, and personality characteristics), and within that framework, we have attempted to illustrate how some traditional issues concerning happiness are amenable to empirical research and resolution. Other approaches to the study of happiness are possible. For example, considerable recent research has been devoted to the effects, as opposed to the causes and correlates, of happiness (e.g., the effects of positive mood on recall and creative problem solving). We cannot review that research here (see Isen, Chapter 27, this volume; Schwarz & Bless, 1991). We therefore conclude this chapter with one final observation. Is happiness the ultimate good, as so often claimed? Our conception of happiness in terms of the proper or optimal functioning of behavioral systems would seem to imply a positive answer. What could be better than optimal functioning? Life, however, is a compromise. Optimal functioning is a theoretical ideal that can seldom be realized in practice; and even if the ideal could be realized, optimizing one function would still entail sacrifices in others. Even theoretically, then, happiness can never be complete, except for fleeting moments before balance must be restored. And perhaps that is for the best: "But a lifetime of happiness! No man alive could bear it: it would be hell on earth" (Shaw, 1905/1963, p. 527).

ACKNOWLEDGMENTS

Preparation of this chapter was supported in part by Grant No. 23-133 from the Forest Service, U.S. Department of Agriculture. Any opinions, findings, and conclusions expressed are our own and do not necessarily reflect the views of the granting agency. Thanks are due Carol Thomas-Knowles for her assistance in reviewing the literature on happiness.

REFERENCES

Abbey, A., & Andrews, F. M. (1986). Modeling the psychological determinants of life quality. In F. M. Andrews (Ed.), *Research on the quality of life* (pp. 85–116). Ann Arbor: University of Michigan, Institute for Social Research.

Andrews, F. M., & Robinson, J. P. (1991). Measures of subjective well-being. In J. P. Robinson, P. R. Shaver, & L. W. Wrightsman (Eds.), *Measures of personality and social psychological attitudes* (pp. 61–114). New York: Academic Press.

Argyle, M. (1987). *The psychology of happiness*. London: Methuen.

Aristotle. (1984a). *Nicomachean ethics* (W. D. Ross, Trans., revised by J. O. Urmson). In J. Barnes (Ed.), *The complete works of Aristotle. Vol. 2* (pp. 1729–1867). Princeton, NJ: Princeton University Press. (Original work written ca. 330 B.C.)

Aristotle. (1984b). *Politics* (B. Jowett, Trans.). In J. Barnes (Ed.), *The complete works of Aristotle. Vol. 2* (pp. 1986–2129). Princeton, NJ: Princeton University Press.

Averill, J. R. (1975). A semantic atlas of emotional concepts. *JSAS: Catalog of Selected Documents in Psychology, 5,* 330. (Ms. No. 1103)

Averill, J. R. (1980). A constructivist view of emotion. In R. Plutchik & H. Kellerman (Eds.), *Emotion: Theory, research and experience: Vol. 1. Theories of emotion* (pp. 305339). New York: Academic Press.

Averill, J. R. (1990). Emotions as related to systems of behavior. In N. L. Stein, B. Leventhal, & T. Trabasso (Eds.), *Psychological and biological approaches to emotion* (pp. 385–404). Hillsdale, NJ: Erlbaum.

Averill, J. R. (1992). The structural bases of emotional behavior: A metatheoretical analysis. In M. S. Clark (Ed.), *Review of personality and social psychology* (Vol. 13, pp. 1–24). Newbury Park, CA: Sage.

Averill, J. R. (1994). I feel, therefore I am—I think. In P. Ekman & R. J. Davidson (Eds.), *The nature of emotion: Fundamental questions* (pp. 379–385). New York: Oxford University Press.

Averill, J. R. (1997). The emotions: An integrative approach. In R. Hogan & J. A. Johnson (Eds.), *Handbook of personality psychology* (pp. 513–541). San Diego, CA: Academic Press.

Bandura, A. (1997). *Self-efficacy: The exercise of control.* New York: Freeman.

Barrick, M. R., Mount, M. K., & Strauss, J. P. (1993). Conscientiousness and performance of sales representatives: Test of the mediating effects of goal setting. *Journal of Applied Psychology, 78,* 715–722.

Bowlby, J. (1982). *Attachment and loss. Vol.1. Attachment* (2nd ed). New York: Basic Books.

Bradburn, N. M. (1969). *The structure of psychological well-being.* Chicago: Aldine.

Brickman, P., & Campbell, D. T. (1971). Hedonic relativism and planning the good society. In M. H. Appley (Ed.), *Adaptation-level theory* (pp. 287–302). New York: Academic Press.

Brickman, P., Coates, D., & Janoff-Bulman, R. (1978). Lottery winners and accident victims: Is happiness relative? *Journal of Personality and Social Psychology, 36,* 917–927.

Buss, D. M., & Craik, K. H. (1984). Acts, dispositions, and personality. In B. A. Maher & W. B. Maher (Eds.), *Progress in experimental personality research* (Vol. 13, pp. 241–301). Orlando, FL: Academic Press.

Campbell, A., Converse, P. E., & Rodgers, W. L. (1976). *The quality of American life: Perceptions, evaluations, and satisfactions.* New York: Russell Sage Foundation.

Costa, P. T., Jr., & McCrae, R. R. (1980). Influence of extraversion and neuroticism on subjective well-being: Happy and unhappy people. *Journal of Personality and Social Psychology, 38,* 668–678.

Costa, P. T., Jr., & McCrae, R. R. (1984). Personality as a lifelong determinant of well-being. In C. Malatesta & C. Izard (Eds.), *Affective processes in adult development and aging* (pp. 141–157). Beverly Hills, CA: Sage.

Csikszentmihalyi, M. (1991). *Flow: The psychology of optimal experience.* New York: HarperCollins.

David, J. P., Green, P. J., Martin, R., & Suls, J. (1997). Differential roles of neuroticism, extraversion, and event desirability for mood in daily life: An integrative model of top-down and bottom-up influences. *Journal of Personality and Social Psychology, 73,* 149–159.

Deci, E. L., & Ryan, R. M. (1985). *Intrinsic motivation and self-determination.* New York: Plenum Press.

DeNeve, K. M., & Cooper, H. (1998). The happy personality: A meta-analysis of 137 personality traits and subjective well-being. *Psychological Bulletin, 124,* 197–229.

Diener, E. (1984). Subjective well-being. *Psychological Bulletin, 95,* 542–575.

Digman, J. M. (1990). Personality structure: Emergence of the five-factor model. *Annual Review of Psychology, 41,* 417–440.

Duncker, K. (1941). On pleasure, emotion, and striving. *Philosophy and Phenomenological Research, 1,* 391–430.

Emmons, R. A. (1996). Striving and feeling: Personal goals and subjective well-being. In P. M. Gollwitzer & J. A. Bargh (Eds.), *The psychology of action: Linking cognition and motivation to behavior* (pp. 313–337). New York: Guilford Press.

Emmons, R. A., & Diener, E. (1985). Personality correlates of subjective well-being. *Personality and Social Psychology Bulletin, 11,* 89–97.

Emmons, R. A., & Diener, E. (1986). Influence of impulsivity and sociability on subjective well-being. *Journal of Personality and Social Psychology, 50,* 1211–1215.

Fehr, B., & Russell, J. A. (1984). Concept of emotion viewed from a prototype perspective. *Journal of Experimental Psychology: General, 113*(3), 464–486.

Fordyce, M. W. (1981). *The psychology of happiness.* Fort Myers, FL: Cypress Lake Media.

Freedman, J. L. (1978). *Happy people.* New York: Harcourt Brace Jovanovich.

Grichting, W. L. (1983). Domain, scope and degree of happiness. *British Journal of Social Psychology, 22,* 247–260.

Headey, B., & Wearing, A. (1989). Personality, life events, and subjective well-being: Toward a dynamic equilibrium model. *Journal of Personality and Social Psychology, 57,* 731–739.

Horace. (1966). *Satires, epistles, ars poetica* (H. R. Fairclough, Trans.). Cambridge, MA: Harvard University Press.

Hotard, S. R., McFatter, R. M., McWhirter, R. M., & Stegall, M. E. (1989). Interactive effects of extraversion, neuroticism, and social relationships on subjective well-being. *Journal of Personality and Social Psychology, 57,* 321–331.

Jones, H. M. (1953). *The pursuit of happiness.* Cambridge, MA: Harvard University Press.

Kekes, J. (1982). Happiness. *Mind, 91*, 358–376.

Kraut, R. (1979). Two conceptions of happiness. *Philosophical Review, 88*, 167–197.

Larsen, R. J., & Ketelaar, T. (1989). Extraversion, neuroticism, and susceptibility to positive and negative mood induction procedures. *Personality and Individual Differences, 10*, 1221–1228.

Lazarus, R. S. (1991). *Emotion and adaptation.* New York: Oxford University Press.

Lewis, C. S. (1982, April). We have no right to happiness. *The Saturday Evening Post*, pp. 42–44. (Original work published 1963)

Locke, E. A., & Latham, G. P. (1990). *A theory of goal setting and task performance.* Englewood Cliffs, NJ: Prentice-Hall.

Lorenz, K. (1971). Part and parcel in animal and human societies (R. Martin, Trans.). In K. Lorenz, *Studies in animal and human behavior* (Vol. 2, pp. 115–195). Cambridge, MA: Harvard University Press.

Lykken, D., & Tellegen, A. (1996). Happiness is a stochastic phenomenon. *Psychological Science, 7*, 186–189.

Maslow, A. H. (1962). Lessons from the peak experiences. *Journal of Humanistic Psychology, 2*, 9–18.

McCrae, R. R. (Ed.) (1992). The five-factor model: Issues and application [Special issue]. *Journal of Personality, 60*(2).

McCrae, R. R., & Costa, P. T., Jr. (1991). Adding *Liebe und Arbeit*: The full five-factor model and well-being. *Personality and Social Psychology Bulletin, 17*, 227–232.

Mencken, H. L. (1930). Editorial: Comfort for the ailing. *American Mercury, 19*, 288–289.

Michalos, A. C. (1985). Multiple discrepancies theory (MDT). *Social Indicators Research, 16*, 347–413.

Michalos, A. C. (1986). Job satisfaction, marital satisfaction, and the quality of life. In F. M. Andrews (Ed.), *Research on the quality of life* (pp. 57–84). Ann Arbor: University of Michigan, Institute for Social Research.

Murray, C. (1988). *In pursuit of happiness and good government.* New York: Simon & Schuster.

Myers, D. G., & Diener, D. (1996). Who is happy? *Psychological Science, 6*, 10–19.

Natsoulas, T. (1991). The concept of consciousness$_2$: The personal meaning. *Journal for the Theory of Social Behaviour, 21*, 339–367.

Novak, M. A., & Suomi, S. J. (1988). Psychological well-being of primates in captivity. *American Psychologist, 43*, 765–773.

Nozick, R. (1989). *The examined life.* New York: Simon & Schuster.

Oswald, A. J. (1997). Happiness and economic performance. *Economic Journal, 107*, 1815–1831.

Parducci, A. (1995). *Happiness, pleasure, and judgment: The contextual theory and its applications.* Mahwah, NJ: Erlbaum.

Power, M., & Dalgleish, T. (1997). *Cognition and emotion: From order to disorder.* Hove, England: Psychology Press.

Russell, B. (1945). *A history of Western philosophy.* New York: Simon & Schuster.

Russell, B. (1950). *The conquest of happiness.* New York: Liveright.

Ryff, C. D. (1989). Happiness is everything, or is it?: Explorations on the meaning of psychological well-being. *Journal of Personality and Social Psychology, 57*, 1069–1081.

Schmutte, P. S., & Ryff, C. D. (1997). Personality and well-being: Reexamining methods and meanings. *Journal of Personality and Social Psychology, 73*, 549–559.

Schwarz, N., & Bless, H. (1991). Happy and mindless, but sad and smart?: The impact of affective states on analytic reasoning. In J. P. Forgas (Ed.), *Emotion and social judgments* (pp. 55–71). Oxford: Pergamon Press.

Seneca, L. A. (1962). *Ad Lucilium epistulae morales, Vol. 2.* (R. M. Gummere, Trans.). Cambridge, MA: Harvard University Press.

Shaver, P., Schwartz, J., Kirson, D., & O'Connor, C. (1987). Emotion knowledge: Further exploration of a prototype approach. *Journal of Personality and Social Psychology, 52*, 1061–1086.

Shaw, G. B. (1963). Man and superman. In G. B. Shaw, *Complete plays with prefaces* (Vol. 3, pp. 483–686). New York: Dodd, Mead. (Original work published 1905)

Simon, H. A. (1990). Invariants of human behavior. *Annual Review of Psychology, 41*, 1–19.

Skinner, B. F. (1986). What is wrong with daily life in the Western world? *American Psychologist, 41*, 568–574.

Smith, R. H., Diener, E., & Wedell, D. H. (1989). Intrapersonal and social comparison determinants of happiness: A range–frequency analysis. *Journal of Personality and Social Psychology, 56*, 317–325.

Strasser, S. (1977). *Phenomenology of feeling* (R. E. Wood, Trans.). Pittsburgh, PA: Duquesne University Press.

Tatarkiewicz, W. (1976). *Analysis of happiness.* Warsaw: Polish Scientific.

Thompson, S. C., Armstrong, W., & Thomas, C. (1998). Illusions of control, underestimations, and accuracy: A control heuristic explanation. *Psychological Bulletin, 123*, 143–161.

Veenhoven, R. (1984). *Conditions of happiness.* Dordrecht, The Netherlands: Reidel.

Vlastos, G. (1985). Happiness and virtue in Socrates' moral theory. *Topoi, 4*, 3–22.

Wallace, J. (1966). An abilities conceptions of personality: Some implications for personality measurement. *American Psychologist, 21*, 132–138.

Wiggens, J. S., & Trapnell, P. D. (1997). Personality structure: The return of the big five. In R. Hogan, J. Johnson, & S. Briggs (Eds.), *Handbook of personality psychology* (pp. 737–765). San Diego: Academic Press.

Willerman, L., Turner, R. G., & Peterson, M. A. (1976). A comparison of the predictive validity of typical and maximal personality measures. *Journal of Research in Personality, 10*, 482–492.

Wills, T. A. (1981). Downward comparison principles in social psychology. *Psychological Bulletin, 90*, 245–271.

CHAPTER 43

Empathy and Sympathy

Nancy Eisenberg

The term "empathy" has been used in many ways at different times. Originally it was used primarily in regard to aesthetics (see Wispe, 1986, 1987) and involved a immediate shared sensory and emotional experience—for example, feeling oneself into a situation (Titchener, 1915). In the 1930s, Mead (1934) defined empathy in a cognitive manner, as "the capacity to take the role of the other and to adopt alternative perspectives vis a vis oneself" (p. 27). Similarly, in the 1950s, 1960s, 1970s, and even sometimes today, some researchers have used the term to refer to the cognitive ability to understand others' mental and emotional states (Borke, 1971, 1973; Deutsch & Madle, 1975) or social insight (Dymond, 1950). In the developmental and social-psychological literature, this ability often has been subsumed, at least in part, under the term "perspective taking" or "role taking" (Underwood & Moore, 1982), and skill at "everyday mind reading" has been labeled "empathic accuracy" (Ickes, 1997, p. 2).

In the clinical literature, empathy has also been defined in a variety of ways. For example, Rogers (1959), in his early work, wrote that empathy means "to perceive the internal frame of reference of another with accuracy, and with the emotional components and meanings which pertain thereto, as if one were the person, but without ever losing the 'as if' condition" (1959, p. 210). Later Rogers expanded his definition to include nonjudgmentally understanding and

communicating one's understanding to another, as well as "checking with him/her as to the accuracy of your sensings, and being guided by the responses you receive" (1975, p. 4). Other clinicians' definitions of empathy have involved shared affect, as well as thinking oneself into another's place and a clear differentiation between self and the other (Katz, 1963; Kohut, 1959; see Strayer, 1987; Wispe, 1986).

At the present time, some social psychologists use empathy to indicate an inferential cognitive process (Ickes, 1987), whereas numerous others have defined empathy as involving affect as well as some basic cognitive processes (Davis, 1994). Based on the work of Feshbach (1978) and Hoffman (1982), a colleague and I (Eisenberg & Strayer, 1987) have defined "empathy" as an affective response that stems from the apprehension or comprehension of another's emotional state or condition, and that is identical or very similar to what the other person is feeling or would be expected to feel. Thus, if a woman sees or hears about a person who is sad and feels sad in response to this information, the woman is experiencing empathy.

In this definition, empathy is believed to involve both cognitive and affective components. It is useful to differentiate empathy from pure emotional contagion; thus we (Eisenberg & Strayer, 1987) have argued that empathy requires at least some differentiation of one's own and another's emotional state or condition (see Feshbach, 1978; Lewis, 1990), and at least a

677

minimal awareness of this difference in specific contexts. According to this perspective, very young infants experience emotional contagion but not empathy, and children and adults can experience either one.

Another important distinction is between empathy and related vicarious emotions. Batson (1991), a social psychologist, has differentiated between empathy (which is really sympathy, not empathy, as defined in this chapter) and personal distress. Although sympathy has been defined in a variety of ways in the past (Wispe, 1986), today sympathy is often defined as involving emotion. For example, I define "sympathy" as an affective response that consists of feeling sorrow or concern for the distressed or needy other (rather than feeling the same emotion as the other person). Sympathy is believed to involve other-oriented, altruistic motivation (Batson, 1991). Although sympathy probably stems primarily from empathy in many contexts, it may also result from cognitive processes such as perspective taking (Batson, 1991; Hoffman, 1982; Eisenberg, Shea, Carlo, & Knight, 1991; Feshbach, 1978) and accessing of information encoded in memory that is relevant to the other person's condition (Eisenberg, Shea, et al., 1991).

In contrast to sympathy, "personal distress" is defined as a self-focused, aversive emotional reaction to another's emotion or condition (e.g., discomfort, anxiety; see Batson, 1991; Eisenberg, Shea, et al., 1991). Like sympathy, personal distress may often stem from empathy or cognitive processing; however, unlike sympathy, it involves the egoistic motive to alleviate one's own distress rather than that of the empathy-inducing individual(s).

The goal of this chapter is to provide a brief overview of theory and research concerning empathy-related responding. Topics salient in contemporary research are emphasized, including (1) temperamental or personality variables related to empathy-related responding; (2) the development of empathy-related responding; (3) the relation of empathy-related reactions to social behavior, including prosocial behavior, aggression, and social competence; (4) gender differences in empathy-related reactions; and (5) socialization correlates. In this review, work from the developmental and social-psychological literature is emphasized (particularly the former), in part because clinicians usually define empathy differently than it is conceptualized in this chapter.

TEMPERAMENTAL OR PERSONALITY VARIABLES RELATED TO EMPATHY-RELATED RESPONDING

Fabes and I (e.g., Eisenberg, Fabes, Murphy, et al., 1994) suggested that sympathy and personal distress involve qualitatively different emotional experiences and are differentially related to several dispositional characteristics linked to emotional experience. Specifically, we hypothesized that empathic overarousal in reaction to another's negative emotion (or condition) is aversive; consequently, it induces a self-focus reaction (Hoffman, 1982) and the egoistic motivation to alleviate that aversive state. In a nutshell, we argued that personal distress is usually the consequence of empathic overarousal. In contrast, we suggested that sympathy is a consequence of either cognitive processes (e.g., perspective taking) or an optimal level of empathic arousal—one that is strong enough to orient the empathizer toward the other person, but is not so strong that it is aversive. Consistent with these hypotheses, negative emotion has been associated with a focus on the self (e.g., Wood, Saltzberg, & Goldsamt, 1990); and people exhibit higher skin conductance or heart rate, and sometimes report more distress, in situations likely to elicit personal distress (in contrast to sympathy or a baseline; Eisenberg, Fabes, Schaller, Miller, et al., 1991; Eisenberg, Fabes, Schaller, Carlo, & Miller, 1991; Eisenberg, Schaller, et al., 1988; see also Strayer, 1993).

On the basis of the aforementioned ideas, we (Eisenberg, Fabes, Murphy, et al., 1994) further argued that aspects of personality or temperament influence whether people are able to maintain their vicarious emotional arousal at a moderate level or become overaroused by negative emotion when confronted with another's negative emotion or situation. Specifically, we suggested that people prone to exhibit sympathy are likely to be those who are dispositionally well regulated (especially in regard to emotion regulation) and prone to intense emotions, be they positive or negative (if they also are well regulated). In contrast, people prone to personal distress were expected to be those low in dispositional regulation (e.g., the ability to shift and focus attention and to manage emotionally based behavior) and high in the intensity and frequency of their experience of negative emotions. These hypotheses have received initial empirical support, particularly when dispositional sympathy and personal distress have been studied. For example, personal distress has been related to low regulation (attentional and/or behavioral) in studies with young adults and older adults (Eisenberg, Fabes, Murphy, et al., 1994; Eisenberg & Okun, 1996). In contrast, dispositional sympathy has been correlated with high regulation (Eisenberg, Fabes, Murphy, et al., 1996; Eisenberg & Okun, 1996; Murphy, Shepard, Eisenberg, Fabes, & Guthrie, 1999), although sometimes only after individual differences in the tendency to experience intense negative emotions have been controlled for (Eisenberg, Fabes, Murphy, et al., 1994).

Consistent with the aforementioned predictions, among adults, dispositional personal distress and sympathy have been associated with self-reported dispositional tendencies to experience intense negative emotions and sadness. The relation of self-reports of frequently experiencing negative emotion with sympathy has been relatively weak (and significant only when social desirability was controlled for), whereas the relation between frequency of negative emotion and personal distress has been relatively strong and consistent. Moreover, friends' reports of negative emotionality (both intensity and frequency) have been related positively to young adults' personal distress, but not to sympathy. Thus adults' personal distress and sympathy have been linked to sadness and intensity of negative emotions when they occur, whereas frequency of negative emotionality has been more clearly associated with personal distress (Eisenberg, Fabes, Murphy, et al., 1994; Eisenberg & Okun, 1996; see also Davis, 1994).

Among children, dispositional regulation, as reported by parents or teachers, also predicts dispositional sympathy (Eisenberg, Fabes, Murphy, et al., 1996; Eisenberg et al., 1998; Murphy et al., 1999). Furthermore, vagal tone, a marker of physiological regulation (Porges, Doussard-Roosevelt, & Maiti, 1994), was positively related to self-reported sympathy for boys (although the relation was negative for girls) (Eisenberg, Fabes, Murphy, et al., 1996). However, in contrast to the findings for adults' self-reported negative emotionality, negative emotionality was negatively related to children's dispositional sympathy, albeit only for boys in early elementary school (and for both sexes by ages 10–12; see Eisenberg et al., 1998; Murphy et al., 1999). It is likely that the re-

versed pattern of findings for children can be attributed to the types of children's negative emotions that are salient to, and reported by, adults who deal with the children on a regular basis. In general, researchers have found that boys exhibit more anger than do girls (see Eisenberg, Martin, & Fabes, 1996), so it is likely that adults' (particularly teachers') reports of children's (especially boys') negative emotionality reflect primarily externalizing emotions such as anger and frustration, as well as other problematic emotions such as overt distress (see Eisenberg, Fabes, Nyman, Bernzweig, & Pinuelas, 1994). These types of negative emotions would not be expected to promote sympathy, and externalizing negative emotions would be expected to undermine sympathetic responding. The fact that other-reports of negative emotionality were negatively related to children's sympathy is somewhat consistent with the relation of other-reports (i.e., friends' reports) of intensity and frequency of adults' negative emotions to adults' personal distress but not sympathy (Eisenberg, Fabes, Murphy, et al., 1994). Moreover, for boys, physiological arousal when exposed to a relatively distressing film clip was related to low dispositional sympathy—a finding supporting the view that negative emotional reactivity is linked to personal distress.

In the same study, adults' reports of children's regulation and emotionality contributed unique as well as overlapping variance to the prediction of children's self-reported and teacher-reported dispositional sympathy (Eisenberg, Fabes, Murphy, et al., 1996). In addition, there was an interaction between general emotional intensity and regulation in predicting teacher-reported child sympathy. "General emotional intensity" was defined as the general tendency to feel emotions strongly, without reference specifically to valence of the emotion (positive or negative). Children low in teacher-reported regulation were low in sympathy, regardless of their general emotional intensity. In contrast, for those children who were moderate or relatively high in regulation, sympathy increased with the level of general emotional intensity. Thus children who were likely to experience positive and negative emotions intensely were sympathetic if they were at least moderately well regulated. These children were likely to experience others' emotions vicariously without becoming overaroused and overwhelmed by their emotions. This finding was partially replicated 2 years later for boys' behavioral regulation and general emotional intensity (Eisenberg et al., 1998).

In brief, across studies, regulation has generally (albeit not always) been correlated with high dispositional sympathy and low dispositional personal distress. The relation of emotionality with empathy-related responding varies, depending upon whether the index is adults' reports of their own emotionality or other people's reports of an individual's negative emotion (e.g., teachers' or parents' reports of children's emotionality, or friends' reports of adults' negative emotionality). In addition, dispositional empathy-related responding is often better predicted by the combination of emotionality and regulation than by either one by itself.

The pattern of relations between *situational* empathy-related responding and regulation and emotionality is not as clear as the findings for dispositional empathy-related reactions, especially in the limited data from adults (Eisenberg, Fabes, Murphy, et al., 1994). In samples of children, measures of situational sympathy (e.g., facial concerned attention in response to an empathy-inducing film, self-reported sympathy, heart rate decline) have sometimes been correlated with adults' reports of children's attentional or behavioral regulation (Eisenberg & Fabes, 1995; Guthrie et al., 1997). Moreover, in one study (Guthrie et al., 1997), situational personal distress (e.g., facial distress) was correlated with high emotionality, whereas situational sympathy was negatively related to ratings of dispositional negative emotionality. However, the strength of these relations has generally been modest, and the overall pattern is often weak and sometimes inconsistent.

THE DEVELOPMENT OF EMPATHY-RELATED RESPONDING

For many years, in part because of Piaget's work, behavioral scientists often assumed that young children were too egocentric to empathize. However, Martin Hoffman's theorizing about empathy challenged the notion that young children are incapable of other-oriented feelings and behavior.

Hoffman (1982) proposed four levels of feelings that result from the coalescence of vicarious affect and the cognitive sense of the other. Hoffman suggested that infants experience empathic distress through one or more simple

mechanisms (e.g., reactive crying to another's distress, conditioning, mimicry) in the first year of life, before they acquire a clear sense of others as separate physical entities. Hoffman hypothesized that because young infants cannot differentiate their own distress from that of another person, they experience global distress—a diffuse and generalized state encompassing both the distressed person and themselves (see also Lewis, 1990).

At Hoffman's next level—egocentric empathy—children are believed to distinguish the self from others, but cannot fully differentiate between their own and another's internal states. Thus they may experience a mixture of sympathy and distress, and they still have difficulty responding sensitively to another's emotions and needs. However, at 2 to 3 years of age, young children become increasingly aware that other people's feelings are independent of, and sometimes different from, their own. Due to increased perspective-taking skills, children can empathize and sympathize with a wider range of emotions than at a younger age, and can respond with empathy/sympathy to information about someone's feelings even when the other person is not physically present. However, until late childhood or early adolescence, children's empathic responses are usually confined to another's immediate, transitory, and situationally specific distress. With greater cognitive maturity and an awareness that people continue to exist over time and contexts, children can empathize with others' general condition. Hoffman hypothesized that this developmental change explains why adolescents are able to understand and respond to the plight of a group or class of people, such as the impoverished or politically oppressed.

There is support for some aspects of Hoffman's theory. For example, there is evidence that, as discussed by Hoffman, newborn infants sometimes display reactive crying to another infant's cry (more so than to a simulated cry), although it is unclear whether such crying reflects primitive empathy, conditioned responses, or emotional contagion (see Thompson, 1987). Moreover, consistent with his expectations, most children do not appear to empathize until 12 to 18 months of age. Six-month-old infants rarely become distressed by the crying of a peer (Hay, Nash, & Pedersen, 1981), although 38- to 61-week-olds sometimes respond to others' distresses that they did not cause with orienting and distress cries or even positive affect

(Zahn-Waxler & Radke-Yarrow, 1982). Distress cries and positive emotion decrease with age in the early years. Moreover, by 12 and 18 months of age, infants sometimes react to others' distress with prosocial interventions suggesting concern (Zahn-Waxler, Radke-Yarrow, & King, 1983). Consistent with Hoffman's theorizing, toddlers who recognize themselves in the mirror—who have a rudimentary sense of self—are relatively empathic and likely to assist others in distress (Bischof-Kohler, 1991; Johnson, 1982; Zahn-Waxler, Radke-Yarrow, Wagner, & Chapman, 1992). Moreover, consistent with the view that rudimentary perspective-taking skills influence the quality of empathy, in the second year of life and at ages 4 to 5 years children's attempts to test hypotheses about why another is distressed have been associated with children's prosocial behavior (Zahn-Waxler, Cole, Welsh, & Fox, 1995; Zahn-Waxler, Robinson, & Emde, 1992).

Although toddlers and preschool children are clearly capable of responding empathically and sympathetically to others' distress, they also often ignore others' distress and sometimes react with avoidance or aggression. Indeed, young children's responsiveness to peers' cries is relatively infrequent (e.g., Howes & Farver, 1987; Phinney, Feshbach, & Farver, 1986). Individual differences in children, situations, and experiential factors appear to influence a particular child's response (Farver & Branstetter, 1994; see Eisenberg & Fabes, 1998).

Children report more empathy with increasing age in the preschool and elementary school years (e.g., Strayer, 1993; see Lennon & Eisenberg, 1987). However, findings pertaining to age changes in empathy-related responding as measured with self-report questionnaires are inconsistent with older children and adolescents. Facial/gestural indices appear to be either inversely related or unrelated to age in the early school years, probably because of increases with age in children's ability to mask their emotions (Lennon & Eisenberg, 1987). In a recent review, we (Eisenberg & Fabes, 1998) found that age-related trends in children's empathy in research were significant and larger for observational and self-report measures than for nonverbal (facial/physiological) or other-report measures (for which the effect sizes were not significant).

There is also evidence that sympathy and empathy are stable interindividually (i.e., are correlated across time) from early adolescence into early adulthood (Davis & Franzoi, 1991; Eisenberg, Carlo, Murphy, & Van Court, 1995). Thus individual differences in empathy-related responding seem to be established by late childhood.

RELATIONS OF EMPATHY-RELATED RESPONDING TO SOCIAL BEHAVIOR

Prosocial Behavior

For many years, psychologists (e.g., Batson, 1991; Feshbach, 1978; Hoffman, 1982) and philosophers (Blum, 1980; Hume, 1748/1975) have proposed that prosocial behavior, particularly altruism (prosocial behavior that is not based on concrete external rewards), is frequently motivated by empathy or sympathy. Moreover, some psychologists believe that links between empathy or sympathy and prosocial behavior exist both within specific contexts and at the dispositional level (i.e., people with a dispositional tendency toward empathy/sympathy are expected to be altruistic in general; Eisenberg & Miller, 1987; Penner, Fritzsche, Craiger, & Freifeld, 1995; Staub, 1979).

According to Hoffman (1982), the development of empathy/sympathy and that of prosocial behavior are intimately related. As young children develop the ability to differentiate between their own negative emotion and that of other people, they are able to experience sympathetic concern for another. This appears to occur to some degree in the second year of life (Zahn-Waxler, Radke-Yarrow, et al., 1992). Initially these efforts often consist of positive physical contact, such as patting the other person.

However, by 18 to 24 months of age, children are increasingly likely to try to provide direct assistance. Young toddlers' prosocial actions may be somewhat inappropriate and egoistic; for example, a young girl may try to comfort a crying peer by bringing her own mother rather than the mother of the peer. However, as children become better at understanding others' perspectives and needs as differentiated from their own (e.g., especially at ages 3 or 4), their prosocial behavior becomes more appropriate and sensitive. Moreover, as children come to understand that others' emotional states and conditions exist over time and beyond the immediate context (at 6 to 9 years of age), they become capable of reacting to others' general condition, as well as to another's immediate distress. Thus they may be sympathetic to the continuing plight of an entire group or class of people, such as the impoverished, oppressed, or disabled.

Despite the common assumption of a link between empathy-related responding and prosocial behavior, Underwood and Moore (1982) found in a meta-analytic review that empathy was virtually unrelated to prosocial behavior. Many of the studies they reviewed involved self-report measures of empathy in which children were presented with a series of short illustrated vignettes about people in emotionally evocative contexts and were asked how they felt. Such measures have proved to be problematic (see Eisenberg & Lennon, 1983; Lennon, Eisenberg, & Carroll, 1983).

Moreover, in the early research on empathy and prosocial behavior, the critical conceptual distinction between sympathy and personal distress was absent. As noted previously, Batson (1991) hypothesized that sympathy (as defined in this chapter), due to its intrinsic other-oriented motivation, is likely to lead to other-oriented, altruistic helping behavior. Moreover, Batson and his colleagues have found that when people experience sympathy, they infer that they value the welfare of persons in need (Batson, Turk, Shaw, & Klein, 1995) and develop more positive attitudes toward members of stigmatized groups (e.g., those with AIDS or the homeless; Batson, Polycarpou, et al., 1997). Thus people experiencing sympathy would be expected to be relatively likely to assist other people, including members of stigmatized groups.

In contrast, Batson (1991) viewed personal distress as involving the egoistic motivation to alleviate one's own distress. Consequently, personal distress is expected to engender prosocial actions only when reducing another's negative emotion or circumstances is the easiest way to alleviate one's own distress. However, if people have the option of easily avoiding contact with the person who elicited the personal distress, they are expected not to assist.

Batson and his colleagues, as well as others (e.g., Schroeder, Dovidio, Sibicky, Matthews, & Allen, 1988), have conducted a series of laboratory studies with adults testing these predictions. In general, they have found that sympathy, in comparison to personal distress, tends to be associated with helping when it is easy for people to escape contact with the person needing assistance (see Batson, 1991, 1998; see also Carlo, Eisenberg, Troyer, Switzer, & Speer, 1991). In most of this work, situationally induced sympathy and personal distress were examined; typically it was induced through some sort of experimental manipulation, and self-reports of emotion were used to assess the success of the manipulation. However, individual differences in sympathy or personal distress to an empathy-inducing stimulus have also been linked to high and low levels of prosocial behavior, respectively, in studies with children and adults (e.g., Carlo et al., 1991; Eisenberg & Fabes, 1991). Moreover, dispositional self-report measures of sympathy and empathy have been associated with older children's and adults' prosocial behavior (Eisenberg & Miller, 1987).

For example, in a series of studies, Fabes, I, and our colleagues demonstrated that children and adults exhibit different heart rate, skin conductance, facial, and (to a more limited degree) self-reported reactions in contexts selected to induce sympathy versus a reaction akin to personal distress. These markers of sympathy and personal distress tended to predict prosocial behavior in situations in which prosocial behavior was anonymous (or relatively anonymous) and potential helpers did not have to deal with the empathy-inducing person if they did not want to do so (Eisenberg et al., 1990, 1993; Eisenberg, Fabes, Miller, et al., 1989; Fabes et al., 1994; Fabes, Eisenberg, & Miller, 1990; Miller, Eisenberg, Fabes, & Shell, 1996). Self-report measures have been less consistently related to children's prosocial behavior than have facial and physiological measures (see Eisenberg & Fabes, 1990, 1998; Holmgren, Eisenberg, & Fabes, 1998; Trommsdorff, 1995; Zahn-Waxler et al., 1995; cf. Roberts & Strayer, 1996). However, in studies of self-reported dispositional empathy or sympathy rather than situational empathy/sympathy, empathy or sympathy tends to be related to self-reported or relatively costly prosocial behavior (Eisenberg, Miller, Shell, McNalley, & Shea, 1991; Eisenberg et al., 1987).

Of course, the predicted relations have not always been obtained. Sometimes the effects of sympathy are moderated by dispositional perspective taking (Knight, Johnson, Carlo, & Eisenberg, 1994) or moral reasoning (Miller et al., 1996), such that prosocial children are high in sympathy *and* perspective taking or moral reasoning. Moreover, preschoolers' personal distress reactions have sometimes been positively related to the children's tendency to engage in compliant, requested prosocial behaviors in other contexts (Eisenberg et al., 1990; Eisenberg, McCreath, & Ahn, 1988). However, such compliant prosocial behavior has been correlated with observed low assertiveness and other behaviors indicative of low social competence with peers. Children high in compliant prosocial behavior (especially boys) appear to be viewed as easy targets by their peers (Eisenberg, Cameron, Tryon, & Dodez, 1981; Eisenberg, McCreath, & Ahn, 1988; Larrieu, 1984), and may engage in requested prosocial actions primarily because they are nonassertive or desire to curtail an unpleasant social interaction.

Moreover, sympathy can sometimes lead to negative moral outcomes. Batson, Klein, Highberger, and Shaw (1995) found that people induced to feel empathy/sympathy were likely to allocate resources preferentially to the individual for whom sympathy was felt, even if they violated principles of justice. Moreover, people may often attempt to forestall feeling sympathy if they are aware that they will be asked to help and the cost of helping is high (Shaw, Batson, & Todd, 1994).

In brief, recent research findings are consistent with the conclusion that sympathy and sometimes empathy (depending on their operationalization) are positively related to prosocial behavior, whereas personal distress is negatively related to prosocial behavior. As might be expected, there is more evidence of associations within contexts than across contexts, although children with a sympathetic disposition appear to be somewhat more prosocial in general than are other children (see Eisenberg & Fabes, 1998).

However, much of this work is not directly relevant to one debate in the field—that of whether sympathy is associated with true altruism (nonegoistically motivated prosocial behavior) or whether the link between sympathy and prosocial behavior is really mediated by egoistic motivations. Batson (1991) argued that sympathy is associated with the selfless desire to benefit another, and that sympathetically motivated altruistic behavior is not due to the desire for external rewards, the desire to avoid guilt, or the expectation of feeling good through vicarious sharing of a person's joy when the person's condition is improved. Although Batson and his colleagues have gathered considerable data consistent with Batson's arguments (e.g., Batson, Sager, et al., 1997), other researchers have data consistent with the view that when people experience sympathy, they help to alleviate their own negative mood (because of perceived oneness with the other person) or to experience empathic joy (Cialdini et al., 1987; Cialdini, Brown, Lewis, Luce, & Neuberg, 1997; Smith, Keating, & Stotland, 1989). Thus the debate regarding whether sympathy (or empathy) ever motivates true altruism is not resolved and may not be in the near future.

Aggression and Social Competence

Theorists have frequently argued that people who tend to empathize or sympathize with another's pain or distress are likely to refrain from or cease aggression because of the emotional discomfort induced by their vicarious response to the victim's emotional (or imagined) reactions (e.g., Feshbach, 1978). Empirical findings are somewhat consistent with this view, although the association between aggression and empathy appears to be modest in strength and varies as a function of the measure of empathy-related responding. In general, self-reported dispositional empathy-related responding has been linked to low aggression in school-age children (Miller & Eisenberg, 1988). For example, Cohen and Strayer (1996) found lower empathy among conduct-disordered than among comparison youths. Moreover, low maternal empathy has been correlated with child abuse (see Miller & Eisenberg, 1988). In contrast, relations of aggression to adolescents' and adults' reports of empathy in experimental contexts and to facial reactions indicative of children's empathy have been nonsignificant (see Miller & Eisenberg, 1988). Thus there appears to be a relation between dispositional empathy and aggression, although evidence of a link between situational empathic responding and aggression is weak. However, stronger relations might be obtained if sympathy rather than empathy were to be assessed.

One of the reasons for the relation between dispositional empathy-related responding and low aggression may be the link between empathy and social competence. Sympathy or empathy has sometimes been considered a component of emotional competence (e.g., Saarni, 1990). Consistent with this view, measures of global empathy have shown modest positive correlations with various measures of social competence (Eisenberg & Miller, 1987). Moreover, children's dispositional sympathy predicts socially appropriate behavior, constructive coping, and low levels of problem behavior as reported by peers, teachers, and mothers, as well as children's enactments of their behavior in social conflicts (Eisenberg, Fabes, Murphy, et al., 1996). Similarly, 4- to 6-year-olds' concerned attention to an empathy-inducing film was correlated with teachers' ratings of children's social skills and with real-life constructive anger reactions (but not sociometric status; Eisenberg & Fabes, 1995). Thus children who experience sympathy in social interactions or are dispositionally sympathetic are relatively likely to behave in socially competent ways.

GENDER DIFFERENCES IN EMPATHY-RELATED RESPONDING

Despite the stereotype that women and girls are more empathic than men and boys, the data pertaining to this issue are complex. Relevant findings in regard to gender differences in empathy and sympathy vary, depending on the definition and measure of empathy-related responding. Lennon and I (Eisenberg & Lennon, 1983; Lennon & Eisenberg, 1987) found large differences favoring females for self-report measures of empathy (or occasionally sympathy), especially for questionnaire measures. No gender differences were obtained when empathy was assessed with either physiological or unobtrusive observations of nonverbal behavior. In more recent work in which sympathy and personal distress were differentiated, investigators have obtained a similar pattern of findings, although occasionally weak sex differences in facial reactions, generally favoring females, have been obtained (see Eisenberg, Fabes, Schaller, & Miller, 1989).

In a recent meta-analysis of relevant studies that were not included in the Eisenberg and Lennon (1983) review (Eisenberg & Fabes, 1998), the sex difference in empathy-related responding was relatively large for self-report studies (significantly larger than in the studies involving other methods), moderate for observational measures (in which a combination of behavioral and facial reactions was generally used), and nonsignificant for nonverbal facial and physiological measures. The sex difference in self-reported empathy/sympathy increased with mean age of the sample (i.e., when participants were older) and when the targets of the empathic response were unspecified/unknown individuals. Sex differences in reported empathy may increase as children become more aware of, and perhaps are more likely to internalize in their self-images, sex-role stereotypes and expectations. The extent to which the gender difference in self-reported empathy-related responding reflects a genuine gender difference rather than the desire to conform with gender stereotypes is unclear at this time. However, the findings from observational studies suggest that there may be a real gender difference, beginning in the first years of life (e.g., Zahn-Waxler, Radke-Yarrow, et al., 1992).

THE ORIGINS OF EMPATHY

Hoffman (1981) hypothesized that empathy has a biological basis and is the biological substrate for prosocial behavior in humans. Consistent with this view, there is evidence from twin studies that some of the individual variation in empathy-related responding is due to genetic factors (Emde et al., 1992; Loehlin & Nichols, 1976; Matthews, Batson, Horn, & Rosenman, 1981; Rushton, Fulker, Neale, Nias, & Eysenck, 1986; Zahn-Waxler, Robinson, & Emde, 1992). For example, Zahn-Waxler, Robinson, and Emde (1992) studied twins at 14 and 20 months and found evidence of a significant genetic contribution to empathic concern (sympathy, perhaps mixed with some distress), responsiveness versus unresponsiveness to others' distresses, and prosocial responding.

However, it is also likely that children's experiences in the home and other social contexts affect their emotional reactions to others (see Plomin et al., 1993). Parents' socialization practices can to some degree reflect parents' genetic makeup, which is passed on to offspring and may affect children's capacity for empathy. Nonetheless, observation of and interactions with socializers also probably contribute to individual differences in empathy-related reactions, above and beyond any contribution made by heredity.

Regardless of the source of any parent–child similarity, there appears to be some relation between parents' reports of their own dispositional sympathy and that of same-sex children. Mothers' sympathy (or perspective taking combined with sympathy) has been positively related to daughters' sympathy (Eisenberg et al., 1992; Eisenberg & McNally, 1993; Fabes et al., 1990) or negatively related to daughters' personal distress (Eisenberg, Fabes, Schaller, Carlo, & Miller, 1991). In contrast, maternal personal distress has sometimes been related to daughters' low empathic responding and/or to sons' and daughters' inappropriate positive emotion in response to distressed or needy others (Eisenberg et al., 1992; Fabes et al., 1990). Mothers' sympathy seldom has been significantly correlated with boys' sympathy (although it was positively related in Eisenberg et al., 1992), whereas fathers' sympathy has been linked with boys' sympathy (Eisenberg, Fabes, Schaller, Carlo, & Miller, 1991).

In contrast, when global empathy (rather than sympathy and personal distress) has been assessed, findings have been rather inconsistent. Some investigators have found little evidence of an association between parent and child empathy (Kalliopuska, 1984; Strayer & Roberts, 1989), whereas others have obtained significant relations (Trommsdorff, 1991) or a complex pattern of correlations (Barnett, King, Howard, & Dino, 1980). In one study in which mothers and children watched an empathy-inducing film together, mothers who tended to exhibit facial distress and heart rate acceleration during the film had children who did likewise (Eisenberg et al., 1992). Of course, it is impossible to determine whether individual differences in parents' empathy-related characteristics caused differences in children's responses, whether children's reactions in the specific situation elicited similar reactions from mothers (or vice versa), or whether constitutional factors were responsible for the similarity in reactions.

Relation between Quality of the Parent–Child Relationship and Children's Vicarious Responding

Although relevant data are scarce, there appears to be a relation between quality of the early parent–child relationship and children's empathy-related reactions. Children who are securely attached, in comparison to insecurely attached children, have been found to be sympathetic with peers at 3½ years of age (Waters, Wippman, & Sroufe, 1979) and to exhibit relatively high levels of empathic prosocial behaviors in preschool (Kestenbaum, Farber, & Sroufe, 1989). Although Iannotti, Cummings,

Pierrehumbert, Milano, and Zahn-Waxler (1992) did not find a relation between quality of attachment and children's empathy, quality of the attachment at age 2 predicted children's prosocial behavior toward peers at 5 years of age. Furthermore, relationships with grandparents and other older people have been linked to higher empathy in children (Bryant, 1987).

It is possible that children with secure attachments attend to and want to please their parents more than other children (Waters, Hay, & Richters, 1986), which may facilitate parental attempts to foster empathy and sympathy. Staub (1992) has argued that the quality of early attachments is important to the development of a sense of connection to others and positive valuing of other people—characteristics likely to foster sympathetic responding.

There is also some evidence of an association between children's empathy and warm, empathic parenting (Trommsdorff, 1991; Zahn-Waxler, Radke-Yarrow, & King, 1979) or parental affection (Barnett, Howard, King, & Dino, 1980; Eisenberg-Berg & Mussen, 1978), although numerous researchers have not found such a relation (e.g., Eisenberg, Fabes, Schaller, Carlo, & Miller, 1991; Janssens & Gerris, 1992; Iannotti et al., 1992). Parental abusive behavior appears to be negatively related to children's empathy (Main & George, 1985; see Miller & Eisenberg, 1988). Bryant (1987) found no relation between general parental support and empathy for 7- and 10-year-olds; however, maternal report of expressions of support during times of stress predicted children's empathy. Maternal support when children are under stress may foster empathy more than overall level of maternal warmth may.

Relations of Parental General Disciplinary Practices to Children's Empathy-Related Responding

Findings regarding links between disciplinary practices and empathy are somewhat inconsistent, perhaps in part because sympathy and personal distress have seldom been differentiated in this research (e.g., Barnett, King, et al., 1980). However, some researchers have obtained evidence suggesting that inductive practices (e.g., parental use of reasoning) are related to children's empathy (e.g., Janssens & Gerris, 1992; Miller, Eisenberg, Fabes, Shell, & Gular, 1989; Zahn-Waxler et al., 1979). Moreover, in a study of children's sympathy and personal distress, mothers' infrequent use of negative control (i.e., nonphysical power assertion or negative appraisals of children), albeit not physical control (physical punishment or physically guiding children's actions), was associated with preschool children's sympathy (Miller et al., 1989). In studies of empathy, parental power assertion has been negatively related (Janssens & Gerris, 1992) or unrelated (Bryant, 1987; Feshbach, 1975) to children's empathy. Finally, parental demandingness (i.e., expectations of mature behavior) and limit setting have been linked to children's empathy (Bryant, 1987; Janssens & Gerris, 1992), whereas paternal (but not maternal) indulgence has predicted low levels of empathy for boys (findings were mixed for girls; Bryant, 1987).

Thus initial evidence is generally consistent with the view that parents who set high standards for their children, who use reasoning for discipline, and who expect mature behavior but are not overcontrolling or punitive are relatively likely to rear empathic or sympathetic children. However, the relevant data are limited in quantity, so further research is required to examine whether the aforementioned findings are robust.

Parental Emotion-Related Disciplinary Practices

Parental reactions to children's emotional displays and emotion-related behavior also appear to be associated with children's sympathy and personal distress reactions.

In general, parental practices that help children to deal constructively with their own negative emotion seen to foster sympathy rather than personal distress. This pattern may hold because children who cannot adequately cope with their emotions may tend to become overaroused and experience a self-focused, aversive response (i.e., personal distress) to others' distress. For example, we (Eisenberg, Fabes, Schaller, Carlo, & Miller, 1991) found that parents' reports of restrictiveness in response to children's expression of self-related anxiety and sadness were associated with facial and physiological markers of boys' distress during a sympathy-inducing film, accompanied by self-reports of low distress in reaction to the film. Thus, these boys seemed prone to experience distress when confronted with others' distress, but denied or did not recognize what they were feeling.

However, the effect of parental restrictiveness may vary with the nature of children's emotion. Parents who discouraged their same-sex elementary school children from expressing emotions hurtful to others had children high in self-reported sympathy (Eisenberg, Fabes, Schaller, Carlo, & Miller, 1991). Parents who try to constrain children's hurtful emotional displays may teach their children to attend to the effects of their emotions on others. However, restrictiveness in regard to the display of hurtful emotions was associated with distress in kindergarten girls. Mothers of these girls appeared less supportive in general; thus, for younger children, this sort of maternal restrictiveness may have reflected age-inappropriate restrictiveness or low levels of support (Eisenberg et al., 1992).

Parents also teach children ways to deal constructively with their negative emotions, and these parental practices have been correlated with children's empathy-related responding. One method of coping with emotional stress that is often viewed as constructive is acting directly upon the problem—that is, trying to change factors in the environment that have caused the distress (Lazarus & Folkman, 1984). In an initial study, boys (but not girls) whose parents encouraged them to deal instrumentally with situations causing their own sadness or anxiety were prone to sympathy rather than personal distress in empathy-inducing contexts (Eisenberg, Fabes, Schaller, Carlo, & Miller, 1991). Boys who are able to deal with their negative emotions in this way may be better able than their peers to regulate their vicarious negative emotion, and thus, more likely to experience sympathy.

Maternal behaviors that direct a child's attention to another's situation and/or help the child to feel the other's distress have also been associated with sympathy (Fabes et al., 1994). For example, mothers' references to their own sympathy and sadness, and their attempts to induce perspective taking or highlight another's feelings or situation, have been associated with boys' reports of sympathy and sadness (Eisenberg et al., 1992).

Findings are mixed in regard to whether the mere discussion of emotions fosters sympathetic tendencies (e.g., Barnett, Howard, et al., 1980; Barnett, King, et al., 1980; Fabes et al., 1994). Parental discussion of emotion may be associated with children's sympathy primarily when parental discussion fosters perspective taking and an understanding of emotion (see Dunn, Brown, & Beardsall, 1991; Dunn, Brown, Slomkowski, Tesla, & Youngblade, 1991), and when such discussion occurs in everyday interactions rather than primarily as a reactive attempt to deal with problematic behavior in children.

Families in which individuals frequently express emotions that are not hurtful or hostile also may encourage children to experience others' emotions (Eisenberg, Fabes, Schaller, Miller, et al., 1991). For example, the expression of soft negative emotions in the home has been correlated with girls' (especially younger girls') sympathy. In contrast, boys and girls from homes in which hostile negative emotions are frequently expressed seem to be prone to personal distress (Eisenberg et al., 1992). It is likely that degree and quality of family expressiveness not only reflect the quality of family interactions, but also implicitly teach children what emotions (and how much emotion) they are expected to display and/or experience (see Halberstadt, 1986), and how to regulate their emotion (Gottman, Katz, & Hooven, 1997).

Findings such as those just reviewed generally support the view that children's tendencies to respond with sympathy versus personal distress are in part learned, although the relevant socialization processes are likely to be complex and may involve genetic factors. Indeed, it is important to note that the emotion-related socialization process is not a one-way street. For example, in one study, mothers' perceptions of how distressed their children became when exposed to others' distress were greater for younger (kindergarten) than for older (second-grade) children. These mothers were warmer and displayed more positive and less negative emotion when telling stories about another in distress to younger than to older children; it appeared that mothers were trying to buffer younger children's reactions to the stories. Indeed, if mothers perceived their kindergartners as emotionally vulnerable, they were especially likely to display positive rather than negative emotion while telling the stories (Fabes et al., 1994). Furthermore, children with difficult temperaments may often elicit negative reactions from their parents when they display negative emotions (Eisenberg & Fabes, 1994; Eisenberg, Fabes, & Murphy, 1996).

In summary, children's empathy-related responding probably emerges as a function of constitutional and environmental factors. However, research on the socialization of empathy-related responding is scarce and is needed to provide an understanding of the origins of empathy and sympathy.

ACKNOWLEDGMENTS

Work on this chapter was supported by Research Scientist Development and Research Scientist Awards from the National Institute of Mental Health (Nos. K02 MH00903 and K05 M801321). I wish to thank Richard Fabes for his collaboration on many of the studies discussed.

REFERENCES

Barnett, M. A., Howard, J. A., King, L. M., & Dino, G. A. (1980). Antecedents of empathy: Retrospective accounts of early socialization. *Personality and Social Psychology Bulletin, 6*, 361–365.

Barnett, M. A., King, L. M., Howard, J. A., & Dino, G. A. (1980). Empathy in young children: Relation to parents' empathy, affection, and emphasis on the feelings of others. *Developmental Psychology, 16*, 243–244.

Batson, C. D. (1991). *The altruism question: Toward a social-psychological answer*. Hillsdale, NJ: Erlbaum.

Batson, C. D. (1998). Altruism and prosocial behavior. In D. T. Gilbert, S. T. Fiske, & G. Lindzey (Eds.), *Handbook of social psychology, Vol. 2* (4th ed., pp. 282–316). New York: McGraw-Hill.

Batson, C. D., Klein, T. R., Highberger, L., & Shaw, L. L. (1995). Immorality from empathy-induced altruism: When compassion and justice conflict. *Journal of Personality and Social Psychology, 68*, 1042–1054.

Batson, C. D., Polycarpou, M. P., Harmon-Jones, E., Imhoff, H. J., Mitchener, E. C., Bednar, L. L., Klein, T. R., & Highberger, L. (1997). Empathy and attitudes: Can feelings for a member of a stigmatized group improve feelings toward the group? *Journal of Personality and Social Psychology, 72*, 105–118.

Batson, C. D., Sager, K., Garst, E., Kang, M., Rubchinsky, K., & Dawson, K. (1997). Is empathy-induced helping due to self–other merging? *Journal of Personality and Social Psychology, 73*, 495–509.

Batson, C. D., Turk, C. L., Shaw, L. L., & Klein, T. R. (1995). Information function of empathic emotion: Learning that we value the other's welfare. *Journal of Personality and Social Psychology, 68*, 300–313.

Bischof-Kohler, D. (1991). The development of empathy in infants. In M. E. Lamb & H. Keller (Eds.), *Infant development: Perspectives from German-speaking countries* (pp. 245–273). Hillsdale, NJ: Erlbaum.

Blum, L. A. (1980). *Friendship, altruism and morality*. London: Routledge & Kegan Paul.

Borke, H. (1971). Interpersonal perception of young children: Egocentricism or empathy? *Developmental Psychology, 5*, 263–269.

Borke, H. (1973). The development of empathy in Chinese and American children between three and six years of age: A cross-cultural study. *Developmental Psychology, 9,* 102–108.

Bryant, B. K. (1987). Mental health, temperament, family, and friends: Perspectives on children's empathy and social perspective taking. In N. Eisenberg & J. Strayer (Eds.), *Empathy and its development* (pp. 245–270). Cambridge, England: Cambridge University Press.

Carlo, G., Eisenberg, N., Troyer, D., Switzer, G., & Speer, A. L. (1991). The altruistic personality: In what contexts is it apparent? *Journal of Personality and Social Psychology, 61,* 450–458.

Cialdini, R. B., Brown, S. L., Lewis, B. P., Luce, C., & Neuberg, S. L. (1997). Reinterpreting the empathy–altruism relationship: When one into one equals oneness. *Personality and Social Psychology, 73,* 481–494.

Cialdini, R. B., Schaller, M., Houlihan, D., Arps, K., Fultz, J., & Beaman, A. L. (1987). Empathy-based helping: Is it selflessly or selfishly motivated? *Journal of Personality and Social Psychology, 52,* 749–758.

Cohen, D., & Strayer, J. (1996). Empathy in conduct-disordered and comparison youth. *Developmental Psychology, 32,* 988–998.

Davis, M. H. (1994). *Empathy: A social psychological approach.* Madison, WI: Brown & Benchmark.

Davis, M. H., & Franzoi, S. (1991). Stability and change in adolescent self-consciousness and empathy. *Journal of Research in Personality, 25,* 70–87.

Deutsch, F., & Madle, R. A. (1975). Empathy: Historic and current conceptualization, measurement, and a cognitive theoretical perspective. *Human Development, 18,* 267–287.

Dunn, J., Brown, J., & Beardsall, L. (1991). Family talk about feeling states and children's later understanding of others' emotions. *Developmental Psychology, 27,* 448–455.

Dunn, J., Brown, J., Slomkowski, C., Tesla, C., & Youngblade, L. (1991). Young children's understanding of other people's feelings and beliefs: Individual differences and their antecedents. *Child Development, 62,* 1352–1366.

Dymond, R. F. (1950). Personality and empathy. *Journal of Consulting Psychology, 14,* 343–350.

Eisenberg, N., Cameron, E., Tryon, K., & Dodez, R. (1981). Socialization of prosocial behavior in the preschool classroom. *Developmental Psychology, 17,* 773–782.

Eisenberg, N., Carlo, G., Murphy, B., & Van Court, P. (1995). Prosocial development in late adolescence: A longitudinal study. *Child Development, 66,* 911–936.

Eisenberg, N., & Fabes, R. A. (1990). Empathy: Conceptualization, assessment, and relation to prosocial behavior. *Motivation and Emotion, 14,* 131–149.

Eisenberg, N., & Fabes, R. A. (1991). Prosocial behavior and empathy: A multimethod, developmental perspective. In P. Clark (Ed.), *Review of personality and social psychology* (Vol. 12, pp. 34–61). Newbury Park: Sage.

Eisenberg, N., & Fabes, R. A. (1994). Mothers' reactions to children's negative emotions: Relations to children's temperament and anger behavior. *Merrill–Palmer Quarterly, 40,* 138–156.

Eisenberg, N., & Fabes, R. A. (1995). The relation of young children's vicarious emotional responding to social competence, regulation, and emotionality. *Cognition and Emotion, 9,* 203–229.

Eisenberg, N., & Fabes, R. A. (1998). Prosocial development. In W. Damon (Series Ed.) & N. Eisenberg (Vol. Ed), *Handbook of child psychology: Vol. 3. Social, emotional, and personality development* (5th ed., pp. 701–778). New York: Wiley.

Eisenberg, N., Fabes, R. A., Carlo, G., Speer, A. L., Switzer, G., Karbon, M., & Troyer, D. (1993). The relations of empathy-related emotions and maternal practices to children's comforting behavior. *Journal of Experimental Child Psychology, 55,* 131–150.

Eisenberg, N., Fabes, R. A., Carlo, G., Troyer, D., Speer, A. L., Karbon, M., & Switzer, G. (1992). The relations of maternal practices and characteristics to children's vicarious emotional responsiveness. *Child Development, 63,* 583–602.

Eisenberg, N., Fabes, R. A., Miller, P. A., Fultz, J., Mathy, R. M., Shell, R., & Reno, R. R. (1989). The relations of sympathy and personal distress to prosocial behavior: A multimethod study. *Journal of Personality and Social Psychology, 57,* 55–66.

Eisenberg, N., Fabes, R. A., Miller, P. A., Shell, C., Shea, R., & May-Plumlee, T. (1990). Preschoolers' vicarious emotional responding and their situational and dispositional prosocial behavior. *Merrill–Palmer Quarterly, 36,* 507–529.

Eisenberg, N., Fabes, R. A., & Murphy, B. C. (1996). Parents' reactions to children's negative emotions: Relations to children's social competence and comforting behavior. *Child Development, 67,* 2227–2247.

Eisenberg, N., Fabes, R. A., Murphy, B., Karbon, M., Maszk, P., Smith, M., O'Boyle, C., & Suh, K. (1994). The relations of emotionality and regulation to dispositional and situational empathy-related responding. *Journal of Personality and Social Psychology, 66,* 776–797.

Eisenberg, N., Fabes, R. A., Murphy, B., Karbon, M., Smith, M., & Maszk, P. (1996). The relations of children's dispositional empathy-related responding to their emotionality, regulation, and social functioning. *Developmental Psychology, 32,* 195–209.

Eisenberg, N., Fabes, R. A., Nyman, M., Bernzweig, J., & Pinuelas, A. (1994). The relations of emotionality and regulation to children's anger-related reactions. *Child Development, 65,* 109–128.

Eisenberg, N., Fabes, R. A., Schaller, M., Carlo, G., & Miller, P. A. (1991). The relations of parental characteristics and practices to children's vicarious emotional responding. *Child Development, 62,* 1393–1408.

Eisenberg, N., Fabes, R. A., Schaller, M., & Miller, P. A. (1989). Sympathy and personal distress: Development, gender differences, and interrelations of indexes. In N. Eisenberg (Ed.), *New directions for child development: Vol. 44. Empathy and related emotional responses* (pp. 107–126). San Francisco: Jossey-Bass.

Eisenberg, N., Fabes, R. A., Schaller, M., Miller, P. A., Carlo, G., Poulin, R., Shea, C., & Shell, R. (1991). Personality and socialization correlates of vicarious emotional responding. *Journal of Personality and Social Psychology, 61,* 459–471.

Eisenberg, N., Fabes, R. A., Shepard, S. A., Murphy, B. C., Jones, J., & Guthrie, I. K. (1998). Contemporaneous and longitudinal prediction of children's sympathy from dispositional regulation and emotionality. *Developmental Psychology, 34,* 910–924.

Eisenberg, N., & Lennon, R. (1983). Gender differences in empathy and related capacities. *Psychological Bulletin, 94,* 100–131.

Eisenberg, N., Martin, C. L., & Fabes, R. A. (1996). Gender development and gender differences. In D. C. Berliner & R. C. Calfee (Eds.), *The handbook of educational psychology* (pp. 358–396). New York: Macmillan.

Eisenberg, N., McCreath, H., & Ahn, R. (1988). Vicarious emotional responsiveness and prosocial behavior: Their interrelations in young children. *Personality and Social Psychology Bulletin, 14,* 298–311.

Eisenberg, N., & McNally, S. (1993). Socialization and mothers' and adolescents' empathy-related characteristics. *Journal of Research on Adolescence, 3,* 171–191.

Eisenberg, N., & Miller, P. (1987). The relation of empathy to prosocial and related behaviors. *Psychological Bulletin, 101,* 91–119.

Eisenberg, N., Miller, P. A., Shell, R., McNalley, S., & Shea, C. (1991). Prosocial development in adolescence: A longitudinal study. *Developmental Psychology, 27,* 849–857.

Eisenberg, N., & Okun, M. A. (1996). The relations of dispositional regulation and emotionality to elders' empathy-related responding and affect while volunteering. *Journal of Personality, 64,* 157–183.

Eisenberg, N., Schaller, M., Fabes, R. A., Bustamante, D., Mathy, R., Shell, R., & Rhodes, K. (1988). The differentiation of personal distress and sympathy in children and adults. *Developmental Psychology, 24,* 766–775.

Eisenberg, N., Shea, C. L., Carlo, G., & Knight, G. (1991). Empathy-related responding and cognition: A "chicken and the egg" dilemma. In W. Kurtines & J. Gewirtz (Eds.), *Handbook of moral behavior and development: Vol. 2. Research* (pp. 63–88). Hillsdale, NJ: Erlbaum.

Eisenberg, N., Shell, R., Pasternack, J., Lennon, R., Beller, R., & Mathy, R. M. (1987). Prosocial development in middle childhood: A longitudinal study. *Developmental Psychology, 23,* 712–718.

Eisenberg, N., & Strayer, J. (1987). Critical issues in the study of empathy. In N. Eisenberg & J. Strayer (Eds.), *Empathy and its development* (pp. 3–13). Cambridge, England: Cambridge University Press.

Eisenberg-Berg, N., & Mussen, P. (1978). Empathy and moral development in adolescence. *Developmental Psychology, 14,* 185–186.

Emde, R. N., Plomin, R., Robinson, J., Corley, R., DeFries, J., Fulker, D. W., Reznick, J. S., Campos, J., Kagan, J., & Zahn-Waxler, C. (1992). Temperament, emotion, and cognition at fourteen months: The MacArthur Longitudinal Twin Study. *Child Development, 63,* 1437–1455.

Fabes, R. A., Eisenberg, N., Karbon, M., Bernzweig, J., Speer, A. L., & Carlo, G. (1994). Socialization of

children's vicarious emotional responding and prosocial behavior: Relations with mothers' perceptions of children's emotional reactivity. *Developmental Psychology, 30,* 44–55.

Fabes, R. A., Eisenberg, N., & Miller, P. (1990). Maternal correlates of children's vicarious emotional responsiveness. *Developmental Psychology, 26,* 639–648.

Farver, J. A. M., & Branstetter, W. H. (1994). Preschoolers' prosocial responses to their peers' distress. *Developmental Psychology, 30,* 334–341.

Feshbach, N. D. (1975). The relationship of child-rearing factors to children's aggression, empathy, and related positive and negative behaviors. In J. DeWit & W. W. Hartup (Eds.), *Determinants and origins of aggressive behavior* (pp. 426–436). The Hague: Mouton.

Feshbach, N. D. (1978). Studies of empathic behavior in children. In B. A. Maher (Ed.), *Progress in experimental personality research* (Vol. 8, pp. 1–47). New York: Academic Press.

Gottman, J. M., Katz, L. F., & Hooven, C. (1997). *Meta-emotion: How families communicate emotionally.* Mahwah, NJ: Erlbaum.

Guthrie, I. K., Eisenberg, N., Fabes, R. A., Murphy, B. C., Holmgren, R., Maszk, P., & Suh, K. (1997). The relations of regulation and emotionality to children's situational empathy-related responding. *Motivation and Emotion, 21,* 87–108.

Halberstadt, A. G. (1986). Family socialization of emotional expression and nonverbal communication styles and skills. *Journal of Personality and Social Psychology, 51,* 827–836.

Hay, D. F., Nash, A., & Pedersen, J. (1981). Responses of six-month-olds to the distress of their peers. *Child Development, 52,* 1071–1075.

Hoffman, M. L. (1981). Is altruism part of human nature? *Journal of Personality and Social Psychology, 40,* 121–137.

Hoffman, M. L. (1982). Development of prosocial motivation: Empathy and guilt. In N. Eisenberg (Ed.), *The development of prosocial behavior* (pp. 281–313). New York: Academic Press.

Holmgren, R. A., Eisenberg, N., & Fabes, R. A. (1998). The relations of children's situational empathy-related emotions to dispositional prosocial behavior. *International Journal of Behavioral Development, 22,* 169–193.

Howes, C., & Farver, J. (1987). Toddlers' responses to the distress of their peers. *Journal of Applied Developmental Psychology, 8,* 441–452.

Hume, D. (1975). *Enquiry into the human understanding* (P. Nidditch, Ed.). Oxford: Clarendon Press. (Original work published 1748)

Iannotti, R. J., Cummings, E. M., Pierrehumbert, B., Milano, M. J., & Zahn-Waxler, C. (1992). Parental influences on prosocial behavior and empathy in early childhood. In J. M. A. M. Janssens & J. R. M. Gerris (Eds.), *Child rearing: Influence on prosocial and moral development* (pp. 77–100). Amsterdam: Swets & Zeitlinger.

Ickes, W. (1997). Introduction. In W. Ickes (Ed.), *Empathic accuracy* (pp. 1–16). New York: Guilford Press.

Janssens, J. M. A. M., & Gerris, J. R. M. (1992). Child rearing, empathy and prosocial development. In J. M. A. M. Janssens & J. R. M. Gerris (Eds.), *Child rearing: Influence on prosocial and moral development* (pp. 57–75). Amsterdam: Swets & Zeitlinger.

Johnson, D. B. (1982). Altruistic behavior and the development of the self in infants. *Merrill–Palmer Quarterly, 28*, 379–388.

Kalliopuska, M. (1984). Relation between children's and parents' empathy. *Psychological Reports, 54*, 295–299.

Katz, R. L. (1963). *Empathy: Its nature and uses.* New York: Free Press.

Kestenbaum, R., Farber, E. A., & Sroufe, L. A. (1989). Individual differences in empathy among preschoolers: Relation to attachment history. In N. Eisenberg (Ed.), *New directions for child development: Vol. 44. Empathy and related emotional responses* (pp. 51–64). San Francisco: Jossey-Bass.

Knight, G. P., Johnson, L. G., Carlo, G., & Eisenberg, N. (1994). A multiplicative model of the dispositional antecedents of a prosocial behavior: Predicting more of the people more of the time. *Journal of Personality and Social Psychology, 66*, 178–183.

Kohut, H. (1959). Instrospection, empathy, and psychoanalysis. *Journal of American Psycholanalytic Association, 7*, 459–483.

Larrieu, J. A. (1984, March). *Prosocial values, assertiveness, and sex: Predictors of children's naturalistic helping.* Paper presented at the biennial meeting of the Southwestern Society for Research in Human Development, Denver, CO.

Lazarus, R. S., & Folkman, S. (1984). *Stress, appraisal, and coping.* New York: Springer.

Lennon, R., & Eisenberg, N. (1987). Gender and age differences in empathy and sympathy. In N. Eisenberg & J. Strayer (Eds.), *Empathy and its development* (pp. 195–217). Cambridge, England: Cambridge University Press.

Lennon, R., Eisenberg, N., & Carroll, J. (1983). The assessment of empathy in early childhood. *Journal of Applied Developmental Psychology, 4*, 295–302.

Lewis, M. (1990). Self-knowledge and social development in early life. In L. A. Pervin (Ed.), *Handbook of personality: Theory and research* (pp. 277–300). New York: Guilford Press.

Loehlin, J. C., & Nichols, R. C. (1976). *Heredity, environment, and personality.* Austin: University of Texas Press.

Main, M., & George, C. (1985). Responses of abused and disadvantaged toddlers to distress in agemates: A study in the day care setting. *Developmental Psychology, 21*, 407–412.

Matthews, K. A., Batson, C. D., Horn, J., & Rosenman, R. H. (1981). Principles in his nature which interest him in the fortune of others: The heritability of empathic concern for others. *Journal of Personality, 49*, 237–247.

Mead, G. H. (1934). *Mind, self, and society.* Chicago: University of Chicago Press.

Miller, P. A., & Eisenberg, N. (1988). The relation of empathy to aggression and externalizing/antisocial behavior. *Psychological Bulletin, 103*, 324–344.

Miller, P. A., Eisenberg, N., Fabes, R. A., & Shell, R.
(1996). Relations of moral reasoning and vicarious emotion to young children's prosocial behavior toward peers and adults. *Developmental Psychology, 32*, 210–219.

Miller, P. A., Eisenberg, N., Fabes, R. A., Shell, R., & Gular, S. (1989). Socialization of empathic and sympathetic responding. In N. Eisenberg (Ed.), *New directions for child development: Vol. 44. Empathy and related emotional responses* (pp. 65–83). San Francisco: Jossey-Bass.

Murphy, B. C., Shepard, S. A., Eisenberg, N., Fabes, R. A., & Guthrie, I. K. (1999). Contemporaneous and longitudinal relations of young adolescents' dispositional sympathy to their emotionality, regulation, and social functioning. *Journal of Early Adolescence, 19*, 66–97.

Penner, L. A., Fritzsche, B. A., Craiger, J. P., & Freifeld, T. S. (1995). Measuring the prosocial personality. In J. Butcher and C. D. Spielberger (Eds.), *Advances in personality assessment* (Vol. 10, pp. 147–163). Hillsdale, NJ: Erlbaum.

Phinney, J., Feshbach, N., & Farver, J. (1986). Preschool children's responses to peer crying. *Early Childhood Research Quarterly, 1*, 207–219.

Plomin, R., Emde, R. N., Braungart, J. M., Campos, J., Corley, R., Fulkner, D. W., Kagan, J., Reznick, J. S., Robinson, J., Zahn-Waxler, C., & DeFries, J. C. (1993). Genetic change and continuity from fourteen to twenty months: The MacArthur Longitudinal Twin Study. *Child Development, 64*, 1354–1376.

Porges, S. W., Doussard-Roosevelt, J. A., & Maiti, A. K. (1994). Vagal tone and the physiological regulation of emotion. In N. A. Fox (Ed.), The development of emotion regulation: Biological and behavioral considerations. *Monographs of the Society for Research in Child Development, 59*(2–3, Serial No. 240), 167–186.

Roberts, W., & Strayer, J. (1996). Empathy, emotional expression, and prosocial behavior. *Child Development, 67*, 449–470.

Rogers, C. R. (1959). A theory of therapy, personality and interpersonal relationships as developed in the client-centered framework. In S. Koch (Ed.), *Psychology: A study of a science. Study 1. Conceptual and systematic: Vol. 3. Formulations of the person in the social context* (pp. 184–256). New York: McGraw-Hill.

Rogers, C. R. (1975). Empathic: An unappreciated way of being. *The Counseling Psychologist, 5*, 2–10.

Rushton, J. P., Fulker, D. W., Neal, M. C., Nias, D. K. B., & Eysenck, H. J. (1986). Altruism and aggression: The heritability of individual differences. *Journal of Personality and Social Psychology, 50*, 1192–1198.

Saarni, C. (1990). Emotional competence: How emotions and relationships become integrated. In R. A. Thompson (Ed.), *Nebraska Symposium on Motivation: Vol. 36. Socioemotional development* (pp. 115–182). Lincoln: University of Nebraska Press.

Schroeder, D. A., Dovidio, J. F., Sibicky, M. E., Matthews, L. L., & Allen, J. L. (1988). Empathic concern and helping behavior: Egoism or altruism? *Journal of Experimental Social Psychology, 24*, 333–353.

Shaw, L. L., Batson, C. D., & Todd, R. M. (1994). Empathy avoidance: Forestalling feeling for another in order to escape the motivational consequences. *Journal of Personality and Social Psychology, 67,* 879–887.

Smith, K. D., Keating, J. P., & Stotland, E. (1989). Altruism revisited: The effect of denying feedback on a victim's status to empathic witnesses. *Journal of Personality and Social Psychology, 57,* 641–650.

Staub, E. (1979). *Positive social behavior and morality: Vol. 2: Socialization and development.* New York: Academic Press.

Staub, E. (1992). The origins of caring, helping, and nonaggression: Parental socialization, the family system, schools, and cultural influence. In P. M. Oliner, L. Baron, L. A. Blum, D. L. Krebs, & M. Z. Smolenska (Eds.), *Embracing the other: Philosophical, psychological, and historical perspectives on altruism* (pp. 390–412). New York: New York University Press.

Strayer, J. (1987). Picture-story indices of empathy. In N. Eisenberg & J. Strayer (Eds.), *Empathy and its development* (pp. 351–355). Cambridge, England: Cambridge University Press.

Strayer, J. (1993). Children's concordant emotions and cognitions in response to observed emotions. *Child Development, 64,* 188–201.

Strayer, J., & Roberts, W. (1989). Children's empathy and role taking: Child and parental factors, and relations to prosocial behavior. *Journal of Applied Developmental Psychology, 10,* 227–239.

Thompson, R. A. (1987). Empathy and emotional understanding: The early development of empathy. In N. Eisenberg & J. Strayer (Eds.), *Empathy and its development* (pp. 119–145). Cambridge, England: Cambridge University Press.

Titchener, E. (1915). *A beginner's psychology.* New York: Macmillan.

Trommsdorff, G. (1991). Child-rearing and children's empathy. *Perceptual and Motor Skills, 72,* 387–390.

Trommsdorff, G. (1995). Person–context relations as developmental conditions for empathy and prosocial action: A cross-cultural analysis. In T. A. Kindermann & J. Valsiner (Eds.), *Development of person–context relations* (pp. 189–208). Hillsdale, NJ: Erlbaum.

Underwood, B., & Moore, B. (1982). Perspective-taking and altruism. *Psychological Bulletin, 91,* 143–173.

Waters, E., Hay, D., & Richters, J. (1986). Infant–parent attachment and the origins of prosocial and antisocial behavior. In D. Olweus, J. Block, & M. Radke-Yarrow (Eds.), *Development of antisocial and prosocial behavior: Research, theories, and issues* (pp. 97–125). Orlando, FL: Academic Press.

Waters, E., Wippman, J., & Sroufe, L. A. (1979). Attachment, positive affect, and competence in the peer group: Two studies in construct validation. *Child Development, 50,* 821–829.

Wispe, L. (1986). The distinction between sympathy and empathy: To call forth a concept, a word is needed. *Journal of Personality and Social Psychology, 50,* 314–321.

Wispe, L. (1987). History of the concept of empathy. In E. Eisenberg & J. Strayer (Eds.), *Empathy and its development* (pp. 17–37). Cambridge, England: Cambridge University Press.

Wood, J. V., Saltzberg, J. A., & Goldsamt, L. A. (1990). Does affect induce self-focused attention? *Journal of Personality and Social Psychology, 58,* 899–908.

Zahn-Waxler, C., Cole, P. M., Welsh, J. D., & Fox, N. A. (1995). Psychophysiological correlates of empathy and prosocial behaviors in preschool children with problem behaviors. *Development and Psychopathology, 7,* 27–48.

Zahn-Waxler, C., & Radke-Yarrow, M. (1982). The development of altruism: Alternative research strategies. In N. Eisenberg (Ed.), *The development of prosocial behavior* (pp. 109–137). New York: Academic Press.

Zahn-Waxler, C., Radke-Yarrow, M., & King, R. A. (1979). Child rearing and children's prosocial initiations toward victims of distress. *Child Development, 50,* 319–330.

Zahn-Waxler, C., Radke-Yarrow, M., & King, R. (1983). Early altruism and guilt. *Academic Psychology Bulletin, 5,* 247–259.

Zahn-Waxler, C., Radke-Yarrow, M., Wagner, E., & Chapman, M. (1992). Development of concern for others. *Developmental Psychology, 28,* 126–136.

Zahn-Waxler, C., Robinson, J., & Emde, R. N. (1992). The development of empathy in twins. *Developmental Psychology, 28,* 1038–1047.

Author Index

"f" indicates a figure; "t" indicates a table; "n" indicates a note

Author Index

Subject Index

"f" indicates a figure; "t" indicates a table; "n" indicates a note